A SOURCE BOOK IN
CHINESE PHILOSOPHY

A SOURCE BOOK IN
CHINESE
PHILOSOPHY

TRANSLATED AND COMPILED BY
WING-TSIT CHAN

PRINCETON, NEW JERSEY
PRINCETON UNIVERSITY PRESS

L.C. Card: 62-7398

ISBN 0-691-01964-9

■

Chapter 7, "The Natural Way of Lao Tzu," with additional notes and comments, has been published as *The Way of Lao Tzu*, copyright © 1963, The Bobbs-Merrill Company.

■

Publication of this book has been aided by
the Ford Foundation program to support publication,
through university presses, of
works in the humanities and social sciences,
as well as by grants from the John Simon Guggenheim
Memorial Foundation, the Edward W. Hazen Foundation,
and the McInerny Foundation.

■

Wing-tsit Chan, now Anna R. D. Gillespie Professor of Philosophy at Chatham College, Pittsburgh, Pennsylvania, is also Professor of Chinese Culture and Philosophy Emeritus at Dartmouth College, Hanover, N.H. He did his undergraduate work at Lingnan University in Canton, China, and received his Ph.D. from Harvard University. He has taught both in China and in this country since 1929, and is the author of many distinguished publications in the field of Chinese philosophy.

■

Printed in the United States of America
by Princeton University Press, Princeton, New Jersey

First PRINCETON PAPERBACK Edition, 1969

Fourth Printing, 1973

TO GREGG M. SINCLAIR

ONE OF THE HOPEFUL SIGNS in these otherwise hectic times in which we are living is the long-overdue realization of the need for mutual understanding between the peoples of the East and those of the West. Genuine understanding of people who are separated from us by great distances or who differ from us in language, in way of life, in social custom, is difficult to achieve, even for those who are sincerely dedicated to this task.

Such understanding is vital—humanly, intellectually, practically— but it cannot be achieved through any superficial assessment of words or actions which are often unrevealing or possibly even misleading. It can be achieved only through a searching and serious study of the dominant ideas, the motivating beliefs that have, down through the ages, shaped the "mind," or over-all philosophy, of a race or a nation.

In getting at this basic philosophy, the only procedure available to the outsider is to study the thought of the intellectual leaders, the molders of the thought of the culture as a whole. And the only way to reach these great minds is through their own words. No amount of second-hand explanation or description or interpretation can assure the student that he is getting at the real mind of the thinker. Studying the original (even in translation), with the aid of knowledgeable guides where necessary— this alone can make for clarity of comprehension and assurance of authenticity.

This Source Book is devoted to the purpose of providing such a basis for genuine understanding of Chinese thought (and thereby of Chinese life and culture, since the relationship between the two is probably more pronounced in China than in any other country). It brings to English-speaking Westerners the basic materials for serious work in Chinese philosophy, which in its profundity and its long historical development is probably less adequately understood than that of any other great civilization in the world today. By virtue of misguided selection of only ancient texts, or popular texts, or texts which are primarily literary rather than technical, the Chinese philosophical tradition has been distorted out of all proportions. The Western philosopher, if he would be a true philosopher in considering all the experiences, insights, and systematic intellectual speculation of mankind as data for his comprehensive philosophical thinking, can no longer remain blind to the important insights of the great Chinese minds of history. The Chinese philosophers have much to contribute in many areas of the broad quest for truth, and it is high time that we in the West overcome our basic ignorance of this field, or at least attempt to correct the limited and possibly distorted interpretations that we now have.

This Source Book is indeed a milestone along the complex and difficult road to significant understanding by Westerners of the Asian peoples, and a monumental contribution to the cause of philosophy. It is the first anthology of Chinese philosophy to cover its entire historical development. It provides substantial selections from all the great thinkers and schools in every period—ancient, medieval, modern, and contemporary —and includes in their entirety some of the most important classical texts. It deals with the fundamental and technical as well as the more general aspects of Chinese thought. With its new translation of source materials (some translated for the first time), its explanatory aids where necessary, its thoroughgoing scholarly documentation, this volume will be an indispensable guide for scholars, for college students, for serious readers interested in knowing the real China.

I must take this opportunity, on behalf of all who are seriously concerned about the development of greater understanding of Asian philosophy, to thank Dr. Chan for producing this significant volume. Dr. Chan has taught Chinese philosophy in both China and the United States and, as far as I know, is the only Chinese philosopher who has taught in the United States in this one field continuously for more than 25 years. He knows thoroughly the needs and problems of students of Chinese philosophy—and, as a public lecturer, he is also well aware of the interests of the educated public. He brings to this work the valuable benefits and advantages of this unique background and experience. The task he has undertaken has been stupendous. Few scholars could have—or would have—undertaken it; no one else could have handled it so well.

As mentioned by Dr. Chan in the preface, this volume is the second in a series of Source Books in Asian philosophy. The first volume, *A Source Book in Indian Philosophy*, edited by Dr. S. Radhakrishnan and myself, was published by Princeton University Press in 1957 and was reissued in 1959. "A Source Book in Buddhist Philosophy," intended as a third volume in this series, is now in preparation.

Charles A. Moore

Honolulu, Hawaii

CHINA has changed more in the twentieth century than in any period in her history. She has overthrown a 3,000-year-old monarchic system. She has replaced the 1,300-year-old examination institution with modern education. Men and women are for the first time equal. And she has embraced Communism. These radical transformations and many more have forced Westerners to ask why they have taken place. The search is no longer one for information but for explanation. Realizing that neither contemporary factors nor external influences alone can provide the answer, they have begun to probe into Chinese thought. And since Chinese thought is predominantly Confucian, they have looked into Confucian teachings with great seriousness.

The study of Confucianism in the West is not new. James Legge's translation of the Confucian Classics began a century ago. Unfortunately, Western studies of Chinese philosophy have been largely confined to ancient Confucianism and its rival systems, as if Chinese Buddhism were not Chinese, Neo-Taoism did not exist, and later Confucianism but a footnote to the Confucian Classics or at best a de luxe edition of them. But the fact is that Chinese thought and the Chinese way of life in the last several hundred years have, generally speaking, been the product of Neo-Confucianism, which thrived from the twelfth to the sixteenth century, and Neo-Confucianism is itself an outgrowth of ancient Confucianism, modified by Taoism and Buddhism. Therefore, in order to understand the mind of China, it is absolutely necessary to understand Chinese thought, especially Neo-Confucianism, in its entire historical development. The present book has been prepared primarily to meet this urgent need.

In attempting to maintain an historical perspective, I have throughout this work tried to strike a balance between the modern, medieval, and ancient periods as well as between Confucianism, Taoism, and Buddhism. The selections presented herein have been chosen with this balance and perspective in view. In the chapters from the *Analects*, for example, special attention has been given to sayings on knowledge, human nature, human destiny, Heaven, and the like—perennial problems in Chinese philosophy—but only to the extent that such selectivity does not distort the total teaching of Confucius. Moreover, my choice of philosophers and schools has been guided by their relative influence on the development of Chinese thought, not by the temporary interest of non-Chinese scholars. Many Western scholars, for example, have been much interested in Wang Ch'ung (27-100?), evidently because of his skepticism and naturalism, but have been little interested in Wang Pi

(226-249). In terms of philosophical influence, however, Wang Ch'ung is almost insignificant whereas Wang Pi is of tremendous importance. I have therefore given much more space to Wang Pi than to Wang Ch'ung in proportion to the amount of their writing. Finally, my introductions to the translations and comments on specific selections were written not only to make the passages more meaningful and stimulating to the reader, but also to show the interconnections between the various periods and between the different schools of Chinese philosophy.

Wherever practicable, I have translated whole pieces. The present work includes four books (the *Great Learning*, the *Doctrine of the Mean*, the *Lao Tzu*, and the *T'ung-shu* [Penetrating the *Book of Changes*]) by Chou Tun-i and thirty-seven chapters or treatises in their entirety[1] besides many chapters almost complete.

I have chosen to translate the entire material myself instead of using existing materials for several reasons. One reason is to achieve consistency in translation, which is absolutely necessary for an adequate understanding of either an individual work or the historical development of Chinese philosophy. Take, for example, the concept of *chung-hsin* (loyalty and faithfulness), a basic concept in the *Analects*.[2] It is clear and definite, and no variation in translation is justified. Translations by Waley, Legge, and Lin Yutang are admirable in many respects but they are not consistent.

The second reason for a fresh translation is that much research has been done and many commentaries have been published since most of the existing translations appeared. Not many existing translations have made use of research scholarship and commentaries in the first place. In any case, recent materials cannot be ignored, for they have thrown much light on various subjects. There are about 350 existing commentaries on the *Lao Tzu* and over a hundred on the *Chuang Tzu*. I have not consulted all of them but have seen a good number although only the most important ones have been mentioned. It is the consultation of commentaries and recent studies that has made me differ from other translations in many places. In cases where alternate interpretations offered by different commentators seem to be of equal merit, I have indicated them in the footnotes.

[1] These are: one from *Mencius* (ch. 3); one from the *Hsün Tzu* (ch. 6); two from the *Chuang Tzu* (ch. 8); three from the *Mo Tzu* (ch. 9); five from the *Kung-sun Lung Tzu* (ch. 10); four by Tung Chung-shu (ch. 14); one by Wang Pi (ch. 19); two by Seng-chao (ch. 21); the *Thirty Verses* of Vasubandhu (ch. 23); three by Chi-tsang (ch. 25); two by Han Yü (ch. 27); one by Chou Tun-i (ch. 28); three by Chang Tsai (ch. 30); two by Ch'eng Hao (ch. 31); two by Ch'eng I (ch. 32); four by Chu Hsi (ch. 34); and one by Wang Yang-ming (ch. 35).

[2] 1:8; 5:27; 7:24; 9:24; 12:10; 15:5.

The third reason for a new translation is that many Chinese technical philosophical terms, especially those of Neo-Confucianism and Buddhism, require a new rendering. Until recently, there had not been sufficient tools to help the translator. Chinese dictionaries and encyclopedias are geared to Chinese literature, not philosophy, and many technical philosophical terms are not included. The publication of the monumental *Daikanwa jiten* (Great Chinese–Japanese Dictonary) in 1955-1960 has been a tremendous help to scholars. But even this great dictionary, with more than half a million terms, leaves some important philosophical terms out.[3] Without adequate tools to help them, many translators have rendered technical terms in their popular meanings. Thus *ching* is often translated as "reverence," which will do so far as its popular sense is concerned but not as a technical term in Neo-Confucianism.[4] Unfortunately there are very few tools to help the translator on Neo-Confucian terms. The situation is much better in Buddhism, for excellent dictionaries do exist. But even these are not complete. The entry *cheng-chü*, does not appear in them, for example. This term ordinarily means "proof," but when one looks into commentaries on Buddhist texts, one finds it to have a special meaning "to show" or "to demonstrate."

Some Chinese terms are so complicated in meaning that there are no English equivalents for them and they therefore have to be transliterated. I have, however, kept these transliterations to a minimum. I prefer to have a term translated even though the translation may not be entirely satisfactory. More about these difficult translations will be said in the Appendix.

I have used what I believe to be the best texts. In almost every text there are variations of individual words. These are noted only when the sense is seriously affected. And I have not noted obvious misprints or misplaced phrases. All titles have been translated. With the exception of some twelve cases, the sources of the 900-odd quotations have been given. Some sources are indicated in the original texts, but in most cases they had to be traced. Since for many of these there is no indication at all that they are quotations, and since indexes for most works are non-existent, to find their origin is often like "fishing up a needle from the bottom of a sea," as the common Chinese saying goes. But the identification of sources is necessary to show the reader the historical and philosophical connections between Chinese thinkers. It also enables him to check the context if he so desires. Those sayings or phrases that have already become established expressions are ordinarily no longer under-

[3] For example, *chih-ming*, or until destiny is fulfilled.
[4] See Appendix.

stood as quotations and there is therefore no need to trace their sources. In most cases where an English translation is available, a specific page reference is given to enable a comparison if desired.

The order of chapters is not strictly chronological but grouped by schools within major periods, so as to give a better picture of the relation of schools. The translated materials in each chapter are, for the most part, arranged in their original order, with the original section or chapter numbers retained. Wherever the original order does not give a logical or well-rounded picture, however, selections are grouped under topics, with consecutive numbers assigned for easy reference.

In many chapters a list of topics and references is given at the end of the introduction. These chapters are indicated by an asterisk at the end of their titles in the Table of Contents. Unless otherwise indicated, all footnotes and insertions in parentheses and brackets are mine. Brackets are intended for extraneous material while parentheses are for explanation and identification. But it is not always easy to draw the line.

Except for some contemporaries who put their personal names before their family names (as I do), Chinese and Japanese names are given in the Chinese order, that is, with the family name first. Chinese and Japanese scholars are not consistent in using the various names of Chinese writers. Here the private names of philosophers, rather than their courtesy or literary names, are used, except in the cases of Lu Hsiang-shan and Wang Yang-ming, who are generally known in China, Japan, and the West by their honorific names. Wherever desirable, courtesy, literary, and other alternate names are given in parentheses to help identification. Chinese words and names are romanized according to the modified Wade-Giles system, save for well-known geographical and personal names which do not conform to it. Unnecessary diacritical marks, however, have been omitted. Dates of persons, if known, are provided in all cases except for those who are mentioned purely incidentally and for Western and contemporary Asian writers. The dates of Confucius, Mencius, Lao Tzu, and Chuang Tzu are given only in the chapters on them. The traditional Chinese calendar year is equated with its corresponding Western year, though the two do not exactly coincide. Thus 1525, for example, refers to the fourth year of the Chia-ching period. In China when a person is said to be fifty, for instance, it means he is in his fiftieth calendar year. I have followed this custom in referring to age.

I T I S D I F F I C U L T to say when the preparation of this book began. In 1948-1949 I was awarded a Guggenheim Fellowship to prepare an anthology on Neo-Confucianism. Part of the material has gone into *Sources of Chinese Tradition* which was compiled by Wm. Theodore de Bary, Burton Watson, and myself and published by Columbia University Press. The entire material now forms part of this book. More work was done in 1955-1956 under a grant from the Rockefeller Foundation. Both Dr. Henry Allen Moe, Vice-President and Secretary-General of the John Simon Guggenheim Memorial Foundation, and Dr. Charles B. Fahs, former Director for the Humanities of the Rockefeller Foundation, have shown great interest and given strong encouragement, for which I am thankful.

I wish also to thank the Harvard-Yenching Library and its Librarian, Dr. K'ai-ming A. Ch'iu, the East Asiatic Library of Columbia University and its Librarian, Mr. Howard P. Linton, the staff of Baker Library, especially its Reference Division, of Dartmouth College, and Miss Naomi Fukuda, Librarian of the International House of Japan, who has been most helpful in locating and microfilming Japanese works for me. The Ford Foundation, The Hazen Foundation, The Guggenheim Foundation, and The McInerny Foundation have generously made grants toward the publication of this book. I am deeply grateful to them. Needless to say, they are neither sponsors of the book nor responsible for its opinions, but their interest in promoting the study of Chinese philosophy is extremely encouraging. I am also grateful to the American Council of Learned Societies and the Social Science Research Council for a research grant in 1959 as well as to Dartmouth College for financial aid in preparing this book. To Columbia University Press I express my appreciation for its kind permission to use certain translations which I contributed to two of its publications, *Sources of Chinese Tradition*, already mentioned, and *Instructions for Practical Living, and Other Neo-Confucian Writings by Wang Yang-ming*, translated by myself. These translations form small parts of present chapters 19, 24, 26, 28-35. I have made some changes in them. Many friends have been keenly interested in this work and have provided much inspiration. I particularly appreciate the encouragement of Professor Edwin A. Burtt of Cornell University and Professor Alban G. Widgery of Duke University. My colleague Professor Arthur Dewing, whom I have interrupted many a time, has been most patient and sympathetic in answering my queries on English usage. Professor Kenneth K. S. Ch'en of Princeton University has given me valuable help on many Sanskrit words, as have Professor

ACKNOWLEDGMENTS

Yuen Ren Chao of the University of California, Professor Tien-yi Li of Yale, and Professors William Hung and Lien-sheng Yang of Harvard on certain Chinese words and expressions. Mrs. Alice W. Weymouth was most helpful in typing the manuscript, which I sincerely appreciate. To Princeton University Press and its Director and Editor, Mr. Herbert S. Bailey, Jr., I wish to express my thanks for their generous aid and effort in the publication of this work, including a substantial contribution from the Press's university press publication fund. Mrs. James Holly Hanford, of Princeton University Press, has given me great help on the arrangement and literary expression of the work.

Above all I am forever indebted to two people. One is my wife. She has given me wholehearted support and in her many unselfish ways has helped to make this work possible. The other is my friend and former colleague Dr. Charles A. Moore of the University of Hawaii, who has kindly written the Foreword. Without him this book would not have been published and probably not even written. In fact, the project was started by us together. We had originally planned a one-volume source book on Asian philosophy and actually did much work on it. It was later found, however, that separate volumes on the several Asian philosophical traditions were necessary. The result has been *A Source Book in Indian Philosophy* by Dr. S. Radhakrishnan and Dr. Moore, Princeton University Press, 1957, and now this anthology.

Dartmouth College
January 1963

WING-TSIT CHAN

CHRONOLOGY OF DYNASTIES

Emperor Yao   (Legendary)   3rd millennium B.C.
Emperor Shun (Legendary)   3rd millennium B.C.
Hsia ⎫   2183-1752 B.C.?
Shang ⎬ (Three Dynasties)   1751-1112 B.C.   (or 1765-1112 B.C.)
Chou ⎭   1111- 249 B.C.   (or 1027- 249 B.C.)
                                                Spring and Autumn .... 722-481 B.C.
                                                Warring States (480-) .... 403-222 B.C.

Ch'in .... (255 B.C.-)   221-206 B.C.

Han .... B.C. 206-220 A.D.   Western (Former) Han B.C. 206- 8 A.D.
                                                    Hsin .... 9- 23 A.D.
                                                    Eastern (Later) Han .... 25-220 A.D.

Wei .... 220-265 A.D.

Three Kingdoms	Wei	220-265
	Shu	221-263
	Wu	222-280

Chin 265-420

Western Chin 265-317
Eastern Chin 317-420

S. and N. Dynasties 420-589

South		North	
Liu Sung	420-479	Later (North) Wei	386-535
Southern Ch'i	479-502	Eastern Wei	534-550
Liang	502-557	Western Wei	535-556
Ch'en	557-589	Northern Ch'i	550-577
		Northern Chou	557-581

Sui 581-618
Tang 618-907
Five Dynasties 907-960

Later Liang	907-923
Later T'ang	923-936
Later Chin	936-947
Later Han	947-950
Later Chou	951-960

Liao (907-) 947-1125
Sung   960-1279

Northern Sung   960-1126
Southern Sung 1127-1279

Hsi-hsia   990-1227
Chin   1115-1234
Yüan (Mongol) .... (1206-) 1271-1368
Ming 1368-1644
Ch'ing (Manchu) 1644-1912
Republic 1912-
People's Republic 1949-

CHRONOLOGY OF PHILOSOPHERS

ANCIENT PERIOD

Confucianism: *Confucius   Great Learning   Mencius*, 371-289 B.C.? ....
             551-479 B.C. *Doc. of the Mean   Hsün Tzu*, fl. 298-238 B.C. ......
Taoism: .... *Lao Tzu*, 6th or 4th cent. B.C.? *Chuang Tzu*, bet. 399 and 295 B.C. ......
Moism: .... *Mo Tzu*, fl. 479–438 B.C.
Logicians: ....*Hui Shih*, 380-305 B.C.
                               Kung-sun Lung, b. 380 B.C.?
Yin Yang: ....*Tsou Yen*, 305-240 B.C. ....
Legalism: ....*Han Fei*, d. 233 B.C. ......

MEDIEVAL PERIOD

Confucianism: *Book of*   *Tung Chung-shu*   *Yang Hsiung*
             Changes   c. 179–c. 104 B.C.   53 B.C.–A.D. 18
             Naturalism .... *Wang Ch'ung*, b. A.D. 27
Taoism and Neo-Taoism: *Huai-nan Tzu*, d. 122 B.C.

                                       Wang Pi, 226-249
                                       Kuo Hsiang, d. 312
                                       Lieh Tzu (Yang Chu)

Buddhism: *Seven Schools*, 4th cent.
             Seng-chao, 384-414
             Three-Treatise School, 4th-7th cent. ....
                Consciousness-Only School, 6th-9th cent. ....
                 T'ien-t'ai School, 6th cent. ....
                     Hua-yen School, 7th cent. ....
                         Zen School, 5th cent. ....
Confucian Revival: *Han Yü*, 768-824
                                 Li Ao, fl. 798

MODERN PERIOD

Sung Neo-Confucianism:
        Chou Tun-i (Chou Lien-hsi), 1017-1073
        Shao Yung, 1011-1077
        Chang Tsai (Chang Heng-ch'ü), 1020-1077
        Ch'eng Hao (Ch'eng Ming-tao), 1032-1085
        Ch'eng I (Ch'eng I-ch'uan), 1033-1107

                          Lu Hsiang-shan (Lu Chiu-yüan), 1139-1193
         School of Principle   *Chu Hsi,* 1130-1200 ....

Ming Neo-Confucianism: School of Mind   *Wang Yang-ming*
                                                  (Wang Shou-jen),
                                                  1472-1529 ....

Ch'ing Confucianism:
        Materialism: .... *Wang Fu-chih (Wang Ch'uan-shan)*, 1619-1692
        Practical Confucianism: .... *Yen Yüan*, 1635-1704
                              Li Kung, 1659-1735

        Principle as Order: .... *Tai Chen (Tai Tung-yüan)*, 1723-1777

CONTEMPORARY PERIOD

.... *K'ang Yu-wei*, 1858-1927
T'an Ssu-t'ung, 1865-1898
.... *Chang Tung-sun*, 1886-1962
.... *Fung Yu-lan*, 1890-
.... *Hsiung Shih-li*, 1885-1968

Communism, 1949-

For more detailed chronological charts, see Wing-tsit Chan,
Historical Charts of Chinese Philosophy, New Haven,
Far Eastern Publications, Yale University, 1955.

CONTENTS

* An analytical content is found at the end of the Introduction to the chapter.

CONTENTS

CONTENTS

A SOURCE BOOK IN
CHINESE PHILOSOPHY

ABBREVIATIONS AND ABRIDGMENTS

CTTC *Chu Tzu ta-ch'üan* (Complete Literary Works
       of Chu Hsi), SPPY
ECCS *Erh-Ch'eng ch'üan-shu* (Complete Works
       of the Two Ch'engs), SPPY
NHCC *Nan-hua chen-ching* (Pure Classic of Nan-hua,
       another name for the *Chuang Tzu*), SPTK
PNP   *Po-na pen* (Choice Works Edition)
SPPY *Ssu-pu pei-yao* (Essentials of the
       Four Libraries) edition
SPTK *Ssu-pu ts'ung-k'an* (*Four Libraries*
       Series) edition
TSD   *Taishō shinshū daizōkyō* (Taishō Edition
       of the Buddhist Canon)
Changes   The Book of Changes
History   The Book of History
Mencius   The Book of Mencius
Odes   The Book of Odes
The Mean The Doctrine of the Mean

Full publication facts for titles abbreviated or abridged
in the footnotes are given in the Bibliography.

THE GROWTH OF HUMANISM

IF ONE WORD could characterize the entire history of Chinese philosophy, that word would be humanism—not the humanism that denies or slights a Supreme Power, but one that professes the unity of man and Heaven. In this sense, humanism has dominated Chinese thought from the dawn of its history.

Humanism was an outgrowth, not of speculation, but of historical and social change. The conquest of the Shang (1751–1112 B.C.) by the Chou in 1111 B.C. inaugurated a transition from tribal society to feudal. To consolidate the empire, the Chou challenged human ingenuity and ability, cultivated new trades and talents, and encouraged the development of experts from all levels of society. Prayers for rain were gradually replaced by irrigation. *Ti*, formerly the tribal Lord, became the God for all. Man and his activities were given greater importance. The time finally arrived when a slave became a prime minister. Humanism, in gradual ascendance, reached its climax in Confucius.

Having overthrown the Shang, founders of the Chou had to justify their right to rule. Consequently, they developed the doctrine of the Mandate of Heaven, a self-existent moral law whose constant, reliable factor was virtue. According to this doctrine, man's destiny—both mortal and immortal—depended, not upon the existence of a soul before birth or after death nor upon the whim of a spiritual force, but upon his own good words and good deeds. The Chou asserted, therefore, that the Shang, though they had received the mandate to rule, had forfeited it because they failed in their duties. The mandate then passed on to the founders of Chou, who deserved it because of their virtue. Obviously, the future of the house of Chou depended upon whether future rulers were virtuous.

The idea that the destiny of man or the future of a dynasty depended upon virtue rather than upon the pleasure of some mysterious, spiritual power marked a radical development from the Shang to the Chou. (Significantly, the term *te* [virtue] is not found in the oracle bones on which Shang ideas and events are recorded, but it is a key word in early Chou documents.) During the Shang, the influence of spiritual beings on man had been almost total, for no important thing could be done without first seeking their approval, but in the Chou (1111–249 B.C.) their dwelling places were regulated by the rulers. As the *Book of Rites* says, "The people of Yin (Shang) honor spiritual beings, serve them, and put them ahead of ceremonies. . . . The people of Chou honor ceremonies and highly value the conferring of favors. They serve the spiritual beings and respect them, but keep them at a distance. They remain near to man and loyal to him."[1]

Similarly, belief in the Lord underwent a radical transformation. In the Shang, he was the supreme anthropomorphic deity who sent blessings or calamities, gave protection in battles, sanctioned undertakings, and passed on the appointment or dismissal of officials. Such belief continued in the early Chou, but was gradually replaced by the concept of Heaven (*T'ien*) as the supreme spiritual reality.[2] This does not mean that either Heaven or spiritual beings did not continue to be highly honored and greatly respected. But their personal power was supplanted by human virtue and human effort, and man, through his moral deeds, could now control his own destiny.

It was in this light that ancestors were regarded in Chou times. During the Shang, great ancestors were either identified with the Lord,[3] or considered as mediators through whom requests were made to the Lord. In the Chou, they were still influential but, as in the case of Heaven, their influence was exerted not through their power but through their moral example and inspiration. They were to be respected but to be kept from interfering with human activities. Individual and social categories were to be stated in moral terms according to a "Great Norm."

The above beliefs are illustrated in the following selections. They are taken from the *Book of History*,[4] the *Book of Odes*,[5] the *Tso chuan* (Tso's Commentary on the *Spring and Autumn Annals*),[6] and the *Kuo-*

[1] *Book of Rites*, "Record of Example," pt. 2. See Legge, trans., *Li Ki*, vol. 1, p. 342.

[2] On this question, see Dubs, "The Archaic Royal Jou (Chou) Religion," *T'oung Pao*, 46 (1959), 218-259.

[3] According to Kuo Mo-jo, *Ch'ing-t'ung shih-tai* (The Bronze Age), 1946, pp. 9-12, and Fu Ssu-nien, *Hsing-ming ku-hsün pien-cheng* (Critical Studies of the Classical Interpretations of the Nature and Destiny), 1940, 2:3a.

[4] The *Book of History*, a basic Confucian Classic, is a collection of documents from the time of legendary Emperor Yao (3rd millennium B.C.) to the early Chou. Twenty-five of the fifty-eight chapters are believed to be forgeries by Wang Su (195-256), Huang-fu Mi (215-282), or Mei Tse (of the Eastern Chin period, 317-420). Of the rest, modern scholars accept only the Chou documents as authentic. The selections presented here are from this group. For English translation, see Legge, trans., *Shoo King*.

[5] The *Book of Odes*, also a basic Confucian Classic, is a collection of 305 poems, including songs sung in religious and early official functions and popular songs from the various states of early Chou times. Five are supposed to have come from the Shang dynasty. Tradition holds that Confucius selected these from three thousand prevailing songs, a belief rejected by modern scholars. It is agreed, however, that many of the songs had been popular and that Confucius knew them. For English translations, see Karlgren, trans., *The Book of Odes*, and Waley, trans., *The Book of Songs*.

[6] This has been traditionally attributed to Tso Ch'iu-ming, a contemporary of

yü (Conversations of the States).[7] The former two contain the oldest material of Chinese literature. Although the latter two are much later works, they record events of pre-Confucian times.

1. ANCESTORS AND THE LORD ON HIGH

Abundant is the year, with much millet and much rice,
And we have tall granaries,
With hundreds of thousands and millions of units.
We make wine and sweet spirits
And offer them to our ancestors, male and female,
Thus to fulfill all the rites,
And bring down blessings to all.

    (*Book of Odes*, ode no. 279, "Abundant is the Year")

Heaven produces the teeming multitude;
As there are things, there are their specific principles (*tse*).
When the people keep to their normal nature,
They will love excellent virtue.
Heaven, looking down upon the House of Chou
Sees that its light reaches the people below,[8]
And to protect the Son of Heaven,
Gave birth to Chung Shan-fu [to help him].[9]

    (*ibid.*, ode no. 260, "The Teeming Multitude")

Comment. Neo-Confucianists, injecting a more metaphysical sense into the second line of this ode, made it mean that inherent in every single thing there are specific principles about its being. There

---

Confucius, and is regarded as a commentary on the *Spring and Autumn Annals* (*Ch'un-ch'iu*) which records the events of the state of Lu during the Spring and Autumn period (722–481 B.C.). The authorship of the *Spring and Autumn Annals* has been ascribed to Confucius, who was a native of Lu. Its records are so brief and often so obscure that commentaries were necessary to supply the background and context and to make the meanings clear. Of three commentaries, the *Tso chuan* is the standard. For English translation, see Legge, trans., *The Ch'un Ts'ew, with The Tso Tsuen*. Modern scholarship, however, holds that the *Tso chuan* is probably an independent work and was not written until the 4th century B.C.

[7] Also attributed to Tso Ch'iu-ming, though not by modern scholars, who believe that the work was probably edited by Liu Hsin (c. 46 B.C.–A.D. 23). However, they accept it as an authentic record of conversations in various states during the Spring and Autumn period. For French translation, see de Harlez, trans., "Koue-Yü," 1st pt., *Journal Asiatique*, vol. 9, no. 1 (1893), 373-419, no. 2 (1894), 5-91; 2nd pt., *Discours des Royaumes*, 1895, pp. 1-268.

[8] The interpretation of this line varies. That of the *Mao-shih cheng-i* (Correct Meanings of the *Book of Odes* Transmitted by Mao) by K'ung Ying-ta (574-648) is followed here.

[9] Chung Shan-fu was Marquis of Fan, according to the *Mao-shih cheng-i*, a very virtuous man, whom Heaven sent out to help King Hsüan (r. 827–782 B.C.).

is no doubt, however, that from very early days the Chinese believed that existence implies a certain principle. Significantly, the word tse[10] means not just principle but *specific* principle, though perhaps it did not have this meaning at the time when the poem was written. In any case, those who believe that, to the Chinese, reality is something like an undifferentiated void should revise their opinion in the light of this long tradition of specific principles for specific things. Mencius, it is to be noted, quoted this poem to support his theory of the originally good nature of man.[11]

2. THE MANDATE OF HEAVEN, ANCESTORS, AND VIRTUE

The Mandate of Heaven,
How beautiful and unceasing!
Oh, how glorious
Was the purity of King Wen's[12] virtue!
With blessings he overwhelms us.
We will receive the blessings.
They are a great favor from our King Wen.
May his descendants hold fast to them.
(*ibid*., ode no. 267, "The Mandate of Heaven")

Comment. Both Cheng Hsüan (127–200)[13] and Chu Hsi (1130–1200)[14] remarked that the Mandate of Heaven (*T'ien-ming*) means the "Way" or the moral order of Heaven (*T'ien-tao*), thus interpreting it in the naturalistic sense. However, in early Chou the belief in an anthropomorphic God was still quite strong.

Thus Duke Chou (d. 1094 B.C.) said, "Prince Shih,[15] Heaven, without pity, sent down ruin on the Yin dynasty (1384–1112 B.C.). Yin having lost the Mandate of Heaven, we, the Chou, have received it. But I dare not say with certainty that our heritage will forever truly remain on the side of fortune. If Heaven renders sincere help, I do not dare say with certainty that the final end will result in misfortune. Oh! you have said, Prince, 'It depends on ourselves.' I also dare not rest in the Mandate of

[10] For a good discussion of the term *tse*, see Needham, *Science and Civilization in China*, vol. 2: *History of Scientific Thought*, pp. 558–562.
[11] *Mencius*, 6A:6.
[12] Founder of Chou (r. 1171–1122 B.C.).
[13] Quoted in *Mao-shih cheng-i*.
[14] See his *Shih-ching chi-chu* (Collected Commentaries on the *Book of Odes*).
[15] Name of Duke Shao (d. 1056 B.C.). Presumably this was written by Duke Chou to dissuade Prince Shih from retiring as chief minister to King Ch'eng (r. 1104–1068 B.C.).

the Lord on High, forever refraining from thinking of the awe-inspiring power of Heaven. At the same time when the péople do not complain, so long are there men [like you]! If our successors should prove utterly unable to reverence Heaven above and the people below, and so bring to an end the glory of their forefathers, could you, by remaining at home, be unaware of it?

"The Mandate of Heaven is not easily [preserved]. Heaven is hard to depend on. Those who have lost the mandate did so because they could not practice and carry on the reverence and the brilliant virtue of their forefathers. As for the present, it is not that I, a little one, have a way of correcting our king. My way of leading him would be merely to make it possible to apply the glory of the forefathers to our young king."

Duke Chou also said, "Heaven is not to be trusted. My way is simply to continue and extend the virtue of our peace-establishing king, and Heaven will not have occasion to remove the mandate received by King Wen. . . ." (*Book of History*, "Prince Shih")

They (descendants of Yin) became subject to Chou.
Heaven's Mandate is not constant.
The officers of Yin were fine and alert.
They assist at the libation in our capital.
In their assisting in the libation,
They always wear skirted robes and close caps [peculiar to Yin].
Oh, you promoted servants of the king,
Don't you mind your ancestors!

Don't you mind your ancestors!
Cultivate your virtue.
Always strive to be in harmony with Heaven's Mandate.
Seek for yourselves the many blessings.
Before Yin lost its army,
Its kings were able to be counterparts to the Lord on High.
In Yin you should see as in a mirror
That the great mandate is not easy [to keep].
      (*Book of Odes*, ode no. 235, "King Wen")

   Comment. The line "Don't you mind your ancestors" has given scholars a great deal of trouble. Because of the deep Chinese reverence for ancestors, they could not see how the advice not to mind the ancestors could be consonant with Confucianism. Therefore Legge had to drop the word "don't" ("Ever think of your ancestors"),[16] Karlgren had to turn it into a question ("Should

---

[16] Legge, trans., *She King*, p. 431.

you not think of your ancestors?"),[17] and Waley had to interpret the term "to mind" to mean "shame."[18] If we realize that humanism was growing strong, and that the emphasis was on self-dependence rather than dependence on Heaven or ancestors, there is no need to twist the original and obvious meaning of the text to conform to any earlier or later custom of ancestor worship.

> The Lord on High said to King Wen:
> "I cherish your brilliant virtue,
> Which makes no great display in sound or appearance,
> Nor is changed with age.[19]
> Without any manipulation or deliberation,[20]
> You follow the principles of the Lord."
>   (*ibid.*, ode no. 241, "August")

"Let the king first bring under his influence the administrators of the affairs of Yin and place them in the midst of the administrators of the affairs of our Chou. Their natures will thus be regulated, and they will improve daily.

"Let the king be serious in what he does. He should not neglect to be serious with virtue." (*Book of History*, "The Announcement of Duke Shao")

> *Comment.* The emphasis on virtue necessarily raises the question of man's original nature. This eventually became one of the most persistent questions, perhaps the most persistent, in the history of Chinese philosophy. But the question was not specifically discussed until Mencius' time. Here is the earliest reference to it. Since nature has to be regulated, especially in the sense of restraint, the implication is that man's nature is originally indifferent or perhaps even evil, which is quite different from the later-established doctrine that human nature is originally good.

3. THE "GREAT NORM"

In the thirteenth year (1121 B.C.) the King [Wu] visited Viscount Chi. The King said, "Oh! Viscount Chi. Heaven, working unseen, has decisively made men with certain hidden springs of character, aiding also the harmonious development of it in their various conditions. I do

[17] *The Book of Odes*, p. 186.

[18] *The Book of Songs*, p. 186.

[19] This is a very obscure line. The interpretation here follows the *Mao-shih cheng-i.*

[20] This is the interpretation of many outstanding commentators, as pointed out by Ch'ü Wan-li, *Shih-ching shih-i* (Meanings of the *Book of Odes* Explained), 1952, p. 214.

not know how the various virtues and their relations should be regulated."[21]

Viscount Chi thereupon replied, "I have heard that of old (Great Yü's father) Kun dammed up the flood and thereby created a chaos among the Five Agents. The Lord (of Heaven) was aroused to anger and did not give him the Great Norm with its Nine Categories. The various virtues and their relations declined in due course, and K'un was executed. Yü thereupon rose to continue the heritage. Heaven gave him the Great Norm with its Nine Categories. And the various virtues and their relations were regulated. . . .

"The first category is the Five Agents (Five Elements); namely, Water, Fire, Wood, Metal, and Earth [which correspond to various human activities]. . . .[22] The second category is the Five Activities; namely, appearance, speech, seeing, hearing, and thinking. The virtue of appearance is respectfulness; that of speech is accordance [with reason]; that of seeing is clearness; that of hearing is distinctness; and that of thinking is penetration and profundity. Respectfulness leads to gravity; accordance with reason, to orderliness; clearness, to wisdom; distinctness, to deliberation; and penetration and profundity, to sageness [all of which should be cultivated by the ruler]. The third category is the Eight Governmental Offices; namely, those of food, commodities, sacrifices, public works, education, and justice, the reception of guests, and the army. [All these functions should be fulfilled in harmony with the next category.] The fourth category is the Five Arrangements of Time, namely, the year, the month, the day, the stars, planets, zodiacal signs, and the calendaric calculations. The fifth category is the Supreme Standard. The sovereign, having established the highest standard, gathers in him the Five Blessings and spreads over his people. Then the people, following your standard, preserve it with you. . . .

"The sixth category is the Three Virtues; namely, correctness and uprightness, strong government, and weak government. In times of peace and tranquillity, apply correctness and uprightness; in times of violence and disorder, apply strong government; and in times of harmony and order, apply weak government.[23] Apply strong government to the reserved and retiring, and apply weak government to the lofty and intelligent. . . . The seventh category is the Examination of Doubts. Select

[21] The interpretation of this passage is based on the *Shang-shu cheng-i* (Correct Meanings of the *Book of History*) by K'ung Ying-ta. An alternate translation would be: "Heaven, working unseen, protects mankind below and helps it to maintain harmony in its abode. I do not know how its eternal principles of human relations should be regulated."

[22] This paragraph in full is found below, ch. 11, sec. 3.

[23] This interpretation also follows the *Shang-shu cheng-i*.

and appoint officers for divination by tortoise shells and by stalks, and command them thus to divine. . . . The calculation of the passage of events is the function of experts whose duty it is to perform the divination. When three of them divine, follow the words of two of them. If you have any doubt about important matters, consult with your own conscience, consult with your ministers and officers, consult with the common people, and consult the tortoise shells and stalks. If you, the tortoise shells, the stalks, the ministers and officers, and the common people all agree, this is called a great concord. There will be welfare to your own person and prosperity to your descendants. The result will be auspicious. If you, the tortoise shells, and the stalks agree but the ministers and officers and the common people oppose, the result will be auspicious. If the ministers and officers, the tortoise shells, and the stalks agree but you and the common people oppose, the result will be auspicious. If the common people, the tortoise shells, and the stalks agree but you and the ministers and the officers oppose, the result will be auspicious. If you and the tortoise shells agree but the stalks, ministers and officers, and the common people oppose, internal operations will be auspicious but external operations will be unlucky. If both the tortoise shells and stalks oppose the views of men, inactivity will be auspicious but active operations will be unlucky.

"The eighth category is the General Verifications [that is, checking governmental measures against natural phenomena], namely, rain, sunshine, heat, cold, wind, and seasonableness [corresponding to the Five Agents]. When the five all come and are complete, and each in its proper order, even the common grain will be luxuriant. . . . The ninth category is the Five Blessings, namely, longevity, wealth, physical and mental health, cultivation of excellent virtue, and an end crowning a good life.

"Negatively, these are the Six Extremities [a punishment for evil conduct]; namely, premature death, sickness, sorrow, poverty, wickedness, and weakness." (*Book of History*, "Great Norm")

> *Comment.* This document is important for two reasons. One is that it contains the doctrine of the Five Agents (which will be dealt with later). The other is that it encompasses early Chinese ideas about the interrelationship of nature (categories nos. 1, 5, 8), the cultivation of personal life (nos. 2 and 6), government (nos. 3, 4, 6), retribution (no. 9), and a central principle, the Supreme Standard (no. 5). Heaven, Earth, and man are correlated, preparing for the later development of the doctrine of the unity of man and Nature that was to dominate the course of Chinese history. Some scholars

think that this document is much later than the twelfth century B.C., but concrete proof is lacking. Besides, its spirit is perfectly consonant with that of the songs of Early Chou, that is, that the power of Heaven is recognized, but the deciding factor is human virtue.

4. SPIRITS, THE SOUL, AND IMMORTALITY

In the fifteenth year (of King Hui, 662 B.C.), a spiritual being descended, and appeared in Hsin. The King asked his minister Kuo, saying, "Why is this? Is there such a thing?"

Kuo replied, "Yes. When a state is about to rise, its ruler is solemn, illustrious, sincere, and correct. He is discriminating, pure, kind, and affable. His virtue is sufficient to make his fragrant offerings manifest, and his kindness is sufficient to unify the people. As the spiritual beings enjoy his offerings and the people listen to him, neither the people nor the spiritual beings have any complaint. Therefore brilliant spiritual beings descend in his state, see the evidence of the virtue of the government, and spread blessings everywhere. When the state is about to perish, its ruler is greedy, reckless, depraved, and perverted. He is lewd, indolent, negligent, and lazy. He is vulgar and cruel. Because his government has a disgusting odor, his offerings do not rise [to reach the spiritual beings]. And because his punishments are imposed on the basis of treachery and slander, his people desert him and divert their loyalty elsewhere. The brilliant spiritual beings no longer give him purification, and his people want to leave him.[24] Both the people and the spiritual beings blame him and hate him, and there is nothing in him for them to cling to. The spiritual beings likewise go to such a state, see the evidence of oppression and evil, and send down calamity." (*Kuo-yü* or Conversations of the States, SPPY, 1:11a-12b)

The Marquis of Chin again (in 655 B.C.) borrowed a way through Yü to attack Kuo. (Great Officer) Kung Chih-ch'i remonstrated with him. . . . The marquis said, "My sacrificial offerings have been abundant and pure. Spiritual beings will comfort me."[25]

Kung Chih-ch'i replied, "I have heard that spiritual beings are not endeared to man as such but cleave only to virtue. Therefore it is said in the 'Book of Chou' that 'August Heaven has no affections; it helps only the virtuous.'[26] It further says, 'It is not the millet that has the fragrance [which attracts the spiritual beings]. Illustrious virtue alone has the

[24] According to the commentary by Wei Chao (of the Wu period, 222-280), to rebel against him.

[25] According to the *Ch'un-ch'iu Tso chuan cheng-i* (Correct Meanings of Tso's Commentary on the *Spring and Autumn Annals*) by K'ung Ying-ta, *chü* here means to comfort.

[26] *History*, "Charge to Chung of Ts'ai." Cf. Legge, *Shoo King*, p. 490.

fragrance.'[27] It also says, 'People have not slighted the things, but it is virtue that makes things acceptable.'[28] Therefore if a ruler acts against virtue, his people will not be attached to him and spiritual beings will not accept his offerings. It is virtue that the spiritual beings will adhere to." (*Tso chuan*, Tso's Commentary on the *Spring and Autumn Annals*, Duke Hsi, 5th year)

[In 535 B.C.] the people of Cheng frightened one another about Po-yu [who was a drunkard],[29] crying, "Po-yu has arrived." They all ran off, not knowing where they were going. In the second month of the year when the criminal code was cast, someone dreamed that Po-yu walked by him in armor and said, "In the year *jen-tzu* I will kill Tai and the next year, the year *jen-yin*, I will kill Tuan. When Ssu Tai did die in the year *jen-tzu*, the terror of the people increased. Then when in the year *jen-yin*, in the month that the Ch'i and Yen states made peace, Kung-sun Tuan died, the terror of the people increased further. It did not stop until the next month when [Prime Minister] Tzu-ch'an appointed Kung-sun Hsieh and [Po-yu's son] Liang-chih [as successors to their fathers] in order to pacify them. Tzu Ta-shu asked him for the reason. Tzu-ch'an replied, "When spiritual beings have a place to return to, they will not become malicious. I have given them a place to return to. . . ."

When Tzu-ch'an went to Chin, Chao Ching Tzu asked him, "Can even Po-yu become a spiritual being?" Tzu-ch'an answered, "Yes, he could. In man's life the first transformations are called the earthly aspect of the soul (*p'o*). After *p'o* has been produced, that which is strong and positive is called the heavenly aspect of the soul (*hun*).[30] If he had an abundance in the use of material things and subtle essentials, his *hun* and *p'o* will become strong. From this are developed essence and understanding until there are spirit and intelligence. When an ordinary man or woman dies a violent death, the *hun* and *p'o* are still able to keep hanging about men and do evil and malicious things. How much more would be the case of Po-yu, a descendant of Duke Mu (r. 659–619 B.C.), the grandson of Tzu-liang, the son of Tzu-erh, all ministers of our state, engaged in government for three generations! Cheng is not a great state but a small, insignificant one; nevertheless, because his family had administered the government for three generations, his use of material things must have been extensive and his enjoyment of subtle essentials

---

[27] *ibid.*, "Prince Ch'en," Legge, p. 539.

[28] *ibid.*, "Hounds of Lü," Legge, pp. 347-348.

[29] For an account of him, see *Tso chuan*, Duke Hsiang, 30th year. Cf. Legge, *The Ch'un Ch'ew, with The Tso Tsuen*, p. 557.

[30] As generally understood, *hun* is the spirit of man's vital force which is expressed in man's intelligence and power of breathing, whereas *p'o* is the spirit of man's physical nature which is expressed in bodily movements.

abundant. Furthermore, his clan is large and there was much to which he could cling. Is it not proper that having died a violent death he should become a spiritual being?" (*ibid.*, Duke Chao, 7th year)

In the spring of the twenty-fourth year (of Duke Hsiang, 546 B.C.), Mu-shu (great officer of Lu) went to Chin. Fan Hsüan Tzu met him, saying, "The ancients had the saying 'Dead but immortal.' What does it mean?"

Before Mu-shu replied, Hsüan Tzu went on to say, "Anciently, the ancestors of our Fan family, from the time of Emperor Shun (3rd millennium B.C.) and earlier, were the Princes of T'ao and T'ang. In the time of Hsia (2183–1752 B.C.?), their ancestors were the lords of Yü-lung. In the time of Shang, they were the lords of Shih-wei. And in the beginning of Chou, they were the lords of T'ang and Tu. Now Chin has achieved the control of the great alliance and become the lords of Fan. Is this [unbroken heritage] what is meant by immortality?"

Mu-shu said, "According to what I have heard, this is called hereditary rank and emolument, not immortality. There was a former great officer of Lu by the name of Tsang Wen-chung. After his death his words remain established. This is what the ancient saying means. I have heard that the best course is to establish virtue, the next best is to establish achievement, and still the next best is to establish words. When these are not abandoned with time, it may be called immortality. As to the preservation of the family name and bestowment of membership in the clan branch in order to preserve ancestral sacrifices uninterrupted from age to age, no state is without these practices. But even those with great emolument cannot be said to be immortal." (*ibid.*, Duke Hsiang, 24th year)

> *Comment.* Chinese belief in the immortality of influence has not changed since ancient times, and is still the conviction of educated Chinese. It is remarkable that a simple and casual utterance made when Confucius was only a child of three should have remained an unalterable conviction for the Chinese for 2,500 years.

2

THE HUMANISM OF CONFUCIUS

CONFUCIUS (551–479 B.C.) can truly be said to have molded Chinese civilization in general. It may seem far-fetched, however, to say that he molded Chinese philosophy in particular—that he determined the direction or established the pattern of later Chinese philosophical developments—yet there is more truth in the statement than is usually realized.

Neo-Confucianism, the full flowering of Chinese thought, developed during the last eight hundred years. Its major topics of debate, especially in the Sung (960-1279) and Ming (1368-1644) periods, are the nature and principle (*li*) of man and things. (For this reason it is called the School of Nature and Principle, or *Hsing-li hsüeh*.) Supplementary to these topics are the problems of material force (*ch'i*); yin and yang (passive and active cosmic forces or elements); *T'ai-chi* (Great Ultimate); being and non-being; substance and function; and the unity of Nature and man. Confucius had nothing to do with these problems, and never discussed them. In fact, the words *li, yin, yang,* and *t'ai-chi* are not found in the *Lun-yü* (Discourses or *Analects*). The word *ch'i* appears several times, but is not used in the sense of material force.[1] And Confucius' pupils said that they could not hear the Master's views on human nature and the Way of Heaven.[2] He did not talk about human nature except once, when he said that "by nature men are alike. Through practice they have become far apart,"[3] but the theory is entirely different from the later orthodox doctrine of the Confucian school that human nature is originally good.

The present discussion is based on the *Analects*, which is generally accepted as the most reliable source of Confucius' doctrines. The subject of "the investigation of things" originated in the *Great Learning* and most of the other topics are mentioned in the *Book of Changes*.[4] But these two Classics are not generally regarded as Confucius' own works. Furthermore, even if they were, the subjects are only briefly mentioned without elaboration. It is correct then to say that the Neo-Confucianists drew their inspiration from them or made use of them to support their

---

[1] *Analects*, 8:4; 10:4 and 8; 16:7. In the rest of this introduction, references to the *Analects* are given only in specific cases. For references on general subjects, see the analytical list at the end of this introduction. For discussion of the *Analects*, see below, n.11.

[2] *Analects*, 5:12.   [3] *ibid.*, 17:2.

[4] For these Classics, see below, ch. 4, n.5, and ch. 13, n.1.

own ideas, but it would be going too far to suggest that they provided an outline or framework for later Chinese philosophy.

However, judging on the basis of the *Analects* alone, we find that Confucius exerted great influence on Chinese philosophical development in that, first of all, he determined its outstanding characteristic, namely, humanism.

As pointed out in the previous chapter, the humanistic tendency had been in evidence long before his time. But it was Confucius who turned it into the strongest driving force in Chinese philosophy. He did not care to talk about spiritual beings or even about life after death. Instead, believing that man "can make the Way (Tao) great," and not that "the Way can make man great,"[5] he concentrated on man. His primary concern was a good society based on good government and harmonious human relations. To this end he advocated a good government that rules by virtue and moral example rather than by punishment or force. His criterion for goodness was righteousness as opposed to profit. For the family, he particularly stressed filial piety and for society in general, proper conduct or *li* (propriety, rites).

More specifically, he believed in the perfectibility of all men, and in this connection he radically modified a traditional concept, that of the *chün-tzu*, or superior man. Literally "son of the ruler," it came to acquire the meaning of "superior man," on the theory that nobility was a quality determined by status, more particularly a hereditary position. The term appears 107 times in the *Analects*. In some cases it refers to the ruler. In most cases, however, Confucius used it to denote a morally superior man. In other words, to him nobility was no longer a matter of blood, but of character—a concept that amounted to social revolution. Perhaps it is more correct to say that it was an evolution, but certainly it was Confucius who firmly established the new concept. His repeated mention of sage-emperors Yao and Shun and Duke Chou[6] as models seems to suggest that he was looking back to the past. Be that as it may, he was looking to ideal men rather than to a supernatural being for inspiration.

Not only did Confucius give Chinese philosophy its humanistic foundation, but he also formulated some of its fundamental concepts, five of which will be briefly commented on here: the rectification of names, the Mean, the Way, Heaven, and *jen* (humanity). In insisting on the rectification of names, Confucius was advocating not only the establishment of a social order in which names and ranks are properly regulated, but also the correspondence of words and action, or in its more philosophical

[5] *Analects*, 15:28.

[6] Yao was a legendary ruler of the 3rd millennium B.C. Shun was his successor. Duke Chou (d. 1094) helped the founder of the Chou dynasty to consolidate the empire and establish the foundations of Chinese culture.

aspect, the correspondence of name and actuality. This has been a perennial theme in the Confucian school, as well as in nearly all other schools. By the Mean, Confucius did not have in mind merely moderation, but that which is central and balanced. This, too, has been a cardinal idea in Chinese thought. In a real sense, the later Neo-Confucian ideas of the harmony of yin and yang and that of substance and function did not go beyond this concept. In his interpretation of Heaven, he departed from traditional belief even more radically. Up to the time of Confucius, the Supreme Power was called *Ti* (the Lord) or *Shang-ti* (the Lord on High) and was understood in an anthropomorphic sense. Confucius never spoke of *Ti*. Instead, he often spoke of *T'ien* (Heaven). To be sure, his Heaven is purposive and is the master of all things. He repeatedly referred to the *T'ien-ming*, the Mandate, will, or order of Heaven. However, with him Heaven is no longer the greatest of all spiritual beings who rules in a personal manner but a Supreme Being who only reigns, leaving his Moral Law to operate by itself. This is the Way according to which civilization should develop and men should behave. It is the Way of Heaven (*T'ien-tao*), later called the Principle of Heaven or Nature (*T'ien-li*).

Most important of all, he evolved the new concept of *jen* which was to become central in Chinese philosophy. All later discussions on principle and material force may be said to serve the purpose of helping man to realize *jen*.[7] The word *jen* is not found in the oracle bones. It is found only occasionally in pre-Confucian texts, and in all these cases it denotes the particular virtue of kindness, more especially the kindness of a ruler to his subjects. In Confucius, however, all this is greatly changed. In the first place, Confucius made *jen* the main theme of his conversations. In the *Analects* fifty-eight of 499 chapters are devoted to the discussion of *jen*, and the word appears 105 times. No other subject, not even filial piety, engaged so much attention of the Master and his disciples. Furthermore, instead of perpetuating the ancient understanding of *jen* as a particular virtue, he transformed it into general virtue. It is true that in a few cases *jen* is still used by Confucius as a particular virtue, in the sense of benevolence. But in most cases, to Confucius the man of *jen* is the perfect man. He is the true *chün-tzu*. He is a man of the golden rule, for, "wishing to establish his own character, he also establishes the character of others, and wishing to be prominent himself, he also helps others to be prominent."[8] In these balanced and harmonized aspects of the self and society, *jen* is expressed in terms of *chung* and *shu*, or conscientious-

[7] For this concept, see Chan, "The Evolution of the Confucian Concept *Jen*," *Philosophy East and West*, 4 (1955), 295-319; also, see below, comment on *Analects* 12:22, and comments on the following: ch. 30, A; ch. 31, secs. 1, 11; ch. 32, sec. 42; ch. 34, A, treatise 1.

[8] *Analects*, 6:28.

ness and altruism, which is the "one thread" running through Confucius' teachings, and which is in essence the golden mean as well as the golden rule. It was the extension of this idea of *jen* that became the Neo-Confucian doctrine of man's forming one body with Heaven, or the unity of man and Nature, and it was because of the character of *jen* in man that later Confucianists have adhered to the theory of the original good nature of man.

It is clear, therefore, that Confucius was a creator as well as a transmitter. He was not a philosopher in a technical sense, but Chinese philosophy would be quite different if he had not lived. He was born in 551 (or 552) B.C. in the state of Lu in modern Shantung. His family name was K'ung, private name Ch'iu, and he has been traditionally honored as Grand Master K'ung (K'ung Fu-tzu, hence the Latinized form Confucius). He was a descendant of a noble but fairly poor family. His father died when Confucius was probably three years old. Evidently a self-made man, he studied under no particular teacher but became perhaps the most learned man of his time.

He began his career in his twenties or thirties. He was the first person in Chinese history to devote his whole life, almost exclusively, to teaching. He sought to inaugurate private education, to open the door of education to all, to offer education for training character instead of for vocation, and to gather around him a group of gentlemen-scholars (thus starting the institution of the literati who have dominated Chinese history and society). *never turned away poor students*

In his younger years Confucius had served in minor posts in Lu. At fifty-one he was made a magistrate, and became minister of justice the same year, perhaps serving as an assistant minister of public works in between. At fifty-six, finding his superiors uninterested in his policies, he set out to travel (for almost thirteen years) in a desperate attempt at political and social reform. He took some of his pupils along with him. Eventually disappointed, he returned, at the age of sixty-eight, to his own state to teach and perhaps to write and edit the Classics. According to the *Shih chi* (Records of the Historian),[9] he had three thousand pupils, seventy-two of whom mastered the "six arts."[10] He died at the age of seventy-three.

[9] These accounts are found in the first—and still the standard—biography of Confucius, ch. 47 of the *Shih chi*. See French translation by Chavannes, *Les mémoires historiques*, vol. 5, pp. 299-300, 391-403, 420; or English translation by Lin Yutang, *The Wisdom of Confucius*, pp. 57, 88-91, 95.

[10] Traditionally believed to refer to the Six Classics, i.e., the Books of *History*, *Odes*, *Changes*, *Rites*, and *Music*, and the *Spring and Autumn Annals*. The *Book of Music* is now lost. For three of the others, see above, ch. 1, nn.4-6. The "six

Many Chinese scholars, especially in the last several decades, have debated such questions as whether he actually made a trip some time in his forties to see Lao Tzu to inquire about ancient rites and ceremonies, whether he wrote the *Ch'un-ch'iu* (*Spring and Autumn Annals*), edited the other ancient Classics, and wrote the "ten wings" or commentaries of one of them, namely, the *Book of Changes*. After having once rejected these claims, many scholars are now inclined to believe them. The controversy has by no means ended. At the same time, the fact that the *Analects* is the most reliable source of Confucius' teachings is accepted by practically all scholars. For this reason, the following selections are made entirely from this book.

Ceremonies and Music: 1:12; 2:5; 3:3-4, 17, 19; 6:25; 8:8
Confucius: 2:4; 5:25; 6:26; 7:1, 2, 7, 8, 16, 18-20, 37; 9:1, 4; 10:9, 14; 14:30, 37, 41; 18:6; 19:24
Education and Learning: 1:1, 6, 8, 14; 2:11, 15; 6:25; 7:7, 2, 24; 15:38; 16:9; 17:8; 19:6
Filial piety: 1:2, 6, 11; 2:5, 7; 4:18, 19, 21
Government: 2:1, 3; 3:19; 8:9, 14; 12:7, 11, 17, 19; 13:3, 6, 16, 29, 30; 14:45; 15:4; 16:1
Heaven, Spirits, Destiny: 2:4; 3:12, 13; 5:12; 6:20, 26; 7:20, 22, 34; 9:1, 5, 6; 11:8, 11; 12:5; 14:37; 16:8; 17:19
Humanism: 6:20; 10:12; 11:11; 12:22; 15:28; 18:6
Humanity (*jen*): 1:2, 3, 6; 3:3; 4:2-6; 6:20, 21, 28; 7:6, 29; 8:7; 12:1, 2, 22; 13:19, 27; 14:30; 15:8, 32, 35; 17:6, 8; 19:6
Knowledge and Wisdom: 2:17, 18; 4:2; 6:18, 20, 21; 7:27; 12:22; 14:30; 15:32; 16:9
Literature and Art: 1:15; 6:25; 7:6; 8:8; 9:5; 15:40; 17:9
Love and Golden rule: 4:2, 15; 5:11; 6:28; 12:2, 5; 14:36, 45; 17:4
Mean and Central thread: 4:15; 15:2
Nature, human: 5:12; 6:17, 19; 16:9; 17:2, 3
Rectification of names: 12:11, 17; 13:3, 6
Righteousness: 2:24; 4:16; 13:3, 6; 15:17
Superior man: 1:2, 8, 14; 2:11, 13; 4:5, 24; 6:16; 9:13; 13:3; 14:30; 15:17, 20, 31; 16:8, 10; contrasted with inferior man: 2:14; 4:11, 16; 8:6; 12:16; 13:23, 26; 14:24; 15:20; 17:23
Virtue: 1:4, 6, 8; 4:12; 7:6; 8:5, 7, 13; 9:4; 13:18, 19; 14:33; 15:8, 17; 16:4, 10; 17:6, 8
Way (Tao): 4:5, 8; 7:6; 15:28, 31; 17:4
Words and Acts: 2:13, 18; 4:24; 13:3; 14:29

THE ANALECTS[11]

1:1. Confucius said, "Is it not a pleasure to learn and to repeat or practice from time to time what has been learned? Is it not delightful to have friends coming from afar? Is one not a superior man if he does not feel hurt even though he is not recognized?"

---

arts" are also understood to mean ceremonies, music, archery, carriage-driving, writing, and mathematics.

[11] The *Analects* is a collection of sayings by Confucius and his pupils pertaining to his teachings and deeds. It was probably put together by some of his pupils and

Comment. Interpretations of Confucian teachings have differed radically in the last 2,000 years. Generally speaking, Han (206 B.C.–A.D. 220) scholars, represented in Ho Yen (d. 249), *Lun-yü chi-chieh* (Collected Explanations of the *Analects*),[12] were inclined to be literal and interested in historical facts, whereas Neo-Confucianists, represented in Chu Hsi (1130-1200), *Lun-yü chi-chu* (Collected Commentaries on the *Analects*) were interpretative, philosophical, and often subjective. They almost invariably understand the Confucian Way (Tao) as principle (*li*), which is their cardinal concept, and frequently when they came to an undefined "this" or "it," they insisted that it meant principle. This divergency between the Han and Sung scholars has colored interpretations of this passage. To Wang Su (195-265), quoted in Ho, *hsi* (to learn) means to recite a lesson repeatedly. To Chu Hsi, however, *hsi* means to follow the examples of those who are first to understand, and therefore it does not mean recitation but practice. In revolt against both extremes, Ch'ing (1644-1912) scholars emphasized practical experience. In this case, *hsi* to them means both to repeat and to practice, as indicated in Liu Pao-nan (1791-1855), *Lun-yü cheng-i* (Correct Meanings of the *Analects*). Thus Ho Yen, Chu Hsi, and Liu Pao-nan neatly represent the three different approaches in the three different periods. Generally speaking, the dominant spirit of Confucian teaching is the equal emphasis on knowledge and action. This dual emphasis will be encountered again and again.[13]

1:2. Yu Tzu[14] said, "Few of those who are filial sons and respectful

---

their pupils. The name *Lun-yü* did not appear until the 2nd century B.C. At that time there were three versions of it, with some variations. Two of these have been lost. The surviving version is that of the state of Lu, where it circulated. It is divided into two parts, with ten books each. In the *Ching-tien shih-wen* (Explanation of Terms in the Classics) by Lu Te-ming (556-627), ch. 24, it is divided into 492 chapters. Chu Hsi combined and divided certain chapters, making a total of 482, one of which is divided into eighteen sections. In translations like Legge's *Confucian Analects*, and Waley's *The Analects of Confucius*, these divisions are taken as chapters, making 499. The same numbering is used in the following selections.

The material is unsystematic, in a few cases repetitive, and in some cases historically inaccurate. However, it is generally accepted as the most authentic and reliable source of Confucian teachings. Chu Hsi grouped it together with the *Book of Mencius*, the *Great Learning*, and the *Doctrine of the Mean* as the "Four Books." Thereupon they became Classics. From 1313 to 1905, they served as the basis for civil service examinations, replacing the earlier Classics in importance.

[12] In the *Lun-yü chu-shu* (Commentary and Subcommentary on the *Analects*) in the Thirteen Classics Series.

[13] See below, comment on *Analects*, 2:18.

[14] Confucius' pupil whose private name was Jo (538–c.457 B.C.), thirteen years (some say thirty-three years) Confucius' junior. In the *Analects*, with minor

brothers will show disrespect to superiors, and there has never been a man who is not disrespectful to superiors and yet creates disorder. A superior man is devoted to the fundamentals (the root). When the root is firmly established, the moral law (Tao) will grow. Filial piety and brotherly respect are the root of humanity (*jen*)."

1:3. Confucius said, "A man with clever words and an ingratiating appearance is seldom a man of humanity."[15]

1:4. Tseng-Tzu[16] said, "Every day I examine myself on three points: whether in counseling others I have not been loyal; whether in intercourse with my friends I have not been faithful; and whether I have not repeated again and again and practiced the instructions of my teacher."[17]

1:6. Young men should be filial when at home and respectful to their elders when away from home. They should be earnest and faithful. They should love all extensively and be intimate with men of humanity. When they have any energy to spare after the performance of moral duties, they should use it to study literature and the arts (*wen*).[18]

1:8. Confucius said, "If the superior man is not grave, he will not inspire awe, and his learning will not be on a firm foundation.[19] Hold loyalty and faithfulness to be fundamental. Have no friends who are not as good as yourself. When you have made mistakes, don't be afraid to correct them."

Comment. The teaching about friendship here is clearly inconsistent with *Analects*, 8:5, where Confucius exhorts us to learn from inferiors. It is difficult to believe that Confucius taught people to be selfish. According to Hsing Ping (932–1010),[20] Confucius meant people who are not equal to oneself in loyalty and faithfulness, assuming that one is or should be loyal and faithful; according to Hsü

---

exceptions, he and Tseng Ts'an are addressed as Tzu, an honorific for a scholar or gentleman, giving rise to the theory that the *Analects* was compiled by their pupils, who supplemented Confucius' sayings with theirs.

[15] Cf. below, 13:27.

[16] Tseng Shen (505–c.436 B.C.), pupil of Confucius, noted for filial piety, to whom are ascribed the *Great Learning* and the *Book of Filial Piety*.

[17] Ho Yen's interpretation: Whether I have transmitted to others what I myself have not practiced. This interpretation has been accepted by many.

[18] *Wen*, literally "patterns," is here extended to mean the embodiment of culture and the moral law (Tao)—that is, the Six Arts of ceremony, music, archery, carriage-driving, writing, and mathematics.

[19] To K'ung An-kuo (fl. 130 B.C.), quoted by Ho Yen, *ku* means "obscure," not "firm." The sentence would read, "If he studies, he will not be ignorant."

[20] *Lun-yü shu* (Subcommentary on the *Analects*). This is part of the *Lun-yü chu-shu*.

Kan (171-218), Confucius simply wanted us to be careful in choosing friends.[21]

1:11. Confucius said, "When a man's father is alive, look at the bent of his will. When his father is dead, look at his conduct. If for three years [of mourning] he does not change from the way of his father, he may be called filial."

Comment. Critics of Confucius have asserted that Confucian authoritarianism holds an oppressive weight on the son even after the father has passed away. Fan Tsu-yü (1041-1098) did understand the saying to mean that the son should observe the father's will and past conduct,[22] but he was almost alone in this. All prominent commentators, from K'ung An-kuo to Cheng Hsüan (127-200),[23] Chu Hsi, and Liu Pao-nan have interpreted the passage to mean that while one's father is alive, one's action is restricted, so that his *intention* should be the criterion by which his character is to be judged. After his father's death, however, when he is completely autonomous, he should be judged by his conduct. In this interpretation, the way of the father is of course the moral principle which has guided or should have guided the son's conduct.

1:12. Yu Tzu said, "Among the functions of propriety (*li*) the most valuable is that it establishes harmony. The excellence of the ways of ancient kings consists of this. It is the guiding principle of all things great and small. If things go amiss, and you, understanding harmony, try to achieve it without regulating it by the rules of propriety, they will still go amiss."

1:14. Confucius said, "The superior man does not seek fulfillment of his appetite nor comfort in his lodging. He is diligent in his duties and careful in his speech. He associates with men of moral principles and thereby realizes himself. Such a person may be said to love learning."

1:15. Tzu-kung[24] said, "What do you think of a man who is poor and yet does not flatter, and the rich man who is not proud?" Confucius replied, "They will do. But they are not as good as the poor man who is happy[25] and the rich man who loves the rules of propriety (*li*)." Tzu-kung said, "*The Book of Odes* says:

[21] *Chung lun* (Treatise on the Mean), pt. 1, sec. 5, SPTK, 1:21b.

[22] Quoted in Chu Hsi's *Lun-yü huo-wen* (Questions and Answers on the *Analects*), 1:20a, in *Chu Tzu i-shu* (Surviving Works of Chu Hsi).

[23] *Lun-yü chu* (Commentary on the *Analects*).

[24] Confucius' pupil, whose family name was Tuan-mu, private name Tz'u, and courtesy name Tzu-kung (520-c.450 B.C.). He was noted for eloquence and was thirty-one years younger than the Master. See *Analects*, 5:8 about him.

[25] An old edition has "happy with the Way."

As a thing is cut and filed,
As a thing is carved and polished. . . .[26]

Does that not mean what you have just said?"

Confucius said, "Ah! Tz'u. Now I can begin to talk about the odes with you. When I have told you what has gone before, you know what is to follow."

1:16. Confucius said, "[A good man] does not worry about not being known by others but rather worries about not knowing them."[27]

2:1. Confucius said, "A ruler who governs his state by virtue is like the north polar star, which remains in its place while all the other stars revolve around it."

> *Comment.* Two important principles are involved here. One is government by virtue, in which Confucianists stand directly opposed to the Legalists, who prefer law and force. The other is government through inaction, i.e., government in such excellent order that all things operate by themselves. This is the interpretation shared by Han and Sung Confucianists alike.[28] In both cases, Confucianism and Taoism are in agreement.[29]

2:2. Confucius said, "All three hundred odes can be covered by one of their sentences, and that is, 'Have no depraved thoughts.'"[30]

2:3. Confucius said, "Lead the people with governmental measures and regulate them by law and punishment, and they will avoid wrong-doing but will have no sense of honor and shame. Lead them with virtue and regulate them by the rules of propriety (*li*), and they will have a sense of shame and, moreover, set themselves right."[31]

2:4. Confucius said, "At fifteen my mind was set on learning. At thirty my character had been formed. At forty I had no more perplexities. At fifty I knew the Mandate of Heaven (*T'ien-ming*). At sixty I was at ease with whatever I heard. At seventy I could follow my heart's desire without transgressing moral principles."

> *Comment.* What *T'ien-ming* is depends upon one's own philosophy.

[26] Ode no. 55. Describing the eloquence of a lover, but here taken by Tzu-kung to mean moral effort.

[27] Similar ideas are found in *Analects*, 14:32; 15:18, 20.

[28] See Ho Yen's *Lun-yü chi-chieh* and Chu Hsi's *Lun-yü chi-chu.*

[29] Cf. *Analects*, 15:4 and *Lao Tzu*, ch. 57.

[30] *Odes*, ode no. 297. Actually there are 305 odes in the book. The word *ssu* means "Ah!" in the poem but Confucius used it in its sense of "thought." For discussion of the *Book of Odes*, see above, ch. 1, n.5.

[31] The word *ko* means both to rectify (according to Ho Yen and most other commentators) and to arrive (according to Cheng Hsüan). In the latter sense, it can mean either "the people will arrive at goodness" or "the people will come to the ruler." See below, ch. 32, comment on sec. 44.

In general, Confucianists before the T'ang dynasty (618-907) understood it to mean either the decree of God, which determines the course of one's life, or the rise and fall of the moral order,[32] whereas Sung scholars, especially Chu Hsi, took it to mean "the operation of Nature which is endowed in things and makes things be as they are."[33] This latter interpretation has prevailed. The concept of *T'ien-ming* which can mean Mandate of Heaven, decree of God, personal destiny, and course of order, is extremely important in the history of Chinese thought. In religion it generally means fate or personal order of God, but in philosophy it is practically always understood as moral destiny, natural endowment, or moral order.

2:5. Meng I Tzu[34] asked about filial piety. Confucius said: "Never disobey." [Later,] when Fan Ch'ih[35] was driving him, Confucius told him, "Meng-sun asked me about filial piety, and I answered him, 'Never disobey.'"[36] Fan Ch'ih said, "What does that mean?" Confucius said, "When parents are alive, serve them according to the rules of propriety. When they die, bury them according to the rules of propriety and sacrifice to them according to the rules of propriety."

2:6. Meng Wu-po[37] asked about filial piety. Confucius said, "Especially be anxious lest parents should be sick."[38]

2:7. Tzu-yu[39] asked about filial piety. Confucius said, "Filial piety nowadays means to be able to support one's parents. But we support even dogs and horses.[40] If there is no feeling of reverence, wherein lies the difference?"

2:11. Confucius said, "A man who reviews the old so as to find out the new is qualified to teach others."

---

[32] See Ch'eng Shu-te *Lun-yü chi-shih* (Collected Explanations of the *Analects*), 1943.

[33] Chu Hsi, *Lun-yü chi-chu.*

[34] A young noble, also styled Meng-sun, once studied ceremonies with Confucius.

[35] Confucius' pupil, whose family name was Fan, private name Hsü, and courtesy name Tzu-ch'ih (b. 515 B.C.).

[36] Not to disobey the principle of propriety, according to Hsing Ping; not to disobey moral principles, according to Chu Hsi; or not to obey parents, according to Huang K'an (448-545), *Lun-yü i-shu* (Commentary on the Meanings of the *Analects*).

[37] Son of Meng I Tzu.

[38] Another interpretation by Ma Jung (79-166), quoted by Ho Yen: A filial son does not do wrong. His parents' only worry is that he might become sick. About half of the commentators have followed him.

[39] Confucius' pupil. His family name was Yen, private name Yen, and courtesy name Tzu-yu (b. 506 B.C.).

[40] Alternative interpretations: (1) Even dogs and horses can support men; (2) Even dogs and horses can support their parents.

2:12. Confucius said, "The superior man is not an implement (*ch'i*)."[41]

> *Comment.* A good and educated man should not be like an implement, which is intended only for a narrow and specific purpose. Instead, he should have broad vision, wide interests, and sufficient ability to do many things.[42]

2:13. Tzu-kung asked about the superior man. Confucius said, "He acts before he speaks and then speaks according to his action."[43]

2:14. Confucius said, "The superior man is broadminded but not partisan; the inferior man is partisan but not broadminded."

2:15. Confucius said, "He who learns but does not think is lost; he who thinks but does not learn is in danger."

2:17. Confucius said, "Yu,[44] shall I teach you [the way to acquire] knowledge?[45] To say that you know when you do know and say that you do not know when you do not know—that is [the way to acquire] knowledge."

2:18. Tzu-chang[46] was learning with a view to official emolument. Confucius said, "Hear much and put aside what's doubtful while you speak cautiously of the rest. Then few will blame you. See much and put aside what seems perilous while you are cautious in carrying the rest into practice. Then you will have few occasions for regret. When one's words give few occasions for blame and his acts give few occasions for repentance—there lies his emolument."

> *Comment.* The equal emphasis on words and deeds has been a strong tradition in Confucianism.[47] Eventually Wang Yang-ming identified them as one.[48]

2:24. Confucius said, "It is flattery to offer sacrifice to ancestral spirits other than one's own. To see what is right and not to do it is cowardice."

3:3. Confucius said, "If a man is not humane (*jen*), what has he to do with ceremonies (*li*)? If he is not humane, what has he to do with music?"

---

[41] Literally "an implement or utensil," *ch'i* means narrow usefulness rather than the ability to grasp fundamentals.

[42] Cf. below, 9:6.   [43] Cf. below, 4:22, 24; 14:29.

[44] Name of Confucius' pupil whose family name was Chung and courtesy name Tzu-lu (542–480 B.C.). He was only nine years younger than Confucius. He was noted for courage.

[45] The sentence may also mean: "Do you know what I teach you?"

[46] Courtesy name of Confucius' pupil, Chuan-sun Shih (503–c.450 B.C.).

[47] See also *Analects*, 4:22, 24; 5:9; 13:3; 14:29; 15:5; 18:8; and *The Mean*, chs. 8, 13.

[48] See below, ch. 35, B, sec. 5.

3:4.   Lin Fang[49] asked about the foundation of ceremonies. Confucius said, "An important question indeed! In rituals or ceremonies, be thrifty rather than extravagant, and in funerals, be deeply sorrowful rather than shallow in sentiment."

3:12.   When Confucius offered sacrifice to his ancestors, he felt as if his ancestral spirits were actually present. When he offered sacrifice to other spiritual beings, he felt as if they were actually present. He said, "If I do not participate in the sacrifice, it is as if I did not sacrifice at all."

3:13.   Wang-sun Chia[50] asked, "What is meant by the common saying, 'It is better to be on good terms with the God of the Kitchen [who cooks our food] than with the spirits of the shrine (ancestors) at the southwest corner of the house'?" Confucius said, "It is not true. He who commits a sin against Heaven has no god to pray to."

3:17.   Tzu-kung wanted to do away with the sacrificing of a lamb at the ceremony in which the beginning of each month is reported to ancestors. Confucius said, "Tz'u![51] You love the lamb but I love the ceremony."

3:19.   Duke Ting[52] asked how the ruler should employ his ministers and how the ministers should serve their ruler. Confucius said, "A ruler should employ his ministers according to the principle of propriety, and ministers should serve their ruler with loyalty."

3:24.   The guardian at I (a border post of the state of Wei) requested to be presented to Confucius, saying, "When gentlemen come here, I have never been prevented from seeing them." Confucius' followers introduced him. When he came out from the interview, he said, "Sirs, why are you disheartened by your master's loss of office? The Way has not prevailed in the world for a long time. Heaven is going to use your master as a bell with a wooden tongue [to awaken the people]."

4:2.   Confucius said, "One who is not a man of humanity cannot endure adversity for long, nor can he enjoy prosperity for long. The man of humanity is naturally at ease with humanity. The man of wisdom cultivates humanity for its advantage."

4:3.   Confucius said, "Only the man of humanity knows how to love people and hate people."[53]

4:4.   Confucius said, "If you set your mind on humanity, you will be free from evil."[54]

---

[49] A native of Lu, most probably not a pupil of Confucius.

[50] Great officer and commander-in-chief in the state of Wei.

[51] Tzu-kung's private name.

[52] Ruler of Confucius' native state of Lu (r. 509–495 B.C.).

[53] Hate here means dislike, without any connotation of ill will. See *Great Learning*, ch. ,10, for an elaboration of the saying.

[54] The word *e*, evil, can also be read *wu* to mean hate or dislike, but it is hardly ever done.

4:5. Confucius said, "Wealth and honor are what every man desires. But if they have been obtained in violation of moral principles, they must not be kept. Poverty and humble station are what every man dislikes. But if they can be avoided only in violation of moral principles, they must not be avoided. If a superior man departs from humanity, how can he fulfill that name? A superior man never abandons humanity even for the lapse of a single meal. In moments of haste, he acts according to it. In times of difficulty or confusion, he acts according to it."

4:6. Confucius said, "I have never seen one who really loves humanity or one who really hates inhumanity. One who really loves humanity will not place anything above it.[55] One who really hates inhumanity will practice humanity in such a way that inhumanity will have no chance to get at him. Is there any one who has devoted his strength to humanity for as long as a single day? I have not seen any one without sufficient strength to do so. Perhaps there is such a case, but I have never seen it."

4:8. Confucius said, "In the morning, hear the Way; in the evening, die content!"

4:10. Confucius said, "A superior man in dealing with the world is not for anything or against anything. He follows righteousness as the standard."

> *Comment.* This is a clear expression of both the flexibility and rigidity of Confucian ethics—flexibility in application but rigidity in standard. Here lies the basic idea of the Confucian doctrine of *ching-ch'üan*, or the standard and the exceptional, the absolute and the relative, or the permanent and the temporary.[56] This explains why Confucius was not obstinate,[57] had no predetermined course of action,[58] was ready to serve or to withdraw whenever it was proper to do so,[59] and, according to Mencius, was a sage who acted according to the circumstance of the time.[60]
>
> The words *shih* and *mo* can be interpreted to mean being near to people and being distant from people, or opposing people and admiring people, respectively, and some commentators have adopted these interpretations.[61] But the majority follow Chu Hsi, as I have done here. Chu Hsi was thinking about the superior man's dealing with things. Chang Shih (Chang Nan-hsien, 1133-1180), on the other hand, thought Confucius was talking about the su-

[55] It is possible to interpret the phrase to mean "will not be surpassed by anyone," but few commentators chose it.
[56] See below, ch. 3, comment on *Mencius*, Additional Selections, 4A:17.
[57] *Analects*, 9:4.
[58] ibid., 18:8.   [59] *Mencius*, 2A:2.   [60] ibid., 5B:1.
[61] See Liu Pao-nan, *Lun-yü cheng-i.*

perior man's state of mind.[62] This difference reflects the opposition between the two wings of Neo-Confucianism, one inclining to activity, the other to the state of mind.[63]

4:11. Confucius said, "The superior man thinks of virtue; the inferior man thinks of possessions.[64] The superior man thinks of sanctions; the inferior man thinks of personal favors."

4:12. Confucius said, "If one's acts are motivated by profit, he will have many enemies."

4:15. Confucius said, "Shen,[65] there is one thread that runs through my doctrines." Tseng Tzu said, "Yes." After Confucius had left, the disciples asked him, "What did he mean?" Tseng Tzu replied, "The Way of our Master is none other than conscientiousness (*chung*) and altruism (*shu*)."

> *Comment.* Confucian teachings may be summed up in the phrase "one thread" (*i-kuan*), but Confucianists have not agreed on what it means. Generally, Confucianists of Han and T'ang times adhered to the basic meaning of "thread" and understood it in the sense of a system or a body of doctrines. Chu Hsi, true to the spirit of Neo-Confucian speculative philosophy, took it to mean that there is one mind to respond to all things. In the Ch'ing period, in revolt against speculation, scholars preferred to interpret *kuan* as action and affairs, that is, there is only one moral principle for all actions.[66] All agree, however, on the meanings of *chung* and *shu*, which are best expressed by Chu Hsi, namely, *chung* means the full development of one's [originally good] mind and *shu* means the extension of that mind to others.[67] As Ch'eng I (Ch'eng I-ch'uan, 1033-1107) put it, *chung* is the Way of Heaven, whereas *shu* is the way of man; the former is substance, while the latter is function.[68] Liu Pao-nan is correct in equating *chung* with Confucius' saying, "Establish one's own character," and *shu* with "Also establish the character of others."[69] Here is the positive version of the Confucian golden rule. The negative version is only one side of it.[70]

[62] See Chu Hsi, *Lun-yü chi-chu*, and Chang Shih, *Lun-yü chieh* (Explanation of the *Analects*).

[63] See Ch'eng Shu-te, *Lun-yü chi-shih*, on this point.

[64] Literally "land," or one's shelter, food, etc.

[65] Private name of Tseng Tzu.

[66] The Ch'ing viewpoint is best represented in Wang Nien-sun (1744-1832), *Kuang-ya shu-cheng* (Textual Commentary on the *Kuang-ya* Dictionary).

[67] Chu Hsi, *Lun-yü chi-chu*. For discussion of *chung-shu*, see Appendix.

[68] *I-shu* (Surviving Works), 21B:1b, in ECCS.

[69] *Lun-yü cheng-i*. He is referring to *Analects*, 6:28.

[70] See other positive versions in *Analects*, 14:45; *The Mean*, ch. 13; *Mencius*,

4:16. Confucius said, "The superior man understands righteousness (*i*); the inferior man understands profit."

> *Comment.* Confucius contrasted the superior man and the inferior in many ways,[71] but this is the fundamental difference for Confucianism in general as well as for Confucius himself. Chu Hsi associated righteousness with the Principle of Nature (*T'ien-li*) and profit with the feelings of man, but later Neo-Confucianists strongly objected to his thus contrasting principle and feelings.

4:18. Confucius said, "In serving his parents, a son may gently remonstrate with them. When he sees that they are not inclined to listen to him, he should resume an attitude of reverence and not abandon his effort to serve them. He may feel worried, but does not complain."

4:19. Confucius said, "When his parents are alive, a son should not go far abroad; or if he does, he should let them know where he goes."

4:21. Confucius said, "A son should always keep in mind the age of his parents. It is an occasion for joy [that they are enjoying long life] and also an occasion for anxiety [that another year is gone]."

4:24. Confucius said, "The superior man wants to be slow in word but diligent in action."

5:11. Tzu-kung said, "What I do not want others to do to me, I do not want to do to them." Confucius said, "Ah Tz'u! That is beyond you."[72]

5:12. Tzu-kung said, "We can hear our Master's [views] on culture and its manifestation,[73] but we cannot hear his views on human nature[74] and the Way of Heaven [because these subjects are beyond the comprehension of most people]."

5:25. Yen Yüan[75] and Chi-lu[76] were in attendance. Confucius said, "Why don't you each tell me your ambition in life?" Tzu-lu said, "I wish to have a horse, a carriage, and a light fur coat[77] and share them with friends, and shall not regret if they are all worn out." Yen Yüan said, "I

1A:7. The negative version is found in *Analects*, 5:11; 12:2; 15:23; in *The Mean*, ch. 13; and in the *Great Learning*, ch. 10.

[71] See *Analects*, 2:14; 4:11, 16; 6:11; 7:36; 12:16; 13:23, 25, 26; 14:7, 24; 15:1, 20, 33; 17:4, 23.

[72] Cf. *Great Learning*, ch. 10.

[73] The term *wen-chang* can also mean literary heritage or simply the ancient Classics.

[74] The word *hsing* (nature) is mentioned elsewhere in the *Analects* only once, in 17:2.

[75] Confucius' favorite pupil, whose family name was Yen, private name Hui, and courtesy name Tzu-yüan (521–490 B.C.). He died at 32.

[76] Tzu-lu.

[77] The word "light" does not appear in the stone-engraved Classic of the T'ang dynasty and is probably a later addition.

wish never to boast of my good qualities and never to brag about the trouble I have taken [for others]."[78] Tzu-lu said, "I wish to hear your ambition." Confucius said, "It is my ambition to comfort the old, to be faithful to friends, and to cherish the young."[79]

5:27. Confucius said, "In every hamlet of ten families, there are always some people as loyal and faithful as myself, but none who love learning as much as I do."

6:5. Confucius said, "About Hui (Yen Yüan), for three months there would be nothing in his mind contrary to humanity. The others could (or can) attain to this for a day or a month at the most."[80]

> Comment. On the basis of this saying alone, some philosophers have concluded that Yen Yüan was a mystic and that Confucius praised mysticism!

6:16. Confucius said, "When substance exceeds refinement (*wen*), one becomes rude. When refinement exceeds substance, one becomes urbane. It is only when one's substance and refinement are properly blended that he becomes a superior man."

6:17. Confucius said, "Man is born with uprightness. If one loses it he will be lucky if he escapes with his life."

> Comment. Although the Confucian tradition in general holds that human nature is originally good, Confucius' own position is not clear. We have read that his doctrine of nature could not be heard,[81] and we shall read his statement that by nature men are alike.[82] But how they are alike is not clear. The saying here can be interpreted to mean that man can live throughout life because he is upright. This is the interpretation of Ma Jung (79-166),[83] which is followed by Wang Ch'ung (27–100?).[84] Most people followed Chu Hsi. He had the authority of Ch'eng Hao (Ch'eng Ming-tao, 1032-1085),[85] who echoed Cheng Hsüan's interpretation that Confucius said that man is *born* upright. This means that Confucius was not only the first one in Chinese philosophy to assume a definite position about human nature, but also the first to teach that human nature is *originally* good.

---

[78] Another interpretation: For his own moral effort.

[79] This is Chu Hsi's interpretation. According to Hsing Ping, it would mean this: The old should be satisfied with me, friends should trust me, and the young should come to me.

[80] We don't know whether this was said before or after Yen Yüan's death.

[81] *Analects*, 5:12.   [82] *Analects*, 17:2.   [83] Quoted by Ho Yen.

[84] *Lun-heng* (Balanced Inquiries), ch. 5, SPPY, 2:2a. For English translation, see Forke, *Lun-heng*, vol. 1, p. 152.

[85] See *Lun-yü chi-chu*.

6:18. Confucius said, "To know it [learning or the Way] is not as good as to love it, and to love it is not as good as to take delight in it."

6:19. Confucius said, "To those who are above average, one may talk of the higher things, but may not do so to those who are below average."

6:20. Fan Ch'ih asked about wisdom. Confucius said, "Devote yourself earnestly to the duties due to men, and respect spiritual beings[86] but keep them at a distance. This may be called wisdom." Fan Ch'ih asked about humanity. Confucius said, "The man of humanity first of all considers what is difficult in the task and then thinks of success. Such a man may be called humane."

> *Comment.* Many people have been puzzled by this passage, some even doubting the sincerity of Confucius' religious attitude—all quite unnecessarily. The passage means either "do not become improperly informal with spiritual beings,"[87] or "emphasize the way of man rather than the way of spirits."[88]

6:21. Confucius said, "The man of wisdom delights in water; the man of humanity delights in mountains. The man of wisdom is active; the man of humanity is tranquil. The man of wisdom enjoys happiness; the man of humanity enjoys long life."

> *Comment.* In the Confucian ethical system, humanity and wisdom are like two wings, one supporting the other.[89] One is substance, the other is function. The dual emphasis has been maintained throughout history, especially in Tung Chung-shu (c.179–c.104 B.C.) and in a certain sense in K'ang Yu-wei (1858-1927).[90] Elsewhere, courage is added as the third virtue,[91] and Mencius grouped them with righteousness and propriety as the Four Beginnings.[92]

6:23. Confucius said, "When a cornered vessel no longer has any corner, should it be called a cornered vessel? Should it?"

> *Comment.* Name must correspond to actuality.[93]

6:25. Confucius said, "The superior man extensively studies literature (*wen*) and restrains himself with the rules of propriety. Thus he will not violate the Way."

---

[86] Meaning especially ancestors.　　　[87] According to *Lun-yü chi-chieh*.

[88] According to Cheng Hsüan, Chu Hsi, and most commentators.

[89] See also *Analects*, 4:2; 12:22; 15:32.

[90] See below, ch. 14, E, sec. 3; ch. 39, sec. 3.

[91] See *Analects*, 9:28; 14:30; *The Mean*, ch. 20.

[92] *Mencius*, 2A:6; 6A:6.

[93] For the Confucian doctrine of the rectification of names, see below, comment on 13:3.

6:26. When Confucius visited Nan-tzu (the wicked wife of Duke Ling of Wei, r. 533–490 B.C.) [in an attempt to influence her to persuade the duke to effect political reform], Tzu-lu was not pleased. Confucius swore an oath and said, "If I have said or done anything wrong, may Heaven forsake me! May Heaven forsake me!"[94]

6:28. Tzu-kung said, "If a ruler extensively confers benefit on the people and can bring salvation to all, what do you think of him? Would you call him a man of humanity?" Confucius said, "Why only a man of humanity? He is without doubt a sage. Even (sage-emperors) Yao and Shun fell short of it. A man of humanity, wishing to establish his own character, also establishes the character of others, and wishing to be prominent himself, also helps others to be prominent. To be able to judge others by what is near to ourselves may be called the method of realizing humanity."[95]

Comment. The Confucian golden rule in a nutshell.

7:1. Confucius said, "I transmit but do not create. I believe in and love the ancients. I venture to compare myself to our old P'eng."[96]

Comment. This is often cited to show that Confucius was not creative. We must not forget, however, that he "goes over the old so as to find out what is new."[97] Nor must we overlook the fact that he was the first one to offer education to all.[98] Moreover, his concepts of the superior man and of Heaven were at least partly new.

7:2. Confucius said, "To remember silently [what I have learned], to learn untiringly, and to teach others without being wearied—that is just natural with me."

7:6. Confucius said, "Set your will on the Way. Have a firm grasp on virtue. Rely on humanity. Find recreation in the arts."

7:7. Confucius said, "There has never been anyone who came with as little a present as dried meat (for tuition)[99] that I have refused to teach him something."

7:8. Confucius said, "I do not enlighten those who are not eager to learn, nor arouse those who are not anxious to give an explanation themselves. If I have presented one corner of the square and they cannot

---

[94] This episode took place when Confucius was 57.

[95] See above comment on 4:15.

[96] An official of the Shang dynasty (1751–1112 B.C.) who loved to recite old stories.

[97] *Analects,* 2:11.

[98] See Fung, *History of Chinese Philosophy,* vol. 1, pp. 46-49.

[99] Cheng Hsüan's interpretation: From young men fifteen years old and upward. Cf. *Analects,* 15:38.

come back to me with the other three, I should not go over the points again."

7:15. Confucius said, "With coarse rice to eat, with water to drink, and with a bent arm for a pillow, there is still joy. Wealth and honor obtained through unrighteousness are but floating clouds to me."

7:16. Confucius said, "Give me a few more years so that I can devote fifty years to study Change.[100] I may be free from great mistakes."

7:17. These were the things Confucius often[101] talked about— poetry, history, and the performance of the rules of propriety. All these were what he often talked about.

7:18. The Duke of She[102] asked Tzu-lu about Confucius, and Tzu-lu did not answer. Confucius said, "Why didn't you say that I am a person who forgets his food when engaged in vigorous pursuit of something, is so happy as to forget his worries, and is not aware that old age is coming on?"[103]

7:19. Confucius said, "I am not one who was born with knowledge; I love ancient [teaching] and earnestly seek it."

7:20. Confucius never discussed strange phenomena, physical exploits, disorder, or spiritual beings.

7:22. Confucius said, "Heaven produced the virtue that is in me; what can Huan T'ui[104] do to me?"

7:24. Confucius taught four things: culture (*wen*), conduct, loyalty, and faithfulness.

7:26. Confucius fished with a line but not a net. While shooting he would not shoot a bird at rest.[105]

7:27. Confucius said, "There are those who act without knowing [what is right].[106] But I am not one of them. To hear much and select

[100] The traditional interpretation of the word *i* (change) is the *Book of Changes*. The ancient Lu version of the *Analects*, however, has *i* (then) instead of *i* (change). Some scholars have accepted this version, which reads ". . . to study, then I may be. . . ." Modern scholars prefer this reading because they do not believe that the *Book of Changes* existed at the time. However, the fact that Confucius was thinking of the *system* of Change instead of the *Book* should not be ruled out.

[101] The word *ya* (often) was understood by Cheng Hsüan as standard, thus meaning that Confucius recited the Books of *Odes*, *History*, and *Rites* in correct pronunciation.

[102] Magistrate of the district She in the state of Ch'u, who assumed the title of duke by usurpation.

[103] According to *Shih chi* (Records of the Historian), PNP, 47:18a, Confucius was 62 when he made this remark. See Chavannes, trans., *Les mémoires historiques*, vol. 5, p. 361.

[104] A military officer in the state of Sung who attempted to kill Confucius by felling a tree. Confucius was then 59 years old.

[105] He would not take unfair advantage.

[106] Other interpretations: Act without the necessity of knowledge; invent stories about history without real knowledge of it; write without knowledge.

what is good and follow it, to see much and remember it, is the second type of knowledge (next to innate knowledge)."

7:29. Confucius said, "Is humanity far away? As soon as I want it, there it is right by me."

> *Comment.* This is simply emphasizing the ever-present opportunity to do good. There is nothing mystical about it. The practice of humanity starts with oneself.[107]

7:34. Confucius was very ill. Tzu-lu asked that prayer be offered. Confucius said, "Is there such a thing?" Tzu-lu replied, "There is. A Eulogy says, 'Pray to the spiritual beings above and below.' " Confucius said, "My prayer has been for a long time [that is, what counts is the life that one leads]."

7:37. Confucius is affable but dignified, austere but not harsh, polite but completely at ease.

> *Comment.* The Confucian Mean in practice.

8:5. Tseng Tzu said, "Gifted with ability, yet asking those without ability; possessing much, yet asking those who possess little; having, yet seeming to have none; full, yet seeming vacuous; offended, yet not contesting—long ago I had a friend [Confucius' most virtuous pupil Yen Yüan?][108] who devoted himself to these ways."

> *Comment.* The similarity to Taoist teachings is striking.

8:6. Tseng Tzu said, "A man who can be entrusted with an orphaned child, delegated with the authority over a whole state of one hundred *li*,[109] and whose integrity cannot be violated even in the face of a great emergency—is such a man a superior man? He is a superior man indeed!"

8:7. Tseng Tzu said, "An officer must be great and strong. His burden is heavy and his course is long. He has taken humanity to be his own burden—is that not heavy? Only with death does his course stop— is that not long?"

8:8. Confucius said, "Let a man be stimulated by poetry, established by the rules of propriety, and perfected by music."

8:9. Confucius said, "The common people may be made to follow it (the Way) but may not be made to understand it."

> *Comment.* Confucianists have taken great pains to explain this saying. Cheng Hsüan said "the common people" refers to ignorant

---

[107] See *Analects*, 12:1.
[108] According to Ma Jung, quoted by Ho Yen, Yen Yüan had died long before.
[109] About one-third of a mile.

people and Chu Hsi said that ordinary people do things without understanding why. There can be no denial that Confucius reflected the feudal society in which it was the duty of ordinary people to follow the elite.

8:13. Confucius said, "Have sincere faith and love learning. Be not afraid to die for pursuing the good Way. Do not enter a tottering state nor stay in a chaotic one. When the Way prevails in the empire, then show yourself; when it does not prevail, then hide. When the Way prevails in your own state and you are poor and in a humble position, be ashamed of yourself. When the Way does not prevail in your state and you are wealthy and in an honorable position, be ashamed of yourself."

8:14. Confucius said, "A person not in a particular government position does not discuss its policies."[110]

9:1. Confucius seldom talked about profit, destiny (*ming* or the Mandate of Heaven), and humanity.

Comment. Few passages in the *Analects* have given commentators as much trouble as this one. It is true that the topic of profit is mentioned in the *Analects* only six times and destiny or fate only ten times, but fifty-eight of the 499 chapters of the *Analects* are devoted to humanity and the word *jen* occurs 105 times. Confucianists have tried their best to explain why Confucius can be said to have seldom talked about them. Huang K'an said these things are so serious that Confucius seldom expected people to live up to them. This line of thought was followed by Juan Yüan (1764-1849).[111] Ho Yen thought that Confucius seldom talked about them because few people could reach those high levels. Hsing Ping, who commented on Ho's commentary, repeated it. Chu Hsi, quoting Ch'eng I, said that Confucius seldom talked about profit, for example, because it is injurious to righteousness, and seldom talked about the others because the principle of destiny is subtle and that of humanity is great.

Other scholars have tried to change the meaning of the passage. Shih Sheng-tsu (fl. 1230) in his *Hsüeh-chai chan-pi* (Simple Observations) interpreted *yü* not as "and" but as "give forth," thus making the sentence say that Confucius seldom talked about profit but gave forth [instructions] on destiny and humanity. Bodde accepts this view.[112] Laufer thinks it should be read: "The Master

[110] The same idea is expressed in 14:27-28.

[111] "Lun-yu lun jen lun" (A Treatise on *Jen* in the *Analects*), *Yen-ching-shih chi* (Collected Works of the Yen-ching Study), 1st collection, 8:21a.

[112] "Perplexing Passage in the Confucian Analects," *Journal of the American Oriental Society*, 53 (1933), 350.

rarely discussed material gains compared with the will of Heaven and compared with humaneness."[113] Chiao Hsün (1763-1820), in his *Lun-yü pu-shu* (Supplementary Commentary on the *Analects*) said that when Confucius occasionally talked about profit, he spoke of it together with destiny or humanity, that is, in the light of either of them. Han Yü (768-824) thought that what Confucius seldom talked about was the *men* of profit, destiny, or humanity, not the three subjects themselves (*Lun-yü pi-chieh,* or Explanations of the *Analects*). According to Huang Shih-nan's *Lun-yü hou-an* (Recent Examinations of the *Analects*, 1844), the word *han* does not mean "seldom," but is an alternate for *hsien*, "elucidation." While this is possible, it seems to be going too far. Most scholars leave the difficulty alone. As K'ang Yu-wei, in his *Lun-yü chu*, says, Confucius talked about the three subjects a great deal, since they are inherently important subjects for discussion.

9:3. Confucius said, "The linen cap is prescribed by the rules of ceremony (*li*) but nowadays a silk one is worn. It is economical and I follow the common practice. Bowing below the hall is prescribed by the rules of ceremony, but nowadays people bow after ascending the hall. This is arrogant, and I follow the practice of bowing below the hall though that is opposed to the common practice."

9:4. Confucius was completely free from four things: He had no arbitrariness of opinion, no dogmatism, no obstinacy, and no egotism.

9:5. When Confucius was in personal danger in K'uang,[114] he said, "Since the death of King Wen,[115] is not the course of culture (*wen*) in my keeping? If it had been the will of Heaven to destroy this culture, it would not have been given to a mortal [like me]. But if it is the will of Heaven that this culture should not perish, what can the people of K'uang do to me?"

9:6. A great official asked Tzu-kung, "Is the Master a sage? How is it that he has so much ability [in practical, specific things]?" Tzu-kung said, "Certainly Heaven has endowed him so liberally that he is to become a sage,[116] and furthermore he has much ability." When Confucius heard this, he said, "Does the great official know me? When I was young, I was in humble circumstances, and therefore I acquired much ability to do the simple things of humble folk. Does a superior

[113] "Lun Yü IX, 1," *ibid.*, 54 (1934), 83.

[114] The people of K'uang, mistaking Confucius for Yang Hu, their enemy whom Confucius resembled in appearance, surrounded him. This happened when Confucius was 56.

[115] Founder of the Chou dynasty.

[116] The term *chiang-sheng* is also understood to mean a great sage, or almost a sage.

man need to have so much ability? He does not." His pupil Lao said, "The Master said, 'I have not been given official employment and therefore I [acquired the ability] for the simple arts.' "[117]

9:13. Confucius wanted to live among the nine barbarous tribes of the East. Someone said, "They are rude. How can you do it?" Confucius said, "If a superior man lives there, what rudeness would there be?"

9:16. Confucius, standing by a stream, said, "It passes on like this, never ceasing day or night!"

> Comment. What was Confucius thinking about? Was he thinking of the unceasing operation of the universe (Chu Hsi and Ch'eng I)? Was he lamenting over the fact that the past cannot be recovered (Hsing Ping)? Was he comparing the untiring effort of a superior man's moral cultivation (Liu Pao-nan)? Was he praising water because its springs continuously gush out (Mencius[118] and Tung Chung-shu[119])? Was he praising water because it has the qualities of virtue, righteousness, courage, and so forth (Hsün Tzu, fl. 298-238 B.C.)?[120] One thing is fairly sure: water to him meant something quite different from what it meant to Indian and Western philosophers, and to some extent to Lao Tzu.[121]

9:25. Confucius said, "The commander of three armies may be taken away, but the will of even a common man may not be taken away from him."

10:9. When his mat was not straight [Confucius] did not sit on it.

10:12. A certain stable was burned down. On returning from court, Confucius asked, "Was any man hurt?" He did not ask about the horses.

10:14. On entering the Ancestral Temple, he asked about everything.

11:8. When Yen Yüan died, Confucius said, "Alas, Heaven is destroying me! Heaven is destroying me!"

11:11. Chi-lu (Tzu-lu) asked about serving the spiritual beings. Confucius said, "If we are not yet able to serve man, how can we serve spiritual beings?" "I venture to ask about death." Confucius said, "If we do not yet know about life, how can we know about death?"

> Comment. A most celebrated saying on humanism.

11:15. Tzu-kung asked who was the better man, Shih[122] or Shang.[123]

---

[117] Cf. Analects, 2:12.　　　　[118] Mencius, 4B:18.

[119] Ch'un-ch'iu fan-lu (Luxuriant Gems of the Spring and Autumn Annals), ch. 73, SPTK, 16:3a.

[120] Hsün Tzu, ch. 28, SPTK, 20:5b-6a.

[121] See below, ch. 7, comment on Lao Tzu, sec. 8.

[122] Name of Confucius' pupil, Tzu-chang.

[123] His family name was Pu and courtesy name Tzu-hsia (507–420 B.C.). Also Confucius' pupil.

Confucius said, "Shih goes too far and Shang does not go far enough." Tzu-kung said, "Then is Shih better?" Confucius said, "To go too far is the same as not to go far enough."

11:21. Tzu-lu asked, "Should one immediately practice what one has heard?" Confucius said, "There are father and elder brother [to be consulted]. Why immediately practice what one has heard?" Jan Yu (Jan Tzu) asked, "Should one immediately practice what one has heard?" Confucius said, "One should immediately practice what one has heard." Kung-hsi Hua[124] said, "When Yu (Tzu-lu) asked you, 'Should one immediately practice what one has heard?' you said, 'There are father and elder brother.' When Ch'iu (Jan Yu) asked you, 'Should one immediately practice what he has heard?' you said, 'One should immediately practice what one has heard.' I am perplexed, and venture to ask you for an explanation." Confucius said, "Ch'iu is retiring; therefore I urged him forward. Yu has more than one man's energy; therefore I kept him back."

11:25. Tzu-lu, Tseng Hsi,[125] Jan Yu, and Kung-hsi Hua were in attendance. Confucius said, "You think that I am a day or so older than you are. But do not think so. At present you are out of office and think that you are denied recognition. Suppose you were given recognition. What would you prefer?" Tzu-lu promptly replied, "Suppose there is a state of a thousand chariots, hemmed in by great powers, in addition invaded by armies, and as a result drought and famine prevail. Let me administer that state. In three years' time I can endow the people with courage and furthermore, enable them to know the correct principles." Confucius smiled at him [with disapproval].

"Ch'iu, how about you?" Jan Yu replied, "Suppose there is a state the sides of which are sixty or seventy *li* wide, or one of fifty or sixty *li*. Let me administer that state. In three years' time I can enable the people to be sufficient in their livelihood. As to the promotion of ceremonies and music, however, I shall have to wait for the superior man."

"How about you, Ch'ih?" Kung-hsi Hua replied, "I do not say I can do it but I should like to learn to do so. At the services of the royal ancestral temple, and at the conferences of the feudal lords, I should like to wear the dark robe and black cap (symbols of correctness) and be a junior assistant."

[Turning to Tseng Hsi,] Confucius said, "How about you, Tien?" Tseng Hsi was then softly playing the zither. With a bang he laid down the instrument, rose, and said, "My wishes are different from what the

[124] Confucius' pupil. His private name was Ch'ih and courtesy name Tzu-hua (b. 509 B.C.). Jan Yu (522–c. 462), whose private name was Ch'iu and courtesy name Jan Tzu, was also a pupil.

[125] Tseng Tzu's father, whose private name was Tien and courtesy name Hsi. He was also a Confucian pupil.

gentlemen want to do." Confucius said, "What harm is there? After all, we want each to tell his ambition." Tseng Hsi said, "In the late spring, when the spring dress is ready, I would like to go with five or six grown-ups and six or seven young boys to bathe in the I River, enjoy the breeze on the Rain Dance Altar, and then return home singing." Confucius heaved a sigh and said, "I agree with Tien."

Comment. Why did Confucius agree with Tseng Hsi? The field is wide open for speculation, and most Confucianists have taken the best advantage of it. Thus it was variously explained that Tseng Hsi was enjoying the harmony of the universe (Wang Ch'ung),[126] that he was following traditional cultural institutions (Liu Pao-nan), that he was wisely refraining from officialdom at the time of chaos (Huang K'an), that he was thinking of the "kingly way" whereas other pupils were thinking of the government of feudal states (Han Yü), that he was in the midst of the universal operation of the Principle of Nature (Chu Hsi), and that he was expressing freedom of the spirit (Wang Yang-ming, 1472-1529).[127] It is to be noted that the last two interpretations reflect the different tendencies of the two wings of Neo-Confucianism, one emphasizing the objective operation of the Principle of Nature, the other emphasizing the state of mind.

12:1. Yen Yüan asked about humanity. Confucius said, "To master[128] oneself and return to propriety is humanity.[129] If a man (the ruler) can for one day master himself and return to propriety, all under heaven will return to humanity.[130] To practice humanity depends on oneself. Does it depend on others?" Yen Yüan said, "May I ask for the detailed items?" Confucius said, "Do not look at what is contrary to propriety, do not listen to what is contrary to propriety, do not speak what is contrary to propriety, and do not make any movement which is contrary to propriety." Yen Yüan said, "Although I am not intelligent, may I put your saying into practice."

[126] *Lun-heng*, ch. 45; SPPY, 15:10a. Cf. Forke, *Lun-Heng*, vol. 2, p. 235.
[127] *Ch'uan-hsi lu* (Instructions for Practical Living), sec. 257. See Chan, trans., *Instructions for Practical Living*.
[128] The word *k'o* was understood by Ma Jung as "to control" but Chu Hsi interpreted it to mean "to master," that is, to conquer the self since it is an embodiment of selfish desires. Here is another example of the sharply different approaches to the *Analects* between the Han Confucianists and the Sung Neo-Confucianists. The Ch'ing Confucianists, such as Juan Yüan, violently opposed Chu Hsi, as is to be expected.
[129] An old saying. Other interpretations: (1) To be able to return to propriety by oneself; (2) to discipline oneself and to act according to propriety.
[130] Other interpretations: (1) Ascribe humanity to him; (2) will follow him.

12:2. Chung-kung[131] asked about humanity. Confucius said, "When you go abroad, behave to everyone as if you were receiving a great guest. Employ the people as if you were assisting at a great sacrifice.[132] Do not do to others what you do not want them to do to you.[133] Then there will be no complaint against you in the state or in the family (the ruling clan)." Chung-kung said, "Although I am not intelligent, may I put your saying into practice."

12:5. Ssu-ma Niu,[134] worrying, said, "All people have brothers but I have none."[135] Tzu-hsia said, "I have heard [from Confucius][136] this saying: 'Life and death are the decree of Heaven (*ming*); wealth and honor depend on Heaven. If a superior man is reverential (or serious) without fail, and is respectful in dealing with others and follows the rules of propriety, then all within the four seas (the world)[137] are brothers.'[138] What does the superior man have to worry about having no brothers?"

12:7. Tzu-kung asked about government. Confucius said, "Sufficient food, sufficient armament, and sufficient confidence of the people." Tzu-kung said, "Forced to give up one of these, which would you abandon first?" Confucius said, "I would abandon the armament." Tzu-kung said, "Forced to give up one of the remaining two, which would you abandon first?" Confucius said, "I would abandon food. There have been deaths from time immemorial, but no state can exist without the confidence of the people."

12.11. Duke Ching of Ch'i[139] asked Confucius about government. Confucius replied, "Let the ruler *be* a ruler, the minister *be* a minister, the father *be* a father, and the son *be* a son." The duke said, "Excellent! Indeed when the ruler is not a ruler, the minister not a minister, the father not a father, and the son not a son, although I may have all the grain, shall I ever get to eat it?"

12:16. Confucius said, "The superior man brings the good things of others to completion and does not bring the bad things of others to completion. The inferior man does just the opposite."

---

[131] Confucius' pupil, whose family name was Jan, private name Yung, and courtesy name Chung-kung. He was noted for excellent character.

[132] Paraphrasing two ancient sayings.

[133] See above, comment on 4:15.

[134] Confucius' pupil, whose family name was Hsiang.

[135] Meaning that his brother Huan T'ui (see above, 7:22) was not worthy to be a brother.

[136] Insertion according to Liu Pao-nan.

[137] Ordinarily meaning China, none doubts that here it means the entire world.

[138] Some say that the last sentence is Tzu-hsia's utterance.

[139] He reigned from 546 to 489 B.C.

12:17. Chi K'ang Tzu[140] asked Confucius about government. Confucius replied, "To govern (*cheng*) is to rectify (*cheng*). If you lead the people by being rectified yourself, who will dare not be rectified?"[141]

12:19. Chi K'ang Tzu asked Confucius about government, saying, "What do you think of killing the wicked and associating with the good?" Confucius replied, "In your government what is the need of killing? If you desire what is good, the people will be good. The character of a ruler is like wind and that of the people is like grass. In whatever direction the wind blows, the grass always bends."

12:22. Fan Ch'ih asked about humanity. Confucius said, "It is to love men." He asked about knowledge. Confucius said, "It is to know man."

> *Comment.* As a general virtue, *jen* means humanity, that is, that which makes a man a moral being. As a particular virtue, it means love. This is the general interpretation during the Han and T'ang times. Later in Neo-Confucianism, it was modified to mean man and Nature forming one body. The doctrine that knowledge of men is power has been maintained throughout the history of Confucianism. This humanistic interest has to a large degree prevented China from developing the tradition of knowledge for its own sake.

13:3. Tzu-lu said, "The ruler of Wei is waiting for you to serve in his administration. What will be your first measure?" Confucius said, "It will certainly concern the rectification of names." Tzu-lu said, "Is that so? You are wide of the mark. Why should there be such a rectification?" Confucius said, "Yu! How uncultivated you are! With regard to what he does not know, the superior man should maintain an attitude of reserve. If names are not rectified, then language will not be in accord with truth. If language is not in accord with truth, then things cannot be accomplished. If things cannot be accomplished, then ceremonies and music will not flourish. If ceremonies and music do not flourish, then punishment will not be just. If punishments are not just, then the people will not know how to move hand or foot. Therefore the superior man will give only names that can be described in speech and say only what can be carried out in practice. With regard to his speech, the superior man does not take it lightly. That is all."

> *Comment.* Most ancient Chinese philosophical schools had a theory about names and actuality. In the Confucian school, however, it assumes special importance because its focus is not metaphysical

---

[140] A great official of the state of Lu. He assumed power of government by usurpation in 492 B.C.
[141] Cf. below, 13:6.

as in Taoism, or logical as in the School of Logicians, or utilitarian as in the Legalist School, but ethical. This means not only that a name must correspond to its actuality, but also that rank, duties, and functions must be clearly defined and fully translated into action. Only then can a name be considered to be correct or rectified. With the ethical interest predominant, this is the nearest the ancient Confucianists came to a logical theory, except in the case of Hsün Tzu, who was the most logical of all ancient Confucianists.

13:6. Confucius said, "If a ruler sets himself right, he will be followed without his command. If he does not set himself right, even his commands will not be obeyed."[142]

13:16. The Duke of She asked about government. Confucius said, "[There is good government] when those who are near are happy and those far away desire to come."[143]

13:18. The Duke of She told Confucius, "In my country there is an upright man named Kung.[144] When his father stole a sheep, he bore witness against him." Confucius said, "The upright men in my community are different from this. The father conceals the misconduct of the son and the son conceals the misconduct of the father. Uprightness is to be found in this."

13:19. Fan Ch'ih asked about humanity. Confucius said, "Be respectful in private life, be serious (*ching*)[145] in handling affairs, and be loyal in dealing with others. Even if you are living amidst barbarians, these principles may never be forsaken."

13:23. Confucius said, "The superior man is conciliatory but does not identify himself with others; the inferior man identifies with others but is not conciliatory."[146]

13:26. Confucius said, "The superior man is dignified but not proud; the inferior man is proud but not dignified."

13:27. Confucius said, "A man who is strong, resolute, simple, and slow to speak is near to humanity."

13:29. Confucius said, "When good men have instructed the people [in morals, agriculture, military tactics][147] for seven years, they may be allowed to bear arms."

---

[142] Cf. above, 12:17.   [143] See below, 16:1.

[144] According to Kung An-Kuo, *kung* is not the name but is used as a noun, meaning the body, and that the man walked erect.

[145] The word *ching* here does not mean reverence, which assumes an object, but seriousness, which is a state of mind. See Appendix.

[146] Cf. above, 2:14.

[147] This is Chu Hsi's understanding, which has been satisfactory to most readers.

13:30.   Confucius said, "To allow people to go to war without first instructing them is to betray them."

14:2.   [Yüan Hsien][148] said, "When one has avoided aggressiveness, pride, resentment, and greed, he may be called a man of humanity." Confucius said, "This may be considered as having done what is difficult, but I do not know that it is to be regarded as humanity."

14:24.   Confucius said, "The superior man understands the higher things [moral principles]; the inferior man understands the lower things [profit]."[149]

14:29.   Confucius said, "The superior man is ashamed that his words exceed his deeds."

14:30.   Confucius said, "The way of the superior man is threefold, but I have not been able to attain it. The man of wisdom has no perplexities; the man of humanity has no worry; the man of courage has no fear." Tzu-kung said, "You are talking about yourself."

14:33.   Confucius said, "He who does not anticipate attempts to deceive him nor predict his being distrusted, and yet is the first to know [when these things occur], is a worthy man."[150]

14:36.   Someone said, "What do you think of repaying hatred with virtue?" Confucius said, "In that case what are you going to repay virtue with? Rather, repay hatred with uprightness and repay virtue with virtue."

Comment. The word for uprightness, chih, is not to be understood as severity or justice, which would imply repaying evil with evil. The idea of repaying hatred with virtue is also found in the Lao Tzu, ch. 63, and some have therefore theorized that the questioner was a Taoist or that the saying was a prevalent one at the time. In any case, by uprightness Confucianists mean absolute impartiality, taking guidance from what is right instead of one's personal preference, however admirable. Obviously this does not satisfy followers of the Christian doctrine of loving one's enemy. As to the golden rule, see above, comment on 4:15.

14:37.   Confucius said, "Alas! No one knows me!" Tzu-kung said,

[148] Confucius' pupil.

[149] This is the general interpretation, based on Huang K'an and commonly accepted before the Sung times. According to Ho Yen, higher things mean the fundamentals and the lower things mean secondary things. Chu Hsi, consistent with his own philosophy, interpreted the word ta not to mean to understand but to reach, and said that the superior man reaches the higher level because he follows the Principle of Nature while the inferior man reaches the lower level because he is carried away by selfish human desires. Cf. below, 14:37.

[150] See Wang Yang-ming, Ch'uan-hsi lu, in Chan, trans., Instructions for Practical Living, secs. 171 and 191 for his discussion of this topic.

"Why is there no one that knows you?" Confucius said, "I do not complain against Heaven. I do not blame men. I study things on the lower level but my understanding penetrates the higher level.[151] It is Heaven that knows me."

14:41. When Tzu-lu was stopping at the Stone Gate[152] for the night, the gate-keeper asked him, "Where are you from?" Tzu-lu said, "From Confucius." "Oh, is he the one who knows a thing cannot be done and still wants to do it?"

14:45. Tzu-lu asked about the superior man. Confucius said, "The superior man is one who cultivates himself with seriousness (*ching*)." Tzu-lu said, "Is that all?" Confucius said, "He cultivates himself so as to give the common people security and peace." Tzu-lu said, "Is that all?" Confucius said, "He cultivates himself so as to give all people security and peace. To cultivate oneself so as to give all people security and peace, even Yao and Shun found it difficult to do."[153]

15:2. Confucius said, "Tz'u (Tzu-kung), do you suppose that I am one who learns a great deal and remembers it?" Tzu-kung replied, "Yes. Is that not true?" Confucius said, "No. I have a thread (*i-kuan*) that runs through it all."[154]

15:4. Confucius said, "To have taken no [unnatural] action[155] and yet have the empire well governed, Shun was the man! What did he do? All he did was to make himself reverent and correctly face south [in his royal seat as the ruler]."

15:8. Confucius said, "A resolute scholar and a man of humanity will never seek to live at the expense of injuring humanity. He would rather sacrifice his life in order to realize humanity."[156]

15:17. Confucius said, "The superior man regards righteousness (*i*) as the substance of everything. He practices it according to the principles of propriety. He brings it forth in modesty. And he carries it to its conclusion with faithfulness. He is indeed a superior man!"

15:20. Confucius said, "The superior man seeks [room for improvement or occasion to blame] in himself; the inferior man seeks it in others."[157]

15:22. Confucius said, "The superior man (ruler) does not pro-

[151] There is a general agreement that the higher level refers to matters of Heaven, such as Heaven's decree (K'ung An-kuo and Huang K'an) and the Principle of Nature (Chu Hsi), and that the lower level refers to mundane matters. Cf. above, 14:24.

[152] The outer gate of the city of Lu. Cf. below, 18:6.

[153] See above, comment on 4:15.

[154] For the idea of a central thread, see above, 4:15.

[155] The term is the same as in Taoism, *wu-wei*. See above, comment on 2:1

[156] Cf. *Mencius*, 6A:10.

[157] Cf. *Great Learning*, ch. 9.

mote (put in office) a man on the basis of his words; nor does he reject his words because of the man."

15:23. Tzu-kung asked, "Is there one word which can serve as the guiding principle for conduct throughout life?" Confucius said, "It is the word altruism (*shu*). Do not do to others what you do not want them to do to you."

15:28. Confucius said, "It is man that can make the Way great, and not the Way that can make man great."

> *Comment.* Humanism in the extreme! Commentators from Huang K'an to Chu Hsi said that the Way, because it is tranquil and quiet and lets things take their own course, does not make man great. A better explanation is found in the *Doctrine of the Mean*, where it is said, "Unless there is perfect virtue, the perfect Way cannot be materialized."[158]

15:31. Confucius said, "The superior man seeks the Way and not a mere living. There may be starvation in farming, and there may be riches in the pursuit of studies. The superior man worries about the Way and not about poverty."

15:32. Confucius said, "When a man's knowledge is sufficient for him to attain [his position][159] but his humanity is not sufficient for him to hold it, he will lose it again. When his knowledge is sufficient for him to attain it and his humanity is sufficient for him to hold it, if he does not approach the people with dignity, the people will not respect him. If his knowledge is sufficient for him to attain it, his humanity sufficient for him to hold it, and he approaches the people with dignity, yet does not influence them with the principle of propriety, it is still not good."

15:35. Confucius said, "When it comes to the practice of humanity, one should not defer even to his teacher."

15:38. Confucius said, "In education there should be no class distinction."

> *Comment.* Confucius was the first to pronounce this principle in Chinese history. Among his pupils there were commoners as well as nobles, and stupid people as well as intelligent ones.[160]

15:40. Confucius said, "In words all that matters is to express the meaning."

16:1. Confucius said, ". . . I have heard that those who administer a state or a family do not worry about there being too few people, but

---

[158] *The Mean*, ch. 27.
[159] According to Pao Hsien (6 B.C.–A.D. 65), quoted by Ho Yen.
[160] Cf. above, 7:7.

worry about unequal distribution of wealth. They do not worry about poverty, but worry about the lack of security and peace on the part of the people. For when wealth is equally distributed, there will not be poverty; when there is harmony, there will be no problem of there being too few people; and when there are security and peace, there will be no danger to the state. . . ."[161]

16:4. Confucius said, "There are three kinds of friendship which are beneficial and three kinds which are harmful. Friendship with the upright, with the truthful, and with the well-informed is beneficial. Friendship with those who flatter, with those who are meek and who compromise with principles, and with those who talk cleverly is harmful."

16:8. Confucius said, "The superior man stands in awe of three things. He stands in awe of the Mandate of Heaven; he stands in awe of great men;[162] and he stands in awe of the words of the sages. The inferior man is ignorant of the Mandate of Heaven and does not stand in awe of it. He is disrespectful to great men and is contemptuous toward the words of the sages."

16:9. Confucius said, "Those who are born with knowledge are the highest type of people. Those who learn through study are the next. Those who learn through hard work are still the next. Those who work hard and still do not learn are really the lowest type."[163]

16:10. Confucius said, "The superior man has nine wishes. In seeing, he wishes to see clearly. In hearing, he wishes to hear distinctly. In his expression, he wishes to be warm. In his appearance, he wishes to be respectful. In his speech, he wishes to be sincere. In handling affairs, he wishes to be serious. When in doubt, he wishes to ask. When he is angry, he wishes to think of the resultant difficulties. And when he sees an opportunity for a gain, he wishes to think of righteousness."

17:2. Confucius said, "By nature men are alike. Through practice they have become far apart."

> *Comment.* This is the classical Confucian dictum on human nature. Neo-Confucianists like Chu Hsi and Ch'eng I[164] strongly argued that Confucius meant physical nature, which involves elements of evil, for since every man's original nature is good, men must be the *same* and therefore cannot be *alike*. Others, however, think that the word *chin* (near or alike) here has the same meaning as in

[161] The historical background in this chapter may be inaccurate, but the teaching in this selection has never been questioned.

[162] Variously interpreted as sages or rulers. It is more likely a Platonic philosopher-king, for in the Confucian system, the sage should be a ruler and the ruler should be a sage.

[163] Cf. *The Mean*, ch. 20.

[164] *I-shu*, 8:2a.

45

Mencius' saying, "All things of the same kind are similar to one another."[165] However, on the surface this saying is indisputably neutral, but all of Confucius' teachings imply the goodness of human nature.[166]

17:3. Confucius said, "Only the most intelligent and the most stupid do not change."

Comment. Advocates of the theory of three grades of nature, notably Wang Ch'ung,[167] Chia I (201–169 B.C.),[168] and Han Yü,[169] have drawn support from this saying by equating the most intelligent with those born good, the most stupid with those born evil, and the rest born neutral. They overlooked the fact that this passage has to do not with nature but only with intelligence. Practically all modern Confucianists are agreed on this point. As Ch'eng I,[170] Wang Yang-ming,[171] Tai Chen (Tai Tung-yüan, 1723-1777),[172] and Juan Yüan[173] all pointed out, it is not that they cannot change. It is simply that they are too intelligent to change downward or too stupid to change upward.

17:4. Confucius went to the city of Wu [where his disciple Tzu-yu was the magistrate] and heard the sound of stringed instruments and singing. With a gentle smile, the Master said, "Why use an ox-knife to kill a chicken [that is, why employ a serious measure like music to rule such a small town]?" Tzu-yu replied, "Formerly I heard you say, 'When the superior man has studied the Way, he loves men. When the inferior man has studied the Way, he is easy to employ.'" Confucius said, "My disciples, what I just said was only a joke."

17:6. Tzu-chang asked Confucius about humanity. Confucius said, "One who can practice five things wherever he may be is a man of humanity." Tzu-chang asked what the five are. Confucius said, "Earnestness, liberality, truthfulness, diligence, and generosity. If one is earnest, one will not be treated with disrespect. If one is liberal, one will win the hearts of all. If one is truthful, one will be trusted. If one is diligent, one

[165] *Mencius*, 6A:7.
[166] See above, comment on 6:17.
[167] See below, ch. 16, first comment.
[168] *Hsin-shu* (New Treatises), ch. 5, sec. 3, SPPY, 5:7a.
[169] See below, ch. 27, sec. 1.
[170] *I-shu*, 18:17b.
[171] *Ch'uan-hsi lu*, sec. 109. See Chan, trans., *Instructions for Practical Living.*
[172] *Meng Tzu tzu-i shu-cheng* (Commentary on the Meanings of Terms in the *Book of Mencius*), sec. 22.
[173] *Hsing-ming ku-hsün* (Classical Interpretations of Nature and Destiny), in *Yen-ching-shih chi*, 1st collection, 10:16b.

will be successful. And if one is generous, one will be able to enjoy the service of others."

17:8. Confucius said, "Yu (Tzu-lu), have you heard about the six virtues[174] and the six obscurations?" Tzu-lu replied, "I have not." Confucius said, "Sit down, then. I will tell you. One who loves humanity but not learning will be obscured by ignorance. One who loves wisdom but not learning will be obscured by lack of principle. One who loves faithfulness but not learning will be obscured by heartlessness. One who loves uprightness but not learning will be obscured by violence. One who loves strength of character but not learning will be obscured by recklessness."

17:9. Confucius said, "My young friends, why do you not study the odes? The odes can stimulate your emotions, broaden your observation, enlarge your fellowship, and express your grievances. They help you in your immediate service to your parents and in your more remote service to your rulers. They widen your acquaintance with the names of birds, animals, and plants."

17:19. Confucius said, "I do not wish to say anything." Tzu-kung said, "If you do not say anything, what can we little disciples ever learn to pass on to others?" Confucius said, "Does Heaven (*T'ien*, Nature) say anything? The four seasons run their course and all things are produced. Does Heaven say anything?"

> *Comment.* This is usually cited to support the contention that Confucius did not believe in an anthropomorphic God but in Heaven which reigns rather than rules. In Neo-Confucianism, Heaven came to be identified with principle (*li*).[175]

17:23. Tzu-lu asked, "Does the superior man[176] esteem courage?" Confucius said, "The superior man considers righteousness (*i*) as the most important. When the superior man has courage but no righteousness, he becomes turbulent. When the inferior man has courage but no righteousness, he becomes a thief."

17:25. Confucius said, "Women and servants are most difficult to deal with. If you are familiar with them, they cease to be humble. If you keep a distance from them, they resent it."

> *Comment.* From Confucius down, Confucianists have always considered women inferior.

[174] The word *yen*, ordinarily meaning saying, here refers to the virtues mentioned below.

[175] Cf. *Lao Tzu*, ch. 23.

[176] In the *Analects* sometimes "superior man" means a ruler and "inferior man" means a common person. It is not clear which is meant here. But the moral is the same.

18:6. Ch'ang-chü and Chieh-ni were cultivating their fields together. Confucius was passing that way and told Tzu-lu to ask them where the river could be forded. Ch'ang-chü said, "Who is the one holding the reins in the carriage?" Tzu-lu said, "It is K'ung Ch'iu (Confucius)." "Is he the K'ung Ch'iu of Lu?" "Yes." "Then he already knows where the river can be forded!" Tzu-lu asked Chieh-ni. Chieh-ni said, "Who are you, sir?" Tzu-lu replied, "I am Chung-yu (name of Tzu-lu)." "Are you a follower of K'ung Ch'iu of Lu?" "Yes." Chieh-ni said, "The whole world is swept as though by a torrential flood. Who can change it? As for you, instead of following one who flees from this man or that man, is it not better to follow those who flee the world altogether?" And with that he went on covering the seed without stopping. Tzu-lu went to Confucius and told him about their conversation. Confucius said ruefully, "One cannot herd with birds and beasts. If I do not associate with mankind, with whom shall I associate? If the Way prevailed in the world, there would be no need for me to change it."[177]

19:6. Tzu-hsia said, "To study extensively, to be steadfast in one's purpose, to inquire earnestly, and to reflect on what is at hand (that is, what one can put into practice)—humanity consists in these."

19:7. Confucius said, "The hundred artisans work in their works to perfect their craft. The superior man studies to reach to the utmost of the Way."

19:11. Tzu-hsia said, "So long as a man does not transgress the boundary line in the great virtues, he may pass and repass it in the small virtues."

Comment. Even Chu Hsi quoted someone who pointed out that this passage is not free from defect.

19:13. Tzu-hsia said, "A man who has energy to spare after studying should serve his state. A man who has energy to spare after serving his state should study."[178]

19:24. Shu-sun Wu-shu[179] slandered Chung-ni (Confucius). Tzu-kung said, "It is no use. Chung-ni cannot be slandered. Other worthies are like mounds or small hills. You can still climb over them. Chung-ni, however, is like the sun and the moon that cannot be climbed over. Although a man may want to shut his eyes to the sun and the moon, what harm does it do to them? It would only show in large measure that he does not know his own limitations."

[177] This episode took place when Confucius was 64. Cf. above, 14:41.
[178] Cf. above, 1:6.   [179] Official-in-chief of Lu.

3

IDEALISTIC CONFUCIANISM: MENCIUS

THE CAREER OF MENCIUS (371–289 B.C.?) was amazingly similar to that of Confucius, whom he proclaimed the greatest sage.[1] Like Confucius, he was born in what is modern Shantung province. Like Confucius, he was a professional teacher, having studied under the pupils of the grandson of Confucius. Like Confucius, he idolized the legendary sage-emperors.[2] Like Confucius, he lived in a period of political struggle, moral chaos, and intellectual conflicts. Like Confucius, he had a sense of mission, if only to suppress "perversive doctrines."[3] To this end he debated with scholars and attacked his opponents, especially the followers of Mo Tzu (fl. 479–438 B.C.) and Yang Chu (440–360 B.C.?).[4] Like Confucius, he traveled for forty years from about 354 B.C. or earlier, to offer advice to rulers for reform.[5] Like Confucius, he once served as an official, in Ch'i from 319 to 312 B.C. Like Confucius, he was a filial son, for while serving in Ch'i, he took three years out to mourn the death of his mother. And like Confucius, he was eventually disappointed, and retired.

One contrast between the two, however, is that we know practically nothing about Mencius' family or his private life. He was a pupil of Confucius' grandson Tzu-ssu's pupil. His dates are uncertain. The most scholars can say is that he lived between 370 and 290 B.C., thus making him contemporaneous with Hsün Tzu, Chuang Tzu, and Plato, with whom he is often compared.

The greatest difference between Mencius and Confucius, however, is in their doctrines. Basically, Mencius' teachings were derived from Confucius. But in the central doctrine of the Confucian school, that of human nature, Mencius took a big step forward, and his new theory colored his other doctrines. While Confucius no more than implied that human nature *is* good, Mencius declared definitely that it is *originally*

[1] *Mencius*, 2A:2; 3B:9; 7B:38.

[2] *ibid.*, 3A:1; 3B:9; 4A:28; 5A:1-3; 7A:16, 30, 35; 7B:33.

[3] See below, comment on 3B:9.

[4] For debates, see *Mencius*, 3B:9; 4A:17; 6A:1-6. For criticisms of Yang and Mo, see *Mencius*, 3A:5; 3B:9; 7A:26; 7B:26. For attack on other schools, see *Mencius*, 3A:4; 3B:10; 6B:1.

[5] So far as scholars can make out, his travel was something like this: He visited the state of Ch'i in or about 357 B.C. He was in Sung around 325 B.C. Some two years later he went to Hsüeh and returned to his native Tsou the next year. At the request of the Duke of T'eng, he went there, staying for three years, probably from 322 to 320 B.C. From T'eng he went to Liang. About 319 B.C. he visited Ch'i once more and served in an official position. In 312 B.C. or soon after, he resigned and left.

good. Moreover, he built his entire philosophy on this tenet, and was the first to do so. Since man is originally good, it logically follows (1) that he possesses the innate knowledge of the good and "innate ability" to do good;[6] (2) that if one "develops his mind to the utmost," he can "serve Heaven" and "fulfill his destiny";[7] (3) that evil is not inborn but due to man's own failures and his inability to avoid evil external influences;[8] (4) that serious efforts must be made to recover our original nature; and (5) that the end of learning is none other than to "seek for the lost mind."[9] His doctrine of the recovery of original nature formed the basis of the philosophy of Li Ao (fl. 798).[10] His doctrine of innate knowledge and ability became the backbone of the idealistic philosophy of Wang Yang-ming (Wang Shou-jen, 1472-1529)[11] and those who followed him for two hundred years. His general theory of the goodness of human nature exercised a tremendous influence on the whole movement of Confucianism in the last millennium, especially on Tai Chen (Tai Tung-yüan, 1723-1777).[12]

Since human nature is good, love is therefore an inborn moral quality. But Mencius insisted that the practice of love must start with the family, and he bitterly opposed the Moist doctrine of universal love without distinctions. For this reason he often advocated humanity (*jen*, love) and righteousness (*i*) together,[13] for to him humanity was necessary to bind people together and righteousness was necessary to make distinctions. In Mencius the ideal of righteousness assumed unprecedented importance. He was the first one to raise righteousness to the highest level in moral values.

In government, too, he felt, humanity and righteousness must be the guiding principles. He strongly advocated "humane government."[14] In fact, he was the first one to use the term. He vigorously opposed righteousness to utility, advantages, and profit. He wanted to overcome the "way of a despot," or the way of force, by the "kingly way," or the way of moral power.

As moral power is inherent in everyone's nature, therefore every individual is "complete in himself"; every individual can become a sage; and everyone is equal to everyone else. For Mencius, people are the most important factor in government, and they have the right to revolt. This idea of revolution was not only novel in Mencius, but it also made him the greatest advocate of political democracy in Chinese history.

Revolutionary as he was, Mencius did not deviate from the general

---

[6] *Mencius*, 7A:15. [7] *ibid.*, 7A:1. [8] *ibid.*, 6A:8.
[9] *ibid.*, 6A:11. [10] See below, ch. 27, sec. 3. [11] See below, ch. 35.
[12] See below, ch. 38, A, secs. 2, 10; and B, sec. 29.
[13] See below, 1A:1; 4A:10, 20, 27; 6A:1, 4, 6, 11.
[14] 1A:1, 5; 2A:5; 3A:3-4.

direction determined by Confucius. What we have in Mencius is therefore orthodox Confucianism, developed along idealistic lines.

The following selections from the *Book of Mencius* consist of Book Six, part 1, in full, which is the most important portion of the book, and selected chapters from other books. Their major topics and references are:

Benevolent government: 1A:1, 5, 7; 1B:5, 7; 2A:5; 3A:3; 4A:14; 5A:5
Equality: 6A:7; 3A:1; 4B:28, 32
Great man: 6A:14, 15; 4B:11, 12
Human relations: 3A:4; 3B:2, 9; 4A:17, 18, 26; 4B:30
Humanity (*jen*) and Righteousness: 6A:1, 4, 8, 10, 11, 18, 19; 1A:1; 2A:2; 4A:10, 20, 27
Nature, human, and Innate virtue: 6A:1-6; 2A:6; 4B:26
People and Revolution: 1B:7, 8; 4B:3
Social classes: 3A:3, 4
Unbearing mind: 1A:7; 2A:6
Undisturbed mind: 2A:2
Yang and Mo: 3A:5; 3B:9; 7A:26

THE BOOK OF MENCIUS[15]

Book Six, Part I

6A:1. Kao Tzu[16] said, "Human nature is like the willow tree, and righteousness is like a cup or a bowl. To turn human nature into humanity and righteousness is like turning the willow into cups and bowls." Mencius said, "Sir, can you follow the nature of the willow tree and make the cups and bowls, or must you violate the nature of the willow tree before you can make the cups and bowls? If you are going to violate the nature of the willow tree in order to make cups and bowls, then must you also violate human nature in order to make it into humanity and righteousness? Your words, alas! would lead all people in the world to consider humanity and righteousness as calamity [because they required the violation of human nature]!"

[15] The *Book of Mencius, Meng Tzu* in Chinese, is divided into seven books, each subdivided into two parts. In all probability it was compiled by pupils of Mencius after his death. Chu Hsi (1130-1200) grouped it with the *Analects*, the *Great Learning*, and the *Doctrine of the Mean* as the "Four Books." From then on they ranked as Classics. These four books and Chu Hsi's commentaries on them were the basis of the civil service examinations from 1313 till 1905, replacing other Classics in importance and influence. For translations of the *Book of Mencius*, see Bibliography.

[16] His dates are c.420–c.350 B.C., but otherwise nothing is known of him. Chao Ch'i (d. 201), in his *Meng Tzu chu* (Commentary on the *Book of Mencius*), says his name was Pu-hai. Chiao Hsün (1763-1820), in his *Meng Tzu cheng-i* (Correct Meanings of the *Book of Mencius*), thought Chao confused him with the Pu-hai who once studied under Mencius. The two different persons merely had the same private name.

6A:2. Kao Tzu said, "Man's nature is like whirling water. If a breach in the pool is made to the east it will flow to the east. If a breach is made to the west it will flow to the west. Man's nature is indifferent to good and evil, just as water is indifferent to east and west." Mencius said, "Water, indeed, is indifferent to the east and west, but is it indifferent to high and low? Man's nature is naturally good just as water naturally flows downward. There is no man without this good nature; neither is there water that does not flow downward. Now you can strike water and cause it to splash upward over your forehead, and by damming and leading it, you can force it uphill. Is this the nature of water? It is the forced circumstance that makes it do so. Man can be made to do evil, for his nature can be treated in the same way."

6A:3. Kao Tzu said, "What is inborn[17] is called nature." Mencius said, "When you say that what is inborn is called nature, is that like saying that white is white?" "Yes." "Then is the whiteness of the white feather the same as the whiteness of snow? Or, again, is the whiteness of snow the same as the whiteness of white jade?" "Yes." "Then is the nature of a dog the same as the nature of an ox, and is the nature of an ox the same as the nature of a man?"

6A:4. Kao Tzu said, "By nature we desire food and sex. Humanity is internal and not external, whereas righteousness is external and not internal." Mencius said, "Why do you say that humanity is internal and righteousness external?" "When I see an old man and respect him for his age, it is not that the oldness is within me, just as, when something is white and I call it white, I am merely observing its external appearance. I therefore say that righteousness is external." Mencius said, "There is no difference between our considering a white horse to be white and a white man to be white. But is there no difference between acknowledging the age of an old horse and the age of an old man? And what is it that we call righteousness, the fact that a man is old or the fact that we honor his old age?" Kao Tzu said, "I love my own younger brother but do not love the younger brother of, say, a man from the state of Ch'in. This is because I am the one to determine that pleasant feeling. I therefore say that humanity comes from within. On the other hand, I respect the old men of the state of Ch'u as well as my own elders. What determines my pleasant feeling is age itself. Therefore I say that righteousness is external." Mencius said, "We love the roast meat of Ch'in as much as we love our own. This is even so with respect to material things. Then are you going to say that our love of roast meat is also external?"

[17] According to Chu Hsi, *Meng Tzu chi-chu* (Collected Commentaries on the *Book of Mencius*), *sheng* refers not to man's inborn nature but to his consciousness and activities, and is comparable to the Buddhist theory that function is nature.

6A:5. Meng Chi Tzu[18] asked Kung-tu Tzu,[19] "What does it mean to say that righteousness is internal?" Kung-tu Tzu said, "We practice reverence, and therefore it is called internal." "Suppose a fellow villager is one year older than your older brother. Whom are you going to serve with reverence?" "I shall serve my brother with reverence." "In offering wine at a feast, to whom will you offer first?" "I shall offer wine to the villager first." Meng Chi Tzu said, "Now you show reverence to one but honor for age to the other. What determines your actions certainly lies without and not within." Kung-tu Tzu could not reply and told Mencius about it. Mencius said, "If you ask him whether he will serve with reverence his uncle or his younger brother, he will say that he will serve with reverence his uncle. Then you ask him, in case his younger brother is acting at a sacrifice as the representative of the deceased, then to whom is he going to serve with reverence? He will say he will serve the younger brother with reverence. Then you ask him 'Where is your reverence for your uncle?' He will then say, '[I show reverence to my younger brother] because he represents the ancestral spirit in an official capacity.' You can then likewise say, '[I show reverence to the villager] because of his position.' Ordinarily, the reverence is due the elder brother, but on special occasions it is due the villager." When Chi Tzu heard this, he said, "We show reverence to uncle when reverence is due him, and we show reverence to the younger brother when reverence is due him. Certainly what determines it lies without and does not come from within." Kung-tu Tzu said, "In the winter we drink things hot. In the summer we drink things cold. Does it mean that what determines eating and drinking also lies outside?"

6A:6. Kung-tu Tzu said, "Kao Tzu said that man's nature is neither good nor evil. Some say that man's nature may be made good or evil, therefore when King Wen and King Wu[20] were in power the people loved virtue, and when Kings Yu and Li[21] were in power people loved violence. Some say that some men's nature is good and some men's nature is evil. Therefore even under (sage-emperor) Yao[22] there was Hsiang [who daily plotted to kill his brother], and even with a bad father Ku-sou, there was [a most filial] Shun[23] (Hsiang's brother

[18] Chu Hsi thinks he was possibly a younger brother of Meng Chung Tzu, pupil of Mencius.

[19] Mencius' pupil.

[20] Sage-kings who founded the Chou dynasty (r. 1171–1122 B.C. and 1121–1116 B.C., respectively).

[21] Wicked kings (r. 781–771 B.C. and 878–842 B.C., respectively).

[22] Legendary ruler (3rd millennium B.C.).

[23] Legendary ruler, successor of Yao.

who succeeded Yao), and even with (wicked king) Chou[24] as nephew and ruler, there were Viscount Ch'i of Wei and Prince Pi-kan.[25] Now you say that human nature is good. Then are those people wrong?"

Mencius said, "If you let people follow their feelings (original nature),[26] they will be able to do good. This is what is meant by saying that human nature is good. If man does evil, it is not the fault of his natural endowment.[27] The feeling of commiseration is found in all men; the feeling of shame and dislike is found in all men; the feeling of respect and reverence is found in all men; and the feeling of right and wrong is found in all men. The feeling of commiseration is what we call humanity; the feeling of shame and dislike is what we call righteousness; the feeling of respect and reverence is what we call propriety (li);[28] and the feeling of right and wrong is what we call wisdom. Humanity, righteousness, propriety, and wisdom are not drilled into us from outside. We originally have them with us. Only we do not think [to find them]. Therefore it is said, 'Seek and you will find it, neglect and you will lose it.'[29] [Men differ in the development of their endowments], some twice as much as others, some five times, and some to an incalculable degree, because no one can develop his original endowment to the fullest extent. The *Book of Odes* says, 'Heaven produces the teeming multitude. As there are things there are their specific principles. When the people keep their normal nature they will love excellent virtue.'[30] Confucius said, 'The writer of this poem indeed knew the Way (Tao). Therefore as there are things, there must be their specific principles, and since people keep to their normal nature, therefore they love excellent virtue.' "

> *Comment.* Mencius is the most important philosopher on the question of human nature, for he is the father of the theory of the original goodness of human nature. In spite of variations and modifications, this has remained the firm belief of the Chinese. Book

[24] King Chou (r. 1175–1112 B.C.) was responsible for the fall of the Shang dynasty (1751–1112 B.C.).

[25] It is not sure whether they were King Chou's uncles. Their good advice to King Chou was rejected.

[26] Note that *ch'ing* here does not mean feelings which are sources of evil desires, as understood by later Confucianists, but feelings proper to the originally good nature of man. As Tai Chen has clearly pointed out in his *Meng Tzu tzu-i shu-cheng* (Commentary on the Meanings of Terms in the *Book of Mencius*), sec. 30, *ch'ing* is the original simple substance, not contrasted with the nature.

[27] The word *ts'ai*, ordinarily meaning ability, is here interchangeable with *ts'ai* meaning raw material.

[28] The word *li* here is not used in its narrow sense of rites and ceremonies but in the broad sense of principle of conduct and the sense of what is proper.

[29] Probably an old saying.

[30] Ode no. 260.

Six, part 1, is almost entirely devoted to the subject. And of all the chapters, this is the most nearly central and the most comprehensive. It records the various theories on human nature in ancient China, except that of Hsün Tzu. It puts Mencius' own theory in direct and simple form. And it also points out that evil or failure is not original but due to the underdevelopment of one's original endowment. Later Confucianists, especially Neo-Confucianists, devoted much of their deliberations to these subjects, but they have never deviated from the general direction laid down by Mencius.

6A:7. Mencius said, "In good years most of the young people behave well.[31] In bad years most of them abandon themselves to evil.[32] This is not due to any difference in the natural capacity endowed by Heaven. The abandonment is due to the fact that the mind is allowed to fall into evil. Take for instance the growing of wheat. You sow the seeds and cover them with soil. The land is the same and the time of sowing is also the same. In time they all grow up luxuriantly. When the time of harvest comes, they are all ripe. Although there may be a difference between the different stalks of wheat, it is due to differences in the soil, as rich or poor, to the unequal nourishment obtained from the rain and the dew, and to differences in human effort. Therefore all things of the same kind are similar to one another. Why should there be any doubt about men? The sage and I are the same in kind. Therefore Lung Tzu[33] said, 'If a man makes shoes without knowing the size of people's feet, I know that he will at least not make them to be like baskets.' Shoes are alike because people's feet are alike. There is a common taste for flavor in our mouths. I-ya[34] was the first to know our common taste for food. Suppose one man's taste for flavor is different from that of others, as dogs and horses differ from us in belonging to different species, then why should the world follow I-ya in regard to flavor? Since in the matter of flavor the whole world regards I-ya as the standard, it shows that our tastes for flavor are alike. The same is true of our ears. Since in the matter of sounds the whole world regards Shih-k'uang[35] as the standard, it shows that our ears are alike. The same is true of our eyes. With regard to Tzu-tu,[36] none in the world did not know that he

[31] Juan Yüan (1764-1849) and Chao Ch'i understood *lai* to mean behaving well. Chiao Hsün, however, interpreted the term *lai* to mean "to become dependent or lazy." See Chiao, *Meng Tzu cheng-i.*

[32] *Pao* is not to be understood in its ordinary meaning of violence, but evil, according to Chao Ch'i.

[33] An ancient worthy.

[34] An ancient famous gourmet, chef of Duke Huan (r. 685-643 B.C.) of Ch'i.

[35] An ancient expert on music, concert master for Duke P'ing (r. 557-532 B.C.) of Chin.

[36] An ancient handsome man.

was handsome. Any one who did not recognize his handsomeness must have no eyes. Therefore I say there is a common taste for flavor in our mouths, a common sense for sound in our ears, and a common sense for beauty in our eyes. Can it be that in our minds alone we are not alike? What is it that we have in common in our minds? It is the sense of principle and righteousness (*i-li*, moral principles). The sage is the first to possess what is common in our minds. Therefore moral principles please our minds as beef and mutton and pork please our mouths."

> *Comment.* In saying that one is of the same kind as the sage, Mencius was pronouncing two principles of utmost significance. One is that every person can be perfect, and the other is that all people are basically equal.[37] Also, in pointing to the moral principle which is common in our minds, he is pointing to what amounts to the Natural Law. Belief in the Natural Law has been persistent in Chinese history. It is called Principle of Nature (*T'ien-li*) by Neo-Confucianists. It is essentially the same as Mencius' *i-li*.

6A:8. Mencius said, "The trees of the Niu Mountain[38] were once beautiful. But can the mountain be regarded any longer as beautiful since, being in the borders of a big state, the trees have been hewed down with axes and hatchets? Still with the rest given them by the days and nights and the nourishment provided them by the rains and the dew, they were not without buds and sprouts springing forth. But then the cattle and the sheep pastured upon them once and again. That is why the mountain looks so bald. When people see that it is so bald, they think that there was never any timber on the mountain. Is this the true nature of the mountain? Is there not [also] a heart of humanity and righteousness originally existing in man? The way in which he loses his originally good mind is like the way in which the trees are hewed down with axes and hatchets. As trees are cut down day after day, can a mountain retain its beauty? To be sure, the days and nights do the healing, and there is the nourishing air of the calm morning which keeps him normal in his likes and dislikes. But the effect is slight, and is disturbed and destroyed by what he does during the day. When there is repeated disturbance, the restorative influence of the night will not be sufficient to preserve (the proper goodness of the mind). When the influence of the night is not sufficient to preserve it, man becomes not much different from the beast. People see that he acts like an animal, and think that he never had the original endowment (for goodness).

---

[37] A similar idea is expressed in *Mencius*, 4B:28 and 32.
[38] Outside the capital of the state of Ch'i.

But is that his true character? Therefore with proper nourishment and care, everything grows, whereas without proper nourishment and care, everything decays. Confucius said, "Hold it fast and you preserve it. Let it go and you lose it. It comes in and goes out at no definite time and without anyone's knowing its direction.' He was talking about the human mind."

6A:9. Mencius said, "Don't suspect that the king[39] lacks wisdom. Even in the case of the things that grow most easily in the world, they would never grow up if they were exposed to sunshine for one day and then to cold for ten days. It is seldom that I have an audience with him, and when I leave, others who expose him to cold arrive. Even if what I say to him is taking root, what good does it do? Now chess playing is but a minor art. One cannot learn it unless he concentrates his mind and devotes his whole heart to it. Chess Expert Ch'iu is the best chess player in the whole country. Suppose he is teaching two men to play. One man will concentrate his mind and devote his whole heart to it, doing nothing but listening to Chess Expert Ch'iu's instructions. Although the other man listens to him, his whole mind is thinking that a wild goose is about to pass by and he wants to bend his bow, adjust the string to the arrow, and shoot it. Although he is learning along with the other man, he will never be equal to him. Is that because his intelligence is inferior? No, it is not."

6A:10. Mencius said, "I like fish and I also like bear's paw. If I cannot have both of them, I shall give up the fish and choose the bear's paw. I like life and I also like righteousness. If I cannot have both of them, I shall give up life and choose righteousness. I love life, but there is something I love more than life, and therefore I will not do anything improper to have it. I also hate death, but there is something I hate more than death, and therefore there are occasions when I will not avoid danger. If there is nothing that man loves more than life, then why should he not employ every means to preserve it? And if there is nothing that man hates more than death, then why does he not do anything to avoid danger? There are cases when a man does not take the course even if by taking it he can preserve his life, and he does not do anything even if by doing it he can avoid danger.[40] Therefore there is something men love more than life and there is something men hate more than death. It is not only the worthies alone who have this moral sense. All men have it, but only the worthies have been able to preserve it.

Suppose here are a small basket of rice and a platter of soup. With

[39] Probably King Hsüan of Ch'i (r. 342–324 B.C.).
[40] Cf. *Analects*, 15:8.

them one will survive and without them one will die. If you offer them in a loud and angry voice, even an ordinary passer-by will not accept them, or if you first tread on them and then offer them, even a beggar will not stoop to take them. What good does a salary of ten thousand bushels do me if I accept them without any consideration of the principles of propriety and righteousness? Shall I take it because it gives me beautiful mansions, the service of a wife and concubines, and the chance gratitude of my needy acquaintances who receive my help? If formerly I refused to accept the offer (of rice and soup) in the face of death and now I accept for the sake of beautiful mansions, if formerly I refused the offer in the face of death and now accept for the sake of the service of a wife and concubines, if formerly I refused the offer and now accept for the sake of the gratitude of my needy acquaintances, is that not the limit? This is called casting the original mind away."[41]

6A:11. Mencius said, "Humanity is man's mind and righteousness is man's path. Pity the man who abandons the path and does not follow it, and who has lost his heart and does not know how to recover it. When people's dogs and fowls are lost, they go to look for them, and yet, when they have lost their hearts, they do not go to look for them. The way of learning is none other than finding the lost mind.

6A:12. Mencius said, "Suppose there is a man whose fourth finger is crooked and cannot stretch out straight. It is not painful and it does not interfere with his work. And yet if there were someone who could straighten out the finger for him, he would not mind going as far as to the states of Ch'in and Ch'u because his finger is not like those of others, yet he does not hate the fact that his mind is not like those of others. This is called ignorance of the relative importance of things."[42]

6A:13. Mencius said, "Anybody who wishes to cultivate the t'ung and tzu trees, which may be grasped by one or both hands, knows how to nourish them. In the case of their own persons, men do not know how to nourish them. Do they love their persons less than the t'ung and tzu trees? Their lack of thought is extreme."

6A:14. Mencius said, "There is not a part of the body that a man does not love. And because there is no part of the body that he does not love, there is not a part of it that he does not nourish. Because there is not an inch of his skin that he does not love, there is not an inch of his skin that he does not nourish. To determine whether his nourishing is good or not, there is no other way except to see the choice he makes for himself. Now, some parts of the body are noble and some

[41] According to Chu Hsi, this is the original mind of shame and dislike.

[42] This interpretation is according to Sun Shih (962-1033), subcommentary on Chao Ch'i's commentary in the Meng Tzu chu-shu (Subcommentary and Commentary on the Book of Mencius) in the Thirteen Classics Series.

are ignoble; some great and some small. We must not allow the ignoble to injure the noble, or the smaller to injure the greater. Those who nourish the smaller parts will become small men. Those who nourish the greater parts will become great men. A gardener who neglects his *t'ung* and *tzu* trees and cultivates thorns and bramble becomes a bad gardener. A man who takes good care of his finger and, without knowing it, neglects his back and shoulders, resembles a hurried wolf.[43] A man who only eats and drinks is looked down upon by others, because he nourishes the smaller parts of his body to the injury of the greater parts. If he eats and drinks but makes no mistake [of injuring the greater parts of his body], how should his mouth and belly be considered merely as so many inches of his body?"

6A:15. Kung-tu Tzu asked, "We are all human beings. Why is it that some men become great and others become small?" Mencius said, "Those who follow the greater qualities in their nature become great men and those who follow the smaller qualities in their nature become small men." "But we are all human beings. Why is it that some follow their greater qualities and others follow their smaller qualities?" Mencius replied, "When our senses of sight and hearing are used without thought and are thereby obscured by material things, the material things act on the material senses and lead them astray. That is all. The function of the mind is to think. If we think, we will get them (the principles of things). If we do not think, we will not get them. This is what Heaven has given to us. If we first build up the nobler part of our nature, then the inferior part cannot overcome it. It is simply this that makes a man great."

> *Comment.* We shall find that the idea of building up the nobler part of our nature became an important tenet in the moral philosophy of Lu Hsiang-shan (Lu Chiu-yüan, 1139-1193), leader of the idealistic school of Neo-Confucianism.[44]

6A:16. Mencius said, "There is nobility of Heaven and there is nobility of man. Humanity, righteousness, loyalty, faithfulness, and the love of the good without getting tired of it constitute the nobility of Heaven, and to be a grand official, a great official, and a high official— this constitutes the nobility of man. The ancient people cultivated the nobility of Heaven, and the nobility of man naturally came to them. People today cultivate the nobility of Heaven in order to seek for the nobility of man, and once they have obtained the nobility of man, they

---

[43] The meaning of the phrase is obscure.
[44] See below, ch. 33, secs. 8 and 24.

forsake the nobility of Heaven. Therefore their delusion is extreme. At the end they will surely lose [the nobility of man] also."

6A:17. Mencius said, "The desire to be honored is shared by the minds of all men. But all men have in themselves what is really honorable. Only they do not think of it. The honor conferred by men is not true honor. Whoever is made honorable by Chao Meng[45] can be made humble by him again. The *Book of Odes* says, 'I am drunk with wine, and I am satiated with virtue.'[46] It means that a man is satiated with humanity and righteousness, and therefore he does not wish for the flavor of fat meat and fine millet of men. A good reputation and far-reaching praise are heaped on him, and he does not desire the embroidered gowns of men."

6A:18. Mencius said, "Humanity subdues inhumanity as water subdues fire. Nowadays those who practice humanity do so as if with one cup of water they could save a whole wagonload of fuel on fire. When the flames were not extinguished, they would say that water cannot subdue fire. This is as bad as those who are inhumane.[47] At the end they will surely lose [what little humanity they have]."

6A:19. Mencius said, "The five kinds of grain are considered good plants, but if they are not ripe, they are worse than poor grains. So the value of humanity depends on its being brought to maturity."

6A:20. Mencius said, "When Master I[48] taught people to shoot, he always told them to draw the bow to the full. The man who wants to learn [the way][49] must likewise draw his bow (his will) to the full. When a great carpenter teaches people, he always tells them to use squares and compasses. The man who wants to learn must likewise use squares and compasses (or moral standards)."

ADDITIONAL SELECTIONS

1A:1. Mencius replied [to King Hui at Liang],[50] "Why must Your Majesty use the term profit? What I have to offer are nothing but humanity and righteousness. If Your Majesty ask what is profitable to your country, if the great officers ask what is profitable to their families, and if the inferior officers and the common people ask what is profitable to themselves, then both the superiors and the subordinates

---

[45] A high official of the Chin state.   [46] Ode no. 247.

[47] This is Chiao Hsün's interpretation. Chao Ch'i and Chu Hsi, however, interpret *yü* not as "the same as" but as "to help," that is, it greatly helps (encourages) the inhumane.

[48] An ancient famous archer.   [49] Insertion according to Chao Ch'i.

[50] Mencius arrived in Liang in 320 B.C. King Hui (r. 370–319 B.C.) assumed the title of king by usurpation.

will try to snatch the profit from one another and the country will crumble."

1A:5. Mencius answered [King Hui], "Even with a territory of a hundred *li*,[51] it is possible to become the true king of the empire. If Your Majesty can practice a humane government to the people, reduce punishments and fines, lower taxes and levies, make it possible for the fields to be plowed deep and the weeding well done, men of strong body, in their days of leisure may cultivate their filial piety, brotherly respect, loyalty, and faithfulness, thereby serving their fathers and elder brothers at home and their elders and superiors abroad. Then you can have them prepare sticks to oppose the strong armor and sharp weapons of the states of Ch'in and Ch'u."

1A:7. Mencius said, "Treat with respect the elders in my family, and then extend that respect to include the elders in other families. Treat with tenderness the young in my own family, and then extend that tenderness to include the young in other families. . . . Let mulberry trees be planted about the homesteads with their five *mou*,[52] and men of fifty will be able to be clothed in silk. Let there be timely care for fowls, pigs, dogs, and swine, and men of seventy will be able to have meat to eat. Let there be no neglect in the timely cultivation of the farm with its hundred *mou*, and the family of eight mouths will suffer no hunger. Let serious attention be paid to education in school, elucidating the principles of filial piety and brotherly respect, and the gray-haired men will not carry burdens on the roads. There has never been a case when men of seventy had silk to wear and meat to eat, when the common people were neither hungry nor cold, and yet the ruler did not become the true king of the empire."

1B:5. King Hsüan of Ch'i said, "I have a weakness. I love wealth." Mencius replied, ". . . If Your Majesty love wealth, let your people enjoy the same, and what difficulty will there be for you to become the true king of the empire?" The King said, "I have a weakness, I love sex." Mencius replied, ". . . If Your Majesty love sex, let your people enjoy the same, and what difficulty will there be for you to become the true king of the empire?"

1B:7. Mencius said [to King Hsüan], ". . . When all your immediate ministers say that a man is worthy, it is not sufficient. When all your great officers say so, it is not sufficient. When all your people say so, look into the case, and if you find him to be worthy, then employ him. When all your immediate ministers say that a man is no good, do not listen to them. When all your great officers say so, do not listen to them.

---

[51] One-third of a mile. [52] One-sixth of an acre.

When all your people say so, look into the case, and if you find him to be no good, then dismiss him. When all your immediate ministers say that a man should be executed, do not listen to them. When all your great officers say so, do not listen to them. When all your people say so, look into the case, and if you find that the person should be executed, then execute him. It is therefore said that the people execute him. Only in this way can a ruler become parent of the people."

> Comment. No one in the history of Chinese thought has stressed more vigorously the primary importance of the people for the state.[53] Mencius considers the people even more important than the ruler or territory. Echoes of this doctrine were especially strong in the seventeenth and twentieth centuries.

1B:8. King Hsüan of Ch'i asked, "Was it a fact that T'ang[54] banished King Chieh[55] and that King Wen punished King Chou?" Mencius replied, "Yes, according to records." The King said, "Is it all right for a minister to murder his king?" Mencius said, "He who injures humanity is a bandit. He who injures righteousness is a destructive person. Such a person is a mere fellow. I have heard of killing a mere fellow Chou, but I have not heard of murdering [him as] the ruler."

> Comment. The doctrine of revolution is here boldly advanced and simply stated. A wicked king has lost the Mandate of Heaven and it should go to someone else. Confucianists have always upheld this doctrine, and it has been used by almost every rebel.[56]

2A:2. [Kung-sun Ch'ou][57] asked, "May I venture to ask, sir, how you maintain an unperturbed mind and how Kao Tzu maintains an unperturbed mind. May I be told?" Mencius answered, "Kao Tzu said, 'What is not attained in words is not to be sought in the mind, and what is not attained in the mind is not to be sought in the vital force.' It is all right to say that what is not attained in the mind is not to be sought in the vital force, but it is not all right to say that what is not attained in words is not to be sought in the mind. The will is the leader of the vital force, and the vital force pervades and animates the body. The will is the highest; the vital force comes next. Therefore I say, 'Hold the will firm and never do violence to the vital force.' "

Ch'ou said, "You said that the will is the highest and that the vital

[53] See below, 7B:14; 4B:3; 5A:5.

[54] Founder of Shang dynasty (r. 1751–1739 B.C.).

[55] A wicked king (r. 1802–1752 B.C.), who was responsible for the fall of the Hsia dynasty (2183–1752 B.C.).

[56] See below, Additional Selections, comment on 4B:3.

[57] Mencius' pupil.

force comes next. But you also say to hold the will firm and never to do violence to the vital force. Why?"

Mencius said, "If the will is concentrated, the vital force [will follow it] and become active. If the vital force is concentrated, the will [will follow it] and become active. For instance, here is a case of a man falling or running. It is his vital force that is active, and yet it causes his mind to be active too."

Ch'ou asked, "May I venture to ask, sir, in what you are strong?"

Mencius replied, "I understand words.[58] And I am skillful in nourishing my strong, moving power."

"May I ask what is meant by the strong, moving power?"

"It is difficult to describe. As power, it is exceedingly great and exceedingly strong. If nourished by uprightness and not injured, it will fill up all between heaven and earth. As power, it is accompanied by righteousness and the Way. Without them, it will be devoid of nourishment. It is produced by the accumulation of righteous deeds but is not obtained by incidental acts of righteousness. When one's conduct is not satisfactory to his own mind, then one will be devoid of nourishment. I therefore said that Kao Tzu never understood righteousness because he made it something external."

> *Comment.* The "strong, moving power" (*hao-jan chih ch'i*) has been likened to "flood breath" or some kind of yoga[59] and mysticism.[60] But as most commentators have pointed out, it is merely a great and strong power.[61] It is comparable to what Confucius said, i.e., that he had no more perplexities at forty.[62]

"Always be doing something without expectation.[63] Let the mind not forget[64] its objective, but let there be no artificial effort to help it grow. Do not be like the man of Sung. There was a man of Sung who was

[58] "I understand people's feelings from their words," according to Chao Ch'i, or "I understand the principles of things as expressed in words," according to Chu Hsi. *who says, the great morale*

[59] Waley, *Three Ways of Thought in Ancient China*, p. 118.

[60] Fung, *History of Chinese Philosophy*, vol. 1, p. 130.

[61] Tung Chung-shu (c.179–c.104 B.C.) saw in the phrase "the force of harmony in the universe." For Yen Shih-ku (581-645), it meant the force of purity and unity. To Liu Liang (1st century), it was the spirit of abandonment and leisure. (See Chiao Hsün, *Meng Tzu cheng-i.*) Chiao, like many others, understood it merely as "great," and Chu Hsi understood it as "strong and moving."

[62] *Analects*, 2:4.

[63] Chiao Hsün read *cheng* ("to correct") as *chih* ("to stop"). I am following Chu Hsi, who interprets *cheng* to mean to expect or to calculate.

[64] It is possible to punctuate after "the mind" so that it reads "stop the mind." However, nothing is gained by this change.

sorry that his corn was not growing, and so he pulled it up. Having been tired out he went home and said to his people, 'I am all tired. I have helped the corn to grow.' When his son ran to look at it, the corn had already withered."

> *Comment.* To Zen Buddhism, the mind must always remain sensitive and sharp. One of their slogans is "Be always alert." Under its impact, Neo-Confucianists similarly stressed "Always be doing something." This is especially true of Wang Yang-ming.[65] The difference between the Buddhists and the Confucianists is that the former emphasize the state of mind while the latter emphasize activity.

2A:3. Mencius said, "A ruler who uses force to make a pretense at humanity is a despot. Such a despot requires a large kingdom. A ruler who practices humanity with virtue is a true king. To become a true king does not depend on a large kingdom. T'ang became so with only seventy *li*, and King Wen with only a hundred. When force is used to overcome people, they do not submit willingly but only because they have not sufficient strength to resist. But when virtue is used to overcome people, they are pleased in their hearts and sincerely submit, as the seventy disciples submitted to Confucius. The *Book of Odes* says:

> From the west, from the east,
> From the south, from the north,
> None wanted to resist.[66]

This is what is meant."

> *Comment.* The foundation of Confucian political philosophy is "humane government," government of the true king, who rules through moral example.[67] His guiding principle is righteousness, whereas that of the despot is profit.[68] This contrast between kingliness and despotism has always remained sharp in the minds of Confucian political thinkers.

2A:5. Mencius said, "If a ruler honors the worthy and employs the competent so that offices are occupied by the wisest, then scholars throughout the world will be delighted to stand in his court. If in the city he levies a rent but does not tax the goods, or enforces certain reg-

[65] *Ch'uan-hsi lu* (Instructions for Practical Living), secs. 147, 163, 186. See Chan, trans., *Instructions for Practical Living.*

[66] Ode no. 244.

[67] See above, Additional Selections, 1A:1, 5; and below, Additional Selections, 2A:5, 3A:3-4, 7A:13.

[68] The contrast is strongly brought out in 1A:1.

ulations but does not levy a rent, then traders throughout the world will be delighted to store goods in his city. If at his frontier passes there will be inspection but no tax, then travelers throughout the world will be delighted to travel on his highways. If farmers are required to give their mutual aid to cultivate the public field but not required to pay tax, then all farmers throughout the world will be delighted to farm in his land. If there is no fine for the idler or the family that fails to meet a certain quota of cloth products, then all people throughout the world will be delighted to become his subjects. If a ruler can truly practice these five things, then the people in the neighboring states will look up to him as a parent. Ever since there has been mankind, none has succeeded in leading children to attack their parents. Thus such a ruler will have no enemy anywhere in the world, and having no enemy in the world, he will be an official appointed by Heaven. There has never been such a person who did not become the true king of the empire."

2A:6. Mencius said, "All men have the mind which cannot bear [to see the suffering of][69] others. The ancient kings had this mind and therefore they had a government that could not bear to see the suffering of the people. When a government that cannot bear to see the suffering of the people is conducted from a mind that cannot bear to see the suffering of others, the government of the empire will be as easy as making something go round in the palm.

"When I say that all men have the mind which cannot bear to see the suffering of others, my meaning may be illustrated thus: Now, when men suddenly see a child about to fall into a well, they all have a feeling of alarm and distress, not to gain friendship with the child's parents, nor to seek the praise of their neighbors and friends, nor because they dislike the reputation [of lack of humanity if they did not rescue the child]. From such a case, we see that a man without the feeling of commiseration is not a man; a man without the feeling of shame and dislike is not a man; a man without the feeling of deference and compliance is not a man; and a man without the feeling of right and wrong is not a man. The feeling of commiseration is the beginning of humanity; the feeling of shame and dislike is the beginning of righteousness; the feeling of deference and compliance is the beginning of propriety; and the feeling of right and wrong is the beginning of wisdom. Men have these Four Beginnings just as they have their four limbs. Having these Four Beginnings, but saying that they cannot develop them is to destroy themselves. When they say that their ruler cannot develop them, they are destroying their ruler. If anyone with these Four Beginnings in him knows how to give them the fullest ex-

[69] According to Chao Ch'i, "cannot bear to do evil to others."

tension and development, the result will be like fire beginning to burn or a spring beginning to shoot forth. When they are fully developed, they will be sufficient to protect all people within the four seas (the world). If they are not developed, they will not be sufficient even to serve one's parents."

Comment. Practically all later Confucianists have accepted the Four Beginnings as the innate moral qualities. In K'ang Yu-wei's philosophy, the "mind that cannot bear" is the starting point.[70]

3A:1. When Duke Wen[71] of T'eng was crown prince, having to go to Ch'u, he went by way of Sung to see Mencius. Mencius discoursed to him on the original goodness of human nature, and when he spoke, he always praised (sage-emperors) Yao and Shun. When the crown prince was returning from Ch'u, he visited Mencius again. Mencius said, "Prince, do you doubt my words? The Way is one and only one. Ch'eng Ch'ien (a brave minister) once said to Duke Ching of Ch'i,[72] 'They are men. I am also a man. Why should I fear them?' and Yen Yüan[73] said, 'Who was Shun and who am I? Anyone who makes the effort will be like him.' Kung-ming I[74] said, 'King Wen is my teacher. (That is, I can be like him.) How should the Duke of Chou[75] deceive me [by those words]?' Now, T'eng, averaging its length and its width, will amount to about fifty *li*. [It is small but] it can still be made to be a good state. The *Book of History* says, 'If medicine does not make the patient dazed, it will not cure his disease.' "[76]

3A:3. Duke Wen of T'eng asked about the proper way of government. Mencius said, "The business of the people should not be delayed. The *Book of Odes* says:

> In the morning go and gather the grass.
> In the evening twist your ropes.
> Then get up soon on the roof [to do the repair],
> For before long the grains have to be sowed.[77]

The way according to which the people conduct their lives is this: If they have a secure livelihood, they will have a secure mind. And if they have no secure livelihood, they will not have a secure mind. And if they have no secure mind, there is nothing they will not do in the way of self-abandonment, moral deflection, depravity, and wild license. When they fall into crime, to pursue and punish them is to entrap them.

---

[70] See below, ch. 39, sec. 3.   [71] Nothing is known of him.
[72] R. 546–489 B.C.
[73] Confucius' most favorite pupil, (521–490 B.C.).
[74] A worthy of the state of Lu.
[75] Younger brother of King Wu (d. 1094 B.C.).
[76] *History*, "Charge to Yüeh." Cf. Legge, trans., *Shoo King*, p. 252.
[77] Ode no. 154.

How can such a thing as entrapping the people be allowed under the rule of a man of humanity? Therefore a worthy ruler will be gravely complaisant and thrifty, showing a respectful politeness to his subordinates, and taking from the people according to regulations. Yang Hu[78] said, 'He who seeks to be rich will not be humane. He who seeks to be humane will not be rich.' The ruler of the Hsia dynasty allotted fifty *mou* of land to a family and required a 'contribution' (amounting to the proceeds of five *mou*). The rulers of Yin (or Shang) allotted seventy *mou* and required an 'aid' (amounting to the proceeds of seven *mou*). The rulers of Western Chou allotted one hundred *mou* and levied a 'take' (amounting to the proceeds of ten *mou*). In reality, in all these cases the payment was a tithe. To 'take' means to take away, and 'aid' means to depend on the people. Lung Tzu said, 'For regulating the land tax, there is no better system than the "aid" system and no worse than the "contribution" system. In the "contribution" system, the normal amount was fixed by taking the average of several years. In prosperous years when the grains lie about in abundance, much might be taken without being oppressive, and the actual exaction would be small. But in bad years, the produce is not sufficient even to repay for the fertilizer, and the system still insists on taking the full amount. When the parent of the people causes the people to look weary, to toil for the whole year without getting enough to support their parents, and to borrow in order to increase their means, so that both old and young are found lying in ditches, how can he be a parent of the people?' As to the system of hereditary salaries, that has already been practiced in T'eng. The *Book of Odes* says:

> May the rain come down on our public field,
> And then upon our private fields.[79]

It was only in the system of 'aid' that there was public land [which was cultivated by the several families and from which the proceeds went to the government as tax]. From this ode we can see that even in the Chou dynasty there was also the system of 'aid.'

"Establish seminaries, academies, schools, and institutes to teach the people. A seminary emphasizes the support of the old; an institute emphasizes instructions on [moral principles and the arts]; and an academy emphasizes archery (etiquette and deportment). In the times of Hsia, the name "institute" was used; in the Yin (Shang) dynasty, the name "academy" was used; in the Western Chou, the name "seminary" was used; and the three dynasties also used the name "school." All [these community] schools were for the purpose of making human relations

---

[78] A minister of the Ch'i family of Lu in the sixth century B.C.
[79] Ode no. 212. Lung Tzu was an ancient worthy.

clear and prominent. If human relations are made clear and prominent above, then the common people below will have affection to one another. When a true king arises, he will surely come to take you as an example, and thus you will be the teacher of kingly rulers. The *Book of Odes* says:

> Although Chou was an old country,
> It received a new mandate [of Heaven].[80]

This refers to King Wen. If you practice these things earnestly, you will also make your kingdom a new one."

The Duke of T'eng sent Pi Chan to Mencius to ask about the "well-field" land system.[81] Mencius said, "Now that your ruler is about to put in practice humane government and has chosen you for this service, you must do your best. Humane government must begin by defining the boundaries of land. If the boundaries are not defined correctly, the division of the land into squares will not be equal, and the produce available for official salaries will not be fairly distributed. Therefore oppressive rulers and corrupt officials are sure to neglect the defining of the boundaries. If the boundaries are correctly defined, the division of land and the regulation of salaries can be settled while you sit.

"Although the territory of T'eng is narrow and small, there must be gentlemen (rulers and nobles) and there must be country men. Without gentlemen, there would be none to rule the country men, and without country men, there would be none to support the gentlemen. I would ask you to divide land in the remoter districts into nine squares and to designate the central square (cultivated by the eight families) as 'aid' (tax), and in the central parts of the state, to let the people pay for themselves one-tenth of their produce. From the chief ministers down, [each family] should have fifty *mou* as sacrificial land, and an additional twenty-five *mou* for each additional male. When there are deaths or moving from one house to another there will be no quitting of the district. In the fields of a district, those who belong to the same nine squares will render friendly service to one another in their going out and coming in, aid one another in keeping watch, and sustain one another in sickness. In this way, the people live in affection and harmony. Each 'well-field' unit is one *li* square and consists of nine hundred *mou*. The center square is public field. The eight households each privately own a hundred *mou* and together they cultivate the public field. Only when

[80] Ode no. 235.

[81] The land was divided into nine squares, with eight families each cultivating its own square and together cultivating the ninth, public square for the government. The shape of the division resembles the Chinese character for "well" and the system was therefore so named.

the public work is done may they attend to their own work. This is where the country men are different [from the gentlemen]. These are the outlines of the system. As to modifying it and adapting it, it is up to you and your ruler."

3A:4. Ch'en Hsiang[82] visited Mencius and repeated the words of Hsü Hsing,[83] saying, "The ruler of T'eng is indeed a worthy ruler. But he has not heard the Way. [According to it], the worthy cultivate the field together with the people for food, and prepare their own meals while they carry on the government. . . ."

Mencius said, ". . . Why does Master Hsü not do the work of the potter and the founder, and supply himself with the articles which he uses solely from his own establishment? Why does he go in great confusion to deal and exchange with the hundred artisans? Why does he mind all the trouble?" "The work of the various artisans can in fact not be done along with farming." "When can the government of the empire alone be done along with farming? There is the work of great men and there is the work of little men. Furthermore, whatever is needed for one single person is supplied by the various artisans. If one must make the things himself before he uses them, this would make the whole empire run about on the road. Therefore it is said, 'Some labor with their minds and some labor with their strength. Those who labor with their minds govern others; those who labor with their strength are governed by others.'[84] Those who are governed by others support them; those who govern them are supported by them. This is a universal principle. . . ."

> *Comment.* Mencius, generally considered the most democratic of Chinese philosophers, has been severely criticized for this undemocratic class distinction. It does not seem to be in harmony with his idea of the basic equality of people.[85] We should not overlook, however, that the distinction is essentially one of function, not of status, for no one is confined to one class by birth.

"According to the way of man,[86] if they are well fed, warmly clothed, and comfortably lodged but without education, they will become almost like animals. The Sage (emperor Shun) worried about it and he appointed Hsieh to be minister of education and teach people human relations, that between father and son, there should be affection; between ruler and minister, there should be righteousness; between husband

---

[82] Pupil of a Confucianist. [83] A theorist on agriculture.
[84] Old sayings.
[85] See below, Additional Selections, comment on 7A:4.
[86] Chu Hsi interpreted the phrase to mean that man possesses moral nature.

and wife, there should be attention to their separate functions; between old and young, there should be a proper order; and between friends, there should be faithfulness. Emperor Yao said, 'Encourage them, lead them on, rectify them, straighten them, help them, aid them, so they discover for themselves [their moral nature], and in addition, stimulate them and confer kindness on them.' When sages were so much concerned with their people, had they the time for farming? . . ."

> *Comment.* The Five Relations have formed the general pattern of Chinese society. It is to be noted that only one of the five is biological, that all are defined in moral terms, and that all are reciprocal.[87] It is often said that these do not include the stranger and the enemy. But to Confucianists, no one is unrelated, and therefore a stranger is inconceivable. He is at least related as older or younger. As to the enemy, there should never be such a person, for all people should be friends.

Ch'en Hsiang said, "If the way of Master Hsü were followed, there would not be two prices in the market. Even if a young boy goes there, none would cheat him. Linen and silk of the same length would be sold at the same price. Bundles of hemp and silk of the same weight would be sold at the same price. Grains of the same quantity would be sold at the same price. And shoes of the same size would be sold at the same price."

Mencius said, "It is the nature of things to be unequal. Some are twice, some five times, some ten times, some a hundred times, and some one thousand or ten thousand times as valuable as others. If you equalize them all, you will throw the world into confusion. If large shoes and small shoes were of the same price, who would make them? If the doctrines of Master Hsü were followed, people would lead one another to practice deceit. How can these doctrines be employed to govern a state?"

> *Comment.* The remark that things are not equal seems to be a casual one, but Neo-Confucianists relied on it heavily for their argument that each thing has its own individual character and that reality is not an undifferentiated continuum.

3A:5. The Moist I Chih[88] sought through Hsü Pei to see Mencius. Mencius said, "Of course I am willing to see him but at present I am still sick. When I get well, I shall go to see him. He need not come."[89]

---

[87] See *The Mean*, ch. 20; *Great Learning*, ch. 3.

[88] Mo Tzu's pupil.

[89] Chao Ch'i considered the last sentence not Mencius' words but a statement saying that I Chih did not go.

The next day I Chih again sought to see Mencius. Mencius said, "I can see him now. If I do not correct his errors, true principles will not be revealed. Let me then correct him. I have heard that I Chih is a Moist. According to the Moists, in the matter of handling funerals, simplicity should be the rule. I Chih wants to change the customs of the world with Moist doctrines. Does he not regard these customs as wrong and not honorable? Nevertheless, he buried his parents in an elaborate manner. This means that he served his parents with what he regarded as dishonorable." Hsü Pei told I Chih about this. I Chih said, "According to the way of the learned, the ancients treated their people as though they were embracing and protecting an infant.[90] What does this saying mean? To me it means that love makes no distinctions, but that its application must begin with one's parents." Hsü Pei told Mencius of this. Mencius said, "Does I Chih really think that a man's affection for the child of his own brother is just like his affection for the child of his neighbor? The saying is an analogy. If an infant crawling around is about to fall into a well, it is no fault of the infant. Furthermore, Heaven produces creatures in such a way as to provide them with one foundation (such as parents being the foundation of men), and I Chih would have two foundations (parents and other people). In great antiquity there were some who did not bury their parents. When their parents died, they took them up and threw them into a ditch. Later when they passed by them and saw foxes and wild cats eating them and flies and gnats eating them, their perspiration started out upon their foreheads, they looked askance and could not bear to look straight. Now the perspiration was not for the sake of other people. It was something at the bottom of their hearts that showed in their expressions. They immediately went home and returned with baskets and spades and covered the bodies. If it was indeed right to cover them, then there must be certain moral principles which made filial sons and men of humanity inter their parents."

Hsü Pei told I Chih what Mencius had said. I Chih seemed at a loss for a moment and then said, "I have learned something from him."[91]

3B:2. Ching Ch'un[92] said, "Are not Kung-sun Yen[93] and Chang I[94] really great men? Let them show anger once and all feudal lords are afraid. Let them live at leisure and peace and the flame of trouble in the world will be extinguished." Mencius said, "How can such men be great

[90] Probably paraphrasing the *Book of History*, "Announcement of K'ang." Cf. Legge, *Shoo King*, p. 389.

[91] See below, Additional Selections, comment on 3B:9.

[92] Nothing is known of him.

[93] Once a prime minister of Ch'in. He was Chang I's contemporary.

[94] Chang I (d. 309 B.C.) was an expert on diplomacy who exerted tremendous influence on the various warring states.

men? Have you not studied the rules of propriety? At the capping of a young man, his father instructs him. At the marriage of a young woman, her mother instructs her. She accompanies the daughter to the door on her leaving and admonishes her, saying, 'Go to your home. Always be respectful and careful. Never disobey your husband.' Thus, to regard obedience as the correct course of conduct is the way for women. [Both Kung-sun and Chang attempted to please their rulers in order to obtain power and were more like women than great men.]

"He who dwells in the wide house of the world, stands in the correct station of the world, walks in the great path of the world; one who practices virtues along with the people when he is successful, and practices the Way alone when he is disappointed; one whose heart cannot be dissipated by the power of wealth and honors, who cannot be influenced by poverty or humble stations, who cannot be subdued by force and might—such a person is a great man."

3B:9. Mencius said, "Do I like to argue? I cannot help it. The world has been in existence for a long time, with a period of order and a period of chaos succeeding each other. . . . After the death of Yao and Shun, the Way of the sages fell into decay. . . . Sage-emperors have ceased to appear. Feudal lords have become reckless and idle scholars have indulged in unreasonable opinions. The words of Yang Chu and Mo Ti[95] fill the world. If the people in their opinions do not follow Yang Chu, they follow Mo Ti. Yang advocated egoism, which means a denial of the special relationship with the ruler. Mo advocated universal love, which means a denial of the special relationship with the father. To deny the special relationship with the father and the ruler is to become an animal. . . . If the principles of Yang and Mo are not stopped, and if the principles of Confucius are not brought to light, perverse doctrines will delude the people and obstruct the path of humanity and righteousness. When humanity and righteousness are obstructed, beasts will be led on to devour men, and men will devour one another. I am alarmed by these things, and defend the doctrines of the ancient kings and oppose Yang and Mo."

> *Comment.* The observation that a period of order and a period of chaos succeed each other represents a belief about history on the part of Confucianists. In a sense, history proceeds in a cycle. Mencius also said that every five hundred years a king or a sage arises to put the world in order.[96]
>
> The dispute between Mencius and the Moists involves a funda-

[95] See below, ch. 9, and ch. 18, Introduction.
[96] See *Mencius*, 2B:13, 7B:38.

mental issue of ethics, namely, whether there should be distinction in love. To the Moists, love should be universal and without distinction. To the Confucianists, on the other hand, while love embraces all relations, it must have an order or procedure, and an order implies relativity of importance or a gradation. Chu Hsi mentions two reasons why there must be distinction in love.[97] One is that parents are the foundation of life and therefore one's moral obligation to them should be greater.[98] The other is that according to Neo-Confucian philosophy, while the principle governing all is one, its manifestations are many. Applied to ethics, this implies that while love is universal, its application to the various relations are different. Human relations should not be the same any more than the myriad things in the world should be identical.[99]

4A:2. Mencius said, "The compass and square are the ultimate standards of the circle and the square. The sage is the ultimate standard of human relations. To be a ruler, one should carry out to the limit the way of the ruler. To be a minister, one should carry out to the limit the way of the minister. They only have to follow the example of Yao and Shun. He who does not serve his ruler as Shun served Yao does not respect his ruler, and he who does not rule his people as Yao ruled his, injures his people.

"Confucius said, 'There are but two ways to follow, that of humanity and that of inhumanity.' A ruler who oppresses his people to the extreme will himself be slain and his kingdom will perish. If he oppresses not to the extreme, even then his life will be in danger and his kingdom will be weakened. They will be called by the names of 'King Yü' (meaning an unenlightened king) and 'King Li' (meaning a cruel king) and though they may have filial sons and affectionate grandsons, they will not be able in a hundred generations to change these names. The *Book of Odes* says:

> The mirror of the Shang dynasty is not far back,
> It was in the time of the Hsia dynasty [whose last, wicked
> king was removed by the founder of Shang].[100]

This is what is meant."

4A:9. Mencius said, "Chieh and Chou lost their empires because they lost the people and they lost the people because they lost the hearts

[97] In his comment on 7A:45. See also 7A:46.
[98] This is the point in 3A:5.
[99] For a lengthy discussion on this question, see Chan, "The Evolution of the Confucian Concept of *Jen*," *Philosophy East and West*, 4 (1955), 300-302, and Fung, *Spirit of Chinese Philosophy*, pp. 37-40.
[100] Ode no. 255.

of the people. There is a way to win the empire. Win the people and you win the empire. There is a way to win the people. Win their hearts and you will win the people. And there is a way to win their hearts. It is to collect for[101] them what they like and do not do to them what they do not like,[102] that is all. The people turn to the humanity [of the ruler] as water flows downward and as beasts run to the wilderness."

4A:10. Mencius said, "It is useless to talk to those who do violence to their own nature, and it is useless to do anything with those who throw themselves away. To speak what is against propriety and righteousness is to do violence to oneself. To say that one cannot abide by humanity and follow righteousness is to throw oneself away. Humanity is the peaceful abode of men and righteousness is his straight path. What a pity for those who leave the peaceful abode and do not live there, and abandon the straight path and do not follow it!"

4A:12. Mencius said, "If those occupying inferior positions do not have the confidence of their superiors, they will not be able to govern the people. There is a way to have the confidence of the superiors. If one is not trusted by his friends, he will not have the confidence of his superiors. There is a way to be trusted by one's friends. If one's service to his parents does not give them pleasure, he will not be trusted by his friends. There is a way to please one's parents. If one examines himself and finds himself to be insincere, he cannot please his parents. There is a way to be sincere with himself. If one does not understand what is good, he will not be sincere with himself. Therefore sincerity is the way of Heaven, and to think how to be sincere is the way of man.[103] There has never been a person who was completely sincere and yet did not move others. Nor has there been a person who was not sincere and yet could move others."

4A:14. Mencius said, "When a ruler failed to practice humane government, all those ministers who enriched him were rejected by Confucius. How much more would he have rejected those who are vehement to fight for their rulers? When they fight for territory, they slaughter so many people that the field is full of them. When they fight for a city, they slaughter so many people that the city is full of them. This is what is called leading on the land to devour human flesh. Death is not enough for such a crime. Therefore those who are skillful in fighting should suffer the heaviest punishment. Those who form alliances with feudal lords should come next. And those who open up uncultivated fields and require the people to cultivate for them should come next after that."

---

[101] The word *yü* is used here in the sense of "for," not "to give."

[102] See above, ch. 2, comment on *Analects*, 4:15.

[103] The passage up to this point also appears with slight variation in *The Mean*, ch. 20.

4A:17.   Shun-yü K'un[104] said, "Is it a rule of propriety that men and women should not touch hands when they give or receive things?"[105] Mencius said, "It is a rule of propriety." "If someone's sister-in-law is drowning, should he rescue her with his hand?" Mencius said, "He who does not rescue his drowning sister-in-law is a wolf. It is a rule of propriety for men and women not to touch hands when giving or receiving things, but it is a matter of expediency to rescue one's drowning sister-in-law with hands." "The whole world is now drowning. Why do you, sir, not rescue it?" Mencius said, "A drowning empire must be rescued with moral principles. Do you wish me to rescue the world with my hand?"

> *Comment.* Here is a classical example of the Confucian theory of *ching-ch'üan*, or the standard and the secondary, the absolute and the relative.[106]

4A:18.   Kung-sun Ch'ou said, "Why is it that the superior man does not teach his son himself?" Mencius said, "The circumstance is such that it cannot be done. To teach is necessarily to inculcate correct principles. When these correct principles are not practiced, anger will follow. As anger follows, feelings will be hurt. [The son would say], 'My master teaches me the correct principles but he himself does not proceed according to correct principles.' This means that the father and son hurt each other's feelings. When father and son hurt each other's feelings, it is bad. The ancients exchanged their sons, one teaching the son of another. Between father and son there should be no reproving admonition to what is good. Such reproofs lead to alienation, and nothing is more inauspicious than alienation."

4A:20.   Mencius said, "It is not enough to remonstrate the government officials, nor is it enough to criticize the governmental measures. It is only the great man who can rectify what is wrong in the ruler's mind. Let the ruler be humane, and all his people will be humane. Let the ruler be righteous, and all his people will be righteous. Let the ruler be correct, and all his people will be correct. Once the ruler is rectified, the whole kingdom will be at peace."

4A:26.   Mencius said, "There are three things which are unfilial, and to have no posterity is the greatest of them all.[107] Shun married with-

[104] A famous debater of Ch'i.

[105] This injunction is found in *Book of Rites*, "Records of Prevention." See Legge, trans., *Li Ki*, vol. 2, p. 299.

[106] Another illustration is found in *Mencius*, 4A:26. See also above, ch. 2, comment on *Analects*, 4:10.

[107] According to Chao Ch'i, the first is to obey parents blindly and cause them to fall into immorality, and the second is not to serve in the government when one's parents are old and poor.

out first informing his parents lest he should have no posterity. Superior men consider this as if he had informed his parents."[108]

4A:27. Mencius said, "The actuality of humanity consists in serving one's parents. The actuality of righteousness consists in obeying one's elder brother. The actuality of wisdom consists in knowing these two things and not departing from them. The actuality of propriety consists in regulating and adorning these two things. The actuality of music consists in rejoicing in these two things. When they are rejoiced in, they will grow. Growing, how can they be stopped? As they cannot be stopped, then unconsciously the feet begin to dance and the hands begin to move."

4B:3. Mencius said to King Hsüan of Ch'i, "If a ruler regards his ministers as his hands and feet, then his ministers will regard him as their heart and mind. If a ruler regards his ministers as dogs and horses, his ministers will regard him as any other man. If a ruler regards his ministers as dirt and grass, his ministers will regard him as a bandit and an enemy."

Comment. After the founder of the Ming dynasty (1368-1644) read this chapter, he was so angry that he ordered the sacrifice to Mencius in the Confucian temple suspended. Eventually his dynasty fell for the very reason Mencius gave here.

4B:10. Mencius said, "Confucius never did anything that went too far."

4B:11. Mencius said, "The great man does not insist that his words be necessarily truthful [at all times and under circumstances] or his actions be necessarily resolute. He acts only according to righteousness."

4B:12. Mencius said, "The great man is one who does not lose his [originally good] child's heart."

4B:26. Mencius said, "All who talk about the nature of things need only [reason from] facts[109] [and principles will be clear]. The fundamental principle [of reasoning] from facts is to follow [their natural tendencies]. What I dislike in your wise men is their forced reasoning. If those wise men would only act as Yü[110] did when he diverted the water to the sea, there would be nothing to dislike in their wisdom. Yü diverted the waters as if he were acting without any special effort [for he followed the natural tendencies]. If wise men would act without any special effort [such as forced reasoning], their wisdom would also be great. Heaven is high and the stars are far away. But if we investigate the facts, we may go back to the solstice of a thousand years while we sit."

4B:28. Mencius said, "The reason why the superior man is dif-

[108] Cf. *Mencius*, 5A:2.

[109] The word *ku* may mean reason, natural course, or what has happened, that is, facts.

[110] Founder of the Hsia dynasty, r. 2183–2175 B.C.(?).

ferent from other men is because of what he preserves in his mind. He preserves humanity and propriety. The man of humanity loves others. The man of propriety respects others. He who loves others is always loved by others, and he who respects others is always respected by them."

4B:30. Mencius said, "There are five things which in common practice are considered unfilial. The first is laziness in the use of one's body without attending to the support and care of one's parents. The second is chess-playing and fondness for wine, without attending to the support and care of one's parents. The third is love of things and money and being exclusively attached to one's wife and children, without attending to the support and care of one's parents. The fourth is following the desires of one's ears and eyes, thus bringing his parents to disgrace. And the fifth is being fond of bravery, fighting, and quarreling, thus endangering one's parents."

4B:32. Master Ch'u[111] said, "The king sends people to spy on you and see whether you are really different from others." Mencius said, "How should I be different from others? Yao and Shun were the same as other men."

5A:5. Wan Chang[112] asked, "Is it true that Yao gave the empire to Shun?" Mencius replied, "No. The emperor cannot give the empire to another person." "Yes, but Shun had the empire. Who gave it to him?" Mencius said, "Heaven gave it to him." "By Heaven's giving it to him, do you mean that Heaven gave it to him in so many words?" "No. Heaven does not speak. It simply shows its will by [Shun's] personal character and his conduct of affairs."

"May I ask how Heaven showed its will by [Shun's] character and his conduct of affairs?" Mencius said, "The emperor can recommend a person to Heaven, but he cannot make Heaven give that man the empire. A feudal lord can recommend a person to the emperor, but he cannot make the emperor make that man a feudal lord. A great officer can recommend a person to a feudal lord, but he cannot make the feudal lord make that man a great officer. In ancient times, Yao recommended Shun to Heaven, and Heaven accepted him. He showed him to the people, and the people accepted him. I therefore say that Heaven did not speak, but that it simply indicated its will by his character and his conduct of affairs."

"May I ask how it was that Yao recommended him to Heaven and Heaven accepted, and that he showed him to the people and the people accepted him?" Mencius said, "He had him preside over the sacrifices, and all the spiritual beings enjoyed them. This means that Heaven accepted him. He had him preside over the conduct of affairs, and the

---

111 A man of Ch'i.   112 Pupil of Mencius.

affairs were well managed, and the people felt satisfied. This means that the people accepted him. It was Heaven that gave the empire to him. It was the people that gave the empire to him. Therefore I said, 'The emperor cannot give the empire to another person.' Shun assisted Yao for twenty-eight years. This was more than a man could do; it was Heaven that did it. After the death of Yao, when the three-year mourning was completed, Shun withdrew from the son of Yao to the south of the South River. The feudal lords of the empire, however, going to court, went not to the son of Yao but to Shun, litigants went not to the son of Yao but to Shun, and singers sang not to the son of Yao but to Shun. Therefore I said, 'Heaven [gave the empire to him].' Only then did he go to the Middle Kingdom (China) and take the emperor's seat. If he had occupied the place of Yao and applied pressure to his son, it would have been an act of usurpation, and not a gift of Heaven. The 'Great Declaration' said, 'Heaven sees as my people see; Heaven hears as my people hear.'[113] This is the meaning."

6B:15. Mencius said, "When Heaven is about to confer a great responsibility on any man, it will exercise his mind with suffering, subject his sinews and bones to hard work, expose his body to hunger, put him to poverty, place obstacles in the paths of his deeds, so as to stimulate his mind, harden his nature, and improve wherever he is incompetent."

7A:1. Mencius said, "He who exerts his mind to the utmost knows his nature. He who knows his nature knows Heaven. To preserve one's mind and to nourish one's nature is the way to serve Heaven. Not to allow any double-mindedness regardless of longevity or brevity of life, but to cultivate one's person and wait for [destiny (*ming*, fate, Heaven's decree or mandate) to take its own course] is the way to fulfill one's destiny."[114]

> *Comment.* In ancient China there were five theories about destiny or the Mandate of Heaven. The first was fatalism: the Mandate of Heaven is fixed and unchangeable. The second was moral determinism: Heaven always encourages virtue and punishes evil; therefore, man can determine his reward and punishment through moral deeds. The third was anti-fatalism, advocated by the Moist School.[115] The fourth was naturalistic fatalism, which means that destiny is not controlled by Heaven in the sense of an anthropomorphic God but by Nature and works automatically. Lastly, there was the

[113] *History*, "Declaration of Ch'in." cf. Legge, *Shoo King*, p. 292.
[114] A similar saying is found in *Mencius*, 7B:33.
[115] See below, ch. 9, C.

Confucian theory of "waiting for destiny."[116] According to this doctrine, man should exert his utmost in moral endeavor and leave whatever is beyond our control to fate. It frankly admits that there are things beyond our control but that is no reason why one should relax in his moral endeavor. The tendency was definitely one of moralism and humanism. The Confucian theory represents the conviction of enlightened Chinese in general.

7A:2. Mencius said, "Everything is destiny (*ming*). A man should accept obediently what is correct [in one's destiny]. Therefore, he who knows destiny does not stand beneath a precipitous wall. Death sustained in the course of carrying out the Way to the limit is due to correct destiny. But death under handcuffs and fetters is not due to correct destiny."

7A:4. Mencius said, "All things are already complete in oneself. There is no greater joy than to examine oneself and be sincere. When in one's conduct one vigorously exercises altruism, humanity is not far to seek, but right by him."[117]

> *Comment.* Confucius carefully balanced the individual and society. This balance is maintained in Mencius as it has been throughout the history of Confucianism. But at many points Mencius seems to emphasize the individual, for he believes that everyone can be a sage[118] and that integrity and will are completely his own.[119] As Hu Shih has pointed out, while the *Great Learning* and the *Doctrine of the Mean* have already raised the position of the individual, Mencius gave him even much more importance.[120]

7A:5. Mencius said, "To act without understanding and do so habitually without examination, following certain courses all their lives without knowing the principles behind them—this is the way of the multitude."

7A:13. Mencius said, "Under a despot, the people look brisk and cheerful [only temporarily and superficially, for the despot's kindness is selfishly motivated]. Under a true king, however, the people feel magnificent and at ease with themselves. Though he punishes them by death, they do not complain, and when he benefits them, they do not

---

[116] For an excellent discussion on this question, see Fu Szu-nien (1896-1950), *Hsing-ming ku-hsün pien-cheng* (Critical Studies of the *Classical Interpretations of the Nature and Destiny*), 1950, 2:14b-24a. See also *Mencius*, 7A:2, 7B:24, 33; *The Mean*, ch. 14.

[117] Cf. above, 4A:10.   [118] See above, comment on 6A:7.

[119] See also *Mencius*, 2A:9; 3A:1; 5B:1; and *Analects*, 9:25.

[120] *Chung-kuo che-hsüeh shih ta-kang* (Outline of the History of Chinese Philosophy), 1919, p. 296.

think of their merit. From day to day they make progress toward the good without knowing who makes them do so. Whenever the superior man passes through, transforming influence follows. Wherever he abides, spiritual influence remains. This forms the same current above and below with that of Heaven and Earth. Is this a small help?"[121]

7A:15. Mencius said, "The ability possessed by men without their having acquired it by learning is innate[122] ability, and the knowledge possessed by them without deliberation is innate knowledge. Children carried in the arms all know to love their parents. As they grow, they all know to respect their elder brothers. To have filial affection for parents is humanity, and to respect elders is righteousness. These feelings are universal in the world, that is all."

> *Comment*. The concepts of innate knowledge and innate ability later formed the keynote of Wang Yang-ming's philosophy.[123]

7A:26. Mencius said, "Yang Chu's choice was 'everyone for himself.' Though he might benefit the entire world by plucking out a single hair, he would not do it. Mo Ti advocated universal love. If by rubbing smooth his whole body from head to foot he could benefit the world, he would do it. Tzu-mo[124] holds the mean between the two, and he is nearer the right. Holding the mean without allowing for special circumstances is like holding on to one particular thing. The reason why I hate holding to one thing is because it destroys the Way. It takes up one point but neglects a hundred others."

7A:30. Mencius said, "Yao and Shun practiced humanity and righteousness because of their nature. King T'ang and King Wu did so because of their personal cultivation. The Five Despots,[125] on the contrary, merely borrowed [the names of humanity and righteousness to adorn their acts]. After they had borrowed them for a long time and did not return them, how could it be known that they did not own them?"

7A:38. Mencius said, "Form and color (our body) are nature endowed by Heaven. It is only the sage who can put his physical form into full use."

7A:45. Mencius said, "In regard to [inferior] creatures, the superior man loves them but is not humane to them (that is, showing them the

---

[121] Cf. above, 2A:3.

[122] Chao Ch'i said that *liang* meant "very," with which Chiao Hsün agreed. Neo-Confucianists understood it to mean "innate."

[123] See below, ch. 35.

[124] A worthy in the state of Lu.

[125] These despots were: Duke Huan of Ch'i (r. 685–643 B.C.), Duke Wen of Chin (r. 636–628 B.C.), Duke Mu of Ch'in (r. 659–619 B.C.), King Chuang of Ch'u (r. 613–589 B.C.), and Duke Hsiang of Sung (r. 650–635 B.C.).

feeling due human beings). In regard to people generally, he is humane to them but not affectionate. He is affectionate to his parents and humane to all people. He is humane to all people and feels love for all creatures."[126]

7A:46. Mencius said, "The man of wisdom knows everything, but he considers the things of immediate importance to be the most urgent. The man of humanity loves all, but he considers the effort to cultivate an affection for the worthy to be the most urgent. Even the wisdom of Yao and Shun did not [actually] extend to everything, but they attended urgently to the most important. Their humanity did not extend to the point of [actually] loving all people, but they urgently cultivated the affection for the worthy."

7B:3. Mencius said, "It would be better to have no Book of History[127] than to believe all of it. In its 'Completion of War' section [for example], I accept only two or three passages.[128] A man of humanity has no enemy in the world. When a most humane person (King Wu) punished a most inhumane ruler (King Chou), how could the blood (of the people) have flowed till it floated the pestles of the mortars?"[129]

7B:14. Mencius said, "[In a state] the people are the most important; the spirits of the land and grain (guardians of territory) are the next; the ruler is of slight importance. Therefore to gain [the hearts of] the peasantry is the way to become an emperor; to gain the [heart of the] emperor is the way to become a feudal lord; and to gain [the heart of the] feudal lord of a state is the way to become a great officer. When a feudal lord (a ruler) endangers the spirits of the land and grain (territory), he is removed and replaced. When sacrificial animals have been well fed, the millet in its vessels has been all pure, and the sacrificial rites have been performed at proper times, if yet there are still droughts and floods [to harm the people], the spirits of the land and grain are removed and replaced."[130]

7B:16. Mencius said, "Humanity is [the distinguishing characteristic of] man.[131] When embodied in man's conduct, it is the Way."

7B:24. Mencius said, "It is due to our nature that our mouths desire sweet taste, that our eyes desire beautiful colors, that our ears desire

[126] See above, comment on 3A:4.

[127] On the Book of History, see ch. 1, n.4.

[128] Literally "slabs." Ancient books consisted of bamboo slabs.

[129] Actually, according to the Book of History, the bloodshed was caused by King Chou's own troops turning against one another. See Legge, Shoo King, p. 315. Commentators have said that Mencius may have thought that there should have been no bloodshed at all, since in his own philosophy, people flocked to a man of humanity as water flows downward. See above, Additional Selections, 4A:9.

[130] Cf. above, Additional Selections, 4B:3; 5A:5.

[131] See comment on The Mean, ch. 20, where a similar saying appears.

pleasant sounds, that our noses desire fragrant odors, and that our four limbs desire ease and comfort. But there is also fate (*ming*) [whether these desires are satisfied or not]. The superior man does not say they are man's nature [and insist on satisfying them]. The virtue of humanity in the relationship between father and son, the virtue of righteousness in the relationship between ruler and minister, the virtue of propriety in the relationship between guest and host, the virtue of wisdom in the worthy, and the sage in regard to the Way of Heaven—these are [endowed in people in various degrees] according to fate. But there is also man's nature. The superior man does not (refrain from practicing them and) say they are matters of fate."[132]

7B:25. Hao-sheng Pu-hai[133] asked, "What sort of man is Yo-cheng?"[134] Mencius said, "He is a good man and a true man." "What is a good man? And what is a true man?" Mencius said, "One who commands our liking [because of his virtue] is called a good man. One who is sincere with himself is called a true man. He [whose goodness] is extensive and solid is called a beautiful man. He [whose goodness] is abundant and is brilliantly displayed is called a great man. When one is great and is completely transformed [to be goodness itself], he is called a sage. When a sage is beyond our knowledge, he is called a man of the spirit."

> *Comment*. It is difficult to say how strong the element of mysticism is in Mencius, but there is no doubt that it is present in him as it is in the *Doctrine of the Mean*. The realm of existence beyond our knowledge is certainly mystical. Fung is right in saying that "forming the same current" with Heaven and Earth is a mystical experience, although in suggesting that "All is complete in me" is also mystical, he has definitely gone too far.[135]

7B:31. Mencius said, "All men have some things which they cannot bear. Extend that feeling to what they can bear, and humanity will be the result. All men have some things which they will not do. Extend that feeling to the things that they do, and righteousness will be the result. If a man can give full development to his feeling of not wanting to injure others, his humanity will be more than what he can ever put into practice. If he can give full development to his feeling of not wanting to break in to steal, his righteousness will be more than what he can ever put into practice. If a man can give full development to his real dislike

[132] See above, Additional Selections, comment on 7A:1.
[133] A man of Ch'i.   [134] An official of Lu.
[135] Fung, *History of Chinese Philosophy*, vol. 1, pp. 129-131. See also his *Spirit of Chinese Philosophy*, pp. 24-27.

of being addressed, 'Hey, you,' he will act according to righteousness wherever he may be. When an officer speaks what he ought not to speak, he is enticing people by speaking. When he does not speak what he ought to speak, he is enticing by not speaking. In both cases he is doing something like breaking in."

7B:33. Mencius said, "With Yao and Shun it was their nature. With T'ang and Wu, it was their effort to return [to their nature]. When all movements and expressions are exactly proper according to the rules of propriety, that shows the highest degree of eminent virtue. The sorrow in weeping for the dead is not for the sake of the living. The regular practice of virtue without any deviation is not to seek emolument. And words should always be sincere not because of any conscious desire to do what is right. The superior man practices principle (Natural Law) and waits for destiny (*ming*, Mandate of Heaven) to take its own course."[136]

[136] See above, comment on 7A:1.

MORAL AND SOCIAL PROGRAMS: THE
GREAT LEARNING

THE IMPORTANCE of this little Classic is far greater than its small size would suggest. It gives the Confucian educational, moral, and political programs in a nutshell, neatly summed up in the so-called "three items": manifesting the clear character of man, loving the people, and abiding in the highest good; and in the "eight steps": the investigation of things, extension of knowledge, sincerity of the will, rectification of the mind, cultivation of the personal life, regulation of the family, national order, and world peace. Moreover, it is the central Confucian doctrine of humanity (*jen*) in application. Confucius said that there is a central thread running through his teachings, and that central principle is conscientiousness and altruism, which are two aspects of humanity.[1] The eight steps are the blueprints for translating humanity into actual living, carefully maintaining the balance and harmony of the individual on the one side and society on the other. It is because of this significance that the *Great Learning* has ranked as a Confucian Classic and has exerted profound influence in the last eight hundred years.

It is no less important from the philosophical point of view. Although the treatise does not discuss metaphysical problems, it does present the investigation of things as the starting point in moral and social life. This is of course perfectly consonant with the Confucian emphasis on learning. However, Confucianists have never agreed on how to learn, and the different interpretations of the investigation of things in this Classic eventually created bitter opposition among Neo-Confucianists. To Chu Hsi (1130-1200), *ko-wu* meant to investigate things,[2] both inductively and deductively, on the premise that principle (*li*), the reason of being, is inherent in things. He believed that only with a clear knowledge of things can one's will become sincere. He therefore rearranged the ancient text of the Classic to have the sections on the investigation of things appear before those on sincerity of the will. Wang Yang-ming (Wang Shou-jen, 1472-1529), on the other hand, believing that principle is inherent in the mind, took *ko* to mean "to correct," that is, to correct what is wrong in the mind. To him, sincerity of the will, without which no true knowledge is possible, must come before the investigation

---

[1] See *Analects*, 4:15. The word *jen* has been variously translated as benevolence, love, human-heartedness, true manhood, etc. For a discussion of *jen*, see Appendix.

[2] *Ta-hsüeh chang-chü* (Commentary on the *Great Learning*), ch. 5.

of things. Therefore he rejected both Chu Hsi's rearrangement of the text and his doctrine of the investigation of things,[3] and based his whole philosophy on the *Great Learning*, with sincerity of the will as its first principle.[4] For centuries Neo-Confucianists of the two schools represented by Chu and Wang debated the issue.

However, they all agreed on another doctrine of the *Great Learning*, that is, that the internal and the external, the fundamental and the secondary, and the first and the last, must be clearly distinguished. No other Confucian Classic has presented this idea so clearly and so forcefully. It is also important because the matter is not just one of procedure but involves the basic question of comparative values. In addition, the concept of being watchful over oneself when alone made a deep impression on the Neo-Confucianists, so much so that none has neglected it and some even built their philosophical systems around it. Since the Classic is important for both practical and theoretical reasons, it is no wonder that, from the early fourteenth century to the twentieth, it was a required text in Chinese education. It is here translated in full, with Chu Hsi's own remarks.

THE GREAT LEARNING[5]

Chu Hsi's Remark. Master Ch'eng I said,[6] "The *Great Learning* is a surviving work of the Confucian school and is the gate through

---

[3] *Ch'uan-hsi lu* (Instructions for Practical Living), sec. 129, 135-137, 172-175, and 201. See Chan, trans., *Instructions for Practical Living.*

[4] His philosophy is summed up in his "Inquiry on the *Great Learning*." See below, ch. 35.

[5] The *Great Learning* is originally ch. 42 of the *Li chi* (*Book of Rites*). Not much attention was paid to it until the time of Ssu-ma Kuang (1019-1086), who wrote a commentary on it, treating it as a separate work for the first time. This commentary is now lost. Ch'eng Hao (Ch'eng Ming-tao, 1032-1085) and his younger brother Ch'eng I (Ch'eng I-ch'uan, 1033-1107) each rearranged the text. Chu Hsi did the same and, moreover, added a "supplement." He further divided the work into one "text" and ten "chapters of commentary," and contended that the former was Confucius' own words handed down by his pupil Tseng Tzu (505–c.436 B.C.) and that the latter were the views of Tseng Tzu recorded by his pupils. There is no evidence for this contention. Recent scholars, equally without evidence, have dated the work as late as around 200 B.C. Regardless of its date and authorship, which has also been attributed to Confucius' grandson Tzu-ssu (492–431 B.C.), it was Chu Hsi who made it important in the last 800 years. He grouped it with the *Analects*, the *Book of Mencius*, and the *Doctrine of the Mean* as the "Four Books" and wrote commentaries on them. Since then they were honored as Classics, and from 1313 till 1905 they were the basis of civil service examinations. Thus they replaced the other Classics in importance and influence.

The Chinese title, *Ta-hsüeh*, literally means education for the adult. In contrast to the education for the young, which consisted of good manners, daily behavior, etc., education for the adult involves moral cultivation and social order. It means, therefore, education for the good man or the gentleman, or using the word in the sense "great," education for the great man.

Among Western translations, that by Hughes in his *The Great Learning and the*

which the beginning student enters into virtue. It is only due to the preservation of this work that the order in which the ancients pursued their learning may be seen at this time. The *Analects* and the *Book of Mencius* are next to it. The student should by all means follow this work in his effort to learn, and then he will probably be free from mistakes."[7]

The Text

The Way of learning to be great (or adult education) consists in manifesting the clear character, loving[8] the people, and abiding (*chih*)[9] in the highest good.

Only after knowing what to abide in can one be calm. Only after having been calm can one be tranquil. Only after having achieved tranquillity can one have peaceful repose. Only after having peaceful repose can one begin to deliberate. Only after deliberation can the end be attained. Things have their roots and branches. Affairs have their beginnings and their ends. To know what is first and what is last will lead one near the Way.

The ancients who wished to manifest their clear character to the world would first bring order to their states. Those who wished to bring order to their states would first regulate their families. Those who wished to regulate their families would first cultivate their personal lives. Those who wished to cultivate their personal lives would first rectify their minds. Those who wished to rectify their minds would first make their wills sincere. Those who wished to make their wills sincere would first extend their knowledge. The extension of knowledge consists in the investigation of things. When things are investigated, knowledge is extended; when knowledge is extended, the will becomes sincere; when the will is sincere, the mind is rectified; when the mind is rectified, the personal life is cultivated; when the personal life is culti-

---

Mean-in-Action follows the ancient text, the one used by Cheng Hsüan (127-200) in his annotation, which is the one in the Thirteen Classics Series and not rearranged by Chu Hsi. Those by Legge, "The Great Learning," and by Lin Yutang, "The Great Learning," follow Chu Hsi's text. This text is called *Ta-hsüah chang-chü,* literally "Punctuation and redivision of the *Great Learning* into Chapters." It contains Chu Hsi's own "Remarks." In the following translation, Chu Hsi's text is used.

[6] What follows is a paraphrase of Ch'eng's words. See his *I-shu* (Surviving Works), 2A:4a, 22A:1a and *Ts'ui-yen* (Pure Words), 1:25a, both in ECCS.

[7] This and the rest of the "Remarks" on the *Great Learning* are by Chu Hsi.

[8] According to Ch'eng I, the character *ch'in* (to love) should be read *hsin* (to renovate). See his revision of the text of the *Great Learning* in *Ching-shuo* (Explanation of the Classics), 5:3a, in ECCS.

[9] The word *chih* is used in this work in its various meanings of abiding, staying, and resting.

vated, the family will be regulated; when the family is regulated, the state will be in order; and when the state is in order, there will be peace throughout the world. From the Son of Heaven down to the common people, all must regard cultivation of the personal life as the root or foundation. There is never a case when the root is in disorder and yet the branches are in order. There has never been a case when what is treated with great importance becomes a matter of slight importance or what is treated with slight importance becomes a matter of great importance.

Chu Hsi's Remark. The above is the text in one chapter. It is the words of Confucius, handed down by Tseng Tzu. The ten chapters of commentary which follow are the views of Tseng Tzu and were recorded by his pupils. In the traditional version there have been some mistakes in its arrangement. Now follows the new version fixed by Master Ch'eng I,[10] and in addition, having examined the contents of the text, I (Chu Hsi) have rearranged it as follows:

Chapters of Commentary

1. In the "Announcement of K'ang" it is said, "He was able to manifest his clear character."[11] In the "T'ai-chia" it is said, "He contemplated the clear Mandates of Heaven."[12] In the "Canon of Yao" it is said, "He was able to manifest his lofty character."[13] These all show that the ancient kings manifested their own character.

Chu Hsi's Remark. The above first chapter of commentary explains manifesting the clear character.

2. The inscription on the bath-tub of King T'ang[14] read, "If you can renovate yourself one day, then you can do so every day, and keep doing so day after day." In the "Announcement of K'ang," it is said, "Arouse people to become new."[15] The *Book of Odes* says, "Although Chou is an ancient state, the mandate it has received from Heaven is new."[16] Therefore, the superior man tries at all times to do his utmost [in renovating himself and others].

[10] Ch'eng I's rearrangement of the work is found in *Ching-shuo*, 5:3a-5b. His elder brother Hao's rearrangement, which is different from his, is found in 5:1a-3a. Actually, Chu Hsi's rearrangement is different from both.
[11] *History*, "Announcement of K'ang." Cf. translation by Legge, *Shoo King*, p. 383.
[12] *ibid.*, "T'ai-chia." Cf. Legge, p. 199.
[13] *ibid.*, "Canon of Yao." Cf. Legge, p. 17.
[14] Founder of the Shang dynasty (r. 1751–1739 B.C.?)
[15] *History*, "Announcement of K'ang." Cf. Legge, p. 388.
[16] Ode no. 235.

Chu Hsi's Remark. The above second chapter of commentary explains the renovating of the people.

3. The *Book of Odes* says, "The imperial domain of a thousand *li*[17] is where the people stay (*chih*)."[18] The *Book of Odes* also says, "The twittering yellow bird rests (*chih*) on a thickly wooded mount."[19] Confucius said, "When the bird rests, it knows where to rest. Should a human being be unequal to a bird?" The *Book of Odes* says, "How profound was King Wen! How he maintained his brilliant virtue without interruption and regarded with reverence that which he abided (*chih*)."[20] As a ruler, he abided in humanity. As a minister, he abided in reverence. As a son, he abided in filial piety. As a father, he abided in deep love. And in dealing with the people of the country, he abided in faithfulness.

The *Book of Odes* says, "Look at that curve in the Ch'i River. How luxuriant and green are the bamboo trees there! Here is our elegant and accomplished prince. [His personal life is cultivated] as a thing is cut and filed and as a thing is carved and polished. How grave and dignified! How majestic and distinguished! Here is our elegant and accomplished prince. We can never forget him!"[21] "As a thing is cut and filed" refers to the pursuit of learning. "As a thing is carved and polished" refers to self-cultivation. "How grave and how dignified" indicates precaution. "How majestic and distinguished" expresses awe-inspiring appearance. "Here is our elegant and accomplished prince. We can never forget him" means that the people cannot forget his eminent character and perfect virtue. The *Book of Odes* says, "Ah! the ancient kings are not forgotten."[22] [Future] rulers deemed worthy what they deemed worthy and loved what they loved, while the common people enjoyed what they enjoyed and benefited from their beneficial arrangements. That was why they are not forgotten even after they passed away.

Chu Hsi's Remark. The above third chapter of commentary explains abiding in the highest good.

4. Confucius said, "In hearing litigations, I am as good as anyone. What is necessary is to enable people not to have litigations at all."[23] Those who would not tell the truth will not dare to finish their words, and a great awe would be struck into people's minds. This is called knowing the root.

Chu Hsi's Remark. The above fourth chapter of commentary explains the root and the branches.

---

[17] About one-third of a mile.   [18] Ode no. 303.   [19] Ode no. 230.
[20] Ode no. 235. King Wen was the founder of the Chou dynasty. He reigned 1171-1122 B.C.   [21] Ode no. 55.   [22] Ode no. 269.   [23] *Analects*, 12:13.

5. This is called knowing the root. This is called the perfecting of knowledge.[24]

Chu Hsi's Remark. The above fifth chapter of commentary explains the meaning of the investigation of things and the extension of knowledge, which is now lost. I have ventured to take the view of Master Ch'eng I and supplement it as follows: The meaning of the expression "The perfection of knowledge depends on the investigation of things (*ko-wu*)"[25] is this: If we wish to extend our knowledge to the utmost, we must investigate the principles of all things we come into contact with, for the intelligent mind of man is certainly formed to know, and there is not a single thing in which its principles do not inhere. It is only because all principles are not investigated that man's knowledge is incomplete. For this reason, the first step in the education of the adult is to instruct the learner, in regard to all things in the world, to proceed from what knowledge he has of their principles, and investigate further until he reaches the limit. After exerting himself in this way for a long time, he will one day achieve a wide and far-reaching penetration. Then the qualities of all things, whether internal or external, the refined or the coarse, will all be apprehended, and the mind, in its total substance and great functioning, will be perfectly intelligent. This is called the investigation of things. This is called the perfection of knowledge.

6. What is meant by "making the will sincere" is allowing no self-deception, as when we hate a bad smell or love a beautiful color. This is called satisfying oneself. Therefore the superior man will always be watchful over himself when alone. When the inferior man is alone and leisurely, there is no limit to which he does not go in his evil deeds. Only

[24] In the Cheng Hsüan text these two sentences come at the end of the "text." Then come sections on sincerity of the will, rectification of the mind, cultivation of the personal life, regulation of the family, order of the state, and peace throughout the world. The first two items, on the investigation of things and perfection of knowledge, are thus missing. This is the reason why Chu Hsi moved the two sentences here and asserted that they are on the investigation of things and the extension of knowledge, and offered a "supplement" to fill in the ideas. Thus he put the investigation of things ahead of sincerity of the will, which is the subject of the next chapter. Chu Hsi's revision here makes the work much more logical, although the revision is arbitrary.

[25] Cheng Hsüan in his commentary on the *Book of Rites* (see the *Li chi cheng-i* or Correct Meaning of the *Book of Rites*, in the Thirteen Classics Series) interprets *ko* to mean to teach, that is, when one has the knowledge of good, good things will reach him. Chu Hsi, in his *Ta-hsüeh chang-chü*, also interprets *ko* as to reach, but according to him, it means to reach things, that is, to get at the principle of things to the utmost. See below, ch. 32, comment on sec. 44 and ch. 34, B, 1g, comment on sec. 30.

when he sees a superior man does he then try to disguise himself, concealing the evil and showing off the good in him. But what is the use? For other people see him as if they see his very heart. This is what is meant by saying that what is true in a man's heart will be shown in his outward appearance. Therefore the superior man will always be watchful over himself when alone. Tseng Tzu said, "What ten eyes are beholding and what ten hands are pointing to—isn't it frightening?" Wealth makes a house shining and virtue makes a person shining. When one's mind is broad and his heart generous, his body becomes big and is at ease. Therefore the superior man always makes his will sincere.

Chu Hsi's Remark. The above sixth chapter of commentary explains the sincerity of the will.

7. What is meant by saying that cultivation of the personal life depends on the rectification of the mind is that when one is affected by wrath to any extent, his mind will not be correct. When one is affected by fear to any extent, his mind will not be correct. When he is affected by fondness to any extent, his mind will not be correct. When he is affected by worries and anxieties, his mind will not be correct. When the mind is not present, we look but do not see, listen but do not hear, and eat but do not know the taste of the food. This is what is meant by saying that the cultivation of the personal life depends on the rectification of the mind.

Chu Hsi's Remark. The above seventh chapter of commentary explains the rectification of the mind in order to cultivate the personal life.

8. What is meant by saying that the regulation of the family depends on the cultivation of the personal life is this: Men are partial toward those for whom they have affection and whom they love, partial toward those whom they despise and dislike, partial toward those whom they fear and revere, partial toward those whom they pity and for whom they have compassion, and partial toward those whom they do not respect. Therefore there are few people in the world who know what is bad in those whom they love and what is good in those whom they dislike. Hence it is said, "People do not know the faults of their sons and do not know (are not satisfied with) the bigness of their seedlings." This is what is meant by saying that if the personal life is not cultivated, one cannot regulate his family.

Chu Hsi's Remark. The above eighth chapter of commentary explains the cultivation of the personal life in order to regulate the family.

9. What is meant by saying that in order to govern the state it is necessary first to regulate the family is this: There is no one who cannot teach his own family and yet can teach others. Therefore the superior man (ruler) without going beyond his family, can bring education into completion in the whole state. Filial piety is that with which one serves his ruler. Brotherly respect is that with which one serves his elders, and deep love is that with which one treats the multitude. The "Announcement of K'ang" says, "Act as if you were watching over an infant."[26] If a mother sincerely and earnestly looks for what the infant wants, she may not hit the mark but she will not be far from it. A young woman has never had to learn about nursing a baby before she marries. When the individual families have become humane, then the whole country will be aroused toward humanity. When the individual families have become compliant, then the whole country will be aroused toward compliance. When one man is greedy or avaricious, the whole country will be plunged into disorder. Such is the subtle, incipient activating force of things. This is what is meant by saying that a single word may spoil an affair and a single man may put the country in order. (Sage-emperors) Yao and Shun[27] led the world with humanity and the people followed them. (Wicked kings) Chieh and Chou[28] led the world with violence and the people followed them. The people did not follow their orders which were contrary to what they themselves liked. Therefore the superior man must have the good qualities in himself before he may require them in other people.[29] He must not have the bad qualities in himself before he may require others not to have them. There has never been a man who does not cherish altruism (*shu*) in himself and yet can teach other people. Therefore the order of the state depends on the regulation of the family.

The *Book of Odes* says, "How young and pretty is that peach tree! How luxuriant is its foliage! This girl is going to her husband's house. She will rightly order her household."[30] Only when one has rightly ordered his household can he teach the people of the country. The *Book of Odes* says, "They were correct and good to their elder brothers. They were correct and good to their younger brothers."[31] Only when one is good and correct to one's elder and younger brothers can one teach the people of the country. The *Book of Odes* says, "His deportment is all correct, and he rectifies all the people of the country."[32] Because he served as a

---

[26] *History*, "Announcement of K'ang." Cf. Legge, *Shoo King*, p. 389.

[27] Legendary rulers of the 3rd millennium B.C.

[28] They (r. 1802–1752 B.C.? and r. 1175–1112 B.C.) caused the downfall of the Hsia and Shang dynasties, respectively.

[29] Cf. *Analects*, 15:20. [30] Ode no. 6.

[31] Ode no. 173. [32] Ode no. 152.

worthy example as a father, son, elder brother, and younger brother, therefore the people imitated him. This is what is meant by saying that the order of the state depends on the regulation of the family.

Chu Hsi's Remark. The above ninth chapter of commentary explains regulating the family to bring order to the state.

10. What is meant by saying that peace of the world depends on the order of the state is this: When the ruler treats the elders with respect, then the people will be aroused toward filial piety. When the ruler treats the aged with respect, then the people will be aroused toward brotherly respect. When the ruler treats compassionately the young and the helpless, then the common people will not follow the opposite course. Therefore the ruler has a principle with which, as with a measuring square, he may regulate his conduct.

What a man dislikes in his superiors, let him not show it in dealing with his inferiors; what he dislikes in those in front of him, let him not show it in preceding those who are behind; what he dislikes in those behind him, let him not show it in following those in front of him; what he dislikes in those on the right, let him not apply it to those on the left; and what he dislikes in those on the left, let him not apply it to those on the right. This is the principle of the measuring square.

The *Book of Odes* says, "How much the people rejoice in their prince, a parent of the people!"[33] He likes what the people like and dislikes what the people dislike. This is what is meant by being a parent of the people. The *Book of Odes* says, "Lofty is the Southern Mountain! How massive are the rocks! How majestic is the Grand Tutor Yin (of Chou)! The people all look up to you!"[34] Thus rulers of states should never be careless. If they deviate from the correct path, they will be cast away by the world. The *Book of Odes* says, "Before the rulers of the Yin (Shang) dynasty[35] lost the support of the people, they could have been counterparts of Heaven.[36] Take warning from the Yin dynasty. It is not easy to keep the Mandate of Heaven."[37] This shows that by having the support of the people, they have their countries, and by losing the support of the people, they lose their countries. Therefore the ruler will first be watchful over his own virtue. If he has virtue, he will have the people with him. If he has the people with him, he will have the territory. If he has the territory, he will have wealth. And if he has wealth, he will have its use. Virtue is the root, while wealth is the branch. If he regards the root as external (or secondary) and the branch as internal

[33] Ode no. 172.   [34] Ode no. 191.   [35] 1384–1112 B.C.
[36] Heaven will accept their sacrifice, according to Cheng Hsüan, or can face Heaven, according to Chu Hsi.
[37] Ode no. 235.

(or essential), he will compete with the people in robbing each other. Therefore when wealth is gathered in the ruler's hand, the people will scatter away from him; and when wealth is scattered [among the people], they will gather round him. Therefore if the ruler's words are uttered in an evil way, the same words will be uttered back to him in an evil way; and if he acquires wealth in an evil way, it will be taken away from him in an evil way. In the "Announcement of K'ang" it is said, "The Mandate of Heaven is not fixed or unchangeable."[38] The good ruler gets it and the bad ruler loses it. In the *Book of Ch'u* it is said, "The State of Ch'u does not consider anything as treasure; it considers only good [men] as treasure. Uncle Fan (maternal uncle to a prince of Chin in exile) said, 'Our exiled prince has no treasure; to be humane toward his parents is his only treasure.' "[39] In the "Oath of Ch'in" it is said, "Let me have but one minister, sincere and single-minded, not pretending to other abilities, but broad and upright of mind, generous and tolerant toward others. When he sees that another person has a certain kind of ability, he is as happy as though he himself had it, and when he sees another man who is elegant and wise, he loves him in his heart as much as if he said so in so many words, thus showing that he can really tolerate others. Such a person can preserve my sons, and grandsons and the black-haired people (the common people). He may well be a great benefit to the country. But when a minister sees another person with a certain kind of ability, he is jealous and hates him, and when he sees another person who is elegant and wise, he blocks him so he cannot advance, thus showing that he really cannot tolerate others. Such a person cannot preserve my sons, grandsons, and the black-haired people. He is a danger to the country."[40] It is only a man of humanity who can send away such a minister and banish him, driving him to live among the barbarian tribes and not allowing him to exist together with the rest of the people in the Middle Kingdom (China). This is what is meant by saying that it is only the man of humanity who can love or who can hate others.[41] To see a worthy and not be able to raise him to office, or to be able to raise him but not to be the first one to do so—that is negligence.[42] To see bad men and not be able to remove them from office, or to be able to remove them but not to remove them as far away as possible—that is a mistake. To love what the people hate and to hate what

[38] *History*, "Announcement of K'ang." Cf. Legge, *Shoo King*, p. 397.

[39] For this story see *Book of Rites*, "T'an-kung," pt. 2. Cf. Legge, trans. *Li Ki*, vol. 1, p. 166.

[40] *History*, "Declaration of Ch'in." Cf. Legge, *Shoo King*, pp. 629-630.

[41] *Analects*, 4:3.

[42] The word *ming*, ordinarily meaning fate, here denotes negligence, according to Cheng Hsüan.

the people love—that is to act contrary to human nature, and disaster will come to such a person. Thus we see that the ruler has a great principle to follow. He must attain it through loyalty and faithfulness and will surely lose it through pride and indulgence.

There is a great principle for the production of wealth. If there are many producers and few consumers, and if people who produce wealth do so quickly and those who spend it do so slowly, then wealth will always be sufficient. A man of humanity develops his personality by means of his wealth, while the inhumane person develops wealth at the sacrifice of his personality. There has never been a case of a ruler who loved humanity and whose people did not love righteousness. There has never been a case where the people loved righteousness and yet the affairs of the state have not been carried to completion. And there has never been a case where in such a state the wealth collected in the national treasury did not continue in the possession of the ruler.

The officer Meng-hsien[43] said, "He who keeps a horse [one who has just become an official][44] and a carriage does not look after poultry and pigs. [The higher officials] who use ice [in their sacrifices] do not keep cattle and sheep. And the nobles who can keep a hundred carriages do not keep rapacious tax-gathering ministers under them. It is better to have a minister who robs the state treasury than to have such a tax-gathering minister. This is what is meant by saying that in a state financial profit is not considered real profit whereas righteousness is considered to be the real profit. He who heads a state or a family and is devoted to wealth and its use must have been under the influence of an inferior man. He may consider this man to be good, but when an inferior man is allowed to handle the country or family, disasters and injuries will come together. Though a good man may take his place, nothing can be done. This is what is meant by saying that in a state financial profit is not considered real profit whereas righteousness is considered the real profit.

> *Chu Hsi's Remark.* The above tenth chapter of commentary explains ordering the state to bring peace to the world. There are altogether ten commentary chapters. The first four generally discuss the principal topics and the basic import. The last six chapters discuss in detail the items and the required effort involved. Chapter five deals with the essence of the understanding of goodness and chapter six deals with the foundation of making the personal life sincere. These two chapters, especially, represent the immediate task, particularly for the beginning student. The reader should not neglect them because of their simplicity.

[43] A worthy officer-in-chief of Lu.
[44] This interpretation follows Cheng Hsüan's commentary.

5

SPIRITUAL DIMENSIONS: THE *DOCTRINE* *OF THE MEAN*

THE *Doctrine of the Mean* and the *Great Learning* are often mentioned together. Both constitute a chapter in the *Li chi* (*Book of Rites*) and were selected by Chu Hsi (1130-1200) to form the "Four Books" with the *Analects* and the *Book of Mencius*. Both became Classics and basic texts for civil service examinations from 1313 until 1905. Both exerted tremendous influence in China in the last eight hundred years, especially on Neo-Confucianism, which looked to them as two of their main sources of inspiration. But they are different in many ways. The *Great Learning* deals with social and political matters, while the *Doctrine of the Mean* is a discourse on psychology and metaphysics. The *Great Learning* discusses the mind but not human nature, whereas with the *Doctrine of the Mean* the opposite is true.[1] The *Great Learning* emphasizes method and procedure, whereas the *Doctrine of the Mean* concentrates on reality. The *Great Learning* is generally rational in tone, but the *Doctrine of the Mean* is religious and mystical. It comes very close to the more mystical aspect of the *Book of Mencius*, and several passages are almost identical in the two works.[2]

Even before this Classic attracted the Neo-Confucianists, its subtle doctrines had strong appeal to both Taoists and Buddhists. From the fourth to the eleventh century, Taoist and Buddhist scholars wrote commentaries on it, and one Buddhist monk in the eleventh century called himself by the name of the book. It formed a bridge between Taoism and Buddhism and the Confucian school and in this way prepared for the influence of Buddhism and Taoism on Confucianism, thus ushering in the Neo-Confucian movement.

What attracted the Taoists, Buddhists, and the Neo-Confucianists were the two main subjects of the book, the very subjects on which Confucius' pupils "could not hear his views,"[3] namely, human nature and the Way of Heaven. Human nature, endowed by Heaven, is revealed through the states of equilibrium and harmony, which are themselves the "condition of the world" and the "universal path." The Way of Heaven transcends time, space, substance, and motion, and is at the same time unceasing, eternal, and evident.

[1] The word "nature" appears only once in the *Great Learning* (ch. 10) and the word "mind" is not found in *The Mean* at all, except in Chu Hsi's and Ch'eng I's remarks.

[2] Cf. *The Mean*, ch. 20 and *Mencius*, 4A:12; 7B:16.

[3] *Analects*, 5:12.

It can readily be seen that the *Doctrine of the Mean* is a philosophical work, perhaps the most philosophical in the whole body of ancient Confucian literature. It is called *chung-yung* in Chinese. In the *Analects*, *chung-yung*, often translated the "Mean," denotes moderation but here *chung* means what is central and *yung* means what is universal and harmonious. The former refers to human nature, the latter to its relation with the universe. Taken together, it means that there is harmony in human nature and that this harmony underlies our moral being and prevails throughout the universe. In short, man and Nature form a unity. Here is an early expression of the theory that was to dominate Chinese thought throughout its history.

The quality that brings man and Nature together is *ch'eng*, sincerity, truth or reality.[4] The extensive discussion of this idea in the Classic makes it at once psychological, metaphysical, and religious. Sincerity is not just a state of mind, but an active force that is always transforming things and completing things, and drawing man and Heaven (*T'ien*, Nature) together in the same current. Insofar as it is mystical, it tends to be transcendental. But its practical aspect has never been forgotten. In fact, if sincerity is to be true, it must involve strenuous effort at learning and earnest effort at practice. After all, *yung* also means the ordinary, and sincerity is to be tested in ordinary words and ordinary deeds and its truth is understandable to the ordinary man. In the final analysis, the *Doctrine of the Mean* is a Confucian document, and as such it has never deviated from its central interest in practical affairs.

It is obvious that the *Doctrine of the Mean* represents an advance over Confucius. It and the *Great Learning* seem to embody two different ancient Confucian tendencies, just as later Mencius and Hsün Tzu (fl. 298–238 B.C.) represented two different schools of thought. Some scholars have suggested that the *Doctrine of the Mean* and the *Great Learning* are offshoots of the teachings of Mencius and Hsün Tzu, respectively.[5] This theory is interesting but not substantiated. Mencius and Hsün Tzu are opposed at many points. The *Doctrine of the Mean* and the *Great Learning* are not, although they are different—one of the reasons why they have been often spoken of together.

Following the list of its major topics and their reference, the work is translated below in full.

   Heaven and Man: 13, 20, 22
   Human relations: 13, 17, 19, 20
   Knowledge and Conduct: 14, 20, 27

[4] *The Mean*, chs. 20-26, 32. Strangely enough, the subject of *ch'eng* is not discussed in the *Analects*.
[5] For example, Fung Yu-lan. See his *History of Chinese Philosophy*, vol. 1, pp. 363, 370.

THE DOCTRINE OF THE MEAN[6]

Chu Hsi's Remark: "Master Ch'eng I (Ch'eng I-ch'uan, 1033-1107) said, 'By *chung* (central) is meant what is not one-sided, and by *yung* (ordinary) is meant what is unchangeable. *Chung* is the correct path of the world and *yung* is the definite principle of the world.' 'This work represents the central way[7] in which the doctrines of the Confucian school have been transmitted.' Fearing that in time errors should arise, Tzu-ssu wrote it down and transmitted it to Mencius. The book 'first speaks of one principle, next it spreads out to cover the ten thousand things, and finally returns and gathers them all under the one principle.' Unroll it, and it reaches in all directions. Roll it up, and it withdraws and lies hidden in minuteness. 'Its meaning and interest are inexhaustible.'[8] The whole of it is solid learning. If the skillful reader will explore and brood over it and apprehend it, he may apply it throughout his life, and will find it inexhaustible."

[6] Originally a chapter in the *Li chi* (*Book of Rites*), evidently it existed in the early Han dynasty (206 B.C.–A.D. 220) independently. Moreover, commentaries in the Han and Liang (502-557) times were written on it as an independent work, although these commentaries are no longer extant. As in the case of the *Great Learning*, great interest in it arose in the Sung period (960-1279). Both Ssu-ma Kuang (1019-1086) and Ch'eng Hao (Ch'eng Ming-tao, 1032-1085) wrote commentaries on it. But it was Chu Hsi who brought it into prominence. He redivided the old text, the one used in Cheng Hsüan's (127-200) commentary, the *Li chi cheng-i* or Correct Meanings of the *Book of Rites* (in the Thirteen Classics Series), into thirty-three sections without altering the order of the text. Thus the text became much clearer. He accepted the account in Ssu-ma Ch'ien's *Shih-chi* (Records of the Historian), ch. 47. (See French translation by Chavannes, *Les mémoires historiques*, vol. 5, p. 431), that Confucius' grandson Tzu-ssu (492–431 B.C.) was the author. Many modern scholars refuse to accept the theory; some have dated it around 200 B.C. The work is not consistent either in style or in thought. It may be a work of more than one person over a considerable period in the fifth or fourth century B.C. English translations by Legge, "The Doctrine of the Mean," and Ku Hung-ming, "Central Harmony," follow Chu Hsi's sectioning, while Hughes, "The Mean-in-Action," follows the Cheng Hsüan text. In our translation, Chu Hsi's arrangement is followed.

[7] The term *hsin-fa* is Buddhist, meaning transmission from mind to mind without the use of words. Ch'eng borrowed the term but used it in an entirely different sense, taking *hsin* (mind) to mean "central," and emphasizing the use of words.

[8] *I-shu* (Surviving Works), 7:3b, 14:1a, 18:30a; *Wai-shu* (Additional Works), 11:1b, both in ECCS.

1. What Heaven (*T'ien*, Nature) imparts to man is called human nature. To follow[9] our nature is called the Way (Tao). Cultivating the Way is called education. The Way cannot be separated from us for a moment. What can be separated from us is not the Way. Therefore the superior man is cautious over what he does not see and apprehensive over what he does not hear. There is nothing more visible than what is hidden and nothing more manifest than what is subtle. Therefore the superior man is watchful over himself when he is alone.

Before the feelings of pleasure, anger, sorrow, and joy are aroused it is called equilibrium (*chung*, centrality, mean). When these feelings are aroused and each and all attain due measure and degree, it is called harmony. Equilibrium is the great foundation of the world, and harmony its universal path. When equilibrium and harmony are realized to the highest degree, heaven and earth will attain their proper order and all things will flourish.

> *Chu Hsi's Remark.* "In the above first chapter, Tzu-ssu relates the ideas which had been transmitted to him, as the basis of discourse. First, it shows clearly that the origin of the Way is traced to Heaven and is unchangeable, while its concrete substance is complete in ourselves and may not be departed from. Next, it speaks of the essentials of preserving, nourishing, and examining the mind. Finally, it speaks of the meritorious achievements and transforming influence of the sage and the spirit man in their highest degree. Tzu-ssu's hope was that the student should hereby return to search within himself to find these truths, so that he might remove his selfish desires aroused by external temptations, and realize in full measure the goodness which is natural to him. This is what scholar Yang meant when he said that this chapter is the quintessence of the whole work.[10] In the following ten chapters, Tzu-ssu quotes Confucius in order fully to develop the meaning of this chapter."

2. Chung-ni (Confucius) said, "The superior man [exemplifies] the Mean (*chung-yung*).[11] The inferior man acts contrary to the Mean. The

[9] Interpretation according to Cheng Hsüan, *Chung-yung chu* (Commentary on the *Doctrine of the Mean*).

[10] Although none of the commentators in the *Chung-yung chang-chü* (Commentary on the *Doctrine of the Mean*) in the *Ssu-shu ta-ch'üan* (Great Collection of Commentaries on the Four Books) mentioned the name of the man, this refers to Yang Shih (Yang Kuei-shan, 1053-1135). In his *Chung-yung huo-wen* (Questions and Answers on the *Doctrine of the Mean*), Chu Hsi repeatedly commented on Yang's theories. The particular remark in question, however, is not found in the *Yang Kuei-shan chi* (Collected Works of Yang Shih). It was probably transmitted orally and was well known to scholars.

[11] The term *chung-yung*, literally "centrality and universality," has been trans-

superior man [exemplifies] the Mean because, as a superior man, he can maintain the Mean at any time. The inferior man [acts contrary to][12] the Mean because, as an inferior man, he has no caution."

3. Confucius said, "Perfect is the Mean. For a long time few people have been able to follow it."[13]

4. Confucius said, "I know why the Way is not pursued. The intelligent go beyond it and the stupid do not come up to it. I know why the Way is not understood.[14] The worthy go beyond it and the unworthy do not come up to it. There is no one who does not eat and drink, but there are few who can really know flavor."

5. Confucius said, "Alas! How is the Way not being pursued!"

6. Confucius said, "Shun[15] was indeed a man of great wisdom! He loved to question others and to examine their words, however ordinary. He concealed what was bad in them and displayed what was good. He took hold of their two extremes, took the mean between them, and applied it in his dealing with the people. This was how he became Shun (the sage-emperor)."

7. Confucius said, "Men all say, 'I am wise'; but when driven forward and taken in a net, a trap, or a pitfall, none knows how to escape. Men all say, 'I am wise'; but should they choose the course of the Mean, they are not able to keep it for a round month."

8. Confucius said, "Hui[16] was a man who chose the course of the Mean, and when he got hold of one thing that was good, he clasped it firmly as if wearing it on his breast and never lost it."

9. Confucius said, "The empire, the states, and the families can be put in order. Ranks and emolument can be declined. A bare, naked weapon can be tramped upon. But the Mean cannot [easily] be attained."

10. Tzu-lu[17] asked about strength. Confucius said, "Do you mean the strength of the South, the strength of the North, or the strength you should cultivate yourself? To be genial and gentle in teaching others and not to revenge unreasonable conduct—this is the strength of the people

---

lated as moderation, the Mean, mean-in-action, normality, universal moral order, etc. According to Cheng Hsüan, *yung* means the ordinary and *chung-yung* means using the Mean as the ordinary way. According to Chu Hsi, it means neither one-sided nor extreme but the ordinary principle of the Mean. The Mean is the same as equilibrium and harmony in ch. 1.

[12] Following Wang Su's (195-256) text.

[13] A similar saying is found in *Analects*, 6:27.

[14] Some eleventh-century scholars thought that the word "pursued" and "understood" should be interchanged, for intelligence and stupidity pertain to understanding while worthiness and unworthiness pertain to action.

[15] Legendary sage-emperor (3rd millennium B.C.).

[16] Name of Confucius' favorite pupil, Yen Yüan (521–490 B.C.).

[17] Confucius' pupil, whose family name was Chung and private name Yu (542–480 B.C.).

of the South. The superior man lives by it. To lie under arms and meet death without regret—this is the strength of the people of the North. The strong man lives by it. Therefore the superior man maintains harmony [in his nature and conduct] and does not waver. How unflinching is his strength! He stands in the middle position and does not lean to one side. How unflinching is his strength! When the Way prevails in the state, [if he enters public life], he does not change from what he was in private life. How unflinching is his strength! When the Way does not prevail in the state, he does not change even unto death. How unflinching is his strength!"

11. "There are men who seek for the abstruse, and practice wonders. Future generations may mention them. But that is what I will not do. There are superior men who act in accordance with the Way, but give up when they have gone half way. But I can never give up. There are superior men who are in accord with the Mean, retire from the world and are unknown to their age, but do not regret. It is only a sage who can do this."

12. "The Way of the superior man functions everywhere and yet is hidden. Men and women of simple intelligence can share its knowledge; and yet in its utmost reaches, there is something which even the sage does not know. Men and women of simple intelligence can put it into practice; and yet in its utmost reaches there is something which even the sage is not able to put into practice. Great as heaven and earth are, men still find something in them with which to be dissatisfied. Thus with [the Way of] the superior man, if one speaks of its greatness, nothing in the world can contain it, and if one speaks of its smallness, nothing in the world can split it. The *Book of Odes* says, 'The hawk flies up to heaven; the fishes leap in the deep.'[18] This means that [the Way] is clearly seen above and below. The Way of the superior man has its simple beginnings in the relation between man and woman, but in its utmost reaches, it is clearly seen in heaven and on earth."

> *Chu Hsi's Remark.* "The above twelfth chapter contains the words of Tzu-ssu, which are meant to clarify and elaborate on the idea of chapter 1 that the Way cannot be departed from. In the following eight chapters, he quotes Confucius here and there to clarify it."

13. Confucius said, "The Way is not far from man. When a man pursues the Way and yet remains away from man, his course cannot be considered the Way. The *Book of Odes* says, "In hewing an axe handle, in hewing an axe handle, the pattern is not far off.'[19] If we take an axe

[18] Ode no. 239.   [19] Ode no. 158.

handle to hew another axe handle and look askance from the one to the other, we may still think the pattern is far away. Therefore the superior man governs men as men, in accordance with human nature, and as soon as they change [what is wrong], he stops. Conscientiousness (*chung*) and altruism (*shu*) are not far from the Way. What you do not wish others to do to you, do not do to them.

"There are four things in the Way of the superior man, none of which I have been able to do. To serve my father as I would expect my son to serve me: that I have not been able to do. To serve my ruler as I would expect my ministers to serve me: that I have not been able to do. To serve my elder brothers as I would expect my younger brothers to serve me: that I have not been able to do. To be the first to treat friends as I would expect them to treat me: that I have not been able to do. In practicing the ordinary virtues and in the exercise of care in ordinary conversation, when there is deficiency, the superior man never fails to make further effort, and when there is excess, never dares to go to the limit. His words correspond to his actions and his actions correspond to his words.[20] Isn't the superior man earnest and genuine?"

> *Comment.* It is often said that Confucianism teaches only the "negative golden rule," not to do to others what one does not want them to do to him. However, the golden rule is here positively stated, that is, to do to others what one expects others to do to him. There is no question about the positive character of the Confucian doctrine which is clearly stated in terms of conscientiousness and altruism.[21]

14. The superior man does what is proper to his position and does not want to go beyond this. If he is in a noble station, he does what is proper to a position of wealth and honorable station. If he is in a humble station, he does what is proper to a position of poverty and humble station. If he is in the midst of barbarian tribes, he does what is proper in the midst of barbarian tribes. In a position of difficulty and danger, he does what is proper to a position of difficulty and danger. He can find himself in no situation in which he is not at ease with himself. In a high position he does not treat his inferiors with contempt. In a low position he does not court the favor of his superiors. He rectifies himself and seeks nothing from others, hence he has no complaint to make. He does not complain against Heaven above or blame men below.[22] Thus it is that the superior man lives peacefully and at ease and waits for his destiny (*ming*, Mandate

---

[20] See above, ch. 2, comment on *Analects*, 2:18.

[21] *ibid.*, comment on *Analects*, 4:15. For a discussion on *chung-shu*, see Appendix.

[22] A similar saying is found in *Analects*, 14:37.

of Heaven, fate),[23] while the inferior man takes to dangerous courses and hopes for good luck. Confucius said, "In archery we have something resembling the Way of the superior man. When the archer misses the center of the target, he turns around and seeks for the cause of failure within himself."

15. The Way of the superior man may be compared to traveling to a distant place: one must start from the nearest point. It may be compared to ascending a height: one must start from below. The *Book of Odes* says, "Happy union with wife and children is like the music of lutes and harps. When brothers live in concord and at peace, the harmony is sweet and delightful. Let your family live in concord, and enjoy your wife and children."[24] Confucius said, "How happy will parents be!"

16. Confucius said, "How abundant is the display of power of spiritual beings! We look for them but do not see them. We listen to them but do not hear them. They form the substance of all things[25] and nothing can be without them. They cause all people in the world to fast and purify themselves and put on the richest dresses to perform sacrifices to them. Like the spread of overflowing water they seem to be above and to be on the left and the right. The *Book of Odes* says, 'The coming of spiritual beings cannot be surmised. How much less can we get tired of them?'[26] Such is the manifestation of the subtle. Such is the impossibility of hiding the real (*ch'eng*)."

17. Confucius said, "Shun was indeed greatly filial! In virtue he was a sage; in honor he was the Son of Heaven (emperor); and in wealth he owned all within the four seas (China). Temple sacrifices were made to him, and his descendants preserved the sacrifices to him. Thus it is that he who possesses great virtue will certainly attain to corresponding position, to corresponding wealth, to corresponding fame, and to corresponding long life. For Heaven, in the production of things, is sure to be bountiful to them, according to their natural capacity. Hence the tree that is well taken care of is nourished and that which is about to fall is overthrown. The *Book of Odes* says, 'The admirable, amiable prince displayed conspicuously his excellent virtue. He put his people and his officers in concord. And he received his emolument from Heaven. It protected him, assisted him, and appointed him king. And Heaven's blessing came again and again.'[27] Therefore he who possesses great virtue will surely receive the appointment of Heaven."

[23] On the doctrine of waiting for destiny, see above, ch. 3, comment on *Mencius*, Additional Selections, 7A:1.

[24] Ode no. 164.

[25] This is Chu Hsi's interpretation of *t'i-wu* in his *Chung-yung chang-ch'ü*. See also below, ch. 30, n.83.

[26] Ode no. 256.   [27] Ode no. 249.

18. Confucius said, "King Wen was indeed the only one without sorrow! He had King Chi for father and King Wu[28] for son. His father laid the foundation of [the great work of the Chou dynasty] and his son carried it on. King Wu continued the enterprise of King T'ai,[29] King Chi, and King Wen. Once he buckled on his armor [and revolted against wicked King Chou of Shang], the world came into his possession, and did not personally lose his great reputation throughout the empire. In honor he was the Son of Heaven, and in wealth he owned all within the four seas. Temple sacrifices were made to him, and his descendants preserved the sacrifices to him.

"King Wu received Heaven's Mandate to rule in his old age. Duke Chou[30] carried to completion the virtue of King Wen and King Wu. He honored T'ai and Chi with the posthumous title of king. He sacrificed to the past reigning dukes of the house with imperial rites. These rites were extended to the feudal lords, great officers, officers, and the common people. If the father was a great officer, and the son a minor officer, when the father died, he was buried with the rite of a great officer but afterward sacrificed to with the rite of a minor officer. If the father was a minor officer and the son was a great officer, then the father was buried with the rite of a minor officer but afterward sacrificed to with the rite of a great officer. The rule for one year of mourning for relatives was extended upward to include great officers, but the rule for three years of mourning was extended upward to include the Son of Heaven. In mourning for parents, there was no difference for the noble or the commoner. The practice was the same."

19. Confucius said, "King Wu and Duke Chou were indeed eminently filial. Men of filial piety are those who skillfully carry out the wishes of their forefathers and skillfully carry forward their undertakings. In spring and autumn they repaired their ancestral temple, displayed their ancestral vessels and exhibited the ancestral robes, and presented the appropriate offerings of the season. The ritual of the ancestral temple is in order to place the kindred on the left or on the right according to the order of descent. This order in rank meant to distinguish the more honorable or humbler stations. Services in the temple are arranged in order so as to give distinction to the worthy [according to their ability for those services]. In the pledging rite the inferiors present their cups to their superiors, so that people of humble stations may have something to do. In the concluding feast, honored places were given people with white hair, so as to follow the order of seniority. To occupy places of

[28] King Wen (r. 1171–1122 B.C.) was the founder of the Chou dynasty. King Wu (r. 1121–1116 B.C.) was his successor.
[29] King Chi's father.　　　　　　　　　　[30] King Wu's brother (d. 1094 B.C.).

their forefathers, to practice their rites, to perform their music, to reverence those whom they honored, to love those who were dear to them, to serve the dead as they were served while alive, and to serve the departed as they were served while still with us: this is the height of filial piety.

"The ceremonies of sacrifices to Heaven and Earth are meant for the service of the Lord on High, and the ceremonies performed in the ancestral temple are meant for the service of ancestors. If one understands the ceremonies of the sacrifices to Heaven and Earth and the meaning of the grand sacrifice and the autumn sacrifice to ancestors, it would be as easy to govern a kingdom as to look at one's palm."

20. Duke Ai[31] asked about government. Confucius said, "The governmental measures of King Wen and King Wu are spread out in the records. With their kind of men, government will flourish. When their kind of men are gone, their government will come to an end. When the right principles of man operate, the growth of good government is rapid, and when the right principles of soil operate, the growth of vegetables is rapid. Indeed, government is comparable to a fast-growing plant.[32] Therefore the conduct of government depends upon the men. The right men are obtained by the ruler's personal character. The cultivation of the person is to be done through the Way, and the cultivation of the Way is to be done through humanity. Humanity (*jen*) is [the distinguishing characteristic of] man,[33] and the greatest application of it is in being affectionate toward relatives. Righteousness (*i*) is the principle of setting things right and proper, and the greatest application of it is in honoring the worthy. The relative degree of affection we ought to feel for our relatives and the relative grades in the honoring of the worthy give rise to the rules of propriety. [If those in inferior positions do not have the confidence of their superiors, they will not be able to govern the people].[34]

> *Comment.* The sentence "Humanity is [the distinguishing characteristic of] man" is perhaps the most often quoted on the subject of humanity (*jen*). In Chinese it is "*jen* is *jen*," the first *jen* meaning humanity and the second referring to man. It is not just a pun, but an important definition of the basic Confucian concept of humanity, for to Confucianists, the virtue of humanity is meaningless unless it is involved in actual human relationships. This is the reason Cheng Hsüan defined it as "people living together," the definition

[31] Ruler of Lu (r. 494–465 B.C.).

[32] Some say that Confucius' words stop here, the rest being Tzu-ssu's elaboration.

[33] Cf. *Mencius*, 7B:16.

[34] Cheng Hsüan correctly pointed out in his commentary that this sentence is duplicated near the end of the chapter and is therefore superfluous.

to which scholars of the Ch'ing dynasty (1644-1912) returned in their revolt against the Neo-Confucianists of the Sung dynasty who interpreted *jen* as a state of mind.[35]

"Therefore the ruler must not fail to cultivate his personal life. Wishing to cultivate his personal life, he must not fail to serve his parents. Wishing to serve his parents, he must not fail to know man. Wishing to know man, he must not fail to know Heaven.

"There are five universal ways [in human relations], and the way by which they are practiced is three. The five are those governing the relationship between ruler and minister, between father and son, between husband and wife, between elder and younger brothers, and those in the intercourse between friends. These five are universal paths in the world.[36] Wisdom, humanity, and courage, these three are the universal virtues. The way by which they are practiced is one.

"Some are born with the knowledge [of these virtues]. Some learn it through study. Some learn it through hard work. But when the knowledge is acquired, it comes to the same thing. Some practice them naturally and easily. Some practice them for their advantage. Some practice them with effort and difficulty. But when the achievement is made, it comes to the same thing."

Confucius said, "Love of learning is akin to wisdom. To practice with vigor is akin to humanity. To know to be shameful is akin to courage. He who knows these three things knows how to cultivate his personal life. Knowing how to cultivate his personal life, he knows how to govern other men. And knowing how to govern other men, he knows how to govern the empire, its states, and the families.

"There are nine standards by which to administer the empire, its states, and the families. They are: cultivating the personal life, honoring the worthy, being affectionate to relatives, being respectful toward the great ministers, identifying oneself with the welfare of the whole body of officers, treating the common people as one's own children, attracting the various artisans, showing tenderness to strangers from far countries, and extending kindly and awesome influence on the feudal lords. If the ruler cultivates his personal life, the Way will be established. If he honors the worthy, he will not be perplexed. If he is affectionate to his relatives, there will be no grumbling among his uncles and brothers. If he respects the great ministers, he will not be deceived. If he identifies himself with the welfare of the whole body of officers, then the officers will repay him heavily for his courtesies. If he treats the common people as his own

---

[35] See Chan, "The Evolution of the Confucian Concept *Jen*," *Philosophy East and West*, 4 (1955), 295-319.

[36] See above, ch. 3, comment on *Mencius*, Additional Selections, 3A:4.

children, then the masses will exhort one another [to do good]. If he attracts the various artisans, there will be sufficiency of wealth and resources in the country. If he shows tenderness to strangers from far countries, people from all quarters of the world will flock to him. And if he extends kindly and awesome influence over the feudal lords, then the world will stand in awe of him.

"To fast, to purify, and to be correct in dress [at the time of solemn sacrifice], and not to make any movement contrary to the rules of propriety—this is the way to cultivate the personal life. To avoid slanderers, keep away seductive beauties, regard wealth lightly, and honor virtue— this is the way to encourage the worthy. To give them honorable position, to bestow on them ample emoluments, and to share their likes and dislikes—this is the way to encourage affection for relatives. To allow them many officers to carry out their functions—this is the way to encourage the great ministers. To deal with them loyally and faithfully and to give them ample emoluments—this is the way to encourage the body of officers. To require them for service only at the proper time [without interfering with their farm work] and to tax them lightly—this is the way to encourage the common masses. To inspect them daily and examine them monthly and to reward them according to the degree of their workmanship—this is the way to encourage the various artisans. To welcome them when they come and send them off when they go and to commend the good among them and show compassion to the incompetent—this is the way to show tenderness to strangers from far countries. To restore lines of broken succession, to revive states that have been extinguished, to bring order to chaotic states, to support those states that are in danger, to have fixed times for their attendance at court, and to present them with generous gifts while expecting little when they come —this is the way to extend kindly and awesome influence on the feudal lords.

"There are nine standards by which to govern the empire, its states, and the families, but the way by which they are followed is one. In all matters if there is preparation they will succeed; if there is no preparation, they will fail. If what is to be said is determined beforehand, there will be no stumbling. If the business to be done is determined beforehand, there will be no difficulty. If action to be taken is determined beforehand, there will be no trouble. And if the way to be pursued is determined beforehand, there will be no difficulties.[37] If those in inferior positions do not have the confidence of their superiors, they will not be able to govern the people. There is a way to have the confidence of the

[37] According to K'ung Ying-ta (574-648; see *Li chi cheng-i*): There will be no limit to its possibility.

superiors: If one is not trusted by his friends, he will not have the confidence of his superiors. There is a way to be trusted by one's friends: If one is not obedient to his parents, he will not be trusted by his friends. There is a way to obey one's parents: If one examines himself and finds himself to be insincere, he will not be obedient to his parents. There is a way to be sincere with oneself: If one does not understand what is good, he will not be sincere with himself. Sincerity is the Way of Heaven. To think how to be sincere is the way of man. He who is sincere is one who hits upon what is right without effort and apprehends without think-ing. He is naturally and easily in harmony with the Way. Such a man is a sage. He who tries to be sincere is one who chooses the good and holds fast to it.

"Study it (the way to be sincere) extensively, inquire into it accurate-ly, think over it carefully, sift it clearly, and practice it earnestly. When there is anything not yet studied, or studied but not yet understood, do not give up. When there is any question not yet asked, or asked but its answer not yet known, do not give up. When there is anything not yet thought over, or thought over but not yet apprehended, do not give up. When there is anything not yet sifted, or sifted but not yet clear, do not give up. When there is anything not yet practiced, or practiced but not yet earnestly, do not give up.[38] If another man succeed by one effort, you will use a hundred efforts. If another man succeed by ten efforts, you will use a thousand efforts. If one really follows this course, though stupid, he will surely become intelligent, and though weak, will surely become strong."

Comment. The five steps of study, inquiry, thinking, sifting, and practice could have come from John Dewey.

21. It is due to our nature that enlightenment results from sincerity. It is due to education that sincerity results from enlightenment. Given sincerity, there will be enlightenment, and given enlightenment, there will be sincerity.

Chu Hsi's Remark. "In the above twenty-first chapter, Tzu-ssu continues Confucius' idea in the preceding chapter of the Way of Heaven and the way of man as a basis for discussion. In the follow-ing twelve chapters, Tzu-ssu reiterates and elaborates the idea of this chapter."

22. Only those who are absolutely sincere can fully develop their nature. If they can fully develop their nature, they can then fully develop

[38] Chu Hsi's interpretation: Either do not study at all, or do not give up until what you studied is all understood, etc.

the nature of others. If they can fully develop the nature of others, they can then fully develop the nature of things. If they can fully develop the nature of things, they can then assist in the transforming and nourishing process of Heaven and Earth. If they can assist in the transforming and nourishing process of Heaven and Earth, they can thus form a trinity with Heaven and Earth.

> *Comment.* Whether this chapter refers to rulers, as Cheng Hsüan and other Han dynasty scholars contended, or to the sage, as Chu Hsi and other Sung scholars thought, is immaterial. The important point is the ultimate trinity with Heaven and Earth. It is of course another way of saying the unity of man and Heaven or Nature, a doctrine which eventually assumed the greatest importance in Neo-Confucianism.[39]

23. The next in order are those who cultivate to the utmost a particular goodness. Having done this, they can attain to the possession of sincerity. As there is sincerity, there will be its expression. As it is expressed, it will become conspicuous. As it becomes conspicuous, it will become clear. As it becomes clear, it will move others. As it moves others, it changes them. As it changes them, it transforms them. Only those who are absolutely sincere can transform others.

24. It is characteristic of absolute sincerity to be able to foreknow. When a nation or family is about to flourish, there are sure to be lucky omens. When a nation or family is about to perish, there are sure to be unlucky omens. These omens are revealed in divination and in the movements of the four limbs. When calamity or blessing is about to come, it can surely know beforehand if it is good, and it can also surely know beforehand if it is evil. Therefore he who has absolute sincerity is like a spirit.

25. Sincerity means the completion of the self, and the Way is self-directing. Sincerity is the beginning and end of things. Without sincerity there would be nothing. Therefore the superior man values sincerity. Sincerity is not only the completion of one's own self, it is that by which all things are completed. The completion of the self means humanity. The completion of all things means wisdom. These are the character of the nature, and they are the Way in which the internal[40] and the external are united. Therefore whenever it is employed, everything done is right.

> *Comment.* In no other Confucian work is the Way (Tao) given such a central position. This self-directing Way seems to be the

---

[39] See below, pp. 524, 666, 752.
[40] It is not clear whether this refers to sincerity, the character of the nature, or the Way.

same as the Tao in Taoism. But the difference is great. As Ch'ien Mu has pointed out, when the Taoists talk about Tao as being natural, it means that Tao is void and empty, whereas when Confucianists talk about Tao as being natural, they describe it as sincerity. This, according to him, is a great contribution of the *Doctrine of the Mean*.[41] It should also be pointed out that with Confucianists, "The Way is not far from man."[42] Contrary to the Tao of Taoism, the Confucian Tao is strongly humanistic.

26. Therefore absolute sincerity is ceaseless. Being ceaseless, it is lasting. Being lasting, it is evident. Being evident, it is infinite. Being infinite, it is extensive and deep. Being extensive and deep, it is high and brilliant. It is because it is extensive and deep that it contains all things. It is because it is high and brilliant that it overshadows all things. It is because it is infinite and lasting that it can complete all things. In being extensive and deep, it is a counterpart of Earth. In being high and brilliant, it is a counterpart of Heaven. In being infinite and lasting, it is unlimited. Such being its nature, it becomes prominent without any display, produces changes without motion, and accomplishes its ends without action.[48]

The Way of Heaven and Earth may be completely described in one sentence: They are without any doubleness and so they produce things in an unfathomable way. The Way of Heaven and Earth is extensive, deep, high, brilliant, infinite, and lasting. The heaven now before us is only this bright, shining mass; but when viewed in its unlimited extent, the sun, moon, stars, and constellations are suspended in it and all things are covered by it. The earth before us is but a handful of soil; but in its breadth and depth, it sustains mountains like Hua and Yüeh without feeling their weight, contains the rivers and seas without letting them leak away, and sustains all things. The mountain before us is only a fistful of straw; but in all the vastness of its size, grass and trees grow upon it, birds and beasts dwell on it, and stores of precious things (minerals) are discovered in it. The water before us is but a spoonful of liquid, but in all its unfathomable depth, the monsters, dragons, fishes, and turtles are produced in them, and wealth becomes abundant because of it [as a result of transportation]. The *Book of Odes* says, "The Mandate of Heaven, how beautiful and unceasing."[44] This is to say, this is

---

[41] *Ssu-shu shih-i* (Explanation of Meanings of the Four Books), 1953.

[42] See above, *The Mean*, ch. 13.

[43] Perhaps this is a step further than described in *The Mean*, ch. 23 and the translation should be "becomes prominent without any display, can change others without moving them, and complete [the self and all things, as in *The Mean*, ch. 25] without any action."

[44] Ode no. 267.

what makes Heaven to be Heaven. Again, it says, "How shining is it, the purity of King Wen's virtue!"[45] This is to say, this is what makes King Wen what he was. Purity likewise is unceasing.

27. Great is the Way of the sage! Overflowing, it produces and nourishes all things and rises up to the height of heaven. How exceedingly great! [It embraces] the three hundred rules of ceremonies and the three thousand rules of conduct. It waits for the proper man before it can be put into practice. Therefore it is said, "Unless there is perfect virtue, the perfect Way cannot be materialized." Therefore the superior man honors the moral nature and follows the path of inquiry and study. He achieves breadth and greatness and pursues the refined and subtle to the limit. He seeks to reach the greatest height and brilliancy and follows the path of the Mean. He goes over the old so as to find out what is new.[46] He is earnest and deep and highly respects all propriety. Therefore when occupying a high position, he is not proud, and when serving in a low position, he is not insubordinate. When the Way prevails in the country, he can rise to official position through his words. When the Way does not prevail in the country, he can preserve himself through silence. The *Book of Odes* says, "Intelligent and wise, he protects his person."[47] This is the meaning.

Comment. The two different approaches through "honoring the moral nature" and "following the path of study and inquiry" represent the two tendencies between the rationalistic Neo-Confucianism of Ch'eng I and Chu Hsi on the one hand and the idealistic Neo-Confucianism of Lu Hsiang-shan (Lu Chiu-yüan, 1139-1193) and Wang Yang-ming (Wang Shou-jen, 1472-1529) on the other. They were the issue between Chu and Lu in their famous debate in 1175.[48]

28. Confucius said, "To be stupid and like to use his own judgment, to be in a humble station and like to dictate, to live in the present world and go back to the ways of antiquity—people of this sort bring calamity on themselves. Unless one is the Son of Heaven, he does not decide on ceremonies [of social order], make regulations, or investigate (determine) the form and pronunciation of characters. In the world today, all carriages have wheels of the same size, all writing is done with the same characters,[49] and all conduct is governed by the same social re-

---

[45] *ibid.*
[46] The same saying appears in *Analects*, 2:11.
[47] Ode no. 260.
[48] See below, ch. 33, sec. 31, and comment on it.
[49] Many modern writers have pointed out that these were not conditions of the fourth century B.C. but of the Ch'in dynasty (221–206 B.C.) when writing and measurements were unified.

lations. Although a man occupies the throne, if he has not the corresponding virtue, he may not dare to institute systems of music and ceremony. Although a man has the virtue, if he does not occupy the throne, he may not dare to institute systems of music and ceremony either."

Confucius said, "I have talked about the ceremonies of the Hsia dynasty (2183–1752 B.C.?), but what remains in the present state of Ch'i (descendant of Hsia) does not provide sufficient evidence. I have studied the ceremonies of the Shang dynasty (1751-1112 B.C.). They are still preserved in the present state of Sung (descendant of Shang). I have studied the ceremonies of the [Western] Chou dynasty (1111–770 B.C.). They are in use today. I follow the Chou."[50]

29. If he who attains to the sovereignty of the world has three important things [ceremonies, regulations, and the form and pronunciation of characters], he will make few mistakes. However excellent may have been the regulations of former times, there is no evidence for them. Without evidence, they cannot command credence, and not being credited, the people would not follow them. However excellent might be the regulations made by one in a low position, his position is not an honored one. The position not being honored does not command credence, and not being credited, the people would not follow them. Therefore the Way of the true ruler is rooted in his own personal life and has its evidence [in the following] of the common people. It is tested by the experience of the Three Kings[51] and found without error, applied before Heaven and Earth and found to be without contradiction in their operation, laid before spiritual beings without question or fear, and can wait a hundred generations for a sage [to confirm it] without a doubt. Since it can be laid before spiritual beings without question or fear, it shows that he knows [the Principle of] Heaven. Since it can wait for a hundred generations for a sage without a doubt, it shows that he knows [the principles of] man. Therefore every move he makes becomes the way of the world, every act of his becomes the model of the world, and every word he utters becomes the pattern of the world. Those who are far away look longingly for him, and those who are near do not get weary of him. The *Book of Odes* says, "There they do not dislike him, here they do not get tired of him. Thus from day to day and night to night, they will perpetuate their praise."[52] There has never been a ruler who did not answer this description and yet could obtain early renown throughout the world.

30. Chung-ni (Confucius) transmitted the ancient traditions of Yao and Shun, and he modeled after and made brilliant the systems of King Wen and King Wu. He conformed with the natural order governing the

---

[50] Cf. *Analects*, 3:9.
[51] Founders of the Hsia, Shang, and Chou dynasties.
[52] Ode no. 278.

revolution of the seasons in heaven above, and followed the principles governing land and water below. He may be compared to earth in its supporting and containing all things, and to heaven in its overshadowing and embracing all things. He may be compared to the four seasons in their succession, and to the sun and moon in their alternate shining. All things are produced and developed without injuring one another. The courses of the seasons, the sun, and moon are pursued without conflict. The lesser forces flow continuously like river currents, while the great forces go silently and deeply in their mighty transformations. It is this that makes heaven and earth so great.

31. Only the perfect sage in the world has quicknesss of apprehension, intelligence, insight, and wisdom, which enable him to rule all men; magnanimity, generosity, benignity, and tenderness, which enable him to embrace all men; vigor, strength, firmness, and resolution, which enable him to maintain a firm hold; orderliness, seriousness, adherence to the Mean, and correctness, which enable him to be reverent; pattern, order, refinement, and penetration, which enable him to exercise discrimination. All embracing and extensive, and deep and unceasingly springing, these virtues come forth at all times. All embracing and extensive as heaven and deep and unceasingly springing as an abyss! He appears and all people respect him, speaks and all people believe him, acts and all people are pleased with him. Consequently his fame spreads overflowingly over the Middle Kingdom (China, the civilized world), and extends to barbarous tribes. Wherever ships and carriages reach, wherever the labor of man penetrates, wherever the heavens overshadow and the earth sustains, wherever the sun and moon shine, and wherever frosts and dew fall, all who have blood and breath honor and love him. Therefore we say that he is a counterpart of Heaven.

32. Only those who are absolutely sincere can order and adjust the great relations of mankind, establish the great foundations of humanity, and know the transforming and nourishing operations of heaven and earth. Does he depend on anything else? How earnest and sincere—he is humanity! How deep and unfathomable—he is abyss! How vast and great—he is heaven! Who can know him except he who really has quickness of apprehension, intelligence, sageliness, and wisdom, and understands character of Heaven?

33. The *Book of Odes* says, "Over her brocaded robe, she wore a plain and simple dress,"[53] for she disliked the loudness of its color and patterns. Thus the way of the superior man is hidden but becomes more

[53] Ode no. 57, actually a paraphrase.

prominent every day,[54] whereas the way of the inferior man is conspicuous but gradually disappears. It is characteristic of the superior man to be plain, and yet people do not get tired of him. He is simple and yet rich in cultural adornment. He is amiable and yet systematically methodical. He knows what is distant begins with what is near. He knows where the winds (moral influence) come from. And he knows the subtle will be manifested. Such a man can enter into virtue.

The *Book of Odes* says, "Although the fish dive and lie at the bottom, it is still quite clearly seen."[55] Therefore the superior man examines his own heart and sees that there is nothing wrong there, and that he is not dissatisfied with himself. The superior man is unequaled in the fact that he [is cautious] in those things which people do not see. The *Book of Odes* says, "Though the ceiling looks down upon you, be free from shame even in the recesses of your own house."[56] Therefore the superior man is reverent without any movement and truthful without any words. The *Book of Odes* says, "Throughout the sacrifice not a word is spoken, and yet [the worshipers are influenced and transformed] without the slightest contention."[57] Therefore the superior man does not resort to rewards and the people are encouraged to virtue. He does not resort to anger and the people are awed. The *Book of Odes* says, "He does not display his virtue, and yet all the princes follow him."[58] Therefore when the superior man is sincere and reverent, the world will be in order and at peace. The *Book of Odes* says, "I cherish your brilliant virtue, which makes no great display in sound or appearance."[59] Confucius said, "In influencing people, the use of sound or appearance is of secondary importance." The *Book of Odes* says, "His virtue is as light as hair."[60] Still, a hair is comparable.[61] "The operations of Heaven have neither sound nor smell."[62]

Chu Hsi's Remark. In the above thirty-third chapter, Tzu-ssu returns to the ideas of "carrying out to the limit" and "exhausting the most refined" (discussed in previous chapters) to search for their source. Furthermore, he extends the discussion to include the effort of the learner who, for his own sake, learns to be careful while alone—an effort which, through earnestness and reverence, culminates in the glory of world peace. Then he further praises the

---

[54] Cf. *Lao Tzu*, ch. 24.   [55] Ode no. 192.   [56] Ode no. 256.

[57] Ode no. 302.   [58] Ode no. 269.   [59] Ode no. 241.

[60] Ode no. 260. Both Chu Hsi and Cheng Hsüan believed that this sentence was uttered by Confucius.

[61] Chu Hsi considered this sentence and the rest to be by Tzu-ssu. Cheng Hsüan and K'ung Ying-ta, however, considered them to be by Confucius.

[62] Ode no. 235.

wonder of all this, and does not stop until he describes it as being without sound or smell. What he does is to pick out the essence of the whole work and talk about it in simple terms. He felt deeply and most earnestly as he instructed people by going over the points again and again. Should the student not apply his mind to the utmost [in studying this work]?"

6

NATURALISTIC CONFUCIANISM: HSÜN TZU

MENCIUS and Hsün Tzu (fl. 298–238 B.C.) have generally been considered as representing the two divergent tendencies of idealistic Confucianism and naturalistic Confucianism in ancient China. Whether these two tendencies were derived, correspondingly, from the *Doctrine of the Mean* and the *Great Learning* is not clear. At any rate, by teaching the doctrine of the original evil nature of man and the necessity for its control through law and rules of propriety (*li*), Hsün Tzu stood diametrically opposed to Mencius whose doctrine professed the original goodness of human nature and moral intuition as the source of political and social development. Generally speaking, Hsün Tzu was naturalistic and Mencius idealistic. In this and other respects, they have been compared with Aristotle and Plato, respectively. Nevertheless, we should not forget that they both believed in the perfectibility of all men, in humanity and righteousness as supreme virtues, in kingly government, and in education. So far as their main difference concerning human nature goes, neither followed Confucius strictly. For the sage, all men were alike in nature but become different through practice.[1]

Hsün Tzu exerted far greater influence up through the Han period (206 B.C.–A.D. 220) than did Mencius. For one thing, both psychology and logic advanced greatly in him, but not in Mencius. His essay on terminology is one of the few Chinese treatises on the subject. In his naturalistic interpretation of Heaven, he came close to Taoism. And in his advocation of control, he contributed to the authoritarianism that resulted in the dictatorship of the Ch'in (221–206 B.C.). As a matter of fact, two of the ministers of the Ch'in, Han Fei (d. 233 B.C.)[2] and Li Ssu (d. 208 B.C.), were his pupils. His influence was extensive in the Han. However, since then he was largely neglected until the nineteenth century. Mencius rather than he was regarded as in the direct line of transmission from Confucius. No commentaries were written on his work until the ninth century, and very few since then. His work was not elevated to the position of a Confucian Classic. Was he too "tough-minded" for the Chinese, who preferred "tender-minded" Mencius? Was he too unorthodox a Confucianist? Or has he been blamed for the Ch'in dictatorship? All these questions aside, because of his naturalism, his realism, his emphasis on logic, his belief in progress, his stress on law, and his sound criticisms of the various philosophical schools, he has a special attraction for the modern Chinese.

[1] *Analects*, 17:2.　　　　　　　　　　[2] See below, ch. 12.

Hsün Tzu, also called Hsün Ch'ing and Hsün K'uang, was a native of Chao.[3] When he was fifty he traveled to Ch'i,[4] where scholars congregated at the time. He was the most eminent of them all. Three times he was honored as the officer for the sacrificial wine offering. Eventually some people slandered him, and he went to Ch'u, where he became a magistrate. Later he lost his position but stayed there and taught until he died. His dates are still subjects for debate, but most scholars agreed that he flourished in the six decades between 298 and 238 B.C. He was contemporaneous with Mencius but there is no evidence that the two ever met. Unlike the *Book of Mencius*, which consists of dialogues, Hsün Tzu's works are made up of self-contained essays on various subjects. The following translations are the complete chapters on Nature and human nature, and parts from the chapter on the rectification of names. These are the three most philosophical questions discussed by him.

THE HSÜN TZU[5]

1. On Nature (ch. 17)

Nature (*T'ien*, Heaven) operates with constant regularity. It does not exist for the sake of (sage-emperor) Yao[6] nor does it cease to exist because of (wicked king) Chieh.[7] Respond to it with peace and order, and good fortune will result. Respond to it with disorder, and disaster will follow. If the foundations of living (*i.e.*, agriculture and sericulture) are strengthened and are economically used, then Nature cannot bring impoverishment. If people's nourishment is sufficient and their labor in keeping with the seasons, then Nature cannot inflict sickness. If the Way

---

[3] In modern Shansi and its vicinity in North China.

[4] Southeast of Chao, in modern Shantung.

[5] The *Hsün Tzu* has thirty-two chapters, which are essays with clear expositions and cogent arguments on such subjects as "Against Physiognomy," "Against the Twelve Philosophers," "On Confucius," "National Wealth," "The Kingly Way versus Despots," "The Removal of Prejudices," and "The Sage-kings." Chapter 27 and subsequent chapters may have been by his pupils and are unimportant. A number of passages of the book also appear in the *Book of Rites*, perhaps for the reason that the latter's compilers selected passages from the *Hsün Tzu* to strengthen discussions on the theoretical and psychological basis of ceremonies in the *Book of Rites*. Since the *Hsün Tzu* did not enjoy the status of a Classic, its influence has been slight. Half of the chapters have been translated into English by Dubs, in *The Works of Hsüntze*. Köster, "*Hsün-tzu* Anschnitt 13," is a translation of ch. 23. Duyvendak, "Hsüntzu on the Rectification of Names," and Mei, "Hsün-tzu on Terminology," are translations of ch. 22. And Legge, *The Works of Mencius*, contains a translation of ch. 23 on the evil nature of man.

[6] Legendary ruler (3rd millennium B.C.).

[7] Chieh (c.1802–1752 B.C.?) was the last ruler of the Hsia dynasty (2183–1752 B.C.). Chinese historians have blamed his wickedness for the fall of the dynasty.

is cultivated[8] without deviation, then Nature cannot cause misfortune. Therefore flood and drought cannot cause a famine, extreme cold or heat cannot cause illness, and evil spiritual beings cannot cause misfortune. But if the foundations of living are neglected and used extravagantly, then Nature cannot make the country rich. If there is meager nourishment and little work, then Nature cannot enable the people to be preserved. If people violate the Way and act foolishly, then Nature cannot give them good fortune. There will be famine before flood or drought approaches, there will be sickness before the thrust of extreme cold or heat, and there will be misfortune before the approach of evil spirits. What the [people in these circumstances] receive from the season (natural factors) is the same as people receive in a period of peace and order and yet the calamities are different from what prevails in the period of peace and order. This cannot be blamed on Heaven; this is how the Way works. Therefore one who understands the distinctive functions of Heaven and man may be called a perfect man.

> *Comment.* Hsün Tzu's concept of Heaven is obviously closer to the Tao of the Taoists than to the *T'ien* (Heaven) of Confucius and Mencius. Their *T'ien* is still purposive, and the source and ultimate control of man's destiny, but Hsün Tzu's *T'ien* is purely Nature so that in most cases the word has to be translated as Nature rather than as Heaven. The marvelous thing is that while he accepted the Taoists' naturalistic view, he was not influenced by their intuitionism and mysticism. In Hsün Tzu, we have rationalism and empiricism instead.

To accomplish without any action and to obtain without effort,[9] this is what is meant by the office of Heaven. This being the case, although the Way of Heaven is deep, the perfect man does not deliberate over it. Although it is great, he does not devote any effort to it. And although it is refined, he does not scrutinize it. This is what is meant by not competing with Heaven. Heaven has its seasons, earth has its wealth, and man has his government. This is how they are able to form a triad.[10] To neglect (human activities) which constitute man's part in the triad and put one's hope in those with which he forms a triad is indeed a mistake.

The fixed stars rotate in succession, the sun and moon shine alternately, the four seasons follow one another, yin (passive cosmic force) and yang (active cosmic force) effect their great transformations, and the

[8] According to Wang Nien-sun (1744-1832), *Tu-shu tsa-chih* (Miscellaneous Notes from Reading), 1933 ed., bk. 11, p. 59, *hsiu* (to cultivate) should read *hsün* (to follow).

[9] A similar saying appears in *Lao Tzu*, ch. 47.

[10] Compare the same idea of forming a triad in *The Mean*, ch. 22.

wind and rain spread over all things. Each of the ten thousand things attains its harmony, and thus grows. Each obtains its nourishment, and thus achieves full development. We do not see their activities but we do see their results. This is what is called spirit. We all know how they attain their full development but none knows that such a process is invisible. This is called Heaven. The sage, however, does not seek to know Heaven. When the office of Heaven is established and the work of Heaven is done, the body will be provided and the spirit born, and the feelings of like, dislike, pleasure, anger, sorrow, and joy embodied. These are called the natural feelings. The ear, the eye, the nose, the mouth, and the body are, each in its own way, able to respond to external things, and cannot be interchanged. These are called natural organs. The heart (mind) occupies the cavity in the center to control the five organs. This is called the natural ruler. To plan and use what is not of one's kind to nourish one's kind—this is called natural nourishment. To act in accord with (the principle and nature of) one's own kind means happiness, and to act contrary to (the principle and nature of) one's own kind means calamity. This is called natural government. To darken one's natural ruler, to confuse the natural organs, to abandon natural nourishment, to act contrary to the natural government, and to violate the natural feelings so as to destroy the work of Nature—this is called great misfortune. The sage purifies his natural ruler, rectifies his natural organs, sufficiently provides for his natural nourishment, follows the natural government, and nourishes his natural feelings so as to bring to completion the work of Nature. In this way he knows what to do and what not to do. Thus he rules heaven and earth and directs the ten thousand things. His actions are all well regulated, his nourishment all well adapted, and his life is not injured—this is called knowing Nature.

Therefore great skill consists in not doing certain things, and great wisdom consists in not deliberating over certain things. What is to be noted about heaven are its visible phenomena, which can help us to foretell things. What is to be noted about earth are its suitable aspects, which can be used for growing things. What is to be noted about the four seasons are their course and their distinctive characteristics, according to which we can manage our affairs. And what is to be noted about yin and yang is their revelation, on the basis of which we can regulate things. The official (astronomer) adheres to [the phenomena of] heaven. As to the sage himself, he adheres to the Way.

Comment. Most ancient Confucianists either emphasized humanity (*jen*) and wisdom equally or stressed humanity. Hsün Tzu, however, emphasizes wisdom. Obviously, inborn humanity has no room in his theory of the innate evil nature of man. As an acquired virtue, humanity is valued. But being a tough-minded realist, he relies on wisdom rather than such an idealistic quality as humanity.

Are order and chaos due to heaven? I say: The sun, the moon, the stars, planets, and auspicious periods of the calendar were the same in the time of (sage-king) Yü as in that of (wicked king) Chieh.[11] Yet Yü brought about order while Chieh brought about chaos. Order and chaos are not due to heaven. Are they due to the seasons? I say: Plants multiply, develop, flourish, and mature in spring and summer. They are collected and stored in the fall and winter. This is also the same at the times of Yü and Chieh. Yet Yü brought about order while Chieh brought about chaos. Order and chaos are not due to the seasons. Are they due to the earth? I say: When a plant is planted in a suitable place, it will grow. When it is planted in an unsuitable place, it will die. This is also the same at the times of Yü and Chieh. Yet Yü brought about order while Chieh brought about chaos. Order and chaos are not due to the earth. The *Book of Odes* says, "Heaven made the high hills. King T'ai extended and cultivated them. He did the pioneering work. (His son) King Wen brought to them peace and prosperity."[12] This is the meaning.

Heaven does not give up the winter because people dislike cold. Earth does not give up its expanse because people dislike distance. The superior man does not give up good conduct because the inferior man rails against him. Heaven has a constant way of action, earth has a constant size, and the superior man has a constant personal demonstration of virtue. The superior man pursues the constant principle, but the inferior man calculates results. The *Book of Odes* says, "[If one makes no mistake about propriety and righteousness], why worry about people's talk?"[13] This is what I mean.

The king of Ch'u had a thousand chariots following him—this is not wisdom. The superior man eats peas and drinks water—this is not stupidity. They do so because it is fitting to the circumstances.[14] As to cultivating one's will, to be earnest in one's moral conduct, to be clear in one's knowledge and deliberations, to live in this age but to set his mind on the ancients (as models), that depends on the person himself.

[11] Yü (c. 2183–2175 B.C.?) was the founder of the Hsia dynasty and has been regarded as a sage-king along with Yao. Chieh (r. 1802–1752 B.C.?) caused the downfall of the Hsia.

[12] Ode no. 270.

[13] This poem is now lost. The addition is made according to Yü Yüeh (1821-1906), "Hsün Tzu shih-shuo" (Explanations on Odes Quoted in the *Hsün Tzu*), in his *Ch'ü-yüan tsa-tsuan* (Miscellaneous Collection of Yü Yüeh), 6:14a-b.

[14] According to Yü Yüeh, *chieh* means to fit.

Therefore the superior man is serious (*ching*)[15] about what lies in himself and does not desire what comes from Heaven. The inferior man neglects what is in himself and desires what comes from Heaven. Because the superior man is serious about what is in himself and does not desire what comes from Heaven, he progresses every day. Because the inferior man neglects what is in himself and desires what comes from Heaven, he retrogresses every day. The reason why the superior man progresses daily and the inferior man retrogresses daily is the same. Here lies the reason for the great difference between the superior man and the inferior man.

When stars fall or trees make a [strange] noise, all people in the state are afraid and ask, "Why?" I reply: There is no need to ask why. These are changes of heaven and earth, the transformation of yin and yang, and rare occurrences. It is all right to marvel at them, but wrong to fear them. For there has been no age that has not had[16] the experience of eclipses of the sun and moon, unreasonable rain or wind, or occasional[17] appearance of strange stars. If the ruler is enlightened and the government peaceful, even if all of these things happen at the same time, they would do no harm. If the ruler is unenlightened and the government follows a dangerous course, even if [only] one of them occurs, it would do no good. For the falling of stars and the noise of trees are the changes of heaven and earth, the transformations of yin and yang, and rare occurrences. It is all right to marvel at them, but wrong to fear them.

Of things that have happened, human portents are the most to be feared. To plough roughly so as to injure the crops, to hoe improperly so as to miss the weed, and to follow a dangerous course in government so as the lose the support to the people, with the result that the fields are full of weeds, the harvest is bad, the price of grain goes up, people starve, and there are dead bodies on the roads—these are what is meant by human portents. When governmental measures and orders are not clear or wise, when activities and handling of affairs are not timely, and when matters concerning the foundation of living are not attended to—these are what is meant by human portents. When propriety and righteousness are not cultivated, when the distinction between the inner (women's) chamber and the outer (men's) chamber is not kept, and

[15] Often translated as "reverent." For a discussion of the translation of this term, see Appendix.

[16] According to Wang Hsien-ch'ien (1842-1917), *Hsün Tzu chi-chieh* (Collected Commentaries on the *Hsün Tzu*), read *ch'ang* (always) as *ch'ang* (has been).

[17] According to Wang Nien-sun, *tang* does not mean frequent, as Yang Liang (fl. 818) contended in his commentary, but means occasional.

when men and women become promiscuous, then father and son distrust each other, the ruler and the ruled will be in conflict and divided, and invasion and disaster will arrive at the same time—these are what is meant by human portents. Portents are born of chaos. When all the three kinds of portents pile upon one another, there will be no order or peace in the state. It is very simple to talk about these portents, but the calamities they bring are most terrible. If conscript labor is employed not at the proper season, [the suffering of the people will so disturb the equilibrium of nature that] cows and horses will breed each other and the six domestic animals will become apparitions.[18] They may be marveled at but should not be feared. The *Record* says, "The classics do not talk about strange phenomena of the ten thousand things."[19] Useless discussions and unnecessary investigations are to be cast aside and not attended to. As to the righteousness between the ruler and minister, affection between father and son, and the distinctive functions between husband and wife, these should be daily cultivated without losing sight of them.

When people pray for rain, it rains. Why? I say: There is no need to ask why. It is the same as when it rains when no one prays for it. When people try to save the sun or moon from being eclipsed, or when they pray for rain in a drought, or when they decide an important affair only after divination, they do so not because they believe they will get what they are after, but to use them as ornament (*wen*) to governmental measures. Hence the ruler intends them to be an ornament, but the common people think they are supernatural. It is good fortune to regard them as ornamental but it is evil fortune to regard them as supernatural.

> *Comment.* The influence of supernatural forces over man is completely ruled out by Hsün Tzu. What he called spirit is but cosmic change and evolution. To him, in religious sacrifice, whether there are really spiritual beings to receive them does not matter. The important thing is one's attitude, especially sincerity, in the performance. Thus sacrifices are "ornaments," or refined manifestation of an inner attitude.

Of the things in heaven, none is brighter than the sun and moon. Of the things on earth, none is brighter than water and fire. Among things, none is brighter than pearls and jade. And among man's virtues, none is brighter than propriety and righteousness. For if the sun and moon

[18] Some commentators contend that this sentence should precede "When propriety and righteousness. . . ." See Wang Hsien-ch'ien, *Hsün Tzu chi-chieh*.
[19] The *Record* is now lost.

were not high, their brightness would not be glorious. If water or fire is not gathered in great quantity, its luster would not be extensive. If pearls and jade were not gleaming on the outside, kings and dukes would not consider them precious. If propriety and righteousness are not applied in the country, their accomplishments and fame would not shine. Therefore the destiny of man lies in Heaven,[20] and the destiny of the state lies in propriety. The ruler who highly exalts propriety and honors the worthy will become a true king, the ruler who stresses law and loves the people will become a despot, the ruler who loves profit and often resorts to deceit will fall, and the ruler who schemes to obtain power, seeks to overthrow others, and is secretive and evil will perish completely.

> Instead of regarding Heaven as great and admiring it,
> Why not foster it as a thing and regulate it?
> Instead of obeying Heaven and singing praise to it,
> Why not control the Mandate of Heaven and use it?
> Instead of looking on the seasons and waiting for them,
> Why not respond to them and make use of them?
> Instead of letting things multiply by themselves,
> Why not exercise your ability to transform [and increase] them?
> Instead of thinking about things as things,
> Why not attend to them so you won't lose them?
> Instead of admiring how things come into being,
> Why not do something to bring them to full development?

Therefore to neglect human effort and admire Heaven is to miss the nature of things.

> *Comment.* Nowhere else in the history of Chinese thought is the idea of controlling nature so definite and so strong. It is a pity that this did not lead to a development of natural science. One explanation is that although Hsün Tzu enjoyed great prestige in the Han dynasty, his theory of overcoming nature was not strong enough to compete with the prevalent doctrine of harmony of man and nature, which both Confucianism and Taoism promoted.

The [moral principles] that have remained unchanged through the time of all kings are sufficient to be the central thread running through the Way. Things come and go, but if they are responded to according to this central thread, one will find that the principle runs through all

---

[20] These words seem to be in opposition to the whole theme of the chapter. It may mean, however, that while certain natural factors are beyond the control of man, it is up to man to adapt himself and control them. What follows clearly says as much.

without any disorder. He who does not know this central thread does not know how to respond to changing conditions. The essential nature of the central thread has never ceased to be. Chaos is the result of a wrong application of the central thread, whereas order is the result of a complete application of it. For what is considered good according to the Way, namely, the Mean, should be followed. What deviates from the Mean should not be done. To be mistaken will lead to great delusion. One who walks in water marks its depth. If the mark is not clear, he will fall into the water. He who governs the people marks the Way. If the mark is not clear, there will be chaos. Rules of propriety are marks. Without propriety, the world will be beclouded. When the world is beclouded, there will be great chaos. Only when the Way is always made clear, when the internal and external aspects are distinctly marked,[21] and when what is manifest and what is hidden remain constant will the suffering of the people be removed.

The ten thousand things are a part of the Way. One thing is a part of the ten thousand things. A stupid man is a part of one thing. But he thinks that he knows the Way. He really does not know. Shen Tzu[22] has insight about following but not about leading. Lao Tzu has insight about bending but not about expansion. Mo Tzu has insight about equality (universal love) but not about inequality (distinction in human relations). And Sung Tzu[23] had insight about having few desires but not about having many desires. If there is only insight on following and not on leading [in the case of a ruler], then the multitude will have no direction to go by.[24] If there is only insight on bending and not on expansion, then noble stations (corresponding to expansion) and humble stations (corresponding to bending) will not be distinguished. If there is only insight on equality and not on inequality, then governmental measures and orders [which are intended to bring about equality and justice] cannot be carried out. If there is only insight on few desires and not on many, then the multitude cannot be transformed [for there would not be sufficient incentive]. The *Book of History* says, "Make no special

[21] The meaning here is obscure. Yang Liang thought that the internal refers to capping and wedding ceremonies and the external refers to etiquettes of tributes and imperial audience. According to Hao I-hsing (1757-1825), *Hsün Tzu pu-chu* (Supplementary Annotations to the *Hsün Tzu*), they refer to rules of propriety. Such interpretations do not help any.

[22] Shen Tao (350–275 B.C.?), was a Legalist who rejected subjectivism in favor of objective knowledge and emphasized actual situations and tendencies. For a brief treatment of his Legalist philosophy, see Fung, *History of Chinese Philosophy*, vol. 1, pp. 153-159, 318.

[23] Sung Hsing (360–290 B.C.?), advocated the prohibition of war and the harboring of few desires. For a brief discussion of him, see Fung, pp. 148-153.

[24] Literally "no gate."

effort to like. Follow the kingly way. Make no special effort to dislike. Follow the kingly path."[25] This is what I mean. (SPTK, 11:15b-25b)

> *Comment.* This is one of the best known classical critiques of ancient Chinese philosophers. There are four other critiques. Two are in the *Hsün Tzu*[26] and the other two in the *Chuang Tzu*[27] and the *Han Fei Tzu*.[28] This shows that Hsün Tzu was the most critical of ancient Chinese philosophers. It also shows that a great variety of thought and extensive freedom of discussion existed in ancient China, a situation comparable to that in ancient Greece.[29]

2. On the Rectification of Names (ch. 22)

... When sage-kings instituted names, the names were fixed and actualities distinguished. The sage-kings' principles were carried out and their wills understood. Then the people were carefully led and unified. Therefore, the practice of splitting terms and arbitrarily creating names to confuse correct names, thus causing much doubt in people's minds and bringing about much litigation, was called great wickedness. It was a crime, like private manufacturing of credentials and measurements, and therefore the people dared not rely on strange terms created to confuse correct names. Hence the people were honest. Being honest, they were easily employed. Being easily employed, they achieved results. Since the people dared not rely on strange terms created to confuse correct names, they single-mindedly followed the law and carefully obeyed orders. In this way, the traces of their accomplishments spread. The spreading of traces and the achievement of results are the highest point of good government. This is the result of careful abiding by the conventional[30] meaning of names.

Now the sage-kings are dead and the guarding of names has become lax, strange terms have arisen, and names and actualities have been confused. As the standard of right and wrong is not clear, even the guardians of law and the teachers of natural principles[31] are in a state of confusion.

---

[25] *History*, "Great Norm." Cf. Legge, trans., *Shoo King*, p. 331.
[26] Chs. 6 and 21. [27] Ch. 33. [28] Ch. 50.
[29] See Hu Shih, (1891-1962) "Chinese Thought," in MacNair, ed. *China*, pp. 221-230, and Dubs, "Comparison of Greek and Chinese Philosophy," *Chinese Social and Political Science Review*, 17 (1933), 307-327.
[30] Yang Liang understood *yüeh* as essential, but according to Liu Shih-p'ei (1884-1919), *Hsün Tzu pu-shih* (Supplementary Explanations of the *Hsün Tzu*), it means to bind, that is, to commit or to agree.
[31] *Shu* is not to be understood in its ordinary meaning of number, as by Duyvendak ("Hsün-tzu on the Rectification of Names," *T'oung Pao*, 23 [1924], p. 228) but in its technical meaning of natural principles or the natural course of things. Hu Shih's rendering as "truth" (*Development of the Logical Method in Ancient China*, p. 160) is not a mistake, as Duyvendak thought.

Should a true king appear, he would certainly retain some old names and create new ones. This being the case, [1] the reason for having names, [2] the causes for the similarities and differences in names, and [3] the fundamental principles on which names are instituted, must be clearly understood.

[1] When different forms are separated from the mind and denote each other, and when different things are made mutually identified in name and actuality,[32] the distinction between the noble and the humble is not clear and similarities and differences are not discriminated. Under such circumstances, there is bound to be danger that ideas will be misunderstood and work will encounter difficulty or be neglected. Therefore men of wisdom sought to establish distinctions and instituted names to indicate actualities, on the one hand clearly to distinguish the noble and the humble and, on the other, to discriminate between similarities and differences. When the distinctions between the noble and the humble are clear and similarities and differences are discriminated, there will be no danger of ideas being misunderstood and work encountering difficulties or being neglected. This is the reason for having names.

[2] What are the causes for the similarities and differences in names? I say: It is because of the natural organs. The organs of members of the same species with the same feelings perceive things in the same way. Therefore things are compared and those that are seemingly alike are generalized. In this way they share their conventional name as a common meeting ground. Forms, bodies, colors, and patterns (*li*) are distinctions made by the eye. Clear and unclear sounds, tunes, leading melodies, and unusual sounds are distinctions made by the ear. Sweet, bitter, salty and insipid, peppery and sour, and unusual tastes are distinctions made by the mouth. Fragrant and putrid smells, fresh and spoiled smells, smells of rotten meat, rancid and sour smells, and unusual smells are distinctions made by the nose. Pain and itching, cold and heat, smooth and rough, light and heavy are distinctions made by the body. Enjoying doing a thing and feeling being forced to do a thing, and the feelings of pleasure, anger, sorrow, joy, like, dislike, and desire are distinctions made by the mind.

The mind collects[33] the knowledge of the senses. It is because the mind collects knowledge that it is possible to know sound through the ear and form through the eye. But the collection of knowledge must also depend on the natural organs first registering it according to its

[32] In the text the twelve Chinese characters form three sentences. Wang Hsien-ch'ien punctuated them to form two sentences. This is correct because they form a parallelism.

[33] Literally *cheng* means to summon or invite, according to Yang Liang. Therefore it is active, not just receiving knowledge passively.

classification. If the five organs register it without knowing what it is, and the mind collects it without understanding it, then everyone says there is no knowledge. These are the causes for the similarities and differences in names.

[3] Then, accordingly, names are given to things. Similar things are given the same name and different things are given different names. When a simple name (e.g., horse) is sufficient to express the meaning, a simple name is used. When a simple name is insufficient, then a compound name (e.g., white horse) is used. When simple and compound concepts do not conflict, then the general name (e.g., tree in general) may be used. Although it is a general name, it does no harm (to the differentiation of things). Knowing that different actualities should have different names, one should let different actualities always have different names. There should not be any confusion in this respect. And similar actualities should always have similar names. For although the myriad things are innumerable, sometimes we want to speak of them as a whole and so we call them "things." "Things" is a great general name. We carry the process further and generalize. In generalizing, we find more things to generalize. We go on and will not stop until there is nothing more general. Sometimes we want to speak of one section of things (e.g., animals), and so we call them "animals." "Animals" is a great particular name. We carry the process further and particularize. In particularizing, we find more things to particularize. We go on and will not stop until there is nothing more particular.

Names have no correctness of their own. The correctness is given by convention. When the convention is established and the custom is formed, they are called correct names. If they are contrary to convention, they are called incorrect names. Names have no corresponding actualities by themselves. The actualities ascribed to them are given by convention. When the convention is established and the custom is formed, they are called names of such-and-such actualities. But some names are felicitous in themselves. When a name is direct, easy to understand, and self-consistent, it is called a felicitous name.

There are things which have the same appearance but are in different places, and there are things which have different appearances but are in the same place (as a person when he is young and when he is old). These can be distinguished. When two things have the same appearance but are in two different places, although they may be grouped together, they are to be called two actualities. When the appearance changes but the actuality is not different, it is called transformation. When there is transformation but no difference in actuality, this is called one actuality. This is the way actualities are examined and their number determined.

126

This is the fundamental principle on which names are instituted. When a latter-day king institutes names, he should clearly understand this.

Comment. Hsün Tzu's latter-day kings are the same as Mencius' ancient kings, namely, founders of the Chou dynasty, especially the Duke of Chou. The significant difference is that Hsün Tzu has a stronger inclination to look to a later period than other philosophers.

[The Three Fallacies] "It is no disgrace to be insulted."[34] "The sage does not love himself."[35] "To kill a robber is not to kill a man."[36] These are examples of the fallacy of so using names as to confuse names. Examine them in the light of [1] "the reason for having names" and see whether any of these statements is applicable. Then you will be able to stop the confusion.

"Mountains are on the same level as marshes."[37] "The desires seek to be few."[38] "Tender meat adds nothing to sweet taste, and the great bell adds nothing to music."[39] These are examples of the fallacy of so using actualities as to confuse names. Examine them by [2] "the cause for the similarities and differences in names" and see which of these statements are harmonious with them. Then you will be able to stop the confusion.

"Fei-erh-yeh, ying-yu-niu" (wrong but visit-a-superior, pillar has ox). "A [white] horse is not a horse."[40] These are examples of the fallacy of so using names as to confuse actualities. Examine them by [3] the convention of names and see how what they have rejected (a horse) contradicts what they have accepted (a white horse), and you will be able to stop the confusion. . . . (SPTK, 16:2b-8b)

Comment. The rectification of names was a common topic of discussion among ancient Chinese philosophical schools. Only in Hsün Tzu, however, did it develop into some sort of systematic logical theory. Whereas in other schools the interest is chiefly social

---

[34] A doctrine of Sung Tzu according to *Chuang Tzu*, ch. 33, NHCC, 10:31a; cf. Giles, trans., *Chuang Tzu*, 1961 ed., p. 317, and *Hsün Tzu*, ch. 18, SPTK, 12:18b; cf. Dubs, trans., *Works of Hsüntze*, p. 207.

[35] Probably referring to *Mo Tzu*, ch. 44, SPTK, 11:1a.

[36] *Mo Tzu*, ch. 45, SPTK, 11:9b.

[37] A doctrine of Hui Shih, as recorded in *Chuang Tzu*, ch. 33, NHCC, 10:38b (cf. Giles, p. 321), and also in *Hsün Tzu*, ch. 3, SPTK, 2:1b (not translated by Dubs).

[38] A doctrine of Sung Tzu, according to *Chuang Tzu*, ch. 33, NHCC, 10:31b (cf. Giles, p. 317), also *Hsün Tzu*, ch. 18, SPTK, 12:22b (cf. Dubs, p. 209).

[39] Yang Liang ascribes the last two doctrines to Mo Tzu, but they have not been traced.

[40] Referring to the *Kung-sun Lung Tzu*, ch. 2. The six Chinese characters preceding this sentence apparently represent two propositions, but no commentator or translator has been able to make any sense out of them without rewriting them.

3. The Nature of Man is Evil (ch. 23)

The nature of man is evil; his goodness is the result of his activity.[41] Now, man's inborn nature is to seek for gain. If this tendency is followed, strife and rapacity result and deference and compliance disappear. By inborn nature one is envious and hates others. If these tendencies are followed, injury and destruction result and loyalty and faithfulness disappear. By inborn nature one possesses the desires of ear and eye and likes sound and beauty. If these tendencies are followed, lewdness and licentiousness result, and the pattern and order of propriety and righteousness disappear. Therefore to follow man's nature and his feelings will inevitably result in strife and rapacity, combine with rebellion and disorder, and end in violence. Therefore there must be the civilizing influence of teachers and laws and the guidance of propriety and righteousness, and then it will result in deference and compliance, combine with pattern and order, and end in discipline. From this point of view, it is clear that the nature of man is evil and that his goodness is the result of activity.

Crooked wood must be heated and bent before it becomes straight. Blunt metal must be ground and whetted before it becomes sharp. Now the nature of man is evil. It must depend on teachers and laws to become correct and achieve propriety and righteousness and then it becomes disciplined. Without teachers and laws, man is unbalanced, off the track, and incorrect. Without propriety and righteousness, there will be rebellion, disorder, and chaos. The sage-kings of antiquity, knowing that the nature of man is evil, and that it is unbalanced, off the track, incorrect, rebellious, disorderly, and undisciplined, created the rules of propriety and righteousness and instituted laws and systems in order to correct man's feelings, transform them, and direct them so that they all may become disciplined and conform with the Way (Tao). Now people who are influenced by teachers and laws, accumulate literature and knowledge, and follow propriety and righteousness are superior men, whereas those who give rein to their feelings, enjoy indulgence, and violate propriety and righteousness are inferior men. From this point of view, it is clear that the nature of man is evil and that his goodness is the result of his activity.

[41] According to Yang Liang, *wei* (artificial) is "man's activity." It means what is created by man and not a result of natural conditions. This is accepted by most commentators, including Hao I-hsing, who has pointed out that in ancient times *wei* (ordinarily meaning false or artificial) and *wei* (activity) were interchangeable.

Comment. In the *Hsün Tzu*, rules of propriety and law are often spoken of together, giving the impression that, unlike Confucius and Mencius who advocated propriety (*li*) as inner control, Hsün Tzu advocated it for external control. Thus rules of propriety shifted from being a means of personal moral cultivation to one of social control.

Mencius said, "Man learns because his nature is good."[42] This is not true. He did not know the nature of man and did not understand the distinction between man's nature and his effort. Man's nature is the product of Nature; it cannot be learned and cannot be worked for. Propriety and righteousness are produced by the sage. They can be learned by men and can be accomplished through work. What is in man but cannot be learned or worked for is his nature. What is in him and can be learned or accomplished through work is what can be achieved through activity. This is the difference between human nature and human activity. Now by nature man's eye can see and his ear can hear. But the clarity of vision is not outside his eye and the distinctness of hearing is not outside his ear. It is clear that clear vision and distinct hearing cannot be learned. Mencius said, "The nature of man is good; it [becomes evil] because man destroys his original nature." This is a mistake. By nature man departs from his primitive character and capacity as soon as he is born, and he is bound to destroy it. From this point of view, it is clear that man's nature is evil.

By the original goodness of human nature is meant that man does not depart from his primitive character but makes it beautiful, and does not depart from his original capacity but utilizes it, so that beauty being [inherent] in his primitive character and goodness being [inherent] in his will are like clear vision being inherent in the eye and distinct hearing being inherent in the ear. Hence we say that the eye is clear and the ear is sharp. Now by nature man desires repletion when hungry, desires warmth when cold, and desires rest when tired. This is man's natural feeling. But now when a man is hungry and sees some elders before him, he does not eat ahead of them but yields to them. When he is tired, he dares not seek rest because he wants to take over the work [of elders]. The son yielding to or taking over the work of his father, and the younger brother yielding to or taking over the work of his older brother—these two lines of action are contrary to original nature and violate natural feeling. Nevertheless, the way of filial piety is the pattern and order of propriety and righteousness. If one follows

---

[42] This and later quotations from Mencius are not really direct but only references to Mencius' debate with Kao Tzu on human nature. See *Mencius,* 6A:1-8.

his natural feeling, he will have no deference or compliance. Deference and compliance are opposed to his natural feelings. From this point of view, it is clear that man's nature is evil and that his goodness is the result of his activity.

Someone may ask, "If man's nature is evil, whence come propriety and righteousness?" I answer that all propriety and righteousness are results of the activity of sages and not originally produced from man's nature. The potter pounds the clay and makes the vessel. This being the case, the vessel is the product of the artisan's activity and not the original product of man's nature. The artisan hews a piece of wood and makes a vessel. This being the case, the vessel is the product of the artisan's activity and not the original product of man's nature. The sages gathered together their ideas and thoughts and became familiar with activity, facts, and principles, and thus produced propriety and righteousness and instituted laws and systems. This being the case, propriety and righteousness, and laws and systems are the products of the activity of the sages and not the original products of man's nature.

As to the eye desiring color, the ear desiring sound, the mouth desiring flavor, the heart desiring gain, and the body desiring pleasure and ease—all these are products of man's original nature and feelings. They are natural reactions to stimuli and do not require any work to be produced. But if the reaction is not naturally produced by the stimulus but requires work before it can be produced, then it is the result of activity. Here lies the evidence of the difference between what is produced by man's nature and what is produced by his effort. Therefore the sages transformed man's nature and aroused him to activity. As activity was aroused, propriety and righteousness were produced, and as propriety and righteousness were produced, laws and systems were instituted. This being the case, propriety, righteousness, laws, and systems are all products of the sages. In his nature, the sage is common with and not different from ordinary people. It is in his effort that he is different from and superior to them.

It is the original nature and feelings of man to love profit and seek gain. Suppose some brothers are to divide their property. If they follow their natural feelings, they will love profit and seek gain, and thus will do violence to each other and grab the property. But if they are transformed by the civilizing influence of the pattern and order of propriety and righteousness, they will even yield to outsiders. Therefore, brothers will quarrel if they follow their original nature and feeling but, if they are transformed by righteousness and propriety, they will yield to outsiders.

People desire to be good because their nature is evil. If one has little, he wants abundance. If he is ugly, he wants good looks. If his circumstances are narrow, he wants them to be broad. If poor, he wants to be rich. And if he is in a low position, he wants a high position. If he does not have it himself, he will seek it outside. If he is rich, he does not desire more wealth, and if he is in a high position, he does not desire more power. If he has it himself, he will not seek it outside. From this point of view, [it is clear that] people desire to be good because their nature is evil.

Now by nature a man does not originally possess propriety and righteousness; hence he makes strong effort to learn and seeks to have them. By nature he does not know propriety and righteousness; hence he thinks and deliberates and seeks to know them. Therefore, by what is inborn alone, man will not have or know propriety and righteousness. There will be disorder if man is without propriety and righteousness. There will be violence if he does not know propriety and righteousness. Consequently by what is inborn alone, disorder and violence are within man himself. From this point of view, it is clear that the nature of man is evil and that his goodness is the result of his activity.

Mencius said, "The nature of man is good." I say that this is not true. By goodness at any time in any place is meant true principles and peaceful order, and by evil is meant imbalance, violence, and disorder. This is the distinction between good and evil. Now do we honestly regard man's nature as characterized by true principles and peaceful order? If so, why are sages necessary and why are propriety and righteousness necessary? What possible improvement can sages make on true principles and peaceful order?

Now this is not the case. Man's nature is evil. Therefore the sages of antiquity, knowing that man's nature is evil, that it is unbalanced and incorrect, and that it is violent, disorderly, and undisciplined, established the authority of rulers to govern the people, set forth clearly propriety and righteousness to transform them, instituted laws and governmental measures to rule them, and made punishment severe to restrain them, so that all will result in good order and be in accord with goodness. Such is the government of sage-kings and the transforming influence of propriety and righteousness.

But suppose we try to remove the authority of the ruler, do away with the transforming influence of propriety and righteousness, discard the rule of laws and governmental measure, do away with the restraint of punishment, and stand and see how people of the world deal with one another. In this situation, the strong would injure the weak and rob them, and the many would do violence to the few and shout them down. The whole world would be in violence and disorder and all would perish in an instant. From this point of view, it is clear that man's nature is evil and that his goodness is the result of his activity.

The man versed in ancient matters will certainly support them with evidences from the present, and he who is versed in [the principles of] Nature will certainly support them with evidences from the world of men. In any discussion, the important things are discrimination[43] and evidence. One can then sit down and talk about things, propagate them, and put them into practice. But now Mencius said that man's nature is good. He had neither discrimination nor evidence. He sat down and talked about the matter but rose and could neither propagate it nor put it into practice. Is this not going too far? Therefore if man's nature is good, sage-kings can be done away with and propriety and righteousness can be stopped. But if his nature is evil, sage-kings are to be followed and propriety and righteousness are to be greatly valued. For bending came into existence because there was crooked wood, the carpenter's square and ruler came into existence because things are not straight, and the authority of rule is instituted and propriety and righteousness are made clear because man's nature is evil. From this point of view, it is clear that man's nature is evil and that his goodness is the result of his activity. Straight wood does not depend on bending to become straight; it is straight by nature. But crooked wood must be bent and heated before it becomes straight because by nature it is not straight. Now, the nature of man is evil. It has to depend on the government of sage-kings and the transforming influence of propriety and righteousness, and then all will result in good order and be in accord with goodness. From this point of view, it is clear that man's nature is evil and that his goodness is the result of his activity.

The questioner may say, "It is by the nature of man that propriety and righteousness [can be produced] through accumulated effort and hence the sages can produce them." I answer that this is not true. The potter pounds the clay and produces the piece of pottery. Is the pottery [inherent] in the nature of the potter? The artisan hews wood and produces a vessel. Is the vessel [inherent] in the nature of the artisan? What the sages have done to propriety and righteousness is analogous to the potter's pounding and producing the pottery. This being the case, is it by the original nature of man that propriety and righteousness are produced through accumulated effort? With reference to the nature of man, it is the same in (sage-emperors) Yao and Shun, (wicked king) Chieh, and (robber) Chih.[44] It is the same in the superior or inferior

[43] According to Yang Liang and Wang Hsien-ch'ien, *pien-ho* literally means a bamboo split into two pieces and yet coming together perfectly. Hence the idea of analysis and discrimination.

[44] Chih was a notorious robber of ancient times.

man. If propriety and righteousness are products of accumulated effort and to be regarded as [inherent] in man's nature, then why are Yao and (sage-king) Yü highly honored, and why is the superior man highly honored? Yao, Yü, and the superior man are highly honored because they can transform nature and arouse effort. As effort is aroused, propriety and righteousness are produced. Thus the relation between the sages and propriety and righteousness produced through accumulated effort, is like the potter pounding the clay to produce the pottery. From this point of view, is it by the nature of man that propriety and righteousness are produced through accumulated effort? Chieh, Chih, and the inferior man are despised because they give rein to their nature, follow their feelings, and enjoy indulgence, and lead to the greed for gain, to quarrels and rapacity. It is clear that man's nature is evil and that his goodness is the result of his activity.

Heaven is not partial to Tseng, Ch'ien, and Hsiao-i[45] and negligent to the common multitude. Then why did Tseng, Ch'ien, and Hsiao-i alone abundantly demonstrate the actuality of filial piety and preserve its good name? It is because they observed propriety and righteousness to the fullest extent. Heaven is not partial to the people of Ch'i and Lu[46] and negligent to the people of Ch'in.[47] Then why is it that in the righteous relation between father and son and the distinction of function between husband and wife, the people of Ch'in are inferior to those of Ch'i and Lu in filial piety and in the mutual respect between husband and wife? It is because the people of Ch'in give rein to their nature and feelings, enjoy indulgence, and neglect propriety and righteousness. Is it because their natures are different?

"Any man in the street can become (sage-king) Yü."[48] What does this ancient saying mean? I say that Yü became sage-king Yü because he practiced humanity, righteousness, laws, and correct principles. This shows that these can be known and practiced. Every man in the street possesses the faculty to know them and the capacity to practice them. This being the case, it is clear that every man can be Yü.

> *Comment.* To all ancient Chinese philosophers, the ideal human being was always an historical person. But whereas Confucius and

[45] Tseng Shen, Min Tzu-ch'ien (both of whom were pupils of Confucius), and Hsiao-i (crown prince of 14th century B.C.), were all distinguished by their filial deeds.

[46] The state of Ch'i produced virtuous rulers and Lu was the native state of Confucius.

[47] Ch'in was a barbarian state which eventually overthrew the Chou, united China, and set up a dictatorship in the third century B.C.

[48] Compare this ancient saying with *Mencius*, 6B:2, to the effect that all men can become Yaos and Shuns.

Mencius idolized Yao and Shun, Hsün Tzu preferred to idolize Yü. Instead of going as far back in history as possible to find the ideal man, as practically all schools did, Hsün Tzu looked to someone later. It is possible that he choose Yü because he was not satisfied with men of perfect morals like Yao and Shun, but sought a man of great practical accomplishments. Yü was such a person, especially noted for his diverting water into nine channels and thus preventing flood.

Shall we consider humanity, righteousness, laws, and correct principles as basically impossible to be known or practiced? If so, even Yü could not have known or practiced them. Shall we consider every man in the street to be without the faculty to know them or the capacity to practice them? If so, at home he would not be able to know the righteous relation between father and son and outside he would not be able to know the correct relation between ruler and minister. But this is not the case. Every man in the street is capable of knowing the righteous relation between father and son at home and the correct relation between ruler and minister outside. It is clear, then, that the faculty to know them and the capacity to practice them are found in every man in the street. Now, if every man's faculty to know and capacity to practice are applied to the fact that humanity and righteousness can be known and practiced, it is clear that he can become Yü. If in his practices and studies day after day for a long time, he concentrates his mind, has unity of purpose, thinks thoroughly and discriminately, and accumulates goodness without stop, he can then be as wise as the gods, and form a trinity with Heaven and Earth. Thus the sage is a man who has reached this state through accumulated effort.

Some one may say, "The sage can reach that state through accumulated effort but not everyone can do so. Why?" I answer that he can, but he does not do it. An inferior man can become a superior man, but he does not want to. A superior man can become an inferior man, but he does not want to. It is not that they cannot become each other. They do not do so because they do not want to. It is possible for every man to become Yü, but it does not follow that every man in the street is able actually to do so. However, the fact that he is not able actually to do so does not destroy the possibility of his doing so. It is possible for a man with feet to walk all over the world and yet so far there has not been any who is able actually to do so. It is possible for the artisan, farmer, or merchant to exchange their professions, and yet there has not been any who is able actually to do so. From this point of view, what is possible is not the same as what is able actually to be done. But not being able actually to be done does not destroy the possibility. There is a great difference between what is possible on the one hand, and what is able actually to be done, on the other. It is clear that they are not interchangeable. . . .[49] (SPTK, 17:1a-12b)

[49] The remaining quarter of the essay deals with the subjects of wisdom, courage, etc. and have nothing to do with the question of human nature.

THE NATURAL WAY OF LAO TZU

CHINESE civilization and the Chinese character would have been utterly different if the book *Lao Tzu* had never been written. In fact, even Confucianism, the dominant system in Chinese history and thought, would not have been the same, for like Buddhism, it has not escaped Taoist influence. No one can hope to understand Chinese philosophy, religion, government, art, medicine—or even cooking—without a real appreciation of the profound philosophy taught in this little book. It is true that, while Confucianism emphasizes social order and an active life, Taoism concentrates on individual life and tranquillity, thus suggesting that Taoism plays a secondary role. But, in reality, by opposing Confucian conformity with non-conformity and Confucian worldliness with a transcendental spirit, Taoism is a severe critic of Confucianism. In its doctrines on government, on cultivating and preserving life, and on handling things, Taoism is fully the equal of Confucianism.

In some respects Taoism goes even deeper into the Way of life, so much so that while every ancient Chinese school taught its own Way (*Tao*)[1] Taoism alone is known by that name. Of course the name "Taoist School" was not used until the first century B.C.,[2] but the teachings of Lao Tzu and Chuang Tzu about Tao were so impressive and influential before that time that the name was inevitable.

Whereas in other schools Tao means a system or moral truth, in this school it is the One, which is natural, eternal, spontaneous, nameless, and indescribable. It is at once the beginning of all things and the way in which all things pursue their course. When this Tao is possessed by individual things, it becomes its character or virtue (*te*).[3] The ideal life for the individual, the ideal order for society, and the ideal type of government are all based on it and guided by it. As the way of life, it denotes simplicity, spontaneity, tranquillity, weakness, and most important of all, non-action (*wu-wei*). By the latter is not meant literally "inactivity" but rather "taking no action that is contrary to Nature"—in other words, letting Nature take its own course.

The Taoist philosophy is perhaps best summed up in the *Chuang Tzu*, which says, "To regard the fundamental as the essence, to regard things as coarse, to regard accumulation as deficiency, and to dwell

---

[1] Literally path, road, way, extended to mean principle, system, truth, Reality, etc.

[2] It was first mentioned in Ssu-ma Ch'ien's (145–86 B.C.?) autobiography in his *Shih chi* (Records of the Historian), PNP, 130:4b.

[3] For a discussion of this term, see Appendix.

quietly alone with the spiritual and the intelligent—herein lie the techniques of Tao of the ancients. Kuan Yin[4] and Lao Tan (Lao Tzu) heard of them and were delighted. They built their doctrines on the principle of eternal non-being and held the idea of the Great One as fundamental. To them weakness and humility were the expression, and openness and emptiness that did not destroy anything were the reality."[5]

One should not be misled by its ideals of weakness and emptiness into thinking that Taoism is a philosophy of negativism or one of absolute quietism. The book advocates not only non-action, but also practical tactics for action. It teaches submission, but strongly opposes oppressive government. The philosophy of the *Lao Tzu* is not for the hermit, but for the sage-ruler, who does not desert the world but rules it with non-interference. Taoism is therefore not a philosophy of withdrawal. Man is to follow Nature but in doing so he is not eliminated; instead, his nature is fulfilled. Any comparison of Taoism with Logos or Brahman must take these facts into account.

All this philosophy is embodied in a small classic of about 5,250 words, called the *Lao Tzu* or *Tao-te ching*[6] (Classic of the Way and its Virtue). No other Chinese classic of such small size has exercised so much influence. More commentaries have been written on it than on any other Chinese classic. About 350 are extant, besides some 350 that are lost or found only in fragments. There are also more English translations of it than of any other Chinese book—already over forty. It is a combination of poetry, philosophical speculation, and mystical reflection. Its vague and cryptic character makes interpretation and translation extremely difficult. Its literary style, grammatical patterns, rhymes, and ideas are in many places inconsistent. Certain terms are indisputably later interpolations. Passages attributed to the *Lao Tzu* in other works are either not found here or are different. On the basis of these facts, some scholars have assigned it to the fourth or third century B.C. or even later. But other scholars, contending that these objections apply to practically all ancient Chinese texts, see sufficient evidence to uphold the traditional sixth-century B.C. date. The argument that the style (e.g., it is not in question-and-answer form) or ideas do not belong to the sixth century B.C. and must come after such and such a style or ideas (as the idea of Tao must follow the idea of the Will of Heaven in the *Mo Tzu*, a

[4] Traditionally believed to be a contemporary of Lao Tzu whose work has been lost.

[5] *Chuang Tzu*, ch. 33, NHCC, 10:34b-35a. See Giles, trans., *Chuang Tzu*, 1961 ed., p. 319. This chapter is the best and oldest critique of ancient philosophical schools. Hsün Tzu (fl. 298–238 B.C.), another excellent critic of ancient philosophical schools, criticized Lao Tzu for "having insight about bending but not about expanding." See above, p. 123.

[6] Literally, the Classic of the Way and its Virtue.

work of the fourth century B.C.), is purely subjective. It is reasonable to believe that the book probably contains the basic teachings of Lao Tzu but was compiled later by more than one person.

As to this person Lao Tzu, opinion has been just as much divided as on the book itself. The *Records of the Historian*[7] states that he was a native of Ch'u (in modern Honan Province), that his family name was Li, private name Erh and posthumous name Tan, that he was a custodian of imperial archives, that Confucius visited him for information on rituals, that at old age he retired to the West and, at the request of a gate keeper, wrote more than 5,000 words on the Way and its virtue. In the midst of this story, the *Records of the Historian* inserted two brief accounts about Lao Lai Tzu, also a native of Ch'u and a contemporary of Confucius, and Tan, an historian of the Chou in the fourth century B.C. It added that no one knew whether they were the same person as Lao Tzu, and said that Lao Tzu's son was a general of Wei.

Obviously, these accounts—of Confucius' visit, generally dated 518 B.C., and of Lao Tzu's son's serving as a general in 273 B.C.—cannot both be true. Chinese tradition has accepted the former and placed Lao Tzu about twenty years senior to Confucius. In the 1920's and 1930's many Chinese and Western scholars rejected tradition and dated Lao Tzu at the fourth or even the third century B.C. But opinions among Chinese scholars were about evenly divided. Since then there has been a tendency to revert to tradition. In mainland China since 1949, however, scholars have held to the later dates.[8] In any case, the theory that Lao Tzu never existed or is merely a legend compounded of three different accounts is no longer seriously entertained. Whether the name Lao means old (hence the translation, "an Old Philosopher"), whether it is a family name, a private name, or the title "viscount" is uncertain.

In view of its importance, the *Lao Tzu* is here translated in full; the following list gives its main concepts and references.

Being and Non-being: 1, 2, 11, 40
Desires: 3, 19, 34, 37, 57
Female, Water: 8, 10, 20, 25, 28, 52, 55, 59, 78
Government: 3, 17, 26, 29-31, 57, 60, 61, 65, 74, 75, 80
Humanity and Righteousness: 18, 19, 38
Knowledge: 3, 70, 71
Name: 1, 25, 32, 41
Natural (*tzu-jan*): 17, 23, 25, 51, 64
Non-strife: 3, 7-9, 22, 24, 66, 73, 81
One: 10, 14, 22, 39, 42
Relativity, Good and Evil, Paradoxes: 2, 7, 20, 36, 45, 58

[7] Ch. 63; 1739 ed., 63:1b.

[8] For a lengthy and systematic discussion of the date of Lao Tzu and the *Lao Tzu*, see Chan, *The Way of Lao Tzu*, Introduction.

Reversal: 14, 16, 28, 40, 52
Simplicity: 19, 28, 32, 37, 57
Tao: 1, 4, 8, 14, 16, 21, 23, 25, 32, 34, 35, 37, 40-42, 51
Tranquillity: 16, 37, 61
Virtue: 10, 21, 23, 38, 51, 65
Weakness: 10, 22, 36, 40, 43, 52, 76, 78
Wu-wei (taking no action): 2, 3, 10, 37, 43, 48, 63, 64

THE LAO TZU (TAO-TE CHING)[9]

1. The Tao (Way) that can be told of is not the eternal Tao;
   The name that can be named is not the eternal name.
   The Nameless is the origin of Heaven and Earth;
   The Named is the mother of all things.
   Therefore let there always be non-being so we may see their subtlety,[10]
   And let there always be being[11] so we may see their outcome.
   The two are the same,
   But after they are produced, they have different names.[12]
   They both may be called deep and profound (*hsüan*).[13]
   Deeper and more profound,
   The door of all subtleties!

Comment. While ancient Chinese philosophical schools differed in many respects, most of them insisted on the correspondence of names and actualities. They all accepted names as necessary and good. Lao Tzu, however, rejected names in favor of the nameless. This, among other things, shows the radical and unique character

---

[9] The *Lao Tzu* was originally not divided, but only later was it separated into two parts containing eighty-one chapters. There are many variations of a minor nature in words and order. The oldest and best text is that used by Wang Pi (226-249), the *Lao Tzu tao-te ching chu* (Commentary on the *Lao Tzu*). The text used by Ho-shang Kung (fl. 179-159 B.C.) in his *Lao Tzu chang-chü* (Commentary on the *Lao Tzu*) is supposed to be older, but its authenticity is doubted. For translations, see Bibliography. The following translation is also published separately with comments on all chapters and many more textual notes. See Chan, *The Way of Lao Tzu*, in Bibliography.

[10] This translation of *miao* as "subtlety" rather than "mystery" is according to Wang Pi.

[11] Ho-shang Kung and Wang Pi punctuated the sentences to mean "have desires" and "have no desires." This interrupts the thought of the chapter. Beginning with Wang An-shih's (1021-1086) *Lao Tzu chu* (Commentary), some scholars have punctuated the two sentences after *wu* (no) and *yu* (to be), thus making them to mean "There is always non-being" and "There is always being." The terms *yu* and *wu* appear in *Lao Tzu*, chs. 2, 11, and 40. I prefer Wang's punctuation.

[12] Ch'en Ching-yüan (d. 1229), in his *Tao-te ching chu* (Commentary), punctuates the sentence after *t'ung* (the same) instead of *t'ung-ch'u* (produced from the same). This punctuation preserves the ancient rhyme of the verse.

[13] The word *hsüan* means profound and mysterious. For a discussion of this term, see Appendix.

of Taoism. To Lao Tzu, Tao is nameless and is the simplicity without names, and when names arise, that is, when the simple oneness of Tao is split up into individual things with names, it is time to stop.[14]

2. When the people of the world all know beauty as beauty,
   There arises the recognition of ugliness.
   When they all know the good as good,
   There arises the recognition of evil.
   Therefore:
   Being and non-being produce each other;
   Difficult and easy complete each other;
   Long and short contrast[15] each other;
   High and low distinguish each other;
   Sound and voice harmonize with each other;
   Front and back follow each other.
   Therefore the sage manages affairs without action
       (*wu-wei*)
   And spreads doctrines without words.
   All things arise, and he does not turn away from them.
   He produces them, but does not take possession of them.
   He acts, but does not rely on his own ability.[16]
   He accomplishes his task, but does not claim credit for it.[17]
   It is precisely because he does not claim credit that his
       accomplishment remains with him.

Comment. The idea of teachings without words anticipated the Buddhist tradition of silent transmission of the mystic doctrine, especially in the Zen School. This is diametrically opposed to the Confucian ideal, according to which a superior man acts and "becomes the model of the world"; he speaks, and "becomes the pattern for the world."[18] It is true that Confucianists say that a superior man "is truthful without any words,"[19] but they would never regard silence itself as virtue.

3. Do not exalt the worthy, so that the people shall not compete.
   Do not value rare treasures,[20] so that the people shall not
       steal.

[14] See *Lao Tzu*, chs. 37, 41, and 32, respectively.
[15] Some texts substitute the character *chiao* for *hsing*, both of which mean to contrast. The former does not rhyme, while the latter appears in the older text.
[16] Ho-shang Kung's interpretation: He does not expect any reward. These last two sentences also appear in *Lao Tzu*, chs. 10, 51, and 77.
[17] This sentence is also found in *Lao Tzu*, ch. 77 with the variation of one word.
[18] *The Mean*, ch. 29.   [19] *ibid.*, ch. 33.
[20] These words also appear in *Lao Tzu*, ch. 64.

Do not display objects of desire, so that the people's hearts
    shall not be disturbed.
Therefore in the government of the sage,
    He keeps their hearts vacuous (hsü),[21]
    Fills their bellies,
    Weakens their ambitions,
    And strengthens their bones,
He always causes his people to be without knowledge (cunning)
    or desire,
And the crafty to be afraid to act.
By acting without action, all things will be in order.

4. Tao is empty (like a bowl),
    It may be used but its capacity is never exhausted.
    It is bottomless, perhaps the ancestor of all things.
    It blunts its sharpness,
    It unties its tangles.
    It softens its light.
    It becomes one with the dusty world.[22]
    Deep and still, it appears to exist forever.
    I do not know whose son it is.
    It seems[23] to have existed before the Lord.

Comment. This chapter shows clearly that, in Taoism, function is
no less important than substance. Substance is further described in
Lao Tzu, chs. 14 and 21, but here, as in *Lao Tzu*, chs. 11 and 45,
function (*yung*, also meaning use) is regarded with equal respect.
There is no renunciation of phenomena as is the case with certain
Buddhist schools.

5. Heaven and Earth are not humane (*jen*).[24]
    They regard all things as straw dogs. → *sacrificed*
    The sage is not humane.   *ceremony*
    He regards all people as straw dogs.   *discarded*
    How Heaven and Earth are like a bellows!
    While vacuous, it is never exhausted.

[21] Literally "empty," *hsü* means absolute peace and purity of mind, freedom
from worry and selfish desires. See Appendix for further comments on it.
[22] These last four lines also appear in *Lao Tzu*, ch. 56.
[23] The word *hsiang* here means "seems" and repeats the feeling expressed in the
word "appear" two lines before. To interpret it as "image," as does Arthur Waley,
would be to make the *Lao Tzu* more metaphysical than it really is. See his translation of the *Lao Tzu*.
[24] Variously rendered as love, benevolence, human-heartedness, true manhood.
For a discussion of this term, see Appendix.

When active, it produces even more.
Much talk will of course[25] come to a dead end.
It is better to keep to the center (*chung*).[26]

Comment. The term "not humane" is of course extremely provocative. It may be suggested that this is Lao Tzu's emphatic way of opposing the Confucian doctrine of humanity and righteousness. Actually, the Taoist idea here is not negative but positive, for it means that Heaven and Earth are impartial, have no favorites, and are not humane in a deliberate or artificial way. This is the understanding of practically all commentators and is abundantly supported by the *Chuang Tzu*.[27] To translate it as unkind, as does Blakney, is grossly to misunderstand Taoist philosophy.

The two Taoist ideas, vacuity (*hsü*) and non-being (*wu*), later employed and elaborated by the Buddhists, were taboos to Confucianists. To them, these ideas are charged with a great danger of nihilism, even if Taoism is not. The Neo-Confucianist Chang Tsai (Chang Heng-ch'ü, 1020-1077) called Reality "Great Vacuity" (*T'ai-hsü*),[28] Chu Hsi (1130-1200) characterized man's nature as *hsü* and intelligent,[29] and Wang Yang-ming (Wang Shou-jen, 1472-1529) described the original mind of man in the same terms.[30] But Chang's Vacuity is equivalent to material force (*ch'i*), which is real and active. To Chu and Wang, as to other Confucianists, vacuity means purity, being devoid of selfish desires, impartiality, and so forth. Even then, they used the term sparingly and with great care.

6. The spirit of the valley never dies.
     It is called the subtle and profound female.
   The gate of the subtle and profound female
     Is the root of Heaven and Earth.
   It is continuous, and seems to be always existing.
   Use it and you will never wear it out.

7. Heaven is eternal and Earth everlasting.
   They can be eternal and everlasting because they
     do not exist for themselves,

[25] The word *shu* means variously number, repeatedly, fate, truth, etc. According to the meaning of truth, the passage would read, "Much talk destroys truth." It seems better to adopt the meaning of repetition (always) here.
[26] The word also means the mean or moderation, but here it means the center.
[27] See below, ch. 8, n.35.
[28] See below, ch. 30, B, 1, secs. 2-9, 16; and C, sec. 63.
[29] In his *Ta-hsüeh chang-chü* (Commentary on the *Great Learning*), comment on the text.
[30] See below, ch. 35, B, sec. 32.

And for this reason can exist forever.
Therefore the sage places himself in the background,
but finds himself in the foreground.
He puts himself away, and yet he always remains.
Is it not because he has no personal interests?
This is the reason why his personal interests
are fulfilled.

8. The best (man) is like water.
Water is good; it benefits all things and does not
compete with them.
It dwells in (lowly) places that all disdain.
This is why it is so near to Tao.
[The best man] in his dwelling loves the earth.
In his heart, he loves what is profound.
In his associations, he loves humanity.
In his words, he loves faithfulness.
In government, he loves order.
In handling affairs, he loves competence.
In his activities, he loves timeliness.
It is because he does not compete that he is
without reproach.

Comment. Water, the female, and the infant are Lao Tzu's famous
symbols of Tao. The emphasis of the symbolism is ethical rather
than metaphysical. It is interesting to note that while early Indians
associated water with creation[31] and the Greeks looked upon it as
a natural phenomenon, ancient Chinese philosophers, whether Lao
Tzu or Confucius,[32] preferred to learn moral lessons from it.
Broadly speaking, these different approaches have characterized
Indian, Western, and East Asian civilizations, respectively.

9. To hold and fill to overflowing
Is not as good as to stop in time.
Sharpen a sword-edge to its very sharpest,
And the (edge) will not last long.
When gold and jade fill your hall,
You will not be able to keep them.
To be proud with honor and wealth
Is to cause one's own downfall.
Withdraw as soon as your work is done.
Such is Heaven's Way.

[31] See *Rig Veda*, 10:129.   [32] See *Analects*, 9:16.

Comment. Note that one should withdraw only *after* his work is done. The Taoist way of life is not that of a hermit, although hermits have taken its name. The idea of withdrawal is not entirely absent even in Confucianism. Mencius said that it was the way of Confucius "to withdraw quickly from office when it was proper to do so."[33]

10. Can you keep the spirit and embrace the One without departing from them?

Can you concentrate your vital force (*ch'i*) and achieve the highest degree of weakness like an infant?

Can you clean and purify your profound insight so it will be spotless?

Can you love the people and govern the state without knowledge (cunning)?

Can you play the role of the female in the opening and closing of the gates of Heaven?

Can you understand all and penetrate all without
taking any action?
To produce things and to rear them,
To produce, but not to take possession of them,
To act, but not to rely on one's own ability,[34]
To lead them, but not to master them—
This is called profound and secret virtue (*hsüan-te*).[35]

Comment. The concentration of *ch'i* (vital force, breath) is not yoga, as Waley thinks it is. Yoga aims at transcending the self and the external environment. Nothing of the sort is intended here. It is true that in the *Huai-nan Tzu*, ch. 12, the story of Yen Hui's "sitting down and forgetting everything"[36] is recited to explain Lao Tzu's saying. But note that "the concentration" is followed by "loving the people" and "governing the state." Because the yoga breathing technique was later promoted by the religious Taoists, some scholars have unjustifiably read it into earlier texts. Wu Ch'eng (1249-1333), for example, thought that the "continuous" operation in ch. 6 was breathing, which is certainly going too far.

11. Thirty spokes are united around the hub to make a wheel,
But it is on its non-being that the utility of the carriage
depends.

[33] *Mencius*, 2A:2.
[34] These last two sentences also appear in *Lao Tzu*, chs. 2 and 51.
[35] These last two sentences also appear in *Lao Tzu*, ch. 51.
[36] SPPY, 12:14a. See Morgan, trans., *Tao, The Great Luminant*, pp. 128-129.

Clay is molded to form a utensil,
　But it is on its non-being that the utility of the utensil
　　depends.
Doors and windows are cut out to make a room,
　But it is on its non-being that the utility of the room
　　depends.
Therefore turn being into advantage, and turn non-being into
　utility.

12. The five colors cause one's eyes to be blind.
The five tones cause one's ears to be deaf.
The five flavors cause one's palate to be spoiled.
Racing and hunting cause one's mind to be mad.
Goods that are hard to get injure one's activities.[37]
For this reason the sage is concerned with the belly and not
　the eyes,
Therefore he rejects the one but accepts the other.

13. Be apprehensive when receiving favor or disgrace.[38]
Regard great trouble as seriously as you regard your body.
What is meant by being apprehensive when receiving
　favor or disgrace?
Favor[39] is considered inferior.
Be apprehensive when you receive them and also be
　apprehensive when you lose them.
This is what is meant by being apprehensive when receiving
　favor or disgrace.
What does it mean to regard great trouble as seriously as
　you regard the body?
The reason why I have great trouble is that I have a body
　(and am attached to it).
If I have no body,
What trouble could I have?
Therefore he who values the world as his body may be
　entrusted with the empire.
He who loves the world as his body may be entrusted with
　the empire.

Comment. On the basis of this attitude toward the body,[40] it is

---

[37] Other interpretations: Impedes one's movements; keeps one on guard; makes
his action violent.
[38] The sentence is obscure. The interpretation here follows that of Chiao Hung
(1540-1620), in *Lao Tzu i* (Aid to the *Lao Tzu*).
[39] Many texts have "disgrace."
[40] Also found in *Lao Tzu*, ch. 44.

difficult to accept the theory that Yang Chu, who would preserve one's own life under any circumstances, was an early Taoist, as Fung has maintained.[41]

14. We look at it and do not see it;
    Its name is The Invisible.
    We listen to it and do not hear it;
    Its name is The Inaudible.
    We touch it and do not find it;
    Its name is The Subtle (formless).
    These three cannot be further inquired into,
    And hence merge into one.
    Going up high, it is not bright, and coming down low, it is not dark.
    Infinite and boundless, it cannot be given any name;
    It reverts to nothingness.
    This is called shape without shape,
    Form (*hsiang*) without object.
    It is The Vague and Elusive.
    Meet it and you will not see its head.
    Follow it and you will not see its back.
    Hold on to the Tao of old in order to master the things of the present.
    From this one may know the primeval beginning [of the universe].
    This is called the bond of Tao.[42]

Comment. Subtlety is an important characteristic of Tao and is more important than its manifestations.[43] The Confucianists, on the other hand, emphasized manifestation. There is nothing more manifest than the hidden (subtle), they said, and a man who knows that the subtle will be manifested "can enter into virtue."[44] The Buddhists and Neo-Confucianists eventually achieved a synthesis and said that "there is no distinction between the manifest and the hidden."[45]

[41] *History of Chinese Philosophy*, vol. 1, p. 137.

[42] *Chi*, literally a thread, denotes tradition, discipline, principle, order, essence, etc. Generally it means the system, principle, or continuity that binds things together.

[43] See also *Lao Tzu*, chs. 1 and 15.

[44] *The Mean*, chs. 1 and 33.

[45] Ch'eng I, preface to the *I chuan* (Commentary on the *Book of Changes*), in ECCS.

15. Of old those who were the best rulers[46] were
    subtly mysterious and profoundly penetrating;
    Too deep to comprehend.
And because they cannot be comprehended,
    I can only describe them arbitrarily:
    Cautious, like crossing a frozen stream in the winter,
    Being at a loss, like one fearing danger on all sides,
    Reserved, like one visiting,
    Supple and pliant, like ice about to melt,
    Genuine, like a piece of uncarved wood,[47]
    Open and broad, like a valley,
    Merged and undifferentiated, like muddy water.

    Who can make muddy water gradually clear through
      tranquillity?
    Who can make the still gradually come to life through
      activity?
    He who embraces this Tao does not want to fill himself
      to overflowing.
    It is precisely because there is no overflowing that he
      is beyond wearing out and renewal.

16. Attain complete vacuity,
    Maintain steadfast quietude.
    All things come into being,
    And I see thereby their return.
    All things flourish,
    But each one returns to its root.
    This return to its root means tranquillity.
    It is called returning to its destiny.
    To return to destiny is called the eternal (Tao).
    To know the eternal is called enlightenment.
    Not to know the eternal is to act blindly to result in disaster.
    He who knows the eternal is all-embracing.
    Being all-embracing, he is impartial.
    Being impartial, he is kingly (universal).[48]

[46] The text has the word *shih* meaning the ruler instead of "Tao." In the text collated by Fu I (555-639), *Chiao-ting ku-pen Lao Tzu* (The Old Text of the *Lao Tzu* Collated), however, the word is *Tao* instead. Ma Hsü-lun in his *Lao Tzu chiao-ku* (*Lao Tzu* collated and explained) and other scholars have preferred to follow Fu I. But the emendation is quite unnecessary.

[47] *P'u*, literally an uncarved wood, has come to mean in Taoism simplicity, plainness, genuineness, etc.

[48] Chiao Hung, *Lao Tzu i*, says that according to one tablet on which the *Lao*

Being kingly, he is one with Nature.[49]
Being one with Nature, he is in accord with Tao.
Being in accord with Tao, he is everlasting,
And is free from danger throughout his lifetime.

Comment. In the philosophy of Lao Tzu, Tao is revealed most fully through tranquillity. The position of the Neo-Confucianists is just the opposite. They said that only through activity can the mind of Heaven and Earth be seen.

17. The best (rulers) are those whose existence is (merely)[50] known by the people.
The next best are those who are loved and praised.
The next are those who are feared.
And the next are those who are despised.
It is only when one does not have enough faith in others that others will have no faith in him.[51]
[The great rulers] value their words highly.
They accomplish their task; they complete their work.
Nevertheless their people say that they simply follow Nature (*Tzu-jan*).[52]

18. When the great Tao declined,
The doctrines of humanity (*jen*) and righteousness (*i*) arose.
When knowledge and wisdom appeared,
There emerged great hypocrisy.
When the six family relationships[53] are not in harmony,
There will be the advocacy of filial piety and deep love to children.[54]

Tzu is inscribed, the word here is not *wang* (kingly) but *chou* (comprehension). Ma Hsü-lun, *Lao Tzu chiao-ku*, notes this approvingly but did not amend the text accordingly. Had he done so, it would not have made any improvement.

[49] Ma thinks that the word *T'ien* (Nature) should have been *ta* (great).

[50] The word "not" does not appear either in the Wang Pi text or in the Ho-shang Kung text, but it appears here in the version used by Wu Ch'eng for his commentary, *Tao-te ching chu* (Commentary on the *Lao Tzu*), in the *Yung-lo ta-tien* (Great Library of the Yung-lo Period, 1403-1424), 1407, and also in the Japanese *Koitsu sōshō* (Collection of Missing Ancient Texts). This version has been accepted by many scholars, including Hu Shih, *Development of the Logical Method in Ancient China*, p. 16. The beginning phrase "the highest" is interpreted by most commentators as "the best ruler," by some as "the highest ruler," and by a few as "ruler of high antiquity."

[51] This sentence is also found in ch. 23.

[52] *Tzu-jan*, literally "self-so," means being natural or spontaneous.

[53] Father, son, elder brother, younger brother, husband, and wife.

[54] Some texts including the *Yung-lo ta-tien* read: "There will be filial sons" instead of "filial piety and deep love."

When a country is in disorder,
There will be praise of loyal ministers.

19. Abandon sageliness and discard wisdom;
    Then the people will benefit a hundredfold.
    Abandon humanity and discard righteousness;
    Then the people will return to filial piety and deep love.[55]
    Abandon skill and discard profit;
    Then there will be no thieves or robbers.
    However, these three things are ornament (*wen*) and not
       adequate.
    Therefore let people hold on to these:
       Manifest plainness,
       Embrace simplicity,
       Reduce selfishness,
       Have few desires.

Comment. The sage as the ideal human being and the ideal ruler
is mentioned thirty times in the book. And yet here sageliness is
condemned. There is no contradiction, for sageliness here means
a particular characteristic, that of broad and extensive learning,
and is therefore mentioned along with wisdom, humanity, and
righteousness. With regard to the sage, it is curious that while
ancient kings were regarded as models by most ancient schools,
and even by Chuang Tzu, they were ignored by Lao Tzu. It is not
that Lao Tzu did not look to the past but rather that to him the
sage transcended time.

20. Abandon learning and there will be no sorrow.[56]
    How much difference is there between "Yes, sir," and "Of
       course not"?
    How much difference is there between "good" and "evil"?
    What people dread, do not fail to dread.
    But, alas, how confused, and the end is not yet.
    The multitude are merry, as though feasting on a day of
       sacrifice,
    Or like ascending a tower at springtime.

---

[55] In some texts, including the *Yung-lo ta-tien*, this sentence precedes the first.
[56] Some scholars have shifted this line to the beginning or the end of the last
chapter. Rearranging the text of *Lao Tzu* has been undertaken by a number of
modern scholars, especially Ma. Duyvendak has done so in his translation. But
such rearrangements have no objective historical or textual foundation and add
little to one's understanding of Taoist philosophy.

I alone am inert, showing no sign (of desires),
Like an infant that has not yet smiled.
Wearied, indeed, I seem to be without a home.
The multitude all possess more than enough,
I alone seem to have lost all.
Mine is indeed the mind of an ignorant man,
Indiscriminate and dull!
Common folks are indeed brilliant;
I alone seem to be in the dark.

Comment. A Confucianist would never say "Abandon learning."
Also he would sharply distinguish between good and evil. The
Neo-Confucianist, Ch'eng Hao (Ch'eng Ming-tao, 1032-1085),
has been severely criticized for his saying that "both good and
evil in the world are both the Principle of Nature,"[57] and Wang
Yang-ming was likewise widely attacked for teaching that "in the
original substance of the mind there is no distinction between
good and evil."[58]

Common folks see differences and are clear-cut;
I alone make no distinctions.
I seem drifting as the sea;
Like the wind blowing about, seemingly without destination.
The multitude all have a purpose;
I alone seem to be stubborn and rustic.
I alone differ from others,
And value drawing sustenance from Mother (Tao).[59]

21. The all-embracing quality of the great virtue (*te*) follows
    alone from the Tao.
  The thing that is called Tao is eluding and vague.
    Vague and eluding, there is in it the form.
    Eluding and vague, in it are things.
  Deep and obscure, in it is the essence.[60]
  The essence is very real; in it are evidences.
  From the time of old until now, its name (manifestations)
    ever remains,
  By which we may see the beginning of all things.
  How do I know that the beginnings of all things are so?
  Through this (Tao).

[57] See below, ch. 31, sec. 8.
[58] See below, ch. 35, sec. 315.
[59] The term "mother" occurs also in *Lao Tzu*, chs. 1, 25, 52, 59. See below, n.97.
[60] The word *ching* (essence) also means intelligence, spirit, life-force.

Comment. Philosophically this is the most important chapter of the book. The sentence "The essence is very real" virtually formed the backbone of Chou Tun-i's (Chou Lien-hsi, 1017-1073) *Explanation of the Diagram of the Great Ultimate*, which centers on the "reality of the Non-Ultimate and the essence of yin and yang."[61] And Chou's work laid the foundation of the entire Neo-Confucian metaphysics. Of course Neo-Confucian metaphysics is more directly derived from the *Book of Changes*, but the concepts of reality in the *Book of Changes* and in this chapter are surprisingly similar.

22. To yield is to be preserved whole.
To be bent is to become straight.
To be empty is to be full.
To be worn out is to be renewed.
To have little is to possess.
To have plenty is to be perplexed.
Therefore the sage embraces the One
And becomes the model of the world.
He does not show himself; therefore he is luminous.
He does not justify himself; therefore he becomes prominent.
He does not boast of himself; therefore he is given credit.
He does not brag; therefore he can endure for long.[62]
It is precisely because he does not compete that the world cannot compete with him.[63]
Is the ancient saying, "To yield is to be preserved whole," empty words?
Truly he will be preserved and (prominence, etc.) will come to him.

23. Nature says few words.[64]
For the same reason a whirlwind does not last a whole morning,
Nor does a rainstorm last a whole day.
What causes them?
It is Heaven and Earth (Nature).
If even Heaven and Earth cannot make them last long,
How much less can man?
Therefore he who follows Tao is identified with Tao.
He who follows virtue is identified with virtue.

[61] See below, ch. 28.
[62] These last four lines are repeated with slight modification in *Lao Tzu*, ch. 24.
[63] This sentence is also found in *Lao Tzu*, ch. 66.
[64] Cf. *Analects*, 17:19.

He who abandons (Tao) is identified with the abandonment
(of Tao).

He who is identified with Tao—Tao is also happy to have
him.

He who is identified with virtue—virtue is also happy to
have him.

And he who is identified with the abandonment (of Tao)—
the abandonment (of Tao) is also happy to abandon him.

It is only when one does not have enough faith in others
that others will have no faith in him.[65]

24. He who stands on tiptoe is not steady.

He who strides forward does not go.

He who shows himself is not luminous.[66]

He who justifies himself is not prominent.

He who boasts of himself is not given credit.

He who brags does not endure for long.[67]

From the point of view of Tao, these are like remnants of
food and tumors of action,

Which all creatures detest.

Therefore those who possess Tao turn away from them.

25. There was something undifferentiated and yet complete,

Which existed before heaven and earth.

Soundless and formless, it depends on nothing
and does not change.

It operates everywhere and is free from danger.

It may be considered the mother of the universe.

I do not know its name; I call it Tao.

If forced to give it a name, I shall call it Great.

Now being great means functioning everywhere.

Functioning everywhere means far-reaching.

Being far-reaching means returning to the original point.

Therefore Tao is great.

Heaven is great.

Earth is great.

And the king[68] is also great.

There are four great things in the universe, and the king is
one of them.

[65] Repeating the sentence in *Lao Tzu*, ch. 17.

[66] Cf. *The Mean*, chs. 26 and 33.

[67] These last four lines virtually repeat *Lao Tzu*, ch. 22.

[68] Both the Wang Pi and Ho-shang Kung texts read "king" instead of "man."
The Fu I text and others have "man" instead. However, "king" is here understood
as the representative of man.

Man models himself after Earth.
Earth models itself after Heaven.
Heaven models itself after Tao.
And Tao models itself after Nature.

Comment. The doctrine of returning to the original is prominent in Lao Tzu.[69] It has contributed in no small degree to the common Chinese cyclical concept, which teaches that both history and reality operate in cycles.

26. The heavy is the root of the light.
    The tranquil is the ruler of the hasty.
    Therefore the sage travels all day
    Without leaving his baggage.[70]
    Even at the sight of magnificent scenes,
    He remains leisurely and indifferent.
    How is it that a lord with ten thousand chariots
    Should behave lightheartedly in his empire?
    If he is lighthearted, the minister will be destroyed.
    If he is hasty, the ruler is lost.

27. A good traveler leaves no track or trace.
    A good speech leaves no flaws.
    A good reckoner uses no counters.
    A well-shut door needs no bolts, and yet it cannot be opened.
    A well-tied knot needs no rope and yet none can untie it.
    Therefore the sage is always good in saving men and
        consequently no man is rejected.
    He is always good in saving things and consequently nothing
        is rejected.
    This is called following the light (of Nature)[71]
    Therefore the good man is the teacher of the bad,
    And the bad is the material from which the good may learn.
    He who does not value the teacher,
    Or greatly care for the material,
    Is greatly deluded although he may be learned.
    Such is the essential mystery.

[69] The doctrine is also encountered in *Lao Tzu*, chs. 14, 16, 28, 40, 52.

[70] The Chinese term for baggage means something heavy.

[71] The word *hsi*, here rendered as "following," is open to various interpretations: To cover, to penetrate, to practice, etc. (according to Ma Hsü-lun, *Lao Tzu chiao-ku*, ch. 52, this *hsi* and the *hsi* meaning practice were interchangeable in ancient times), but it is most commonly understood as "following," an interpretation which is supported by the *Chuang Tzu*, ch. 2, where the terms "letting Nature follow its own course" (that is, following Nature) and "using the light" are repeatedly used.

28. He who knows the male (active force) and keeps to the
      female (the passive force or receptive element)
    Becomes the ravine of the world.
    Being the ravine of the world,
    He will never depart from eternal virtue,
    But returns to the state of infancy.
    He who knows the white (glory) and yet keeps to the
      black (humility),
    Becomes the model for the world.
    Being the model for the world,
    He will never deviate from eternal virtue,
    But returns to the state of the Ultimate of Non-being.
    He who knows glory but keeps to humility,
    Becomes the valley of the world.
    Being the valley of the world,
    He will be proficient in eternal virtue,
    And returns to the state of simplicity (uncarved wood).
    When the uncarved wood is broken up, it is turned into
      concrete things (as Tao is transformed into the myriad
      things).
    But when the sage uses it, he becomes the leading official.
    Therefore the great ruler does not cut up.

29. When one desires to take over the empire and act on it
      (interfere with it),
    I see that he will not succeed.
    The empire is a spiritual thing,[72] and should not be acted on.
    He who acts on it harms it.
    He who holds on to it loses it.
    Among creatures some lead and some follow.
    Some blow hot and some blow cold.
    Some are strong and some are weak.
    Some may break and some may fall.
    Therefore the sage discards the extremes, the extravagant,
      and the excessive.

30. He who assists the ruler with Tao does not dominate the
      world with force.
    The use of force usually brings requital.
    Wherever armies are stationed, briers and thorns grow.
    Great wars are always followed by famines.
    A good (general) achieves his purpose and stops,

[72] For Wang Pi's explanation of this term, see below, ch. 19, sec. 3.

But dares not seek to dominate the world.

He achieves his purpose but does not brag about it.

He achieves his purpose but does not boast about it.

He achieves his purpose but is not proud of it.

He achieves his purpose but only as an unavoidable step.

He achieves his purpose but does not aim to dominate.

(For) after things reach their prime, they begin to grow old,

Which means being contrary to Tao.

Whatever is contrary to Tao will soon perish.[73]

31. Fine weapons are instruments of evil.

They are hated by men.

Therefore those who possess Tao turn away from them.

The good ruler when at home honors the left (symbolic of good omens).

When at war he honors the right (symbolic of evil omens).

Weapons are instruments of evil, not the instruments of a good ruler.

When he uses them unavoidably, he regards calm restraint as the best principle.

Even when he is victorious, he does not regard it as praiseworthy,

For to praise victory is to delight in the slaughter of men.

He who delights in the slaughter of men will not succeed in the empire.

In auspicious affairs, the left is honored.

In unauspicious affairs, the right is honored.

The lieutenant-general stands on the left.

The senior general stands on the right.

That is to say that the arrangement follows that of funeral ceremonies.[74]

For the slaughter of the multitude, let us weep with sorrow and grief.

For a victory, let us observe the occasion with funeral ceremonies.

---

[73] These last two sentences also appear in *Lao Tzu*, ch. 55.

[74] Most commentators agree that these last five sentences are commentaries interpolated in the text by mistake. They interrupted the preceding and following passages. They contain the terms "lieutenant-general" and "senior general" which did not appear until the Han (206 B.C.–A.D. 220) times, and this is the only chapter in Wang Pi's text which contains no comments, indicating that these five sentences were commentaries, although his commentaries in other chapters are more philosophical and more plentiful. It should be noted that the mention of Han generals is the only anachronism in the *Lao Tzu*.

32. Tao is eternal and has no name.
Though its simplicity seems insignificant, none in the world can master it.
If kings and barons would hold on to it, all things would submit to them spontaneously.
Heaven and earth unite to drip sweet dew.
Without the command of men, it drips evenly over all.
As soon as there were regulations and institutions, there were names (differentiation of things).
As soon as there are names, know that it is time to stop.
It is by knowing when to stop that one can be free from danger.
Analogically, Tao in the world (where everything is embraced by it), may be compared to rivers and streams running into the sea.

33. He who knows others is wise;
He who knows himself is enlightened.
He who conquers others has physical strength.
He who conquers himself is strong.
He who is contented is rich.
He who acts with vigor has will.
He who does not lose his place (with Tao) will endure.
He who dies but does not really perish enjoys long life.

Comment. What is it that dies but does not perish? Wang Pi said it was Tao on which human life depended, and Wu Ch'eng said it was the human mind. Other commentators have given different answers. Most of them, however, believe that Lao Tzu meant the immortality of virtue. Thus the Taoists conformed to the traditional belief which had already been expressed in the *Tso chuan* (Tso's Commentary on the *Spring and Autumn Annals*), namely, the immortality of virtue, achievement, and words,[75] and which has continued to be the typical Chinese idea of immortality.[76] It is to be noted that unlike Chuang Tzu, Lao Tzu showed no tendency to believe in earthly immortals (*hsien*, a fairy), although his exaltation of everlasting life undoubtedly contributed to the development of the belief.

[75] See above, ch. 1, sec. 4.
[76] Erkes thinks that death meant that a dead man still possessed power to influence the living and that perishing means that this power is gone as the body has been dissolved. Dubs rejects this interpretation and insists that Lao Tzu meant immortality of influence. (See Erkes, *Ssu erh pu-wang* in *Asia Major*, 3:2 [1952], 156-159; note by Dubs, *ibid.*, 159-161; Erkes' reply, *ibid.*, 4:1 [1954], 149-150.) Most Chinese scholars would support Dubs.

34. The Great Tao flows everywhere.
    It may go left or right.
    All things depend on it for life, and it does not turn away
       from them.
    It accomplishes its task, but does not claim credit for it.
    It clothes and feeds all things but does not claim to be
       master over them.
    Always without desires, it may be called The Small.
    All things come to it and it does not master them;
       it may be called The Great.
    Therefore (the sage) never strives himself for the great, and
       thereby the great is achieved.[77]

35. Hold fast to the great form (Tao),[78]
    And all the world will come.
    They come and will encounter no harm;
    But enjoy comfort, peace, and health.
    When there are music and dainties,
    Passing strangers will stay.
    But the words uttered by Tao,
    How insipid and tasteless!
    We look at Tao; it is imperceptible.
    We listen to it; it is inaudible.
    We use it; it is inexhaustible.

36. In order to contract,
       It is necessary first to expand.
    In order to weaken,
       It is necessary first to strengthen.
    In order to destroy,
       It is necessary first to promote.
    In order to grasp,
       It is necessary first to give.
    This is called subtle light.
    The weak and the tender overcome the hard and the strong.
    Fish should not be taken away from water.
    And sharp weapons of the state should not be displayed
       to the people.

Comment. The Confucianists have never excused Lao Tzu for
teaching such a doctrine of "deceit."

[77] This sentence also appears in *Lao Tzu*, ch. 63, with some variation.
[78] The term "great form" also appears in ch. 41.

37. Tao invariably takes no action, and yet there is nothing left undone.

    If kings and barons can keep it, all things will transform spontaneously.

    If, after transformation, they should desire to be active, I would restrain them with simplicity, which has no name.

    Simplicity, which has no name, is free of desires.

    Being free of desires, it is tranquil.

    And the world will be at peace of its own accord.

38. The man of superior virtue is not (conscious of) his virtue, And in this way he really possesses virtue.

    The man of inferior virtue never loses (sight of) his virtue, And in this way he loses his virtue.

    The man of superior virtue takes no action, but has no ulterior motive to do so.

    The man of inferior virtue takes action, and has an ulterior motive to do so.

    The man of superior humanity takes action, but has no ulterior motive to do so.

    The man of superior righteousness takes action, and has an ulterior motive to do so.

    The man of superior propriety[79] takes action,

    And when people do not respond to it, he will stretch his arms and force it on them.

    Therefore, only when Tao is lost does the doctrine of virtue arise.

    When virtue is lost, only then does the doctrine of humanity arise.

    When humanity is lost, only then does the doctrine of righteousness arise.

    When righteousness is lost, only then does the doctrine of propriety arise.

    Now, propriety is a superficial expression of loyalty and faithfulness, and the beginning of disorder.

    Those who are the first to know have the flowers (appearance) of Tao but are the beginning of ignorance.

    For this reason the great man dwells in the thick (substantial), and does not rest with the thin (superficial).

    He dwells in the fruit (reality), and does not rest with the flower (appearance).

    Therefore he rejects the one, and accepts the other.

---

[79] In a narrow sense, *li* means rites, ritual, ceremonies, etc., but in a broad sense it means rules of behavior or principles of conduct.

Comment. Wang Pi, who wrote the best and most philosophical commentary on the *Lao Tzu*, wrote the longest of his comments on this chapter.[80] It is in this commentary that the important Chinese concepts of *t'i-yung* (substance and function) first appeared. Han Fei Tzu, the first commentator on the *Lao Tzu*,[81] wrote one of his longest and best comments on this chapter also.

39. Of old those that obtained the One:
Heaven obtained the One and became clear.
Earth obtained the One and became tranquil.
The spiritual beings obtained the One and became divine.
The valley obtained the One and became full.
The myriad things obtained the One and lived and grew.
Kings and barons obtained the One and became rulers[82] of the empire.
What made them so is the One.[83]
If heaven had not thus become clear,
It would soon crack.
If the earth had not thus become tranquil,
It would soon be shaken.
If the spiritual beings had not thus become divine,
They would soon wither away.
If the valley had not thus become full,
It would soon become exhausted.
If the myriad things had not thus lived and grown,
They would soon become extinct.
If kings and barons had not thus become honorable and high in position,
They would soon fall.
Therefore humble station is the basis of honor.
The low is the foundation of the high.
For this reason kings and barons call themselves the orphaned, the lonely ones, the unworthy.
Is this not regarding humble station as the basis of honor?
Is it not?

[80] See below, ch. 19, sec. 3.
[81] For his elaboration on the concept of Tao, see below, ch. 12, sec. 2.
[82] The word *cheng*, ordinarily meaning upright or firm, here denotes a ruler.
[83] Both the Wang Pi and Ho-shang Kung texts do not have the word "One" but most others have.

Therefore enumerate all the parts of a chariot as you may,
and you still have no chariot.[84]
Rather than jingle like the jade,
Rumble like the rocks.

40. Reversion is the action of Tao.
Weakness is the function of Tao.
All things in the world come from being.
And being comes from non-being.

41. When the highest type of men hear Tao,
They diligently practice it.
When the average type of men hear Tao,
They half believe in it.
When the lowest type of men hear Tao,
They laugh heartily at it.
If they did not laugh at it, it would not be Tao.
Therefore there is the established saying:
The Tao which is bright appears to be dark.
The Tao which goes forward appears to fall backward.
The Tao which is level appears uneven.
Great virtue appears like a valley (hollow).
Great purity appears like disgrace.
Far-reaching virtue appears as if insufficient.
Solid virtue appears as if unsteady.
True substance appears to be changeable.
The great square has no corners.
The great implement (or talent) is slow to finish (or mature).
Great music sounds faint.
Great form has no shape.
Tao is hidden and nameless.
Yet it is Tao alone that skillfully provides for all and
brings them to perfection.

42. Tao produced the One.
The One produced the two.
The two produced the three.
And the three produced the ten thousand things.
The ten thousand things carry the yin and embrace the
yang,[85] and through the blending of the material force
(*ch'i*)[86] they achieve harmony.

[84] The Wu Ch'eng text reads "Supreme praise is no praise." This substitution of
words does not improve the meaning.

[85] Yin is the passive, female cosmic principle or force while yang is the active
or male principle.

[86] Variously translated as matter, matter-energy, vital force, breath, etc.

People hate to be the orphaned, the lonely ones, and the
   unworthy.
And yet kings and lords call themselves by these names.
Therefore it is often the case that things gain by
   losing and lose by gaining.
What others have taught, I teach also:
"Violent and fierce people do not die a natural death."[87]
I shall make this the father (basis or starting point)
   of my teaching.

Comment. It is often understood that the One is the original
material force or the Great Ultimate, the two are yin and
yang, the three are their blending with the original material force,
and the ten thousand things are things carrying yin and embracing
yang. However, there is no need to be specific. The important
point is the natural evolution from the simple to the complex
without any act of creation. This theory is common to practically
all Chinese philosophical schools.[88]

43. The softest things in the world overcome the hardest
      things in the world.
   Non-being penetrates that in which there is no space.
   Through this I know the advantage of taking no action.
   Few in the world can understand teaching without words
      and the advantage of taking no action.

44. Which does one love more, fame or one's own life?
   Which is more valuable, one's own life or wealth?
   Which is worse, gain or loss?
   Therefore he who has lavish desires will spend extravagantly.
   He who hoards most will lose heavily.
   He who is contented suffers no disgrace.
   He who knows when to stop is free from danger.
   Therefore he can long endure.

45. What is most perfect seems to be incomplete;
   But its utility is unimpaired.
   What is most full seems to be empty;
   But its usefulness is inexhaustible.
   What is most straight seems to be crooked.
   The greatest skills seems to be clumsy.
   The greatest eloquence seems to stutter.

---

[87] An ancient saying.
[88] See below, ch. 17, sec. 3 and ch. 28, sec. 1.

Hasty movement overcomes cold,
(But) tranquillity overcomes heat.
By being greatly tranquil,
One is qualified to be the ruler of the world.

46. When Tao prevails in the world, galloping horses are turned
    back to fertilize (the fields with their dung).
    When Tao does not prevail in the world, war horses
    thrive in the suburbs.
    There is no calamity greater than lavish desires.[89]
    There is no greater guilt than discontentment.
    And there is no greater disaster than greed.
    He who is contented with contentment is always contented.

47. One may know the world without going out of doors.
    One may see the Way of Heaven without looking through
    the windows.
    The further one goes, the less one knows.
    Therefore the sage knows without going about,
    Understands[90] without seeing,
    And accomplishes without any action.

48. The pursuit of learning is to increase day after day.
    The pursuit of Tao is to decrease day after day.
    It is to decrease and further decrease until one reaches the
    point of taking no action.
    No action is undertaken, and yet nothing is left undone.
    An empire is often brought to order by having no activity
    (laissez-faire).
    If one (likes to)[91] undertake activity, he is not qualified to
    govern the empire.

49. The sage has no fixed (personal) ideas.
    He regards the people's ideas as his own.
    I treat those who are good with goodness,
    And I also treat those who are not good with goodness.
    Thus goodness is attained.[92]
    I am honest to those who are honest,

[89] This sentence does not appear in the Wang Pi text but appears in numerous texts, including the Ho-shang Kung and Fu I texts.

[90] The word *ming* ordinarily means "name" but is interchangeable with *ming* meaning to understand.

[91] This interpretation follows Ho-shang Kung's commentary.

[92] Read *te* (to attain) instead of *te* (virtue), according to the Fu I text. Actually in ancient times the two words were interchangeable.

And I am also honest to those who are not honest.

Thus honesty is attained.

The sage, in the government of his empire, has no subjective viewpoint.[93]

His mind forms a harmonious whole with that of his people.

They all lend their eyes and ears,[94] and he treats them all as infants.

50. Man comes into life and goes out to death.

Three out of ten are companions of life.

Three out of ten are companions of death.

And three out of ten in their lives lead from activity to death.[95]

And for what reason?

Because of man's intensive striving after life.

I have heard that one who is a good preserver of his life will not meet tigers or wild buffalos,

And in fighting will not try to escape from weapons of war.

The wild buffalo cannot butt its horns against him,

The tiger cannot fasten its claws in him,

And weapons of war cannot thrust their blades into him.

And for what reason?

Because in him there is no room for death.

51. Tao produces them (the ten thousand things).

Virtue fosters them.

Matter gives them physical form.

The circumstances and tendencies complete them.

Therefore the ten thousand things esteem Tao and honor virtue.

Tao is esteemed and virtue is honored without anyone's order.

They always come spontaneously.

Therefore Tao produces them and virtue fosters them.

They rear them and develop them.

They give them security and give them peace.

They nurture them and protect them.

(Tao) produces them but does not take possession of them.

It acts, but does not rely on its own ability.

[93] This is Wang Pi's interpretation.

[94] The Wang Pi text does not have these words but the Fu I text does.

[95] Han Fei Tzu understood "ten-three" not as three out of ten but thirteen and identified the four limbs and the nine external cavities as factors that sustain life, lead to death, or lead through activity to death. Few commentators follow him. See *Han Fei Tzu*, ch. 20, SPTK, 6:8a, or Liao, trans., *Han Fei Tzu*, vol. 1, p. 196.

It leads them but does not master them.
This is called profound and secret virtue.[96]

52. There was a beginning of the universe
Which may be called the Mother of the Universe.
He who has found the mother (Tao)[97]
And thereby understands her sons (things)
And having understood the sons,
Still keeps to its mother,
Will be free from danger throughout his lifetime.
Close the mouth.
Shut the doors (of cunning and desire).[98]
And to the end of life there will be (peace) without toil.
Open the mouth.
Meddle with affairs,
And to the end of life there will be no salvation.
Seeing what is small is called enlightenment.
Keeping to weakness is called strength.
Use the light.
Revert to enlightenment,
And thereby avoid danger to one's life—
This is called practicing the eternal.

53. If I had but little[99] knowledge
I should, in walking on a broad way,
Fear getting off the road.
Broad ways are extremely even,
But people are fond of by-paths.
The courts are exceedingly splendid,
While the fields are exceedingly weedy,
And the granaries are exceedingly empty.
Elegant clothes are worn,
Sharp weapons are carried,
Foods and drinks are enjoyed beyond limit,
And wealth and treasures are accumulated in excess.

[96] These last four sentences appear in *Lao Tzu*, ch. 10, where the subject is the sage rather than Tao. The first two of these four sentences also appear in ch. 2. The third is repeated in ch. 77.
[97] According to the earliest commentary on the *Lao Tzu*, *Han Fei Tzu*, ch. 20, SPTK, 6:5a (Liao, p. 183), "mother" means Tao.
[98] These two lines are also found in *Lao Tzu*, ch. 56.
[99] Ho-shang Kung understood *chieh-jan* as great, but in *Lieh Tzu*, ch. 7, it means small. See Yang Po-chün, *Lieh Tzu chi-shih* (Collected Explanations of the *Lieh Tzu*), 1958, p. 138.

This is robbery and extravagance.

This is indeed not Tao (the way).[100]

54. He who is well established (in Tao) cannot be pulled away.

He who has a firm grasp (of Tao) cannot be separated from it.

Thus from generation to generation his ancestral sacrifice will never be suspended.

When one cultivates virtue in his person, it becomes genuine virtue.

When one cultivates virtue in his family, it becomes overflowing virtue.

When one cultivates virtue in his community, it becomes lasting virtue.

When one cultivates virtue in his country, it becomes abundant virtue.

When one cultivates virtue in the world, it becomes universal.

Therefore the person should be viewed as a person.

The family should be viewed as a family.

The community should be viewed as a community.

The country should be viewed as a country.

And the world should be viewed as the world.[101]

How do I know this to be the case in the world?

Through this (from the cultivation of virtue in the person to that in the world).

55. He who possesses virtue in abundance

May be compared to an infant.

Poisonous insects will not sting him.

Fierce beasts will not seize him.

Birds of prey will not strike him.

His bones are weak, his sinews tender, but his grasp is firm.

He does not yet know the union of male and female,

But his organ is aroused.

This means that his essence is at its height.

He may cry all day without becoming hoarse,

This means that his (natural) harmony is perfect.

[100] Using the term *tao* both as an abstract noun and a concrete noun.

[101] The Chinese merely reads: From person see person, etc. Wang Pi says "The Tao in the person may be seen from the person's own state of mind," etc. Hoshang Kung says "From the person who cultivates the Tao, the person who does not cultivate Tao may be seen," etc. Wei Yüan (1794-1856), *Lao Tzu pen-i* (Original Meanings of the *Lao Tzu*), says, "By one's own person, other persons may be seen," etc.

To know harmony means to be in accord with the eternal.
To be in accord with the eternal means to be enlightened.
To force the growth of life means ill omen.
For the mind to employ the vital force without restraint
    means violence.
After things reach their prime, they begin to grow old,
Which means being contrary to Tao.
Whatever is contrary to Tao will soon perish.[102]

56. He who knows does not speak.
    He who speaks does not know.
    Close the mouth.
    Shut the doors (of cunning and desires).[103]
    Blunt the sharpness.
    Untie the tangles.
    Soften the light.
    Become one with the dusty world.[104]
    This is called profound identification.
    Therefore it is impossible either to be intimate and close to
        him or to be distant and indifferent to him.
    It is impossible either to benefit him or to harm him,
    It is impossible either to honor him or to disgrace him.
    For this reason he is honored by the world.

57. Govern the state with correctness.
    Operate the army with surprise tactics.
    Administer the empire by engaging in no activity.
    How do I know that this should be so?
    Through this:
        The more taboos and prohibitions there are in the world,
            The poorer the people will be.
        The more sharp weapons the people have,
            The more troubled the state will be.
        The more cunning and skill man possesses,
            The more vicious things will appear.
        The more laws and orders are made prominent,
            The more thieves and robbers there will be.

[102] These two sentences are also found in *Lao Tzu*, ch. 30. Ma Hsü-lun thinks they are misplaced here. But repetition does not necessarily mean misplacement. Since in ancient times books consisted of bamboo or wooden slabs containing some twenty characters each, it was not easy for these sentences of twelve words to be added by mistake. The *Lao Tzu* is not a systematic treatise. Repetitions are found in more than one place.

[103] These last two sentences also appear in *Lao Tzu*, ch. 52.

[104] These last four sentences also appear in ch. 4.

Therefore the sage says:

I take no action and the people of themselves are transformed.

I love tranquillity and the people of themselves become correct.

I engage in no activity and the people of themselves become prosperous.

I have no desires and the people of themselves become simple.

Comment. Laissez-faire government. Even Confucius shared this ideal.[105]

58. When the government is non-discriminative and dull,
The people are contented and generous.
When the government is searching and discriminative,
The people are disappointed and contentious.
Calamity is that upon which happiness depends;
Happiness is that in which calamity is latent.
Who knows when the limit will be reached?
Is there no correctness (used to govern the world?)
Then the correct again becomes the perverse
And the good will again become evil.[106]
The people have been deluded for a long time.
Therefore the sage is as pointed as a square but does not pierce.
He is as acute as a knife but does not cut.
He is as straight as an unbent line but does not extend.
He is as bright as light but does not dazzle.

59. To rule people and to serve Heaven there is nothing better than to be frugal.
Only by being frugal can one recover quickly.
To recover quickly means to accumulate virtue heavily.
By the heavy accumulation of virtue one can overcome everything.
If one can overcome everything, then he will acquire a capacity the limit of which is beyond anyone's knowledge.
When his capacity is beyond anyone's knowledge, he is fit to rule a state.
He who possesses the Mother (Tao)[107] of the state will last long.

---

[105] See *Analects*, 15:4. [106] These three lines are very obscure.
[107] See above, n.97.

This means that the roots are deep and the stalks are firm,
which is the way of long life and everlasting existence.[108]

60. Ruling a big country is like cooking a small fish.[109]
If Tao is employed to rule the empire,
Spiritual beings will lose their supernatural power.
Not that they lose their spiritual power,
But their spiritual power can no longer harm people.
Not only will their supernatural power not harm people,
But the sage also will not harm people.
When both do not harm each other,
Virtue will be accumulated in both for the benefit [of the
people].[110]

61. A big country may be compared to the lower part of a river.
It is the converging point of the world;
It is the female of the world.
The female always overcomes the male by tranquillity,
And by tranquillity she is underneath.
A big state can take over a small state if it places itself below
the small state;
And the small state can take over a big state if it places itself
below the big state.
Thus some, by placing themselves below, take over (others),
And some, by being (naturally) low, take over (other
states).

After all, what a big state wants is but to annex and herd
others,
And what a small state wants is merely to join and serve
others.
Since both big and small states get what they want,
The big state should place itself low.

62. Tao is the storehouse[111] of all things.
It is the good man's treasure and the bad man's refuge.
Fine words can buy honor,
And fine deeds can gain respect from others.[112]

---

[108] Meaning everlasting existence.
[109] Too much handling will spoil it.
[110] This interpretation follows *Han Fei Tzu*, ch. 20, SPTK, 6:6a; see Liao, p.
187.
[111] Literally the southwestern corner of the house, where treasures were stored.
[112] The punctuation and interpretation of this sentence follow Wei Yüan, who
has the authority of *Huai-nan Tzu*, chs. 12 and 18, SPPY, 12:11b and 18:9a, as
well as the Fu I text. The sentence is missing from Morgan's translation, *Tao. The
Great Luminant*, p. 123.

Even if a man is bad, when has (Tao) rejected him?

Therefore on the occasion of crowning an emperor or installing the three ministers,[113]

Rather than present large pieces of jade preceded by teams of four horses,

It is better to kneel and offer this Tao.

Why did the ancients highly value this Tao?

Did they not say, "Those who seek shall have it and those who sin shall be freed"?

For this reason it is valued by the world.

63. Act without action.

Do without ado.

Taste without tasting.

Whether it is big or small, many or few,[114] repay hatred with virtue.

Prepare for the difficult while it is still easy.

Deal with the big while it is still small.

Difficult undertakings have always started with what is easy,

And great undertakings have always started with what is small.

Therefore the sage never strives for the great,

And thereby the great is achieved.[115]

He who makes rash promises surely lacks faith.

He who takes things too easily will surely encounter much difficulty.

For this reason even the sage regards things as difficult,

And therefore he encounters no difficulty.

Comment. The Taoist doctrine of walking the second mile,[116] which was unacceptable to Confucius.[117]

64. What remains still is easy to hold.

What is not yet manifest is easy to plan for.

What is brittle is easy to crack.

What is minute is easy to scatter.

Deal with things before they appear.

Put things in order before disorder arises.

A tree as big as a man's embrace grows from a tiny shoot.

---

[113] Grand tutor, grand preceptor, and grand protector.

[114] The text reads "big small, many few" and can therefore be open to many interpretations.

[115] Repeats the sentence in *Lao Tzu*, ch. 34.

[116] Also taught in ch. 49.   [117] See *Analects*, 14:36.

A tower of nine storeys begins with a heap of earth.
The journey of a thousand *li*[118] starts from where one stands.
He who takes an action fails.
He who grasps things loses them.
For this reason the sage takes no action and therefore does not fail.
He grasps nothing and therefore he does not lose anything.
People in their handling of affairs often fail when they are about to succeed.
If one remains as careful at the end as he was at the beginning, there will be no failure.
Therefore the sage desires to have no desire.[119]
He does not value rare treasures.[120]
He learns to be unlearned,[121] and returns to what the multitude has missed (Tao).
Thus he supports all things in their natural state but does not take any action.

65. In ancient times those who practiced Tao well
Did not seek to enlighten the people, but to make them ignorant.
People are difficult to govern because they have too much knowledge.
Therefore he who rules the state through knowledge is a robber of the state;
He who rules a state not through knowledge is a blessing to the state.
One who knows these two things also (knows) the standard.
Always to know the standard is called profound and secret virtue.
Virtue becomes deep and far-reaching,
And with it all things return to their original natural state.
Then complete harmony will be reached.

66. The great rivers and seas are kings of all mountain streams
Because they skillfully stay below them.
That is why they can be their kings.

---

[118] A *li* is about one-third of a mile.
[119] Ho-shang Kung interpreted "desire not desire" to mean that the sage desires what the multitude does not desire.
[120] This sentence repeats the one in *Lao Tzu*, ch. 3.
[121] "Learn not learn": Wang Pi understood the expression to mean that the sage learns without learning, and Ho-shang Kung interpreted it to mean that the sage learns what the multitude cannot learn.

Therefore, in order to be the superior of the people,
    One must, in the use of words, place himself below them.
And in order to be ahead of the people,
    One must, in one's own person, follow them.
Therefore the sage places himself above the people and they
    do not feel his weight.
He places himself in front of them and the people do not
    harm him.
Therefore the world rejoices in praising him without getting
    tired of it.
It is precisely because he does not compete that the world
    cannot compete with him.[122]

67. All the world says that my Tao is great[123] and does not seem
    to resemble (the ordinary).[124]
It is precisely because it is great that it does not resemble
    (the ordinary).
If it did resemble, it would have been small for a long time.
I have three treasures. Guard and keep them:
    The first is deep love,
    The second is frugality,
    And the third is not to dare to be ahead of the world.
Because of deep love, one is courageous.
Because of frugality, one is generous.
Because of not daring to be ahead of the world, one becomes
    the leader of the world.
Now, to be courageous by forsaking deep love,
To be generous by forsaking frugality,
And to be ahead of the world by forsaking following
    behind—
    This is fatal.
For deep love helps one to win in the case of attack,
    And to be firm in the case of defense.
When Heaven is to save a person,
    Heaven will protect him through deep love.

68. A skillful leader of troops is not oppressive with his military
    strength.[125]

[122] Repeating *Lao Tzu*, ch. 22.

[123] The second sentence clearly shows that the first should not be punctuated after the word "great" and it should not be translated as "greatly," as is done in some translations.

[124] The term *pu-hsiao* is open to many possible interpretations: unworthy, seems to be like folly, indescribable, cannot be distinguished, etc.

[125] The interpretation of this sentence follows Wang Pi.

A skillful fighter does not become angry.

A skillful conqueror does not compete with people.

One who is skillful in using men puts himself below them.

This is called the virtue of not-competing.

This is called the strength to use men.

This is called matching Heaven, the highest principle of old.[126]

69. The strategists say:

"I dare not take the offensive but I take the defensive;
I dare not advance an inch but I retreat a foot."

This means:

To march without formation,

To stretch one's arm without showing it,

To confront enemies without seeming to meet them,

To hold weapons without seeming to have them.

There is no greater disaster than to make light of the enemy.

Making light of the enemy will destroy my treasures.[127]

Therefore when armies are mobilized and issues joined,

The man who is sorry[128] over the fact will win.

70. My doctrines are very easy to understand and very easy to practice,

But none in the world can understand or practice them.

My doctrines have a source (Nature); my deeds have a master (Tao).

It is because people do not understand this that they do not understand me.

Few people know me, and therefore I am highly valued.

Therefore the sage wears a coarse cloth on top and carries jade within his bosom.

71. To know that you do not know is the best.[129]

To pretend to know when you do not know is a disease.

Only when one recognizes this disease as a disease can one be free from the disease.

The sage is free from the disease.

Because he recognizes this disease to be disease, he is free from it.

[126] Most commentators agree that "of old" here is spurious.

[127] We are not sure if the treasures referred to are those in *Lao Tzu*, ch. 67. According to Ho-shang Kung, the latter part does not mean "will destroy my treasures" but "will destroy my body right here."

[128] To Wang Pi, *ai* here does not mean sorrow but kindness.

[129] Ho-shang Kung's interpretation: To know Tao and say you do not know is the best.

Comment. Note the similarity with the Confucian teaching: say that you know when you do know and say that you do not know when you do not know.[130]

72. When the people do not fear of what is dreadful,[131]
   Then what is greatly dreadful will descend on them.
   Do not reduce the living space of their dwellings.
   Do not oppress their lives.
   It is because you do not oppress them that they are not oppressed.
   Therefore the sage knows himself but does not show himself.
   He loves himself but does not exalt himself.
   Therefore he rejects the one but accepts the other.

73. He who is brave in daring will be killed.
   He who is brave in not daring will live.
   Of these two, one is advantageous and one is harmful.
   Who knows why Heaven dislikes what it dislikes?
   Even the sage considers it a difficult question.
   The Way of Heaven does not compete, and yet it skillfully achieves victory.
   It does not speak, and yet it skillfully responds to things.
   It comes to you without your invitation.
   It is not anxious about things and yet it plans well.
   Heaven's net is indeed vast.
   Though its meshes are wide, it misses nothing.

Comment. The analogy of Heaven's net has strongly strengthened the Chinese belief in retribution and formed the basis of popular Taoist religious treatises such as the *T'ai-shang kan-ying p'ien* (Tract of Influence and Responses of the Most Exalted One).

74. The people are not afraid of death.
   Why, then, threaten them with death?
   Suppose the people are always afraid of death and we can seize those who are vicious and kill them,
   Who would dare to do so?
   There is always the master executioner (Heaven) who kills.
   To undertake executions for the master executioner is like hewing wood for the master carpenter.
   Whoever undertakes to hew wood for the master carpenter rarely escapes injuring his own hands.

[130] *Analects*, 2:17.
[131] According to Chiao Hung, *wei*, ordinarily meaning power, here means to be dreadful. According to Ho-shang Kung, however, it means what is harmful.

75. The people starve because the ruler eats too much tax-grain.
    Therefore they starve.
    They are difficult to rule because their ruler does too many
        things.
    Therefore they are difficult to rule.
    The people take death lightly because their ruler strives for
        life too vigorously.
    Therefore they take death lightly.
    It is only those who do not seek after life that excel in making
        life valuable.

76. When man is born, he is tender and weak.
    At death, he is stiff and hard.
    All things, the grass as well as trees, are tender and supple
        while alive.
    When dead, they are withered and dried.
    Therefore the stiff and the hard are companions of death.
    The tender and the weak are companions of life.
    Therefore if the army is strong, it will not win.
    If a tree is stiff, it will break.
    The strong and the great are inferior, while the tender and
        the weak are superior.

77. Heaven's Way is indeed like the bending of a bow.
    When (the string) is high, bring it down.
    When it is low, raise it up.
    When it is excessive, reduce it.
    When it is insufficient, supplement it.
    The Way of Heaven reduces whatever is excessive and
        supplements whatever is insufficient.
    The way of man is different.
    It reduces the insufficient to offer to the excessive.
    Who is able to have excess to offer to the world?
    Only the man of Tao.
    Therefore the sage acts, but does not rely on his own ability.[132]
    He accomplishes his task, but does not claim credit for it.[133]
    He has no desire to display his excellence.

78. There is nothing softer and weaker than water,
    And yet there is nothing better for attacking hard and
        strong things.
    For this reason there is no substitute for it.

[132] This sentence is found also in *Lao Tzu*, chs. 2, 10, 51.
[133] Repeating the sentence in ch. 2 with the variation of one word.

All the world knows that the weak overcomes the strong and
the soft overcomes the hard.
But none can practice it.
Therefore the sage says:
He who suffers disgrace for his country
Is called the lord of the land.
He who takes upon himself the country's misfortunes
Becomes the king of the empire.
Straight words seem to be their opposite.

79. To patch up great hatred is surely to leave some hatred
behind.
How can this be regarded as good?
Therefore the sage keeps the left-hand portion (obligation)
of a contract
And does not blame the other party.
Virtuous people attend to their left-hand portions,
While those without virtue attend to other people's mistakes.
"The Way of Heaven has no favorites.
It is always with the good man."[134]

80. Let there be a small country with few people.
Let there be ten times and a hundred times[135] as many
utensils
But let them not be used.
Let the people value their lives highly and not migrate far.
Even if there are ships and carriages, none will ride in them.
Even if there are armor and weapons, none will display
them.
Let the people again knot cords and use them (in place of
writing).
Let them relish their food, beautify their clothing, be content
with their homes, and delight in their customs.
Though neighboring communities overlook one another
and the crowing of cocks and barking of dogs can be heard,
Yet the people there may grow old and die without ever
visiting one another.

81. True words are not beautiful;
Beautiful words are not true.

[134] A common ancient proverb.
[135] According to Yu Yüeh (1821-1906) *Chu-tzu p'ing-i* (Textual Critique of
the Various Philosophers), ch. 8, 1898 ed., 8:22 a-b, *shih-po* (ten, hundred) also
means military weapons.

A good man does not argue;
He who argues is not a good man.
A wise man has no extensive knowledge;
He who has extensive knowledge is not a wise man.
The sage does not accumulate for himself.
The more he uses for others, the more he has himself.
The more he gives to others, the more he possesses of his own.
The Way of Heaven is to benefit others and not to injure.
The Way of the sage is to act but not to compete.

8

THE MYSTICAL WAY OF CHUANG TZU

CHUANG TZU (bet. 399 and 295 B.C.) has always fascinated the Chinese mind. He takes his readers to undreamed of lands and stimulates them through conversations of the shadow, the skeleton, and the north wind. His freshness of insight and broadness of vision are in themselves inspiring. He seems to transcend the mundane world, yet he is always in the very depth of daily life. He is quietistic, yet for him life moves on like a galloping horse. He is mystical, but at the same time he follows reason as the leading light.

All this is a direct product of his concept of Nature. To him, Nature is not only spontaneity but nature in the state of constant flux and incessant transformation. This is the universal process that binds all things into one, equalizing all things and all opinions. The pure man makes this oneness his eternal abode, in which he becomes a "companion" of Nature and does not attempt to interfere with it by imposing the way of man on it. His goal is absolute spiritual emancipation and peace, to be achieved through knowing the capacity and limitations of one's own nature, nourishing it, and adapting it to the universal process of transformation. He abandons selfishness of all descriptions, be it fame, wealth, bias, or subjectivity. Having attained enlightenment through the light of Nature, he moves in the realm of "great knowledge" and "profound virtue." Thus he is free. As the *Chuang Tzu* itself says of him, "Alone he associates with Heaven and Earth and spirit, without abandoning or despising things of the world. He does not quarrel over right or wrong and mingles with conventional society. . . . Above, he roams with the Creator, and below he makes friends with those who transcend life and death and beginning and end. In regard to the essential, he is broad and comprehensive, profound and unrestrained. In regard to the fundamental, he may be said to have harmonized all things and penetrated the highest level. However, in his response to change and his understanding of things, his principle is inexhaustible, traceless, dark and obscure, and unfathomable."[1]

It is interesting to note that the above account is separate from that on Lao Tzu.[2] Although it has been customary to speak of Lao Tzu and Chuang Tzu together as Lao-Chuang, actually the practice did not begin

---

[1] Ch. 33, NHCC, 10:37a-38a. Cf. Giles, trans., *Chuang Tzu*, 1961 ed., pp. 318-321.

[2] See above, ch. 7, n.5.

until the fifth century.[3] Clearly, just as Mencius did not merely elaborate on Confucius' doctrines but presented something new, so Chuang Tzu definitely advanced beyond Lao Tzu. The Tao in Lao Tzu is still worldly, whereas in Chuang Tzu it becomes transcendental. While Lao Tzu emphasizes the difference between glory and disgrace, strength and weakness, and so forth, and advocates the tender values, Chuang Tzu identifies them all. Lao Tzu aims at reform, but Chuang Tzu prefers to "travel beyond the mundane world." His concept of te as Tao individualized in the nature of things is much more developed and more clearly stated. There is in him a greater stress on following one's nature, nourishing it, and adapting it to environment. Thus there is a stronger emphasis on the individual, which eventually led to the over-all importance of particular nature in particular things in Neo-Taoism, especially in his first, and still the best commentator, Kuo Hsiang (d. 312). Furthermore, the idea of self-tranformation takes on a central focus in Chuang Tzu, which presents life and reality as dynamic and ever-changing, thus making a comparison with him and Heraclitus or Hegel stimulating as well as instructive. To regard transformation as the final abode of life is certainly a new note in Chinese philosophy.

In Chuang Tzu, too, differences between Confucianism and Taoism become much sharper. The Confucianists teach full development of one's nature, fulfillment of one's destiny, and participation in the creative work of Nature. Chuang Tzu, on the other hand, believes in nourishing nature, returning to destiny, and enjoying Nature. The Confucianists want people transformed through education, but Chuang Tzu leaves transformation to things themselves. These differences from Confucianism of course make Chuang Tzu all the more Taoistic. It is not wrong, after all, to link Lao Tzu and Chuang Tzu together, although it must be borne in mind that he certainly carried Taoism to new heights.

By and large Confucianists have been critical of Chuang Tzu. Hsün Tzu (fl. 298–238 B.C.) said that he was "prejudiced in favor of Nature and does not know man."[4] Ssu-ma Ch'ien (145–86 B.C.?), the famous historian and the first biographer of Chuang Tzu, characterized his work as "empty talk not based on facts . . . primarily aimed at pleasing himself and useless to rulers of men."[5] And Chu Hsi (1130-1200), the leading Neo-Confucianist, complained, "Lao Tzu still wanted to do something, but Chuang Tzu did not want to do anything at all. He even said that he knew what to do but just did not want to do it."[6] As a matter

---

[3] In the *Hou-Han shu* (History of the Later Han Dynasty, 25-220), by Fan Yeh (398-445), ch. 90, pt. 1, PNP, 90A:1a.

[4] *Hsün Tzu*, ch. 21, SPTK, 15:5b. Cf. Dubs, trans., *Works of Hsüntze*, p. 264.

[5] *Shih chi* (Records of the Historian), PNP, 63:5a.

[6] *Chu Tzu yü-lei* (Classified Conversations of Chu Hsi), 1880 ed., 125:4a.

of fact, he was so much rejected by Chinese thinkers that since the fifth century, his doctrines have never been propagated by any outstanding scholar.

This does not mean that he has not been influential, however. On the contrary, his impact on Buddhism has been tremendous, especially in the development of the Zen School. He has been a main source of inspiration in Chinese landscape painting and poetry. As part of Taoism, his philosophy helped to transform ancient and medieval Confucianism into Neo-Confucianism, which is Chu Hsi's own philosophy. His revolt against traditionalism and conventional standards, his poetic mysticism, his subtle individualism, his insight into human nature, his profound interest in how to live and how to respond to all things, and his broad view of things remained inexhaustible sources of inspiration for the Chinese.

We don't know much about him, except that according to Ssu-ma Ch'ien's account his personal name was Chou, he was once a small official, and he declined an offer to become a prime minister in order to retain his freedom. His dates are uncertain, probably between 399 and 295 B.C. He and Mencius were contemporaries, but evidently neither was aware of the other, in all likelihood because of geographical separation.

The following selections include chapters 2 and 6 in full from the *Chuang Tzu*. The former reveals his philosophy, the latter his way of life.

THE CHUANG TZU[7]

A. The Equality of Things (ch. 2)

Tzu-chi of Nan-kuo sat leaning on a low table. Looking up to heaven, he sighed and seemed to be at a loss as if his spirit had left him. Yen Ch'eng Tzu-yu (his pupil), who was standing in attendance in front of him, said, "What is the matter? The body may be allowed to be like dry wood but should the mind be allowed to be like dead ashes? Surely the man leaning on the table now is not the same man leaning on the table before."

Comment. The *Chuang Tzu* is a rich reservoir of imageries. The dry wood and dead ashes have become common idioms in Chinese

---

[7] The *Chuang Tzu*, also called the *Nan-hua chen-ching* (Pure Classic of Nan-hua, the meaning of the term "nan-hua" being unknown), is in 33 chapters. Most scholars accept the first seven, the so-called "inner chapters," as Chuang Tzu's own works, the other fifteen "outer" chapters and the eleven "miscellaneous" chapters as works by his pupils or other people later, although some passages may well be from Chuang Tzu's own hand. For English translations, see Bibliography.

literature and philosophy. They represent the persistent questions whether man is a spirit and whether the mind is alert.

"Aren't you asking a good question!" Tzu-chi replied. "Do you know that I have just lost myself? You have heard the music of man but not the music of earth. You may have heard the music of the earth but not the music of heaven."

"I beg to ask about its composition," said Tzu-yu.

"The breath of the universe is called wind," said Tzu-chi. "At times it is inactive. But when active, angry sounds come from thousands of hollows. Have you never listened to its prolonged roar? The peaks and heights[8] of mountains and forests, and the hollows and cavities of huge trees many a span in girth are like nostrils, mouths, ears, beam-sockets, goblets, mortars, puddles, and pools. [The wind rushes into them,] rushing, whizzing, making an explosive and rough noise, or a withdrawing and soft one, shouting, wailing, moaning, and crying. The wind that comes ahead sings 'yü' and the wind that follows echoes 'yung.' When the winds are gentle, the harmony is small, and when the winds are violent, the harmonies are great. When the fierce gusts stop, all hollows become empty and silent. Have you never witnessed how the trees swing and bend [after the wind is gone]?"

Tzu-yu said, "Since the music of earth consists of sounds produced in the various hollows, and the music of man consists of sounds produced in a series of flutes, what is the music of heaven?"

"The wind blows in a thousand different ways," replied Tzu-chi, "but the sounds are all produced in their own way. They do so by themselves. Who is there to rouse them to action?"

Great knowledge is leisurely and at ease,[9] (or all-embracing and extensive)[10] whereas small knowledge is inquisitive (or partial and discriminative).[11] Great speech is simple (as in simple taste) whereas small speech is full of details. Whether in sleep when the various elements of the spirit are interlocked in dreams, or when awake when the body is free to move and act, in all their contacts and associations, some of our minds are leisurely, some are deep, and some are serious. We scheme and fight with our minds. When we have small fears we are worried, and when we have great fears we are totally at a loss. One's mind shoots

[8] The reading here follows the commentary by Wang Hsien-ch'ien (1842-1917), *Chuang Tzu chi-chieh* (Collected Commentaries on the *Chuang Tzu*).

[9] This is the interpretation of Lu Ch'ang-keng (fl. 1566), *Nan-hua chen-ching fu-mo* (Commentary on the *Chuang Tzu*).

[10] According to Chang Ping-lin (Chang T'ai-yen, 1868-1936), *Ch'i-wu lun shih* (Explanations of "The Equality of Things"), the interpretation is: all embracing and extensive.

[11] Chang's interpretation.

forth like an arrow to be the arbiter of right and wrong. Now it is reserved like a solemn pledge, in order to maintain its own advantage. Then, like the destruction of autumn and winter, it declines every day. Then it is sunk in pleasure and cannot be covered. Now it is closed like a seal, that is, it is old and exhausted. And finally it is near death and cannot be given life again. Pleasure and anger, sorrow and joy, anxiety and regret, fickleness and fear, impulsiveness and extravagance, indulgence and lewdness come to us like music from the hollows or like mushrooms from damp. Day and night they alternate within us but we don't know where they come from. Alas! These are with us morning and evening. It's here where they are produced![12]

Without them (the feelings mentioned above) there would not be I. And without me who will experience them? They are right near by. But we don't know who causes them. It seems there is a True Lord who does so, but there is no indication of his existence.

> *Comment.* This sentence has exerted profound influence on Chinese thought and has fortified the long tradition of agnosticism. Later Chuang Tzu speaks of the Creator, but as it will be pointed out later, that does not mean a God directing the operation of the universe. Demiéville thinks that questions in the *Chuang Tzu* about the existence of the Creator are not to deny his existence but, rather, a peculiar way to indicate, without a name, the principle which has a strongly religious character.[13] The naturalism in Chuang Tzu is so strong that Demiéville is right only if by principle he means Nature. Any personal God or one that directs the movement of things is clearly out of harmony with Chuang Tzu's philosophy.

There is evidence of activity (of the self?) but we do not see its physical form. It has reality but no physical form.[14] The hundred bones, the nine external cavities and the six internal organs are all complete in the body. Which part shall I love best? Would you say to love them all? But there is bound to be some preference. Do they all serve as servants of someone else? Since servants cannot govern themselves, do they serve as master and servant by turn? Surely there must be a true ruler who controls them![15]

[12] Commentators do not agree on what this means. The tendency has been to interpret this to mean that the self is the source of these psychological conditions.

[13] "Enigmes taoïstes," Kaizuka Shigeki, ed., *Silver Jubilee Volume of Zinbun-Kagaku-Kenkyusyo,* pp. 54-60.

[14] We are not sure whether these descriptions refer to the emotions, the True Lord, or the Way (Tao). In ch. 6 of the *Chuang Tzu,* NHCC, 3:10a (Giles, trans., *Chuang Tzu,* 1961 ed., p. 76) it says that "Tao has reality and evidence but no action or physical form." See Fung, trans., *Chuang Tzu,* p. 117.

[15] Some commentators turned this into a question. There is no justification for

But whether we discover its reality or not, it does not affect its being true. Once it received the bodily form complete, it does not fail to function until the end. Whether in conflict or in harmony with things, it always pursues its course like a galloping horse which no one can stop. Is this not pitiful indeed? To toil all one's life without seeing its success and to be wearied and worn out without knowing where to end—is this not lamentable? People say there is no death. But what is the use? Not only does the physical form disintegrate; the mind also goes with it. Is that not very lamentable? Are men living in this world really so ignorant? Or am I alone ignorant while others are not?

If we are to follow what is formed in our mind as a guide, who will not have such a guide? Not only those who know the succession [of day and night] and choose them by exercising their own minds have them (opinions). Stupid people have theirs too. To have opinions as to right or wrong before [the feelings] are produced in the mind is as mistaken as to say that "one goes to the state of Yüeh today and arrives there yesterday."[16] This is to turn what is not into what is. Even Yü[17] with his spiritual intelligence cannot know how to turn what is not into what is. How can I?

For speech is not merely the blowing of breath. The speaker has something to say, but what he says is not final. Has something been said? Or has something not been said? It may be different from the chirping of chickens. But is there really any difference? Or is there no difference?

How can Tao be so obscured that there should be a distinction of true and false? How can speech be so obscured that there should be a distinction of right and wrong? Where can you go and find Tao not to exist? Where can you go and find speech impossible? Tao is obscured by petty biases and speech is obscured by flowery expressions. Therefore there have arisen the controversies between the Confucianists and the Moists, each school regarding as right what the other considers as wrong, and regarding as wrong what the other considers as right. But to show that what each regards as right is wrong or to show that what each regards as wrong is right, there is no better way than to use the light (of Nature).

There is nothing that is not the "that" and there is nothing that is not the "this." Things do not know that they are the "that" of other things; they only know what they themselves know. Therefore I say that the "that" is produced by the "this" and the "this" is also caused by the

doing so. But whether this "true ruler" is the True Lord mentioned above or the self is not clear.

[16] One of Hui Shih's paradoxical sayings. See below, ch. 10, A, 7.

[17] Founder of Hsia dynasty (2183–1752 B.C.?).

"that." This is the theory of mutual production.[18] Nevertheless, when there is life there is death,[19] and when there is death there is life. When there is possibility, there is impossibility, and when there is impossibility, there is possibility. Because of the right, there is the wrong, and because of the wrong, there is the right. Therefore the sage does not proceed along these lines (of right and wrong, and so forth) but illuminates the matter with Nature. This is the reason.

The "this" is also the "that." The "that" is also the "this." The "this" has one standard of right and wrong, and the "that" also has a standard of right and wrong. Is there really a distinction between "that" and "this"? Or is there really no distinction between "that" and "this"? When "this" and "that" have no opposites,[20] there is the very axis of Tao. Only when the axis occupies the center of a circle can things in their infinite complexities be responded to. The right is an infinity. The wrong is also an infinity. Therefore I say that there is nothing better than to use the light (of Nature).

> *Comment.* Things are not only relative, they are identical, for opposites produce each other, imply each other, are identical with each other, and are both finite series. In some respects Chuang Tzu is surprisingly similar to Hegel and Nāgārjuna (c. 100–200).[21] It must be quickly added, however, that both the dialectic of Hegel and the relativity of Nāgārjuna are much more conceptual than Chuang Tzu's synthesis of opposites.

To take a mark (*chih*) to show that a mark is not a mark is not as good as to take a non-mark to show that a mark is not a mark. To take a horse to show that a [white] horse is not a horse (as such) is not as good as to take a non-horse to show that a horse is not a horse.[22] The universe is but one mark, and all things are but a horse. When [people say], "All right," then [things are] all right. When people say, "Not all right," then [things are] not all right. A road becomes so when people

[18] According to Ch'ien Mu, *Chuang Tzu tsuan-chien* (Collected Commentaries on the *Chuang Tzu*), 1951, *fang-sheng* means simultaneously coming into being. It means simultaneous production or causation. The idea is that one implies or involves the other, or coexistence. The emphasis here, however, is the causal relation rather than coexistence.

[19] The same saying appears in Hui Shih's (380–305 B.C.) paradoxes. See below, ch. 10, A, 4.

[20] Interpretation following Kuo Hsiang, whose commentary on *Chuang Tzu* is the most important of all. However, Kuo's commentary is more a system of his own philosophy than explanation of the text. For his philosophy, see below, ch. 19, sec. 6.

[21] See below, ch. 22, comment on sec. 1.

[22] This is clearly a criticism of Kung-sun Lung (b. 380 B.C.?). See below, ch. 10, B.

walk on it,[23] and things become so-and-so [to people] because people call them so-and-so. How have they become so? They have become so because [people say they are] so. How have they become not so? They have become not so because [people say they are] not so. In their own way things are so-and-so. In their own way things are all right. There is nothing that is not so-and-so. There is nothing that is not all right. Let us take, for instance, a large beam and a small beam, or an ugly woman and Hsi-shih (famous beauty of ancient China), or generosity, strangeness, deceit, and abnormality. The Tao identifies them all as one. What is division [to some] is production [to others], and what is production [to others] is destruction [to some]. Whether things are produced or destroyed, [Tao] again identifies them all as one.

Only the intelligent knows how to identify all things as one. Therefore he does not use [his own judgment] but abides in the common [principle]. The common means the useful and the useful means identification. Identification means being at ease with oneself. When one is at ease with himself, one is near Tao. This is to let it (Nature) take its own course.[24] He has arrived at this situation,[25] and does not know it. This is Tao.

Those who wear out their intelligence to try to make things one without knowing that they are really the same may be called "three in the morning." What is meant by "three in the morning"? A monkey keeper once was giving out nuts and said, "Three in the morning and four in the evening." All the monkeys became angry. He said, "If that is the case, there will be four in the morning and three in the evening." All the monkeys were glad. Neither the name nor the actuality has been reduced but the monkeys reacted in joy and anger [differently]. The keeper also let things take their own course. Therefore the sage harmonizes the right and wrong and rests in natural equalization. This is called following two courses at the same time.

> *Comment.* The doctrine of following two courses at the same time has become a cardinal one in practically all Chinese philosophical schools. We have read in the *Doctrine of the Mean* that several courses can be pursued without conflict.[26] The reference there is to the rotation of heavenly bodies, but the Chinese have taken it to mean life in general. In the *Book of Changes*, it is said that "in the world there are many different roads but the destination is the same."[27] The upshot is that most Chinese follow the three systems

[23] According to Wang Hsien-ch'ien, *tao* here does not mean Tao but a road.

[24] Other interpretations: (1) This is because he relies on this (that is, Tao); (2) he stops with this.

[25] Another interpretation: He has stopped.

[26] Ch. 30.

[27] "Appended Remarks," pt. 2, ch. 5. Cf. Legge, trans., *Yi King*, p. 389.

of Confucianism, Taoism, and Buddhism, and usually take a multiple approach to things.

The knowledge of the ancients was perfect. In what way was it perfect? There were those who believed that nothing existed. Such knowledge is indeed perfect and ultimate and cannot be improved. The next were those who believed there were things but there was no distinction between them. Still the next were those who believed there was distinction but there was neither right nor wrong. When the distinction between right and wrong became prominent, Tao was thereby reduced. Because Tao was reduced, individual bias was formed. But are there really production and reduction? Is there really no production or reduction? That there are production and reduction is like Chao Wen[28] playing the lute [with petty opinions produced in his mind]. That there is no production or reduction is like Chao Wen not playing the lute,[29] [thus leaving things alone]. Chao Wen played the lute. Master K'uang[30] wielded the stick to keep time. And Hui Tzu[31] leaned against a drayanda tree [to argue]. The knowledge of these three gentlemen was almost perfect, and therefore they practiced their art to the end of their lives. Because they liked it, they became different from others, and they wished to enlighten others with what they liked. They were not to be enlightened and yet they insisted on enlightening them. Therefore Hui Tzu lived throughout his life discussing the obscure doctrines of hardness and whiteness.[32] And Chao Wen's son devoted his whole life to his heritage but ended with no success. Can these be called success? If so, even I am a success. Can these not be called success? If so, then neither I nor anything else can be called a success. Therefore the sage aims at removing the confusions and doubts that dazzle people. Because of this he does not use [his own judgment] but abides in the common principle. This is what is meant by using the light (of Nature).

Suppose we make a statement. We don't know whether it belongs to one category or another. Whether one or the other, if we put them in one, then one is not different from the other. However, let me explain. There was a beginning. There was a time before that beginning. And there was a time before the time which was before that beginning. There was being. There was non-being. There was a time before that non-being. And there was a time before the time that was before that non-being.

---

[28] Identity unknown.
[29] Kuo Hsiang said in his commentary, "Not all sounds can be produced."
[30] Ancient musician famous for his sharpness in listening.
[31] Hui Shih. See below, ch. 10, A.
[32] In ch. 5 of the *Chuang Tzu*, NHCC, 2:44a, Giles, pp. 69-70, Chuang Tzu refers to Hui Tzu's discussion and doctrines.

Suddenly there is being and there is non-being, but I don't know which of being and non-being is really being or really non-being. I have just said something, but I don't know if what I have said really says something or says nothing.

There is nothing in the world greater than the tip of a hair that grows in the autumn, while Mount T'ai is small.[33] No one lives a longer life than a child who dies in infancy, but P'eng-tsu (who lived many hundred years) died prematurely. The universe and I exist together, and all things and I are one. Since all things are one, what room is there for speech? But since I have already said that all things are one, how can speech not exist? Speech and the one then make two. These two (separately) and the one (the two together) make three. Going from this, even the best mathematician cannot reach [the final number]. How much less can ordinary people! If we proceed from nothing to something and arrive at three, how much more shall we reach if we proceed from something to something! Let us not proceed. Let us let things take their own course.[34]

> *Comment.* The Taoist goal is to become one with all things and to coexist with Heaven and Earth. It is obviously not a philosophy of life negation. One does not reject the world. Instead, he enlarges it to include the whole universe.

In reality Tao has no limitation, and speech has no finality. Because of this there are clear demarcations. Let me talk about clear demarcations. There are the left and the right. There are discussions and theories. There are analyses and arguments. And there are competitions and quarrels. These are called the eight characteristics. What is beyond the world, the sage leaves it as it exists and does not discuss it. What is within the world, the sage discusses but does not pass judgment. About the chronicles of historical events and the records of ancient kings, the sage passes judgments but does not argue. Therefore there are things which analysis cannot analyze, and there are things which argument cannot argue. Why? The sage keeps it in his mind while men in general argue in order to brag before each other. Therefore it is said that argument arises from failure to see [the greatness of Tao].

Great Tao has no appellation. Great speech does not say anything. Great humanity (*jen*) is not humane (through any special effort).[35]

---

[33] This is similar to Hui Shih's paradox no. 3. See below, ch. 10, A.

[34] Another interpretation is: Let us stop.

[35] It means that a man of humanity is not humane in a deliberate or artificial way, and that he is not partial. See above, ch. 7, comment on *Lao Tzu*, ch. 5. The word *jen* is often rendered as love, kindness, human-heartedness, true mankind, etc. In its broad sense, it denotes the general virtue. For a discussion of the term, see Appendix.

Great modesty is not yielding. Great courage does not injure. Tao that is displayed is not Tao. Speech that argues is futile. Humanity that is specially permanent or specially attached to someone or something will not be comprehensive.[36] Modesty that is too apparent is not real. Courage that injures the nature of things will not succeed. These five are all-comprehensive and all-embracing but tend to develop sharp edges. Therefore he who knows to stop at what he does not know is perfect. Who knows the argument that requires no speech or the Tao that cannot be named? If anyone can know, he is called the store of Nature (which embraces all). This store is not full when more things are added and not empty when things are taken out. We don't know where it comes from. This is called dimmed light.[37]

Of old Emperor Yao said to Shun,[38] "I want to attack the states of Tsung, Kuei, and Hsü-ao. Since I have been on the throne, my mind has not been free from them. Why?"

"The rulers of these states are as lowly as weeds," replied Shun. "Why is your mind not free from them? Once there were ten suns shining simultaneously and all things were illuminated. How much more can virtue illuminate than the suns?"

Nieh Ch'üeh asked Wang I,[39] "Do you know in what respect all things are right?"

"How can I know?" replied Wang I.

"Do you know that you do not know?"

Wang I said, "How can I know?"

"Then have all things no knowledge?"

"How can I know?" answered Wang I. "Nevertheless, I will try to tell you. How can it be known that what I call knowing is not really not knowing and that what I call not knowing is not really knowing? Now let me ask you this: If a man sleeps in a damp place, he will have a pain in his loins and will dry up and die. Is that true of eels? If a man lives up in a tree, he will be frightened and tremble. Is that true of monkeys? Which of the three knows the right place to live? Men eat vegetables and flesh, and deer eat tender grass. Centipedes enjoy snakes, and owls and crows like mice. Which of the four knows the right taste? Monkey mates with the dog-headed female ape and the buck mates with the doe, and eels mate with fishes. Mao Ch'iang[40] and Li Chi[41] were considered by

[36] This is Kuo Hsiang's interpretation.

[37] This phrase is obscure. Each commentator has his own interpretation, which is mostly subjective.

[38] Legendary sage-emperors (3rd millennium B.C.).

[39] A virtuous man at the time of Yao, and teacher of Nieh Ch'üeh.

[40] Concubine of a king of Yüeh, which state ended in 334 B.C.

[41] Favorite of Duke Hsien (r. 676–651 B.C.) of Chin.

men to be beauties, but at the sight of them fish plunged deep down in the water, birds soared high up in the air, and deer dashed away. Which of the four knows the right kind of beauty? From my point of view, the principle of humanity and righteousness and the doctrines of right and wrong are mixed and confused. How do I know the difference among them?"

Comment. Chuang Tzu's spirit of doubt has substantially contributed to China's long tradition of skepticism.

"If you do not know what is beneficial and what is harmful," said Nieh Ch'üeh, "does it mean that the perfect man does not know them also?"

"The perfect man is a spiritual being," said Wang I. "Even if great oceans burned up, he would not feel hot. Even if the great rivers are frozen, he would not feel cold. And even if terrific thunder were to break up mountains and the wind were to upset the sea, he would not be afraid. Being such, he mounts upon the clouds and forces of heaven, rides on the sun and the moon, and roams beyond the four seas. Neither life nor death affects him. How much less can such matters as benefit and harm?"

Ch'ü-ch'iao Tzu asked Ch'ang-wu Tzu,[42] "I have heard from my grand master (Confucius) that the sage does not devote himself to worldly affairs. He does not go after gain nor avoid injury. He does not like to seek anything and does not purposely adhere to Tao. He speaks without speaking, and he does not speak when he speaks. Thus he roams beyond this dusty world. My grand master regarded this as a rough description of the sage, but I regard this to be the way the wonderful Tao operates. What do you think, sir?"

"What you have said would have perplexed even the Yellow Emperor," replied Ch'ang-wu Tzu. "How could Confucius be competent enough to know?" Moreover, you have drawn a conclusion too early. You see an egg and you immediately want a cock to crow, and you see a sling and you immediately want to roast a dove. Suppose I say a few words to you for what they are worth and you listen to them for what they are worth. How about it?

Comment. It is interesting that to Chuang Tzu, the wisest man was

[42] The identities of these men have not been established. Most probably they are fictitious, products of Chuang Tzu's creative imagination. Yü Yüeh (1821-1906), in his *Chu-tzu p'ing-i* (Textual Critiques of the Various Philosophers), ch. 17, 1899 ed., 17:6b, argues that since the term "grand master" which is the honorific for Confucius, is used, the questioner must have been a pupil of Confucius. This is not necessarily the case, for Chuang Tzu freely put words into the mouths of people, historic or imaginary.

neither Yao nor Shun, idols of Confucianists, but the Yellow Emperor of far greater antiquity. Although it is true that ancient Chinese schools competed in going as far back in history as possible to find their heroes, it would be a great mistake to interpret Chuang Tzu as backward-looking. He was purposely not following any popular tradition. Like Lao Tzu, he does not glorify any particular ancient sage-king.

"The sage has the sun and moon by his side. He grasps the universe under the arm. He blends everything into a harmonious whole, casts aside whatever is confused or obscured, and regards the humble as honorable. While the multitude toil, he seems to be stupid and non-discriminative. He blends the disparities of ten thousand years into one complete purity. All things are blended like this and mutually involve each other.

"How do I know that the love of life is not a delusion? And how do I know that the hate of death is not like a man who lost his home when young and does not know where his home is to return to? Li Chi was the daughter of the border warden of Ai. When the Duke of Chin first got her, she wept until the bosom of her dress was drenched with tears. But when she came to the royal residence, shared with the duke his luxurious couch and ate delicate food, she regretted that she had wept. How do I know that the dead will not repent having previously craved for life?

"Those who dream of the banquet may weep the next morning, and those who dream of weeping may go out to hunt after dawn. When we dream we do not know that we are dreaming. In our dreams we may even interpret our dreams. Only after we are awake do we know we have dreamed. Finally there comes a great awakening, and then we know life is a great dream. But the stupid think they are awake all the time, and believe they know it distinctly. Are we (honorable) rulers? Are we (humble) shepherds? How vulgar! Both Confucius and you were dreaming. When I say you were dreaming, I am also dreaming. This way of talking may be called perfectly strange. If after ten thousand generations we could meet one great sage who can explain this, it would be like meeting him in as short a time as in a single morning or evening.

"Suppose you and I argue. If you beat me instead of my beating you, are you really right and am I really wrong? If I beat you instead of your beating me, am I really right and are you really wrong? Or are we both partly right and partly wrong? Or are we both wholly right and wholly wrong? Since between us neither you nor I know which is right, others are naturally in the dark. Whom shall we ask to arbitrate? If we ask someone who agrees with you, since he has already agreed with you, how can he arbitrate? If we ask someone who agrees with me, since he has already agreed with me, how can he arbitrate? If we ask someone who disagrees with both you and me to arbitrate, since he has already disagreed with you and me, how can he arbitrate? If we ask someone who agrees with both you and me to arbitrate, since he has already agreed with you and me, how can he arbitrate? Thus among you, me, and others, none knows which is right. Shall we wait for still others? The great variety of sounds are relative to each other just as much as they are not relative to each other. To harmonize them in the functioning of Nature[43] and leave them in the process of infinite evolution is the way to complete our lifetime."[44]

"What is meant by harmonizing them with the functioning of Nature?"

"We say this is right or wrong, and is so or is not so. If the right is really right, then the fact that it is different from the wrong leaves no room for argument. If what is so is really so, then the fact that it is different from what is not so leaves no room for argument. Forget the passage of time (life and death) and forget the distinction of right and wrong. Relax in the realm of the infinite and thus abide in the realm of the infinite."

The Shade asks the Shadow, "A little while ago you moved, and now you stop. A little while ago you sat down and now you stand up. Why this instability of purpose?"

"Do I depend on something else to be this way?" answered the Shadow. "Does that something on which I depend also depend on something else? Do I depend on anything any more than a snake depends on its discarded scale or a cicada on its new wings? How can I tell why I am so or why I am not so?"

Once I, Chuang Chou, dreamed that I was a butterfly and was happy as a butterfly. I was conscious that I was quite pleased with myself, but I did not know that I was Chou. Suddenly I awoke, and there I was, visibly Chou. I do not know whether it was Chou dreaming that he was a butterfly or the butterfly dreaming that it was Chou. Between Chou and the butterfly there must be some distinction. [But one may be the other.] This is called the transformation of things. (NHCC, 1:18a-48b)

Comment. A beautiful story in itself, it is a complete rejection of

[43] This interpretation follows Kuo Hsiang. Ma Hsü-lun in his *Chuang Tzu i-cheng* (Textual Studies of the Meaning of the *Chuang Tzu*), 1930, 2:23b, says that it means the revolving process of Nature.

[44] In the text these two sentences follow the next four. Following some editions, I have shifted them here. It seems a most logical thing to do.

the distinction between subject and object and between reality and unreality.

B. The Great Teacher (ch. 6)

He who knows the activities of Nature (*T'ien*, Heaven) and the activities of man is perfect. He who knows the activities of Nature lives according to Nature. He who knows the activities of man nourishes what he does not know with what he does know, thus completing his natural span of life and will not die prematurely half of the way. This is knowledge at its supreme greatness.

However, there is some defect here. For knowledge depends on something to be correct, but what it depends on is uncertain and changeable. How do we know that what I call Nature is not really man and what I call man is not really Nature?

Furthermore, there must be the pure man before there can be true knowledge. What is meant by a pure man? The pure man of old did not mind having little, did not brag about accomplishments, and did not scheme about things. If [the opportunity] had gone, he would not regret, and if he was in accord [with his lot in life] he did not feel satisfied with himself. Being of this character, he could scale heights without fear, enter water without getting wet, and go through fire without feeling hot. Such is the knowledge that can at last[45] ascend to Tao.

The pure man of old slept without dreams and awoke without anxiety. He ate without indulging in sweet tastes and breathed deep breaths. The pure man draws breaths from the great depths of his heels, the multitude only from their throats. People defeated (in argument) utter words as if to vomit, and those who indulge in many desires have very little of the secret of Nature.

> *Comment.* It is tempting to equate Chuang Tzu's reference to breathing with Indian yoga. But there is a great deal of difference between them. What Chuang Tzu means is that we must go to the depth (the heels) of things. It is there that the "secret of Nature" (*t'ien-chi*) begins. By this secret is meant the secret operation of Nature, the way in which things spring forth. One should not try to get away from Nature but go to its depth. The idea of *t'ien-chi* has had a strong influence on Neo-Confucianists.[46]

[45] Following Wang K'ai-yün's (1832-1916) commentary.

[46] Especially Ch'eng I (Ch'eng I-ch'uan, 1033-1107). See *I-shu*, (Surviving Works), 2A:22a and *Wai-shu* (Additional Works), 12:8a, 14b, 15b, both in ECCS; and Wang Yang-ming (Wang Shou-jen, 1472-1529). See his *Ch'uan-hsi lu* (Instructions for Practical Living), secs. 202, 212, in Chan, trans., *Instructions for Practical Living*.

The pure man of old knew neither to love life nor to hate death. He did not rejoice in birth, nor did he resist death. Without any concern he came and without any concern he went, that was all. He did not forget his beginning nor seek his end. He accepted [his body] with pleasure, and forgetting [life and death], he returned to [the natural state]. He did not violate Tao with his mind, and he did not assist Nature with man. This is what is meant by a pure man.

> *Comment.* The doctrine of identifying life and death as one is not peculiar to Taoism, for it was common among several schools at Chuang Tzu's time. The point to note is that Taoism never glorifies death, as it is sometimes mistakenly understood.

Such being the pure man, his mind is perfectly at ease.[47] His demeanor is natural. His forehead is broad. He is as cold as autumn but as warm as spring. His pleasure and anger are as natural as the four seasons. He is in accord with all things, and no one knows the limit thereof. Therefore the sage, in employing an army, can destroy a country without losing the affection of the people. His benefits may be extended to ten thousand generations without any [partial] love for any man.

Therefore he who takes special delight in understanding things is not a sage. He who shows [special] affection [to anyone] is not a man of humanity (*jen*, love). He who calculates opportunity is not a worthy person. He who does not see through benefits and injuries is not a superior man. He who seeks fame and thus loses his own nature is not learned. And he who loses his own nature and thus misses the true way is not one who can have others do things for him. Such men as Hu Pu-chieh (who drowned himself rather than accept the throne from Yao), Wu Kuang (who also drowned himself instead of accepting the throne from T'ang), Po-i and Shu-ch'i (who, as citizens of the Shang, refused to eat the grains of the Chou and chose to starve to death), the viscount of Chi (who pretended to be mad and became a slave because the wicked King Chou did not accept his advice), Hsü Yü (a recluse who painted his body and pretended to be mad),[48] Chi T'o (who drowned himself when he heard that Wu Kuang had declined the throne and King T'ang might offer it to him), and Shen-t'u Ti (of the Shang, who drowned himself),[49] did things as others would have them do, took

---

[47] This is Kuo Hsiang's interpretation of the word *chih*. Others like Chiao Hung (1541-1620) in his *Chuang Tzu i* (An Aid to the *Chuang Tzu*) read *chih* as *wang*, forgetful, that is, being without thought.

[48] Possibly the same madman who ridiculed Confucius for his desperate efforts at reform (see *Analects*, 18:5) or Pi-kan who remonstrated with wicked King Chou (r. 1175-1112 B.C.), and was executed (see *Analects*, 18:1).

[49] Most of these figures are legendary.

delight in what others would delight, and did not take delight in what would be delightful to themselves.

The pure man of old was righteous[50] but impartial, and humble but not subservient. He was naturally independent but not obstinate. His humility was manifest but not displayed. Smiling, he seemed to be happy. He acted as if he had to. His countenance improved further and further in richness, and his virtue rested more and more in the [highest good]. His efforts seemed to be those of the common people, but his loftiness could not be restrained. Deep and profound, he seemed to be like a closed door (unfathomable). Without any attachment, he seemed to have forgotten what he said. He considered law as part of the nature [of government and not of his making], ceremonies as an aid [wanted by people themselves], knowledge as a [product of] time, and virtue as people's observance. To regard law as part of the nature of government means to be broad-minded when it comes to killing. To regard ceremonies as an aid to people themselves means that they prevail in the world [like conventions]. To regard knowledge as a product of time means to respond to events as if they had to be. And to regard virtue as people's observance means that it is comparable to the fact that anyone with two feet can climb a hill, but people think that a pure man makes diligent effort to do so. Therefore what he liked was one and what he did not like was also one. That which was one was one and that which was not one was also one. He who regards all things as one is a companion of Nature. He who does not regard all things as one is a companion of man. Neither Nature nor man should overcome the other. This is what is meant by a pure man.

Life and death are due to fate (*ming*, destiny) and their constant succession like day and night is due to Nature, beyond the interference of man. They are the necessary character of things. There are those who regard Heaven as their father and love it with their whole person. How much more should they love what is more outstanding than Heaven [that is, self-transformation itself]?[51] There are those who regard the ruler as superior to themselves and would sacrifice their lives for him. How much more should they sacrifice for what is more real than the ruler (Nature)?[52]

When the springs are dried up, the fishes crowd together on the land. They moisten each other with the dampness around them and keep one another wet by their spittle. It is better for them to forget each other

---

[50] According to Yü Yüeh, *Chu-tzu p'ing-i*, 17:15b, the word *i* (righteousness) here should be interpreted to mean lofty.

[51] Interpretation according to Kuo Hsiang.

[52] This interpretation also follows Kuo Hsiang.

in rivers and lakes.[53] Rather than praise (sage-emperor) Yao and con-demn (wicked king) Chieh,[54] it is better to forget both and to trans-form their ways [which give rise to conventional standards of right and wrong].[55]

The universe gives me my body so I may be carried, my life so I may toil, my old age so I may repose, and my death so I may rest. To regard life as good is the way to regard death as good. A boat may be hidden in a creek or a mountain in a lake. These may be said to be safe enough. But at midnight a strong man may come and carry it away on his back. An ignorant person does not know that even when the hiding of things, large or small, is perfectly well done, still something will escape you. But if the universe is hidden in the universe itself, then there can be no escape from it. This is the great truth of things in general. We possess our body by chance and we are already pleased with it. If our physical bodies went through ten thousand transformations without end, how in-comparable would this joy be! Therefore the sage roams freely in the realm in which nothing can escape but all endures. Those who regard dying a premature death, getting old, and the beginning and end of life as equally good are followed by others. How much more is that to which all things belong and on which the whole process of transformation de-pends (that is, Tao)?

Tao has reality and evidence but no action or physical form. It may be transmitted but cannot be received. It may be obtained but cannot be seen. It is based in itself, rooted in itself. Before heaven and earth came into being, Tao existed by itself from all time. It gave spirits and rulers their spiritual powers. It created heaven and earth. It is above the zenith but it is not high. It is beneath the nadir but it is not low. It is prior to heaven and earth but it is not old. It is more ancient than the highest antiquity but is not regarded as long ago. Emperor Hsi-wei[56] obtained it and so he set the universe in order. Emperor Fu-hsi[57] obtained it and with it he was united with the source of material force. The Great Dipper obtained it and has therefore never erred from its course. The sun and moon obtained it and so they have never ceased to revolve. The deity K'an-pi obtained it and was therefore able to enter the high K'un-lun mountains. F'eng I (a river immortal) obtained it and was therefore

[53] These three sentences also appear in ch. 14 of the *Chuang Tzu* where they are put in the mouth of Lao Tzu. See NHCC, 5:46b and Giles, p. 148.

[54] Chieh (r. 1802–1752 B.C.?). He was responsible for the ruin of the Hsia dynasty (2183–1752 B.C.?).

[55] A similar sentence appears in *Chuang Tzu*, ch. 26, NHCC, 9:6a and Giles, p. 262.

[56] Legendary emperor of antiquity.

[57] Legendary emperor credited with the invention of the Eight Trigrams.

able to roam in the great rivers. Chien-wu (a mountain immortal) obtained it and was therefore able to dwell on Mount T'ai. The Yellow Emperor obtained it and with it he ascended heaven high in the clouds. Emperor Chuan-hsü[58] obtained it and with it he dwelt in the Dark Palace. The deity Yü-ch'iang[59] obtained it and so he was established in the North Pole. The Queen Mother of the West obtained it and so she secured her seat in the vast empty space of the west, and no one knows when that began or will end. P'eng-tsu[60] obtained it and so he lived from the time of Emperor Shun[61] until the time of the five lords.[62] Fu Yüeh obtained it and with it he became prime minister of King Wu-ting[63] and in a grand manner extended his rule to the whole empire. [After he dies, his spirit], charioting upon one constellation and drawn by another, has taken its position as one of the heavenly stars.

> *Comment.* One of the most important passages on Tao. Note the stress on reality and evidence, remarkably similar to *Lao Tzu*, ch. 21. There is nothing negative about it.

Nan-po Tzu-k'uei[64] asked Nü-yü,[65] "Sir, you are old but have the look of a child. How is this?"

"I have learned Tao," replied Nü-yü.

"Can Tao be learned?" Nan-po Tzu-k'uei said.

"Ah! How can it?" replied Nü-yü. "You are not the type of man. Pü-liang I[66] had the ability of the sage but did not know the teachings. I knew all the teachings but did not have his ability. I wanted to teach him so he could become a sage. But that was not such a simple case. It seemed easy to teach the doctrines of a sage to a man with his ability. But I still had to wait to teach him. It was three days before he was able to transcend this world. After he transcended this world, I waited for seven days more and then he was able to transcend all material things. After he transcended all material things, I waited for nine days more and then he was able to transcend all life. Having transcended all life, he became as clear and bright as the morning. Having become as clear and bright as the morning, he was able to see the One. Having seen the One, he was then able to abolish the distinction of past and

---

[58] Grandson of the Yellow Emperor, who, according to legend, obtained Tao and became the ruling deity of the northern quarter, which is dark.

[59] Also grandson of the Yellow Emperor, according to legend.

[60] China's famous man of longevity.

[61] Emperor Yao's successor.

[62] Lords of the Hsia, Shang (1751–1112 B.C.), and Chou (from 1111 B.C.) dynasties.

[63] King (r. 1339–1281 B.C.) of the Shang dynasty.

[64] The same as Tzu-chi of Nan-kuo in *Chuang Tzu*, ch. 2?

[65] Unidentified. Said by some to be a woman.

[66] Unidentified.

present. Having abolished the past and present, he was then able to enter the realm of neither life nor death. Then, to him, the destruction of life did not mean death and the production of life did not mean life. In dealing with things, he would not lean forward or backward to accommodate them. To him everything was in the process of destruction, everything was in the process of perfection. This is called tranquillity in disturbance. Tranquillity in disturbance means that it is especially in the midst of disturbance that [tranquillity] becomes perfect."

> *Comment.* Like many of Chuang Tzu's phrases, "not to lean forward or backward" has become a favorite dictum among later Chinese thinkers, especially Neo-Confucianists. It does not mean moderation or indifference but absolute spontaneity and impartiality in dealing with things and complete naturalness in response to things.

"Where did you learn this?" asked Nan-po Tzu-k'uei.

"I learned it from the son of Writing the Assistant (for writing is no more than an aid)," Nü-yü said. "The son of Writing the Assistant learned it from the grandson of Repeated Recitation (which preceded writing), the grandson of Repeated Recitation learned it from Clear Understanding, Clear Understanding learned it from Whispering, Whispering learned it from Earnest Practice, Earnest Practice learned it from Joyful Singing, Joyful Singing learned it from Noumenon (*hsüan-ming*),[67] Noumenon learned it from Penetration of Vacuity, and Penetration of Vacuity learned it from Doubtful Beginning."

Tzu-ssu, Tzu-yü, Tzu-li, and Tzu-lai[68] were conversing together, saying, "Whoever can make non-being the head, life the backbone, and death the buttocks, and whoever knows that life and death, and existence and non-existence are one, that man shall be our friend." The four looked at each other and smiled, completely understood one another, and thus became friends.

Soon afterward Tzu-yü fell ill and Tzu-ssu went to see him. "Great is the Creator!" said the sick man. "See how he (or it) has made me crumbled up like this!"

> *Comment.* The term "Creator" (*Tso-wu che*) seems to suggest a personal God. But as Kuo Hsiang points out, this means Nature, which also creates.

His back was hunched and his backbone was protruding. His internal organs were on the top of his body. His cheeks were level with his

---

[67] For a discussion of the translation of this term, see Appendix.
[68] All fictitious.

navel. His shoulders were higher than his head. The hair on top of his head pointed up toward the sky. The yin and yang (passive and active cosmic forces) in him were out of order, but his mind was at ease as though nothing had happened. He limped and walked quickly to the well and looked at his reflection, and said, "Alas! The Creator has made me crumbled up like this!"

"Do you dislike it?" asked Tzu-ssu.

"No," said Tzu-yü, "why should I dislike it? Suppose my left arm is transformed into a cock. With it I should herald the dawn. Suppose my right arm is transformed into a sling. With it I should look for a dove to roast. Suppose my buttocks were transformed into wheels and my spirit into a horse. I should mount them. What need do I have for a chariot? When we come, it is because it was the occasion to be born. When we go, it is to follow the natural course of things. Those who are contented and at ease when the occasion comes and live in accord with the course of Nature cannot be affected by sorrow or joy. This is what the ancients called release from bondage. Those who cannot release themselves are so because they are bound by material things. That material things cannot overcome Nature, however, has been a fact from time immemorial. Why, then, should I dislike it?"

> *Comment.* Release here means spiritual freedom and is to be sharply differentiated from Buddhist Nirvāṇa.

Soon afterward Tzu-lai fell ill, was gasping for breath and was about to die. His wife and children surrounded him and wept. Tzu-li went to see him. "Go away," he said. "Don't disturb the transformation that is about to take place." Then, leaning against the door, he continued, "Great is the Creator! What will he make of you now? Where will he take you? Will he make you into a rat's liver? Will he make you into an insect's leg?"

Tzu-lai said, "Wherever a parent tells a son to go, whether east, west, south, or north, he has to obey. The yin and yang are like man's parents. If they pressed me to die and I disobeyed, I would be obstinate. What fault is theirs? For the universe gave me the body so I may be carried, my life so I may toil, my old age so I may repose, and my death so I may rest. Therefore to regard life as good is the way to regard death as good.

"Suppose a master foundryman is casting his metal and the metal leaps up and says, 'I must be made into the best sword (called *mo-yeh*).' The master foundryman would certainly consider the metal as evil. And if simply because I possess a body by chance, I were to say, 'Nothing but a man! Nothing but a man!' the Creator will certainly regard me as evil. If I regard the universe as a great furnace and creation as a master foundryman, why should anywhere I go not be all right? When the body is formed, we sleep. With it visibly there, we wake."[69]

Tzu Sang-hu, Meng Tzu-fan, and Tzu Ch'in-chang[70] were friends. They said to each other, "Who can live together without any special effort to live together and help each other without any special effort to help each other? Who can ascend to heaven, roam through the clouds, revolve in the realm of the infinite, live without being aware of it, and pay no attention to death?" The three looked at each other and smiled, completely understood each other, and thus became friends.

After a short while of silence, Tzu Sang-hu died. Before he was buried, Confucius had heard about it and sent (his pupil) Tzu-kung to take part in the funeral. One of the friends was composing a song and the other was playing a lute and they sang in harmony, saying, "Alas! Sang-hu. Alas! Sang-hu. You have returned to the true state but we still remain here as men!"

Tzu-kung hurried in and said, "I venture to ask whether it is in accord with the rules of propriety to sing in the presence of a corpse."

The two men looked at each other, laughed, and said, "How does he know the idea of rules of propriety?" Tzu-kung returned and told Confucius, asking him, "What sort of men are those? There is nothing proper in their conduct, and they looked upon their bodies as external to themselves. They approached the corpse and sang without changing the color of countenance. I don't know what to call them. What sort of men are they?"

"They travel in the transcendental world," replied Confucius, "and I travel in the mundane world. There is nothing common between the two worlds, and I sent you there to mourn! How stupid! They are companions of the Creator, and roam in the universe of one and original creative force (ch'i). They consider life as a burden like a tumor, and death as the cutting off of an abscess. Such being their views, how do they care about life and death or their beginning and end? To them life is but a temporary existence of various elements in a common body which they borrow. They are unaware of their livers and gall (emotions) and oblivious of their ears and eyes (sensation). They come and go, and begin and end and none will know when all these will stop. Without any attachment, they stroll beyond the dusty world and wander in the original state of having no [unnatural] action (wu-wei). How can they take the trouble to observe the rules of propriety of popular society in order to impress the multitude?"

[69] This sentence is very obscure. No commentator has offered a satisfactory explanation. All agree that it means that life and death are one. The translation here, while quite literal, is already a subjective interpretation.

[70] Fictitious.

Comment. Chuang Tzu distinguished traveling in the transcendental world, or *fang-wai* (literally, "outside the sphere" of human affairs), and traveling in the mundane world, or *fang-nei* (literally, "inside the sphere"). Later the former came to mean Buddhism and the latter Confucianism. The first distinction was made here. To consider life as a temporary existence of various elements is highly Buddhistic, for in Buddhism an entity is but a temporary grouping of five elements. But Taoism is free from the quietism of Buddhism and emphasizes non-action. As Kuo Hsiang emphatically stated, however, taking no action does not mean doing nothing but simply doing nothing unnatural.[71]

Tsu-kung asked, "If that is the case, which world would you follow?"
"I am Nature's prisoner," said Confucius. "But let me share something with you."
Tzu-kung said, "May I ask which is your world?"
Confucius said, "Fishes attain their full life in water and men attain theirs in the Tao. Those fish which attain a full life in water will be well nourished if a pool is dug for them, and those men who attain a full life in the Tao will achieve calmness of nature[72] through inaction. Therefore it is said, 'Fishes forget each other (are happy and at ease with themselves) in rivers and lakes and men forget each other in the workings of Tao.'"
"May I ask about those strange people?" said Tzu-kung.
Replied Confucius, "Those strange people are strange in the eyes of man but are equal to Nature. Therefore it is said, 'The inferior man to Nature is a superior man to men, and the superior man to men is an inferior man to Nature.'"

Yen Hui asked (his master) Confucius, "When Meng-sun Ts'ai's[73] mother died, he wept without sniveling, his heart felt no distress, and he wore mourning but showed no sorrow. Yet, although wanting in these three essential demonstrations of filial piety, he is known all over the state of Lu as an excellent mourner. Is it possible that without actuality one can obtain the name? I am rather puzzled."
Confucius said, "Meng-sun is perfect. He is more advanced than the wise ones. [Ordinary people] cannot minimize [their expressions of sorrow], and in doing so they already minimize [their true nature].[74] Meng-

[71] See below, ch. 19, sec. 6, selection 31.
[72] *Sheng* (life) is here interpreted in the sense of nature, *hsing*, according to Wang Hsien-ch'ien.
[73] According to Li I (of Chin, 265-420), quoted in Lu Te-ming (556-627), *Ching-tien shih-wen* (Explanations of Words in the Classics), he was a descendant of Meng-sun, and traced his ancestry to Duke Huan (r. 711–694 B.C.) of Lu.
[74] This interpretation follows Yao Nai (1731-1815), *Chuang Tzu chang-i* (Meaning of the *Chuang Tzu*).

sun does not know how life comes about and does not know how death comes about. He does not prefer the one or the other. He lets himself be transformed into whatever it may be, and waits for further transformations which are not yet known. Moreover, how can one in the midst of transformation know that he will not be transformed? And how can one not being transformed know that he has already been transformed? Perhaps you and I are dreaming and have not wakened. Moreover, to him there has been a change of physical form but no decline in the spirit. There has been a change of lodging but no real death. Meng-sun, having awakened, wept when he saw that others wept. This is natural with him.

"People say to each other, 'I am I.' How do they know that their 'I' is the real 'I'? Suppose you say you dream you are a bird and fly way up in the sky or you dream you are a fish and dive deep into the ocean. We cannot know whether the man now speaking is awake or is dreaming. As we reach the point of satisfaction, [we are so at ease with ourselves] that we do not even smile. When a smile does come forth, we do not even think of manipulating for it to come. We put ourselves at the manipulation [of Nature] and ignore all transformations. With this we enter into the realm of vacuous nature which is one."

I-erh Tzu went to see Hsü Yu.[75] Hsü Yu said, "What has Yao benefited you?"

"Yao said to me that I must personally practice humanity and righteousness," replied I-erh Tzu, "and talk clearly about right and wrong."

Hsü Yu said, "Then why have you come here? Yao has already treated you like criminals by branding you with humanity and righteousness and cutting off your nose with right and wrong. How can you travel on the road of freedom, ease, and flexibility?"

"Be that as it may," said I-erh Tzu. "Still I like to travel along its edge."

"No," said Hsü Yu, "when a man is blind, he has nothing to do with the beauty of a human face or the colors of embroidered robes."

I-erh Tzu said, "The ancient beauty Wu-chuang disregarded her beauty, strong man Chü-liang disregarded his strength, and the Yellow Emperor abandoned his wisdom. All these resulted from filing and hammering. How do you know the Creator may not remove my branding and repair my nose so that I may again be perfect in form and follow you, sir?"

"That I don't know," replied Hsü Yu. "But let me tell you the essentials. Ah! my master, my master! He tears all things to pieces but did

---

[75] A recluse who, when offered the empire by Emperor Yao, ran away and washed his ears.

not specially make up his mind to be just. His blessing reaches the ten thousand generations but he has no partial love for anyone. He is more ancient than the highest antiquity but is not old. He covers heaven and supports the earth, and fashions the shapes of all things and yet he is not purposely skillful. This is the way he roams around."

Yen Hui said, "I have made some progress."

"What do you mean?" asked Confucius.

"I have forgotten humanity and righteousness," replied Yen Hui.

"Very good, but that is not enough," said Confucius.

On another day Yen Hui saw Confucius again and said, "I have made some progress."

"What do you mean?" asked Confucius.

"I have forgotten ceremonies and music," replied Yen Hui.

"Very good, but that is not enough," said Confucius.

Another day Yen Hui saw Confucius again and said, "I have made some progress."

"What do you mean?" asked Confucius.

Yen Hui said, "I forget everything while sitting down."

Confucius' face turned pale. He said, "What do you mean by sitting down and forgetting everything?"

"I cast aside my limbs," replied Yen Hui, "discard my intelligence, detach from both body and mind, and become one with Great Universal (Tao).[76] This is called sitting down and forgetting everything."

> *Comment.* This is not a cult of unconsciousness. Lu Ch'ang-keng has correctly said, "To forget means to have one's mind in all things but not to have any mind about oneself, and to have one's feelings in accord with all things but not to have any feelings of oneself." Lu is here quoting Ch'eng Hao (Ch'eng Ming-tao, 1032-1085), who said that "there is nothing better than to become broad and extremely impartial and to respond spontaneously to all things as they come."[77] In fact, Chuang Tzu's doctrine of "sitting down and forgetting everything" strongly stimulated Neo-Confucian thought.

Confucius said, "When you become one with the Great Universal you will have no partiality, and when you are part of the process of transformation, you will have no constancy (rigidity). You are really a worthy man. I beg to follow your steps."

Tzu-yü and Tzu-sang were friends. Once it had rained continuously

---

[76] According to Ch'eng Hsüan-ying (fl. 647-663), *Chuang Tzu shu* (Commentary on the *Chuang Tzu*), this means identifying with Tao, and according to Hsi T'ung's (1876-1936) *Chuang Tzu pu-chu* (Supplementary Annotations on the *Chuang Tzu*), this means the Great Transformation.

[77] See below, ch. 31, sec. 2.

for ten days. Tzu-yü said, "Maybe Tzu-sang has become sick." So he packed up some food and went to feed him. Arriving at the door, he heard something between singing and wailing accompanied by the lute, saying "O father! O mother! Is this due to Nature? Is this due to man?" It seemed that the voice was broken and the words faltered. Tzu-yü went in and asked, "Why are you singing like this?"

"I tried to think who has brought me to this extreme [poverty]," answered Tzu-sang, "but have found no answer. Would my father and mother want me to be poor? Heaven covers all things without partiality and the earth supports all things without partiality. Would heaven and earth make me so poor in particular? This is what I have tried to find out but have failed. Then it must have been fate that has brought me to such an extreme." (3:1a-27b)

C. Additional Selections

1. The Nature and Reality of Tao

In the great beginning, there was non-being.[78] It had neither being nor name. The One originates from it; it has oneness but not yet physical form. When things obtain it and come into existence, that is called virtue (which gives them their individual character). That which is formless is divided [into yin and yang], and from the very beginning going on without interruption is called destiny (*ming*, fate). Through movement and rest it produces all things. When things are produced in accordance with the principle (*li*) of life, there is physical form. When the physical form embodies and preserves the spirit so that all activities follow their own specific principles, that is nature. By cultivating one's nature one will return to virtue. When virtue is perfect, one will be one with the beginning. Being one with the beginning, one becomes vacuous (*hsü*, receptive to all), and being vacuous, one becomes great. One will then be united with the sound and breath of things. When one is united with the sound and breath of things, one is then united with the universe. This unity is intimate and seems to be stupid and foolish. This is called profound and secret virtue, this is complete harmony.[79] (ch. 12, NHCC, 5:8b-9b)

> *Comment.* This is an important passage on metaphysics. It bears striking similarity to the philosophy of the *Book of Changes*.[80] More than one Neo-Confucianist has commended Chuang Tzu for

[78] The punctuation here follows that of Fung, *History of Chinese Philosophy*, vol. 1, p. 224.

[79] Cf. *Lao Tzu*, chs. 10 and 65.

[80] See below, ch. 13, especially sec. 4, Selections from "Remarks on Certain Trigrams," ch. 1.

having really understood in this passage the substance of Tao. Chuang Tzu's use of principle (*li*), of course, is after the hearts of Neo-Confucianists, whose whole philosophy is that of principle.

2. *Tao Everywhere*

Tung-kuo Tzu asked Chuang Tzu, "What is called Tao—where is it?"

"It is everywhere," replied Chuang Tzu.

Tung-kuo Tzu said, "It will not do unless you are more specific."

"It is in the ant," said Chuang Tzu.

"Why go so low down?"

"It is in the weeds."

"Why even lower?"

"It is in a potsherd."

"Why still lower?"

"It is in the excrement and urine," said Chuang Tzu. Tung-kuo gave no response.

> *Comment.* Compare this with a most celebrated Buddhist dialogue:
> Question: What is the Buddha?
> Answer: It is the dried human excrement-removing stick.[81]

"Sir," said Chuang Tzu. "Your question does not touch the essential. When inspector Huo asked the superintendent of markets about the fatness of pigs, the tests were always made in parts less and less likely to be fat. Do not insist on any particular thing. Nothing escapes from Tao. Such is perfect Tao, and so is great speech. The three, Complete, Entire, and All, differ in name but are the same in actuality. They all designate (*chih*, mark) the One." (ch. 22, NHCC, 7:49a-50a)

3. *Constant Flux*

"Is the sky revolving around? Is the earth remaining still? Are the sun and the moon pursuing each other? Who prescribes this? Who directs this? Who has the leisure to push them to go on? Is there perhaps some mechanical arrangement so that they cannot help moving? Or is it perhaps that they keep revolving and cannot stop themselves? Do clouds cause the rain or does the rain cause the clouds? Who makes them rise and sends them down? Who has the leisure and delights in promoting such things? The wind rises from the north. It now blows east and now west, and now it whirls upward. Who is sucking and blowing it alternately? Who has the leisure to shake it about like this? Please tell me why?"

[81] A famous saying by Zen Master Wen-yen (d. 949). See Ogato, *Zen for the West*, p. 109. The translation "dirt cleaner" by Ogato for the dried human excrement-removing stick is evidently a Zen accommodation to Western decency!

Wu-hsien waved to him and said, "Come, let me tell you. There are in nature the six ultimates and five constancies.[82] When rulers follow them there will be order. When they disobey them, there will be calamity." (ch. 14, NHCC, 5:35a-36a)

4. Evolution

All species have originative or moving power (*chi*).[83] When they obtain water, they become small organisms like silk. In a place bordering water and land, they become lichens. Thriving on the bank, they become moss. On the fertile soil they become weeds. The roots of these weeds become worms, and their leaves become butterflies. Suddenly the butterfly is transformed into an insect, which is born under the stove (for its heat), and which has the appearance of having its skin shed. Its name is called *chü-t'o*. After a thousand days, *chü-t'o* becomes a bird called *kan-yü-ku*. The spittle of the *kan-yü-ku* becomes an insect called *ssu-mi*. The *ssu-mi* becomes a wine fly, which produces the insect called *i-lu*. The insect *huang-k'uang* produces the insect called *chiu-yu*. Mosquitos come from the rotten insects called *huan*. The plant *yang-hsi* paired with the bamboo which for a long time has had no shoot, produces the insect called *ch'ing-ning*. The *ch'ing-ning* produces the insect called *ch'eng, ch'eng* produces the horse, and the horse produces men. Man again goes back into the originative process of Nature. All things come from the originative process of Nature and return to the originative process of Nature. (ch. 18, NHCC, 6:36a-b)

> *Comment.* Is this natural evolution? Hu Shih (1891-1962) thinks so.[84] Whether it is or not, it cannot be doubted that Chuang Tzu conceived reality as ever changing and as developing from the simple to the complex.

5. Tao as Transformation and One

Although the universe is vast, its transformation is uniform. Although the myriad things are many, their order is one. Although people are

---

[82] Commentators do not agree on what these are. The theory that the six ultimates means the six directions and that the five constancies means the Five Agents of Metal, Wood, Water, Fire, and Earth seems to be the most reasonable.

[83] Wang Hsien-ch'ien quoting Ch'eng Hsüan-ying, interpreted the word *chi* to mean "how many." Hu Shih understands it to mean "the minutest form" or germs, partly on the authority of the *Book of Changes* (see his *Development of the Logical Method in Ancient China*, p. 136). Following Yen Fu (1853-1921), *Chuang Tzu p'ing* (Critique of the *Chuang Tzu*), I read *chi* as *chi* (originative or moving power). This is the word used at the end of the paragraph. This interpretation seems to be more in keeping with Chuang Tzu's concept of the incessant transformation of nature.

[84] See his *Development of the Logical Method in Ancient China*, pp. 131-139.

numerous, their ruler is the sovereign. The sovereign traces his origin to virtue (*te*, individual and essential character), and attains his perfection in Nature. Therefore it is said that in the cases of sovereigns of high antiquity, no [unnatural] action (*wu-wei*) was undertaken and the empire was in order. That was because of their natural virtue. When speech is seen through the point of Tao, the name of the sovereign of the world becomes correct. When functions and ranks are seen through Tao, the distinction between the ruler and the minister becomes clear. When ability is seen through Tao, the offices of the empire become regulated. When all things in general are seen through Tao, the response of things to each other becomes complete. Therefore it is virtue that penetrates Heaven and Earth, and it is Tao that operates in all things. Government by the ruler means human affairs, and when ability is applied to creative activities, it means skill. Skill is commanded by human affairs, human affairs are commanded by the distinction of functions, distinction is commanded by virtue, virtue is commanded by Tao, and Tao is commanded by Nature. Therefore it is said that ancient rulers of empires had no [selfish] desires and the empire enjoyed sufficiency. They undertook no [unnatural] action and all things were transformed. They were deep and tranquil and all their people were calm. The *Record* says, "When one is identified with the One, all things will be complete with him. When he reaches the point of having no subjective feelings, spiritual beings will submit to him."[85]

The Grand Master[86] said, "Tao covers and supports all things. How overflowingly great! The ruler should cast away his [selfish] mind. To act without taking an [unnatural] action means Nature. To speak without any action means virtue. To love people and benefit all things means humanity (*jen*). To identify with all without each losing his own identity means greatness. To behave without purposely showing any superiority means broadness. To possess an infinite variety means richness. Therefore to adhere to virtue is called discipline. To realize virtue means strength. To be in accord with Tao means completeness. And not to yield to material things is called perfection. If a superior man understands these ten points, he surely makes up his mind and all the world will come to him like rushing water." (ch. 12, NHCC, 5:1a-3a)

6. Nature vs. Man

The Spirit of the North Sea said to Uncle River,[87] "A huge beam can knock down a city wall but cannot repair a breach which shows that

---

[85] This work is now lost.

[86] Wang Hsien-ch'ien said, "From the fact that later in the chapter it is said, 'The Grand Master asked Lao Tzu. . .' we know this refers to Confucius."

[87] Same as Feng I in *Chuang Tzu*, ch. 6.

different things have different capacities. Famous horses can travel a thousand *li*[88] in one day, but for catching rats they are not equal to a fox or a wild cat, which shows that different things have different skills. An owl can catch fleas at night, and sees the tip of a hair, but in the daytime even with its eyes wide open it cannot see a mountain, which shows that different things have different natures. Therefore it is said, 'Why not let us follow the right instead of the wrong, and follow order instead of chaos?' This is to misunderstand the principle (*li*) of nature and the reality of things. It is like following heaven but not earth, and following yin but not yang. It is clear that it will not do. But people keep on saying that without stop. They must be either stupid or wrong.

"Emperors and kings yielded their thrones in different ways, and the Three Dynasties[89] succeeded each other under different conditions. One who is out of step with the times and goes against the tide is a usurper, but one who is in keeping with the times and follows the tide is a man of high character. Better keep quiet, Uncle River. How do you know the distinction between noble and humble families and between the great and small houses?"

"Then what shall I do?" asked Uncle River. "What shall I not do? Should I accept or reject, advance or withdraw?"

The Spirit of the North Sea said, "From the point of view of Tao, what is noble and what is humble? They all merge into one. Never stick to one's own intention and thus handicap the operation of Tao. What is much and what is little? They replace and apply to each other. Never follow one stubborn course of action and thus deviate from Tao. Be serious as the ruler is to his people who is impartial in his kindness. Be as at ease as the sacrifice at the Spirit of Earth, where blessings are asked for all. And be as comprehensive as the four directions which know no limit and have no boundaries. Embrace all things without inclining to this or that way. This means not tending to any direction.

"All things are one. Which is short and which is long? Tao has neither beginning nor end. Things are born and die, and their completion cannot be taken for granted. They are now empty and now full, and their physical form is not fixed in one place. The years cannot be retained. Time cannot be arrested. The succession of decline, growth, fullness, and emptiness go in a cycle, each end becoming a new beginning. This is the way to talk about the workings of the great principle and to discuss the principle of all things. The life of things passes by like a galloping horse. With no activity is it not changing, and at no time is it not moving. What shall we do? What shall we not do? The thing to do is to leave it to self-transformation."

[88] About one-third of a mile.   [89] The Hsia, Shang, and Chou.

Uncle River said, "In that case, what is the value of Tao?"

"One who knows Tao will surely penetrate the principle of things," said the Spirit of the North Sea, "and one who penetrates the principle of things will surely understand their application in various situations. He who understands their application in various situations will not injure himself with material things. A man of perfect virtue cannot be burnt by fire, nor drowned by water, nor hurt by the cold of winter or the heat of summer, or harmed by animals. It does not mean that he puts himself in these situations. It means that he discriminates between safety and danger, remains calm whether he suffers calamity or enjoys blessing, and is careful about taking or not taking an action, so that none can harm him. Therefore it is said that what is natural lies within and what is human lies without, and virtue abides in the natural. Know the action of Nature and man, follow Nature as the basis and be at ease with one's own situation, then one can expand or contract as times may require. This is the essential of learning and the ultimate of truth."

"What do you mean by Nature and what do you mean by man?"

The Spirit of the North Sea replied, "A horse or a cow has four feet. That is Nature. Put a halter around the horse's head and put a string through the cow's nose, that is man. Therefore it is said, 'Do not let man destroy Nature. Do not let cleverness destroy destiny. And do not sacrifice your name for gain.' Guard carefully your nature and do not let it go astray. This is called returning to one's true nature." (ch. 17, NHCC, 6:17b-21b)

7. Calmness of Mind

Do not be the possessor of fame. Do not be the storehouse of schemes. Do not take over the function of things. Do not be the master of knowledge (to manipulate things). Personally realize the infinite to the highest degree and travel in the realm of which there is no sign. Exercise fully what you have received from Nature without any subjective viewpoint. In one word, be absolutely vacuous (*hsü*).[90]

The mind of the perfect man is like a mirror. It does not lean forward or backward in its response to things. It responds to things but conceals nothing of its own. Therefore it is able to deal with things without injury to [its reality]. (ch. 7, NHCC, 3:35b-36a)

> *Comment.* The mirror is an important symbol for the mind both in Zen Buddhism and in Neo-Confucianism. The difference is that with Buddhism, external reality is to be transcended, whereas with Chuang Tzu and Neo-Confucianists, external reality is to be re-

[90] Empty in the sense of having no bias or selfish desires. For a discussion of this term, see Appendix.

sponded to naturally and faithfully, like a mirror objectively reflecting all.[91]

8. Sageliness and Kingliness

The evolution of the Tao of Nature goes on without obstruction. Therefore all things are produced. The evolution of the Tao of the sovereign goes on without obstruction and therefore the whole empire comes to him. The evolution of the Tao of the sage goes on without obstruction and therefore the whole world pays him homage. He who understands Nature penetrates the way of the sage, and possesses the virtue of emperors and kings to the extent of the six directions (space) and the four seasons (time) will be able to leave things to take their own course, to be dimmed in his brilliancy, and to be tranquil in all respects. The sage is tranquil not because he says to himself, "It is good to be tranquil," and therefore became tranquil. He is tranquil because nothing disturbs him.

When water is tranquil, its clearness reflects even the beard and the eyebrows. It remains definitely level, and master carpenters take it as their model. If water is clear when it is tranquil, how much more so is the spirit? When the mind of the sage is tranquil, it becomes the mirror of the universe and the reflection of all things.

Vacuity, tranquillity, mellowness, quietness, and taking no action characterize the things of the universe at peace and represent the ultimate of Tao and virtue. Therefore rulers and sages abide in them. Abiding leads to vacuity (embracing all). Vacuity leads to actuality. Actuality leads to the establishment of order among all things. Vacuity leads to tranquillity, tranquillity leads to activity, and activity leads to adjustment. Tranquillity leads to taking no action, and taking no action leads to everyone fulfilling his duty. Because one takes no action, one is at peace himself, and when one is at peace himself, no worry or sorrow can affect him and he enjoys long life.

Vacuity, tranquillity, mellowness, quietness, and taking no action are the root of all things. To understand them and to rule with them was how Yao was an emperor, and to understand them and to serve with them was how Shun was a minister. These are the virtue of rulers and emperors when they manage things above. They are the way of the profound mysterious sage and the uncrowned king[92] when they manage things below. When a person retires with these virtues and roams at leisure, all the scholars in the rivers and seas and hills and forests will

[91] See Paul Demiéville, "Le miroir spirituel," *Sinologica* 1 (1948), especially pp. 117-119.
[92] References to Lao Tzu and Confucius, respectively?

admire him. If one assumes office with them to pacify the world, his achievements will be great and his fame will be prominent, and the empire will become unified. In tranquillity he becomes a sage, and in activity he becomes a king. He takes no action and is honored. He is simple and plain and none in the world can compete with him in excellence. For such a one understands this virtue of Heaven and Earth. He is called the great foundation and the great source of all being and is in harmony with Nature. One who is in accord with the world is in harmony with men. To be in harmony with men means human happiness, and to be in harmony with Nature means the happiness of Nature. (ch. 13, NHCC, 5:21b-24a)

> *Comment.* The equal importance of tranquillity and activity expressed here should dispel once and for all any doubt that the philosophy of Chuang Tzu is not the quietism of the Buddhist type. The idea that one should have sageliness within and kingliness without also means a balanced life. This latter idea later became a central one in Neo-Taoism.

9. *The Equality of Life and Death*

Chuang Tzu's wife died and Hui Tzu went to offer his condolence. He found Chuang Tzu squatting on the ground and singing, beating on an earthen bowl. He said, "Someone has lived with you, raised children for you and now she has aged and died. Is it not enough that you should not shed any tear? But now you sing and beat the bowl. Is this not too much?"

"No," replied Chuang Tzu. "When she died, how could I help being affected? But as I think the matter over, I realize that originally she had no life; and not only no life, she had no form; not only no form, she had no material force (*ch'i*). In the limbo of existence and non-existence, there was transformation and the material force was evolved. The material force was transformed to be form, form was transformed to become life, and now birth has transformed to become death. This is like the rotation of the four seasons, spring, summer, fall, and winter. Now she lies asleep in the great house (the universe). For me to go about weeping and wailing would be to show my ignorance of destiny. Therefore I desist." (ch. 18, NHCC, 6:31b-32a)

10. *Subjectivity*

Chuang Tzu and Hui Tzu were taking a leisurely walk along the dam of the Hao River. Chuang Tzu said, "The white fish are swimming at ease. This is the happiness of the fish."

"You are not fish," said Hui Tzu. "How do you know its happiness?"

"You are not I," said Chuang Tzu. "How do you know that I do not know the happiness of the fish?"

Hui Tzu said, "Of course I do not know, since I am not you. But you are not the fish, and it is perfectly clear that you do not know the happiness of the fish."

"Let us get at the bottom of the matter," said Chuang Tzu. "When you asked how I knew the happiness of the fish, you already knew that I knew the happiness of the fish but asked how. I knew it along the river." (ch. 17, NHCC, 6:28a-29a)

11. The Inner Spirit

When Prince Yüan of Sung was about to have a portrait painted, all official painters came, bowed, and at the royal command stood waiting, licking their brushes and mixing their ink. Half of them were outside the room. One official came late. He sauntered in without hurrying himself, bowed at the royal command and would not remain standing. Thereupon he was given lodging. The prince sent a man to see what he did. He took off his clothes and squatted down bare-backed. The ruler said, "He will do. He is a true painter." (ch. 21, NHCC, 7:36b)

> Comment. In this simple story lies a basic principle of Chinese art. It is expressed in the phrase "taking off clothes and squatting down bare-backed," which has become a key phrase in essays on Chinese aesthetics. It means that art is dedicated to the expression of the inner spirit instead of physical verisimilitude and that painting should be a spontaneous and instantaneous flow of the brush.

9

MO TZU'S DOCTRINES OF UNIVERSAL LOVE, HEAVEN, AND SOCIAL WELFARE

STUDENTS OF CHINESE thought are likely to think that Confucianism and Taoism have been the two outstanding indigenous philosophical systems in China. This is true so far as the last two thousand years are concerned. In ancient China, up to the beginning of the Han dynasty (206 B.C.–A.D. 220), the greatest schools were Confucianism and Moism.[1] They dominated the intellectual scene from the fifth to at least the third century B.C. And they vigorously attacked each other.

The two were bitter enemies because in their doctrines they were diametrically opposed. While Confucius took the Western Chou (1111–770 B.C.) as his model, Mo Tzu looked to the Hsia (2183–1752 B.C?) instead. The whole Confucian ethical system is based on the concept of humanity (*jen*), whereas Mo Tzu (fl. 479–438 B.C.)[2] based his on the concept of righteousness (*i*). Both are of course human values. But while Confucianists kept humanity essentially a human value, Mo Tzu traced righteousness to the will of Heaven. To the Confucianists, Heaven does not directly exert its will but leaves the moral law to operate by itself. To Mo Tzu, however, the will of Heaven determines all. Mo Tzu strongly condemns ceremonies, music, elaborate funerals, and the belief in fate (*ming,* destiny), all of which were promoted by Confucius and his followers. For Confucius, moral life is desirable for its own sake, whereas for Mo Tzu it is desirable because of the benefits it brings. Even his concept of the will of Heaven is colored by this utilitarian approach.

The greatest divergence between Confucianism and Moism, however, is on the issue of human relations. What distinguishes the Moist movement is its doctrine of universal love: other people's parents, families, and countries are to be treated like one's own. This is of course absolutely incompatible with the basic Confucian doctrine of love with distinctions: while love should embrace all, it must start with love for one's parents; therefore, one has a special obligation of filial piety to parents. Thus there is a gradation or degree in human relations. If the Moist doctrine were adopted, the whole Confucian system would be destroyed from its very foundation. This was the reason why Mencius attacked Moism mercilessly.[3]

The Moists challenged the Confucianists not only in theory, but also

---

[1] Often spelled "Mohism," although the "h" is entirely superfluous.
[2] The name Mo Tzu has been variously written as Moh-tse, Meh-tse, Micius, etc.
[3] *Mencius*, 3A:5, 3B:9.

in actual practice. Like Confucius, Mo Tzu traveled from one state to another offering help to rulers. He did not hesitate to walk for ten days and ten nights in an effort to dissuade a ruler from making war, for he strongly condemned war. One might even say that the Confucianists and the Moists represented two entirely different groups of people. While Confucian followers came from all classes of society and Confucianism is basically equalitarian, they represented and aimed at producing an élite. We are not sure who the Moists were. The name Mo may have been a family name or may have denoted a form of punishment. The fact that Mo Tzu's followers were ascetics and had "elders" suggests that they might have been prisoners or slaves. All speculation aside, the fact remains that they may have represented the working class. If this is correct, then the opposition between Confucianism and Moism is a foregone conclusion.

We know very little about Mo Tzu himself. His private name was Ti. He was a native of either Sung or Lu, Confucius' native state. He was once the chief officer of Sung. Some say he was at first a follower of Confucianism and then turned to be an opponent. Eventually he had about three hundred followers. His dates are uncertain except that probably he was born before Confucius died and died before Mencius was born. Aside from continuing his ethical teachings, his followers also developed some epistemological interest and evolved a crude system of definition and argumentation, perhaps in order to defend their peculiar doctrines. Both of these teachings disappeared soon after the third century B.C. Ever since then, no Moist philosopher has appeared. The centuries of war in which Moism thrived was no time for intellectual hair-splitting and sophistry, and their condemnation of war did not endear them to rulers. Their asceticism and utilitarianism were too extreme to be practicable. But why did their lofty doctrine of universal love fail to continue? Was it too idealistic for the Chinese? Or was it inherently weak because it is largely motivated by the benefits it would bring?[4] The question is open to speculation. One thing is certain, and that is, philosophically Moism is shallow and unimportant. It does not have the profound metaphysical presuppositions of either Taoism or Confucianism. Consequently it was only a temporary challenge to other schools, though a strong one. In the last two thousand years, it was philosophically profound Taoism and Buddhism, and not Moism, that provided Confucianism with stimulation and challenge. Modern interest in Moism arose in China because of its utilitarian spirit, and in the West because of its superficial resemblance to the Christian teachings of the will of God and universal love. This

[4] On this question, see Dubs, "The Development of Altruism in Confucianism," *Philosophy East and West*, 1 (1951), pp. 48-55.

interest is likely to be temporary. However, to understand ancient Chinese thought, a study of Moism is indispensable. The following translations include the three most important chapters and additional selections of Mo Tzu's work.

THE MO TZU[5]

A. Universal Love, Pt. 2 (ch. 15)

Mo Tzu said: What the man of humanity devotes himself to surely lies in the promotion of benefits for the world and the removal of harm from the world. This is what he devotes himself to.

But what are the benefits and the harm of the world?

Mo Tzu said: Take the present cases of mutual attacks among states, mutual usurpation among families, and mutual injuries among individuals, or the lack of kindness and loyalty between ruler and minister, of parental affection and filial piety between father and son, and of harmony and peace among brothers. These are harms in the world.

But when we examine[6] these harms, whence did they arise? Did they arise out of want of mutual love?

Mo Tzu said: They arise out of want of mutual love. At present feudal lords know only to love their own states and not those of others. Therefore they do not hesitate to mobilize their states to attack others. Heads of families know only to love their own families and not those of others. Therefore they do not hesitate to mobilize their families to usurp others. And individuals know only to love their own persons and not those of others. Therefore they do not hesitate to mobilize their own persons to injure others. For this reason, as feudal lords do not love one another, they will fight in the fields. As heads of families do not love one another, they will usurp one another. As individuals do not love one another, they will injure one another. When ruler and minister do not love each other, they will not be kind and loyal. When father and son do not love each other, they will not be affectionate and filial. When brothers do not love one another, they will not be harmonious and peaceful. When nobody

[5] The *Mo Tzu* is similar to the *Hsün Tzu* and later philosophical works in style in devoting each chapter to a particular subject. Originally there were seventy-one chapters but only fifty-three are extant. They cover subjects like "Condemnation of Confucianists," "Condemnation of War," etc., and military defense. Chapters 40-45 are on dialects, including the definition of terms and the explanations of major and minor causes, and are believed to have been by Mo Tzu's pupils. There was no commentary until the eighteenth century. For English translation, see Mei, *Ethical and Political Works of Motse*, which contains most of the chapters. Some chapters have also been translated by others. For a German translation of chapters 40-45, not translated by Mei, see Forke, *Mei Ti*.

[6] Read *ch'ung* (honor) as *ch'a* (examine), according to Yü Yüeh (1821-1906), *Chu-tzu p'ing-i* (Critique of the Various Philosophers), ch. 9, 1899 ed., 9:18b.

in the world loves any other, the strong will surely overcome the weak, [The many will oppress the few],[7] the rich will insult the poor. The honored will despise the humble, and the cunning will deceive the ignorant. Because of want of mutual love, all the calamities, usurpations, hatred, and animosity in the world have arisen. Therefore the man of humanity condemns it.

Now that it is condemned, what should take its place?

Mo Tzu said: It should be replaced by the way of universal love and mutual benefit.

What is the way of universal love and mutual benefit?

Mo Tzu said: It is to regard other people's countries as one's own. Regard other people's families as one's own. Regard other people's person as one's own. Consequently, when feudal lords love one another, they will not fight in the fields. When heads of families love one another, they will not usurp one another. When individuals love one another, they will not injure one another. When ruler and minister love each other, they will be kind and loyal. When father and son love each other, they will be affectionate and filial. When brothers love each other, they will be peaceful and harmonious. When all the people in the world love one another, the strong will not overcome the weak, the many will not oppress the few, the rich will not insult the poor, the honored will not despise the humble, and the cunning will not deceive the ignorant. Because of universal love, all the calamities, usurpations, hatred, and animosity in the world may be prevented from arising. Therefore the man of humanity praises it.

But now gentlemen of the world would say: Yes, it will be good if love becomes universal. Nevertheless, it is something distant and difficult to practice.

Mo Tzu said: This is simply because gentlemen of the world fail to recognize its benefit and understand its reason. Now, to besiege a city, to fight in the fields, and to sacrifice one's own life for fame are what all people consider difficult. And yet when a ruler likes them, his multitude can do them. Besides, to love one another universally and to benefit one another mutually is different from these. Those who love others will be loved by others. Those who benefit others will be benefited by others. Those who hate others will be hated by others. And those who harm others will be harmed by others. Then, what difficulty is there with this universal love? Only the ruler does not make it his governmental measure and officers do not make it their conduct.

[7] According to Sun I-jang (1848-1908), *Mo Tzu chien-ku* (Explanation and Commentary on the *Mo Tzu*), these words are probably missing from the original text.

Comment. The motive of benefits is behind all Moist doctrines. Confucianists throughout history have condemned benefits as motivation instead of righteousness. For Confucius, a main difference between a superior man and an inferior man is that the former is after righteousness and the latter after benefits.[8] Not that Confucianism renounces benefits. On the contrary, it promotes them. But they should be the *results* of good deeds, not the *motivation* for them. Mo Tzu does emphasize righteousness, but to him righteousness is to be understood in terms of beneficial results.

Formerly, Duke Wen[9] of Chin liked his officers to wear coarse clothing. Therefore all his ministers wore [simple] sheepskin garments, carried their swords in [unadorned] leather girdles, and put on hats of plain cloth. Thus attired, they appeared before the ruler inside and walked around the court outside. What was the reason for this? It was because the ruler liked it and therefore the ministers could do it. Formerly, King Ling[10] of Ch'u wanted people to have slender waists. Therefore all his ministers limited themselves to one meal a day. They exhaled before they tied their belts. They leaned against the wall before they could stand up. Within a year all at court looked thin and dark. What was the reason for this? It was because the ruler liked it and therefore the ministers could do it. Formerly, King Kou-chien[11] of Yüeh liked his officers to be brave. He trained his ministers, gathered them together, set his palace boat on fire and, to test his officers, said that all the treasure of Yüeh was there. The King of Yüeh himself beat the drum to urge them on. As the officers heard the drum, they rushed in disorder. More than a hundred stepped into the fire and died. Then the King of Yüeh beat the gong to let them retreat.

Therefore Master Mo said: Now, to eat little, to wear coarse clothing, and to sacrifice one's life for fame are things all people in the world consider difficult. But if the ruler likes them, the multitude can do them. Besides, universal love and mutual benefit are different from these. Those who love others will thereby be loved by them. Those who benefit others will thereby be benefited by them. Those who hate others will thereby be hated by them. And those who harm others will thereby be harmed by them. What difficulty is there in this (universal love)? Only the ruler does not make it his governmental measure and officers do not make it their conduct.

Comment. Universal love is promoted by Moism because of its beneficial results. There is no conviction that it is dictated by the

---

[8] See *Analects*, 4:11, 16; 15:17; 17:23.
[9] R. 636–628 B.C.   [10] R. 530–527 B.C.   [11] Fl. 452 B.C.

inherently good nature of man or by the inherent goodness of the act. Although Confucianism teaches love with distinctions, it also teaches love for all, but it does so on the grounds of moral necessity and of the innate goodness of man.[12]

But now gentlemen of the world would say: Yes, it will be good if love becomes universal. Nevertheless, it is something impracticable. It is like grappling with Mount T'ai and leaping over the Chi River.[13]

Mo Tzu said: The analogy is wrong. To grapple with Mount T'ai and leap across River Chi would be truly an extreme feat of strength. From antiquity down to the present day none has been able to do it. Besides, universal love and mutual benefit are different from this. Ancient sage-kings did practice them. How do we know this to be the case? In ancient times, when Yü[14] was ruling the empire, he dug the West and the Yü-tou Rivers in the west to release the water from the Ch'ü-sun-huang River. In the north he built a dam across the Yüan-ku River in order to fill the Hou-chih-ti and Hu-ch'ih Rivers. Mount Ti-chu was used as a water divide and a tunnel was dug through Lung-men Mountain. All this was done for the benefit of the Yen, Tai, Hu, and Ho tribes and the people west of the Yellow River. In the east, he drained the great plain and built dikes around the Meng-chu marshes and the water was divided into nine canals in order to regulate the water in the east and to benefit the people of the district of Chi. In the south he regulated the Yangtze, Han, Huai, and Ju Rivers so their water flowed eastward and emptied into the Five Lakes, in order to benefit the peoples of Ching, Ch'u, Kan, and Yüeh and the barbarians of the south. This is the story of Yü's accomplishments. This shows that my doctrine of universal love has been practiced.

Comment. While Confucianists cited historical examples for inspiration and as models, Mo Tzu cited them to show that his teachings had been demonstrated. The difference between the idealistic and practical approach is clear.

In ancient times, when King Wen[15] ruled the Western Land, he shone like the sun and the moon all over the four quarters as well as the Western Land. He did not permit a big state to oppress a small state, or the multitude to oppress the widow or widower, or the ruthless and powerful to rob people's grains or live stocks. Heaven recognized his deeds and visited him with blessings. Consequently, the old and childless

[12] See above, ch. 3, comment on *Mencius*, 3B:9 for a discussion on the doctrine of love with distinctions in relation to the doctrine of universal love.

[13] This is a reference to *Mencius*, 1A:7.

[14] Founder of the Hsia dynasty (r. 2183–2175 B.C.?).

[15] Founder of the Chou dynasty (r. 1751–1739 B.C.).

were well adjusted and enjoyed their full life span, the lonely and brotherless had opportunity to fulfill their work among mankind,[16] and the orphaned had the support to grow up. This is the story of King Wen's accomplishment. It shows that my doctrine of universal love has been practiced.

In ancient times when King Wu[17] was about to sacrifice to Mount T'ai, it was recorded, he said, "Mount T'ai, virtuous descendent King of the Chou assumed a great undertaking [to remove wicked King Chou[18] of the Shang] and now the great undertaking has been accomplished. Men of humanity have arisen, and I pray the Lord on High to save the people of the Middle Kingdom (China) and the various barbarian tribes. Although King Chou had his near relatives, they cannot compare with my men of humanity. If there is any blame anywhere, the responsibility rests with me alone."[19] This is the story of King Wu's accomplishment. It shows that my doctrine of universal love has been practiced.

Therefore Mo Tzu said: If rulers of the world today really want the empire to be wealthy and hate to have it poor, want it to be orderly and hate to have it chaotic, they should practice universal love and mutual benefit. This is the way of the sage-kings and the principle of governing the empire, and it should not be neglected. (SPTK, 4:3a-8a.)

B. The Will of Heaven, Pt. 1 (ch. 26)

Mo Tzu said: Gentlemen of the world today know small things and do not know great things. How do we know? We know from their conduct at home. If in their conduct at home they should offend their elders, there are still the homes of neighbors to which to flee. Yet relatives, brothers, and acquaintances all warn and admonish them, saying, "You must be cautious. You must be careful. How can it be to offend elders in one's conduct at home?" Not only is this true of conduct at home. It is also true of conduct in the state. If in one's conduct in the state one should offend the ruler, there are still the neighboring states to which to flee. Yet relatives, brothers, and acquaintances all warn and caution him, saying, "You must be cautious. You must be careful. How can it be to offend the ruler in one's conduct in the state?" These are people who have places to flee. Yet the warning and caution to them are strong like this. Should the warning and caution not be much stronger for those who have no place to flee? There is a saying: "If one commits a sin in daylight, where can he flee?" I say: There is no place to flee. For Heaven

[16] The word *tse* means to fulfill or accomplish, said Sun I-jang.
[17] Son of King Wen (r. 1121–1116 B.C.).
[18] R. 1175–1112 B.C. He was responsible for the fall of the Shang dynasty (1751–1112 B.C.).
[19] Cf. *Analects*, 20:1.

should not be regarded as a forest, a valley, or an obscure gate[20] where no one is present. It will surely see the evil action clearly. But with regard to Heaven, gentlemen of the world today are all negligent and do not warn and caution one another. This is how we know that the gentlemen in the world know small things but do not know great things.

Now what does Heaven want and what does Heaven dislike? Heaven wants righteousness and dislikes unrighteousness. Therefore, in leading the people in the world to engage in practicing righteousness, I should be doing what Heaven wants. When I do what Heaven wants, Heaven also does what I want. Now, what do I want and what do I dislike? I want happiness and wealth, and dislike calamities and misfortunes. [If I do not do what Heaven wants and do what Heaven does not want,] then I should be leading the people in the world to devote themselves to calamities and misfortunes. But how do we know that Heaven wants righteousness and dislikes unrighteousness? I say: With righteousness the world lives and without righteousness the world dies, with it the world becomes rich and without it the world becomes poor, with it the world becomes orderly and without it the world becomes chaotic. Now, Heaven wants to have the world live and dislikes to have it die, wants to have it rich and dislikes to have it poor, and wants to have it orderly and dislikes to have it chaotic. Therefore I know Heaven wants righteousness and dislikes unrighteousness.

Comment. Even the will of Heaven and righteousness are explained in terms of practical results.

Moreover, righteousness is the standard.[21] It is not to be given by the subordinate to the superior but must be given from the superior to the subordinate. Therefore, the common people should attend to their work with all their might, and should not forthwith[22] set up the standard themselves. There are minor officials to give them the standard. Minor officials should attend to their work with all their might and should not forthwith set the standard themselves. There are great officials to give them the standard.[23] Great officials should attend to their work with all their might and should not forthwith set the standard themselves. There are the three

---

[20] Wang Nien-sun (1744-1832), *Tu-shu tsa-chih* (Miscellaneous Notes from Reading), 1933 ed., bk. 9, p. 71, reads *men* (gate) as *hsien* (leisure) and Pi Yüan (1730-1797), *Mo Tzu chu* (Commentary on the *Mo Tzu*) reads it as *chien* (brook), both without improving the text.

[21] *Cheng*, ordinarily meaning to govern, here means to be correct or to be a standard, according to Wang Nien-sun, *Tu-shu tsa-chih, ibid.*, and Sun I-jang, *Mo Tzu hsien-ku*, ch. 7.

[22] Sun I-jang interprets *tz'u* as forthwith but Pi Yüan reads it as *tzu*, to indulge in.

[23] The text says "generals and officials" but Sun I-jang says that means great officials.

ministers[24] and the several feudal lords to give them the standard. The three ministers and the several feudal lords should attend to government with all their might and should not forthwith set the standard themselves. There is the Son of Heaven (emperor) to give them the standard. The emperor should not forthwith set the standard himself. There is Heaven to give him the standard. Gentlemen of the world of course clearly understand that the emperor gives the standard to the three ministers, the several feudal lords, the minor officials, and the common people, but the common people of the world do not clearly understand that Heaven gives the standard to the emperor. Therefore the ancient sage-kings of the Three Dynasties,[25] Yü, T'ang,[26] and Wu, desiring to make it clear to the common people that Heaven gives the standard to the emperor, all fed oxen and sheep with grass and dogs and pigs with grain, and cleanly prepared pastry and wine to sacrifice to the Lord on High and spiritual beings and pray to Heaven for blessing. But I have not heard of Heaven praying to the emperor for blessing. I therefore know that Heaven gives the standard to the emperor.

Thus the emperor is the most honorable in the world and the richest in the world. Therefore those who desire honor and wealth cannot but obey the will of Heaven. Those who obey the will of Heaven love universally and benefit each other, and will surely obtain rewards. Those who oppose the will of Heaven set themselves apart from each other, hate each other, and injure each other, and will surely incur punishment. Now, who were those who obeyed the will of Heaven and obtained rewards and who were those who opposed the will of Heaven and incurred punishment?

Mo Tzu said: The ancient sage-kings of the Three Dynasties, Yü, T'ang, Wen, and Wu, were those who obeyed the will of Heaven and obtained rewards. The wicked kings of the Three Dynasties, Chieh,[27] Chou, Yu,[28] and Li,[29] were those who opposed the will of Heaven and incurred punishment.

Well, how did Yü, T'ang, Wen, and Wu obtain rewards? Mo Tzu said: On the highest level they honored Heaven, on the middle level they served spiritual beings, and on the lower level they loved the people. Thereupon the will of Heaven proclaimed, "They love universally those whom I love. They benefit universally those whom I benefit. Such love of people is really universal and such benefit to people is really substantial." Therefore Heaven caused them to have the honor of being

---

[24] The grand protector, the grand preceptor, and the grand tutor.
[25] Hsia, Shang, and Chou.
[26] Founder of the Shang dynasty (r. 1751–1739 B.C.?).
[27] He (r. 1802–1752 B.C.) lost the Hsia dynasty.
[28] R. 781–771 B.C.   [29] R. 878–842 B.C.

Sons of Heaven and possess the wealth of the whole empire. Their heritages were continued by the descendants of ten thousand generations, who continually praised their good deeds. They spread [benefits] all over the world, and people praise them to this day, calling them sage-kings.

Well, how did Chieh, Chou, Yu, and Li incur punishment? Mo Tzu said: On the highest level they blasphemed against Heaven, on the middle level they blasphemed against spiritual beings, and on the lower level they injured the people. Thereupon the will of Heaven proclaimed, "They set themselves apart from those whom I love and hated them. They injure all those whom I benefit. Such hatred of people is really universal and such injury to people is really substantial." Therefore Heaven caused them not to live out their life-span or to survive their generation. They are condemned to this day and are called wicked kings.

But how do we know that Heaven loves all the people in the world? Because it enlightens them all. How do we know that it enlightens them all? Because it possessses them all. How do we know that it possesses them all? Because it feeds them all. How do we know that it feeds them all? I say: Within the four seas (the world) all grain-eating (civilized) people feed oxen and sheep with grass and dogs and pigs with grain, and cleanly prepare pastry and wine to sacrifice to the Lord on High and spiritual beings. Possessing all people, how could Heaven not love them? Moreover, I declare that for the murder of one innocent person, there will surely be one misfortune. Who is it that murders the innocent person? It is man. Who is it that sends down misfortune? It is Heaven. If it is thought that Heaven does not love the people of the world, why does it send misfortune because a man murders a man? This is why I know that Heaven loves the people of the world.

To obey the will of Heaven is to use righteousness as the method of control. To oppose the will of Heaven is to use force as the method of control.[30] What will happen if righteousness is used as a method of control? Mo Tzu said: A ruler of a big state will not attack a small state. A ruler of a large family will not usurp a small family. The strong will not plunder the weak. The honored will not despise the humble. And the cunning will not deceive the ignorant. This is beneficial to Heaven on the highest level, beneficial to spiritual beings on the middle level, and beneficial to man on the lower level. Being beneficial to these three means being beneficial to all. Therefore the whole world gives them a good name and calls them sage-kings.

Comment. In teaching obedience to the will of Heaven, Mo Tzu

---

[30] According to Sun I-jang, *cheng*, which ordinarily means to govern, should be *cheng*, meaning the way to control.

was the most religious of ancient Chinese philosophers. No one else relied on religious sanction as much as he did. Some scholars even suggested that he founded a religion, assuming that his followers formed some sort of a religious group. If so, he was the only personal religious founder in ancient China.

Those who use force as the way of control will act differently. Their words will be different and their action will be the opposite, like galloping back to back. A ruler of a large state will attack a small state. A ruler of a large family will usurp a small family. The strong will plunder the weak. The honorable will despise the humble. And the cunning will deceive the ignorant. This is not beneficial to Heaven on the highest level, not beneficial to spiritual beings on the middle level, and not beneficial to people on the lower level. Not being beneficial to these three means not being beneficial to all. Therefore the whole world gives them a bad name and calls them wicked kings.

Mo Tzu said: The will of Heaven to me is like the compasses to the wheelwright and the square to the carpenter. The wheelwright and the carpenter apply their square and compasses to measure all square and circular objects in the world. They say that those that fit are correct and those that do not fit are not correct. The writings of the scholars and gentlemen of the world today cannot all be loaded in carts and the many doctrines they teach cannot all be enumerated. They try to persuade the feudal lords above and various minor officials below. But as to humanity and righteousness, they are far, far off the mark. How do I know? I say: I have the shining model in the world (the will of Heaven) to measure them. (SPTK, 7:1a-6a)

C. Attack on Fatalism, Pt. 1 (ch. 35)

Mo Tzu said: In ancient times kings, dukes, and great officials, who ruled the state all wanted their country to be rich, their population to be large, and their administration of government to be orderly. But instead of wealth they got poverty, instead of a large population they got a small population, and instead of order they got chaos. Fundamentally this is to lose what they desired but to get what they disliked. What is the reason? Mo Tzu said: It was due to the large number of fatalists among the people.

The fatalists say: When fate (*ming*) decrees that the country shall be wealthy, it will be wealthy. When it decrees that it shall be poor, it will be poor. When fate decrees that the population shall be large, it will be large. When it decrees that it shall be small, it will be small. When it decrees that the country shall be orderly, it will be orderly. When it decrees that it shall be chaotic, it will be chaotic. When fate decrees that one shall enjoy longevity, one will enjoy longevity. And when fate decrees that one will suffer brevity of life, he will suffer brevity of life. What is the use of exerting strong [effort]?[31] With this doctrine they tried to persuade the kings, dukes, and great officials above and to prevent the common people from doing their work. Therefore the fatalists are not men of humanity. Their doctrine must be clearly examined.

> *Comment.* Both Confucianists and Taoists discussed *ming* in its more fundamental aspect of destiny, that is, man's endowment and function in relation to the total existence of the universe. Mo Tzu, however, looked at *ming* only in its narrow meaning of fate, and he discussed it primarily from the point of view of its effects. The deeper philosophical and religious phases did not interest him.

Now, how is this doctrine to be clearly examined? Mo Tzu said: For any doctrine some standard must be established. To expound a doctrine without a standard is like determining the directions of sunrise and sunset on a revolving potter's wheel. In this way the distinction of right and wrong and benefit and harm cannot be clearly known. Therefore for any doctrine there must be the three standards.[32] What are the three standards? Mo Tzu said: [1] There must be a basis or foundation. [2] There must be an examination. [3] And there must be practical application. [1] Where to find the basis? Find it in the [will of Heaven and the spirits and][33] the experiences of the ancient sage-kings above. [2] How is it to be examined? It is to be examined by inquiring into the actual experience of the eyes and ears of the people below. [3] How to apply it? Put[34] it into law and governmental measures and see if they bring about benefits to the state and the people. These are called the three standards.

> *Comment.* A surprisingly scientific procedure: basis, examination, and application. A theory is to be verified and tested in actual experience. One cannot help sensing a strongly pragmatic flavor.

[1] But some of the gentlemen of the world today believe that there is fate. Why not look into the experiences of the sage-kings? In ancient times the chaos created by King Chieh was taken over by King T'ang

---

[31] The idea of effort is found in pts. 2 and 3, or chs. 27 and 28 of the *Mo Tzu.*

[32] In chs. 36 and 37 of the *Mo Tzu, fa* is used instead of *piao* as it is here. According to Sun I-jang, they all have the same meaning as *i,* which is translated as "standard" above.

[33] These inserted words appear in a similar passage in the opening paragraph of *Mo Tzu,* ch. 36.

[34] According to Wang Nien-sun, *ibid.,* p. 87, *fei* and *fa* were interchangeable, meaning to issue forth.

and replaced by order, and the chaos created by King Chou was taken over by King Wu and turned into order. The times were the same and the people were not different, and yet the empire was a chaos under Chieh and Chou but an orderly state under T'ang and Wu. How can it be said that there is fate?

[2] But some of the gentlemen of the world today believe that there is fate. Why not look into the written records of past rulers? In the written records of past rulers what were issued to the whole country and distributed among the people were the laws. Did any of them say that blessings cannot be invoked and calamities cannot be averted, or that reverence does no good and cruelty does no harm? What were employed to settle litigations and mete out punishment were the laws. Did any of them say that blessings cannot be invoked and calamities cannot be averted, or that reverence does no good and cruelty does no harm? What were used to organize armies and order soldiers were the declarations. Did any of them say that blessings cannot be invoked and calamities cannot be averted, or that reverence does no good and cruelty does no harm? Mo Tzu said: I have not enumerated all[35] the records. The good records of the world are innumerable. Generally speaking, they are the three types.[36] Try as we may, we cannot find there the doctrine of those who believe in fate. Should the doctrine not be abandoned?

[3] To adopt the doctrine of those who believe in fate is to upset righteousness in the world. To upset righteousness in the world is to establish fate. This means sorrow for the people. And to be delighted in people's sorrow is to destroy them. Now, why do we want men of righteousness in the government? The answer is that when men of righteousness are in the government the world will be in order, the Lord on High, mountains and rivers, and spiritual beings will be sacrificed to by their proper sacrificers, and the people will receive great benefits from them. How do we know? Mo Tzu said: In ancient times T'ang was conferred a fief at Po. Making allowance for the irregular boundary lines, his territory was one hundred li[37] in width and length. He and his people loved one another universally and benefited one another mutually. They shared the wealth when there was abundance. He led his people to honor Heaven and serve spiritual beings above. Consequently Heaven and spiritual beings enriched them, the feudal lords befriended them, the people loved them, and the worthy scholars came to them. Within a generation he became king of the empire and leader[38] of the feudal lords.

In ancient times King Wen was conferred a fief at the Chou district

[35] According to Pi Yüan, the word *yen* (salt) is a misprint for *chin* (all).

[36] The text has "five" but it should have been three, according to Pi Yüan.

[37] A *li* is about one-third of a mile.

[38] Sun I-jang said that *cheng* here means to be a leader.

at the foot of Ch'i Mountain. Making allowance for the irregular boundary lines, his territory was one hundred *li* in width and length. He and his people loved one another universally and benefited one another mutually. Therefore those near him were contented with his government and those far away came to the fold of his virtue. Those who heard of King Wen all rose up and rushed to him. The weak, the unworthy, and the paralyzed remained where they were and expressed their desires, saying, "Why is King Wen's land not extended to include us? Wouldn't we then enjoy the same benefits as the subjects of King Wen?" Therefore Heaven and spiritual beings enriched them, the feudal lords befriended them, the people loved them, and the worthy scholars came to them. Within a generation he became king of the empire and leader of the feudal lords. I have said, when men of righteousness are in the government, the world will be in order, the Lord on High, mountains and rivers, and spiritual beings will be sacrificed to by their proper sacrificers, and the people will receive great benefits from them. From these ancient experiences I know what I said is true.

Therefore ancient sage-kings propagated laws and issued edicts, and offered rewards and punishments to encourage virtue [and check wickedness].[39] Consequently, people showed filial piety and deep love to their parents at home and respect to their elders in the community. They followed a standard in their conduct, observed discipline in their movements, and maintained the distinction between men and women. When they were ordered to manage official treasuries, they would not steal. When they were ordered to defend a city, they would not desert or rebel. When their ruler met with death, they sacrificed their own lives. When their ruler fled, they followed him. This is what the superior rewarded and the common people praised. But those who believe in fate say, "Whoever is rewarded by the superior is of course rewarded by fate. It is not because of virtue that he is rewarded. Whoever is punished is of course punished by fate. It is not because of his cruelty that he is punished." In consequence people do not show filial piety and deep love to their parents at home or respect to their elders in the community. They do not follow any standard in their conduct, observe discipline in their movements, or maintain the distinction between men and women. Therefore when they manage the official treasuries, they would steal. When they defend a city, they would desert or rebel. When their ruler meets with death, they would not sacrifice their lives. When their ruler flees, they would not follow him. This is what the superior will punish and the common people will condemn. But those who believe in fate say,

---

[39] According to Sun I-jang, these words should have been added to the text.

"Whoever is punished by the superior is of course punished by fate. It is not because of his cruelty that he is punished. Whoever is rewarded by the superior is of course rewarded by fate. It is not because of his virtue that he is rewarded." As a ruler he who holds this doctrine will not be righteous. As a minister he will not be loyal. As a father he will not be deeply loving. As a son he will not be filial. As an elder brother he will not be brotherly. And as a younger brother he will not be respectful. The unreasoning adherence to this doctrine is the source of evil ideas and the way of the wicked man.

How do we know that fatalism is the way of the wicked man? Poor people of ancient times were greedy in drinking and eating but lazy in their work. Therefore their resources for food and clothing were inadequate, and the troubles of hunger and cold were approaching. They did not know enough to say, "We are weak and unworthy. We did not work hard." But they would say, "It is originally our fate that we are poor." The wicked kings of ancient times did not check the indulgence of their ears and eyes and the depravity of their minds. They did not obey their ancestors and consequently they lost their countries and ruined their states. They did not know to say, "We are weak and unworthy. Our government has not been good." But they would say, "It is originally our fate that we lost them." The "Announcement of Chung-hui" says, "I have heard that the man of the Hsia (King Chieh) issued orders to the world and falsely claimed them to be the Mandate of Heaven (T'ien-ming). The Lord on High was for this reason displeased and [ordered King T'ang] to destroy his armies."[40] This tells how King T'ang showed Chieh's belief in fate to be wrong. The "Great Oath" says, "King Chou abides squatting on the floor, not serving the Lord on High or spiritual beings. He neglected his ancestors and did not sacrifice to them. Thereupon he said, 'I [have] the people and I have the mandate (fate).' He neglected his duty.[41] Heaven also cast him away and withdrew its protection.[42] This tells how King Wu (who removed King Chou) showed Chou's belief in fate to be wrong.

If the doctrine of the fatalist is put into practice, the ruler above would not attend to government, and people below would not attend to their work. If the ruler does not attend to government, then law and government will be disorderly. If the people do not attend to their work, wealth and resources will not be adequate. Then on the higher level there will

[40] Paraphrasing *History*, "Announcement of Chung-hui. Cf. trans., Legge, *Shoo King*, p. 178.
[41] The text of this sentence is obscure. This is Pi Yüan's interpretation based on the phraseology of a similar passage at the end of ch. 36.
[42] The whole quotation is a paraphrase of *History*, "Great Oath." Cf. Legge, p. 286. The last sentence does not appear in *History*.

not be the supply of pastry and wine to offer in sacrifice to the Lord on High and spiritual beings, and on the lower level there will be nothing to satisfy and comfort the worthy scholars of the world. Externally, there will be nothing to entertain the feudal lords as guests, and internally, there will be nothing to feed the hungry, clothe the cold, support the aged and protect the weak. Therefore on the higher level fatalism is not beneficial to Heaven, on the middle level it is not beneficial to spiritual beings, and on the lower level it is not beneficial to men. The unreasoning adherence to this doctrine is the source of evil ideas and the way of the wicked man. Therefore Mo Tzu said: If the gentlemen of the world today really want the world to be rich and dislike it to be poor, and want the world to be orderly and dislike it to be chaotic, they must condemn the doctrine of fatalism. It is a great harm to the world. (SPTK, 9:1a-6b.)

D. Additional Selections

1. Utilitarianism

Mo Tzu said: Any word or action that is beneficial to Heaven, spiritual beings, and the people is to be undertaken. Any word or action that is harmful to Heaven, spiritual beings, and the people is to be rejected. Any word or action that is in accord with the sage-kings of the Three Dynasties, sage-emperors Yao and Shun,[43] and sage-kings Yü, T'ang, Wen, and Wu is to be undertaken. Any word or action that is in accord with the wicked kings of the Three Dynasties, Chieh, Chou, Yu, and Li, is to be rejected.

Mo Tzu said: Any doctrine that can elevate conduct should be perpetuated. Any doctrine that cannot elevate conduct should not be perpetuated. To perpetuate those doctrines that cannot elevate conduct is a waste of speech. (ch. 47, SPTK, 12:2b-3a.)

When a sage rules a state, the benefits of that state may be doubled. When he extends his rule to the empire, those of the empire may be doubled. This twofold increase is not the result of appropriating land from outside, but that of doing away with useless expenditure in the state. In issuing orders, promoting any undertaking, employing the people, or expending wealth, the sage-kings in their administration never do anything that is not useful. Therefore resources are not wasted and the people can[44] be free from being overworked, and many benefits will be promoted. . . .

In ancient times the sage-kings formulated laws which said, "No man of twenty should dare to remain single, no girl of fifteen should dare

---

[43] Legendary rulers (3rd millennium B.C.).
[44] According to Sun I-jang, te (virtue) is to be read te (can).

to be without her master." This was the law of sage-kings. Now that the sage-kings have passed away, the people do what they want. Those who like to have a family early sometimes marry at twenty. Those who like to have a family later sometimes marry at forty. When the late marriages are made up by the early marriages, the average is still later by ten years than the legal age decreed by the sage-kings. Suppose there is one birth in three full years, then there would be two or three children born [by the time men now marry]. This does not only show that if people are caused to marry early, the population can be doubled.

But that is not all. Rulers of today reduce the population in more ways than one. They overwork the people in employing them, and impose heavy burdens by levying taxes. People's resources become insufficient and innumerable people die of hunger and cold. Moreover, great officials mobilize armies to invade neighboring states, for a whole year in long expeditions or for a few months in quicker ones. For a long time, husbands and wives would not see each other. These are ways in which population is reduced. . . . (ch. 20, SPTK, 6:1a-2b.)

2. The Condemnation of War

Now does it mean that to annex a state and destroy an army, injure and oppress the people, and throw the heritages of sages into confusion will benefit Heaven? But to recruit the people of Heaven to attack the cities of Heaven is to murder the people of Heaven, smash altars, demolish shrines, and kill sacrificial animals. In this way, on the higher level no benefit to Heaven can be attained. Does it mean to benefit spiritual beings? But people of Heaven are murdered and spiritual beings are denied their patron sacrifices. The spirits of past rulers are neglected. The multitude are injured and oppressed and the people are scattered. Thus on the middle level no benefit to spiritual beings can be attained. Does it mean to benefit the people? The benefit to the people from killing the people of Heaven is slight[45] indeed! And calculate its cost! This is the root of destruction of life. It exhausts the people to an immeasurable degree. Thus on the lower level no benefit to the people can be attained. (ch. 19, SPTK, 5:9a-9b.)

3. The Condemnation of Wasteful Musical Activities

The reason why Mo Tzu condemns music is not because the sounds of the big bells, resounding drums, harps, and pipes are not delightful. . . . But set against the past it is not in accord with the deeds of the sage-kings and checked with the present it is not in accord with the benefits

[45] Read po (extensive) as po (thin), according to Yü Yüeh, Chu-tzu p'ing-i (Textual Critiques of the Various Philosophers) ch. 9, 1899 ed., 9:20a.

of the people. Therefore Mo Tzu said: To engage in music is wrong. . . .

Mo Tzu said: To levy heavy taxes on the people in order to produce the sounds of big bells, resounding drums, harps, and pipes does not help the promotion of benefits and the removal of harms in the world. Therefore Mo Tzu said: To engage in music is wrong. . . . To have men engage in music is to waste their time for ploughing and planting. To have women engage in music is to waste their effort for weaving and spinning. Now, kings, dukes, and great officials engage in music. To strike musical instruments to produce music, they loot the people's resources for food and clothing to such an extent! Therefore Mo Tzu said: To engage in music is wrong.

Now, the sounds of big bells, resounding drums, harps, and pipes are produced. It is no pleasure for the great lords to play and listen alone. They must enjoy it either with the common people or with the rulers. If with the rulers, it will cause them to neglect their attention to government. If with the common people, it will cause them to neglect their work. Now kings, dukes, and great officials engage in music. To strike musical instruments they loot the people's resources for food and clothing to such an extent! Therefore Mo Tzu said: To engage in music is wrong.

Formerly Duke K'ang[46] of Ch'i promoted music and dance. The dancers[47] were not to wear coarse garments or eat coarse food. They said that if food was not good, their appearance and complexion would not be good to look at, and if clothing was not beautiful the body and its movements would not be good to observe. Therefore their food had to consist of grain and meat and their clothing of beautiful patterns and embroidery. This is not to produce material for food and clothing but to live on others all the time. Therefore Mo Tzu said: Now, kings, dukes, and great officials engage in music. To strike musical instruments they loot the people's resources for food and clothing to such an extent! Therefore Mo Tzu said: To engage in music is wrong. . . .

Now, kings, dukes, and great officials love music and listen to it, they certainly cannot go to court early and retire late in order to listen to litigations and administer the government. Therefore the country is in chaos and the state in danger. . . . Therefore Mo Tzu said: To engage in music is wrong. (ch. 32, SPTK, 8:14a-18b)

4. The Condemnation of Elaborate Funerals

Now the gentlemen on the world still doubt whether elaborate funerals and extended mourning are right or wrong, beneficial or harmful. Therefore Mo Tzu said: I have inquired into the matter. If the doctrines

---

[46] R. 404–379 B.C.

[47] Following Sun I-jang, read wan (ten thousand) as wu (to dance).

of those who advocate elaborate funerals and extended mourning are followed in the affairs in the country, it will mean that whenever a king, duke, or great official dies, there would be layers of coffin, the burial would be deep, the shrouding would be plenty, the embroidery covering would be elaborate, and the grave mound would be massive. . . . Mourners would weep in a confused manner to the point of choking, wear sackcloth on the breast and flax on the head, keep the snivel dangling, live in a mourning hut, sleep on straw, and rest their heads on a lump of earth. . . . All this is to last for three years.

If such a doctrine is followed and such a principle is practiced, kings, dukes, and great officials practicing it cannot go to court early [and retire late to administer their government, and attend to the] five offices and six departments[48] and develop agriculture and forestry and fill the granaries, farmers practicing it cannot start out early and return late to plough and plant, artisans practicing it cannot build vehicles and make utensils, and women practicing it cannot rise early and retire late to weave and spin. So, much wealth is buried in elaborate funerals and long periods of work are suspended in extended mourning. Wealth that is already produced is carried to be buried and wealth yet to be produced is long delayed. To seek wealth in this way is like seeking a harvest by stopping farming. . . . (ch. 25, SPTK, 6:7b-9a)

5. Elevating the Worthy to Government Positions

How do we know elevating the worthy is the foundation of government? The answer is: When the honorable and the wise run the government, the ignorant and the humble remain orderly, but when the ignorant and the humble run the government, the honorable and the wise become rebellious. Therefore we know that elevating the worthy is the foundation of government.

The ancient sage-kings greatly valued the elevation of the worthy and employed the capable. They did not side with their fathers and brothers. They were not partial toward people of wealth and high position. They had no special love for the good-looking. They raised and promoted the worthy, gave them wealth and high position, and made them leading officials. They demoted and rejected the unworthy, caused them to be poor and humble, and made them servants. In this way all people were encouraged by rewards and scared by punishment. They led one another to become worthy. The result was that many were worthy and few were unworthy. Such is the advancing of the worthy. . . .

Now, when kings, dukes, and great officials cannot make a coat, they

---

[48] The five offices were those of education, war, public works, civil personnel, and justice. The six departments were divisions in the treasury.

will depend on an able tailor. When they cannot kill an ox or sheep, they will depend on an able butcher. . . . If kings, dukes, and great officials really want to put the state in order and make it permanent and secured, why do they not understand that elevating the worthy is the foundation of government? . . . (ch. 9, SPTK, 2:4a-9a)

6. Agreement with the Superior

How is order brought about in the empire? There is order in the empire because the emperor can bring about a unified and agreed concept of right in the empire. If the people all agree with the emperor but not with the Heaven, then calamity still remains. Now, the frequent arrival of hurricanes and torrents are the punishment from Heaven upon the people for their failure to agree with Heaven. . . . (ch. 11, SPTK, 3:3b)

How do we know that the principle of agreement with the superior can be used to govern the empire? Well, why not examine the theory of the origin of the government? In the beginning when man was created, there was no ruler. People existed as individuals. As they existed as individuals, there was one concept of right for a hundred men, a thousand concepts of right for a thousand men, and so on until there were a countless number of concepts of right for a countless number of men. All of them considered their own concepts of right as correct and other people's concepts as wrong. And there were strife among the strong and quarrels among the weak. Thereupon Heaven wished to unify all concepts of right in the world. The worthy was therefore selected and made an emperor. The emperor, realizing his inadequate wisdom and ability to govern alone, selected the next best in virtue and appointed them as the three ministers. The three ministers, realizing their inadequate wisdom and ability to assist the emperor alone, divided the country into states and set up feudal lordships. The feudal lords, realizing their inadequate wisdom and ability to govern the land within the four borders by themselves, selected the next best in virtue. . . . Therefore, in appointing the three ministers, the feudal lords, the great officers, the prime minister, the village elders, and the heads of households, the emperor of old did not select them because of their wealth, high position, or leisure, but employed them to assist in bringing political order and administering the government. . . . When order prevails in the empire, the emperor further unifies all concepts of right as one in the empire and makes it agree with [the will of] Heaven. Therefore the principle of agreement with the superior can be applied by the emperor to govern the empire, by the feudal lords to govern the state, and heads of households to govern the family. . . . (ch. 13, SPTK, 3:13b-18a)

Comment. Mo Tzu has been criticized for absolutism. The danger is certainly present. The requirement for conformity is strict. We must not forget, however, that the final authority is Heaven. In this sense, it is not essentially different from the Confucian theory of the Mandate of Heaven. In both cases, whether the Mandate of Heaven is fulfilled is determined by whether the people are happy and society in good order. Still Confucianists were thinking of moral obligations, while Mo Tzu was thinking of practical results.

10

DEBATES ON METAPHYSICAL CONCEPTS:
THE LOGICIANS

PRACTICALLY all major ancient Chinese philosophical schools were greatly concerned with the relationship between names and actuality, whether for its social and moral significance (as in Confucianism), for its metaphysical import (as in Taoism), or for political control (as in Legalism). None of them was interested in the logical aspect of the problem. Hsün Tzu's (fl. 298–238 B.C.) rectification of names comes close to it, but his objective was still moral and social. The only school that was primarily devoted to logical considerations was the Logicians, who constituted one of the smallest schools and exercised no influence whatsoever after their own time.

The name "Logicians" is used only to emphasize their intellectual character. Actually, they neither evolved any syllogism nor discovered any law of thought. They expressed themselves in dialogues, aphorisms, and paradoxes instead of systematic and cogent argumentation. Nevertheless, they were the only group devoted to such problems as existence, relativity, space, time, quality, actuality, and causes. Although the Chinese name for them is Ming-chia (School of Names), or Ming-pien (Scholars of Names and Debaters), they were not confined to the correspondence of names and actuality. Their metaphysical and epistemological concepts are primitive, but they represent the only tendency in ancient China toward intellectualism for its own sake. They subscribed to the Moist doctrine of universal love, and therefore may be considered to have gone into a discussion of concepts in order to support this doctrine. But if so, they must have detoured a long way to do so. There is every indication that their purely intellectual interest was genuine and primary. In this they were singular in Chinese history.

The group is not so easily identified as other schools such as the Confucianists or the Moists. It consisted of a number of minor thinkers. Among them Hui Shih (380–305 B.C.?) and Kung-sun Lung (b. 380 B.C.?) were the most prominent. They were not unanimous in their opinions. Hui Shih and his friend Chuang Tzu both believed that all things formed one body and that there was the great unit or great One. But Chuang Tzu sought to know these through mystical experience, whereas Hui Shih attempted to do so through rational knowledge. Hui Shih and Kung-sun Lung were opposed to each other at more than one point. To Hui Shih things were relative, but to Kung-sun Lung they were absolute. The former emphasized change, while the latter stressed universality and permanence. These are also basic problems underlying the twenty-one paradoxes of the Debaters. A number of these paradoxes seem to side with Hui Shih in stressing the relativity of space and time, but others side with Kung-sun Lung in stressing universality and permanence.

The question is inevitably asked why the intellectual tendency of this school did not develop in China. The answer is to be found partly in the fact that the Chinese have not been interested in the science of logic, and partly in the fact that the period of upheaval in which the Logicians lived was not conducive to logical studies. Moreover, the common emphasis of the major schools on solving human problems, as well as the attempts of some thinkers to strive for social reform, made the Logicians look like idle debaters. As Chuang Tzu said of them, "They are able to subdue other people's mouths, but cannot win their hearts. This is where their narrowness lies."[1]

A. THE PARADOXES OF HUI SHIH AND
THE DEBATERS

Hui Shih had many tricks. His books filled five carts. His doctrines are contradictory and his sayings miss the truth. Referring to the nature of things, he said:

1. The greatest has nothing beyond itself; it is called the great unit.[2] The smallest has nothing within itself; it is called the small unit.

   Comment. Was Hui Shih thinking of the atom?

2. That which has no thickness cannot have any volume, and yet in extent it may cover a thousand *li*.[3]

3. Heaven is as low as the earth; mountains and marshes are on the same level.

4. When the sun is at noon, it is setting; when there is life, there is death.

5. A great similarity is different from a small similarity; this is

---

[1] *Chuang Tzu*, ch. 33, NHCC, 10:24b. Cf. Giles, trans., *Chuang Tzu*, 1961 ed., p. 314. For further criticism of the Logicians, see *Hsün Tzu*, chs. 6 and 21, SPTK, 3:14b, 15:5a (see Dubs, trans., *The Works of Hsüntze*, pp. 79 and 262), and Ssu-ma Ch'ien (145–86 B.C.?), *Shih chi* (Records of the Historian), PNP, 130:3b–4a. Little is known of Hui Shih except that he was a native of Sung, was once prime minister to King Hui (r. 371–320 B.C.) of Liang, and often debated with his friend Chuang Tzu. Kung-sun Lung, a native of Chao, was a guest of Prince P'ing-yüan who treated him well, but finally rejected him.

[2] Cf. *Chuang Tzu*, chs. 24 and 33, NHCC, 8:42a, 10:35a. See Giles, pp. 246 and 319.

[3] A *li* is about one-third of a mile.

called the lesser similarity-and-difference. All things are similar to one another and different from one another; this is called the great similarity-and-difference.[4]

6. The South has no limit and yet has a limit.
7. One goes to the state of Yüeh today and arrives there yesterday.[5]
8. Joint rings can be separated.
9. I know the center of the world: it is north of the state of Yen (in the north) and south of the state of Yüeh (in the south).
10. Love all things extensively. Heaven and earth form one body.[6]

Comment. Chang Ping-Lin (Chang T'ai-yen, 1868-1936), foremost modern scholar on ancient Chinese philosophy, especially on Chuang Tzu, regards paradoxes nos. 1, 2, 3, 6, 8, and 9 as arguing for the theory that all quantitative measurements and all spatial distinctions are illusory and unreal, that nos. 4 and 7 are arguing for the unreality of time, and that nos. 5 and 10 are arguing for the unreality of all apparent similarities and differences between things.[7] This seems to be a reasonable interpretation. Hu Shih (1891-1962), however, thinks the first nine paradoxes are intended to prove a monistic theory of the universe, which is expressed in the last paradox.[8] Is this not reading too much modern philosophy into an ancient text?

Hui Shih considered these to be the great insights of the world and tried to enlighten the debaters. And they enjoyed it. [They said]:

1. The egg has hair.
2. A chicken has three legs.[9]
3. Ying (capital of Ch'u) contains the whole world.
4. A dog can be a sheep.
5. The horse has eggs.
6. The frog has a tail.
7. Fire is not hot.
8. Mountains produce mouths.
9. The wheel never touches the ground.

[4] Cf. this with Hsün Tzu's great general name and great particular name. See *Hsün Tzu*, ch. 22, SPTK, 16:6a-b. Cf. Dubs, *The Works of Hsüntze*, p. 286.

[5] This sentence also appears in *Chuang Tzu*, ch. 2, NHCC, 1:25b. See Giles, p. 36.

[6] Cf. *Chuang Tzu*, ch. 2, NHCC, 1:34a, Giles, p. 41.

[7] *Kuo-ku lun-heng* (Balanced Inquiries on Classical Studies), pp. 192-193.

[8] *Development of the Logical Method in Ancient China*, p. 113.

[9] The two physical legs and the spirit that moves them. See Wang Hsien-ch'ien (1842-1917) *Chuang Tzu chi-chieh* (Collected Explanations of the *Chuang Tzu*), ch. 33. In the *Kung-sun Lung Tzu*, ch. 4 (below, B, 3), the meaning seems to be the two legs and the leg as such.

10. The eye does not see.

11. The pointing of the finger[10] does not reach [a thing]; the reaching never ends.

12. The tortoise is longer than the snake.

13. The carpenter's square is not square in shape and a compass cannot draw a circle.

14. The mortise does not surround the bit of a chisel.

15. The shadow of a flying bird never moves.

16. The arrow is flying so fast that there are moments when it is neither in motion nor at rest.

17. A puppy is not a dog.

18. A brown horse and a dark ox make three.[11]

19. A white dog is black.

20. An orphan colt has never had a mother.

21. Take a stick one foot long and cut it in half every day and you will never exhaust it even after ten thousand generations.

With these propositions the debaters argued with Hui Shih all their lives without coming to an end. (*Chuang Tzu*, ch. 33, NHCC, 10:38a-42b)

Comment. Hu Shih has grouped twenty of these paradoxes[12] into four groups: nos. 3, 9, 15, 16, and 21 arguing for the unreality of distinctions in space and time; nos. 1, 5, 6, 12, 13, 14, and 17 arguing for the relativity of all similarities and differences; nos. 2, 7, 10, 11, and 18 discussing problems of knowledge; and nos. 4, 19, and 20 on names.[13] Most students would agree. In any case, the similarity of nos. 16 and 21 with Zeno's third and second arguments against motion should be obvious to students of philosophy.

B. THE KUNG-SUN LUNG TZU[14]

1. On the White Horse (ch. 2)

A. "Is it correct to say that a white horse is not a horse?"

B. "It is."

A. "Why?"

---

[10] *Chih*, literally meaning finger or pointing, has been interpreted as "marks," "signs," "attributes," etc. Since all the other paradoxes deal with concrete things, I prefer to translate it literally as a concrete noun rather than interpreting it too philosophically.

[11] The two colors and the animal.

[12] No. 8 is not included because it is not clear.

[13] *Chung-kuo che-hsüeh shih ta-kang* (An Outline of the History of Chinese Philosophy), 1919, p. 239. Cf. his *Development of the Logical Method in Ancient China*, pp. 118-128.

[14] The *Kung-sun Lung Tzu* is a short treatise in six chapters. Much of it is so corrupt that it is impossible to make it completely intelligible, and no such at-

B. "Because 'horse' denotes the form and 'white' denotes the color. What denotes the color does not denote the form. Therefore we say that a white horse is not a horse."

A. "There being a horse, one cannot say that there is no horse. If one cannot say that there is no horse, then isn't [it] a horse?[15] Since there being a white horse means that there is a horse, why does being white make it not a horse?"

B. "Ask for a horse, and either a yellow or a black one may answer. Ask for a white horse, and neither the yellow horse nor the black one may answer. If a white horse were a horse, then what is asked in both cases would be the same. If what is asked is the same, then a white horse would be no different from a horse. If what is asked is no different, then why is it that yellow and black horses may yet answer[16] in the one case but not in the other? Clearly the two cases are incompatible. Now the yellow horse and the black horse remain the same. And yet they answer to a horse but not to a white horse. Obviously a white horse is not a horse."

A. "You consider a horse with color as not a horse. Since there is no horse in the world without color, is it all right [to say] that there is no horse in the world?"

B. "Horses of course have color. Therefore there are white horses. If horses had no color, there would be simply horses. Where do white horses come in? Therefore whiteness is different from horse. A white horse means a horse combined with whiteness. [Thus in one case it is] horse and [in the other it is] a white horse. Therefore we say that a white horse is not a horse."

A. [Since you say that] before the horse is combined with whiteness, it is simply a horse, before whiteness is combined with a horse it is simply whiteness, and when the horse and whiteness are combined they are collectively called a white horse, you are calling a combination by what is not a combination. This is incorrect.[17] Therefore it is incorrect to say that a white horse is not a horse."

tempt is made in the following translation. Commentators and translators have made so many emendations in an attempt to make the work perfectly understandable that they almost turned it into their own essays. In a number of cases they have changed "is" into "is not" in order to make sense. Chapter 1 deals with Kung-sun Lung's life, and is of no philosophical interest. It is therefore omitted from the translation. For another English translation, see Bibliography.

[15] The word *ju* (if) here was interchangeable with *erh* (yet). See Ch'ien Mu, *Hui Shih Kung-sun Lung* (On Hui Shih and Kung-sun Lung), 1931, p. 49.

[16] Read *yeh* (final positive article) as *yeh* (final interrogative article), according to Yü Yüeh (1821-1906), "Tu Kung-sun Lung Tzu" ("Notes on the *Kung-sun Lung Tzu*"), in *Yü-lou tsa-tsuan* (Miscellaneous Collections of Yü Tower), p. 2a.

[17] This sentence is not clear. None of the many emendations by commentators and translators seems satisfactory.

B. "If you regard a white horse as a horse,[18] is it correct to say that a white horse is a yellow horse?"

A. "No."

B. "If you regard a white horse as different from a yellow horse, you are differentiating a yellow horse from a horse. To differentiate a yellow horse from a horse is to regard the yellow horse as not a horse. Now to regard a yellow horse as not a horse and yet to regard a white horse as a horse is like a bird flying into a pool or like the inner and outer coffins being in different places. This would be the most contradictory argument and the wildest talk."

A."[When we say that] a white horse cannot be said to be not a horse, we are separating the whiteness from the horse. If [the whiteness] is not separated from [the horse], then there would be a white horse and we should not say that there is [just] a horse. Therefore when we say that there is a horse, we do so simply because it is a horse and not because it is a white horse. When we say that there is a horse, we do not mean that there are a horse [as such] and another horse [as the white horse]."

B. "It is all right to ignore the whiteness that is not fixed on any object. But in speaking of the white horse, we are talking about the whiteness that is fixed on the object. The object on which whiteness is fixed is not whiteness [itself]. The term 'horse' does not involve any choice of color and therefore either a yellow horse or a black one may answer. But the term 'white horse' does involve a choice of color. Both the yellow horse and the black one are excluded because of their color. Only a white horse may answer. What does not exclude [color] is not the same as what excludes [color]. Therefore we say that a white horse is not a horse." (SPPY, 3b-5b)

2. On Marks (chih) and Things (ch. 3)

All things are marks. But marks are no marks [for themselves]. If there were no marks in the world, nothing could be called a thing. If there were no marks, can things in the world be spoken of as marks? Marks are what do not exist in the world, but things are what do exist in the world. It is incorrect to consider what does exist in the world to be what does not exist in the world.

[If] there are no marks in the world, things cannot be called marks. What cannot be called marks are not marks. Not being marks, all things are marks. [To say that if] there are no marks in the world things cannot be called marks, does not mean that there are [things] without marks. There not being [things] without marks means that all things are

---

[18] The SPPY edition has "not a horse."

marks. All things being marks means that marks are not marks. That there are no marks in the world is due to the fact that all things have their own names which do not serve as marks. To call them marks when they do not serve as marks, is to consider them all as marks for another and really no marks. It is incorrect to consider what is not a mark as a mark.

Furthermore, marks serve as marks for each other. That there are no marks in the world means that things cannot be said to be without marks. That things cannot be said to be without marks means that there are none which are not marks. As there are none which are not marks, then all things are marks. Marks are different from what are not marks. Marks and things combined are different from marks. If there were no marks of things in the world, who could say that [x] are not marks? If there were nothing in the world, who could say that [x] are marks? If there were marks in the world but no marks of things, who could say that [x] are not marks, or that all things are not marks? Furthermore, marks are in themselves not marks. Why do they have to be combined with a thing in order to be marks? (SPPY, 5b-6b)

> *Comment.* The word *chih* has so many meanings that scholars have found it easy and even tempting to read their own philosophies into Kung-sun Lung. Those who affirm universals would interpret *chih* to mean universal concepts, while nominalists would insist on its common meaning or finger or designation. Equally ready opportunities are open to others. But the text is simply too corrupt to enable anyone to be absolutely sure.

3. On the Explanation of Change (ch. 4)

A. "Is one contained in two?"
B. "One is not in two."
A. "Is right contained in two?"
B. "Right is not in two."
A. "Is left contained in two?"
B. "Left is not contained in two."
A. "Can right be called two?"
B. "No."
A. "Can left be called two?"
B. "No."
A. "Can left and right together be called two?"
B. "Yes."
A. "Is it correct to say that what changes is not what does not change?"
B. "Yes."

A. "If right is combined [with something], is it correct to say that it has changed?"

B. "Yes."

A. "What has it changed to be?"[19]

B. "Right."

A. "If right has changed, how can it still be called right? And, if it has not changed, how can you say that it has changed?"

B. "If two has no left it will also have no right. Left and right together are two. How is it? A ram and an ox together are not a horse. An ox and a ram together are not a fowl."

A. "Why?"

B. "A ram is definitely different from an ox. A ram has upper front-teeth and an ox has none. Yet it is incorrect to say that an ox is not a ram or that a ram is not an ox. For they might not both have [those particular teeth] and yet belong to the same species. A ram has horns and an ox also has horns. Yet it is incorrect to say that an ox is a ram or that a ram is an ox. For they might both have [horns] and yet belong to different species. Both a ram and an ox have horns, but a horse none. A horse has a mane but both a ram and an ox have none. Therefore I say that a ram and an ox together are not a horse. By that I mean that there is no horse [in this case]. As there is no horse, neither a ram nor an ox is two, but a ram and an ox are two. Consequently it is correct to say that a ram and an ox together are not a horse. If such a case were presented as correct, it would be like putting different things in the same species. The cases of left and right are similar to this.

"Both an ox and a ram have hair, while a fowl has feathers. When we speak of fowl's leg [as such], it is one. But when we count the [particular] legs of a fowl, they are two. Two and[20] one put together make three.[21] When we speak of an ox's or a ram's leg [as such], it is one. But when we count their [particular] legs, they are four. Four and one put together makes five. Thus a ram or an ox has five legs while a fowl has three. Therefore I say that an ox or a ram together are not a fowl. There is no other reason that [an ox or a ram] is not a fowl.

"A horse is better than a fowl [for the purpose of illustration]. Regardless of the ability of a horse and the lack of ability of a fowl, however, the fact is obvious that they are different in species [from an ox or a ram]. To give these cases as examples [of being one with an ox or a ram] is called a confusion of terms; it is giving an absurd case."

[19] Read *chih* (classifier for a bird) as *hsi* (what, how), according to Yü Yüeh, *ibid.*, p. 6a.

[20] According to Ch'ien Mu, *Hui Shih Kung-sun Lung*, p. 64, *erh* (yet) here means "and."

[21] See above, paradox, second group, no. 2.

A. "Then let us use some other illustrations."

B. "Green and[22] white are not yellow; white and green are not blue."

A. "Why?"

B. "Because green and white cannot be combined, and if you combined them, they would stand in contrast to each other. They do not occupy adjacent positions; but if you made them so, that would not, however, injure their positions. This is so because while [green and white] stand in contrast to each other [in quality], they do not interfere with each other in position. This may be seen from the case of left and right, which cannot be mixed.[23] Therefore it is impossible to unite [white] with green, nor is it possible to unite [green] with white. Then where does yellow come in? Yellow is a standard color, and can be given as a correct case. This is like the relation between the ruler (corresponding to white) and the minister (corresponding to green) in the state (corresponding to yellow).[24] Hence there are health and long life.

"Furthermore, when green is mixed with white, white does not dominate [green]. It should but it does not. This means that the element of wood (corresponding to green) is injuring the element of metal (corresponding to white). This is [like] the color blue, and blue is not a correct example [of standard colors]. Green and white [originally] cannot be combined. When they are combined, one does not dominate the other, and both stand out. When they compete in standing out, [it is like] the color blue.

"Yellow is better than blue [for the purpose of illustration]. The case of yellow is [like] the case of a horse. Yellow has something in common [with green and white]. On the other hand, the case of blue is [like] the case of a fowl. It is in conflict[25] with [green and white]. If a ruler and ministers are in conflict, both would compete and stand out. When both stand out, the result is darkness, and darkness is not a correct example. By not being a correct example is meant that names do not correspond to actuality. Mixed colors (colors that are not standard) come to shine out in brilliancy. This is what is meant by both standing out. When both stand out, truth fades away beyond rectification." (SPPY, 6b-9a)

4. On Hardness and Whiteness (ch. 5)

A. "Is it correct that hardness, whiteness, and stone are three?"

B. "No."

[22] According to Ch'ien Mu, ibid., p. 66, the word i (by) here means "and."
[23] The word li is very obscure. To understand it as mixed is the best commentators can do.
[24] The correspondence of colors is according to the commentary by Hsieh Hsi-shen (of Sung, 960-1279).
[25] Pao is here interpreted as conflict, following Ch'ien Mu, ibid., p. 70.

A. "Is it correct that they are two?"

B. "Yes."

A. "Why?"

B. "When whiteness but not hardness is perceived, we have a case of two. When hardness but not whiteness is perceived, we have a case of two."

A. "When whiteness is perceived, it is incorrect to say that there is no whiteness. When hardness is perceived, it is incorrect to say that there is no hardness. The stone is by nature so [hard and white]. Does that not make it three?"

B. "When seeing does not perceive hardness but whiteness, there is no hardness to speak of. When touching perceives not whiteness but hardness, there is no whiteness to speak of."

A. "If there were no whiteness in the world, one could not see a stone. If there were no hardness in the world, one could not speak of a stone. Hardness, whiteness, and stone do not exclude each other. How could the three be hidden?"

B. "Some are hidden by themselves, [such as whiteness is hidden from touch]. They are not hidden because someone has hidden them."

A. "Whiteness and hardness are necessary attributes of the stone that pervade each other. How is it possible that they hide themselves?"

B. "Whether one perceives the whiteness [of the stone] or perceives the hardness [of the stone] depends on whether one sees or not. Seeing and not seeing are separate from each other. Neither one pervades the other, and therefore they are separate. To be separate means to be hidden."

> Comment. Fung Yu-lan thinks that to say that a thing is hidden or concealed seems to be another way of saying that it subsists. This is reading the *Kung-sun Lung Tzu* in the framework of the Neo-realists to whom particulars exist while universals subsist. To make his interpretation consistent, he has to interpret *chih* as universal.[26] But the meaning of *chih* is too uncertain to justify any definite conclusion.

A. "[The whiteness] is the whiteness of the stone and [the hardness] is the hardness of the stone. Whether one perceives them or not, the two together [with the stone] make three. They pervade each other as width and length do in a surface. Is this not a [clear] case?"

B. "Some thing may be white, but whiteness is not fixed on it. Some thing may be hard, but hardness is not fixed on it. What is not fixed on anything is universal. How can it be [in] the stone?"

[26] *History of Chinese Philosophy*, vol. 1, p. 209.

A. "According to the nature of the stone,[27] without it (hardness) there cannot be the stone, and without the stone we cannot be talking about the white stone. That [they] are not separated from each other is so by nature and will forever be so."

B. "Stone is one; hardness and whiteness are two. But in the stone one of them can be felt and the other cannot; one of them can be seen and the other cannot. What is felt and what is not felt are separate from each other; the seen and the unseen are hidden from each other. As they are hidden, who can say that they are not separate?"

A. "The eye cannot perceive hardness nor the hand perceive whiteness. But one cannot say that there is no hardness or whiteness. [The organs] have different functions and cannot substitute for each other. Hardness and whiteness reside in the stone. How can they be separated?"

B. "Hardness does not have to be combined with stone to be hardness; it is common to many things. As it does not have to be combined with things to be hardness, it is hardness by necessity of its being hardness. As it is hardness without being the hardness of the stone or other things, it seems there is no such hardness in the world. [Actually] it is hidden.

"If whiteness is from the beginning not whiteness in itself, how can it make the stone and other things white? If whiteness is necessarily white, it is then white not because it is the whiteness of a thing. It is the same with yellow and black. However, the stone is no longer there. How can we speak of a hard stone or a white stone? Therefore they are separate. For this reason they are separate. For this reason it is better to follow this (natural separateness) than to determine [their separateness] by the use of strength and knowledge.[28]

"Furthermore, whiteness is perceived by the eye because of light. But light itself does not see. Neither the light nor the eye sees; it is the mind that sees. The mind does not see either. Seeing is something separate [from them]. Hardness is [perceived] by the hand, and the hand [perceives] by the stroke. But the stroke itself does not feel. Neither the hand nor the stroke feels; it is the mind that feels. The mind does not feel either.[29] This means that they are separate. [Things] being separate, this is the only correct thing in the world." (SPPY, 9a-11b)

Comment. The problems discussed are strikingly similar to those of seventeenth-century philosophers in Europe, namely, primary and secondary qualities.

[27] Another interpretation: When we touch the stone.
[28] While most commentators agree in this interpretation, the original sentence is quite obscure.
[29] The whole passage is not clear.

5. On Names and Actuality (ch. 6)

Heaven, earth, and their products are all things. When things possess the characteristics of things without exceeding them, there is actuality. When actuality actually fulfills its function as actuality, without wanting, there is order. To be out of order is to fall into disorder. To remain in order is to be correct. What is correct is used to rectify what is incorrect. [What is incorrect is not used to][30] doubt what is correct. To rectify is to rectify actuality, and to rectify actuality is to rectify the name corresponding to it.

If the name is rectified, then "this" and "that" are restricted. If the designation "that" is not restricted to that, then the "that" will not do. If the designation "this" is not restricted to this, then the "this" will not do. This is because the non-equivalent is regarded as the equivalent. What is not equivalent will lead to disorder. If that "that" is equivalent to that and is therefore restricted to that, then the designation will do for that. When this "this" is equivalent to this and is therefore restricted to this, then the designation will do for this. This is because the equivalent is correct. Therefore it is correct that "that" is limited to that and this "this" is limited to this. But it is incorrect to apply "that" to this and even to regard "that" as this, or to apply "this" to that and even to regard "this" as that.

A name is to designate an actuality. If we know that this is not this and know that this is not here, we shall not call it ["this"]. If we know that that is not that and know that that is not there, we shall not call it ["that"].

Perfect were the wise kings of old. They examined names and actualities and were careful in their designations. Perfect were the wise kings of old. (SPPY, 11b-12b)

[30] These words appear in certain editions.

11

THE YIN YANG SCHOOL

THE YIN YANG doctrine is very simple but its influence has been extensive. No aspect of Chinese civilization—whether metaphysics, medicine, government, or art—has escaped its imprint. In simple terms, the doctrine teaches that all things and events are products of two elements, forces, or principles: yin, which is negative, passive, weak, and destructive, and yang, which is positive, active, strong, and constructive. The theory is associated with that of the Five Agents or Elements (*wu-hsing*,[1] Metal, Wood, Water, Fire, and Earth) which may be taken as an elaboration of the yin yang idea but actually adds the important concept of rotation, i.e. that things succeed one another as the Five Agents take their turns.

The two concepts of the yin yang and the Five Agents go far back to antiquity and to quite independent origins. Much obscurity still surrounds their history. For example, we are not sure whether the terms "yin" and "yang" originally referred to physical phenomena (clouds shading the sun and the sun shining, respectively) or the female and male. We do not know anything about their early representatives or works, if any. Tsou Yen (305–240 B.C.?) is often mentioned as the representative thinker of this school, but his work is lost and all that we have about him is a brief account of his life and thought in the *Shih chi* (Records of the Historian) by Ssu-ma Ch'ien (145–86 B.C.?).[2] However, long before Tsou Yen's time, both the ideas of yin yang and the Five Agents had been discussed by various philosophers. The yin yang idea is present in the *Tso chuan*, *Lao Tzu*, *Chuang Tzu*, and *Hsün Tzu*,[3] and the Five Agents idea is present in the *Book of History*, *Mo Tzu*, *Hsün Tzu*, *Tso chuan*, and *Kuo-yü*.[4] Curiously enough, they are not found in the *Analects*, the *Book of Mencius*, the *Doctrine of the Mean* or the *Great Learning*. In other words, of all ancient Confucian Classics, they are not mentioned

---

[1] Literally "five actions or operations." Therefore the rendering "Five Agents" is preferred.

[2] Ch. 74.

[3] *Tso chuan* (Tso's Commentary on the *Spring and Autumn Annals*), Duke Hsi, 16th year, Duke Hsiang, 28th year, and Duke Chao, 4th, 7th, and 21st years. See Legge, trans., *Ch'un Ts'ew*, pp. 540, 597, 618, 688; *Lao Tzu*, ch. 42; *Chuang Tzu*, chs. 2, 4, 6, 11, 13, 16, 21, 24, 25, 33, passim; and *Hsün Tzu*, chs. 9 and 17, passim.

[4] *History*, "Oath of Kan" and "Great Norm" (Legge, trans., *Shoo King*, pp. 173, 320); *Mo Tzu*, chs. 41 and 43; *Hsün Tzu*, ch. 6 (SPTK, 3:14b [not translated in Dubs, *The Works of Hsüntze*]); *Tso chuan*, Duke Chao, 20th and 25th years (See Legge, trans., *Ch'un Ts'ew*, p. 708); *Kuo-yü* (Conversations of the States), ch. 4 (SPPY, 4:7b).

except in the *Hsün Tzu*. And yet Hsün Tzu (fl. 298-238 B.C.) himself said that Confucius' grandson Tzu-ssu (492–431 B.C.) advanced the Five Agents theory and Mencius followed it.[5] The possible explanation is that in Tsou Yen's promotion of the theory, there is explicitly the exaltation of virtue, the stress on personal cultivation, especially on the part of the ruler, and the emphasis on humanity and righteousness, all of which are moral objectives of Confucianists.

Briefly, both the yin yang and the Five Agents doctrines may be regarded as early Chinese attempts in the direction of working out a metaphysics and a cosmology. Questions of the process through which things in the world have come to be and the fundamental stuff of which they are made have captivated men's minds since time immemorial. These Chinese proposals indicate reality as a pair of opposites in the one case, and as a group of five items in the other. Whether two or five, they are understood better as forces, powers, and agents than as material elements. The emphasis is on principles and laws of operation. The outlook is dynamic and not static. And the end is an ordered nature rather than chaos. In point of process, there is contradiction as well as harmony, and in point of reality, there is unity in multiplicity. The apparent dualism and pluralism are, in each case, a dynamic monism through the dialectic.

By the time of Tsou Yen, the two concepts, which had much in common, were thought of together. As a matter of fact, he is usually credited as the one who combined the two independent currents into one. The one is now the expression of the other, and both operate in cycles of rise and fall and in a universal pattern, thus uniting man and Nature. There developed also the ideas of mutual production and mutual overcoming among the Five Agents, as well as the correspondence of them with five colors, five tones, five tastes, and the like. When this interest in correspondence was extended to the realm of political affairs, there emerged a cyclical philosophy of history on the one hand and the mutual influence between man and Nature on the other. Just as the seasons rotate, so does history; since man and Nature correspond to each other, they are expressions of the same force and therefore can influence each other.

The cyclical theory of history exercised a tremendous influence in the Han dynasty (206 B.C.–A.D. 220), especially over Tung Chung-shu (c.179–c.104 B.C.). It turns into a definite theory Mencius' simple idea that in every five hundred years a true king will arise.[6] This cyclical interpretation of history has been a persistent one in Chinese thought.

The idea of the cycle is not limited to the interpretation of history,

---

[5] *Hsün Tzu*, ch. 6 (SPTK, 3:14b [not translated in Dubs]).
[6] *Mencius*, 2B:13.

of course. It is thought to characterize all changes. In the cyclical process, the idea of one force overcoming another was soon replaced by that of one producing another. This idea was particularly strong in the Han. Eventually, however, it is the idea that all forces are harmonized that has become the typical Chinese conception.

The theory of the mutual influence of man and Nature is hinted at in the *Doctrine of the Mean* where it is said, "When a nation or family is about to flourish, there are sure to be lucky omens. When a nation or family is about to perish, there are sure to be unlucky omens."[7] The Confucianists intended this to be a moral lesson, but the theory eventually led to fatalism and much superstition. Philosophically, however, it resulted not only in the concept of a common law governing both man and Nature but also in a most important doctrine that has dominated Chinese philosophy in the last eight hundred years, namely, the unity of man and Nature, or "Nature and man forming one body."[8]

Aside from these significant impacts, the yin yang theory has also put Chinese ethical and social teachings on a cosmological basis. It has helped to develop the view that things are related and that reality is a process of constant transformation. The harmony of yin and yang accounts for much of the central emphasis on harmony in Chinese life and thought, and it has reinforced the doctrine of the Mean common to Confucianism, Taoism, and Buddhism. It formed the backbone of Neo-Confucian metaphysics.

The importance of the yin yang theory is indeed incalculable. Paradoxically, there is not a single ancient treatise on it or even a good passage embodying its essence. Consequently we have to resort to an account of Tsou Yen's life and thought and passages from the *Book of Changes*,[9] the *Book of History*,[10] and the *Lü-shih ch'un-ch'iu* (Mr. Lü's Spring and Autumn Annals)[11] in which the doctrines of yin yang and the Five Agents are stated in simple outline.

1. TSOU YEN

In the state of Ch'i there were three scholars named Tsou. . . . The second of these was Tsou Yen, who came after Mencius. He saw that the rulers were ever more unrestrained and were unable to exalt virtue, as

[7] Ch. 24.

[8] See below, ch. 31, comment on sec. 1.

[9] For this book, see below, ch. 13, n.1.

[10] For this book, see below, ch. 1, n.4.

[11] A book in 26 chapters, supposedly written by Lü Pu-wei (d. 235 B.C.) but actually a collective work of scholars who were his retainers. It deals with various subjects and contains the doctrines of many schools, especially the Confucian and the Taoist. There is a German translation by Richard Wilhelm. See Bibliography.

does a real gentleman,[12] who correctly practices it himself and applies it in dealing with the common people. He therefore examined deeply into the increase and decrease of yin and yang and wrote essays totaling more than one hundred thousand words about the phenomenon of extraordinary change and the rise and fall of great sages. His words were exaggerating and unorthodox. He invariably examined small objects and extended this to larger and larger ones until infinity. He first described the present and then traced back to the Yellow Emperor,[13] all of which has been recorded by scholars. Then following the general outline[14] of the rise and fall of the ages he [observed the times and explained the events]. Thereupon he recorded their good and evil fortunes and institutions. He extended his survey way backward to the time before heaven and earth came into existence, to what was obscure and abstruse, and on which no more inquiry was possible.

He first made a list of China's famous mountains, great rivers, deep valleys, birds and animals, things produced on land and sea, and select objects. On the basis of these he extended his survey to what is beyond the seas, to what men are unable to see. He mentioned and cited the fact that ever since the separation of heaven and earth the Five Powers (Five Agents) have been in rotation. The reign of each power was quite appropriate and how has it corresponded to fact!

He maintained that what scholars called the Middle Kingdom (China) constituted only one eighty-first of the world. He called the Middle Kingdom the Divine Continent of the Red Region within which are nine districts. These are the nine districts with which Yü had formed a system [by controlling floods and directing the flow of water].[15] But these are not to be counted among the continents.

Besides the Middle Kingdom there are continents similar to the Divine Continent of the Red Region totaling nine, which are the so-called Nine Continents. Around each of these is a small encircling sea. People and beasts cannot pass from one to another, thus making each a separate

---

[12] *Ta-ya* has been interpreted to refer to the section of the *Book of Odes* by that title and more especially to ode no. 240, which extols the moral influence of King Wen (r. 1171–1122 B.C.). But this interpretation is not based on any evidence. In none of the editions which have special marks for titles is *ta-ya* treated as a title. Its ordinary meaning of "a gentleman" is both natural and clear here.

[13] A legendary emperor of the 3rd millennium B.C.

[14] Insertion following the *Shih chi so-yin* (Tracing the Hidden Meanings of the *Records of the Historian*), by Ssu-ma Chen (fl. 727). According to both the *Shih chi so-yin* and the *Shih chi cheng-i* (Correct Meanings of the *Records of the Historian*), by Chang Shou-chieh (fl. 737), *ta-pang* (not pronounced *ta-ping*) means following the general outline.

[15] Founder of the traditional Hsia dynasty (2183–1752 B.C.?), who spent nine years in conquering China's great flood.

247

district, which makes a continent. There are nine of these. Around them is a large encircling sea, and this sea is where heaven and earth meet.

His methods and system were all of this sort. But in the final analysis they all end up in the virtues of humanity, righteousness, restraint, frugality, and the practice of the proper relations of ruler and minister, superior and inferior, and the six family relations.[16] It is only at the beginning that his [theories] exceeded the proper bounds.[17]

When the rulers and great officials first saw his system, they were struck with awe, reflected on it, and followed it, but eventually they were unable to practice it. . . . (*Shih chi*, SPTK, 74:1a-b)

> *Comment*. This is the first attempt in Chinese history to put government, society, history, astronomy, and geography under one definite formula based on practical observation. Tsou Yen's "extension" may be an imagination rather than a logical inference, but his general theory is the result of postulation, however crude it may be. His use of the here and now as the starting point sharply distinguishes him from his predecessors or contemporaries who used the past as the standard.

2. YIN AND YANG

Heaven is high, the earth is low, and thus *ch'ien* (Heaven) and *k'un* (Earth) are fixed. As high and low are thus made clear, the honorable and the humble have their places accordingly. As activity and tranquillity have their constancy, the strong and the weak are thus differentiated. Ways come together according to their kinds, and things are divided according to their classes. Hence good fortune and evil fortune emerge. In the heavens, forms (heavenly bodies) appear and on earth shapes (creatures) occur. In them change and transformation can be seen. Therefore the strong and the weak interact and the Eight Trigrams activate each other. Things are stimulated by thunder and lightning and enriched by the influence of wind and rain. Sun and moon revolve on their course and cold and hot seasons take their turn. The way of *ch'ien* constitutes the male, while the way of *k'un* constitutes the female. *Ch'ien* knows the great beginning, and *k'un* acts to bring things to completion. *Ch'ien* knows through the easy, and *k'un* accomplishes through the simple. (*Book of Changes*, "Appended Remarks," pt. 1, ch. 1)

The Master (Confucius) said, "*Ch'ien* and *k'un* are indeed the gate of Change! *Ch'ien* is yang and *k'un* is yin. When yin and yang are united

---

[16] Between father and son, elder brother and younger brother, and husband and wife.

[17] According to the *Shih chi so-yin*, this sentence means, "These are the source and foundation for later ages," a rather far-fetched interpretation.

in their character, the weak and the strong attain their substance. In this way the products of Heaven and Earth are given substance and the character of spiritual intelligence can be penetrated. . . . (*ibid.*, pt. 2, ch. 6)

Ch'ien is heaven. It is round, it is the ruler, the father, jade, metal, cold, ice, deep red, a good horse, an old horse, a lean horse, a piebald horse, tree fruit. *K'un* is the earth, the mother, cloth, kettle, frugality, the level, a young heifer, a large carriage, fiber, multitude, a handle, and black soil among the various kinds of soil. . . . (*ibid.*, "Remarks on Certain Trigrams," ch. 11)

3. THE FIVE AGENTS

Heaven gave him (Great Yü) with its Nine Categories. And the various virtues and their relations were regulated. . . .

The first category is the Five Agents; namely, Water, Fire, Wood, Metal, and Earth. The nature of Water is to moisten and descend; of Fire, to burn and ascend; of Wood, to be crooked and straight; of Metal, to yield and to be modified; of Earth, to provide for sowing and reaping. That which moistens and descends produces saltiness; that which burns and ascends produces bitterness; that which is crooked and straight produces sourness; that which yields and is modified produces acridity; that which provides for sowing and reaping produces sweetness.

The second category is the Five Activities; namely, appearance, speech, seeing, hearing, and thinking. The virtue of appearance is respectfulness; that of speech is accordance [with reason]; that of seeing is clearness; that of hearing is distinctness; and that of thinking is penetration and profundity. Respectfulness leads to gravity; accordance with reason, to orderliness; clearness, to wisdom; distinctness, to deliberation; and penetration and profundity, to sageness [all of which should be cultivated by the ruler]. . . .

The fourth category is the Five Arrangements of Time; namely, the year, the month, the day, the stars and planets and the zodiacal signs, and the calendaric calculations. . . . The ninth category is the Five Blessings; namely, longevity, wealth, physical and mental health, love of virtue, and an end crowning life [which will be bestowed by Heaven if the ruler is good.] (*Book of History*, "Great Norm")[18]

Comment. These are but a few correlations of the Five Agents. Almost all possible sets of five things—the five directions, five musical notes, five colors, five grains, five sense organs, five atmospheric

[18] For a fuller translation of the "Great Norm," see above, ch. 1, sec. 3.

conditions, five metals, five ancient emperors, five virtues, five feelings, five social relations—have been equated with them.

Whenever an emperor or king is about to rise, Heaven will always first manifest some good omen to the common people. In the time of the Yellow Emperor, Heaven made a large number of earthworms and mole crickets appear. The Yellow Emperor said, "The force of Earth is dominant." As the force of Earth was dominant, he chose yellow as his color and Earth as the model for his activities.

When it came to the time of Yü, Heaven first made grass and trees appear which did not die in the autumn and winter. Yü said, "The force of Wood is dominant." As the force of Wood was dominant, he chose green as his color and Wood as the model for his activities.

When it came to the time of T'ang[19] (r. 1751–1739 B.C.?), Heaven first made some metal blades appear in the water. T'ang said, "The force of Metal is dominant." As the force of Metal was dominant, he chose white as his color and Metal as the model for his activities.

When it came to the time of King Wen,[20] Heaven first made fire appear, while red birds holding a red book in their bills gathered on the altar of the soil of the House of Chou. King Wen said, "The force of Fire is dominant." As the force of Fire was dominant, he chose red as his color and Fire as the model for his activities.

Water will inevitably replace Fire. Now Heaven will first make the dominance of Water manifest. As the force of water is dominant, black will be chosen as the color and Water the model for activities. The force of Water reaches its limit without people realizing it. The course is now completed, and the process will revert to Earth. (*Lü-shih ch'un-ch'iu*, ch. 13, sec. 2, SPPY, 13:4a)

> *Comment.* Under the influence of Lü, who was a prime minister of Ch'in, the First Emperor (r. 246–210 B.C.) of the dynasty actually used the black color for his costumes, banners, and the like, and claimed Water to be the model for his activities. If he had respected water's qualities of softness and weakness, he would not have established the most severe and ruthless dictatorship in Chinese history. But the Warring States period (403–222 B.C.) of the Chou dynasty was certainly characterized by Fire, and the First Emperor needed a rationalization for his conquest of the Chou.

[19] Founder of the Shang dynasty (1751–1112 B.C.).
[20] Founder of the Chou dynasty (1111–249 B.C.).

12

LEGALISM

THE LEGALIST SCHOOL was the most radical of all ancient Chinese schools. It rejected the moral standards of the Confucianists and the religious sanction of the Moists in favor of power. It accepted no authority except that of the ruler and looked for no precedent. Its aim was political control of the state and the population, a control to be achieved through an intensive set of laws, backed up by generous rewards and severe punishments. According to their theory, aggression, war, and regimentation would be used without hesitation so long as they contributed to the power of the ruler.

It can be readily seen that Legalism is entirely incompatible with other schools, especially Confucianism, which it bitterly attacked. The Confucianists were dedicated to the cultivation of virtue, the development of individual personality, government for the people, social harmony, and the use of moral principles, moral examples, and moral persuasion. On the contrary, the Legalists were primarily interested in the accumulation of power, the subjugation of the individual to the state, uniformity of thought, and the use of force. It is not surprising that they were instrumental in setting up the dictatorship of Ch'in (221–206 B.C.), in unifying China in 221 B.C., and in instituting the tightest regimentation of life and thought in Chinese history.

The brutality and violence of the Ch'in brought its early downfall in 206 B.C., and the Chinese, fearful of the ruthlessness of the Legalists, have ever since that time rejected them. There has been no Legalist School in China in the last two thousand years, or even any Legalist scholar of any prominence. When the *Ssu-k'u ch'üan-shu* (Four Libraries) was compiled late in the eighteenth century, of the 3,457 works included, only eight were Legalist. The totalitarian goal and authoritarian methods promoted by the Legalists have been revived periodically by despots, of course. But there has been no continuous Legalist tradition comparable to that of the Confucianists and Taoists. It might seem, therefore, that Legalist philosophy was entirely negative. Such however, is not the case, for it has its positive aspects. It was the only ancient school that was consistently and vigorously anti-ancient. It worshiped no sage-emperors like Yao and Shun[1] of the Confucianists or Great Yü[2] of the Moists. It looked to the present rather than the past, and to changing circumstances rather than any prescribed condition. It denounced moral

---

[1] Legendary rulers (3rd millennium B.C.).
[2] Founder of the Hsia dynasty (r. 2183–2175 B.C.?).

platitudes and vain talks. Instead, it demanded actual accomplishments and concrete results. It was strongly objective and realistic. In place of vague moral doctrines it advocated the novel idea that law must be written, uniform, and publicly proclaimed to the people. While it shared the Confucian concept that ranks and duties must be clearly differentiated, it insisted that laws must be applicable to all. Thus in spite of their suppression of the rights and desires of the people, they unwittingly promoted the doctrine of equality in which close or distant relationships are overlooked and high or low stations are ignored.

The term "Legalist School" (Fa-chia) did not appear until 90 B.C.[3] but the Legalist movement had been going on for some five hundred years. The first prominent Legalist was Kuan Chung (d. 645 B.C.), prime minister of Ch'i, whom Confucius greatly admired. The work *Kuan Tzu* attributed to him is spurious but contains unmistakable Legalist ideas. The movement took on great momentum in Shang Yang (Kung-sun Yang) or Lord Shang (d. 338 B.C.), prime minister of Ch'in who made Ch'in a strong state and who stressed the importance of law. The *Book of Lord Shang*[4] may or may not have been his. The momentum was enhanced in Shen Pu-hai (d. 337 B.C.), prime minister of the state of Han, who emphasized statecraft, techniques, methods, and the like, summed up in the word *shu*, and in Shen Tao (Shen Tzu, 350–275 B.C?), who emphasized power, circumstances, and natural tendencies, all summed up in the word *shih*. Only fragments of their works have survived. The three tendencies—law, statecraft, and power—were synthesized in Han Fei Tzu (d. 233 B.C.), prince of Han. He offered his services to the powerful king of Ch'in, but through intrigue by his schoolmate Li Ssu (d. 208 B.C.), he had to commit suicide. The following selections are from his work, the *Han Fei Tzu*, in which Legalist doctrines are synthesized. In addition, there is also a selection on Han Fei's interpretation of Tao. In it he took the Taoist philosophy to new heights.

THE HAN FEI TZU[5]

1. The Synthesis of Legalistic Doctrine

The dominant systems of learning of our time are Confucianism and Moism. . . . Both Confucius and Mo Tzu transmitted the doctrines of (sage-emperors) Yao and Shun. Although they differed in what they

---

[3] In Ssu-ma Ch'ien's (145–86 B.C.?) autobiography in the *Shih chi* (Records of the Historian), ch. 130, PNP, 130:3b. For the term *fa*, see Appendix.

[4] English translation by Duyvendak, *Book of Lord Shang*.

[5] The work consists of fifty-five chapters in twenty books. For a complete translation, see Bibliography. An incomplete translation of chs. 49 and 50 by Y. P. Mei is found in de Bary, *Sources of Chinese Tradition*, pp. 138-150.

accepted or rejected, they each claimed to represent the true teachings of Yao and Shun. Now Yao and Shun cannot come to life again. Who is going to determine the truth of Confucianism or Moism? It has been more than seven hundred years from the Yin and Chou times, and more than two thousand years from the times of Yao and Shun.[6] If we are unable to determine the truth of Confucianism or Moism and yet wish to determine the doctrines of Yao and Shun of three thousand years ago, I believe it is impossible to be sure of anything. To be sure of anything without corroborating evidences is stupidity, and to base one's argument on anything about which one cannot be sure is perjury. Therefore those who openly base their arguments on the authority of the ancient kings and who are dogmatically certain of Yao and Shun are men either of stupidity or perjury. Such learning, characterized by stupidity and perjury, and such an unrefined and conflicting [doctrine] practiced [by the Confucianists and Moists] are unacceptable to an enlightened ruler. . . .

The severe household has no fierce slaves, but it is the affectionate mother who has spoiled sons. From this I know that awe-inspiring power can prohibit violence and that virtue and kindness are insufficient to end disorder. When the sage rules the state, he does not depend on people to do good for him, but utilizes their inability to do wrong. If he depends on people to do good for him, we cannot even count ten within the state, but if he utilizes the people's inability to do wrong, the whole country may be regulated. A ruler makes use of the majority and neglects the minority, and so he does not devote himself to virtue but to law.

If we had to depend[7] on an arrow being absolutely straight by nature, there would be no arrow in a hundred generations. If we had to depend on a piece of wood being perfectly round by nature, there would not be any wheel in a thousand generations. There is not one naturally straight arrow or naturally round piece of wood in a hundred generations, and yet in every generation people ride carriages and shoot birds. Why? Because of the application of the methods of straightening and bending. Although there is a naturally straight arrow or a naturally round piece of wood [once in a hundred generations] which does not depend on any straightening or bending, the skilled workman does not value it. Why?

[6] Ch'en Ch'i-t'ien, in his *Han Fei Tzu chiao-shih* (Collation and Explanation of the *Han Fei Tzu*), 1958, pp. 4-5, thinks the numbers of years should be interchanged. This was done by Liao in *The Complete Works of Han Fei Tzu*, vol. 2, p. 299. However, Yin dated from 1384 to 1112 B.C., and Chou started in 1111 B.C. It was just about 700 years to Han Fei's time. From the time of Yao to Han Fei Tzu it was just a little over two thousand years. Therefore no interchange of dates is necessary.

[7] According to Wang Hsien-shen, *Han Fei Tzu chi-chieh* (Collected Commentaries on the *Han Fei Tzu*), 1895, 19:16a, the word *shih* (to depend) should read *tai* (to wait for). Such emendation is quite unnecessary.

Because it is not just one person who wishes to ride and not just one shot that the archer wishes to shoot. Similarly, the enlightened ruler does not value people who are naturally good and who do not depend on reward and punishment. Why? Because the laws of the state must not be neglected and government is not for only one man. Therefore the ruler who has the technique does not follow the good that happens by chance but practices the way of necessity. . . . (*Han Fei Tzu*, ch. 50, SPTK, 19:7b-8a, 9b-10a)

> *Comment.* In the necessity of straightening and bending, note the similarity to Hsün Tzu (fl. 298–238 B.C.).[8] The theory of the originally evil nature of man is a basic assumption of the Legalists. But whereas the straightening and bending in Hsün Tzu consist of ceremonies and music, education, and the rectification of names, those of the Legalists consist of reward and punishment. Hsün Tzu had a firm faith in man's moral reform but the Legalists had no such faith. Although both Han Fei and Li Ssu were pupils of Hsün Tzu, master and pupils were utterly different in their attitudes toward man as a moral being. It is misleading, at least, to say, as Fung does, that Han Fei Tzu based his doctrines on the teachings of Hsün Tzu.[9]

There are four things that enable the enlightened ruler to achieve accomplishments and establish fame; namely, timeliness of the seasons, the hearts of the people, skill and talents, and position of power. Without the timeliness of the seasons, even the Yaos cannot grow a single ear of grain in the winter. Acting against the sentiment of the people, even Meng Pen and Hsia Yü (famous men of great strength)[10] could not make them exhaust their efforts. Therefore with timeliness of the seasons, the grains will grow of themselves. If the ruler has won the hearts of the people, they will exhort themselves without being pressed. If skill and talents are utilized, results will be quickly achieved without any haste. If one occupies a position of power, his fame will be achieved without pushing forward. Like water flowing and like a boat floating, the ruler follows the course of Nature and enforces an infinite number of commands. Therefore he is called an enlightened ruler. . . . (ch. 28, SPTK, 8:10b-11a)

> *Comment.* Of all the ideas of the Legalists, perhaps the most philosophical is that of following Nature, which was derived from the

[8] See above, ch. 6, sec. 3.

[9] Fung, *History of Chinese Philosophy*, vol. 1, p. 320.

[10] Both of the Chou period. Meng Pen was probably from Wei, once served Ch'in.

Taoists. The famous historian Ssu-ma Ch'ien is correct in saying that Han Fei Tzu's doctrines can be traced to Lao Tzu.[11] Han Fei Tzu commented and elaborated on the *Lao Tzu*.[12]

The Taoist ideal of taking no action (*wu-wei*) had a strong appeal to the Legalists because if laws worked effectively at all times, there would be no need for any actual government. The various Taoist tactics, such as withdrawing before advancing,[13] must have impressed the Legalists as clever techniques. And Chuang Tzu's advice to respond to different situations in different ways must also have been attractive to them. These were certainly some of the reasons why the Legalists did not attack the Taoists while they bitterly attacked the Confucianists and the Moists. But it must be remembered that differences between Taoism and Legalism far outweigh their similarity, which is both apparent and remote, to say the least. Control, violence, superiority of the state, and so forth are entirely incompatible with Taoism.

The questioner asks, "Of the doctrines of the two schools of Shen Pu-hai and Shang Yang, which is of more urgent need to the state?" I reply: "They cannot be evaluated. A man will die if he does not eat for ten days. He will also die if he wears no clothing during the height of a severe cold spell. If it is asked whether clothing or food is more urgently needed by a man, the reply is that he cannot live without either, for they are both means to preserve life."

Shen Pu-hai advocated statecraft and Shang Yang advocated law. Statecraft involves appointing officials according to their abilities[14] and demanding that actualities correspond to names. It holds the power of life and death and inquires into the ability of all ministers. These are powers held by the ruler. By law is meant statutes and orders formulated by the government, with punishments which will surely impress the hearts of the people. Rewards are there for those who obey the law and punishments are to be imposed on those who violate orders. These are things the ministers must follow. On the higher level, if the ruler has no statecraft, he will be ruined. On the lower level, if ministers are without laws, they will become rebellious. Neither of these can be dispensed with. They both are means of emperors and kings. . . . (ch. 43, SPTK, 17:4b-5a)

---

[11] *Shih chi*, ch. 63, SPTK, 63:1b.

[12] *Han Fei Tzu*, ch. 20, "*Lao Tzu* Explained," and ch. 21, "Examples for the *Lao Tzu*."

[13] *Lao Tzu*, chs. 36 and 77.

[14] *Jen* here means ability. See Ch'en Ch'i-yu, *Han Fei Tzu chi-shih* (Collected Explanations of the *Han Fei Tzu*), 1958, p. 908.

The important thing for the ruler is either laws or statecraft. A law is that which is enacted into the statute books, kept in government offices, and proclaimed to the people. Statecraft is that which is harbored in the ruler's own mind so as to fit all situations and control all ministers. Therefore for law there is nothing better than publicity, whereas in statecraft, secrecy is desired. . . . (ch. 38, SPTK, 16:5b-6a)

The means[15] by which the enlightened ruler controls his ministers are none other than the two handles. The two handles are punishment and kindness (*te*). What do we mean by punishment and kindness? To execute is called punishment and to offer congratulations or rewards is called kindness. Ministers are afraid of execution and punishment but look upon congratulations and rewards as advantages. Therefore, if a ruler himself applies punishment and kindness, all ministers will fear his power and turn to the advantages. As to treacherous ministers, they are different. They would get [the handle of punishment] from the ruler [through flattery and so forth] and punish those whom they hate and get [the handle of kindness] from the ruler and reward those whom they love. If the ruler does not see to it that the power of reward and punishment proceeds from himself but instead leaves it to his ministers to apply reward and punishment, then everyone in the state will fear the ministers and slight the ruler, turn to them and get away from the ruler. This is the trouble of the ruler who loses the handles of punishment and kindness.

For the tiger is able to subdue the dog because of its claws and fangs. If the tiger abandons its claws and fangs and lets the dog use them, it will be subdued by the dog. Similarly, the ruler controls his ministers through punishment and kindness. If the ruler abandons his punishment and kindness and lets his ministers use them, he will be controlled by the ministers. . . .

> *Comment.* Confucius was not unaware of the "two handles" of the government.[16] But whereas the Confucianists put virtue ahead of punishment, the Legalists put punishment ahead of virtue. In fact, virtue in the true sense of the word is rejected by the Legalists, for *te* as used here by Han Fei Tzu no longer denotes moral virtue but merely kindness in the sense of rewards and favors. Even these are to be bestowed with an ulterior motive.

Whenever a ruler wants to suppress treachery, he must examine the correspondence between actuality and names.[17] Actuality and names

---

[15] According to Yü Yüeh (1821-1906), *Chu-tzu p'ing-i* (Textual Critiques of the Various Philosophers), ch. 21, 1899 ed., 21:7b-8a, *tao*, ordinarily meaning "the way," here means "the way by which."

[16] See *Analects*, 2:3.

[17] The term *hsing-ming*, often mistranslated as "punishment and names," means

refer to the ministers' words and deeds. When a minister presents his words, the ruler assigns him a task in accordance with his words and demands accomplishments specifically from that work. If the results correspond to the task and the task to the words, he should be rewarded. If the accomplishments do not correspond to the task or the task not to the words, he will be punished. If the minister's words are big but his accomplishment is small, he will be punished. The punishment is not for the small accomplishment but for the fact that the accomplishment does not correspond to the words. If the minister's words are small and his accomplishments are big, he will also be punished. It is not that the ruler is not pleased with the big accomplishments but he considers the failure of the big accomplishments to correspond to the words worse than the big accomplishments themselves. Therefore he is to be punished. . . . (ch. 7, SPTK, 2:4a-5a)

> *Comment.* Like practically all ancient Chinese schools, the Legalists emphasized the theory of the correspondence of names and actualities. But while the Confucianists stressed the ethical and social meaning of the theory and the Logicians stressed the logical aspect, the Legalists were interested in it primarily for the purpose of political control. With them the theory is neither ethical nor logical but a technique for regimentation.

Indeed customs differ between the past and the present. Old and new things are to be applied differently. To try to govern the people of a chaotic age with benevolent and lenient measures is like to drive wild horses without reins or whips. This is the trouble of the lack of wisdom.

At present the Confucianists and Moists all praise ancient kings for their universal love for the whole world, which means that they regarded the people as parents [regard their children]. How do we know this to be the case? Because they say, "When the minister of justice carries out an execution, the ruler will stop having music"[18] and that "when the sovereign gets the report of a capital punishment, he sheds tears."[19] These are their praises of ancient kings. Now, to hold that rulers and ministers act toward each other like father and son and consequently there will necessarily be orderly government, is to imply that there are no disorderly fathers or sons. According to human nature, none are more affectionate

---

the same as *ming-shih*, or name and actuality. The word *hsing*, ordinarily meaning punishment, is interchangeable with *hsing* meaning shape or form, that is, the concrete or the actual as contrasted with name. For further discussion on the term, see Appendix.

[18] *Tso chuan* (Tso's Commentary on the *Spring and Autumn Annals*), Duke Chuang, 20th year. See Legge, trans., *Ch'un Ts'ew*, p. 99.

[19] Source not identified.

than parents who love all children, and yet not all children are necessarily orderly. Although the parents' love is deep, why should they cease to be disorderly? Now the love of ancient kings for their people could not have surpassed that of parents for their children. Since children do [not] necessarily cease to be disorderly, then why should the people be orderly? Furthermore, if the ruler sheds tears when punishment is carried out according to law, that is a way to show humanity but not the way to conduct a government. For it is humanity that causes one to shed tears and wish for no punishment, but it is law that punishments cannot be avoided. Ancient kings relied on laws and paid no heed to tears. It is clear that humanity is not adequate for a government.

Moreover, people are submissive to power and few of them can be influenced by the doctrines of righteousness. Confucius was a sage known throughout the empire. He cultivated his own character and elucidated his doctrines and traveled extensively within the four seas (China). People within the four seas loved his doctrine of humanity and praised his doctrine of righteousness. And yet only seventy people became his devoted pupils. The reason is that few people value humanity and it is difficult to practice righteousness. That was why in the wide, wide world there were only seventy who became his devoted pupils and only one (Confucius) who could practice humanity and righteousness. On the other hand, Duke Ai[20] of Lu was an inferior ruler. When he sat on the throne as the sovereign of the state, none within the borders of the state dared refuse to submit. For people are originally submissive to power and it is truly easy to subdue people with power. Therefore Confucius turned out to be a subordinate and Duke Ai, contrary to one's expectation, became a ruler. Confucius was not influenced by Duke Ai's righteousness; instead, he submitted to his power. Therefore on the basis of righteousness, Confucius would not submit to Duke Ai, but because of the manipulation of power, Confucius became a subordinate to him. Nowadays in trying to persuade rulers, scholars do not advocate the use of power which is sure to win, but say that if one is devoted to the practice of humanity and righteousness, one will become a true king. This is to expect that every ruler must be equal to Confucius and that all people in the world are equal to his [seventy-odd] followers. This is absolutely impossible. . . .

What are mutually incompatible should not exist together. To reward those who kill their enemies in battle and at the same time to exalt acts of kindness and benevolence, to bestow honors and offices to those who capture cities and at the same time to believe in the doctrine of universal love, to sharpen weapons and strengthen troops as preparation for emergency and at the same time to praise the style of flowing robes and ornamental girdles (worn by the literati), to enrich the state through agriculture and to depend on the army to resist the enemy and at the same time highly to value men of letters, to neglect the people who respect the ruler and are afraid of the law and at the same time to support men like knights-errant and assassins—how can an orderly and strong state result from such self-contradictory acts? The state supports scholars and knights-errant in time of peace, but when emergency arises it has to use soldiers. Thus those who have been benefited by the government cannot be used by it and those used by it have not been benefited. This is the reason why those who serve take their work lightly and the number of traveling scholars increases every day. This is the reason why the world has become disorderly.

What is now called a worthy person is one who practices correctness and faithfulness. What is called wisdom consists of subtle and unfathomable doctrines. Such subtle and unfathomable doctrines are difficult even for men of highest intelligence to understand. If what men of highest intelligence find to be difficult to understand is used to become laws for the people, the people will find them impossible to understand. When you have not even coarse rice to eat, don't look for refined grains and meat. When you don't even have rags to wear, don't wait for fancy embroidery. For in governing a state, when urgent matters have not been accomplished, efforts should not be directed toward things that can wait. If in governmental measures one neglects ordinary affairs of the people and what even the simple folks can understand, but admires the doctrines of the highest wisdom, that would be contrary to the way of orderly government. Therefore subtle and unfathomable doctrines are no business of the people. . . . Therefore the way of the enlightened ruler is to unify all laws but not to seek for wise men and firmly to adhere to statecraft but not to admire faithful persons. Thus laws will never fail and no officials will ever commit treachery or deception.

In regard to the words [of traveling scholars], rulers of today like their arguments but do not find out if they correspond to facts. In regard to the application of these words to practice, they praise their fame but do not demand accomplishment. Therefore there are many in the world whose talks are devoted to argumentation and who are not thorough when it comes to practical utility. That is why even when the hall of the ruler is full of scholars who praise ancient kings and preach humanity and righteousness, the government is still not free from disorder. In their deeds scholars struggle for eminence but there is nothing in them that is suitable for real accomplishment. Therefore wise scholars withdraw to caves and decline the offering of positions. Inevitably armies become weak and the government becomes disorderly. What is the reason? The reason is that what the people praise and what the ruler respects are those techniques that bring disorder to the state. . . .

Therefore in the state of the enlightened ruler, there is no literature of books and records but the laws serve as the teaching. There are no sayings of ancient kings but the officials act as teachers. And there are no rash acts of the assassin; instead, courage will be demonstrated by those who decapitate the enemy [in battle]. Consequently, among the people within the borders of the state, whoever talks must follow the law, whoever acts must aim at accomplishment, and whoever shows courage must do so entirely in the army. Thus the state will be rich when at peace and the army will be strong when things happen. These are the materials for the true king. Having stored up these materials and taken advantage of the enemy's moments of weakness, this is surely the method to surpass the Five Emperors and match the Three Kings. . . .[21] (ch. 49, SPTK, 19:2b-3a, 4b, 5a-b)

> *Comment.* The advocation of prohibiting the propagation of private doctrines eventually led to the Burning of Books in 213 B.C. and in the periodic prohibition of the propagation of personal doctrines throughout Chinese history.

2. Interpretations of Tao

Tao is that by which all things become what they are. It is that with which all principles are commensurable.[22] Principles are patterns (*wen*) according to which all things come into being, and Tao is the cause of their being. Therefore it is said that Tao puts things in order (*li*).[23] Things have their respective principles and cannot interfere[24] with each other. Since things have their respective principles and cannot interfere with each other, therefore principles are controlling factors in things. Everything has its own principle different from that of others, and Tao is commensurate with all of them [as one]. Consequently, everything has to go through the process of transformation. Since everything has to go through the process of transformation, it has no fixed mode of life. As it has no fixed mode of life, its life and death depend on the en-

[21] The Five Emperors refer to five legendary rulers of antiquity. There are three different sets, two of which include Yao and Shun. The Three Kings are King Yü (r. 2183–2175 B.C.?), King T'ang (r. 1751–1739 B.C.?), and King Wen (r. 1171–1122 B.C.), founders of the Hsia, Shang, and Chou dynasties, respectively.

[22] The word *chi* is here used in the sense of combining or being equivalent. See Ch'en Ch'i-t'ien, *Han Fei Tzu chiao-shih*, p. 749.

[23] The word *li*, meaning principle, when used as a verb means to put things in order.

[24] According to Wang Hsien-ch'ien (1842-1917), quoted in Wang Hsien-shen, *Han Fei Tzu chi-shih*, 6:13a, the word *po* means to oppress or invade.

dowment of material force (*ch'i*) [by Tao]. Countless wisdom depends on it for consideration. And the rise and fall of all things are because of it. Heaven obtains it and therefore becomes high. The earth obtains it and therefore can hold everything. . . .[25]

Men seldom see a living elephant. They obtain the skeleton of a dead elephant and imagine a living one according to its features. Whatever people use for imagining the real is called form (*hsiang*). Although Tao cannot be heard or seen, the sage decides and sees its features on the basis of its effects. Therefore it is called [in the *Lao Tzu*] "shape without shape and form without objects."[26]

In all cases principle is that which distinguishes the square from the round, the short from the long, the coarse from the refined, and the hard from the brittle. Consequently, it is only after principles become definite that Tao can be realized. According to definite principles, there are existence and destruction, life and death, flourish and decline. Now, a thing which first exists and then becomes extinct, now lives and then dies, or flourishes at first and declines afterward cannot be called eternal. Only that which exists from the very beginning of the universe and neither dies nor declines until heaven and earth disintegrate can be called eternal. What is eternal has neither change nor any definite particular principle itself. Since it has no definite principle itself, it is not bound in any particular locality. This is why [it is said in the *Lao Tzu*] that it cannot be told.[27] The sage sees its profound vacuity (*hsü*) and utilizes its operation everywhere. He is forced to give it the name Tao.[28] Only then can it be talked about. Therefore it is said, "The Tao that can be told of is not the eternal Tao."[29] (ch. 20, SPTK, 16:7a-8a)

> *Comment.* This is one of the earliest and most important discussions on Tao. It is of great importance for two reasons. First, principle (*li*) has been the central concept in Chinese philosophy for the last eight hundred years, and Han Fei was one of the earliest to employ the concept. Secondly, to him Tao is not an undifferentiated continuum in which all distinctions disappear. On the contrary, Tao is the very reason why things are specific and determinate. This is a radical advance and anticipated the growth of Neo-Taoism along this direction in the third and fourth centuries A.D.

[25] Cf. *Lao Tzu*, ch. 39.   [26] Ch. 14.   [27] Ch. 1.
[28] Cf. *Lao Tzu*, ch. 25.   [29] *Lao Tzu*, ch. 1.

13

THE PHILOSOPHY OF CHANGE

THE *Book of Changes (I Ching)*[1] grew out of the ancient practice of divination. Its text is very cryptic and no definite philosophical conclusion can be drawn from it. In the commentaries, however, which have been ascribed to Confucius by tradition but to unknown writers three or four centuries later by some scholars, there is a clear outline of a rational approach to a well-ordered and dynamic universe. It is a universe of constant change, and whatever issues from it is good. One is reminded of "perfect sincerity" in the *Doctrine of the Mean*, which is the source of the good and is unceasing.[2]

Change is simple and easy. (The Chinese word for change, *i*, also

[1] The *Book of Changes* is one of the basic Confucian Classics. It is also much cherished by the Taoists. It is divided into the texts and commentaries. The texts consist of sixty-four hexagrams and judgments on them. These hexagrams are based on the Eight Trigrams, each of which consists of three lines, divided or undivided, the divided representing the weak, or yin, and the undivided representing the strong, or yang. Each of these eight corresponds to a direction, a natural element, a moral quality, etc. For example, *ch'ien* (Heaven) ☰ is heaven, *k'un* (Earth) ☷ is earth, *chen* (activity) ☳ is thunder, *sun* (bending) ☴ is wind, *k'an* (pit) ☵ is water, *li* (brightness) ☲ is fire, *ken* (to stop) ☶ is mountain, and *tui* (pleasure) ☱ is a collection of water. Each trigram is combined with another, one upon the other, thus making sixty-four hexagrams. These hexagrams symbolize all possible situations. For example, the hexagram with the water trigram over the fire trigram symbolizes conquest, success, etc.

Each hexagram is followed by two texts, namely (1) the *kua-tz'u* or the explanation of the text of the whole hexagram and (2) the *yao-tz'u* or the explanation of the component lines. The commentaries number seven. First is (3) the *tuan-chuan* or the commentary on (1) and then there is (4) the *hsiang* or abstract meaning of (1) and (2). For the first two hexagrams (the *ch'ien* or Heaven and *k'un* or Earth), there are in addition (5) the *wen-yen* or commentary on the first two texts to stress their philosophical or ethical meaning. Following these sixty-four hexagrams and their discussions, there are (6) the *hsi-tz'u* or the appended remarks, (7) the remarks on certain trigrams, (8) the remarks on the order of the hexagrams, and (9) the random remarks on the hexagrams. Nos. 3, 4, and 6, each in two parts, and nos. 5, 7, 8, and 9 form the "ten wings" of the book.

The most important parts are the texts (1 and 2) and discussions (5) on the first two hexagrams, the appended remarks (6), and the remarks on the trigrams (7). It is here that much of Chinese philosophical speculation has been based.

Tradition has ascribed the Eight Trigrams to legendary Fu-hsi, the sixty-four hexagrams to King Wen (r. 1171–1122 B.C.), the two texts (1 and 2) to him or Duke Chou (d. 1094 B.C.) and the "ten wings" to Confucius. Most modern scholars have rejected this attribution, but they are not agreed on when and by whom the book was produced. Most probably it is a product of many hands over a long period of time, from the fifth or sixth century B.C. to the third or fourth century B.C.

For English translations, see Bibliography.

[2] Ch. 26.

means easy.) It engenders the two forces, yin, the passive or the female element, and yang, the active or the male element, and their interaction in turn gives rise to all multiplicity. Whether this idea of interaction between yin and yang is originally a borrowing from the interaction of the male and the female is unimportant. The important point is that the universe is not just a well-ordered state of existence in which all things are correlated and man and Nature form a unity, as envisaged by the Yin Yang School. What is more, it is a continuous change, for things are forever interfused and intermingled. The universe is a realm of perpetual activity.

In certain respects, the activity takes the form of cycles, as in the Yin Yang School. But the far more important aspect of the interaction of yin and yang is its progressive direction leading to the development of society, morality, and civilization. In the beginning there is the Great Ultimate (*T'ai-chi*). It engenders yin and yang, which in their turn give rise to the four forms. These refer to major and minor yin and yang. But the word for form (*hsiang*) also connotes symbols, patterns, and ideas. This means that out of the interaction of the two cosmic forces, all patterns, ideas, systems, and culture are evolved. The earlier trigrams are now given an entirely new interpretation. Their divided and undivided lines are no longer considered elements of good and evil fortune, but cosmic forces. When the Eight Trigrams, each containing three lines, multiply themselves to become sixty-four hexagrams, they are taken to represent all possible forms of change, situations, possibilities, and institutions. Thus a complex civilization is conceived of as a process of systematic and progressive development which can be traced to its simplest beginning. The cosmology may be naïve and crude, but the philosophical spirit is clear. Instead of a universe controlled by spiritual beings whose pleasures can only be discovered through divination, we have a natural operation of forces which can be determined and predicted objectively. The word "spirit" does not denote spiritual beings any more but natural forces or, as one is tempted to say, natural law. It is interesting that things are even assigned numbers in an attempt to reduce existence to the simplest formula. As we shall see, the rational character of the book had a tremendous appeal to Neo-Confucianists, who quoted it frequently. Philosophically speaking, it has exerted more influence than any other Confucian Classic.

1. SELECTIONS FROM THE COMMENTARIES
ON THE *BOOK OF CHANGES*

Hexagram No. 1, Ch'ien (Heaven)

Great is *ch'ien*, the originator! All things obtain their beginning from it. It unites and commands all things under heaven.[3] The clouds move and the rain is distributed, and the various things are evolved in their respective forms. Thus the beginning and the end are profoundly understood,[4] and the six positions of the hexagram[5] are achieved at the proper time.

[*Ch'ien*] at all times rides the six dragons (*ch'i* or material forces) [of the six lines] and controls all things under heaven. The way of *ch'ien* is to change and to transform so that everything will obtain its correct nature and destiny (*ming*) and the great harmony [of natural forces] will be self-proficient. There the result will be the advantage [derived from the harmony of all things] and firmness [throughout their existence]. [*Ch'ien*] towers above the myriad things [like a king] and all states enjoy peace. . . .

The character of the great man is identical with that of Heaven and Earth; his brilliance is identical with that of the sun and the moon; his order is identical with that of the four seasons, and his good and evil fortunes are identical with those of spiritual beings. He may precede Heaven and Heaven will not act in opposition to him. He may follow Heaven, but will act only as Heaven at the time would do. . . .

Hexagram No. 2, K'un (Earth)

Being straight means correctness, and being square means righteousness. The superior man applies seriousness (*ching*)[6] to straighten the internal life and righteousness to square the external life. As seriousness and righteousness are established, one's virtue will not be an isolated instance. Straight, square, and great, [the superior man] works his operations without repeated effort, and is in every respect advantageous.

---

[3] This interpretation follows Wang Pi's (226-249) commentary in the Thirteen Classics Series.

[4] This does not refer to the understanding of any sage or holy man, as Legge, *Yi King*, p. 213, and Richard Wilhelm, *I Ching*, vol. 2, p. 3 have it, but to the operation of the Principle of Nature. See subcommentary by K'ung Ying-ta (574-648), *Chou-i cheng-i* (Correct Meanings of the *Book of Changes*), ch. 1, in the Thirteen Classics Series.

[5] See above, n.1. Since the hexagram consists of two trigrams, it therefore consists of six lines in their six positions.

[6] This word is not to be interpreted in the ordinary sense of reverence, which assumes an object. See Appendix.

Comment. The two complementary ethical formulae, seriousness to straighten the internal life and righteousness to square the external life, eventually became the keystone in the method of moral cultivation for many Neo-Confucianists, especially Ch'eng I (Ch'eng I-ch'uan, 1033-1107).

2. SELECTIONS FROM THE "APPENDED REMARKS," PT. 1

Ch. 1. Heaven is high, the earth is low, and thus *ch'ien* (Heaven) and *k'un* (Earth) are fixed. As high and low are thus made clear, the honorable and the humble have their places accordingly. As activity and tranquillity have their constancy, the strong and the weak are thus differentiated. Ways come together according to their kind, and things are divided according to their classes. Hence good fortune and evil fortune emerge. In the heavens, forms (heavenly bodies) appear and on earth shapes (creatures) occur. In them change and transformation can be seen. Therefore the strong and the weak interact and the Eight Trigrams activate each other. Things are stimulated by thunder and lightning and enriched by the influence of wind and rain. Sun and moon revolve on their course and cold and hot seasons take their turn. The way of *ch'ien* constitutes the male, while the way of *k'un* constitutes the female. *Ch'ien* knows the great beginning, and *k'un* acts to bring things to completion. *Ch'ien* knows through the easy, and *k'un* accomplishes through the simple.

Ch. 4. The system of Change[7] is tantamount to Heaven and Earth, and therefore can always handle and adjust the way of Heaven and Earth. Looking up, we observe the pattern of the heavens; looking down, we examine the order of the earth. Thus we know the causes of what is hidden and what is manifest. If we investigate the cycle of things, we shall understand the concepts of life and death.

Essence and material force (*ch'i*) are combined to become things. The wandering away of spirit (force) becomes change. From this we know that the characteristics and conditions of spiritual beings are similar to those of Heaven and Earth and therefore there is no disagreement between them. The knowledge [of spirit] embraces all things and its way helps all under heaven, and therefore there is no mistake. It operates freely and does not go off course. It rejoices in Nature (*T'ien*, Heaven) and understands destiny. Therefore there is no worry. As [things] are contented in their stations and earnest in practicing kindness, there can be love. It molds and encompasses all

---

[7] Many commentators have taken this to mean the *Book of Changes*.

transformations of Heaven and Earth without mistake, and it stoops to bring things into completion without missing any. It' penetrates to a knowledge of the course of day and night.[8] Therefore spirit has no spatial restriction and Change has no physical form.

> *Comment.* Exactly what is meant by "spirit" is not clear, but it is surely not the spirit of a deceased person that influences human affairs. Traditionally *kuei-shen* means either simply spirits of ancestors or spiritual beings. In the latter case, it may mean either good or evil spirits or the positive and negative aspects of the soul, respectively. But here it is simply the unfathomable force behind all transformations. Later in Neo-Confucianism, it is to be understood purely as the spontaneous activity of yin and yang.[9]

Ch. 5. The successive movement of yin and yang constitutes the Way (Tao). What issues from the Way is good, and that which realizes it is the individual nature. The man of humanity (*jen*)[10] sees it and calls it humanity. The man of wisdom sees it and calls it wisdom. And the common people act according to it daily without knowing it. In this way the Way of the superior man is fully realized.[11] It [spirit] is manifested in humanity but is concealed in its functioning. It promotes all things without sharing the anxiety of the sage. How perfect is its eminent virtue and great achievement! Its achievement is great because it possesses everything, and its virtue is abundant because it renovates things every day.

> *Comment.* The idea of renewing every day has already been found in the *Great Learning*[12] and will be reiterated again and again in the Neo-Confucian philosophy.[13]

Changes mean production and reproduction. *Ch'ien* means the completion of forms, and *k'un* means to model after them. Divination means to go to the utmost of the natural course of events in order to know the future. Affairs mean to adapt and accommodate accordingly. And that which is unfathomable in the operation of yin and yang is called spirit.

[8] According to Han K'ang-po (of Chin, 265-420), the foregoing descriptions refer to spirit, whereas K'ung Ying-ta thought they refer to the sage. See the *Chou-i cheng-i*. Sun Hsing-yen (1753-1818), in his *Chou-i chi-chieh* (Collected Explanations of the *Book of Changes*), supports Han K'ang-po.

[9] See below, ch. 30, B, 10, 11, 31, 56; ch. 32, sec. 65, 70, 73, 78; ch. 34, B, 130-133.

[10] Variously rendered as benevolence, love, human-hearted, etc.

[11] The word *hsien* here does not mean few, as all translators have understood it, but means to the fullest extent. See Sun Hsing-yen, *Chou-i chi-chieh*.

[12] Ch. 2.   [13] See below, pp. 558, 693, 752, 760.

Comment. The concept of production is new and will form an important part of Neo-Confucianism. Both change and the characteristic of the universe are described in terms of life-giving.

Ch. 10. . . . Change has neither thought nor action, because it is in the state of absolute quiet and inactivity, and when acted on, it immediately penetrates all things. If it were not the most spirit-like thing in the world, how can it take part in this universal transformation? The system of Change is that by which the sage reaches the utmost of things and examines their subtle emergence (*chi*, subtle activating force). Only through depth can the will of all men be penetrated; only through subtle activation can all undertakings in the world be brought to completion; and only through spirit is there speed without hurry and the destination reached without travel. . . .

Comment. What is quiet is substance and what penetrates things is function. This sets the pattern for the Neo-Confucian theory of substance and function.

Ch. 11. . . . Therefore *k'un* means closing and *ch'ien* means opening. The succession of closing and opening constitutes transformation. The alternate going and coming [of yin and yang] is called penetration. What is manifested is called form (*hsiang*). What has taken physical form is called a concrete thing (*ch'i*).[14] To control and use things is called method. And [when they are] used to advantage, either in this or that way, so all people utilize them, that is called spirit.

Therefore in the system of Change there is the Great Ultimate. It generates the Two Modes (yin and yang). The Two Modes generate the Four Forms (major and minor yin and yang). The Four Forms generate the Eight Trigrams. The Eight Trigrams determine good and evil fortunes. And good and evil fortunes produce the great business [of life]. . . .

Ch. 12. . . . The system of Change is indeed intermingled with the operations of *ch'ien* and *k'un*. As *ch'ien* and *k'un* take their respective positions, the system of Change is established in their midst. If *ch'ien* and *k'un* are obliterated, there would be no means of seeing the system of Change. If the system of Change cannot be seen, then *ch'ien* and *k'un* would almost cease to operate.

Therefore what exists before physical form [and is therefore without it][15] is called the Way. What exists after physical form [and is therefore with it] is called a concrete thing. That which transforms things and

14 Literally an implement, a utensil, a particular thing. For a discussion of this term, see Appendix.
15 About this translation, see Appendix, comment on *Hsing-erh-shang*.

controls them is called change. That which extends their operation is called penetration. To take them and apply them to the people of the world is called the business of life. . . .

3. SELECTIONS FROM THE "APPENDED REMARKS," PT. 2

Ch. 1. . . . The great characteristic of Heaven and Earth is to produce. The most precious thing for the sage is [the highest] position. To keep his position depends on humanity. How to collect a large population depends on wealth. The right administration of wealth, the rectification of terms, and prohibiting people from wrong doing constitute righteousness.

Ch. 5. It is said in the Change, "Full of anxious thought you come and go. [Only] friends will follow you and think of you." The Master[16] said, "What is there in the world to think about or to deliberate about? In the world there are many different roads but the destination is the same. There are a hundred deliberations but the result is one. What is there in the world to think about or to deliberate about?"

> Comment. The idea of a hundred roads to the same destination is a direct expression of the spirit of synthesis which is extremely strong in Chinese philosophy. It is the Confucian version of Chuang Tzu's doctrine of following two courses at the same time.[17]

After the sun goes, the moon comes. After the moon goes, the sun comes. The sun and the moon push each other in their course and thus light appears. After the winter goes, the summer comes. After the summer goes, the winter comes. The winter and the summer push each other and thus the year is completed. To go means to contract and to come means to expand. Contraction and expansion act on each other and thus advantages are produced. The looper caterpillar coils itself up (contracts) in order to stretch out (expand). Dragons and snakes hibernate (contract) in order to preserve life (expand). Investigate the principles of things with care and refinement until we enter into their spirit, for then their application can be extended, and utilize that application and secure personal peace, for then our virtue will be exalted. What goes beyond this is something we can hardly know. To investigate spirit to the utmost and to understand transformation is the height of virtue. . . .

Ch. 6. The Master (Confucius) said, "*Ch'ien* and *k'un* are indeed the

---

[16] Traditionally identified as Confucius.
[17] See comment on it on p. 184.

gate of Change! *Ch'ien* is yang and *k'un* is yin. When yin and yang are united in their character, the weak and the strong attain their substance. In this way the products of Heaven and Earth are given substance and the character of spiritual intelligence can be penetrated. . . .

4. SELECTIONS FROM "REMARKS ON CERTAIN TRIGRAMS"

Ch. 1. In ancient times in instituting the system of Change, the sages, with the hidden assistance of spiritual intelligence, created the system of divination by the use of milfoil stalks. The number 3 was assigned to heaven, 2 to earth, and from these other numbers were established.[18] They observed the changes in yin and yang (divided and the undivided lines) and form the trigrams. From the movements that took place in the weak and strong [lines], they produced [the principles of] the individual lines. They harmonized [these principles] with the Way and virtue, and laid down the order of moral principles. [Their teaching is to] investigate principle (*li*) to the utmost and fully develop one's nature until destiny is fulfilled.

> *Comment.* The three subjects of principle, nature, and destiny cover practically the whole philosophy of the Neo-Confucian movement. In fact, the movement is called the Philosophy of Nature and Principle. In essence, the teaching is no different from Mencius' teaching of fully developing one's mind, knowing Heaven, and fulfilling one's destiny.[19] But Mencius did not provide the metaphysical basis for Neo-Confucianism as does the *Book of Changes*. It is also to be noted that unlike the Taoists who require vacuity (*hsü*) of mind for one to become identified with Nature, here Confucianists advocate the fulfillment of one's own nature to achieve the same objective.

Ch. 2. In ancient times, the sages instituted the system of Change in order to follow the principle of the nature and destiny. Therefore yin and yang were established as the way of Heaven, the weak and the strong as the way of Earth, and humanity and righteousness as the way of man. [Each hexagram] embraced those three powers (Heaven, Earth, and man) and doubled them. Therefore in the system of Change a hexagram is complete with six lines. They are distinguished as yin and yang and the weak and the strong are employed in succession. Thus in

[18] This is open to various interpretations. The interpretation by Wang Su (195-256) is adopted here. See Sun Hsing-yen, *Chou-i chi-chieh.*
[19] *Mencius,* 7A:1.

the system of Change there are six positions and the pattern is complete.

Ch. 11. *Ch'ien* is heaven. It is round, the ruler, the father, jade, metal, cold, ice, deep red, a good horse, an old horse, a lean horse, a piebald horse, tree fruit. *K'un* is the earth, the mother, cloth, kettle, frugality, the level, a young heifer, a large carriage, fibre, multitude, a handle, and black soil among the various kinds of soil. . . .

14

YIN YANG CONFUCIANISM: TUNG CHUNG-SHU

ON THE SURFACE, Tung Chung-shu (c.179–c.104 B.C.) seems to be of only minor philosophical interest, but historically he is of the utmost importance. He was chiefly instrumental in making Confucianism the state doctrine in 136 B.C. This supremacy excluded other schools, and lasted until 1905. But a closer examination of his philosophy reveals some extremely significant developments. In the Yin Yang School, the universe is conceived of as a well-coordinated system in which every thing is related to everything else. In the *Book of Changes* this order is conceived of as a process of transformation. In Tung Chung-shu, however, both ideas took a step forward: the universe is treated as an organic whole. In his belief, not only are things related generally, but they are so in exact detail; and not only do things change, but they activate each other. The theory that things of the same kind energize one another presupposes an organic structure and a pre-established harmony. The correspondence of man and Nature is now reduced to numbers. Nature can always influence man through portents because the same material forces of yin and yang govern both of them. In fact, to Tung man is the universe in miniature: man is the microcosm, Nature the macrocosm.

Since things are always activating one another, the universe is not static but dynamic. This idea is underscored by the concept of the origin (*yüan*), a concept not much different from that of Change. But as the Great Ultimate in the system of Change is confined to the metaphysical realm, Tung's concept of the origin finds its richest meaning in history and human affairs. To him, origin means foundation, and nothing can be correct unless its foundation is correct. This is why, according to him, the *Spring and Autumn Annals* records events beginning with the first of the year. According to tradition, Confucius wrote the Classic to record the affairs of his native state of Lu from 722 to 481 B.C., which eventually came to be known as the Period of Spring and Autumn. Confucius did record the events in such a way as to suggest certain judgment upon them. But Tung regarded the book as laws for future dynasties. In his eyes, names used in the book are incidents of the rectification of names from which moral and political correctness can be discerned. Moreover, the book is the embodiment of the Natural Law. One suspects that the reason why Tung honored the *Spring and Autumn Annals* the most highly of all Confucian Classics stems at least partly from the fact that in this book human affairs are viewed in the perspective of the origin and what follows from it—that is, in the perspective of time.

Likewise, the time element has an unusual bearing on his doctrine of history. He views history as going in a cycle of three periods, symbolized by black, white, and red. This in itself is not much different from Tsou Yen's (305–240 B.C.?) theory of the revolution of the Five Powers.[1] What is unique is that the correct period must begin at the right time.

In this scheme of things, the supreme position belongs to the king. When imperial power was fast growing in the Han (206 B.C.–A.D. 220), this is not surprising. People, born with greed as well as with humanity, are considered to be unenlightened by nature, and require a king to instruct them. Applied to human relations, this becomes Tung's Three Bonds according to which the ruler, the father, and the husband are to be the standards of the ruled, the son, and the wife. Some scholars have maintained that it was precisely because of this authoritarianism that the Han rulers welcomed Confucianism as the state ideology. Be that as it may, it must be pointed out that in Tung's system there are factors that would check the ruler. After all, he can rule only if he receives the mandate from Heaven, and the will of Heaven is to be discovered not by an astrologer to whom the king might dictate but through portents, which are expressions of the natural cosmic forces of yin and yang. In the final analysis it was Confucius, according to Tung, who understood the origin of things, of which portents as well as human and natural events are manifestations, and who taught humanity (*jen*) and righteousness rooted in Heaven. Thus the final power of interpreting what is correct or not rests with Confucian scholars. Hu Shih (1891-1962) has suggested that Tung was probably the first man to make an appeal to the Law of God in his attack on the nobles and officials of the empire.[2]

Tung was a professor of the national university, a very high honor, as well as twice a chief minister. He was the greatest Confucianist of his time, and for several hundred years afterward. Once he studied and taught so hard that for three years he did not see his garden.[3] The follow-

---

[1] See above, ch. 11, sec. 1.

[2] "The Natural Law in the Chinese Tradition," in *Natural Law Institute Proceedings*, vol. 5, p. 148.

[3] According to the *Ch'ien-Han shu* (History of the Former Han Dynasty, 206 B.C.–A.D. 8), ch. 56, Tung devoted himself to the *Spring and Autumn Annals* in his youth. In 140, 136, or 134 B.C. he was the top scholar commanded to answer questions by Emperor Wu (r. 140–87 B.C.). It was largely through his influence that non-Confucian scholars were dismissed from the government and Confucianism was made state dogma by Emperor Wu. In 140 B.C. Tung was appointed chief minister to a prince. Because he applied his belief in portents to governmental measures, he was attacked and dismissed. Later he was chief minister to another prince. At old age he retired to write.

ing are selections, including four full chapters, from his work the *Ch'un-ch'iu fan-lu* (Luxuriant Gems of the *"Spring and Autumn Annals"*)

LUXURIANT GEMS OF THE SPRING AND AUTUMN ANNALS[4]

A. The Profound Examination of Names and Appellations (ch. 35)

. . . . The present generation is ignorant about human nature. Speakers on the subject differ from each other. Why not try to go back to the term "nature" (*hsing*)? Does not the term "nature" mean what is inborn (*sheng*)?[5] If it means what is inborn, then the basic substance naturally endowed is called man's nature. Nature is the basic substance. If we inquire into the basic substance of nature by applying the term "good," will that be correct? If not, why still say that the basic substance is good? The term "nature" cannot be separated from the basic substance. When it is separated from the basic substance, as in the case of hair, it will no longer be nature. This should be clearly understood. The *Spring and Autumn Annals* examines the principles of things and rectifies their names. It applies names to things as they really are, without making the slightest mistake. Therefore in mentioning [the strange event of] falling meteorites, it mentions the number five afterward [because the meteorites were seen first and their number discovered later], whereas in mentioning the [ominous event of] fishhawks flying backward, it mentions the number six first [because six birds were first seen flying away and upon a closer look it was then found that they were fishhawks].[6] Such is the care of the Sage (Confucius, its author) to rectify names. [As he himself said], "With regard to his speech, the superior man does not take it lightly."[7] His statements about the five meteorites and the six fishhawks are good illustrations of this.

[4] The *Ch'un-ch'iu fan-lu* (Luxuriant Gems of the *Spring and Autumn Annals*) consists of eighty-two short essays on philosophical and political subjects. For a French translation of chs. 44 and 74 see Bibliography. The word *lu* is often translated literally as "dew." According to one interpretation, *fan-lu* means luxuriant dew, that is, the richness of meaning in Confucius' *Spring and Autumn Annals*. But the more common interpretation is that of gems hanging down from a cap, symbolizing the connecting links between the use of terms in the Classic and the event it describes. For the *Spring and Autumn Annals*, see above, ch. 1, n.6.

[5] The character of nature, *hsing*, contains as its chief component the character for "birth," *sheng*, to produce, to create. Furthermore, they sound very much alike. In the Chinese language two words pronounced the same or very much alike often connote each other. It is not to be dismissed simply as a pun.

[6] According to the *Spring and Autumn Annals*, five meteorites fell in the state of Sung and six fishhawks flew backward over its capital in the 16th year of Duke Hsi (642 B.C.). See Legge, trans., *Ch'un Ts'ew*, p. 170. The *Kung-yang Commentary* explains why the number is given first in the one case but last in the other.

[7] *Analects*, 13:3.

It is the mind that keeps the various evil things weak within so that they cannot be expressed outside. Therefore the mind (*hsin*) is called the weak (*jen*).[8] If in the endowment of material force (*ch'i*) one is free from evil, why should the mind keep anything weak? From the name of the mind I know the real character of man. In his real character man has both humanity (*jen*)[9] and greed. The material forces responsible for both humanity and greed are found in his person. What is called the person is received from Heaven (*T'ien*, Nature). Heaven has its dual operation of yin and yang (passive and active cosmic forces), and the person also has his dual nature of humanity and greed. There are cases when Heaven restricts the operation of yin and yang, and there are cases when the person weakens his feelings and desires. [The way of man] and the Way of Heaven are the same. Consequently as yin functions, it cannot interfere with spring or summer (which correspond to yang), and the full moon is always overwhelmed by sunlight, so that at one moment it is full and at another it is not. This is the way Heaven restricts the operation of yin. How can [man] not reduce his desires and stop his feelings (both corresponding to yin) in order to respond to Heaven? As the person restricts what Heaven restricts, it is therefore said that the person is similar to Heaven. To restrict what Heaven restricts is not to restrict Heaven itself. We must know that without training our nature endowed by Heaven cannot in the final analysis make [the feelings and desires] weak. If we examine actuality to give names, when there has been no training, on what ground can nature be so called (as good)?

> *Comment.* It is absurd to draw conclusions on human nature from similarity in pronunciation of words. The question of human nature, however, is a serious one, for it was a central problem during the entire history of Confucianism, and with Tung it enters upon a new stage. In saying that nature means what is inborn, he seems to be repeating Kao Tzu (c.420–c.350 B.C.), and in asserting the dual nature of humanity and greed, he seems to be suggesting the theory that human nature is a mixture of good and evil. Actually neither is true. The theory of mixed nature did not develop until Yang Hsuing (53 B.C.–A.D. 18).[10] Tung's own theory is unique: there is goodness in human nature, but it is only the beginning of goodness and it requires training to be realized. His whole emphasis is on education.

Therefore man's nature may be compared to the rice stalks and goodness to rice. Rice comes out of the rice stalk but not all the stalk be-

---

[8] *Hsin* and *jen* were pronounced much alike.

[9] *Jen* is often translated as love, goodness, benevolence, etc. For comments on translations of this term, see Appendix.

[10] For Kao Tzu, see above, ch. 3, *Mencius*, 6A:1-6, and for Yang Hsuing, see below, ch. 15.

comes rice. Similarly, goodness comes out of nature but not all nature becomes good. Both goodness and rice are results of human activity in continuing and completing the creative work of Heaven, which is outside of Heaven's own operation, and are not inherent in what Heaven has produced, which is within its operation. The activity of Heaven extends to a certain point and then stops. What stops within the operation of Heaven is called human nature endowed by Heaven, and what stops outside the operation of Heaven is called human activity. Man's activity lies outside of his nature, and yet it is inevitable that [through training] his nature will become virtuous. The term "people" (*min*) is derived from the term "sleep" (*ming*, ignorant, literally, closing one's eyes).[11] If nature is already good [at birth], why are people so called? Take the case of meteorites. If they were not supported in place, they would be rolling wild. How can they be good?

Man's nature may be compared to the eyes. In sleep they are shut and there is darkness. They must await the awakening before they can see. Before the awakening it may be said that they possess the basic substance (quality) to see, but it cannot be said that they see. Now the nature of all people possesses this basic substance but it is not yet awakened; it is like people in sleep waiting to be awakened. It has to be trained before it becomes good. Before it is awakened, it may be said to possess the basic substance to become good but it cannot be said that it is already good. It is the same as the case of the eyes being shut and becoming awakened. If we leisurely examine this matter with a calm mind, the truth becomes evident. Man's nature being in sleep, as it were, and before awakening is the state created by Heaven (Nature). To follow what Heaven has done and give it a name, we call the creatures "people" (*min*). By that is meant that they are in sleep (*ming*). If we inquire into principles according to their names and appellations, we shall understand. Thus names and appellations are to be rectified in accordance with [the principles] of Heaven and Earth. Nature and feelings are produced by Heaven and Earth. Both nature and feelings are the same in a state of sleep. Feelings are [part of] nature. If we say that nature is already good, what can we say about feelings [which are sources of evil]? Therefore the Sage never said that nature is good, for to say so would be to violate the correctness of the name.

That the person possesses nature and feelings is similar to the fact that Heaven has yin and yang. To say that there is no feeling in man's basic substance is like saying that there is yang in Heaven but no yin. Such absurd ideas are never acceptable.[12] What we call nature does not

---

[11] Another case of words pronounced alike with similar meaning.
[12] The sentence is obscure.

refer to the highest type of man nor to the lowest, but to the average. The nature of man is like a silk cocoon or an egg. An egg has to be hatched to become a chicken, and a silk cocoon has to be unravelled to make silk. It is the true character of Heaven that nature needs to be trained before becoming good. Since Heaven has produced the nature of man which has the basic substance for good but which is unable to be good [by itself], therefore it sets up the king to make it good. This is the will of Heaven. The people receive from Heaven a nature which cannot be good [by itself], and they turn to the king to receive the training which completes their nature. It is the duty of the king to obey the will of Heaven and to complete the nature of the people.

> *Comment.* Tung's idea of three types of man seems to anticipate the theory of three grades of human nature which originated with Hsün Yüeh (148-209).[13] That theory was a prevalent one during the whole Eastern Han period (25-220). During the Western Han (206 B.C.–A.D. 8), however, the prevalent theory was that human nature is good whereas feelings are evil, and Tung was the one who initiated it. To him, everyone has the beginning of goodness in his nature, which also involves evil. The highest type not only has the beginning but almost goodness in its activity, and the lowest type has almost no beginning at all. Nevertheless, nature as an equivalent to yang is good, whereas feelings as equivalent to yin are evil. Thus humanity belongs to nature, and greed belongs to feelings. But since feelings are included in nature, it is correct to say that greed also belongs to nature. Tung tries to resolve the conflict between nature and feelings through education. However, philosophically it was not resolved until Neo-Confucianism.

Now to claim on the basis of the true character of the basic substance of man that man's nature is already good [at birth] is to lose sight of the will of Heaven and to forgo the duty of the king. If the nature of all people were already good, then what duty is there for the king to fulfill when he receives the mandate from Heaven? To give an incorrect name and as a consequence to abandon one's solemn duty and to violate the great Mandate of Heaven is not to use any word in an exemplary way. In using terms the *Spring and Autumn Annals* approaches from the external aspect of a thing if its internal aspect depends on the external aspect [for its full meaning]. Now the nature of all people depends on training, which is external, before it becomes good. Therefore goodness has to do with training and not with nature. If it had to do with nature, it would be much involved and lack refinement, and everyone would be-

---

[13] See below, ch. 27, comment on sec. 1.

come perfect by himself and there would be no such people as worthies and sages. This is an erroneous doctrine of highly respected people of our time but not the way in which terms are used in the *Spring and Autumn Annals*. Unexemplary words and unfounded doctrines are avoided by the superior man. Why utter them?

Someone says, "Since nature contains the beginning of goodness and since the mind possesses the basic substance of goodness, how can nature still not be regarded as good?"

I reply, "You are wrong. The silk cocoon contains [potential] silk but it is not yet silk, and the egg contains the [potential] chicken but it is not yet a chicken. If we follow these analogies, what doubt can there be? Heaven has produced mankind in accordance with its great[14] principle, and those who talk about nature should not differ from each other. But there are some who say that nature is good and others who say that nature is not good. Then what is meant by goodness differs with their various ideas. There is the beginning of goodness in human nature. Let us activate it and love our parents. And since man is better than animals, this may be called good—this is what Mencius meant by goodness.[15] Follow the Three Bonds[16] and the Five Relationships.[17] Comprehend the principles of the Eight Beginnings.[18] Practice loyalty and faithfulness and love all people universally. And be earnest and deep and love propriety.[19] One may then be called good—this is what the Sage meant by goodness."

> *Comment.* Although the Confucian five human relations are established on the basis of mutual moral obligation, at the same time the thought was inherent in the Confucian system that the ruler, the father, and the husband are superior to the ruled, the son, and the wife. This distinction is strengthened by Tung Chung-shu, for by "bond" is meant not merely a relationship but a standard. Ever since Han times, in the Confucian ethic, the ruler has become the "standard" of the ruled, and so forth. In view of the fact that to him yang is superior to yin, it is logical to say that the ruler, who

[14] Read *liu* (six) as *ta* (great), according to Su Yü, *Ch'un-ch'iu fan-lu i-cheng* (Textual Studies of the *Luxuriant Gems of the Spring and Autumn Annals*).

[15] See *Mencius*, 2A:6; 4B:19; 6A:7, 8.

[16] The Three Bonds are those binding the ruler with the minister, the father with the son, and the husband with the wife.

[17] According to Ling Shu, *Ch'un-ch'iu fan-lu chu* (Commentary on the *Luxuriant Gems of the Spring and Autumn Annals*) Tung means the Six Relationships, namely, paternal uncles, brothers, fellow clansmen, maternal uncles, teachers, and friends.

[18] Mencius spoke of the Four Beginnings: the feeling of commiseration is the beginning of love; the feeling of right and wrong, that of righteousness; the feeling of deference and compliance, that of propriety; and the feeling of shame and dislike, that of wisdom. Tung probably meant all eight of these.

[19] *The Mean*, ch. 27.

corresponds to yang, is superior to the ruled. The same is true of the other relations. Thus the double standard is put on a natural basis.

Therefore Confucius said, "A good man it is not mine to see. If I could see a man of constant virtue, I would be content."[20] From this we know that what the Sage called goodness is not easy to match. It is not simply because we are better than animals that we may be called good. If merely activating the beginning and being better than animals may be called goodness, why is it not evident [from the beginning]? That being better than animals is not sufficient to be called goodness is the same as being wiser than plants is not sufficient to be called wisdom. The nature of people is better than that of animals but may not be regarded as good. The term knowledge (wisdom) is derived from the word sageliness. What the Sage ordered is accepted by the world as correct. To correct the course of day and night depends on the polar star, and to correct suspicions and doubts depends on the Sage. From the point of view of the Sage, the generation without a king and people without training cannot be equal to goodness. Such is the difficulty to match goodness. It is too much to say that the nature of all people can be equal to it. If evaluated in comparison with the nature of animals, the nature of man is of course good. But if evaluated in comparison with the goodness according to the way of man [as it should be], man's nature falls short. It is all right to say that human nature is better than that of animals, but it is not all right to say that their nature is what the Sage calls goodness. My evaluation of life and nature differs from that of Mencius. Mencius evaluated on the lower level the behavior of animals and therefore said that man's nature is good [at birth]. I evaluate on the higher level what the Sage considers to be goodness, and therefore say that man's nature is not good to start with. Goodness is higher than human nature, and the sage is higher than goodness. The *Spring and Autumn Annals* is concerned with the great origin. Therefore it is very careful in the rectification of names. If a name does not come from its proper origin, how can we talk about nature not being good or already being good?" (SPTK, 10:3b-7a)

Comment. Tung Chung-shu actually departs from Confucius and Mencius in the matter of education. Early Confucianists emphasized self-education, although teachers and rulers are helpful and even necessary. But Tung insists that people by nature and by their very name are in the dark (in sleep) and cannot be good without instructions from the ruler. Then he offers human nature as a justi-

[20] Paraphrasing *Analects*, 7:25.

fication for authoritarianism. In this he goes even further than Hsün Tzu (fl. 298–238 B.C.).

B. The Meaning of the Five Agents (ch. 42)

Heaven has Five Agents (i.e. Elements): the first is Wood; the second, Fire; the third, Earth; the fourth, Metal; and the fifth, Water. Wood is the beginning of the cycle of the Five Agents, Water is its end, and Earth is its center. Such is their natural sequence. Wood produces Fire, Fire produces Earth, Earth produces Metal, Metal produces Water, and Water produces Wood. Such is their father-and-son relationship. Wood occupies the left, Metal occupies the right, Fire occupies the front, Water occupies the rear, and Earth occupies the center. Such is their order as that of father and son, and the way in which they receive from each other and spread out. Therefore Wood received from Water, Fire from Wood, Earth from Fire, Metal from Earth, and Water from Metal. Those that give are fathers and those that receive are sons. It is the Way of Heaven that the son always serves his father. Therefore when Wood is produced, Fire should nourish it, and after Metal perishes, Water should store it. Fire enjoys Wood and nourishes it with yang, but Water overcomes Metal and buries it with yin. Earth serves Heaven with the utmost loyalty. Therefore the Five Agents are the actions of filial sons and loyal ministers. The Five agents are so called because they are tantamount to five actions. That is how the term was derived. The sage knows this and therefore he shows much love and little sternness, and is generous in supporting the living and serious in burying the dead. This is to follow the system of Heaven. It is the function of the son to receive and to fulfill. For him to support is like Fire enjoying Wood, to bury one's father is like Water overcoming Metal, and serving the ruler is like Earth showing respect to Heaven. People like these may be said to be good in their actions.

> *Comment.* Unlike the Yin Yang School which puts the Five Agents on the same level or in a cycle, Tung arranges them lineally. He did so partly because of his strong emphasis on the idea of the origin which means that things proceed in time on a straight-line sequence, and partly because of his strong feeling for hierarchy. It is no wonder that loyalty and filial piety are on the forefront, for that is where the ruler and the father are to be found.

Each of the Five Agents succeeds the others according to its order. Each of them performs its official function by fulfilling its capacity. Thus Wood occupies the eastern quarter and controls the forces (*ch'i*) of spring, Fire occupies the southern quarter and controls the forces of summer, Metal occupies the western quarter and controls the forces of autumn, and Water occupies the northern quarter and controls the forces of winter. For this reason Wood controls production, Metal controls destruction, Fire controls heat, and Water controls cold. It is the course of Nature that people must be employed according to their order and officials appointed according to their capacity. Earth occupies the center and is the natural benefactor. It is the helper of Heaven. Its character is abundant and beautiful and cannot be identified with the affairs of any single season. Therefore among the Five Agents and the four seasons, Earth includes them all. Although Metal, Wood, Water, and Fire each have their own functions, their positions would not be established were it not for Earth, just as sourness, saltiness, acridness, and bitterness would not become tastes were it not for savoriness. Savoriness is the basis of the five tastes, and Earth is the controlling factor of the Five Agents. The controling factor of the Five Agents is the material force of Earth. It is like the fact that with savoriness the five tastes cannot help being tastes. Therefore among the actions of the sage, nothing is more valuable than loyalty, for it is the character of Earth. The great office of men, the function of which need not be mentioned, is that which they receive from each other. The great office of Heaven, the origin of which need not be mentioned, is Earth. (SPTK, 11:2b-3b)

C. The Correspondence of Man and the Numerical Categories of Heaven (ch. 56)

Heaven is characterized by the power to create and spread things, Earth is characterized by its power to transform, and man is characterized by moral principles. The material force of Heaven is above, that of Earth below, and that of man in between. Spring produces and summer grows, and all things flourish. Autumn destroys and winter stores, and all things are preserved. Therefore there is nothing more refined than material force, richer than Earth, or more spiritual than Heaven. Of the creatures born from the refined essence of Heaven and Earth, none is more noble than man. Man receives the mandate from Heaven and is therefore superior to other creatures.[21] Other creatures suffer troubles and defects and cannot practice humanity and righteousness; man alone can practice them. Other creatures suffer troubles and defects and cannot match Heaven and Earth; man alone can match them. Man has 360 joints, which match the number of Heaven (the round number of days in a year). His body with its bones and flesh matches the thickness of Earth. He has ears and eyes above, with their keen sense of hearing and seeing, which resemble the sun and moon. His body has its orifices and

[21] This reading follows the commentary by Lu Wen-ch'ao (1717-1795).

veins, which resemble rivers and valleys. His heart has feelings of sorrow, joy, pleasure, and anger, which are analogous to the spiritual feelings (of Heaven). As we look at man's body, how much superior it is to that of other creatures and how similar to Heaven! Other creatures derive their life from the yin and yang of Heaven in a non-erect way, but man brilliantly shows his patterns and order. Therefore with respect to the physical form of other creatures, they all move about in a non-erect and incumbent position. Man alone stands erect, looks straight forward, and assumes a correct posture. Thus those who receive little from Heaven and Earth take the non-erect posture, while those receiving much from them take the correct posture. From this we can see that man is distinct from other creatures and forms a trinity with Heaven and Earth.

Therefore in the body of man, his head rises up and is round and resembles the shape of heaven.[22] His hair resembles the stars and constellations. His ears and eyes, quick in their senses, resemble the sun and the moon. The breathing of his nostrils and mouth resembles the wind. The penetrating knowledge of his mind resembles the spiritual intelligence [of Heaven]. His abdomen and womb, now full and now empty, resemble the myriad things. The myriad things are nearest to the earth. Therefore the portion of the body below the waist corresponds to earth. As the body resembles heaven and earth, the waist serves as a sash. What is above the neck is noble and majestic in spirit, which is to manifest the feature of heaven and its kind. What is below the neck is full and humble, comparable to the soil. The feet are spread out and square, resembling the shape of the earth. Therefore in wearing ceremonial sash and girdle, the neck must be straight to distinguish it from the heart. What is above the sash (the waist) is all yang and what is below the sash is all yin, each with its own function. The yang is the material force of heaven, and the yin is the material force of the earth. Therefore when yin and yang become operative and cause man to have ailment in the foot or numbness in the throat [for example], the material force of the earth rises to become clouds and rain. Thus there is resemblance in the correspondence. The agreement of heaven and earth and the correspondence between yin and yang are ever found complete in the human body. The body is like heaven. Its numerical categories and those of heaven are mutually interwoven, and therefore their lives are interlocked. Heaven completes the human body with the number of days

[22] The Chinese believe heaven to be round and the earth to be square. Many of the comparisons between the human body and heavenly bodies are found in the *Huai-nan Tzu* (late 2nd cent. B.C.), ch. 7, SPPY, 7:2a-b. See Morgan, trans., *Tao, The Great Luminant*, pp. 59-60. They are also found in the apocryphal literature of Tung Chung-shu's time or shortly afterward. Evidently they were commonly held at the time.

in a full year. Consequently the body's 366 lesser joints correspond to the number of days in a year, and the twelve larger joints correspond to the number of months. Internally the body has the five viscera,[23] which correspond to the number of the Five Agents. Externally there are the four limbs, which correspond to the four seasons. The alternating of opening and closing of the eyes corresponds to day and night. The alternating of strength and weakness corresponds to winter and summer. And the alternating of sorrow and joy corresponds to yin and yang. The mind has calculations and deliberations, which fact corresponds to that of periods of time and number of degrees of distance. Man's conduct follows the principles of human relations, which fact corresponds to the relationship of heaven and earth. All this, whether obscure or obvious in the body, is born with man. When it is matched with heaven and earth and compared, it is found to be fitting. In what may be numbered, there is correspondence in number. In what may not be numbered, there is correspondence in kind. They are all identical and correspond to Heaven. Thus [Heaven and man] are one. Therefore present the formed so as to make manifest the formless and get hold of what may be numbered to [make manifest what may not be numbered]. Spoken of in this way, it is quite proper for things to correspond to each other in kind. It is like the form [of the body]. Its [correspondence to heaven] is correct by virtue of its numerical categories. (SPTK, 13:1b-3b)

> *Comment.* To match the number of bones in the human body with the number of days in the year sounds ridiculous and suggests that it is no more than a leftover of primitive divination. What is not so ridiculous, however, is the possibility of knowledge of the formless from the formed and through numbers. This involves the belief that all things of the same kind are reducible to the same pattern and the same numerical category. Behind all this is the idea of uniformity of nature and knowledge by inference, quite aside from the mere doctrine of correspondence of man and Nature or their unity.

D. *Things of the Same Kind Activate Each Other* (ch. 57)

If now water be poured on level ground, it will avoid the dry area and run to the wet area, whereas if two identical pieces of firewood are exposed to fire, the fire will avoid the wet piece and go to the dry one.[24] All things avoid what is different from them and follow what is similar to them. Therefore similar forces come together and matching tones

---

[23] Heart, liver, stomach, lungs, and kidneys.
[24] As Hsün Tzu has said. See *Hsün Tzu*, ch. 27, SPTK, 19:23a.

respond to each other.[25] This is clear from evidence. Suppose the seven-stringed and the twenty-five stringed lutes are tuned and played. When the note F in the one is struck, the note F on the other will respond to it, and when the note G in the one is struck, the note G in the other will respond to it. Among the five notes each one that matches will sound of itself. There is nothing supernatural in this. It is their natural course that they do so. A beautiful thing calls forth things that are beautiful in kind and an ugly thing calls forth things that are ugly in kind, for things of the same kind arise in response to each other. For example, when a horse neighs, it is horses that will respond, [and when an ox lows, it is oxen that will respond]. Similarly, when an emperor or a king is about to rise, auspicious omens will first appear, and when he is about to perish, unlucky omens will first appear.[26] Therefore things of the same kind call forth each other. Because of the dragon, rain is produced, and by the use of the fan, the heat is chased away. Wherever armies are stationed, briers and thorns grow.[27] All beautiful and ugly things have their origins and have their lives accordingly. But none knows where these origins are.

> *Comment.* The belief in portents is as old as Chinese thought. What is new in Tung Chung-shu is that he explains it in terms of natural law. Instead of expressions of the pleasure or displeasure of spiritual beings, portents are results of the cosmic material forces of yin and yang.

When the sky is dark and it is about to rain, a person's sickness affects him first, because the force of yin rises in response. When the sky is dark and it is about to rain, people want to sleep, because the material force of yin is at work. People who are sad want to lie down, because the yin of sadness and lying down seek each other. And people who are happy do not want to lie down because the yang of happiness and staying up require each other. Because of the night, the water level rises in some degree. Because of the east wind, the wine becomes further fermented.[28] When the night comes, the sick person's sickness becomes worse. When the day is about to dawn, cocks all crow and press on each other, their force becoming more and more refined. Therefore the yang reinforces the yang and the yin reinforces the yin, for the forces of yin and yang can naturally augment or diminish things because of their similarity in kind.

Heaven possesses yin and yang and man also possesses yin and yang.

[25] Paraphrasing *Lü-shih ch'un-chiu* (Mr. Lü's *Spring and Autumn Annals*), ch. 20, sec. 4, SPPY, 20:7b.
[26] The doctrine is taught in *The Mean*, ch. 24.
[27] Paraphrasing *Lao Tzu*, ch. 30.
[28] Paraphrasing *Huai-nan Tzu*, ch. 6, SPPY, 6:2b.

When the universe's material force of yin arises, man's material force of yin arises in response. Conversely, when man's material force of yin arises, that of the universe should also arise in response. The principle is the same. He who understands this, when he wishes to bring forth rain, will activate the yin in man in order to arouse the yin of the universe. When he wishes to stop rain, he will activate the yang in man in order to arouse the yang of the universe. Therefore the bringing forth of rain is nothing supernatural. People suspect that it is supernatural because its principle is subtle and wonderful. It is not only the material forces of yin and yang that can advance or withdraw according to their kind. Even the way misfortunes, calamities, and blessings are produced follows the same principle. In all cases one starts something himself and other things become active in response according to their kind. Therefore men of intelligence, sageliness, and spirit introspect and listen to themselves, and their words become intelligent and sagely. The reason why introspection and listening to oneself alone can lead to intelligence and sageliness is because one knows that his original mind lies there. Therefore when the note of F is struck in the seven-stringed or twenty-one stringed lute, the F note in other lutes sound of themselves in response. This is a case of things being activated because they are similar in kind. Their activity takes place in sound and is invisible. Not seeing the form of their activity, people say that they sound of themselves. Furthermore, since they activate each other invisibly, it is thought that they do so themselves. In reality, it is not that they do so themselves, but that there is something that causes them. In reality things are caused, but the cause is invisible. According to the tradition mentioned in the commentary of the *Book of History*, when the House of Chou was about to arise, some big red crows holding some seeds of grain in their bills gathered on the roof of the king's house. King Wu (r. 1121–1116 B.C.?) was happy and all great officials were glad. The Duke of Chou (d. 1094 B.C.) said, "Make greater effort. Make greater effort. Heaven shows this in order to exhort us."[29] The duke was afraid that people depended on [Heaven]. (SPTK, 13:3b-5a)

E. Additional Selections

1. The Origin (Yüan)

Why does the *Spring and Autumn Annals* value the origin highly and talk about it?[30] The origin means the beginning. It means that the foun-

---

[29] *Shang-shu ta-chuan* (Great Commentary on the *Book of History*), attributed to Fu Sheng (fl. 220 B.C.), 2:1b.

[30] Confucius, in writing the *Spring and Autumn Annals*, began with the first year (*yüan*, first) of each ruler.

dation must be correct. It expresses the kingly way. The king is the beginning of man. If the king is correct, then the original material force will be harmonious, wind and rain will be timely, lucky stars will appear, and the yellow dragon will descend. If the king is not correct, then strange transformations will take place in heaven above and bandits will appear. . . . (ch. 6, SPTK, 4:1a)

It is only the Sage who can relate the myriad things to the One and tie it to the origin. If the source is not traced and the development from it followed, nothing can be accomplished. Therefore in the *Spring and Autumn Annals* the first year is changed to be called the year of *yüan* (origin). The origin is the same as source (*yüan*).[31] It means that it accompanies the beginning and end of Heaven and Earth. Therefore if man in his life has a beginning and end like this, he does not have to respond to the changes of the four seasons. Therefore the origin is the source of all things, and the origin of man is found in it. How does it exist? It exists before Heaven and Earth. Although man is born of the force of Heaven and receives the force of Heaven, he may not partake the origin of Heaven, or rely on its order and violate what it does. Therefore the first month of spring is a continuation of the activities of Heaven and Earth, continuing the activities of Heaven and completing it. The principle is that [Heaven and man] accomplish together and maintain the undertaking. How can it be said to be merely the origin of Heaven and Earth? What does the origin do? How does it apply to man? If we take the connections seriously, we shall understand the order of things. The Sage did not want to talk about [the behavior] of animals and such. What he wanted to talk about was humanity and righteousness so as to put things in order. . . . (ch. 13, SPTK, 5:8a-b)

> *Comment.* What Jesus did for the West—i.e., form a bridge between God and man—Tung would have Confucius do—i.e., form a bridge between the myriad things and the One or the origin. Actually in the Western Han there was an effort to deify him, but it was short-lived. What prevented Confucius' permanent deification was his primary concern with a perfect moral life, that of humanity and righteousness.

2. Humanity and Righteousness

What the *Spring and Autumn Annals* regulates are others and the self. The principles with which to regulate others and the self are humanity and righteousness. Humanity is to give others peace and security and righteousness is to rectify the self. Therefore the word "humanity" (*jen*)

---

[31] The two different Chinese characters are pronounced the same and have similar meanings.

means others (people, *jen*)[32] and the word "righteousness" means the self.[33] The distinction is made in the terms themselves. . . . The principle of humanity consists in loving people and not in loving oneself, and the principle of righteousness consists in rectifying oneself and not in rectifying others. If one is not rectified himself, he cannot be considered righteous even if he can rectify others, and if one loves himself very much but does not apply his love to others, he cannot be considered humane. . . . (ch. 29, SPTK, 8:8b-9a)

> *Comment.* This understanding of humanity (*jen*) as love is found in ancient philosophers, notably in Mo Tzu (fl. 479–438 B.C.),[34] Chuang Tzu,[35] Hsün Tzu[36] and Han Fei Tzu (d. 233 B.C.).[37] But for them it was one of several possible meanings, but in Tung Chungshu it is *the* meaning. This interpretation is characteristic of practically all Han Confucianists, and Tung was the first.

3. Humanity and Wisdom

Love without wisdom means love without discrimination. Wisdom without humanity means knowledge not translated into action. Therefore humanity is to love mankind and wisdom is to remove its evil.

What is meant by humanity? The man of humanity loves people with a sense of commiseration. He is careful and agreeable and does not quarrel. His likes and dislikes are harmonized with human relations. He does not harbor the feeling of hate or a desire to hurt. He has no intention to conceal or to evade. He has no disposition of jealousy. He has no desires that lead to sadness or worry. He does not do anything treacherous or cunning. And he does not do anything depraved. Therefore his heart is at ease, his will is peaceful, his vital force is harmonious, his desires are regulated, his actions are easy, and his conduct is in accord with the moral law. It is for this reason that he puts things in order peacefully and easily without any quarrel. This is what is meant by humanity.

What is meant by wisdom? It is to speak first and then act accordingly. It is to weigh with one's wisdom whether to act or not and then pro-

---

[32] As *The Mean*, ch. 20, says, "Humanity is the distinguishing characteristic of man."

[33] The word "righteousness" (*i*) contains the component *wo*, which means the self.

[34] *Mo Tzu*, chs. 40 and 42, SPTK, 10:1a, 6b.

[35] *Chuang Tzu*, ch. 12, NHCC, 5:2b. See Giles, trans., *Chuang Tzu*, 1961 ed., p. 118.

[36] *Hsün Tzu*, ch. 27, SPTK, 19:5a.

[37] *Han Fei Tzu*, ch. 20, SPTK, 6:1a. See Liao, trans., *Complete Works of Han Fei Tzu*, vol. 1, p. 171.

ceed accordingly. When one's weighing is correct, what he does will be proper, what he handles will be appropriate, his action will bring result, his fame will become glorious, benefits will gather around him with no trouble, blessings will reach his offspring, and benefits will be bestowed on all his people. Such were the cases of wise kings T'ang and Wu.[38] When one's weighing is wrong, what he does will be improper, what he handles will be inappropriate, his action will bring no result, his name will become a shame, injuries will gather around him, his posterity will be cut off, and his state will be ruined. Such were the cases of [wicked kings Chieh and Chou].[39] . . . (ch. 30, SPTK, 8:12b-13a)

> *Comment.* The equal emphasis on humanity and wisdom exercised a tremendous influence on K'ang Yu-wei (1858-1927).[40]

4. Historical Cycles

One becomes a king only after he has received the Mandate of Heaven. As the king, he will determine which day is to be the first day of the year for his dynasty, change the color of clothes worn at court, institute systems of ceremonies and music, and unify the whole empire. All this is to show that the dynasty has changed and that he is not succeeding any human being, and to make it very clear that he has received the mandate from Heaven. . . . Therefore T'ang received the mandate and became king. In response to Heaven he abolished the Hsia dynasty [whose system was symbolized by red]. He called his dynasty Yin (Shang). The system was corrected to be that symbolized by white. . . . King Wu received the mandate. . . . Therefore [in the beginning of] the Ch'un-ch'iu period [of the Chou dynasty], in response to Heaven, he undertook the business of a new king. The system was corrected to be that symbolized by black. . . . The Three Correct Systems[41] began with the system symbolized by black. . . . The material force (*ch'i*), integrated by Heaven, begins to penetrate and transform things. It is evident that buds beginning to appear in plants are black (or dark, still closed). Therefore the color of clothes worn at court is black. . . . In the system symbolized by white. . . . the material force integrated by Heaven begins to form things. They begin to sprout. The color is white. Therefore the color of clothes worn at court is white. . . . In the system symbolized by red. . . .

---

[38] T'ang (r. 1751–1739 B.C.) was the founder of the Shang (1751–1112 B.C.) and Wu was the founder of the Chou (1111–249 B.C.).

[39] They were responsible for the fall of the Hsia (2183–1752 B.C.?) and Shang dynasties, respectively.

[40] See below, ch. 39, sec. 3.

[41] *San-cheng* in Chinese. It is also called *san-t'ung*, Three Systems, *t'ung* meaning a system which is based on a certain correct principle that integrates and directs all things within it. For this doctrine in K'ang Yu-wei, see below, ch. 39, sec. 1.

[the material force integrated by Heaven extends to all things and things begin their activity. The color is red].[42] . . . The reason why the Three Systems are called the Three Correct Systems is because they make things operate. When the integration is extended to cover the material force of all things, their will all will respond [to Heaven]. As the correct system is rectified, everything else will be rectified. . . . (ch. 23, SPTK, 7:3b-6a)

[42] According to Lu Wen-ch'ao, these words are missing from the text.

15

TAOISTIC CONFUCIANISM: YANG HSIUNG

YANG HSIUNG (53 B.C.–A.D. 18) is usually given a position in the history of Chinese thought, though a minor one, because of his doctrine of human nature as a mixture of good and evil. The theory is asserted only in a sentence and is not elaborated upon or argued. Still it represents a real advance because it avoids the extremes of Mencius and Hsün Tzu (fl. 298–238 B.C.) and the arbitrary division into the two levels of nature and feelings by Tung Chung-shu (c. 179–c. 104 B.C.), and offers a significant alternative. It also underlines the fact that the problem of human nature remained a major one throughout the history of Chinese philosophy.

As to his metaphysics, by which he is identified with the term *T'ai-hsüan* (the Supremely Profound Principle or Great Mystery), he does no more than repeat Taoism, except that he combines it with Confucian ethics, in which his real interests lay. In this respect, he reflects the syncretic spirit of the Han period (206 B.C.-A.D. 220). At the same time, he exhibits a certain independent quality in refusing to accept the Confucian doctrine of the periodic appearance of sages, which was explicit in Mencius and implicit in Tung Chung-shu. He also rejects the popular belief in immortals. A man of extensive learning and high integrity, he endured poverty and led an undistinguished public life.[1] The following selections are from his two books, the *Fa-yen* (Model Sayings) and the *T'ai-hsüan ching* (Classic of the Supremely Profound Principle).[2]

SELECTIONS

Man's nature is a mixture of good and evil. He who cultivates the good in it will become a good man and he who cultivates the evil in it will become an evil man. The material force (*ch'i*) [with which one is endowed] is the driving force[3] that leads one to good or evil. . . . Therefore the superior man studies hard and practices earnestly. He

---

[1] For details of his life, see *Ch'ien-Han shu* (History of the Former Han Dynasty, 206 B.C.–A.D. 8), ch. 87.

[2] The *Fa-yen* consists of questions and answers on ethics, history, and other typically Confucian subjects, and to this extent is an imitation of the *Analects*. But, unlike the classic, it has thirteen chapters devoted to thirteen subjects. For translations, see Bibliography. The *T'ai-hsüan ching* is made up of fifteen essays and is an imitation of the *Book of Changes* in form. There is no European translation so far.

[3] Literally, a horse.

waits till his good becomes a rare treasure before he sells it. He cultivates his personal life before he makes friends. And he plans well before
he acts. This is the way to fulfill the Way. . . . (*Fa-yen*, SPPY, 3:1a-b)

> *Comment.* According to Wang Ch'ung (27–100 A.D.?), the theory
> of the mixture of good and evil nature had been advanced long be-
> fore Yung Hsiung.[4] But Wang Ch'ung wrote long after Yang
> Hsiung. There can be no doubt that Yang's theory was original.
> In any event, he has been considered the originator of the theory
> and has been severely criticized by Confucianists.

Someone asks, "Is it true that every five hundred years a sage will
appear?"[5]

I reply, "Yao,[6] Shun,[7] and Yü[8] were rulers and ministers, and they
came one after another. (Sages) King Wen,[9] King Wu,[10] and the Duke of
Chou[11] were father and sons, and they lived at the same time. King
T'ang[12] and Confucius lived several hundred years [after the previous
sage]. Inferring the future on the basis of the past, we do not know
whether one sage will appear in a thousand years or a thousand sages
will appear in one year."[13] (SPPY, 8:1a)

Someone asks, "Don't the dragon, the tortoise, and the wild swan live
very long?"

I say, "They live very long."

"Can man live very long?"

"Creatures live long because of their nature. Man does so because of
his humanity (*jen*)." . . .

Someone asks, "If there are no immortals in the world, why do people
talk about them?"

I reply, "Isn't all this talk hubbub? Because it is hubbub, it can make
what is nonexistent seem to exist."

Someone then asks about the actual truth about immortals.

I say, "I shall have nothing to do with the question. Their existence
or nonexistence is not something to talk about. What should be asked
are questions on loyalty and filial piety." (SPPY, 12:4b-5a)

[4] See below, ch. 16, A.
[5] So said Mencius. See *Mencius*, 2B:13.
[6] Legendary sage-emperor (3rd millennium B.C.).
[7] Yao's successor.
[8] Founder of the Hsia dynasty (r. 2183–2175 B.C.?).
[9] Founder of the Chou dynasty (r. 1171–1122 B.C.).
[10] King Wen's son (r. 1121–1116 B.C.).
[11] Younger brother of King Wu, who died in 1094 B.C.
[12] Founder of the Shang dynasty (r. 1751–1739 B.C.?).
[13] This interpretation follows the commentary by Li Kuei (of Eastern Chin,
317-420). The text merely says "thousand one" and can mean that a sage may
appear in a thousand years or in one year.

Comment: A typical Confucian attitude toward life after death. The belief in immortals was being promoted by a religious cult worshipping the legendary Yellow Emperor of high antiquity and Lao Tzu. But to seek to live forever is contrary to the Taoist philosophy of indifference to life and death and to letting things take their own course. Therefore the belief had no place in Taoist philosophy but only in a popular cult which later assumed the name of Taoist religion.

The Supremely Profound Principle deeply permeates all species of things but its physical form cannot be seen. It takes nourishment from vacuity (*hsü*) and nothingness (*wu*) and derives its life from Nature.[14] It correlates matters of spiritual intelligence and determines the natural course of events. It penetrates the past and present and originates the various species. It operates yin and yang (passive and active cosmic forces) and starts the material force in motion. As yin and yang unite, all things are complete in heaven and earth. The sky and the sun rotate and the weak and the strong interact. They return to their original positions and thus the beginning and end are determined. Life and death succeed each other and thus the nature and destiny are made clear. Looking up, we see the forms of the heavens. Looking down, we see the condition of the earth. We examine our nature and understand our destiny. We trace our beginning and see our end. . . . Therefore the Profound Principle is the perfection of utility. To see and understand is wisdom. To look and love is humanity. To determine and decide is courage. To control things universally and to use them for all is impartiality. To be able to match all things is penetration. To have or not to have the proper circumstance is destiny. The way by which all things emerge from vacuity is the Way. To follow the principles of the world without altering them and to attain one's end is virtue. To attend to life, to be in society, and to love universally is humanity. To follow order and to evaluate what is proper is righteousness. To get hold of the Way, virtue, humanity, and righteousness and put them into application is called the business of life. To make clear the achievement of Nature and throw light on all things is called yang. To be hidden, without form, deep and unfathomable is called yin. Yang knows yang but does not know yin. Yin knows yin but does not know yang. The Profound Principle alone knows both yin and yang, both going and stopping, and both darkness and light. . . . (*T'ai-hsüan ching*, ch. 9, SPTK, 7:5a-9b)

[14] Both punctuation and interpretation of this sentence follow the commentary by Fan Weng (of Chin, 265-420).

··· 16 ···

THE NATURALISM OF WANG CH'UNG

CONSIDERABLE INTEREST in Wang Ch'ung (27-100?) has been aroused in the last several decades. In our age of critical spirit, skepticism, scientific method, demand for evidence, and revolt against the past, this is perfectly natural, for Wang Ch'ung represents all these. A thoroughly independent thinker, he was not identified with any school and has often been classified as a member of the Miscellaneous School. In his metaphysics, he is definitely Taoistic, somewhat modified by the idea of the interfusion and intermingling of the yin and yang forces in the *Book of Changes*. But even here he is different, for while Taoism is very much interested in metaphysics but not much in human institutions, Wang took the opposite position. Actually he is neither creative nor significant so far as metaphysics is concerned. His chief contribution to the history of Chinese thought is to clear the atmosphere of superstition and enhance the critical and rational spirit that was already incipient.

When Wang was born, Confucianism had been the supreme doctrine in China for more than a hundred years. Influenced by popular priest-magicians who spread superstitions and performed miracles, the essentially rationalistic Confucian doctrine of the unity of man and Nature had degenerated into one of mutual influence, often of a mysterious kind. Furthermore, in an attempt to make Confucius more than the supreme sage, efforts were made to deify him, and he was considered the "uncrowned king" appointed by Heaven. The beginning of this tendency was already evident in Tung Chung-shu (c.179–c.104 B.C.). During the Western Han period (206 B.C.–A.D. 8) a whole body of apocryphal literature grew up to supplement the basically humanistic and rationalistic Confucian Classics, a literature with fantastic interpretation of the Classics in order to support the belief in portents and prophecies. The influence of this literature was particularly strong between the Western Han and the Eastern Han (25-220). It was very popular during the reign of Emperor Wu (r. 140–87 B.C.), and Wang Mang, ruler of Hsin dynasty (9-23), loved it exceedingly. The intellectual situation at Wang Ch'ung's time was therefore something like this: (1) Confucianism was supreme; (2) it was being debased into a mysterious and superstitious doctrine; (3) the unity of man and Nature was turned into one of mutual influence; (4) these influences were thought to be exerted through strange phenomena and calamities; (5) Heaven, though not anthropomorphic, was purposive, asserting its will through prodigies as warning to men; and (6), on a smaller scale spiritual beings exercised similar influence.

Wang Ch'ung rose in revolt against all these prevalent beliefs. In clear, critical, and strong terms, he declared that Heaven takes no action, that natural events, including prodigies, occur spontaneously, that there is no such thing as teleology, that fortune and misfortune come by chance, and that man does not become a ghost at death. In addition, he insisted that any theory must be tested by concrete evidence, and he himself argued in a strictly rational manner supporting his theories with one fact after another. For him, the past is no sure guidance, for there is no fact to prove that the past is better than the present. Thus in one stroke he rejected the total body of beliefs and dogma accumulated over several centuries. In doing so, he raised the pitch of skepticism and naturalism to a height never before reached in Chinese history. In this way he prepared for the growth of rationalism and naturalism in the Wei-Chin period (220-420) which probably would not have come about without him. Wang's contribution, then, does not lie in any original thought but in the fostering of a new spirit.

Wang grew up in a very poor family and had to read books in a bookstore. He was a quiet scholar and devoted teacher, and was known as one of three geniuses in his time.[1] The following selections are from his extant work, the *Lun-heng* (Balanced Inquiries).

THE BALANCED INQUIRIES[2]

A. On Original Nature (ch. 13)

Man's feelings and nature are the root of government by men and the source of ceremonies and music. Therefore as we investigate the matter, we find that ceremonies are employed to check the excess of the nature and feelings and music is used to regulate them. In man's nature there are the qualities of humbleness, modesty, deference, and compliance. Hence ceremonies have been instituted to adjust them to their proper expression. In men's feelings there are the qualities of like and dislike, pleasure and anger, and sorrow and joy. Hence music has been created to enable their feeling of reverence to be expressed everywhere. Nature and feelings are therefore the reason why systems

---

[1] An orphan, Wang started school at the age of eight. After studying at the national university in the national capital, he returned home to teach. Later he served successively as a district officer, a prefect officer in charge of educational and ceremonial affairs, and an assistant to an inspecting censor. Eventually he resigned and went home. See *Lun-heng*, ch. 85.

[2] This consists of eighty-four chapters in thirty books. Most chapters are devoted to an attack on current beliefs. There are special chapters criticizing Confucius, Mencius, and Han Fei Tzu (d. 233 B.C.). For translation, see Bibliography. Most people, emphasizing Wang's critical spirit, have translated *lun-heng* as "critical essays," but by Wang's own words (ch. 30), his work aimed at a "balanced (or fair) discussion."

of ceremonies and music have been created. Scholars in the past have written essays and treatises to discuss the subjects but none of them was final or correct.

Shih Shih[3] of the Chou (1111–249 B.C.) maintained that in nature some are born good and some are born evil. Take the good nature and cultivate it, and goodness will develop. Take the evil nature and cultivate it, and evil will develop. Thus in nature some belong to yin (passive cosmic force) and some belong to yang (active cosmic force), and some are good and some are evil. It all depends on cultivation. Therefore Master Shih wrote the "Book on Cultivating [Nature]."[4] People like Mi Tzu-chien, Ch'i Tiao-k'ai, and Kung-sun Ni-tzu[5] also discussed the subjects of man's feelings and nature. They varied from Master Shih somewhat, and all said that in nature some are good and some are evil. Mencius wrote an essay on the goodness of human nature and thought that the nature of all men is originally good and that if they are evil, it is because material circumstances upset them.[6] . . . According to Mencius, all people are good in childhood. . . . When (wicked king) Chou[7] was a child, the viscount of Wei saw the evil nature in him. His evil nature was no worse than that of the ordinary people, but as he grew up, he did violence to it instead of transforming it. . . . What Mencius said about the feelings and nature is not true. . . . Kao Tzu was a contemporary of Mencius. In his discussion on human nature, he said that it is neither good nor evil. . . .[8] When Kao Tzu used the analogy of breaching water [to the east or west as nature can be made good or evil], he was referring to average people but not to those extremely good or extremely evil. Confucius said, "By nature men are alike. Through practice they have become far apart."[9] . . . And also, "Only the most intelligent and the most stupid do not change."[10] Nature in some is good and in some is evil, and can no longer be changed by the influence of sages or the teachings of worthies. . . . Therefore I know that what Kao Tzu said is not true.

Hsün Tzu (fl. 298–238 B.C.) opposed Mencius and wrote "The Nature

---

[3] He was a pupil of a Confucian pupil. His book in twenty-one chapters is no longer extant, though fragments have survived.

[4] The word "nature" is added according to Kao Su-yüan, Lun-heng, 1935, p. 17. Huang Hui, however, does not think so. See his Lun-heng chiao-shih (Balanced Inquiries Collected and Annotated), 1938, p. 124.

[5] The first two were Confucius' pupils and the latter was pupil of a pupil. Their works disappeared long ago, though fragments of Mi's have survived.

[6] Mencius, 6A:1-7.

[7] R. 1175–1112 B.C. Chinese historians have held him responsible for the fall of the Shang dynasty (1751–1112 B.C.).

[8] Mencius, 6A:1-6.

[9] Analects, 17:2.

[10] ibid., 17:3.

of Man Is Evil."[11] . . . According to his words, men are not good in childhood. But when Chi (worthy minister of sage-emperor Yao,[12] who taught people agriculture) was a boy he played planting trees, and as soon as Confucius could walk, he performed sacrificial rites for fun.[13] A stone is hard as soon as it is produced, and an orchid is fragrant as soon as it comes into being. . . . What Hsün Tzu said is not true. . . .

Tung Chung-shu read the works of Mencius and Hsün Tzu and originated the theory of human nature and feelings saying, ". . . nature is born of yang and feelings are born of yin. The force of yin results in greed and that of yang results in humanity. Those who say that nature is good have insight about yang and those who say that nature is evil have insight about yin."[14] What Tung Chung-shu means is that Mencius had insight about yang and Hsün Tzu had insight about yin. So far as he asserts that each of them had his own insight, he is correct. But his theory does not settle the matter of the nature and the feelings. It is not true that the nature and the feelings of all men are both good and evil. For both man's nature and his feelings are products of yin and yang. Being products of yin and yang, some are rich and some are poor. Jades are products of stone. Some are pure and some are impure. How can nature and feelings, being [products of] yin and yang, be purely good? What Tung Chung-shu said is not true.

Liu Tzu-cheng (77–6 B.C.) said, "Man's nature is inborn. It is in man and is not expressed. His feelings, on the other hand, are what come into contact with things. They are revealed externally. What is revealed externally is called yang and what is not expressed is called yin."[15] . . . According to his words, nature is yin (evil) and feelings are yang (good). But don't man's endowed feelings, after all, have both good and evil elements? . . .

The truth is that in nature, some people are born good and some born evil. It is just as some people's capacity is high and some people's is low. High capacity cannot be made low and low capacity cannot be made high. To say that human nature is neither good nor evil is like saying that man's capacity is neither high nor low. . . . At bottom I consider Mencius' doctrine of the goodness of human nature as referring to people above the average, Hsün Tzu's doctrine of evil nature of man

[11] *Hsün Tzu*, ch. 23.

[12] Legendary emperor (3rd millennium B.C.).

[13] These stories are found in the *Shih chi* (Records of the Historian), PNP, 4:1b and 47:2a. For Chi, see Chavannes, *Les mémoires historiques*, vol. 1, 210.

[14] These words are not found in Tung's extant works; cf. above, ch. 14, A.

[15] His name was Hsiang. He was a high governmental official and the author of many works, including the *Hsin-hsü* (New Narrations) and *Shuo-yüan* (Collection of Discourses). But the quotation is not found in his extant works.

as referring to people below the average, and Yang Hsiung's (53 B.C.–A.D. 18) doctrine that human nature is a mixture of good and evil[16] as referring to average people. Insofar as their doctrines return to moral principles and accord with truth, they may be used to teach people. As to principles of nature, however, they have not been able to investigate them to the utmost. (SPPY, 3:12a-16a)

> *Comment.* Wang Chung sums up practically all previous theories on human nature: (1) that some people are born good and some are born evil (Shih Shih);[17] (2) that man is born good (Mencius); (3) that man is originally neither good nor evil (Kao Tzu); (4) that man is born evil (Hsün Tzu); (5) that man has the beginning of goodness and his nature is good but his feelings are evil (Tung Chung-shu); (6) that man's nature is evil but his feelings are good (Liu Hsiang); and (7) that man's nature is a mixture of good and evil (Yang Hsiung). He also criticized Lu Chia (216-176 B.C.), but Lu merely repeated Mencius except that instead of fully developing one's nature as Mencius had urged, he advocated "examining one's nature." Actually he did not represent any new theory.
>
> Wang's own theory is new but it is not a real advance, for the presence of either good or evil is not explained. In accepting Yang Hsiung's theory of mixture as referring to average people, he seems to believe in three grades of human nature. This would have anticipated Hsün Yüeh (148-209).[18] However, his main thesis is dualism. Inasmuch as the entire Western Han period is characterized by a dualistic approach to human nature, in terms of good nature and evil feelings, Wang's own dualism, in terms of good and evil natures, shows little progress.

B. On Spontaneity (ch. 54)

When the material forces (*ch'i*)[19] of Heaven and Earth come together, all things are spontaneously produced, just as when the vital forces (*ch'i*) of husband and wife unite, children are naturally born. Among the things thus produced, blood creatures are conscious of hunger and cold. Seeing that the five grains are edible, they obtain and eat them. And seeing that silk and hemp can be worn, they obtain and wear them. Some say that Heaven produces the five grains in order to feed man and produces silk

[16] See above, ch. 15.

[17] Perhaps he was the one whom Kao Tzu referred to. See *Mencius*, 6A:6.

[18] See comment on Han Yü's theory, ch. 27, sec. 1.

[19] This word means variously material force or energy, vital force, power, breath, and so forth and has to be translated variously. For a discussion on it, see Appendix.

and hemp in order to clothe man. This is to say that Heaven becomes a farmer or a mulberry girl for the sake of man. This is contrary to spontaneity. Therefore their ideas are suspect and should not be followed.

Let us discuss these concepts according to Taoism. Heaven (*T'ien*, Nature) gives forth and distributes material force universally into all things. Grains overcome hunger and silk and hemp save people from cold. Consequently people eat grains and wear clothing of silk and hemp. Now, that Heaven does not purposely produce the five grains and silk and hemp in order to feed and clothe man is very much like the fact that there are calamities and strange transformations but not for the purpose of reprimanding man. Things are spontaneously produced and man eats them and wears them, and material forces spontaneously change [in strange ways] and people are afraid of them. To talk otherwise may be agreeable to the minds of people. But if lucky influences from Heaven are intentional, where would spontaneity be, and where would non-action (*wu-wei*) be found?

How do we [know] that Heaven is spontaneous? Because it has neither mouth nor eyes. Those who engage in [purposive] action are something like those with mouth and eyes. The mouth desires to eat and the eyes desire to see. When something is desired inside, that desire is expressed outside, and the mouth and eyes seek for that thing, considering it an advantage to have it. This is the activity of desire. Now that there is no desire in the mouth or the eyes, there is no demand for things. What is any [intentional] act for?

How do we know that Heaven has neither mouth nor eyes? We know it from Earth. The body of Earth is made up of dirt, and dirt of course has neither mouth nor eyes. Heaven and Earth are like husband and wife. Since the body of the Earth has neither mouth nor eyes, we know that Heaven also has neither mouth nor eyes. If Heaven consists of a body, it should be similar to that of the Earth. If Heaven consists of vital force, it would be clouds and fog. How can things like clouds and fog have a mouth or an eye?

Someone says: Everything that moves is from the beginning engaged in action.[20] It moves because it has desires. Since it moves, it is engaged in action. Now, the activities of Heaven are similar to those of man. How can we say that it takes no action?

I reply: The activities of Heaven consist in the giving forth and distributing of the material force. As the body moves, the material force issues forth, and things are then produced. It is like the fact that as one's vital force is moved, his body moves, the vital force issues forth, and a

---

[20] The text has the word "no" before "action." As Sun Jen-ho suggested, it is superfluous. See his *Lun-heng chü-cheng* (*Balanced Inquiries* Corrected), 1924, p. 156.

child is produced. When man gives forth and distributes his vital force, it is not for the purpose of producing a child. As the vital force is distributed, a child is born spontaneously. Heaven moves without the desire to produce things and yet things are produced of themselves. That is spontaneity. When material force is given forth and distributed without the purpose of producing things and yet things are produced of themselves, that is non-action. What do we mean when we say that Heaven is spontaneous and takes no action? It is material force. It is tranquil, without desire, and is engaged in neither action nor business. . . .

When the Taoists talk about spontaneity, they do not know how to recite facts to prove their theory or practice. That is why their doctrine of spontaneity has not yet found credence. However, in spite of spontaneity, there must also be activity to help. Ploughing, tilling, weeding, and sowing in the spring are human activities. After the grains have entered the soil, they grow by day and night. It is not something man can do. If someone tries to do it, that would be a way to spoil them. A man of Sung was sorry that his corn was not growing. He went and pulled them up. The next day it dried up and died.[21] Those who take action to be spontaneous are like the man of Sung.

Someone asks: Man is born from Heaven and Earth. Since Heaven and Earth take no action and since man is endowed with the nature of Heaven [and Earth], he should take no action either. And yet he does take action. Why?

I reply: A person who is rich and pure in perfect virtue is endowed with a large quantity of vital force and is therefore able to approximate Heaven in being spontaneous and taking no action. Those who are endowed with little vital force do not follow moral principles and do not resemble Heaven and Earth. They are therefore called unworthy. By that is meant that they are not similar to Heaven and Earth. Since they do not resemble Heaven and Earth, they do not belong to the same class as sages and worthies and therefore take action.

Heaven and Earth are like a furnace. Their work is creation. Since the endowment of the vital force is not the same in all cases, how can all be worthy?. . .

The Way of Heaven is to take no action. Therefore in the spring it does not act to start life, in summer it does not act to help grow, in autumn it does not act to bring maturity, and in winter it does not act to store up. When the material force of yang comes forth itself, things naturally come to life and grow. When the material force of yin arises of itself, things naturally mature and are stored up. When we draw water from wells or breach water over a dam in order to irrigate fields and

[21] Referring to the story in *Mencius*, 2A:2.

gardens, things will also grow. But if rain falls like torrents, soaking through all stalks, leaves, and roots, in an amount equivalent to that in a pond, who would prefer drawing water from wells or breaching water over a dam? Therefore to act without acting is great. Originally no result is sought, and yet results are achieved. Originally no fame is sought, and yet fame is attained. Great indeed is the achievement and fame of abundant rain. Yet Heaven and Earth do not act for them. When the material forces are united in harmony, the rain gathers of itself. . . .

Since Heaven takes no action, it does not speak. When the time comes for calamities and strange transformations, the material force produces them spontaneously. Heaven and Earth cannot do it and cannot know it. When there is a cold in the stomach, it aches. It is not that man causes it. Rather, the vital force does it spontaneously. The space between heaven and earth is comparable to that between the back and the stomach. If we say that it is Heaven that causes all calamities and strange transformations, shall we say that all prodigies, big or small, substantial or light, are all made by Heaven? Suppose a cow gives birth to a horse or a peach tree produces a plum. Does it mean, according to their theory, that the spirit of Heaven enters the belly of the cow to create a horse or takes the seed of the plum and places it on the peach tree? . . . (SPPY, 18:1a-6b)

> *Comment.* The net effect of Wang Ch'ung's naturalism is to depersonalize Heaven and to deny the existence of design in any form. One would expect that his rationalism and naturalism would promote the development of natural science in China. Joseph Needham, however, has suggested that instead of fostering the development of science, Wang actually deterred it, for according to Needham, there must be a lawgiver before there can be natural laws. If Wang Ch'ung were alive, the first question he would ask would be, "What is your evidence to prove it?"[22]

C. A Treatise on Death (ch. 62)

People today say that when men die they become spiritual beings (*kuei*, ghosts), are conscious, and can hurt people. Let us try to prove by means of the species of creatures that the dead do not become spiritual beings, do not possess consciousness, and cannot hurt people. How shall we prove this? We do so by means of other creatures. Man and other creatures are all creatures. When other creatures die, they do not become spiritual beings. Why should man alone become a spiritual being

[22] See Needham, *Science and Civilisation in China*, vol. 2: *History of Scientific Thought*, pp. 371, 528.

when he dies? If people can make a distinction between man and other creatures as to which cannot become a spiritual being, they will still find it difficult to make clear why [man] becomes a spiritual being but [other creatures] do not. If they cannot make a distinction, then how do they know that men become spiritual beings [inasmuch as other creatures do not]?

Man can live because of his vital forces. At death his vital forces are extinct. What makes the vital forces possible is the blood. When a person dies, his blood becomes exhausted. With this his vital forces are extinct, and his body decays and becomes ashes and dust. What is there to become a spiritual being?

If a man has neither ears nor eyes (senses), he will have no consciousness. Hence men who are dumb and blind are like plants and trees. When the vital forces have left man, is it simply like a man without ears or eyes? [The whole body] decays and disappears. It becomes diffused and invisible, and is therefore called a spiritual being (*kuei-shen*, earthly and heavenly spirits). When people see the shape of spiritual beings, they of course do not see the vital forces of the dead. Why? Because the very name "spiritual being" means what is diffused and invisible. When a man dies, his spirit ascends to heaven and his flesh and bones return (*kuei*) to earth, and that is why an earthly spiritual being (*kuei*) [and a heavenly spiritual being (*shen*)][23] are so-called. To be an earthly spiritual being (*kuei*) means to return (*kuei*). . . . To be a heavenly spiritual being (*shen*) means to expand (*shen*). When the expansion reaches its limit, it ends and begins again. Man is born of spiritual forces. At death he returns to them. Yin and yang are called *kuei-shen*. After people die, they are also called *kuei-shen*.

The vital forces produce man just as water becomes ice. As water freezes into ice, so the vital forces coagulate to form a man. When ice melts, it becomes water. When a man dies, he becomes spirit again. He is called spirit just as melted ice changes its name to water. As people see that its name has changed, they say that it has consciousness, can assume physical form, and can hurt people. But they have no basis for saying so.

People see ghosts with the form of living men. From the fact that they appear in the form of living men, we know that they are not spirits of the dead. How can we show that to be true? When a sack is filled with rice or a bag with millet the rice will stay in the sack or the millet in the bag. It will be full and firm, standing up and visible. When people look at it, they know that it is a sack of rice or a bag of millet. How? Because the

[23] Additions according to Huang Hui, *Lun-heng chiao-shih*, p. 869. For a discussion of *kuei-shen*, see Appendix.

contents of the sack or bag can be clearly discerned from the shape. If the sack has a hole and the rice runs out, or if the bag is torn and the millet is lost, the sack or bag will either be thrown away or folded up. When people look at it, it can no longer be seen. The spirit of man is stored up inside the body in the same way as the millet is in the bag or rice in the sack. At death the body decays and the vital forces disintegrate like the sack having a hole or the bag having been torn and the rice running out or the millet being lost. When the rice has run out or the millet is lost, the sack or bag no longer keeps its shape. How can the vital forces of man still possess a body and be seen by men when they have disintegrated and become extinct?. . .

Since the beginning of the universe and rulers of high antiquity, people who died according to their allotted time or died at middle age or prematurely have numbered in the hundreds of millions. The number of men living today is not as great as that of the dead. If everyone who dies becomes an earthly spirit, there should be an earthly spirit at every pace on the road. If men see spirits when they are about to die, they should see millions and millions filling the hall and crowding the road instead of only one or two. . . .

Now, people say that a spiritual being is the spirit of a dead man. If the earthly spirit is really the spirit of a dead man, then when people see it, they ought to see the form of a nude, for there is no reason why they should see any garments. Why? Because garments have no spirit. When a man dies, they decay along with his body. How can they be worn by a spirit? . . .

Man is intelligent and wise because he possesses the forces of the Five Constant Virtues (of humanity, righteousness, propriety, wisdom, and faithfulness). The five forces are in him because there are the five internal organs in his body (namely, heart, liver, stomach, lungs, and kidneys, which correspond to the five virtues). If the five organs are unimpaired, he is wise. If they become diseased, he becomes hazy and confused. Being hazy and confused, he becomes stupid and foolish. When a man dies, the five organs rot and decay. As they rot and decay, the Five Constant Virtues will have nothing to attach to. What embodies wisdom will be destroyed, and what exercises wisdom will be gone. The body needs the vital forces in order to be complete, and the vital forces need the body in order to have consciousness. There is in the world no fire burning from itself. How can there be a spirit in the world that has consciousness from itself but is without a body?. . .

Before a person dies, his wisdom and spirit are calm. When he is sick, he is dull and confused, because his spirit is disturbed. Now, death is sickness much intensified. Since in sickness, which is but a mild form of death, one is already dull and confused, how much more would he be when it is intensified? When the spirit is disturbed, one loses consciousness. How much more when the spirit disintegrates? Man's death is like the extinction of fire. When a fire is extinguished, its light shines no longer, and when a man dies, his consciousness has no more understanding.[24] The two cases are the same in reality and properly so.[25] If people still maintain that the dead has consciousness, they are all deluded. What is the difference between a sick man about to die and the fire about to be extinguished? After the fire is extinguished and the light disappears, only the candle remains. After a man dies, his vital forces become extinct but only his body remains. To say that a man has consciousness after death is to say that a fire still has light after the fire is extinguished. . . .

After a man dies he does not become a spiritual being, has no consciousness, and cannot speak. He therefore cannot hurt people. How can we prove it? When a man gets angry, he utilizes his vital forces. When he hurts people, he has to apply strength. In order to apply strength, his sinews and bones must be strong. If they are strong, he can hurt people. . . . After a man dies, his hands and arms decay and can no longer hold a blade. His teeth have all fallen and he can no longer bite. How can he hurt people?. . . (SPPY, 20:9a-14a)

> *Comment.* In arguing against the existence of ghosts, Wang Ch'ung has offered more reasons than has any other Chinese thinker. For almost two thousand years now no one has been able to refute him, although some of his arguments sound very naïve.

D. Additional Selections

1. Accidents vs. Necessity

In their conduct, some men are worthy and some men are stupid. In encountering calamity or blessing, some are fortunate and some are unfortunate. In their action, some are right and some are wrong. When they meet with reward or punishment, some are lucky and some are unlucky. Many people may encounter war together, but those who hide themselves do not get hit. Several plants may be affected by frost on the same day, but the one that is covered does not get injured. Those that get hit or injured are not necessarily evil, and those that hide or are covered

[24] *Hui*, ordinarily meaning wisdom, here means understanding.
[25] Leslie, in his "Contribution to a New Translation of the *Lun Heng*," *T'oung Pao*, 44 (1956), p. 128, says *tung-i-shih* means "the same kind" and thinks Forke is wrong in translating it as "the nature of both is the same." Actually Forke's "nature" is closer to the meaning of *shih* (reality) whereas Leslie's "kind" is not.

are not necessarily good. Those that hide or are covered are lucky and those that get hit or are injured are unlucky. Many people may want to offer loyalty. But some are rewarded and some punished. Many people may want to do some good. But some are trusted and some doubted. Those rewarded and trusted are not necessarily genuine and those punished and doubted are not necessarily insincere. The rewarded and trusted ones are lucky and the punished and doubted ones are unlucky. . . .

Crickets and ants creep on the ground. A man lifts his foot and walks across it. Those crickets and ants he steps on are pressed to death, whereas those he does not step on remain completely alive and unhurt. When fires sweep through wild grass, that which has been pressed down[26] by wheels does not burn. Some ordinary folks are delighted and call it lucky grass. Now, what the feet do not step on and what the fire does not reach are not necessarily good, for the lifting of the foot and the spread of the fire are accidental. (ch. 5, SPPY, 2:1a-b)

2. Strange Phenomena

Those who talk about calamities and strange phenomena have themselves already doubted the theory that Heaven uses calamities and prodigies as a means of reprimanding people. So they alter their argument to say that calamities and prodigies come because the ruler, through his governmental measures, moves Heaven to do so. Heaven activates the material force to respond to him. It is like beating a drum with something or striking a bell with a hammer. The drum is like Heaven, the hammer like the governmental measures, and the sound of the drum or bell like Heaven's response. As the ruler acts below, the material force of Heaven comes after man accordingly. But I say: This is also doubtful. For Heaven can activate things, but how can things activate Heaven? Why? Because man and things are bound by Heaven and Heaven is the master of man and things. . . . Therefore man living in the universe is like a flea or louse being inside a garment or a cricket or an ant inside a hole or a crack. Can the flea, louse, cricket, or ant, by being obedient or disobedient, cause the material force inside the garment or the hole to move or to change? Since the flea, louse, cricket, and ant cannot do so, to say that man alone can is to fail to understand the principle of the material force of things. As the wind comes, trees' branches swing. But tree branches cannot cause the wind. (ch. 43, SPPY, 15:1a-b)

3. Fate

With respect to man's appointment of fate, when his parents give forth their vital forces, he already gets his fortunes and misfortunes. Man's

---

[26] Liu P'an-sui is correct in this understanding. See Liu's *Lun-heng chi-chieh* (Collected Explanations of the *Balanced Inquiries*), 1932, p. 19.

nature is different from his fate. There are people whose nature is good but whose fate is unlucky, and there are others whose nature is evil but whose fate is lucky. Whether one is good or evil in his conduct is due to his nature, but calamities and blessings, and fortunes and misfortunes, are due to fate. Some people do good but get calamities. This is a case of good nature but unlucky fate. Some people do evil but get blessings. This is a case of evil nature but lucky fate. Nature may be good or evil, and fate may be lucky or unlucky. A person with lucky fate does not necessarily miss blessings even if he does no good, and a person with unlucky fate does not necessarily escape calamity even if he makes good efforts in his conduct. (ch. 6, SPPY, 2:5a-b)

4. The Equality of Past and Present

The world was well governed in earlier ages because of sages. It was well governed in later ages because of sages. The virtue of sages earlier or later was not different, and therefore good government in earlier ages and today is not different. The Heaven of earlier ages was the same as the Heaven of later ages. Heaven does not change, and its material forces do not alter. The people of earlier ages were the same as those of later ages. All were endowed with the original material forces, which are pure and harmonious and are not different in earlier or later ages. . . . In ancient times there were unrighteous people, and today there are gentlemen of established integrity. Good and evil intermingle. What age is devoid of them? (ch. 56, SPPY, 18:13b, 16a)

THE TAOISM OF HUAI-NAN TZU

HUAI-NAN TZU (d. 122 B.C.) was the most prominent Taoist philosopher between ancient Taoism of the fourth century B.C. and Neo-Taoism of the third and fourth centuries A.D. His originality is negligible, but he maintained Taoism at the time when Confucianism had just assumed the dominant and exclusive role in government as well as in the realm of thought. Although his ideas are no more than reiteration and elaboration of Lao Tzu and Chuang Tzu, at least he kept the fire of Taoism burning and helped to make possible the emergence of Neo-Taoism. Because of his essentially rational approach to metaphysics and cosmogony, it may be said that he indirectly, at least, prepared for that rationalistic critic Wang Ch'ung (27-100?).

His name was Liu An. As Prince of Huai-nan, he had thousands of scholars under his patronage. He plotted rebellion, failed, and committed suicide.

The following selections are from the work which is a joint product of himself and his guests.

THE HUAI-NAN TZU[1]

1. The Nature of Tao

Tao covers Heaven and supports Earth. It is the extent of the four quarters of the universe and the dimensions of the eight points of the firmament. There is no limit to its height, and its depth is unfathomable. It encloses Heaven and Earth and endows things [with their nature] before they have been formed. . . . Compressed, it can expand. Hidden, it can be manifest. Weak, it can be strong. Soft, it can be firm. . . . With it the mountain becomes high and the abyss becomes deep. Because of it, animals run and birds fly. Sun and moon shine and the planets revolve by it. Through it the unicorn emerges and the phoenix soars. . . . After having been polished and cut, it returns to simplicity. It acts without action and is in accord with Tao. It does not speak and is identified with virtue. Perfectly at leisure and without pride, it is at home with harmony. The myriad things are all different but each suits its own nature. Its spirit may be set on the tip of an autumn hair, but its greatness combines the entire universe. Its virtue softens Heaven and Earth and har-

---

[1] The *Huai-nan Tzu* is a lengthy work of twenty-one long chapters on metaphysics, astronomy, government, military strategy, etc. Morgan's translation is both incomplete and inaccurate.

monizes yin and yang (passive and active cosmic forces). It regulates the four seasons and harmonizes the Five Agents (Metal, Wood, Water, Fire, and Earth). . . . Therefore those who understand Tao return to tranquillity and those who have investigated things ultimately rest with non-action. (SPPY, 1:1a-2a, 6b)

2. The Beginning of Reality

(1) There was a beginning. (2) There was a time before that beginning.[2] (3) There was a time before the time which was before the beginning. (4) There was being. (5) There was non-being. (6) There was a time before that non-being. (7) There was a time before the time which was before that non-being.

(1) What is meant by "There was a beginning" is that there was accumulation which has not sprung unto activity. There were signs of sprouts and shoots but no physical form.[3] Like insects moving,[4] they are about to spring into life but their species have not yet been formed.

(2) At the time before that beginning, the material force (ch'i) of Heaven began to descend and that of Earth began to ascend. Yin and yang interacted and united, competing leisurely to expand in the universe. Embracing genuine character and containing harmony, they were interfused and stayed together.[5] They wanted to come in contact with other things but they had not yet had physical form.

(3) At the stage when there was a time before the time which was before the beginning, Heaven contained harmony but had not yet descended, and Earth embraced the material force but had not yet ascended. It was empty, quiet, desolate, and dark, there was nothing which was even indistinct. At last the material force greatly penetrated the realm of darkness.

(4) "There was being" means that the myriad things appeared[6] in great numbers. The roots, stems, branches, and leaves of plants were young, luxuriant, flourishing, and colorful. Insects flew, moved, crawled, and breathed. They could be touched and grasped and they could be counted in quantities.

(5) "There was non-being" means that the eye looked at it but could not see any form. The ear listened to it but could not hear any sound. The hand touched it but could not feel anything tangible. And as one

[2] The term *wei-shih* merely means there has not been, and does not mean anterior to a beginning.

[3] Interpretation according to Wang Nien-sun (1744-1832), *Tu-shu tsa-chih* (Miscellaneous Notes from Reading), 1933 ed., bk. 12, p. 58.

[4] Interpretation according to Liu Wen-tien, *Huai-nan hung-lieh chi-chieh* (Collected Commentaries on the *Huai-nan Tzu*), 1926, vol. 2, p. 1a.

[5] This is the understanding of Kao Yu's (fl. 205) commentary.

[6] Literally, to fall [upon the earth].

looked at it, its limit could not be reached. Great and extensive, it could not be measured and was identical with light.

(6) At the time before that non-being, Heaven and Earth were enclosed and the myriad things were molded and produced. The great universal (Tao)[7] was undifferentiated and noumenal. Nothing, however deep, extensive, vast, or great, existed beyond it. Even the minutest hair and the sharpest point could not exist within it. It was space without surrounding walls. It produced the root of being and non-being.

(7) At the time before the time which was before that non-being, heaven and earth had not come into existence and yin and yang had not been distinguished. The four seasons had not yet separated and the myriad things had not yet been born. It was extremely peaceful and very tranquil. Forms were not yet visible. It was like light in the midst of non-being which retreats and is lost sight of.[8] (SPPY, 2:1a-2a)

> *Comment.* The seven stages were first mentioned by Chuang Tzu[9] but Huai-nan Tzu provided them with a content. Hu Shih (1891-1962) has arranged them in this order: 7, 3, 6, 2, 1, 4, 5.[10] Huai-nan Tzu's view may not be scientific or logical. It is remarkable, however, that in an age of prevalent superstitions and common belief in prodigies, he should have maintained an absolutely naturalistic attitude toward creation.

3. Centrifugal Cosmogony

Before heaven and earth took shape, there was only undifferentiated formlessness. Therefore it was called the great beginning.[11] Tao originated from vacuity and vacuity produced the universe (of space and time).[12] The universe produced the material force. The material force was extremely secure.[13] That which was clear and light drifted up to become heaven, and that which was heavy and turbid solidified to form earth. It was especially easy for the clear and refined to unite but ex-

[7] The Great Universal is Tao, according to Kao Yu. The term, *ta-t'ung*, comes from *Chuang Tzu*, ch. 6, NHCC, 3:26b. See Giles, trans., *Chuang Tzu*, 1961 ed., p. 85.

[8] There is no need to change *chien* (space) to *wen* (to ask) in order to conform to the story of Light asking Non-being in *Chuang Tzu*, ch. 22, NHCC, 7:53B, Giles, p. 217, as suggested by Ch'en Kuan-lou, quoted in Wang Nien-sun, *Tu-shu tsa-chih, ibid.*, p. 76.

[9] *Chuang Tzu*, ch. 2, NHCC, 1:33b. See Giles, p. 41.

[10] *Huai-nan Wang shu* (On Huai-nan Tzu), 1934, pp. 26-27.

[11] Read *chao* (light) as *shih* (beginning), according to Wang Nien-sun, *ibid.*, p. 89.

[12] According to Kao Yu, *yü-chou* (universe) means space (*yü*) and time (*chou*).

[13] Instead of translating the Chinese phrase as "having limits" as practically all other translators have done, I have followed Kao Yu's interpretation.

tremely difficult for the heavy and turbid to solidify. Therefore heaven was formed first and the earth became definite later. The material forces[14] of Heaven and Earth combined to form yin and yang. The concentrated forces of yin and yang became the four seasons, and the scattered forces of the four seasons became the myriad things. When the hot force of yang accumulated, fire was produced and the essence of the material force of fire became the sun. When the cold force of yin accumulated, water was produced and the essence of the material force of water became the moon. The excess of the essence of the sun and moon became the stars and planets. Heaven received the sun, moon, and stars, while earth received water and soil. (SPPY, 3:1a)

> *Comment.* In its broad outline this cosmogony has remained the orthodox doctrine among Chinese philosophers, including Neo-Confucianists.

4. Macrocosm and Microcosm

Heaven, earth, infinite space, and infinite time are the body of one person, and the space within the six cardinal points is the form of one man.[15] Therefore he who understands his nature will not be threatened by Heaven and Earth, and he who comprehends evidences will not be fooled by strange phenomena. Therefore the sage knows the far from what is near, and to him all multiplicity is one. Men of old were one with the universe in the same material force, and were in harmony with the age. (SPPY, 8:3a-b)

[14] *Ching* means material force, according to Kao Yu.

[15] Read *chi* (system) as *hsing* (form), according to Wang Nien-sun, *ibid.*, bk. 13, p. 47. See also Liu Chia-li, *Huai-nan chi-cheng* (Collected Textual Commentaries on the *Huai-nan Tzu*), 1924, 8:6a.

··· 18 ···

NEGATIVE TAOISM IN THE *LIEH TZU*
AND THE "YANG CHU CHAPTER"

THE TAOISM OF LAO TZU, Chuang Tzu, and Huai-nan Tzu (d. 122 B.C.), were all positive in that each represents something new. The Taoism in the *Lieh Tzu* and its "Yang Chu Chapter," however, is purely negative.

The ideas of the equality of all things, indifference to life and death, following one's nature, and accepting one's fate are all original ingredients of Taoism. But the hedonistic philosophy in the "Yang Chu Chapter" is directly opposed to the Taoist philosophy of having no desire. In the *Lieh Tzu*, the Taoist doctrine of inaction, i.e., taking no artificial action, has degenerated into a complete abandonment of effort. Spontaneity is confused with resignation. And the Taoist doctrine of nourishing one's nature is forgotten. Perhaps the only constructive aspect is the strong sense of skepticism, which, as in the case of Wang Ch'ung (27-100?), did help to set the Chinese mind free from dogmas and traditions.

Lieh Tzu lived in the fifth century B.C. and was a follower of Taoism, but the present book under his name is surely not original.[1] Yang Chu (440-360 B.C.?) was known for his doctrine of self-preservation to the point of not plucking out a single hair even if he could benefit the entire world by doing so, according to Mencius.[2] It was for this egoism that Mencius strongly attacked him.[3] Records elsewhere confirm this teaching.[4] This idea is reproduced in the "Yang Chu Chapter." But other parts of the chapter contradict it, for self-preservation and indifference

---

[1] This book, SPTK, called *Ch'ung-hsü chih-te chen-ching* (Pure Classic of the Perfect Virtue of Simplicity and Vacuity), is in eight chapters. Since the majority of its material came from other books, chiefly the *Chuang Tzu*, obviously it cannot have been the original work of Lieh Tzu, which was lost in the second century B.C. For the same reason, the seventh chapter, entitled "Yang Chu," cannot be the work of Yang Chu. It was probably a separate work from the *Lieh Tzu* and somehow got included in it. In both cases, however, some original teachings of the two philosophers have been incorporated. For example, the "Yang Chu" briefly discusses the problem of names and actualities. As Hu Shih (1891-1962) has pointed out, this is a common topic of discussion during the Warring States period (403-222 B.C.) but not in later times. (See his *Chung-kuo che-hsüeh shih ta-kang*, or Outline of the History of Chinese Philosophy, 1919, p. 176.) For translations, see Bibliography.

[2] *Mencius*, 7A:26.   [3] *ibid.*, 3B:9.

[4] See *Lü-shih ch'un-ch'iu* (Mr. Lü's Spring and Autumn Annals), ch. 17, sec. 6, SPPY, 17: 16a, and *Huai-nan Tzu*, ch. 13, SPPY, 13:7b. See Morgan, trans., *Tao, The Great Luminant*, p. 155.

to life and death are obviously incompatible. Besides, indulging in sensuous pleasure was not Yang Chu's way of preserving nature.[5] In the opinion of many scholars, what happened was that at the time of political chaos in the third century, some writers, trying to escape from intolerable situations, utilized the names of Lieh Tzu and Yang Chu and took refuge under the purely negative aspects of Taoism.

A. THE "YANG CHU CHAPTER"

Yang Chu said, "One hundred years is the limit of a long life. Not one in a thousand ever attains it. Suppose there is one such person. Infancy and feeble old age take almost half of this time. Rest during sleep at night and what is wasted during waking hours in the daytime take almost half of that. Pain and sickness, sorrow and suffering, death [of relatives], and worry and fear take almost half of the rest. In the ten and some years that is left, I reckon, there is not one moment in which we can be happily at ease without worry.

"This being the case, what is life for? What pleasure is there? For beauty and abundance, that is all. For music and sex, that is all. But the desire for beauty and abundance cannot always be satisfied, and music and sex cannot always be enjoyed. Besides, we are prohibited by punishment and exhorted by rewards, pushed by fame and checked by law. We busily strive for the empty praise which is only temporary, and seek extra glory that would come after death. Being alone ourselves, we pay great care[6] to what our ears hear and what our eyes see, and are much concerned with what is right or wrong for our bodies and minds. Thus we lose the great happiness of the present and cannot give ourselves free rein for a single moment. What is the difference between that and many chains and double prisons?

"Men of great antiquity knew that life meant to be temporarily present and death meant to be temporarily away. Therefore they acted as they pleased and did not turn away from what they naturally desired. They would not give up what could amuse their own persons at the time. Therefore they were not exhorted by fame. They roamed as their nature directed and would not be at odds with anything. They did not care for a name after death and therefore punishment never touched them. They took no heed of fame, being ahead or being behind, or the span of life."

Yang Chu said, "The myriad creatures are different in life but the same in death. In life they may be worthy or stupid, honorable or humble. This is where they differ. In death they all stink, rot, disinte-

---

[5] According to the *Huai-nan Tzu*, *ibid.*, Yang Chu would not injure the nature with material desires.

[6] *Shun* (to follow) and *shen* (to care) were interchangeable.

grate, and disappear. This is where they are the same. However, being worthy, stupid, honorable, or humble is beyond their power, and to stink, rot, disintegrate, and disappear is also beyond their power. Thus life, death, worthiness, stupidity, honor, and humble station are not of their own making. All creatures are equal in these, [that is, they all return to nature].[7] The one who lives for ten years dies. The one who lives for a hundred years also dies. The man of virtue and the sage both die; the wicked and the stupid also die. In life they were (sage-emperors) Yao and Shun;[8] in death they were rotten bones. In life they were (wicked kings) Chieh[9] and Chou;[10] in death they were rotten bones. Thus they all became rotten bones just the same. Who knows their difference? Let us hasten to enjoy our present life. Why bother about what comes after death?". . .

Yang Chu said, "Po-ch'eng Tzu-kao[11] refused to pluck one hair to benefit things. He gave up his kingdom and became a hermit farmer.[12] Great Yü[13] refused to benefit himself [but instead devoted his energies to diverting floods to rivers and the sea], and his body was half paralyzed. Men of antiquity did not prefer to sacrifice one single hair to benefit the world. Nor did they choose to have the world support them. If everyone refrains from sacrificing even a single hair and if everyone refrains from benefiting the world, the world will be in order." (SPTK, 7:1b-4b)

B. THE LIEH TZU

1. Skepticism

King T'ang[14] of Yin[15] asked Hsia Chi,[16] "Were there things in high antiquity?" Hsia Chi said, "If there were nothing in high antiquity, how could there be things today? Would it be all right for people in the future to say that there is nothing now?" "In that case," said T'ang, "don't things have before or after?" "There is no ultimate in the be-

[7] This is the interpretation of Chang Chan (fl. 310). See his commentary on the *Lieh Tzu*.

[8] Legendary rulers (3rd millennium B.C.).

[9] R. 1802–1752 B.C.(?). He caused the downfall of the Hsia dynasty (2183–1752 B.C.?).

[10] R. 1175–1112 B.C. He caused the downfall of the Shang dynasty (1751–1112 B.C.).

[11] A feudal lord at the time of Emperor Yao.

[12] For the legend, see *Chuang Tzu*, ch. 12, NHCC, 5:7b-8a. See Giles, trans., *Chuang Tzu*, 1961 ed., p. 121.

[13] Founder of the Hsia dynasty (r. 2183–2175 B.C.?).

[14] Founder of Shang dynasty (r. 1751–1739 B.C.?).

[15] Part of Shang dynasty (1384–1112 B.C.).

[16] A great official under T'ang. For the pronunciation of his name, see Yang Po-chün, *Lieh Tzu chi-shih* (Collected Explanations of the *Lieh Tzu*), 1958, p. 92.

ginning or end of things," said Hsia Chi. "The beginning may be the end and the end may be the beginning. Who knows their order? As to what exists outside of things or before the beginning of events, I do not know."

"Is there any limit to the above, the below, or the eight directions?" asked T'ang. Hsia Chi answered, "I don't know." As T'ang persisted in asking, Hsia Chi said, "If there is nothing, then it is infinite. If there is something, then there must be a limit. How do I know? But beyond infinity there is no more infinity and within the unlimited there is no more unlimitedness. Infinity is followed by no more infinity, and the unlimited is followed by no more unlimitedness. From this I know there are infinity and the unlimited and do not know that there are the finite and the limited."

"What is there beyond the four seas (China)?" T'ang further asked. Hsia Chi replied, "It is just like the district of Ch'i (same as China)."[17] "How can you prove it?" asked T'ang. "I traveled east to Ying, where the inhabitants were the same as those here. I inquired about the countries further east and found that they were no different from Ying. I traveled west to Pin where the inhabitants were the same as those here. I inquired about the countries further west and found that they were no different from Pin. From this I know the regions within the four seas, the four wildernesses, and the four outermost regions are no different. Thus the lesser is always enclosed by a greater, and so on without end. Heaven and earth, which enclose the myriad things, are themselves enclosed. The enclosing of the myriad things never reaches a limit. Likewise, the enclosing of heaven and earth never reaches an end. How do I know that there is not a greater universe outside our own? This is something I do not know." (SPTK, 5:1a-b)

Those who maintain that heaven and earth are destructible are wrong and those who maintain that they are indestructible are also wrong. Whether they are destructible or indestructible, I do not know. However, it is the same in one case and also the same in the other.[18] The living do not know the dead and the dead do not know the living. What is gone does not know what is to come and what is to come does not know what is gone. Why should I be concerned whether they are destructible or indestructible? (SPTK, 1:6b)

2. Fatalism

Effort said to Fate (*Ming*, Destiny), "How can your achievement be

---

[17] According to the commentary of Chang Chan.

[18] According to Chang Chan, this means that "the one" refers to destructibility and "the other" to indestructibility, and that regardless of which is true, we should not be affected.

equal to mine?" "What effect do you have on things," replied Fate, "that you wish to compare with me?" "Well," said Effort, "longevity and brevity of life, obscurity and prominence, honorable and humble stations, and poverty and richness, are all within my power."

Fate said, "P'eng-tsu[19] was not superior to (sage-emperors) Yao and Shun in wisdom and yet he lived to an age of eight hundred. Yen Yüan (virtuous pupil of Confucius) was not inferior to the ordinary people in ability but he lived only to eighteen.[20] Confucius was not inferior to the feudal lords in virtue, but he was in trouble between Ch'en and Ts'ai.[21] (Wicked king) Chou of the Yin dynasty was not superior to the three men of virtue[22] in conduct, but he occupied the throne. Chicha[23] had no noble rank in Wu but T'ien Heng[24] had the state of Ch'i all for himself. Po-i and Shu-ch'i starved at Shou-yang Mountain [rather than serve the conquerors of the Shang], whereas the Chi family (who controlled the state of Lu) were richer than Chan-ch'in (worthy official of Lu noted for integrity).[25] If what you mentioned were all within your power, how is it that one enjoyed longevity while the other suffered brevity of life, that the sage was obscure while a violator of virtue was in a prominent position, that the worthy had a humble station while the stupid enjoyed honor, and that the good were poor but the wicked were rich?"

Effort said, "If, as you say, I have no effect on things, then are things, being what they are,[26] the result of your control?"

"Since you already speak of it as fate," replied Fate, "how can there be any control? As for me, if a thing is straight, I push it straighter, and if it is crooked, I let it remain so. Longevity, brevity of life, obscurity, prominence, humble and honorable stations, and richness and poverty all come of themselves. How can I know them? How can I know them?" (SPTK, 6:1a)

---

[19] A legendary figure supposed to have been an official under Yao and Shun.

[20] Other texts have "four times eight," which is nearer to the truth.

[21] He was surrounded between Ch'en and Ts'ai by officials of those states to prevent him from going to Ch'u, their enemy state. He and his pupils were out of food and many became sick. See Ssu-ma Ch'ien (145–86 B.C.?), *Shih chi* (Records of the Historian), PNP, 47:19a. See also translation by Chavannes, *Les mémoires historiques*, vol. 5, pp. 364-371.

[22] The viscounts Wei and Chi and Pi Kan who offered good advice to Chou but were exiled, imprisoned, and executed by him, respectively. See *Analects*, 13:1.

[23] He declined the throne in 561 B.C. and became a farmer.

[24] He usurped the throne in 386 B.C.

[25] He is better known as Liu-hsia Hui, whom Confucius highly praised. See *Analects*, 15:13.

[26] According to T'ao Hung-ch'ing, quoted in Yang Po-chün, *Lieh Tzu chi-shih*, 1958, p. 121, the first *yeh* (interrogative article) is to be read as *yeh* (final positive article).

19

NEO-TAOISM

TOO OFTEN the intellectual movement in the Wei-Chin period (220-420) is described as purely an escape from reality. Political conditions at the time certainly tend to support such a conclusion. During the last four decades of the Han dynasty (206 B.C.–A.D. 220), China was divided into three states. In addition to continuous warfare, there were repeated floods and droughts. Population was reduced to perhaps the lowest point in twenty-five centuries. Eunuchs and royal relatives controlled the court, which was marked by intrigue and murders. The founder of the Wei (220-265) came to power through usurpation, and his court repeated the ugly drama of the Han. Many scholars of integrity refused to serve such corrupt governments, and others, looking for freedom and security, preferred to withdraw in search of transcendental values. Consequently, the whole intellectual movement was marked by a transcendental quality, with emphasis on non-being, vacuity, and the noumenal world.

But the movement was negative only on the surface, for there were positive forces at work. One of these was the sharp reaction against the intellectual trends of the Han. For several hundred years Confucian teachings on ranks, functions, and various social and moral dogmas had been accumulating weight. The minute and endless studies of Confucian Classics had turned the study of Confucian thought into sheer scholasticism. The belief in mutual influence of Nature and man, dominant since the time of Tung Chung-shu (c. 179–c. 104 B.C.), was no longer satisfactory as an explanation of events. At the same time, the popular religious movement under the name of Huang-Lao—the legendary Yellow Emperor Huang-ti and Lao Tzu—in combination with the Yin Yang philosophy, astrology, and divination, had been so influential that philosophy was degenerating into occultism. All of these deteriorating developments called for revolt, and for some years after A.D. 190 several thousand scholars, gathered in Ching-chou,[1] turned away from scholasticism in their study of Classics.

The other positive force at work was perhaps even more significant, for it pointed not to the past but to the future, and it grew from within the intellectual movement itself. In the first and second centuries, a bitter controversy between the Ancient Script School and Modern Script School centered on the two versions of Confucian Classics. The Modern Script School insisted that Confucius was destined as a savior of the

---

[1] In present Hupeh.

world and a throneless king whose subtle doctrines lay behind his written words. The Ancient Script School, on the other hand, maintained that Confucius was essentially an ancient teacher who transmitted the wisdom of the past, and rejected the position of the Modern Script School as subjective, unhistorical, and corrupted by the belief in prodigies. Regardless of the issues of the controversy, it had created a spirit of free inquiry, critical study, and independent thinking. It was impossible for this new spirit not to seek new frontiers.

Furthermore, after two hundred years of Confucian supremacy, the revival of a study of ancient philosophers was long overdue. It was no accident, therefore, that scholars were now attracted to Lao Tzu, Chuang Tzu, Mo Tzu (fl. 479–438 B.C.), and the Logicians. Since Moists and the Logicians distinguished themselves as debaters, they exerted considerable influence on Wei-Chin scholars who loved nothing better than a debate and obviously enjoyed demolishing "objections," whether from others or from themselves. But they went a step further than the ancient debaters, for instead of being satisfied with argumentation they looked for a universal ground on which to base their arguments, and they found this in principle (*li*, reason) which eventually became a central concept of Chinese thought.

The study of the *Lao Tzu* and *Chuang Tzu* was of course an aid to escape, and Taoism was a natural reaction to Confucianism. But here again the Wei-Chin scholars discovered something positive: non-being (*wu*), as no longer simply a contrast to being but as the ultimate of all, or pure being, the one and the undifferentiated. Thus the whole movement was charged with tremendous possibilities for the future.

The movement expressed itself in two facets, the Light Conversation or Pure Conversation (*Ch'ing-t'an*) and the Metaphysical Schools (*Hsüan-hsüeh*),[2] one involving the other. Most of the members were the younger generation. In their conversations they avoided the vulgarism of politics or traditional mores and concentrated on the pure or light aspect of matters, whether sex or poetry, in such a way as to free the spirit and sharpen the imagination, and to display a lofty ideal and a philosophical wit. Many of them acted in a most unconventional and carefree manner. The whole outlook was a romantic wandering over the universe, as Chuang Tzu would put it, and an intimate union with ultimate reality. The most famous group of the Light Conversationists were the Seven Worthies of the Bamboo Grove, including Jüan Chi (210-263), who in his *Ta-jen hsien-sheng chuan* (Biography of Mr. Great Man) advocated becoming one with the universe and transcend-

---

[2] The word *hsüan* means profound, deep, dark, abstruse, mysterious. See Appendix for further comments.

315

ing all distinctions between right and wrong, wealth and poverty, high and humble stations, and Hsi K'ang (223-262), who in his essays expressed similar sentiments. These men often met in bamboo groves to drink, write poems, and talk and behave with utter disregard for social conventions or worldly values.

The more important facet, however, was the metaphysical. As already indicated, Han thought was strongly characterized by the doctrine of the correspondence of Nature and man and their mutual influence. It was therefore greatly concerned with natural phenomena. The Metaphysical Schools of Wei-Chin, on the contrary, went beyond phenomena to find reality beyond space and time. They found this in the non-being of Lao Tzu and Chuang Tzu but gave it a new meaning. Hence these schools are called by modern scholars Neo-Taoism. But these philosophers are not exclusively Taoistic. Like philosophers of the Han, they are syncretic. While they are Taoistic in their metaphysics, they are Confucian in their social and political philosophy.

The most outstanding Neo-Taoists were Wang Pi (226-249), Ho Yen (d. 249), and Kuo Hsiang (d. 312). Wang Pi traced his intellectual heritage to Ching-chou. He was once a minister in the Wei government and wrote commentaries on both the *Book of Changes* and the *Lao Tzu*, that on the latter being the oldest in existence. Before he died at the early age of twenty-four, he had already inaugurated a new movement, for he raised the level of Chinese thought to that of metaphysics. Han thought was primarily concerned with cosmology and cosmogony, but Wang Pi went beyond the realms of names and forms to ultimate reality, namely, original non-being (*pen-wu*). According to his theory, which is developed in his commentary on the *Lao Tzu*, original non-being transcends all distinctions and descriptions. It is the pure being, original substance (*pen-t'i*), and the one in which substance and function are identified. It is whole and strong. And it is always correct because it is in accord with principle. This emphasis on principle is very conspicuous in his commentaries. Where Lao Tzu had destiny (*ming*, fate), Wang Pi would substitute principle, thus anticipating the Neo-Confucianists, who preferred to speak of the Principle of Nature (*T'ien-li*) instead of destiny decreed by Heaven (*T'ien-ming*).

The idea that there is the one underlying and uniting all phenomena is also vigorously stressed in his essay on the *Book of Changes*.[8] This book, consisting of hexagrams made up of six broken lines (representing yin or passive cosmic force) and unbroken lines (representing yang or active cosmic force), was used in ancient times for divination but later used by Confucianists to discern principles underlying events. It had

[8] For this book, see above, ch. 13, n.1.

been the custom to equate each of the sixty-four hexagrams with a particular object, but Wang argues that this is unnecessary because there is a general principle behind all particular objects. This principle is discoverable in one of the six lines, so that the other five become secondary. In short, he stresses the over-all principle which unites and commands all particular concepts and events. It is remarkable that in a time of disunity and confusion he should insist on a united system based on one fundamental reality, original non-being.

Like Wang Pi, Ho Yen was known as a brilliant young man, was once a minister, and was fond of Taoism. While he never developed the concept of non-being to the level of Wang Pi, he brought out more strongly the idea that non-being is nameless and is beyond words and forms. In their social and political thought, both he and Wang Pi were Confucian. Confucius, rather than Lao Tzu, was the sage, for in their view, he and not Lao Tzu was the one who demonstrated the highest truth within human society.

Kuo Hsiang was also a high government official and an enthusiast for Taoism. Unlike Wang Pi who commented on the *Lao Tzu*, however, he commented on the *Chuang Tzu*. Evidences show that he incorporated much of Hsiang Hsiu's (fl. 250) commentary into his own—thus indicating plagiarism, of which he was not at all incapable. Some scholars speak of Hsiang-Kuo instead of Kuo Hsiang alone. However, their ideas are not different, and all texts still name Kuo Hsiang as the commentator.

Just as Wang Pi went beyond Lao Tzu, so Kuo Hsiang went beyond Chuang Tzu. The major concept is no longer Tao, as in Chuang Tzu, but Nature (*Tzu-jan*). Things exist and transform themselves spontaneously and there is no other reality or agent to cause them. Heaven is not something behind this process of Nature but is merely its general name. Things exist and transform according to principle, but each and every thing has its own principle. Everything is therefore self-sufficient and there is no need of an over-all original reality to combine or govern them, as in the case of Wang Pi. In other words, while Wang Pi emphasizes non-being, Kuo emphasizes being, and while Wang Pi emphasizes the one, Kuo emphasizes the many. To Wang Pi, principle transcends things, but to Kuo, it is immanent in them.

However, Kuo Hsiang and Wang Pi are similar in that both consider that the sage rises above all distinctions and contradictions. He remains in the midst of human affairs although he accomplishes things by taking no unnatural action. But he is not someone who "folds his arms and sits in silence in the midst of some mountain forest." To such a sage, all transformations are the same and in dealing with things he has "no deliberate mind of his own" (*wu-hsin*) but responds to them spontaneously without any discrimination. Confucius, and not Lao Tzu or Chuang Tzu, was such a sage.

In their philosophy of life, Kuo Hsiang differed greatly from Wang Pi in one respect. Kuo was a fatalist while Wang was not. Since according to Kuo everything has its own nature and ultimate principle, everything is determined and correct. Therefore he taught contentment in whatever situation one may find himself. Neither free will nor choice has meaning in his system.

How much influence did Neo-Taoism have in the development of Chinese thought? This is not an easy question to answer. Neither Chinese Buddhism nor Neo-Confucianism can be said to have owed their development to Neo-Taoism. Nevertheless, as we shall see, its influence on early Chinese Buddhist schools is definite and clear.[4] Besides, such concepts as principle, original reality, substance, and function may well be considered to have set the pattern for later Buddhists and Neo-Confucianists. The following selections are designed to show their influence as well as their own thoughts.

1. WANG PI'S

SIMPLE EXEMPLIFICATIONS OF THE PRINCIPLES OF THE BOOK OF CHANGES

An Explanation of The Explanations of Hexagrams[5]

What is an explanation of a hexagram as a whole? It discusses generally the substance of a hexagram and makes clear the controlling principle out of which it is developed. Now, the many cannot be regulated by the many. They are regulated by the smallest in number (the one). Activity cannot be controlled by activity. They are controlled by that which is firmly rooted in the one.[6] The reason why the many can exist is that their ruling principle returns always to the one and all activities can function because they have all come from the same source. Things never err; they always follow their principle. There is the chief to unite them, and there is the leader to group them together. Therefore, though complex, they are not chaotic, and though many, they are not confused.

[4] See below, ch. 20, Introduction.

[5] This is pt. 1 and the most important part of his *Chou-i lüeh-li* (Simple Exemplifications of the Principles of the *Book of Changes*), a brief essay in six parts. The essay is included in the *Han-Wei ts'ung-shu* (Collection of Works of the Han and Wei Dynasties, 206 B.C.–A.D. 265). There are annotations by Hsing Shou (of T'ang, 618-907), but they are inferior. Pt. 4 of this work has been translated by Hellmut Wilhelm in his *Change*, pp. 87-88.

[6] Paraphrasing the *Book of Changes*, "Appended Remarks," pt. 2, ch. 1. Cf. Legge, *Yi King*, p. 380. See also *Lao Tzu*, ch. 39.

Hence the intermingling of the six lines in a hexagram can be understood by taking up one [of them, for one is always the ruling factor of the six] and the interaction of weakness (yin) and strength (yang) can be determined by having the basic controlling principle well established. Therefore, "for gathering things together, enumerating qualities, and distinguishing right and wrong, there would be insufficiency if there were not one line among [the six as the ruling factor]."[7] Therefore if we investigate things by approaching them as a united system, although they are many, we know we can handle them by adhering to the one, and if we view them from the point of view of the fundamental, although their concepts are broad, we know we can cover all of them under a single name. If we view the great heavenly movements through an astronomical instrument, we shall not wonder at the movements of heaven and earth, and if we occupy the central point to view whatever may come, then all things coming in from the six directions will not be beyond control. Therefore when the name of the hexagram is mentioned, we have the ruling factor of all its concepts, and as soon as we read the explanation of a hexagram, we understand more than half of the ideas involved.

Although past and present are not the same and armies and states appear different, we must not neglect the application of the central principle [in considering them]. Differences vary in a thousand ways, but the leading, ruling principle remains. This is the thing most highly valued in the explanation of a hexagram.

The little is valued by the plentiful, and the few are the leaders of the many. If there are five yang (undivided lines) and one yin (undivided), the yin is the ruling factor. If there are five yin and one yang, the one yang is the ruling factor. For yin seeks after yang and yang seeks after yin. If yang is one and unified, how can all the five yin help returning to it? If yin is singular, how can all the five yang help following it? Thus although the yin is lowly, yet it is the controlling principle of the hexagram because it occupies the position of the least. Some people discard the lines and split the substance of a hexagram, but does the substance of the hexagram not depend on the lines? Although things are complex, there is no worry about their becoming chaotic, and although they change, there is no worry about their being confused. That which broadens is preserved by that which restricts, and the many is helped by the simple. The explanation of hexagrams alone can [show this]. Unless the explanation represents the most subtle and profound [principle] in the world, how can it avoid confusion in chaos and alteration in the process of change? If we view an explanation of a hexagram in this way, its concepts will become readily clear.

[7] *Changes*, "Appended Remarks," pt. 2, ch. 9. Cf. Legge, p. 400.

2. WANG PI'S

COMMENTARY ON THE BOOK OF CHANGES

Only because there is ultimate principle in the world is it possible to employ strength and uprightness completely and to drive far away those who ingratiate by flattery. . . . If we understand the activities of things, we shall know all the principles which make them what they are. (Commentary on hexagram no. 1, *ch'ien* or Heaven in the *Book of Changes*)

Taking the position of the superior and contending with the subordinate are things that can be changed. Therefore they are not great faults. If one can return to obey the fundamental principle and alter the command [to violate moral principles], rest with the firm and correct, refrain from drifting away from the Way, and practice humanity beginning with oneself,[8] good fortune will follow him. (Commentary on hexagram no. 6, *sung* or contention)

If one is agreeable but does not follow indiscriminately and is joyful without deviating from the Mean, one will be able to associate with superiors without flattery and with subordinates without disrespect. As he understands the causes of fortune and misfortune, he will not speak carelessly, and as he understands the necessary principles, he will not change his good conduct. (Commentary on hexagram no. 16, *yü* or happiness)

[A superior man sees] similarity in general principles but diversity in functions and facts. (Commentary on hexagram no. 38, *k'uei* or to part)

> *Comment*. Note the contrast between principle and facts. Later, in Chinese Buddhism, the realm of principles and the realm of facts constitute the two realms of existence. They are, however, not to be sharply contrasted, for they involve each other and are ultimately identical. This one-is-all and all-is-one philosophy is a common heritage of all Chinese philosophical systems—Confucian, Taoist, and Buddhist.

If a thing has any fault, it will not be [in accord with] its principle. A concept is the same as principle. (Commentary on hexagram no. 40, *chieh* or to remove)

To return is to revert to the original [substance]. The original [substance] is the mind of Heaven and Earth. Whenever activity ceases, there is tranquillity, but tranquillity is not opposed to activity. Whenever speech ceases, there is silence, but silence is not opposed to speech. Thus

---

[8] Referring to *Analects*, 12:1.

although Heaven and Earth are vast, possessing the myriad things in abundance, where thunder moves and winds circulate, and while there is an infinite variety of changes and transformations, yet its original [substance] is absolutely quiet and perfect non-being. Therefore only with the cessation of activities within Earth can the mind of Heaven and Earth be revealed. If being were to be the mind [of Heaven and Earth], things of different categories will not be able to exist together. (Commentary on hexagram no. 24, *fu* or to return)

> *Comment.* Wang Pi is characteristically Taoistic in saying that only in a state of tranquillity can the mind of Heaven and Earth be seen. Like Wang Pi, Neo-Confucianists paid a great deal of attention to this hexagram in the *Book of Changes.* But they maintained that the mind of Heaven and Earth is to be seen in a state of activity instead of tranquillity. As Ch'eng I (Ch'eng I-ch'uan, 1033-1107) said, "Former scholars all said that only in a state of tranquillity can the mind of Heaven and Earth be seen. They did not realize that the mind of Heaven and Earth is found in the beginning of activity."[9]

3. WANG PI'S

COMMENTARY ON THE LAO TZU

All being originated from non-being. The time before physical forms and names appeared was the beginning of the myriad things. After forms and names appear, Tao (the Way) develops them, nourishes them, and places them in peace and order; that is, becomes their Mother. This means that Tao produces and completes things with the formless and nameless. Thus they are produced and completed but do not know why. Indeed it is the mystery of mysteries. (*Lao Tzu chu*, or Commentary on the *Lao Tzu*, ch. 1)

Man does not oppose Earth and therefore can comfort all things, for his standard is the Earth. Earth does not oppose Heaven and therefore can sustain all things, for its standard is Heaven. Heaven does not oppose Tao and therefore can cover all things, for its standard is Tao. Tao does not oppose Nature and therefore it attains its character of being. To follow Nature as its standard is to model after the square while within the square and the circle while within the circle, and not to oppose Nature in any way. By Nature is meant something that cannot be labeled and something ultimate. To use knowledge is not as good as to have no knowledge. Body and soul are not as good as essence and form. Essence

[9] *I ch'uan* (Commentary on the *Book of Changes*), ECCS, 2:33a.

and form are not as good as the formless. That with modes is not as good as that without modes. Hence these model after one another. Because Tao obeys Nature, Heaven relies on it. Because Heaven models after Tao, Earth follows Heaven as its principle. Because Earth models after Heaven, man uses Earth as his form. (*ibid.*, ch. 25)

The sage does not institute forms and names to restrain things. He does not formulate standards of advance so that the degenerate will be discarded. Instead he assists all things in their natural state and does not play the part of their originator. This is why it is said that the sage never discards anyone. "Do not exalt the worthy, so that the people shall not compete. Do not value rare treasures, so that the people shall not steal. Do not display objects of desire, so that the people's hearts shall not be disturbed."[10] If people are always enabled to free their minds from doubts and desires, they will not be discarded. (*ibid.*, ch. 27)

When essence is scattered, its different dispositions produce multiplicity, and species come into being as concrete things. Because they are scattered, the sage institutes rules for them, lets good be their teacher and evil be their material [as object lessons], changes their way of life, and transforms their customs so they will return to the one. (*ibid.*, ch. 28)

Spirit has no physical form and has no spatial restrictions, whereas concrete things (*ch'i*) are produced through an integration of elements. When there is an integration without form, it is therefore called a spiritual thing. The nature of the myriad things is spontaneity. It should be followed but not interfered with. . . . The sage understands Nature perfectly and knows clearly the conditions of all things. Therefore he goes along with them but takes no unnatural action. He is in harmony with them but does not impose anything on them. He removes their delusions and eliminates their doubts. Hence the people's minds are not confused and things are contented with their own nature. (*ibid.*, ch. 29)

How is virtue to be attained? It is to be attained through Tao. How is virtue to be completely fulfilled? It is through non-being as its function. As non-being is its function, all things will be embraced. Therefore in regard to things, if they are understood as non-being all things will be in order, whereas if they are understood as being, it is impossible to avoid the fact that they are products (phenomena). Although Heaven and Earth are extensive, non-being is the mind, and although sages and kings are great, vacuity (*hsü*) is their foundation. Therefore it is said that by returning and seeing [absolute quiet and perfect non-being], the mind of Heaven and Earth will be revealed.[11] . . . Tao is indeed the ultimate of

[10] *Lao Tzu*, ch. 3.
[11] See above, sec. 2, Wang's comment on hexagram no. 24.

greatness. Anything beyond it is not worth honoring. Although [Heaven and Earth] are engaged in great undertakings and have great wealth in possessing the myriad things, each thing still has its own character. Although it is valuable to have non-being as its function, nevertheless there cannot be substance without non-being. . . . (*ibid.*, ch. 38)

> *Comment.* This is the first time in the history of Chinese thought that substance (*t'i*) and function (*yung*) are mentioned together. In the *Book of Changes*, it is said that "the state of absolute quiet and inactivity. . . when acted on, immediately penetrates all things."[12] Neo-Confucianists interpreted the two states as substance and function, but they are so only by implication. The concepts of substance and function definitely originated with Wang Pi. They were to become key concepts in Chinese Buddhism and Neo-Confucianism.

One is the beginning of number and the ultimate of things. All things are produced by the one and this is why it is the master of all. And all things achieve their completion because of the one. (*ibid.*, ch. 39)

All things in the world came from being, and the origin of being is based on non-being. In order to have being in total, it is necessary to return to non-being. (*ibid.*, ch. 40)

The ten thousand things have ten thousand different forms but in the final analysis they are one. How did they become one? Because of non-being. . . . Therefore in the production of the myriad things, I know its master. Although things exist in ten thousand different forms, their material forces are blended as one. The multitude have their own minds, and different countries have different customs. But if the one is attained, there will be kings and dukes as their masters. One is the master. How can it be abandoned? The greater the number, the further we go astray. We are nearer to [truth] if the number is reduced. When it is reduced to the least (one), we shall arrive at the ultimate. . . . Follow Nature and place perfect principle in the forefront. If we follow it, there will be fortune, and if we disobey it, there will be misfortune. (*ibid.*, ch. 42)

There is a basis for all affairs and a foundation for all things. There may be many roads but their destination is the same, and there may be a hundred deliberations but the result is the same.[13] There is a great constancy in Tao and there is a generality in principle. By holding on to the Tao of old, we can master the present.[14] Although we live in the present age, we can know the past. This is why it is said [in this chapter]

[12] "Appended Remarks," pt. 1, ch. 10. Cf. Legge, p. 370.
[13] Paraphrasing *Changes*, "Appended Remarks," pt. 2, ch. 5. Cf. Legge, p. 389.
[14] Paraphrasing *Lao Tzu*, ch. 14.

that one may know [the world] without going out of doors or looking through the windows. Non-being is inherent in the one. But when we look for it in the multiplicity of things, it is like Tao which can be looked for but not seen, listened to but not heard, reached for but not touched. If we know it, we do not need to go out of doors. If we do not know it, the further we go, the more beclouded we become. If we know the general principle of things, we can know through thinking even if we do not travel. If we know the basis of things, even if we do not see them, we can point to the principle of right and wrong [which governs them]. (*ibid.*, ch. 47)

4. HO YEN'S

TREATISE ON TAO

Being, in coming into being, is produced by non-being. Affairs, as affairs, are brought into completion by non-being. When one talks about it and it has no predicates, when one names it and it has no name, when one looks at it and it has no form, and when one listens to it and it has no sound—that is Tao in its completeness. Hence it is able to make sounds and echoes brilliant, to cause material force (*ch'i*) and material objects to stand out, to embrace all physical forms and spiritual activity, and to display light and shadow. Because of it darkness becomes black and plainness becomes white. Because of it the carpenter's square draws a square and the compass draws a circle. The compass and square obtain forms but Tao has no form. Black and white obtain names but Tao has no name. (*Tao lun*, or Treatise on Tao, quoted by Chang Chan (fl. 310) in his commentary on the *Lieh Tzu*, (SPTK, 1:2b)

> *Comment.* It is characteristic of both the Light Conversation movement and the Metaphysical School to reject all words and forms as descriptions of the ultimate reality. These may be used, then forgotten, as the fish trap is forgotten once the fish is caught.[15] The whole spirit is to get at the ultimate totally, which is not to be limited even by a name.

5. HO YEN'S

TREATISE ON THE NAMELESS

Those accorded fame by the people have names. Those not given fame have no names. As to the sage, his name is really no name, and

---

[15] This metaphor comes from the *Chuang Tzu*, ch. 26, NHCC, 9:11a. It is a favorite metaphor for Chinese philosophers. See Giles, trans., *Chuang Tzu*, 1961 ed., p. 265.

his fame really no fame. When one realizes that the nameless is Tao and the fameless is great, then the nameless may be spoken of as having a name and the fameless may be spoken of as having fame. But is the sage similar to those who can be accorded names or fame? It is like possessing nothing and thereby possessing everything. However, in possessing things one should be in harmony with possessing nothing, and be different from those who possess what they have. No matter how far apart things are, things of the same kind respond to one another, and no matter how near they are, things of different kinds do not violate each other. It is like the yang (active cosmic force) in the yin (passive cosmic force) or the yin in the yang. Each attracts and responds to its own kind. The sun in the summer is yang but at night it is yin in the same way as the sun in far-off winter is yin. The sun in the winter is yin but in the daytime it is yang in the same way as the sun in far-off summer is yang. They are all different while nearby, but similar while far away. Only when such similarity and difference are fully comprehended can the discourse on the nameless be understood. How does it happen to be this way? Now Tao never possesses anything. But since the beginning of the universe it has possessed all things and yet it is still called Tao because it can exercise its ability not to possess them. Therefore although it dwells in the realm of the namable, it shows no sign of the nameless. It is like a substance at a distance characterized by yang forgetting that it has a distant counterpart in yin. Hsia-hou Hsüan[16] said, "Heaven and Earth rotate spontaneously, and the sage functions spontaneously." By spontaneity is meant Tao. Essentially speaking, Tao has no name. This is why Lao Tzu said that he was "forced to give it a name."[17] Confucius praised (sage-emperor) Yao, saying, "The people could find no name for him," but continued to say, "How majestic" was "his accomplishment!"[18] It is clear that to give a name perforce is merely to give an appellation on the basis of only what people know. If one already has a name, how can it be said that people could find no name for him? It is only because he has no name that all possible names in the world can be used to call him. But are these really his names? If from this analogy one still does not understand, it would be like looking at the loftiness and eminence of Mount T'ai and yet saying that the original material force [which makes the productions of things possible] is not overwhelming or extensive. (*Wu-ming lun*, or Treatise on the Nameless, quoted by Chang Chan, *ibid.*, 4:2b-3a)

[16] He was born in 209. For his biography, see *Wei chih* (History of the Wei Dynasty, 220-265), ch. 9, PNP, 9:7b.

[17] *Lao Tzu*, ch. 25.

[18] Yao was a legendary emperor (3rd millennium B.C.). See *Analects*, 8:19.

6. KUO HSIANG'S

COMMENTARY ON THE CHUANG TZU

Topics and Reference:

Following one's nature and Contentment: 2, 4, 9, 13, 15, 20, 21, 27, 28, 30, 31

Having no mind of one's own: 8, 14, 29

Lao Tzu and Chuang Tzu: 5

Multiplicity of things: 10, 18

Natural self-transformation: 3, 4, 11, 12, 19, 32, 34, 39

Past and present, difference of: 22, 36, 37

Principle (*li*): 1, 9, 12, 13, 16, 17, 19, 23, 25, 27-29, 32, 34

Sage: 5, 7, 8, 29

Sagely government: 5, 24, 26, 38

Transcendental and mundane worlds: 5, 29

1. A big thing necessarily comes about in a big situation, and a big situation necessarily comes about with a big thing. It is because of principle that it is naturally so. We need not worry that this will fail. Why be anxious about it? (*Chuang Tzu chu* or Commentary on the *Chuang Tzu*, ch. 1, NHCC, 1:2a)

2. The flight of the fabulous (*p'eng*) bird may take half a year and will not stop until it gets to the Celestial Lake. The flight of a small bird takes only half of the morning and stops at getting from tree to tree. So far as capacities are concerned, there is a difference. But in adapting to their nature, they are the same. (ch. 1, NHCC, 1:2b)

3. The fabulous (*p'eng* bird) and the small (quail) have different interests. Are their interests different because the birds knowingly differ? No, they are naturally different and no one knows why. To be natural means not to take any unnatural action. This is the general idea of [what Chuang Tzu means by] roaming leisurely or freedom. Everything has its own nature and each nature has its own ultimate. (ch. 1, NHCC, 1:4b-5a)

> *Comment.* Kuo Hsiang practically anticipated the Neo-Confucianists, who maintained that there is a Great Ultimate in each and every thing.

4. The universe is the general name for all things. They are the substance of the universe while Nature is their norm. Being natural means to exist spontaneously without having to take any action. Therefore the fabulous *p'eng* bird can soar high and the quail can fly low, the cedrela can live for a long time and the mushroom for a short time. They are capable of doing these not because of their taking any action but because of their being natural. (ch. 1, NHCC, 1:8b)

5. It is he who does no governing that can govern the empire. There-fore Yao governed by not governing. It was not because of his governing that his empire was governed. Now (the recluse) Hsü Yu[19] only realized that since the empire was well governed, he should not replace Yao. He thought it was Yao who did the actual governing. Consequently he said to Yao, "You govern the empire." He should have forgotten such words and investigated into that condition of peace. Someone may say, "It was Yao who actually governed and put the empire in good order but it was Hsü Yu who enabled Yao to do so by refusing to govern himself." This is a great mistake. Yao was an adequate example of governing by not governing and acting by not acting. Why should we have to resort to Hsü Yu? Are we to insist that a man fold his arms and sit in silence in the middle of some mountain forest before we will say he is practicing non-action? This is why the words of Lao Tzu and Chuang Tzu are rejected by responsible officials. This is why responsible officials insist on remain-ing in the realm of action without regret. . . . For egotistical people set themselves up against things, whereas he who is in accord with things is not opposed to them. . . . Therefore he profoundly and deeply re-sponds to things without any deliberate mind of his own and follows whatever comes into contact with him. He is like an untied boat drifting, claiming neither the east nor the west to be its own. He who is always with the people no matter what he does is the ruler of the world wherever he may be. (ch. 1, NHCC, 1:10a-10b)

> Comment. Practically all commentators praise or defend their authors. Kuo Hsiang, on the contrary, criticized Lao Tzu and Chuang Tzu. Like Wang Pi, he inclined to Taoism in his meta-physics but adhered to Confucianism in social and political philoso-phy. For this reason, he rated Confucius far above these Taoist philosophers.[20]

6. The cook, the boy impersonating the dead at sacrificial rites, and the officer of prayer each is contented with his duties. Birds and animals and the myriad things are contented with their endowment. Emperor Yao and Hsü Yu were tranquil in their circumstances. This is the perfect reality of the universe. When everything attains its reality, why should it take any action? Everything will be contented and at ease. Therefore, although Yao and Hsü Yu and Heaven and Earth are different, their freedom is the same. (ch. 1, NHCC, 1:11a)

7. Although the sage is in the midst of government, his mind seems to be in the mountain forest. . . . His abode is in the myriad things, but

---

[19] According to legend, Yao yielded the throne to him but he refused it.
[20] See below, comment on sec. 29.

it does not mean that he does not wander freely. (ch. 1, NHCC, 1:11b-14b)

8. The mind of the sage penetrates to the utmost the perfect union of yin and yang and understands most clearly the wonderful principles of the myriad things. Therefore he can identify himself with changes and harmonize with transformations, and finds everything all right wherever he may go. He embraces all things and thus nothing is not in its natural state. The world asks him [to rule] because of disorder. He has no deliberate mind of his own. Since he has no deliberate mind of his own, why should he not respond to the world? He who identifies himself with the profoundly mysterious state and understands its wonder to the utmost, appreciates the nature of all things, partakes in the creative and transforming process of the universe, and fulfills the fame of Yao and Shun.[21] He can do so because he acts by taking no [unnatural] action. (ch. 1, NHCC, 1:13b)

9. If one is contented wherever he goes, he will be at ease wherever he may be. Even life and death cannot affect him. How much less can flood or fire? The perfect man is not besieged by calamities, not because he escapes from them but because he advances the principles of things and goes forward and naturally comes into union with good fortune. (ch. 1, NHCC, 1:14a)

10. Pipes and flutes differ in length and the various notes differ in pitch. Hence the multiplicity and complexity of long and short, low and high, tones. Although tones vary in a thousand ways, the principle of their natural endowment is the same. (ch. 2, NHCC, 1:19a)

11. The music of Nature is not an entity existing outside of things. The different apertures, the pipes and flutes and the like, in combination with all living beings, together constitute Nature. Since non-being is non-being, it cannot produce being. Before being itself is produced, it cannot produce other beings. Then by whom are things produced? They spontaneously produce themselves, that is all. By this is not meant that there is an "I" to produce. The "I" cannot produce things and things cannot produce the "I". The "I" is self-existent. Because it is so by itself, we call it natural. Everything is what it is by nature, not through taking any action. Therefore [Chuang Tzu] speaks in terms of Nature. The term Nature (literally "Heaven") is used to explain that things are what they are spontaneously, and not to mean the blue sky. But someone says that the music of Nature makes all things serve or obey it. Now, Nature cannot even possess itself. How can it possess things? Nature is the general name for all things. Nature does not set its mind for or against anything. Who is the master to make things obey? Therefore all things

---

[21] Yao's successor.

exist by themselves and come from nature. This is the Way of Heaven. (ch. 2, NHCC, 1:21a)

12. Everything is natural and does not know why it is so. The further things differ in physical form, the further they are alike in being natural .... Heaven and Earth and the myriad things change and transform into something new every day and so proceed with time. What causes them? They do so spontaneously. . . . What we call things are all what they are by themselves; they did not cause each other to become so. Let us then leave them alone and principle will be perfectly realized. The ten thousand things are in ten thousand different conditions, and move forward and backward differently, as if there is a True Lord to make them do so. But if we search for evidences for such True Lord, we fail to find any. We should understand that things are all natural and not caused by something else. (ch. 2, NHCC, 1:22b-23a)

13. If people with the capacity of attendants are not contented with the responsibilities of attendants, it will be a mistake. Therefore we know that whether one is a ruler or a minister, a superior or an inferior, and whether it is the hand or the foot, the inside or the outside, it is naturally so according to the Principle of Nature. Is it really due to the activity of man? Attendants should merely be contented with their stations and then they will never fail to govern each other. Mutually governing each other is like the four limbs and the various parts of the body each having its own function and at the same time employing and utilizing each other. (ch. 2, NHCC, 1:24a)

14. "This" and "that" oppose each other but the sage is in accord with both of them. Therefore he who has no deliberate mind of his own is silently harmonized with things and is never opposed to the world. This is the way to occupy the central position and to be in union with the profoundly mysterious ultimate in order to respond with things from any direction they may come. (ch. 2, NHCC, 1:28B)

15. When their physical forms are compared, Mount T'ai is larger than an autumn hair. But if everything is in accord with its nature and function, and is silently in harmony with its ultimate capacity, then a large physical form is not excessive and a small one is not inadequate. If the nature of everything is sufficient, the autumn hair will not alone consider its smallness as small and Mount T'ai will not alone consider its largeness as large. If whatever is sufficient in its nature is considered large, then nothing under heaven is more sufficient than the autumn hair. If whatever is sufficient in nature is not considered as large, then even Mount T'ai may be called small. This is why [Chuang Tzu says, "There is nothing in the world greater than the tip of hair that grows in the autumn; while Mount T'ai is small." If even Mount T'ai is regarded as

small, nothing in the world is large, and if the autumn hair is regarded as large, nothing in the world is small. As there is nothing small or large, and nothing enjoys longevity or suffers brevity of life, therefore the chrysalis does not admire the cedrela but is happy and contented with itself, and the quail does not value the Celestial Lake and its desire for glory is thus satisfied. If I am satisfied with what comes from Nature and am contented with my nature and destiny, even Heaven and Earth will not be considered as lasting but will be considered as coexisting with me, and the myriad things will not be considered different but will be considered to be at ease with me. This being the case, why can't everything coexist with Heaven and Earth and all things at ease with themselves be unified as one? (ch. 2, NHCC, 1:34a-b)

16. Everything has its principle and every affair has its proper condition. (ch. 2, NHCC, 1:35b)

17. Things have their spontaneity and principle has its ultimate. If one follows them and advances forward, one will deeply and silently come into accord with them. (ch. 2, NHCC, 1:40b)

18. The ordinary people will consider it lack of simplicity to harmonize all the changes throughout ten thousand years. With a tired body and a frightened mind, they toil to avoid this and to take that. The sage alone has no prejudice. He therefore proceeds with utter simplicity and becomes one with transformation and always roams in the realm of unity. Therefore, although the irregularities and confusions over millions of years result in a great variety and infinite multiplicity, as "Tao operates and given results follow," the results of the past and the present are one. And as "things receive names and are what they are," the myriad things are one in being what they are. Since there is nothing which is not what it is, and since there is no time in which results are not brought about, it may be called simplicity. (ch. 2, NHCC, 1:41b-42a)

19. If we insist on the conditions under which things develop and search for the cause thereof, such search and insistence will never end, until we come to something that is unconditioned, and then the principles of self-transformation will become clear. . . . There are people who say that shade is conditioned by the shadow, the shadow by the body, and the body by the Creator. But let us ask whether there is a Creator or not. If not, how can he create things? If there is, he is incapable of materializing all the forms. Therefore before we can talk about creation, we must understand the fact that all forms materialize by themselves. If we go through the entire realm of existence, we shall see that there is nothing, not even the shade, that does not transform itself behind the phenomenal world. Hence everything creates itself without the direction of any Creator. Since things create themselves, they

are unconditioned. This is the norm of the universe. (ch. 2, NHCC, 1:46b-47a)

> *Comment.* The denial of a Creator is complete. Whereas Chuang Tzu raised the question whether there is a Creator or not, Kuo Hsiang unreservedly denied its existence. Given the theory that all things come into existence by themselves and that their transformation is also their own doing, this is the inevitable outcome. Thus Taoist naturalism is pushed to its ultimate conclusion.

20. When a person is perfectly at ease with his spirit and his physical power, whether he lifts something heavy or carries something light, it is due to the fact that he uses his strength to a desired degree. When a person loves fame and is fond of supremacy and is not satisfied even when he has broken his back in the attempt, it is due to the fact that human knowledge knows no limit. Therefore what is called knowledge is born of losing sight of what is proper and will be eliminated when one is in silent harmony with his ultimate capacity. Being silently in harmony with one's ultimate capacity means allowing one's lot to reach its highest degree, and [in the case of lifting weights] not adding so much as an ounce. Therefore though a person carries ten thousand pounds, if it is equal to his capacity he will suddenly forget the weight upon his body. Though a person attends to ten thousand matters, [if his capacity is equal to them] he will be utterly unaware that the affairs are upon him. These are the fundamentals for the cultivation of life. . . . If one attains the Mean and silently reaches the proper limit, everything can be done. The cultivation of life is not to exceed one's lot but to preserve the principle of things and to live out one's allotted span of life. (ch. 3, NHCC, 2:1a-2a)

21. Joy and sorrow are results of gains and losses. A gentleman who profoundly penetrates all things and is in harmony with their transformations will be contented with whatever time may bring. He follows the course of Nature in whatever situation he may be. He will be quietly harmonized and united with Creation. He will be himself wherever he may be. Where does gain or loss, life or death, come in? Therefore, if one lets what he has received from Nature take its own course, there will be no place for joy or sorrow. (ch. 3, NHCC, 2:6a-b)

22. Man in society cannot get away from his fellow beings. The changes in society vary from generation to generation according to different standards. Only those who have no deliberate minds of their own and do not use their own judgment can adapt themselves with changes and not be burdened by them. (ch. 4, NHCC, 2:7a)

23. By being a companion with Nature, Chuang Tzu meant to rely

on the Principle of Nature and apply it to one's own nature and destiny, like a child's going straight forward. (ch. 4, NHCC, 2:12a)

24. When a thousand people gather together without a person as their leader, they will be either disorderly or disorganized. Therefore when there are many virtuous people, there should not be many rulers, but when there is no virtuous person, there should be a ruler. This is the Way of Heaven and the most proper thing to do. (ch. 4, NHCC, 2:16b)

25. Things happen by necessity, and principle, of course, prevails at all times. Therefore if we leave things alone, they will accomplish their purpose. As things have accomplished their purpose, there has never been a case where one's life is not preserved. What is the use of being anxious about one's life? (ch. 4, NHCC, 2:17b)

26. When the king does not make himself useful in the various offices, the various officials will manage their own affairs. Those with clear vision will do the seeing, those with sharp ears will do the listening, the wise will do the planning, and the strong will provide protection. What need is there to take any action? Only profound silence, that is all. (ch. 4, NHCC, 2:25a)

27. Allow the foot to walk according to its capacity, and let the hand grasp according to its strength. Listen to what the ear hears and see what the eye sees. In knowing, stop at what cannot be known. In action, stop at what cannot be done. Employ [the faculties] as they would use themselves. Do things that would be done by themselves. Be unrestrained within your lot but do not attempt the least outside of it. This is the easiest way of taking no unnatural action. There has never been a case where no unnatural action is taken and yet one's nature and destiny have not been preserved, and I have never heard of such a principle according to which the preservation of nature and life is not a blessing. (ch. 4, NHCC, 2:28a)

28. The principles of things are from the very start correct. None can escape from them. Therefore a person is never born by mistake, and what he is born with is never an error. Although heaven and earth are vast and the myriad things are many, the fact that I happen to be here is not something that spiritual beings of heaven and earth, sages and worthies of the land, and people of supreme strength or perfect knowledge can violate. . . . Therefore if we realize that our nature and destiny are what they should be, we will have no anxiety and will be at ease with ourselves in the face of life or death, prominence or obscurity, or an infinite amount of changes and variations, and will be in accord with principle. (ch. 5, NHCC, 2:40a)

Comment. Determinism and fatalism are here explained in terms of principle and correctness. Fate is not merely something beyond human control or understanding; it is necessary truth. Nowhere else in Chinese thought is it asserted so strongly.

29. To cry as people cry is a manifestation of the mundane world. To identify life and death, forget joy and sorrow, and be able to sing in the presence of the corpse is the perfection of the transcendental world. . . . Therefore principle has its ultimate, and the transcendental and the mundane world are in silent harmony with each other. There has never been a person who has roamed over the transcendental world to the utmost and yet was not silently in harmony with the mundane world, nor has there been anyone who was silently in harmony with the mundane world and yet did not roam over the transcendental world. Therefore the sage always roams in the transcendental world in order to enlarge the mundane world. By having no deliberate mind of his own, he is in accord with things. (ch. 6, NHCC, 3:19a-b)

> Comment. As pointed out before, neither Wang Pi nor Kuo Hsiang considered Lao Tzu or Chuang Tzu a sage. Instead, their sage was Confucius. This is amazing, but the reason is really not far to seek. For to Kuo Hsiang, especially, the ideal person is a sage who is "sagely within and kingly without" and who travels in both the transcendental and mundane worlds. According to the Neo-Taoists, Lao Tzu and Chuang Tzu traveled only in the transcendental world and were therefore one-sided, whereas Confucius was truly sagely within and kingly without.

30. The expert driver utilizes the natural capacity of horses to its limit. To use the capacity to its limit lies in letting it take its own course. If forced to run in rapid pace, with the expectation that they can exceed their capacity, horses will be unable to bear and many will die. On the other hand, if both worn-out and thoroughbred horses are allowed to use their proper strength and to adapt their pace to their given lot, even if they travel to the borders of the country, their nature will be fully preserved. But there are those who, upon hearing the doctrine of allowing the nature of horses to take its own course, will say, "Then set the horses free and do not ride on them," and there are those who, upon hearing the doctrine of taking no action, will immediately say, "It is better to lie down than to walk." Why are they so much off the track and unable to return? In this they have missed Chuang Tzu's ideas to a very high degree. (ch. 9, NHCC, 4:11b)

31. By taking no action is not meant folding up one's arms and closing one's mouth. If we simply let everything act by itself, it will be

contented with its nature and destiny. To have no alternative but [to rule an empire] is not to be forced into doing so by power or punishment. Straightly speaking, if only Tao is embraced and simplicity cherished, and if what has to be is allowed to run its maximum course, the world will naturally be contented with itself. (ch. 11, NHCC, 4:29a)

32. There is no preconceived give and take in things or in their principles of being. If things are natural, they will transform themselves without taking any action. (ch. 11, NHCC, 4:38b)

33. The two sages [the Great Yü and King Wen] had to govern their empires because there was disorder. [Emperor Shun] bowed and yielded the throne to [Yü] whereas [King Wen] had to resort to military expeditions [to take away the power from despotic King Chou] because the situations of the time were different. Neither of the two procedures is necessarily superior to the other. (ch. 12, NHCC, 5:17a)

34. In cutting a tree the workman does not take any action; the only action he takes is in plying the axe. In the actual managing of affairs, the ruler does not take any action; the only action he takes is in employing his ministers. If the ministers can manage affairs, the ruler can employ ministers, the axe can cut the tree, and the workman can use the axe, each corresponding to his capacity, then the Principle of Nature will operate of itself, not because someone takes action. If the ruler does the work of his ministers, he will no longer be the ruler, and if the ministers control the ruler's employment, they will no longer be ministers. Therefore when each attends to his own responsibility, both ruler and the ruled will be contented and the principle of taking no action is attained. We must not fail to discern the term "taking no action." In ruling an empire, there is the activity of ruling. It is called "taking no action" because the activity is spontaneous and follows the nature of things. And those who serve the empire also do so spontaneously. In the case of ministers managing affairs, even Shun and Yü, as ministers, would still be regarded as taking action. Therefore when the superior and inferior are contrasted, the ruler is tranquil and the minister is active. . . . But in each case they allowed their nature to work and their destiny to unfold itself in its wonderful way. Thus neither the superior nor the inferior, neither antiquity nor the later period takes any action. Who then will? (ch. 13, NHCC, 5:25a-b)

35. Events that took place in the past have disappeared with the past. Some may be transmitted to us [in writing], but can this make the past exist in the present? The past is not in the present and every present event is soon changed. Therefore only when one abandons the pursuit of knowledge and lets Nature take its own course, and changes with the times, can he be perfect. (ch. 13, NHCC, 5:35a)

36. The ceremonies of ancient kings were intended to meet the needs of the time. When the time is past and the ceremonies are still not cast away, they will become an evil influence on the people and serve to hasten the start of affectations and imitation. (ch. 14, NHCC, 5:42a)

37. Humanity and righteousness are principles of human nature. Human nature undergoes changes and is different past and present. If one takes a temporary abode in a thing and then moves on, he will silently understand [the reality of things]. If, however, he stops and is confined to one place, he will develop prejudices. Prejudices will result in hypocrisy, and hypocrisy will result in many reproaches. (ch. 14, NHCC, 5:44b)

38. Although [Yao] ruled the empire, he delegated his government to his many officials and left matters to the myriad things themselves without interfering with them. This means he did not employ others for his own purpose. He was in accord with the people and let things take their own course without toiling himself. This means he was not employed by others as a servant. (ch. 20, NHCC, 7:18a)

39. Not only is it impossible for non-being to be changed into being. It is also impossible for being to become non-being. Therefore, although being as a substance undergoes infinite changes and transformations, it cannot in any instance become non-being. . . . What came into existence before there were things? If I say yin and yang came first, then since yin and yang are themselves entities, what came before them? Suppose I say Nature came first. But Nature is only things being themselves. Suppose I say perfect Tao came first. But perfect Tao is perfect non-being. Since it is non-being, how can it come before anything else? Then what came before it? There must be another thing, and so on *ad infinitum*. We must understand that things are what they are spontaneously and not caused by something else. (ch. 22, NHCC, 7:54b-55b)

20

THE SEVEN EARLY BUDDHIST SCHOOLS

WHEN BUDDHISM first arrived in China,[1] it was mixed up with popular religious beliefs and practices. As translation of Buddhist scriptures began in the middle of the second century,[2] Buddhist thought started to develop in China. By the first quarter of the third century, there had been two Buddhist movements of thought: *dhyāna* (concentration) and *prajñā* (wisdom). The objective of *dhyāna* was so to meditate and to achieve calmness of mind as to remove ignorance and delusions, while that of *prajñā* was to gain the wisdom that things possess no self-nature (*svabhāva*).

As time went on, more and more *prajñā* literature became available in China and the movement became as prevalent as it was influential. This spread brought the Buddhists, the *prajñā* scholars especially, into contact with the Chinese literati. Although in the beginning this contact was slight, records show that Buddhist monks came under the influence of the Light Conversation[3] movement and the metaphysical discussions of the Chinese literati, and followed the vogue. When Lo-yang, in the north (the capital of Chin, 265-420), fell to invaders and the government moved to the south, many of the literati and Buddhist monks also migrated south. Both groups being refugees, they became intimate and the interchange of ideas became free and frequent.

Before the exodus to the south, there had already been the practice of "matching concepts" of Buddhism and Taoism,[4] in which a Buddhist concept is equated with one in Chinese thought. Thus *tathatā* (thusness, ultimate reality) was translated by the Taoist term "original non-being" (*pen-wu*, pure being). Now close contacts between the Buddhists and Neo-Taoists in the south reached a very high philosophical level. As the fundamental problem of Neo-Taoism was that of being and non-being, and since Neo-Taoists conceived fundamental reality to be original non-being, the Buddhists similarly centered their own thoughts along these lines. Seven schools developed, all in the south except the School of Original Non-being, which arose in the north. Like the Neo-Taoists,

---

[1] In 2 B.C. a Chinese official received instructions on a Buddhist scripture from a foreign envoy. This is the earliest record of Buddhism in China.

[2] Tradition ascribes the translation of the *Forty-Two-Chapter Scripture* to an earlier period but most scholars believe that it is a work of the Wei-Chin times (220-420).

[3] See above, ch. 19, Introduction.

[4] For this system, called *ko-i*, or matching concepts, see T'ang Yung-t'ung, "On 'Ko-yi,'" in Inge, *Radhakrishnan*, pp. 276-286.

the Buddhists regarded ultimate reality as transcending all being, names, and forms, and as empty and quiet in its nature. As in the case of Neo-Taoism this is not nihilism, for non-being thus understood is really pure being or reality undifferentiated.

Records about the seven schools are scanty and the tenets of several of them are not quite clear. They did not exert much influence on later Buddhists. Nevertheless the records are sufficient to show several things. One is that Neo-Taoism was instrumental in the growth of the earliest Chinese Buddhist philosophical schools and not vice versa. Second, these schools were essentially Chinese both in thought and in language. As Liebenthal has aptly put it, "The so-called schools were originated by the Chinese and had no relation to Indian controversies. The Chinese asked all the questions and Indian Buddhist revelation supplied the answers."[5] Third, they showed that in the Eastern Chin (317-420) the arena of Chinese philosophy was dominated by Buddhists rather than by Confucian or Taoist thinkers. From now on for several hundred years, the story of Chinese philosophy was that of Buddhism. Fourth, the schools laid down the direction of philosophical discussion in the Six Dynasties (222-589), for the problems of being and non-being remained basic.

Furthermore, the schools generally fell into two groups. The School of Original Non-being and its Variant School may be labeled as schools of non-being, whereas the other five may be labeled as schools of being, for while they maintain that matter is empty, they do not deny its conditional existence. It happens that later Buddhist schools are usually classified into the two categories of being and non-being. It would be far-fetched to say that the seven schools set the pattern, but one cannot help pointing out that the basic issue remained the same, namely, that between being and non-being. As has already been pointed out, the Neo-Taoism of Wang Pi (226-249) affirms the one while that of Kuo Hsiang (d. 312) affirms the many.[6] Since these Buddhist philosophers lived much nearer to the time of Kuo Hsiang than to that of Wang Pi, is it unreasonable to suggest that the Neo-Taoist spirit of "saving the appearance" in Kuo Hsiang had some bearing on their thought?

The following selection is from the *Chung-kuan lun shu* (Commentary on the *Treatise on the Middle Doctrine, Mādhyamika śāstra*) by Chi-tsang, 549-623.

[5] Liebenthal, trans., *Book of Chao*, p. 147.
[6] See above, ch. 19, Introduction.

THE CHUNG-KUAN LUN SHU

Before Master Kumārajīva[7] arrived in Ch'ang-an[8] [in 401[9]], there were originally three schools of thought.

1. The first was the monk Tao-an (312-385)[10] who propagated the doctrine of original non-being. He said that non-being existed before the myriad things evolved and transformed, and that Emptiness[11] was the beginning of all beings with forms. What obstructs man's [mind] are derived entities.[12] If the mind finds its abode[13] in original non-being, erroneous thoughts will cease. Teacher of the Law Seng-jui (352-436)[14] said, "The method of matching Buddhist concepts with those of Taoism is off the mark and misinterprets the original meaning. The [following] six schools are all one-sided and have not touched the truth. Our Master said, 'I, Monk Tao-an, cut a desert path to open up a track, and signal to the world the doctrine of the emptiness of the nature of things as a profound concept.' Tested by the actual results the schools have produced, the School of the Emptiness of the Nature of Things alone attains the truth in the highest degree."[15] If we understand this idea fully, we realize that according to Master Tao-an's explanation of original non-being, all dharmas (elements of existence)[16] are in their original nature empty and void (tranquil and devoid of differentiated character). Hence the name original non-being (pure being).[17] This doctrine is no different from those taught in the Mahāyāna scriptures and treatises as well as by schools of Kumārajīva and Seng-chao (384-414).[18]

[7] For his biography, see below, ch. 21, Introduction. [8] Present Sian.

[9] He arrived in the last month of the lunar year corresponding to 401 but that month actually fell in early 402.

[10] Tao-an was an orphan, joined the Buddhist order at twelve, and became a pupil of Fo T'u-ch'eng (233-248). He became a leading Buddhist in Ch'ang-an, with several thousand followers. Extremely earnest in propagating the Buddhist faith, he sent followers to various parts of China. For his biography, see the *Kao-seng chuan* (Biographies of Eminent Monks), ch. 5, TSD, 50:351-354.

[11] The Chinese translated *śūnya* as *k'ung*, empty or void. It means the unreality of all phenomena or anything that is caused or created. It is the Absolute.

[12] *Mo-yu*, opposed to original non-being (*pen-wu*).

[13] Read *ch'a* (boast) as *chai* (abode). This is supported by the quotation of the sentence in the biography of T'an-chi (fl. 458), in the *Ming-seng chuan ch'ao* (Biographies and Excerpts from Famous Monks). See *Zokuzōkyō* (Supplement to the Buddhist Canon), collection, pt. 2, B, case 7, vol. 1, p. 9b.

[14] Tao-an's pupil.

[15] See Seng-yu (445-518), *Ch'u san-tsang chih-chi* (Collection of Records of Translation of the Buddhist Canon), TSD, 55:59.

[16] About translation of the word *dharma*, see Appendix, comment of *Fa*.

[17] It is a great mistake to interpret non-being as nihilism. It is really pure being, a positive concept.

[18] See below, ch. 21, sec. 2, and n.2.

Comment. T'ang Yung-t'ung has pointed out the similarity of Tao-an's theory of original non-being to that of Wang Pi.[19] We should also note that Tao-an's way to realize the original non-being is through the calmness of mind. Thus in effect he synthesized the *dhyāna* and *prajñā* movements.

2. The next is [the Variant School of Original Non-being of] Teacher of the Law Fa-shen (286-374).[20] He said that by original non-being is meant that before there was any dharma of form (or matter),[21] there was first of all non-being. Therefore being came out of non-being. That is, non-being existed before being and being came into existence after non-being. This is why it is called original non-being.

This theory has been demolished by Master Seng-chao in his treatise "The Emptiness of the Unreal,"[22] and has not been taught in the scriptures or treatises. If non-being existed before being, then the original nature of what is not existent is non-being. This means that there was first non-being and then being, and that things will return from being back to non-being. The scripture says, "If dharmas first exist and then cease to exist, then all Buddhas and bodhisattvas[23] have erred and sinned [because coming into existence and going out of existence constitute suffering]. If they are non-being at first and then become being, all Buddhas and bodhisattvas will also have erred and sinned."[24] Therefore the scripture is not in agreement with this doctrine.

3. The second school is that of the theory of matter as it is (*chi-se*, "matter as we find it" or actual things).[25] There are two representatives. One is the theory of matter as it is of the Kuan-nei area,[26] which ex-

[19] *Wei-Chin hsüan-hsüeh lun-kao* (Preliminary Treatise on the Metaphysical Schools of the Wei-Chin Period, 220-420), 1957, p. 50.

[20] He was Chu Ch'ien. This doctrine was pronounced in 365. For his biography, see *Kao-seng chuan*, ch. 4, TSD, 50:347-348.

[21] This is *se* in Chinese, which is the translation for the Sanskrit *rūpa*. It means appearance, matter, color, form, thing.

[22] See below, ch. 21, sec. 2.

[23] A bodhisattva is one who has dedicated himself to achieve enlightenment and salvation for all.

[24] I have not been able to trace the source of this quotation. It may refer to scriptures in general.

[25] The term *chi-se* literally means "matter right here." As explained by T'ang Yung-t'ung, it is not substantive but matter as apprehended immediately as it exists, or appearance. The school maintains that matter has no self-nature but depends on external causes and conditions for its existence, and is therefore empty. But it does have a conditional or temporary existence, which the school holds to be real and not empty. The name probably came from the title of the treatise mentioned in the next paragraph. See T'ang's *Han Wei Liang-Chin Nan-pei-ch'ao Fo-chiao shih* (History of Chinese Buddhism from 206 B.C. to A.D. 589), 1938, p. 261.

[26] Modern Shensi. Concerning this school, see T'ang, *ibid.*, p. 260.

plains that matter as it is is empty. The explanation for this is that matter has no self-nature. [That is, it does not exist by its own nature but through external causes and conditions. But as such it does have a conditional existence which is not empty]. The theory says that matter as it is is empty but does not say that matter as it is is in its very nature empty. This doctrine has been criticized by Master Seng-chao. He said that this theory understands that "matter has no self-nature but does not understand that matter [including its conditional existence] is really not matter at all."[27]

The other representative is Chih Tao-lin (314-366).[28] He wrote "Roaming in the Supremely Profound State (*Hsüan*) Inherent in Matter As It Is"[29] to explain that matter as it is is empty [because it depends on certain conditions for its existence]. This is why he called the treatise "Roaming in the Supremely Profound State Inherent in Matter As It Is." This means that he speaks of the true state without rejecting temporary names (derived or transitory entities which depend on causes for their production). This is no different from Master Tao-an's theory of the emptiness of original nature.

> *Comment.* According to T'ang Yung-t'ung, while Tao-an's theory of original non-being corresponds to that of Wang Pi, Chih Tao-lin's theory of matter as it is corresponds to the doctrine of Kuo Hsiang.[30] In saying that Chih Tao-lin's theory is no different from that of Tao-an, Chi-tsang is correct only insofar as the emptiness of original nature is concerned. According to Tao-an, as original non-being is realized, the conditional existence of matter becomes equally empty; according to Chih Tao-lin, on the other hand, it remains real, though conditionally so. T'ang Yung-t'ung is therefore correct in likening Chih Tao-lin to Kuo Hsiang.

4. The third school is that of Teacher of the Law Fa-wen (fl. 374)[31] who advocated the theory of the non-being of mind.[32] By the non-being of mind is meant that one should not have any deliberate mind toward the myriad things. The myriad things in themselves, however, are not

---

[27] See below, ch. 21, sec. 2.

[28] He was a nobleman turned monk. He wrote extensively, including commentaries on the *Lao Tzu* and *Chuang Tzu*, and helped to make Buddhism popular through the synthesis of Taoist and Buddhist ideas. All his works are lost except an introduction. For his biography, see *Kao-seng chuan*, ch. 4, TSD, 50:348-349.

[29] This work is no longer extant. According to Yüan-k'ang (fl. 627–649), the reference is to Chih Tao-lin's *Miao-kuan chang* (Essay on Subtle Insight). For Yüan-k'ang, see below, ch. 21, n.14.

[30] *Wei-Chin hsüan-hsüeh lun-kao*, p. 53.

[31] Pupil of Fa-shen. For his biography, see *Kao-seng chuan*, ch. 4, TSD, 50:348.

[32] Actually the theory was first propagated by Chih Min-tu (fl. 326–342).

nonexistent. The explanation of this idea is this: The scriptures say that all dharmas are empty because it is intended to enable the substance of our minds not to cling to anything unreal or imaginary. This is why the non-being of the mind is spoken of. The theory does not assert that external things are empty. In other words, it does not hold that the objective sphere[33] of the myriad things is empty. As Master Seng-chao has well said, "The theory is right about the tranquillity of the spirit but it is wrong in not realizing the vacuity of things."[34] The idea of his refutation is that the theory recognizes the emptiness of mind but still holds that things exist. Thus it is right in one respect but wrong in another.

> *Comment.* One is reminded of the teaching of "having no deliberate mind of one's own (*wu-hsin*)" in Kuo Hsiang and Chuang Tzu.[35] In all cases, the emphasis is on the state of mind which should be such that it no longer clings to or is affected by external things.

The above four masters established their theories in the Chin period (265-420). When it came to the Liu Sung period (420-479), Teacher of the Law T'an-chi of the Ta Chuang-yen Temple wrote the "Treatise on the Seven Schools" and recounted the four masters of four different schools.

5. The fifth is the theory of consciousness being contained [in the spirit][36] founded by Yü Fa-k'ai (fl. 364).[37] [According to him], the Three Worlds (of desires, matter, and pure spirit)[38] is an abode of a long night (of worldly existence), and the mind is the basis of a great dream. All that we see is seen in this dream. When we awaken from the great dream, and the long night gets to be dawn, then the consciousness that produces illusions will be extinguished and the Three Worlds will be seen to be all empty. At this time nothing is produced [from the mind] and yet nothing is not produced from it.

Objection: If what is asserted is correct, then at the time of great awakening, nothing will be seen and that would not be in accord with

---

[33] See ch. 23, n.8.

[34] See below, ch. 21, sec. 2.

[35] See above, ch. 19, sec. 6, selections 8, 14, 29.

[36] According to T'ang Yung-tung, Yü Fa-k'ai distinguished between the spirit and consciousness, and held that consciousness is the function of the spirit. The awakening refers to that of the spirit. See *Han Wei Liang-Chin Nan-pei-ch'ao Fo-chiao shih*, p. 265.

[37] He was of the Liu Sung period and famous as a medical practitioner. See his biography in *Kao-seng chuan*, ch. 4, TSD, 50:350.

[38] The world of sensuous desires (which includes the six heavens of desires), the world of matter (various heavens which are free of desires), and the world of pure spirit (the highest level, where the mind dwells in deep and mystical meditation).

worldly (relative, common) truth.[39] Then what do the five kinds of eyes[40] of the Tathāgata (Buddha)[41] see?

6. The sixth school is that of Teacher of the Law Tao-i (d. 401).[42] He said all dharmas of worldly truth are illusory. This is why the scripture says that from the very beginning there have never been any [such dharmas].[43]

Objection: According to the scriptures, activities of illusory products have neither merit nor demerit. If all dharmas are equally illusory, what is the difference between an illusory person and a real person? Furthermore, the scripture merely makes use of what is vacuous to refute what is actual. Now to give up what is vacuous when what is actual is gone is to misunderstand the idea of the scripture.

7. The seventh is the theory of casual union propagated by Yü Tao-sui.[44] He said that [dharmas] are casual unions (results of a combination of causes) and as such are called worldly truth. As the causes dissipate the dharmas cease to exist. That is called the highest (absolute) truth.

Objection: The scriptures talk about the true nature of dharmas without destroying temporary names (dependent entities). Why must there be the dissipation of causes before there is the true non-being? The non-being that is possible only with the dissipation of causes is only the non-being of the realm of worldly affairs. (*Chung-kuan lun shu*, ch. 2, TSD, 42:29)

[39] The theory taught in most Buddhist schools is that there are two levels of truth: worldly truth, i.e., relative truth or truth pertaining to the phenomenal world, and the highest truth, i.e., absolute truth. These are the Two Levels of Truth, *paramārthasatya* and *laukikasatya*.

[40] The human vision, that of heavenly things, Hīnayāna wisdom, bodhisattva truth, and Buddha-vision or omniscience.

[41] Literally "thus come" or "thus go," one of the ten titles of the Buddha. It means that the Buddha comes as all things come, that is, through causation, but he achieves perfect wisdom and attains Buddhahood. It also means that he has come by the way of "thus come" to the Three Worlds to preach and save sentient beings.

[42] He held that while the dharmas of worldly truth are illusory, the spirit is not. See his biography in *Kao-seng chuan*, ch. 5, TSD, 50:357.

[43] Quoting the *Ta-chi ching* (Scripture of the Great Assembly of Bodhisattvas), ch. 9, TSD, 13:58.

[44] He studied under the same teacher with Yü Fa-k'ai. He was also a medical practitioner. He accompanied his teacher on his journey to India, reached Annam, fell sick and died at 31. For his biography, see *Kao-seng chuan*, ch. 4, TSD, 50:350.

21

SENG-CHAO'S DOCTRINE OF REALITY

THE SEVEN SCHOOLS discussed in the preceding chapter represent individual philosophers and isolated theories without any systematic philosophy. Moreover, they are largely Chinese. With Seng-chao (384-414), however, Chinese Buddhist philosophy entered upon a new stage: for the first time there was a systematic philosophy. Moreover, his philosophy helped to root firmly on Chinese soil a Buddhist philosophy from India, namely, the Three-Treatise or the Middle Doctrine School.

The credit for the growth of systematic development of Buddhist philosophy in China must go to Kumārajīva (344-413), for it was he who first translated the really philosophical texts into Chinese and it was his disciples who developed the philosophies. He was half-Indian and half-Kuchen, and became a monk at seven years of age. He had such a great reputation in the western regions that in 384 a king of Former Ch'in (351-394) sent a general to bring him back to China. After the general had kept him in northwestern China for seventeen years, a king of Later Ch'in (384-417) dispatched an army to bring him to the capital of Ch'ang-an in 401.[1] There he enjoyed the highest honors and had the highest title of National Teacher conferred on him. Over a thousand monks sat in his daily lectures. In the course of about ten years, he translated into excellent Chinese seventy-two works in 384 chapters. Among his pupils were the famous Ten Philosophers. Of these, Seng-chao was his first disciple, and philosophically the most outstanding.

Seng-chao was born in a poor family and had to earn his living by repairing and copying books. This enabled him to read extensively in literature and history, and he took a special liking to Lao Tzu and Chuang Tzu. However, after he read the translation of the *Vimalakīrti-nirdeśa sūtra* (Scripture Spoken by Vimalakīrti), he was convinced of the superiority of Buddhism, and became a monk. His name spread over the Shensi area even when he was still a young boy. Around 398, when he was hardly fifteen years old, having heard of the fame of Kumārajīva, he went far west to become his pupil and later returned with him to Ch'ang-an. Besides helping his master in the translations, he wrote a number of treatises of his own. Of these, the two translated below are the most important. When he died he was barely thirty-one.[2]

---

[1] Actually he arrived in the last month of the lunar year, which happened to fall in the beginning of 402. Ch'ang-an is present Sian.

[2] For his life, see *Kao-seng chuan* (Biographies of Eminent Monks), ch. 6, TSD, 50:365-366.

343

He felt that previous Chinese Buddhist schools were one-sided insofar as they still adhered to being or non-being. This is the gist of his criticism of the schools. To him, substance and function are identical, and activity and tranquillity are the same. He believed that the self-nature of things is vacuous, and therefore things defy any determination. All dharmas (elements of existence)[3] are merely temporary names (dependent entities), as they come into existence through causes and conditions and not through any nature of their own. Being temporary names, they are unreal, and being unreal, they are empty.

Such a conclusion is, of course, strictly Buddhistic. In his theory of the immutability of things, he follows not only Buddhism in general, but a particular school, that of the Middle Doctrine of Nāgārjuna (c.100–200), which was then very prominent in India. This school was introduced into China by Kumārajīva, where it was also known as the Three-Treatise School. The ideal of the school is the Absolute or Ultimate Emptiness. Its logical weapon was the famous Four Points of Argumentation,[4] that is, refuting an idea as being, as non-being, as both being and non-being, and as neither being nor non-being. Seng-chao accepted this doctrine of Nāgārjuna's through Kumārajīva and applied it fully to his treatise on immutability. Thus he prepared for Chi-tsang (549-623) who elaborated on the doctrine and made it a major school in China until it declined in the ninth century.

In spite of this purely Indian character, however, Seng-chao was still a bridge between Taoism and Buddhism. His fondness for Lao Tzu and Chuang Tzu had a lasting influence on him. The Taoist ideas of vacuity and the sage having no deliberate mind of his own have a prominent place in his philosophy. In this way he not only incorporated Taoism into his system but also harmonized the Middle Doctrine philosophy with that of the *prajñā* (wisdom) movement which aims at achieving the wisdom of realizing that things in their own self-nature are unreal.

The following two chapters are from the *Chao lun* (Seng-chao's Treatises).[5]

SENG-CHAO'S TREATISES

1. The Immutability of Things (ch. 1)

That birth and death alternate, that winter and summer repeatedly succeed each other, and that all things move on like a current is an ordinary belief of men. But I think that it is not the case.

[3] See Appendix, comment on *Fa*, for note on the term *dharma*.

[4] For this school, see ch. 22, Introduction.

[5] This book consists of four chapters. For an English translation, see Bibliography. There is a very important study of it in Japanese, the *Jōron kenkyū* (Studies on *Seng-chao's Treatises*), compiled by Tsukamoto Zenryu, 1955.

The *Fang-kuang ching* (Scripture of the Shedding of the Light of the Buddha) says, "There is no dharma that goes or comes, or moves to change its position."[6] As we investigate the meaning of not moving, does it mean to cast aside motion (activity) in order to seek rest (tranquillity)? No, rest must be sought right in motion. As rest must be sought right in motion, therefore there is eternal rest in spite of motion, and as motion is not to be cast aside in order to seek rest, therefore although there is rest, it is never separated from motion. This being the case, motion and rest are from the beginning not different, but deluded people consider them to be dissimilar. Consequently, the true words [of Buddhism] are obstructed by their competitive arguments and the orthodox path is deflected by their fondness of heterodoxy. Thus it is not easy to speak about the ultimate [relation] between rest and motion.[7] Why? Because when one speaks the truth, he goes against the common folks, but if he follows them, he will violate the truth. When one violates the truth, he will be deluded about the [original] nature [of things] and will be forever lost, and when he goes against the common folks, his words will be insipid and tasteless.[8] Consequently, when the average type of men [hear the truth] they half believe in it and half doubt it, and the lowest type of men clap their hands (in glee) and ignore it completely.[9] Indeed, the [original] nature of things is something near at hand but difficult to know. But I cannot help setting my mind on the relation between motion and rest. I dare not say that my ideas are necessarily true, but I shall try to discuss them.

The *Tao-hsing ching* (Scripture on Learning and Practicing the Way) says, "In reality dharmas do not come from anywhere or go anywhere."[10] The *Chung lun* (Treatise on the Middle Doctrine) says, "From one's own point of view one knows that a thing has gone away, but what is [thought to have] gone does not arrive anywhere."[11] Both of these show that rest must be sought right in motion. From this we know that it is clear that things are immutable.

Comment. In both Taoist and early Buddhist thought, the unreality of things is often argued from the fact that things are in constant

---

[6] *Fang-kuang ching* (Scripture of the Shedding of the Light of the Buddha, *Pañcaviṁśatisāhasrikāprajñāpāramitā sūtra*, or Scripture of Perfection of Wisdom in 25,000 Stanzas), ch. 5, TSD, 8:32. The quotation is not literal.

[7] It is significant that the two peculiar terms for tranquillity and activity or rest and motion are those used in *Lao Tzu*, ch. 26.

[8] Quoting *Lao Tzu*, ch. 35.   [9] Paraphrasing *Lao Tzu*, ch. 41.

[10] *Tao-hsing ching* (Scripture on Learning and Practicing the Way, *Daśasāhasrikāprajñāpāramitā sūtra* or Scripture of Perfection of Wisdom in 10,000 Stanzas), ch. 10, TSD, 8:475.

[11] Paraphrasing *Chung lun* (Treatise on the Middle Doctrine, *Mādhyamaka śāstra*) by Nāgārjuna, ch. 1, sec. 2, TSD, 30:3.

flux. Seng-chao, on the other hand, attempts to show that this flux itself is unreal. This is a new approach.

What other people mean by motion is that because things of the past [have gone away] and do not reach the present, therefore they are said to have moved and are not at rest (continue to exist). What I mean by rest is that, similarly, because things of the past do not reach the present, therefore they may be said to be at rest and have not moved. [Other people believe] things move but are not at rest because [past things] have not come down (continue to exist) to the present. [I believe] things are at rest and do not move because [past things] have not gone anywhere. Thus the situation [that past things have neither come to the present nor have gone anywhere] remains the same but our viewpoints are different. People who go against [the truth] will call [that situation] a barrier but those who follow [the truth] will call it a passage. If one has found the right way, what is there to obstruct him?

It is sad that people have been deluded in their views for such a long time. Truth is right before their eyes but they do not realize it. They already know that past things cannot come [to the present] but still maintain that present things can go (pass on). As past things cannot come [to the present], where do present things go? Why? If we look for past things in the past, we find that they are never nonexistent in the past, but if we search for past things in the present, we find that they are never existent there. That they are never existent in the present shows that they never come, and that they are never nonexistent in the past shows that they do not go away from it. If we turn our attention to investigate the present, we know that the present, too, does not go anywhere. This means that past things by their very nature exist in the past and have not gone there from the present, and present things by their nature exist in the present and have not come here from the past. This is why Confucius said, "Hui,[12] [every day] I see something new. [Although you and I have been associated with each other for a long time], in a single moment you are no longer the same as before."[13] Thus it is clear that [past] things do not come and [present] things do not go. As there is not even a subtle sign of going or returning, what thing can there be that can move? This being the case, the raging storm that uproots mountains is always tranquil (at rest), rivers rushing to the sea do not flow, the fleeting forces moving in all directions and pushing about do not move, and the sun and moon

12 Yen Hui, Confucius' favorite pupil.
13 Alluding to the story told in *Chuang Tzu*, ch. 21, NHCC, 7:32a. See Giles, trans., *Chuang Tzu*, 1961 ed., pp. 200-201. The philosophical idea of impermanence is ascribed to this story by Kuo Hsiang (d. 312) in his commentary on the *Chuang Tzu*. Seng-chao is here following Kuo Hsiang.

revolving in their orbits do not turn round. What is there to wonder about any more?

Alas, the Sage has said, "Man's life passes away quickly, more quickly than the stream current."[14] Therefore by realizing the impermanence of things the Buddha's ordinary disciples (*śrāvaka*, those who attain to their own salvation by hearing the Buddha's teaching) attain enlightenment, and the Buddhas-for-themselves (*pratyekabuddha*, who attain enlightenment by their own exertions),[15] by realizing that causes [which make an entity a dependent being] can be removed, become identified with the real. If all motions (activities) of things are not changes, why should they seek after [the principle] of change in order to ascend the steps to enlightenment? [However], if we again investigate the saying of the Sage, we shall find its meaning to be subtle, hidden, and unfathomable. Things seem to move but are really at rest, and they seem to go away but really remain. Such things can only be understood by the spirit and cannot be discovered in ordinary facts. Therefore when the Sage said that things go, he did not mean that they really go; he merely wanted to prevent ordinary thoughts, and when he said that things remain in the same state,[16] he did not mean that they really remain; he merely wanted to discard what ordinary people call the passing (impermanence) of things. He did not mean to say that by going is meant something being sent away and by remaining something being retained. Therefore the *Ch'eng-chü ching* (Scripture on Producing and Completing the Light) says, "The bodhisattva,[17] living in the midst of people who believe in permanence, propagates the doctrine of impermanence."[18] And the *Mo-ho-yen lun* (Treatise of Great Wisdom) says, "Dharmas do not move. They neither go anywhere nor come to anywhere."[19] All these are intended to lead the common folks to reach enlightenment. The two different sayings aim

[14] Yüan K'ang (fl. 627–649), in his *Chao lun shu* (Commentary on *Seng-chao's Treatises*), TSD, 45:168, thought this is a quotation from the *Nirvāṇa sūtra*. The *Chao lun Chung-wu chih-chieh* (Commentaries on *Seng-chao's Treatises* Collected by Pi-ssu of Chung-wu [in present Kiangsu]), edited by his pupil Ching-yüan (1011-1088), refers to the same scripture. But as Liebenthal has pointed out, this scripture was probably not known to Seng-chao. (*Book of Chao*, p. 49.) He thinks that the reference is to *Analects*, 9:16. Japanese scholars think the same. See Tsukamoto Zenryu, *Jōron kenkyū*, p. 10.

[15] See below, ch. 25, n.14.

[16] This word, *sthiti* in Sanskrit and *chu* in Chinese, has been variously rendered as abiding, dwelling, stagnation, permanence. It is one of the four characteristics of all things: coming into existence, remaining in the same state, change, and going out of existence.

[17] A bodhisattva is a saint who is strongly determined to seek salvation for himself and others.

[18] *Ch'eng-chü kuang-ming ching* (Scripture on Producing and Completing the Light), TSD, 15:451.

[19] *Mahāprajñāpāramitā śāstra*, ch. 51, TSD, 25:427.

at the same thing. Shall we say that because they differ in language they are contradictory in objectives? Although permanence is mentioned, it does not mean remaining in the same state, and although going is mentioned, it does not mean instability. Since dharmas are not mutable, they are always at rest even though they have gone, and because they do not remain, they are always gone even though they are at rest. As they are always gone although at rest, they do not mutate while being gone, and as they are always at rest while they are gone, they do not remain while at rest. When Chuang Tzu said that [it is impossible to] hide a mountain [in a lake for at midnight a strong man may come and carry it away on his back][20] and when Confucius stood by the stream [and said, "It passes on like this, never ceasing day or night"],[21] both expressed the feeling that what is gone cannot be retained. Did they say that [things] can cast aside the present and pass on? Thus we see that the minds of the sages are different from the views of the common people. Why? They say that a man possesses the same body in youth and in old age and that the same substance persists over a hundred years. They only know that the years pass on but do not realize that the body follows. A young ascetic seeking Nirvāṇa left his family and when his hair had turned white, returned home. When his neighbors saw him and asked, "Is the man of the past still living?" he replied, "I look like the man of the past but I am not he." The neighbors were all startled and rejected his words.[22] [When Chuang Tzu] said that a strong man comes and carries it away on his back but an ignorant man does not know this,[23] this is the meaning.

The Tathāgata (Buddha),[24] in accordance with the obstruction in the common people's views, speaks appropriate words to dispel their delusions. He exercises his true mind which transcends any duality and preaches various doctrines which need not be the same [but which vary according to circumstances].[25] The words of the Sage are indeed conflicting but are never different [from the Middle Path]. Therefore when he talks about truth, he speaks in terms of [things being] immutable, but when he wants to lead the ordinary folk, he talks in terms of [things] moving on like a current. Although there are a thousand paths and a variety of tunes, they all converge at the same point.

But people who rely on the letter, when they hear of immutability,

[20] *Chuang Tzu*, ch. 6, NHCC, 3:8b. See Giles, p. 75.

[21] *Analects*, 9:16.

[22] The source of this story is unknown, even to Yüan-k'ang. See his commentary in TSD, 45:169.

[23] *Chuang Tzu*, ch. 6, NHCC, 3:8b, Giles, p. 75.

[24] See ch. 20, n.41.

[25] This interruption follows that in the *Chao lun Chung-wu chi-chieh*.

believe that things of the past cannot reach the present, and when they hear of things moving on like a current, believe that things of the present can reach the past. Since they have already made the distinction of past and present, how can things pass on between them? To say that [things] have gone does not necessarily mean that they have gone away. Both the past and the present exist permanently because they do not move. To say that [things] go does not necessarily mean that they really go, for the past cannot be reached from the present, since [the past] does not come [to the present]. As [things] do not come, there cannot be any shifting between past and present, and since they do not move, every thing, in accordance with its nature, remains for one period of time. This being the case, although the various books differ in language and the many schools differ in theory, if we find out where they converge, how can different expressions delude us?

What people call remaining, I call passing on, whereas what people call passing on, I call remaining. Although passing on and remaining are different, ultimately they are the same. This is why it is said in the scripture, "Straight words seem to be their opposite. Who will believe them?"[26] There is reason for this saying.

What shall we say? People seek the past in the present. [Since it is not found in the present], they say that it does not remain. I seek the present in the past. [Since it is not in the past], I know that it does not go anywhere. If the present passes on to the past, then there should be the present in the past. If the past reaches to the present, then there should be the past in the present. Since there is no past in the present, we know that it does not come, and since there is no present in the past, we know that it does not go. As neither does the past reach to the present nor does the present reach to the past, every thing, according to its nature, remains for only one period of time. What thing is there to come and go?

> *Comment.* This is the central issue of the problem, for motion and rest imply time. Throughout the essay, Seng-chao follows closely the logic of Nāgārjuna. According to him, time is unreal. For example, the present cannot be either in the past or not in the past. If it is in the past, it is obviously not present, and if it is not in the past, there would be nothing to cause its present existence. Since it is neither in the past nor not in the past, it is unreal. The same is true of the past and the future. This is argued in chapter nineteen

[26] *P'u-yao ching* (*Lalitavistara sūtra* or Scripture of a Detailed Narration of the Sport [of the Buddha]), ch. 7, TSD, 3:527. The first sentence also appears in *Lao Tzu*, ch. 78.

of his treatise. By arguing that time is impossible, Seng-chao concludes that motion is illusory, since motion depends on time.

This being the case, although the four seasons are as fleeting as the wind and although the polar star revolves with lightning speed, if we understand the least bit [that things do not move], we will realize that, quick as they are, they do not move.

For the above reason, the merit[27] of the Tathāgata continues for countless generations and exists permanently, and his truth remains firmer after having gone through a hundred aeons. The completion of a mountain lies in the first basket,[28] and arriving at the destination of a long journey depends on the first step.[29] The reason, surely, is that merit is immortal.

Since merit is immortal, it does not change though it is in the past. Since it does not change, it is immutable. And since it is immutable, it is clear that [merit remains] tranquil. Therefore the scripture says, "Although the three calamities [of fire, water, and wind] extend everywhere, the merit remains tranquil."[30] How true are these words! Why? The effect does not exist together with causes,[31] because the effect is produced by the causes. Since the result is produced by the causes, the causes could not have been extinguished in the past. Since the result and the causes do not exist simultaneously, the causes do not come to the present. As they neither perish nor come to the present, the conclusion that they are immutable is clear. Why should we be deluded about [things] going or remaining any more, or be undecided as to whether [things] move or are at rest? Thus even if heaven and earth turn upside down, it does not mean that they are not at rest, and even if floods overflow heaven, it does not mean that they are in motion. If one's spirit is harmonized with things as they are found, one can realize [the principle of the immutability of things] right where he is. (TSD, 45:151)

2. The Emptiness of the Unreal (ch. 2)

The Supreme Vacuity which neither comes into [nor goes out of] existence is probably the subtle principle in the reflection of the mysterious mirror of *prajñā* (wisdom) and the source of all existence. Unless one possesses the intelligence and special penetrating power of a sage, how can he harmonize his spirit with the realm of neither existence nor nonexistence? Therefore the perfect man penetrates the infinite with

[27] A good deed brings merit which influences the future favorably. This is the doctrine of karma.

[28] Alluding to *Analects*, 9:18.   [29] Alluding to *Lao Tzu*, ch. 64.

[30] Source unidentified.

[31] In Buddhist philosophy, a result is due to more than one cause.

his wonderful mind and the finite cannot obstruct him. He applies to the utmost his ears to listen and his eyes to see, and sound and color cannot restrict him. Is this not because he leaves the vacuous self-nature of things as it is and therefore they cannot affect his spiritual intelligence? Therefore the sage exercises his true mind and is in accord with principle (*li*), and there is no obstruction which he cannot pass through. He views the transformation of all things with the clear understanding that [they are all of] one material force[32] and therefore he is in accord with whatever he may encounter. Since there is no obstruction which he cannot pass through, therefore he can mix with the impure and achieve purity, and since he is in accord with whatever he encounters, he sees the unity of things as he comes in contact with them. Since this is the case, although the ten thousand forms (phenomenal things) seem to be different, they are not so in themselves. As they are not different in themselves, it follows that these [apparent] forms are not the real forms. As these forms are not the real forms, although they [appear to be] forms, they are not [real] forms at all.

> *Comment.* This description of the mind of the sage is strikingly similar to those by Chuang Tzu and Kuo Hsiang.[33] The desired state is practically identical with Chuang Tzu's becoming one with the universe and Kuo Hsiang's quiet harmony with all things. In all cases there is "no more deliberate mind of one's own" (*wu-hsin*) and consequently there is no obstruction between the self and the other but complete harmony without distinction.

Thus things and I sprang from the same root, and right and wrong come out of the same breath. [This principle] is deep, subtle, abstruse, and hidden, and it is well nigh impossible for ordinary people to understand completely.

This is the reason why in the brief discussion of today everybody has his own opinion when it comes to the profound, fundamental doctrine [of *prajñā*]. But if agreement is to be arrived at through adhering to differences of opinion, what common ground is there for agreement? Therefore different theories have come up in competition with one another, and by their very nature they cannot agree.

There is the School of Non-being of Mind.[34] [It says that] "one should not have any deliberate mind toward the myriad things. The myriad things themselves, however, are not nonexistent." This theory is right

---

[32] The term "one material force" comes from *Chuang Tzu*, ch. 6, NHCC, 3:20a, Giles, p. 81. See also Yüan-k'ang's commentary, TSD, 45:171.

[33] See above, ch. 19, sec. 6, selections 8, 14, 29.

[34] For this and the following two schools, see above, ch. 20, secs. 1-4.

about the tranquillity of the spirit but is wrong in not realizing the emptiness of things.

Then there is the School of Matter[35] As It Is. It explains that matter has no self-nature [but depends on external causes and conditions for its existence] and therefore, although it is [called] matter, it is not really matter [since it has only conditional existence and is therefore empty]. When we speak of matter, we should regard matter as it is [in its conditional existence] to be matter. Why must we wait till [a self-nature] has transformed it into matter [of absolute existence] before it can be called matter?[36] This theory merely says that matter has no self-nature but does not understand that matter [including its conditional existence] is really not matter at all.

[Finally] there is the School of Original Non-being. This school is very fond of non-being.[37] Regardless of what is said, it tends to say that it is non-being. Therefore [when the scriptures say that things] are not existent, it immediately interprets existence as non-being, and [when the scriptures say that things] are not nonexistent, it immediately interprets nonexistence as being non-being also. If we look into the original meaning of the sayings, we shall find that they merely mean to say that nonexistence means having no real (absolute) existence, and that no nonexistence means having no real (absolute) nonexistence. Why must having nonexistence be interpreted to mean that [this particular thing] has no existence, and not nonexistence be interpreted to mean that that [particular thing] has no nonexistence? This theory is nothing but a talk partial to non-being. How can it be said to be in accord with things or express their true nature?

As a thing is a thing because it becomes so in relation to other things, what is thus made may be called a thing. But since a thing caused by another thing is not really a thing, it is not really a thing although it is so called [inasmuch as it has no nature of its own].

> *Comment.* Another borrowing from Chuang Tzu. The phraseology itself comes from him.[38]

Therefore the actuality of things cannot be equated with their names, and names in their true meanings cannot be matched by things. This being so, absolute truth remains tranquil outside of any elucidation

---

[35] *Rūpa* in Sanskrit and *se* in Chinese, variously translated as form, color, phenomenon, etc.

[36] According to Yüan-k'ang, statements of the theory end here. See TSD, 45:171.

[37] This is Yüan-k'ang's punctuation (TSD, 45:171). In the text the word *to* (very much, frequently) belongs to the next sentence, making it read, "Frequently, regardless. . . ." Actually, the difference is not important.

[38] *Chuang Tzu*, chs. 11 and 12, NHCC, 4:40a, 7:55a, Giles, pp. 114, 218.

through names. How can it be expressed by letters and words? But I cannot remain silent. Let me, then, employ words to offer some suggestions and try to discuss the matter as follows:

The *Mo-ho-yen lun* says, "The dharmas have neither the character of existence nor the character of nonexistence."[39] The *Chung lun* says, "The dharmas have neither existence nor nonexistence."[40] [These statements express] the absolute truth. As we go into the matter, when we say that there is neither existence nor nonexistence, does it mean to wipe out all the myriad things, blot out our seeing and hearing, and be in a state without sound, form, or substance before we can call it absolute truth? Truly, [absolute truth is] in accord with things as they are and therefore is opposed by none. The false is regarded as false and the true is regarded as true, and therefore their nature cannot alter the absolute truth. As it cannot be altered by the nature of anything, although it seems to be nonexistent, it is really existent. And as it is not opposed by anything, although it seems to be existent, it is really nonexistent. As it is nonexistent although it seems to be existent, it is the same as being nonexistent, and as it is existent although it seems to be nonexistent, it is the same as not being nonexistent. Thus not being existent and not being nonexistent do not mean that there are no things, but that all things are not things in the real (absolute) sense. As all things are not things in the real sense, what is there in relation to which a thing can be so-called? Therefore the scripture says, "Matter is empty by virtue of its own nature; it is not empty because it has been destroyed."[41] This is to make clear that the sage, in his attitude toward the myriad things, leaves the vacuous nature of things as it is and does not need to disintegrate it before he can penetrate it. This is why it is said that the sickness of Vimalakīrti is unreal,[42] and the *Ch'ao-jih ching* (Scripture [on Calmness] Outshining Sunshine) says that [the four elements of Earth, Water, Fire, and Wind] are all empty.[43] Thus although the language in the Buddhist Canon varies, what combines and unites it is one.

The *Fang-kuang ching* says, "According to the absolute truth, no affair is accomplished and no thing is attained, but according to worldly (relative) truth, affairs are accomplished and things are attained."[44] Now, accomplishment is a false name [indicating the relative aspect of] accomplishment, and non-accomplishment is the real name [indicating the absolute aspect of] accomplishment. Since it is the true name, al-

---

[39] Ch. 6, TSD, 25:105.   [40] Ch. 2, sec. 5, TSD, 30:7.

[41] *Vimalakīrtinirdeśa sūtra* (Scripture Spoken by Vimalakīrti), sec. 9, TSD, 14:551.

[42] *ibid.*, sec. 3, TSD, 14:545.

[43] *Ch'ao-jih-ming san-mei ching*, sec. 1, TSD, 15:532.

[44] Ch. 5, TSD, 8:36.

though it is true, accomplishment does not exist. And since it is a false name, although it is false, accomplishment is not nonexistent. Therefore what is said to be true (absolute) is not necessarily existent, and what is said to be false (relative) is not necessarily nonexistent. The two terms are not the same but the principles are not different. Therefore the scripture says, "Are absolute truth and worldly truth different? The answer is, 'No'."[45] This scripture directly elucidates the absolute truth to make clear that [things] are not existent, and elucidates worldly truth to make clear that [things] are not nonexistent. Does it mean to say that because there are the two levels of absolute and worldly truth, there are two different kinds of things?

Thus there are truly reasons why things are nonexistent and why they are not nonexistent. As there are reasons why they are not existent, therefore although they [appear to] exist, they are really not existent, and as there are reasons why they are not nonexistent, therefore although they [appear to] be nonexistent, they are really not nonexistent. Since things [appear to be] nonexistent but are really not nonexistent, the non-existence is not absolutely vacuous, and since things [appear to be] existent but are really not existent, the existence is not true (absolute) existence. Since the existent as it is is not true and the nonexistent is not entirely obliterated without any trace, although they are called differently, their ultimate meaning is the same.

Therefore the youth [in the *Scripture Spoken by Vimalakīrti*] says with a sigh of admiration, "[The Buddha] has said that dharmas are neither existent nor nonexistent, because they are produced by causes."[46] The *Ying-lo ching* (Necklace Scripture) says, "When [the bodhisattva] turns the Wheel of Law [to preach], there is neither turning nor no turning. This means to turn where there is nothing to be turned."[47] These are the subtle words of various scriptures.

What shall we say? Shall we say that things are nonexistent? Then the heterodox view [that things are annihilated] would not be erroneous. Shall we say that things are existent? Then the view that things are eternal would be correct. Because things are not nonexistent, the heterodox view is therefore erroneous, and because things are not existent, therefore the eternalist's view is incorrect. Thus the true words of the absolute truth are that things are neither existent nor nonexistent.

The *Tao-hsing ching* says, "The mind is neither existent nor nonexistent."[48] The *Chung lun* says, "Things are nonexistent because they originate from causes, but because they arise through causation, they are not nonexistent."[49] If we pursue the truth, we shall find these to be true.

The reason for this is this: If the existence of things is true (absolute)

---

[45] *Mahāprajñāpāramitā sūtra*, ch. 22, TSD, 8:378.   [46] Sec. 1, TSD, 14:537.
[47] The *Bodhisattva-keyūra sūtra*, ch. 13, TSD, 16:108.   [48] Ch. 1, TSD, 8:425.
[49] Ch. 4, sec. 16, TSD, 30:33.

existence, this existence should be eternal by its own nature and should not depend on causes to be existent. If the nonexistence of things were absolute nonexistence, it should be eternal nonexistence by its own nature and should not depend on causes to be nonexistent. If existence is not existence by its own nature but depends on causes to be existent, we know that although it [appears to] exist, it has no true existence. Since it has no true existence, it cannot be called existence in the real sense although it exists.

As to [what the scriptures describe as] not nonexistent, what is non-existent is tranquil and does not move, and may be called nonexistent. If the myriad things were nonexistent, they should not originate (rise). If they arise, they are not nonexistent. It is clear that "because things arise through causation, therefore they are not nonexistent."

The *Mo-ho-yen lun* says, "Since all dharmas arise through causation, therefore they should have [only relative] existence. [Likewise] since all dharmas arise through causation, therefore they should not have [absolute] existence. Since all nonexistent dharmas arise through causation, they should have [only relative] existence. And since all existent dharmas arise through causation, they should have no [absolute] existence."[50] As we think about it, are these words about existence and nonexistence merely intended for disagreement?

If by saying that a thing "should have existence" is meant that it actually has existence, then it should not be said that it is nonexistent. If by saying that a thing "should have nonexistence" is meant that it is actually nonexistent, then it should not be said that it is actually existent. The reason why it is said to be existent [or nonexistent] is to make clear, by employing the concept of existence, that it is not non-existent, and by employing the concept of nonexistence, that it is not existent. Here the fact[51] is one but the statements are two. The expressions seem to be different, but if we appreciate their identical points, there are no differences which are not the same.

Thus there are reasons why all dharmas are nonexistent and therefore cannot be considered to be existent, and there are reasons why they are not nonexistent and therefore cannot be considered to be nonexistent. Why? Suppose we say that they are existent. Such existence is not true (or absolute). Or suppose we say that they are nonexistent. But phe-nomena have already taken shape. Inasfar as things have already taken shape, they cannot be said to be nonexistent, and since they have no true existence, they cannot be said to be really existent. From this, the principle of the emptiness of the unreal should become clear.

Therefore the *Fang-kuang ching* says, "All dharmas are temporary

---

[50] Ch. 80, TSD, 8:425.
[51] The Yüan-k'ang text has "principle" instead of "fact."

names and not real. They resemble a man produced by magic."[52] This man is not nonexistent, but it is a man produced by magic and not a real man.

If we look for a thing through a name, we shall find that there is no actuality in that thing which would correspond to the name, and if we look for the name through a thing, we shall find that the name is not capable of helping us to discover a thing. A thing that has no actuality corresponding to a name is not a thing, and a name that is not capable of discovering a thing is not a name. Consequently, a name does not correspond to an actuality and an actuality does not correspond to a name. As name and actuality do not correspond to each other, where do the myriad things exist?

The *Chung lun* says, "Things are neither this nor that."[53] But one man will consider "this" to be "this" and "that" to be "that," while another man considers "this" to be "that" and "that" to be "this." Thus "this" and "that" do not definitely refer to a particular name, but deluded people would believe that they necessarily do. This being the case, [the distinction] between "this" and "that" is from the beginning nonexistent, but to the deluded it is from the beginning not nonexistent. If we realize that "this" and "that" do not exist, is there anything that can be regarded as existent? Thus we know that things are not real; they are from the beginning only temporary names. This is why the *Ch'eng-chü ching* utters the expression that names are given perforce,[54] and the *Chuang Tzu* resorted to the similes of marks and horses [which are but names].[55] Thus profound doctrines [about the relationship between existence and nonexistence] can be found anywhere.

The sage moves within the thousand transformations but does not change, and travels on ten thousand paths of delusion but always goes through. This is so because he leaves the vacuous self-nature of things as it is and does not employ the concept of vacuity to make things vacuous. Therefore the scripture says, "Marvellous, the World-Honored One (Buddha). You establish all dharmas in their places without disturbing Reality."[56] He does not depart from reality in order to establish them in their places; reality is right where they are established. This being so, is the Way far away? Reality is wherever there is contact with things. Is the sage far away? Realize him in one's life and there will be spiritual intelligence. (TSD, 45:152-153)

[52] Ch. 18, TSD, 8:128.
[53] According to Yüan-k'ang, TSD, 45:174, this refers to the general idea of the treatise but may also be considered to refer specifically to ch. 3, sec. 12, TSD, 30:17.
[54] TSD, 15:454. See also *Lao Tzu*, ch. 25.
[55] *Chuang Tzu*, ch. 2, NHCC, 1:29a, Giles, p. 38.
[56] *Fang-kuang ching*, ch. 20, TSD, 8:140.

22

THE PHILOSOPHY OF EMPTINESS: CHI-TSANG
OF THE THREE-TREATISE SCHOOL

THE Three-Treatise School and the Consciousness-Only School represented the two major developments of Mahāyāna or Great Vehicle philosophy in India. The former insists that dharmas (elements of existence)[1] and their causes are unreal and has therefore been known as the School of Non-being, while the latter insists that they are real and has therefore been known as the School of Being. Both were introduced into China by outstanding philosophers. Both had something profound and subtle to offer which China had never known. Both lasted for several centuries. But both failed to exert lasting influence on Chinese thought. It is important to understand why this has been the case.

The Three-Treatise School, called Mādhyamika (Middle Doctrine) in Sanskrit, was founded in India by Nāgārjuna (c.100–200 A.D.). Kumārajīva (344-413) introduced it into China by translating Nāgārjuna's two most important treatises, the *Mādhyamika śāstra* (Treatise on the Middle Doctrine)[2] and the *Dvādaśanikāya śāstra* (Twelve Gates Treatise) and his disciple Āryadeva's *Śata śāstra* (One Hundred Verses Treatise).[3] Hence the school is called the Three-Treatise School.[4]

The central concept of the school is Emptiness (*Śūnyata*) in the sense that the nature and characters of all dharmas, together with their causation, are devoid of reality. Thus all differentiations, whether being or non-being, cause or effect, or coming-into-existence or going-out-of-existence are only "temporary names" and are empty in nature. The only reality is Emptiness itself, which is the Absolute, Ultimate Void, the Original Substance, or in Chinese terminology, the correct principle (*cheng-li*). As such it is equivalent to Nirvāṇa and the Dharma-body.[5]

The doctrine was transmitted in China through Kumārajīva's pupil Seng-chao (384-414) and played a dominant role there from the fourth to the seventh century. It had a tremendous attraction for the Chinese because its philosophy of Emptiness suited the temper of Chinese intellectuals of Wei-Chin times (220-420), who were then propagating the Taoist doctrine of non-being. Its highly developed and systematic method

---

[1] For note on this translation of "dharma," see Appendix, comment on *Fa*.
[2] See Bibliography for a German translation by Walleser and a partial English translation by Stcherbatsky.
[3] For an English translation by Tucci, see Bibliography.
[4] *San-lun* in Chinese and *sanron* in Japanese.
[5] For this concept, see below, ch. 26, n.44.

of reasoning was a stimulating novelty to the Chinese. Its spirit of criticism and refutation gave the rebellious Chinese philosophers, including the Neo-Taoists, a sense of emancipation. Its nominalism reinforced the Chinese opposition to the Confucian doctrine of ranks and names, especially in the sixth century. In addition to all this, it had the great fortune of having as its systematizer the outstanding figure, Chi-tsang (549-623).

This thinker, who had a Parthian father and a Chinese mother, joined the Buddhist order when he was seven, and eventually became one of the greatest systematizers of Chinese Buddhist thought and one of the most outstanding Chinese commentators on Buddhist texts. In him the Three-Treatise School reached its highest development. He wrote in excellent prose. His literary activity, including commentaries on the three treatises, is unparalleled in his age or before, and it is remarkable that all this was achieved during a period of continuous warfare.[6]

Ironically, Chi-tsang's success was at the same time the failure of his school, for it became less and less Chinese. As mentioned before,[7] Seng-chao was still a bridge between Taoism and Buddhism. He combined the typical Chinese concept of identity of substance and function, for example, with the Buddhist concepts of temporary names and Emptiness. In Chi-tsang, substance and function are sharply contrasted instead. In that, he was completely Indian in viewpoint, although he quoted Taoists. As a systematizer and transmitter of Indian philosophy, he brought about no cross-fertilization between Buddhist and Chinese thought. And it happened that the Indian thought which he promoted was so utterly unacceptable to the Chinese that the school declined in the ninth century. It was introduced into Japan in 625 where it has never existed as an independent school, although its doctrine has remained an important object of learning even to this day.

The reason for its decline is not so much its metaphysics as its approach to it. Its goal of Emptiness is not essentially different from that of other Mahāyāna schools. Its distinction rather lies in its three basic doctrines, namely, the Two Levels of Truth, refutation of erroneous views, and Eightfold Negation. According to the theory of Two Levels of Truth, it is worldly truth (*laukikasatya*) or common or relative truth that things exist provisionally as dependent beings or temporary names, but it is absolute truth (*paramārthasatya*) that all dharmas are empty.[8] The doctrine is by no means unique to this school. What distinguishes it is that

[6] For his biography, see *Hsü kao-seng chuan* (Supplement to the *Biographies of Eminent Monks*), ch. 11, TSD, 50:513-515. He was born in Nanking. Throughout his career he was highly honored by both Sui and T'ang emperors.

[7] See above, ch. 21, Int oduction.

[8] Or universal relativity, as Stcherbatsky interprets it.

while the Consciousness-Only School, for instance, affirms dependent existence as real, this school insists that it is unreal. Actually this school denies both existence and nonexistence, for both are results of causation and as such are regarded as empty. The theory of being is looked upon as one extreme and that of non-being is looked upon as another. This opposition must be synthesized but the synthesis itself is a new extreme which has its own antithesis. At the end only the highest synthesis, the True Middle, or Emptiness, is true. Hence the school was originally known as Mādhyamika or the Middle Doctrine School.

This is the inevitable outcome of the logical methods developed by the school, namely, those of refutation and negation. To this school, refutation of erroneous views is essential for and indeed identical with the elucidation of right views. But when a right view is held in place of a wrong one, the right view itself becomes one-sided and has to be refuted. It is only through this dialectic process that Emptiness can be arrived at, which alone is free from names and character and is "inexplicable in speech and unrealizable in thought." The specific method in this dialectic process is Nāgārjuna's Middle Path of Eightfold Negations, which denies that dharmas come into existence or go out of existence, that they are permanent or come to an end, that they are the same or different, and that they come or go away. The basis of all arguments is the so-called Four Points of Argumentation. By the use of this method of argument, a dharma as being, as non-being, as both being and non-being, and as neither being nor non-being are all refuted and proved to be untrue. Chi-tsang illustrates this method fully in his refutation of causation.

It is obvious that this approach is as nihilistic as it is destructive. The school had little new substance to offer and nothing constructive. It is true that Emptiness as the Absolute is as pure and perfect as anything conceivable, but being devoid of specific characters and divorced from mundane reality, it becomes too abstract for the Chinese. It might be hoped that its novel and radical method of reasoning at least aroused the Chinese mind and led to a new approach to life and reality, but it did not. That opportunity was left to the Zen (Meditation, Ch'an) School.

The writings of Chi-tsang are extremely schematic in presentation and highly summary in content, without thorough discussion or sustained argumentation. They do, however, represent the essence of the doctrines of this school. The following are from two of his most important works, a selection from his *Erh-ti chang* (Treatise on the Two Levels of Truth), a short essay in three parts, and several selections from his *San-lun hsüan-i* (Profound Meaning of the Three Treatises), a longer work in two parts.

TREATISE ON THE TWO LEVELS OF TRUTH

1. The Two Levels of Truth

The three kinds of Two Levels of Truth all represent the principle of gradual rejection, like building a framework from the ground. Why? Ordinary people say that dharmas, as a matter of true record, possess being, without realizing that they possess nothing. Therefore the Buddhas propound to them the doctrine that dharmas are ultimately empty and void.

When it is said that dharmas possess being, it is ordinary people who say so. This is worldly truth, the truth of ordinary people. Saints and sages, however, truly know that dharmas are empty in nature. This is absolute truth, the truth of sages. This principle [of worldly versus absolute truth is taught] in order to enable people to advance from the worldly to the absolute, and to renounce [the truth of] ordinary people and to accept that of the sages. This is the reason for clarifying the first level of twofold truth.

Next comes the second stage, which explains that both being and non-being belong to worldly truth, whereas non-duality (neither being nor non-being) belongs to absolute truth. It shows that being and non-being are two extremes, being the one and non-being the other. From these to permanence and impermanence, and the cycle of life-and-death and Nirvāṇa these are both two extremes. Because the absolute [truth of non-being] and the worldly [truth of being] and the cycle of life-and-death and Nirvāṇa are both two extremes, they therefore constitute worldly truth, and because neither-the-absolute-nor-the-worldly, and neither-the-cycle-of-life-and-death-nor-Nirvāṇa are the Middle Path without duality, they constitute the highest truth.

Next comes the third stage in which both duality and non-duality are worldly truth, whereas neither-duality-nor-non-duality is the highest truth. Previously it has been explained that the worldly and the absolute and the cycle of life-and-death and Nirvāṇa are two extremes and one-sided and therefore constitute worldly truth, whereas neither-the-worldly-nor-the-absolute and neither-the-cycle-of-life-and-death-nor-Nirvāṇa are the Middle Path without duality and therefore constitute the highest truth. But these two are also two extremes. Why? Duality is one-sided while non-duality is central. But one-sidedness is an extreme and centrality is also an extreme. One-sidedness and centrality, after all, are two extremes. Being two extremes, they are therefore called worldly truth. Only neither-one-sidedness-nor-centrality can be regarded as the Middle Path or the highest truth. (*Erh-ti chang*, pt. 1, TSD, 45:90-91)

Comment. The similarity of this dialectic is strikingly similar to that of Hegel and Chuang Tzu.[9] With Chuang Tzu, both the right or the wrong, or the "this" or the "that" are infinite series and are to be synthesized in the all-inclusive Tao. It has been said that while the dialectic of Hegel includes all in the Absolute, that of Nāgārjuna excludes everything from Emptiness. This is not correct, for worldly truth is not denied but accepted as such. However, like Hegel, every new synthesis is regarded as higher, and worldly truth is therefore considered inferior. In this respect, Taoism is different from both of them, for Taoism grants equality to all things, whether worldly or not.

PROFOUND MEANING OF THE THREE TREATISES

2. Causes and Effects

Question: What does it mean to say that there are erroneous causes and erroneous effects?

Answer: Some heterodoxical schools say that the Great Lord of Heaven[10] can produce the myriad things, and that when they perish, they return to the original Heaven. Therefore they say that if the Great Lord is angry, all the four kinds of living beings[11] will suffer, and if the Great Lord is pleased, there will be happiness in all the Six Stages of Existence.[12] But Heaven is not the cause of things and things are not the effects of Heaven. They are imagined by an erroneous mind and are therefore called erroneous causes and erroneous effects.

The objection is this: Good deeds invite happy reward, and evil influence brings fruits of suffering. For [this world] is the home of inter-actions [of cause and effect] and the realm of retribution. These schools do not understand this principle and therefore produce such falsehood. Furthermore, the species of man produces man, and the species of things produces things. Since the species of man produces man, man, after all, resembles man, and since the species of things produces things, things, after all, resemble things. This is the way of one member of the species producing another. But to say that a single cause, Heaven, can produce ten thousand species as retribution—is that not a falsehood?

Question: What does it mean to say that there are no causes but effects?

Answer: There are other heterodoxical schools that have exhaustively

[9] See ch. 8, comment on p. 183.

[10] Maheśvara, the Great Lord of the Universe, who can make all things free and at ease.

[11] Those produced from the womb, from eggs, from moisture, and through metamorphosis.

[12] Those of hells, hungry ghosts, beasts, demons, human beings, and deities.

traced the origin of the myriad things and have found that they are derived from nothing. Therefore they say that there are no causes, but that if we presently look at the various dharmas we should know that there are effects. Take, for example, Chuang Tzu's story about the Shade asking the Shadow.[13] The shadow exists because of the body, and the body exists because of the Creator. But the Creator originated from nowhere. If the root exists of itself, it means that the branches are not caused by anything else. Therefore there are no causes but there are effects.

Question: What is the difference between the absence of cause and spontaneity (*tzu-jan*)?

Answer: Absence of cause is based on the fact that no cause exists, whereas spontaneity shows that the effect exists. While in the strictest sense they are different, they still represent the same erroneous conception.

Our objection to it is this: Cause and effect produce each other very much like long and short contrast each other.[14] If there is already an effect, how can there be no cause? If there is no cause, how can there be the effect alone? If there had to be no cause but had to be effect, then good deeds would invite hell and evil deeds would result in going to Paradise.

Question: Someone says that spontaneity may have a cause or it may not. The myriad things differ, but they all spontaneously exist. Therefore there is no such error as you have just stated.

Answer: The falsehood arises because the matter has not been examined carefully. If one examines carefully, one will find that according to reason the conclusion will be otherwise. For spontaneity means not [having been caused] by another thing. If a thing has been caused by another, it cannot be said to be spontaneous. Therefore given spontaneity, there will be no cause, and given a cause, there will be no spontaneity. To have asserted a cause and then spontaneity also is to be self-contradictory.

Question: What does it mean to say that there are causes but no effects?

Answer: According to those who hold the view that things will come to an end,[15] there is only the present but no future. Plants, for example, last for one season only.

Our objection to the theory is this: The spiritual principle (Buddhism)

[13] *Chuang Tzu*, ch. 2, NHCC, 1:46b. See Giles, trans., *Chuang Tzu*, 1961 ed., p. 47.

[14] Quoting *Lao Tzu*, ch. 2.

[15] This view, and the view that things are eternal, are considered two heterodoxical extremes.

is abstruse and profound, but deluded people are very much deceived. Moral principles have been gone through by Confucius but are still not clear.[16] Principle has been gone through by Duke Chou[17] but it is still in the dark. Buddhism alone can show its utmost. The scripture says:

> Suppose a bird is inside a vase,
> Whose opening is covered with silk.
> When the silk is torn and the bird flies away,
> The body is destroyed but the spirit has gone away.[18]

Hui-yüan (334-416) of K'uang-shan[19] said, "The transmission of fire in the firewood is similar to the transmission of the spirit in the body. Fire is transmitted to another piece of firewood in the same way as the spirit is transmitted to another body. The earlier firewood is not the same as the later one. From this we know that the art is wonderful for fingers to supply no more [firewood while the fire is transmitted elsewhere].[20] The former body is not the later body. From this we realize that the feeling about man's destiny[21] is deep. When we see that the body of one life perishes, we must not say that consciousness and spirit die with it, and when we see the fire ending with one piece of wood, we must not say that the time is up and all is finished."[22] A latter-day scholar[23] quoted the words of the Yellow Emperor,[24] saying, "Although the body has decomposed, the spirit does not disintegrate. It goes along with the transformations [of the universe] and changes infinitely."[25] Although the saying does not explicitly talk about the three periods (past, present and future periods of existence), the idea is clear that [the past, the present, and] the future are continuous.

[16] Confucius was believed to have edited the Classics and thus expounded moral principles. The point here is that Confucius and Duke Chou understood moral and mundane principles but not spiritual principles.

[17] D. 1094 B.C. He was highly praised by Confucius and was a sage to Confucianists. He was credited with having written the text and explanations of the lines in the *Book of Changes* in which natural principles are subtly explained.

[18] *Ch'i-nü ching* (Scripture on the Seven Princesses), TSD, 85:1459.

[19] Another name for Mount Lu, the famous center for Buddhism at Hui-yüan's time.

[20] Referring to *Chuang Tzu*, ch. 3, NHCC, 2:6b. See Giles, p. 50.

[21] *Ch'ing-shu*, the allotted number or fate of sentient beings.

[22] *Hung-ming chi* (Essays Elucidating the Doctrine), SPPY, 5:10a.

[23] The phrase "the questioner asked" at the head of this sentence is superfluous, according to the *San-lun hsüan-i yu-meng* (Instructions for Beginners on the *Profound Meaning of the Three Treatises*), pt. 2, TSD, 70:534. In Hui-yüan's treatise, the scholar's name Wen Tzu is mentioned (*Hung-ming chi*, 5:10a). He was a mythical figure supposed to have been Lao Tzu's pupil.

[24] Legendary emperor of great antiquity.

[25] *Hung-ming chi*, 5:10a. In the present *Wen Tzu*, sec. 13 (SPPY, pt. 1, p. 21a), the words are attributed not to the Yellow Emperor but to Lao Tzu.

Question: What does it mean to say that there are neither causes nor effects?

Answer: It means that the idea of receiving the fruits of action in a later life is rejected and that there are also no present causes. This is why the six teachers[26] said that there are no evil deeds or their recompense, and there are no good deeds or their recompense. Of the four perverse doctrines, this is the most harmful. It cuts off good for the present and produces an evil state of life for the future.... (*San-lun hsüan-i*, pt. 1, TSD, 45:1)

> *Comment.* We see here the Four Points of Argumentation at work. The various theories on cause and effect are reduced to four: theories of ens, of non-ens, of both ens and non-ens, and neither ens nor non-ens. This pattern of thought is prominent not only in the Three-Treatise School but in other Buddhist schools as well. Some Buddhist scholars maintain that, generally speaking, Western thought has not gone beyond the third stage, that of "both-and," whereas the fourth stage of "neither-nor" has been reached in Emptiness which defies all descriptions. But does not the Absolute in Western thought include all, the negative as well as the positive?

3. The Four Subsidiary Causes

Question: Why does the study of Abhidharma[27] result in a perverse view?

Answer: If one says [as does the Abhidharma School] that the Four Causes produce all the dharmas, then who produces the Four Causes? If the Four Causes are produced by something else, then that something

---

[26] Pūraṇa Kāśyapa, Maskarī-Gośāliputra, Sañjaya, Vairāṭīputra, Ajita Keśakambala, Kakuda Kātyāyana, and Nirgrantha Jñatiputra, all contemporaries of the Buddha. See *Vimalakīrtinirdeśa sūtra* (Scripture Spoken by Vimalakīrti), sec. 3, TSD, 14:540.

[27] The Abhidharma School is an old Hīnayāna (Small Vehicle) school whose origin is traced to the third century B.C. It was introduced into China in the fourth century A.D. It maintains that all dharmas are real and that they are produced by the Six Primary Causes and Four Subsidiary Causes. The Six Primary Causes are (1) the Active Cause, or the leading factor, (2) the Coexistent Cause, or a cause working with another, (3) the Similar-species Cause, or a cause helping other causes of its kind, (4) the Concomitant Cause, or a cause making an effect arise under any circumstance, (5) the Universally Prevalent Cause, a cause always connected with wrong views which produce all the errors of men, and (6) the Cause Ripening at Later Times, a cause which produces its effect later. The Four Subsidiary Causes are (1) the Cause Condition, or the chief condition which acts as the chief cause, for example, the wind and water that cause the wave, (2) the Immediate Condition, which immediately follows a preceding condition, such as waves following one another, (3) the Objective Condition, or the objective environment, like the basis or the boat, and (4) the Upheaving Condition, the condition that brings all conditions to the climax, such as the last wave that upsets the boat.

else must be produced by something else again, and so on to infinity. If the Four Causes exist of themselves and are not produced by something else, then the myriad things, too, must not be produced by the Four Causes, and should fall into the condition of having no cause at all. Therefore if things are produced by something else, the process would be unlimited, and if there is a limit, there is no cause. From these two points, one may not believe in the existence of causes or effects. Therefore if one studies the Abhidharma for long, a perverse view will result . . . . (*ibid.*, TSD, 45:3)

> *Comment.* The problem of causality is one of the most important in Buddhist schools. It is central in the Three-Treatise School, because its basic concept of Emptiness is untenable unless causality is rejected. The four causes here remind one of Aristotle and Scholasticism. They also underlie the fact that all Buddhist schools think of plurality of causes and effects instead of the one-to-one relationship between cause and effect. They, of course, all reject the First Cause. It is also interesting to note that the argument against the First Cause here is practically the same as that advanced by Taoists. As the Shadow in the *Chuang Tzu* asks, "Do I depend on something else to be this way? Does this something on which I depend also depend on something else?"[28]

4. *Existence, Nonexistence, and Emptiness*

Question: If both other Buddhist schools and heterodoxical schools are denounced and both the Mahāyāna (Great Vehicle) and Hīnayāna (Small Vehicle) are refuted, what is the basis of your discussion?

Answer: If one's mind still dwells on Buddhist or heterodoxical schools or if one's feelings still linger around the Mahāyāna or Hīnayāna, one will fall into one-sided perversion and lose sight of correct principle (*li*). If correct principle is lost sight of, correct view will not arise. If correct view does not arise, then the views that things come to an end and that they are eternal will not be eliminated. If they are not eliminated, the wheel of suffering will forever turn, for only when both Buddhist and heterodoxical schools are taken out of sight[29] and both the Mahāyāna and Hīnayāna are silenced can there be anything called correct principle. As this correct principle is understood, correct view will arise. And when correct view arises, then nonsensical discussion will cease. When nonsensical discussion ceases, the wheel of suffering will be destroyed. This is the general principle of the Three Treatises. It summarizes all conclusions of the various schools and combines the spiritual

[28] See above, p. 190.
[29] The word *ming* means literally dark or to disappear.

storehouses (merits) of the many sages. Do people who love the Way not rest on this principle?

Question: If both other Buddhist schools and heterodoxical schools are rejected and both the Mahāyāna and Hīnayāna are refuted, this is a [perverse] view that things come to an end. How can it be called a correct doctrine?

Answer: Once they are taken out of sight, then both theories that things come to an end and that things are eternal are silenced. When the two extremes are abandoned, is that not correct doctrine?

Objection: As things come to an end or are eternal, we say that they exist, and as they neither come to an end nor are eternal, we say that they are nonexistent. Since [you virtually say] they are nonexistent, how can [your view] be separated from the view that things come to an end?

Answer: Once the theories that things come to an end or are eternal are silenced, then existence, nonexistence, and so forth, are all eliminated. One may no longer say that our doctrine is defiled by the concept of non-existence.

Objection: Although you have this way out, at the end you cannot escape objection. When there is the existence of being and when there is the existence of non-being, we say there is existence. And when there is nonexistence of either being or non-being, there is then great nonexistence. Since you have already fallen into the concept of nonexistence, how can you be separated from the view that things come to an end?

Answer: The idea of nonexistence is presented primarily to handle the disease of the concept of existence. If that disease disappears, the useless medicine is also discarded. Thus we know that the Way of the sage has never held to either existence or nonexistence. What obstacle can there be?

Objection: To affirm both existence and nonexistence is a double affirmation. To negate both existence and nonexistence is a double negation. Since you have fallen into affirmation and negation, you are, after all, the same as the Confucianists and Moists.[30]

Answer: Our double negation is primarily intended to negate the double affirmation. Once the double affirmation is forgotten, the double negation also ceases. Thus we know that to negate an affirmation is also to negate a negation.

Objection: To negate both an affirmation and a negation is after all to fall into a double negation. How can you escape negation?

---

[30] This refers to *Chuang Tzu*, ch. 2, NHCC, 1:26b-27a, Giles, p. 37. Chuang Tzu severely criticized the Confucianists and Moists for their one-sided opinions, on the basis of which they engaged in extensive controversy.

Answer: A double affirmation produces a dream tiger, and a double negation reveals a flower in the air. Thus we know that originally there is nothing to affirm and there is not now anything to negate.

Objection: If there is neither affirmation nor negation, then there is neither perverseness nor correctness. Why in the beginning section do you call it "demolishing the perverse" and "showing the correct"?

Answer: It is considered perverse to affirm or negate. It is said to be correct only when there is neither affirmation nor negation. We therefore called the section "explaining the demolition of perverseness and the showing of correctness."

Objection: Since you say there are perverseness to demolish and correctness to show, then you have the intention of clinging or discarding. How can you say you are not attached to anything?

Answer: We are forced to use the word "correct" in order to stop the perverseness. Once perverseness has been stopped, correctness will no longer remain. Therefore the mind is attached to nothing.

Objection: If one wants both perverseness and correctness to disappear, is this not a view of Emptiness [itself an affirmation]?

Answer: The *Cheng-kuan lun* (Treatise on the Correct View) says:

> The Great Sage preached the Law of Emptiness
> In order to free men from all [personal] views.
> If one still holds the view that Emptiness exists,
> Such a person the Buddhas will not transform.[31]

If, while ordinarily fire can extinguish fire, now it produces fire instead, what shall we use to destroy it? The view that things come to an end or are eternal is fire, and Emptiness can destroy it. But if one is still attached to Emptiness, then there is no medicine that can eliminate the disease.

Objection: Since one is attached to the disease of Emptiness, why talk about giving up his transformation instead of giving him the medicine of existence?

Answer: If one tries to transform by means of the concept of existence, one becomes impeded by it instead. If, on the other hand, one goes so far as to forget all words, one will then become attached to the view that things come to an end. How can persons like these be transformed?

Question: What is wrong for the mind to have attachment?

Answer: If the mind is attached to something, it is bound to it and cannot be emancipated from birth and old age, sickness and death, sorrow and grief, and suffering and distress. Therefore the *Lotus Scripture* says, "I (the Buddha) have used an infinite number of convenient means

[31] Also called *Chung lun* (*Mādhymika śāstra*), ch. 6, sec. 24, TSD, 30:32-33.

to lead sentient beings and to enable them to be free from various attachments."[32] The *Ching-ming* (Fame for Purity) says:

> [The Buddha] is unattached to the mundane world and is
>   like the lotus flower.
> He is always skillful in entering into the paths of emptiness
>   and silence.
> He penetrates the characters of the various dharmas and
>   has no more impediment or obstruction.
> Bow your head [to Him who is] like space and leans to
>   nothing. . . .[33]

(*ibid.*, TSD, 45:6-7)

5. Substance and Function

Question: How many kinds of correctness are there?

Answer:. . . The first is correctness in substance and the second is correctness in function. Correctness in substance means that it is neither absolute nor worldly, and correctness in function means being both absolute and worldly. The reason for this is that the true nature[34] of all dharmas is entirely inexplicable in speech and unrealizable in thought. As it has never been either absolute or worldly, it is therefore called substance. It is regarded as correct because it is completely cut off from all kinds of one-sidedness and perverseness. This is why we speak of correctness in substance. The reason why we speak of correctness in function is that if substance is completely cut off from names and words, things cannot be understood. Although it is neither existent nor nonexistent, we are forced to speak of it as absolute and worldly. Therefore we called it function. It is regarded as correct because this being both absolute and worldly is not one-sided or perverse. Therefore we called it correctness in function.

Question: Since you have already spoken of being absolute and being worldly, it means two extremes. How can you call that correctness?

Answer: Things are produced by causes and therefore have dependent existence. That is regarded as worldly. But dependent existence should not be said to be definitely existent, nor should it be said to be definitely nonexistent. This type of dependent existence is far from the two ex-

---

[32] *Saddharmapuṇḍarīka sūtra*, ch. 1, TSD, 9:5. Cf. Soothill, trans., *The Lotus of the Wonderful Law*, p. 65. The point has not been brought out in Soothill's paraphrase.

[33] Ch. 1, TSD, 14:538. *Fame for Purity* is another title for the *Vimalakīrtinirdés sūtra* (Scripture Spoken by Vimalakīrti). It is what the name Vimalakīrti means.

[34] This is *lakshaṇa* in Sanskrit, meaning character, features, form, appearance, etc. True character, however, means essential character, that is, nature.

tremes and is therefore called correctness. Worldly existence being what it is and absolute nonexistence also being what it is, dependent nonexistence should not be said to be either definitely nonexistent or definitely existent. It is far from the two extremes, and is therefore regarded as correct. . . . (*ibid.*, TSD, 45:7)

23

BUDDHIST IDEALISM: HSÜAN-TSANG OF THE CONSCIOUSNESS-ONLY SCHOOL

IN SUBTLETY of concepts and refinement of analysis, the Consciousness-Only School[1] is the most philosophical of Buddhist schools. Originally called Yogācāra (way of yoga), it was founded by Asaṅga (c.410–c.500) for the purpose of mystical enlightenment through metaphysical reflections. When his younger brother Vasubandhu (c.420–c.500) systematized and developed its philosophical views, he designated its tenet as Consciousness-Only. It and the Three-Treatise School dominated the Chinese intellectual scene and rivaled each other from the fifth to the seventh century.

The school first existed as the She-lun School[2] but was eventually replaced by the Consciousness-Only School of Hsüan-tsang[3] (596-664). Not being satisfied with the conflicting doctrines of his time, he went to India in 629 and for sixteen years studied and debated with the greatest Indian scholars. When he returned in 645, he brought, among other things, 657 Buddhist works, and under imperial patronage he and a large group of assistants, in the largest translation project in Chinese history, devoted some twenty years to translating seventy-five of them, mostly Yogācāra works.[4]

The essentials of the Yogācāra School are summed up in Vasubandhu's *Vijñatimātratātrimśika* (Treatise in Thirty Verses on Consciousness-Only).[5] Ten Indian philosophers, including Dharmapāla (439-507), elaborated on the meaning of these verses. Hsüan-tsang selected, summarized, and systematized their interpretations, following chiefly Dharmapāla, and the result is his famous *Ch'eng-wei-shih lun* (*Vijñaptimātratāsiddhi*, or Treatise on the Establishment of the Doctrine of

---

[1] *Wei-shih* in China, *yuishiki* in Japanese, and *vijñaptimātra* in Sanskrit.

[2] Named after Asaṅga's *Mahāyānasamparigraha* (Acceptance of the Great Vehicle) annotated by Vasubandhu, translated into Chinese in 531, 563, and 648-649 (this time by Hsüan-tsang), and known as the *She ta-ch'eng lun* (Treatise on Acceptance of the Great Vehicle). For a French translation, see Bibliography.

[3] Variously spelled as Hsüan-chang, Hiuen-tsang, etc.

[4] He entered a monastery of the Pure Land School at thirteen. From 618 he went to monasteries in Ch'ang-an, Ch'eng-tu, and other places and studied the doctrines taught in those places. In search of the true doctrine, he left China against imperial order. But when he returned he was given an overwhelming welcome at the capital and when he died the emperor suspended audiences for three days. For his biography see *Hsü kao-seng chuan* (Supplement to the *Biographies of Eminent Monks*), chs. 4-5, TSD, 50:446-459.

[5] The Chinese title for this is *Wei-shih san-shih lun*. For translations, see Bibliography.

Consciousness-Only).[6] His prose is excellent, and he created such a neat and consistent vocabulary that his works are directly comprehensible without resorting to the original Sanskrit. Nevertheless, the Chinese language was ill equipped to translate the intricate and difficult philosophy. During the translation, his pupil K'uei-chi (632-682)[7] took many notes, which come to sixty long chapters. Without his *Ch'eng-wei-shih lun shu-chi* (Notes on the *Treatise on the Establishment of the Doctrine of Consciousness-Only*), it is impossible to get at the real meaning of Hsüan-tsang's treatise. Even with it, we are not sure whether the Consciousness-Only philosophy presented by Hsüan-tsang is originally Vasubandhu's, for it has now gone through two interpretations, first by Dharmapāla and then by Hsüan-tsang. This fact is of tremendous importance. Does his very selection not indicate the direction in which Buddhist philosophy was developing in China?

The central doctrine of the school is that of eight consciousnesses. No other philosophy has ever analyzed the mind into so many parts. According to the school, the eight consciousnesses, that is, the five sense-consciousnesses, the sixth or sense-center consciousness (*manovijñāna*) which forms conceptions, the seventh or thought-center consciousness (*manasvijñāna*) which wills and reasons on a self-centered basis, and the eighth or storehouse consciousness (*ālaya*), are in perpetual change which involves a threefold transformation. The first transformation is the storehouse consciousness. It is so called because it stores the "seed" or effects of good and evil deeds which exist from time immemorial and become the energy to produce manifestation. This storehouse consciousness is in constant flux, constantly "perfumed" (influenced) by incoming perceptions and cognitions from external manifestations. At the same time, it endows perceptions and cognitions with the energy of the seeds, which in turn produce manifestations. According to the stock saying of the school:

> A seed produces a manifestation;
> A manifestation perfumes a seed;
> The three elements (seed, manifestation, and perfuming)
>   turn on and on;
> The cause and effect occur at one and the same time.

This is the basic consciousness. All others are "stored" in it and depend on it for their own transformation. The second transformation, which constitutes the seventh or thought-center consciousness, trans-

[6] For a French translation, see Bibliography.

[7] For K'uei-chi's biography, see *Sung Kao-seng chuan* (Biographies of Eminent Monks Compiled in the Sung Period [988]), ch. 4, TSD, 50:725-726.

forms with the storehouse consciousness and, unlike the first six consciousnesses, has as its object not the external world but the *ālaya* itself. Its special function is intellectual deliberation, which clings to the *ālaya* consciousness and considers it to be the self. Its operation is deep and uninterrupted and is always accompanied by the evils of self-interest.

The third transformation consists of the five sense-consciousnesses and the sixth or sense-center consciousness. They are characterized by discrimination and differentiation out of which the external world appears. The difference between the sixth and the first five is that while each of the five has its own sphere of objects,[8] the sixth takes the external world as a whole as its object. In this sense it is self-centered but not to the degree of the seventh, which is free from the external world. Because these six consciousnesses have external things as their objects, they are conditioned by them and are therefore crude, superficial, and discontinuous.

All these transformations take place at the same time and influence each other. They are all governed by cause and effect. The law of cause and effect is a cardinal one in Buddhism, but in no other school is it so closely bound with its central thesis. It must be noted, however, that this law is applied here purely in a speculative fashion, with neither historical nor scientific support.

The school further analyzes each consciousness into four functional portions, namely, the objective portion, the subjective portion, the self-witnessing portion, and the rewitnessing portion. That is to say that each idea not only involves the seeing and the seen, but the witnessing of the experience by the self, which witnessing will then be witnessed once more. It is out of this complicated process of deliberation and discrimination that the external world appears. The result is a world of differentiated dharmas (elements of existence)[9] each with its own specific characters.[10] It is to these dharma-characters that the school has directed its attention. Of Vasubandhu's thirty verses, the first twenty are devoted to them. Consequently the school is also known as the Fa-hsiang or Dharma-character School.

The characters of dharmas are classified into three different kinds. Those "conceived by vast imagination," like horns of a rabbit, are purely illusory and therefore have only false existence. Those which "depend on others for production" have purely temporary or dependent

---

[8] *Vishaya* in Sanskrit and *ching* in Chinese, meaning the sphere or realm in which the mind gropes for an object which is its own imagination. In its various contexts, it means the external world, external objects, the sphere of color and the eye, the sphere of sound and ear, etc., domain of perception, and the like.

[9] For the translation of "dharma," see Appendix, comment on *Fa*.

[10] *Lakshaṇa in Sanskrit*. See Appendix, comment on *Hsiang*.

existence, for they depend on causes for their production and have no nature of their own. Only those of the "nature of perfect reality" have true existence. This perfect reality transcends all specific characters. It is simply Thusness or Suchness (*Tathatā*), the Ultimate Reality.[11] This reality will be realized when through discipline and enlightenment the pure seeds in the storehouse consciousness are cultivated and the impure aspect of the storehouse is overcome.

This type of philosophy is completely alien to the Chinese tradition so that, like the Three-Treatise School, it was merely an Indian system transplanted on Chinese soil. However, its emphasis on dharma-characters, that is, on the mundane world, may have been due to the mundane character of Chinese thought. As indicated before, it may have been Hsüan-tsang's own choice. Unfortunately, in spite of this mundane tendency, it did not survive the Chinese climate and rapidly declined since the ninth century. The persecution of Buddhism in 845 dealt all Buddhist schools a serious blow. Within Buddhism itself, forces were at work to bring about its decline. In the seventh century, the Consciousness-Only and the Zen (Meditation or Ch'an) Schools were the two major movements in Chinese Buddhism, one essentially a classical movement and the other romantic.[12] The romantic movement, because of its affinity with Taoism, gradually soared to great heights and overshadowed the Consciousness-Only School. At the same time the Hua-yen School, which was growing in influence, relegated it to the position of "elementary doctrine" in the Mahāyāna (Great Vehicle) far below other Buddhist schools, because it advocated that some people, being devoid of Buddha-nature, can never achieve Buddhahood, thus clearly betraying the Mahāyāna ideal of universal salvation. Its own philosophy was too abstract for the practical Chinese mind. Its texts are the most difficult to read (and to translate!). Above all, its hair-splitting analysis was not harmonious with the Chinese spirit of synthesis. Besides, its most important texts were lost and forgotten during the Yüan period (1271-1368). With these basic works gone, both knowledge and interest evaporated. Its influence on Neo-Confucianism is negligible, if any. Wang Fu-chih (1619-1692) showed an interest in it but few other scholars did until the late nineteenth century. In the 1880's, a number of Buddhist texts were brought back to China from Japan, including K'uei-chi's *Notes*. This aroused immediate and strong interest. The leading authority on Chinese studies, Chang Ping-lin (Chang T'ai-yen, 1868-1936) wrote a commentary on the second chapter of the *Chuang Tzu*

[11] On this concept, see below, ch. 24, n.19.

[12] This characterization is by Hu Shih (1891-1962). See his *Chung-kuo chung-ku ssu-hsiang shih ti t'i-yao* (Essentials of the History of Medieval Chinese Thought), 1932, p. 28a.

in terms of Consciousness-Only philosophy. China was by this time on the eve of the Intellectual Renaissance. New systems of thought were being introduced, and European idealism was becoming popular. The new scientific spirit made analysis attractive. Two Buddhist scholars, layman Ou-yang Ching-wu (1871-1943) and Abbot T'ai-hsü (1889-1947) revived the philosophy and created two strong movements in the twentieth century.[13] Actually they contributed little that was new except to revive the old. It is in Hsiung Shih-li that the Consciousness-Only philosophy has been used constructively, that is, as a stimulation to his idealism which is his reconstruction of Neo-Confucian idealistic philosophy.[14]

The following are selections from Hsüan-tsang's *Ch'eng wei-shih lun*, including all the thirty verses by Vasubandhu.

THE TREATISE ON THE ESTABLISHMENT OF THE DOCTRINE OF CONSCIOUSNESS-ONLY

1. The Nonexistence of the Self

1. Because the ideas of the self (*atman*) and dharmas are
       [constructions produced by causes and therefore][15] false,
    Their characters of all kinds arise.[16]
    These characters are [constructions] based on the transfor-
       mations of consciousness,
    Which are of three kinds.

2a. They are the consciousness (the eighth or storehouse
       consciousness) whose fruits (retribution) ripen at later
       times,
    The consciousness (the seventh or thought-center con-
       sciousness) that deliberates, and the consciousness (the
       sense-center consciousness and the five sense conscious-
       ness) that discriminates spheres of objects.

The Treatise says:

Both the world and sacred doctrines declare that the self and dharmas are merely constructions based on false ideas and have no reality of their

---

[13] For their movements, philosophies, and controversy, see Chan, *Religious Trends in Modern China*, pp. 105-126.

[14] See below, ch. 43.

[15] This insertion is based on K'uei-chi's *Ch'eng wei-shih lun shu-chi*, Nanking edition, 1901, 2:82. This work is included in TSD, 43:229-606. The Nanking edition is used here for more precise reference.

[16] *Chuan*, literally to change, to turn, to transform, means "to become different because of the constructions," according to Hsüan-tsang, p. 1, and "to arise," according to K'uei-chi, 2:17a.

own. . . . On what basis are [the self and dharmas] produced?[17] Their characters are all constructions based on the evolution and transformation of consciousness. . . .

How do we know that there is really no sphere of objects but only inner consciousness which produces what seem to be the external spheres of objects? Because neither the real self nor the real dharma is possible.

Why is the real self impossible? Theories of the self held by the various schools may be reduced to three kinds. The first holds that the substance of the self is eternal, universal, and as extensive as empty space.[18] It acts anywhere and as a consequence enjoys happiness or suffers sorrow. The second holds that although the substance of the self is eternal, its extension is indeterminate, because it expands or contracts according to the size of the body.[19] The third holds that the substance of the self is eternal and infinitesimal like an atom, lying deeply and moving around within the body and thus acts.[20]

The first theory is contrary to reason. Why? If it is held that the self is eternal, universal, and as extensive as empty space, it should not enjoy happiness or suffer sorrow along with the body. Furthermore, being eternal and universal, it should be motionless. How can it act along with the body? Again, is the self so conceived the same or different among all sentient beings? If it is the same, when one being acts, receives the fruits of action, or achieves salvation, all beings should do the same. But this would of course be a great mistake. If it is different, then the selves of all sentient beings would universally penetrate one another and their substance would be mixed, and since the field of abode of all selves is the same, the acts of one being or the fruits of action received by him should be the act or fruits of all beings. If it is said that action and fruits belong to each being separately and there would not be the mistake just described, such a contention is also contrary to reason, because action, fruits, and body are identified with all selves and it is unreasonable for them to belong to one self but not to another. When one is saved, all should be saved, for the Dharma (truth) practiced and realized would be identical with all selves.

The second theory is also contrary to reason. Why? If in substance the self always remains in the same state, it should not expand or contract along with the body. If it expands or contracts like wind in a bag or a pipe, it is not always remaining in the same state. Furthermore, if the

[17] Addition according to K'uei-chi, 2:17b.

[18] The Sāṁkhya and Vaiśeshika schools, etc., according to K'uei-chi, 3:11b. See nn.30 and 34.

[19] The Nirgrantha school, etc., according to K'uei-chi, 3:12a. See n.36.

[20] The Pāśupata school, etc., according to K'uei-chi, 3:12b.

self follows the body, it would be divisible. How can it be held that the substance of the self is one? What this school says is like child's play.

The last theory is also contrary to reason. Why? Since the self is infinitesimal like an atom, how can it cause the whole big body [that extends throughout the world of form][21] to move? If it is said that although it is small it goes through the body like a whirling wheel of fire so that the whole body seems to move, then the self so conceived is neither one nor eternal, for what comes and goes is neither eternal nor one.

Furthermore, there are three additional theories of the self. The first holds that the self is identical with the aggregates[22] (namely, matter,[23] sensation, thought, disposition, and consciousness).[24] The second holds that it is separated from the aggregates.[25] And the third holds that it is neither identical with nor separated from the aggregates.[26] The first theory is contrary to reason, for the self would be like the aggregates and is therefore neither eternal nor one. Furthermore, the internal matters (the five senses) are surely not the real self, for they are physically obstructed (or restricted) like external matters. The mind and mental qualities are not the real self either, for they are not always continuous and depend on various causes to be produced. Other conditioned things and matters are also not the real self, for like empty space they are without intelligence.

The second theory is also contrary to reason, for the self would then be like empty space, which neither acts nor receives fruits of action.

The last theory is also contrary to reason. This theory allows that the self is based on the aggregates but is neither identical with nor separated from them. The self would then be like a vase [which depends on clay] and has no reality of its own. Also, since it is impossible to say whether it is produced from causes or not produced from causes, it is also impossible to say whether it is a self or not. Therefore the real self conceived in the theory cannot be established.

Again, does the substance of the real self conceived by the various schools think or not? If it does, it would not be eternal, because it does not think all the time. If it does not, it would be like empty space, which neither acts nor receives fruits of action. Therefore on the basis of reason, the self conceived by the theory cannot be established.

[21] Interpretation according to K'uei-chi, 3:18b.

[22] In Buddhist philosophy, a thing is but a combination of these five aggregates or *skandhas*.

[23] Matter, *rūpa* in Sanskrit and *se* in Chinese, refers to form, color, appearance, phenomenon, etc.

[24] The Yogācāra school, according to K'uei-chi, 3:19b.

[25] The three theories refuted above, according to K'uei-chi, *ibid.*

[26] The Vātsīputrīya school, according to K'uei-chi, *ibid.*

Again, does this substance of the real self conceived by the various schools perform any function or not? If it does, it would be like hands and feet and would not be eternal. If it does not, it would be like [illusory] horns of a hare and not the real self. Therefore in either case, the self conceived by them cannot be established.

Again, is the substance of the real self conceived by the various schools an object of the view of the self or not? If it is not, how do advocates of the theory know that there is really a self? If it is, then there should be a view of the self that does not involve any perversion, for that would be knowledge of what really is. In that case, how is it that the perfectly true doctrines believed in by those holding the theory of the self all denounce the view of the self and praise the view of the non-self? [Advocates of the theory themselves][27] declare that the view of the non-self will lead to Nirvāṇa while clinging to the view of the self will lead to sinking in the sea of life and death (transmigration). Does an erroneous view ever lead to Nirvāṇa and a correct view, on the contrary, lead to transmigration?

Again, the various views of the self [actually] do not take the real self as an object, because it has objects [which are not itself] like the mind takes others [such as external matters][28] as objects. The object of the view of the self is certainly not the real self, because it [the view] is an object like other dharmas. Therefore the view of the self does not take the real self as an object. Only because the various aggregates are transformed and manifested by inner consciousness, all kinds of imagination and conjecture result in accordance with one's own erroneous opinions . . . . (ch. 1, TSD, 31:1-2).

> *Comment.* The denial of the ego is the starting point of Buddhist philosophy in general and the Consciousness-Only School in particular. The idealism of Berkeley and that of this school are very much alike. But while Berkeley's philosophy is built on the assumption of individual minds and therefore finds itself in an "ego-centric predicament," Buddhist idealism rejects the ego to start with and is therefore able to be free from solipsism.

2. The Nonexistence of Dharmas

Although the variety of heterodoxical schools is great, their theories of existent dharmas[29] are only of four kinds. The first, like the Sāṁkhyas[30]

---

[27] Insertion following K'uei-chi, 4:5a.

[28] This insertion according to K'uei-chi, 4:6a.

[29] Dharmas of being, in contrast with dharmas of non-being, like horns of a rabbit.

[30] One of the Six Systems of philosophy in India, probably the oldest. Its name means number, because it interprets reality in terms of a number of categories. It

and others, holds that existent dharmas and the nature of being[31] and so forth[32] are definitely identical in substance. Their theory is contrary to reason. Why? Because it must not be held that all dharmas are identical with the nature of being. If they are all the same as the nature of being, there would be no difference in their substance. This would contradict [the Sāṁkhya theory that][33] the three qualities [of goodness, activity, negativity of matter], the self, and so forth are different in substance. It would also contradict the fact that in the world the various dharmas are different. Furthermore, if color and so forth are identical with the nature of color and so forth, they should not be differentiated as green, yellow, and the like.

The second, like the Vaiśeshika[34] and so forth, holds that existent dharmas and the nature of being and so forth are definitely different in substance. Their theory is also contrary to reason. Why? Because it must not be held that dharmas are different from the nature of being. If they are extinct and no longer exist, they cannot possess any substance. This would contradict [the Vaiśeshika theory that][35] substance and other categories are not without nature of their own. It would also contradict the fact that in the world things evidently exist. Furthermore, if color and so forth are not identical with the nature of color and so forth they, like sound, would not be objective spheres of vision.

The third, like the Nirgrantha[36] and others, holds that existent dharmas

---

holds that primal matter (*prakṛti*), the ultimate cause of the world of objects, whether physical or psychical, is moved by spirit (*purusha*), another ultimate principle, to interact with it, thus evolving the world. The products of this evolution are successively the intellect, the ego, the five organs of perception, the five motor organs, the five generic essences of sound, touch, smell, color, and taste, and the five gross physical elements of earth, water, fire, air, and ether. These, plus the two ultimate principles of spirit and matter, constitute the 25 categories.

[31] Meaning the categories of substance, quality, and action of the Vaiśeshika School described in n.34.

[32] According to K'uei-chi (6:21b), these are the Vaiśeshika categories of generality and particularity.

[33] According to K'uei-chi, 6:22a.

[34] Another of the Six Systems. It is an atomistic philosophy stressing particularity or differentiation, which is what the name means. According to the school, the world of multiplicity is the product of the combination of material atoms of various kinds and qualities. It is described in terms of six positive categories, namely, substances (nine kinds such as earth and water), qualities (24 kinds, such as color, smell, pleasure, pain, desire, and tendency), action (five kinds), generality, particularity, and inherence. Besides these there are negative categories. At the same time the school is theistic, for in its theory the world is created and destroyed by God according to the moral deserts of individual souls, although He is not the author of the order of nature or the atoms, minds, and souls.

[35] Following K'uei-chi, 6:23a.

[36] A minor school, called the Shameless School, which believed that sorrow and happiness depend on the Great Lord of the Universe (Maheśvara, Great Self-Existent Heaven) and one is not responsible for one's moral action and therefore should be shameless.

and the nature of being and so forth are both identical and different. Their theory is wrong. Why? Because they are mistaken about identity as the first theory and about difference as the second. The two characters of identity and difference are mutually exclusive and should be differentiated in substance, and it is impossible for identity and difference to share the same substance. It must not be held that all dharmas are of the same substance or that they should be simultaneously identical and different. This view is false and not true but is held to be true. It is certainly contrary to reason.

The fourth, like the Ajivikas[37] and others, holds that existent dharmas are neither identical with nor different from the nature of beings and so forth. Their theory is contrary to reason. Why? Because the theory that existent dharmas are neither identical with nor different from the nature of beings is virtually the same as the theory that existent dharmas are both identical with and different from the nature of beings. Is the expression "neither identical with nor different from" an affirmation or a denial? If it is an affirmation, the double negation should not be used. If it is purely a denial, then no theory should be held. If it is both an affirmation and a denial, it is self-contradictory. And if it is neither an affirmation nor a denial, it is nonsense. Furthermore, such a doctrine contradicts the fact that the whole world knows that one thing differs from another. It also contradicts the doctrine of the schools themselves, which hold that existent dharmas such as color are definitely real. . . . (ch. 1, TSD, 31:3-4)

> *Comment.* The Four Points of Argumentation are here employed to refute the doctrines of existence of dharmas.[38] Whether the logic is sound or not, it cannot be denied that Buddhist thinking is rational and methodical, absolutely contrary to the common belief, even among some scholars, that the only mental activity of the Buddhist is intuition. It is significant that in a school chiefly concerned with the thinking process, the rationalistic and methodical elements are so strong.

3. The First Transformation of Consciousness

From what is said above it is clear that the self and dharmas separated from consciousness conceived by the heterodoxical and other schools are all unreal. . . . From this we ought to know that there is really no external sphere of objects. There is only inner consciousness which produces what seems to be the external sphere. . . .

The characters transformed by consciousness are infinite in variety,

---

[37] Literally, people who live on others by improper means.
[38] For the Four Points, see above, ch. 22, comment in sec. 2.

but the consciousnesses that transform can be divided into three kinds. The first is the consciousness where fruits ripen at a later time. It is the eighth consciousness. [It is so called] because it possesses in abundance the nature to ripen at later times. The second is called deliberation. It is the seventh consciousness. [It is so called] because it is continuously in the process of deliberation. The third is called the consciousness that discriminates spheres of objects. It is the same as the first six consciousnesses (the five sense-consciousnesses and the sense-center consciousness). [It is so called] because it discriminates gross spheres of objects....

2b. First of all, the storehouse consciousness (ālaya),
   Which brings into fruition all seeds (effects of good and evil deeds).
3. [In its state of pure consciousness] it is not conscious of its clingings and sensations.
   In both its objective and subjective functions it is always associated with contact,
   Volition, sensation, thought, and cognition.
   But it is always indifferent to its associations.
4. It is not affected by the darkness of ignorance or by an indifference to good and evil.
   The same is true in the case of touch and so forth.
   It is always flowing like a torrent,
   And is renounced in the state of the arhat (a saint who enters Nirvāṇa).[39]

The Treatise says:

The first transformation of consciousness is called storehouse in both the Mahāyāna and Hīnayāna. . . . Why are the seeds so called? They mean that functions and differentiations in the root consciousness (the eighth) spontaneously produce their own fruition. These are neither the same with nor different from the root consciousness itself or their fruition. . . . (ch. 2, TSD, 31:7-8)

In this way the other consciousnesses which "perfume" (affect) it and the consciousness which is perfumed arise and perish together, and the concept of perfuming is thus established. The act of enabling the seeds that lie within what is perfumed (the storehouse consciousness) to grow, as the hemp plant is perfumed, is called perfuming. As soon as the seeds are produced, the consciousnesses which can perfume become in their turn causes which perfume and produce seeds. The three dharmas (the

---

[39] Arhat or arhan, the worthy or saint, who is no longer bound in the cycle of life and death or transmigration. He is the ideal being in the Hīnayāna or Small Vehicle.

seeds, the manifestations, and perfuming) turn on and on, simultaneously acting as cause and effect. . . . (ch. 2, TSD, 31:9-10)

Comment. Did this idea of seeds as a generative force have any influence on Ch'eng Hao (Ch'eng Ming-tao, 1032-1085) and his brother Ch'eng I (Ch'eng I-ch'uan, 1033-1107) who saw the universe as a process of "production and reproduction" and *jen*[40] (humanity) as growth (*sheng*)?[41] The Consciousness-Only School was still active in the city of Lo-yang where the Ch'eng brothers lived. Furthermore, they both studied Buddhism for almost a decade before they returned to Confucianism. They had Buddhist friends. Their pupil Hsieh Liang-tso (1050-1103) came very close to Buddhism and actually said that "the seeds of peaches and apricots that can grow are called *jen* because they produce."[42] Ch'eng I himself said, "The mind is like seeds of grain. Their nature of growth is *jen*."[43] The resemblance of these ideas to those of Buddhism is amazing.

It can be argued, of course, that there is a fundamental difference between Buddhism and Neo-Confucianism in this respect. In Buddhism the seeds mutually "perfume" one another and hence the process is circular, whereas in Neo-Confucianism *jen* is a continuous development. Furthermore, the Ch'engs and Hsieh were critical of Buddhism.[44] Most important of all, there is no evidence that they had derived the idea of seeds from any Buddhist text or Buddhist thinker.

Nevertheless, Buddhist influence on Neo-Confucianism is deep and extensive. There is at least an evidence of contact. Hsieh specifically pointed out that the Buddhists knew the meaning of seeds although he criticized them for ignoring moral efforts in cultivating them.[45] In the opinion of Professor Paul Demiéville, there is no doubt that the idea is taken from Buddhist philosophy in which it was so common that no precise reference is needed.[46]

Does the storehouse consciousness come to an end or is it eternal? It

[40] Variously translated as goodness, benevolence, human-heartedness, etc. See Appendix.

[41] For a fuller discussion, see below, ch. 32, comment on sec. 22, and also Chan, "The Neo-Confucian Solution of the Problem of Evil," *Bulletin of the Institute of History and Philology*, 28 (1957), 773-791.

[42] *Shang-ts'ai yü-lu* (Recorded Sayings of Hsieh Liang-tso), *Cheng-i-t'ang ch'üan-shu* (Complete Library of the Hall of Rectifying the Way) ed., pt. 1, p. 2b.

[43] *I-shu* (Surviving Works), ECCS, 18:2a.

[44] See below, ch. 31, secs. 21, 32, 46, 76, 77; ch. 32, secs. 23, 25, 52-55; *Shang-ts'ai yü-lu*, pt. 1, p. 12b; pt. 2, p. 4b; pt. 3, p. 1a.

[45] *ibid.*, pt. 1, p. 2b.

[46] In a personal letter to me in September 1957.

neither comes to an end nor is eternal, for it is in perpetual transformation. By "perpetual" is meant that this consciousness, from time immemorial, has continued in the same way without any interruption. For it is the basis of the constructions in the [four] realms [which form the substance of existence], the [five] stages of transmigration, and the [four] kinds of living beings,[47] and its nature is so firm that it holds the seeds without losing them. By "transformation" is meant that this consciousness, from time immemorial, comes into and goes out of existence every moment and changes both before and after, for while it goes out of existence as cause, it comes into existence as effect, and thus is neither permanent nor one. In this way it can be perfumed by the other transforming consciousnesses and produce seeds. The term "perpetual" denies the idea that things come to an end, while the term "transformation" affirms the idea that things are not eternal. It is like a violent torrent, for it is naturally so because of cause and effect. Being like a violent torrent, it neither comes to an end nor is eternal. As it continues for a long time, some sentient beings will float and others will sink. It is the same with this consciousness. . . .

This consciousness has been in perpetual transformation like a torrent from time immemorial. In what state will it be finally renounced? Only in the state of the arhat will it be finally renounced. It means that saints are called arhats when they completely cut off all obstacles of defilement. At that time all seeds of defilement in this consciousness are forever eliminated. . . . (ch. 3, TSD, 31:12-13)

> Comment. The theory that consciousness is a constant stream of ideas inevitably reminds one of Hume. The comparison between him and the Consciousness-Only School has been made by Fung Yu-lan, among others.[48] Both the school and Hume hold that the mind is nothing but a stream of ideas, that ideas are governed by a causal relationship, and that the external world is ultimately unreal. But Buddhism is free from the skepticism of Hume, for Nirvāṇa is realizable through spiritual cultivation. Furthermore, in Buddhism, but not in Hume, the source of ideas is known and can be controlled.

[47] In Buddhism, there are the four realms which constitute the substances of all existence: earth, water, fire, and air; the five stages of transmigration: the hells, those of ghosts, animals, human beings, and heavenly beings; and four kinds of beings: those produced from the womb, from eggs, from moisture, and through metamorphosis. The Consciousness-Only School, because it denies the reality of the self and dharmas, regards all these as constructions of consciousness.

[48] History of Chinese Philosophy, vol. 2, p. 339.

4. The Second Transformation of Consciousness

5. The second transformation of consciousness
Is called the thought-center consciousness,
Which transforms with that [storehouse consciousness] as
the basis and has it as an object.
It has the nature and character of deliberation.

6. It is always accompanied by the four evil defilements,
Namely, self-delusion, self-view [as being real and perma-
nent],
Self-conceit, and self-love,
And by contact and so forth [volition, feeling, sensation,
thought, and cognition].

7. It is free from an indifference to good and evil but not from
the darkness of ignorance.
It follows its objects in their emergence and dependence,
In [the state of] the arhat, in the state of complete extinction [of thought and mental qualities of the thought-
center consciousness]
Or in the stage free from mundane delusions, [these defile-
ments] do not exist.

The Treatise says:

. . . Spontaneously this thought-center consciousness perpetually takes
the storehouse consciousness as an object and is associated with the
four basic defilements. What are the four? They are self-delusion, self-
view, self-conceit and self-love. These are the four. Self-delusion means
ignorance, lack of understanding of the character of the self, and
being unenlightened about the principle of the non-self. Therefore it is
called self-delusion. Self-view means clinging to the view that the self
exists, erroneously imagining certain dharmas to be the self that are not
the self. Therefore it is called self-view. Self-conceit means pride. On the
strength of what is clung to as the self, it causes the mind to feel superior
and lofty. It is therefore called self-conceit. Self-love means a greedy
desire for the self. It develops deep attachment to what is clung to as the
self. It is therefore called self-love. . . . These four defilements constantly
arise and pollute the inner mind and cause the [six][49] other transforming
consciousnesses to be continuously defiled. Because of this, sentient
beings are bound to the cycle of life and death and transmigration and
cannot be free from them. Hence they are called defilements. . . . (ch. 4,
TSD, 31:19-22)

[49] The consciousness of the five senses and the sense-center consciousness. K'uei-
chi, 28:3a.

5. The Third Transformation of Consciousness

8. Next comes the third transforming consciousness
   Which consists of the last six categories of discrimination
      (the consciousness of touch, sight, hearing, smell, taste,
      and the sense-center consciousness).
   Their nature and character consist in the discrimination
      of spheres of objects.
   They are neither good nor evil.

Comment. Note the equal emphasis on the nature and characters of dharmas, here as well as in verse 5. This equal emphasis gives special meaning to the school's acceptance of the doctrine of Two Levels of Truth.[50] However, the primary concern of the school has always been on characters of dharmas. In accepting them as real, the school is not quite Mahāyāna and has therefore been regarded as quasi-Hīnayāna which, generally speaking, accepts the external world as real. One wonders if the Chinese refusal to regard the world as illusory did not have something to do with the school's position.

With how many mental qualities are these six consciousnesses associated? The verse says:

9. The mental qualities are: general mental qualities,
   Particular mental qualities, good mental qualities, mental
      qualities of defilement,
   Derived mental qualities of defilement, and indeterminate
      mental qualities.[51]
   They are all associated with the mind which is impressed in
      three ways [of joy, of sorrow, and of indifference].
10. First, general mental qualities are touch and so forth
      (volition, feeling, thought, cognition).
   Next, particular mental qualities refer to desire,
   Resolve, remembrance, calmness, and wisdom.
   The things that constitute their objects are not the same.
11. Good mental qualities refer to belief, sense of shame, sense
      of integrity.
   The three roots of absence of covetousness and so forth
      (absence of anger and absence of delusions),

[50] See below, first comment in sec. 7.

[51] These are the six categories of mental qualities, which have fifty-one dharmas mentioned in verses 10-14. Besides there are eight dharmas of mind, eleven dharmas of matter, twenty-four dharmas not associated with mind, and six dharmas not produced by cause, making a total of one hundred dharmas in five divisions. For this school these make up all the elements of existence.

Diligence, repose of mind, vigilance,
Equanimity, and non-injury.

12. Mental qualities of defilement are covetousness, anger,
Delusion, conceit, doubt, and false view.
Derived mental qualities of defilement are fury,
Enmity, concealment, affliction, envy, parsimony.

13. Deception, fraudulence, injury, pride,
Absence of a sense of shame, absence of a sense of integrity,
Agitation, low-mindedness,
Unbelief, indolence.

14. Idleness, forgetfulness,
Distraction, and non-discernment.
Indeterminate mental qualities refer to regret, drowsiness,
Inquisitiveness, and investigativeness, the former two com-
posing a different class from the latter.[52]

15. Based on the root consciousness (the eighth consciousness)
The five consciousnesses (of the senses) manifest themselves in accordance with various causes.
Sometimes [the senses manifest themselves] together, and
sometimes not,
Just as waves [manifest themselves] depending on water
conditions.

16. The sense-center consciousness always arises and manifests
itself,
Except when born in the realm of absence of thought,
In the two forms of calmness, namely, calmness in which
there is no more activity of thought [and calmness in
which there is the complete extinction of sensation and
thought].
In sleep, and in that state where the spirit is depressed or
absent.

The Treatise says:

The root consciousness is the storehouse consciousness because it is
the root from which all pure and impure consciousnesses grow. . . . By
"causes" are meant rising activities of the mind, the sense organs, and
spheres of objects. It means that the five consciousnesses arise and manifest themselves, internally based on the root consciousness and externally
as a result of a combination of the causes like the rising activities of the
mind, the five sense organs, and spheres of objects. These conscious-

---

[52] According to Hsüan-tsang, there are two other interpretations: (1) the latter
two may be either pure or impure; (2) all mental qualities and derived mental
qualities have the nature of evil and indifference to good and evil.

nesses manifest themselves sometimes together and sometimes separately. This is so because the external causes may be combined suddenly or gradually. . . . (chs. 5-7, TSD, 31:26-37)

6. Consciousness-Only

17. Thus the various consciousnesses transform and change.
      Both discrimination (consciousnesses) and the object of discrimination
      Are, because of this, unreal.
      For this reason, everything is consciousness only.

The Treatise says:

"The various consciousnesses" refer to the three transforming consciousnesses previously discussed and their mental qualities. They can all transform and appear as the perceiving and the perceived portions. The term "transformation" is thus employed. The perceiving portion of the transformation is called discrimination because it can grasp the perceived portion (as the object of perception). The perceived portion of the transformation is called the object of discrimination because it is grasped by the perceiving portion. According to this correct principle, apart from being transformations of consciousness, the self and dharmas are both definitely nonexistent, because apart from what grasps and what is grasped, there is nothing else, and because there are no real things separated from the two portions.

Therefore everything produced from causes, everything not produced from causes, and everything seemingly real or unreal, are all inseparable from consciousness. The word "only" is intended to deny that there are real things separated from consciousness, but not to deny that there are mental qualities, dharmas, and so forth inseparable from consciousness. The word "transform" means that the various inner consciousnesses transform and manifest the characters which seem to be the external spheres of the self and dharmas. This process of transformation and change is called discrimination because it is its own nature to make erroneous discriminations [that things are real]. It refers to the mind and mental qualities in the Three Worlds.[53] These, what it holds to be spheres of objects, are called objects of discrimination, that is, the self and dharmas which it erroneously holds to be real. Because of this discrimination, which evolves characters which seem to be the external spheres of the false self and dharmas, what is discriminated as the real self and dharmas are all absolutely nonexistent. This theory has been extensively refuted by the doctrines [of our teachers] already cited.

Therefore everything is consciousness only, because erroneous dis-

[53] See above, ch. 20, n.38.

crimination in itself is admitted as a fact. Since "only" does not deny the existence of dharmas not separated from consciousness, therefore true Emptiness [mental qualities][54] and so forth have the nature of being. In this way we steer far away from the two extremes of holding that dharmas are real [although they have no nature of their own] or holding that dharmas are unreal [although they do function as causes and effects], establish the principle of Consciousness-Only, and hold correctly to the Middle Path.

7. Nine Objections to the Consciousness-Only Doctrine and Their Answers

(1) *Objection*: On the basis of what doctrines is the principle of Consciousness-Only established?

Answer: Have we not already explained? However, the explanations are not sufficient. One's own principle cannot be established by demolishing those of others. One should definitely present his own doctrine in order to establish it.

The true scriptures[55] declare that "in the Three Worlds there is nothing but mind,"[56] that objects are but manifestations of consciousness-only,[57] that all dharmas are not separated from the mind,[58] that sentient beings become pure or impure in accordance with the mind,[59] that bodhisattvas[60] (saints of the Mahāyāna) who perfected the Four Wisdoms will, following their awakening, penetrate the truth of consciousness-only and the absence of spheres of objects.[61]

The Four Wisdoms are: first, the wisdom that contradictory consciousnesses are but characters. This means that the same thing perceived by ghosts, human beings, and deities appear differently to them in accordance with their past deeds. If there is really an external sphere, how can this be possible? Second, the wisdom that consciousness takes non-being as its object. This means that the past, the future, images in dreams,

---

[54] Addition according to K'uei-chi, 42:6a.

[55] Literally, the scriptures that teach correct principles.

[56] *Shih-ti ching* (*Daśabhūmi sūtra* or Ten-Stage Scripture), ch. 4, sec. 6, TSD, 10:533. See K'uei-chi, 42:7b.

[57] *Chieh shen-mi ching* (*Sandhinirmocana sūtra* or Scripture Explaining the Deep and the Secret), ch. 2, sec. 4-5, TSD, 16:693; see K'uei-chi, 42:8a.

[58] *Ju Leng-chia ching* (*Laṅkāvatāra sūtra* or Scripture about [the Buddha] Entering into Laṅka), ch. 5, TSD, 16:543. See translation by Suzuki, *Laṅkāvatāra sūtra*, pp. 171-175. See K'uei-chi, 42:8b.

[59] *Shuo Wu-kou-ch'eng ching* (*Vimalakīrtinirdeśa sūtra* or Scripture Spoken by Vimalakīrti), ch. 1, TSD, 14:559. See K'uei-chi, 42:8b.

[60] A bodhisattva is one who has a strong determination to seek enlightenment and salvation for all.

[61] The name of this scripture is uncertain. See de la Vallée Poussin, *la siddhe de Hiuan-tsang*, p. 421, n.1. K'uei-chi was not sure (42:9a).

and things imagined have no real, objective basis. They are possible because they are manifestations of consciousness. If these objective bases are nonexistent, the rest is also nonexistent. The third is the wisdom that naturally there should be no perversion of truth. This means that if the intelligence of ordinary people is able to perceive the real spheres of objects, they should naturally achieve freedom from perversion and should be able to achieve emancipation without any effort. [Since they are not emancipated, it shows that the objective spheres they perceive are not real at all.][62] The fourth is the wisdom changing with three wisdoms:

a) Changing with the wisdom of the one who is free and at ease. This means that he who has realized the freedom and the ease of mind can change and transform earth [into gold] and so forth without fail according to his desires. If there was really an external sphere, how can these transformations be possible?

b) Changing with the wisdom of the one who meditates and sees clearly. This means that when one who has achieved supreme calmness and has practiced the meditation on the Law meditates on one sphere of objects, its various characters appear in front of him. If the sphere is real, why does it change according to his mind?

c) Changing with the wisdom of no discrimination. This means that as the non-discriminating wisdom which realizes truth arises, all spheres of objects and their characters will cease to appear. If there are real spheres of objects, why should they do so? The bodhisattva who achieves the Four Wisdoms will definitely understand and penetrate the principle of consciousness-only.

Furthermore, the hymn says:

> The objects of mind, thought-center consciousness, and [the
> other six] consciousnesses
> Are not distinct from their own nature.
> Therefore I declare that all things
> Are consciousness only and there is nothing else [which is
> external to the mind]. . . .[63]

(2) *Objection*: If what seem to be external spheres are simply the products of the inner consciousness, why is it that what we see in the world, whether sentient beings or non-sentient objects, are definite with

[62] According to K'uei-chi, 42:10a.

[63] *Hou-yen ching* (*Ghanavyūha sūtra* or Rich and Splendid (Scripture), according to K'uei-chi, 42:11b. The title *Hou-yen ching* is that of the Tibetan translation. The two Chinese translations of the scripture are both entitled *Ta-ch'eng mi-yen ching* (Secret and Splendid Scripture of the Mahāyāna), but I cannot find the passage in them. The general idea, however, runs through the scripture, especially in sec. 8 of the first version, TSD, 16:740.

respect to space [for example, a certain mountain is always seen in a certain place] and time but indefinite with respect to people [for example, when many people see the same mountain at the same time, their consciousness of it is not determined by any one of them] and function [for example, food has real function in waking life but not in a dream]?

Answer: Your doubt may be dispelled with reference to the world of dreams.

(3) *Objection*: Why did the World-Honored One (Bhagavat, the Buddha) teach the Twelve Bases (the five senses, the mind, and their organs)?

Answer: These are transformations based on consciousness. They are not real things separated from consciousness. In order to introduce [his disciples] to the truth of the emptiness of the self, He spoke to the six internal bases and six external bases, just as He spoke of the continuity of sentient beings in order to deny the [false] view that things come to an end. And in order to introduce them to the truth of the emptiness of dharmas, He also spoke of consciousness-only, so they know that external dharmas are also nonexistent.

(4) *Objection*: Is the nature of consciousness-only not also empty?

Answer: No. Why? Because it is not a matter of clinging? We say dharmas are empty because the [so-called] real dharmas erroneously conceived on the basis of transformations of consciousness are contrary to reason. We do not say dharmas are empty because there is no nature of consciousness-only realized by correct and indescribable wisdom. If there were no such consciousness, there would be no worldly (relative) truth, and if there were no worldly truth, there would be no absolute truth, for the Two Levels of Truth are established on the basis of each other. To reject the Two Levels of Truth is to have evil ideas of Emptiness, a disease the Buddhas consider to be incurable. We should realize that some dharmas [which are imagined] are empty and some [which depend on something else, i.e., cause, to be complete][64] are not, and that is why Maitreya[65] recited the two verses above [to the effect that some dharmas are empty and some are not].

> *Comment*. It is interesting to note that the position of this school with reference to the Two Levels of Truth is somewhere between that of the Three-Treatise School, which subordinates worldly truth to absolute truth, and the Hua-yen School, which identifies them. Although this school represents the doctrine of being, actually it aims at a synthesis of both being and non-being. Consequently both

[64] According to K'uei-chi, 43:7a.
[65] The next Buddha, who is to come in the future to save the world.

character and nature of dharmas are emphasized and both inner and external spheres are stressed.

(5) *Objection*: If the bases of the various forms of matter are consciousness in substance, why do the various consciousnesses of matter appear and manifest themselves in the semblance of characters of matter —homogeneous, unchangeable—and transform continuously?

Answer: Because [these manifestations] arise through the force of the influence of names and words [residing in the body from time immemorial], and are based on pure and impure dharmas. If there were none [of these characters], there would be no perversion of truth, and thus there would be neither dharmas of defilement nor pure dharmas. This is why the various consciousnesses appear in the semblance of matter. . . .

Comment. Like any idealistic philosophy, Consciousness-Only faces the most difficult task of explaining the regularity, consistency, and continuity of ideas. Instead of resorting to a belief in God, as Berkeley did, who assumes that God is the giver of them, this school treats regularity and so forth as simply characters of dharmas and as such, to be explained in terms of cause and effect. In this process of mutual cause and effect, certain seeds regularly perfume in a certain way, and therefore people with similar seeds in them are perfumed in the same way. The answer to the second objection above is no evasion, for dreams, like ideas in waking life, are governed by the law of cause and effect. By the use of this law, idealistic Buddhism has avoided the necessity of a belief in God as it has avoided the necessity of a belief in an ego.[66]

(6) *Objection*: The external spheres of color and so forth are clearly and immediately realized. How can what is perceived through immediate apprehension be rejected as nonexistent?

Answer: At the time the external spheres are realized through immediate apprehension, they are not taken as external. It is later that the sense-center consciousness discriminates and erroneously creates the notion of externality. Thus the objective spheres immediately apprehended are the perceived portion of the consciousnesses themselves. Since they are transformations of consciousness, we say they exist. But since color and so forth, which the sense-center consciousness conceives as external and real, are erroneously imagined to be existent, we say they are nonexistent. Furthermore, objective spheres of color and so forth are not colors but appear to be color, and are not external but appear

[66] For a fuller answer to these objections, see Vasubandhu's *Viṁśatikā*, trans. by Hamilton, *Wei Shih Er Shih Lun*.

390

to be external. They are like objects in a dream, and should not be taken as real, external color.

(7) *Objection*: If color and so forth perceived when we are awake are all like objects in a dream and inseparable from consciousness, then as we awake from a dream, we know that they are only mental. Why is it that when we are awake we do not know that the objective sphere of color perceived by ourselves is not consciousness only?

Answer: We do not realize ourselves [that objects in a dream are unreal] as long as we have not awakened from the dream. It is only after we have awakened that we, in retrospect, come to realize it. We should know that the same is true of our knowledge of the objective sphere of color in our waking life. Before we reach the state of true awakening, we do not ourselves know it, but when we reach the state of true awakening, we can also, in retrospect, come to realize it. Before we achieve true awakening, we are perpetually in the midst of a dream. This is why the Buddha spoke of the long night of transmigration, because of our failure to understand that the objective spheres of color [and so forth] are consciousness only.

(8) *Objection*: If external matter is really nonexistent, it may be granted that it is not a sphere of objects for one's inner consciousness. But the mind of another person really exists. Why is it not an object of one's own consciousness?

Answer: Who says that another person's mind is not a sphere of objects for one's own consciousness? We only say that it is not its immediate and direct object. This means that when the consciousness [of another person's mind] arises, it has no real function. The case is different from that of the hands and so forth which grasp an external thing immediately and directly, or that of the sun and so forth, which spread their light and by direct contact shine on external spheres immediately and directly. The consciousness is merely like a mirror, in which what seems to be an external sphere appears. It is in this sense that it is called the mind that discriminates another. But it cannot discriminate [another mind] immediately and directly. What it discriminates immediately and directly are its own transformations. Therefore the true scripture[67] says that not the least dharma [one's own mind] can grasp other dharmas [other minds].[68] It is only when consciousness is produced that it manifests a character similar to that of another thing. This is called grasping another thing. It seems like taking another person's mind as an object. The same is true of matter and so forth.

(9) *Objection*: Since there is [another mind] distinct from [one's

[67] Interpretation according to K'uei-chi, 43:15a.
[68] *Chieh shen-mi ching*, ch. 3, sec. 6, TSD, 16:698.

own] sphere of objects,[69] how can you say there is consciousness only?

Answer: How extraordinarily obstinate! You raise doubts at every point. Does the doctrine of Consciousness-Only assert that there is only one individual consciousness? No, it does not. Why? Please listen carefully.

If there were only one individual consciousness, how is it that there is a variety of ordinary people, saints, the honored ones and lowly ones, and causes and effects in the ten cardinal directions? Who would then expound teachings to whom? What dharmas would there be? And what goal is there to seek? Therefore there is a deep purpose in saying there is consciousness only.

The word "consciousness" generally expresses the idea that all human beings each possess eight consciousnesses, six categories of mental quali-ties,[70] the perceiving portion and perceived portion which are products of transformation, the different categories of [dharmas of consciousness, dharmas of matter and mind, and dharmas not associated with the mind], and True Thusness (True Reality)[71] revealed by the principle of the emptiness [of the self and dharmas].

Because consciousnesses are their own characters, because conscious-nesses are associated with mental qualities, because of the transforma-tions of the perceiving portion and perceived portion, because of the three categories of dharmas, and because of these four true realities, all dharmas are inseparable from consciousness and the general term "consciousness" has been set up. The word "only" is employed merely to deny what ordinary people take to be real matter definitely separated from the various consciousnesses. . . .

If there is consciousness only and no external causes, how did the various discriminations arise? The verse says:

18. Because consciousness involves all kinds of seeds,
    Different transformations take place.
    Because of their power to turn on and on,
    All sorts of discriminations are produced.

The Treatise says:

By consciousness evolving all kinds of seeds is meant that functions and differentiations in the root consciousness spontaneously produce their own fruition. . . . (ch. 7, TSD, 31:38-40)

> *Comment*. The Consciousness-Only philosophy is permeated with the concepts of change and transformation like the *Book of*

[69] These interpretations are K'uei-chi's, 43:15b.
[70] These six categories are mentioned in verses 9-14, above.
[71] See below, ch. 24, n.19.

Changes. However, certain fundamental differences should not be overlooked. The change in this philosophy takes place in consciousness, whereas that of Change operates in the objective world. In both philosophies change operates in the pattern of opposition—in perfuming by pure or impure seeds in the one and in the alteration of yin and yang (passive and active cosmic forces) in the other. But while the direction of perfuming is circular, that of yin yang is progressive—from yin yang to the Four Forms (major and minor yin and yang) and the myriad things. Most important, change in Buddhism leads finally to quietness and silence in Nirvāṇa, but transformation in Confucianism is an eternal process of "production and reproduction."

8. *The Three Natures of Being, Three Natures of Non-being, and Thusness*

19. Due to the force of habit of various pervious deeds
    The force of habit of the six sense organs and that of their objects[72] working on each other both ways [by being influenced and also by producing their own functions within the eighth consciousness].[73]
    As the previous ripening-at-later-times is completed,
    Succeeding ripenings-at-later-times are produced.

20. Because of a variety of vast imagination,
    Various things [like the hair of a tortoise][74] are vastly imagined.
    What is conceived by this vast imagination
    Has no nature of its own whatsoever.

21. The self-nature which results from dependence on others
    Consists of discriminations produced by various causes.
    The difference between Perfect Reality and the nature of being dependent on others,
    Is that the former is eternally free from being conceived by vast imagination [whereas the latter is merely defiled by imagination].

22. Thus Perfect Reality and the dependent
    Are neither the same nor different.
    As in the cases of impermanence and so forth,
    It is not that when one is not understood, the other can.

[72] According to K'uei-chi, 47:4a-5b, this is only one of eight interpretations of *erh-ch'ü*, literally "two-take."

[73] Insertion following K'uei-chi, 47:5b.

[74] K'uei-chi, 51:3b.

If there is the Threefold Nature of Being (Being Conceived by Vast Imagination, Being Dependent on Others for Production, and Being of Perfect Reality), why did the World-Honored One say that all dharmas are without nature of their own? The verse says:

23. On the basis of the Threefold Nature of Being
Threefold Nature of Non-being is established.
Therefore the Buddha said earnestly
That all dharmas have no nature [of their own].

24. The first is the Non-being of Characters [since they are but products of imagination].
The second is the Non-being of Self-existence [since it is the result of discrimination].
The last is [Non-being in the Highest Sense].
They are forever separated from the self and dharmas previously conceived.

25. In the highest sense all these dharmas
Are nothing other than True Thusness (True Reality).
They are forever true to their nature,
Which is the true nature of consciousness-only.

26. As long as the consciousness (of wisdom) has not arisen
To seek to remain[75] in the state of consciousness-only
The six sense organs and their objects and the seeds of evil desires
Cannot be overcome and annihilated.

27. To hold something before oneself,
And to say that it is the nature of consciousness-only,
Is really not to remain in the state of consciousness-only,
Because it is the result of grasping.

28. When in the [sphere of] objects
There is nothing for the wisdom [which no longer discriminates] to grasp,
The state of consciousness-only is realized,
Since the six sense organs and their objects are no longer present.

29. Without grasping, mysterious, and indescribable,
This is supramundane wisdom.
Because of the abandonment of the force of habits of various previous deeds and the six sense organs as well as their objects,
The transformation [of the seeds of defilement] into the abiding with [perfect wisdom] will be realized.

[75] Literally "seeking after."

30. This is the realm of the absence of afflictions (end of
   transmigration),
   Which is beyond description, is good, and is eternal,
   Where one is in the state of emancipation, peace, and joy.
   This is the Law of "Great Silence."[76]

(chs. 8-10, TSD, 31:43-57)

Comment. In the final analysis, Buddhism is mysticism and a religion. All speculation is but a way to Nirvāna.

---

[76] The Law realized by the Great Buddha, Śākyamuni, the sage who realized it through silence—that is, freedom from words, relative knowledge, and mistakes.

24

THE T'IEN-T'AI PHILOSOPHY
OF PERFECT HARMONY

ALL BUDDHIST SCHOOLS claim to teach the Middle Path of the Buddha but they differ radically in their interpretations. For the Three-Treatise School, it connotes absolute Emptiness without specific characters. For the Consciousness-Only School, it is identified with Thusness,[1] which also transcends all specific characters.[2] The Middle Path of both these schools is transcendent although the latter attempts to arrive at a middle ground between realism and nihilism. In the T'ien-t'ai School, however, the Middle Path means a synthesis of phenomenon and noumenon, in which transcendence and immanence are harmonized so that "every color or fragrance is none other than the Middle Path." This tendency toward synthesis had been characteristic of Chinese thought, especially in the *Book of Changes* and in Neo-Taoism. Its further development in Buddhism is only natural.

The central doctrines of the T'ien-t'ai School may be summed up in its three common sayings, namely, "the true nature of all dharmas (elements of existence)";[3] "the perfect harmony of the Three Levels of Truth;" and "the three thousand worlds immanent in an instance of thought." By the perfect harmony of the Three Levels of Truth is meant that all dharmas are empty because they have no nature of their own but depend on causes for their production. This is the Truth of Emptiness. But dharmas *are* produced and do possess temporary and dependent existence. This is Temporary Truth. Being both empty and temporary is the very nature of dharmas. This is the Truth of the Mean. The three involve each other, for Emptiness renders dharmas really empty, dependent existence makes them relatively real, and the Mean embraces both. Consequently the three are one and one is three. This mutual identity is the true state of all dharmas.

In the realm of Temporary Truth, that is, the phenomenal world, there are ten realms: Buddhas, bodhisattvas,[4] buddhas-for-themselves,[5] direct disciples of the Buddha,[6] heavenly beings, spirits, human beings,

[1] See below, n.19.

[2] *Hsiang* in Chinese and *lakshana* in Sanskrit, meaning characteristics.

[3] For the translation of dharma, see Appendix, comment on *Fa*.

[4] A bodhisattva is one with strong determination to seek enlightenment and salvation for himself and others.

[5] *Pratyekabuddhas*, who attain to their personal enlightenment by their own exertion in an age in which there is no Buddha.

[6] *Śravākas*, who attain to their own salvation by hearing the Buddha's preaching.

departed beings, beasts, and depraved men. Since each of these involves the others, there are thus one hundred realms. Each of these in turn possesses the Ten Characters of Thusness: character, nature, substance, energy, activity, cause, condition, effect, retribution, and being ultimate from beginning to end, that is, each is "thus-caused," "thus-natured," and so forth. Each of these consists of living beings, of space, and of aggregates (matter, sensation, thought, disposition, and consciousness). The result is three thousand worlds, which is the totality of manifested reality.

This does not mean a pluralistic universe but one in which one is all and all is one. The worlds are so interpenetrated that they are said to be "immanent in a single instant of thought." This is not to say that they are produced by any mind, for production implies a sequence in time. Nor are they to be thought of as being included in an instant of thought, for inclusion implies space. Rather, it means that all the possible worlds are so much identified that they are involved in every moment of thought. In other words, all phenomena are manifestations of the Mind of Pure Nature and each manifestation is the Mind in its totality.

This Mind is to be carefully differentiated from that of the Consciousness-Only School. The world is not consciousness itself but the manifestation of the Mind. It is not in constant transformation as is the Mind of the Consciousness-Only School. Instead, it does not change. Since it involves all, it cannot, like the Consciousness-Only School, exclude a certain group of people from salvation. In fact, one of the outstanding features of T'ien-t'ai is the doctrine of universal salvation. Since everything involves everything else, it follows that all beings possess Buddha-nature and are therefore capable of salvation. The logical position of the T'ien-t'ai School cannot tolerate any different position, although the Confucian doctrine that everyone can become a sage definitely prepared for it.[7] As to methods for salvation, the school lays dual emphasis on concentration and insight.

The school can be traced to Kumārajīva,[8] but the founder was really Chih-i (538-597)[9] who lived and taught in the T'ien-t'ai (Heavenly Terrace) Mountain in Chekiang. Hence the school is called T'ien-t'ai.[10] This fact is significant because it indicates that the school is essentially Chinese. It is true that it was founded by Chih-i on the authority of the

---

[7] See *Mencius*, 6B:2.

[8] See above, ch. 21, Introduction.

[9] He was the most outstanding and the most highly revered Buddhist priest of his time. He was repeatedly invited by rulers of the various dynasties to lecture. In 583 he lectured in the palace at Nanking. Thirty-two pupils spread his doctrines in various parts of China. For his biography, see *Hsü kao-seng chuan* (Supplement to the *Biographies of Eminent Monks*), ch. 21, TSD, 50:264-268.

[10] Tendai in Japan.

397

Indian text, the *Lotus Scripture*,[11] that the doctrine of the Ten Characters of Thusness comes from this scripture, and that the idea that dharmas, Emptiness, and the Middle Path are identical is taught in the *Chung lun* (Treatise on the Middle Doctrine) of the Three-Treatise School.[12] But it was Hui-wen (550-577) who discovered the idea in that treatise and developed it into a central doctrine. The idea of three thousand worlds immanent in a single instant of thought was Chih-i's own.

The philosophical ideas underlie the basic scriptures of the school but they are not expressed in lengthy passages. Chih-i's works are mostly devoted to spiritual cultivation.

The following selections are from the *Ta-ch'eng chih-kuan fa-men*[13] (The Method of Concentration and Insight) ascribed to Hui-ssu (514-577),[14] Hui-wen's pupil and Chih-i's teacher, which is perhaps the most philosophical of all. Its authenticity has been questioned because it quotes a scripture which appeared earlier.[15] But it is a work in which the equal emphasis of the school on the Mind as the totality of the universe and on the method of concentration and insight is made.

THE METHOD OF CONCENTRATION AND INSIGHT

1. The Various Aspects of the Mind

By concentration is meant to know that all dharmas (elements of existence), from the very beginning have no nature of their own. They neither come into nor go out of existence. Because they are caused by illusion and imagination, they exist without real existence. But the existence of existent dharmas is the same as nonexistence. They are only the one mind, whose substance admits no differentiation. Those who hold this view can stop the flow of erroneous thought. This is called concentration.[16]

[11] *Saddharmapuṇḍarīka sūtra* (Scripture of the Lotus of the Good Law). For English translation, see Bibliography.

[12] *Mādhyamika śāstra*, ch. 6, TSD, 30:33.

[13] The word *men* has the meanings of both gate and divisions or kinds. Thus it means different approaches, methods, variety, etc. This is the idea behind the term *fa-men*, or "gates of dharmas," for dharmas are various. But *fa* also means model, that is, the way that can be taken as a model, referring to the path travelled by Buddhas and saints.

[14] *Hsü kao-seng chuan*, ch. 17, TSD, 50:562-564. The second patriarch of the T'ien-t'ai School, he was particularly attracted to the *Lotus Scripture*.

[15] See below, n. 20.

[16] *Chih* in Chinese, literally "to stop," or to bring the mind to a rest, the Chinese translation for the Sanskrit, *śamatha*, which means calmness of mind and cessation of erroneous thoughts.

By insight[17] is meant that although we know that [things] originally do not come into existence and at present do not go out of existence, nevertheless they were caused to arise out of the mind's nature and hence are not without a worldly function of an unreal and imaginative nature. They are like illusions and dreams which [seem to] exist but really do not. This is therefore called insight. . . . It means to base and concentrate on the one mind in order to practice concentration and insight. . . .

This mind is the same as the Mind of Pure Self-nature, True Thusness, Buddha-nature, Dharma-body, the Storehouse of the Thus-come (Tathāgata), the Realm of Dharmas, and Dharma-nature. . . .

Question: Why is it called the Mind of Pure Self-nature?

Answer: Although this mind has been obscured from time immemorial by contaminating dharmas based on ignorance,[18] yet its nature of purity has never changed. Hence it is called pure. Why? Because contaminating dharmas based on ignorance are from the beginning separated from the mind. Why do we say that they are separated? Because dharmas with ignorance as their substance are nonexistent dharmas. Their existence is the same as nonexistence. Since they are nonexistent, they cannot be associated with the mind. Therefore we say they are separated. Since there are no contaminating dharmas based on ignorance to be associated with it, therefore it is called pure in nature. Being central (without going to the extreme) and real, it is originally awakened. It is therefore called the mind. For these reasons it is called the Mind of Pure Self-nature.

Question: Why is it called True Thusness (True Reality)?[19]

Answer: All dharmas depend on this mind for their being and take the mind as their substance. When it is compared with dharmas all of them are unreal and imaginary, and their existence is the same as nonexistence. Contrasted with these unreal and false dharmas, the mind is regarded as true.

Furthermore, although dharmas are really nonexistent, because they are caused by illusion and imagination, they have the character of coming into and going out of existence. When unreal dharmas come into existence, this mind does not come into existence, and when the dharmas go out of existence, this mind does not go out of existence. Not coming

---

[17] *Kuan* in Chinese and *vipaśyanā* in Sanskrit, which means to contemplate, to examine, to look into, so as to gain insight of true Thusness.

[18] Especially the ignorance of facts and principles of dharmas.

[19] As indicated in the following passage, True Thusness or Suchness (*tathatā* in Sanskrit and *chen-ju* in Chinese) means truth and it-is-so. As truth, it is antithesis to illusion and falsehood, and "being so" it is eternal, unchangeable, indestructible, without character or nature, and is not produced by causes. It is the Absolute, Ultimate Reality, or True Reality, the Storehouse of the Thus-come, the Realm of Dharmas, Dharma-nature, and Perfect Reality.

into existence, it is therefore not increased, and not going out of existence, it is therefore not decreased. Because it neither comes into nor goes out of existence and is neither increased nor decreased, it is called true. The Buddhas of the three ages (past, present, and future) and all sentient beings have this one Pure Mind as their substance. All ordinary and saintly beings and dharmas each have their own differences and differentiated characters. But this True Mind has neither differentiation nor characters. It is therefore called Thusness.

Furthermore, by True Thusness is meant that all dharmas, being thus real, are merely this one mind. Therefore this one mind is called True Thusness. If there are dharmas outside of the mind, they are neither real nor thus so, but are false and differentiated characters. This is why the *Awakening of Faith* says, "From the very beginning all dharmas are free from the characters of words and speech, from the characters of terms and concepts, and from the characters of mental causation (groping for objects). At bottom they are all the same, without differentiation, do not change or become different, and cannot be destroyed. They are only one mind. Therefore it is called True Thusness."[20] Because of this meaning, the Mind of Pure Self-nature is also called True Thusness.

> *Comment.* We have here the major doctrines of the school in a nutshell: the Three Levels of Truth, namely, that dharmas are differentiated (Temporary Truth), that the True Mind is not differentiated (the Truth of Emptiness), and that True Thusness means that dharmas are real in this way (the Truth of the Mean). Furthermore, all this is but the one mind.

Question: Why is this mind also called Buddha-nature?

Answer: The word "buddha" means awakening, and nature means the mind. Because the substance of this Pure Mind is not unawakened, it is described as the awakened mind.

Question: How do you know that this true mind is not unawakened?

Answer: Unawakening is the basis of ignorance. If this Pure Mind were ignorance, then when all sentient beings attain Buddhahood and ignorance is annihilated, there would be no true mind. Why? Because the mind is ignorance. Since ignorance is naturally annihilated, the Pure Mind naturally exists. We therefore know that the Pure Mind is not unawakening. Furthermore, only when unawakening is annihilated can the Pure Mind be realized. From this we know that the mind is not unawakening. (ch. 1, TSD, 46:642)

---

[20] *Ta-ch'eng ch'i-hsin lun* (*Mahāyānaśraddhotpāda śāstra*, or Treatise on the Wakening of Faith in the Mahāyāna) by Aśvaghoṣa (c. 100 A.D.), TSD, 32:576; cf. Suzuki, p. 57. Suzuki's translation is of a different Chinese version from the one quoted here.

Question: Why is this mind called Dharma-body?[21]

Answer: The meaning of dharma consists in functioning, and the body means a place to depend and rest upon. Because the substance of this mind has the function of being affected by contamination, it is influenced by all contaminating dharmas. Precisely because this mind is affected by contamination, it can get hold of and control the power of this influence and also can, on the basis of this influence, manifest the contaminating dharmas. That is to say, the two functions—to hold and to manifest—which this mind by its nature possesses, and the two types of contaminating dharmas—the held and the manifested—are all established on the basis of this one mind, and are neither the same with nor different from it. Therefore this mind is called Dharma-body. . . .

Question: Why is this mind also called the Storehouse of the Thus-come (Tathāgata)?[22]

Answer: . . . . Because it embodies both the nature and the fact of contamination as well as the nature and the fact of purity without obstacle. Therefore it is called the storehouse by virtue of its ability to store. Because the substance of the storehouse is the same and not differentiated, it is called "thus." And because all causations arise in the same way, it is called "come" . . . . Because this True Mind is stored (covered) by the shell of ignorance, it is described as the storehouse that is stored. As the substance of the storehouse has neither differentiation nor characters, it is called "thus," and as its substance fully possesses both functions of contamination and purity, it is called "come." Therefore it is called the storehouse by virtue of what is stored in it. . . . It is called "thus" because contamination and purity are the same and not differentiated, and it is called "come" because it can produce both contamination and purity. Therefore it is called the Storehouse of Thus-come by virtue of its ability to produce.

> *Comment*. The spirit of synthesis is here carried to the point of maintaining that both nature (substance) and fact (function) involve contamination and purity at the same time. Fung Yu-lan suggests that this is a dualistic theory of human nature.[23] This is true only insofar as the world of phenomenon is concerned, for underlying contamination and purity there is always the Mind of Pure Nature. Applied to the question of salvation, the idea of the coexistence of contamination and purity provides a logical basis for the idea that ordinary people and the Buddhas possess the nature

[21] See below, ch. 26, n.44.
[22] See above, ch. 20, n.41.
[23] *History of Chinese Philosophy*, vol. 2, p. 363.

of each other, but through concentration and insight, all can realize Buddha nature and be saved.

Question: Why is the Pure Mind also called the Realm of Dharmas?[24]

Answer: Because dharmas are naturally what they are and because the realm means that in which the natures of dharmas are differentiated. Because the substance of this mind naturally makes all dharmas fully sufficient, it is therefore described as the Realm of Dharmas.

Question: Why is this Pure Mind called Dharma-nature?

Answer: Dharma refers to all dharmas and by nature is meant the differentiation of substance. Because this Pure Mind possesses the nature to differentiate, it can become the substance of all dharmas. Furthermore, by nature is meant that the substance is really unchanged, for all dharmas take this mind as their substance. The characters of all dharmas spontaneously come into and go out of existence. Therefore they are called unreal and imaginary, and because this mind is real, unchangeable, and indestructible, it is called Dharma-nature. . . .

As to the substance and features of the mind, there are three: . . . (1) From the very beginning this mind has been free from all kinds of character. It is the same without differentiation and is in the state of Nirvāṇa. It is not with characters. It is not without characters. It is not either with or without characters. And it is not neither with nor without characters. . . .

(2) Although it has been explained above that the Pure Mind is free from the characters of all discriminative minds and sense objects, nevertheless these characters are not different from the Pure Mind. Why? Although the substance of this mind is the same and not differentiated, it originally possesses both functions of being contaminated and remaining pure. Furthermore, because of the power of ignorance and imagination to influence it from time immemorial, both its substance and its function of being contaminated manifest themselves according to the influence. These unreal characters have no substance; they are but the Pure Mind. Hence it is said that [substance and features] are not different.

But at the same time they are not the same. Why? Because, although it possesses the two functions of contamination and purity, the substance of the Pure Mind does not have the character of distinction between the two. It is simply the same and undifferentiated. Simply depending on the unreal characters manifested by the power of influence, there are varying degrees of difference. But these unreal characters come into and go out of existence, whereas the substance of the Pure Mind is eternal: it neither comes into nor goes out of existence, and endures forever without change.

---

[24] *Dharmadhātu*, the universe.

Hence it is said that [substance and features] are not the same. . . . (ch. 1, TSD, 46:644-645)

(3) The substance of the storehouse is the same and undifferentiated, and in fact has no differentiation. In this respect it is the Storehouse of the Thus-come of Emptiness. However, because the substance of this storehouse also has mysterious functions, it possesses all dharma natures to the fullest extent, including their differentiations. In this respect, it is the Storehouse of the Thus-come of Non-emptiness, that is, the differentiation of non-differentiation.

What does this mean? It means that it does not, like a lump of clay, possess many particles of dust. Why? The lump of clay is false, whereas the particles of dust are real. Therefore each particle has its own distinctive material. But since they are combined to form a lump of clay, it possesses the distinctiveness of the various particles. But the Storehouse of the Thus-come is different from this. Why? Because the Storehouse of the Thus-come is the Real Dharma. It is perfectly harmonious without duality. Therefore the Storehouse of the Thus-come, in its totality, is the nature of a single hair-pore of a single being, and at the same time the nature of all hair-pores of that being. And as in the case of the nature of the hair-pore, so in that of the nature of every dharma in the world. . . . (ch. 2, TSD, 46:648).

2. Three Ages as an Instant; Substance and Function

Question: Is an instant of thought on my part an equivalent to the three ages? Is what is seen as a particle of dust the equivalent of the ten cardinal directions?

Answer: Not only is an instant of thought equivalent to the three ages; we may say that it *is* the full span of the three ages. Not only is a particle of dust equivalent to the ten cardinal directions; we may say that it *is* the world of ten directions. Why? Because all dharmas are but one mind. Therefore there is no differentiation in itself, for differentiation is the one mind. As the mind involves all functions, the one mind is differentiation. They are always the same and always different. The Realm of Dharmas [the universe] is naturally so. . . .

> *Comment*. The all-in-one and one-in-all theory is further developed in the Hua-yen School. T'ien-t'ai exerted a strong influence on it, and through it on Neo-Confucianism.

Question: If substance and function are not different, it can only be said that the Two Levels of Truth (worldly or relative truth and absolute truth) involve each other. How can worldly truth also involve worldly events?

Answer: By saying substance and function are not different, one does not mean collecting the different functions of many particles of dust to form the one substance of the lump of clay. It merely means that within the level of worldly truth, every event or character is the total substance of absolute truth. Therefore we say that substance and function are not different. Because of this meaning, if absolute truth involves completely all events and characters within the level of worldly truth, at the same time every single event or character within the level of worldly truth also involves completely all events and characters within the level of worldly truth. (ch. 2, TSD, 46:650)

> *Comment*. Because the school advocates the doctrine of the harmony of the Three Levels of Truth, it is a definite advance beyond the doctrine of the Two Levels of Truth of other schools. The intention here is not to affirm Two Levels of Truth but to stress the idea that one involves all and all involve one.

3. The Function of Concentration and Insight

As to the function of concentration and insight: It means that because of the accomplishment of concentration, the Pure Mind is realized in substance, the nature which is without duality is harmonized through principle (*li*, rational nature of things), these and all sentient beings are harmoniously identified to form a body of one single character. Thereupon the Three Treasures[25] are merged together without being three, and because of this the Two Levels of Truth are fused without being two. How calm, still, and pure! How deep, stable, and quiet! How pure and clear the inner silence! It functions without the character of functioning, and acts without the character of acting. It is so because all dharmas are from the very beginning the same and not differentiated and because the nature of the mind is naturally so. This is the substance of the most profound Dharma-nature.

It also means that because of the accomplishment of insight, the substance of the Pure Mind is manifested, and the function of the Realm of Dharmas, which is without obstacle, naturally produces all capabilities to be contaminated and to be pure. . . . Again, owing to the accomplishment of concentration, one's mind is the same and not differentiated and one no longer remains within the cycle of life and death. Yet owing to the accomplishment of insight, one's characteristics and functions arise from causation and one does not enter Nirvāṇa. Moreover, owing to the accomplishment of concentration, one remains in the great Nirvāṇa, and yet owing to the attainment of insight, one dwells in the realm of life

[25] The Three Bodies of a Buddha. See below, ch. 26, n.44.

and death. Furthermore, owing to the accomplishment of concentration, one is not contaminated by the world, but owing to the attainment of insight, one is not bogged down in the realm of extinction [of passions, that is, Nirvāṇa]. Further, owing to the accomplishment of concentration, one achieves eternal extinction in the process of functioning, and owing to the attainment of insight, one achieves eternal function in the state of extinction. Further, owing to the accomplishment of concentration, one knows that the cycle of life and death is the same as Nirvāṇa, and owing to the attainment of insight, one knows that Nirvāṇa is the same as the cycle of life and death. Further, owing to the accomplishment of concentration, one knows that the cycle of life and death and Nirvāṇa cannot be attained at the same time, but owing to the attainment of insight, one knows that transmigration is the cycle of life and death and the absence of transmigration is Nirvāṇa. (ch. 4, TSD, 46:661)

> *Comment.* Concentration and insight are but two of the stages in Indian meditation, but T'ien-t'ai treats them as the total process. Furthermore, the two are regarded as two wings of a bird, functioning at the same time. The equal emphasis on the volitional and intellectual aspects of the mind is itself indicative of the School's spirit of synthesis. To a certain extent this reflects the intellectual climate of the time, for in sixth-century China, Buddhist thought was intellectual in character in the south while contemplative in the north. The dual method, however, is dictated by the philosophy of the school itself. This is why the two not only go together but reinforce each other. Contemplation assists understanding, and understanding assists contemplation.

25

THE ONE-AND-ALL PHILOSOPHY: FA-TSANG
OF THE HUA-YEN SCHOOL

THE Hua-yen philosophy represents the highest development of Chinese Buddhist thought. It is the most syncretic, and with the philosophy of T'ien-t'ai, forms the metaphysical basis of Chinese Buddhism in the last millennium. Except for the Zen School, it is the most Chinese and has exercised the greatest influence on Neo-Confucian thought.

The teachings of the school are based on the *Hua-yen ching* (Flowery Splendor Scripture)[1] and for this reason the school is called Hua-yen (Flowery Splendor).[2] But in India it never existed as a school. It was in China that it became a movement and a strong one. For a century after the treatise was first translated in 420, it attracted little attention. Eventually interest was aroused. Tu-shun (557-640) lectured and wrote on it and became the nominal founder of the school. The real founder, however, was Fa-tsang (643-712), who built up an elaborate and well-coordinated system on the simple ideas of the scripture.

Fa-tsang became a monk at twenty-eight. There is a record that he assisted Hsüan-tsang (596-664) in his translations,[3] but finally left because he did not agree with him. Since Hsüan-tsang died before Fa-tsang was twenty or had joined the order, the record is probably fiction. But the point the story is intended to make is significant, for the doctrines of the Hua-yen and the Consciousness-Only Schools are strongly opposed at many points. Fa-tsang wrote some sixty works, the most important of which are devoted to the exposition of the Hua-yen philosophy. He enjoyed the strong favor and support of Empress Wu (r. 684-705), who commanded him to lecture on the new translation of the *Avataṁsaka* in 699 in a temple. According to the story, his lecture was so moving that "even the earth shook"! About 704 he lectured before the empress' palace and, finding philosophy too abstruse for her to comprehend, used

[1] *Avataṁsaka sūtra* in Sanskrit. There are three Chinese translations: the 60-chapter version of 420 by Buddhabhadra (359-429), TSD, 9:395-788, which is the standard text; the 80-chapter version of 699 by Śikshānanda (652-710), TSD, 10:1-444; and the 40-chapter version of 798 by Prajña (date unknown), TSD, 10:661-851. The last version is but one of the 40 sections of the former two scriptures, and of which alone there is in existence the Sanskrit original, called the *Gaṇḍavyūha* (Detailed Description of Flowery Splendor). The following references are to the 60-chapter version.

[2] It is called Kegon in Japanese, *kegon* being the Japanese pronunciation of *hua-yen*.

[3] See above, ch. 23, Introduction.

the figure of a lion in the palace architecture to illustrate his points. The result is the famous treatise by its name.[4]

The whole Hua-yen philosophy centers around its fundamental concept, the Universal Causation of the Realm of Dharmas (elements of existence).[5] The Realm of Dharmas (*Dharmadhātu*) connotes the whole universe, which in the belief of the school, is fourfold. It involves the Realm of Facts, the Realm of Principle (*Li*), the Realm of Principle and Facts harmonized, and the Realm of All Facts interwoven and mutually identified. Principle is static, spaceless, formless, characterless, Emptiness, the noumenon; while facts are dynamic, have specific forms and specific characters, are in an unceasing process of transformation, and constitute the phenomenal world. They interact and interpenetrate and thus form a Perfect Harmony.

The basic principle underlying this perfect harmony is the simple idea of interpenetration and mutual identification. It is based on the theory of the Ten Mysterious Gates, according to which all things are coexistent, interwoven, interrelated, interpenetrating, mutually inclusive, reflecting one another, and so on. This doctrine in turn rests on the theory of the Six Characters to the effect that each dharma possesses the six characteristics of universality, specialty, similarity, difference, integration, and disintegration, so that each dharma is at once one and all and the world is in reality a Perfect Harmony. Consequently, when one dharma rises, all dharmas rise with it, and vice versa. In short, the entire universe rises at the same time. This is the meaning of the Universal Causation of the Realm of Dharmas.

So far the Hua-yen system seems to be identical with that of T'ien-t'ai or at most an elaboration of it. Actually, it is a definite advance. The Perfect Harmony in T'ien-t'ai is arrived at through the mutual inclusion of their Ten Characters of Thusness. That of Hua-yen, on the other hand, is arrived at not only through mutual inclusion but, more important, through mutual implication. Dharmas do not merely depend on and correspond to each other. They imply each other as well, for their character of specialty, for example, implies generality, and vice versa. It is this type of interrelationship that makes the one, all, and the all, one, and the entire universe a complete concord. Since dharmas have no substance of their own, they are empty. It is precisely this Emptiness that combines them in these mutual relationships. In a real sense, dharmas exist only in

---

[4] For Fa-tsang's biography and these stories, see *Sung kao-seng chuan* (Biographies of Eminent Monks Compiled in the Sung Period [988]), ch. 5, TSD, 50:732. His family was originally from Sogdiana in present Sinkiang and Russian Central Asia. Before he joined the Buddhist order, he had studied the Hua-yen philosophy extensively.

[5] See Appendix, comment on *Fa* for the meaning of dharma.

relation to each other and to the entire universe, which is a set of inter-relationships. It is too much to suggest that this is organic philosophy, but it certainly points to that direction. Hua-yen exercised considerable influence on Neo-Confucianism chiefly because of this organic character. Its famous metaphor of the big ocean and the many waves was borrowed, with modification, by Chu Hsi (1130-1200).[6] The main concepts of Neo-Confucianism, those of principle and material force, were derived through, if not from, those of principle and fact in Hua-yen. Its one-is-all and all-is-one philosophy shows unmistakable Hua-yen imprints.

Nevertheless, with respect to the relationship between principle and fact, Hua-yen and Neo-Confucianism are diametrically opposed. For Hua-yen, all phenomena are manifestations of the mind but this is not so in the rationalistic Neo-Confucianism of Ch'eng I (Ch'eng I-ch'uan, 1033-1107) and Chu Hsi. It may be said that the idealistic Neo-Con-fucianism of Lu Hsiang-shan (Lu Chiu-yüan, 1139-1193) and Wang Yang-ming (Yang Shou-jen, 1472-1529), which identifies principle with mind, is similar to the idealism of Hua-yen. But historically the Buddhist influence on the Lu-Wang School came by way of the Zen School rather than Hua-yen. In both rationalistic and idealistic Con-fucianism, it is in accordance with principle that the universe "produces and reproduces." The universe is therefore daily renewed. This creative element is lacking in the Universal Causation of Hua-yen.

In comparing the idealistic position of Hua-yen and that of the Con-sciousness-Only School, Fung Yu-lan has observed that inasmuch as Fa-tsang regards the permanent and unchanging mind as the basis of all phenomena, his system is one of objective idealism—implying thereby that the system of Hsüan-tsang is one of subjective idealism.[7] Gen-erally speaking, this is true. The fact remains, however, that in both schools, the external world, called external sphere by Hsüan-tsang and the Realm of Facts by Fa-tsang, is considered manifestations of the mind. In both schools, these manifestations have universal and ob-jective validity, although the degree of validity is higher in Hua-yen. The interesting thing is that Hua-yen presupposes a preestablished harmony while the Consciousness-Only School does not.

Fa-tsang's works are very systematic but unfortunately too summary. The following translations, the *Chin-shih-tzu chang* (Treatise on the Golden Lion) in its entirety and two chapters from his *Hua-yen- i-hai po-men* (Hundred Gates to the Sea of Ideas of the *Flowery Splendor Scripture*) in which he summarized the Hua-yen philosophy in one hundred points, are from his two most important works.

---

[6] See below, ch. 34, sec. 116.
[7] *History of Chinese Philosophy*, vol. 2, p. 359.

A. TREATISE ON THE GOLDEN LION

1. Clarifying the fact that things arise through causation

It means that gold has no nature of its own. As a result of the conditioning of the skillful craftsman, the character[8] of the lion consequently arises. This arising is purely due to causes. Therefore it is called arising through causation.

2. Distinguishing matter and Emptiness

It means that the character of the lion is unreal; there is only real gold. The lion is not existent, but the substance of the gold is not nonexistent. Therefore they are [separately] called matter and Emptiness. Furthermore, Emptiness has no character of its own; it shows itself by means of matter. This does not obstruct its illusory existence. Therefore they are [separately] called matter[9] and Emptiness.

3. Simply stating the Three Natures

The lion exists because of our feelings. This is called [the nature] arising from vast imagination.[10] The lion seems to exist. This is called [the nature of] dependence on others (gold and craftsman) [for production].[11] The nature of the gold does not change. This is therefore called [the nature of] Perfect Reality.[12]

> Comment. In name these Three Natures are not different from those of the Consciousness-Only School.[13] But there is a radical difference. For the Consciousness-Only School, Perfect Reality, as consciousness-only, is in perpetual transformation, whereas for Hua-yen, Perfect Reality does not change.

4. Showing the nonexistence of characters

It means that as the gold takes in the lion in its totality, apart from the gold there is no character of the lion to be found. Therefore it is called the nonexistence of characters.

5. Explaining non-coming-into-existence

It means that at the moment when we see the lion come into existence, it is only gold that comes into existence. There is nothing apart from the gold. Although the lion comes into existence and goes out of existence,

---

[8] *Hsiang* in Chinese and *lakshana* in Sanskrit, meaning feature, form, appearance, etc. It is contrasted with the nature of a thing.

[9] *Rūpa*, meaning form, appearance, phenomenon, color, etc.

[10] *Parikalpita.* [11] *Paratantra.* [12] *Parinishpanna.*

[13] See above, ch. 23, sec. 8.

the substance of the gold at bottom neither increases nor decreases. Therefore we say that [dharmas] do not come into existence [nor go out of existence].

6. Discussing the Five Doctrines

(1) Although the lion is a dharma produced through causation, and comes into and goes out of existence every moment, there is really no character of the lion to be found. This is called the Small Vehicle (Hīnayāna) Doctrine of Ordinary Disciples [that is, the Hīnayāna schools].[14]

(2) These dharmas produced through causation are each without self-nature. It is absolutely Emptiness. This is called the Initial Doctrine of the Great Vehicle (Mahāyāna) [that is, the Three-Treatise and Conscious-Only Schools].

(3) Although there is absolutely only Emptiness, this does not prevent the illusory dharmas from being clearly what they are. The two characters of coming into existence through causation and dependent existence coexist. This is called the Final Doctrine of the Great Vehicle [that is, the T'ien-t'ai School].

(4) These two characters eliminate each other and both perish, and [consequently] neither [the products of] our feelings nor false existence remain. Neither of them has any more power, and both Emptiness and existence perish. Names and descriptions will be completely discarded and the mind will be at rest and have no more attachment. This is called the Great Vehicle's Doctrine of Sudden Enlightenment [that is, the Zen School].

(5) When the feelings have been eliminated and true substance revealed, all becomes an undifferentiated mass. Great function then arises in abundance, and whenever it does, there is surely Perfect Reality. All phenomena are in great profusion, and are interfused but not mixed (losing their own identity). The all is the one, for both are similar in being nonexistent in nature. And the one is the all, for [the relation between] cause and effect is perfectly clear. As the power [of the one] and the function [of the many] embraces each other, their expansion and contraction are free and at ease. This is called the Rounded (inclusive) Doctrine of the One [all-inclusive] Vehicle. [The Hua-yen School.]

14 This refers to one of the Three Vehicles in Buddhism, namely, the Vehicle of Buddha's Direct Disciples (Śrāvaka), or Hīnayāna disciples who attain their own salvation by hearing the Buddha's teachings; the Vehicle of the Self-enlightened Ones (Pratyekabuddha), who attain to their personal enlightenment by their own exertion; and the Vehicle of Bodhisattvas, who are strongly determined to achieve enlightenment for all people.

Comment. The classification of schools is similar to that of the T'ien-t'ai School, which divides the doctrines of the Buddha into five periods, with Hīnayāna literature as elementary and Mahāyāna literature as advanced but that of T'ien-t'ai, the *Lotus Scripture*, as final. It is no surprise that Hua-yen considers itself the culmination of other schools. The sectarian spirit is undeniable. But sectarianism in Buddhism has been mild and free from hostility. The real significance of the classification is its syncretism, which considers an all-inclusive doctrine as the highest truth.

7. *Mastering the Ten Mysteries* [*Gates*][15]

(1) The gold and the lion exist simultaneously, all-perfect and complete in their possession. This is called the gate of simultaneous completion and mutual correspondence.

(2) If the eye of the lion completely takes in the lion, then the all (the whole lion) is purely the eye (the one). If the ear completely takes in the lion, then the all is purely the ear. If all the sense organs simultaneously take in [the lion] and all are complete in their possession, then each of them is at the same time mixed (involving others) and pure (being itself), thus constituting the perfect storehouse. This is called the gate of full possession of the attributes of purity and mixture by the various storehouses.

(3) The gold and the lion are mutually compatible in their formation, the one and the many not obstructing each other. In this situation the principle (the one or the gold) and facts (the many or the lion) are each different, but whether the one or the many, each remains in its own position. This is called the gate of mutual compatibility and difference between the one and the many.

(4) Since the various organs and each and every hair of the lion completely take in the lion by means of the gold, each and every one of them penetrates the whole. The eye of the lion is its ear, its ear is its nose, its nose is its tongue, and its tongue is its body. They each exist freely and easily, one not hindering or obstructing the other. This is called the gate of mutual identification of all dharmas existing freely and easily.

(5) If we look at the lion [as lion], there is only the lion and no gold. This means that the lion is manifest while the gold is hidden. If we look

[15] For the idea of "gates," see above, ch. 24, n.13. The idea behind the theory of the Ten Mysterious Gates originated with Tu-shun, but it was his pupil Chih-yen (602-668) who formulated it. This is called the old Ten Mysterious Gates. Fa-tsang adopted it and changed its order and supplied his own contents. This is called the new Ten Mysterious Gates. Actually the orders in his two pertinent works are somewhat different. Here he explains them in terms of the gold and lion, following the order in one of these two works but again changing the titles of nos. 2 and 10. The purport of all the versions is practically the same.

at the gold, there is only the gold and no lion. This means that the gold is manifest while the lion is hidden. If we look at them both, then both are manifest and both hidden. Being hidden, they are secret, and being manifest, they are evident. This is called the gate of the completion of the secret, the hidden, and the manifest.

(6) The gold and the lion may be hidden or manifest, one or many, definitely pure or definitely mixed, powerful or powerless, the one or the other. The principal and the companion mutually shine. Principle and fact appear together and are completely compatible with each other. They do not obstruct each other's peaceful existence, and thus the subtle and the minute are accomplished. This is called the gate of the compatibility and peaceful existence of the subtle and the minute.

(7) In each of the lion's eyes, ears, limbs, joints, and in each and every hair, there is the golden lion. All the lions embraced by all the single hairs simultaneously and instantaneously enter a single hair. Thus in each and every hair there are an infinite number of lions, and in addition all the single hairs, together with their infinite number of lions, in turn enter into a single hair. In this way the geometric progression is infinite, like the jewels of Celestial Lord Indra's net.[16] This is called the gate of the realm of Indra's net.

(8) The lion is spoken of in order to show the meaning of ignorance[17] while its golden substance is spoken of in order to make sufficiently clear the true nature. And principle and fact are discussed together as a description of the storehouse consciousness[18] so that correct understanding may be created. This is called the gate of relying on facts in order to explain dharmas and create understanding.

(9) The lion is a dharma produced from causes, coming into existence and going out of existence at every moment. Each of these instants is divided into three periods, that is, past, present, and future, and each of these periods contains past, present, and future. Altogether there are three times three units, thus forming nine ages, and these, grouped together, become the total gate [to truth]. Although there are nine ages, each separate from the other, yet, since they are formed because of one another, they are harmoniously merged and mutually penetrated without obstacle and together constitute one instant of time. This is called the gate of different formation of separate dharmas in ten ages (the nine ages separately and all of them together).

[16] Indra is King of Heaven in Hinduism, who fights demons with his thunderbolt. Buddhism adopted him as its defender, but he is considered to be inferior to the Buddha. His net is a favorite Buddhist metaphor. The net is decorated with a bright jewel on each knot of the mesh. Each of these many jewels reflects not only the image of every other jewel, but all the other jewels, and so on to infinity.

[17] Avidya, notably ignorance of facts and principles about dharmas.

[18] This is ālaya consciousness. For its characterization, see above, ch. 23, sec. 3.

(10) The gold and the lion may be hidden or manifest, and may be one or many. Neither has self-nature. They are [always] turning and transforming in accordance with the mind. Whether spoken of as fact or principle, there is the way (the mind) by which they are formed and exist. This is called the gate of the excellent completion through the turning and transformation of the mind only.

8. Putting together the Six Characters

The lion represents the character of universality. The five sense organs, being various and different, represent the character of specialty. The fact that they all arise from one single cause represents the character of similarity. The fact that its eyes, ears, and so forth do not exceed their bounds represents the character of difference. Since the combination of the various organs becomes the lion, this is the character of integration. And as each of the several organs remains in its own position, this is the character of disintegration.

9. Achieving perfect wisdom (bodhi)

"Bodhi" means in Chinese the Way or enlightenment.[19] It means that when we look at the lion, we see right away that all dharmas produced through causes, even before disintegration, are from the very beginning quiescent and extinct.[20] By being free from attachment or renunciation one will flow right along this way into the sea of perfect knowledge. Therefore it is called the Way. One understands right away that from time immemorial all afflictions resulting from passions originally have no reality. This is called enlightenment. The ultimate possession of the wisdom that knows all[21] is called the achievement of perfect wisdom.

10. Entering Nirvāṇa

When we look at the lion and the gold, the two characters both perish and afflictions resulting from passions will no longer be produced. Although beauty and ugliness are displayed before the eye, the mind is as calm as the sea. Erroneous thoughts all cease, and there are no compulsions. One gets out of bondage and is free from hindrances, and for-

[19] These are the two translations of the word. It denotes perfect wisdom.

[20] That is, in the state of Thusness (*Tathātā*), devoid of characters.

[21] *I-ch'ieh-chung chih* in Chinese; it means that one knows from one kind of knowledge all the ways of the various Buddhas. It is the highest of the Three Wisdoms, namely, the wisdom of Buddha's Direct Disciples, who know the character of universality of the emptiness of all dharmas; the wisdom of bodhisattvas or saints, who know the character of specialty, that is, differences and diversities; and the wisdom of the Buddhas, who know both. Thus the last types of wisdom include the preceding two.

ever cuts off the source of suffering. This is called entry into Nirvāṇa. (TSD, 45:663-667)

B. HUNDRED GATES TO THE SEA OF IDEAS OF THE FLOWERY SPLENDOR SCRIPTURE

1. All That Come into Existence Through Causation End Together in Quiescence (ch. 1)

All beings arise through causation, and being is necessarily manifested in many varieties. On the other hand, the absence of [self] nature is a singular principle, and principle shows itself in many characteristics. If we analyze their power and function, the meaning of their expansion and contraction can then be easily seen, and only when we examine their profound principle can the twofold division of principle (*li*) and fact be understood. We shall now, from the point of view of substance and function, briefly discuss ten different principles.

(1) Understanding the fact that things arise through causation

For example, when dust (that is, a small particle of matter) is perceived, it is a manifestation of one's own mind. Since it is manifested by one's own mind, it means that one's own mind is the cause. It is only because the cause reveals [objects] before us that dharmas of the mind arise. This is why the dust is called a dharma arising through causation. The scripture says, "All dharmas arise through causation. Without causes, they will not arise."[22] The causes for our sinking in the sea of suffering do not exist externally. In the final analysis there is no dharma outside the mind that can serve as its cause. Although the dust is distinct, it still clings to no [external] cause. But the character of this round small particle of dust arises on the basis of dharma, is a false construction, and seems to exist, but ultimately has no real substance. One can neither be attached to it[23] nor renounce it, and because one cannot be attached to it or renounce it, we know that the substance of the dust is empty and devoid of all things. Now that we understand that causes are really not causes, any arising will be wonderful. So long as the substance of things arising through causation is void, there will never be any arising even though there seems to be, and if it is understood that substance is in accord with causes, there will always be arising even though there seems to be none. Such a view is called real knowledge and perception.

[22] Source unidentified. A similar saying is found in *Hua-yen ching*, sec. 10, pt. 1, TSD, 9:442.

[23] The word *ch'ü* here is not to be understood as to take, apprehend, seize, or accept, but to cling to or to be attached to.

Comment. The doctrine of all things arising through causation is comparable to the T'ien-t'ai doctrine of all dharmas in their True Nature. Both are manifestations of the mind and both are identical with Thusness.[24] However, to T'ien-t'ai all things are immanent and complete and sufficient in each other, whereas to Hua-yen, all things arise. In this respect, Hua-yen is closer to the dynamic philosophy of the Consciousness-Only School.

(2) Apprehending the realm of dharmas

This little particle of dust arises through causes. This means a dharma. This dharma is manifested in accordance with wisdom and possesses a variety of function. This implies a realm. Because this dharma has no nature [of its own], it can be neither divided nor equalized. It is harmonious without the twofold character of similarity and difference and is identical with reality. It is like the realm of empty space, which extends everywhere, permeates everything, manifests itself wherever it may be, and is always very clear. But this one particle of dust and all other dharmas do not know each other. Nor do they perceive each other. Why? Because each of them is a completely perfect realm of dharmas, universally involving everything, and apart from it there is no other realm of dharmas. Therefore they no longer know or perceive each other. Even if we speak of knowing or perceiving, it is none other than the realm of dharmas knowing and perceiving [itself], and at bottom there is no other realm of dharmas to be known or to be perceived. The scripture says, "The realm of dharmas is at the same time no realm of dharmas. A realm of dharmas does not know [another] realm of dharmas."[25] If neither nature nor character exists, it becomes the realm of dharmas of principle. When both fact and character are clearly in existence without obstacle, it becomes the realm of dharmas of facts. When principle and fact are combined without obstacle, the two are at the same time one and one is at the same time two. This is the realm of dharmas.

Comment. The dual concepts of principle and fact are essentially similar to those of nature and character, substance and function, and the Two Levels of Truth (worldly or relative truth and absolute truth) common in all Mahāyāna schools, especially T'ien-t'ai. The two terms occur often in T'ien-t'ai literature. But in no other place have they occupied such a dominant position as in Hua-yen.

The two concepts can be traced to Neo-Taoism and the Early

24 For this concept, see above, ch. 24, n.19.
25 I have not been able to trace the source of this quotation.

Seven Buddhist Schools where the dual concepts of being and non-being enjoyed their central attention. The idea of principle was already prominent in Neo-Taoism.[26] After it was developed in Buddhism, it eventually became the basic idea in Neo-Confucian thought.

(3) Discerning not-coming-into-existence

It means that the dust is a subsidiary cause of the mind and the mind is the primary cause of the dust. Only when these causes are combined do illusory characters come into existence. Because they come into existence through causation, they surely have no nature of their own. Why? Because the dust is not self-caused but necessarily depends on the mind. Similarly, the mind does not come from itself, but also depends on subsidiary causes. Since they depend on each other, they do not come into existence through any fixed causes. This being the case, we refer to them as not-coming-into-existence. We are not speaking of not-coming-into-existence apart from coming-into-existence through causation. The treatise says, "A primary cause does not by itself cause anything to come into existence but needs subsidiary causes to do so. Subsidiary causes do not by themselves cause anything to come into existence, but need primary causes to do so."[27] Since a thing can be said to come into existence only because it does so through causation, only when we understand that coming-into-existence has no nature [of its own] can we affirm that there is no coming-into-existence. But coming-into-existence and not-coming-into-existence fulfill and negate each other. When negated, there is no coming-into-existence, and when fulfilled, there is coming into existence through causation. Because there is simultaneous fulfillment and negation, therefore at the time of coming into existence there is no coming into existence. He who understands this understands not-coming-into-existence.

(4) Having a correct view of the absence of characters

For example, the characters of this small and round particle of dust arise from the transformations of one's own mind. They are false constructions without reality. Now that one cannot be attached to them, we know that they are unreal and nonexistent. They are produced by the mind and have no self-nature at all. This is called the absence of characters. The scripture says, "All dharmas are originally empty in their nature and have not the least character."[28]

---

[26] See above, ch. 19, introduction.
[27] I have not been able to trace the source of this quotation.
[28] *Hua-yen ching*, sec. 22, pt. 3, TSD, 9:558.

However, although character cannot be attached to, that does not exhaust the idea of nonexistence. From the fact that character has no substance, the nature of dharma is established. Because the character of dharma is not lost inasmuch as the dharma is the basis of its absence, therefore character is at the same time no character and non-character is at the same time character. There is really no difference between character and the absence of character. This idea of the absence of character is similar to the rope appearing as a snake. We say there is no snake at all, but we should realize that the rope is the basis of the absence of snake. As dharma is the basis of the absence of character, character [exists] entirely because dharma possesses no character.

(5) Discriminating formation and destruction

For example, the dust arises through causation. That is formation. But at the same time its substance does not become dust. That is destruction. Now, having discriminated the fact that causes are really not causes, we may use the term "formation through causation," and having discriminated the fact that destruction is really not destruction, we may use the term "destruction through causation." Because destruction does not hinder the initial formation of the dharma, therefore the time of destruction is precisely the time of formation. And because in formation there is nothing to be had, therefore the time of formation is precisely the time of destruction. They are simultaneously established, neither earlier nor later than each other. If there were formation without destruction, that would mean that dharmas exist because of their own nature, and if there were destruction without formation, it would mean that dharmas become empty through cessation.[29] As formation and destruction are identical, characters are thereby manifested.

(6) Showing the hidden and the manifest

When we contemplate the characters of the dust and fail to find them, it means that characters have ceased to be and Emptiness is manifest. It is because when we observe characters we have not directly grasped the principle that it is hidden while the facts are manifest. Furthermore, this dust and other dharmas depend on and involve each other. They differ in their existence or nonexistence. If the dust involves the others, then the others become hidden and the dust becomes manifest. If the others involve the dust, then the dust becomes hidden while the others become manifest. Being hidden and being manifest are identical, for at the moment of being manifest it is already hidden. Why? Because at the

---

[29] To Buddhists, the view that things come to an end is a great heresy, as wrong as the view that things are eternal.

time [the one] is manifest, [the others] are all hidden, which makes it possible [for the one] to be manifest, and at the time [the one] is hidden, [the others] are all manifest, which makes it possible [for the one] to be hidden. As being hidden and being manifest establish each other, therefore the time of being hidden is precisely the time of being manifest and the time of being manifest is precisely the time of being hidden.

(7) Revealing perfect wisdom (bodhi)

It means that the fact that this dust is identical with the Nirvāṇa of quiescence and extinction (devoid of characters) and is without nature [of its own] is revealed by the perfect wisdom of the Buddha. Because of the discrimination and understanding of the principle that all living beings, dust, hair, and so forth have no nature [of their own], the perfect wisdom of the Buddha is achieved. Therefore the teaching for all living beings to achieve Buddhahood can be seen in the wisdom of the Buddha itself. Furthermore, all living beings, dust, hair, and so forth become so because of the principle of the Buddha's perfect wisdom. Therefore the Buddha's resolve to achieve perfect wisdom and to cultivate the deeds of the bodhisattva[30] can be seen in the wisdom of all living beings itself. We should know the perfect wisdom of the Buddha and should have no heretical views. The Buddha is now preaching to all living beings in the world and all living beings are receiving the Buddha's preaching in this world. Therefore the Buddha is the Buddha of all living beings and living beings are living beings of the Buddha. Although they do not exactly coincide, they are at bottom not different. To hold such a view is to resolve to achieve perfect wisdom, to arouse the great compassion which considers all as one body with oneself and to teach and transform all living beings.

(8) Explaining Nirvāṇa

This means that not having understood the manifestations of the dust, one is deluded by manifestation and regards it as coming-into-existence. He in turn sees that the dust is hidden, and being deluded by it, he regards it as going-out-of-existence. Thus on the basis of the characters of coming-into- and going-out-of-existence, which move on like a current, he takes the dust as an object. Transformations arise from this deluded mind, and he considers them to be true and real. Now that in our search for the characters of coming-into- and going-out-of-existence, we find that after all nothing arises and there is nothing to be found, perturbed thoughts naturally cease and erroneous discriminations are annihilated. As these are annihilated, there is great Nirvāṇa. Therefore the scripture

---

[30] One who has dedicated himself to seek salvation for himself and others.

says, "To move on like a current means transmigration. Absolute quiescence means Nirvāṇa."[31]

(9) Investigating going and coming

It means that when the dust follows the wind to the east, its character of going is not to be found, and when it follows the wind to the west, its character of coming is not to be found either. This is all due to the fact that the dharma of dust at bottom has no character of coming or going for it is not real. When it comes, it comes from nowhere, and when it goes, it goes nowhere. The scripture says, "Dharmas neither go nor come, for they never remain [at any point from which to go or to come]."[32] Because the fact that the coming and going of the dust has no substance is understood, therefore the coming or going is at the same time not-coming or not-going, and not-coming or not-going is always coming or going. They are established as one without any difference as between "this" or "that." Therefore the scripture says, "The bodhisattva comes without the character of coming. He goes without the character of going."[33] Therefore although the position of the dust does not change, it reaches the ten cardinal directions, and although the ten cardinal directions remain where they are, they can always enter into the dust. At all times there is neither going nor coming, but the extent of coming and going equals the entire realm of dharmas.

(10) Seeing clearly activity and tranquillity

It means when the dust floats gently around following the wind, that is activity, and when it is absolutely quiet and does not arise, that is tranquillity. Now, because at the time of tranquillity activity does not cease to be, that means tranquillity is entirely formed by activity, and because at the time of activity tranquillity does not cease to be, that means activity is entirely formed by tranquillity. Because they completely form each other, therefore the time of activity is precisely the time of tranquillity, and the time of tranquillity is precisely the time of activity. It is like the wind which is originally not active but can activate all things. If there were activity to start with, it would lose its own substance and be active no more. Think of it.

From the above principles, the theory of things coming into existence through causation is unfathomable; thus its many gates are universally alone. All things are exhaustively combined as one, and all infinities are

---

[31] *Hua-yen ching*, sec. 10, pt. 2, TSD, 9:443.

[32] *ibid.*, sec. 20, TSD, 10:101.

[33] *Vimalakīrtinirdeśa sūtra* (Scripture Spoken by Vimalakīkti), sec. 5 (with slight alteration), TSD, 14:544. I am grateful to Professor Nakamura Hajime of the University of Tokyo and Professor Mou Tsung-san of Hong Kong for this information.

embraced to form a totality. If we investigate its mystery, although [coming-into-existence through causation] may occupy a narrow position, it is always broad, and if we wish to investigate its source, we find that the deeper it is, the shallower it becomes. The principle of coming-into-existence through causation is great indeed! (TSD, 45:627-628)

2. Harmonious Combination and Spontaneity (ch. 4)

The sea of the nature of things has no shore, and because of that, its characteristics have become many and extensive. Coming-into-existence through causation is unfathomable; thus its many gates are universally prevalent and open. [All things] turn on and on in ten thousand different ways, but the form of expansion and contraction accords with wisdom. Harmoniously combined as one, the conditions of their opening and closing follow the mind. As [the mind is as clear as] shining and does not give rise to incipient [and disturbing] activity, although there are varieties and differences, it is always in harmony with them. And since function does not pervert substance, although [things] are of one flavor, they are always free and without obstacle. We shall now, from the point of view of substance and tendency, briefly discuss ten different principles.

(1) Appreciating principle and fact

For example, the dust has the characters of roundness and smallness. This is fact. Its nature is empty and nonexistent. This is principle. Because facts have no substance, they merge together in accordance with principle. And because the dust has no substance, it universally penetrates everything. For all facts are no different from principle and they are completely manifested in the dust. Therefore the scripture says, "The wide world is the same as the narrow world, and the narrow world is the same as the wide world."[34]

(2) Discerning matter and Emptiness

For example, dust is formed through causation; this is matter. Matter has no substance; this is Emptiness. If Emptiness is spoken of apart from matter, it would mean that there is no false matter in the realm of worldly truth, and that because of false matter there is the True Emptiness in the realm of absolute truth. If matter is spoken of apart from Emptiness, it would mean that there is no True Emptiness in the realm of absolute truth, and that because of True Emptiness there is false matter in the realm of worldly truth. Now, it is only necessary to understand that True Emptiness means that matter is false and has no substance. Emptiness is not so called because there is no matter. The scripture says,

[34] *Hua-yen ching*, sec. 13, TSD, 9:450.

"Matter is empty not because it has been destroyed, but because it is of itself empty.[35]

(3) Penetrating the big and the small

For example, dust has the character of roundness; this is smallness. Mount Sumeru is high and wide; this is bigness. But this dust and that mountain, though one is big and the other small, contain each other, turn on and on in accordance with the mind, and neither come into nor go out of existence. For example, when one sees a mountain as high and wide, it is his own mind that manifests it as large; there is no largeness distinct from it. When one sees the dust as round and small, it is also his own mind that manifests it as small; there is no smallness distinct from it. Thus when we see this dust, it is entirely the dust manifested by the mind which sees the mountains as high and wide. Therefore the large is contained right in the small. The scripture says, "The number of Hard Iron Enclosing Mountains[36] is infinite. All of them can be placed at the tip of a hair. In order to understand the largest and the smallest phenomena the bodhisattva therefore begins his resolution [to seek perfect wisdom]."[37]

(4) Taking in both the far and the near

It means that this dust is near and the world of the ten cardinal directions is far away. But as the dust has no substance, it fully penetrates all the ten cardinal directions. In other words, the ten directions are all those of the dust. Therefore the far is always near. However, although the ten directions are far away, they are merely those of the nature of dust. Even though they go beyond a world which cannot be described, they still do not go outside the nature of dust. Why? Because the extension of dust has no substance. It is similar to space and cannot be transcended. Therefore all the ten cardinal directions are but manifestations of the nature of dust. Furthermore, although one leaves this dust and goes to the ten directions, one still sees this dust. Why? Because the dust has no substance, and facts [of which dust is an instance] are clearly manifested in accordance with principle. Therefore when the nature of the dust universally pervades everything, the dust as a fact is also manifested at the same time. This means that in one particle of dust everything is manifested and both the near and the far are clearly before our eyes. As the ten directions enter into one particle of dust, they are always near although they are far, and as the dust universally pervades all the ten

[35] *Vimalakīrtinirdeśa sūtra*, sec. 9, TSD, 14:551.
[36] These mountains are believed to encircle the earth.
[37] *Hua-yen ching*, sec. 11, TSD, 9:447.

directions, it is always far although it is near. Both the dust and the ten directions, and both the far and the near, are clearly identical without any difference. Think of it.

(5) Understanding the pure and the mixed

It means that inasmuch as the dust does not come into existence, all dharmas do not come into existence. This is purity. Nevertheless, in the idea itself that the dust does not come into existence, both principle and fact are fully contained. It is both Emptiness and matter, and both perfect wisdom and Nirvāṇa. This is a case of what is mixed. Principle never obstructs fact, for what is pure is always mixed. Fact always fulfills principle, for the mixed is always pure. Because both principle and fact are free and at ease, they do not obstruct each other.

(6) Comprehending the instant and the infinitely long period

For example, when the dust is perceived, it is a manifestation of the mind for an instant. This manifestation of the mind for an instant is entirely the same as hundreds and thousands of infinitely long periods. Why? Because all these periods are originally formed from an instant. Since they establish each other, both lack substance or nature. Because an instant has no substance, it penetrates the infinitely long periods, and because these periods have no substance, they are fully contained in a single instant. Since both the instant and the long periods have no substance, the characters of length and shortness are naturally harmonized. All worlds, whether far or near, the Buddhas, living beings, and all things in the three ages (past, present, and future) are manifested in one instant. Why? Because all things and dharmas are manifested in accordance with the mind. As there is no obstruction to the instant [of thought], all dharmas are consequently harmonized. Therefore in an instant [of thought] all facts and things in the three ages are clearly seen. The scripture says, "Any instant is the same as hundreds and thousands of infinitely long periods, and hundreds and thousands of infinitely long periods are the same as a single instant."[38]

> *Comment.* One cannot help recalling the T'ien-t'ai doctrine of three thousand worlds immanent in one single instant of thought. In fact, the ideas of the two schools are so close that they have formed a common foundation for Chinese Buddhist teachings. As the saying goes, "The Hua-yen and T'ien-t'ai Schools for doctrines, and the Zen and Pure Land Schools for practice."

[38] *ibid.*, sec. 13, TSD, 9:451.

(7) Discriminating the one and the many

For example, the dust's own character is one. It is because its own one-ness is quiescent and calm that it can universally respond to become many. If its own oneness is perturbed, it will lose its universal corre-spondence [to others] and the many [to which it universally responds] cannot be formed. The same is true of the two, the three, and so forth.

Furthermore, the one and the many established each other. Only when the one is completely the many can it be called the one, and only when the many is completely the one can it be called the many. There is not a separate one outside the many, for we clearly know that it is one within [coincides with] the many. There are not the many outside of the one, for we clearly know they are the many within the one. The reason is that they are not many [separately] and yet they can be many [coincid-ing with] the one, and that it is not [independently] the one and yet it can be one [coinciding with] the many. Only when we understand that [dharmas] have no nature [of their own] can we have the wisdom about the one and the many. The scripture says, "It is like calculation. From one gradually to ten down to infinity, all comes from the basic number. When viewed with wisdom, there is no difference."[39]

(8) Appreciating the unrestricted and the restricted

It means that the dust has the character of smallness; that is restric-tion. But the very character has no substance; this is non-restriction. Now, an infinite number of lands and seas are always manifested in the dust. This means the unrestricted is always restricted. But one particle of dust universally pervades all lands and seas. This means the restricted is al-ways unrestricted. Furthermore, the small need not be destroyed to con-tain the large, which means that the mysterious particle of dust extensively contains the lands [and seas] of the Buddha. The large need not be destroyed in order to dwell in the small, which means that the mysterious lands and seas of the Buddha are always manifested in the dust. This is the non-obstruction between the unrestricted and the re-stricted.

(9) Understanding expansion and contraction

It means that the dust has no nature [of its own]. When substance comes to the fore and completely permeates the ten cardinal directions, that is expansion. The ten directions have no substance and are entirely manifested in the dust through causation—that is contraction. The scripture says, "One land of the Buddha fills the ten directions, and the

[39] *ibid.*, sec. 16, TSD, 9:465, a paraphrase.

ten directions enter into the one [land] without residue."[40] When contracted, all things are manifested in one particle of dust. When expanded, one particle of dust will universally permeate everything. Expanding is the same as ever contracting, for a particle of dust involves everything. Contracting is the same as ever expanding, for everything involves the one particle of dust. This is what is meant by saying that expansion and contraction are free and at ease.

(10) Grasping perfect harmony

It means that as the character of the dust has already ceased to be, deluded consciousness also perishes. Because fact has no substance, it follows principle and becomes perfectly harmonized with it. Because substance involves facts, therefore principle follows fact and is in complete accord with it. Thus they always exist but are at the same time ever empty, for Emptiness does not destroy existence. They are always empty but at the same time ever existent, for existence does not obstruct Emptiness. The Emptiness that does not obstruct existence can harmonize all phenomena, and the existence that does not destroy Emptiness can complete everything. Therefore all phenomena clearly exist before us and one does not obstruct the other.

From the above principles, the tendency of harmonious combination becomes unrestricted because it has no nature, and all phenomena which exist spontaneously can be combined because they rise through causation. As the one and the many totally involve each other, we look at one particle of dust and [everything] suddenly becomes manifest. As the "this" takes in the "other," we look at a tiny hair and all things appear together. The reason is that, when the mind understands, all dharmas can be free and at ease, and because the principle is clear, great wisdom can be achieved. Among seekers after wisdom, who will examine its source? People talking about it seldom investigate its mystery to the limit. What can match the function of spontaneity? (TSD, 45:630-631)

---

[40] *ibid.*, sec. 2, pt. 3, TSD, 9:414.

26

THE ZEN (CH'AN) SCHOOL OF SUDDEN
ENLIGHTENMENT

THE CH'AN MOVEMENT, better known as Zen, has been described by Hu Shih (1891-1962) as a "reformation or revolution in Buddhism,"[1] and by Suzuki as a movement in which "the Chinese mind completely asserted itself, in a sense, in opposition to the Indian mind. Zen could not rise and flourish in any other land or among any other people."[2] The two outstanding scholars sharply differ in their approaches to Zen: the one, historical; the other, religious and mystical. But they reinforce each other in characterizing Zen's development in Chinese history, for it was through a revolution that Ch'an came completely into its own.

Literally, the name of the school should be Meditation, for the Sanskrit *dhyāna*, pronounced in Chinese "ch'an" and in Japanese "zen," means that. But meditation changed its character in China almost from the very inception of Buddhism, although the typically Indian form of sitting in meditation and concentrating one's mind to the point of ignoring the external world has continued in Chinese Buddhist schools. When Buddhism first came to China, it was mixed up with the Yellow Emperor–Lao Tzu cult. As a result, meditation was not understood in the Indian sense of concentration but in the Taoist sense of conserving vital energy, breathing, reducing desire, preserving nature, and so forth. This was the meditation taught by early Buddhist Masters like An Shih-kao (c.A.D. 150), Kumārajīva (344-413), Tao-an (312-385), and Hui-yüan (334-416). In the end, meditation meant neither sitting in meditation nor mental concentration, but simply the direct enlightenment of the mind.

Tradition traces the beginning of the school to Bodhidharma (fl. 460-534), whose historicity has been questioned in the West. Most Chinese and Japanese scholars, however, are satisfied that he did come to China.[3] But a clear picture of the school did not emerge until Hung-

---

[1] Hu Shih, "Ch'an (Zen) Buddhism in China: Its History and Method," *Philosophy East and West*, 3 (1953), p. 12.

[2] Suzuki, "Zen: A Reply to Hu Shih," *ibid.*, p. 40.

[3] See Hu Shih, *Hu Shih lun-hsüeh chin-chu* (Recent Essays on Learned Subjects by Hu Shih), 1931, pp. 486-487, T'ang Yung-t'ung, *Han Wei Liang-Chin Nan-pei-ch'ao Fo-chiao shih* (History of Chinese Buddhism from 206 B.C. to A.D. 589), Shang-hai, 1938, pp. 779-780, and Lo Hsiang-lin, *T'ang-tai wen-hua shih* (History of the Civilization of the T'ang Dynasty, 618-907), Taiwan, 1955, pp. 110-123. Tradition said that Bodhidharma came to Canton in 520 or 527. Hu rejects these dates and said he came during 470-475. Lo believes he arrived between 465 and 524. T'ang thinks he died in China before 534. For his biography see *Hsü kao-seng chuan*

jen (601-674).⁴ With him the history of Zen in China took a radical turn. According to tradition, Bodhidharma handed down the *Laṅkāvatāra sūtra* (Scripture about [The Buddha] Entering into Laṅka)⁵ whereas Hung-jen taught the *Diamond Scripture*.⁶ The central emphasis of the former is Ultimate Reality or the true nature of dharmas (elements of existence), whereas the emphasis of the latter is on the mind, and it is the mind rather than Ultimate Reality that has become the central focus of Chinese Zen. Hung-jen's two outstanding disciples, Shen-hsiu (605?–706) in the north⁷ and Hui-neng (638-713)⁸ in the south, developed divergent tendencies. Shen-hsiu stressed gradual enlightenment of the mind whereas Hui-neng stressed sudden enlightenment.

For decades Shen-hsiu had been a celebrated Zen Master in the north. In 700, at the age of ninety, he was invited to the capital by Empress Wu (r. 684–705), who did him the extraordinary honor of curtseying to him.

(Supplement to the *Biographies of Eminent Monks*), ch. 19, TSD, 50:551 and *Ching-te ch'uan-teng lu* (Records of the Transmission of the Lamp Compiled during the Ching-te Period, 1004-1107), SPTK, 3:1b-9b. It is not certain whether he was a Persian or the son of an Indian prince. He first came and settled in a monastery in Canton. Unproved traditional accounts have added that he was invited by the emperor to go to the capital at Nanking. When the emperor asked if there was any merit in building temples or copying scriptures, he said no. Realizing that the emperor did not understand, he left and went to Lo-yang. For forty or fifty years he propagated the Laṅka doctrine in North China and attracted many followers.

⁴ For his biography, see *Sung kao-seng chuan* (Biographies of Eminent Monks Compiled in the Sung Period [988]), ch. 8, TSD, 50:54, and *Ching-te ch'uan-teng lu*, 3:14b-16a. Accounts of his life are mostly legends. It is agreed that he was a bright boy and that after he joined the Buddhist order he spent most of his time in spiritual cultivation and teaching. In 659 he was favored with an imperial audience.

⁵ See translation by Suzuki, *Laṅkāvatāra Sūtra*. It is from the existing Sanskrit text. The scripture that Bodhidharma is said to have transmitted is one of the four Chinese translations which were evidently made from different Sanskrit texts that are lost.

⁶ The *Chin-kang ching* or *Vajracchedikā*, perhaps the most popular Buddhist scripture in China. Among English translations, see Conze, *Buddhist Wisdom Books*, pp. 21-71, with commentary, and Shao Chang Lee, *Popular Buddhism in China*, pp. 27-52.

⁷ For his biography, see *Sung kao-seng chuan*, ch. 8, TSD, 50:755-756, and *Ching-te ch'uan-teng lu*, 4:15a-b. He was quite a student of Chinese philosophy before he joined the Buddhist order, having thoroughly studied Lao Tzu, Chuang Tzu, and the *Book of Changes*. He became a monk probably at fifteen or older and Hung-jen's pupil in 669 when he was at least fifty years old. He was therefore Hung-jen's pupil for six years until the latter died. He was an abbot in a monastery in Hupei in central China until he was called by the empress. See Lo Hsiang-lin, *T'ang-tai wen-hua shih*, pp. 105-108, 136-143.

⁸ See *Sung kao-seng ch'uan*, ch. 8, TSD, 50:754-755 and *Ching-te ch'uan-teng lu*, 5:3a-5b. His life story told in the following selections is probably legendary. He was a native of Kwangtung. It is fairly certain that he was an orphan at three, went to visit Hung-jen at thirty-four, and became a Buddhist priest in Canton at thirty-nine. See Lo Hsiang-lin, *ibid.*, pp. 143-156.

Shen-hsiu's prestige and influence soared to great heights. He was honored as "the Lord of the Law at the Two National Capitals of Ch'ang-an and Lo-yang, and the Teacher of Three Sovereigns." His movement, later known as the Northern School of Zen, almost completely dominated the religious and intellectual life of the time.

Some years before these triumphant events, Hui-neng, originally an illiterate fuel-wood peddler, preached radically new doctrines in Ts'aohsi, about 120 miles north of Canton. In 734, his pupil Shen-hui (670-762)[9] who, like Shen-hsiu before him, enjoyed strong support from the aristocrats and had a large following, openly attacked Shen-hsiu's school in the north. The freshness and the challenging spirit of their teachings became an irresistible attraction. A stampede was soon on, and their school, later known as the Southern School, eventually overshadowed the Northern School and from the ninth century onward, the story of Zen has been that of the Southern School.

The two schools are usually distinguished by the fact that while the Northern School advocates gradual enlightenment, the Southern School advocates sudden enlightenment. As a matter of emphasis, this is certainly correct. But Shen-hsiu did not rule out sudden enlightenment and neither Hui-neng nor Shen-hui rejected gradual enlightenment altogether. The contrast between the two schools is much deeper. It lies in the different concepts of the mind.

Both schools started from the major premise that Nirvāṇa is identical with the original substance of the Buddha-mind, which is the same as Buddha-nature, and that Buddha-nature is in all men so that all can become Buddhas. So far both schools remain within the Buddhist traditions of idealism and universal salvation. But while the Northern School teaches that the pure mind arises from absolute quietude and does so only after erroneous thoughts are eliminated, the Southern School insists that the mind cannot be split into parts and that all its activities are functions of Thusness (True Reality).[10] Consequently, the mind cannot be divided into the true mind without differentiation, on the one hand, and the false mind with differentiation, on the other. Furthermore, the

[9] For his biography see *Sung kao-seng chuan*, ch. 8, TSD, 50:756-757 and *Ching-te ch'uan-teng lu*, 5:24a-b. His dates are usually given as 668-760, but after recent research Hu Shih decided on 670-762. See *Bulletin of the Institute of History and Philology, Academica Sinica*, 29 (1958), p. 875; extra vol. 4 (1960), p. 6. He studied Confucianism and Taoism before be became a Buddhist priest. After he was thirty, he went south to see Hui-neng. Much affected, he returned north to preach the doctrine of sudden enlightenment. In 720 he was appointed to be a priest in Honan and in 745 he was invited to live in a temple in the eastern capital, Lo-yang. Eight years later he was banished to Kiangsi because he was suspected of "gathering large crowds with harmful motives."

[10] For this concept, see above, ch. 24, n.19.

Northern School considers the mind in its undisturbed state as calmness (*samādhi*) and the senses in their undisturbed state as wisdom (*prajñā*), but the Southern School refuses to accept the distinction, regarding both as of one substance and not two. In fact, it affirms the unity not only of the mind but of everything else. The Buddha-mind is everywhere so that anything can be an occasion for its realization at any moment and this realization can take place in any way. It was out of this major concept that the peculiar Zen methods have evolved.

The standard sayings of the school are: "Point directly to the human mind" and "See one's nature and become a Buddha." Everything other than the cultivation of the mind, such as reading scriptures, making offerings to the Buddha, reciting His name, joining the monastic order, are regarded as unnecessary. The total effect is to minimize, if not to wipe out, the whole Buddhist organization, creed, and literature and to reduce Buddhism to a concern with one's mind alone. The logical conclusions are that everyone can achieve enlightenment and become a Buddha, since everyone possesses the Buddha-nature,[11] that he can do so immediately, and that he can do so "in this very body." No matter how one looks at this movement, it was revolutionary in the true sense of the word.

Since the chief concern of the school is the Buddha-mind in everything, various methods were developed to realize it. Shen-hui himself taught "the absence of thought" so that the mind will return to its original state of tranquillity. Another Zen Master (though he cannot be said to belong to either the Northern or Southern tradition) emphasized "forgetting our feelings" so as to remove selfish clingings and evil desires. Still another Zen Master advocated "letting the mind take its own course" so it can be at ease and not be disturbed either by its own differentiated characters or by the phenomenal world, for both of these are, after all, manifestations of the Buddha-mind. The influence of Neo-Taoism and early Buddhism on this development is obvious.

So far these methods are still traditional. From the ninth century to the eleventh, however, novel and unconventional techniques were developed, and vigorously, if only occasionally, applied. One was travel, which was calculated to broaden one's perspective and deepen one's insight. When one's experience is enriched, one day he will suddenly intuit truth at the singing of a bird, the blooming of a flower, or a drop of rain. Another method was "never to tell too plainly,"[12] for the obvious reason that the student must discover truth himself.

The more interesting, more radical, and perhaps most misunderstood

---

[11] For the doctrine of universal salvation, see above, ch. 24 Introduction.
[12] *Pu-shuo-p'o*.

technique is the *koan*.[13] Literally *koan* means an official document on the desk, connoting a sense of important decision and the final determination of truth and falsehood. To this end Zen Masters made use of any story, problem, or situation, the more shocking the better. But more often than not, the method consists of a question and an enigmatic answer. It is often believed that such answers are due to the belief that truth is so mysterious, irrational, or paradoxical that only an illogical answer can reveal it. Nothing is farther from the truth. When a pupil asked, "Whenever there is any question, one's mind is confused. What is wrong?" and the answer was, "Kill! Kill!" this may sound absurd.[14] But when a pupil asked what the Buddha was, and the Master answered, "Three pounds of flax," it is not as silly as one may think.[15] Any alert mind will soon realize that conceptualization can never discover what the Buddha is and that he should return to his spontaneous mental faculty to look for the answer himself.

But the most puzzling technique is that of shouting and beating. Even these are not madness or dramatics but an unorthodox way of shocking the pupil out of his outmoded mental habits and preconceived opinions so that his mind will be pure, clear, and thoroughly awakened. In short, the whole philosophy of the various methods is to broaden a person's vision, sharpen his imagination, and sensitize his mind so that he can see and grasp truth instantly any time and anywhere. This type of mental training is utterly Chinese. Nothing like it can be found in the tradition of Indian meditation. In Indian meditation, the mind tries to avoid the external world, ignores outside influence, aims at intellectual understanding, and seeks to unite with the Infinite. Chinese meditation, on the other hand, works with the aid of external influence, operates in this world, emphasizes quick wit and insight, and aims at self-realization.

It was inevitable that such a philosophy would exercise a profound influence. Its impact on Chinese philosophy was great. The new doctrine of seriousness (*ching*)[16] in Neo-Confucianism was one of its direct products, and the whole idealistic Neo-Confucian movement of several hundred years, initiated by Lu Hsiang-shan (Lu Chiu-yüan, 1139-1193) and culminating in Wang Yang-ming (Wang Shou-jen, 1472-1529), was so much influenced by it that it has often been called Zen in Confucian

[13] *Kung-an* in Chinese and *koan* in Japanese.

[14] *Ts'ao-shan Pen-chi Ch'an-shih yü-lu* (Recorded Conversations of Zen Master Pen-chi, 840-901), TSD, 47:539.

[15] *Ching-te ch'uan-teng lu*, 19:14b. One of the most famous *koans*. *Pi-yen lu* (Records of the Green Cave), no. 12.

[16] See Appendix for comments on *Ching*. Also see below, ch. 34, comment on sec. 12, and lists of topics in chs. 31 and 32.

disguise. Even the Neo-Confucian tradition of compiling and publishing the recorded sayings of philosophers is an imitation of those of Zen.

The basic teachings of Zen are recorded in the *Liu-tsu t'an-ching* (Platform Scripture of the Sixth Patriarch). The following includes selections from it and also some from the *Shen-hui yü-lu* (Recorded Conversations of Shen-hui). In addition, there are selections from the *Lin-chi Hui-chao Ch'an-shih yü-lu* (Recorded Conversations of Zen Master I-hsüan, d. 867). He was the founder of the Lin-chi School, one of the seven schools that developed within the Southern School in the ninth century. Each had its peculiar method, but the Lin-chi "lightning" technique was the most radical of all.

A. THE PLATFORM SCRIPTURE[17]

3. Priest Hung-jen asked me (Hui-neng), "Whence have you come to this mountain to pay reverence to me? What do you wish from me?"

I answered, "Your disciple is a native of Ling-nan,[18] a citizen of Hsin-chou. I have purposely come a great distance to pay you reverence. I seek nothing other than to practice the Law of the Buddha."

The Great Master reproved me, saying, "You are from Ling-nan, and, furthermore, you are a barbarian. How can you become a Buddha?"

I answered, "Although people are distinguished as northerners and southerners, there is neither north nor south in the Buddha-nature. The

---

[17] These selections are made from the oldest version of the *Liu-tsu t'an-ching* discovered in a Tun-huang cave in 1900. In 1907 Sir Aurel Stein brought it to the British Museum. It contains about 11,000 Chinese characters and is included in TSD, no. 2007, 48:337-345. There are many mistakes in the Tun-huang copy. In these selections, the most obvious mistakes have been corrected. Minor corrections, however, have not been noted in footnotes. Sectioning follows the collated edition by Suzuki Teitarō and Kuda Rentarō, published in Tokyo in 1934, entitled *Tonkō shutsudo Rokuso dankyō* (The Platform Scripture of the Sixth Patriarch Uncovered at Tun-huang). For a complete translation and a lengthy discussion of this Tun-huang manuscript, see Wing-tsit Chan, trans., *The Platform Scripture, The Basic Classic of Zen Buddhism*, St. John's University Press, 1963.

There are five later versions of the *Liu-tsu t'an-ching*. The latest version (TSD no. 12008, 48:345-365) is dated 1291. It is included in the Ming dynasty (1368-1644) editions of the Buddhist Canon of 1420-1440 and is therefore generally called the Ming Canon version. It has been in general use for centuries. For two English translations and a partial German version, see Bibliography under "Hui-neng." The Tun-huang version bears a very long title, of which *Liu-tsu . . . . t'an-ching* is only a part, and ascribes it to Hui-neng. Dr. Hu Shih thinks that it was probably by an eighth-century monk, most likely a follower of Shen-hui's school (*Philosophy East and West*, 3 [1953], p. 11). In any case, the later the version was, the more additions and interpolation, so that the Ming Canon version is twice as long as the oldest text. However, elaboration does not alter the general story or the fundamental teachings.

[18] Literally "South of the mountain ranges," in the region of present Canton in South China.

physical body of the barbarian and [that of][19] the monk are different. But what difference is there in their Buddha-nature?"

The Great Master intended to argue with me further, but, seeing people around, said nothing more. He ordered me to attend to duties among the rest. Then a lay attendant ordered me to the rice-pounding area[20] to pound rice. This I did for more than eight months.

4. One day the Fifth Patriarch (Hung-jen) suddenly called all his pupils to come to him. When we had already[21] assembled, he said, "Let me say this to you: Life and death are serious matters. You disciples are engaged all day in making offerings, going after fields of blessings[22] only, and you make no effort to achieve freedom from the bitter sea of life and death. If you are deluded in your own nature, how can blessings save you? Go to your rooms, all of you, and think for yourselves. Those who possess wisdom use the wisdom (*prajñā*) inherent in their own nature. Each of you must write a verse and present it to me. After I see the verses, I will give the robe and the Law to the one who understands the basic idea [of the Law preached by the Buddha] and will appoint him to be the Sixth Patriarch. Hurry, hurry!"

6. . . . . At midnight Head Monk Shen-hsiu, holding a candle, wrote a verse on the wall of the south corridor, without anyone knowing about it, which said:

> The body is the tree of perfect wisdom (*bodhi*)
> The mind is the stand of a bright mirror.
> At all times diligently wipe it.
> Do not allow it to become dusty.

7. . . . . The Fifth Patriarch said, "The verse you wrote shows some but not complete understanding. You have arrived at the front door but you have not yet entered it. Ordinary people, by practicing in accordance with your verse, will not fail. But it is futile to seek the supreme perfect wisdom while holding to such a view. One must enter the door and see his own nature. Go away and come back after thinking a day or two. Write another verse and present it to me. If then you have entered the door and have seen your own nature, I will give you the robe and the Law." Head Monk Shen-hsiu went away and for several days could not produce another verse.

8. . . . . I (Hui-neng) also composed a verse. . . . My verse says:

[19] Insertion according to Ui Hakuju, *Zenshūshi kenkyū* (Studies in the History of Zen), vol. 2, Tokyo, 1941, p. 119.
[20] A *fang*, which could be a sizable area or simply a room.
[21] Read *chi* (record) as *ch'i* (already), according to Ui, *ibid*., p. 120.
[22] Where the blessings will keep on growing.

Fundamentally perfect wisdom has no tree.
Nor has the bright mirror any stand.
Buddha-nature is forever clear and pure.
Where is there any dust?

Another verse, which says:

The mind is the tree of perfect wisdom.
The body is the stand of a bright mirror.
The bright mirror is originally clear and pure.
Where has it been defiled by any dust?

Monks in the hall were all surprised at these verses. I, however, went back to the rice-pounding area. The Fifth Patriarch suddenly realized that I alone had the good knowledge and understanding of the basic idea, but he was afraid lest the rest learn it. He therefore told them, "He does not understand perfectly after all."

9. The Fifth Patriarch waited till midnight, called me to come to the hall, and expounded the *Diamond Scripture*. As soon as I heard this, I understood. That night the Law was imparted to me without anyone's knowing it, and thus the method of sudden enlightenment and the robe were transmitted to me. "You are now the Sixth Patriarch. This robe is the testimony of transmission from generation to generation. As to the Law, it is to be transmitted from mind to mind. Let people achieve enlightenment through their own effort."

The Fifth Patriarch said, "Hui-neng, from the very beginning, in the transmission of the Law one's life is as delicate as hanging by a thread. If you remain here, someone might harm you. You must leave quickly."

Comment. The praise of the *Diamond Scripture* may conflict with the doctrine of total rejection of literature enunciated below. The important point, however, is that before Hui-neng, the most important scripture in Zen was the *Laṅkāvatāra sūtra* (Scripture about [the Buddha] Entering into Laṅka).[23] Hui-neng praised the *Diamond Scripture* instead. This in itself was a revolt.

12. Then I came and stayed in this place (the Canton region) and associated with government officials, disciples who have renounced their families, and lay folk. This, after all, was due to causes operating over many long periods of time. The doctrine has been handed down from past sages; it is not my own wisdom. Those who wish to hear the teachings of past sages must purify their hearts. Having heard them, they

---

[23] English translation by Suzuki, *Laṅkāvatāra Sūtra.* Laṅka is an island south of India, popularly identified with Ceylon.

must vow to rid themselves of delusions and thereby to become enlightened as[24] the former sages. (This is the method described below.)[25]

Great Master Hui-neng declared, "Good and learned friends, perfect wisdom is inherent in all people. It is only because they are deluded in their minds that they cannot attain enlightenment by themselves. They must seek the help of good and learned friends of high standing to show them the way to see [their own] nature. Good and learned friends, as soon as one is enlightened, he attains wisdom."

13. "Good and learned friends, calmness (*samādhi*) and wisdom (*prajñā*) are the foundations of my method.[26] First of all, do not be deceived into thinking that the two are different. They are one substance and not two. Calmness is the substance of wisdom and wisdom is the function of calmness. Whenever wisdom is at work, calmness is within it. Whenever calmness is at work, wisdom is within it. Good and learned friends, the meaning here is that [calmness and] wisdom are identified. Seekers of the Way, arouse your minds. Do not say that wisdom follows[27] calmness or vice versa, or that the two are different. To hold such a view [would imply that] the dharmas (elements of existence) possess two different characters. In the case of those whose words are good but whose hearts are not good, wisdom and calmness are not identified. But in the case of those whose hearts and words are both good and in whom the internal and the external are one, calmness and wisdom are identified. Self-enlightenment and practice do not consist in argument. If one is concerned about which comes first, he is a [deluded][28] person. If he is not freed from the consideration of victory or defeat, he will produce the dharmas as real entities[29] and cannot be free from the Four Characters [of coming into existence, remaining in the same state, change, and going out of existence]."

> *Comment.* This spirit of synthesis is characteristic of the Southern School. We have already seen this synthetic character of the mind in Hua-yen and T'ien-t'ai. In fact, this goes back to early Taoism and Neo-Taoism, and it is no wonder that Zen writers employed many Taoist and Neo-Taoist terms, such as "substance" and "function" and "original substance." Shen-hui as a youth studied the *Lao Tzu* and *Chuang Tzu*.

[24] Read *yü* (in) as *ju* (as). The popular (Ming Canon) version, sec. 2, has *ju*.
[25] Original note in the text.
[26] This is *fa-men* in Chinese. See above, ch. 24, n.13.
[27] Read *fa* (start) as *hou* (afterward).
[28] Insertion following Suzuki and Kuda. See n.17.
[29] The popular version, sec. 4, has "self dharma," that is, the dharma of self, instead of dharma-self, or dharmas and the self. In this case the four characters become those of a self, a human being, a being among men, and a being with a definite span of life.

16. "Good and learned friends, in method there is no distinction between sudden enlightenment and gradual enlightenment. Among men, however, some are intelligent and others are stupid. Those who are deluded understand gradually, while the enlightened achieve understanding suddenly. But when they know their own minds, then they see their own nature, and there is no difference in their enlightenment. Without enlightenment, they remain forever bound in transmigration."

17. "Good and learned friends, in this method of mine, from the very beginning, whether in the sudden-enlightenment or gradual-enlightenment tradition, absence-of-thought has been instituted as the main doctrine, absence-of-characters as the substance, and nonattachment as the foundation. What is meant by absence-of-characters? Absence-of-characters means to be free from characters while in the midst of them. Absence-of-thought means not to be carried away by thought in the process of thought. Nonattachment is man's original nature. Thought after thought goes on without remaining. Past, present, and future thoughts continue without termination. But if we cut off and terminate thought one instant, the dharma-body (Law-body or spiritual body)[30] is freed from the physical body. At no time should a single instant of thought be attached to any dharma. If one single instant of thought is attached to anything, then every thought will be attached. That is bondage. But if in regard to dharmas no thought is attached to anything, that is freedom. [This is] the meaning of having nonattachment as the foundation.

"Good and learned friends, to be free from all characters means the absence of characters. Only if we can be free from characters will the substance of our nature be pure. That is the meaning of taking the absence-of-character as the substance.

"Absence-of-thought means not to be defiled by external objects.[31] It is to free our thoughts from external objects and not to have thoughts arise over dharmas. But do not[32] stop thinking about everything and eliminate all thought. As soon as thought stops, one dies[33] and is reborn elsewhere. Take heed of this, followers of the Way. If[34] one does not think[35] over the meaning of the Law and becomes mistaken himself, that is excusable. How much worse is it to encourage others to be

[30] See below, n.44.
[31] Or spheres of objects. See above, ch. 23, n.8.
[32] The popular version, sec. 4, has "if merely" instead of "don't", which makes the sentence say the opposite.
[33] Read *wu* (no) as *ssu* (die), following the popular version, sec. 4.
[34] Reading *mo* (none) as *jo* (if), following *ibid*.
[35] Read *hsi* (stop) as *ssu* (to think), following Suzuki and Kuda.

[mistaken]! Deluded, he does not realize that he is so, and he even blasphemes the scripture and the Law! That is the reason why absence-of-thought is instituted as the doctrine. Because people who are deluded have thoughts about the spheres of objects, perverse views arise[36] in them, and all sorts of afflictions resulting from passions and erroneous thoughts are produced.

> *Comment.* The doctrine of the absence of thought is no cult of unconsciousness. Nor is it a Zen invention. It goes back to Taoism, Neo-Taoism, and the Early Seven Schools of Buddhism, all of which taught "having no mind of one's own," that is, having no mental attachment which would keep the mind in bondage.

"However, this school has instituted absence-of-thought as the doctrine. When people of the world are free from erroneous views, no thoughts will arise. If there are no thoughts, there will not even be an 'absence-of-thought.' Absence means absence of what? Thought means thought of what? Absence-of-thought means freedom from the character of the duality (existence or nonexistence of characters) and from all afflictions resulting from passions. [Thought means thought of the true nature of True Thusness (True Reality).][37] True Thusness is the substance of thought and thought is the function of True Thusness. It is the self-nature that gives rise to thought. Therefore in spite of the functioning of seeing, hearing, sensing, and knowing, self-nature is not defiled by the many spheres of objects and always remains free and at ease. As the *Wei-mo-chieh* [*so-shuo*] *ching* (Scripture Spoken by Vimalakīrti) says, "Externally it skillfully differentiates the various dharma-characters while internally it abides immovably in the First Principle."[38]

18. "Good and learned friends, according to this method sitting in meditation is at bottom neither looking at[39] the mind nor looking at purity. Nor do we say that there should be imperturbability.[40] Suppose we say to look at the mind. The mind is at bottom false. Since being false is the same as being illusory, there is nothing to look at. Suppose we say to look at purity. Man's nature is originally pure. It is by false thoughts that True Thusness is obscured. Our original nature is pure as long as it is free from false thoughts. If one does not realize that his own nature is originally pure and makes up his mind to look at purity, he is

---

[36] Read *ch'ü* (go) as *ch'i* (arise), following *ibid.*

[37] See ch. 24, n.19. Insertion according to the popular version, sec. 4.

[38] *Vimalakīrtinirdésa sūtra*, sec. 1, TSD, 14:537. The words "externally" and "internally" do not appear in the original scripture.

[39] Read *chao* (to attach) as *k'an* (to look at). The reason is obvious from what follows.

[40] This interpretation accords with the sense in the popular version, sec. 5.

creating a false purity. Such purity has no objective existence. Hence we know that what is looked at is false. Purity has neither physical form nor character, but some people set up characters of purity and say that this is the object of our task. People who take this view hinder their own original nature and become bound by purity. If those who cultivate imperturbability would ignore people's mistakes and defects, their nature would not be perturbed. Deluded people may not be perturbed physically themselves, but whenever they speak, they criticize others and thus violate the Way. Thus looking at the mind or at purity causes a hindrance to the Way."

19. "Now, this being the case, in this method, what is meant by sitting in meditation? In this method, to sit means to be free from all obstacles, and externally not to allow thoughts to rise from the mind[41] over any sphere of objects. To meditate means to realize the imperturbability of one's original nature. What is meant by meditation and calmness? Meditation means to be free from all characters externally; calmness means to be unperturbed internally. If there are characters outside and the inner mind is not disturbed, one's original nature is naturally pure and calm. It is only because of the spheres of objects that there is contact, and contact leads to perturbation. There is calmness when one is free from characters and is not perturbed. There is meditation when one is externally free from characters, and there is calmness when one is internally undisturbed. Meditation and calmness mean that external meditation is attained and internal calmness is achieved. The *Wei-mo-chieh* [*so-shuo*] *ching* says, 'Immediately we become completely clear and recover our original mind.'[42] The *P'u-sa chieh ching* (Scripture of Disciplines for Bodhisattvahood) says, 'We are originally pure in our self-nature.'[43] Good and learned friends, realize that your self-nature is naturally pure. Cultivate and achieve for yourselves the Law-body of your self-nature. Follow the Way of the Buddha yourselves. Act and achieve Buddhahood for yourselves."

20. "Good and learned friends, you must all go through the experience yourselves and receive the discipline that frees you from the attachment to differentiated characters. Follow me at the same time and repeat my slogans. They will enable you, good and learned friends, to see that the Three Bodies[44] of the Buddha are within you: 'We take

[41] Read *shang* (up) as *hsin* (mind), according to the popular version, sec. 5.

[42] Sec. 3, TSD, 14:541.

[43] The scripture is part of sec. 10 of the *Bramajāla sūtra* (*Fan-wang ching*, or Brahma-net Scripture). See TSD, 24:1003.

[44] Buddhism conceives a Buddha to have a threefold body, namely, the Law-body or spiritual body (*Dharmakāya*), the Reward-body or Enjoyment-body (*Sambhogakāya*), and the Transformation-body or body of incarnation (*Nir-*

refuge in the pure Law-body of the Buddha with our own physical bodies. We take refuge in the Myriad Transformation-body with our own physical bodies. We take refuge in the Perfect Reward-body with our own physical bodies.' (The above is to be chanted three times.)[45] The physical body is like an inn and cannot be spoken of as a refuge. It has always been the case that the Three Bodies lie in one's own nature. Everyone has them, yet because they are deluded they do not see, and they seek the Three [Bodies] of the Tathāgata (Thus-come Buddha)[46] externally, without realizing that the Three Bodies are inherent in one's own physical body. Good and learned friends, listen to your good friend. If you, good and learned friends, now see in your own physical bodies the self-nature that involves the Three Bodies of the Buddha, these Three Bodies will arise from your nature.

Comment. The doctrine of "becoming a Buddha in this very body" is a far cry from the original Indian idea that the body is a hindrance to freedom. One cannot help recalling that the Confucianists have always regarded the body as a gift from parents and as such it is a sacred trust and therefore to be well taken care of, and that for centuries the Taoists religion had tried in many ways, including medicine, diets, exercise, sex technique, and breath control, to make the body suitable for everlasting life on earth. These are some of the roots that make Zen essentially Chinese.

"What is meant by the Pure [Law][47] of the Buddha? Good and learned friends, our nature is originally pure. All dharmas lie in this self-nature. If we think of all kinds of evil deeds, we will practice evil. If we think of all kinds of good deeds, we will do good. Thus we know that all dharmas lie in one's self-nature. Self-nature is always pure, just as the sun and moon are always shining. It is only when they are obscured by clouds that there is brightness above but darkness below and the sun, the moon, and the stars cannot be seen. But when suddenly a gentle wind blows and scatters all clouds and fog, all phenomena are abundantly spread out before us, all appearing together. The purity of people's

---

māṇakāya). The Law-body is the Buddha-body in its self-nature, the body of the Dharma or truth, the body of reality, the body of principle. This "body" has no bodily existence. It is identical with truth. In various schools it is identical with the Realm of Dharma (*Dharmadhātu*), Buddha-nature, or the Storehouse of the "Thus-come" (*Tathāgatagarbha*). The Reward-body is the person embodied with real insight, enjoying his own enlightenment or that of others. The Transformation-body is a body variously appearing to save people. The three bodies are three in one, are possessed of all Buddhas, and are potential to all men.

[45] Original note in the text.
[46] See above, ch. 20, n.41.
[47] This word has been added according to the popular version, sec. 6.

nature is comparable to the clear sky, their wisdom comparable to the sun, and sagacity comparable to the moon. Their sagacity and wisdom are always shining. It is only because externally people are attached to spheres of objects[48] that erroneous thoughts, like floating clouds, cover the self-nature so that it is not clear. Therefore when they meet a good and learned friend who reveals to them the true method and scatters delusions and falsehood, then they are thoroughly illumined both internally and externally, and all dharmas reveal the free and easy character in their own nature. This is called the Pure Law-body. By taking refuge ourselves is meant to remove evil deeds. This is called taking refuge.

"What is meant by the Myriad Transformation-body? When there is no thought, one's nature is empty of differentiated characters and is tranquil, but when there is thought, that is self-transformation. When one thinks of evil dharmas, the transformation becomes hell, but when one thinks of good dharmas, the transformation becomes Paradise. What is poisonous and harmful is transformed into beasts. What is compassionate is transformed into bodhisattvas.[49] What is sagacious and wise is transformed into the higher realm. What is ignorant and deluded is transformed into the lower region. The transformations of self-nature are many,[50] but deluded people do not know this themselves. If one has a single good thought, sagacity and wisdom arise.

"What is meant by the Perfect Reward-body? One light can illuminate the darkness of a thousand years, and one bit of wisdom can destroy the ignorance of ten thousand years. Never mind looking back to the past; always consider the future, and always make future thoughts good. This is called the Reward-body. The reward of one evil thought will remove[51] the good of a thousand years, and the reward of one good thought will destroy the evil of a thousand years. At all times make the next thought a good one. This is called the Reward-body. Thinking on the basis of the Law-body is the same as the Transformation-body, and making every thought good is the same as the Reward-body. Achieving enlightenment oneself and practicing [the Law] oneself is called taking refuge. Skin and flesh constitute the physical body. It is an inn and cannot be spoken[52] of as a refuge. If a person understands the Three Bodies, he will recognize my basic idea."

30. "All scriptures and writings, both Mahāyāna and Hīnayāna, and

---

[48] Read *k'an-ching* (see reverence) as *chao-ching* (attach to sphere), according to Suzuki and Kuda, and also Ui, p. 130.

[49] A bodhisattva is one who is strongly determined to seek enlightenment and salvation for all.

[50] Read *ming* (name) as *to* (much), according to Suzuki and Kuda.

[51] Read *hsin* (mind) as *wang* (to destroy), according to Suzuki and Kuda.

[52] Read *tsai* (in) as *yen* (saying), according to TSD, 48:140.

the twelve sections of the scriptures are provided for [men].[53] It is because man possesses the nature of wisdom that these were instituted. If there were no men in the world, there would naturally not be any dharmas.[54] We know, therefore, that dharmas exist because of man and that there are all these scriptures because there are people to preach them.

"The reason is that among men some are wise and others are stupid. The stupid are inferior, whereas the wise are superior. The deluded consult the wise and the wise explain the Law to the stupid and enable them to understand and to open up their minds.[55] When deluded people understand and open up their minds, they are no longer different from the superior and the wise. Hence we know that without enlightenment, a Buddha is no different from other living beings. With enlightenment, even in a single instant of thought, all living beings become the same as a Buddha. Hence we know that all dharmas are immanent in one's mind and person. Why not seek in one's own mind the sudden realization of the original nature of True Thusness? The *P'u-sa chieh ching* says, 'We are originally pure in our self-nature. If we understand our minds and see our nature, we shall achieve Buddhahood ourselves.'[56] [And the *Wei-mo-chieh* (*so-shuo*) *ching* says] 'Immediately we become completely clear and recover our original mind.' "[57]

31. "Good and learned friends, when I was at Priest Hung-jen's place, I understood immediately as soon as I heard him, and suddenly realized the original nature of True Thusness. For this reason I propagate this doctrine so that it will prevail among later generations and seekers of the Way will be able to achieve perfect wisdom through sudden enlightenment, each to see his own mind, and to become suddenly enlightened through his own original nature. If they are not able to enlighten themselves, they should seek good and learned friends of high standing to show them the way to see their nature.

"What is meant by a good and learned friend of high standing? A good and learned friend of high standing is one who can explain to people the very best method and can directly show them the correct way. That is a good and learned friend of high standing. That is a great cause. That is to [say],[58] he will teach and direct people so they can see their own nature. For all good dharmas arise because of him. [The wisdom] of the past, present, and future Buddhas as well as

[53] Insertion according to *ibid.*
[54] This reading follows the popular version.
[55] Read *jan* (infected) as *hsin* (mind), to conform with the sentence that follows.
[56] See n.43.   [57] See n.42.
[58] Read *wei* (to act) as *wei* (to say), according to the popular version, sec. 2.

439

the twelve sections of the scripture are all immanent in human nature. It originally possesses them to the fullest extent. Those who cannot enlighten themselves should have good and learned friends to show them the way to see their nature. Those who can enlighten themselves, however, need not depend on good and learned friends. If they seek outside for good and learned friends and hope for emancipation, they will get nowhere. Understanding coming from the good and learned friend inside a person's own mind, however, will lead him to emancipation. But if one's own mind is perverse and deluded, [full of] erroneous thoughts and perversions, even if good and learned friends from the outside offer instructions, no salvation can be attained.[59] If you have not been able to enlighten yourselves, you should arouse your wisdom illuminatingly to examine [facts and principles]. Then in an instant all erroneous thoughts will vanish. This is your true and really good and learned friend, who as soon as he is enlightened immediately realizes Buddhahood."

B. THE RECORDED CONVERSATIONS OF SHEN-HUI[60]

The priest (Shen-hui) said, "There are mundane mysteries and also supramundane mysteries. When a commoner suddenly becomes a sovereign, for example, it is mundane mystery. If in the first stage of one's spiritual progress which consists of ten beliefs,[61] in one's initial resolve to seek perfect wisdom, an instant of thought corresponds with truth, one will immediately achieve Buddhahood. This is supramundane mystery. It is in accord with principle. What is there to wonder about? This clarifies the mystery of sudden enlightenment." (p. 100)

The priest said, "The resolve [to seek perfect wisdom] may be sudden or gradual, and delusion and enlightenment may be slow or rapid. Delusion may continue for infinitely long periods, but enlightenment takes but a moment. This principle is difficult to understand. Let me first give an analogy and then clarify the principle, and then you may perhaps understand through this example. Suppose there are individual strands of light green silk each consisting of numerous threads. If they are twisted to become a rope and are placed on a board, one cut with a sharp sword will sever all threads at the same time. Although the

[59] This clause is added according to *ibid.*

[60] These are from the "Recorded Sayings" in the *Shen-hui Ho-shang i-chi* (Surviving Works of Priest Shen-hui), ed. by Hu Shih, Shanghai, 1930. For a French translation, see Bibliography.

[61] There are 52 grades, divided into six stages, toward Buddhahood. The first stage consists of ten grades, namely, faith, unforgetfulness, serious effort, wisdom, calmness, non-retrogression, protection of the Law, the mind to reflect the light of the Buddha, discipline, and free will. Ordinarily one has to go through all six stages before achieving Buddhahood.

number of silk threads is large, it cannot stand the sword. It is the same with one who resolves to seek perfect wisdom. If he meets a truly good friend who by the use of [various][62] convenient means shows him True Thusness directly, and if he uses the diamond wisdom (which by its reality overcomes all illusory knowledge) to cut off all afflictions in the various stages, he will be completely enlightened, and will realize by himself that the nature of dharmas is originally empty and void. As his wisdom has become sharp and clear, he can penetrate everything and everywhere without obstacle. At this moment of realization, all causes [that give rise to attachment to external objects] will perish, and erroneous thoughts as numerous as sand in the Ganges will suddenly vanish altogether. Unlimited number of merits will be complete at the appropriate time. Once the diamond wisdom issues forth, why can't [Buddhahood] be achieved?" (pp. 120-121)

Teacher of the Law Chih-te[63] asked, "Zen Master, you teach living beings to seek only sudden enlightenment. Why not follow the gradual cultivation of Hīnayāna? One can never ascend a nine-story tower without going up the steps gradually."

Answer: "I am afraid the tower you talk about ascending is not a nine-story tower but a square tomb consisting of a pile of earth. If it is really a nine-story tower, it would mean the principle of sudden enlightenment. If one directs one's thought to sudden enlightenment as if one ascends a nine-story tower with the necessity of going through the steps gradually, one is not aiming right but sets up the principle of gradual enlightenment instead. Sudden enlightenment means satisfying both principle (*li*) and wisdom. The principle of sudden enlightenment means to understand without going through gradual steps, for understanding is natural. Sudden enlightenment means that one's own mind is empty and void from the very beginning. It means that the mind has no attachment. It means to enlighten one's mind while leaving dharmas as they are and to be absolutely empty in the mind. It means to understand all dharmas. It means not to be attached to Emptiness when one hears about it and at the same time not to be attached to the absence of Emptiness. It means not to be attached to the self when one hears about it and at the same time not to be attached to the absence of the self. It means entering Nirvāṇa without renouncing life and death. Therefore the scripture says, '[Living beings] have spontaneous wisdom and wisdom without teacher.'[64] He who issues from principle approaches the Way rapidly, whereas he who cultivates externally approaches slowly.

---

[62] One word here is missing in the text. [63] Nothing is known of him.
[64] *Saddharmapuṇḍarika sūtra* (Scripture of the Lotus of the Good Law), ch. 3, TSD, 9:13. See Soothill, trans., *The Lotus of the Wonderful Law*, p. 93.

People are surprised and skeptical when they hear that there is supramundane mystery. There are sudden mysteries in the world. Do you believe it?"

Comment. Note the equal emphasis on wisdom and principle. The rational element of principle, which occupies an important place in Hua-yen and later in Neo-Confucianism, also has an important role in Zen. Intuition does not preclude intellectual understanding.

Question: "What do you mean?"

Answer: "For example, Duke Chou (d. 1094 B.C.)[65] and Fu Yüeh[66] were originally a fisherman and a mason, respectively. 'The choice laid in the minds of the rulers.'[67] Consequently, they rose as simple folks and suddenly ascended to the position of a prime minister. Is this not a wonderful thing in the mundane world? As to wonderful things in the mundane world, when living beings whose minds are clearly full of greed, attachment, and ignorance, meet a truly good friend and in one instant of thought correspond [with truth], they will immediately achieve Buddhahood. Is this not a wonderful thing in the mundane world?

"Furthermore, [the scripture][68] says, 'All living beings achieve Buddhahood as they see their own nature.' Also, Nāgakanyā, daughter of the Dragon King, achieved Buddhahood at the very moment she resolved to seek perfect wisdom.[69] Again, in order to enable living beings to penetrate the knowledge and perception of the Buddha but not to allow sudden enlightenment, the Tathāgata everywhere spoke of the Five Vehicles (leading to their corresponding destinations for human beings, deities, ordinary disciples, the self-enlightened ones, and bodhisattvas).[70] Now that the scriptures do not speak of the Five Vehicles but merely talk about penetrating the knowledge and perception of the Buddha, in the strict sense they only show the method of sudden enlightenment. It is to harbor only one thought that corresponds with truth but surely not to go through gradual steps. By corresponding is meant the understanding of the absence of thought, the understanding of self-nature, and being absolutely empty in the mind. Because the mind is absolutely

[65] He assisted his brother, King Wu (r. 1121–1116 B.C.) in founding the Chou dynasty and later became prime minister during the reign of King Wu's son. He used to fish.

[66] Fu Yüeh was helping people build dykes when the sovereign Wu-ting (r. 1339–1281 B.C.) heard of him and later appointed him prime minister.

[67] This is a quotation from *Analects*, 20:1.

[68] Hu Shih (*Shen-hui Ho-shang i-chi*, p. 131) thinks that what follows is probably a quotation from some scripture.

[69] Referring to the story in *Saddharmapuṇḍarika sūtra*, ch. 12, TSD, 9:35. See Soothill, p. 174.

[70] For the last three vehicles, see above, ch. 25, n.14. For bodhisattvas, see n.74.

empty, that is Tathāgata Meditation. The *Wei-mo-chieh* [*so-shuo*] *ching* says, "I contemplate my own body in the sense of real character. I contemplate the Buddha in the same way. I see the Tathāgata as neither coming before, nor going afterward, and not remaining at present."[71] Because it does not remain (no attachment), it is Tathāgata Meditation." (pp. 130-132)

Question: "Why is ignorance[72] the same as spontaneity (*tzu-jan*)?"

Answer: "Because ignorance and Buddha-nature come into existence spontaneously. Ignorance had Buddha-nature as the basis and Buddha-nature has ignorance as the basis. Since one is basis for the other, when one exists, the other exists also. With enlightenment, it is Buddha-nature. Without enlightenment, it is ignorance. The *Nieh-p'an ching* (Nirvāṇa Scripture) says, 'It is like gold and mineral. They come into existence at the same time. After a master founder has smelted and refined the material, gold and the mineral will presently be differentiated. The more refined, the purer the gold will become, and with further smelting, the residual mineral will become dust.'[73] The gold is analogous to Buddha-nature, whereas mineral is analogous to afflictions resulting from passions. Afflictions and Buddha-nature exist simultaneously. If the Buddhas, bodhisattvas,[74] and truly good friends teach us so we may resolve to cultivate perfect wisdom, we shall immediately achieve emancipation."

Question: "If ignorance is spontaneity, is that not identical with the spontaneity of heretics?"

Answer: "It is identical with the spontaneity of the Taoists, but the interpretations are different."

Question: "How different?"

Answer: "In Buddhism both Buddha-nature and ignorance are spontaneous. Why? Because all dharmas depend on the power of Buddha-nature. Therefore all dharmas belong to spontaneity. But in the spontaneity of Taoism, 'Tao produced the One. The One produced the two. The two produced the three. And the three produced the ten thousand things.'[75] From the One down, all the rest are spontaneous. Because of this the interpretations are different." (pp. 98-99)

The assistant to the governor said, "All palace monks serving the emperor speak of causation instead of spontaneity, whereas Taoist

---

[71] *Wei-mo-chieh ching*, sec. 12, TSD, 14:554.

[72] *Avidyā*, particularly ignorance of facts and principles about dharmas.

[73] Paraphrasing a passage in *Nirvāṇa sūtra*, ch. 26, TSD, 12:788.

[74] Bodhisattvas are beings who are enlightened and are ready to become Buddhas but because of their compassion they remain in the world to save all sentient beings.

[75] *Lao Tzu*, ch. 42.

priests over the world only speak of spontaneity and do not speak of causation."

Answer: "It is due to their stupid mistake that monks set up causation but not spontaneity, and it is due to their [stupid] mistake that Taoist priests only set up spontaneity but not causation."

The assistant to the governor asked: "We can understand the causation of the monks, but what is their spontaneity? We can understand the spontaneity of the Taoists, but what is their causation?"

Answer: "The spontaneity of the monks is the self-nature of living beings. Moreover, the scripture says, "Living beings [have] spontaneous wisdom and wisdom without teacher.' This is called spontaneity. But in the case of causation of the Taoists, Tao can produce the One, the One can produce the two, the two can produce the three, and the three produce all things. All are produced because of Tao. If there were no Tao, nothing will be produced. Thus all things belong to causation." (pp. 143-144)

C. THE RECORDED CONVERSATIONS
OF ZEN MASTER I-HSÜAN[76]

1. The Prefect, Policy Advisor Wang,[77] and other officials requested the Master to lecture. The Master ascended the hall and said, "Today it is only because I, a humble monk, reluctantly accommodate human feelings that I sit on this chair. If one is restricted to one's heritage in expounding the fundamental understanding [of salvation], one really cannot say anything and would have nothing to stand on.[78] However, because of the honorable general advisor's strong request today, how can the fundamental doctrines be concealed? Are there any talented men or fighting generals to hurl their banners and unfold their strategy right now? Show[79] it to the group!"

A monk asked, "What is the basic idea of the Law preached by the Buddha?" Thereupon the Master shouted at him. The monk paid reverence. The Master said, "The Master and the monk can argue all right."

Question: "Master, whose tune are you singing? Whose tradition are you perpetuating?"

---

[76] For his biography see *Sung kao-seng chuan*, ch. 12, TSD, 50:779. Not much is known of him. His school is called the Lin-chi school (Rinsai in Japanese) because he lived in the Lin-chi monastery in Hopei.

[77] He was Wang Ching-ch'u, prefect of the Honan Prefecture, and a Buddhist lay pupil of Zen Master Ling-yu (771-853).

[78] Commentators are not agreed on the meaning of this sentence. The present interpretation is harmonious with the spirit of independence and revolt of the Zen School.

[79] The phrase *cheng-chü* here does not mean evidence but to make clear.

The Master said, "When I was a disciple of Huang-po,[80] I asked him three times and I was beaten three times."

As the monk hesitated about what to say, the Master shouted at him and then beat him, saying, "Don't nail a stick into empty space."[81]

2. The Master ascended the hall and said, "Over a lump of reddish flesh there sits a pure man who transcends and is no longer attached to any class of Buddhas or sentient beings. He comes in and out of your sense organs all the time. If you are not yet clear about it, look, look!"

At that point a monk came forward and asked, "What is a pure man who does not belong to any class of Buddhas or sentient beings?" The Master came right down from his chair and, taking hold of the monk, exclaimed, "Speak! Speak!" As the monk deliberated what to say, the Master let him go, saying, "What dried human excrement-removing stick is the pure man who does not belong to any class of Buddhas or sentient beings!" Thereupon he returned to his room. (TSD, 47:496)

> *Comment.* This is one of the most famous *koans*. The nonsensical answer in the *koan* is a new Zen device, but witty and shocking conversations have their precedents in Taoism and Neo-Taoism. One can find many in the *Chuang Tzu* and the *Shih-shuo hsin-yü* (New Discourse on the Talk of the Times), to mention only two well-known examples.
>
> The mention of excrement is no vulgarism. It is derived from Chuang Tzu who said that Tao is even in human excrement and urine.[82] Japanese scholars have invariably avoided direct translation of the term and used such expressions as "dried stick of dirt" instead. In doing so, they have missed the extremely important point in Taoism and seem to forget that the Buddha, like Tao, is everywhere.

3. The Master ascended the hall. A monk asked, "What is the basic idea of the Law preached by the Buddha?" The Master lifted up his swatter. The monk shouted, and the Master beat him.

[The monk asked again], "What is the basic idea of the Law preached by the Buddha?" The Master again lifted up his swatter. The monk shouted, and the Master shouted also. As the monk hesitated about what to say, the Master beat him.

> *Comment.* The swatter was originally used to hit mosquitoes but

---

[80] This refers to Zen Master Hsi-yün (d. 850) who lived in the Huang-po Mountain. For his work, see Bibliography.

[81] One gets nowhere in so doing.

[82] *Chuang Tzu*, ch. 22, HHCC, 7:49b. cf. Giles trans., *Chuang Tzu*, 1961 ed., p. 215. See above, ch. 8, comment on C, 2.

in Zen it is used to needle the mind. Hu Shih and Suzuki are diametrically opposed in their interpretations of such a technique. For Hu Shih, the apparently nonsensical Zen gestures are calculated to force the student to think for himself, "a method of education by the hard way."[83] For Suzuki, the swatter and various forms of gestures represent Zen's "persistent and often violent opposition to words and then to the intellect which deals exclusively in words."[84] Suzuki added that Zen has no prescribed methods. We may add that in the typical Buddhist fashion of the Four Points of Argumentation,[85] the swatter may mean this, it may mean that, it may mean both this and that, and it may mean neither this nor that.

Thereupon the Master said, "Listen, men. Those who pursue after the Law will not escape from death. I was in my late Master Huang-po's place for twenty years. Three times I asked him about the basic idea of the Law preached by the Buddha and three times he bestowed upon me the staff. I felt I was struck only by a dried stalk. Now I wish to have a real beating. Who can do it to me?"

One monk came out of the group and said, "I can do it."

The Master picked up the staff to give him. As he was about to take it over, the Master beat him. (TSD, 47:496-497)

4. The Master ascended the hall and said, "A man stands on top of a cliff, with no possibility of rising any further. Another man stands at the crossroad, neither facing nor backing anything. Who is in the front and who is in the back? Don't be like Vimalakīrti (who was famous for his purity), and don't be like Great Gentleman Fu (who benefited others).[86] Take care of yourselves." (TSD, 47:497)

5. The Master told the congregation: "Seekers of the Way. In Buddhism no effort is necessary. All one has to do is to do nothing, except to move his bowels, urinate, put on his clothing, eat his meals, and lie down if he is tired. The stupid will laugh at him, but the wise one will understand. An ancient person said, 'One who makes effort externally is surely a fool.' "[87] (TSD, 47:498)

6. *Question*: "What is meant by the mind's not being different at different times?"

[83] Hu Shih, "Ch'an (Zen) Buddhism in China: Its History and Method," *Philosophy East and West*, 3 (1953) p. 21.

[84] Suzuki, "Zen: A Reply to Hu Shih," *ibid.*, p. 36.

[85] See above, ch. 22, Introduction.

[86] Fu Hsüan-feng (b. A.D. 28) put the fish he caught in a basket and submerged it under water so those fish which wished to escape could do so. He and his wife worked in the farm for others.

[87] This saying and part of what precedes immediately come from a song by Zen Master Ming-tsan (fl. 788) in TSD, 49:606.

The Master answered, "As you deliberated to ask the question, your mind has already become different. Therefore the nature and character of dharmas have become differentiated. Seekers of the Way, do not make any mistake. All mundane and supramundane dharmas have no nature of their own. Nor have they the nature to be produced [by causes]. They have only the name Emptiness, but even the name is empty. Why do you take this useless name as real? You are greatly mistaken! . . . If you seek after the Buddha, you will be taken over by the devil of the Buddha, and if you seek after the patriarch, you will be taken over by the devil of the patriarch. If you seek after anything, you will always suffer. It is better not to do anything. Some unworthy priests tell their disciples that the Buddha is the ultimate, and that he went through three infinitely long periods, fulfilled his practice, and then achieved Buddhahood. Seekers of the Way, if you say that the Buddha is the ultimate, why did he die lying down sidewise in the forest in Kuśinagara after having lived for eighty years? Where is he now?. . . Those who truly seek after the Law will have no use for the Buddha. They will have no use for the bodhisattvas or arhats.[88] And they will have no use for any excellence in the Three Worlds (of desires, matter, and pure spirit).[89] They will be distinctly free and not bound by material things. Heaven and earth may turn upside down but I shall have no more uncertainty. The Buddhas of the ten cardinal directions may appear before me and I shall not feel happy for a single moment. The three paths (of fire, blood, and swords) to hell may suddenly appear, but I shall not be afraid for a single moment. Why? Because I know that all dharmas are devoid of characters. They exist when there is transformation [in the mind] and cease to exist when there is no transformation. The Three Worlds are but the mind, and all dharmas are consciousness only. Therefore [they are all] dreams, illusions, and flowers in the air. What is the use of grasping and seizing them?. . .

"Seekers of the Way, if you want to achieve the understanding according to the Law, don't be deceived by others and turn to [your thoughts] internally or [objects] externally. Kill anything that you happen on. Kill the Buddha if you happen to meet him. Kill a patriarch or an arhat if you happen to meet him. Kill your parents or relatives if you happen to meet them. Only then can you be free, not bound by material things, and absolutely free and at ease. . . . I have no trick to give people. I merely cure disease and set people free. . . . My views are

[88] An arhat or arhan is the ideal being in Hīnayāna or Small Vehicle, a saint or worthy who is no longer subject to incarnation.
[89] For the Three Worlds, see above, ch. 20, n.38.

few. I merely put on clothing and eat meals as usual, and pass my time without doing anything. You people coming from the various directions have all made up your minds to seek the Buddha, seek the Law, seek emancipation, and seek to leave the Three Worlds. Crazy people! If you want to leave the Three Worlds, where can you go? 'Buddha' and 'patriarchs' are terms of praise and also bondage. Do you want to know where the Three Worlds are? They are right in your mind which is now listening to the Law." (TSD, 47:499-500)

> *Comment.* This "doing nothing" philosophy means more than the Taoist philosophy of leaving things alone and being absolutely spontaneous. It assumes that Ultimate Reality is everywhere and can be discovered without any special searching. Eating, sweeping the floor, simply walking, or anything will do.

7. Ma-ku[90] came to participate in a session. As he arranged his seating cushion, he asked, "Which face of the twelve-face Kuan-yin[91] faces the proper direction?"

The Master got down from the rope chair. With one hand he took away Ma-ku's cushion and with the other he held Ma-ku, saying, "Which direction does the twelve-face Kuan-yin face?"

Ma-ku turned around and was about to sit in the rope chair. The Master picked up the staff and beat him. Ma-ku having grasped the staff, the two dragged each other into the room.

8. The Master asked a monk: "Sometimes a shout is like the sacred sword of the Diamond King.[92] Sometimes a shout is like a golden-haired lion squatting on the ground. Sometimes a shout is like a rod or a piece of grass [used to attract fish]. And sometimes a shout is like one which does not function as a shout at all. How do you know which one to use?"

As the monk was deliberating what to say, the Master shouted. (TSD, 47:504)

9. When the Master was among Huang-po's congregation, his conduct was very pure. The senior monk[93] said with a sigh, "Although he is young, he is different from the rest!" He then asked, "Sir, how long have you been here?"

[90] Zen Master Pao-ch'e of Ma-ku Mountain.
[91] Avalokiteśvara, the bodhisattva "who sees the world's sound," or the cries of suffering. The name may also mean the one who sees reality as it is, free and at ease. Characterized by compassion, this Buddhist saint assumes many forms, has many faces and hands the better to see and help sentient beings toward salvation. In popular Chinese religion, the saint had assumed a feminine form and has come to be known in the West as Goddess of Mercy.
[92] A bodhisattva in the diamond-realm, the realm of wisdom as contrasted with the realm of principle, the two realms representing those of effect and cause, respectively.
[93] Huang-po's disciple Ch'en Mu-chou.

The Master said, "Three years."

The senior monk said, "Have you ever gone to the head monk (Huang-po) and asked him questions?"

The Master said, "I have not. I wouldn't know what to ask."

The senior monk said, "Why don't you go and ask the head monk what the basic idea of the Law preached by the Buddha clearly is?"

The Master went and asked the question. But before he finished, Huang-po beat him. When he came back, the senior monk asked him how the conversation went. The Master said, "Before I finished my question, he already had beaten me. I don't understand." The senior monk told him to go and ask again.

The Master did and Huang-po beat him again. In this way he asked three times and got beaten three times. . . . Huang-po said, "If you go to Ta-yü's[94] place, he will tell you why."

The Master went to Ta-yü, who asked him, "Where have you come from?"

The Master said, "I am from Huang-po's place."

Ta-yü said, "What did Huang-po have to say?"

The Master said, "I asked three times about the basic idea of the Law preached by the Buddha and I was beaten three times. I don't know if I was mistaken."

Ta-yü said, "Old kindly Huang-po has been so earnest with you and you still came here to ask if you were mistaken!"

As soon as the Master heard this, he understood and said, "After all, there is not much in Huang-po's Buddhism." (TSD, 47:504)

> Comment. Not only is there not much in Huang-po's Buddhism; there is not much in Buddhism itself![95] This saying has been repeated time and again by Zen Buddhists. It expresses not only a spirit of revolt, but also the determination to wipe out anything in the way of the mind's direct and immediate intuition of truth, including Buddhism itself. Fung Yu-lan is right in considering this point as one of the five most important in Zen.[96]

[94] This monk lived in the Ta-yü Mountain in Kiangsi Province.

[95] This was actually said in the same story recorded in *Ching-te ch'uan-teng lu*, 12:3b.

[96] *History of Chinese Philosophy*, vol. 2, 1953, p. 401.

27

THE REVIVAL OF CONFUCIANISM:
HAN YÜ AND LI AO

HAN YÜ (768-824) and Li Ao (fl. 798) are usually considered as forerunners of the Neo-Confucianism that developed in the eleventh century. Actually, they were more than that. For they were not merely precursors of a movement; they did much to determine its direction.

As philosophers they are quite negligible. There is nothing new in their theories of human nature, and their dualism of good nature and evil feelings is but a continuation of a worn-out theory some eight hundred years old. Han Yü's discussion of the Way is superficial and, unlike that of the Taoists and Buddhists, does not touch upon its deeper aspects. And yet they were key figures in the transition from the Confucianism of medieval China to Neo-Confucianism. Han Yü, especially, stood out like a giant in the history of Confucianism from the second century B.C. to the tenth. He was of course one of the greatest literary masters China ever produced. So far as Chinese thought is concerned, his greatness and that of Li Ao lie in the fact that they saved Confucianism from its possible annihilation by Taoism and Buddhism and that they defined the direction and nature of its resurgence.

They accomplished this remarkable task in several ways. First of all, attacking Taoism and Buddhism, which were then at their height, Han Yü reversed the tide of Confucian decline. Second, both he and Li Ao concentrated on the central problem in the history of Confucianism, namely, human nature, and thus kept it central in later Confucianism. Significantly, Neo-Confucianism is called the study of human nature and destiny. Their study was specifically urged by Li Ao.[1] Third, by quoting from the *Great Learning*, the *Doctrine of the Mean*, and the *Book of Changes*, they discovered their importance and laid the foundation for Neo-Confucianists whose ideas were largely based on these Classics. Fourth, both of them singled out Mencius as the person through whom the true doctrines of Confucius were transmitted to later ages. Han Yü was particularly vehement about this "correct transmission." He rejected Hsün Tzu (fl. 298–238 B.C.) and Yang Hsiung (53 B.C.–A.D. 18) as unworthy of it. However dogmatic he may have been, this "correct transmission" as fixed by Han Yü has been accepted by Confucianists ever since.

Last, and perhaps the most important, by attacking Taoist inaction

[1] *Li Wen Kung chi* (Collected Works of Li Ao), "Recovery of the Nature," pt. 1, SPTK, 1:7a-8a.

and Buddhist silence and annihilation instead of their metaphysics, Han Yü prevented Confucianism from developing along the line of speculative philosophy in order to compete with them, and helped confine Confucian objectives to the traditional goal of a moral being and a moral society. This may have been a misfortune for Confucianism, for although Neo-Confucianists did base their whole movement on the metaphysical concept of principle (*li*), metaphysics is not one of their distinctions. But in emphasizing the Confucian Way of having action and of sustaining and supporting the life of one another, as Han Yü did, and in reiterating the ancient Confucian ideal of the sincerity of the will, the rectification of the mind, the cultivation of the personal life, the regulation of the family, ordering the state, and bringing peace to the world, as both Han and Li did, they did much to retain the real strength of the Confucian system.

Han was an orphan at three and grew up in difficult circumstances, but he eventually rose to be a vice-minister in the ministry of civil personnel. In 819 he protested against welcoming a Buddhist relic, supposed to be a bone of the Buddha, to the palace and almost lost his life because of it. Li Ao was his friend, or, according to some, his pupil.[2] The following selections are from their collected works.

1. AN INQUIRY ON HUMAN NATURE, BY HAN YÜ

The nature of man comes into existence with birth,[3] whereas the feelings are produced when there is contact with external things. There are three grades of human nature, and what constitute that nature are five. There are three grades of feelings, and what constitute feelings are seven. What are these? I say: The three grades of nature are: superior, the medium, and the inferior. The superior is good, and good only. The medium may be led to be either superior or inferior. The inferior is

---

[2] Han's courtesy name was T'ui-chih and his posthumous title was Wen (Culture). He had a "presented scholar" degree and served in many governmental posts, i.e., professor of the national university, censor, assistant departmental chief, and divisional chief. He was demoted several times. As a result of his protest against the Buddhist relic in 819, he was banished to Ch'ao-chou in South China, where, it is said, he successfully told the crocodiles to leave the place. In the next year he was made director of education. Later he became vice-minister in the ministry of the army, then censor, and finally vice-minister in the ministry of civil personnel.

Li Ao's courtesy name was Hsi-chih and his posthumous title was also Wen. He held a "presented scholar" degree and rose to be a professor at the directorate of education. Later he served as divisional chief, censor, and vice-minister in the ministry of justice and then in the ministry of revenues and population.

For more information on the two men, see the *Hsin-T'ang shu* (New History of the T'ang Dynasty, 618-907), chs. 176-177.

[3] Compare this with Kao Tzu's theory. See *Mencius*, 6A:1-6.

evil, and evil only. Human nature consists in five virtues, namely, humanity (*jen*), propriety (*li*), faithfulness, righteousness (*i*), and wisdom.[4] In the superior grade, one[5] of these five is the ruling factor while the other four also are practiced. In the medium grade, there is more or less of one of the five while the other four are not pure.[6] In the inferior grade, one rebels against one of these and is out of accord with the other four. The relation of nature to feelings depends on its grade.

Similarly, there are three grades of feelings: the superior, the medium, and the inferior, and what constitute the feelings are seven: pleasure, anger, sorrow, fear, love, hate, and desire. In the superior grade, when any of these seven becomes active, it abides by the Mean. In the medium grade, some of the seven are excessive and some are deficient but there is an effort to be in accord with the Mean. In the inferior grade, whether they are excessive or deficient, action is directed by whichever feeling happens to be predominant. The relation between feelings and nature depends on their grade.

In discussing human nature, Mencius said, "Man's nature is good." Hsün Tzu said, "Man's nature is evil." And Yang Hsiung said, "Man's nature is a mixture of good and evil."[7] Now to say that nature is good at first but subsequently becomes evil, or bad at first and subsequently becomes good, or mixed at first and is now either good or evil, is to mention only the medium grade and leave the superior and inferior grades out of account and to take care of one case but to lose sight of the other two.

When Shu-yü was born, his mother knew, as soon as she looked at him, that he would die of love of bribes.[8] When Yang I-wo[9] was born, Shu-hsiang's mother knew, as soon as she heard him cry, that he would cause the destruction of all his kindred.[10] When Yüeh-chiao was born, Tzu-wen considered it a great calamity, knowing that because of him the

---

[4] These five are the traditional Five Constant Virtues. Other editions have them in the usual order: humanity, righteousness, propriety, wisdom, and faithfulness. The commentary says that the present propriety and faithfulness are nearer to humanity than righteousness and wisdom. Chu Hsi (1130-1200) thought that this is correct, and added that Han Yü often liked to be different. See commentary on the *Han Ch'ang-li ch'üan-chi* (Complete Works of Han Yü). It was carefully collated by Chu Hsi and contains Chu's as well as other people's comments.

[5] According to Chu Hsi, the meaning here is one of the five, not the first of the five.

[6] This is Chu Hsi's interpretation.

[7] See *Mencius*, 6A:6; *Hsün Tzu*, ch. 23. For Yang Hsiung's doctrine, see above, ch. 15.

[8] For this story, see *Kuo-yü* (Conversations of the States), ch. 14, SPPY, 14:3a. See de Harlez, trans., *Kuoe-yü*, pt. 2, p. 152.

[9] Pronunciation according to the commentary.

[10] See *Tso chuan* (Tso's Commentary on the *Spring and Autumn Annals*), Duke Chao, 28th year. See Legge, trans., *Ch'un Ts'ew*, p. 727.

ghosts of the Jo-ao family would be famished.[11] [With all these evidences] can we say that human nature is good?

When Hou-chi was born, his mother did not suffer. As soon as he began to creep, he displayed understanding and intelligence.[12] When King Wen was in his mother's womb, she had no trouble.[13] After he was born, those who assisted him did not have to work hard, and those who taught him did not have to labor. [With all these evidences] can we say that human nature is evil?

Emperor Yao's son Chu, Emperor Shun's son Chün,[14] and King Wen's sons Kuan and Ts'ai were not without good in their practice, but they eventually became wicked. Ku-sou's son Shun and Kun's son Yü[15] were not without evil in their practice but they eventually became sages. [With all these evidences,] can we say that human nature is a mixture of good and evil?

I therefore say that the three philosophers, in their theories on human nature, mentioned the medium grade and left the superior and inferior grades out of account. They took care of one case but lost sight of the other two.

It may be asked: In that case, does it mean that the nature of the superior and inferior grades can never be changed?

I reply: The nature of the superior grade becomes more intelligent through education. The nature of the inferior grade comes to have few faults through an awe of power. Therefore the superior nature can be taught and the inferior nature can be controlled. But their grades have been pronounced by Confucius to be unchangeable.[16]

It may be asked, Why are those who talk about human nature today different from this?

I reply: Those who talk about human nature today have confused their theories with Buddhism and Taoism. Since they have confused their theories with Buddhism and Taoism, how can they speak without being different from me? (*Yüan-hsing* or an Inquiry on Human nature, *Han Ch'ang-li ch'üan-chi*, or Collected Works of Han Yü, SPPY, 11:5b-7b)

> *Comment.* Han Yü has often been credited with originating the theory of the three grades of human nature. It is true that he was the first to use the term "three grades" in connection with man's

[11] *ibid.*, Duke Hsüan, 4th year. See Legge, p. 296.

[12] *Odes*, no. 245.

[13] See *Kuo-yü*, ch. 10, SPPY, 10:19a. Cf. de Harlez, trans., *Kuoe yü*, p. 120. King Wen (r. 1171–1122 B.C.) was the founder of the Chou dynasty.

[14] Yao and Shun were legendary sage-emperors (3rd millennium B.C.).

[15] Founder of the Hsia dynasty (r. 2183–2175 B.C.?).

[16] See above, ch. 2, comment on *Analects*, 17:3.

nature, but the term is found in several places in the Classics, and Hsün Yüeh (148-209) six hundred years before him had propounded the theory of three grades of human destiny.[17] The theory of three grades of human nature itself had been taught in Buddhism, specifically in the *Ch'eng-wei-shih lun* (*Vijñaptimātratāsiddhi*, or Treatise on the Establishment of the Doctrine of Consciousness-Only), which was translated into Chinese by Hsüan-tsang (596-664) about a hundred and fifty years before.[18] The actual source of Han Yü's theory may have been Wang Ch'ung (27-100?)[19] whom he admired. In any case, the originality of Han Yü has been overrated.

2. AN INQUIRY ON THE WAY (TAO), BY HAN YÜ

Universal love is called humanity. To practice this in the proper manner is called righteousness. To proceed according to these is called the Way. To be sufficient in oneself without depending on anything outside is called virtue. Humanity and righteousness are definite values, whereas the Way and virtue have no substance in themselves [but depend on humanity and righteousness for it]. Thus we have the Way of the superior man [as in Confucianism] and the Way of the inferior man [as in Taoism] and there are the inauspicious virtue [as in Taoism] and auspicious virtue [as in Confucianism]. Lao Tzu belittled humanity and righteousness not because he destroyed them but because his viewpoint was small. If a man sits at the bottom of a well, looks up at the sky, and says, "The sky is small," it does not mean that the sky is really small. Lao Tzu considered little acts [of kindness] as humanity and isolated deeds [of good] as righteousness. It is no wonder that he belittled them. What he called the Way was only the Way as he understood it and not what I call the Way. What he called virtue was only the virtue as he understood it and not what I call virtue. What I call the Way and virtue always involve both humanity and righteousness, which is the opinion shared by the whole world. What Lao Tzu called the Way and virtue was devoid of humanity and righteousness, which was the private opinion of one man. . . .

> *Comment.* In declaring that "universal love is called humanity," was Han Yü under the influence of the Moist doctrine of universal love or the Buddhist gospel of compassion for all? One would think that the Confucian teaching of love with distinctions was not al-

[17] *Shen-chien* (A Mirror Extensively Used), ch. 5, SPPY, 5:2b.
[18] Ch. 5, TSD, 31:23. See La Vallée Poussin, trans., *le siddhi de Hsüan Tsang*, p. 265.
[19] See above, ch. 16, A.

truistic enough to compete with Buddhism and that Han Yü had to yield to the doctrine of a system which he strongly attacked. It is significant, however, that he avoided the Moist term "mutual love" (*chien-ai*) and the Buddhist term "compassion" but used *po-ai* (universal love) instead. The term first appeared in the commentary on the *Kuo-yü*[20] of the third century and then in the *Book of Filial Piety*[21] and was used by Hsü Kan (171-218) to describe humanity.[22] The idea of *po* had been well understood all along, and the very word appears in *Analects* 6:28. Thus Han Yü was merely reiterating a Confucian tradition.[23]

Now the method [of the Taoists and Buddhists] is to insist on discarding the relationship between ruler and ministers, doing away with the relationship between father and son, and stopping the process of sustaining and supporting the life of one another, in order to seek for what they call silence and annihilation. . . . The *Record* says, "The ancients who wished to manifest their clear character to the world would first bring order to their states. Those who wished to bring order to their states would first regulate their families. Those who wished to regulate their families would first cultivate their personal lives. Those who wished to cultivate their personal lives would first rectify their minds. Those who wished to rectify their minds would first make their wills sincere."[24] Thus what the ancients meant by rectifying the mind and making the will sincere was to engage in activity [as against the inaction of the Taoists and Buddhists]. But now [the Taoists and Buddhists] seek to govern their hearts by escaping from the world, the state, and the family. They destroy the natural principles of human relations so that the son does not regard his father as a father, the minister does not regard his ruler as a ruler, and the people do not attend to their work. . . . Now, they take the ways of barbarism and elevate them above the teachings of our ancient kings. Does this not almost make all of us barbarians?

What were the teachings of our ancient kings? Universal love is called humanity. To practice this in the proper manner is called righteousness. To proceed according to these is called the Way. To be sufficient in oneself without depending on anything outside is called virtue. Their literature comprised the Books of *Odes*, *History*, *Changes*, and the *Spring and Autumn Annals*. Their methods consisted of rules of propriety,

[20] Ch. 3, SPPY, 3:3a.
[21] Ch. 7. See Makre, trans., *Hsiao King*, p. 7.
[22] *Chung lun* (A Treatise on the Mean), ch. 9, SPTK, 1:34a.
[23] See above, ch. 3, comment on *Mencius*, Additional Selections, 3B:9 on the question of love with distinctions versus universal love.
[24] The text of the *Great Learning*.

music, laws, and governmental measures. Their people were the four classes of scholars, farmers, artisans, and merchants. Their relationships were those between ruler and minister, father and son, teacher and friend, guest and host, elder and younger brother, and husband and wife. Their clothing was hemp and silk. Their dwellings were halls and houses. Their food consisted of grain and rice, fruit and vegetables, fish and meat. As methods theirs were easy to understand and as teachings theirs were easy to practice. Employed to conduct oneself, they brought harmony and blessing, and employed to deal with others, love and impartiality. Employed to cultivate the mind, they gave peace and harmony, and employed to deal with the world, the state, and the family, they were always fitting no matter where they were applied. Consequently, in life people were able to express their feelings, and at death the eternal relations between them and their descendants were fulfilled [by the latter]. They offered sacrifices to Heaven and the gods came to receive them. They offered sacrifices to their ancestors and the ancestors enjoyed them. What Way is this? I say: This is what I call the Way, and not what the Taoists and the Buddhists called the Way. . . . (*Yüan-tao* or Inquiry on the Way, SPPY, 11:1a-4b)

3. THE RECOVERY OF THE NATURE, PT. 2, BY LI AO

Someone asked: Man has been darkened for a long time. If he is to recover his original nature, he must do so gradually. May I ask what the method should be?

Answer: Without deliberation and without [anxious] thought, the feelings will not arise. When the feelings do not arise, thought becomes correct. Correct thought means having neither deliberation nor [anxious] thought. The *Book of Changes* says, "What is there in the world to think about or to deliberate about?"[25] It also says, "Guarding against depravity, he preserves his sincerity."[26] And the *Book of Odes* says, "Have no depraved thoughts."[27]

Question: Is that all?

Answer: No. This is the fasting of the mind. It is not yet free of tranquillity. As there is tranquillity, it will necessarily be followed by activity, and when there is activity, it will necessarily be followed by tranquillity. The unceasing alternation of tranquillity and activity means the feelings. The *Book of Changes* says, "Fortune and misfortune, occasion for re-

---

[25] "Appended Remarks," pt. 2, ch. 5. Cf. Legge, trans., *Yi King*, p. 389.
[26] Commentary on hexagram no. 1, *ch'ien* (Heaven). Cf. Legge, p. 410.
[27] No. 297. See above, ch. 2, n.30.

pentance or regret, all arise from activity."[28] Under such conditions, how can one recover his nature?

Question: What can be done?

Answer: At the time of tranquillity, to know that there is no thought in the mind is the fasting of the mind, to realize that originally there is no thought in the mind and that it is completely free from tranquillity and activity, and to be in the state of absolute quiet and inactivity—that is absolute sincerity. The *Doctrine of the Mean* says, "Given sincerity, there will be enlightenment."[29] And the *Book of Changes* says, "All activities in the world obtain their firm nature from one principle."[30]

Question: During the time when there is neither deliberation nor thought, things attack from outside and the feelings respond to them from the inside, how can one stop the feelings? Is it possible to stop feelings with feelings?

Answer: Man's feelings are the evil aspect of his nature. If one realizes that they are evil, then this evil will not exist in the first place. If the mind is in the state of absolute quiet and inactivity, depraved thoughts will cease of themselves. If human nature shines clearly, how can depravity arise? If one is to stop feelings with feelings, that is to magnify the feelings. When feelings are used to stop one another, will there be an end to it? The *Book of Changes* says, "The son of the Yen family,[31] whenever he did anything wrong, never failed to realize it, and having realized it, he never did it again. As it is said in the *Book of Changes*, 'Returning after not having gone (astray) very far, there is no occasion for repentance. There will be great fortune.' "[32]

> *Comment.* There were no new theories about human nature after the Western Han (206 B.C.–A.D. 8) when Confucianists developed the theory that human nature was good but the feelings were evil, thus forming two levels. For several hundred years, then, there was no new concept about human nature. In this period both Buddhism and Taoism soared to great heights in their discussions of this question. Under the stimulation and challenge of Buddhism and in order to compete with it, Li Ao sought a compromise doctrine, found it in the Western Han Confucianists, and combined it with Mencius' doctrine of originally good human nature, the idea of tranquil nature in the *Book of Changes*, and the idea of the full development

[28] "Appended Remarks," pt. 2, ch. 1. Cf. Legge, p. 380.

[29] Ch. 21.

[30] See n.28.

[31] This refers to Yen Hui, Confucius' favorite pupil. See "Appended Remarks," pt. 2, ch. 5. Cf. Legge, pp. 392-393.

[32] Commentary on hexagram no. 24, *fu* (to return). Cf. Legge, p. 108.

of human nature in both Mencius and the *Doctrine of the Mean*. It is this originally good nature that he advocates recovering.

Question: You said that originally there is no thought in the mind and that it is completely free from activity and tranquillity. But is one, then, not to hear the sound that comes or to see the thing that appears?

Answer: If we were not to see anything or to hear anything, one would not be a man. But to see and hear clearly and yet not to be aroused by what is seen or heard—that will be all right. To know everything, to do everything, to be absolutely quiet in the mind, and yet to have its light illumine heaven and earth—that is the enlightenment resulting from sincerity. The *Great Learning* says, "the extension of knowledge consists in the investigation of things."[33] And the *Book of Changes* says, "In the operation of Change, there is neither thought nor action, because it is the state of absolute quiet and inactivity, and when acted on, it immediately penetrates all things. If it were not the most spirit-like thing under heaven, how can it be like this?"[34]

Question: May I ask what is meant by "the extension of knowledge consists in the investigation of things (*ko-wu*)"?

Answer: By things is meant the myriad things, and by *ko* is meant arriving or reaching. When things come before one, his mind clearly sifts them and yet he does not respond to (or is not affected by) them. This is the extension of knowledge. This is the perfecting of knowledge. As knowledge is perfected, the will becomes sincere. As the will is sincere, the mind becomes rectified. As the mind is rectified, the personal life becomes cultivated. As the personal life is cultivated, the family becomes regulated. As the family is regulated, the state will be in order. As the state is in order, the world will be at peace.[35] This is how a person can form a trinity with Heaven and Earth. . . . (*Fu-hsing shu* or The Recovery of the Nature, in *Li Wen Kung chi*, or Collected Works of Li Ao, SPTK, 1:8a-9b)

> *Comment*. Both the idea of recovering one's nature and that of the fasting of one's mind come from Chuang Tzu.[36] In trying to eliminate both activity and tranquillity, Li Ao goes even further than Chuang Tzu, who still wants activity and tranquillity harmonized.[37] Li Ao's dictum, "having no thought," sounds very much like those of Zen Buddhism. For this reason he has been described as Buddhistic.

[33] The text.

[34] "Appended Remarks," pt. 1, ch. 10. Cf. Legge, p. 370.

[35] Paraphrasing the text of the *Great Learning*.

[36] *Chuang Tzu*, chs. 16 and 4, respectively, NHCC, 6:5b, 8a, and 2:13a, respectively. See Giles, trans., *Chuang Tzu*, 1961 ed., pp. 156-157 and 54, respectively.

[37] *ibid.*, ch. 13, NHCC, 5:24a-b. See Giles, pp. 132-133.

While a certain amount of Buddhist influence cannot be denied, he remains essentially Confucian in culminating his doctrine in personal cultivation, social harmony, and world peace through the investigation of things and the extension of knowledge. What he means by having no thought is at bottom no different from what Mencius meant by the undisturbed mind.[38] However, Mencius' undisturbed mind is meant to be a condition for action, whereas Li Ao was more concerned with a state of mind. It is to be noted that while he was profoundly influenced by the idea of sincerity in the *Doctrine of the Mean*, he does not seem to have been particularly impressed by the doctrine of earnest practice in the same book.[39]

[38] *Mencius*, 2A:2.　　　　　　　　[39] *The Mean*, ch. 20.

28

THE NEO-CONFUCIAN METAPHYSICS
AND ETHICS IN CHOU TUN-I

NEO-CONFUCIANISM may be traced to earlier Confucianists, but the one who really opened its vista and determined its direction was Chou Tun-i (Chou Lien-hsi,[1] 1017-1073), who is generally called the pioneer of Neo-Confucianism. In two short treatises, the *T'ai-chi-t'u shuo* (An Explanation of the Diagram of the Great Ultimate) and the *T'ung-shu* (Penetrating the *Book of Changes*), he laid the pattern of metaphysics and ethics for later Neo-Confucianism. Whether he got the diagram from a Taoist priest is a debatable point, but the strong Taoist influence on him is unmistakable. The very concept of the Ultimate of Non-being (*Wu-chi*) comes from Lao Tzu.[2] But his diagram is not exactly like any diagram of the Taoists, and in his evolutionary process of creation from the Great Ultimate through the passive cosmic force, yin, and the active cosmic force, yang, to the myriad things, he faithfully followed the *Book of Changes*[3] rather than Taoism. Actually what he did was to assimilate the Taoist element of non-being to Confucian thought, but in so doing, he discarded the fantasy and mysticism of Taoism. The diagram had been used by Taoists in their attempt to obtain elixir for immortal life, but Chou Tun-i used it for rational philosophy. In this way he restored Chinese philosophy to a healthier climate.

The fact that he relies on the *Book of Changes* is important, for although many Neo-Confucianists before him had written commentaries on the Classic and thus brought the book to the fore, he based his entire philosophy on it. From then on the book assumed unusual importance in Neo-Confucianism.

Furthermore, he developed the idea that "the many are [ultimately] one, and the one is actually differentiated into the many," and that "the one and many each has its own correct state of being," thus starting another fundamental concept of Neo-Confucianism and anticipating Ch'eng I (Ch'eng I-ch'uan, 1033-1107).[4] He also spoke of principle (*li*), the nature, and destiny together, which eventually became the three cardinal concepts in Neo-Confucian thought. But he never explained the nature of the Great Ultimate, the relation between it and principle,

---

[1] Also pronounced Chou Lien-ch'i.

[2] *Lao Tzu*, ch. 28; also *Chuang Tzu*, ch. 11, NHCC, 4:36a, Giles, trans., *Chuang Tzu*, 1961 ed., p. 112.

[3] For this book, see above, ch. 13, n.1.

[4] See below, ch. 32, sec. 75.

or the relation between them and sincerity (*ch'eng*). The clarification of their relationships had to wait for Chu Hsi (1130-1200).

The idea of sincerity of course comes from the *Doctrine of the Mean*.[5] In describing it as tranquil he betrays more Taoist influence. But to him sincerity is not just tranquillity. It is the foundation of moral nature and the source of all activities. It is true substance and unerring. It is pure and perfectly good. The concept is so important that it has often been considered the foundation of his teaching.[6] Equally significant is his idea that sincerity is the state in which one can detect the subtle, incipient, activating force (*chi*) of good and evil and make the choice either for good or for evil. In Chou Tun-i's mind, sincerity in its reality is tranquil but in its function is dynamic, and this is a far cry from Taoism. In this way he rejected the Taoist over-emphasis on the internal to the neglect of the external. For him, the ideal being is the sage, and the highest ideal, the Mean. The sage "settles human affairs by the principles of the Mean, correctness, humanity (*jen*) and righteousness," which means that the sage equally stresses the internal and the external life. This equal emphasis paved the way for Ch'eng Hao's (Ch'eng Ming-tao, 1032-1085) and his brother Ch'eng I's doctrine of "seriousness to straighten the internal life and righteousness to square the external life."[7]

From the foregoing, it is clear that to call him a pioneer of Neo-Confucianism is an understatement, although to call him the founder of the philosophy, as some have done, is certainly going too far. Perhaps the most accurate evaluation is that of Huang Po-chia (fl. 1695), who said, "Since the time of Confucius and Mencius, Han (206 B.C.–A.D. 220) Confucianists merely had textual studies of the Classics. The subtle doctrines of the Way and the nature of man and things have disappeared for a long time. Master Chou rose like a giant. . . . Although other Neo-Confucianists had opened the way, it was Master Chou who brought light to the exposition of the subtlety and refinement of the mind, the nature, and moral principles."[8]

Chou was a native of Tao-chou in present Hunan. His personal name

[5] Chs. 16, 20-26, 32.

[6] Notably by Huang Tsung-hsi (1610-1695) and Huang Kan (Huang Mien-chai, 1152-1221). See Huang Tsung-hsi *et al.*, *Sung-Yüan hsüeh-an* (Anthology and Critical Accounts of the Neo-Confucianists of the Sung and Yüan Dynasties, 960-1368), SPPY, 12:17a, 18a.

[7] See below, ch. 31, secs. 18, 32, 46, 50; ch. 32, sec. 46.

[8] *Sung-Yüan hsüeh-an*, SPPY, 11:2a. Graham, in his *Two Chinese Philosophers*, pp. 152-175, argues that Chou had little influence on the Ch'eng brothers and should not be regarded as the founder of Neo-Confucianism. In view of what has been said, his statements like "The philosophy of the Ch'engs is not a development of that of Chou Tun-yi; it is based on quite different premises" (p. 162) are untenable. See my review of Graham's book in the *Journal of the American Oriental Society*, 79 (1959), p. 154.

was Tun-i and courtesy name Mao-shu. He named his study after the stream Lien-hsi (Stream of Waterfalls) which he loved, and posterity has honored him by calling him Master of Lien-hsi.

He loved lotus flowers ardently, evidently because of their purity and tranquillity. His love for life was so strong that he would not cut the grass outside his window.[9] The two Ch'eng brothers had once studied under him (in 1046-1047) and were much influenced by him. Because of his influence the brothers did not take the civil service examination or hunt.[10] He was a great admirer of Buddhism, and Ch'eng I called him "poor Zen fellow."[11] But strangely, Buddhist influence on him is negligible. In fact, he may be said to have set the course for Neo-Confucianism in such a way that neither Buddhist nor Taoist influence changed its fundamentally Confucian character.[12]

Below, following the list of major concepts and chapter references of the *T'ung-shu*, are the *T'ai-chi-t'u shuo*[13] and the *T'ung-shu*[14] translated in full from the *Chou Tzu ch'üan-shu* (Complete Works of Chou Tun-i).

Activity and Tranquillity: 2, 4, 5, 9, 12, 16, 20, 35, 40
Cosmology and Metaphysics: 1, 11, 16, 36
Good and Evil: 3, 7, 15
Government: 12, 32
Humanity and Righteousness: 3, 5, 6, 11, 12
Impartiality: 20, 21, 37
Incipient activating force: 3, 4, 9
Mean: 6, 7, 17
Nature and Destiny: 1, 3, 22

[9] *I-shu* (Surviving Works), 3:2a, in ECCS.
[10] *ibid.*, 2A:2b, 7:1a, 3:1b; *Ts'ui-yen* (Pure Words), 2:13b, in ECCS.
[11] *I-shu*, 6:4a.
[12] Chou had a busy official career. He was district keeper of records (1040), magistrate in various districts (1046-1054), prefectural staff supervisor (1056-1059), professor of the directorate of education and assistant prefect (1061-1064), among others. It was when he was assistant prefect that he built his study, "Stream of Waterfalls." He resigned from his governmental position in 1072, the year before he died. See *Sung shih* (History of the Sung Dynasty, 960-1279), SPTK, 427:2b-5a and Bruce, *Chu Hsi and His Masters*, pp. 18-24.
[13] This short essay is found in many other collections and has been translated into several European languages. The diagram, of which the essay is an explanation, is not necessary for the understanding of the philosophical ideas in general or for the understanding of the essay in particular.
[14] There are many editions. The *Cheng-i-t'ang ch'üan-shu* (Complete Library of the Hall of Rectifying the Way) edition of 1869 has commentaries by Chu Hsi. That in the *Chou Tzu ch'üan-shu* (Complete Works of Chou Tun-i) contains comments by other Neo-Confucianist also. For a German version by Grube, see Bibliography. Other translations are: de Harlez, *L'École philosophique moderne de la Chine*, pp. 25-32 (partial); P. C. Hsü, *Ethical Realism in Neo-Confucian Thought*, Appendix, pp. i-iv (partial); and Chow Yih-Ching, *La philosophie morale dans le Néo-Confucianisme*, pp. 163-188. The *Wan-yu wen-k'u* (Universal Library) edition of the *Chou Tzu ch'üan-shu* is used here.

Principle: 22
Propriety and Music: 13, 17, 18, 19
Sincerity: 1, 2, 3, 4, 35

1. AN EXPLANATION OF THE DIAGRAM OF
THE GREAT ULTIMATE

The Ultimate of Non-being and also the Great Ultimate (*T'ai-chi*)!
The Great Ultimate through movement generates yang. When its activity
reaches its limit, it becomes tranquil. Through tranquillity the Great
Ultimate generates yin. When tranquillity reaches its limit, activity begins
again. So movement and tranquillity alternate and become the root
of each other, giving rise to the distinction of yin and yang, and the two
modes are thus established.

By the transformation of yang and its union with yin, the Five Agents
of Water, Fire, Wood, Metal, and Earth arise. When these five material
forces (*ch'i*) are distributed in harmonious order, the four seasons run
their course.

The Five Agents constitute one system of yin and yang, and yin and
yang constitute one Great Ultimate. The Great Ultimate is fundamentally the Non-ultimate. The Five Agents arise, each with its specific nature.

When the reality of the Ultimate of Non-being and the essence of yin,
yang, and the Five Agents come into mysterious union, integration
ensues. *Ch'ien* (Heaven) constitutes the male element, and *k'un* (Earth)
constitutes the female element. The interaction of these two material
forces engenders and transforms the myriad things. The myriad things
produce and reproduce, resulting in an unending transformation.

It is man alone who receives (the Five Agents) in their highest
excellence, and therefore he is most intelligent. His physical form appears, and his spirit develops consciousness. The five moral principles
of his nature (humanity or *jen*, righteousness, propriety, wisdom, and
faithfulness) are aroused by, and react to, the external world and engage
in activity; good and evil are distinguished; and human affairs take
place.

The sage settles these affairs by the principles of the Mean, correctness, humanity, and righteousness (for the way of the sage is none other
than these four),[15] regarding tranquillity as fundamental. (Having
no desire, there will therefore be tranquillity.) Thus he establishes himself as the ultimate standard for man. Hence the character of the sage is
"identical with that of Heaven and Earth; his brilliancy is identical with
that of the sun and moon; his order is identical with that of the four

---

[15] This insertion and that immediately following the sentence are Chou's own
annotations.

seasons; and his good and evil fortunes are identical with those of spiritual beings."[16] The superior man cultivates these moral qualities and enjoys good fortune, whereas the inferior man violates them and suffers evil fortune.

Therefore it is said that "yin and yang are established as the way of Heaven, the weak and the strong as the way of Earth, and humanity and righteousness as the way of man."[17] It is also said that "if we investigate the cycle of things, we shall understand the concepts of life and death."[18] Great is the *Book of Changes*! Herein lies its excellence! (*Chou Tzu ch'üan-shu*, chs. 1-2, pp. 4-32)

Comment. This *Explanation* has provided the essential outline of Neo-Confucian metaphysics and cosmology in the last eight hundred years. Few short Chinese treatises like this have exerted so much influence. Although the whole concept owes much to the *Book of Changes*, it is to be noted that it rejected the idea of the Eight Trigrams of the *Book of Changes* and used the Five Agents instead, thus showing that the system was the product of Chou Tun-i's own speculation.

A great amount of literature has grown up on the history of the diagram and on the concept of the Great Ultimate. So far as philosophy is concerned, most Neo-Confucianists have followed Chou although they have differed in many details. However, two of Chou's ideas have aroused considerable criticism. One is the idea of the Non-ultimate. One of the famous debates between Chu Hsi and Lu Hsiang-shan (Lu Chiu-yüan, 1139-1193) was over this idea. The word *erh* in the opening sentence means "and also" or "in turn." But it can be interpreted in the sense of "and then," in which case, the Non-ultimate and the Great Ultimate would be two separate entities. This was precisely what Lu Hsiang-shan was objecting to, as he saw in Chou Tun-i a bifurcation of reality as two.[19] On the other hand, Chu Hsi claimed that Chou never meant that there is a Non-ultimate outside of the Great Ultimate,[20] that the Non-ultimate is the state of reality before the appearance of forms whereas the Great Ultimate is the state after the appear-

[16] *Changes*, commentary on hexagram no. 1, *ch'ien* (Heaven). Cf. Legge, trans., *Yi King*, p. 417.

[17] *ibid.*, "Remarks on Certain Trigrams," ch. 2. Cf. Legge, p. 423.

[18] *ibid.*, "Appended Remarks," pt. 1, ch. 4. Cf. Legge, p. 353.

[19] *Hsiang-shan ch'üan-chi* (Complete Works of Lu Hsiang-shan), SPPY, 2:6a, 9a.

[20] *Chu Tzu yü-lei* (Classified Conversations of Chu Hsi), 1876 ed., 94:2a-b.

ance of forms, and that the two form a unity.[21] This interpretation has been accepted by most Neo-Confucianists, including most prominent ones like Ts'ao Tuan (Ts'ao Yüeh-ch'uan, 1376-1434) and Hsüeh Hsüan (Hsüeh Ching-hsien, 1392-1464).[22]

The other idea that has attracted much criticism is the Taoistic idea of tranquillity. Chu Hsi took pains to explain that Chou meant tranquillity to be the basis for activity, and that of the four moral qualities of the sage (the Mean, humanity, correctness, and righteousness), the first two connote activity while the latter two connote tranquillity. This explanation is both arbitrary and unconvincing.[23] Similarly, Li Kuang-ti (1642-1718) tried to justify Chou by saying that his statement in the *Explanation*, "Having no desire, there will therefore be tranquillity," means the same thing as his statement in the *T'ung-shu*, "Having no desire, one is vacuous while tranquil and straightforward while in action,"[24] and that in Chou's mind tranquillity is never divorced from activity.[25] It is true that in the *T'ung-shu* itself, activity and tranquillity are spoken of together.[26] In fact, activity is mentioned alone several times[27] and tranquillity not even once alone. But so far as the *Explanation* is concerned, the emphasis on tranquillity is undeniable. It is far better to admit his Taoist influence and to point out that in spite of it, he steered Neo-Confucianism away from it.

2. PENETRATING THE BOOK OF CHANGES

Ch. 1. Sincerity, Pt. 1

Sincerity (*ch'eng*)[28] is the foundation of the sage. "Great is the *ch'ien*, the originator! All things obtain their beginning from it."[29] It is the source of sincerity. "The way of *ch'ien* is to change and transform

---

[21] *Chu Tzu wen-chi* (Collection of Literary Works of Chu Hsi), CTTC, 36:8a-12a. For Chu Hsi's and other comments on this controversy, see *Sung-Yüan hsüen-an*, SPPY, 12:3a-9a.

[22] See *Chou Tzu ch'üan-shu*, 1937 ed., pp. 81 and 89. For other Neo-Confucianists' discussions of the "Explanations," see *Sung-Yüan hsüeh-an*, SPPY, 12:1b-15a.

[23] *Chou Tzu ch'üan-shu*, p. 24.

[24] *T'ung-shu*, ch. 20.

[25] *Jung-ts'un T'ung-shu p'ien* (Essay on *Penetrating the Book of Changes*) appended to the *Chou Tzu T'ung-shu* (Penetrating the *Book of Changes* by Master Chou), SPPY, p. 2a.

[26] Chs. 4, 5, 9, 16, 20.

[27] Chs. 2, 31, 32.

[28] This word means not only sincerity in the narrow sense, but also honesty, absence of fault, seriousness, being true to one's true self, being true to the nature of being, actuality, realness.

[29] *Changes*, commentary on hexagram no. 1, *ch'ien*. Cf. Legge, p. 213.

so that everything will obtain its correct nature and destiny."[30] In this way sincerity is established. It is pure and perfectly good. Therefore "the successive movement of yin and yang constitutes the Way (Tao). What issues from the Way is good, and that which realizes it is the individual nature."[31] Origination and flourish characterize the penetration of sincerity, and advantage and firmness are its completion (or recovery). Great is the Change, the source of nature and destiny!

Ch. 2. Sincerity, Pt. 2

Sagehood is nothing but sincerity. It is the foundation of the Five Constant Virtues (humanity, righteousness, propriety, wisdom, and faithfulness) and the source of all activities. When tranquil, it is in the state of non-being, and when active, it is in the state of being. It is perfectly correct and clearly penetrating. Without sincerity, the Five Constant Virtues and all activities will be wrong. They will be depraved and obstructed. Therefore with sincerity very little effort is needed [to achieve the Mean].[32] [In itself] it is perfectly easy but it is difficult to put into practice. But with determination and firmness, there will be no difficulty. Therefore it is said, "If a man can for one day master himself and return to propriety, all under heaven will return to humanity."[33]

Ch. 3. Sincerity is the Subtle, Incipient, Activating Force (Chi) of Virtue

Sincerity [in its original substance] engages in no activity, but is the subtle, incipient, activating force giving rise to good and evil. The virtue of loving is called humanity, that of doing what is proper is called righteousness, that of putting things in order is called propriety, that of penetration is called wisdom, and that of abiding by one's commitments is called faithfulness. One who is in accord with his nature and acts with ease is a sage. One who returns to his nature and adheres to it is a worthy. And one whose subtle emanation cannot be seen and whose [goodness] is abundant and all-pervasive without limit is a man of the spirit.[34]

> *Comment.* The first sentence of this chapter occasioned a great deal of discussion among Neo-Confucianists.[35] Chou seems to contradict himself, for sincerity, being the original state of man's moral nature, is perfectly good and yet it gives rise to both good and evil.

[30] *ibid.*

[31] *ibid.*, "Appended Remarks," pt. 1, ch. 5. Cf. Legge, pp. 355-356.

[32] Chu Hsi is followed in this interpretation. See *Chou Tzu ch'üan-shu*, p. 124.

[33] *Analects*, 12:1. [34] Cf. *Mencius*, 7B:25.

[35] See *Chou Tzu ch'üan-shu*, pp. 126-133.

Actually the problem of evil had bothered Confucianists right along and there was no solution until Chang Tsai (Chang Heng-ch'ü, 1020-1077).[36] Chou adheres to the traditional Confucian position that human nature is inherently good but as one's nature comes into contact with external things, good and evil appear. Whereas both Taoism and Buddhism maintain that this external influence corrupts, Confucianism puts the responsibility on man himself by holding that evil appears when man fails to adhere to the Mean.[37] Thus the good moral nature is substance, and good and evil appear only in its function. This doctrine was upheld throughout the history of Neo-Confucianism. As Sun Ch'i-feng (1584-1675) has observed in commenting on this chapter, Chou teaches that good results from one's being correct and evil from one's being one-sided, a theory quite different from that of Hu Hung (Hu Wu-feng, 1100-1155), who said that both good and evil proceed from nature.[38] Chou Tzu's important contribution in this connection is his idea of subtle, incipient activation. It is also found in chapters four and nine and, according to Chu Hsi, is implicit in chapter twenty-seven.[39]

The word *chi* means an originating power, an inward spring of activity, an emergence not yet visible, a critical point at which one's direction toward good or evil is set. It is here and now that one must be absolutely sincere and true to his moral nature so he will not deviate from it either in going too far or not going far enough. Thus Chou turns a quietistic state into a dynamic one.

Ch. 4. Sagehood

"The state of absolute quiet and inactivity" is sincerity. The spirit is that which, "when acted on, immediately penetrates all things."[40] And the state of subtle incipient activation is the undifferentiated state between existence and nonexistence when activity has started but has not manifested itself in physical form. Sincerity is infinitely pure and hence evident. The spirit is responsive and hence works wonders. And incipient activation is subtle and hence abstruse. The sage is the one who is in the state of sincerity, spirit, and subtle incipient activation.

[36] See Chan, "The Neo-Confucian Solution of the Problem of Evil," *Studies Presented to Hu Shih on His Sixty-fifth Birthday*, pp. 773-791.

[37] See chs. 7 and 22.

[38] *Li-hsüeh tsung-ch'uan* (Orthodox Transmission of Neo-Confucianism), 1880 ed., 1:9a.

[39] *Chou Tzu ch'üan-shu*, p. 178.

[40] *Changes*, "Appended Remarks," pt. 1, ch. 10. Cf. Legge, p. 370.

Ch. 5. Caution about Activity

When activity is directed along its correct course, we have the Way. When its operations are harmonized, we have virtue. The violation of humanity, of righteousness, of propriety, of wisdom, and of faithfulness is depravity. Any activity of depravity is disgraceful. When pushed to a high degree, it is even dangerous. Consequently, the superior man is cautious about his activity.

Ch. 6. The Way

The way of the sage is nothing but humanity, righteousness, the Mean, and correctness. Preserve it and it will be ennobling. Practice it and it will be beneficial. Extend it and it will match Heaven and Earth. Is it not easy and simple? Is it hard to know? (If so), it is because we do not preserve, practice, and extend it.

> Comment. Note that "humanity, righteousness, the Mean, and correctness" is a quotation from the Explanation of the Diagram. This treatise repeats the Explanation four times (chs. 6, 16, 20, 22). As a matter of fact, as Chu Hsi has said, the entire treatise is an elaboration on the Explanation.[41]

Ch. 7. Teachers

Someone asked, "How can good be promoted in the world?"
I said, "Through teachers."
"How is that?"
I said, "In human nature there are only strength, weakness, good, evil, and the Mean."
The questioner did not understand.
I explained, "Righteousness, uprightness, decisiveness, strictness, and firmness of action are examples of strength that is good, and fierceness, narrow-mindedness, and violence are examples of strength that is evil. Kindness, mildness, and humility are examples of weakness that is good, and softness, indecision, and perverseness are examples of weakness that is evil. Only the Mean brings harmony. The Mean is the principle of regularity, the universally recognized law of morality, and is that to which the sage is devoted. Therefore the sage institutes education so as to enable people to transform their evil by themselves, to arrive at the Mean and to rest there. Therefore those who are the first to be enlightened should instruct those who are slower in attaining enlightenment, and the ignorant should seek help from those who understand. Thus the way of teachers is established. As the way of teachers is established, there will

---

[41] Chou Tzu ch'üan-shu, p. 120.

be many good people. With many good people, the government will be correct and the empire will be in order."

> *Comment.* Chou Tzu's doctrines on education here and on government, ceremonies, and music below are traditional and there is nothing new. The same is true of later Neo-Confucianists. The important philosophical point here is that the Mean is considered the highest good. According to Chu Hsi, strength and weakness and good and evil refer to physical nature, not original nature.[42]

Ch. 8. Fortune

It is a misfortune in one's life that he is not told his mistakes, and it is a great misfortune not to have a sense of shame. Only with a sense of shame can one be educated, and if one is told his mistakes, it will make it possible for him to become a worthy.

Ch. 9. Thought

It is said in the "Great Norm" that "thought should be penetrating and profound. . . . Such thinking leads to sageliness."[43] Having no thought is the foundation, and thinking penetratively is its function. With subtle incipient activation becoming active on the one hand, and with sincerity becoming active in response, on the other—having no thought and yet penetrating all—thus is one a sage.

One cannot penetrate subtlety without thought, and cannot penetrate all without profound thought. Thus the ability to penetrate all comes from the ability to penetrate subtlety, and the ability to penetrate subtlety comes from thinking. Therefore thinking is the foundation of the sage's effort and is also the subtle, incipient activation of good and evil. It is said in the *Book of Changes*, "The superior man acts as soon as he sees the subtle, incipient activating force [giving rise to good and evil] without waiting for the end of the day."[44] It is again said, "One who knows subtle incipient activation is a man of the spirit."[45]

> *Comment.* Under Taoist influence, Chou Tun-i emphasized tranquillity. Unlike the Taoists, however, he stressed thinking also. It is thinking that keeps one alert to the subtle, incipient activation of good and evil. Clearly, there is a fundamental difference between his tranquillity and that of the Taoists. However, about thinking itself, Chou has said very little.

[42] *Chu Tzu yü-lei*, 94:32b.
[43] *History*, "Great Norm." Cf. Legge, trans., *Shoo King*, p. 327.
[44] "Appended Remarks," pt. 2, ch. 5. Cf. Legge, *Yi King*, p. 392.
[45] *ibid.*

Ch. 10. The Will to Learn

The sage aspires to become Heaven, the worthy aspires to become a sage, and the gentleman aspires to become a worthy. I-yin and Yen Yüan were great worthies. I-yin was ashamed that his ruler would not become a sage-emperor like Yao and Shun,[46] and if a single person in the empire was not well adjusted, he felt as if he himself were as disgraced as if he had been whipped in public. Yen Yüan[47] "did not transfer his anger; he did not repeat a mistake,"[48] and "for three months there would be nothing in his mind contrary to humanity."[49] If one desires what I-yin desired and learns what Yen Yüan learned, he will become a sage if he reaches the highest degree and a worthy if he reaches the proper degree. Even if he does not, he will not miss a good reputation.

Ch. 11. Harmony and Transformation

Heaven produces the ten thousand things through yang and brings them to completion through yin. To produce is humanity, and to bring to completion is righteousness. Therefore when the sage administers an empire, he cultivates all things with humanity and sets all people right with righteousness. As the Way of Heaven operates, all things are in harmony. As the virtue of the sage-ruler is cultivated, all people are transformed. The great harmony and great transformation leave no trace, and no one knows how they come to be: This is called spirit. Therefore, the foundation of the multitude lies in one person. Is the Way far away? Need there be many methods [other than humanity and righteousness]?

Ch. 12. Government

In governing a hamlet of ten families, it is impossible to complete the task even if one teaches everybody most earnestly to the point of whispering to his ears. How much more difficult in an extensive empire with millions of people. The answer is this: Purify the heart, that is all. By purity is meant that one, whether he is active or tranquil, does not violate humanity, righteousness, propriety, and wisdom in his speech, appearance, seeing, or listening. When one's heart is pure, men of virtue and talents will come to help him. With the help of such men the empire will be governed. Purity of heart is indeed important, and the employment of men of virtue and talents is an urgent matter.

---

[46] I-yin was a minister who helped T'ang found the Shang dynasty (1751-1112 B.C.). T'ang's grandson, T'ai-chia (r. 1738–1727 B.C.) was not a good ruler and banished I-yin. Yao and Shun were 3rd millennium B.C. legendary sages for Confucianists. For the story about I-yin, see *History*, "Charge to Yüeh," pt. 3 (Legge, trans., *Shoo King*, p. 262).

[47] Confucius' favorite pupil. [48] *Analects*, 6:2.
[49] *ibid.*, 6:5.

Ch. 13. Ceremony and Music

Ceremonies are intended to establish order (*li*) and music means to harmonize. Only when yin and yang operate according to order can they be in harmony. Then the ruler will truly be the ruler, the minister will truly be the minister, the father will truly be the father, the son will truly be the son, brothers will truly be brothers, and husband and wife will truly be husband and wife. All things must fulfill their principle before they are in harmony. Therefore ceremonies come first and music afterward.

Ch. 14. Devotion to Actuality

When actuality (substance) dominates, it is good, but when name dominates, it is shame. Therefore the superior man advances his virtue and cultivates all aspects of his task with unceasing diligence, for he wants actuality to dominate. If his virtue or task has not become prominent, he fears with a sense of alarm that the fact may become known, for he wants to be as far away from shame as possible. On the other hand, the inferior man is simply insincere. Therefore the superior man is at ease at all times whereas the inferior man is anxious at all times.

Ch. 15. Love and Reverence

"Suppose I do not measure up to the goodness of others. [What shall I do?]"

"If you do not measure up to it, learn to do so."

"What if others do evil?"

"If they do evil, tell them that it is evil and, furthermore, exhort them, saying, 'Suppose you change your ways. You will then be a superior man.' If one person does good and two do evil, learn from the one and exhort the two. If someone should say, 'So-and-so does evil but it is not a great wrong,' you should say, 'Who does not make mistakes? How do we know that they cannot be corrected? If one corrects his mistakes, he will be a superior man. If he does not correct them, that will be wrong, and Heaven dislikes the wrong. Does he not fear Heaven? How do we know he cannot correct his mistakes?' "[50] Therefore the superior man possesses all virtues and is loved and revered by all.

Ch. 16. Activity and Tranquillity

Things cannot be tranquil while active or active while tranquil. Spirit, however, can be active without activity and tranquil without tranquil-

[50] According to the commentary by Chu Hsi, the answer ends here, not earlier.

lity.[51] Being active without activity and tranquil without tranquillity does not mean that spirit is neither active nor tranquil.[52] Things cannot penetrate each other but spirit works wonders with all things. The passive material force of Water is rooted in yang and the active material force of Fire is rooted in yin. The Five Agents are nothing but yin and yang and these in turn are the Great Ultimate. The four seasons run their course, and all things have their beginnings and ends. How undifferentiated! How extensive! And how infinite!

Ch. 17. Music, Pt. 1

In ancient times sage-kings instituted ceremonies and cultivated moral education. They rectified the Three Bonds (of ruler and minister, father and son, and husband and wife) and put in order the Nine Categories (of the Great Norm).[53] Consequently all people were in perfect harmony and all things were in concord. Thereupon the sage-kings created music to give expression to the winds (people's sentiments) coming from the eight directions and to appease the feelings of the people. This is the reason why the sound of music is calm and not harmful, and is harmonious without being licentious. As it enters the ear and affects the heart, everyone becomes calm and peaceful. Because of calmness, one's desires will be appeased, and because of harmony, one's impetuousness will disappear. Peace, calmness, and moderation—these are the height of virtue. As the world is transformed and brought to completion,[54] government reaches its perfection. This is what is meant by moral principles which match Heaven and Earth and which are the ultimate standard of the ancients.[55]

Later generations have neglected ceremonies. Their governmental measures and laws have been in disorder. Rulers have indulged their material desires without restraint, and consequently the people below them have suffered bitterly. Rulers have claimed that ancient music is not worth listening to and replaced it by or changed it into modern music, which is seductive, licentious, depressive, and complaining. It arouses desires and increases bitterness without end. Therefore there have been cases of people destroying their rulers, casting away their fathers, taking life lightly, and ruining human relations, and it has been impossible to put an end to such atrocities. Alas! Ancient music appeased the heart but

[51] In his commentary Chu Hsi says, "Spirit does not leave physical form but is not restricted by it."

[52] Chu Hsi said, "There is tranquillity in activity and there is activity in tranquillity."

[53] See above, ch. 1, sec. 3.

[54] Chu Hsi said that according to some, the word *chung* (middle) should read *ch'eng* (to complete).

[55] Paraphrasing *Lao Tzu*, ch. 68.

modern music enhances desires. Ancient music spread a civilizing influence, but modern music increases discontent. To hope for perfect government without restoring ancient and changing modern music is to be far off the mark.

Ch. 18, Music, Pt. 2

Music is based on government. As the government is good and the people are happy, the hearts of all will be harmonious. The sage therefore creates music to give expression to this harmony in their hearts. As it penetrates heaven and earth, their vital force (*ch'i*) will be affected and there will be great harmony. As there is harmony throughout heaven and earth, all things will be in concord. Therefore spiritual beings will come to enjoy sacrifices offered them, and all animals will become tamed.

Ch. 19. Music, Pt. 3

As the sound of music is calm, the heart of the listener becomes peaceful, and as the words of the music are good, those who sing them will admire them. The result will be that customs are transformed and mores are changed. The influence of seductive sounds and passionate words is equally great.

Ch. 20. Learning to Be a Sage

"Can one become a sage through learning?"

"Yes."

"Is there any essential way?"

"Yes."

"Please explain it to me."

"The essential way is to [concentrate on] one thing. By [concentrating on] one thing is meant having no desire. Having no desire, one is vacuous (*hsü*, being absolutely pure and peaceful) while tranquil, and straightforward while in action. Being vacuous while tranquil, one becomes intelligent and hence penetrating. Being straightforward while active, one becomes impartial and hence all-embracing. Being intelligent, penetrating, impartial, and all-embracing, one is almost a sage."

> *Comment.* Confucianists had never advocated having no desire. Mencius merely advocated having few desires.[56] The Taoist influence here is obvious. Hitherto, it was only a Taoist and Buddhist method of moral cultivation, but from now on, it became a Confucian method too. But as Chu Hsi said,[57] Chou went too far, and as the prerequisite for concentrating on one thing, Ch'eng had to

[56] *Mencius*, 7B:35.   [57] *Chou Tzu ch'üan-shu*, p. 165.

substitute seriousness (*ching*) for desirelessness,[58] evidently in order to eliminate this Taoist influence.

Ch. 21. Impartiality and Understanding

Whoever is impartial toward himself will be impartial toward others. There has never been a person who is partial toward himself and yet impartial toward others. Doubt arises when understanding is not perfect. With understanding there will be no doubt. To say that to be able to doubt is to understand is as far wrong as a thousand miles off the mark.

Ch. 22. Principle, Human Nature, and Destiny

Only the intelligent can understand the manifestations and concealments (of the operations of yin and yang). Strength may be good or it may be evil. The same is true of weakness. The ideal is the Mean.

The myriad things are created and transformed out of the two material forces and the Five Agents. These Five Agents are the basis of their differentiation while the two material forces constitute their actuality. The two forces are fundamentally one. Consequently, the many are [ultimately] one and the one is actually differentiated in the many. The one and the many each has its own correct state of being. The great and the small each has its definite function.

> *Comment.* This is the most important chapter, because, as the title indicates, it deals with the three basic subjects in Neo-Confucianism: human nature, principle, and destiny. Strangely enough, none of the words appears in the chapter. According to Chu Hsi, the first sentence deals with principle, the next three deal with nature, and the rest deals with destiny.[59] But as Sun Ch'i-feng pointed out, destiny refers to the endowment by Heaven and nature refers to what is inherent in man and things, and both are principle.[60] Chu Hsi identifies the one with the Great Ultimate. The fundamental Neo-Confucian tenet, that substance is one but its manifestations are many, is here succinctly stated. As Chu Hsi said, "The one and the many each having its own correct state of being means that principle is one but its manifestations are many."[61] Thus in this

[58] See below, ch. 32, secs. 32 and 46.
[59] *Chou Tzu ch'üan-shu*, pp. 168-169.
[60] *ibid.*, p. 169. According to Lü Nan (1479-1542), the chapter is primarily intended to show that nature and destiny follow the same principle. See his *Sung ssu-tzu ch'ao-shih* (Excerpts from Four Masters of Sung, 960-1279, Explained), *Hsi-yin-hsien ts'ung-shu* (Hall of Being-Careful-with-Time Collection) ed., sec. on Master Chou, 1:8a.
[61] *Chu Tzu yü-lei*, 94:41b.

chapter are found the three major subjects of Neo-Confucianism and one of its most fundamental tenets.

Ch. 23. Yen Tzu

Yen Tzu (Yen Yüan) had only a single bamboo dish of rice, a single gourd dish of drink, and lived in his mean narrow lane. Others could not have endured this distress but he did not allow his joy to be affected by it.[62] Now, wealth and honor are what people love. Yen Tzu did not love or seek them but instead enjoyed poverty. What is the idea? There are the highest honor and the greatest [wealth to][63] love and seek. But he acted differently because he saw what was great and ignored what was small. Since he saw the great, his mind was at peace. His mind being at peace, he had no discontent. Having no discontent, he treated wealth, honor, poverty, or humble station in the same way. As he treated them in the same way, he could transform them and equalize them.[64] This is why Yen Tzu has been regarded as second to the Sage.

Ch. 24. Teachers and Friends, Pt. 1

The most honorable thing in the world is moral principle, and the most valuable thing is virtue. Man is most precious. What makes him most precious is his possession of moral principles and virtue. Without the help of teachers and friends, it is impossible for one to possess in his person what makes man the most precious.

Ch. 25. Teachers and Friends, Pt. 2

Moral principles are honorable and valuable only when they are possessed by man. At birth man is ignorant. He remains stupid when he grows up if he has no teachers or friends to help him. Thus moral principles become valuable and honorable when they are possessed by man through the help of teachers and friends. Is the meaning not important? Is man's possession not enjoyable?

Ch. 26. Mistakes

Tzu-lu[65] was happy to hear about his mistakes[66] and his good reputation was unlimited. Nowadays when people have faults they do not like others to correct them. It is as though a man should hide his illness and

---

[62] Analects, 6:9.

[63] Chu Hsi thought that these words should be added to the text.

[64] Chu Hsi (Chou Tzu ch'üan-shu, p. 172) thought the word ch'i (equal) is out of place or it means to be equal to the sage. But there is nothing wrong in accepting the word in its ordinary meaning "to equalize." Is it because Chu Hsi did not want to associate Master Chou with Chuang Tzu's doctrine of equality of things?

[65] Confucius' pupil, 542-480 B.C.

[66] Mencius, 2A:8.

avoid a physician. He would rather destroy his life than awake. How lamentable!

Ch. 27. Tendencies

The most important things in the world [with regard to the subtle, incipient activation of things][67] are tendencies. Tendencies may be strong or weak. If a tendency is extremely strong, it cannot be controlled.[68] But it is possible to control it quickly if one realizes that it is strong. To control it requires effort. If one does not realize early enough, it will not be easy to apply effort. If one has exerted his effort and does not succeed, that is due to Heaven, but if one either does not realize or does not apply effort, that is due to man. Is it due to Heaven? No, it is due to man. Why complain?

Ch. 28. Literary Expressions

Literature is a vehicle of moral principles. If wheels and shafts of carriages are decorated but are not used, they would have been decorated for nothing. How much less useful would an undecorated carriage be!

Literary expressions are art and moral principles are substance. If one is earnest about substance and writes it down with art, it will be beautiful and loved. As it is loved, it will be transmitted to posterity. The worthy can then learn it and achieve its object. This is education. This is why it is said, "Words without literary quality will not go very far."[69] But unworthy people will not learn even if their parents supervise them or if teachers and tutors exhort them. They will not obey even if they are forced to. They do not know to devote themselves to moral principles and virtue and merely apply their ability to literary expressions. This is no more than art. Alas! This defect has existed for a long time.

Ch. 29. The All-Embracing Depth of the Sage

[Confucius said,] "I do not enlighten those who are not eager to learn, nor arouse those who are not anxious to give an explanation themselves. If I have presented one corner of the square and they cannot come back to me with the other three, I should not go over the points again."[70] He also said, "I do not wish to say anything. . . . Does Heaven say anything? The four seasons run their course and all things are produced."[71] Thus the all-embracing depth of Confucius could be seen only by Yen Tzu. He was the one who discovered the all-embracing depth of the Sage and taught the ten thousand generations without end. A sage is equal to

[67] Chu Hsi is followed in this interpretation.
[68] Literally "to recover."
[69] *Tso chuan* (Tso's Commentary on the *Spring and Autumn Annals*), Duke Hsiang, 25th year. See Legge trans., *Ch'un Ts'ew*, p. 517.
[70] *Analects*, 7:8.   [71] *ibid.*, 17:19.

Heaven. Is he not profound? When an ordinary person hears or knows anything, he is afraid that others will not quickly know that he has it. How superficial it is to make haste to let people know and to seek a name!

Ch. 30. The Refinement and All-Embracing Depth of the Sage

The refinement of the Sage is revealed in the hexagrams, and the all-embracing depth of the Sage is expressed through them. If the hexagrams had not been drawn, it could not have been possible to reveal the refinement of the Sage. And if there were no hexagrams, it would almost be impossible to know all about the all-embracing depth of the Sage. The *Book of Changes* is not only the source of the Five Classics;[72] it is the deep and dark abode of Heaven, Earth, and spiritual beings.

Ch. 31. The Hexagrams of Ch'ien (Heaven), Sun (Decrease) I (Increase),[73] and Activity

"The superior man is active and vigilant and is unceasing in his sincerity." But he must "restrain his wrath and repress his desires," "move toward good," and "correct his mistakes"[74] before he can achieve his objective. Among the functions of *ch'ien*, none is better than to achieve this, and the greatness of *sun* and *i* does not go beyond this.[75] It is the greatness of *sun* and *i*, and there is nothing superior. The thought of the Sage is deep indeed! "Good fortune, evil fortune, occasion for repentance, and reason for regret all arise from activity."[76] Alas! good fortune is only one out of four. Should we not be careful about activity?

Ch. 32. The Hexagrams of Chia-jen (Family), K'uei (To Part), Fu (To Return), and Wu-wang (Absence from Falsehood)[77]

There is a foundation for the government of the world. It is the ruler's person. There is a model for the government of the world. It is the family. The foundation must be correct. To make the foundation correct, there is no other way than to make the heart sincere. The model must be good. In order for the model to be good, there is no other way than to maintain harmony among kin. It is difficult to govern a family whereas it is easy to govern the world, for the family is near while the world is distant. If members of the family are separated, the cause surely

[72] *Books of History, Odes, Rites,* and the *Spring and Autumn Annals,* besides the *Book of Changes.*

[73] Hexagrams nos. 1, 41, and 42, respectively.

[74] These phrases are from the sections on the three hexagrams. Cf. Legge, *Yi King,* pp. 317, 319, 410.

[75] Read *ch'i* (that) as *mo* (none), according to Chu Hsi.

[76] *Changes,* "Appended Remarks," pt. 2, ch. 1. Cf. Legge, p. 380.

[77] Hexagrams nos. 37, 38, 24, and 25, respectively.

lies with women. This is why *k'uei* follows *chia-jen*, for "when two women live together, their wills move in different directions."[78] This was why (sage-emperor) Yao, having put his empire in order, gave his two daughters in marriage to Shun in order to test him and see whether the throne should be given to him. Thus it is that, in order to see how a ruler governs his empire, we observe the government of his family. In order to see how he governs his family, we observe how he governs himself. To be correct in one's person means to be sincere in one's heart. And to be sincere in one's heart means to return from (turn away from) evil activities. Evil activities represent falsehood. When it has been turned away, there will be none. Being free from it, one is sincere. This is the reason why *wu-wang* comes after *fu*. And it is said, "The ancient kings made their regulations in complete accordance with the seasons, thereby nourishing all things."[79] How profound!

Ch. 33. Wealth and Honor

The superior man considers a rich possession of moral principles to be honor and peace in his person to be wealth. Therefore he is always at peace and is never discontented. To him carriages and ceremonial caps (symbols of honor) are as light as a cash, and gold and jade are as tiny as a speck of dust. Nothing can be added to the great value [of rich possession of moral principle and peace in the person].

Ch. 34. Vulgarity

The way of the Sage is to be heard through the ear, to be preserved in the heart, to be deeply embraced there and to become one's moral character, and to become one's activities and undertakings when it is put into practice. Those who are engaged purely in literary expressions are vulgar people.

Ch. 35. Consideration and Deliberation

Perfect sincerity leads to activity. Activity leads to change. And change leads to transformation. Hence it is said, "One will consider before he speaks and deliberate before he acts. By such consideration and deliberations he undertakes to complete all changes and transformations."[80]

Ch. 36. Punishment

Heaven produces all things in the spring and stops producing in the autumn. All things have been produced and matured and it would be

[78] *ibid.*, commentary on hexagram no. 38, *kuei*. Cf. Legge, p. 243.
[79] *ibid.*, commentary on hexagram no. 25, *wu-wang*. Cf. Legge, p. 299.
[80] "Appended Remarks," pt. 1, ch. 8. Cf. Legge, p. 361.

a mistake not to stop. Therefore there is the autumn to complete the process. The sage models after Heaven in governing and nourishing all people. So he regulates them with punishment. As people have abundance, their desires are aroused. Their feelings become dominant and they are guided by advantages and disadvantages. Consequently they would attack one another without cease. They would destroy themselves and human relations would be ruined. Therefore they receive punishment [from the sage] so that they may become regulated.

Feelings are not genuine but are obscure. They change in a thousand ways. They cannot be regulated except by a person who is characterized by the Mean, correctness, intelligence, penetration, courage, and firmness. The explanation of the hexagram *sung* (contention) says, "It will be advantageous to see the great man". . . for the strong has occupied the central position.[81] The explanation of the hexagram *shih-ho* (biting and uniting) says, "It will be advantageous to use legal restraint"[82] for it is an activity with intelligence. Ah! Those who administer punishment control the lives of the people throughout the empire. Should their appointment not be careful?

Ch. 37. Impartiality

The way of the sage is nothing other than absolute impartiality.
Someone asked, "What does that mean?"
I said, "Heaven and Earth are nothing other than absolute impartiality."

Ch. 38. Confucius, Pt. 1

The *Spring and Autumn Annals*[83] is to set the kingly way correct and to make clear the fundamental principles of government. Confucius wrote it for the benefit of kings of later generations, and, by recording the capital punishments of rebellious ministers and villainous sons in the past, to warn ministers and sons that were to come. It is fitting that for ten thousand generations without end kings have offered sacrifice to Confucius to repay his infinite kindness and contributions.

Ch. 39. Confucius, Pt. 2

Confucius was the only one who possessed virtue in abundance, who exercised an unlimited amount of civilizing influence, and who could really form a trinity with Heaven and Earth and be equal to the four seasons.

[81] Commentary on hexagram no. 6, *sung*. Cf. Legge, p. 69.
[82] Commentary on hexagram no. 21, *shih-ho*. Cf. Legge, p. 230.
[83] For this Classic, see above, ch. 1, n.6.

Ch. 40. The Hexagrams of Meng (Obscure) and Ken (To Stop)[84]

"The youthful and ignorant comes and seeks me."[85] I follow the correct way and determine his conduct as in the case of divination. Divination is to seek advice from spirits. "To ask for the second or third time [thus showing lack of concentration] would be to indicate doubt. In that case, the spirits would not give him any advice."[86] [The hexagram represents] a spring issuing forth beneath a mountain.[87] It will be clear if it is still, but if it is disturbed, it will be confused. Being confused, it loses its destination. One must be careful. The only right thing to do is to be timely and to follow the Mean.

"Stop in the back of a thing."[88] The back is not seen. If one is tranquil, one will stop [at the right point]. To stop means not to do anything [deliberate], for if one does anything [deliberate], one will not be able to stop [at the right point]. The truth [in these hexagrams] is deep indeed!

[84] Hexagrams nos. 4 and 52, respectively.
[85] ibid., commentary on hexagram no. 4, meng. Cf. Legge, p. 64.
[86] ibid. Cf. Legge, p. 216.
[87] ibid. Cf. Legge, p. 271.
[88] ibid., commentary on hexagram no. 52, ken. Cf. Legge, p. 175.

29

THE NUMERICAL AND OBJECTIVE TENDENCIES
IN SHAO YUNG

IN SPITE OF its metaphysics, Neo-Confucianism as a whole is homocentric. It proceeds from man to embrace the whole universe. In the case of Shao Yung (Shao K'ang-chieh, Shao Yao-fu, 1011-1077), however, the direction is reversed. To him, man is only one of many creatures, though the most important one, and he is only part of an extensive process of universal operation. This is clear from his major concepts.

Shao's fundamental concepts are three. First, there are the supreme principles governing the universe. Second, these principles can be discerned in terms of numbers. And third, the best knowledge of them is the objective, that is, viewing things from the viewpoint of things. In holding that all things have principles in them, he is not different from other Neo-Confucianists. To this concept, he devoted his major work, the *Huang-chi ching-shih shu* (Supreme Principles Governing the World). However, while he followed the same pattern of cosmic evolution in the *Book of Changes* as most other Neo-Confucianists did, that is, the evolution from the Great Ultimate through yin and yang or negative and positive cosmic force, to the myriad things, he added the element of number. To him universal operation, or Change, is due to spirit, which gives rise to number, number to form, and form to concrete things. The whole process works according to principle and is natural. Man is the most intelligent of the products of natural evolution, but like all other things he is governed by numbers.

The concept of number is not new. It is present in the *Lao Tzu*, the *Book of Changes*, the Five Agents School, the apocryphal literature of the Western Han period (206 B.C.–A.D. 8), and Yang Hsiung (53 B.C.–A.D. 18), but he was the first one to base his whole philosophy on it and build a system of numerical progression. Evidently under the influence of the *Book of Changes* in which the Great Ultimate engenders the four forms of major and minor cosmic forces yin and yang, he used the number 4 as the basis of classification of all phenomena. Thus there are the four heavenly bodies (sun, moon, stars, and zodiacal space), the four earthly substances (water, fire, earth, and stone), the four kinds of creatures (animals, birds, grass, and plants), the four sense organs (eye, ear, nose, and mouth), the four ways of transforming the world (by truth, virtue, work, and effort), the four kinds of rulers, the four kinds of Mandate of Heaven, and so forth. The whole scheme is neat and systematic but also mechanical and arbitrary. However, in its progression from 4 to 64, which is the number of hexagrams in the *Book of Changes*, it clearly indicates the evolutionary development from the one to the many. Furthermore, since the process is essentially the work of spirit, which expresses itself in interpenetrating activity and in the tranquillity of yin and yang, the universal operation is conceived of as opening (expansion) and closing (contraction) and thus the dynamic character of Change is dominant. What is new in the numerical approach is that things are definite and that by mathematical calculation they can be predicted. He applied this to history and equated it with the four seasons with calculable beginning and predictable end.

In this scheme of things, objective viewing of things is not only desirable but necessary. To view things this way meant not to be subjective but to follow principle which is inherent in things, and to maintain the mean in one's emotions so they would not lead one to partiality.

In such ideas as these, he comes close to other Neo-Confucianists. Generally speaking, however, he stands in a class by himself. Historians of Chinese philosophy usually refer to the "Five Masters of the early Sung period," namely, Chou Tun-i (Chou Lien-hsi, 1017-1073), Shao Yung, Chang Tsai (Chang Heng-ch'ü, 1020-1077), Ch'eng Hao (Ch'eng Ming-tao, 1032-1085), and Ch'eng I (Ch'eng I-ch'uan, 1033-1107). They were contemporaries and friends. But in his anthology of early Sung philosophy, Chu Hsi (1130-1200) did not include Shao Yung. The other outstanding anthologies do include him but put him after Chang Tsai, although he was nine years senior to Chang and both died in the same year.[1] The reason for this is that Chu Hsi fixed the line of the orthodox transmission of Neo-Confucianism from Chou Tun-i through the Ch'eng brothers to Chang Tsai. Later Neo-Confucianists included Chu Hsi but not Shao Yung.[2]

[1] The *Chin-ssu lu* (Reflections on Things at Hand) contains selections from the works of the other four but not Shao. The other anthologies are: the *Hsing-li ta-ch'üan* (Great Collection of Neo-Confucianism) compiled by Hu Kuang (1370-1418) *et al.*, 1405; Sun Ch'i-feng (1584-1675), *Li-hsüeh tsung-ch'uan* (Orthodox Transmission of Neo-Confucianism), 1666; and the *Hsing-li ching-i* (Essentials of Neo-Confucianism), compiled by Li Kuang-ti (1642-1718), 1717. In the *Sheng-hsüeh tsung-ch'uan* (Orthodox Transmission of the Doctrine of the Sage), compiled by Chou Ju-teng (1547-1629), 1605, however, Shao Yung is included and comes before Chang Tsai. Chou belonged to the idealistic school of Neo-Confucianism, that of Wang Yang-ming (1472-1529), which is directly opposed to the rationalistic school of Chu Hsi. Also in the *Sung-Yüan hsüeh-an* (Anthology and Critical Accounts of the Neo-Confucianists of the Sung and Yüan Dynasties, 960-1368), compiled by Huang Tsung-hsi (1610-1695) *et al.*, Shao precedes Chang. Huang also belonged to the Wang Yang-ming school.

[2] For example, in the *Tao-t'ung lu* (Record of the Transmission of the Way) by Chang Po-hsing (1651-1725), Chou, the Ch'engs, Chang, and Chu are included but not Shao. Chang Po-hsing was an ardent follower of Chu Hsi.

This belittling of Shao is partly due to the partisan spirit of Chu Hsi and other Neo-Confucianists. All records agree that Shao received his learning from a Taoist. But the more important reason for not considering him important is his failure to discuss such central Confucian problems as humanity and righteousness. As Hsieh Liang-tao (Hsieh Shang-ts'ai, 1050-1103) has remarked, "He had insight on the principle of progress and retrogression of the universe and the rise and fall of all things . . . but had not devoted himself to the task of studying things on the lower level (human affairs) before penetrating things on the higher level."[3] One may say in Shao's defense that he does regard man as the most important creature, that for him as for other Neo-Confucianists the sage is the ideal man, and that nature, destiny, and principle are for him as for other Neo-Confucianists basic problems. There is no denial, however, that he was not as much concerned with social and moral problems as his fellow Neo-Confucianists. It was primarily because of this that he exercised little influence on his contemporaries and had no followers and that his doctrine has not been propagated by later Neo-Confucianists.

As a man, he was much respected. For forty years he lived in Lo-yang in poverty. He was offered two minor offices but he declined. When he approached in a small cart, all people, whether adults or children, welcomed him with warm smiles.[4] He wrote a number of works, but the most important is the *Huang-chi ching-shih shu* (Supreme Principles Governing the World).[5]

[3] *Shang-ts'ai yü-lu* (Recorded Sayings of Hsieh Liang-tso), *Cheng-i-t'ang ch'üan-shu* (Complete Library of the Hall of Rectifying the Way) ed., pt. 1, 8a. Ch'eng Hao also said that Shao's philosophy was "castle in the air." *I-shu* (Surviving Works), 7:1b, in ECCS.

[4] According to the *Sung shih* (History of the Sung Dynasty, 960-1279), PNP, 427:18b-21b, Shao learned from Li Chih-ts'ai, a magistrate from Pei-hai in modern Shantung, certain diagrams connected with the *Book of Changes*, out of which Shao's theory of diagrams and numbers evolved. Li learned them from the Taoist Ch'en T'uan (c. 906-989). Shao supported himself by farming and called himself "Mr. Happiness" and his place "Happy Nest." Out of respect, many prominent scholars and officials, including eminent Ssu-ma Kuang (1019-1086), often visited him. Ch'eng Hao and Ch'eng I were his great friends. About 1060 he was appointed keeper of records in the board of public works and about a decade later a militia judge. In both occasions he refused to assume office. See Bruce, *Chu Hsi and His Masters*, pp. 31-35.

[5] This is the most important work by Shao Yung. The number of chapters varies from eight to seventeen. There are many editions, including one in the *Tao-tsang* (Taoist Canon), chs. 705-718. The one used here is the SPPY edition, in nine chapters. Chs. 5 and 6 make up the "Inner Chapters on the Observation of Things" and chs. 7A to 8B the "Outer Chapters on the Observation of Things." Selections are from these chapters. Selected passages have been translated by de Harlez, *L'École philosophique modern de la Chine*, pp. 82-110.

Following the list of its major topics and references are selections from it.

SUPREME PRINCIPLES GOVERNING THE WORLD

1. Heaven is born of activity and Earth is born of tranquillity. The interaction of activity and tranquillity gives full development to the Way of Heaven and Earth. At the first appearance of activity, yang is produced. As activity reaches its limit, yin is produced. The interaction of yin and yang gives full development to the functions of Heaven. At the first appearance of tranquillity, the element of weakness is produced. When weakness reaches its limit, the element of strength is produced. The interaction of these two elements gives full development to the functions of Earth. Greater activity is called major yang, while greater tranquillity is called major yin. Lesser activity is called minor yang, while lesser tranquillity is called minor yin. Major yang constitutes the sun; major yin, the moon; lesser yang, the stars; and lesser yin, the zodiacal spaces. The interaction of the sun, moon, stars, and zodiacal spaces gives full development to the substance of Heaven. Greater tranquillity is called major weakness, while lesser tranquillity is called minor weakness. Greater activity is called major strength, while lesser activity is called minor strength. Lesser weakness constitutes water; major strength, fire; lesser weakness, earth; and lesser strength, stone. The interaction of water, fire, soil, and stone gives full development to substance of Earth.

The sun constitutes heat, the moon constitutes cold, the stars constitute daylight, and the zodiacal spaces constitute the night. The interaction of heat, cold, daylight, and night gives full development to the transformations of Heaven. Water constitutes rain, fire constitutes wind, earth constitutes dew, and stone constitutes thunder. The interaction of rain, wind, dew, and thunder gives full development to the changes of Earth. The transformations of heat result in the dormant nature of things; those of cold, their manifested nature; those of daylight, the physical forms of things; and those of night, their substance. The interaction of the dormant nature, manifested nature, physical form, and substance of things gives full development to the external influence on plants and animals. Rain affects animals; wind, birds; dew, grass; and thunder, plants. The interaction of animals, birds, grass, and plants gives full development to the response of animals and plants to external influence. (5:1b-2b)

2. Man is the most intelligent of all things because his eyes can perceive the colors of all things, his ears can perceive the sounds of all things, his nose can perceive the smell of all things, and his tongue can perceive the tastes of all things. Color, sound, smell, and taste are the substance of things and the four senses are the functions of all men. Substance has no definite function—its function is to transform itself. Function has no definite substance—its substance is change itself. In the interaction of substance and function, the principles of man and things are complete. (5:5a)

3. It is said in the *Book of Changes*, "Investigate principle (*li*) to the utmost and fully develop nature, until destiny is fulfilled."[6] By principle is meant the principle inherent in things. By nature is meant nature endowed by Heaven (*T'ien*, Nature). And by destiny is meant to abide in principle and one's nature. How else can we abide in principle and our nature except through the Way?

From this we know that the Way is the basis of Heaven and Earth, and that Heaven and Earth are the basis of all things. Viewed from Heaven and Earth, the myriad things are the myriad things (that is, individual entities). When Heaven and Earth are viewed from the Way, then they themselves are also the myriad things. The principle of the Way finds its full development in Heaven; the principle of Heaven, in Earth; the principle of Earth, in the myriad things; and that of the myriad things, in man. One who knows how the principles of Heaven, Earth, and all things find their full development in man can give full development to his people. (5:7a)

4. With truth, virtue, work, and effort, the august sovereigns transformed the people, the emperors educated the people, the kings encouraged the people, and the despots led them. (5:14a)

5. The past and the present in the universe is comparable to morning and evening. When the present is viewed from the past, it is called the present, but when viewed from posterity, it will become the past. When the past is viewed from the present, it is called the past, but when viewed from the past itself, it would be its present. Thus neither the present nor the past is necessarily the present or the past as such. The

---

[6] *Changes*, "Remarks on Certain Trigrams," ch. 1. Cf. Legge trans., *Yi King*, p. 422.

distinction is entirely due to our subjective points of view. People generations ago and people generations to come all have this subjective viewpoint. (5:14b)

6. Therefore from the times of old, in the administration of their empires, rulers have had four kinds of Mandates of Heaven, namely, correct mandate (given by Heaven), accepted mandate (given by man), modified mandate (such as revolution), and substituted mandate (such as a minister acting for a ruler).[7] Correct mandate is that which is completely followed. Accepted mandate is that which is followed with certain changes. Modified mandate is mostly changed but partly followed. And substituted mandate is that which is changed completely. That which is followed completely is augmented further and further. That which is followed with certain changes is augmented with some diminution. That which is mostly changed but partly followed is diminished with some augmentation. That which is changed completely is diminished further and further. That which is changed completely is work meant for one generation. That which is mostly changed but partly followed is work meant for ten generations. That which is mostly followed but partly changed is work meant for a hundred generations. That which is followed completely is work meant for a thousand generations. That which follows what ought to be followed and changes what ought to be changed is work meant for countless generations. Work meant for one generation, is this not the way of the Five Despots?[8] Work meant for ten generations, is this not the way of the Three Kings?[9] Work meant for a hundred generations, is this not the way of the Five Emperors?[10] Work meant for a thousand generations, is this not the way of the Three August Sovereigns?[11] Work meant for countless generations, is this not the way of Confucius? Thus we know that the despots, kings, emperors, and sovereigns had what were called mandates for a limited number of

[7] Explanations in parentheses are by Shao Po-wen (1057-1134) in his commentary in the *Hsing-li ta-ch'üan* (Great Collection of Neo-Confucianism), 9:34a. Chu Pi (fl. 1279), however, thinks that accepted mandate means hereditary rule, modified mandate means either reform or revolution, and substituted mandate means expedient and temporary rule. See his *Kuan-wu p'ien chieh* (Explanation of the *Chapter on Viewing Things*), *Ssu-k'u ch'üan-shu chen-pen* (Rare Editions of the *Four Libraries*) ed., 5:44b.

[8] They were: Duke Huan (r. 685–643 B.C.) of Ch'i, Duke Wen (r. 636–628 B.C.) of Chin, Duke Mu (r. 659–619 B.C.) of Ch'in, King Chuang (r. 613–589 B.C.) of Ch'u, and Duke Hsiang (r. 650–635 B.C.) of Sung.

[9] Founders of the three dynasties, Hsia (2183–1752 B.C.?), Shang (1751–1112 B.C.), and Chou (1111–249 B.C.).

[10] There are three different sets of Five Emperors in the various Classics, all of whom were legendary rulers of the third millennium B.C. Sage emperors Yao and Shun are included in two of these sets.

[11] Fu-hsi, Shen-nung, and the Yellow Emperor, legendary rulers before the Five Emperors.

generations. But the mandate of Confucius transcends generations. (5:15a-b)

7. The period of the Three August Sovereigns [when cultural institutions were quietly formed] was the spring of history; that of the Five Emperors [when they grew], the summer; that of the Three Kings [when they matured], the autumn; and that of the Five Despots [when they were destroyed], the winter.[12] As to the Seven States,[13] they were the tail end of winter. (6:15a)

> *Comment.* Shao was one of the few Chinese philosophers who tried to formulate a metaphysical theory of history. Like most others, he could not get away from the concept of cycles. By combining the idea of cycles with his own theory of numbers, he viewed history as an infinite series of cycles. Starting with the traditional unit of 30 years for a generation, he held that a revolution consists of 12 generations (like a day with 12 periods), or 360 years, that an epoch consists of 30 revolutions (like a month with 30 days), or 10,800 years, and that a cycle consists of 12 epochs (again like 12 months in a year), or 129,600 years. The first three epochs, according to him, correspond to the first three months of the year or the first three periods of the day in which yang begins to rise and things grow gradually. Thus the first three epochs are the periods of the birth of heaven, earth, and man, successively. By the end of the sixth epoch (64,800 years), or June, yang reaches its height. This is the time of sage-emperors Yao and Shun. In his own time (75,600 years), or the eleventh century, yang begins to decline and yin rises. Eventually, after 129,600 years, the whole cycle would end and another cycle would begin all over.
>
> The whole scheme is as arbitrary as it is superficial. The idea that one world succeeds another is evidently Buddhist-influenced, for Buddhism conceives existence in terms of an infinite series of worlds, whereas the Chinese idea of cycles means rise and fall within the history of this world.

8. By viewing things is not meant viewing them with one's physical eyes but with one's mind. Nay, not with one's mind but with the principle inherent in things. There is nothing in the universe without principle, nature, and destiny. These can be known only when principle has been investigated to the utmost, when nature is completely developed, and when destiny is fulfilled. The knowledge of these three is true knowl-

[12] Interpretation according to Shao Po-wen's commentary, in *Hsing-li ta-ch'üan*, 10:23b.

[13] Warring states during the Warring States period (403–222 B.C.).

edge. Even the sage cannot go beyond it. Whoever goes beyond it cannot be called a sage.

A mirror reflects because it does not obscure the physical form of things. But water (with its purity) does even better because it reveals the universal character of the physical form of things as they really are. And the sage does still better because he reflects the universal character of the feelings of all things. The sage can do so because he views things as things view themselves; that is, not subjectively but from the viewpoint of things. Since he is able to do this, how can there be anything between him and things? (6:26a-b)

> *Comment.* Shao Yung's doctrine of viewing things from the standpoint of principle has received particular emphasis by Neo-Confucianists not so much for its merit as to offset his reputation as one who could foretell future events. He has not been described as a Taoist magician or diviner but he was very popular as a prophet. Wang Chih (b. 1685) thinks that Shao Yung purposely emphasized viewing things from the standpoint of principle in order to correct any wrong impression of him.[14] Huang Po-chia (fl. 1695) took care to point out that Shao's prophecies were results of his insight into the principle of things and not occultism.[15] But Chu Hsi insisted that although Shao Yung saw principle, he did not pay enough attention to it.[16] The whole effort of later Neo-Confucianists has been to minimize any element of occultism in Shao Yung's philosophy. Such is the rationalism of Neo-Confucianist thought.

9. The numbers of Heaven are five (1, 3, 5, 7, 9). The numbers of Earth are also five (2, 4, 6, 8, 10). Together they form the ten numbers in all. Heaven differentiates from 1 (Great Ultimate) to 4 (the Four Forms of greater and lesser yin and yang). Earth also differentiates from 1 to 4 (the Four Forms of greater and lesser strength and weakness). The four are physical, but the one is not. This is the ultimate distinction of being and non-being. The substance of Heaven numbers 4 (Four Forms), but its function numbers only 3 (minus greater yin). The same is true of Earth (minus greater strength).[17] (7A:1a)

---

[14] *Huang-chi ching-shih ch'üan-shu chieh* (Commentary on the *Supreme Principle Governing the World*), 6:65b.

[15] *Sung-Yüan hsüeh-an,* SPPY, 9:2b.

[16] *Chu Tzu yü-lei* (Classified Conversations of Chu Hsi), 1876 ed., 100:1b.

[17] These explanations follow Shao Po-wen's commentary in *Hsing-li ta-ch'üan,* 11:1b. Function numbers 3 because yin does not operate in Heaven and greater strength does not operate in Earth. Huang Yüeh-chou (of Ming, 1368-1644), in his commentary, said that function is the interaction of corporeality and incor-

10. Yang is superior and spiritually powerful. Being superior, it can control the external world. Being spiritually powerful, it can preserve its unlimited efficiency. For this reason the Way creates heaven and earth and all things without showing itself. All these are patterned after the Way. Yang is the function of the Way, while yin is its substance. Yin and yang operate on each other. When yang is the function, yin becomes superior. When yin is the function, yang becomes superior. (7A:16a)

11. Yang cannot exist by itself; it can exist only when it is supported by yin. Hence yin is the foundation of yang. Similarly, yin cannot alone manifest itself; it can manifest itself only when accompanied by yang. Hence yang is the expression of yin. Yang controls the origination and enjoys the completion [of things] while yin follows the way [yang produces] and completes the work of yang. (7A:17a)

12. As the Great Ultimate becomes differentiated, the Two Modes (yin and yang) appear. Yang descends and interacts with yin, and yin rises to interact with yang, and consequently the Four Forms (major and minor yin and yang) are constituted. Yin and yang interact and generate the Four Forms of Heaven: the element of weakness and the element of strength interact and generate the Four Forms of Earth; and consequently the Eight Elements (heaven, water, fire, thunder, wind, water in motion, mountain, and earth) are completed. The Eight Elements intermingle and generate the myriad things. Therefore the one is differentiated into the two, two into four, four into eight, eight into sixteen, sixteen into thirty-two, and thirty-two into sixty-four. Thus it is said (in the *Book of Changes*) that "they are distinguished as yin and yang and the weak and the strong are employed in succession. Thus in the system of Change there are six positions and the pattern is complete."[18] Ten is divided to become 100, 1,000, and 10,000. This is similar to the fact that the root engenders the trunk; the trunk, branches; and the branches, leaves. The greater the division, the smaller the result, and the finer the division, the more complex. Taken as a unit, it is one. Taken as diffused development, it is the many. Hence the hexagrams *ch'ien* (Heaven) divides, *k'un* (Earth) unites; *chen* (activity) augments, and *sun* (bending) diminishes. Augmentation leads to division, division leads to diminution, and diminution leads to closing. (7A:24b)

13. Material force is one. It is produced by *ch'ien* (the Principle of Heaven). Spirit is also one. Through material force it changes and transforms, and operates freely in the realm of existence and non-

---

poreality. As incorporeality is involved in corporeality (4) itself, the net result is 3. (*Huang-chi ching-shih shu*, 7A:1a-b).

[18] *Changes*, "Remarks on Certain Trigrams," ch. 2. Cf. Legge, *Yi King*, p. 423.

existence as well as in the realm of life and death. It has no spatial restrictions and is unfathomable. (7B:2b)

14. The origin of Heaven and Earth is based on the principle of the Mean (the central principle). Thus *ch'ien* and *k'un* never deviate from this central principle of existence although they are engaged in incessant transformation. Man is central in the universe, and the mind is central in man. The sun is most glorious and the moon is full when they are in the central position. Therefore, the superior man highly values the principle of centrality. (7B:4a)

15. In the human being, *ch'ien* constitutes the male element while *k'un* constitutes the female element. On the infra-human, *ch'ien* constitutes yin while *k'un* constitutes yang. (7B:7a)

16. Forms come from physical shapes, and number comes from substance. Names come from language, while concepts come from function. All numbers in the world are derived from principle. If principle is violated, they will be degenerated into divination techniques. Ordinary people associate numbers with divination techniques and therefore they are not associated with principle. (7B:19b)

> *Comment.* Insofar as Shao Yung's number is calculable and is not left to the whims of spirits, his system is sharply different from occultism. But a numerical interpretation of things like his is too rigid and too mechanical to leave any room for any human effort. There is no doubt that this mechanism was one factor for the unpopularity of his philosophy among Neo-Confucianists. Ch'eng I associated with him for thirty years and discussed with him many subjects but never touched on the subject of numbers.[19]

17. Internal forms and numbers are what exist naturally and cannot be changed. The rest is all external forms and numbers.

What exists naturally is due to Heaven. Only the sage can investigate it. Man follows it as the model. But if man can act or not act [as principle dictates][20] even though he is a man, he would be [equivalent to] Heaven.

Change has internal forms and external forms. The former are principles and numbers while the latter refer to individual, concrete, unchanging objects. (7B:20a-b)

[19] Chu Hsi, *I-Lo yüan-yüan lu* (Record of the Origins of the Schools of the Two Ch'engs), *Cheng-i-t'ang ch'üan-shu* (Complete Library of the Hall of Rectifying the Way) ed., 5:7a.

[20] This interpretation follows Chang Hsing-ch'eng (fl. 1170), *Huang-chi ching-shih kuan-wu wai-p'ien yen-i* (Elaboration of the Meanings of the Outer Chapter on Viewing Things of the *Supreme Principles Governing the World*), *Ssu-k'u ch'üan-shu chen-pen* ed., 8:2a.

18. Spirit is the master of Change. It therefore has no spatial restriction. Change is the function of spirit. Therefore it has no physical form. "Spirit has no spatial restriction and Change has no physical form."[21] If spirit is impeded spatially, it would not be able to effect transformation and would cease to be spirit. If Change had a definite, physical form, it would not be able to penetrate things and would cease to be Change. Although Change seems to have physical form, it is but a symbol by which physical form is manifested. Actually Change itself has no physical form. (7B:21a-b)

19. By its nature, the Great Ultimate is unmoved. When it is aroused, it becomes spirit. Spirit leads to number. Number leads to form. Form leads to concrete things. Concrete things undergo infinite transformations, but underlying them is spirit to which they must be resolved. (7B:23b)

20. Forms and numbers in the universe can be calculated, but their wonderful operations cannot be fathomed. The universe can be fully investigated through principles but not through physical forms. How can it be fully investigated through external observation? (8A:16b)

21. The numerical principle of Change penetrates the universe from its beginning to end. Someone asked, "Does the universe have a beginning and an end?"

Answer: "Since it is involved in the process of augmentation and diminution, how can it be without a beginning and an end? Although heaven and earth are vast, they are also physical forms and concrete things. As such they are two individual entities." (8A:31b)

22. The law (of history) began with Fu-hsi, completed in Emperor Yao, modified in the period of the Three Kings, reached its limit in the period of the Five Despots, and disappeared in the time of Ch'in (221–206 B.C.). This is the track of the cycle of peace and chaos throughout the ten thousand generations. (8A:32a)

23. Everything follows the evolutionary order of the Great Ultimate, the Two Modes (of yin and yang), the Four Forms, and the Eight Elements. Everything also possesses the two forms of time, the past and the present. As form is externalized in physical form, the result is physical substance, for substance is derived from physical form. As form contains the dormant nature of things, the result is their manifested nature, for manifested nature is the expression of dormant nature. In fire, the nature is fundamental, while its physical substance is secondary, whereas in water the opposite is true. Each of the Eight Elements has its own nature and physical substance, but none can exist outside of the operation of *ch'ien* and *k'un*. Thus all things receive their nature from

[21] *Changes*, "Appended Remarks," pt. 1, ch. 4. Cf. Legge, p. 354.

Heaven but the nature of each is peculiar to it. In man it becomes human nature. In animals and plants it becomes the nature of animals and plants. (8B:9b)

24. Our nature views things as they are, but our feelings cause us to see things subjectively and egotistically. Our nature is impartial and enlightened, but our feelings are partial and deceived. When the material endowment in man is characterized by equilibrium and harmony, the elements of strength and weakness in him will be balanced. If yang predominates, he will be off balance toward strength, and if yin predominates, he will be off balance toward weakness. As knowledge directed toward the nature of man increases, the knowledge directed toward things will decrease.

Man occupies the most honored position in the scheme of things because he combines in him the principles of all species. If he honors his own position and enhances his honor, he can make all species serve him.

The nature of all things is complete in the human species.

The spirit of man is the same as the spirit of Heaven and Earth. Therefore, when one deceives himself, he is deceiving Heaven and Earth. Let him beware!

Spirit is nowhere and yet everywhere. The perfect man can penetrate the minds of others because he is based on the One. Spirit is perforce called the One and the Way. It is best to call it spirit. (8B:16a-17a)

25. Without physical substance, the nature (of man and things) cannot be complete. Without nature, physical substance cannot be produced. The yang has the yin as its physical substance and the yin has the yang as its nature. Nature is active but physical substance is tranquil. In heaven, yang is active while yin is tranquil, whereas in earth yang is tranquil while yin is active. When nature is given physical substance, it becomes tranquil. As physical substance follows nature, it becomes active. Hence yang is at ease with itself but yin is fast moving without control. (8B:22a)

26. The Great Ultimate is the One. It produces the two (yin and yang) without engaging in activity.[22] The two (in their wonderful changes and transformations) constitute the spirit. Spirit engenders

---

[22] Forke, *Geschichte der neueren chinesischen Philosophie*, p. 22, and Fung, *History of Chinese Philosophy*, vol. 2, p. 458 and *Short History of Chinese Philosophy*, p. 276, all mispunctuated the sentence to read, in effect, that "the Great Ultimate does not move. It produces. . . ." This is to separate the phrases "not move" and "it produces" and thereby the two ideas. This is a serious mistake because the emphasis here is that the Great Ultimate produces without engaging in any activity. This point is made quite clear in the commentary. Furthermore, in Wang Chih, *Huang-chi ching-shih ch'üan-shu chieh*, 8:73a, the text is punctuated as I have translated here.

number, number engenders form, and form engenders concrete things. (8B:23a)

> *Comment.* In saying that the Great Ultimate produces without activity, Shao Yung is different from Chou Tun-i who said that the Great Ultimate generates yang through movement.[23] Shao did not want to differentiate activity and tranquillity or yin and yang sharply as in the case of Chou. As Huang Yüeh-chou said in his commentary, the point is that spirit produces the two not as two separate entities but the two embraced in the One, namely, the Great Ultimate.[24]

27. The mind is the Great Ultimate. The human mind should be as calm as still water. Being calm, it will be tranquil. Being tranquil, it will be enlightened.

In the study of prior existence[25] sincerity[26] is basic. Perfect sincerity can penetrate all spirits. Without sincerity, the Way cannot be attained.

Our nature comes from Heaven, but learning lies with man. Our nature develops from within, while learning enters into us from without. "It is due to our nature that enlightenment results from sincerity,"[27] but it is due to learning that sincerity results from intelligence.

The learning of a superior man aims precisely at enriching his personality. The rest, such as governing people and handling things, is all secondary.

Without sincerity, one cannot investigate principle to the utmost.

Sincerity is the controlling factor in one's nature. It is beyond space and time.

He who acts in accordance with the Principle of Nature will have the entire process of creation in his grip. When the Principle of Nature is achieved, not only his personality, but his mind also, are enriched. And not only his mind but his nature and destiny are enriched. To be in accord with principle is normal, but to deviate from principle is abnormal. (8B:25a-26a)

28. When one can be happy or sad with things as though he were the things themselves, one's feelings may be said to have been aroused and to have acted to a proper degree. (8B:26a)

---

[23] See above, ch. 28, sec. 1.

[24] Commentary in *Huang-chi ching-shih shu*, 8B:23b.

[25] The Chinese term for *a priori* existence literally means existence preceding Heaven. According to Yu Pen (1482-1529), *Huang-chi-ching-shih shih-i* (Explanation of the Meanings of the *Supreme Principles Governing the World*), 1934 ed., 2:74a, it means existence before things came into existence.

[26] The Chinese word *ch'eng* means not only sincerity in the ordinary sense, but also absence of fault, seriousness, being true to one's real self, being true to the nature of things, actuality, and realness.

[27] *The Mean*, ch. 21.

29. We can handle things as they are if we do not impose our ego on them. The sage gives things every benefit and forgets his own ego.

To let the ego be unrestrained is to give rein to feelings; to give rein to feelings is to be beclouded; and to be beclouded is to be darkened. To follow the natural principles of things, on the other hand, is to grasp their nature; to grasp their nature is to be in possession of spiritual power; and to possess spiritual power is to achieve enlightenment. (8B:27b)

30. When the mind retains its unity and is not divided, it can respond to all things. Thus the mind of the superior man is vacuous (absolutely pure and peaceful) and is not disturbed.

The Way is in all events, whether great or little. They conform to the Way when they are contented with their state of being. They violate the Way when they are in discord with their state of being. (8B:29a)

31. The principles governing Heaven (Nature) and man are found in all events, great or little. It is the duty of man to cultivate his person, but whether he enjoys good fortune or suffers from evil fortune is up to Heaven. The way to obey Heaven is to remain undisturbed whether one succeeds or fails, but one disobeys Heaven when he takes to a dangerous course and hopes for luck.[28] It is the duty of man to seek, but whether he gets or not is up to Heaven. The way to obey Heaven is not to be disturbed whether he gets or not, but one violates the Principle of Nature if he tries to obtain by force. Calamity will fall on those who violate the Principle of Nature. (8B:31b)

[28] Paraphrasing *The Mean*, ch. 14.

30

CHANG TSAI'S PHILOSOPHY OF
MATERIAL FORCE

LIKE OTHER Neo-Confucianists, Chang Tsai (Chang Heng-ch'ü, 1020-1077) drew his inspiration chiefly from the *Book of Changes*. But unlike Chou Tun-i (Chou Lien-hsi, 1017-1073) according to whom evolution proceeds from the Great Ultimate through the two material forces (yin and yang) and the Five Agents (Metal, Wood, Water, Fire, and Earth) to the myriad things, and unlike Shao Yung (1011-1077) according to whom evolution proceeds from the Great Ultimate through the two material forces and other stages to concrete things, Chang Tsai identifies material force (*ch'i*) with the Great Ultimate itself. He discards both yin and yang and the Five Agents as generative forces. To him, yin and yang are merely two aspects of material force, and as such are basically one. As substance, before consolidation takes place, material force is the Great Vacuity. As function, in its activity and tranquillity, integration and disintegration, and so forth, it is the Great Harmony. But the Great Vacuity and the Great Harmony are the same as the Way (Tao), the One. As contraction and expansion, the two aspects of material force are *kuei-shen,* or negative and positive spiritual forces. Here Chang replaces the traditional theory of spiritual beings or spirits of deceased persons and things with a completely rationalistic and naturalistic interpretation, and establishes a doctrine from which later Neo-Confucianists have never deviated. Also, believing existence to be perpetual integration and disintegration, he strongly attacked Buddhist annihilation and Taoist non-being. In this process of perpetual integration and disintegration, certain fundamental laws of the universe follow. Evolution abides by definite principles and has a certain order. Nothing is isolated. And yet everything is distinct from others.

The universe is one but its manifestations are many. This is a fundamental idea in Chang Tsai, an idea that exercised a tremendous influence over his contemporaries and later Neo-Confucianists. As applied to the way of life, this idea becomes the concept of Heaven and Earth as universal parents and love for all in the "Western Inscription." This is one of the most celebrated essays in Neo-Confucian literature. Each human relation has its specific moral requirement, but love embraces them all. At the end, the man of love not only has affection for all men but identifies himself with Heaven and Earth. Here we have another fundamental idea of his, which has also exercised an extensive influence over his contemporaries and over later Neo-Confucianists.

Chang was a native of Ch'ang-an in modern Shensi, four years junior to Chou Tun-i. In his youth he loved military craft. As he was not satisfied with Confucian learning, he turned to study Buddhism and Taoism for years but finally returned to Confucian Classics, especially the *Book of Changes* and the *Doctrine of the Mean*, which eventually formed the basis of his own philosophy. When he lectured on the *Book of Changes* in the capital, his students included the outstanding Neo-Confucian scholar and statesman, Ssu-ma Kuang (1019-1086), and his two nephews, Ch'eng Hao (Ch'eng Ming-tao, 1032-1085) and Ch'eng I (Ch'eng I-ch'uan, 1033-1107) who became his critics and central figures in the Neo-Confucian movement. In his political views, he was at odds with the reformer Wang An-shih (1021-1086), for he insisted on reviving ancient Confucian economic systems, including the "well-field" system in which a field was divided into nine squares with eight families each cultivating one square separately for its own support and one square jointly for governmental revenues. He retired from minor governmental positions to teach in his home and actually attempted to have other scholars join him to put the "well-field" system into practice.[1]

Among Chang's works, the most important are the short treatise *Hsi-ming* (Western Inscription) and the longer one, *Cheng-meng* (Correcting Youthful Ignorance). The first in its entirety and the two most important chapters of the second are translated below, plus a selection from Chang's other works. A list of major topics and references is provided here for easy reference.

Being and Non-being: 3, 4, 6, 7, 29, 63
Buddhism and Taoism: 3, 4, 60, 61, 63, 64, 67
Cosmology and Metaphysics: 5, 12, 13, 16, 17, 56-58
Knowledge: 20, 25, 34, 47, 59
Material force: 2-9, 16, 30, 36, 42, 43
Mind: 9, 37, 59, 68
Nature and Destiny: 3, 4, 9, 18, 25-33, 35, 37, 39, 40, 42, 43, 45, 46, 51-53, 55, 61, 63
One and Many: 3, 12-14, 17-19
Physical nature: 40-43, 50, 59, 66

---

[1] Chang was son of a prefect. At twenty-one he wrote to and then saw the outstanding scholar official, Fan Chung-yen (989-1052), who told him to study the *Doctrine of the Mean*. This started his search from Confucianism through Buddhism and Taoism and back to Confucianism. He obtained a "presented scholar" degree in 1057 and was appointed a magistrate. In 1069 he pleased the emperor with his orthodox Confucian answers to questions on government and was appointed a collator in the imperial library. But he disapproved of the radical reforms of Wang An-shih, and eventually resigned. In 1077 he was a director of the board of imperial sacrifices but was unhappy and resigned. He became sick and died on his way home. See *Sung shih* (History of the Sung Dynasty, 960-1279), PNP, 427:15b-18b and Bruce, *Chu Hsi and His Masters*, pp. 50-52.

Principle: 3, 7, 22, 34, 35, 43, 48, 51, 54, 55, 61, 63, 65, 67
Sincerity: 20-24, 54
Spirit: 1, 8, 15, 16, 44
Spiritual forces: 10, 11, 31, 56, 64
Vacuity: 2-9, 16, 63
Yin yang: 1-5, 10, 17, 18, 22, 31, 56

A. THE WESTERN INSCRIPTION[2]

Heaven is my father and Earth is my mother, and even such a small creature as I finds an intimate place in their midst.

Therefore that which fills the universe I regard as my body and that which directs the universe I consider as my nature.

All people are my brothers and sisters, and all things are my companions.

The great ruler (the emperor) is the eldest son of my parents (Heaven and Earth), and the great ministers are his stewards. Respect the aged —this is the way to treat them as elders should be treated. Show deep love toward the orphaned and the weak—this is the way to treat them as the young should be treated. The sage identifies his character with that of Heaven and Earth, and the worthy is the most outstanding man. Even those who are tired, infirm, crippled, or sick; those who have no brothers or children, wives or husbands, are all my brothers who are in distress and have no one to turn to.[3]

When the time comes, to keep himself from harm—this is the care of a son. To rejoice in Heaven and to have no anxiety—this is filial piety at its purest.

He who disobeys [the Principle of Nature] violates virtue. He who destroys humanity is a robber. He who promotes evil lacks [moral] capacity. But he who puts his moral nature into practice and brings his physical existence into complete fulfillment can match [Heaven and Earth].

One who knows the principles of transformation will skillfully carry forward the undertakings [of Heaven and Earth], and one who penetrates spirit to the highest degree will skillfully carry out their will.[4]

Do nothing shameful in the recesses of your own house[5] and thus bring

[2] This is originally part of ch. 17 of the *Cheng-meng*. It was inscribed on the west window of Chang's lecture hall. There are several European translations, including an English version by Bodde, in Fung, *History of Chinese Philosophy*, vol. 2, pp. 493-495. The *Chang Tzu ch'üan-shu* (Complete Works of Master Chang), SPPY, is used in this and the following translations.

[3] For treating the young, the crippled, etc., see *Mencius*, 1A:7, 1B:5.

[4] Cf. *The Mean*, ch. 19.

[5] Quoting *Odes*, ode no. 256. The recesses refer to the northwest corner, the darkest in the house.

no dishonor to them. Preserve your mind and nourish your nature and thus (serve them) with untiring effort.

The Great Yü hated pleasant wine but attended to the protection and support of his parents.[6] Border Warden Ying brought up and educated the young and thus extended his love to his own kind.[7]

Shun's merit lay in delighting his parents with unceasing effort,[8] and Shen-sheng's reverence was demonstrated when he awaited punishment without making an attempt to escape.[9]

Tsang Shen received his body from his parents and reverently kept it intact throughout life,[10] while Po-ch'i vigorously obeyed his father's command.[11]

Wealth, honor, blessing, and benefits are meant for the enrichment of my life, while poverty, humble station, and sorrow are meant to help me to fulfillment.

In life I follow and serve [Heaven and Earth]. In death I will be at peace. (1:1a-6b)

> Comment. Just as Chou Tun-i's short essay on the diagram of the Great Ultimate has become the basis of Neo-Confucian metaphysics, so Chang's "Western Inscription" has become the basis of Neo-Confucian ethics. Ch'eng I was not exaggerating when he said that there was nothing like it since Mencius.[12] It is important because, as Ch'eng I said, it deals with the substance of humanity (*jen*).[13] Its primary purpose, as Yang Shih (Yang Kuei-shan, 1053-1135) pointed out, was to urge students to seek *jen*.[14]
>
> The development of the concept of *jen* is a long and continuous one in the history of Confucianism. It progressed from Confucius'

[6] Founder of the Hsia dynasty (r. 2183-2175 B.C.?). The story refers to *Mencius*, 4B:20.

[7] The story is found in the *Tso chuan* (Tso's Commentary on the *Spring and Autumn Annals*), Duke Yin, 1st year. See Legge, trans., *Ch'un Ts'ew*, p. 4.

[8] Legendary sage-emperor (3rd millennium B.C.). The story refers to *Mencius*, 4A:28.

[9] Heir-apparent of the state of Chin who committed suicide because he was falsely accused of attempting to poison his father, Duke Hsien (r. 676-651 B.C.). See *Book of Rites*, "T'an-kung," pt. 1 (Legge, trans., *Li Ki*, vol. 1, pp. 126-127).

[10] Tseng Tzu (505-c.436 B.C.), pupil of Confucius, was well known for his filial piety. In the *Book of Filial Piety* (*Hsiao ching*), falsely attributed to him, it is said, "Our bodies—to every hair and bit of skin—are received by us from our parents, and we must not presume to injure or wound them." See Makre, trans., *Hsiao King*, p. 3.

[11] Yin Po-ch'i was a ninth century B.C. prince. He obediently accepted his father's expulsion of him at the instigation of his stepmother who wanted her own son to be the crown prince. See annotation on the eulogy at the end of ch. 79 of the *Ch'ien-Han shu* (History of the Former Han dynasty, 206 B.C.–A.D. 8).

[12] *Chang Tzu ch'üan-shu*, 15:1b.   [13] *ibid.*, 15:1a.

[14] *Kuei-shan yü-lu* (Recorded Sayings of Yang Shih), SPTK, 3:28a.

doctrine of *jen* as the general virtue through *jen* as love in the Han times (206 B.C.–A.D. 220) to Han Yü's "universal love."[15] So far Confucian *jen* has been largely confined to the mundane world. Chang, however, extended it to encompass the entire universe. There is no doubt that the idea reflects Buddhist influence, for the object of moral consciousness in Buddhism is the entire realm of existence. Yang Shih thinks that Chang's doctrine comes from Mencius' saying, "The superior man . . . loves all things,"[16] but "things" in the quotation refers only to living beings whereas Chang extended *jen* to cover the whole universe. The outcome of this extension is the doctrine of "forming one body with the universe"—an all-important doctrine throughout Neo-Confucianism.

The question whether this universal love is similar to that of Buddhism and Moism raises an important issue; for if it were, it would destroy the orthodox Confucian doctrine of love with distinctions.[17] Yang Shih himself objected that the essay deals only with the substance of *jen* but not its function, but as Ch'eng I explained to him, it is precisely in harmonizing substance and function that the "Western Inscription" is of great significance to Confucian ethics. Underlying the essay, according to Ch'eng, is Chang's epoch-shaking theory that "Principle is one but its manifestations are many."[18] The universal love, as Ch'en Ch'un (Ch'en Pei-hsi, 1153-1217) has observed, is not mere identification with all things, but the actual operation of principle which combines all as one.[19] It is principle that love should be universal (as substance), but it is also principle that there should be special affection for parents (as function) because they are the root of one's life. Thus the doctrine of universal love and that of the traditional Confucian doctrine of love with distinctions are harmonized. Yang Shih himself has said, "As we know, the principle is one, and that is why there is love. The functions are many, and that is why there is righteousness. . . . Since functions are different, the applications [of *jen*] cannot be without distinctions."[20] Or as Chu Hsi (1130-1200) put it:

"There is nothing in the entire realm of creatures that does not regard Heaven as the father and Earth as the mother. This means that the principle is one. . . . Each regards his parents as his own parents and his son as his own son. This being the case, how can

[15] See above, comment on ch. 21, sec. 2.

[16] *Mencius*, 7A:45; Yang Shih, *Kuei-shan yü-lu*, 2:18b.

[17] See above, ch. 3, comment on *Mencius*, Additional Selections, 3B:9.

[18] *I-ch'uan wen-chi* (Collection of Literary Works by Ch'eng I), 5:12b, in ECCS. See below, ch. 32, sec. 2.

[19] *ibid.*, 1:9b. [20] *Kuei-shan yü-lu*, 2:18b.

principle not be manifested as many? . . . When the intense affection for parents is extended to broaden the impartiality that knows no ego, and absolute sincerity in serving one's parents leads to the understanding of the way to serve Heaven, then everywhere there is the operation that 'the principle is one but its manifestations are many.'[21] As Neo-Confucianists see it, there is a vast difference between Chang's doctrine and that of the Moists, for the latter recognizes no distinctions and therefore fails to understand function."[22]

Actually the "Western Inscription" does not say anywhere that "the principle is one but its manifestations are many," and only five or six of its sentences can be taken to imply it. But in the view of Chu Hsi and others, the references to father, mother, and other human relations clearly point to differentiation. In any case, in the understanding of Neo-Confucianists, the "Western Inscription," in thus preserving the harmony of substance and function of *jen* and putting it on the metaphysical basis, carries the doctrine of *jen* to a level higher than before. It also paves the way for the culmination of Neo-Confucian theories of *jen* in Chu Hsi.[23]

B. CORRECTING YOUTHFUL IGNORANCE[24]

1. Great Harmony (ch. 1)

1. The Great Harmony is called the Way (Tao, Moral Law). It embraces the nature which underlies all counter processes of floating and sinking, rising and falling, and motion and rest. It is the origin of the process of fusion and intermingling, of overcoming and being overcome, and of expansion and contraction. At the commencement, these processes are incipient, subtle, obscure, easy, and simple, but at the end they are extensive, great, strong, and firm. It is *ch'ien* (Heaven) that begins with the knowledge of Change, and *k'un* (Earth) that models after simplicity. That which is dispersed, differentiated, and capable of assuming form becomes material force (*ch'i*), [25] and that which is pure,

---

[21] Chu Hsi's commentary on the "Western Inscription," *Chang Tzu ch'üan-shu,* 1:7a.

[22] *ibid.,* 1:8a.

[23] See Chan, "The Evolution of the Confucian Concent of *Jen*," *Philosophy East and West,* 4 (1955), 305-308. Also see below, ch. 34, comment on treatise 1; ch. 31, secs. 1 and 11; ch. 32, sec. 42; ch. 40, Introduction.

[24] This book is in seventeen chapters. There are many commentaries on it by prominent Neo-Confucianists. Some selected passages have been translated in de Harlez, *L'École philosophique moderne de la Chine,* pp. 36-76, and in Graf. *Djin-si lu, passim.* See above, n.2.

[25] For a discussion of this term, see Appendix.

penetrating, and not capable of assuming form becomes spirit. Unless the whole universe is in the process of fusion and intermingling like fleeting forces moving in all directions, it may not be called Great Harmony. When those who talk about the Way know this, then they really know the Way, and when those who study Change (or the *Book of Changes*) understand this, then they really understand Change. Otherwise, even though they possess the admirable talents of Duke Chou,[26] their wisdom is not praiseworthy.

2. The Great Vacuity (*Hsü*)[27] has no physical form. It is the original substance of material force. Its integration and disintegration are but objectifications caused by Change. Human nature at its source is absolutely tranquil and unaffected by externality. When it is affected by contact with the external world, consciousness and knowledge emerge. Only those who fully develop their nature can unify the state of formlessness and unaffectedness, and the state of objectification and affectedness.

3. Although material force in the universe integrates and disintegrates, and attracts and repulses in a hundred ways, nevertheless the principle (*li*) according to which it operates has an order and is unerring.

As an entity, material force simply reverts to its original substance when it disintegrates and becomes formless. When it integrates and assumes form, it does not lose the eternal principle (of Change).

The Great Vacuity of necessity consists of material force. Material force of necessity integrates to become the myriad things. Things of necessity disintegrate and return to the Great Vacuity. Appearance and disappearance following this cycle are a matter of necessity. When, in the midst [of this universal operation] the sage fulfills the Way to the utmost, and identifies himself [with the universal processes of appearance and disappearance] without partiality (*i.e.*, lives the best life and takes life and death objectively), his spirit is preserved in the highest degree. Those (the Buddhists) who believe in annihilation expect departure without returning, and those (the Taoists) who cling to everlasting life and are attached to existence expect things not to change. While they differ, they are the same in failing to understand the Way. Whether integrated or disintegrated, it is my body just the same. One is qualified to discuss the nature of man when he realizes that death is not annihilation.

Comment. As Chang Po-hsing (1651-1725) has noted, to say that death is not annihilation is dangerously close to Buddhist transmigration. He quickly points out, however, that what Chang meant

[26] Duke Chou (d. 1044 B.C.) was greatly praised by Confucius. See *Analects*, 8:11.

[27] For a discussion of this term, see Appendix.

is neither Buddhist transmigration nor Taoist immortality on earth but the indestructibility of material force whether it is integrated or disintegrated. What is not annihilated, then, is not the person but principle, according to which material force operates.[28]

4. When it is understood that the Vacuity, the Void, is nothing but material force, then existence and nonexistence, the hidden and the manifested, spirit and eternal transformation, and human nature and destiny are all one and not a duality. He who apprehends integration and disintegration, appearance and disappearance, form and absence of form, and trace them to their source, penetrates the secret of Change.

If it is argued that material force is produced from the Vacuity, then because the two are completely different, the Vacuity being infinite while material force is finite, the one being substance and the other function, such an argument would fall into the naturalism of Lao Tzu who claimed that being comes from non-being and failed to understand the eternal principle of the undifferentiated unity of being and non-being. If it is argued that all phenomena are but things perceived in the Great Vacuity, then since things and the Vacuity would not be mutually conditioned, since the physical form and the nature of things would be self-contained, and since these, as well as Heaven and man, would not be interdependent, such an argument would fall into the doctrine of the Buddha who taught that mountains, rivers, and the total stretch of land are all subjective illusions. This principle of unity is not understood because ignorant people know superficially that the substance of the nature of things is the Vacuity, the Void, but do not know that function is based on the Way of Heaven (Law of Nature). Instead, they try to explain the universe with limited human knowledge. Since their undertaking is not thorough, they falsely assert that the universal operation of the principles of Heaven and Earth is but illusory. They do not know the essentials of the hidden and the manifest, and jump to erroneous conclusions. They do not understand that the successive movements of the yin and the yang (passive and active cosmic forces) cover the entire universe, penetrate day and night,[29] and form the central standard of Heaven, Earth, and man. Consequently they confuse Confucianism with Buddhism and Taoism. When they discuss the problems of the nature (of man and things) and their destiny or the Way of Heaven, they either fall into the trap of illusionism or are determined that being comes from non-being, and re-

[28] Chang Po-hsing's commentary on the *Cheng-meng* in *Chang Heng-ch'ü chi* (Collected Works of Chang Tsai), *Cheng-i-t'ang ch'üan-shu* (Complete Library of the Hall of Rectifying the Way) ed., 2:4a.

[29] Paraphrasing *Changes*, "Appended Remarks," pt. 1, ch. 4. Cf. Legge, trans., *Yi King*, "Appended Remarks," p. 354.

gard these doctrines as the summit of philosophical insight as well as the way to enter into virtue. They do not know how to choose the proper method for their investigation. This clearly shows they are obscured by one-sided doctrines and fall into extremes.

5. As the Great Vacuity, material force is extensive and vague. Yet it ascends and descends and moves in all ways without ever ceasing. This is what is called in the *Book of Changes* "fusion and intermingling"[30] and in the *Chuang Tzu* "fleeting forces moving in all directions while all living beings blow against one another with their breath."[31] Here lies the subtle, incipient activation of reality and unreality, of motion and rest, and the beginning of yin and yang, as well as the elements of strength and weakness. Yang that is clear ascends upward, whereas yin that is turbid sinks downward. As a result of their contact and influence and of their integration and disintegration, winds and rains, snow and frost come into being. Whether it be the countless variety of things in their changing configurations or the mountains and rivers in their fixed forms, the dregs of wine or the ashes of fire, there is nothing (in which the principle) is not revealed.

6. If material force integrates, its visibility becomes effective and physical form appears. If material force does not integrate, its visibility is not effective and there is no physical form. While material force is integrated, how can one not say that it is temporary? While it is disintegrated, how can one hastily say that it is non-being? For this reason, the sage, having observed phenomena and examined above and below, only claims to know the causes of what is hidden and what is manifest but does not claim to know the causes of being and non-being.

What fills the universe is but molds and forms (copies). With our insight (or clarity of mind), the system and principles of the universe cannot be examined. When there are physical forms, one may trace back to the causes of that which is hidden, and when there is no physical form, one may trace back to the cause of that which is manifested.

7. The integration and disintegration of material force is to the Great Vacuity as the freezing and melting of ice is to water. If we realize that the Great Vacuity is identical with material force, we know that there is no such thing as non-being. Therefore, when discussing the ultimate problems of the nature of things and the Way of Heaven, the sage limits himself to the marvelous changes and transformations of yin and yang and the Five Agents (of Metal, Wood, Water, Fire, and Earth). The doctrine of those superficial and mistaken philosophers who draw the

[30] *ibid.*, pt. 2, ch. 5. Cf. Legge, p. 393.
[31] *Chuang Tzu*, ch. 1, NHCC, 1:2b. See Giles, trans., *Chuang Tzu*, 1961 ed., p. 27.

distinction between being and non-being is not the way to investigate principle to the utmost.

> *Comment.* Chang's theory of material force exercised considerable influence on Wang Fu-chih (Wang Ch'uan-shan, 1619-1692), whose philosophy of principle as inherent in material force is as materialistic as the philosophy of Chang. It is easily understandable why Wang was an admirer of Chang but a severe critic of Chu Hsi and Ch'eng I, who contrasted principle and material force too sharply to suit him. As to Chang's own theory of material force, he has never explained why some is clear and some is turbid. Neither has he made his idea of the nature clear. For these, we have to wait till Ch'eng and Chu.

8. The Great Vacuity is clear. Being clear, it cannot be obstructed. Not being obstructed, it is therefore spirit. The opposite of clearness is turbidity. Turbidity leads to obstruction. And obstruction leads to physical form. When material force is clear, it penetrates; and when it is turbid, it obstructs. When clearness reaches its limit, there is spirit. When spirit concentrates, it penetrates like the breeze going through the holes (of musical instruments), producing tones and carrying them to great distances. This is the evidence of clearness. As if arriving at the destination without the necessity of going there, penetration reaches the highest degree.

9. From the Great Vacuity, there is Heaven. From the transformation of material force, there is the Way. In the unity of the Great Vacuity and material force, there is the nature (of man and things). And in the unity of the nature and consciousness, there is the mind.[32]

> *Comment.* Although Chang made it quite clear that the Great Vacuity is identical with material force (before its integration) and is nothing like the Taoist non-being, still the concept is too Taoistic to be acceptable to Neo-Confucianists, for vacuity is a typical and prominent Taoist concept.[33] Ch'eng I thought that reality should not be described simply as clear and vacuous, but should also be considered turbid and substantial.[34] Chu Hsi thought that to describe reality purely as integration and disintegration of material force would be to view it as a great process of transmigration.[35] These criticisms are by no means unfair. There is no doubt that Chang's materialistic philosophy tends to be one-sided and me-

[32] For Chu Hsi's criticism of this idea, see below, ch. 34, sec. 80.
[33] Hsün Tzu did use the term *hsü* but he used it to describe a state of mind (*Hsün Tzu*, ch. 21, SPTK, 15:7b. See Dubs, trans., *Works of Hsüntze*, p. 267).
[34] *Chang Tzu ch'üan-shu*, 2:1a.   [35] *ibid.*, 2:1b.

chanical. At any rate, his philosophy of vacuity has never been propagated by any later Neo-Confucianist.

10. The negative and positive spiritual forces (*kuei-shen*)[36] are the spontaneous activity of the two material forces (yin and yang). Sagehood means absolute sincerity[37] forming a unity with Heaven, and spirit means the Great Vacuity in its wondrous operation and response. All molds and forms in the universe are but dregs of this spiritual transformation.

> *Comment.* This is a completely new interpretation of *kuei* and *shen*. The rationalistic approach to *kuei-shen*, which had meant spiritual beings, is evident in the *Book of Changes*,[38] but no one before Chang had understood *kuei-shen* as the spontaneous activity of material force and incorporated the concept into a coherent metaphysical system.

11. The Way of Heaven is infinite but does not go beyond the succession of summer and winter [for example]. The activities of things are infinite but do not go beyond expansion and contraction. The reality of the negative and positive spiritual forces does not go beyond these two fundamental elements (of yin and yang).

12. If yin and yang do not exist, the One (the Great Ultimate)[39] cannot be revealed. If the One cannot be revealed, then the function of the two forces will cease. Reality and unreality, motion and rest, integration and disintegration, and clearness and turbidity are two different substances. In the final analysis, however, they are one.

13. Only after [the One] is acted upon will it begin to penetrate [through yin and yang]. Without the two forces there cannot be the One. Hence the sage establishes the two principles of strength and weakness as the foundation of things. "If *ch'ien* and *k'un* are obliterated, there would be no means of seeing the system of Change."[40]

14. Material force moves and flows in all directions and in all manners. Its two elements unite and give rise to the concrete. Thus the multiplicity of things and human beings is produced. In their ceaseless successions the two elements of yin and yang constitute the great principles of the universe.

15. "The sun and moon push each other in their course and thus light

---

[36] For a discussion of these terms, see Appendix. See also secs. 11 and 56.

[37] The word *ch'eng* means more than sincerity in the ordinary sense. It means absence of fault, seriousness, being true to one's nature and the nature of things, actuality, reality, etc.

[38] "Appended Remarks," pt. 1, ch. 4. Cf. Legge, p. 353.

[39] Chu Hsi is followed in this interpretation.

[40] *Changes, ibid.*, ch. 12. Cf. Legge, p. 377.

appears. The winter and summer push each other and thus the year is completed."[41] Spirit has no spatial restrictions and Change has no physical form.[42] "The successive movement of yin and yang" and "unfathomable is the movement of yin and yang."[43] These describe the way in which day and night are penetrated.

16. Day and night are but a moment of the universe, and winter and summer but its day and night. According to the Way of Heaven, material force changes as spring and autumn succeed each other, just as man's soul exists in different states between waking and sleeping hours. In such alternating states, dreams are completed and a great variety of feelings are expressed in utter confusion. This and the contrasting waking hours constitute the day and night of a person. Material force enters into a new state in the spring and the myriad things flourish in profusion. This and its contrasting autumn constitute the day and night of Heaven. In its original state of Great Vacuity, material force is absolutely tranquil and formless. As it is acted upon, it engenders the two fundamental elements of yin and yang, and through integration gives rise to forms.[44] As there are forms, there are their opposites. These opposites necessarily stand in opposition to what they do. Opposition leads to conflict, which will necessarily be reconciled and resolved. Thus the feelings of love and hate are both derived from the Great Vacuity, and they ultimately result in material desires. Suddenly to bring into existence and promptly to bring to completion without a moment's interruption—this is indeed the wonderful operation of spirit.

17. No two of the products of creation are alike. From this we know that although the number of things is infinite, at bottom there is nothing without yin or yang [which differentiate them]. From this we know also that the transformations and changes in the universe are due to these two fundamental forces.

18. The multiple forms and appearances of the myriad things are the dregs of spirit. The nature and the Way of Heaven are but Change. The mind varies and differs in a thousand ways because it is acted on by the external world in various ways. Heaven is vast and there is nothing outside of it. What acts on the mind are the two fundamental processes of fusion and intermingling.

19. In the mutual interaction of things, it is impossible to know the

---

[41] *ibid.*, pt. 2, ch. 5. Cf. Legge, p. 389.

[42] Paraphrasing *ibid.*, pt. 1, ch. 4. Cf. Legge, p. 354.

[43] *ibid.*, ch. 5. Cf. Legge, pp. 355, 357.

[44] Generally referring to physical forms and specifically referring to the Four Secondary Forms or Modes variously identified as Metal, Wood, Water, and Fire, or yin, yang, strength, and weakness, or major and minor yang and major and minor yin.

directions of their operation and of their appearance and disappearance. This is the wonder that lies in all things. These are principles by which material force and the will, as well as Heaven and man, overcome each other. When the sage-ruler reigns above, all his subjects follow his good example. This demonstrates the principle that when material force is concentrated and acts, it moves the will. When the male and female phoenix arrive and perform their ceremonial dance (peace and order prevail).[45] This demonstrates the principle that when the will concentrates and acts, it moves material force. (SPPY, 2:1b-5b)

2. Enlightenment Resulting from Sincerity (ch. 6)

20. Knowledge gained through enlightenment which is the result of sincerity[46] is the innate knowledge[47] of one's natural character. It is not the small knowledge of what is heard or what is seen.[48]

21. When the Way of Heaven [or principle] and the nature of man [or desires][49] function separately, there cannot be sincerity. When there is a difference between the knowledge obtained by following (the Way of) Heaven and that obtained by following (the nature of) man, there cannot be perfect enlightenment. What is meant by enlightenment resulting from sincerity is that in which there is no distinction between the Way of Heaven as being great and the nature of man as being small.

22. When moral principles and human destiny are united in harmony, they will be preserved and abide in principle. When humanity and wisdom are united in harmony, they will be preserved and abide in the sage. When activity and tranquillity are united in harmony, they will be preserved and abide in spirit. When yin and yang are united in harmony they will be preserved and abide in the Way. And when the nature of man and the Way of Heaven are united in harmony, they will be preserved and abide in sincerity.

23. Sincerity is the way according to which heaven can last for long

---

[45] According to ancient beliefs, the appearance of these mystical birds is a good omen that right principles are going to triumph in the world. See *History*, "I and Chi." Cf. Legge, trans., *Shoo King*, p. 88. Confucius said, "The Phoenix does not come. It is all over with me." (*Analects*, 9:8)

[46] This phrase is derived from *The Mean*, ch. 21.

[47] The term *liang-chih* is from *Mencius*, 7B:15. It means native knowledge of the good.

[48] See also sec. 59.

[49] The interpretation here follows Wang Fu-chih, *Chang Tzu cheng-meng chu* (Commentary on the *Correcting Youthful Ignorance* by Master Chang), 3:6b, in *Ch'uan-shan i-shu* (Surviving Works of Wang Fu-chih), 1933 ed. Liu Chi (fl. 1513), however, did not contrast Heaven and man so sharply. To him Heaven meant principle as it originally is and man meant imperfect realization of principle. See his *Cheng-meng hui-kao* (Commentary on the *Correcting Youthful Ignorance* Drafted at a Meeting), *Hsi-yin-hisen ts'ung-shu* (Hall of Being-Careful-with-Time Collection) ed., 2:6b.

and is unceasing. The reason why the man of humanity and the filial son can serve Heaven and be sincere with himself is simply that they are unceasing in their humanity and filial piety. Therefore for the superior man sincerity is valuable.

24. Sincerity implies reality.[50] Therefore it has a beginning and an end. Insincerity implies absence of reality. How can it have a beginning or end? Therefore it is said, "Without sincerity, there will be nothing."[51]

25. By "sincerity resulting from enlightenment"[52] is meant to develop one's nature fully through the investigation of things to the utmost, and by "enlightenment resulting from sincerity"[53] is meant to investigate things to the utmost through fully developing one's nature.

26. One's nature is the one source of all things and is not one's own private possession. It is only the great man who is able to know and practice its principle to the utmost. Therefore, when he establishes himself, he will help others to establish themselves. He will share his knowledge with all. He will love universally. When he achieves something, he wants others to achieve the same. As for those who are so obstructed themselves [by selfishness][54] as not to understand this principle of mine, nothing can be done.

27. Nature connotes what one can do by natural endowment. Ability connotes what one can do through his own planning. In fully developing his nature, the great man does not consider the ability endowed by Heaven to be ability but considers man's planning to be ability. This is why it is said, "Heaven and earth have their fixed positions and the sages are able to carry out and complete their abilities."[55]

28. Only through fully developing one's nature can one realize that he possesses nothing in life and loses nothing at death.

29. There has never been any substance which is nonexistent. Nature means examining and practicing the substance.

30. Nature endowed by Heaven completely permeates the Way. It cannot be obscured by the material force (one's physical nature) whether it is clear or dark. What has been decreed by Heaven (*ming*, destiny, fate) completely permeates one's nature. It cannot be destroyed by one's fortune, whether it is good or evil. If they are obscured or destroyed, it is because one has neglected to learn. Nature permeates beyond the material force and destiny operates within the material force. But the material force is neither internal nor external. We speak in this

---

[50] *Ch'eng* means both being real and being sincere.   [51] *The Mean*, ch. 25.
[52] *ibid.*, ch. 21.   [53] *ibid.*
[54] According to Chiang Yung (1681-1762), the obstruction means that one only thinks of himself. See his *Chin-ssu lu chi-chu* (Collected Commentaries on the *Reflections on Things at Hand*), SPPY, 1:17b.
[55] *Changes*, "Appended Remarks," pt. 2, ch. 12. Cf. Legge, p. 405.

way only because it temporarily assumes physical form. Therefore those who wish to know [the way of] man must know [the nature endowed by] Heaven. Only when one has fully developed his nature can one fulfill his destiny.

31. If one knows his nature and Heaven, then [all the operations] of yin and yang and negative and positive spiritual forces are all part of my lot.

32. The Heavenly endowed nature in man is comparable to the nature of water in ice. It is the same whether the ice freezes or melts. Water's reflection of light may be much or little, dark or bright, but in receiving the light, it is the same in all cases.

33. The innate ability endowed by Heaven is fundamentally my own innate ability. Only I may have lost some of it.

> *Comment.* Wang Fu-chih has observed that whereas Mencius stressed both innate ability and innate knowledge,[56] Chang stressed only innate ability and Wang Yang-ming later stressed only innate knowledge.[57]

34. Those who understand the higher things return to the Principle of Nature (*T'ien-li*, Principle of Heaven) while those who understand lower things[58] follow human desires.

> *Comment.* Chang was the first Confucianist to have made a clear-cut distinction between the Principle of Nature and human desires. The sharp distinction was maintained through Sung (960-1279) and Ming (1368-1644) Neo-Confucianism until Ch'ing (1644-1912) Confucianists vigorously revolted against it.

35. It is the function of nature to combine. In so doing it unites the two.[59] It is the function of destiny to receive. In receiving it follows spe-

---

[56] *Mencius*, 7A:15.

[57] Wang Fu-chih, *Chang Tzu cheng-meng chu*, 3:10b.

[58] Cf. *Analects*, 14:24.

[59] Just what "the two" are is not clear. As Huang Po-chia (fl. 1695) has pointed out, scholars from Chu Hsi down have found this puzzling. Huang understood "the two" in the sense of destiny, on the one hand, and nature, on the other. That is, despite the inequalities in men's destinies, everyone can fulfill his destiny if he fully develops his nature, since it is the embodiment of principle and combines all. See Huang Tsung-hsi (1610-1695), *et al.*, *Sung-Yüan hsüeh-an* (Anthology and Critical Accounts of the Neo-Confucianists of the Sung and Yüan Dynasties, 960-1368), SPPY, 17:20b. According to Liu Chi, the nature combines all principles and the two means multiplicity (*Cheng-meng hui-kao*, 2:12a). To Li Kuang-ti (1642-1718), "the two" refers to yin and yang, weak and strong, humanity and righteousness. (*Cheng-meng chu*, or Commentary on the *Correcting Youthful Ignorance*, *Jung-ts'un ch'üan-shu*, or Complete Works of Li Kuang-ti ed., 1:46b.) Ch'ien Mu, however, offered probably the best explanation when he said "the two" refers to Great Vacuity and material force, for it is said in

cific principles. If the fundamental principle of combining (the highest good)[60] is not applied to the utmost, the lot received cannot be perfectly understood. When in the full development of my nature and the investigation of things to the utmost there are things that cannot be changed, they would be in accord with principles applied to me. Destiny is that whose operation even Heaven cannot stop, and the nature of man is necessarily affected by the external world. Therefore the sage does not allow what he should worry about (the state of affairs that affects his nature) to be confused with what he should not worry about (the natural operation of destiny). There is the principle of assisting [Heaven] in its task of production and bringing things to perfection. That depends on me.

36. Stillness and purity characterize the original state of material force. Attack and seizure characterize it when it becomes desire [upon contact with things]. The relation between the mouth and the stomach on the one hand and food on the other, and between the nose and tongue on the one hand and smell and taste on the other are all cases of [physical] nature's attacking and seizing. He who understands virtue will have a sufficient amount, that is all. He will not allow sensual desires to be a burden to his mind, the small to injure the great, or the secondary to destroy the fundamental.

37. If one's mind can fully develop one's nature, it shows that "it is man that can make the Way great." If one's nature does not know how to discipline one's mind, it shows that "it is not the Way that can make man great."[61]

38. One who can fully develop his nature can also develop the nature of other people and things. He who can fulfill his destiny can also fulfill the destiny of other people and things,[62] for the nature of all men and things follows the Way and the destiny of all men and things is decreed by Heaven. I form the substance of all things[63] without overlooking any, and all things form my substance, and I know that they do not overlook anything. Only when one fulfills his destiny can he bring himself and things into completion without violating their principle.

39. To consider what is inborn as one's nature is to fail to penetrate to a knowledge of the course of day and night.[64] Furthermore, that doc-

---

sec. 9 that in the unity of these two there is nature. See his "Cheng-meng ta-i fa-wei" (Revealing the Subtleties of the Great Principles of the *Correcting Youthful Ignorance*), *Ssu-hsiang yü shih-tai* (Thought and the Age), 48 (1947), p. 13.

[60] According to Chang Po-hsing's commentary in *Chang Heng-ch'ü chi*, 3:6b.
[61] Both quotations in this section are from *Analects*, 15:28.
[62] Cf. *The Mean*, ch. 22.
[63] See n.83.
[64] Paraphrasing *Changes*, "Appended Remarks," pt. 1, ch. 4. Cf. Legge, p. 354.

trine considers man and things to be equal. Therefore the mistake of Kao Tzu[65] must not be left unrefuted.

40. Nature in man is always good. It depends on whether man can skillfully return to it or not. To exceed the transforming operation of Heaven and Earth (such as food and sex) means not to return skillfully. Destiny in man is always correct. It depends on whether or not one obeys it. If one takes to dangerous courses and hopes for good luck, he is not obeying his destiny.[66]

41. With the existence of physical form, there exists physical nature. If one skillfully returns to the original nature endowed by Heaven and Earth, then it will be preserved. Therefore in physical nature there is that which the superior man denies to be his original nature.[67]

Comment. Chu Hsi said, "The doctrine of physical nature originated with Chang and Ch'eng (Ch'eng I). It made a tremendous contribution to the Confucian School and is a great help to us students. None before them had enunciated such a doctrine. Hence with the establishment of the doctrine of Chang and Ch'eng, the theories [of human nature] of all previous philosophers collapse."[68] Chu Hsi is correct because for the first time Confucianism has found an at least tentatively satisfactory answer to the question of evil. Mencius gave no answer because he merely put the responsibility on man himself. Han and T'ang (618-907) Confucianists ascribed evil to feelings, but they never explained why feelings should be evil. There was no convincing answer until Chang, and his answer is physical nature.

In his theory, Reality is one but its manifestations are many. In the state of differentiatedness, there is bound to be opposition, discrimination, conflict, and imbalance. These characteristics are attendant in one's endowment of physical nature by the very fact of its differentiatedness. Such imbalance leads to excess in the natural transformation process, that is, deviation from the Mean, and that is evil. It is not that physical nature as such is evil, for that would be following the Buddhist doctrine that the world is an illusion. Rather, in the physical nature is the occasion for evil, and how to use this occasion depends on man.[69]

[65] *Mencius,* 6A:3.

[66] Cf. *The Mean,* ch. 14.

[67] Cf. *Mencius,* 7B:24. Physical nature means the nature of man and things conditioned by the material force and concrete stuff of the universe.

[68] Chu's commentary on the *Cheng-meng, Chang Tzu ch'üan-shu,* 2:19a. Also *Chu Tzu yü-lei,* 4:15a.

[69] See Chan, "The Neo-Confucian Solution to the Problem of Evil," *Studies Presented to Hu Shih on His Sixty-fifth Birthday,* pp. 780-783.

42. Man's strength, weakness, slowness, quickness, and talent or lack of talent are due to the one-sidedness of the material force. Heaven (Nature) is originally harmonious and not one-sided. If one cultivates this material force and returns to his original nature without being one-sided, one can then fully develop his nature and [be in harmony with] Heaven. Before man's nature is formed, good and evil are mixed. Therefore to be untiring in continuing the good which issues [from the Way][70] is good. If all evil is removed, good will also disappear [for good and evil are relative and are necessary to reveal each other]. Therefore avoid just saying "good" but say, "That which realizes it (the Way) is the individual nature."[71]

43. When moral character does not overcome the material force, our nature and destiny proceed from the material force. But when moral character overcomes the material force, then our nature and destiny proceed from moral character. If one investigates principle to the utmost and fully develops his nature, then his nature will be in accord with the character of Heaven and his destiny will be in accord with the Principle of Heaven (Nature). Only life, death, and longevity and brevity of life are due to the material force and cannot be changed.

Therefore, in discussing life and death, [Confucius said] that they "are the decree of Heaven," referring to material force, and in discussing wealth and honor he said that they "depend on Heaven"[72] referring to principle. This is why a man of great virtue (the sage ruler) always receives the Mandate of Heaven (T'ien-ming). He is in accord with the easy and simple Principle of Heaven and Earth, and occupies the central position in the universe. What is meant by the Principle of Heaven is the principle which can make the hearts of all people happy and give free expression to the will of the whole world. As it can make the world happy and free in their expression, the world will all turn to him. If some do not do so, it would be because of differences in circumstances and opportunities, as in the cases of Confucius [who never had a chance to be a ruler] and those rulers who succeeded [sage rulers in spite of their own wickedness].

[Confucius said,] "Shun and Yü held possession of the empire as if it were nothing to them."[73] This was because they achieved the Principle of Heaven through moral effort and not because they were entitled to rule because of their endowment in physical nature or because they obtained it through their ambition. Shun and Yü were mentioned by Confucius because the rest of the rulers did not come to the throne through natural tendencies but because they sought it.

[70] Changes, "Appended Remarks" pt. 1, ch. 5. Cf. Legge, p. 356.
[71] Quoting Changes, ibid.   [72] Analects, 12:5.   [73] Analects, 8:18.

44. Spirit moves smoothly, whereas a material object is obstructed. Therefore because of their physical form wind and thunder cannot be as quick as the mind. However, the mind is limited by what one sees and hears and is therefore not as great as the nature.

45. Because they have departed from their nature too far, the most intelligent and the most stupid cannot change.[74]

46. If one removes even the slightest evil, goodness will become his nature. If he fails to detect evil completely, although his nature is good, it will become impure.

47. "Without awareness or knowledge, follow the principle of the Lord."[75] If one does so consciously or knowingly, one will lose the [Principle of] Heaven. What belongs to the nature of the superior man forms the same current with Heaven and Earth. He merely acts differently [from the ordinary man].

48. By "being on the left and on the right of the Lord"[76] is meant to understand the Principle of Heaven whether one is on the left or on the right. The Principle of Heaven operates according to the circumstances of time and according to moral principle. When a superior man teaches others, he presents the Principle of Heaven and explains it to them. In his own conduct, he follows the Principle of Heaven according to the circumstances of the time.

49. Peace and joy are the beginning of the Way. Because it is peaceful, it can be great, and because it is joyous, it can be lasting. The nature of Heaven and Earth is nothing other than being great and lasting.

50. Everything is due to Heaven. If yang that is clear dominates, one's moral nature will function. If yin that is turbid dominates, one's material desires will have their way. To "remove evil and complete the good"[77] surely depends on learning.

51. Can a person who is not sincere [within] and grave [without] be said to be able to develop his nature fully and investigate principle to the utmost? The character of one's nature is never insincere or disrespectful. Therefore, I know that he who is not free from insincerity or disrespect does not know his nature.

52. If effort is needed to be sincere or grave, that is not our nature. To be sincere or grave without effort may be said of the superior man who "is truthful without any words" and "does not resort to anger and the people are awed."[78]

53. If one is upright in his life and follows principle, then all his

---

[74] See above, ch. 2, comments on *Analects*, 17:2-3.

[75] *Odes*, ode no. 241.   [76] *ibid.*, ode no. 235.

[77] *Book of Rites*, "Confucius at Home at Leisure." Cf. Legge, trans., *Li Ki*, vol. 2, p. 271.

[78] *The Mean*, ch. 33.

good and evil fortunes are correct. If one is not upright in his life, either he enjoys blessings that are evil or he shirks from danger.

54. "Contraction and expansion act on each other and thus advantages are produced."[79] This is so because they are influenced by sincerity. "Truthfulness and insincerity act on each other and advantages and disadvantages are produced."[80] This is so because insincerity is mixed with sincerity. A person with perfect sincerity obeys principle and finds advantages, whereas a man of insincerity disobeys principle and meets harm. If one obeys the principle of nature and destiny, then all the good and evil fortunes are correct. If one violates principle, then evil fortune is of his own choice and good fortune is luck obtained by taking to a dangerous course.

55. "Everything is destiny. A man should accept obediently what is correct [in his destiny]."[81] If one obeys the principles of his nature and destiny, he will obtain what is correct in them. If one destroys principle and indulges in desires to the limit, he will be inviting evil fortune. (SPPY, 2:17a-21a)

C. ADDITIONAL SELECTIONS FROM THE WORKS OF CHANG TSAI

56. The life of animals is based on heaven [for their heads tend upward]. Their transition from integration to disintegration depends on their inhalation and exhalation of breath. The life of plants is based on earth [for their roots grow downward]. Their transition from integration to disintegration depends on the rise and fall of yin and yang. When a thing first comes into existence, material force comes gradually into it to enrich its vitality. As it reaches its maturity, material force gradually reverts to where it came from, wanders off and disperses. Its coming means positive spiritual force (shen), because it is expanding (shen). Its reversion means negative spiritual force (kuei), because it is returning (kuei). (Cheng-meng, ch. 5, Chang Tzu ch'üan-shu, SPPY, 2:16a)

57. In the process of production, some things come first and some afterward. This is Heaven's sequence. They coexist and contrast one another in their different sizes and levels. This is Heaven's orderliness. In the production of things, there is sequence, and in their existence in physical forms, there is orderliness. Only when sequence is understood

[79] Changes, "Appended Remarks," pt. 2, ch. 5. Cf. Legge, p. 389.
[80] ibid., ch. 12. Cf. Legge, p. 405.
[81] Mencius, 7A:2. See above, ch. 3, comment on Mencius, Additional Selections, 7A:1.

will moral principles be correct, and only when orderliness is understood will the principle of propriety operate. (ch. 5, SPPY, 2:16b)

58. According to principle nothing exists alone. Unless there are similarity and difference, contraction and expansion, and beginning and end among things to make it stand out, it is not really a thing although it seems to be. To become complete (to attain individuality), a thing must have a beginning and an end. But completion cannot be achieved unless there is mutual influence between similarity and difference (change) and between being and non-being (becoming). If completion is not achieved, it is not really a thing although it seems to be. Therefore it is said, "Contraction and expansion act on each other and thus advantages are produced."[82] (ibid.)

59. By enlarging one's mind, one can enter into all the things in the world [to examine and understand their principle].[83] As long as anything is not yet entered into, there is still something outside the mind. The mind of ordinary people is limited to the narrowness of what is seen and what is heard. The sage, however, fully develops his nature and does not allow what is seen or heard to fetter his mind. He regards everything in the world to be his own self. This is why Mencius said that if one exerts his mind to the utmost, he can know nature and Heaven.[84] Heaven is so vast that there is nothing outside of it. Therefore the mind that leaves something outside is not capable of uniting itself with the mind of Heaven. Knowledge coming from seeing and hearing is knowledge obtained through contact with things. It is not knowledge obtained through one's moral nature. Knowledge obtained through one's moral nature does not originate from seeing or hearing. (ch. 7, SPPY, 2:21a)

60. The Buddhists do not understand destiny decreed by Heaven and think that the production and annihilation of the universe are due to the elements of existence (dharmas) created by the mind. They regard the small (human consciousness) as the cause of the great (reality), and the secondary as the cause of the fundamental. Whatever they cannot understand thoroughly, they regard as illusion or error. They are indeed [summer insects] which doubt the existence of ice. (ibid., 2:22b)

61. Confucianists investigate principle and therefore can follow their nature. This constitutes the Way. Buddhists, on the other hand, do not know how to investigate principle and arbitrarily consider [Emptiness]

[82] Changes, "Appended Remarks," pt. 2, ch. 5. Cf. Legge, p. 389.

[83] Chu Hsi's interpretation. In his commentary, Chu Hsi says t'i-wu here means entering into things, unlike the term in sec. 38 and in The Mean, 16 (see above, ch. 5, n.25), where it means forming the substance of things. Some commentators, Wang Fu-chih, for example, prefer the latter meaning here. Both meanings are possible.

[84] Mencius, 7A:1.

as the true nature. Consequently their theory cannot prevail. (ch. 8, SPPY, 2:26a)

62. In one's words there should be something to teach others. In one's activities there should be something to serve as model for others. In the morning something should be done. In the evening something should be realized. At every moment something should be nourished. And in every instant something should be preserved. (ch. 12, SPPY, 3:9a)

63. It is according to one's nature that being and non-being, and reality and unreality pervade a thing. If they are not united as one, nature cannot be developed fully. Food and sex are both nature. How can they be obliterated? Thus being and non-being are both nature. How can there be no opposition? The Taoists and Buddhists have for long maintained that there is none. Do they really understand truth? (ch. 17, SPPY, 3:21b)

64. In trying to understand spirits, Buddhists say that beings with consciousness die and are born in cycles. They are therefore tired of suffering and seek to escape from it. Can they be said to understand spiritual beings? They consider human life as a delusion. Can they be said to understand man? Heaven and man form a unity, but they accept one (the ultimate nature of Heaven) and reject the other (human affairs). Can they be said to understand Heaven? What Confucius and Mencius called Heaven, they call the Path. "The wandering away of the spirit (material force) [as it disintegrates] becomes change,"[85] but the deluded Buddhists call this transmigration. They just don't think. (ibid., 3:22a)

> Comment. Neo-Confucianists attacked Buddhism on all fronts. Chang did so mostly on philosophical grounds. Other Neo-Confucianists, like Ch'eng Hao, Ch'eng I, and Wang Yang-ming (1472-1529), stressed the social and ethical aspects by emphasizing Buddhist escape from social responsibility and selfish desire for personal salvation.

65. Things should be investigated gradually. By seeing more and more things and investigating their principles more and more, one can fully develop the nature of things. ("Recorded Sayings," ibid., 12:1b)

66. The great benefit of learning is to enable one to transform his physical nature himself. Otherwise he will have the defect of studying in order to impress others, in the end will attain no enlightenment, and cannot see the all-embracing depth of the sage. (ibid., 12:3a.)

> Comment. The phrase, "transform the physical nature," has been hailed by Neo-Confucianists as an outstanding contribution and

[85] Changes, "Appended Remarks," pt. 1, ch. 4. Cf. Legge, p. 353.

has remained a golden teaching in the Confucian School. The doctrine holds man himself responsible, and puts faith in education. Philosophically, the significant point is that evil can be transmuted to be good. As he said before, when virtue overcomes material force, one's nature and destiny are controlled and determined by virtue. Only life and death are material forces that cannot be changed. As to method, the best is to enlarge the mind.[86]

67. Everything has principle. If one does not know how to investigate principle to the utmost, he would be dreaming all his life. Buddhists do not investigate principle to the utmost. They consider everything to be the result of subjective illusion. Chuang Tzu did understand principle, but when he went to its utmost, he also considered things to be a dream. Therefore in referring to Confucius and Yen Yüan,[87] he said that they both were dreaming.[88] (*ibid.*)

68. The mind commands man's nature and feelings. ("Additional Sayings on the Nature and Principle," *ibid.*, 14:2a)

Comment. This is a simple saying but the doctrine became a major one in Neo-Confucianism because it not only restores feeling to a position of equality with nature; it also makes the mind the master of a person's total being. What is more, Neo-Confucianists were very insistent that reality and function, and in this theory substance (nature) and function (feelings), are harmonized by the mind.

[86] See Chan's article noted in n.69.
[87] Confucius' pupil.
[88] *Chuang Tzu*, ch. 6, NHCC, 3:23a. See Giles, trans., *Chuang Tzu*, p. 83.

31

THE IDEALISTIC TENDENCY
IN CH'ENG HAO

THE TWO Ch'eng brothers (Ch'eng Hao, also called Ch'eng Ming-tao, 1032-1085, and Ch'eng I, also called Ch'eng I-ch'uan, 1033-1107) represent a unique and an extremely interesting case in the history of Chinese philosophy. Both brothers became outstanding philosophers, reminding one of the two brothers, Asaṅga (c.410–c.500) and Vasubandhu (c.420–c.500) in the history of Indian philosophy. They were students of Chou Tun-i (Chou Lien-hsi, 1017-1073), friends of Shao Yung (1011-1077), and nephews of Chang Tsai (Chang Heng-ch'ü, 1020-1077).[1] These five are often called the Five Masters of eleventh-century Chinese philosophy. As noted before, the two brothers set the pattern for Neo-Confucianism. They were of utterly different temperament, and yet they agreed essentially in their philosophies. Many of the sayings in the *I-shu* (Surviving Works) and *Wai-shu* (Additional Works) of the *Erh-Ch'eng ch'üan-shu* (Complete Works of the Two Ch'engs) are assigned to both, and in most cases scholars do not agree to which brother they should be ascribed. When Chu Hsi (1130-1200) referred to "Master Ch'eng," most of the time he meant Ch'eng I, oftentimes Ch'eng Hao, but sometimes both.

This does not mean that there are no differences between them. In fact, Ch'eng I is so much more rationalistic than Ch'eng Hao and Ch'eng Hao is so much more idealistic than Ch'eng I that it is permissible to say that Ch'eng Hao inaugurated the idealistic wing of Neo-Confucianism while his brother inaugurated the rationalistic wing, although their differences have been exaggerated in recent years. Their similarities and dissimilarities will be brought out in the comments and in the next chap-

---

[1] Ch'eng Hao's courtesy name was Po-ch'un and he was called Master Ming-tao (Illuminating the Way). His father was a chief officer. After he obtained the "presented scholar" degree in 1057, he became a keeper of records (assistant magistrate) and scored a great success in averting a famine by saving the dikes. Later he was a magistrate for three years (1065-1067), brought peace and order, and gained the great affection of the populace. In 1069 he became undersecretary of the heir apparent. Emperor Shen-tsung (r. 1068-1085) gave him a number of audiences and was much impressed with his recommendations. But he strongly opposed Wang An-shih (1021-1086) in his radical reforms. In 1070 he was demoted to be an assistant prefect. In 1078-1080 he was again a magistrate but his political enemies finally had him dismissed. The new emperor, Che-tsung (r. 1086-1093) appointed him a bureau assistant executive, but before he took office he died. See *Sung shih* (History of the Sung Dynasty, 960-1279), PNP, 247:5a-10a, *I-ch'uan wen-chi* (see n.21), 7:1a-7a, the introduction to the next chapter, and Bruce, *Chu Hsi and His Masters*, pp. 41-45.

ter.[2] But their fundamental agreement, which forms the keynote to their philosophy in particular and to Neo-Confucianism in general, namely, the concept of principle (*li*), must be pointed out right away.

The concept of principle is found in ancient Chinese philosophy, in Neo-Taoism, and in Buddhism,[3] but the Ch'eng brothers were the first ones to build their philosophy primarily on it. More especially for Ch'eng Hao, principle is the Principle of Nature (*T'ien-li*, Principle of Heaven). As conceived and understood by the brothers, principle is self-evident and self-sufficient, extending everywhere and governing all things. It cannot be augmented or diminished. It is many but it is essentially one, for all specific principles are but principle. It is possessed by all people and all things. Even a very small thing has principle. It is laid before our very eyes. Man and all things form one body because all of them share this principle. To be sincere is to be sincere to it, and to be serious is to be serious about it. In short, it is one and all. It is identical with the mind and it is identical with the nature. All things exist because of it and can be understood through it. It is universal truth, universal order, universal law. Most important of all, it is a universal process of creation and production. It is dynamic and vital.

It can easily be seen that to the Ch'eng brothers this principle means both natural principles and moral principles, and both general principles and specific principles. They were not much concerned with abstract reality, for they were primarily interested in the meaning of principle for man. Thus they turned Neo-Confucianism from speculation on cosmology to concentrate on the problems of principle and human nature, thereby making Neo-Confucianism truly a School of Nature and Principle (*Hsing-li hsüeh*).

What is equally even more significant is that Ch'eng Hao (and also his brother) used the term *T'ien-li*. As Hu Shih has pointed out, it stands for the Natural Law.[4] Where did the Ch'engs get their ideas? Much of their philosophy may be traced to ancient Confucian Classics. As Ch'eng I said of his brother, "From the time when, at fifteen or sixteen, he heard Chou Tun-i discourse on the Way, he got tired of preparing for civil service examinations and arduously made up his mind to seek the Way. Not knowing the essential steps, he drifted among the various schools of thought and went in and out of the Taoist and Buddhist schools for almost ten years. Finally he returned to the Six Classics[5] and only then did he find the Way."[6] Of these Classics, the

---

[2] See below, ch. 32, Introduction.

[3] See above, pp. 122, 131, 202, 260, 269, 318, 323, 326, 412, 415.

[4] Hu Shih (1891-1962), "The Natural Law in the Chinese Tradition," *Natural Law Institute Proceedings*, 5 (1953): 119-153.

[5] The *Books* of *History, Odes, Changes, Rites*, the *Chou-li* (Rites of Chou) and

Book of Changes and the *Doctrine of the Mean*, which is part of the *Book of Rites*, are the ones to which he often turned. But so far as the concept of the Principle of Nature is concerned, he got no help from them. The term *T'ien-li* appears in the *Book of Rites*.[7] However, there it means the principle endowed in man by Heaven and does not have the connotation of universal truth or natural law. As related by his follower Hsieh Liang-tso (Hsieh Shang-ts'ai, 1050-1103), Ch'eng himself once said, "Although I have learned some of my doctrines from others, the concept of the Principle of Nature, however, has been realized by myself."[8] What is said of Ch'eng Hao could have been said of Ch'eng I.

This does not mean that they developed their philosophy in a vacuum. Chou Tun-i's influence on their ideas and personality has already been pointed out.[9] Some people have denied this influence. Ch'üan Tsu-wang (1705-1755), for example, said that "while the two Ch'engs studied with Chou in their youth, what they achieved did not come from him. . . . Throughout their life the two Masters Ch'eng never praised Chou very much. . . . Chu Hsi was the first one to decide definitely that the philosophy of the two Ch'engs came from Chou and later generations followed him. . . . But the two Ch'engs never transmitted the doctrines of Chou."[10] In his *I-Lo yüan-yüan lu* (Record of the Origin of the School of the Two Ch'engs)[11] Chu Hsi places Chou first, then the two brothers, and then Shao Yung and Chang Tsai, and others, thus implying that the Ch'eng philosophy originated with Chou and was transmitted through Shao and Chang. This line of transmission is too simple and direct to be true and Ch'üan was correct in rejecting it. But to deny Chou's influence on the Ch'engs[12] is to ignore certain indisputable facts. The two brothers certainly did study with Chou.[13] It has been suggested that their relationship was not that of teacher and pupil, because the Ch'engs always

---

the *Spring and Autumn Annals*. The ancient Six Classics included the *Book of Music*, now lost, instead of the *Chou-li*.

[6] *I-ch'uan wen-chi*, 7:6a. See n.21.

[7] "Record of Music." See trans. by Legge, *Li Ki*, ch. 17, p. 96.

[8] *Shang-ts'ai yü-lu* (Recorded Conversations of Hsien Liang-tso), *Cheng-i-t'ang ch'üan-shu* (Complete Library of the Hall of Rectifying the Way) ed., pt. 1, p. 5b, also *Wai-shu*, 12:4a. (See n.21)

[9] See above, pp. 461-462.

[10] Huang Tsung-hsi (1610-1695) *et al.*, *Sung-Yüan hsüeh-an* (Anthology and Critical Accounts of the Neo-Confucianists of the Sung and Yüan Dynasties, 960-1368), SPPY, 11:1a.

[11] The term "I-Lo" refers to the I and Lo Rivers in which area Lo-yang is located. Both brothers lived and taught there.

[12] As Graham does. See his *Two Chinese Philosophers*, pp. 152-168. See my review of it in the *Journal of American Oriental Society*, 79 (1959), p. 154.

[13] *I-shu*, 2A:2b, 3:1b; *I-ch'uan wen-chi*, 7:6a; *Ts'ui-yen*, 1:24b. See n.21.

referred to his courtesy name, Mao-shu,[14] and once even called him "poor Zen fellow,"[15] not very respectful ways to refer to a teacher. However, it is not entirely unknown, though unusual, for pupils to call their teachers by courtesy names. For example, Hu Yüan (993-1059), Ch'eng I's teacher, was referred to by his courtesy name An-ting.[16] It is also argued that the Ch'engs never mentioned the Great Ultimate,[17] perhaps the central concept in Chou's philosophy. This is certainly a puzzle. But their failure to mention the term does not necessarily mean that Chou had had no influence on them, any more than it meant that the *Book of Changes* did not have any influence on them. It had enough influence on Ch'eng I for him to write a commentary on it, although he never mentioned the Great Ultimate, which is one of the basic concepts in the book. They did not mention the Great Ultimate perhaps because they wanted to avoid Taoist influence, since Chou's "Diagram of the Great Ultimate" came from the Taoist tradition. Ch'üan Tsu-wang is correct in contending that the Ch'engs did not transmit the philosophy of Chou, but it is still true that the basic problems and the general direction of their philosophy were within the broad outline of Chou's philosophy, including the concept of principle.

All this does not remove the fact that it was the Ch'eng brothers' own idea to make principle the central focus of their philosophy. While the two brothers shared common ideas about it, they also had different emphases. As will be shown, Ch'eng I stressed the doctrine that principle is one but its manifestations are many. Compared with his brother, Ch'eng Hao has emphasized more strongly the idea of production and reproduction as the chief characteristic of the universe. He saw the spirit of life in all things. To him, this creative quality is *jen* (humanity),[18] which removes all distinctions between the self and the other and combines Heaven, Earth, and man as one.

As the great virtue of Heaven and Earth is to produce, whatever is produced in man, that is, whatever is inborn in him, is his nature. To him this is identical with material force (*ch'i*). In its original, tranquil state, human nature is neither good nor evil. The distinction arises when human nature is aroused and is manifested in feelings and actions, and when these feelings and actions abide by or deviate from the mean. The chief task of moral and spiritual cultivation is to calm one's nature, through absolute impartiality and the identification of internal and ex-

[14] For example, *I-shu*, 2A:2b, 3:1b, 2a, 6:4a, 7:1a, 22A:1b; *Wai-shu*, 2:4b, 10:4b. See Graham, p. 173, n.38.

[15] *I-shu*, 6:4a.   [16] For example, *I-shu*, 2A:4a, 4:3b.

[17] It is mentioned in a preface to Ch'eng I's *I chuan* (see n.21), but as Graham has well shown (p. 144), this preface is unauthentic.

[18] For a discussion of this term, see Appendix.

ternal life. Any opposition between the internal and the external, he said, must be forgotten. In fact, he rejects dichotomy of any kind, whether between the human mind and the moral mind, between the Principle of Nature and human desires, or between human nature and feelings. To achieve unity, he advocated sincerity and seriousness (*ching*),[19] that is, concentrating on one thing and not getting away from it.

There can be no denial that in advocating such a method of moral cultivation he tended to quietism. Whether he was influenced by Chou Tun-i or by Zen Buddhists or both is a moot point. We must not forget, however, that he looked upon Chou Tun-i's doctrine of tranquillity as unbalanced and substituted for it seriousness. Moreover, to him the universe is a great current of production. Whatever quietism there is in him, then, is not Buddhist emptiness and silence but a vital, if gentle and quiet, process. Like the Buddhists, however, he almost exclusively emphasizes the mind. To him, "Principle and the mind are one,"[20] and he stresses holding on to the mind with seriousness and preserving the mind as fundamental steps to moral perfection. In thus stressing the mind, he and his brother, who stressed more strongly the extension of knowledge, moved in different directions, he the idealistic, later developed by Lu Hsiang-shan (Lu Chiu-yüan, 1139-1193) and Wang Yang-ming (Wang Shou-jen, 1472-1529), the other the rationalistic, later culminated in Chu Hsi.

Following the list of major topics and references are selections from the *Erh-Ch'eng ch'üan-shu* (Complete Works of the Two Ch'engs).

Buddhism: 21, 32, 46, 76, 77
Goodness; Good and Evil: 7, 8, 15, 19, 64
Human Nature; Destiny: 1, 2, 5, 7, 12, 36, 51, 56, 67
Jen (Humanity): 1, 11, 13, 23, 27, 28, 40, 50, 51, 65
Life, Spirit of; Origination; Production: 19, 21, 27-29, 38, 39, 51
Material force (*ch'i*) and Physical form: 5, 7, 36, 37, 42, 58, 75
Mean, Equilibrium, and Centrality: 4, 8, 34, 61, 69, 73, 74
Nature and man forming one body: 1, 4, 11, 18, 21, 35, 48, 51, 54
Principle of Nature (Heaven): 3, 8, 15, 16, 18, 20-24, 26, 33, 34, 37, 53, 60, 62, 64, 65, 67, 69, 70-72, 75
Seriousness (*ching*): 1, 10, 18, 20, 23, 30, 32, 45, 46, 49, 50, 66, 69
Sincerity: 1, 5, 6, 17, 20, 41, 45, 66, 68
Way, the: 1, 5, 19, 32, 41, 42, 44, 50

[19] For comment on this term, see *ibid.*
[20] *I-shu*, 5:1a.

CH'ENG HAO

THE COMPLETE WORKS OF THE TWO CH'ENGS[21]

1. On Understanding the Nature of Jen (Humanity)

The student must first of all understand the nature of *jen*. The man of *jen* forms one body with all things without any differentiation. Righteousness, propriety, wisdom, and faithfulness are all [expressions of] *jen*.

[One's duty] is to understand this principle (*li*) and preserve *jen* with sincerity and seriousness (*ching*), that is all. There is no need for caution and control. Nor is there any need for exhaustive search. Caution is necessary when one is mentally negligent, but if one is not negligent, what is the necessity for caution? Exhaustive search is necessary when one has not understood principle, but if one preserves *jen* long enough, it will automatically dawn on him. Why should he have to depend on exhaustive search?

Nothing can be equal to this Way (Tao, that is, *jen*). It is so vast that nothing can adequately explain it. All operations of the universe are our operations. Mencius said that "all things are already complete in oneself" and that one must "examine oneself and be sincere (or absolutely real)" and only then will there be great joy.[22] If one examines himself and finds himself not yet sincere, it means there is still an op-

---

[21] This is the *Erh-Ch'eng ch'üan-shu*, which includes (1) the *I-shu* (Surviving Works), consisting of conversations of the brothers, (2) the *Wai-shu* (additional Works), consisting of additional conversations of theirs, (3) the *Ming-tao wen-chi* (Collection of Literary Works by Ch'eng Hao), consisting of poems, letters, and the like, (4) the *I-ch'uan wen-chi* (Collection of Literary Works by Ch'eng I), (5) the *I ch'uan* (Commentary on the *Book of Changes*) by Ch'eng I, (6) his *Ching-shuo* (Explanations of the Classics), and (7) the *Ts'ui-yen* (Pure Words), which contains additional conversations of the two brothers, mostly duplicates of the *I-shu* and the *Wai-shu*. (*Ts'ui-yen* has sometimes been mistranslated as "choice sayings" and "collected sayings.") For the present work, the SPPY edition is used. It is interesting to note that the *Ts'ui-yen* is put at the end of the *Complete Works*. For a good account of these works, see Tsai, *The Philosophy of Ch'eng I*, pp. 27-61. Tsai is sometimes too skeptical and used untenable arguments. For example, he said that the *Ts'ui-yen* is unreliable because it is in the literary style whereas the editor of this work, Yang Shih (Yang Kuei-shan, 1053-1135) always referred to it as *yü-lu* or "recorded sayings in the vernacular" (p. 60). But *yü-lu* merely means recorded sayings and does not necessarily mean sayings in the vernacular. The *Chang Tzu yü-lu* (Recorded Conversations of Chang Tsai), for example, is in the literary style. Besides, not all the recorded conversations of the Ch'eng brothers are in the vernacular. They are vernacular in the *I-shu* but literary in the *Wai-shu*, which was compiled by Chu Hsi.

None of the above works has been translated into any European language. A good number of sayings of both brothers has been translated by Graham in his book and a considerable number of sayings by Ch'eng I has been translated by Ts'ai in his work. Chu Hsi's selections from the two brothers in his *Chin-ssu lu* (Reflections on Things at Hand) have been translated into German by Graf, *Djin-sï lu, passim*.

[22] *Mencius*, 7A:4.

position between the two (the self and the non-self). Even if one tries to identify the self with the non-self, one still does not achieve unity. How can one have joy?

The purpose of (Chang Tsai's) "Western Inscription"[23] is to explain this substance (of complete unity) fully. If one preserves it (*jen*) with this idea, what more is to be done? "Always be doing something without expectation. Let the mind not forget its objective, but let there be no artificial effort to help it grow."[24] Not the slightest effort is exerted! This is the way to preserve *jen*. As *jen* is preserved, the self and the other are then identified.

For our innate knowledge of good and innate ability to do good are originally not lost. However, because we have not gotten rid of the mind dominated by habits, we must preserve and exercise our original mind, and in time old habits will be overcome. This principle[25] is extremely simple; the only danger is that people will not be able to hold on to it. But if we practice it and enjoy it, there need be no worry of our being unable to hold to it. (*I-shu*, 2A:3a-b)

> *Comment.* As has been pointed out, in Chang Tsai's "Western Inscription," *jen* is universalized to include the whole universe.[26] It was in the Ch'eng brothers, however, that the Neo-Confucian doctrine of man and the universe forming one body took root and became a cardinal concept. In this little essay, which has been a *vade mecum* for many a Chinese scholar, unity of man and Nature (*T'ien*, Heaven) is affirmed on the basis of the elimination of all opposition between the self and the other. In section 11 of *Selected Sayings*, below, unity is also argued on the basis of the all-loving character of *jen*. His brother also said that "The man of *jen* regards Heaven and Earth and all things as one body."[27] And the doctrine is later fully developed in Wang Yang-ming.[28]
>
> Strangely enough, Chu Hsi left this essay out of his *Chin-ssu lu* (Reflections on Things at Hand)[29] because it is "too broad" and "may easily be misunderstood."[30] Evidently the teaching that there is no need for caution, control, or exhaustive search sounds dangerous. But in defense of Ch'eng, Liu Tsung-chou (1578-1645) has pointed out that Ch'eng did not teach people to meditate out of

[23] See above, ch. 30, sec. 1.   [24] *Mencius*, 2A:2.
[25] The text has *shih* (fact) instead of *li* (principle).
[26] See above, ch. 30, comment on sec. 1.
[27] *Ts'ui-yen*, 1:7b.
[28] See below, ch. 35, B, secs. 89, 93, 274, and 337.
[29] The *Chin-ssu lu* is an anthology of the Ch'eng brothers, Chou Tun-i and Chang Tsai.
[30] *Chu Tzu yü-lei* (Classified Conversations of Chu Hsi), 1876 ed., 97:5b-6a.

a vacuum but merely stressed the fundamental as the first step.[31] Nevertheless, as Ch'ien Mu has noted, Ch'eng did not tell in detail how to know the substance of *jen* except to advise us to preserve it according to the idea in the "Western Inscription." This task was left to his brother.[32]

2. Reply to Master Heng-ch'ü's Letter on Calming Human Nature[33]

I have received your letter in which you said that nature in the state of calmness cannot be without activity and must still suffer from the influence of external things. This problem has been ardently pondered by a worthy [like you]. What need is there for a humble person like myself to say anything? However, I have gone over the matter in my mind, and dare present my ideas to you. By calmness of nature we mean that one's nature is calm whether it is in a state of activity or in a state of tranquillity. One does not lean forward or backward to accommodate things, nor does he make any distinction between the internal and external.[34] To regard things outside the self as external, and force oneself to conform to them, is to regard one's nature as divided into the internal and the external. Furthermore, if one's nature is conceived to be following external things, then, while it is outside what is it that is within the self? To conceive one's nature thus is to have the intention of getting rid of external temptations, but to fail to realize that human nature does not possess the two aspects of internal and external. Since one holds that things internal and things external form two different bases, how can one hastily speak of the calmness of human nature?

The constant principle of Heaven and Earth is that their mind is in all things, and yet they have no mind of their own. The constant principle of the sage is that his feelings are in accord with all creation, and yet he has no feelings of his own. Therefore, for the training of the superior man there is nothing better than to become broad and extremely impartial and to respond spontaneously to all things as they come. The *Book of Changes* says, "Firm correctness brings good fortune and prevents all occasions for repentance. If he is hesitant in his movements, only his friends will follow his purpose."[35] If one merely attempts to remove external temptations, then no sooner do some disappear in the

[31] *Sung-Yüan hsüeh-an*, SPPY, 13:3b.

[32] *Chung-kuo ssu-hsiang shih* (History of Chinese Thought), 1952, p. 138.

[33] According to Chu Hsi, this was written when Ch'eng Hao was twenty-two or twenty-three. See *Chu Tzu yü-lei*, 93:9a.

[34] Indirectly quoting *Chuang Tzu*, ch. 22, NHCC, 7:55b. See Giles, trans., *Chuang Tzu*, 1961 ed., p. 219.

[35] Commentary of hexagram no. 31, *hsien* (influence). Cf. Legge, trans., *Yi King*, p. 123.

east than others will arise in the west. Not only is one's time limited, but the source of temptation is inexhaustible and therefore cannot be removed.

Everyone's nature is obscured in some way and as a consequence he cannot follow the Way. In general the trouble lies in resorting to selfishness and the exercise of cunning. Being selfish, one cannot take purposive action to respond to things, and being cunning, one cannot be at home with enlightenment. For a mind that hates external things to seek illumination in a mind where nothing exists, is to look for a reflection on the back of a mirror. The *Book of Changes* says, "Stop in the back of a thing. See not the person. Walk in the hall and do not see the people in it."[36] Mencius also said," What I dislike in your wise men is their forced reasoning."[37] Instead of looking upon the internal as right and the external as wrong, it is better to forget the distinction. When such a distinction is forgotten, the state of quietness and peace is attained. Peace leads to calmness and calmness leads to enlightenment. When one is enlightened, how can the response to things become an impediment? The sage is joyous because according to the nature of things before him he should be joyous, and he is angry because according to the nature of things before him he should be angry. Thus the joy and anger of the sage do not depend on his own mind but on things. Does not the sage in this way respond to things? Why should it be regarded wrong to follow external things and right to seek what is within? Compare the joy and anger of the selfish and cunning man to the correctness of joy and anger of the sage. What a difference! Among human emotions the easiest to arouse but the most difficult to control is anger. But if in time of anger one can immediately forget his anger and look at the right and wrong of the matter according to principle, he will see that external temptations need not be hated, and he has gone more than halfway toward the Way. My subtle ideas cannot be expressed in words. On top of my usual lack of skill in writing, my official duties have kept me busy, so that I have not given the finest thought to this matter. Whether I am correct or not, I pray you to let me know. However, I believe I am not far from the truth in essential points. The ancients considered it wrong to seek afar when the truth lies nearby. Will you, a man of wisdom and intelligence, draw your own conclusions. (*Ming-tao wen-chi*, 3:1a-b)

> *Comment.* As Liu Tsung-chou has well pointed out, this essay is essentially an elaboration of Chou Tun-i's doctrine of "considering tranquillity to be fundamental."[38]

[36] The text of hexagram no. 52, *ken* (to stop). Cf. Legge, pp. 175-176.
[37] *Mencius*, 4B:26.
[38] *Sung-Yüan hsüeh-an*, 13:8a. For Chou's doctrine, see above, ch. 28, sec. 1.

SELECTED SAYINGS[39]

3. There is no creature in the world that does not possess sufficient principle. I have always thought that rulers and ministers, fathers and sons, brothers, and husbands and wives have somewhat failed to fulfill their functions.[40] (1:2a)* c ch s

4. Man is not the only perfectly intelligent creature in the universe. The human mind (in essence) is the same as that of plants and trees, birds and animals. It is only that man receives at birth the Mean of Heaven and Earth (balanced material force). (1:3a)* c m s

5. "The operations of Heaven (Nature) have neither sound nor smell."[41] Their substance is called Change; their principle, the Way; and their function, spirit. What Heaven imparts to man is called the nature. To follow the law of our nature is called the Way (Tao). Cultivation according to the Way is called education. . . .[42] What exists before physical form [and is therefore without it] constitutes the Way. What exists after physical form [and is therefore with it] constitutes concrete things. Nevertheless, though we speak in this way, concrete things are the Way and the Way is concrete things. So long as the Way obtains, it does not matter whether it is present or future, or whether it is the self or others. (1:3a-b)* c ch m

6. Sincerity is the way to unify the internal and the external. "Without sincerity there will be nothing."[43] (1:7a)* m

7. "What is inborn is called nature."[44] Nature is the same as material force and material force is the same as nature. They are both inborn.

---

[39] All these sayings are from the *I-shu*. The asterisk following the page reference indicates that the saying is ascribed in the *I-shu* to the "two Masters" without specifying which of the two. The letters c, ch, l, m, and s indicate that it has been taken to be Ch'eng Hao's saying in the anthologies represented by them as follows. With two exceptions, to be pointed out, none of these anthologies ascribes any of these sayings to Ch'eng I:

c. Chu Hsi, *Chin-ssu lu* (Reflections on Things at Hand).
ch. Ch'en Lung-cheng (1585-?), *Ch'eng Tzu hsiang-pen* (Detailed and Classified Anthology of Masters Ch'eng).
l. Sun Ch'i-feng (1584-1675), *Li-hsüeh tsung-ch'uan* (Orthodox Transmission of Neo-Confucianism).
m. Shen Kuei (of Ming, 1368-1644), *Ming-tao ch'üan-shu* (Complete Works of Ch'eng Hao).
s. Huang Tsung-hsi (1610-1695) *et al., Sung-Yüan hsüeh-an* (Anthology and Critical Accounts of the Neo-Confucianists of the Sung and Yüan Dynasties, 960-1368).

[40] According to Yeh Ts'ai (fl. 1248), function means here what is correct according to principle. See *Djin-sï lu*, trans. by Graf, vol. 2, p. 58.
[41] *The Mean*, ch. 33.
[42] *ibid.*, ch. 1.
[43] *ibid.*, ch. 25.
[44] A saying by Kao Tzu (c.420–c.350 b.c.). *Mencius*, 6A:3.

According to principle,[45] there are both good and evil in the material force with which man is endowed at birth. However, man is not born with these two opposing elements in his nature to start with. Due to the material force with which men are endowed some become good from childhood and others become evil.[46] Man's nature is of course good, but it cannot be said that evil is not his nature. For what is inborn is called nature. "By nature man is tranquil at birth."[47] The state preceding this cannot be discussed. As soon as we talk about human nature, we already go beyond it. Actually, in our discussion of nature, we only talk about (the idea expressed in the *Book of Changes* as) "What issues from the Way is good."[48] This is the case when Mencius speaks of the original goodness of human nature. The fact that whatever issues from the Way is good may be compared to the fact that water always flows downward. Water as such is the same in all cases. Some water flows onward to the sea without becoming dirty. What human effort is needed here? Some flows only a short distance before growing turbid. Some travels a long distance before growing turbid. Some becomes extremely turbid, some only slightly so. Although water differs in being clean or turbid, we cannot say that the turbid water (evil) ceases to be water (nature). This being the case, man must make an increasing effort at purification. With diligent and vigorous effort, water will become clear quickly. With slow and lazy effort, water will become clear slowly. When it is clear, it is then the original water. Not that clear water has been substituted for turbid water, nor that turbid water has been taken out and left in a corner. The original goodness of human nature is like the original clearness of water. Therefore it is not true that two distinct and opposing elements of good and evil exist in human nature and that each of them issues from it. This principle is the Mandate of Heaven. For anyone to obey and follow it is the Way. For anyone to follow it and cultivate it so that he attains his function [corresponding to his nature] is education. From the Mandate of Heaven to education, one can neither augment nor diminish [this function]. Such is the case of Shun, who [obeying and

[45] According to Sun Ch'i-feng, *Li-hsüeh ts'ung-ch'uan*, 1880 ed., 2:11b, the word "principle" should read "nature."

[46] "Such as Hou-chi having an outstanding appearance and when Tzu-yüeh-chiao was born, people knew that he would destroy his own clan," says Ch'eng Hao's own note. Hou-chi was Emperor Shun's (3rd millennium B.C.) minister, who is described in the *Book of Odes*, ode no. 245, as having an outstanding appearance at birth, thus indicating his inborn virtue. The reference to Tzu-yüeh-chiao is found in the *Tso chuan*, Duke Hsüan, 4th year.

[47] *Book of Rites*, "Record of Music." Cf. Legge, trans., *Li Ki*, vol. 1, p. 96.

[48] *Changes*, "Appended Remarks," pt. 1, ch. 5. Cf. translation by Legge, *Yi King*, p. 353.

following the Way], possessed his empire as if it were nothing to him.[49] (1:7b-8a)* C L M S

> *Comment.* This passage has aroused considerable critical comments. In the *Chu Tzu yü-lei* (Classified Conversations of Chu Hsi), there is more discussion on it than on almost any other subject concerning the Ch'engs.[50] Ch'eng Hao used the expression "What is inborn is called nature," which is the same as Kao Tzu's saying, and thus seems to follow Kao Tzu's theory that by nature man is born morally neutral or that his nature is a mixture of good and evil. But as Chu Hsi has pointed out, no such idea is intended. From the fact that water is clear originally, and turbid only when flowing has started, it is clear that Ch'eng meant two natures, namely, man's basic nature, which is originally good, and his physical nature, which involves evil.[51] Actually Ch'eng Hao did not depart from the general Neo-Confucian position so far as human nature is concerned. The trouble arises from ambiguity in the passage. One possible explanation for his using an expression identical with Kao Tzu's is perhaps that its emphasis was on the process of production and reproduction.

8. Good and evil in the world are both the Principle of Nature. What is called evil is not original evil. It becomes evil only because of deviation from the Mean. Yang Chu (440–360 B.C.?) and Mo Tzu (fl. 479–438 B.C.)[52] are examples of this. (2A:1b)

> *Comment.* This utterance has been most severely condemned by Neo-Confucianists. It seems to destroy one of the foundations of Neo-Confucian metaphysics, namely, that nature, which is identical with principle, is good, and it also seems to tolerate evil. Judged by his whole philosophy, nothing is further from his mind. He merely echoed Mencius' contention that things are unequal (see sec. 15). He accepted evil as a fact, but insisted on removing it. This is obvious in the preceding section.

9. The student should completely preserve his mind [so it will not be overcome by selfish desires].[53] Although his studies may not be complete, as things come to him he should not fail to respond, but should respond according to his capacity. If he does not hit the mark, he will not be far from it. (2A:2a)* C M

---

[49] Paraphrasing *Analects*, 8:18. [50] *Chu Tzu yü-lei*, 95:11a-18a.
[51] *ibid.*, 95:11a-b.
[52] See above, ch. 3, *Mencius*, Additional Selections, 3A:5, 3B:9.
[53] This is Chu Hsi's understanding. See *Chu Tzu yü-lei*, 96:1b.

10. The student should hold fast to the mind with seriousness. He should not be anxious. Instead he should nourish and cultivate it deeply and earnestly, immerse and soak himself in it. Only then can he be at ease with himself. If one seeks anxiously, that is merely selfishness. In the end he will not be able to understand the Way. (2A:2a)* CH M

11. A book on medicine describes paralysis of the four limbs as absence of jen.[54] This is an excellent description. The man of jen regards Heaven and Earth and all things as one body. To him there is nothing that is not himself. Since he has recognized all things as himself, can there be any limit to his humanity? If things are not parts of the self, naturally they have nothing to do with it. As in the case of paralysis of the four limbs, the vital force no longer penetrates them, and therefore they are no longer parts of the self. Therefore, to be charitable and to assist all things is the function of a sage. It is most difficult to describe jen. Hence Confucius merely said that the man of jen, "wishing to establish his own character, also establishes the character of others, and wishing to be prominent himself, also helps others to be prominent. To be able to judge of others by what is in ourselves may be called the method of realizing jen."[55] The hope was that by looking at it this way, we might get at the substance of humanity. (2A:2a-b)

> Comment. The all-important concept of jen went through radical developments in Neo-Confucianism, especially in Chang Tsai and the Ch'eng brothers.[56] In the I-shu of the brothers, jen is discussed more than any other topic. In section 1, righteousness, propriety, wisdom, and faithfulness are considered as expressions of jen. This is a new development, for traditionally the five are called the Five Constant Virtues, all being equal, whereas he and his brother, who developed the idea further, regarded jen as embracing the other four. Here jen is understood as a feeling for life, an even more radical interpretation of jen. As Chu Hsi explained, jen is the mind of Heaven and Earth to produce things. Since man has received this mind to be his own mind, he and Heaven and Earth and all things share the same mind. It is for this reason that there is penetration through all things.[57]

[54] Su-wen (Question on the Original Simplicity), sec. 42, Erh-shih-erh tzu (Twenty-two Philosophers) ed., 12:2a. The meaning of the title is not clear, but according to the commentary in the book (1:1a), su refers to the original substance, and therefore does not mean purity or plainness.

[55] Analects, 6:28.

[56] See above, ch. 30, comment on sec. 1, and below, ch. 32, comment on sec. 42.

[57] Chu Tzu yü-lei, 95:10a. For further comment on jen, see sec. 1; also see above, ch. 30, sec. 1; and see below, ch. 32, comment on sec. 42; ch. 34, comment on treatise 1; and ch. 40, Introduction.

12. The investigation of principle to the utmost, the full development of nature, and the fulfillment of destiny (*ming*, fate)—these three things are to be accomplished simultaneously. There is basically no time sequence among them. The investigation of principle to the utmost should not be regarded merely as a matter of knowledge. If one really investigates principle to the utmost, even one's nature and destiny can be fulfilled. (2A:2b)

13. A student should understand the substance of *jen* (namely, the Principle of Nature)[58] and make it concretely part of his own self. Then all that is necessary is to nourish it with moral principles. All such things as seeking the meanings of the Classics are meant to nourish it. (2A:-2b)* C M

14. Formerly when [we] received instructions from Chou Mao-shu (Chou Tun-i),[59] he often told [us] to find out wherein Confucius and Yen Tzu[60] found their joy. (2A:2b)* C CH L M S

> *Comment.* Neither Chou nor the Ch'eng brothers ever indicated where Confucius or Yen Tzu found his joy. In *Analects*, 6:9, Confucius praised his pupil for enjoying extremely simple life and in 7:15, Confucius said he himself found joy in having only coarse rice to eat, water to drink, and his bent arm for a pillow. But Neo-Confucianists were not contented with such a general expression of love of virtue, and so each of them described joy in his own way— as extensive study of literature and self-restraint with rules of conduct, self mastery, enjoying the Way, complete elimination of selfish desires, following the Principle of Nature, and so forth. This is an excellent example of how Neo-Confucianists always went back to ancient Classics for authority and expressions but always interpreted them in their own way.[61]

15. Good and evil among things are both Principle of Nature. In the Principle of Nature, some things must be good and others bad, for "It is the nature of things to be unequal."[62] We should examine the matter and should not enter into evil ourselves and be dragged by any particular thing. (2A:3b)

16. We should know the origin of life and death, and existence and extinction, and be very clear and absolutely sure about them. There is

---

[58] Interpretation according to Sun Ch'i-feng, *Li-hsüeh tsung-ch'uan*, 2:20b.

[59] For Chou Tun-i, see above, ch. 28.

[60] Confucius' most virtuous pupil (521-490 B.C.). The reference is to *Analects,* 6:9.

[61] For Chu Hsi's various interpretations, see Chiang Yung (1681-1762), *Chin-ssu lu chi-chu* (Collected Commentaries on the *Reflections on Things at Hand*), SPPY, 2:8b.

[62] *Mencius*, 3A:4.

only this principle governing them. When Confucius said, "If we do not yet know about life, how can we know about death?",[63] he spoke in a general way. The matter of death is part of life. There is no separate principle [governing it]. (2A:4a)

17. Wisdom, humanity, and courage are "the three universally recognized virtues," but "the way by which they are practiced is one."[64] As it is one there is sincerity. It merely means to make three virtues real. Apart from these three virtues, there is no other kind of sincerity. (2A:5a)* M

18. The student need not seek afar but search right here in himself. All he has to do is to understand the Principle of Nature and be serious. This is where restraint lies [as against extensive learning]. In the section on the *ch'ien* (Heaven) hexagram of the *Book of Changes*, the learning of the sage is discussed, and in the section on the *k'un* (Earth) hexagram the learning of the worthy is discussed. They only say that "seriousness is to straighten one's internal life and righteousness is to square one's external life"[65] and that "as seriousness and righteousness are established, one's virtue will not be an isolated instance."[66] Even for a sage this is all; there is no other way. To force things and to drag things along is naturally not to be in accord with the Way and principle. Therefore when the Way and principle are followed, Heaven and man will be one and can no longer be separable. The great moving power is my own power. If it is nourished and not injured, it fills up all between heaven and earth.[67] However, as soon as it is obscured by selfish ideas, it will be diminished and feeble. From this we know it is small. "Have no depraved thoughts."[68] "Never lack seriousness."[69] If one follows only these two teachings and puts them into practice, how can he make any mistake? Any mistake is due to the lack of seriousness and to incorrectness of thought. (2A:5b-6a)

19. "Change means production and reproduction."[70] This is how Heaven becomes the Way. To Heaven, the Way is merely to give life. What follows from this principle of life-giving is good. Goodness involves the idea of origination (*yüan*), for origination is the chief quality of goodness. All things have the impulses of spring (spirit of growth) and this is goodness resulting from the principle of life. "That which realizes it is the individual nature."[71] Realization is possible only when the myriad things fully realize their own nature. (2A:12b)* M S

---

[63] *Analects*, 11:11.
[64] *The Mean*, ch. 20.
[65] Cf. Legge, *Yi King*, p. 420.
[66] *ibid.*
[67] Quoting *Mencius*, 2A:2.
[68] *Analects*, 2:2.
[69] *Book of Rites*, "Summary of Ceremonies," pt. 1. Cf. Legge, *Li Ki*, vol. 1, p. 61.
[70] *Changes*, "Appended Remarks," pt. 1, ch. 5. Cf. Legge, *Yi King*, p. 356.
[71] *ibid.*

Comment. To look upon the universe as an unceasing process of life-giving is a new development in Chinese thought and gives Neo-Confucianism a distinctive character. Few developments are as important as this. It is significant that the Ch'eng brothers did not talk about the idea of the Great Ultimate in the *Book of Changes* but instead they talked about Origination. The universe is conceived to be a continuous process of production, creation, and growth. This is a far cry from the Buddhist concept of annihilation or cycles and a definite advance over Chou Tun-i's idea of the interaction of yin and yang and Chang Tsai's idea of perpetual interfusing and intermingling of the material forces. Where did the idea come from? What is its bearing on the central Neo-Confucian doctrines of *jen*, and man forming one body with the universe? These are discussed elsewhere.[72] It suffices to note here that running through the apparently quietistic philosophy of Ch'eng Hao there is this dynamic, vital, and creative life-giving concept.

20. As to the meaning of the Principle of Nature: To be sincere is to be sincere to this principle, and to be serious is to be serious about this principle. It is not that there is sincerity by itself and there is further seriousness by itself. (2A:13b)* M

21. The reason why it is said that all things form one body is that all have this principle, simply because they all have come from it. "Change means production and reproduction."[73] In production, once a thing is produced, it possesses this principle complete. Man can extend this principle to others, but because their material force with which they are endowed is dark, things cannot do so. But we must not say that they do not share principle with others. Simply because of selfishness, man thinks in terms of his own person, and therefore, from the point of view of principle, belittles them. If he lets go this person of his and views all things in the same way, how much[74] joy would there be! Because the Buddhists do not know this, they think in terms of the self. As they cannot cope with it, they become disgusted and want to get rid of sense-perception, and because the source of their mind is not calm, they want to be like dry wood and dead ashes. But this is impossible. It is possible only with death. The Buddhists say all that because they in reality love their own persons and cannot let go. They are like those worms that carry things on their backs which are already unable to bear their load, and still add more things on their bodies, or like a man who sinks in a river

[72] See comment on sec. 11, and below, ch. 32, comments on secs. 22 and 42.

[73] *Changes,* "Appended Remarks," pt. 1, ch. 5. Cf. Legge, *Yi King,* p. 356.

[74] According to Chiang Yung, *Chin-ssu lu chi-chu,* 13:3a, *ta-hsiao-ta* is a Sung period (960-1279) colloquial meaning "so much."

holding a rock, and although its weight makes him sink deeper, never thinks of letting the rock go but merely resents its weight. (2A:15b)* M

22. "All things are already complete in oneself."[75] This is not only true of man but of things also. Everything proceeds from the self, only things cannot extend [the principle in them] to others whereas man can. However, although man can extend it, when has he augmented it to any extent? And although things cannot extend it, when have they diminished it to any extent? All principles exist in complete sufficiency and are openly laid before us. How can we say that (sage-emperor) Yao,[76] in fulfilling the Way of the ruler, added anything to it, or Shun,[77] in fulfilling the Way of the son, added anything to it? They are always there as ever before. (2A:16a)* L M S

23. There is only one principle in the world. You may extend it over the four seas and it is everywhere true. It is the unchangeable principle that "can be laid before Heaven and Earth" and is "tested by the experience of the Three Kings."[78] Therefore to be serious is merely to be serious with this principle. To be humane (*jen*) is to be humane with this principle. And to be faithful is to be faithful to this principle. (Confucius) said, "In times of difficulty or confusion, [a superior man] acts according to it."[79] (His pupil) also said, "I do not yet have the confidence to do so."[80] They could say this much. Principle is extremely difficult to describe. (2A:19a)* M

24. The principles of things are most enjoyable. (2A: 19b)* M

25. There is nothing in the world which is purely yin (passive cosmic force) or purely yang (active cosmic force), as yin and yang are interfused and irregular. Nevertheless, there cannot be anything without the distinction between rising and falling, and between birth and extinction. (2A:19b-20a)* M

26. By "the state of absolute quiet and inactivity" and "that which when acted upon immediately penetrates all things,"[81] is meant that the Principle of Nature is self-sufficient and from the very beginning lacks nothing. It does not exist because of sage-emperor Yao nor does it cease to exist because of wicked Chieh.[82] The constant principle governing the relations of father and son and of ruler and minister are unchangeable. When has it moved? Because the Principle of Nature is unmoved, there-

[75] *Mencius*, 7A:4.
[76] Legendary ruler (3rd millennium B.C.).
[77] Legendary ruler, Yao's successor.
[78] *The Mean*, ch. 29. The Three Kings were founders of the three dynasties (Hsia, 2183–1752 B.C.?; Shang, 1751–1112 B.C.; and Chou, 1111–249 B.C.).
[79] *Analects*, 4:5. [80] *ibid.*, 5:5.
[81] *Changes*, "Appended Remarks," pt. 1, ch. 10. Cf. Legge, p. 370.
[82] The last king of Hsia (r. 1802–1752 B.C.), who caused the downfall of the dynasty.

fore it is described as absolutely quiet. Although it is unmoved, when acted on it reacts and penetrates, for the influence is not from without. (2A:22b)* CH M S

27. Feeling the pulse is the best way to embody *jen*. (3:1a)

28. Observe the chicks. (One can see *jen* in this way.)[83] (3:1a)

29. Chou Mao-shu (Chou Tun-i) did not cut the grass growing outside his window. When asked about it, he said that he felt toward the grass as he felt toward himself. (When Tzu-hou [Chang Tsai] heard the cry of a donkey he said the same thing.)[84] (3:2a)

> *Comment*. Like Chou, Ch'eng also refused to cut the grass outside his window. When asked why, he said that he wanted always to see the spirit of creation. He also kept several small fish and frequently observed them. When asked for his reason, he said, "I wish to see that all things are at ease with themselves."[85] It is clear that Chou's love of life had a definite influence on him.[86]

30. When I practice calligraphy, I am very serious. My objective is not that the calligraphy must be good. Rather my practice is the way of moral training. (3:2a)

31. What fills the whole body is the feeling of commiseration. (3:3a)

32. There is nothing outside of the Way, and there is no Way outside of things. Thus within heaven and earth there is nowhere without the Way. Right in the relation of father and son, the way of father and son lies in affection, and right in the relation between ruler and minister, the way of ruler and minister lies in seriousness.[87] From these to being husband and wife, elder and younger, and friends, there is no activity that is not the Way. This is why "The Way cannot be separated from us for a moment."[88] This being the case, to renounce human relations and to do away with the Four Elements (Earth, Water, Fire, and Wind) [as the Buddhists try to do] is to deviate very far from the Way. Therefore "a superior man in dealing with the world is not for anything or against anything. He follows righteousness as the standard."[89] If one is for or against anything, there will be distinction between him and the Way and that would not be Heaven and Earth in their completeness. In the learning of the Buddhists there is seriousness to straighten the internal life but no righteousness to square the external life. Therefore those who

[83] This sentence in parentheses is Ch'eng Hao's own.

[84] This additional saying is Ch'eng Hao's own.

[85] *Sung-Yüan hsiieh-an*, SPPY, 14:5b.

[86] For Chou's additional influence on the personality of the Ch'eng brothers, see above, ch. 28, Introduction.

[87] One version has "reverence" instead.

[88] *The Mean*, ch. 1. [89] *Analects*, 4:10.

are rigid become like dry wood and those who are relaxed end up in recklessness. This is why Buddhism is narrow. Our Way is different. It is to follow our nature, that is all. The Sage has fully explained this in the *Book of Changes*. (4:4b)* C L M

33. Principle and the mind are one, and man cannot put them together as one. (5:1a)* M

34. When none of the myriad things is not adjusted, that is the Mean maintained at all times according to the Principle of Nature.[90] (5:1b)* M

35. Nature and man are basically not two. There is no need to speak of combining them. (6:1b)* C L M

36. It would be incomplete to talk about the nature of man and things without including material force and unintelligible to talk about material force without including nature. (It would be wrong to consider them as two.)[91] (6:2a)* CH L M[92]

37. Due to (the interaction of) the two material forces (yin and yang) and the Five Agents (of Metal, Wood, Water, Fire, and Earth), things vary as weak and strong in thousands of ways. What the sage follows, however, is the one principle. People must return to their original nature, [Which is identical with principle]. (6:2b)* M S

38. Observe the disposition of all living things within heaven and earth. (So viewed Chou Mao-shu.)[93] (6:3a)* C M S

Comment. This advocacy of observing dispositions is common to the Ch'eng brothers. Ch'eng I urged the observation of the disposition of the Sage.[94] Their follower, Chu Hsi's teacher, Li T'ung (Li Yen-p'ing, 1088-1163), taught people to observe the disposition before the feelings are aroused.[95] All this was certainly a tendency toward quietism. Evidently being aware of this, Chu Hsi said that Master Ch'eng merely happened to have said it and that one should not simply keep observing the disposition of living things.[96] While Chu Hsi is correct, it should not be forgotten that Ch'eng is primarily interested in the spirit of life in things, as the following selection indicates. To him everything is full of life, and

[90] Another version: That is the Principle of Nature.

[91] Ch'eng's own note.

[92] It is not explicitly stated in the *I-shu* whether this is Ch'eng Hao's or Ch'eng I's saying. It is attributed to Ch'eng I in *Chu Tzu yü-lei*, 95:12a but to Ch'eng Hao in *ibid.*, 62:14b and *Chu Tzu wen-chi*, 44:19b. In his *Meng Tzu chi-chu*, ch. 11, comment on *Mencius*, 6B:6, Chu Hsi quotes this saying and another from *I-shu*, 18:17b as those of "Master Ch'eng." Since the latter saying is definitely Ch'eng I's, this saying must also be his. In *Chin-ssu lu*, ch. 2, sec. 30, it seems to belong to Ch'eng I.

[93] Ch'eng's own note.   [94] *I-shu*, 22A:5b, 9a.

[95] *Li Yen-p'ing chi* (Collected Works of Li T'ung), *Cheng-i-t'ang ch'üan-shu* ed., 2:16a-b.

[96] *Chu Tzu yü-lei*, 96:17b-18a.

this is *jen*, which can be seen by feeling the pulse or watching the chicks. (secs. 27-28)

39. When one observes the myriad things after one becomes tranquil, they will all naturally show their impulses of spring. (6:4a)* C M S

40. Humanity implies impartiality, that is, to make (the moral principle) human. Righteousness means what is proper, the standard for weighing what is of greater or smaller importance. Propriety means to distinguish (to determine ranks and functions). Wisdom is to know. And faithfulness (belief) means "We have it." All things have nature.[97] These Five Constant Virtues are nature. As to commiseration and so forth (the sense of shame, the sense of deference and compliance, and the sense of right and wrong),[98] they are all feelings. Whatever is aroused is called feeling. (One's nature is naturally self-sufficient. Faithfulness merely means "We have it." It shows itself only because of disbelief. Therefore faithfulness is not mentioned among the Four Beginnings.)[99] (9:1a)* M

41. There is one basis for the Way. Some have said that it is better to embrace the mind with sincerity than to embrace sincerity with the mind, and it is better to enter into man and things with sincerity than to become a triad with Heaven and Earth with it. That would mean two bases. To know that there are not two bases is the way to be genuinely respectful and to bring peace to the world. (11:1b)

42. "What exists before physical form [and is therefore without it] is called the Way. What exists after physical form [and is therefore with it] is called a concrete thing."[100] If anyone regards purity, vacuity, oneness, and greatness as the Way of Nature, he is speaking in terms of concrete things and not the Way. (11:1b)

43. "Heaven and earth have their fixed positions and yet the system of Change operates in them."[101] Why not say man operates in them? Because man is also a thing. If we say spirit operates in them, people would look for it only in spiritual beings. It is also all right to say principle or sincerity operates in them. Change is purposely mentioned in order that people may silently remember it and realize for themselves. (11:1b)

44. In the "Appended Remarks," (of the *Book of Changes*) it is said, "What exists before physical form [and is therefore without it] is called the Way. What exists after physical form [and is therefore with it] is

---

[97] The text has "faithfulness" instead of "nature." Obviously a misprint.
[98] Referring to the Four Beginnings discussed in *Mencius*, 2A:6.
[99] Ch'eng's own note.
[100] *Changes*, "Appended Remarks," pt. 1, ch. 12. Cf. Legge, p. 377.
[101] *ibid*., ch. 7. Cf. Legge, p. 360.

called a concrete thing.[102] It is also said, "Yin and yang are established as the Way of Heaven; the weak and the strong as the way of Earth; and humanity and righteousness as the Way of man."[103] It further says, "The successive movement of yin and yang constitutes the Way."[104] Yin and yang also exist after physical form, and yet here they are called the Way. This expression clearly distinguishes what exist before and after physical form. From the beginning the Way is nothing but this. The important thing is that man must in his own mind appreciate this truth. (11:1b)

45. "Heaven and earth have their fixed positions and yet the system of Change operates in them." This is nothing but seriousness. With seriousness, there will be no interruption. To form the substance of all things and nothing can be without it[105] means nothing but sincerity and seriousness, for "without sincerity there will be nothing."[106] The *Book of Odes* says, "The Mandate of Heaven, how beautiful and unceasing. How shining is it, the purity of King Wen's virtue!"[107] "Purity is also unceasing."[108] With purity, there will be no interruption. (11:2a)

46. "Seriousness is to straighten one's internal life and righteousness is to square one's external life." This is the way to unify internal and external life. (The Buddhist way of internal and external life is incomplete.)[109] (11:2a)

47. Between substance and function there is neither earlier nor later. (11:2b)

48. There is no division between Nature and man. (11:2b)

49. Seriousness overcomes all evil. (11:2b)

50. Mencius said, "Humanity is the distinguishing character of man. When embodied in man's conduct it is the Way."[110] This is what the *Doctrine of the Mean* means when it says that "to follow human nature is called the Way."[111] *Jen* is to humanize. "Seriousness is to strengthen the internal life and righteousness is to square the external life."[112] This means *jen*. If one purposely uses seriousness to straighten his internal life, it will not be straightened. Must one be [purposely] straight in the

---

[102] *ibid.*, ch. 12. Cf. Legge, p. 377.

[103] "Remarks on Certain Trigrams," ch. 2. Cf. Legge, p. 423.

[104] "Appended Remarks," pt. 1, ch. 5. Cf. Legge, p. 355.

[105] Quoting *The Mean*, ch. 16.

[106] *ibid.*, ch. 25.

[107] Ode no. 267. King Wen (r. 1171–1122 B.C.) was founder of the Chou dynasty.

[108] *The Mean*, ch. 26, commenting on the ode.

[109] Ch'eng's own note. The quotation is from *Changes*, commentary on hexagram no. 2, *k'un* (Earth). Cf. Legge, p. 426.

[110] *Mencius*, 7B:16.

[111] Ch. 1.

[112] *Changes*, commenting on hexagram no. 2, *k'un*. Cf. Legge, p. 420.

practice of humanity and righteousness? If one is "always doing something without expectation,"[113] one will be straight. For if one can practice seriousness to straighten the internal life and righteousness to square the external life, one can be harmonious with things. This is why it is said that "as seriousness and righteousness are established, one's virtue will not be an isolated instance."[114] Thus the man of *jen* has nothing in opposition to him. He can wander over the four seas and always hits the mark. (11:3a)

51. "The great characteristic of Heaven and Earth is to produce."[115] "In the fusion and intermingling of Heaven and Earth, the ten thousand things are transformed and attain their purity."[116] What is inborn is called one's nature. The most impressive aspect of things is their spirit of life. This is what is meant by origination being the chief quality of goodness.[117] This is *jen*. Man and Heaven and Earth are one thing. Why should man purposely belittle himself? (11:3a-b)[118]

52. Only because it is spirit that is swiftness without hurrying and arrives without having traveled.[119] Spirit is neither swift nor arrives. We speak of it in this way because otherwise we cannot describe it. (11:3b)

53. According to the Principle of Heaven and Earth and all things, nothing exists in isolation but everything necessarily has its opposite. All this is naturally so and is not arranged or manipulated. (11:3b)

54. The cold of winter and the heat of summer are due to yin and yang, and what causes movement and transformation is spirit. Spirit has no spatial restriction and Change itself has no physical form.[120] If someone should separately establish Nature and say that man cannot embrace it, there would be spatial restriction. There would be two bases. (11:3b)

55. "By thoroughly investigating spirit, transformation may be understood."[121] Spirit is the mystery of transformation. (11:3b)

56. The investigation of principle to the utmost, the full development of one's nature, and the fulfillment of destiny are one thing. (11:3b)

Comment. These three things remained for the Ch'eng brothers, as for practically all Neo-Confucianists, the chief objectives in their philosophy. In this they did not depart from the *Book of Changes*

---

[113] *Mencius*, 2A:2.

[114] *Changes, ibid.*

[115] *ibid.*, "Appended Remarks," pt. 2, ch. 1. Cf. Legge, p. 381.

[116] *ibid.*, ch. 5. Cf. Legge, p. 393.

[117] *Changes*, commentary on hexagram no. 1, *ch'ien* (Heaven). Cf. Legge, p. 408.

[118] In *Chu Tzu yü-lei*, 95:19a, Chu Hsi's pupil mistakenly ascribed this saying to Ch'eng I.

[119] *Changes*, "Appended Remarks," pt. 1, ch. 10. Cf. Legge, p. 370.

[120] *ibid.*, ch. 4. Cf. Legge, 354.

[121] *ibid.*, pt. 2, ch. 5. Cf. Legge, p. 390.

from which these concepts have been derived.[122] However, whereas in the *Book of Changes* and in Chang Tsai, for example, the fulfillment of destiny always follows the two other steps,[123] the Ch'eng brothers stressed their simultaneity. They were the first ones to do so. But Chang criticized them as too high sounding, for according to him, the full development of nature involves the nature not only of oneself but of all men and even things, and therefore there must be a sequence.[124]

57. "Heaven and earth have their fixed positions and yet the system of Change operates in them."[125] This is because of spirit. (11:4a)

58. There is no spirit outside of material force and there is no material force outside of spirit. If it is said that the pure is spirit, does it mean that the turbid is not spirit? (11:4a)

59. When one says that there is non-being, the word "is" is superfluous. When one says that there is not being, the term "is not" is superfluous. Being and non-being are comparable to activity and tranquillity. Before winter solstice, when heaven and earth seem to close up, tranquillity prevails, and yet the sun, the moon, and the stars move by themselves without cease. Can it be said to be without activity? Only people do not understand the true nature of being and non-being, and activity and tranquillity! (11:4a)

60. Loyalty and faithfulness are spoken of with reference to man. Essentially, they are concrete principles. (11:4a)

61. The principle of the Mean is perfect. Nothing can be produced with yin or yang alone. Those who possess them partially are animals and barbarians, while those who possess them in balanced proportions are men. (11:4b)

62. All things have their principle. It is easy for a thing to function if it is in accord with principle but difficult if it violates it. When everything follows its own principle, what is the necessity of one's own hard toil? (11:5a)

63. Every human mind possesses knowledge. Only when it is obscured by human desires does it forget the Principle of Nature.[126] (11:5a)

64. All the myriad things have their opposites. When there is yin,

---

[122] "Remarks on Certain Trigrams," ch. 1. Cf. Legge, p. 422.

[123] See Chang's *Cheng-meng* (Correcting Youthful Ignorance), ch. 6, in *Chang Heng-ch'ü chi* (Collected Works of Chang Tsai), *Cheng-i-t'ang ch'üan-shu* ed., 3:5a.

[124] See *I-shu*, 10:5a.

[125] *Changes*, "Appended Remarks," pt. 1, ch. 7. Cf. Legge, p. 360.

[126] The text has "virtue" but one version has "principle." It is used here for the contrast between human desires and the Principle of Nature that was to play a great role in the controversy among Neo-Confucianists.

there is yang. When there is good, there is evil. As yang increases, yin decreases, and as goodness is augmented, evil is diminished. This principle can be extended far and wide. Man only needs to know this principle. (11:5a-b)

65. *Jen* means to devote oneself to the benefit of other people and things. Altruism means putting oneself in their position. Conscientiousness and altruism form the central thread running through all conduct. Conscientiousness is the Principle of Nature whereas altruism is the way of man. Conscientiousness is unerring and altruism is the way to practice that conscientiousness. Conscientiousness is substance, while altruism is function. They are the great foundation and universal way of life. (11:5b)

66. To be sincere is the way of Heaven (Nature). To be serious is the basis of human affairs. (Seriousness is function.)[127] One who is serious will be sincere. (11:7b)

67. To use oxen for carts and horses for chariots is to do so in accordance with their nature. Why not use oxen for chariots and horses for carts? Because principle does not permit this. (11:8a)

68. "All things are already complete in oneself. There is no greater joy than to examine oneself and be sincere (or absolutely real).[128] If one lacks sincerity, one will violate the principle of things and will not be in harmony with them. (11:9a)

69. The Mean is the great foundation of the universe. It is the correct principle of all under heaven which is central and straight. Any deviation from it is wrong. Only when one cultivates it with seriousness without fail can one fully preserve it. (11:11a)

70. Nature is identical with principle. By spirit is meant the mystery of the ten thousand things. The Lord is so-called because it is the master of things. (11:11b)

71. "Heaven produced the virtue that is in me."[129] "Since the death of King Wen, is not the course of culture (*wen*) in my keeping?"[130] In saying this the Sage absolutely and decisively based it on principle. (11:11b)

> *Comment.* It had always been understood that Confucius was thinking of fate (*ming*, destiny) but Ch'eng Hao substituted principle for it. This testifies to the rationalism in Neo-Confucian thought.

72. Principle and righteousness are substance and function, respectively. (11:12a)

---

[127] Ch'eng's own note.　　[128] *Mencius*, 7A:4.
[129] *Analects*, 7:22.　　[130] *ibid.*, 9:5.

73. Men are born with the endowment of the Mean from Heaven and Earth. This is what is meant by "What Heaven imparts to man is called human nature."[131] [When Confucius said], "Man is born with uprightness,"[132] he meant the same. (12:1a)

74. With reference to what is called centrality (the Mean), if it means the center of a square, then is there no centrality in the four sides? If centrality means the middle between the inside and outside, then is there no centrality on the outside? "Change means production and re-production. . . ."[133] Thus can we only consider the *Book of Changes* to be Change! Let us call what is central, central, but we must not hold on to that point as centrality. (12:1a)

75. Even sweeping the floor and answering questions belong to the realm of what exists before physical form, for in principle there is neither great nor small. Therefore the superior man should simply be watchful over himself when alone. (13:1b)

76. The Buddhists do not understand yin and yang, day and night, life and death, or past and present. How can it be said that their meta-physics is the same as that of the Sage? (14:1b)

77. The Sage extends his mind of impartiality and exhausts the principle of Heaven, Earth, and all things to the utmost, each according to its proper function. But the Buddhists are all devoted to their own selfishness. How can their doctrines be the same as that of the Sage? The Sage follows principle and therefore his doctrines are even, straight and can easily be practiced. But the machination of the heterodox school re-quires so much effort. It is not natural. Therefore it is far, far wrong. (14:2a)

> *Comment.* Like other Neo-Confucianists, Ch'eng Hao was not unattracted to Buddhism at first. As pointed out before, he "went in and out of the Taoist and Buddhist Schools for almost ten years,"[134] and once when he visited a Buddhist temple and saw the marvelous etiquette, he exclaimed, "All the decorum of the Three Dynasties[135] is found here!" But he must not be made to ap-pear Buddhistic as Tokiwa has done.[136] After all he was a severe

---

[131] *The Mean*, ch. 1.   [132] *Analects*, 6:17.

[133] *Changes*, "Appended Remarks," pt. 1, ch. 5. Cf. Legge, p. 356.

[134] See above, Introduction.   [135] Hsia, Shang, and Chou.

[136] Tokiwa Daijō, *Shina ni okeru bukkyō to jukyō dōkyō* (Buddhism in Re-lation to Confucianism and Taoism in China), 1930. Here Ch'eng's doctrine of calming one's nature is considered as a result of his understanding, though not experience, of Buddhism, and his doctrine of "there is nothing outside the Way and there is no Way outside of things" (sec. 32) as similar to the Buddhist doc-trine that matter and emptiness are identical! (pp. 277, 297)

critic of Buddhism. To him, the Buddhists were selfish, limited, and partisan in their views, incapable of handling human affairs, and threatening people with the cycle of birth and death.[137] While he offered no unusual argument, his antagonism is unmistakable.

[137] *I-shu*, 13:1a-b.

32

THE RATIONALISTIC TENDENCY IN CH'ENG I

THE GREAT IMPORTANCE of Ch'eng I (Ch'eng I-ch'uan, 1033-1107) and his elder brother Ch'eng Hao (Ch'eng Ming-tao, 1032-1085) in the history of Chinese philosophy, the origin of their ideas, and their fundamental agreement in their basic concept of principle (*li*) have been dealt with in the previous chapter. As indicated there, with reference to principle, while Ch'eng Hao emphasizes its aspect of production and reproduction, Ch'eng I emphasizes the aspect of the harmony of one and many. His saying, "Principle is one but its manifestations are many,"[1] has become one of the most celebrated philosophical statements in China. It also sums up Neo-Confucian metaphysics in brief.[2] There is a strong probability that the idea came from Buddhism, particularly the Hua-yen School, for its similarity to the Hua-yen doctrine of harmony of principle and facts is too close to be dismissed as coincidence.[3]

As to the relation between principle and material force (*ch'i*), it is popular to contrast Ch'eng I as dualistic and Ch'eng Hao as monistic. It is true that Ch'eng Hao said, "There is no spirit outside of material force and there is no material force outside of spirit,"[4] while Ch'eng I said material force exists after physical form [and is therefore with it] whereas the Way exists before form [and is therefore without it].[5] But Ch'eng I also said that there is no yin or yang (material forces or passive and active cosmic forces) outside the Way.[6] For him the two realms are not widely separate or sharply different. As he said, "What makes [the material force] yin or yang is the Way."[7] In other words, principle and material force are merely two aspects. Whatever dualism there may be, it is superficial.

Fung Yu-lan has asserted that to Ch'eng I, principle is comparable to the "idea" or "form" in ancient Greek philosophy, whereas to Ch'eng Hao, it is "nothing more than the natural tendency or force inherent in any concrete object."[8] In view of their common ideas of principle, it is difficult to understand this diametric opposition. Carsun Chang is right in taking Fung to task.[9] As Chang has pointed out, both brothers main-

[1] See secs. 2 and 75; also *Ts'ui-yen* (Pure Words), 1:23b-24a, in ECCS.

[2] For the application of the theory to Chinese ethics, see above, ch. 30, comment on sec. 1.

[3] See above, ch. 25, Introduction; A, 7; B, 1; B, 2, (1).

[4] See above, ch. 31, sec. 58.   [5] See sec. 36.   [6] *ibid.*   [7] *ibid.*

[8] *History of Chinese Philosophy*, vol. 2, pp. 507-508.

[9] *Development of Neo-Confucian Thought*, pp. 192-194.

tained that the Way cannot be found outside of material force. A thing involves both the corporeal (material force) and incorporeal (principle) aspects. This is what Ch'eng I meant by one manifesting as many.

It should be apparent that while the Ch'eng brothers resemble Chang Tsai (Chang Heng-ch'ü, 1020-1077) in emphasizing material force, with them it is no longer the basis of existence as with Chang[10] but only the corporeal aspect. Also, while Chang conceived material force to be perpetual contraction and expansion, to the Ch'eng brothers each operation is new. This is a new note in Chinese philosophy, a note more strongly struck by Ch'eng I than by his brother. Again and again he underlines the fact that in each new production fresh material force is used. Thus as the universe is a perpetual process of production and reproduction, new material force is perpetually generated by Origination. But exactly how this process works has never been explained.

To both brothers this creative process is jen. To Ch'eng Hao, jen is a matter of feeling, but Ch'eng I conceives it to be a seed that grows.[11] This obviously reflects his idea of the universe as production and reproduction. It also indicates that while Ch'eng Hao is more subjective and tends toward the internal, Ch'eng I tends to the external as well and is more objective. In his emphasis on seriousness (ching),[12] he seems to stress the internal as does Ch'eng Hao, although for both of them "Seriousness to straighten the internal life and righteousness to square the external life" must go hand in hand. However, while Ch'eng Hao more or less concentrates on self-cultivation, Ch'eng I insists that self-cultivation and the extension of knowledge must be pursued at the same time. Here lies perhaps the greatest divergence between the two brothers. Ch'eng Hao said very little about the investigation of things. Ch'eng I, on the contrary, makes the investigation of things a cardinal concept in his system. Besides, for Ch'eng Hao, the investigation of things means to correct the mind of bad habits, but for Ch'eng I it means inductive and deductive study and handling human affairs, for, according to him, everything, however small, contains principle and is to be investigated. This is the rationalistic spirit that characterizes his whole philosophy and later that of his follower, Chu Hsi (1130-1200), so that their school, called the Ch'eng-Chu School, may properly be called the Rationalistic School.

The two brothers are as widely different in temperament as can be imagined. Ch'eng Hao was warm, always at ease, tolerant, agreeable, understanding, amiable, and never angry for as long as twenty years.

[10] For Chang, see above, ch. 30, secs. 2-9, 16, 30, 36, 42, and 43.

[11] See above, ch. 31, sec. 11, and ch. 32, sec. 42. See also comment on the latter For comments on the term jen, see Appendix.

[12] For a discussion on this term, see Appendix.

Ch'eng I, on the other hand, was stern, grave, straight, not hesitating to shout at people, and so strong in self control that when the boat in which he was riding was about to sink, he was not disturbed at all. Perhaps the most dramatic event that shows the differences between the two brothers is that once when they entered a hall, all people followed Ch'eng Hao on one side but none followed Ch'eng I on the other.[13]

Both brothers exerted a tremendous influence on the philosophical and political thinking of their time, having, as they did, prominent official scholars as their followers. Ch'eng I's influence was comparatively greater because he enjoyed a long life. Although he declined high official positions, he openly and freely criticized those in power and in this way was to no small degree responsible for the rise of bitter struggle between his and opposing parties.[14] His teachings were prohibited most of the time from 1103, five years before his death, to 1155. The antagonism of the rulers against his moralistic lectures was so strong that only four people were courageous enough to attend his funeral.[15] However, his philosophy contained too many sound ideas to be suppressed forever. By 1155, Chu Hsi was already twenty-five years old. Within a decade, he was already expounding a philosophy that made him Ch'eng I's greatest follower. The Ch'eng-Chu School developed rapidly.

[13] *Wai-shu* (Additional Works), 11:5b, 12:3b, 5b, 6b, in ECCS; *I-Lo yüan-yüan lu* (Record of the Origin of the School of the Two Ch'engs), *Cheng-i-t'ang ch'üan-shu* (Complete Library of the Hall of Rectifying the Way) ed., 2:15a, 4:15a.

[14] Ch'eng I's courtesy name was Cheng-shu. Because he and his brother lived in the I River area in Honan, he was called Master I-ch'uan (I River). In 1056 he and his brother entered the national university where he was so outstanding that a schoolmate treated him as a teacher. At twenty-five (1057) he memorialized the emperor to practice the Confucian kingly way. Two years later he obtained the "presented scholar" degree. He lived and taught in Lo-yang, and repeatedly declined high offices, including a professorship at the directorate of education in 1085. In 1086 he was appointed expositor in waiting, and he lectured in great seriousness on Confucian principles to the emperor. He did this for twenty months and attracted many followers. But his uncompromising attitude, his critical opinions, and his attack on many things created bitter enemies, particularly Su Shih (Su Tung-po, 1036-1101), leader of the Szechuan group. This led to the bitter factional struggle between it and the Lo-yang group led by Ch'eng I. In 1087 he was appointed director of the directorate of education in the western capital but resigned a few months later. When he was supervisor of the directorate in 1092, censors repeatedly petitioned for his impeachment. He finally resigned and returned to Lo-yang. In 1097 his teachings were prohibited, his land was confiscated, and he was banished to Fu-chou in modern Szechuan. He was pardoned three years later and resumed his position at the directorate. By that time, government persecution of factions had become severe. Both he and Su Shih, along with several hundred scholars, were blacklisted. His followers left him. In 1103 his books were destroyed and teachings prohibited. He was pardoned again in 1106, a year before he died. See *Sung shih* (History of the Sung Dynasty, 960-1279), PNP, 427:10a-15b, Yao Ming-ta, *Ch'eng I-ch'uan nien-p'u* (Chronological Biography of Ch'eng I), 1937, and Bruce, *Chu Hsi and His Masters*, pp. 45-47.

[15] Yao Ming-ta, *Ch'eng I-ch'uan nien-p'u*, pp. 262, 273-283.

Below are selections of Ch'eng I's sayings covering various subjects as follows:[16]

Buddhism and Taoism: 23, 25, 50-55
Good and Evil: 58, 63, 66, 71
Investigation of things: 14, 16, 17, 31, 44, 47, 62
Jen (humanity): 6, 7, 28, 40-42, 71, 74
Knowledge: 4, 11, 38, 67, 68
Material force (*ch'i*): 12, 13, 21, 33, 35-37, 39, 63
Mind: 3, 58, 64
Moral cultivation: 1, 15, 18, 20, 24, 45, 56
Nature and Destiny: 8, 12, 49, 58-61, 63, 66, 67, 72
Principle (*li*): 2, 17, 18, 24, 31, 34, 47, 48, 58, 62, 66, 75-77
Production and reproduction: 21, 22, 39, 64, 70
Seriousness (*ching*): 5, 9, 15, 29, 32, 43, 45, 46
Spiritual forces: 65, 70, 73, 78
Way (Tao): 10, 13, 22, 26, 30, 33, 36, 57, 69, 73, 78

THE COMPLETE WORKS OF THE TWO CH'ENGS[17]

1. A Treatise on What Yen Tzu[18] Loved to Learn

When Master Ch'eng studied at the national university as a young man [1056],[19] Hu An-ting (Hu Yüan, 993-1059) examined his students on this subject. When he read this treatise, he was greatly amazed. He immediately asked to meet him and forthwith appointed him to an academic position.[20]

In the school of Confucius, there were three thousand pupils. Yen Tzu alone was praised as loving to learn. It is not that the three thousand scholars had not studied and mastered the Six Classics such as the *Book of Odes* and the *Book of History*. Then what was it that Yen Tzu alone loved to learn? *Answer*: It was to learn the way of becoming a sage.

Can one become a sage through learning? *Answer*: Yes. What is the way to learn? *Answer*: From the essence of life accumulated in Heaven and Earth, man receives the Five Agents (Water, Fire, Wood, Metal, and Earth) in their highest excellence. His original nature is pure and tranquil. Before it is aroused, the five moral principles of his nature, called humanity, righteousness, propriety, wisdom, and faithfulness, are

---

[16] All the sayings are from ECCS.

[17] For this work, see above, ch. 31, n.21.

[18] Yen Hui, Confucius' favorite pupil. Confucius once remarked that the pupil loved learning more than anyone else. See *Analects*, 6:2.

[19] Chu Hsi said that this was written when Ch'eng I was eighteen, that is, in 1060. See *Chu Tzu yü-lei* (Classified Conversations of Chu Hsi), 1880 ed., 93:9a. Yao Ming-ta, however, in his *Ch'eng I-ch'uan nien-p'u*, p. 16, contends with convincing evidence that the date was 1056.

[20] This note is in the text.

complete. As his physical form appears, it comes into contact with external things and is aroused from within. As it is aroused from within, the seven feelings, called pleasure, anger, sorrow, joy, love, hate, and desire, ensue. As feelings become strong and increasingly reckless, his nature becomes damaged. For this reason the enlightened person controls his feelings so that they will be in accord with the Mean. He rectifies his mind and nourishes his nature. This is therefore called turning the feelings into the [original] nature. The stupid person does not know how to control them. He lets them loose until they are depraved, fetter his nature, and destroy it. This is therefore called turning one's nature into feelings.

The way to learn is none other than rectifying one's mind and nourishing one's nature. When one abides by the Mean and correctness and becomes sincere, he is a sage. In the learning of the superior man, the first thing is to be clear in one's mind and to know where to go[21] and then act vigorously in order that one may arrive at sagehood. This is what is meant by "sincerity resulting from enlightenment."[22]

Therefore the student must exert his own mind to the utmost. If he does so, he will know his own nature. And if he knows his own nature, examines his own self and makes it sincere, he becomes a sage. Therefore the "Great Norm" says, "The virtue of thinking is penetration and profundity. . . . Penetration and profundity lead to sageness."[23] The way to make the self sincere lies in having firm faith in the Way. As there is firm faith in the Way, one will put it into practice with determination. When one puts it into practice with determination, he will keep it securely. Then humanity, righteousness, loyalty, and faithfulness will never depart from his heart. In moments of haste, he acts according to them. In times of difficulty or confusion, he acts according to them.[24] And whether he is at home or outside, speaking or silent, he acts according to them. As he holds on to them for a long time without fail, he will then be at home with them and in his movements and expressions, he will always be acting in a proper manner, and no depraved thought will arise in him. This is the reason why Yen Tzu, in his behavior, "did not see what was contrary to propriety, did not listen to what was contrary to propriety, did not speak what was contrary to propriety, and did not make any movement which was contrary to propriety."[25] Confucius praised him, saying, "When he got hold of one thing that was good, he clasped it firmly, as if wearing it on his breast, and never lost it."[26] He also said, "[Hui] did not transfer his anger; he did not repeat a mistake."[27] "Whenever he did anything wrong, he never

---

[21] One version has "what to nourish."   [22] *The Mean*, ch. 21.
[23] *History*, "Great Norm." Cf. translation by Legge, *Shoo King*, p. 327.
[24] *Analects*, 4:5.   [25] *ibid.*, 12:1.
[26] *The Mean*, ch. 8.   [27] *Analects*, 6:2.

failed to realize it. Having realized it, he never did it again."[28] This is the way he earnestly loved and learned.

All [Yen Hui's] seeing, listening, speaking, and movement were in accord with propriety. Therein he differed from a sage in that whereas a sage "apprehends without thinking, hits upon what is right without effort, and is easily and naturally in harmony with the Way,"[29] Yen Tzu had to think before apprehending, and had to make an effort before hitting upon what was right. Hence it has been said, "The difference between Yen Tzu and the sage is as little as a moment of breathing."[30]

Mencius said, "He [whose goodness] is abundant and is brilliantly displayed is called a great man. When one is great and is completely transformed [to be goodness itself], he is called a sage. When a sage is beyond our knowledge, he is called a man of the spirit."[31] The virtue of Yen Tzu may be said to be abundant and brilliantly displayed. What was lacking in him was that he held on to [goodness] but was not yet completely transformed [into goodness itself]. Since he loved to learn, had he lived longer,[32] he would have achieved transformation in a short time. Therefore Confucius said, "[Hui] unfortunately lived a short life."[33] Confucius was lamenting the fact that he did not reach the state of the sage.

What is meant by being transformed [to be goodness itself] is to enter into the spirit and be natural with it, so that one can apprehend without thinking and hit upon what is right without effort. When Confucius said, "At seventy I could follow my heart's desire without transgressing moral principles," he meant this.[34]

Someone asks: A sage is one who is born with knowledge. Now you say that sagehood can be achieved through learning. Is there any basis for this contention? *Answer*: Yes, Mencius said, "Sage-emperors Yao and Shun[35] [practiced humanity and righteousness] because of their nature, and Kings T'ang and Wu[36] [practiced them] because of their effort to return (to their nature)."[37] Those who do so by nature are those born with the knowledge (of the good), and those who return to their nature are those who obtain knowledge (of the good) through learning. It is also said, "Confucius was born with such knowledge but Mencius

[28] *Changes*, "Appended Remarks," pt. 2, ch. 5. Cf. translation by Legge, *Yi King*, p. 392.

[29] *The Mean*, ch. 20.

[30] This is probably Ch'eng I's own statement. In *Ch'eng I-ch'uan nien-p'u*, p. 17, this saying is not in quotation marks while actual quotations are.

[31] *Mencius*, 7B:25.   [32] He died at thirty-two.

[33] *Analects*, 6:2.   [34] *Analects*, 2:4.

[35] Legendary rulers (3rd millennium B.C.).

[36] Founders of the Shang (1751–1112 B.C.) and Chou (1111–249 B.C.) dynasties, respectively.

[37] *Mencius*, 7A:30.

obtained it through learning."[38] Not understanding the true meaning of this, in later years people thought that sagehood was basically due to inborn knowledge (of the good) and could not be achieved through learning. Consequently the way to learn has been lost to us. Men do not seek within themselves but outside themselves and engage in extensive learning, effortful memorization, clever style, and elegant diction, making their words elaborate and beautiful. Thus few have arrived at the Way. This being the case, the learning of today and the learning that Yen Tzu loved are quite different. (*I-ch'uan wen-chi*, 4:1a-2a)

2. Letter in Reply to Yang Shih's[39] Letter on the Western Inscription

The opinions expressed in the ten essays on history which you sent me are quite correct. Soon after I looked at them, they were borrowed from me. I shall have to read them again carefully. Your opinions on the "Western Inscription," however, are incorrect. It is true that Chang Tsai has sometimes gone too far in what he says, notably in his *Cheng-meng* (Correcting Youthful Ignorance).[40] As a written work, however, the "Western Inscription" extends principle to cover all in order to preserve righteousness (what is correct and proper in specific social relations), thus expounding on something that previous sages has not expressed. In this his contribution is equal to that of Mencius' doctrines on the original goodness of human nature and on nourishing the strong moving power.[41] (Both of these had also not been expressed by previous sages.)[42] How can there be any comparison with Mo Tzu (fl. 479–438 B.C.)? The "Western Inscription" makes it clear that principle is one but its manifestations are many, but Mo Tzu's teachings involve two bases without differentiation. (To treat the elders in one's own family with respect and the young with tenderness and then extend that respect and tenderness to include the elders and young in other families shows that principle is one, whereas Mo Tzu's doctrine of universal love without distinction means that there are two bases [one's own parents as the source of life and also other people's parents]). The fault of

[38] Probably referring to *Mencius*, 2A:2. It is not a quotation from any work. In his translation of the treatise, P. C. Hsü omitted the phrase "It is also said" (*Ethical Realism in Neo-Confucian Thought*, p. xviii).

[39] Yang Kuei-shan (1053-1135) was one of the outstanding pupils of the Ch'eng brothers and a prominent Neo-Confucianist. For an account of him and his thought, see Forke, *Geschichte der neueren chinesischen Philosophie*, pp. 104-110; also Huang Tsung-hsi (1610-1695) *et al.*, *Sung-Yüan hsüeh-an* (Anthology and Critical Accounts of the Neo-Confucianists of the Sung and Yüan Dynasties, 960-1368), ch. 25. Yang's letter to Ch'eng is found in the *Yang Kuei-shan Hsiensheng chi* (Collected Works of Master Yang Shih), 1707 ed., 16:6a-b. For the "Western Inscription," see above, ch. 30, A.

[40] See above, ch. 30, B.   [41] *Mencius*, 6A:2, 2A:2.

[42] This and the following sentence in parentheses are Ch'eng's own insertions.

having [only] the many manifestations [that is, distinctions in human relations but no universal principle underlying them] is that selfishness will dominate and humanity (*jen*) will be lost. On the other hand, the sin of having no manifestations is that there will be universal love for all without righteousness. To establish the many manifestations and to extend the one principle in order to check the tendency of being dominated by selfishness, is the method of *jen*. To make no distinction in human relations and to be deluded in universal love to the extreme of recognizing no special relationship with the father,[43] is to do violent injury to righteousness. You are mistaken in comparing and equating them. Furthermore, you said that the "Western Inscription" speaks of substance [*jen*] without including function [its specific application in various human relations according to righteousness]. But its intention is to enable people to extend [principle] and put it into practice. The purpose is primarily for its function (practice). And yet you said that it does not include function. How strange! (*ibid.*, 5:12b)

SELECTED SAYINGS[44]

3. The mind of one man is one with the mind[45] of Heaven and Earth. The principle of one thing is one with the principle of all things. The course of one day is one with the course of a year. (2A:1a)

4. True knowledge and ordinary knowledge are different. I once saw a farmer who had been wounded by a tiger. When someone said that a tiger was hurting people, everyone was startled. But in his facial expression the farmer reacted differently from the rest. Even a young boy knows that tigers can hurt people, but his is not true knowledge. It is true knowledge only if it is like the farmer's. Therefore when men know evil and still do it, this also is not true knowledge. If it were, they would surely not do it. (2A:2b-3a)*[46]

To devote oneself to investigate principle to the utmost does not mean that it is necessary to investigate the principle of all things in the world to the utmost nor does it mean that principle can be understood merely by investigating one particular principle. It is necessary to accumulate much and then one will naturally come to understand principle. (2A:22b)* CH[47]

---

[43] This is Mencius' criticism of Mo Tzu's doctrine of universal love. See *Mencius*, 3B:9.

[44] Unless otherwise indicated, all sayings are from the *I-shu*. See above, ch. 31, nn.21 and 39. Here the letters indicate that the sayings have been taken to be Ch'eng I's in the anthologies represented by the letters.

[45] One version has *t'i* (substance) instead of "mind."

[46] Ch'eng I said virtually the same thing in *I-shu* 15:4a. For an explanation of the asterisk, see above, ch. 31, n.39.

[47] For an explanation of this and other letters, see above, ch. 31, n.39.

5. Seriousness without fail is the state of equilibrium before the feelings of pleasure, anger, sorrow, and joy are aroused.[48] Seriousness is not equilibrium itself. But seriousness without fail is the way to attain equilibrium. (2A:23b)* s CH M[49]

6. With *jen* (humanity) there will be unity. Without *jen*, there will be duality. (3:3b)

7. The way of *jen* is difficult to describe. Impartiality alone is close to it. But impartiality is not identical with *jen*. (3:3b)

8. One's nature cannot be spoken of as internal or external. (3:4a)

9. Only after one forgets seriousness can he be serious at all times. (3:5b)

10. "The successive movement of yin and yang (passive and active cosmic forces) constitutes the Way (Tao)."[50] The Way is not the same as yin and yang but that by which yin and yang succeed each other. It is like Change, which is the succession of closing (contracting) and opening (expanding). (3:6a)

11. The source of learning is thought. (6:1a)* c

12. It would be incomplete to talk about the nature of man and things without including material force and unintelligible to talk about material force without including nature. (It would be wrong to consider them as two.)[51] (6:2a)* c s

13. All that has physical form is identical with material force. Only the Way is formless. (6:2b)* M

14. The extension of knowledge consists in the investigation of things.[52] As things approach, knowledge will arise. Leave things as they are and do not labor your knowledge of them. Then you will be sincere and not disturbed. As the will is sincere, it will naturally be calm and the mind will be rectified. This is the task of beginning to learn. (6:3b)* s

15. If one concentrates on one thing and does not get away from it and be serious in order to straighten the internal life, he will possess strong, moving power. (15:1a)

16. If one extends knowledge to the utmost, one will have wisdom. Having wisdom, one can then make choices. (15:1a)

17. A thing is an event. If the principles underlying the event are investigated to the utmost, there all principles will be understood. (15:-1a)

---

[48] *The Mean*, ch. 1.

[49] It is not clear whether this saying is assigned to Ch'eng I or Ch'eng Hao in Chu Hsi's *Chin-ssu lu* (Reflections on Things at Hand), ch. 4, but Chu Hsi in his *Chu Tzu wen-chi* (Collection of Literary Works by Chu Tzu), CTTC, 64:29a, quotes part of this as Ch'eng I's.

[50] *Changes*, "Appended Remarks," pt. 1, ch. 5. Cf. Legge, *Yi King*, p. 355.

[51] Ch'eng's own note. See above, ch. 31, n.92.

[52] Quoting the text of the *Great Learning*.

18. If one does not look, listen, speak, or move in violation of principle, that is propriety, for propriety is none other than principle. What is not of the Principle of Nature (*T'ien*, Heaven) is of human (selfish) desire. In that case, even if one has the intention to do good, it will still be contrary to propriety. When there is no human (selfish) desire, then all will be the Principle of Nature. (15:1b)

19. Where there is impartiality, there is unity, and where there is partiality, there is multiplicity. The highest truth is always revolved into a unity, and an essential principle is never a duality. If people's minds are as different as their faces are, it is solely due to partiality. (15:1b)

20. In nourishing the mind there is nothing better than having few desires. Without desires, there will be no delusion. One does not need to be submerged in desires. Merely to have the intention is already desire. (15:2b)

21. If we say that the material force which has already returned [to Nature] must be needed to become once more the expanding material force, such a theory would be entirely at odds with the transformation of Heaven and Earth. The transformation of Heaven and Earth naturally produces and reproduces without end. What is the need for any physical form that has perished or material force that has returned [to Nature] to constitute creation? Let us take an example near at hand in our own body. The opening and closing, going and coming [of the material or vital force] can be seen in breathing. It is not necessary to depend on inhaling the already exhaled breath for the second time in order to breathe out. Material (vital) force naturally produces it. The material force of man is produced from the true source (*chen-yüan*, true origin). The material force of Nature also naturally produces and reproduces without end. Take, for example, the case of tides. They dry up because yang (the sun) is very strong. When yin (the moon) is strong and tides are produced, it is not that the dried-up water is used to produce them. They are produced by themselves. Going and coming, and expansion and contraction, are but principle. As there is growth, there is decline; as there is morning, there is evening; and as there is going, there is coming. The universe is like a vast furnace. What cannot be burned up? (15:4b-5a)

22. The Way spontaneously produces all things. What has grown in the spring and what has matured in the summer are all productions of the Way. When things grow in the next season, we should not say that the material force already used for production now produces again. It is the Way that spontaneously produces and reproduces without end. (15:5b)

Comment. The significance of this new idea of the universe as production and reproduction has been indicated.[53] Where did this idea come from? The idea that the characteristic of Heaven and Earth is to give life comes from the *Book of Changes.*[54] But why did it suddenly occur with the Ch'eng brothers after having been dormant for a thousand years? In all likelihood, Chou Tun-i's love of life and, through his influence, Ch'eng Hao's love of the spirit of life certainly had something to do with it. Perhaps the Buddhist doctrine of "seeds" was a contributing factor. According to the Consciousness-Only School of Buddhism, the mind is a storehouse of "seeds" or effects of good and evil deeds which exist from time immemorial and become the energy to produce manifestations that make up the world. The Ch'engs had been for years interested in Buddhism, and it is not unreasonable to suppose that the idea of the generative "seeds" might have made some impression on them although there is no concrete evidence to prove the point.[55] The most important factor, however, is the fact that the idea of "sustaining and supporting the life of one another" had been a long tradition in the Confucian School. Han Yü (768-824) brought it to the fore when he attacked Buddhism and Taoism in his celebrated essay, *Yüan-tao* (An Inquiry on the Way). From that idea it was a logical step to the concept of giving life or production and reproduction, not only as way of man's life, but of the universe as well.[56] All these ideas are expressed by the word *sheng.*

23. The doctrines of Buddhism are not worthy of matching the doctrines of our Sage. One need only compare them and having observed that they are different, leave Buddhism alone. If one tries to investigate all its theories, it is probably an impossible task. Before one has done that, he will already have been transformed into a Buddhist. But let us take a look at Buddhism from the point of view of facts. In deserting his father and leaving his family, the Buddha severed all human relationships. It was merely for himself that he lived alone in the forest. Such a person should not be allowed in any community. Generally speaking, he did to others what he himself despised. Such is not the mind of the sage, nor is it the mind of a superior man. The Buddhists themselves will not abide by the principles of the relationship between the ruler and minister, between father and son, and between husband and wife, and criticize

---

[53] See above, ch. 31, comment on sec. 19.

[54] "Appended Remarks," pt. 2, ch. 1. Cf. trans. by Legge, p. 381.

[55] See above, ch. 23, comment on sec. 3.

[56] For a more lengthy discussion of the idea, see Chan, "The Neo-Confucian Solution of the Problem of Evil," *Studies Presented to Hu Shih on His Sixty-fifth Birthday,* pp. 787-791.

others for not doing as they do. They leave these human relationships to others and have nothing to do with them. They set themselves apart as a special class. If this is the way to lead the people, it will be the end of the human race. As to their discourse on principle and the nature of things, it is primarily for the sake of life and death. Their feelings are basically love of life and fear of death. This is selfishness. (15:5b)

24. If one guards against depravity, that of course constitutes [con-concentration on][57] one thing. But if one concentrates on one thing, there will be no need to speak of being on guard against depravity. There are some who think that singlemindedness is difficult to recognize and not easy to work for, and do not know what to do. Singlemindedness is nothing but orderliness and graveness. With these the mind will be concentrated. As it is concentrated, it will naturally not do anything wrong. If one cultivates the mind for a long time, the Principle of Nature will become clear to him. (15:6b)

25. You cannot say that the teachings of the Buddhists are ignorance, for actually they are extremely lofty and profound. But essentially speaking, they can finally be reduced to a pattern of selfishness. Why do we say this? In the world there cannot be birth without death or joy without sorrow. But wherever the Buddhists go, they always look for an opportunity to tell subtle falsehood and exercise deception, and to preach the elimination of birth and death and the neutralization of joy and sorrow. In the final analysis this is nothing but self-interest. The teachings of the Taoists even carry with them an element of treachery, as evidenced in their sayings that the purpose of giving is to take away and the purpose of opening is to close.[58] Furthermore, their general intention is to fool the people and to be wise themselves. When the ruler of Ch'in (221-206 B.C.) fooled his people, his tricks probably derived from the Taoists. (15:7b)

26. Within heaven and earth there is only the process of action and response. What else is there? (15:7b)

27. Empty and tranquil, and without any sign, and yet all things are luxuriantly present.[59] The state before there is any response to it is not an earlier one, and the state after there has been response to it is not a later one. It is like a tree one hundred feet high. From the root to the branches and leaves, there is one thread running through all. We should

[57] This appears in one version. [58] *Lao Tzu*, ch. 36.

[59] Many Japanese historians of Chinese philosophy have asserted that this saying is of Buddhist origin but none has given any direct reference. Yamazaki Ansai (1618-1682), in his essay on the saying (*Zoku Yamazaki Ansai zenshū*, or Supplement to the *Complete Works of Yamazaki Ansai*, pt. 2, pp. 78-86), has listed all quotations of this saying and discussions of it by Neo-Confucianists but did not say a word about its Buddhist origin. The *Daikanwa jiten* (Great Chinese-Japanese Dictionary), the fullest dictionary of its kind so far, gives Ch'eng I as its author and not any Buddhist.

not say that the state described above, which has neither form nor sign, depends on man to manipulate it when the occasion requires, in order to pull it into a track. Tracks are, after all, tracks.[60] Actually there is only one track.[61] [That is to say, all specific principles or tracks come from the same source.][62] (15:8a)

> *Comment.* The first sentence is one of the most important sayings by Ch'eng I, and has been much quoted and discussed. Chu Hsi said that the passage is "nothing more than an explanation of [Chou Tun-i's (1017-1073) dictum], 'The Ultimate of Non-being and also the Great Ultimate.' "[63] This was said in spite of the fact that Ch'eng I never mentioned the Great Ultimate once! Chu Hsi usually saw in the philosophy of the two Ch'engs more of Chou's philosophy than is justified.

28. Essentially speaking, the way of *jen* may be expressed in one word, namely, impartiality. However, impartiality is but the principle of *jen*; it should not be equated with *jen* itself. When one makes impartiality the substance of his person, that is *jen*. Because of his impartiality there will be no distinction between himself and others. Therefore a man of *jen* is a man of both altruism and love. Altruism is the application of *jen*, while love is its function. (15:8b)

29. "When you go abroad, behave to everyone as if you were receiving a great guest. Employ the people as if you were assisting at a great sacrifice."[64] [When Confucius said that], he meant nothing other than seriousness. Seriousness means unselfishness. As soon as one lacks seriousness, thousands of selfish desires arise to injure his humanity. (15:-9a)

30. In the state of absolute quiet and inactivity,[65] all things are luxuriantly present. When it is "acted upon and it immediately penetrates all things,"[66] the action is merely action from within. It is not that there is something outside with which to act on it. (15:9a)

31. To investigate things in order to understand principle to the utmost does not mean that it is necessary to investigate all things in the world. One has only to investigate the principle in one thing or one event to the utmost and the principle in other things or events can then be in-

---

[60] Interpretation according to Chu Hsi, *Chu Tzu yü-lei*, 95:22a.

[61] Chu Hsi thought that possibly the recorder of the saying missed some words, but he was not sure. *ibid.*, 95:22b.

[62] This is Chu Hsi's interpretation, *ibid.*, 95:22a.

[63] *ibid.*, 95:22b. For Chou's dictum, see above, ch. 28, sec. 1.

[64] *Analects*, 12:2.

[65] Quoting *Changes*, "Appended Remarks," pt. 1, ch. 10. Cf. Legge, *Yi King*, p. 370.

[66] *ibid.*

ferred. For example, when we talk about filial piety, we must find out what constitutes filial piety. If principle cannot be investigated to the utmost in one event, investigate another. One may begin with either the easy or the most difficult, depending on the degree of one's capacity. There are thousands of tracks and paths to go to the capital. Yet one can enter if he has found just one way. Principle can be investigated to the utmost [in this way] because all things share the same principle. Even the most insignificant of things and events has this principle. (15:-11a)

32. One who is serious is naturally vacuous (absolutely pure and peaceful, not being disturbed by incoming impression) and tranquil. But vacuity and tranquillity cannot be called seriousness. If one dwells in seriousness, one naturally behaves with an easy feeling. But if one "dwells in an easy feeling in order to carry it out in his practice,"[67] there will not be an easy feeling, for what he dwells in is already too excessive. (15:11a)

33. "The successive movement of yin and yang constitutes the Way."[68] This principle is very profound and cannot be explained. The Way is that through which yin and yang operate. The very term "material force" implies a duality and the very expression "opening and closing" implies one thing acting on another. Wherever there is a duality, there is always such an action. The Way is that through which opening and closing operate, and opening and closing are the same as yin and yang. It is wrong for the Taoists to say that material force comes from the vacuity. There is no time sequence in yin and yang or in opening and closing. It should not be said that there is yin today and yang tomorrow. Take, for example, man's body and shadow. As they are simultaneous, it should not be said that a man has his body today and his shadow tomorrow. To have them is to have them at the same time. (15:13b)

34. To know the Mandate of Heaven means to understand the Principle of Heaven (Nature). Surely to receive the mandate (*ming*, destiny) means to get the retribution of Heaven. Destiny is what has been decreed by Heaven. It is like a command. The retribution of Heaven is always like a shadow or an echo. It is normal to have its retribution and it is abnormal not to get the retribution. However, upon careful examination, we know that retribution is inevitable. Only because people seek it with shallow and limited views, they say that it is irregular. Furthermore, the Mandate of Heaven cannot be changed except by a man of virtue. (15:14a)

35. A meteor is not produced from any species; its species is the material force. Likewise, the unicorn is not produced from any species;

<hr />

[67] *Analects*, 6:1.
[68] *Changes*, "Appended Remarks," pt. 1, ch. 5. Cf. Legge, p. 355.

it is also evolved from material force. The same is true of the origin of man in the beginning. When, for example, a sandbank rises from the beach, many insects, animals, and plants will grow there. They are not produced from any species. This, however, is something we can see. But in a fairly large island away out in the sea where we cannot see, who knows that there are not men living there who were not produced from any species? Ever since mankind came into existence, however, surely no man has evolved from material force. (15:14b)

36. There is no Way independent of yin and yang. What makes [the material force] yin or yang is the Way. Yin and yang are material force. Material force is what exists after physical form [and is with it], whereas the Way is what exists before physical form [and is without it]. What exists before physical form is hidden. (15:14b-15a)

37. When a thing disintegrates, its material force is forthwith exhausted. There is no such thing as material force returning to its source. The universe is like a vast furnace. Even living things will be burned to the last and no more. How can material force that is already disintegrated still exist? Furthermore, what is the need of such a disintegrated material force in the creative process of the universe? It goes without saying that the force used in creation is vital and fresh. (15:15b)

38. When knowledge is profound, action will be thorough. No one ever knows without being able to act. If one knows without being able to act, the knowledge is superficial. Because they know the danger, people do not eat poisonous herbs when hungry and do not tread on water or fire. People do evil simply because they do not know. (15:16b)

Comment. Both Huang Tsung-hsi[69] and Sun Ch'i-feng (1584-1675)[70] maintained that Ch'eng I anticipated Wang Yang-ming's (Wang Shou-jen, 1472-1529) famous doctrine of the unity of knowledge and action.[71] However, Ch'eng merely says that true knowledge will lead to action but does not say that action leads to knowledge, as Wang does. It is significant to note, however, that the relationship between knowledge and action has always been of great concern to the Confucianists.[72] Ch'eng also distinguishes two types of knowledge, that obtained through information and that obtained through the exercise of moral nature,[73] thus echoing Chang Tsai.[74] This does not mean intuitive knowledge, but knowledge obtained through experience.[75]

[69] *Sung-Yüan hsüeh-an*, SPPY, 15:10a.
[70] *Li-hsüeh tsung-ch'uan* (Orthodox Transmission of Neo-Confucianism), 1880 ed., 3:17a.
[71] See below, ch. 35.
[72] See below, ch. 35, comment on sec. 5.
[73] See sec. 67.
[74] See above, ch. 30, secs. 20 and 59.
[75] See sec. 4.

39. The material force of the true source is the source from which material force is produced and is not mixed with external force. It is nourished and cultivated only by external force. It is like fish in water. The life and nature of fish are not made by the water, but they must be nourished and cultivated by water in order that they may live. Man's position in the force of the universe is not different from that of fish in water. As to the nourishment of food, it is a way in which man is nourished and cultivated by external force. And as to inhaling and exhaling of breath, it is only the operation of opening and closing. The breath that has just been exhaled is not the material force that is inhaled in the next breath. But the true source can create material force by itself. The material force that is inhaled simply enters the human body when the body closes. This material force is not needed to assist the true source. (15:17b)

40. When asked about humanity, the Teacher said: It is up to you gentlemen to think for yourselves, gather and examine what the sages and worthies have said about it, and personally realize what humanity is. Because Mencius said, "The feeling of commiseration is what we call humanity,"[76] later scholars have therefore considered love to be humanity. The feeling of commiseration is of course [an expression of] love. But love is feeling whereas humanity is the nature. How can love be taken exclusively as humanity? Mencius said that the feeling of commiseration is humanity because he had said that the feeling of commiseration is the beginning of humanity.[77] Since it is called the beginning of humanity, it should not be called humanity itself. It is wrong for Han Yü to say universal love is humanity.[78] A man of humanity of course loves universally. But one may not therefore regard universal love as humanity. (18:1a)

41. *Question*: "Filial piety and brotherly respect are the root of humanity."[79] Does that mean that *jen* can be achieved through filial piety and brotherly respect? *Answer*: No. It means that the practice of humanity begins with filial piety and brotherly respect. Filial piety and brotherly respect are items in the practice of humanity. It is all right to say that they are the root of the practice of humanity but not all right to say that they are the root of humanity itself. For humanity is nature,[80] while filial piety and brotherly respect are its function. There are in our nature only humanity, righteousness, propriety, and wisdom. Where

[76] *Mencius*, 6A:6.
[77] *ibid.*
[78] *Yüan-tao* (Inquiry on the Way), *Han Ch'ang-li ch'üan-chi* (Collected Works of Han Yu), SPPY, 11:1a. See above, ch. 27, sec. 2.
[79] *Analects*, 1:2.
[80] One edition has "the root" instead of "the nature."

do filial piety and brotherly respect come in?[81] The controlling factor of humanity is love, and there is no greater love than to love parents. Hence it is said, "Filial piety and brotherly respect are the root of *jen!*" (18:1b)

42. *Question*: What is the difference between *jen* and the mind? *Answer*: The mind is comparable to seeds of grain. The nature of growth is *jen*. (18:2a)

> *Comment*. The concept of *jen* has gone through many stages of development. From the earliest idea of *jen* as a specific virtue, notably benevolence, Confucius changed it to the general virtue (humanity). Throughout the ages it has been variously interpreted as affection, love, universal love, impartiality, consciousness, unity with Heaven and Earth, and so forth, but the idea that *jen* is "seed," which is life-giving, is a unique contribution of Ch'eng I. As such it brought the concept of *jen* to the highest stage of development up to this time. It is more than a pun on the word *jen*, meaning seed. It is the generative force of all virtues. It is this life-giving quality that enables man to form a unity with Heaven, Earth and all things and makes it possible for him to overcome evil. This is the reason why the Ch'eng brothers said that *jen* embraces the four virtues of righteousness, propriety, wisdom, and faithfulness instead of treating all five virtues on an equal basis and calling them the Five Constant Virtues as has been done in tradition.[82] Chu Hsi hits the right note in saying that *jen* embraces the four virtues because of its spirit of life and because it is originating.[83] No doubt the Ch'eng brothers' general concept of the universe as a process of production and reproduction has contributed to the idea.[84]

43. *Question*: What about people who devote all their effort to seriousness in order to straighten the internal life but make no effort to square the external life? *Answer*: What one has inside will necessarily be shown outside. Only worry that the internal life is not straightened. If it is straightened, then the external life will necessarily be square. (18:3a)

44. Someone asked what the first step was in the art of moral cultivation. *Answer*: The first thing is to rectify the mind and make the will sincere. The sincerity of the will depends upon the extension of knowledge and the extension of knowledge depends upon the investigation

[81] In the Chao edition, "Where do all these miscellaneous items come in?"
[82] See sec. 71. [83] *Chu Tzu yü-lei*, 6:8b-9a.
[84] See sec. 22. See also above, ch. 30, sec. 1; ch. 31, comment on secs. 1 and 11; ch. 34, comment on treatise 1; and, ch. 40, Introduction.

of things. The word *ko* (investigate) means to arrive, as it is used in the saying "the spirits of imperial progenitors have arrived."[85] There is principle in everything, and one must investigate principle to the utmost. There are many ways to do this. One way is to read books and elucidate moral principles. Another way is to discuss people and events of the past and present, and to distinguish which are right and which are wrong. Still another way is to handle affairs and settle them in the proper way. All these are ways to investigate the principle of things exhaustively.

Someone asked: In investigating things, is it necessary to investigate every thing or can one know all principles by investigating only one thing? *Answer*: How can one understand everything like this? Even Yen Tzu[86] would not dare say he could readily understand all principles by investigating only one thing. One must investigate one item today and another item tomorrow. When one has accumulated much knowledge he will naturally achieve a thorough understanding like a sudden release. (18:5b)

> *Comment*. The doctrine of the investigation of things is a cardinal one in the Ch'eng-Chu system. More will be said about it when we come to Chu Hsi.[87] At least three important observations can now be made. First, just as the Ch'eng brothers were the first ones in the history of Chinese philosophy to make principle the basis of their philosophy, so were they the first ones to employ the investigation of things as the method. Before the Sung dynasty (960-1279), no one had ever written an essay on the subject of the investigation of things. The first one to do so was Ssu-ma Kuang (1019-1086),[88] but the Ch'eng brothers were the first ones to use the investigation of things as an important means for moral cultivation.
>
> Secondly, he and Chu gave a new interpretation to the term *ko*. The term *ko-wu* of course comes from the *Great Learning*.[89] According to one source, from Han times (206 B.C.–A.D. 220) there have been seventy-two explanations of the term *ko-wu*.[90] Four of these have become prominent. The first is the interpretation by

---

[85] *History*, "I and Chi." Cf. Legge, *Shoo King*, p. 87.

[86] When he knew one part, he knew all about the subject. See *Analects*, 5:8.

[87] See below, ch. 34, comment on sec. 30.

[88] See his "A Treatise on the Extension of Things Consisting in the Investigation of Things," in the *Ssu-ma Wen Kung wen-chi* (Collection of Literary Works by Ssu-ma Kuang), SPPY, 13:66-72.

[89] The text.

[90] *Ching-i ts'ung-ch'ou* (Excerpts on the Meaning of the Classics), in *Huang-Ch'ing ching-chieh* (Explanations of Classics by Scholars of the Ch'ing Dynasty, 1644-1912), vol. 1388, p. 25a.

Cheng Hsüan (127-200), who took *ko* to mean to come, the idea being that when one's knowledge of the good is perfect, good things will come.[91] His interpretation became standard. The second interpretation was given by Ssu-ma Kuang, who asserted that *ko* meant to ward off or to resist. "Only when external things are warded off can ultimate truth be known," he said.[92] The third interpretation is that of rectification or *cheng* as used in the *Analects*[93] and the *Book of Mencius*.[94] The fourth interpretation is that of *ko* as a model or measure, as given in the *Yü-p'ien* (Book of Jade), a dictionary of A.D. 1386.[95] The important thing to note in these interpretations is that they are all ethical. Furthermore, they all have one thing in common, namely, they stressed the point that knowledge is to be achieved by the mind without the aid of external things. Ch'eng I and Chu Hsi, however, took a completely new approach. They understood *ko* as to arrive, but to arrive means to investigate to the utmost the principles of all things we come into contact with. The third observation is that the doctrine of the investigation of things has become a major tenet in all Neo-Confucian schools, although each interpreted it differently. As to whether it is scientific, the matter will be taken up when we comment on Chu Hsi.

45. Self-cultivation requires seriousness; the pursuit of learning depends on the extension of knowledge. (18:5b)

Comment. This represents the basic formula of Ch'eng's method of cultivation and is often quoted as a summary statement of his teachings. It bears a striking resemblance to the Buddhist twofold formula of meditation (*dhyāna*) and wisdom (*prajñā*). Perhaps Hu Shih has gone too far in calling it a new version of the Buddhist method.[96] But the similarity is unmistakable. It must be quickly added, however, that this formula has the rationalistic flavor totally absent in its Buddhist counterpart. Besides, even seriousness is to acquire meaning in the world of human affairs, quite different from the Buddhist inward, personal meditation.[97]

Huang Tsung-hsi said that Ch'eng Hao substituted seriousness for Chou Tun-i's tranquillity because he felt tranquillity was an

[91] In his commentary on the text of the *Great Learning*.

[92] *Ssu-ma Wen Kung wen-chi*, 13:72. This interpretation was followed by Yen Yüan (1635-1704). See below, ch. 37.

[93] *Analects*, 2:3.   [94] *Mencius*, 4A:20.

[95] *Yü-p'ien* (Book of Jade), SPPY, 2:13a.

[96] "Religion and Philosophy in Chinese Philosophy," in Sophia Zen, ed., *Symposium on Chinese Culture*, p. 57.

[97] See the next section.

extreme. Likewise, Ch'eng I felt that seriousness alone was not enough and therefore he supplemented it with the extension of knowledge.[98] This is a keen observation. It may be added that with regard to seriousness, while Ch'eng Hao is primarily concerned with the mental state of seriousness, Ch'eng I pays attention to its external aspect also, such as orderliness of dress. Even regarding the mental state, Ch'eng I offers more ideas, like guarding against depravity, concentration on one thing, and so forth.

46. *Someone asked*: Is it necessary to exert the will in order to be serious? *Answer*: In the beginning, how can one not exert the will? If it is possible not to exert the will, then there will be nothing. *Further question*: Is seriousness not tranquillity? *Answer*: As soon as you speak of tranquillity, you fall into the doctrine of Buddhism. Don't use the word "tranquillity." Only use the word "seriousness." As soon as you use the word "tranquillity," you imply forgetfulness. Mencius said, "Always be doing something without expectation. Let the mind not forget its objective, but let there be no artificial effort to help it grow."[99] Always be doing something means [presence of] mind. Not to forget and not to expect means not to help it grow. (18:6b)

47. *Question*: Do observation of things and self examination mean returning to the self and seeing [principles] after [some principles] have been discovered in things? *Answer*: You do not have to say it in this way. Things and the self are governed by the same principle. If you understand one, you understand the other, for the truth within and the truth without are identical. In its magnitude it reaches the height of heaven and the depth of earth, but in its refinement it constitutes the reason of being in every single thing. The student should appreciate both. *Further question*: In the extension of knowledge, how about seeking first of all in the Four Beginnings (of our nature, namely, humanity, righteousness, propriety, and wisdom)? *Answer*: To seek in our own nature and feelings is indeed to be concerned with our own moral life. But every blade of grass and every tree possesses principle and should be examined. (18:8b-9a)

48. All things under heaven can be understood in the light of their principle. As there are things, there must be their specific principles.[100] One thing necessarily has one principle. (18:9a)

49. The investigation of principle to the utmost, the full development of the nature, and the fulfillment of destiny are only one thing. As principle is investigated to the utmost, one's nature is fully developed, and as one's nature is fully developed, destiny is fulfilled. (18:9a)

[98] *Sung-Yüan hsüeh-an*, SPPY, 16:10a.   [99] *Mencius*, 2A:2.
[100] Paraphrasing *Odes*, ode no. 260.

50. *Question*: About the theory of immortals—are there such beings? *Answer*: I don't know. If you mean such things as people ascending to heaven in clear daylight, there is none. But if you mean people living in mountain forests to preserve their physical form and to imbibe energy to prolong life, then there are. It is like fire in a stove. If it is placed in the wind, it will be easily blown out. But if it is placed in a tightly closed room, it will not be easily blown out. This is in accordance with principle. *Further question*: Yang Hsiung (53 B.C.–A.D. 18) said that "the sage does not learn from immortals, for their art is not a normal one."[101] Can sages practice the art of immortals? *Answer*: An immortal is a thief in the world. If he does not steal the secret of creation, how can he extend life forever? If sages cared to do it, Duke Chou[102] and Confucius would have done it. (18:10a)

51. *Question*: How about hating external things? *Answer*: This is due to ignorance of the Way. How can things be hated? That is the doctrine of the Buddhists. They want to cast aside affairs, and do not ask whether according to [principle] they exist or not. If they exist, how can you cast them aside? If they do not exist, they naturally are not there. What is there to be cast aside? Those who live outside the mundane world carelessly devote themselves to tranquillity and set their feet far away in mountains and forests. They don't understand principle. And yet the world thinks they are lofty. The world is fooled. (18:10b)

52. The Buddhists have the doctrine of renunciation of the family and the world. Fundamentally the family cannot be renounced. It is of course possible for them to run away inasmuch as they do not treat their fathers as fathers and their mothers as mothers. But as to the world, how can they escape from it? As they have already claimed to have renounced it, that is possible only when they no longer stand under heaven or upon the earth. But they still drink when thirsty and eat when hungry, and still stand under heaven and set their feet on the earth. (18:10b)

53. The Buddhists talk about formation, remaining in the same state, deterioration, and extinction. This indicates that they are ignorant of the Way. There are only formation and deterioration but no remaining or extinction. Take plants, for example. When they are first produced, they are already formed. As they approach the highest point of growth, they immediately begin to decay. The Buddhists think that in the life of plants, they grow until they reach maturity, remain in that state for some time, and then gradually deteriorate. But nothing in the world

[101] *Fa-yen* (Model Sayings), ch. 12, SPPY, 12:4b-5a. For Yang Hsiung, see above, ch. 15.

[102] Duke Chou (d. 1094 B.C.) helped found the Chou dynasty and was greatly admired by Confucius for his virtue.

remains in the same state. Any day added to the life of an infant means a day spent. Since when can one stay in the same state? (18:10b-11a)

54. Someone asked about the Buddhist doctrine of obstruction by principle. *Answer*: The Buddhists do have such a doctrine. By this they mean that when one understands principle and is attached to it, principle becomes an obstruction. This shows they have misunderstood principle. There is only one principle in the universe. If it is understood, what is there to obstruct? If principle is understood as an obstruction, there would be a dichotomy of principle and the self (which principle obstructs). (18:11a)

55. Followers of Zen Buddhism always talk about the realms of human nature and human destiny in high-sounding words. As to human affairs, very often some of them are just totally ignorant. This is simply because they really achieve nothing by their talk. (18:11a)

> *Comment*. Ch'eng criticized Buddhism on many grounds, but mostly on ethical ones. In this he differs from Chang Tsai, who attacked Buddhism more on philosophical grounds.[103]

56. Su Chi-ming[104] asked: Is the principle of equilibrium the same as the equilibrium before the feelings of pleasure, anger, sorrow, and joy are aroused?[105] *Answer*: No. Before the feelings of pleasure, sorrow, and joy are aroused, equilibrium is in that state. The same word "equilibrium" is used but differently. *Someone asked*: Is it all right to seek equilibrium before the feelings of pleasure, anger, sorrow, and joy are aroused? *Answer*: No. Thinking of seeking it before the feelings of pleasure, anger, sorrow, and joy are aroused is already thought, and thought is an aroused state (like the four feelings). The aroused state may be described as harmony but not as equilibrium. *Further question*: Academician Lü[106] said that one should seek in the state before the feelings are aroused. If we follow his words, I am afraid there will be nothing to hold on. What can we do? *Answer*: We must understand the basic meaning of the saying. If it means to preserve and nourish oneself before his feelings are aroused, that will be all right. But if it means to seek equilibrium in the state before feelings are aroused, that is incorrect.

---

[103] See above, ch. 30, comment on sec. 64.

[104] Pupil of the two Ch'engs, who first studied under Chang Tsai. He became a professor of the national university and an official but was eventually banished to South China because his recommendations offended those in power. He recorded the conversations in bk. 10 of the *I-shu*.

[105] *The Mean*, ch. 1.

[106] Lü Yü-shu (Lü Ta-lin, 1044-1090), one of the Ch'engs' outstanding pupils. He recorded the sayings in bk. 2 of the *I-shu*. For an account of him, see Forke, *Geschichte der neueren chinesischen Philosophie*, pp. 116-119, and *Sung-Yüan hsüeh-an*, ch. 31. This doctrine of his is found in 31:9a of the latter.

Further question: A student should of course exert effort to discipline himself as his feelings are aroused. How should he apply his effort before feelings are aroused? *Answer*: How can we seek anything before our feelings are aroused? The only thing to do is to cultivate oneself every day. After a sufficient period of time, feelings will naturally attain due measure and degree when they are aroused. *Someone said*: Then there is an equilibrium before the feelings are aroused and another equilibrium after they are aroused. *Answer*: No. The state after the feelings are aroused is harmony. It is of course equilibrium when feelings are aroused and attain due measure and degree (such as equilibrium at all times), but when we speak of equilibrium and harmony separately, the state after feelings are aroused is harmony. (18:14b-15a)

57. Su Chi-ming asked: You said that in the sentence, "Before the feelings of pleasure, anger, sorrow, and joy are aroused, it is called equilibrium,"[107] equilibrium means being in the center. I do not know what that means. *Answer*: Equilibrium is simply the state in which the feelings of pleasure, anger, sorrow, and joy have not been aroused. *Question*: Does that mean that equilibrium has no physical form or body but only a subject in the discussion about the Way? *Answer*: No. What physical form has equilibrium? However, since it is called equilibrium it must possess some feature. *Question*: At the moment of equilibrium, is it true that the ear hears nothing and the eye sees nothing? *Answer*: Although the ear hears nothing and the eye sees nothing, nevertheless the principle of hearing and seeing must be already there before hearing and seeing are possible. . . . Suppose you describe the condition of tranquillity. Chi-ming said: One cannot say that there is anything.[108] But one is naturally conscious of something. The Teacher said: Since there is consciousness, there is activity. How can it be said to be tranquillity? When people explain the sentence "In the *fu* (to return) hexagram we see the mind of Heaven and Earth," they all say that in the state of perfect tranquillity we can see the mind of Heaven and Earth.[109] This is wrong. The line at the bottom of the hexagram *fu* indicates activity. How can we say that it is tranquillity? From ancient times scholars all have said that the mind of Heaven and Earth can be seen in a state of tranquillity, but I say that the mind of Heaven and Earth can be seen in a state of activity. (18:15a)

58. *Question*: Are there good and evil in the mind? *Answer*: What is

[107] *The Mean*, ch. 1.

[108] Chu Hsi said (*Chu Tzu yü-lei*, 96:9a) that "there is nothing" in the text should read "there is anything." This is confirmed by *Ts'ui-yen*, 1:6a.

[109] The quotation is from *Changes*, commentary on hexagram no. 24, *fu* (to return). Cf. Legge, *Yi King*, p. 233. Wang Pi (226-249) is the chief exponent of the theory. See above, ch. 19, sec. 2.

received by man and things from Heaven are called destiny. What is inherent in things[110] is called principle. What is endowed in man is called nature. And as the master of the body it is called the mind. In reality they are all one. The mind is originally good. As it is aroused and expresses itself in thoughts and ideas, there is good and evil. When the mind has been aroused, it should be described in terms of feelings, and not as the mind in itself. For instance, water is water. But as it flows and branches off, some to the east and some to the west, it is called streams and branches. (18:17a)

59. *Question*: Do joy and anger come from one's nature? *Answer*: Yes, of course. As soon as there is consciousness, there is nature. As there is nature, there must be feelings. Without nature, how can there be feelings? *Further question*: [Suppose you say that] joy and anger come from the outside. How is that? *Answer*: They do not come from the outside. They arise from within under external influence. *Question*: Are joy and anger to man's nature as waves are to water? *Answer*: Yes. It is the nature of water to be clear, level, and tranquil like a mirror. But when it strikes sand and stone, or when the ground underlying it is not level, it immediately begins to move violently. Or perhaps wind moves over it, and it immediately gives rise to waves and currents. But are these the nature of water? In man's nature there are only the Four Beginnings and not the various forms of evil. But without water, how can there be waves? Without man's nature, how can there be feelings? (18:17b)

60. *Question*: Since man's nature is originally clear, why is there obscuration? *Answer*: This must be investigated and understood. Mencius was correct in saying that man's nature is good.[111] Even Hsün Tzu (fl. 298–238 B.C.) and Yang Hsiung failed to understand man's nature. Mencius was superior to other Confucianists because he understood man's nature. There is no nature that is not good. Evil is due to capacity. Man's nature is the same as principle, and principle is the same from the sage-emperors Yao and Shun[112] to the common man in the street. Capacity is an endowment from material force. Material force may be clear or turbid. Men endowed with clear material force are wise, while those endowed with turbid material force are stupid. *Further question*: Can stupidity be changed? *Answer*: Yes. Confucius said, "The most intelligent and the most stupid do not change."[113] But in principle they

---

[110] The text has *i* (moral principle) but Chu Hsi thought it should be "things." In the *Honan Ch'eng-shih i-shu* (Surviving Works of the Ch'engs of Honan), another edition of the work, *Kuo-hsüeh chi-pen ts'ung-shu* (Basic Sinological Series) ed., p. 226, there is a note by Chu Hsi to this effect.

[111] *Mencius*, 6A:2-8.

[112] Legendary rulers (3rd millennium B.C.).

[113] *Analects*, 17:3.

can. Only those who ruin themselves and cast themselves away do not change. *Question*: Is it due to their capacity that the most stupid ruin and throw themselves away? *Answer*: Certainly. But it cannot be said that they cannot be changed. Since all have the same basic nature, who cannot be changed? Because they ruin and cast themselves away and are not willing to learn, people are unable to change. If they are willing to learn, in principle they can change. (18:17b)

61. [Someone asked: Confucius said,] "By nature men are alike. Through practice they have become far apart."[114] Nature is one. Why should it be said to be alike? *Answer*: This refers to physical nature, as in popular phrases, "quick by nature," "slow by nature," and so forth. How can nature itself be slow or quick? The word "nature" used here is the same as the one used in "What is inborn is called nature."[115]

Further question: [Confucius said,] "The most intelligent and the most stupid do not change."[116] Is this due to the nature? *Answer*: This is due to capacity. We must understand the difference between the nature and capacity. *Further question*: [Confucius said,] "To those who are above average, one may talk of the higher things, but may not do so to those who are below the average."[117] Is this due to capacity? *Answer*: Of course it is, but this is only speaking generally. It means that it is all right to talk with men above the average on things near the high level but not all right to talk with men below the average on things near the high level. As to the saying, "What is inborn is the nature," whenever the nature is talked about, we must see what the objective of the speaker is. When, for example, [Mencius] said that human nature is good,[118] he was referring to the fundamental character of nature. But when [Kao Tzu (c.420–c.350 B.C.) said] that what is inborn is nature, he meant what is endowed in man. Confucius said that man's nature is alike. How can one say so if he is thinking of the fundamental character of nature? Confucius only referred to man's endowment. What Kao Tzu said is of course in answer to Mencius' question. But what he said is wrong. (18:19b)

62. *Question*: In the investigation of things, should these be external things or things within our nature and function? *Answer*: It does not matter. All that is before our eyes is nothing but things, and all things have principle. For example, from that by which fire is hot or water is cold to the relations between ruler and minister, and father and son, are all principle. *Further question*: If one investigates only one thing, does he understand only one thing or does he understand the various principles? *Answer*: We must seek to understand all. However, even Yen

---

[114] *Analects*, 17:2.
[116] *Analects*, 17:3.
[115] *Mencius*, 6A:3. This is Kao Tzu's doctrine.
[117] *Analects*, 6:19.
[118] *Mencius*, 6A:2-8.

Tzu could understand only ten points when he heard one.[119] When one finally understands principle, even millions of things can be understood. (19:1a)

63. Nature comes from Heaven, whereas capacity comes from material force. When material force is clear, capacity is clear. When material force is turbid, capacity is turbid. Take, for instance, wood. Whether it is straight or crooked is due to its nature. But whether it can be used as a beam or as a truss is determined by its capacity. Capacity may be good or evil, but the nature is always good. (19:4b)

64. The mind is the principle of production. As there is the mind, a body must be provided for it so it can produce. The feeling of commiseration is the principle of production in man. (21B:2a)

> *Comment.* A great deal of doubt has been raised about this. As Chu Hsi explains it, "The mind is the principle of production, and the sense of commiseration is man's principle of production. That means that man creates because he has received the mind of Heaven to do so."[120] But as Chiang Yung (1681-1762) has observed, "Chu Hsi also said that the mind belongs to Heaven and Earth and not to a person. I am afraid this is not Chu Hsi's final conclusion."[121]

65. *Further question*: The *Book of Changes*[122] says [that a sage knows] the features of positive and negative spiritual forces (*kuei-shen*).[123] Are there really such features? *Answer*: Yes. *Further question*: If there are features there must be spiritual beings. [Is that right?] *Answer*: Positive and negative spiritual forces referred to in the *Book of Changes* are the same as production and transformation. *Further question*: How is it that famous mountains and great rivers can give rise to clouds and cause rain to fall? *Answer*: They are the results of material force rising as vapor. *Question*: Since there are the sacrifices [to these mountains and rivers], must there not be their spirits? *Answer*: Material force itself is spirit. Nowadays people are ignorant of this principle. They go to temples and pray for rain as soon as there is a drought. (22A:8a-b)

66. The nature is the same as principle. This is what we call rational nature. Traced to their source, none of the principles in the world is not good. Before they are aroused, have pleasure, anger, sorrow, and joy ever been found to be not good? As they are aroused and attain due

---

[119] *Analects*, 5:8.   [120] *Chu Tzu yü-lei*, 95:25a.
[121] See his *Chin-ssu lu chi-chu*, ch. 1, SPPY, 1:16a. His reference to Chu Hsi is to *Chu Tzu yü-lei*, 95:25b.
[122] "Appended Remarks," pt. 1, ch. 4. Cf. Legge, *Yi King*, p. 253.
[123] For a discussion of this term, see Appendix.

measure and degree, they are good. no matter in what connection. Whenever we speak of good and evil, good always precedes evil. Whenever we speak of good and evil fortune, good fortune always precedes evil fortune. And whenever we speak of right and wrong, right always precedes wrong. (22A:11a)

67. The knowledge obtained through hearing and seeing is not the knowledge obtained through moral nature. When a thing (the body) comes into contact with things, the knowledge so obtained is not from within. This is what is meant by extensive learning and much ability today. The knowledge obtained from moral nature does not depend on seeing and hearing. (25:2a)

68. A student must first of all learn to doubt. (*Wai-shu*, 11:2b)

69. Substance and function come from the same source, and there is no gap between the manifest and the hidden.[124] (Preface to *I chuan*)

70. Spoken of as one, Heaven is the Way (Tao). This is the meaning when it is said that "Heaven will not be in opposition."[125] Spoken of in its different aspects, it is called heaven with respect to its physical body, the Lord (*Ti*) with respect to its being master, negative and positive spiritual forces with respect to its operation, spirit (*shen*) with respect to its wonderful functioning, and *ch'ien* with respect to its nature and feelings. *Ch'ien* is the beginning of all things. Therefore it is Heaven, yang, father, and ruler. Origination, flourish, advantage, and firmness are called the Four Moral Qualities. Origination is the beginning of all things, flourish the growth of all things, advantage the success of all things, and firmness the completion of all things. (*I chuan*, 1:1a)

71. Origination in the Four Moral Qualities is comparable to humanity in the Five Constant Virtues (humanity, righteousness, propriety, wisdom, and faithfulness). Separately speaking, it is one of the several, but collectively speaking, it embraces all the four. (*ibid.*, 1:2b)

---

[124] Japanese sources (e.g., *Daikanwa jiten* or Great Chinese-Japanese Dictionary) maintain that the first half of the saying originated with Ch'eng-kuan (c.760-838) in his commentary on *Hua-yen ching* (*Avataṁsaka sūtra*, or Flower Splendor Scripture), but as Ōta Kinjō (1765-1825) has pointed out (*Gimon roku*, or Records of Questioning, 1831 ed., pt. 1, p. 6), it does not appear here or in any of Ch'eng-kuan's works. It is possible that it was in the portion of his commentary which is now lost, but if so, no one has given any specific source. However, Ch'eng-kuan virtually said the same thing rather extensively, though in slightly different words, in his commentary (*Zokuzōkyō*, or Supplement to the Buddhist Canon, 1st collection, case 88, 3:35a-b). By the eleventh century, the saying was common among both Buddhists and Neo-Confucianists. As T'ang Shun-chih (1507-1560) said, "Both Buddhists and Confucianists said the same thing and none could tell whose words they were." (*T'ang Ching-ch'uan chi*, or Collected Works of T'ang Shun-chih, 1553 ed., 6:2b.) As to the second half of the saying, Ōta said that it is Fa-tsang's (643-712), but he gave no specific reference.

[125] *Changes*, commentary on hexagram no. 1, *ch'ien* (Heaven). Cf. Legge, p. 417.

72. Destiny is what is endowed by Heaven and the nature is what things have received from Heaven. (*ibid.*, 1:2b)

73. In identifying himself with Heaven and Earth, sun and moon, the four seasons, and positive and negative spiritual forces, the great man identifies himself with the Way. Heaven and Earth are the Way. Positive and negative spiritual forces are traces of creation. (*ibid.*, 1:7b-8a)

74. Humanity is universal impartiality; it is the foundation of goodness. (*ibid.*, 2:34a)

75. Principle in the world is one. Although there are many roads in the world, the destination is the same, and although there are a hundred deliberations, the result is one.[126] Although things involve many manifestations and events go through infinite variations, when they are united by the one, there cannot be any contradiction. (*ibid.*, 3:3b)

76. According to the principle of the world, nothing can last forever without activity. With activity, a thing will begin again when it ends, and can therefore last forever without limit. Among things in the universe, even as solid and dense as huge mountains, nothing can remain unchanged. Thus being long lasting does not mean being in a fixed and definite state. Being fixed and definite, a thing cannot last long. The way to be constant is to change according to circumstances. This is a common principle. . . . Unless one knows the Way, how can he understand the constant and lasting way of the universe and the constant and lasting principle of the world? (*ibid.*, 3:6a)

77. That which is inherent in things is principle. That by which things are managed is moral principles. (*ibid.*, 4:20b)

78. The beginning and ending of all things are nothing but integration and disintegration. Positive and negative spiritual forces are the function of creation. If viewed from the causes of what is hidden and what is manifest, from the principle of life and death, and from the features of positive and negative spiritual forces, the Way of Heaven and Earth can be understood. . . . Activity and tranquillity have no beginning and yin and yang have no starting point. Unless one knows the Way, how can he understand this? Activity and tranquillity cause each other and thus changes and transformation are produced. What follows this Way is good. . . . Heaven and Earth do not share the anxiety of the sage. For Heaven and Earth do not act as master whereas the sage has a mind of his own. Heaven and Earth create and transform without having any mind of their own. The sage has a mind of his own but does not take an [unnatural] action. How perfect is the eminent virtue and great achievement of Heaven and Earth and the sage![127] (*Ching-shuo* or Explanations of the Classics, 1:1b-2a)

[126] Quoting *Changes*, "Appended Remarks," pt. 2, ch. 5. Cf. Legge, p. 389.
[127] Quoting *Changes*, "Appended Remarks," pt. 1, ch. 5. Cf. Legge, p. 356.

33

THE UNITY OF MIND AND PRINCIPLE
IN LU HSIANG-SHAN

WE HAVE SEEN that in the Ch'eng brothers there was a strong emphasis on the single and the fundamental. For Lu Hsiang-shan (Lu-Chiu-yüan, 1139-1193),[1] these formed the very bases of his philosophy and methodology as well as his personality.

As a man, he led a simple life, devoting much of it to lecturing on moral principles. Thousands of scholars gathered to listen to his simple and straight lectures, which always went directly into the fundamentals. In his lecture on righteousness versus profit, in 1183, he moved his audience to tears. In methodology, he rejected details and superfluous writing and advocated the concentration on the most essential. In both moral cultivation and intellectual pursuit, he simply relied on the mind.

The mind is conceived by him to be morally self-sufficient, and endowed with innate knowledge of the good and innate ability to do good. It is one and indissoluble. It fills the whole universe. As such it is identical with principle (*li*). The investigation of things means nothing more than to investigate this mind.

This doctrine was simply put forth with no literary embellishment and little logical deliberations, but it started a strong current that was to oppose the rationalism of the Ch'eng-Chu School for several hundred years. It can readily be seen that he is opposed to Chu Hsi (1130-1200) at every point. To Chu Hsi, principle and the element that gives being its substance and physical form, namely material force (*ch'i*), are sharply different. To Lu, on the contrary, there is nothing outside the Way (Tao) and there is no Way outside things. Chu Hsi discussed human nature extensively. Lu hardly mentioned the subject. To Chu Hsi, mind

---

[1] Lu's courtesy name was Tzu-ching. He obtained the "presented scholar" degree in 1.172 and in 1174 served as a district keeper of records (assistant magistrate). Three years later he and Chu engaged in one of the most famous debates in Chinese history (see sec. 31). In 1179 he was district keeper of records again and in 1182 he became a professor of the national university. For four years he lectured there and attracted much following. Minor posts followed. After he resigned he returned to his home in Kiangsi and lived in Hsiang-shan (Elephant Mountain) to teach and lecture. Hence the honorary title "Master Hsiang-shan." In 1190 he was appointed a magistrate and gave an excellent account of himself. He died while he was in office. Throughout his life he mostly taught and lectured. He wrote no books, for his emphasis was not on them. Even the Classics, he said, were his footnotes only. (See sec. 20.) He died in the third year of the Shao-hsi period, which is ordinarily equated with 1192. But he died on the fourteenth day of the twelfth month, which happened to fall on January 10, 1193. This fact has been pointed out in Siu-chi Huang, *Lu Hsiang-shan*, p. 9, n.2.

is the function of human nature, and human nature is identical with principle. To Lu, however, mind *is* principle. Although both philosophers insisted that mind is one, Chu Hsi made the distinction between the human mind, which is in a precarious position because it is liable to mistakes, and the moral mind, which always follows the Way. Lu refused to accept such a distinction. To him, the mind is one and the same, and it is the same whether in each individual or in the entire universe. Chu Hsi considered the Great Ultimate above physical forms and yin and yang (passive and active cosmic forces) within physical forms. Lu rejected such a dichotomy, declaring that yin and yang are already above the realm of corporeality. While both philosophers agreed that human nature is originally good, Chu Hsi contrasted the Principle of Nature (*T'ien-li*, Principle of Heaven) with human desires. To Lu, such a contrast is untenable. For Chu Hsi, the investigation of things means investigating the principle in things. For Lu, investigation means investigating the mind, for to him all principles are inherent and complete in the mind.

These philosophical differences are as sharp as they are incompatible. Their opposition in the way of life, however, is even more direct. In Lu's opinion, the way of Chu Hsi was one of divided mind, aimless drifting, and devotion to isolated details that meant little to life. Instead, he advocated the simple, easy, and direct method of recovering one's original good nature, by having a firm purpose, by establishing the nobler part of one's nature, and by coming to grips with fundamentals. In short, Chu's way is that of "following the path of inquiry and study," while Lu's way is that of "honoring the moral nature."[2] Thus they intensified the different emphasis of Ch'eng I (Ch'eng I-ch'uan, 1033-1107) and his brother Ch'eng Hao (Ch'eng Ming-tao, 1032-1085) and formed the two wings of Neo-Confucianism, the rationalistic or the School of Principle and the idealistic or the School of Mind, that were to flourish for several centuries. While in the long run the influence of Lu was not anywhere so great as that of Chu, the idealism of Lu culminated in the philosophy of Wang Yang-ming (Wang Shou-jen, 1472-1529) that overshadowed the rationalistic movement in the Ming period (1368-1644), as we shall see.

Following the list of topics and references are selections from the *Hsiang-shan ch'üan-chi* (Complete Works of Lu Hsiang-shan).[3]

Book learning: 20, 34
Buddhism: 4

[2] These two ways are taught in *The Mean*, ch. 27 as complementary.

[3] This is in thirty-six chapters, consisting of letters, short essays, poems, official documents, and recorded conversations. A selection from the letters and conversations has been made by Cady. See Bibliography.

THE COMPLETE WORKS OF LU HSIANG-SHAN

1. Principle is endowed in me by Heaven, not drilled into me from outside. If one understands that principle is the same as master and really makes it his master, one cannot be influenced by external things or fooled by perverse doctrines. (1:3a)

2. The mind is one and principle is one. Perfect truth is reduced to a unity; the essential principle is never a duality. The mind and principle can never be separated into two. That is why Confucius said, "There is one thread that runs through my doctrines,"[4] and Mencius said, "The Way is one and only one."[5] (Quoting Confucius), Mencius also said, "There are but two ways to be pursued, that of humanity (*jen*) and that of inhumanity."[6] To do in a certain way is humanity. Not to do in a certain way is the opposite of humanity. Humanity is the same as the mind and principle. "Seek and you find it"[7] means to find this principle. "Those who are the first to know" know this principle, and "those who are the first to understand"[8] understand this principle. It is this principle that constitutes the love for parents, reverence for elders, and the sense of alarm and commiseration when one sees a child about to fall into a well. It is this principle that makes people ashamed of shameful things and hate what should be hated. It is this principle that enables people to know what is right to be right and what is wrong to be wrong. It is this principle that makes people deferential when deference is due and humble when humility is called for. Seriousness (*ching*)[9] is this principle. Righteousness is also this principle. What is internal is this principle. What is external is also this principle. Therefore it is said, "Straight, square, and great, (the superior man) works his operation, without repeated effort, (and is) in every respect advantageous."[10] Mencius said, "The ability possessed by men without their having acquired it by learning is innate ability, and the knowledge possessed by them without de-

---

[4] *Analects*, 4:15.   [5] *Mencius*, 3A:1.   [6] *ibid.*, 4A:2.
[7] *ibid.*, 6A:6.   [8] *ibid.*, 5A:7.
[9] *Ching* is here not used in the sense of respect for people but in the sense of absolute equanimity and absolute steadfastness. See Appendix.
[10] *Changes*, commenting on hexagram no. 2, *k'un* (Earth). Cf. translation by Legge, *Yi King*, p. 420.

liberation is innate knowledge."[11] These are endowed in us by Heaven. "We originally have them with us," and "they are not drilled into us from outside."[12] Therefore Mencius said, "All things are already complete in oneself. There is no greater joy than to examine oneself and be sincere (or absolutely real)."[13] (1:3b-4a)

3. The Way fills the universe. It does not hide or escape from anything. With reference to Heaven, it is called yin and yang (passive and active cosmic forces). With reference to Earth, it is called strength and weakness. With reference to man, it is called humanity and righteousness. Thus humanity and righteousness are the original mind of man. Mencius said, "Is there not a heart of humanity and righteousness originally existing in man?"[14] He also said, "We originally have them with us (the senses of humanity and righteousness, propriety, and wisdom)" and "they are not drilled into us from outside."[15] The stupid and the unworthy do not come up to them and thus they are obscured with selfish desires and lose their original mind. The worthy and the wise go beyond them and thus are obscured by subjective viewpoints and lose their original mind.[16] (1:6b)

4. I use these two words, righteousness and profit, to distinguish between Confucianism and Buddhism. I also use the terms "public-spiritedness" and "selfishness", but actually they mean righteousness and profit. The Confucianists consider man, living in the world, as more intelligent than the myriad things and more noble than the myriad things, and that man and Heaven and Earth coexist as three ultimates. For Heaven there is the Way of Heaven, for Earth there is the Way of Earth, and for man there is the way of man. Unless man fully practices the Way of man, he will not be qualified to coexist with Heaven and Earth. Man has five senses and each sense has its own function. From this [common experience of mankind] we have the right and wrong and success and failure, and we have education and learning. This is the basis on which Confucian doctrines have been founded. Therefore we call them righteous and public-spirited. Buddhists, on the other hand, consider man, living in the world, as consisting of a chain of birth and death, a wheel of transmigration, and afflictions resulting from passions, and regard them as most painful, and seek to escape from them. Those who realize the truth and achieve awakening realize that there is originally no chain of birth and death, no transmigration, and no afflictions resulting from passions. Therefore they say, "The matter of the chain of birth and death is important." What you[17] called resolution to become a bodhi-

---

[11] *Mencius*, 7A:15. [12] *ibid.*, 6A:6. [13] *ibid.*, 7A:4.
[14] *ibid.*, 6A:8. [15] *ibid.*, 6A:6.
[16] For the deviation from the Mean, see *The Mean*, ch. 4.
[17] This selection is part of a letter Lu Hsiang-shan wrote to Wang Po-shun.

sattva (a Buddhist saint) is merely for the sake of this important matter. This is the basis on which Buddhist doctrines are founded. Therefore we call them profit-seeking and selfish. It is precisely because of righteousness and public-spiritedness that we Confucianists are engaged in putting the world in order, and because of their desire for profit and selfishness that the Buddhists withdraw from the world. Even when Confucianists reach to the realms of (Heaven) which has neither sound nor smell,[18] (spirit) which is not spatially restricted, and (Change) which has no physical form,[19] they always emphasize putting the world in order. Although the Buddhists would save all people in the future, they always emphasize withdrawing from the world. Now, those who follow Buddhism are all human beings. As they are human beings, how can they cast aside our Confucian humanity and righteousness? Although they renounce the family, they still want to repay the Four Kindnesses (of parents, teachers, the king, and benefactors).[20] Thus in their daily life they of course sometimes preserve this principle which is rooted in the human mind and cannot be obliterated. However, their doctrines did not arise in order to preserve it. Therefore whether it is preserved or not is of no sufficient importance to those who are advanced in the Buddhist way of life. We Confucianists, on the other hand, say that "That whereby man differs from the lower animals is but small. The ordinary people cast it away, while the superior man preserves it."[21] The Buddhists pity people because they have not escaped the wheel of transmigration but continue in the chain of birth and death, regarding them as floating and sinking in the sea of life and death. Do sages and worthies in Confucianism merely float and sink in this sea of life and death of theirs. Our sages and worthies are free from that which the Buddhists pity. Their doctrines did not arise for the sake of escaping from it and therefore their teachings do not emphasize it. Therefore our Confucian sages and worthies are free from that which the Buddhists pity, but Buddhist sages and worthies are not free from those things for which we Confucianists show concern. If we judge the Buddhist sages and worthies by the law of the *Spring and Autumn Annals* [which demands putting the world in order], even a boy knows that they cannot get away from its condemnation. From the point of view of the origin of their respective doctrines, we see that the distinction between the Confucianists and the Buddhists as one for public-spiritedness and righteousness and the other for selfishness and profit is perfectly clear and that they are absolutely incompatible. (2:-1b-2a)

[18] *The Mean*, ch. 30.
[19] *Changes*, "Appended Remarks," pt. 1, ch. 4. Cf. Legge, *Yi King*, p. 354.
[20] For the layman, the four kindnesses are those of parents, all sentient beings, the king, and the Three Treasurers (Buddha, the Law, and the Order).
[21] *Mencius*, 4B:19.

Comment. Many writers, past and present, have described Lu Hsiang-shan as Buddhistic. Chu Hsi said that Lu taught the doctrines of Zen Buddhism in Confucian disguise like a salt smuggler who covers his load with salted fish.[22] Ch'en Chien (Ch'en Ch'ing-lan, 1497-1567), strong defender of the Chu Hsi School and severe critic of Lu Hsiang-shan and Wang Yang-ming, ruthlessly attacked both as advocates of Zen throughout his book, *Hsüeh-pu t'ung-pien* (General Critique of Obscurations of Learning). To the extent that Lu over-emphasized the mind, the criticisms are valid. But he is far more different from Zen than he is similar to it. His doctrine of the mind, for example, has none of the profound mystery of Zen. He stressed thinking, doubt, and judgment, and that is a far cry from Zen. In the above discussion, he pointed out a key difference between him and Buddhists. Whatever similarities exist between his philosophy and Buddhism are superficial. Incidentally, many writers, including such outstanding scholars as Tokiwa Daijō, have exaggerated the similarities between Neo-Confucianism and Buddhism.[23]

5. In your (Chu Hsi's) second letter [to my brother Lu Tzu-mi] you also said that the Ultimate of Non-being is the same as the absence of physical form and the Great Ultimate is the same as the presence of principle, and that Master Chou Tun-i (Chou Lien-hsi, 1017-1073)[24] for fear that students might misunderstand the Great Ultimate to be a separate entity and therefore applied the name Ultimate of Non-being to clarify the matter.[25] In the "Appended Remarks" of the *Book of Changes*, it is said, "What exists before physical form [and is without it] is the Way."[26] It is also said, "The successive movement of yin and yang (passive and active cosmic forces) constitutes the Way."[27] The successive movement of yin and yang already exists before physical forms. How much more is the Great Ultimate!. . .

The *Explanation of the Diagram of the Great Ultimate* begins with the term "ultimate of non-being," but the entire *T'ung-shu* (Penetrating

[22] *Chu Tzu yü-lei* (Classified Conversations of Chu Hsi), 1880 ed., 124:11a.

[23] This is true of Tokiwa Daijō's (1870-1945) *Shina ni okeru bukkyō to jukyō dōkyō* (Buddhism in Relation to Confucianism and Taoism in China), 1930, and Kubota Ryōon's *Shina judōbutsu kōshōshi* (The Interrelations between Confucianism, Taoism, and Buddhism in China), 1943. However, the latter's *Shina judōbutsu sankyō shiron* (Historical Discussion of the Three Systems of Confucianism, Taoism, and Buddhism in China), 1931, brings out the Neo-Confucianists' criticism of Buddhism rather fully.

[24] For Chou's doctrine on the Great Ultimate, see ch. 28, sec. 1.

[25] This letter is found in the *Chu Tzu wen-chi* (Collection of Literary Works by Chu Hsi), CTTC, 36:4b-5b.

[26] Pt. 1, ch. 12. Cf. Legge, *Yi King*, p. 377.

[27] Pt. 1, ch. 5. Cf. Legge, p. 355.

the *Book of Changes*)[28] makes not a single mention of the term. The two Ch'engs (Ch'eng Hao and Ch'eng I) both said and wrote much, but never used the term "ultimate of non-being." Even if Master Chou at first really had such a diagram, from the fact that later he never mentioned the ultimate of non-being, it is clear that he had advanced in his thought and no longer considered his earlier position correct. (2:6a-b)

6. In your (Chu Hsi) letter [to me] you maintained that the term "ultimate of non-being" (in Chou Tun-i's *Explanation of the Diagram of the Great Ultimate*) is intended to clarify principle. In essence, you said that "it clearly shows the true substance of the Great Ultimate."[29] I am afraid that you do not really know the Great Ultimate. If you did, you would realize that it is entirely unnecessary to precede the term "great ultimate" with "ultimate of non-being" or follow it with "true substance." To add "ultimate of non-being" is really, [as you said], to "put a bed above a bed" and to follow it with "true substance" is really, [as you said], to "build a house under a house."[30]. . . . Lao Tzu regarded non-being as the beginning of Heaven and Earth and being as the mother of all things, and tried to see the subtlety of things through eternal non-being and to see the outcome of things through eternal being.[31] To add "non-being" to "ultimate" is precisely to follow the teaching of Lao Tzu. How can this be denied? Primarily because the Taoists were beclouded in this way that they have degenerated into indulging in divination and magic and have become unscrupulous. Principle exists in the universe from the very beginning. How can it be said to be non-being? If it is considered non-being, then the ruler [since there is no principle of the ruler] would not be the true ruler, the minister not the true minister, the father not the true father, and the son not the true son. (2:9a-b)

7. Of course study should not be without thought. But the way to think should emphasize reflection on things at hand, and should be done in a free, easy, and leisurely manner. With reflection on things at hand, the self will not be at a loss, and with free and leisurely thinking one will not be impeded by material things. (3:1b-2a)

8. This principle existing throughout the universe is hidden from nothing and nothing can escape from it. Heaven and Earth are what they are because they follow this principle without partiality. Man coexists with Heaven and Earth as the three ultimates. How can man be selfish and disobey principle? Mencius said, "First build up the nobler part of your nature and then the inferior part cannot overcome it."[32] It

[28] See above, ch. 28, sec. 2.

[29] In Chu Hsi's letter to Lu. See *Chu Tzu wen-chi*, CTTC, 36:8a.

[30] *ibid.*, 36:9a.

[31] *Lao Tzu*, ch. 1. Lu Hsiang-shan understood the sentences in this way because he followed a certain punctuation. See ch. 7, n.11.

[32] *Mencius*, 6A:15.

is because people fail to build up the nobler part of their nature that it is overcome by the inferior part. In consequence they violate principle and become different from Heaven and Earth. (11:1a)

> *Comment.* Lu Hsiang-shan quoted Mencius even more than Confucius. The quotation here is his favorite one. And it is also the keynote of his philosophy.

9. This principle fills the universe. Even Heaven and Earth and spiritual beings cannot deviate from it. How much less can man? (11:-4a)

10. Mencius said, "That whereby man differs from the lower animals is but small. The ordinary people cast it away, while the superior man preserves it."[33] What is cast away is the mind. That is why Mencius said that some people "cast their original mind away."[34] What is preserved is this mind. That is why Mencius said that "The great man is one who does not lose his child's heart."[35] (What Mencius referred to as) the Four Beginnings (of humanity, righteousness, propriety, and wisdom, that is, the sense of commiseration, the sense of shame, the sense of deference and compliance, and the sense of right and wrong)[36] are this mind. It is what Heaven has endowed in us. All men have this mind, and all minds are endowed with this principle. The mind *is* principle. (11:-5b-6a)

11. There is of course concrete principle in the universe. The value of study lies in understanding this principle. If it is understood, concrete action and concrete accomplishments will naturally result. (14:1a)

12. This principle fills the universe. Who can escape from it? Those who follow it will enjoy good fortune and those who violate it will encounter calamities. People (whose minds) are obscure and beclouded are darkened and stupid, and those (whose minds) are penetrative and discerning are intelligent and wise. The darkened and stupid do not see this principle and therefore they often violate it and suffer calamity. The intelligent and wise understand this principle and are therefore able to follow it and achieve good fortune. Commentators of the *Book of Changes* say that yang is honorable while yin is lowly, and the element of strength is bright while the element of weakness is dark. It is quite true. (21:1a)

13. The four directions plus upward and downward constitute the spatial continuum (*yü*). What has gone by in the past and what is to come in the future constitute the temporal continuum (*chou*). The universe (these continua) is my mind, and my mind is the universe.

---

[33] *Mencius,* 4B:19.   [34] *ibid.,* 6A:10.
[35] *ibid.,* 4B:12.   [36] *ibid.,* 2A:6.

Sages appeared tens of thousands of generations ago. They shared this mind; they shared this principle. Sages will appear tens of thousands of generations to come. They will share this mind; they will share this principle. Over the four seas sages appear. They share this mind; they share this principle. (22:5a)

> *Comment.* This is Lu's philosophy in a word. Chu Hsi is correct in saying that all Lu talked about was the one mind.[37] Unfortunately, Lu has never explained the mind fully beyond saying that it is the mind of everyone, that it is the original mind, that it is equivalent to *jen* (humanity),[38] and that it consists of the Four Beginnings of humanity, righteousness, propriety, and wisdom taught by Mencius. In short, he added nothing to what Mencius had taught. His importance in the history of Chinese philosophy does not lie in his philosophical originality but in the fact that he made the mind the center of a philosophical movement.

14. The affairs in the universe (*yü-chou*) are my own affairs. My own affairs are affairs of the universe. (22:5a)

15. The human mind is most intelligent and principle is most clear. All people have this mind and all minds contain this principle in full. (22:5a)

16. Moral principles inherent in the human mind are endowed by Heaven and cannot be wiped out. Those who are beclouded by material desires so as to pervert principles and violate righteousness, do so because they do not think, that is all. If they can truly examine themselves and think, their sense of right and wrong and their choice between right and wrong will have the qualities of quiet alertness, clear-cut intelligence, and firm conviction. (32:4a)

17. The Teacher always said that outside of the Way there are no events and outside of events there is no Way. (34:1a)

18. When has the Way existing in the universe any defect? Only men themselves have defects. Sages and worthies of all ages merely remove the defects of man. How can the Way be augmented or diminished? (34:1a)

19. Moral principles are nothing but those moral principles right before our eyes. Even when our understanding reaches the level of sages, they are nothing but moral principles right before our eyes. (34:-1a)

20. If in our study we know the fundamentals, then all the Six Classics[39] are my footnotes. (34:1b)

---

[37] *Chu Tzu yü-lei*, 124:4b.   [38] For a discussion of this term, see Appendix.
[39] The *Books of Odes, History, Rites, Changes,* the *Chou-li* (Rites of Chou),

Comment. A most daring statement by a Confucianist! This revolt against the heavy weight of literature has nothing to do with the Zen doctrine of having no use for words or literature. He rejected commentaries, but he still read the original. This is in line with his philosophy of ignoring details and concentrating on fundamentals. It is true, however, that, generally speaking, he did not care for reading or writing. Among Neo-Confucianists only he and Ch'eng Hao did not write anything except letters, prefaces, and the like. As in the case of Ch'eng, his philosophy was expressed chiefly in letters and conversations. If they lack systematic presentation and logical arguments, they are products of actual living and are meant not for academic debate but for the guidance of everyday life.

21. The theory that principle is due to Nature (*T'ien,* Heaven) whereas desire is due to man is, without saying, not the best doctrine. If principle is due to Nature and desire due to man, then Nature and man must be different. This theory can be traced to Lao Tzu. In the "Record of Music" it is said, "By nature man is tranquil at birth. When, influenced by external things, he begins to be active, that is desire arising from his nature. As one becomes conscious of things resulting from this impact, one begins to have likes and dislikes. . . . When [as a result of these likes and dislikes] one is unable to return to his original mind, the Principle of Nature is destroyed."[40] Here is the origin of the theory that principle is from Nature whereas desire is from man. And the words of the "Record of Music" are based on the Taoists.[41] If it is said that only tranquillity is inborn nature, is activity not inborn nature also? It is said in the *Book of History* that "the human mind is precarious, the moral mind is subtle."[42] Most interpreters have explained the human mind (which is liable to make mistakes) as equivalent to [selfish] human desires and the moral mind (which follows the Way, the Moral Law) as equivalent to the Principle of Nature. This interpretation is wrong. The mind is one. How can man have two minds? (34:1b)

22. Someone asked, "In learning your doctrines, where should one begin?" The Teacher answered, "Genuine and personal concern, self-examination, correcting one's mistakes, reforming to do good. That is all." (34:4b)

---

and the *Spring and Autumn Annals.* The ancient Six Classics had the *Book of Music,* now lost, instead of the *Chou-li.*

[40] *Book of Rites,* "Record of Music." Cf. translation by Legge, *Li Ki,* p. 96.

[41] The term Principle of Nature of course does not appear in the *Lao Tzu.* Lu was evidently thinking of the general Taoist doctrine of having no or few desires in chs. 3, 19, 34, 37, 57.

[42] "Counsels of the Great Yü." Cf. translation by Legge, *Shoo King,* p. 61.

23. Chu Yüan-hui (Chu Hsi) once wrote to one of his students saying, "Lu Tzu-ching (Lu Hsiang-shan) taught people only the doctrine of 'honoring the moral nature.'[43] Therefore those who have studied under him are mostly scholars who put their beliefs into practice. But he neglected to follow the path of study and inquiry.[44] In my teaching is it not true that I have put somewhat more emphasis on 'following the path of study and inquiry'? As a consequence, my pupils often do not approach his in putting beliefs into practice." From this it is clear that Yüan-hui wanted to avoid two defects (failure to honor the moral nature and failure to practice) and combine the two merits (following the path of study and inquiry and practicing one's beliefs). I do not believe this to be possible. If one does not know how to honor his moral nature, how can he talk about following the path of study and inquiry? (34:4b-5a)

24. My learning is different from that of others in the fact that with me every word comes spontaneously. Although I have uttered tens of thousands of words, they all are expressions of what is within me, and nothing more has been added. Recently someone has commented of me that aside from [Mencius'] saying, "First build up the nobler part of your nature,"[45] I had nothing clever. When I heard this, I said, "Very true indeed." (34:5a)

25. My brother Fu-chai one day asked me, "Where do you devote your efforts now?" I answered: "I devote my efforts to the area of human feelings and human affairs, practical situations, and principles of things." He nodded, that was all. When a person knows whether the prices of goods are high or low and can discriminate whether a thing is beautiful or ugly and genuine or false, I cannot say that he is not an able man. However, what I call making effort does not refer to these. (34:5a)

26. Men living in the world all share the same material force. It is in accordance with moral principles that they should support each other in doing good and stop each other from doing evil. Why should there be any idea to divide one another? And why should there be any idea of imposing one's own will? (34:5a)

27. The universe has never separated itself from man. Man separates himself from the universe. (34:5b)

28. When the Teacher resided in the Hsiang-shan, he often said to his pupils, "Your hearing is by nature distinct and your vision is by nature clear. By natural endowment you are capable of serving your father with filial piety and your elder brother with respect. Fundamentally there is nothing wanting in you. There is no need to seek elsewhere. All depends on your establishing yourself in life." (34:10b)

[43] *The Mean*, ch. 27.   [44] *ibid.*   [45] *Mencius*, 6A:15.

29. Someone said that the Teacher's doctrines concern morality, human nature and destiny, and what exists before physical form, whereas the doctrines of Chu Hsi concern the names, varieties, and systems of things and what exist after physical form, and that a student should learn the doctrines of both teachers. The Teacher said, "Chu Hsi would not be satisfied with what you have said about him. He himself said that there is one thread running through his doctrines. However, he has not understood the Way clearly and in the end there is no thread running through them. I once wrote him and said, 'When imagination and imitation are skillful and copying and borrowing are close, their particulars are enough to make one self-confident, and their details enough to give him self-comfort.'[46] These words cut into the very heart of his doctrines." (34:18b)

30. The Teacher said that all things are luxuriantly present in the mind. What permeates the mind, emanates from it, and extends to fill the universe is nothing but principle. (34:21a)

31. Lü Po-kung (Lü Tsu-ch'ien, 1137-1181)[47] arranged a meeting at the Goose Lake Temple.[48] My late elder brother Fu-chai said to me, "Po-kung has invited Yüan-hui (Chu Hsi) to meet us particularly because we differ from him in doctrines.". . . [Chu Hsi] was debating with my brother. I said, "On the way I wrote a poem. . . :

Work that is easy and simple will in the end be lasting and great,
Understanding that is devoted to isolated details will end up in
    aimless drifting. . . ."

When I recited my poem up to these lines, Yüan-hui's face turned pale. (34:24a-b)

> Comment. This meeting in 1175 was one of the most celebrated in Chinese history. It was a dramatic meeting of the three leading scholars of the time. More important, it was an encounter of two sharply different ways of life—one for "honoring the moral nature" and the other for "following the path of inquiry and study." As Huang Tsung-hsi (1610-1695) has said, these two ways are, respectively, the foundations of Lu Hsiang-shan's and Chu Hsi's

[46] *Hsiang-shan ch'üan-chi,* 2:9a.

[47] He was a high official and a prominent scholar, to whom Chu Hsi wrote many letters discussing various philosophical problems. These letters are found in the *Chu Tzu wen-chi,* chs. 33-35. For an account of him, see Forke, *Geschichte der neueren chinesischen Philosophie,* pp. 226-229 or Huang Tsung-hsi et al., *Sung-Yüan hsüeh-an* (Anthology and Critical Accounts of the Neo-Confucianists of the Sung and Yüan Dynasties, 960-1368), ch. 51. Hu, Chu, and Lu represented the most outstanding currents of thoughts at this time. His system is a synthesis of Chu's rationalism and Lu's idealism.

[48] In present Kiangsi Province.

systems.[49] This diametrical opposition is not the only one between the two, as already pointed out in the introduction. They also debated over metaphysics (sec. 6). That debate, which took place in 1188, is equally famous, although it was not as dramatic because it was conducted through correspondence.

32. A student must make up his mind. To read books and merely understand their literal meanings means not to have made up one's mind. (35:1b)

33. The Way in the universe cannot be augmented or diminished. Neither can it be taken or be given away. Man must find this out for himself. (35:3a)

34. Li Po-mien[50] asked how to investigate things. The Teacher said, "Study the principles of things." Po-mien said, "There are so many things in the world. How can one study all of them?" The Teacher said, " 'All things are already complete in oneself.'[51] It is only necessary to understand principle. . . . In the past I did not read the writings of the I-Lo School of Ch'eng Hao and Ch'eng I.[52] Only recently have I read them. I find there are incorrect ideas in them. Nowadays when people read, they pay no attention to what is simple and easy, but devote their vigorous efforts to study what can arouse people's admiration. When did ancient sages aim to arouse people's admiration? It is because the Way has not prevailed that when people see something unusual, their admiration is aroused. . . . When I read, I merely look at ancient annotations, and the words of the sages are clear of themselves. Take the saying, 'Young men should be filial when at home and respectful to their elders when away from home.'[53] This clearly means that when at home you are to be filial and when away from home you are to be respectful. What is the need for commentaries? Students have exhausted their energies in them and therefore their burden has become even heavier. When they come to me, I simply reduce the burden for them. This alone means the investigation of things." (35:7b-8a)

> *Comment.* It is correct to say that Ch'eng I and Chu Hsi represented the rationalistic wing of Neo-Confucianism while Ch'eng Hao, Lu Hsiang-shan, and Wang Yang-ming represented the idealistic wing. But we must not say that Lu's philosophy is an

[49] *Sung-Yüan hsüeh-an*, SPPY, 58:2a.

[50] Among Lu's pupils, he studied with him for the longest period. He recorded the conversations in *Hsiang-shan ch'üan-chi*, 35:5a-11b.

[51] *Mencius*, 7A:4.

[52] So-called because the two Ch'eng brothers lived and taught in the I River area and Lo-yang. Later the term also applied to Chu Hsi, that is, the Ch'eng-Chu School as a whole.

[53] *Analects*, 1:6.

offshoot of that of Ch'eng Hao. There was little historical connection between Lu and Ch'eng Hao. Ch'üan Tsu-wang (1705-1755) said that Lu represented the full development of the Ch'eng Hao School through Hsieh Liang-tso (Hsieh Shang-ts'ai, 1050-1103)[54] but he offered no evidence.[55] Chu Hsi confessed that he did not know who Lu's teachers were.[56] And Lu Hsiang-shan himself said that he conceived his ideas from reading the *Book of Mencius*.[57] As in the case of Ch'eng Hao, any realization was achieved through his own effort. This is the very foundation for the spirit of independence in his thought.

In a way, Lu went too far in his independent thinking. As was to be expected, Lu had little to say about the investigation of things. His theory that it is nothing but understanding principle, which is identical with mind, is surely an extreme. For this he had no support from Mencius and offered no logical justification.

35. [In answer to Li Po-mien the Teacher said], "Students of today only pay attention to details and do not search for what is concrete. Mencius said, 'He who exerts his mind to the utmost knows his nature. He who knows his nature knows Heaven (Nature).'[58] There is only one mind. My mind, my friends' mind, the mind of the sages thousands of years ago, and the mind of sages thousands of years to come are all the same. The substance of the mind is infinite. If one can completely develop his mind, he will become identified with Heaven. To acquire learning is to appreciate this fact. This is what is meant by the saying, 'Sincerity means the completion of the self, and the Way is self-directing.'[59] When is it necessary to depend on words?"

Po-mien asked, "What is meant by exerting the mind to the utmost? What is the difference between mind, capacity, the nature, and feeling?"

The Teacher said, "What you say is also details. However, this is not your fault, my friend; it is the defect of the entire world. When scholars read today, they only try to understand words and do not go further to find out what is vital. As to feeling, the nature, mind, and capacity, they are all one thing in general and simply happen to be expressed differently."

Po-mien said, "Is it that they 'are the same, but after they are produced, they have different names'?"[60]

---

[54] One of the most outstanding pupils of the Ch'eng brothers and a prominent Neo-Confucianist. For an account of his philosophy see Forke, *Geschichte der neueren chinesischen Philosophie*, pp. 110-116, or *Sung-Yüan hsüeh-an*, ch. 24.

[55] *Sung-Yüan hsüeh-an*, SPPY, 58:1a.   [56] *Chu Tzu yü-lei*, 124:1a.

[57] *Hsiang-shan ch'üan-chi*, 35:29a.   [58] *Mencius*, 7A:1.

[59] *The Mean*, ch. 25.   [60] Quoting *Lao Tzu*, ch. 1.

The Teacher said, "You do not have to talk about them. If you do, you will be wrong, and in the future you will only depend on words, and study not for your own sake but to impress others. If you pay attention to what is concrete to yourself, you will eventually understand. But if you insist on talking about them, you may say that with respect to Heaven, it is the nature, and with respect to man, it is the mind." (35:-10a-b)

36. Principle exists in the universe without any obstruction. It is only that you sink from it, hide yourself in darkness as in the trap, and lose all sense of what is high and far beyond. It is imperative that this trap be decisively broken and the confining net be penetrated and destroyed. (35:15b-16a)

37. Collect your spirit. Be your own master. "All things are already complete in oneself."[61] What is it that is lacking? When I should be commiserative, I am naturally commiserative. When I should be ashamed, liberal, generous, affectionate, tender, or strong and firm, I am naturally so. (35:18a)

38. Establish yourself in life and respect yourself. Don't follow other people's footsteps nor repeat their words. (35:22a)

39. The Four Beginnings (of humanity, righteousness, propriety, and wisdom) are all originally present in the self. Nothing need be added from the outside. (35:22a)

40. It is wrong to say that the human mind is identical with human artificiality whereas the moral mind is identical with the Principle of Nature [as suggested in the saying, "The human mind is precarious (liable to make mistakes), and the moral mind is subtle"].[62] By the human mind is meant the mind of everyone. To be subtle means [for the mind] to be refined, and that if it is coarse to any extent, it will not be refined. To say that one is human desires and the other the Principle of Nature is wrong. There are good and evil in man, and there are also good and evil in Nature [such as eclipses and evil stars].[63] How can it be correct to ascribe all good to Nature and all evil to man? (35:23a)

41. The theory of the distinction between the Principle of Nature and human desires is extremely defective. Since it was enunciated in the *Book of Rites* people have repeated it. In the "Record of Music" it is said that "By nature man is tranquil at birth. When influenced by external things, he begins to be active, which is desire."[64] If all this is good, then both activity and tranquillity are good. Is there any distinction

---

[61] *Mencius*, 7A:4.
[62] *History*, "Counsels of the Great Yü." Cf. Legge, *Shoo King*, p. 62.
[63] Lu's own insertion.
[64] Cf. Legge, *Li Ki*, vol. 1, p. 97.

between the Principle of Nature and human desires in this respect? If it is not good, then tranquillity is also not good. What is there between tranquillity and activity? (35:31b)

42. The Way refers to existence before physical form [and is without it], whereas concrete things refer to existence after physical form [and is with it]. Both heaven and earth are concrete things. What they produce and support necessarily have principle in them. (35:32b)

34

THE GREAT SYNTHESIS IN CHU HSI

NO ONE has exercised greater influence on Chinese thought than Chu Hsi (Chu Yüan-hui, 1130-1200), except Confucius, Mencius, Lao Tzu, and Chuang Tzu. He gave Confucianism new meaning and for centuries dominated not only Chinese thought but the thought of Korea and Japan as well.

Our philosopher early distinguished himself as a patriot-scholar, having repeatedly petitioned the emperor to practice the Confucian principles of "the investigation of things" and "the extension of knowledge," to impeach inefficient officials, and not to make peace with the invading enemy. But he preferred a life of peace and poverty. From 1163 to 1178, he declined official positions and devoted his time to scholarship. Eventually he spent nine years in public service, and gave an excellent account of himself in promoting education and agriculture. He revived the intellectual center at the White Deer Grotto in present Kiangsi Province, and his lectures there attracted all prominent scholars of the time. But his philosophical views were too radical for the rulers to accept. He was repeatedly dismissed from office. In 1196, his teachings were prohibited, and someone even demanded his execution. He continued to write after his dismissal from government service, and in so doing made tremendous contributions.[1]

[1] Chu Hsi was a native of Fukien. For several years he studied under his father who was head of various departments but eventually left the capital because he opposed accepting humiliating peace terms from the northern invaders. In 1154-57, Chu Hsi was a district keeper of records. But he preferred quiet study. From 1158 he studied under Li T'ung (Li Yen-p'ing, 1088-1163) who continued the tradition of the Neo-Confucianism of Ch'eng Hao and Ch'eng I. Most of his life, Chu Hsi was off and on a guardian of some temple, utilizing the peace and quiet to study, write, and talk with the most prominent scholars of the day. His official life, other than the guardianship, was intermittent and turbulent, for he strongly opposed concluding peace and repeatedly memorialized the throne to criticize officials and policies. Time and again he declined official positions. In 1179 he was appointed a prefect. In 1182 he was demoted to a minor post because he incurred the anger of the emperor by attacking the incompetency of officials on all levels. In 1188 he was appointed vice minister of the army department, but the vice-minister himself vigorously attacked him and he was shifted to a small position. Later in the year he was appointed a junior expositor in waiting to expound the Classics to the emperor, but he declined. In 1190 he became a prefect in Fukien and in 1194 a prefect in Hunan for one month. Later that year he became expositor in waiting but because he memorialized to attack the wicked but powerful officials he was dismissed and given the sinecure of a temple guardian. Two years later a censor accused him of ten crimes, including refusing to serve and spreading false learning, and someone even petitioned for his execution. All his posts were taken away. Although the attack on "false learning" was severe,

His contributions were by no means confined to philosophy, although that is the most important. He synthesized Confucius' concept of *jen* (humanity), Mencius' doctrines of humanity and righteousness, the idea of the investigation of things in the *Great Learning*, the teaching of sincerity in the *Doctrine of the Mean*, the yin yang (passive and active cosmic forces) and the Five Agents (Water, Fire, Wood, Metal, Earth) doctrines of Han times (206 B.C.–A.D. 220), and practically all the important ideas of the Neo-Confucianists of early Sung (960-1279), as we shall point out later on. His breadth of insight and his scholarship are equalled by few men in Chinese history. Rightly or wrongly, he was the one who established the orthodox line of transmission of the Confucian School from Confucius through Mencius, Chou Tun-i (Chou Lien-hsi, 1017-1073), Chang Tsai (Chang Heng-ch'ü, 1020-1077), Ch'eng Hao (Ch'eng Ming-tao, 1032-1085), and his brother Ch'eng I (Ch'eng I-ch'uan, 1033-1107).[2] He inaugurated new tendencies in textual criticisms. Among other things, he considered the *Book of Changes* as a book primarily for divination, thus radically differing from other Neo-Confucianists who depended on it for much of their philosophical inspiration. His most radical innovation was to select and group the *Analects*, the *Book of Mencius*, the *Great Learning*, and the *Doctrine of the Mean* (both of which are chapters of the *Book of Rites*), as the Four Books, wrote commentaries on them, interpreted them in new lights, and made them the foundation of his social and ethical philosophy. From 1313 to 1905 the Four Books were the basis of the civil service examinations. As a result, they have exercised far greater influence on Chinese life and thought in the last six hundred years than any other Classic. Through his interpretations of the Four Books, he made Neo-Confucianism truly Confucian, stripped of the Buddhist and Taoist influence which had been conspicuous in previous Neo-Confucianists.

Generally speaking, while he reaffirmed the basic doctrines of Confucianism, he brought its development over the centuries, especially during the Sung period, into a harmonious whole and gave it a new complexion.

Up to this time, Neo-Confucianism was characterized by six major concepts advocated by the different philosophers, namely, the Great

almost a thousand people attended his funeral when he died. For greater details, see Wang Mou-hung (1668-1741), *Chu Tzu nien-p'u* (Chronological Biography of Chu Hsi), *Kuo-hsüeh chi-pen ts'ung-shu* (Basic Sinological Series), ed., *Sung shih* (History of the Sung Dynasty, 960-1279), ch. 429, and Bruce, *Chu Hsi and His Masters*, pp. 56-96.

[2] In his *I-Lo yüan-yüan lu* (Record of the Origin of the School of the Two Ch'engs), he placed Chou Tun-i ahead of the two Ch'engs, thus asserting that Chou was the founder of Neo-Confucianism and the two Ch'engs more or less transmitted his doctrines. For comments on this matter, see above, pp. 482, 520.

Ultimate, principle (*li*), material force (ch'i),[3] the nature, the investigation of things, and humanity. All of these were developed, systematized, and synthesized in the greatest of Neo-Confucianists, Master Chu.

Assimilating the concepts of the Great Ultimate advocated by Chou Tun-i and combining it with the concept of principle of Ch'eng Hao and his brother Ch'eng I, Chu Hsi held that the Great Ultimate has no physical form but consists of principle in its totality. All actual and potential principles are contained in the Great Ultimate, which is complete in all things as a whole and in each thing individually. The relationship between the Great Ultimate in the universe and the Great Ultimate in each individual thing is not one of whole and part, but one similar to moonlight shining on objects. Each object has its own moonlight but this moonlight is moonlight as a whole.

It is the principle of things to be actualized, and actualization requires principle as its substance and material force as its actuality. Thus the Great Ultimate involves both principle and material force. The former is necessary to explain the reality and universality of things. It is incorporeal, one, eternal and unchanging, uniform, constituting the essence of things, always good, but it does not contain a dichotomy of good and evil, does not create things. The latter is necessary to explain physical form, individuality, and the transformation of things. It is physical, many, transitory and changeable, unequal in things, constituting their physical substance, involving both good and evil (depending on whether its endowment in things is balanced or partial), and is the agent of creation.

While seemingly dualistic, principle and material force are never separate. Principle needs material force in order to have something to adhere to, and material force needs principle as its own law of being. The fact that they always work together is due to the direction of the mind of the universe, which is the universe itself. In man this mind becomes, on the one hand, the moral mind, which is the principle of his original nature, and on the other, the human mind, which is the principle of original nature mixed with physical endowment and human desires. The principle of a thing or man is his very nature, real and concrete, unlike the nature in Buddhism, which is Emptiness. Original mind is principle in itself, unmoved, and perfectly good, while physical nature, on the other hand, is principle mixed with material force; it is the aroused state, involving both good and evil. The two natures, however, are always interfused, one the substance and the other, function. As substance, it is the nature, and as function, it is the feelings. That which unites and commands both human nature and feelings, according to Chang Tsai,

[3] See Appendix for a discussion of these two terms.

is the mind. By unifying and commanding is meant the mind unifying itself by harmonizing man's nature and his feelings and by transforming the human mind into the moral mind. Hence the possibility of morality. Moreover, all human beings and things have a mind, and this mind is in essence identical with the mind of the universe. Therefore there is the possibility of knowledge and the mutual influence and response among things and human beings, whether living or dead. Hence the investigation of things and religious sacrificial rites.

In his doctrine of the investigation of things, Chu Hsi follows closely Ch'eng I, as he does in the doctrine of principle. Indeed he was a fourth-generation pupil of the two Ch'eng brothers; and of the two, Ch'eng I was his main source of ideas. But he did not merely follow him or elaborate on him. He differs from him at many points. For example, while to Ch'eng I physical nature is outside principle, to Chu Hsi they are intermingled. Like Ch'eng, he taught seriousness (*ching*)[4] as the psychological prerequisite for true knowledge and exhaustive investigation as the method. But he was careful to emphasize equally both the deductive and inductive methods and both objective observation and intuitive understanding.

The greatest understanding to be achieved is that of *jen*,[5] an idea close to the hearts of all Confucianists. It was one of the most persistent subjects in the history of Chinese philosophy, and its long evaluation finally culminated in Chu Hsi's famous description that it is "the character of man's mind and the principle of love." The significance and implications of this idea as well as of other ideas of his will be elaborated in the comments. Suffice it to say here that virtually every cardinal Confucian concept was brought to a higher peak by Chu Hsi.

Such a well organized and freshly envigorated philosophy could not but overwhelm the Chinese. Although not without opposition from such outstanding Neo-Confucianists as Lu Hsiang-shan (Lu Chiu-yüan, 1139-1192), his philosophy and that of Ch'eng I, that is, the Ch'eng-Chu School of Principle, dominated the intellectual life of the Southern Sung period (1127-1279). In the Yüan dynasty (1271-1368) that followed, the supremacy of the Ch'eng-Chu School remained unchallenged. With a few exceptions, great scholars were all exponents of Chu Hsi's rationalism. Even those who attempted to reconcile the conflicts between him and Lu Hsiang-shan were essentially faithful disciples of his. In the Ming period (1318-1644), before the idealism of Wang Yang-ming (Wang Shou-jen, 1472-1529) emerged as the leading philosophy, his rationalism was the strongest intellectual current. Even during the fif-

---

[4] For comment on this term, see *ibid.*

[5] See *ibid.* for a discussion of the term.

teenth and sixteenth centuries when Wang overshadowed him, it did not entirely disappear. There were philosophers like members of the Tung-lin School who defended it and others like Liu Tsung-chou (1578-1645) who tried to synthesize it with the idealism of Wang. Consequently as opposition against idealism grew in the seventeenth century, Chu's philosophy was revived in strength. This period was one of independent and critical thinking, but some of the most outstanding scholars of the time, notably Ku Yen-wu (1613-1682) and Wang Fu-chih (1619-1692) were greatly influenced by and strongly inclined toward Chu Hsi. While eventually the critical spirit overthrew the speculative philosophies of both Wang and Chu, the latter had left a permanent imprint on the philosophical life of China. From the beginning of the fourteenth century on, his and Ch'eng I's interpretation of the Confucian Classics were officially held as the orthodox doctrines, and as already mentioned they formed the basis of civil service examinations and were therefore the intellectual standards for the Chinese literati until 1905 when the examination system was abolished. His philosophy survived the Intellectual Revolution of 1917 and became in the thirties the foundation of Professor Fung Yu-lan's new rationalism. His influence was not limited to China. It became an orthodoxy in Korea and the outstanding school of thought in the history of Japan.

The following selections include three short essays and a letter from the *Chu Tzu wen-chi* (Collection of Literary Works by Chu Hsi),[6] and a number of sayings from the *Chu Tzu ch'üan-shu* (Complete Works of Chu Hsi).[7]

[6] This work, dated 1532, consists of letters, official documents, short essays, poems, and the like in 121 chapters (36 vols.). The SPPY edition of 1930, entitled *Chu Tzu ta-ch'üan* (Complete Literary Works of Chu Hsi), is used.

[7] The 1714 edition is used. The title "Complete Works" is misleading, for actually it consists of selected passages from the *Chu Tzu wen-chi* and sayings from the *Chu Tzu yü-lei* (Classified Conversations of Chu Hsi) of 1270 which is in 140 chapters (40 vols.). It was compiled by imperial command in 1713 in a topical arrangement in 66 chapters (25 vols.) and published in 1714. It is worth noting that in the arrangement, moral cultivation comes first and metaphysics comes very much later. In practically all anthologies of Chu Hsi's works in Chinese, this characteristic dominates. The best example is the *Hsü Chin-ssu-lu* (Supplement to the *Reflections on Things at Hand*) by Chang Po-hsing (1651-1725). Even sayings on metaphysics are selected with moral cultivation in mind, as can be seen by his annotations. In our selections, the original topical arrangement is followed simply to keep the original order.

Chapters 42-48 of this work have been translated by Bruce into English, called *The Philosophy of Human Nature*, and ch. 49 has been rendered in European languages several times, the most recent in French by Pang Ching-Jen, in his *L'idée de Dieu chez Malebranche et l'idée de Li chez Tchou Hi*, pp. 73-119.

A. Treatises:
1. A Treatise on *Jen*
2. A Treatise on Ch'eng Ming-tao's Discourse on the Nature
3. First Letter to Gentlemen of Hunan on Equilibrium and Harmony
4. A Treatise on the Examination of the Mind

B. Selection of Sayings:

A. TREATISES

1. A Treatise on Jen

Original note: In the Chekiang edition, the "Treatise on *Jen*" by Chang Shih (Chang Nan-hsien, 1133-1180) is erroneously considered to be by Master Chu and Master Chu's treatise is considered to be a preface to Chang's essay. There is also a note saying that this treatise is perhaps a preface to Chang's essay. This is a mistake and is here corrected.

"The mind of Heaven and Earth is to produce things."[8] In the production of man and things, they receive the mind of Heaven and Earth as their mind. Therefore, with reference to the character of the mind, although it embraces and penetrates all and leaves nothing to be desired,

---

[8] *Wai-shu* (Additional Works), 3:1a, in ECCS. There is no indication which of the two brothers said this. It is considered to be Ch'eng Hao's in the *Ming-tao ch'üan-shu* (Complete Works of Ch'eng Hao) by Shen Kuei (of Ming, 1368-1644).

nevertheless, one word will cover all of it, namely, *jen* (humanity). Let me try to explain fully.

The moral qualities of the mind of Heaven and Earth are four: origination, flourish, advantages, and firmness.[9] And the principle of origination unites and controls them all. In their operation they constitute the course of the four seasons, and the vital force of spring permeates all. Therefore in the mind of man there are also four moral qualities—namely, *jen*, righteousness, propriety, and wisdom—and *jen* embraces them all. In their emanation and function, they constitute the feeling of love, respect, being right, and discrimination between right and wrong—and the feeling of commiseration pervades them all. Therefore in discussing the mind of Heaven and Earth, it is said, "Great is *ch'ien* (Heaven), the originator!" and "Great is *k'un* (Earth), the originator."[10] Both substance and function of the four moral qualities are thus fully implied without enumerating them. In discussing the excellence of man's mind, it is said, "*Jen* is man's mind."[11] Both substance and function of the four moral qualities are thus fully presented without mentioning them. For *jen* as constituting the Way (Tao) consists of the fact that the mind of Heaven and Earth to produce things is present in everything. Before feelings are aroused this substance is already existent in its completeness. After feelings are aroused, its function is infinite. If we can truly practice love and preserve it, then we have in it the spring of all virtues and the root of all good deeds. This is why in the teachings of the Confucian school, the student is always urged to exert anxious and unceasing effort in the pursuit of *jen*. In the teachings (of Confucius, it is said), "Master oneself and return to propriety."[12] This means that if we can overcome and eliminate selfishness and return to the Principle of Nature, (*T'ien-li*, Principle of Heaven), then the substance of this mind (that is, *jen*) will be present everywhere and its function will always be operative. It is also said, "Be respectful in private life, be serious in handling affairs, and be loyal in dealing with others."[13] These are also ways to preserve this mind. Again, it is said, "Be filial in serving parents," "Be respectful in serving elder brothers."[14] and "Be loving in dealing with all things."[15] These are ways to put this

[9] *Changes*, commentary on hexagram no. 1, *ch'ien* (Heaven). Cf. translation by Legge, *Yi King*, p. 57.

[10] *ibid.*, commenting on hexagram nos. 1 and 2, *k'un* (Earth). See Legge, pp. 213-214.

[11] *Mencius*, 6A:11.   [12] *Analects*, 12:1.   [13] *ibid.*, 13:19.

[14] Both quotations from *Book of Filial Piety*, ch. 14. See Makre, trans., *Hsiao Ching* p. 31.

[15] This is not a quotation from early Confucian texts but Ch'eng I's interpretation of the Confucian concept of altruism. See *I-shu* (Surviving Works), 11:5b, in ECCS.

mind into practice. It is again said, "They sought *jen* and found it,"[16] for (Po-i) declined a kingdom and left the country (in favor of his younger brother, Shu-ch'i) and they both remonstrated their superior against a punitive expedition and chose retirement and hunger,[17] and in doing so, they prevented losing this mind. Again it is said, "Sacrifice life in order to realize *jen*."[18] This means that we desire something more than life and hate something more than death, so as not to injure this mind. What mind is this? In Heaven and Earth it is the mind to produce things infinitely. In man it is the mind to love people gently and to benefit things. It includes the four virtues (of humanity, righteousness, propriety, and wisdom) and penetrates the Four Beginnings (of the sense of commiseration, the sense of shame, the sense of deference and compliance, and the sense of right and wrong).

Someone said: According to our explanation, is it not wrong for Master Ch'eng[19] to say that love is feeling while *jen* is nature and that love should not be regarded as *jen*?[20]

Answer: Not so. What Master Ch'eng criticized was the application of the term to the expression of love. What I maintain is that the term should be applied to the principle of love. For although the spheres of man's nature and feelings are different, their mutual penetration is like the blood system in which each part has its own relationship. When have they become sharply separated and been made to have nothing to do with each other? I was just now worrying about students' reciting Master Ch'eng's words without inquiring into their meaning, and thereby coming to talk about *jen* as clearly apart from love. I have therefore purposely talked about this to reveal the hidden meaning of Master Ch'eng's words, and you regard my ideas as different from his. Are you not mistaken?

Someone said: The followers of Master Ch'eng have given many explanations of *jen*. Some say that love is not *jen*, and regard the unity of all things and the self as the substance of *jen*. Others maintain that love is not *jen* but explain *jen* in terms of the possession of consciousness by the mind. If what you say is correct, are they all wrong?

Answer: From what they call the unity of all things and the self,[21] it can be seen that *jen* involves love for all, but unity is not the reality

---

[16] *Analects*, 7:14.

[17] When their father left the throne to Shu-ch'i, he declined in deference to his elder brother Po-i, but Po-i would not violate the order of his father and therefore chose to flee. Later, when King Wu (r. 1121–1116 B.C.) overthrew the Shang dynasty in spite of their remonstration, and founded the Chou dynasty, they would not eat the grains of Chou and starved to death.

[18] *Analects*, 15:8.   [19] Presumably Ch'eng I.

[20] *I-shu*, 18:1a.

[21] Referring to Yang Kuei-shan (Yang Shih, 1053-1135), in the *Kuei-shan yü-lu* (Recorded Conversations of Yang Shih), SPTK, 2:28a.

which makes *jen* a substance. From what they call the mind's possession of consciousness,[22] it can be seen that *jen* includes wisdom, but that is not the real reason why *jen* is so called. If you look up Confucius' answer to (his pupil) Tzu-kung's question whether conferring extensive benefit on the people and bringing salvation to all (will constitute *jen*)[23] and also Master Ch'eng's statement that *jen* is not to be explained in terms of consciousness,[24] you will see the point. How can you still explain *jen* in these terms?

Furthermore, to talk about *jen* in general terms of the unity of things and the self will lead people to be vague, confused, neglectful, and make no effort to be alert. The bad effect—and there has been—may be to consider other things as oneself. To talk about love in specific terms of consciousness will lead people to be nervous, irascible, and devoid of any quality of depth. The bad effect—and there has been—may be to consider desire as principle. In one case, (the mind) forgets (its objective). In the other (there is artificial effort to) help (it grow).[25] Both are wrong. Furthermore, the explanation in terms of consciousness does not in any way approach the manner of (a man of *jen* who) "delights in mountains" (while a man of wisdom delights in water)[26] or the idea that (*jen* alone) "can preserve" (what knowledge has attained),[27] as taught his pupil by Confucius. How then can you still explain love in those terms? I hereby record what they said and write this treatise on *jen*. (*Chu Tzu wen-chi*, or "Collection of Literary Works of Chu Hsi," CTTC, 67:20a-21b)

> *Comment.* This short treatise is both a criticism of certain theories and the incorporation of others into a harmonious whole. In addition, as Sun Ch'i-feng (1584-1675) has said, it expresses what the Ch'eng brothers had not expressed.[28] As can readily be seen, the central point is the synthesis of substance and function. In a way Chang Heng-ch'ü had implied it,[29] but the relationship between substance and function of *jen* was not clear until Chu.
>
> In ignoring the nature of *jen* and confining his teachings only to

[22] This is a reference to Hsieh Shang-ts'ai (Hsieh Liang-tso, 1050-1103), who described *jen* as consciousness. See *Shang-ts'ai yü-lu* (Recorded Conversations of Hsieh Liang-tso), *Cheng-i-t'ang ch'üan-shu* (Complete Library of the Hall of Rectifying the Way) ed., pt. 1, 2a-b. See also Forke, *Geschichte der neueren chinesischen Philosophie*, pp. 110-116.

[23] For the answer to Tzu-kung (520–c. 450 B.C.), see *Analects*, 6:28 (in ch. 2, above).

[24] *I-shu*, 24:3a.

[25] Quoting *Mencius*, 2A:2.

[26] *Analects*, 6:21.

[27] *ibid.*, 15:32.

[28] *Li-hsüeh tsung-ch'uan* (Orthodox Transmission of Neo-Confucianism), 1880 ed., 6:17a-b.

[29] See above, ch. 30, comment on sec. A.

its practice, Confucius taught only the function of *jen*. In a sense Mencius was the first to stress both substance and function when he laid equal emphasis on *jen* and righteousness. In interpreting *jen* as love, Han Confucianists viewed it almost exclusively from the point of view of function. Early Neo-Confucianists, on the other hand, whether in their doctrines of *jen* as impartiality, as forming one body with Heaven and Earth, or as consciousness, viewed *jen* almost exclusively from the point of view of substance. Here Chu Hsi gives substance and function equal importance, as they are synthesized neatly in the saying that *jen* is "the character of the mind" and "the principle of love."[30] This has become a Neo-Confucian idiom. It means that, as substance, *jen* is the character of man's mind, and, as function, it is the principle of love.

Since *jen* is the character of the mind, it is the nature of every man, and as such, universal nature. Thus it includes wisdom, propriety, and righteousness. The reason for this is the generative character of *jen*, which he got from the Ch'eng brothers.[31]

2. A Treatise on Ch'eng Ming-tao's Discourse on the Nature

[Master Ch'eng Hao also said,] "What is inborn is called nature. . . . They (nature and material force, *ch'i*) are both inborn."[32] [His meaning is this]: What is imparted by Heaven (Nature) to all things is called destiny (*ming*, mandate, fate). What is received by them from Heaven is called nature. But in the carrying out of the Mandate of Heaven, there must first be the interaction, mutual influence, consolidation, and integration of the two material forces (yin and yang) and the Five Agents (of Metal, Wood, Water, Fire, and Earth) before things can be produced. Man's nature and destiny exist before physical form [and are without it], while material force exists after physical form [and is with it]. What exists before physical form is the one principle harmonious and undifferentiated, and is invariably good. What exists after physical form, however, is confused and mixed, and good and evil are thereby differentiated. Therefore when man and things are produced, they have in them this material force, with the endowment of which they are produced. But the nature endowed by Heaven is therein preserved. This is

---

[30] These phrases appear separately in the treatise. However, they form one sentence in his *Lun-yü chi-chu* (Collected Commentaries on the *Analects*), ch. 1, commentary on *Analects*, 1:2. For a refutation of the theory that these phrases were borrowed from a Buddhist, see Yamaguchi Satsujō, *Jin no kenkyū* (An Investigation on *Jên*), 1936, pp. 370-372.

[31] On *jen*, see above, ch. 30, sec. 1, ch. 31, comment on secs. 1 and 11, and ch. 32, comment on sec. 42.

[32] *I-shu*, 1:7b. In the beginning sentence, Ch'eng is quoting Kao Tzu (c.420– c.350 B.C.) See *Mencius*, 6A:3.

how Master Ch'eng elucidated the doctrine of Kao Tzu that what is inborn is called nature, and expressed his own thought by saying that "One's nature is the same as material force and material force is the same as nature."[33]

[Master Ch'eng also said,] "[According to principle, there are both good and evil] in the material force with which man is endowed at birth. . . . [Nature is of course good], but it cannot be said that evil is not nature."[34] It is the principle of nature that the material force with which man is endowed necessarily has the difference of good and evil. For in the operation of material force, nature is the controlling factor. In accordance with its purity or impurity, material force is differentiated into good and evil. Therefore there are not two distinct things in nature opposing each other. Even the nature of evil material force is good, and therefore evil may not be said to be not a part of nature. The Master further said, "Good and evil in the world are both the Principle of Nature. What is called evil is not original evil. It becomes evil only because of deviation from the mean."[35] For there is nothing in the world which is outside of one's nature. All things are originally good but degenerated into evil, that is all.

[The Master further said,] "For what is inborn is called one's nature. . . . [The fact that whatever issues from the Way is good may be compared to] water always flowing downward."[36] Nature is simply nature. How can it be described in words? Therefore those who excel in talking about nature only do so in terms of the beginning of its emanation and manifestation, and what is involved in the concept of nature may then be understood in silence, as when Mencius spoke of the Four Beginnings (of humanity, righteousness, propriety, and wisdom).[37] By observing the fact that water necessarily flows downward, we know the nature of water is to go downward. Similarly, by observing the fact that the emanation of nature is always good, we know that nature involves goodness.

[The Master further said,] "Water as such is the same in all cases. . . . [Although they differ in being turbid or clear, we cannot say that the turbid water ceases to be water. . . . The original goodness of human nature is like the original clearness of water. Therefore it is not true that two distinct and opposing elements of good and evil exist in human nature and that] each issues from it." This is again using the clearness and turbidity of water as an analogy. The clearness of water is comparable to the goodness of nature. Water flowing to the sea without getting dirty is similar to one whose material force with which he is endowed

---

[33] *I-shu*, 1:7b.   [34] *ibid.*   [35] *ibid.*, 2A:1b.
[36] *ibid.*, 1:7b. The same for all the following quotations from Ch'eng Hao.
[37] *Mencius*, 2A:6.

is pure and clear and who is good from childhood. In the case of a sage it is his nature to be so and he preserves his Heavenly endowment complete. Water that flows only a short distance and is already turbid is like one whose material endowment is extremely unbalanced and impure and is evil from childhood. Water that flows a long distance before becoming turbid is like one who, as he grows up, changes his character as he sees something novel and attractive to him, and loses his child's heart. That water may be turbid to a greater or smaller extent is similar to the fact that one's material force may be dark or clear and pure or impure in varying degrees. "We cannot say that the turbid water ceases to be water" means that it cannot be said that evil is not nature. Thus although man is darkened by material force and degenerates into evil, nature does not cease to be inherent in him. Only, if you call it nature, it is not the original nature, and if you say it is not nature, yet from the beginning it has never departed from it. Because of this, man must increase his effort at purification. If one can overcome material force through learning, he will know that this nature is harmonious and unified and from the beginning has never been destroyed. It is like the original water. Although the water is turbid, the clear water is nevertheless there, and therefore it is not that clear water has been substituted by turbid water. When it is clear, it is originally not turbid, and therefore it is not that turbid water has been taken out and laid in a corner. This being the case, the nature is originally good. How can there be two distinct, opposing, and parallel things existing in nature?

[Master Ch'eng finally said,] "This principle is the Mandate of Heaven. [To obey and follow it is the Way. . . . One can neither augment nor diminish this function which corresponds to the Way.] Such is the case of Shun[38] who, [obeying and following the Way], possessed the empire as if it were nothing to him.[39] The sentence "This principle is the Mandate of Heaven" includes the beginning and ending, and the fundament and the secondary. Although the cultivation of the Way is spoken of with reference to human affairs, what is cultivated is after all nothing but the Mandate of Heaven as it originally is and is nothing man's selfishness or cunning can do about it. However, only the sage can completely fulfill it. Therefore the example of Shun is used to make the meaning clear. (*Chu Tzu wen-chi*, 67:16b-18a)

> *Comment.* In this essay, Chu Hsi not only removes the ambiguity in Ch'eng Hao's original treatise, which uses the same term, "nature," for basic nature—which is perfectly good—in the first part, and for physical nature—which involves both good and

[38] Legendary sage-emperor (3rd millennium B.C.)
[39] Paraphrasing *Analects*, 8:18.

evil—in the second part. He also harmonizes all theories of human nature before him, whether Mencius' theory of original goodness, Hsün Tzu's (fl. 298–238 B.C.) theory of original evil, or Chang Tsai's theory of physical nature.[40] Evil can now be explained, while the key Confucian teaching that evil can be overcome is reaffirmed. In addition, the ambiguity in Ch'eng Hao's statement that there are both good and evil in man's nature, which led to severe criticism of him, is now removed.[41]

3. First Letter to the Gentlemen of Hunan[42] on Equilibrium and Harmony

Concerning the meaning in the *Doctrine of the Mean* that equilibrium (*chung*, centrality, the Mean) is the state before the feelings of pleasure, anger, sorrow, and joy are aroused and that harmony is that state after they are aroused,[43] because formerly I realized the substance of the operation of the mind, and, furthermore, because Master Ch'eng I had said that "whenever we talk about the mind, we refer to the state after the feelings are aroused,"[44] I looked upon the mind as the state after the feelings are aroused and upon nature as the state before the feelings are aroused. However, I have observed that there are many incorrect points in Master Ch'eng's works. I have therefore thought the matter over, and consequently realized that in my previous theory not only are the [contrasting] terms "mind" and "nature" improper but the efforts in my daily task also completely lack a great foundation. Therefore the loss has not been confined to the meanings of words.

The various theories in Master Ch'eng's *Wen-chi* (Collection of Literary Works) and *I-shu* (Surviving Works) seem to hold that before there is any sign of thought or deliberation and prior to the arrival of

[40] See above, ch. 30, sec. 41.

[41] See above, ch. 31, comments on secs. 7-8.

[42] According to Wang Mou-hung, *Chu Tzu nien-p'u*, p. 37, this letter was written in 1169 when Chu Hsi was forty. The Hunan friends included Chang Nan-hsien (Chang Shih, also called Chang Ching-fu and Chang Ch'ien-fu, 1133-1180), with whom Chu Hsi carried on extensive correspondence on equilibrium and harmony and other subjects. (*Chu Tzu wen-chi*, chs. 31-33). For an account of him, see Forke, *Geschichte der neueren chinesischen Philosophie*, pp. 260-264 or *Sung-Yüan hsüen-an*, ch. 50. Chang was a resident of Hunan. According to the *Chu Tzu nien-p'u*, in 1167 when Chu Hsi was thirty-eight, he and Chang visited Mount Heng in Hunan. The group also included Lin Tse-chih with whom Chu Hsi once visited Chang in Ch'ang-sha, Hunan, and with whom he also corresponded extensively, chiefly on equilibrium and harmony (*Chu Tzu wen-chi*, 43-17a-32b). In a letter to Lin, Chu Hsi mentioned "Human friends" and also Chang (*ibid.*, 43:30b), who is also mentioned in other letters to Lin.

[43] *The Mean*, ch. 1.

[44] *I-ch'uan wen-chi* (Collection of Literary Works by Ch'eng I), 5:12a, in ECCS.

[stimulus] of external things, there is the state before the feelings of pleasure, anger, sorrow, and joy are aroused. At this time, the state is identical with the substance of the mind, which is absolutely quiet and inactive, and the nature endowed by Heaven should be completely embodied in it. Because it is neither excessive nor insufficient, and is neither unbalanced nor one-sided, it is called equilibrium. When it is acted upon and immediately penetrates all things, the feelings are then aroused.[45] In this state the functioning of the mind can be seen. Because it never fails to attain the proper measure and degree and has nowhere deviated from the right, it is called harmony. This is true because of the correctness of the human mind and the moral character of the feelings and nature.

However, the state before the feelings are aroused cannot be sought and the state after they are aroused permits no manipulation. So long as in one's daily life the effort at seriousness and cultivation is fully extended and there are no selfish human desires to disturb it, then before the feelings are aroused it will be as clear as a mirror and as calm as still water, and after the feelings are aroused it will attain due measure and degree without exception. This is the essential task in everyday life. As to self-examination when things occur and seeking understanding through inference when we come into contact with things, this must also serve as the foundation. If we observe the state after the feelings are aroused, what is contained in the state before the feelings are aroused can surely be understood in silence. This is why in his answers to Su Chi-ming, Master Ch'eng discussed and argued back and forth in the greatest detail and with extreme care, but in the final analysis what he said was no more than the word "seriousness" (*ching*).[46] This is the reason why he said, "Seriousness without fail is the way to attain equilibrium,"[47] and "For entering the Way there is nothing better than seriousness. No one can[48] ever extend knowledge to the utmost without depending on seriousness,"[49] and again, "Self-cultivation requires seriousness; the pursuit of learning depends on the extension of knowledge."[50]

Right along, in my discussions and thinking, I have simply considered the mind to be the state after the feelings are aroused, and in my daily efforts I have also merely considered examining and recognizing the clues [of activities of feelings] as the starting points. Consequently I have neglected the effort of daily self-cultivation, so that the mind is disturbed

---

[45] Generally stating the ideas in *Changes*, "Appended Remarks," pt. 1, ch. 10. Cf. Legge, *Yi King*, p. 370.

[46] The discussions are found in *I-shu*, 18:14b-16a.

[47] *ibid.*, 2A:23b.

[48] This word is added according to the *I-shu*.

[49] *I-shu*, 3:5b.   [50] *ibid.*, 18:5b.

in many ways and lacks the quality of depth or purity. Also, when it is expressed in speech or action, it is always characterized by a sense of urgency and an absence of reserve, and there is no longer any disposition of ease or profoundness. For a single mistake in one's viewpoint can lead to as much harm as this. This is something we must not overlook.

When Master Ch'eng said that "whenever we talk about the mind, we refer to the state after the feelings are aroused," he referred [only] to the mind of an infant [whose feelings have already been aroused]. When he said "whenever we talk about the mind," he was mistaken in the way he expressed it and therefore admitted the incorrectness and corrected himself [by saying, "This is of course incorrect, for the mind is one. Sometimes we refer to its substance (namely, the state of absolute quietness and inactivity) and sometimes we refer to its function (namely, its being acted on and immediately penetrating all things). It depends on one's point of view"].[51] We should not hold on to his saying which he had already corrected and on that basis doubt the correctness of his various theories, or simply dismiss it as incorrect without examining the fact that he was referring to something else. What do you gentlemen think about this? (*Chu Tzu wen-chi*, 64:28b-29b)

> *Comment.* As Liu Tsung-chou (Liu Ch'i-shan, 1578-1645) has pointed out, this letter represents Chu Hsi's final doctrine on moral efforts.[52] Chou Lien-hsi had taught tranquillity. Chu Hsi's own teacher, Li T'ung (Li yen-p'ing, 1088-1163) had taught sitting in meditation. Chu Hsi was at first much convinced. But after he learned the doctrine of seriousness from the Ch'eng brothers, he felt, as the Ch'engs did, that tranquillity was an extreme, and in seriousness one maintains the balance of internal and external life. In this letter, Chu Hsi emphasizes the point that the key to moral cultivation is to have a great foundation. Once the foundation is firm, tranquillity, sitting in meditation, and seriousness are all helpful. This is not only a synthesis of the teachings of his predecessors but a new approach.

4. A Treatise on the Examination of the Mind

Someone asked whether it is true that the Buddhists have a doctrine of the examination of the mind.

Answer: The mind is that with which man rules his body. It is one and not a duality, is subject and not object, and controls the external

---

[51] *I-ch'uan wen-chi*, 5:12a. The insertions in parentheses are Ch'eng's own.

[52] See Liu's comment on this letter in the *Sung-Yüan hsüeh-an*, (Anthology and Critical Accounts of the Neo-Confucianists of the Sung and Yüan Dynasties, 960-1368), ed. by Huang Tsung-hsi (1610-1695) *et al.*, SPPY, 48:9a.

world instead of being controlled by it. Therefore, if we examine external objects with the mind, their principles will be apprehended. Now (in the Buddhist view), there is another thing to examine the mind. If this is true, then outside this mind there is another one which is capable of controlling it. But is what we call the mind a unity or a duality? Is it subject or object? Does it control the external world or is it controlled by the external world? We do not need to be taught to see the fallacy of the Buddhist doctrine.

Someone may say: In the light of what you have said, how are we to understand such expressions by sages and worthies as "absolute refinement and singleness (of mind),"[53] "Hold it fast and you preserve it. Let it go and you lose it,"[54] "Exert the mind to the utmost and know one's nature. . . . Preserve one's mind and nourish one's nature,"[55] and "(Standing) let a man see (truthful words and serious action) in front of him, and (riding in a carriage), let him see them attached to the yoke."[56]

Answer: These expressions and (the Buddhist doctrine) sound similar but are different, just like the difference between seedlings and weed, or between vermilion and purple, and the student should clearly distinguish them. What is meant by the precariousness of the human mind is the budding of human selfish desires, and what is meant by the subtlety of the moral mind is the all-embracing depth of the Principle of Heaven (Nature).[57] The mind is one; it is called differently depending on whether or not it is rectified. The meaning of the saying, "Have absolute refinement and singleness (of mind)" is to abide by what is right and discern what is wrong, as well as to discard the wrong and restore the right. If we can do this, we shall indeed "hold fast the Mean,"[58] and avoid the partiality of too much or too little. The saying does not mean that the moral mind is one mind, the human mind another, and then still a third one to make them absolutely refined and single. By "holding it fast and preserving it" is not meant that one mind holds fast to another and so preserves it. Neither does "letting it go and losing it" mean that one mind lets go another and so loses it. It merely means that if the mind holds fast to itself, what might be lost will be saved, and if the mind does not hold fast but lets itself go, then what is preserved will be lost. "Holding it fast" is another way of saying that we should not allow our conduct during the day to fetter and destroy our innate mind characterized by humanity and righteousness.[59] It does not mean that we

[53] *History*, "Counsels of Great Yü." Cf. translation by Legge, *Shoo King*, p. 62.
[54] *Mencius*, 6A:8.   [55] *ibid.*, 7A:1.
[56] *Analects*, 15:5.   [57] *History, ibid.* Cf. Legge, p. 62.
[58] *ibid.*   [59] Paraphrasing *Mencius*, 6A:8.

should sit in a rigid position to preserve the obviously idle consciousness and declare that "This is holding it fast and preserving it!" As to the exerting of the mind to the utmost, it is to investigate things and study their principles to the utmost, to arrive at broad penetration, and thus to be able fully to realize the principle (*li*) embodied in the mind. By preserving the mind is meant "seriousness (*ching*) to straighten the internal life and righteousness to square the external life,"[60] a way of cultivation similar to what has just been called absolute refinement, singleness, holding fast, and preserving. Therefore one who has fully developed his mind can know his nature and know Heaven,[61] because the substance of the mind is unbeclouded and he is equipped to search into principle in its natural state, and one who has preserved the mind can nourish his nature and serve Heaven,[62] because the substance of the mind is not lost and he is equipped to follow principle in its natural state. Is this the same as using one mind fully to develop another, or one mind to preserve another, like two things holding on to each other and refusing to let go?

The expressions "in front of him" and "attached to the yoke" are intended to teach loyalty, faithfulness, earnestness, and seriousness,[63] as if saying that if these moral qualities are always borne in mind, we will see them no matter where we may go. But it does not mean that we observe the mind. Furthermore, suppose the body is here while the mind is in the front beholding it, and the body is in the carriage while the mind is attached to its yoke. Is that not absurd? Generally speaking, the doctrine of the sage is to base one's mind on investigating principle to the utmost and to respond to things by following it. It is like the body using the arm and the arm using the finger. The road will be level and open, the abiding place will be broad and easy, and the principle concrete and its operation natural.

According to the doctrine of the Buddhists, one seeks the mind with the mind, one employs the mind with the mind, like the mouth gnawing the mouth or the eye seeing the eye. Such an operation is precarious and oppressive, the road dangerous and obstructed, and the principle empty and running against its own course. If their doctrine seems to have something similar (to the Confucian), in reality it is different like this. But unless one is a superior man who thinks accurately and sifts clearly, how can he avoid being deluded in this matter? (*Chu Tzu wen-chi*, 67:18b-20a).

---

[60] *Changes*, commentary on hexagram no. 2. *k'un* (Earth). Cf. Legge, *Yi King*, p. 420.
[61] *Mencius*, 7A:1.   [62] *ibid.*   [63] *Analects*, 15:5.

B. THE COMPLETE WORKS OF CHU HSI

1. Moral Cultivation

a. How to Study

1. *Question*: Does what is called the fundamental task consist only in preserving the mind, nourishing the nature, and cultivating and controlling them?

Answer: Both the effort of preserving and nourishing and that of the investigation of principle to the utmost must be thorough. However, the effort of investigating principle to the utmost is already found within that of preserving and nourishing, and the effort of preserving and nourishing is already found within that of the investigation of principle to the utmost. To investigate principle to the utmost is the same as investigating to the utmost what is preserved, and to preserve and nourish is the same as nourishing what has been investigated. (1:18b-19a)

2. Now there is nothing for the student to do except to examine all principles with his mind. Principle is what is possessed by the mind. Always preserve this mind to examine all principles. These are the only things to do. (1:19a)

3. Although literature cannot be abolished, nevertheless the cultivation of the essential and the examination of the difference between the Principle of Nature (*T'ien-li*, Principle of Heaven) and human selfish desires are things that must not be interrupted for a single movement in the course of our daily activities and movement and rest. If one understands this point clearly, he will naturally not get to the point where he will drift into the popular ways of success and profit and expedient schemes. I myself did not really see the point until recently. Although my past defect of emphasizing fragmentary and isolated details showed different symptoms from these ways of life, yet the faults of forgetting the self, chasing after material things, leaving the internal empty, and greedily desiring the external remain the same. Master Ch'eng said, "One must not allow the myriad things in the world to disturb him. When the self is established, one will naturally understand the myriad things in the world."[64] When one does not even know where to anchor his body and mind, he talks about the kingly way and the despotic way, and discusses and studies the task of putting the world in order as if it were a trick. Is that not mistaken? (1:30a-b)

4. I have heard the sayings of Master Ch'eng I, "Self-cultivation re-

[64] *I-shu*, 6:2a.

quires seriousness. The pursuit of learning depends on the extension of knowledge."[65] These two sayings are really the essentials for the student to advance in establishing himself in life. And the two efforts have never failed to develop each other. However, when Master Ch'eng taught people to hold fast to seriousness, he meant nothing more than the primary importance of being orderly in clothing and appearance, and by the extension of knowledge he meant no more than to find out, in reading books and history and in dealing with things, where their principles are. The teachings are nothing like the absurd, wild, and unreasonable theories of recent times. (1:37b-38a)

b. Preserving the Mind and Nourishing the Nature

5. If one can in his daily life and at leisurely moments decidedly collect his mind right here, that is the equilibrium before the feelings of pleasure, anger, sorrow, and joy are aroused, and is the undifferentiated Principle of Nature. As things and affairs approach, the mind can clearly see which is right and which is wrong accordingly. What is right is the Principle of Nature, and what is wrong is in violation of the Principle of Nature. If one can always collect the mind like this, it would be as if he holds the scale and balance to measure things. (2:2a)

6. The mind embraces all principles and all principles are complete in this single entity, the mind. If one is not able to preserve the mind, he will be unable to investigate principle to the utmost. If he is unable to investigate principle to the utmost, he will be unable to exert his mind to the utmost. (2:4b)

7. *Someone asked*: How about guarding against depravity and concentrating on one thing? *Answer*: Concentrating on one thing is similar to "holding the will firm," and guarding against depravity is similar to "never doing violence to the vital force."[66] To guard against depravity merely means to prevent depraved forces from entering [the mind], whereas in concentrating on one thing one protects it from the inside. Neither should be unbalanced in any way. This is the way the internal and the external mutually cultivate each other. (2:8b)

c. Holding Fast to Seriousness (Ching)

8. The task of seriousness is the first principle of the Confucian School. From the beginning to the end, it must not be interrupted for a single moment. (2:21b)

9. Seriousness merely means the mind being its own master. (2:22a)

10. If one succeeds in preserving seriousness, his mind will be tranquil and the Principle of Nature will be perfectly clear to him. At no

---

[65] *ibid.*, 18:5b.   [66] *Mencius*, 2A:2.

point is the slightest effort exerted, and at no point is the slightest effort not exerted. (2:22a)

11. To be serious does not mean to sit still like a blockhead, with the ear hearing nothing, the eye seeing nothing, and the mind thinking of nothing, and only then it can be called seriousness. It is merely to be apprehensive and careful and dare not give free rein to oneself. In this way both body and mind will be collected and concentrated as if one is apprehensive of something. If one can always be like this, his dispositions will naturally be changed. Only when one has succeeded in preserving this mind can he engage in study. (2:22a)

12. It is not necessary to talk much about the doctrine of holding fast to seriousness. One has only to brood over thoroughly these sayings [of Ch'eng I], "Be orderly and dignified,"[67] "Be grave and austere,"[68] "Be correct in movement and appearance and be orderly in thoughts and deliberations,"[69] and "Be correct in your dress and dignified in your gaze,"[70] and make real effort. Then what [Ch'eng] called straightening the internal life and concentrating on one thing will naturally need no manipulation, one's body and mind will be serious, and the internal and external will be unified. (2:22a-b)

> Comment. Like Ch'eng I, Chu Hsi struck the balance between seriousness and the investigation of things in moral cultivation. He said that seriousness is the one important word transmitted in the Confucian School, that it is the foundation in Ch'eng I's teachings, and that it is Ch'eng's greatest contribution to later students.[71] His own contribution in this regard is to have steered the doctrine away from the subjective emphasis evident in Ch'eng Hao toward a unity of internal and external life.

d. Tranquillity

13. In the human body there is only a [combination of] activity and tranquillity. Tranquillity nourishes the root of activity and activity is to put tranquillity into action. There is tranquillity in activity. For example, when the feelings are aroused and all attain due measure and degree, that is tranquillity in activity. (2:38a)

14. About response to things. Things and the principle [inherent] in my mind are fundamentally one. Neither is deficient in any degree. What

[67] *I-shu*, 15:5a.
[68] *ibid.*, 15:21a; originally from the *Book of Rites*, "Meaning of Sacrifices." Cf. translation by Legge, *Li Ki*, vol. 2, p. 216.
[69] *I-shu*, 15:5a; the first half originally from *Analects*, 8:4.
[70] *I-shu*, 18:3a.
[71] See *Chu Tzu ch'üan-shu*, 2:17b-18b, 2:21b.

is necessary is for me to respond to things. Things and the mind share the same principle. To be calm is to be tranquil. To respond is to be active. (2:38b)

15. Ch'eng I sometimes also taught people sitting in meditation. But from Confucius and Mencius upward, there was no such doctrine. We must search and investigate on a higher plane and see that sitting in meditation and the examination of principle do not interfere with each other, and then it will be correct. (2:44a-b)

e. The Examination of the Self and Things

16. There is dead seriousness and there is living seriousness. If one merely adheres to seriousness in concentrating on one thing and, when things happen, does not support it with righteousness to distinguish between right and wrong, it will not be living seriousness. When one becomes at home with it, then wherever there is seriousness, there is righteousness, and wherever there is righteousness, there is seriousness. When tranquil, one examines himself as to whether one is serious or not, and when active, one examines himself as to whether he is righteous or not. Take, for example, the cases of "going abroad and behaving to everyone as if you were receiving a guest and employing the people as if you were assisting at a great sacrifice."[72] What would happen if you were not serious? Or the cases of "sitting as if one is impersonating an ancestor, and standing as if one is sacrificing."[73] What would happen if you were not serious? Righteousness and seriousness must support each other, one following the other without beginning or end, and then both internal and external life will be thoroughly penetrated by them. (3:1b-2a)

17. If the Principle of Nature exists in the human mind, human selfish desires will not, but if human selfish desires win, the Principle of Nature will be destroyed. There has never been a case where both the Principle of Nature and human selfish desires are interwoven and mixed. This is where the student must realize and examine for himself. (3:3a)

18. "Thinking alone can check passionate desires."[74] What do you think of the saying? *Answer*: Thinking is the same as examining. It means that when one is angry, if one can directly forget his anger and examine the right and wrong according to principle, then right and wrong will be clearly seen and desires will naturally be unable to persist. (3:3b)

19. To say that one must examine at the point where the feelings are about to be aroused means to be careful when thoughts and deliberations

---

[72] *Analects*, 12:2.

[73] *Book of Rites*, "Summary of Ceremonies," pt. 1. Cf. Legge, *Li Ki*, vol. 1, p. 62.

[74] Ch'eng I's saying. *I-shu*, 25:3a-b.

are just beginning, and to say that one must examine after the feelings have been aroused means that one must examine one's words and actions after they have taken place.[75] One must of course be careful about thoughts and deliberations when they begin, but one must not fail to examine his words and action after they have taken place. (3:7a)

f. Knowledge and Action

20. Knowledge and action always require each other. It is like a person who cannot walk without legs although he has eyes, and who cannot see without eyes although he has legs. With respect to order, knowledge comes first, and with respect to importance, action is more important. (3:8a)

21. The efforts of both knowledge and action must be exerted to the utmost. As one knows more clearly, he acts more earnestly, and as he acts more earnestly, he knows more clearly. Neither of the two should be unbalanced or discarded. It is like a person's two legs. If they take turn to walk, one will be able gradually to arrive at the destination. If one leg is weak and soft, then not even one forward step can be taken. However, we must first know before we can act. This is why the *Great Learning* first talks about the extension of knowledge,[76] the *Doctrine of the Mean* puts wisdom ahead of humanity and courage,[77] and Confucius first of all spoke of knowledge being sufficient to attain its objective.[78] But none of extensive study, accurate inquiry, careful thinking, clear sifting, and vigorous practice[79] can be omitted. (3:8b)

22. When one knows something but has not yet acted on it, his knowledge is still shallow. After he has experienced it, his knowledge will be increasingly clear, and its character will be different from what it was before. (3:12b)

23. Generally speaking, in any matter there is only one right or wrong. When the right or wrong is determined, one should choose the right and keep acting on it. How can one expect that by wavering he can win approval from everyone? Whether a thing is right or wrong will eventually become definite of itself. For the moment what is important is that one is satisfied within himself, so that looking up, he has no occasion for shame, and looking down, he has no occasion to blush.[80] Never mind whether other people say they like it or not. (3:12b-13a)

24. Throughout a person's handling of affairs and dealing with

[75] The question of examination before and after the feelings are aroused was extensively discussed by Chu Hsi and his friends. See *Chu Tzu wen-chi*, 53:18a-21a.
[76] The text.   [77] Ch. 20.   [78] *Analects*, 15:32.
[79] The five efforts taught in *The Mean*, ch. 20.
[80] Quoting *Mencius*, 7A:20.

things, there is no point at which moral principles are not present. Although one cannot know all of them, in all likelihood he has heard the great essentials. The important point is to put into action vigorously what he has already known and make efforts to go beyond it. In this way he can go from the near to the far and from the coarse to the refined, methodically and in an orderly manner, and observable effect can be achieved every day. (3:22b-23a)

g. The Extension of Knowledge

25. What sages and worthies call extensive learning means to study everything. From the most essential and most fundamental about oneself to every single thing or affair in the world, even the meaning of one word or half a word, everything should be investigated to the utmost, and none of it is unworthy of attention. Although we cannot investigate all, still we have to keep on devoting our attention to them in accordance with our intelligence and ability, and in time there will necessarily be some accomplishment. Is this not better than not to pay attention at all? If we absolutely pay no attention, even ignoring things passing before us whose names are unknown to us, is that the way to investigate things to the utmost? (3:26a)

26. Ch'i-yüan[81] asked: In investigating the principles of things and affairs to the utmost, should one investigate exhaustively the point where all principles converge? What do you think? *Answer*: There is no need to talk about the converging point. All that is before our eyes is things and affairs. Just investigate one item after another somehow until the utmost is reached. As more and more is done, one will naturally achieve a far and wide penetration. That which serves as the converging point is the mind. (3:26a-b)

27. Moral principles are quite inexhaustible. No matter what past scholars have said, they have not necessarily exhausted the subject. We must examine them this way and that way ourselves. The more deeply we go into them, the more we shall discover. (3:27a)

28. Pay no attention to names. We must investigate into the reason things are as they are. (3:27b)

29. There is no other way to investigate principle to the utmost than to pay attention to everything in our daily reading of books and handling of affairs. Although there may not seem to be substantial progress, nevertheless after a long period of accumulation, without knowing it one will be saturated [with principle] and achieve an extensive harmony

---

[81] There is no record of any of Chu Hsi's pupils by this name. He was probably Ts'ao Shu-yüan, whose courtesy name was Ch'i-yüan, and who as a young man was a follower of Ch'en Fu-liang (1137-1203). In one of Chu Hsi's letters to Ch'en (*Chu Tzu wen-chi*, 38:46a), he mentioned a visit of Ts'ao Ch'i-chih.

and penetration. Truly, one cannot succeed if one wants to hurry. (3:33b)

30. To investigate principle to the utmost means to seek to know the reason for which things and affairs are as they are and the reason according to which they should be, that is all. If we know why they are as they are, our will will not be perplexed, and if we know what they should be, our action will not be wrong. It does not mean to take the principle of something and put it in another. (3:34a)

> *Comment.* The philosophical basis for all these sayings on the investigation of things and the extension of knowledge is that principle is universal. The mind can investigate things because both share the same principle. Furthermore, since all things have the same principle, investigation can therefore exhaust all things. One major difference between Ch'eng I and Chu Hsi is that while Ch'eng largely confined investigation to the mundane world, Chu Hsi extended it to cover the entire universe. This is stated in his commentary on the *Great Learning*, which is not only a clear summary of his doctrine but also the most important statement on the investigation of things in the history of Chinese thought.[82]
>
> The significance of the Ch'eng-Chu doctrine of investigation has been indicated.[83] The whole spirit of their doctrine, involving both induction and deduction, is definitely consonant with science. Chu Hsi himself discovered the nature of fossils.[84] Early Neo-Confucianists wrote on pharmaceutical botany, the magnetic compass, fossils, mathematics, geography, cartography, and so forth.[85] And yet his doctrine in particular and Neo-Confucian in general did not develop natural science in China. Many theories have been advanced, especially those to the effect that Neo-Confucianists were more concerned with moral training than objective study of nature and they depended too much on books.[86] In this connection, what Hu Shih has to say is worth repeating. According to him, the Neo-Confucianists had the scientific spirit but not the scientific method. Their methods were observation and reflection. Without a scientific tradition such as the Greeks and the medieval doctors bequeathed to modern Europe, these Chinese philosophers were greatly handi-

[82] See above, ch. 4, Chu's remarks on sec. 5.

[83] See above, ch. 32, comment on sec. 44.

[84] See his theory about the mountains being formerly waves in sec. 124.

[85] Needham, *Science and Civilisation in China*, vol. 2. *History of Scientific Thought*, pp. 494-495.

[86] For a lengthy discussion of Neo-Confucianism and science, see Needham, *ibid.*, pp. 455-495, and Chan, "Neo-Confucianism and Chinese Scientific Thought," *Philosophy East and West*, 6 (1957), 309-332.

capped. The result was that to "investigate things" came to mean understanding right and wrong and handling human affairs. In the seventeenth century, the Ch'eng-Chu scientific spirit brought on an age of scientific scholarship in the critical study of classical and historical literature, an age ushered in by Chu Hsi himself. This new critical scholarship reached its maturity in the seventeenth century under the leadership of Ku Yen-wu (1613-1682), founder of the science of Chinese phonology, and Yen Jo-ch'ü (1636-1704), founder of the science of higher criticism of the classics. Ku once offered 160 cases as evidence to prove the ancient pronunciation of a single word. The similarity in the scientific spirit and the methods used by these masters is striking. But even then they were working with books, words, and documents, when their contemporaries in Europe were working with natural phenomena. Nevertheless, the tradition of the scientific spirit since their day has never been broken. Because of this tradition, the modern Chinese have not found themselves at sea in the scientific age.[87]

2. The Relation between the Nature of Man and Things and Their Destiny

31. *Question*: About the distinction between Heaven (Nature), destiny (*ming*, fate), nature, and principle. Heaven refers to what is self-existent; destiny refers to that which operates and is endowed in all things; nature refers to the total substance and that by which all things attain their being; and principle refers to the laws underlying all things and events. Taken together, Heaven is principle, destiny is nature, and nature is principle. Is this correct?

Answer: Yes. Nowadays, it is maintained that Heaven does not refer to the blue sky. In my view it cannot be left out of account. (42:1a-b)

32. Principle is the substance of Heaven, while destiny is the function of principle. One's nature is what is endowed in man. And one's feelings are the function of one's nature. (42:1b)

33. I-ch'uan (Ch'eng I) said that destiny is that which is endowed by Heaven and nature is what things have received from Heaven.[88] Principle is one. As endowed by Heaven in all things it is called destiny. As received by creatures from Heaven, it is called nature. The difference lies really in the different points of view. (42:2b)

34. On being asked about (Chang Tsai's) section on moral character failing to overcome material force,[89] (Chu Hsi) said: Master Chang Tsai merely said that both man's nature and material force flow down

---

[87] Hu Shih (1891-1962), *The Chinese Renaissance*, pp. 64-74.
[88] *I-shu*, 6:8a.   [89] See above, ch. 30, sec. 43.

from above. If my moral character is not adequate to overcome material force, then there is nothing to do but to submit to material force as endowed by Heaven. If my moral character is adequate to overcome material force, however, then what I receive from the endowment is all moral character. Therefore if I investigate principle to the utmost and fully develop my nature, then what I have received is wholly Heaven's moral character, and what Heaven has endowed in me is wholly Heaven's principle. The cases in which material force cannot be altered are life, death, longevity and brevity of life, for these, and poverty and wealth, and honor and humble station, all depend on material force. On the other hand, the practice of righteousness between the ruler and his ministers and the exercise of humanity between father and son, are what we call matters of fate. But there is also man's nature. The superior man does not say they are matters of fate."[90] They must proceed from myself, not from fate. (42:3a-b)

35. *Question*: [Chang Tsai said,] "If one investigates principle to the utmost and fully develops his nature, then his nature will be in accord with the character of Heaven and his destiny will be in accord with the Principle of Heaven."[91] How are nature and destiny to be distinguished?

Answer: Nature refers to what is stabilized whereas destiny refers to what is operating. Destiny, for example, refers to water flowing, while nature refers to water contained in a bowl. A big bowl contains more water, whereas a small one contains less. The water in a clean bowl will be clear, whereas that in a dirty bowl will be turbid. (42:3b)

36. *Question*: Destiny is what Heaven endows in man and things and nature is what they receive from Heaven. But nature and destiny each has two aspects. From the point of view of their principle, the principle that is destined in man and things by Heaven is called destiny, and the principle received by them from Heaven is called their nature. From the point of view of material force, the material force that is destined in man and things by Heaven is also called destiny and the material force received by them from Heaven is also called their nature. Is this correct?

Answer: Material force cannot be called the nature or destiny. They exist because of it, that is all. When the nature of Heaven and Earth are spoken of, it refers to principle only; when the physical nature is spoken of, it refers to principle and material force combined. Material force is not to be referred to as nature or destiny. (42:4b)

37. "Heaven produces the teeming multitude. As there are things, there are their specific principles."[92] This means that at the very time when a person is born, Heaven has already given him his nature. Man's

[90] *Mencius*, 7B:24.   [91] See above, ch. 30, sec. 43.
[92] *Odes*, ode no. 260.

nature is nothing but principle. It is called nature because it is endowed in man. It is not a concrete entity by itself which is to be destined as nature and which neither comes into nor goes out of existence. As I once illustrated, destiny (mandate) is like an appointment to office by the throne, and nature is like the office retained by the officer. This is why Master I-ch'uan (Ch'eng I) said, "Destiny is what is endowed by Heaven and nature is what things receive."[93] The reason is very clear. Therefore when ancient sages and worthies spoke of nature and destiny, they always spoke of them in relation to actual living. For example, when they spoke of the full development of human nature, they mean the complete realization of the moral principles of the Three Bonds (between ruler and minister, father and son, and husband and wife) and the Five Constant Virtues (that is, righteousness on the part of the father, love on the part of the mother, brotherliness on the part of the elder brother, respect on the part of the younger brother, and filial piety on the part of the son),[94] covering the relationships between the ruler and ministers and between father and son. When they spoke of nourishing our nature, they mean that we should nourish these moral principles without doing them any harm. This central truth runs through the most subtle principles and the most obvious facts, with nothing left uncovered. These are not empty words. (42:5a)

3. The Nature of Man and Things

38. The Way (Tao, Moral Law) is identical with the nature of man and things and the nature is identical with the Way. They are one and the same but we must understand in what connection it is called the nature and in what connection it is called the Way. (42:6a)

39. [Ch'eng I said,] "The nature is the same as principle."[95] In relation to the mind, it is called the nature. In relation to events, it is called principle. (42:6a)

40. The principle of life is called the nature. (42:6b)

41. The nature consists of innumerable principles created by Heaven. (42:6b)

42. The nature consists of concrete principle, complete with humanity, righteousness, propriety, and wisdom. (42:6b)

> *Comment.* Chu Hsi liked to quote Ch'eng I's statement that nature is the same as principle. This does not mean that he was merely repeating Ch'eng. As a matter of fact, the Neo-Confucian doctrine

[93] *I-shu*, 6:8a.

[94] In other connections the Five Constant Virtues are humanity, righteousness, propriety, wisdom, and faithfulness.

[95] *I-shu*, 22A:11a.

of nature was not quite clear until Chu Hsi made it so. With him, the relationships between nature and the Way, between nature and the feelings, and between basic nature and physical nature became well defined. In his system it is quite clear that nature refers to what is endowed in man and things, whereas the Way (principle) refers to that which is inherent in all existence. That is to say, generally and objectively speaking, it is the Way, while particularly and subjectively speaking it is nature. Likewise, the distinction between nature and the feelings is unmistakable, for nature is the substance, the form, the state before activity takes place, whereas the feelings are the function, the phenomena, the state after activity has started. Through the doctrine that principle is one but its manifestations are many, any conflict or bifurcation is eliminated.[96]

43. After reading some essays by Hsün[97] and others on nature, the Teacher said that in discussing nature it is important to know first of all what kind of entity it really is. (At bottom nature has neither physical form nor shadow. It is merely the moral principle possessed by the mind.)[98] Master Ch'eng I put it best when he said that "nature is the same as principle." Now if we regard it as principle, then surely it has neither physical form nor shadow. It is nothing but this very principle. In man, humanity, righteousness, propriety and wisdom are his nature, but what physical form or shape have they? All they have are the principles of humanity, righteousness, propriety, and wisdom. As they possess these principles, many deeds are carried out, and man is enabled to have the feelings of commiseration, shame, deference and compliance, and right and wrong. Take for example the nature of drugs, such as their property of increasing or decreasing heat (vigor, strength, vitality). There is no external form of this nature to be found in the drugs. Only after the drug is taken, heat or cold is produced—this is their nature. In man, nature is merely humanity, righteousness, propriety, and wisdom. According to Mencius, humanity, righteousness, propriety, and wisdom are rooted in the mind.[99] When, for example, he speaks of the mind of commiseration, he attributes feeling to the mind.

The Teacher further said: Shao Yao-fu (Shao Yung, 1011-1077) said that "nature is the concrete embodiment of the Way and the mind

[96] For the relationship between basic nature and physical nature, see above, ch. 30, comment on sec. 41.
[97] Huang Hsün, 1147-1212, Chu Hsi's pupil who recorded his conversation in 1188. For a brief account of him, see *Sung-Yüan hsüeh-an*, SPPY, ch. 69:12a.
[98] This sentence is added in the record by pupil Wu Pi-ta (fl.1188) who recorded the conversations in 1188-1189. For a brief account of him, see *Sung-Yüan hsüeh-an*, 69:33b.
[99] *Mencius*, 7A:21.

615

is the enclosure of the nature."[100] This theory is very good. For the Way itself has no physical form or body; it finds it only in man's nature. But if there were no mind, where could nature be? There must be mind before nature can be gotten hold of and put forth into operation, for the principles contained in man's nature are humanity, righteousness, propriety, and wisdom, and these are concrete principles. We Confucianists regard nature as real, whereas Buddhists regard it as unreal. However, it is incorrect to equate mind with nature. Nowadays people often explain nature in terms of mind. They should first understand before they talk. (If they consider consciousness as nature, they are only talking about the mind.)[101] For example, wherever there is the nature as endowed by Heaven, there is also the physical nature. If we regard the nature endowed by Heaven as rooted in the mind, then where will you place the physical nature? When, for example, it is said that "the human mind is precarious (liable to make mistakes), the moral mind is subtle (the mind that follows Tao, the Moral Law),"[102] the word "mind" is used in both cases. It is incorrect to say that the mind following the Moral Law is mind whereas the mind of the natural man is not mind. (42:6b-7a)

44. The Teacher asked how the nature is concrete embodiment of the Way. Ch'un[103] replied: The Way is principle inherent in the nature. The Teacher said: The term Way is used with reference to a universal order, whereas the term nature is used with reference to an individual self. How do we know that the Way operates in the world? Simply by putting it into operation in one's own experience.[104] Wherever nature is, there is the Way. The Way is the principle inherent in things, whereas nature is the principle inherent in the self. But the principle in all things is also in the principle inherent in the self. One's nature is the framework of the Way. (42:9b)

45. Chi-sui,[105] adhering to the doctrine of his family, said that nature cannot be spoken of as good, for the goodness that is originally

[100] Preface to his *Chi-jang chi* (Striking Earthen Musical Instruments—a Collection of Poems), *Shao Tzu ch'üan-shu* (Complete Works of Shao Yung), 1606 ed., 18:2a.

[101] This sentence in parentheses is added in Wu Pi-ta's record.

[102] *History*, "Counsels of the Great Yü." Cf. Legge, *Shoo King*, p. 62.

[103] Ch'en Ch'un (Ch'en Pei-hsi, 1153-1217). For an account of him, see *Sung-Yüan hsüeh-an*, ch. 68. Also Forke, *Geschichte der neueren chinesischen Philosophie*, pp. 211-225.

[104] As recorded by Liu Ti (fl. 1173-1190), who recorded the conversations of 1190, this sentence read: By returning to our own persons and seeking it there. For an account of him, see *Sung-Yüan hsüeh-an*, ch. 69:34a.

[105] Hu Chi-sui, grandson of Hu An-kuo (1073-1138), and son of Hu Hung (1100-1155), founder and expounder, respectively, of the Hu school of Neo-Confucian philosophy. See *Sung-Yüan hsüeh-an*, chs. 34 and 42.

so has no opposite. As soon as you describe nature as good, you are already contrasting it with evil, and when you speak of it in terms of the opposites of good and evil, it is no longer the original nature you are talking about. Original nature is transcendent, absolute, and beyond comparison, whereas goodness applies to the mundane world. The moment you say it is good, you are contrasting it with evil and you are no longer talking about original nature. When Mencius said that nature is good, he did not mean that nature is morally good, but simply used the language of admiration, like saying "How fine the nature!" just as the Buddha exclaimed, "Excellent is the Path!"[106]

I have criticized this theory and said that it is true that original nature is an all-pervading perfection not contrasted with evil. This is true of what Heaven has endowed in the self. But when it operates in man, there is the differentiation between good and evil. When man acts in accord with it, there is goodness. When man acts out of accord with it, there is evil. How can it be said that the good is not the original nature? It is in its operation in man that the distinction between good and evil arises, but conduct in accord with the original nature is due to the original nature. If, as they say, there is the goodness that is originally so and there is another goodness contrasted with evil, there must be two natures. Now what is received from Heaven is the same nature as that in accordance with which goodness ensues, except that as soon as good appears, evil, by implication, also appears. Therefore good and evil must be spoken of as contrast. But it is not true that there is originally an evil existing out there, waiting for the appearance of good to oppose it. We fall into evil only when our actions are not in accordance with the original nature. (42:9b-10a)

46. Again, referring to Master Shao's saying, "Man's nature is the concrete embodiment of the Way," the Teacher said: The Way exists everywhere, but how are we to find it? Simply by returning to the self and discovering it within one's nature and function. From the fact that we possess the principles of humanity, righteousness, propriety, and wisdom, we know that others also possess them. Of the thousands and tens of thousands of human beings and of all things, there is none independent of these moral principles. Even if extended to include all existence, you will find none to be independent of them. He put it very well when he said that "The nature is the concrete embodiment of the Way." (42:13a-b)

---

[106] This is Hu An-kuo's doctrine but more developed by his son Hu Hung in his *Chih-yen* ("Understanding Words"), on which Chu Hsi wrote lengthy critical comments, especially on Hu's theory that the nature is neither good nor evil. See *Sung-Yüan hsüeh-an*, ch. 42:3a-8a. Also Forke, pp. 122-135.

47. It is said that the word "good" in the expression "Nature is good" is different from the good as contrasted with evil. On that theory I hold that the good traced to the source of our being and the good in the process of life involving both good and evil are not two different things. They merely refer to two different states before and after it has emanated into activity. But it is the same good whether before it has emanated or afterward when it becomes contrasted with evil. Only after its emanation is it intermingled with evil. But the good in this state is the same good that emanates from the source of our being. (42:13b-14a)

48. In your (Ho Shu-ching's) letter you say that you do not know whence comes human desire. This is a very important question. In my opinion, what is called human desire is the exact opposite of the Principle of Nature. It is permissible to say that human desire exists because of the Principle of Nature, but it is wrong to say that human desire is the same as the Principle of Nature. For in its original state the Principle of Nature is free from human desire. It is from the deviation in the operation of the Principle of Nature that human desire arises. Master Ch'eng Hao says that "Good and evil in the world are both the Principle of Nature. What is called evil is not originally evil. It becomes evil only because of deviation from the mean."[107] Your quotation, "But it cannot be said that evil is not nature,"[108] expresses the same idea. (42:14b-15a)

49. Before material force exists, there is already nature. There is a time when material force does not exist, but nature is eternal. Although it is implanted in material force, yet material force is still material force and nature is still nature, the two not being confused. As to nature being inherent in all things and existing everywhere, there is no material force, whether refined or coarse, without principle. It is incorrect to regard the more refined part of material force as nature and the coarser part of nature as material force. (42:18b)

50. It is true that nature cannot be without activity, but its all-inclusiveness is not due to its inevitable activity. Even if it were without activity, is there anything wanting in its all-inclusiveness? The fallacy of the Buddhists lies in their erroneously regarding the heavenly and earthly aspects of the soul (hun-p'o) as nature and not in their ignorance of the fact that nature does not become all-inclusive through activity. (42:19a)

51. Master Ch'eng I said that nature is the same as principle and Master Shao Yung said that nature is the concrete embodiment of the Way.[109] These two sayings explain each other. But in your (Chiang Shu-ch'üan's) deliberation you consider one better than the other. In this,

[107] I-shu, 2A:1b.   [108] I-shu, 1:7b.   [109] See above, n.100.

you not only have failed to grasp Master Shao's idea, but I fear you also have not reached the depth of Master Ch'eng's expression. When Mr. Fang Pin-wang says that "the Way is Heaven as the self-existent and that nature is what Heaven has endowed in all things and what they have received from Heaven,"[110] he is transmitting the old doctrines of past scholars. While in reality nature and the Way are not two different things, yet there is a difference in the two terms which must be distinguished. Furthermore, in the passage that [immediately] follows, he says, "Although nature is received from Heaven, it is no more or less as compared with Heaven as such." This clearly shows that he does not cut them into pieces. However, he says, "The substance of the Way has no activity, whereas the human mind does have activity."[111] This means, that nature (which is the concrete embodiment of the Way) and the mind operate in two different spheres, a theory hardly tenable. Master Shao is nearer to the truth when he says that "The mind is the enclosure of nature."[112] However, the meaning of such an expression is much too unrefined. We must know that the mind is the master of the body, and nature is the moral principle inherent in the mind, and then we will not be wrong. (42:19b-20a)

52. "Nature is the same as principle." If you regard it as the source of the ten thousand principles, it would seem to be a different thing. Master K'ang-chieh (Shao Yung) said, "Man's nature is the concrete embodiment of the Way." His statement seems to the point. He also said, "Although the nature remains tranquil, but if we do not know how to preserve it, it will not attain the mean."[113] Now, the nature should necessarily attain the Mean, just as water should necessarily be cold and fire be hot. But the Mean is sometimes not attained because man loses his original nature and beclouds it by habits engendered by material force. It is not that nature fails to attain the Mean. (42:21b)

53. "Nature is the concrete embodiment of the Way" is a sentence in (Shao Yung's) preface to his *Chi-jang ko* (Striking Earthen Musical Instruments; A Collection of Poems). Its meaning is that nature is the concrete substance of what man receives from Heaven while the Way is the principle by which things are as they are. The principle of things is, of course, inherent in their nature, but when it is spoken of as the Way, it means something indefinite, boundless, and different in infinite variety, where concreteness is not to be seen. Only when we look into nature—and nowhere else—do we find the Way in its concreteness.

---

[110] Fang's letter to Chu Hsi. See *Chu Tzu wen-chi*, 56:10b.
[111] *ibid.*
[112] See above, n.100.
[113] I cannot trace the source of this saying. It is not found in the existing works of Shao Yung. It was probably orally transmitted.

When the *Doctrine of the Mean* says "To follow human nature is called the Way,"[114] it means this. (42:21b-22a)

54. "Nature is the concrete embodiment of the Way." When it is spoken of as the Way, it means something to spread over all things, with no clue for us to find it. But if we look for it in the mind, we shall find that all the principles inherent in it have definite substance and are unchangeable. These principles inherent in the mind are what we call nature. Therefore Master Shao goes on to say, "The mind is the endowment of nature." If you examine the matter in this way, the truth or error of what you (Fang Pin-wang) say can readily be seen. (42:22a)

4. The Nature of Man and the Nature of Things Compared

55. *Question*: Do all the Five Agents (Metal, Wood, Water, Fire, and Earth) possess the Great Ultimate?

Answer: They all do.

Question: Does man embody all the Five Agents while things embody only one of them?

Answer: Things also embody all the Five Agents, except that they embody them partially. (42:25a)

56. *Question*: Man and things are all endowed with the principle of the universe as their nature, and receive the material force of the universe as their physical form. The difference in personality is of course due to the various degrees of purity and strength of the material force. But in the case of things, are they as they are because of the incompleteness of the principle with which they are endowed or because of the impurity and beclouding character of the material force endowed in them?

Answer: The principle received by things is precisely in the same degree as the material force received by them. For example, the physical constitution of dogs and horses being what it is, they know how to do only certain things.

Further question: If each individual thing possesses its own Great Ultimate in its completeness, then principle can never be incomplete. [In this case, how is it that things possess principle only to a limited degree?]

Answer: You may consider it complete or you may consider it partial. From the point of view of principle, it is always complete, but from the point of view of material force, it cannot help being partial. This is why Lü Ta-lin (Lü Yü-shu, 1044-1090) said that in certain cases the nature

[114] Ch. 1.

of things approximates to the nature of man and in some cases the nature of man approximates that of things.[115] (42:26b-27a)

57. *Question*: Physical nature differs in the degree of purity. Does the nature bestowed by Heaven differ in the degree of its completeness?

Answer: No, there is no difference in the degree of its completeness. It is like the light of the sun and moon. In a clear, open field, it is seen in its entirety. Under a mat-shed, however, some of it is hidden and obstructed so that part of it is visible and part of it is not. What is impure is due to the impurity of material force. The obstruction is due to the self, like the mat-shed obstructing itself. However, man possesses the principle that can penetrate this obstruction, whereas in birds and animals, though they also possess this nature, it is neverthless restricted by their physical structure, which creates such a degree of obstruction as to be impenetrable. In the case of love, for example, in tigers and wolves, or in the sacrificial rites in the wolf and otter,[116] or in the righteousness in bees and ants, only the obstruction to a particular part of their nature is penetrated, just as light penetrates only a crack. As to the monkey, whose bodily form resembles that of man, it is the most intelligent among other creatures except that it cannot talk. (42:27a-b)

58. Chi[117] submitted to the Teacher the following statement concerning a problem in which he was still in doubt: The nature of man and the nature of things are in some respects the same and in other respects different. Only after we know wherein they are similar and wherein they are different can we discuss nature. Now, as the Great Ultimate begins its activity, the two material forces (yin and yang, passive and active cosmic forces) assume physical form, and as they assume physical form, the myriad transformations of things are produced. Both man and things have their origin here. This is where they are similar. But the two material forces and the Five Agents, in their fusion and intermingling, and in their interaction and mutual influence, produce innumerable changes and inequalities. This is where they are different. They are similar in regard to principle, but different in respect to material force. There must be principle before there can be that which constitutes the nature of man and things. Consequently, what makes them similar can-

---

[115] To Chu Hsi, he was the most outstanding of the Ch'engs' pupils. He recorded the conversations in bk. 2 of the *I-shu*. For an account of Lü, see Forke, *Geschichte der neueren chinesischen Philosophie*, pp. 116-119, or *Sung-Yüan hsüeh-an*, ch. 31. The saying here referred to is not found in the *Sung-Yüan hsüeh-an* or in any of Lü's existing works. It was probably orally transmitted.

[116] These animals would often catch more prey than they could devour at once and would spread it, walk around it, and watch it, as though devoutly performing a sacrificial rite. Ancient Confucianists drew a moral lesson from such animal behavior. See *Book of Rites*, "Monthly Order" (Legge, trans., *Li Ki*, ch. 22, p. 251).

[117] Ch'en Chi, a pupil from Foochow.

not make them different. There must be material force before there can
be that which constitutes their physical form. Consequently, what makes
them different cannot make them similar. For this reason, in your
Ta-hsüeh huo-wen (Questions and Answers on the Great Learning),
you said, "From the point of view of principle, all things have one
source, and of course man and things cannot be distinguished as higher
and lower creatures. From the point of view of material force, that
which receives it in its perfection and is unimpeded becomes man, while
those that receive it partially and are obstructed become things. Because
of this, they cannot be equal, but some are higher and others are
lower."[118] However, while in respect to material force they are unequal,
they both possess it as the stuff of life, and while in respect to principle
they are similar, in receiving it to constitute his nature, man alone
differs from other things. This consciousness and movement proceed
from material force while humanity, righteousness, propriety, and wisdom proceed from principle. Both man and things are capable of consciousness and movement, but though things possess humanity, righteousness, propriety, and wisdom, they cannot have them completely.
Now Kao Tzu (c.420–c.350 B.C.) pointed to material force and neglected principle. He was confined to what is similar and ignorant of
what is different, and was therefore attacked by Mencius.[119] In your
[*Meng Tzu*] *chi-chu* (Collected Commentaries on the *Book of Mencius*)
you maintain that "in respect to material force, man and things do not
seem to differ in consciousness and movement, but in respect to principle, the endowment of humanity, righteousness, propriety, and wisdom are necessarily imperfect in things."[120] Here you say that man and
things are similar in respect to material force but different in respect to
principle, in order to show that man is higher and cannot be equaled
by things. In the *Ta-hsüeh huo-wen*, you say that man and things are
similar in respect to principle but different in respect to material force,
in order to show that the Great Ultimate is not deficient in anything and
cannot be interfered with by any individual. Looked at this way, there
should not be any question. When someone was puzzled by the discrep-
ancies in the *Ta-hsüeh huo-wen* and the *chi-chu*, I explained it in this
way. Is this correct?

The Teacher commented: On this subject you have discussed very
clearly. It happened that last evening a friend talked about this matter
and I briefly explained it to him, but not as systematically as you have
done in this statement. (42:27b-29a)

[118] *Ta-hsüeh huo-wen*, p. 8b.
[119] *Mencius*, 6A:1-4, 6.
[120] *Meng Tzu chi-chu*, ch. 1, commenting on *Mencius*, 6A:3.

59. *Question*: How is it that dry and withered things also possess the nature?

Answer: Because from the very beginning they possess this nature. This is why we say so. There is not a single thing in the universe that is outside nature.

Thereupon the Teacher walked up the step and said: The bricks of these steps have in them the principle of bricks. Then he sat down and said: A bamboo chair has in it the principle of the bamboo chair. It is correct to say that dry and withered things have no spirit of life, but it is incorrect to say that they have no principle of life. For example, rotten wood is useless except as fuel—there is in it no spirit of life. But when a particular kind of wood is burned, a particular kind of force is produced, each different from the other. This is so because of the principle originally inherent in it. (42:29b-30a)

60. *Question*: Principle is what is received from Heaven by both man and things. Do things without feelings also possess principle?

Answer: They of course have principle. For example, a ship can go only on water while a cart can go only on land. (42:30a)

61. *Question*: Man and birds and animals all have consciousness, although with varying degrees of penetration or impediment. Do plants also have consciousness?

Answer: Yes, they also have. Take a pot of flowers, for example. When watered, they flourish gloriously, but if broken off, they will wither and droop. Can they be said to be without consciousness? Chou Mao-shu (Chou Tun-i) did not cut the grass growing outside his window and said that he felt toward the grass as he felt toward himself.[121] This shows that plants have consciousness [in so far as it has the spirit of life]. But the consciousness of animals is inferior to that of man, and that of plants is inferior to that of animals. Take also the example of the drug rhubarb, which, when taken, acts as a purgative, and the drug aconite, which, when taken, produces heat (vitality and strength). In these cases, the consciousness acts in one direction only.

When asked further whether decayed things also have consciousness, the Teacher said: They also have, as when burned into ashes, made into broth, and drunk, they will be caustic or bitter. (42:31b-32a)

5. Physical Nature

62. Nature is principle only. However, without the material force and concrete stuff of the universe, principle would have nothing in which to inhere. When material force is received in its state of clearness, there will be no obscurity or obstruction and principle will express itself freely.

121 *I-shu*, 3:2a.

If there is obscurity or obstruction, then in its operation of principle, th Principle of Heaven will dominate if the obstruction is small and humai selfish desire will dominate if the obstruction is great. From this we know that original nature is perfectly good. This is the nature describec by Mencius as "good,"[122] by Master Chou Tun-i as "pure and perfectly good,"[123] and by Master Ch'eng I as "the fundamental character of our nature"[124] and "the nature traced to the source of our being."[125] However, it will be obstructed if physical nature contains impurity. Hence, [as Chang Tsai said] "In physical nature there is that which the superior man denies to be his original nature," and "If one learns to return to the original nature endowed by Heaven and Earth, then it will be preserved."[126] In our discussion of nature, we must include physical nature before the discussion can be complete. (43:2b-3a)

63. When we speak of the nature of Heaven and Earth, we refer to principle alone. When we speak of the physical nature, we refer to principle and material force combined. Before material force existed, basic nature was already in existence. Material force does not always exist, but nature is eternal. Although nature is implanted in material force, yet material force is still material force and nature is still nature, without being confused or mixed up. As to its immanence in things and universal existence, regardless of whether material force is refined or coarse, there is nothing without its principle. (43:3a-b)

64. The physical nature is no different from the nature of Heaven and Earth. The point is that the nature of Heaven and Earth runs through the physical nature. For example, the good nature is like water. The physical nature is as though you sprinkled some sauce and salt in it and it then acquired a peculiar flavor. (43:4a)

65. The nature of all men is good, and yet there are those who are good from their birth and those who are evil from their birth. This is because of the difference in material force with which they are endowed. The revolutions of the universe consist of countless variety and are endless. But these may be seen: If the sun and moon are clear and bright, and the climate temperate and reasonable, the man born at such a time and endowed with such material force, which is clear, bright, well-blended, and strong, should be a good man. But if the sun and moon are darkened and gloomy, and the temperature abnormal, all this is evidence of violent material force. There is no doubt that if a man is endowed with

[122] *Mencius*, 6A:1-6.
[123] *T'ung-shu* (On Understanding the *Book of Changes*), ch. 1.
[124] *I-shu*, 18:19b, 22A:10b.
[125] *ibid.*, 3:3b.
[126] *Cheng-meng* (Correcting Youthful Ignorance), ch. 6, *Chang Tzu ch'üan-shu* (Complete Works of Master Chang), SPPY, 2:18b.

such material force, he will be a bad man. The objective of learning is to transform this material endowment. (43:4b)

66. Nature is like water. If it flows in a clean channel, it is clear, if it flows in a dirty channel, it becomes turbid. When physical nature that is clear and balanced is received, it will be preserved in its completeness. This is true of man. When physical nature that is turbid and unbalanced is received, it will be obscured. This is true of animals. Material force may be clear or turbid. That received by men is clear and that received by animals is turbid. Men mostly have clear material force; hence the difference between them and animals. However, there are some whose material force is turbid, and they are not far removed from animals. (43:7a-b)

67. Someone asked about the inequality in the clearness of the material endowment. The Teacher said: The differences in the material endowment are not limited to one kind and are not described only in terms of clearness and turbidity. There are men who are so bright that they know everything. Their material force is clear, but what they do may not all be in accord with principle. The reason is that their material force is not pure. There are others who are respectful, generous, loyal, and faithful. Their material force is pure, but in their knowledge they do not always penetrate principle. The reason is that their material force is not clear. From this you can deduce the rest. (42:8a)

68. Although nature is the same in all men, it is inevitable that [in most cases] the various elements in their material endowment are unbalanced. In some men the material force of Wood predominates. In such cases, the feeling of commiseration is generally uppermost, but the feeling of shame, of deference and compliance, and of right and wrong are impeded by the predominating force and do not emanate into action. In others, the material force of Metal predominates. In such cases, the feeling of shame is generally uppermost, but the other feelings are impeded and do not emanate into action. So with the material forces of Water and Fire. It is only when yin and yang are harmonized and the five moral natures (of humanity, righteousness, propriety, wisdom, and good faith) are all complete that a man has the qualities of the Mean and correctness and becomes a sage. (43:8a-b)

69. *Question*: Men often differ in the degree of clearness and purity. These are of course due to material endowment. By necessity their minds differ depending on their material endowment. Now, the mouth, the ear, and the eye, as well as the mind are all organs. Why is it that Heaven, in imparting the physical nature, invests the qualities of clearness and turbidity and purity and impurity only in the mind but not in the mouth, ear, or eye?. . . . *Answer*: The mouth, ear, and eye also differ

in clearness and turbidity and in purity and impurity. For example, people like I-ya (famous cook of the seventh century B.C.), the music-master Kuang[127] (music-master shortly before Confucius), and Li-lou (legendary figure famous for power of vision)[128] preserved clearness in the highest degree. It is the same with the mind. (43:17a-b)

70. Question about man's nature and destiny. *Answer*: If those born wise are completely and perfectly good, material force is there as material force and principle is there as principle, without any connection between each other. In such cases, there is no need to speak of the physical nature. But in the cases of men inferior to those born wise, [those who learn through study to be wise, those who learn through hard work, and those who work hard but still do not learn],[129] even the Principle of Nature is not deficient. Nevertheless it is tied up with material force. When material force is clear, principle will be obvious. When material force is turbid, principle will be obscured. The two—material force and principle—always go together, and therefore we designate this state as physical nature. It means that principle advances or retards depending on material force, and not to consider physical nature as the nature and destiny.

Answer: In the cases of those who are born wise, material force is extremely clear and principle is not obstructed. In the cases of those who learn to be wise and those below them, the clearness or turbidity of material force varies in degree. Whether principle is complete or incomplete depends on this. (43:18a)

6. Destiny

71. *Question*: You, sir, say that there are two kinds of destiny, one determining wealth and poverty, honor or humble station, life or death, and longevity or brevity of life, the other determining clearness or turbidity, partiality or balance, the wise or the stupid, and the worthy or the unworthy. The former pertains to material force, while the latter pertains to principle. As I (Hsien)[130] see it, both seem to pertain to material force, for the wise or the stupid, the worthy or the unworthy, clearness or turbidity, or partiality or balance are all caused by material force.

Answer: That is of course true. However, nature consists of the principles of destiny (principles underlying wisdom, stupidity and so forth). (43:27a)

72. *Question*: (The Confucian pupil) Yen Yüan [because of fate] unfortunately lived a short life.[131] When (another pupil) Po Niu died,

---

[127] *Mencius*, 4A:1.   [128] *ibid.*   [129] *Analects*, 16:9.
[130] Chou Hsien. Nothing is known of this pupil.   [131] *Analects*, 6:2.

Confucius said, "Alas! It is fate (*ming*, also meaning destiny, mandate).[132] And in regard to his obtaining office or not, he said, "That depends on fate."[133] Is there no difference between fate (destiny) in these cases and the fate (decree) in the sentence "What Heaven imparts (decrees) to man is called human nature"?[134]

Answer: Correct destiny proceeds from principle, whereas modified destiny proceeds from physical nature. Essentially in both cases it is imparted by Heaven. Mencius said, "That which happens without man's causing it to happen is the Mandate of Heaven."[135] However, man ought to fulfill his duty, and then whatever mandate he meets with is correct mandate.

Thereupon the question: At present the school of occultism (divination and the use of numbers), such as that of Shao Yung, asserts that all is predetermined and cannot be changed. What do you say?

Answer: They can only show the general course in which the principle of the prosperity and decline and the augmentation and diminution of yin and yang is revealed. Such theories were not held by sages or worthies. At present people expounding Shao Yung's [system based on] number assert that he said that everything and every event succeeds or fails at a predetermined point of time. Such exposition is superficial. (43:28b-29a)

73. *Question*: Yin and yang should be equal and therefore the number of worthy and unworthy people should be equal. Why is it that there are always fewer superior men and more inferior men?

Answer: Naturally things and events are confused and mixed. How can they be equal?. . .

Further question: Although things and events are confused and mixed, nevertheless they are nothing but the successive movement of the material forces of yin and yang. How is it that they are not equal?

Answer: It is not as you say. If there were only a single yin and a single yang, everything would be equal. But because of the great complexity and infinite transformation of things, it is impossible to have everything just right.

Further question: If so, then Heaven produces sages and worthies only accidentally and not with any intention.

Answer: When does Heaven say that it purposely wanted to produce a sage or a worthy? The mere fact is that whenever the courses of material force reach certain point and meet, a sage or a worthy is born. After he is born, it does seem that Heaven had such an intention. (43:30-a-b)

---

[132] *ibid.*, 6:8.   [133] *Mencius*, 5A:8.
[134] *The Mean*, ch. 1.   [135] *Mencius*, 5A:6.

74. In the *I-shu* (Surviving Works) where destiny is discussed (by Ch'eng I), [his own] note says that "It is not that the sage does not know destiny, but he must do his very best."[136] What do you say of this?

Answer: It is true that each man has his destiny, but he should not fail to obey the correct destiny. For example, the man who understands destiny will not stand beneath the precipitous wall.[137] If he should say that everything depends on the Mandate of Heaven and goes to stand under a precipitous wall, and if by any chance the wall should crumble and crush him, he cannot blame it on destiny. Whenever a man has done his very best, there he has his destiny alone. (43:33a-b)

7. The Mind

75. The principle of the mind is the Great Ultimate. The activity and tranquillity of the mind are the yin and yang. (44:1b)

76. Mind alone has no opposite. (44:1b)

77. *Question*: Is consciousness what it is because of the intelligence of the mind or is it because of the activity of material force?

Answer: Not material force alone. [Before material force existed], there was already the principle of consciousness. But principle at this stage does not give rise to consciousness. Only when it comes into union with material force is consciousness possible. Take, for example, the flame of this candle. It is because it has received this rich fat that there is so much light.

Question: Is that which emanates from the mind material force?

Answer: No, that is simply consciousness. (44:2a)

78. *Question*: Mind is consciousness and the nature is principle. How do the mind and principle pervade each other and become one?

Answer: They need not move to pervade each other. From the very start they pervade each other.

Question: How do they pervade each other from the very start?

Answer: Without the mind, principle would have nothing in which to inhere. (44:2a)

79. *Question*: Mind as an entity embraces all principles. The good that emanates of course proceeds from the mind. But the evil that emanates is all due to selfish material desires endowed by material force. Does it also proceed from the mind?

Answer: It is certainly not the original substance of the mind, but it also emanates from the mind.

Further question: Is this what is called the human mind?[138]

Answer: Yes.

---

[136] *I-shu*, 18:20b.   [137] *Mencius*, 7A:2.

[138] Such contrast is made in the *Book of History*, "The Counsels of Yü." Cf. Legge, *Shoo King*, p. 61.

Thereupon Ch'ien Tzu-sheng[139] asked: Does the human mind include both good and evil?

Answer: Both are included. (44:2b-3a)

80. Master Chang Tsai said that "in the unity of the nature and consciousness, there is the mind."[140] I am afraid this idea is not free from error, as though there was a consciousness outside our nature. (44:5a)

81. *Question*: The mind is essentially an active thing. It is not clear to me whether before (feelings) are aroused the mind is completely quiet and tranquil or whether its tranquillity contains within it a tendency toward activity.

Answer: It is not that tranquillity contains within it a tendency toward activity. Master Chou Tun-i said that "when tranquil, it is in the state of non-being. When active, it is in the state of being."[141] Tranquillity is not non-being as such. Because it has not assumed physical form, we call it non-being. It is not because of activity that there is being. Because (activity makes) it visible, we call it being. Heng-ch'ü's (Chang Tsai's) theory that "the mind commands man's nature and feelings"[142] is excellent. The nature is tranquil while feelings are active, and the mind involves both tranquillity and activity. Whether these refer to its substance or its function depends on one's point of view. While it is in the state of tranquillity, the principle of activity is already present. Ch'eng I said that in the state of equilibrium (before the feelings are aroused), "Although the ear hears nothing and the eye sees nothing, nevertheless the principles of hearing and seeing must be already there before hearing and seeing are possible."[143] When activity takes place, it is the same tranquillity that becomes active. (44:6b-7a)

82. In the passage, "By enlarging one's mind, one can enter into all things in the world,"[144] the expression "enter into" is like saying that humanity enters into all events and is all-pervasive. It means that the operation of the principle of the mind penetrates all as blood circulates and reaches the entire body. If there is a single thing not yet entered, the reaching is not yet complete and there are still things not yet embraced. This shows that the mind still excludes something. For selfishness separates and obstructs, and consequently one and others stand in opposition. This being the case, even those dearest to us may be excluded. "Therefore the mind that leaves something outside is not capable of uniting itself with the mind of Heaven."[145] (44:12b)

[139] This pupil recorded the conversations of 1197.

[140] *Cheng-meng*, 2:7b.   [141] *T'ung-shu*, ch. 2.

[142] *Chang Tzu ch'üan-shu*, 14:2b.   [143] *I-shu*, **18:15a.**

[144] *Chang Tsai, Cheng-meng*, ch. 7, *Chang Tzu ch'üan-shu*, 2:21a. See above, ch. 30, n.83.

[145] *ibid.*

83. *Question*: How can the mind by means of moral principles (Tao) penetrate all things without any limit?

Answer: The mind is not like a side door which can be enlarged by force. We must eliminate the obstructions of selfish desires, and then it will be pure and clear and able to know all. When the principles of things and events are investigated to the utmost, penetration will come as a sudden release. Heng-ch'ü (Chang Tsai) said, "Do not allow what is seen or heard to fetter the mind." "By enlarging one's mind one can enter into all things in the world." This means that if penetration is achieved through moral principles, there will be penetration like a sudden release. If we confine (the mind) to what is heard and what is seen, naturally our understanding will be narrow. (44:13a-b)

84. "The mind is the principle of production. . . . The feeling of commiseration is the principle of production in man."[146] This is because man is born with the mind of Heaven. The mind of Heaven is to produce things. (44:14a)

> *Comment*. The Ch'eng brothers' doctrine that the character of Heaven and Earth is to produce is here applied to the character of the mind. This concept underlies all Chu Hsi's ideas about the mind. It is this creative force of the mind that makes it the master of the universe, unites principle and material force, and enables consciousness to function without end in its activity and tranquillity.

8. The Mind, the Nature, and the Feelings

85. The nature is comparable to the Great Ultimate, and the mind to yin and yang. The Great Ultimate exists only in the yin and yang, and cannot be separated from them. In the final analysis, however, the Great Ultimate is the Great Ultimate and yin and yang are yin and yang. So it is with nature and mind. They are one and yet two, two and yet one, so to speak. Philosopher Han Yü (768-824) described nature as humanity, righteousness, propriety, wisdom, and faithfulness and the feelings as pleasure, anger, sorrow, and joy.[147] This is an advance over other philosophers on the problem of human nature. As to his division of human nature into three grades (superior, medium, and inferior),[148] he has only explained material force but not nature. (45:1a)

86. Although nature is a vacuity, it consists of concrete principles. Although the mind is a distinct entity, it is vacuous, and therefore embraces all principles. This truth will be apprehended only when people examine it for themselves. (45:2a)

[146] Ch'eng I's saying. *I-shu*, 21B:2a.
[147] *Yüan-hsing* (Inquiry on Human Nature). See above, ch. 27, sec. 1.
[148] *ibid*.

87. Nature consists of principles embraced in the mind, and the mind is where these principles are united. (45:2a)

88. Nature is principle. The mind is its embracement and reservoir, and issues it forth into operation. (45:2a)

89. Some time ago I read statements by Wu-feng (Hu Hung, 1100-1155) in which he spoke of the mind only in contrast to nature, leaving the feelings unaccounted for.[149] Later when I read Heng-ch'ü's (Chang-tsai's) doctrine that "the mind commands man's nature and feelings,"[150] I realized that it was a great contribution. Only then did I find a satisfactory account of the feelings. His doctrine agrees with that of Mencius. In the words of Mencius, "the feeling of commiseration is the beginning of humanity."[151] Now humanity is nature, and commiseration is feeling. In this, the mind can be seen through the feelings. He further said, "Humanity, righteousness, propriety, and wisdom are rooted in the mind."[152] In this, the mind is seen through nature. For the mind embraces both nature and the feelings. Nature is substance and feelings are function. (45:3a-b)

90. Nature is the state before activity begins, the feelings are the state when activity has started, and the mind includes both of these states. For nature is the mind before it is aroused, while feelings are the mind after it is aroused, as is expressed in [Chang Tsai's] saying, "The mind commands man's nature and feelings." Desire emanates from feelings. The mind is comparable to water, nature is comparable to the tranquillity of still water, feeling is comparable to the flow of water, and desire is comparable to its waves. Just as there are good and bad waves, so there are good desires, such as when "I want humanity,"[153] and bad desires which rush out like wild and violent waves. When bad desires are substantial, they will destroy the Principle of Heaven, as water bursts a dam and damages everything. When Mencius said that "feelings enable people to do good,"[154] he meant that the correct feelings flowing from our nature are originally all good. (45:4a)

91. The mind means master. It is master whether in the state of activity or in the state of tranquillity. It is not true that in the state of tranquillity there is no need of a master and there is a master only when the state becomes one of activity. By master is meant an all-pervading control and command existing in the mind by itself. The mind unites and apprehends nature and the feelings, but it is not united with them as a vague entity without any distinction. (45:4a-b)

92. In his reply to Heng-ch'ü's dictum that "nature in the state

[149] *Chih-yen*, ch. 3. See also *Sung-Yüan hsüeh-an*, 42:2a.
[150] *Chang Tzu ch'üan-shu*, 14:2b.   [151] *Mencius*, 2A:6, 6A:6.
[152] *ibid.*, 7A:21.   [153] *Analects*, 7:29.
[154] *Mencius*, 6A:6.

of calmness cannot be without activity," Ming-tao's (Ch'eng Hao's) idea is that we should not hate things and events nor chase after them. Nowadays people who hate things avoid them completely, and who chase after them are continuously lured away by them. The best thing is neither to shun away from things nor to drift with them, but to face and respond to them in various ways. For Heng-ch'ü's idea was to cut ourselves from the external world and achieve calmness internally, whereas Ming-tao's idea was that the internal and the external must be harmonized and unified. If (as Ming-tao said) that nature is calm "whether it is in a state of activity or in a state of tranquillity,"[155] then in our response to things we will naturally not be bound by them. If nature can be calmed only in a state of tranquillity, I am afraid that in time of activity it will be tempted and carried away by external things. (45:11b-12a)

93. *Question*: Is it correct to suppose that sages never show any anger?

Answer: How can they never show anger? When they ought to be angry, they will show it in their countenances. But if one has to punish someone for his crime and purposely smiles, that would be wrong.

Question: In that case, does it not show some feeling of wrath?

Answer: When Heaven is angry, thunder is also aroused. When sage-emperor Shun executed the four cruel criminals,[156] he must have been angry at that time. When one becomes angry at the right time, he will be acting in the proper degree. When the matter is over, anger disappears, and none of it will be retained. (45:14b-15a)

94. *Question*: "How can desires be checked? Simply by thought. In learning there is nothing more important than thought. Only thought can check desires."[157] Someone said that if thought is not correct, it will not be adequate to check desires. Instead, it will create trouble. How about "having no depraved thoughts"?[158]

Answer: Thoughts that are not correct are merely desires. If we think through the right and wrong, and the ought and ought-not of a thing, in accordance with its principle, then our thought will surely be correct. (45:19b)

9. Jen

95. Whenever and wherever humanity (*jen*) flows and operates, righteousness will fully be righteousness and propriety and wisdom will

---

[155] For both Chang's dictum and Ch'eng's response, see *Ming-tao wen-chi* (Collection of Literary Works by Ch'eng Hao), 3:1a, in ECCS.

[156] Accounts of this vary. According to the *Book of History*, "Canon of Shun" (Legge, p. 40), he banished or imprisoned them.

[157] Ch'eng I's saying, *I-shu*, 25:3a-b. [158] *Analects*, 2:2.

fully be propriety and wisdom. It is like the ten thousand things being stored and preserved. There is not a moment of cessation in such an operation for in all of these things there is the spirit of life. Take for example such things as seeds of grain or the peach and apricot kernels. When sown, they will grow. They are not dead things. For this reason they are called *jen* (the word *jen* meaning both kernel and humanity). This shows that *jen* implies the spirit of life. (47:3a)

96. *Jen* is spontaneous, altruism (*shu*) is cultivated. *Jen* is natural, altruism is by effort. *Jen* is uncalculating and has nothing in view, altruism is calculating and has an object in view. (47:6a-b)

97. *Jen* is the principle of love, and impartiality is the principle of *jen*. Therefore, if there is impartiality, there is *jen*, and if there is *jen*, there is love. (47:6b)

98. *Question*: Master Ch'eng Hao said, " 'Seriousness is to straighten the internal life and righteousness is to square the external life.' This means *jen*."[159] How can these be sufficient to be regarded as *jen*?

Answer: These two are *jen*. Wherever selfish desires can be entirely eliminated and the Principle of Nature freely operates, there is *jen*. For example, if one can "study extensively," be "steadfast in one's purpose," "inquire earnestly," and "reflect on things at hand (that is, what one can put into practice)," then "humanity (*jen*) consists in these."[160] "To master oneself and return to propriety"[161] is also *jen*. "When you go abroad, behave to everyone as if you were receiving a great guest. Employ the people as if you were assisting at a great sacrifice"[162]—this is also *jen*. To "be respectful in private life, be serious in handling affairs, and be loyal in dealing with others"[163]—these are also *jen*. All these depend on what path you follow. Once you have entered that path, exert effort until the limit is reached—all this is *jen*. (47:14b)

99. "When one makes impartiality the substance of his person, that is *jen*."[164] *Jen* is the principle originally inherent in man's mind. With impartiality, there is *jen*. With partiality, there is no *jen*. But impartiality as such should not be equated with *jen*. It must be made man's substance before it becomes *jen*. Impartiality, altruism, and love are all descriptions of *jen*. Impartiality is antecedent to *jen*; altruism and love are subsequent. This is so because impartiality makes *jen* possible, and *jen* makes love and altruism possible. (47:19b-20a)

---

159 *I-shu*, 11:3a. Ch'eng was quoting *Changes*, commentary on hexagram no. 2, *k'un*. See Legge, *Yi King*, p. 420.
160 *Analects*, 19:6.   161 *ibid.*, 12:1.   162 *ibid.*, 12:2.
163 *ibid.*, 13:19.   164 *I-shu*, 15:8b.

10. Principle (Li) and Material Force (Ch'i)

100. In the universe there has never been any material force without principle or principle without material force. (49:1a)

101. *Question*: Which exists first, principle or material force?

Answer: Principle has never been separated from material force. However, principle "exists before physical form [and is therefore without it]" whereas material force "exists after physical form [and is therefore with it]."[165] Hence when spoken of as being before or after physical form, is there not the difference of priority and posteriority? Principle has no physical form, but material force is coarse and contains impurities. (49:1a-b)

102. Fundamentally principle and material force cannot be spoken of as prior or posterior. But if we must trace their origin, we are obliged to say that principle is prior. However, principle is not a separate entity. It exists right in material force. Without material force, principle would have nothing to adhere to. As material force, there are the Agents (or Elements) of Metal, Wood, Water, and Fire. As principle, there are humanity, righteousness, propriety, and wisdom. (49:1b)

> *Comment.* Much discussion has taken place on the question whether Chu Hsi is a dualist. No one can doubt that principle is a universal, that there is a distinction between what exists before physical form and is therefore without it and what exists after form and is therefore with it, and that principle and material are different in many respects. As already suggested, Ch'eng Hao tended more to the monistic view while Ch'eng I tended more to the dualistic view, but it was also noted that whatever dualism there was, was superficial.[166] What Chu Hsi did was to harmonize the two trends of the Ch'eng brothers. In his system, principle has not only a logical priority. It actually exists before physical form and is without it because it is the principle of being. But it is not something outside of material force that imparts a principle of being into it. This is the reason why he said that principle has never been separate from material force. Thus principle is both immanent and transcendent. In other words, he is neither a monist nor a dualist, or he is both a monist and a dualist. Perhaps one may say that with respect to ultimate reality, he is a monist but with respect to phenomena he is a dualist. But since principle and material force are never separate, they do not exist independently of each other, much less in

---

[165] *Changes*, "Appended Remarks," pt. 1, ch. 12. Cf. Legge, *Yi King*, p. 377. About this translation, see Appendix, comment on "*Hsing-erh-shang.*"
[166] See above, p. 544.

CHU HSI

opposition. The fact is that any contrast of monism and dualism does not apply to his philosophy.

103. Question about the relation between principle and material force.

Answer: I-ch'uan (Ch'eng I) expressed it very well when he said that principle is one but its manifestations are many.[167] When heaven, earth, and the myriad things are spoken of together, there is only one principle. As applied to man, however, there is in each individual a particular principle. (49:1b)

104. *Question*: What are the evidences that principle is in material force?

Answer: For example, there is order in the complicated interfusion of the yin and the yang and of the Five Agents. Principle is there. If material force does not consolidate and integrate, principle would have nothing to attach itself to. (49:2b)

105. *Question*: May we say that before heaven and earth existed there was first of all principle?

Answer: Before heaven and earth existed, there was after all only principle. As there is this principle, therefore there are heaven and earth. If there were no principle, there would also be no heaven and earth, no man, no things, and in fact, no containing or sustaining (of things by heaven and earth) to speak of. As there is principle, there is therefore material force to operate everywhere and nourish and develop all things.

Question: Is it principle that nourishes and develops all things?

Answer: As there is this principle, therefore there is this material force operating, nourishing, and developing. Principle itself has neither physical form nor body. (49:3a-b)

106. K'o-chi[168] asked: When the creative process disposes of things, is it the end once a thing is gone, or is there a principle by which a thing that is gone may return?

Answer: It is the end once a thing is gone. How can there be material force that has disintegrated and yet integrates once more? (49:3b-4a)

107. *Question*: "The Lord on High has conferred even on the inferior people a moral sense."[169] "When Heaven is about to confer a great responsibility on any man. . ."[170] "Heaven, to protect the common people, made for them rulers."[171] "Heaven, in the production of things, is sure

[167] *Ts'ui-yen* (Pure Words), 1:24a; in ECCS. Also *I chuan* (Commentary on the Book of Changes), 3:3b.
[168] Lu K'o-chi, a pupil. Otherwise nothing is known of him.
[169] *History*, "Announcement of T'ang." Cf. Legge, *Shoo King*, p. 185.
[170] *Mencius*, 6B:15.   [171] *History*, "Great Oath." Cf. Legge, p. 286.

to be bountiful to them, according to their natural capacity."[172] "On the good-doer, the Lord on High sends down all blessings, and on the evil-doer, He sends down all miseries."[173] "When Heaven is about to send calamities to the world, it will always first produce abnormal people as a measure of their magnitude."[174] In passages like these, does it mean that Heaven has no personal consciousness and the passages are merely deductions from principle?

Answer: These passages have the same meaning. It is simply that principle operates this way. (49:4a)

108. Principle attaches to material force and thus operates. (49:4b)

109. Throughout the universe there are both principle and material force. Principle refers to the Way, which exists before physical form [and is without it] and is the root from which all things are produced. Material force refers to material objects, which exists after physical form [and is with it]; it is the instrument by which things are produced. Therefore in the production of man and things, they must be endowed with principle before they have their nature, and they must be endowed with material force before they have physical form. (49:5b)

Comment. Needham correctly understands Neo-Confucian philosophy, especially as developed by Chu Hsi, as essentially organic. As he aptly summarizes it: "The Neo-Confucians arrive at essentially an organic view of the universe. Composed of matter-energy [material force] and ordered by the universal principle of organization [principle], it was a universe which, though neither created nor governed by any personal deity, was entirely real, and possessed the property of manifesting the highest human values (love, righteousness, sacrifice, etc.) when beings of an integrative level sufficiently high to allow of their appearance, had come into existence."[175] Surely the Neo-Confucian conception of the universe is that of a single organism. All things exist in relations, and all relations follow a definite pattern according to which things are organized on various levels. That the universe is a set of relations goes far back to the *Book of Changes*, for Change itself is but relation. Tao as the principle of being is basically a principle of relationship. Impressed with this relational character of Chinese philosophy, Needham saw a striking similarity between Chinese organism and that of Whitehead. He also has made a most illuminating study of Chu Hsi's influence on Leibniz and the philoso-

[172] *The Mean*, ch. 17.
[173] *History*, "Instructions of I." Cf. Legge, p. 198.
[174] Source not traced.
[175] *Science and Civilisation in China*, vol. 2: *History of Scientific Thought*, p. 412.

phy of organism.[176] We must remember, however, that in Chu Hsi's philosophy, the world is more than just an organism, for principle is metaphysical. Moreover, while the many similarities between Neo-Confucianism and Whitehead's organism as pointed out by Needham are surprising, there is absent in Neo-Confucianism Whitehead's God, who, as the principle of concretion, is ultimate irrationality.

110. What are called principle and material force are certainly two different entities. But considered from the standpoint of things, the two entities are merged one with the other and cannot be separated with each in a different place. However, this does not destroy the fact that the two entities are each an entity in itself. When considered from the standpoint of principle, before things existed, their principles of being had already existed. Only their principles existed, however, but not yet the things themselves. Whenever one studies these aspects, one should clearly recognize and distinguish them, and consider both principle and material force from the beginning to the end, and then one will be free from error. (49:5b-6a)

111. There is principle before there can be material force. But it is only when there is material force that principle finds a place to settle. This is the process by which all things are produced, whether large as heaven and earth or small as ants. Why should we worry that in the creative process of Heaven and Earth, endowment may be wanting? Fundamentally, principle cannot be interpreted in the senses of existence or nonexistence. Before Heaven and Earth came into being, it already was as it is. (49:6a)

112. Considering the fact that all things come from one source, we see that their principle is the same but their material force different. Looking at their various substances, we see that their material force is similar but their principle utterly different. The difference in material force is due to the inequality of its purity or impurity, whereas the difference in principle is due to its completeness or partiality. If you will please examine thoroughly, there should be no further doubt. (49:7a)

113. The nature of man and things is nothing but principle and cannot be spoken of in terms of integration and disintegration. That which integrates to produce life and disintegrates to produce death is only material force.[177] What we called the spirit, the heavenly and earthly aspects of the soul (hun-p'o),[178] and consciousness are all effects of ma-

---

[176] ibid., pp. 291, 454, 466, 474, 496-505, 562.

[177] This sentence does not appear in the text but in Chu Tzu wen-chi, 45:19b from which the passage is selected.

[178] For a description of hun-p'o, see above, ch. 1, n.30.

terial force. Therefore when material force is integrated, there are these effects. When it is disintegrated, there are no more. As to principle, fundamentally it does not exist or cease to exist because of such integration or disintegration. As there is a certain principle, there is the material force corresponding to it, and as this material force integrates in a particular instance, its principle is also endowed in that instance. (49:8a)

11. The Great Ultimate

114. The Great Ultimate is nothing other than principle. (49:8b)

Comment. This is the central idea in Chu Hsi's philosophy.[179] He considered Chou Tun-i's doctrine of the Great Ultimate as based on principle instead of material force, as was the case before Chou's time. The concept was implied in Chou but firmly established in Chu Hsi.

115. Question: The Great Ultimate is not a thing existing in a chaotic state before the formation of heaven and earth, but a general name for the principles of heaven and earth and the myriad things. Is that correct?

Answer: The Great Ultimate is merely the principle of heaven and earth and the myriad things. With respect to heaven and earth, there is the Great Ultimate in them. With respect to the myriad things, there is the Great Ultimate in each and every one of them. Before heaven and earth existed, there was assuredly this principle. It is the principle that "through movement generates the yang." It is also this principle that "through tranquillity generates the yin."[180] (49:8b-9a)

116. Question: [You said,] "Principle is a single, concrete entity, and the myriad things partake it as their substance. Hence each of the myriad things possesses in it a Great Ultimate."[181] According to this theory, does the Great Ultimate not split up into parts?

Answer: Fundamentally there is only one Great Ultimate, yet each of the myriad things has been endowed with it and each in itself possesses the Great Ultimate in its entirety. This is similar to the fact that there is only one moon in the sky but when its light is scattered upon rivers and lakes, it can be seen everywhere. It cannot be said that the moon has been split. (49:10b-11a)

---

179 This was pointed out by Shih Huang (fl. 1705) in commenting on the saying in his *Wu-tzu chin-ssu lu fa-ming* (Exposition of the *Reflections on Things at Hand by Five Philosophers*), 1:34b.

180 Chou Tun-i, *An Explanation of the Diagram of the Great Ultimate*.

181 Chu Hsi's commentary on Chou Tun-i's *T'ung-shu*, ch. 22. See *Chou Tzu ch'üan-shu* (Complete Works of Chou Tun-i), *Wan-yu wen-k'u* (Universal Library) ed., p. 170.

Comment. The idea that principle is one but its manifestations are many is derived from Ch'eng but the doctrine was not fully developed until Chu Hsi. Its similarity with the doctrine of one and many in the Hua-yen School of Buddhism has been noted. Chu's analogy of the moon is a specific, though indirect, borrowing of the Hua-yen analogy of the moon and its many reflections.[182] According to Fung Yu-lan, it is similar to the Hua-yen metaphor of "the realm of Indra's net" which contains many jewels each of which reflects not only the image of every other jewel but also all the multiple images reflected in each of those other jewels. However, Fung correctly adds that while according to the Hua-yen School within any given individual concrete object all other concrete objects are actually present, to Chu Hsi, each concrete object has within it the Great Ultimate, that is, the principles of all things but not the physical objects themselves.[183]

117. The Great Ultimate has neither spatial restriction nor physical form or body. There is no spot where it may be placed. When it is considered in the state before activity begins, this state is nothing but tranquillity. Now activity, tranquillity, yin, and yang all exist only after physical form [and are with it]. However, activity is after all the activity of the Great Ultimate and tranquillity is also its tranquillity, although activity and tranquillity themselves are not the Great Ultimate. This is why Master Chou Tun-i only spoke of that state as Non-ultimate.[184] While the state before activity begins cannot be spoken of as the Great Ultimate, nevertheless the principles of pleasure, anger, sorrow, and joy are already inherent in it. Pleasure and joy belong to yang and anger and sorrow belong to yin. In the initial stage the four are not manifested, but their principles are already there. As contrasted with the state after activity begins, it may be called the Great Ultimate. But still it is difficult to say. All this is but a vague description. The truth must be personally realized by each individual himself. (49:11a-b)

Comment. The difference between Chou Tun-i and Chu Hsi is that for Chou the Great Ultimate involves activity and tranquillity, whereas for Chu, it has only the principle of activity and tranquillity, for the Great Ultimate is absolute and is therefore above phenomenal manifestations. Actually, Chou's Great Ultimate is identical with material force, whereas Chu's Great Ultimate is identical with principle. As to how the Great Ultimate can produce the two material forces (yin and yang), Chu's answer is vague.

.[182] See above, ch. 25, introduction. Cf. *Hua-yen ching*, verse in ch. 23.
[183] Fung, *History of Chinese Philosophy*, vol. 2, pp. 541-542.
[184] See above, ch. 28, sec. 1.

118. Someone asked about the Great Ultimate. *Reply*: The Great Ultimate is simply the principle of the highest good. Each and every person has in him the Great Ultimate and each and every thing has in it the Great Ultimate. What Master Chou calls the Great Ultimate is a name to express all the virtues and the highest good in Heaven and Earth, man, and things. (49:11b)

> *Comment.* Commenting on this passage, Fung Yu-lan said, "The Supreme Ultimate is very much like what Plato called the Idea of the Good, or what Aristotle called God."[185] Previously, Bruce had asserted that Chou Tun-i's doctrine of the Supreme Ultimate was expanded and interpreted by the Ch'eng brothers and Chu Hsi along lines suggestive of Plato and Aristotle.[186] Recently, Carsun Chang compared Chu Hsi and Aristotle in the greatest detail so far. He pointed out that Chu Hsi agrees with Aristotle that Ideas do not exist for themselves, that the Idea as the one does not exist apart from the many, that matter exists in the sense of possibility or capacity, that matter and form exist together, that there is an eternal principle, that it is at once form, end, and moving cause, that matter is the ultimate source of the imperfection in things and that it is the principle of individuation and plurality, that an entity (God or Heaven) exists which imparts motion but is itself unmoved, and that it is pure energy, eternal, and good *per se*. However, he added that although Chu Hsi is an Aristotelian in the field of nature, he is a Platonist in the field of moral values, recognizing that there exists an eternal, unchanging truth.[187]
>
> Needham, however, rejects any comparison with Aristotle. He says: "It is true that form was the factor of individuation, that which gave rise to the unity of any organism and its purposes; so was *Li*. But there the resemblance ceases. The form of the body was the soul; but the great tradition of Chinese philosophy had no place for souls. . . Again, Aristotelian form actually conferred substantiality on things, but . . . the *ch'i* [material force] was not brought into being by *Li*, and *Li* had only a logical priority. *Ch'i* did not depend upon *Li* in any way. Form was the 'essence' and 'primary substance' of things, but *Li* was not itself substantial or any form of *ch'i*. . . . I believe that *Li* was not in any strict sense metaphysical, as were Platonic ideas and Aristotelian forms, but rather the invisible organizing fields or forces existing at all levels within the natural world. Pure form and pure actuality was God,

185 Fung, vol. 2, p. 537.
186 Bruce, *Chu Hsi and His Masters*, pp. 48-49.
187 Carsun Chang, *Neo-Confucian Thought*, pp. 255-256.

but in the world of *Li* and *ch'i* there was no *Chu-Tsai* [Director] whatsoever."[188]

These comparisons show that in any comparative study similarities are usually accompanied by dissimilarities. The important point to note is that Chu Hsi is neither Platonic nor Aristotelian. The usual Western polarities do not apply in Chinese philosophy.

119. The Great Ultimate is similar to the top of a house or the zenith of the sky, beyond which point there is no more. It is the ultimate of principle. Yang is active and yin is tranquil. In these it is not the Great Ultimate that acts or remains tranquil. It is simply that there are the principles of activity and tranquillity. Principle is not visible; it becomes visible through yin and yang. Principle attaches itself to yin and yang as a man sits astride a horse. As soon as yin and yang produce the Five Agents, they are confined and fixed by physical nature and are thus differentiated into individual things each with its nature. But the Great Ultimate is in all of them. (49:14a)

120. The Great Ultimate contains all principles of the Five Agents and yin and yang. It is not an empty thing. If it were a void, it would approach the Buddhist theory of dharma-nature (which maintains that the nature of dharmas, that is, elements of existence, are void). (49:14a)

121. *Question*: Is the Great Ultimate the highest principle of the human mind?

Answer: There is an ultimate in every thing or event. That is the ultimate of principle.

Someone asked: Like humanity on the part of the ruler and respect on the part of ministers. These are ultimates.

Answer: These are ultimates of a particular thing or event. When all principles of heaven and earth and the myriad things are put together, that is the Great Ultimate. The Great Ultimate originally has no such name. It is merely a name to express its character. (49:14b-15a)

122. There is no other event in the universe except yin and yang succeeding each other in an unceasing cycle. This is called Change. However, for these activity and tranquillity, there must be the principles which make them possible. This is the Great Ultimate. (49:16a)

12. Heaven and Earth

123. In the beginning of the universe there was only material force consisting of yin and yang. This force moved and circulated, turning this way and that. As this movement gained speed, a mass of sediment was compressed (pushed together), and since there is no outlet for

---

[188] *Science and Civilisation in China*, vol. 2: *History of Scientific Thought*, p. 475.

this, it consolidated to form the earth in the center of the universe. The clear part of material force formed the sky, the sun, and moon, and the stars and zodiacal spaces. It is only on the outside that the encircling movement perpetually goes on. The earth exists motionless in the center of the system, not at the bottom. (49:19a)

124. In the beginning of the universe, when it was still in a state of undifferentiated chaos, I imagine there were only water and fire. The sediment from water formed the earth. If today we climb the high mountains and look around, we will see ranges of mountains in the shape of waves. This is because the water formed them like this, though we do not know in what period they solidified. The solidification was at first very soft, but in time it became hard.

Question: I imagine it is like the tide rushing upon and making waves in the sand.

Answer: Yes. The most turbid water formed the earth and the purest fire became wind, thunder, lightning, the stars, and the like. (49:19b-20a)

125. *Question*: From the beginning of the universe to this day, it has not yet been ten thousand years. I do not know how things looked before then.

Answer: The past is to be understood in the same way.

Further question: Can the universe be destroyed?

Answer: It is indestructible. But in time man will lose all moral principles and everything will be thrown together in a chaos. Man and things will all die out, and then there will be a new beginning.

Further question: How was the first man created?

Answer: Through the transformation of material force. When the essence of yin and yang and the Five Agents are united, man's physical form is established. This is what the Buddhists call production by transformation. There are many such productions today, such as lice. (49:-20a)

> *Comment*. This is a curious compromise between the traditional Confucian human cycles within the world and the Buddhist doctrine of cycle of the world itself.

126. *Question*: With reference to the mind of Heaven and Earth and the Principle of Heaven and Earth. Principle is moral principle. Is mind the will of a master?

Answer: The mind is the will of a master, it is true, but what is called master is precisely principle itself. It is not true that outside of the mind there is principle, or that outside of principle there is a mind. (49:23a)

127. Heaven and Earth have no other business except to have the

mind to produce things. The material force of one origin (the Great Ultimate including principle and material force) revolves and circulates without a moment of rest, doing nothing except creating the myriad things.

Question: Master Ch'eng I said, "Heaven and Earth create and transform without having any mind of their own. The sage has a mind of his own but does not take any [unnatural] action."[189]

Answer: That shows where Heaven and Earth have no mind of their own. It is like this: The four seasons run their course and the various things flourish. When do Heaven and Earth entertain any mind of their own? As to the sage, he only follows principle. What action does he need to take? This is the reason why Ming-tao (Ch'eng Hao) said, "The constant principle of Heaven and Earth is that their mind is in all things and yet they have no mind of their own. The constant principle of the sage is that his feelings are in accord with all creation, and yet he has no feelings of his own."[190] This is extremely well said.

Question: Does having their mind in all things not mean to pervade all things with their mind without any selfishness?

Answer: Heaven and Earth reach all things with this mind. When man receives it, it then becomes the human mind. When things receive it, it becomes the mind of things (in general). And when grass, trees, birds, animals receive it, it becomes the mind of grass, trees, birds, and animals (in particular). All of these are simply the one mind of Heaven and Earth. Thus we must understand in what sense Heaven and Earth have mind and in what sense they have no mind. We cannot be inflexible. (49:23b-24a)

128. When the myriad things are born and grow, that is the time when Heaven and Earth have no mind. When dried and withered things desire life, that is the time when Heaven and Earth have mind. (49:24a)

129. The Lord (*Ti*) is principle acting as master. (49:25a)

13. Spiritual Beings and Spiritual Forces (Kuei-Shen)

130. Someone asked whether there are spiritual beings (*kuei-shen*)?[191]

Answer: How can this matter be quickly explained? Even if it could, would you believe it? You must look into all principles of things and gradually understand, and then this puzzling problem will be solved by itself. When Fan Ch'ih asked about wisdom, Confucius said, "Devote oneself earnestly to the duties due to men, and respect spiritual beings

---

[189] *Ching-shuo* (Explanation of the Classics), in ECCS, 1:2a.
[190] *Ming-tao wen-chi*, 3:1a.
[191] For a discussion on *kuei-shen*, see above, ch. 30, comment on sec. 10.

but keep them at a distance. This may be called wisdom."[192] Let us attend to those things that should be attended to. Those that cannot be attended to, let us set aside. By the time we have attended thoroughly to ordinary daily matters, the principles governing spiritual beings will naturally be understood. This is the way to wisdom. [When Confucius said], "If we are not yet able to serve man, how can we serve spiritual beings?"[193] he expresses the same idea. (51:2a)

131. Is expansion positive spiritual force (*shen*) and contraction negative spiritual force (*kuei*)?

The Teacher drew a circle on the desk with his hand and pointed to its center and said: Principle is like a circle. Within it there is differentiation like this. All cases of material force which is coming forth belong to yang and are positive spiritual force. All cases of material force which is returning to its origin belong to yin and are the negative spiritual force. In the day, forenoon is the positive spiritual force, afternoon is the negative spiritual force. In the month, from the third day onward is the positive spiritual force; after the sixteenth day, it is the negative spiritual force.

T'ung Po-yü[194] *asked*: Is it correct when speaking of the sun and moon as opposites, to say that the sun is the positive spiritual force and the moon is the negative spiritual force?

Answer: Yes, it is. Plants growing are the positive spiritual force, plants declining are the negative spiritual force. A person from childhood to maturity is the positive spiritual force, while a man in his declining years and old age is the negative spiritual force. In breathing, breath going out is the positive spiritual force, breath coming in is the negative spiritual force. (51:6b)

132. The positive and negative spiritual forces are so called with respect to function. Spirit is so-called with respect to the wonderful functioning. In the cases of positive and negative spiritual forces, like yin and yang, contraction and expansion, going and coming, and diminution and augmentation, there are rough traces that can be seen. In the case of spirit which is so-called because of the mysterious functioning, it happens all of a sudden and is unfathomable. It suddenly comes, suddenly goes; it is suddenly here, suddenly there. (51:7b)

133. Question about the principles of life and death and spiritual beings. (*Question*: Although we know that spiritual beings and life and death are governed by one and the same principle, we do not understand the exact point. *Answer*: "Essence and material force are combined

---

[192] *Analects*, 6:20.   [193] *ibid.*, 11:11.

[194] Chu Hsi's pupil. People in his community called him "Master of Respect for Moral Principles." For a brief account of him, see *Sung-Yüan hsüeh-an*, 69:39a.

to be things. The wandering away of the spirit becomes change."[195]
This is the principle of life and death. The questioner did not understand. *Further remark*: Essence and material force consolidate to become man, and as they disintegrate, they become a spiritual being.

Further question: When essence and material force consolidate, is this principle attached to material force?)[196]

Answer: As the Way of Heaven operates, the myriad things develop and grow. There is (logically) principle first and then material force. Although they coexist at the same time, in the final analysis principle is basic. Man receives it and thus possesses life. (But material force may be clear or turbid.) The clear part of material force becomes his vital force (*ch'i*), while the turbid part becomes his physical nature. (The clear part belongs to yang while the turbid part belongs to yin.) Consciousness and movement are due to yang, while physical form and body (bones and flesh, skin and hair) are due to yin. The vital force belongs to the heavenly aspect of the soul (*hun*) and the body is governed by the earthly aspect of the soul (*p'o*). In his commentary on the *Huai-nan Tzu*, Kao Yu (fl. 205) said, "*Hun* is the spirit of yang and *p'o* is the spirit of yin."[197] By spirit is meant the master of the body and the vital force. Man is born as a result of integration of essence and material force. He possesses this material force only in a certain amount, which in time necessarily becomes exhausted. (This is what is meant by physicians when they say that yin or yang no longer rises or falls.) When exhaustion takes place, the heavenly aspect of the soul and the vital force return to Heaven, and the earthly aspect of the soul and the body return to the Earth, and the man dies. When a man is about to die, the warm material force leaves him and rises. This is called the *hun* rising. The lower part of his body gradually becomes cold. This is called the *p'o* falling. Thus as there is life, there is necessarily death, and as there is beginning, there must be an end. What integrates and disintegrates is material force. As to principle, it merely attaches itself to material force, but from the beginning it does not consolidate into a separate thing by itself. However, whatever in one's functioning that is correct is principle. It need not be spoken of in terms of integration and disintegration. When a man dies, his material force necessarily disintegrates. However, it does not disintegrate completely at once. Therefore in religious sacrifices we have the principle of spiritual influence and response. Whether the material force (or vital force) of ancestors of many generations ago is still there or not cannot be known. Nevertheless, since those who perform the sacrificial rites are

---

[195] *Changes*, "Appended Remarks," pt. 1, ch. 4. Cf. Legge, p. 353.
[196] Passages in parentheses in this section are added in the record by Chou Mingtso, Chu Hsi's pupil, who recorded his conversations after 1192.
[197] SPPY, 7:6a.

their descendants, the material force between them is after all the same. Hence there is the principle by which they can penetrate and respond. But the material force that has disintegrated cannot again be integrated. And yet the Buddhists say that man after death becomes a spiritual being and the spiritual being again becomes a man. If so, then in the universe there would always be the same number of people coming and going, with no need of the creative process of production and reproduction. This is decidedly absurd. (51:18b-19b)

14. Buddhism

134. *Question*: What is the difference between Buddhist non-being and Taoist non-being?

Answer: For the Taoists, there is still being after all. For example, the saying, "Let there [always] be non-being so we may see their subtlety, and let there [always] be being so we may see their outcome,"[198] is an evidence of this. The Buddhists, however, consider heaven and earth as illusory and erroneous and the Four Elements (Earth, Water, Fire, and Wind) as temporary (unreal) aggregates. This means complete non-being. (60:12b)

135. The mistake of the Buddhists arises from their dislike [of the world] which is the result of their selfishness, and the mistake of the Taoists arises from their trickery which is the result of their selfishness. The mistake of the Buddhists is to dislike and take lightly human affairs and therefore wish completely to turn everything into a void. The mistake of the Taoists is to take advantage of critical situations and opportunities and to resort to tricks and expediency, thus exploiting all kinds of schemes and crafts in the world. That is why military strategy, the art of calculation, and the technique of debate[199] today are mostly based on Taoist ideas. (60:12b-13a)

136. It is not necessary to examine the doctrines of Buddhism and Taoism deeply to understand them. The mere fact that they discard the Three Bonds (between ruler and minister, father and son, and husband and wife) and the Five Constant Virtues (righteousness on the part of the father, deep love on the part of the mother, friendliness on the part of the elder brother, respect on the part of the younger brother, and filial piety on the part of the son) is already a crime of the greatest magnitude. Nothing more need be said about the rest. (60:13a)

137. Where the Buddhists have lofty views, they are really lofty. Someone asked why they only talk about Emptiness. The Teacher said:

[198] *Lao Tzu*, ch. 1.
[199] *Hsing-ming* in Chinese, meaning actuality and name. For a discussion of this term, see Appendix.

They talk about Stubborn Emptiness[200] and also True Emptiness. Stubborn Emptiness means that there is Emptiness without anything, whereas True Emptiness means that there is still something. The latter theory is somewhat similar to our Confucian doctrine. However, the Buddhists ignore the universe completely and only pay attention to the mind, very much like the Taoists, who also merely want to preserve the spirit and power [of the mind].[201] I-ch'uan (Ch'eng I) said that we can draw a final conclusion [that Buddhism and Confucianism are different] from the manifestations[202] of Buddhism alone.[203] I do not know what use there is for such doctrines as these. (60:13a-b)

138. Someone talked about the harm of Chuang Tzu, Lao Tzu, Zen, and [orthodox] Buddhism. The Teacher said: The doctrines of Zen are the most harmful to the Way. Chuang Tzu and Lao Tzu still did not completely destroy moral principles. In the case of [orthodox] Buddhism, human relations are already destroyed. When it comes to Zen, however, from the very start it wipes out all moral principles completely. Looked at this way, Zen has done the greatest harm.

After a moment he said again: Generally speaking, actually [these schools are all harmful] just the same. In the matter of doing harm, there has never been a case which does not proceed from the smaller to the greater degree. (60:13b)

139. Ts'ao[204] asked how to tell the difference between Confucianism and Buddhism. The Teacher said: Just take the doctrine, "What Heaven imparts to man is called human nature."[205] The Buddhists simply do not understand this, and dogmatically say that nature is empty consciousness. What we Confucianists talk about are concrete principles, and from our point of view they are wrong. They say, "We will not be affected by a single speck of dust [such as distinction of right and wrong or subject and object]. . . . and will not discard a single element of existence (dharma) [such as the minister's loyalty to the ruler or the son's filial piety to the father]."[206] If one is not affected by any speck of dust, how is

[200] *Wan-k'ung*, literally "stubborn emptiness," which is so stubborn as to resist and therefore negate everything.
[201] The term *shen-ch'i* has many meanings, such as the mysterious force that produces all things, the essence of the Five Agents, feeling and disposition, expression, spirit and power of the mind. The latter is a Taoist concept, and is contrasted with the body. See *Chuang Tzu*, ch. 12, NHCC, 5:13a, or Giles, trans., *Chuang Tzu*, 1961 ed., p. 125.
[202] *Chi*, literally trace or track, means manifestation, sign, effect, evidence, or fact.
[203] *I-shu*, 15:10a.
[204] Most likely one of Chu Hsi's three pupils with such a family name.
[205] *The Mean*, ch. 1.
[206] A saying by Zen Master Ling-yu (771-853). According to him, on the level of absolute truth there is only One Nature, which is free of any contamination

it possible for him not to discard a single element of existence? When he arrives at what is called the realm of Emptiness, he does not find any solution. Take the human mind, for example. There is necessarily in it the Five Relations between father and son, ruler and minister, old and young, husband and wife, and friends. When the Buddhists are thorough in their action, they will show no affection in these relationships, whereas when we Confucianists are thoroughgoing in our action, there is affection between father and son, righteousness between ruler and minister, order between old and young, attention to their separate functions between husband and wife, and faithfulness between friends.[207] We Confucianists recognize only the moral principles of sincerity and genuineness. Sincerity is the essence of all good deeds. (60:14a)

140. The only difference between the Confucianists and Buddhists in their discourses on the nature is that the Buddhists talk about emptiness whereas the Confucianists talk about concreteness, and whereas the Buddhists talk about non-being, the Confucianists talk about being. (60:14b)

141. The Buddhists are characterized by vacuity, whereas we Confucianists are characterized by concreteness. The Buddhists are characterized by duality (of Absolute Emptiness and the illusory world), whereas we Confucianists are characterized by unity (one principle governing all). The Buddhists consider facts and principles as unimportant and pay no attention to them. (60:14b)

142. With us Confucianists, although the mind is vacuous, principle is concrete. The Buddhists, on the other hand, go straightly to their destination of emptiness and void. (60:14b)

143. We consider the mind and principle as one but they consider the mind and principle as two. It is not that the two groups purposely [differ] like this; it is the result of their different points of view. From their point of view, the mind is empty and is without principle, while from our point of view, although the mind is empty, all the principles are complete in it. However, although [we] say that the mind and principle are one, [we] fail to discern the selfishness resulting from material desires with which man is endowed in their physical nature. It is because

---

such as the distinction between right and wrong or subject and object, but on the level of worldly truth, Buddhism does not discard any element of existence and therefore exhorts the minister to be loyal and the son to be filial. See *Wu-teng hui-yüan* (Five Lamps Combined), ch. 8, in *Zokuzōkyō* (Supplement to the Buddhist Canon), pt. collection, pt. 2, B, case 24, p. 426a, and *Ching-te ch'uan-teng lu* (Records of the Transmission of the Lamp Compiled During the Ching-te Period, 1004-1007), SPTK, 9:3a.

[207] Quoting *Mencius*, 3A:4.

[we] do not see correctly that [we] have this defect. This is why the *Great Learning* highly values the investigation of things.[208] (60:15a-b)

144. Hsü Tzu-jung[209] has a theory that dry and withered things have [only physical] nature but not [the basic] nature [that is identical with principle]. The Teacher said: The nature is merely principle. As there is a thing, there is a principle for it. Where Tzu-jung is wrong is to have mistaken the mind for the nature. This is just like the Buddhists, except that the Buddhists polish the mind to the highest degree of refinement. It is like a lump of something. Having peeled off one layer of skin, they peel off another, until there is no more layer of skin to peel. When the mind is polished to the point of having nothing [else but its true nature], they recognize it as the nature. They do not realize that is precisely what the Sage called the mind. Therefore Hsieh Shang-ts'ai said, "What the Buddhists call the nature is precisely what the Sage called the mind, and what the Buddhists call the mind is precisely what the Sage called the will."[210] The mind is simply to embrace principle. At bottom the Buddhists do not understand this part, namely principle, and look upon consciousness and movement as the nature. Take the cases of seeing, hearing, speaking, and appearance. With the Sage, in seeing there is the principle of seeing, in hearing there is the principle of hearing, in speaking there is the principle of speaking, in acting there is the principle of acting, and in thinking there is the principle of thinking, as what Viscount Chi called clearness [in seeing], distinctness [in hearing], accordance [with reason in speech], respectfulness [in appearance], and penetration and profundity [in thought].[211] The Buddhists recognize only that which can see, hear, speak, think, and move, and consider that to be the nature. Whether the seeing is clear or not, whether the hearing is distinct or not, whether the speech is in accord with reason or not, and whether the thought is penetrating and profound or not, they do not care at all. No matter whether it goes this way or that way, they always accept it as nature. They are most afraid of the very mention of the word principle, and want to get rid of it also. This is exactly Kao Tzu's doctrine that "What is inborn is called nature."[212]

Shen Hsien[213] asked: Zen Buddhists also regard "raising the eyebrow

[208] For the doctrine of the investigation of things in the *Great Learning*, see above, ch. 4, sec. 5.

[209] He was Chu Hsi's pupil, whom the Teacher highly praised for his integrity. See *Chu Tzu wen-chi*, 58:12a. His doctrine and Chu Hsi's criticism of it are found in the latter's letter to him, *ibid.*, 58:13a-14b.

[210] Paraphrasing Hsieh Liang-tso, *Sheng-ts'ai yü-lu*, pt. 2, p. 7a.

[211] *History*, "Great Norm." Cf. Legge, *Shoo King*, pp. 326-327.

[212] *Mencius*, 6A:3.

[213] Chu Hsi's pupil who recorded the conversations of 1198 and those after.

and winking the eye,"[214] and consciousness and movement as "playing with the spirit"[215] and condemn it. Why?

Answer: Simply because it is playing with the spirit. It is merely polishing the spirit to be so refined that it is brilliant and no longer coarse.

Hsien asked: The Buddhists say that all things will be annihilated. The Law-body (*Dharmakāya*) alone remains forever and will not be extinct. Is this the only one they call the Law-body?

Answer: Yes. But I do not know how you can foretell that this thing remains forever. Both heaven and earth are destructible. How can you foretell that this thing is permanent and will not be extinct?

Question: They probably want to regard Emptiness as the substance. They say that heaven, earth, and all things will finally be reduced to Emptiness. This Emptiness is their substance.

Answer: They do not want to regard Emptiness as substance either. They merely say that the inside of this thing is fundamentally empty and not a single thing can be attached to it. (60:16b-17a)

145. Asked about the Buddhist practice of meditation and the Taoist practice of counting breath, the Teacher said: All they want is tranquillity, so that they will not err in their response to and dealing with things. Mencius also wanted to preserve the restorative influence of the night. But in order to do so, one has to pay attention to what he does during the day, [for if the originally good mind is disturbed by what one does during the day, the restorative influence of the night will not be sufficient to preserve the proper goodness of the mind].[216]

Question: Why don't we Confucianists imitate them in doing these?

Answer: [It is useless], for as soon as they open their eyes from meditation, what they try to get hold of is again gone from them as before. They just stubbornly cling to it. It is not as good as our Confucian ways of not seeing, hearing, speaking or acting what is contrary to propriety,[217] being cautious over what one does see and apprehensive over what one does not hear,[218] and being serious to straighten the internal life and righteous to square the external life.[219] They want to block everything from the outside.

Question: Is it correct that the Buddhists merely refrain from seeing

[214] See *Hsü-t'ang yü-lu* (Recorded Conversations of Hsü-t'ang), ch. 4, TSD, 47:1002.

[215] See commentary on the *Pi-yen chi* (Green Cave Collection), sec. 1, TSD, 48:140.

[216] *Mencius*, 6A:8.   [217] *Analects*, 12:1.   [218] *The Mean*, ch. 1.

[219] *Changes*, commentary on hexagram no. 2, *k'un*. Cf. Legge, *Yi King*, p. 420.

and hearing as such and make no effort whatever [to avoid] what is contrary to propriety?

Answer: Yes.

Thereupon Ts'ai Chi-t'ung[220] said: Things in the world must be handled by men. If we sit in meditation like them, what can be done? The sun and moon must circulate, and heaven and earth must rotate. The Teacher said: In not circulating and not rotating, the Buddhists are of course wrong. Here we do circulate; we do rotate. But in our circulation and rotation we make mistakes. Now we are happy for no reason and are angry for no reason. Is that not a mistake? They go to the excess, while nowadays people do not go far enough [in the control of the mind]. (60:21a-b)

146. The *I-Shu* (of Master Ch'eng Hao) says that the Buddhists have the teaching of exerting the mind to the utmost and knowing the nature but do not have the teaching of preserving the mind and nourishing the nature[221] [whereas Mencius taught all four].[222] I am afraid there is some mistake in the record of the conversation. Generally speaking, the Buddhists merely see a little bit of the shadow of the mind and the nature in a confused situation and have not been able to see in detail the mind and the nature in their reality and concreteness. That is why they do not see the many moral principles inherent in them. Even[223] if they have made an effort at preserving and nourishing, they can only preserve and nourish the shadow they see. Of course we cannot say that they see nothing. Nor can we say that they cannot nourish anything. But what they see and nourish is not the reality of the mind or the nature. (60:-30a-b)

147. Although there is a slight resemblance between the doctrines of the Buddhists and our own Confucian doctrines, they are really what is called similar in appearance but different in spirit, or appearing to be so but actually not. This must be clearly understood. Master Ming-tao (Ch'eng Hao) said, "Every sentence [of theirs] is similar [to ours] and every thing fits in. But we are different."[224] This is really very interesting. If he had not seen the matter very closely, how did he dare pass a judgment like this?

---

[220] Ts'ai Chi-t'ung (Ts'ai Yüan-ting, 1135-1198) was one of Chu Hsi's outstanding pupils and a prominent scholar in his own right. For his philosophy and life, see Forke, *Geschichte der neueren chinesischen Philosophie*, pp. 203-205, or *Sung-Yüan hsüeh-an*, ch. 62.

[221] *I-shu*, 13:1b.   [222] *Mencius*, 7A:1.

[223] *Cheng* in Chinese. Ordinarily meaning government, it is interchangeable with *cheng* (correct) and is used here in the sense of precisely or truly.

[224] Ōta Kinjō in his *Gimon Roku* (Records of Questioning), 1831 ed., pt. 2, p. 19, said that this is Ch'eng Hao's saying in the *I-shu*, but I have been unable to find it there. Chu Hsi was probably repeating Ch'eng's idea rather than quoting his exact words.

In what the Confucian School calls hearing the Way,[225] hearing merely means to see, hear, reflect, brood over and acquire the Way by oneself, and the Way is simply the self-evident principle governing the daily activities in the relations between ruler and minister and father and son [and so forth]. There is nothing deep, mysterious, or unfathomable in them similar to what the Buddhists describe as a wide and far-reaching great awakening or the whole body sweating. Now there is no need to devote one's effort elsewhere but to hold fast to seriousness in order to investigate things. People today often misinterpret the Confucian saying, "(Standing), let a man see (truthful words and serious action) in front of him, (riding in a carriage), let him see them attached to the yoke,"[226] and have therefore repeatedly drifted into Buddhist doctrines. When the ancient Sage said this, he merely meant for us "to be surely loyal and faithful in our words and surely earnest and serious in our action"[227] and for us not to forget in every moment of our thoughts, but to seem to see these two things at all times and in all places without allowing them to get away from our minds or our eyes. Taking the sayings "Seeing Emperor Yao[228] in the soup" and "Seeing Emperor Yao on the wall,"[229] does it mean that my mind sees itself as another thing outside of myself? The substance of the mind is originally without thought or activity. Before it is acted on by external things, it has the ability to remain so. When acted on, it immediately penetrates all things. I am afraid it is not like what you have described.[230] As to your contention that in Zen, entering into meditation is to cut off thought and to reveal the Principle of Nature completely, that is especially wrong. When thinking is correct, there is the Principle of Nature. In all operations and functioning, there is none which is not a revelation of the Principle of Nature. Does it need to wait to have all thoughts cut off before the Principle of Nature can be revealed? Furthermore, what is this that we call the Principle of Nature? Are humanity, righteousness, propriety, and wisdom (the four moral qualities natural to man) not the Principle of Nature? Are the five human relations between ruler and minister, between father and son, between old and young, between husband and wife, and between friends not the Principle of Nature? If the Buddhists have really seen the Principle of Nature, why should they violate and confuse [truth] like this, destroy

[225] *Analects*, 4:8.   [226] *ibid.*, 15:5.   [227] *ibid.*

[228] Legendary sage-ruler (3rd millennium B.C.).

[229] According to *Hou-Han shu* (History of Later Han, 25–220 A.D.), PNP, 63:13a. Emperor Shun admired Yao so much that for three years after Yao's death, he saw Yao on the wall whenever he sat down and saw Yao in the soup whenever he ate.

[230] This selection is part of Chu Hsi's reply to a letter from Wu Tou-nan, which is found in *Chu Tzu wen-chi*, 59:22a-24b. What Wu had to say, however, is not repeated in this reply and is nowhere recorded.

everything, and darken and delude their original mind without realizing it themselves? All these (Buddhistic doctrines) are great defects of recent generations which have fallen and degenerated into depraved doctrines. I am surprised that an enlightened person (like you) cannot avoid the popular trend and express such ideas. (60:31a-32a)

> *Comment.* Chu Hsi's knowledge of Buddhism was very superficial and in saying that Buddhist ideas came from the *Chuang Tzu* and the *Lieh Tzu*, for example, he revealed both his prejudice and ignorance.[231] But his attack on Buddhism was more comprehensive than his predecessors', for he criticized Buddhism from all points of view—ethical, theoretical, practical, historical, and textual.[232] In his philosophical criticism, he concentrated on two points, namely that the Buddhists divide the mind into two so that one examines the other,[233] and that the Buddhists identify the mind with nature, thus leading to the erroneous conclusion that the world is empty. The first criticism may well be applied to the Neo-Confucian doctrine of self-examination itself, which Chu Hsi advocated. As to the second, Chu Hsi had in mind that to the Buddhists only the mind in its pure consciousness can be called nature whereas all phenomena, being imagination of the mind, are devoid of true nature. On the other hand, to the Confucianists, all things have their nature. There is no question whether they have nature or not but only whether nature is balanced or not. Therefore he said the Buddhist position is empty but the Confucian position is concrete. Actually he confused the Buddhist single meaning of nature as true reality and the Confucian twofold meaning of nature as both consciousness and physical nature. He also ignored the fact that, in the Hua-yen School of Buddhism, principle and facts are harmonized so that no fact needs to be sacrificed for the sake of principle.[234]

[231] *Chu Tzu yü-lei*, 126:1a-7b.

[232] See Sargent, *Tchou Hi contre le Bouddhisme*, pp. 10-39.

[233] This point is stressed in his "Treatise on the Examination of the Mind." See above, treatise 4.

[234] For Hua-yen doctrines, see above, ch. 25, especially A, 7, (3), (6), and (8), and B, 2, (1).

35

DYNAMIC IDEALISM IN WANG YANG-MING

THE DYNAMIC IDEALISM of Wang Yang-ming (Wang Shou-jen, 1472-1529)[1] dominated China during his lifetime and for 150 years thereafter. Confucius, Mencius, Chu Hsi (1300-1200) and others have exerted stronger influence on Chinese thought, but they had prominent rivals whereas Wang shone alone.

The reason for his strong impact lies in the dynamic quality of his philosophy. It was the result of the unhealthy state of Chu Hsi's philosophy, on the one hand, and the bitterness of Wang's own life and time, on the other.

Since 1313 Chu Hsi's interpretation of Confucianism had been made orthodox and the basis of the civil service examinations. Its spirit of rational inquiry and genuine search for fundamental principles had, by Wang's time, degenerated into trifling with what Wang called "fragmentary and isolated details and broken pieces." What was worse, the examinations were no longer an avenue for serving the people and bringing peace to the world but for personal profit and success. To Wang, the source of the trouble was the erroneous theory of the investigation of

---

[1] Wang was a native of Yüeh in present Chekiang. His private name was Shou-jen and courtesy name Po-an. His father was an earl and a minister of civil personnel. In his youth he was with his father in Nanking and then Peking. In 1492 he obtained the "recommended person" degree and in 1499 the "presented scholar" degree. He then served in the government as an executive assistant in one department after another. In 1506, because he offended a eunuch, he was banished to modern Kueichow where he stayed for more than two years.

In 1510 he was appointed a magistrate in Kiangsi, where he built up a remarkable record of administration in seven months. From late 1510 through 1516, he served in various posts in Peking and Nanking. From 1517 to 1519, he suppressed several rebellions in Kiangsi and Fukien, including the one by Prince Ning. He also established schools, rehabilitated the rebels, and reconstructed the economy. He was awarded the title Earl of Hsin-chien and promised certain hereditary privileges, but his enemies at court accused him of conspiring with the prince and he was therefore ostracized by them. From 1521 to 1527 he was in virtual retirement in his native Yüeh.

In 1527, he was called to suppress rebellions in Kwangsi, which he did successfully. On his return he died on the way in the seventh year of the Chia-ching period at the age of fifty-seven. Ordinarily this year is equated with 1528, but his death actually occurred on January 10, 1529.

Now he was accused of spreading false doctrines and opposing Chu Hsi. His hereditary privileges were revoked. It was not until 1567, thirty-eight years after his death, that he was given the title Marquis of Hsin-chien and honored with the posthumous title of Wen-ch'eng (Completion of Culture). In 1584 by imperial decree it was ordered that he be offered sacrifice in the Confucian temple. This was the highest honor for a scholar. Only four scholars were so honored during the whole Ming period.

things propagated by Ch'eng I (Ch'eng I-ch'uan, 1033-1107) and Chu Hsi. In insisting that every blade of grass and every tree possesses principle and therefore should be investigated,[2] the theory diverted people from the basic principles of things and the fundamentals of life. Moreover, by saying that the mind should go to things to investigate the principles inherent in them, the theory considered things as external and separated the mind and principle. As a result, according to Wang, the mind lost its direction and its motivating power. If principles were outside the mind, he said, then the principle of filial piety and therefore the desire to be filial would cease to be as soon as the parents die.[3] To him, principle and the mind are one and the principle of filial piety is nothing but the exercise of the mind. Things (and affairs), too, are not external, for they are likewise inside the mind.

By the mind Wang meant essentially the will. There would be no principle or things unless the mind were determined to realize it. This is the reason why Wang insisted that the sincerity of the will must precede the investigation of things. In this he directly opposed Chu Hsi who shifted the chapters of the *Great Learning* so that that on the investigation of things comes before that on the sincerity of the will. Wang rejected this rearrangement and returned to the old text as it is found in the *Book of Rites* where the chapter on the sincerity of the will comes first.

The fundamental difference between Chu and Wang lies in the fact that while Chu's approach is intellectual, Wang's is moral. Chu Hsi interpreted the term *ko-wu* as the rational and objective investigation of things, but Wang preferred to interpret it to mean to "eliminate what is incorrect in the mind so as to preserve the correctness of its original substance."[4] That is to say, to investigate things or affairs is to do good and to remove evil.[5]

Actually Wang's theory is entirely subjective and confuses reality with value. It is difficult to accept his version of *ko-wu*, for if the term means to rectify the mind, why should it be *ko-wu* (to *ko* things) instead of *ko-hsin* (to *ko* the mind)? His interpretation is of course based on the theory that the mind and things are one. But this theory of his is founded on very shaky grounds. When he was asked what the mind has to do with blossoming trees on the high mountains, he merely answered that their colors show up when you look at them.[6] The point, however, is that his whole emphasis is on moral values. He was convinced that if the mind is divided or devoted to external things, it will be concerned only with frag-

---

[2] *I-shu* (Surviving Works), 18:9a, ECCS. Also see above, ch. 32, comment on sec. 30.

[3] *Ch'uan-hsi-lu* (Instructions for Practical Living), sec. 135.

[4] *ibid.*, secs. 7, 85, 174.   [5] *ibid.*, sec. 315.   [6] *ibid.*, sec. 275.

mentary details and will lack the essentials. Scholars with such a mind will trifle with things and lose their purpose in life. For him this was the reason for the decline of the Confucian teachings, which in turn brought on the intellectual, political, and moral decay of his time.

What was Wang's remedy for this sad situation? The remedy is his greatest contribution to Chinese philosophy, namely, the doctrine of the extension of the innate knowledge of the good (chih liang-chih). The idea of the extension of knowledge comes from the *Great Learning*[7] and the idea of innate knowledge of the good from Mencius.[8] Wang's theory is not merely a combination of the two but it gives them a new meaning which gives a new complexion to Chinese thought.

Wang describes innate knowledge as "the original substance of the mind," "the Principle of Nature," "the pure intelligence and clear consciousness of the mind," the mind that is "always shining" and reflects things as they come without being stirred, the spirit of creation, which "produces heaven, earth, spiritual beings and the Lord," and "man's root which is intelligent. . . . It naturally grows and grows without cease."[9] In short, it is the Principle of Nature (T'ien-li), which is not only the principle of right and wrong but also the principle that naturally extends. The mind in its original substance naturally knows the principle of filial piety, for example, when one sees one's parents, and naturally extends it into action.

This leads to another major contribution he made to Chinese philosophy, namely, the doctrine of the unity of knowledge and action. The Confucianists have always stressed the correspondence and equal importance of knowledge and action,[10] but Wang was the first to identify them as one. According to him, knowledge is the beginning of action and action the completion of knowledge.[11] No one really knows food unless he has tasted it, he argued. He was thinking only of a particular kind of knowledge, but his total emphasis on the will is clear. In his doctrine of the identity of the mind and principle, he was following Lu Hsiang-shan (Lu Chiu-yüan, 1139-1193), but in his doctrine of the unity of knowledge and action, he offered something neither Lu nor anyone else in Chinese history ever thought of. Ordinarily the idealistic movement in Neo-Confucianism is called the Lu-Wang School, in contrast to the rationalistic Ch'eng-Chu School. But it was Wang's doctrines, rather than Lu's, that had the tremendous impact in the Ming dynasty (1368-1644). His doctrines demand forthright, direct, and spontaneous action.

[7] *Great Learning*, ch. 5.
[8] *Mencius*, 7A:15.
[9] *Ch'uan-hsi lu*, secs. 152, 135, 137, 151, 261, and 244, respectively.
[10] See above, ch. 32, comment on sec. 38 and n.72.
[11] *Ch'uan-hsi lu*, sec. 5.

As said before, his philosophy is partly a product of the bitterness of his own life and time. China in the fifteenth century was externally harassed by semi-nomadic tribes in the north. Internally, China was ruled by incompetent rulers who allowed eunuchs to usurp power and to suppress scholars. Great domains were established for court favorites and members of the imperial family. Heavy taxes drove many people to become bandits. Even a prince was in revolt. The cultural brilliancy and economic prosperity of the first half of the Ming dynasty had turned into decadence and chaos. Many scholars struggled hard to find a solution but were persecuted for so doing.

Wang had a searching mind from his youth. It is said that on his wedding day, he became so absorbed in talking to a Taoist priest about everlasting life that he did not go home until the next morning. At first he studied military crafts. In 1492 he began to study Chu Hsi's philosophy. Following Chu Hsi's doctrine of the investigation of things, he and a friend sat in front of bamboos to try to investigate their principles, only to become ill after seven days. After trying the writing of flowery compositions, he went back to military crafts and then to Taoist techniques of nourishing everlasting life. Only after having found all these to be futile did he return to Confucianism.

He started his official career at twenty-eight. In the next several years he developed his own philosophy and began to attract disciples. He lectured on the primary importance of making up one's mind to become a sage, and he severely attacked the current habits of recitation and flowery compositions. This did not please the rulers or conservative scholars. In 1506, when he protested the imprisonment of a scholar official by a powerful eunuch, he was beaten forty times before the emperor and then banished to modern Kueichow which was then inhabited by aborigines. There, having to face in isolation political, natural, as well as cultural hardships, he was driven to search within his own mind. One night in 1508, he suddenly understood the doctrine of the investigation of things and the extension of knowledge. A year later, he realized the unity of knowledge and action. Later, in 1514-1516, when he was an official at Nanking, his fame spread and many scholars became his followers, including one of his superior officials. But his radical doctrines, including his insistence on following the old text of the *Great Learning* instead of the one rearranged by Chu Hsi, attracted more and more criticism. From 1516 to 1519 he was ordered to suppress several rebellions, which he successfully did. But the combination of his blunt personality, his attack on orthodoxy, and his novel ideas worked against him. Instead of being rewarded for his accomplishments, he became *persona non grata*. From 1521 to 1527 he was in virtual retirement in his native place. Hundreds of scholars from all over China came to him. It was in 1521, when he was fifty, that he arrived at the doctrine of the extension of innate knowledge which culminated his philosophy, and it was about 1527, a little over a year before his death, that he wrote down the *Inquiry on the Great Learning* which embodies virtually all of his major doctrines. During this last decade of his life, attack and ridicule on him grew in extent and intensity, but they only served to reinforce his search for fundamental values. As he said, his doctrines were "achieved from a hundred deaths and a thousand sufferings."[12] This is why he demanded determination, firm purpose, self-examination and self-mastery, "always be doing something," "polishing and training in the actual affairs of life," and realization of truth through personal experience.

Both his teachings and technique are new and challenging. But his final goal—forming one body with all things—and his basic value—humanity (*jen*)—are typically Confucian. He has many similarities with Zen Buddhism and has been attacked for centuries because of this, but any superficial similarity is far outweighed by his stress on active involvement in human affairs and a dynamic approach to the mind.

His influence extended to Japan where his school, known as the Yōmeigaku, rivaled the Chu Hsi School (Shushigaku) from the seventeenth through the nineteenth century and provided strong leadership for the Meiji Restoration in 1868. In China itself, Wang's followers disagreed on their interpretations of his teachings, especially on the meaning of innate knowledge. This led to division and confusion. Moreover, some of his followers became socially uncomformative and intellectually undisciplined. In many cases they even committed evil in the name of innate knowledge. Many historians have gone too far in blaming the collapse of the Ming dynasty on his degenerated followers, but there is no doubt that the Wang School had allowed the pitfalls of an unorthodox system to spoil itself. However, the dynamic quality and the purposefulness of his philosophy appealed to modern thinkers like Sun Yat-sen (1866-1925), T'an Szu-t'ung (1865-1898), and Hsiung Shih-li (1885—).[13] As in the fifteenth century, the contemporary situation, in the eyes of many, requires a solution that only a dynamic and idealistic system like Wang's can offer.

The following selections include the *Inquiry on the Great Learning* in its entirety and some selections from the *Ch'uan-hsi lu* (Instructions for Practical Living) which consists of conversations with his pupils, letters, and several short essays.[14]

[12] *Wang Wen-ch'eng Kung ch'üan-shu* (Complete Works of Wang Yang-ming), preface, SPTK, p. 15b.

[13] See below, chs. 40 and 43.

[14] Both of these are included in the *Wang Wen-ch'eng Kung ch'üan-shu* and

Chu Hsi: 6, 33, 135, 319
Extension of knowledge and Investigation of things: A, 6, 7, 89, 135, 262, 315, 319, 331
Forming one body with all things: A, 89, 93, 274, 337
Highest good, Good and evil: A, 3, 6, 34, 53, 101, 228, 308, 315
Humanity (*jen*): A, 89, 93, 133
Innate knowledge: A, 135, 155, 262, 274, 315, 331
Knowledge and action: 5, 26, 132, 133
Methods of cultivation: A, 53, 93, 101, 132, 155, 262, 315, 331
Mind: A, 3, 5, 6, 32, 33, 34, 78, 94, 108, 135, 228, 275, 277, 315, 337
Principle: A, 3, 6, 32, 33, 34, 94, 133, 135
Principle of Nature: 7, 53, 101, 135, 228
Sincerity of the will: A, 6, 101

A. INQUIRY ON THE GREAT LEARNING

Question: The *Great Learning* was considered by a former scholar [Chu Hsi] as the learning of the great man.[15] I venture to ask why the learning of the great man should consist in "manifesting the clear character"?[16]

Master Wang said: The great man regards Heaven and Earth and the myriad things as one body. He regards the world as one family and the country as one person. As to those who make a cleavage between objects and distinguish between the self and others, they are small men. That the great man can regard Heaven, Earth, and the myriad things as one body is not because he deliberately wants to do so, but because it is natural to the humane nature of his mind that he do so. Forming one body with Heaven, Earth, and the myriad things is not only true of the great man. Even the mind of the small man is no different. Only he himself makes it small. Therefore when he sees a child about to fall into a well, he cannot help a feeling of alarm and commiseration.[17] This shows that his humanity (*jen*) forms one body with the child. It may be objected that the child belongs to the same species. Again, when he observes the pitiful cries and frightened appearance of birds and animals about to be slaughtered, he cannot help feeling an "inability to bear" their suffering.[18] This shows that his humanity forms one body with birds and

---

have been translated by Chan in his *Instructions for Practical Living, and Other Neo-Confucian Works by Wang Yang-ming*, New York, Columbia University Press, 1963. The section numbers of the *Ch'uan-hsi lu* are retained in the following selections.

[15] Chu Hsi, *Ta-hsüeh chang-chü* (Commentary on the *Great Learning*), the text. Actually by "great learning" (*ta-hsüeh*) Chu Hsi meant "education for the adult," but the Chinese phrase can also mean the learning of the great man. Wang preferred this latter interpretation.

[16] The text of the *Great Learning*.   [17] *Mencius*, 2A:6.
[18] *ibid*.

animals. It may be objected that birds and animals are sentient beings as he is. But when he sees plants broken and destroyed, he cannot help a feeling of pity. This shows that his humanity forms one body with plants. It may be said that plants are living things as he is. Yet even when he sees tiles and stones shattered and crushed, he cannot help a feeling of regret. This shows that his humanity forms one body with tiles and stones. This means that even the mind of the small man necessarily has the humanity that forms one body with all. Such a mind is rooted in his Heaven-endowed nature, and is naturally intelligent, clear, and not beclouded. For this reason it is called the "clear character." Although the mind of the small man is divided and narrow, yet his humanity that forms one body can remain free from darkness to this degree. This is due to the fact that his mind has not yet been aroused by desires and obscured by selfishness. When it is aroused by desires and obscured by selfishness, compelled by greed for gain and fear of harm, and stirred by anger, he will destroy things, kill members of his own species, and will do everything. In extreme cases he will even slaughter his own brothers, and the humanity that forms one body will disappear completely. Hence, if it is not obscured by selfish desires, even the mind of the small man has the humanity that forms one body with all as does the mind of the great man. As soon as it is obscured by selfish desires, even the mind of the great man will be divided and narrow like that of the small man. Thus the learning of the great man consists entirely in getting rid of the obscuration of selfish desires in order by his own efforts to make manifest his clear character, so as to restore the condition of forming one body with Heaven, Earth, and the myriad things, a condition that is originally so, that is all. It is not that outside of the original substance something can be added.

Question: Why, then, does the learning of the great man consist in loving the people?

Answer: To manifest the clear character is to bring about the substance of the state of forming one body with Heaven, Earth, and the myriad things, whereas loving the people is to put into universal operation the function of the state of forming one body. Hence manifesting the clear character consists in loving the people, and loving the people is the way to manifest the clear character. Therefore, only when I love my father, the fathers of others, and the fathers of all men can my humanity really form one body with my father, the fathers of others, and the fathers of all men. When it truly forms one body with them, then the clear character of filial piety will be manifested. Only when I love my brother, the brothers of others, and the brothers of all men can my humanity really form one body with my brother, the brothers of others, and the brothers of all men. When it truly forms one body with them, then the clear character of brotherly respect will be manifested. Everything from ruler, minister, husband, wife, and friends to mountains, rivers, spiritual beings, birds, animals, and plants should be truly loved in order to realize my humanity that forms one body with them, and then my clear character will be completely manifested, and I will really form one body with Heaven, Earth, and the myriad things. This is what is meant by "manifesting the clear character throughout the empire."[19] This is what is meant by "regulation of the family," "ordering the state," and "bringing peace to the world."[20] This is what is meant by "full development of one's nature."[21]

Question: Then why does the learning of the great man consist in "abiding in the highest good"?[22]

Answer: The highest good is the ultimate principle of manifesting character and loving people. The nature endowed in us by Heaven is pure and perfect. The fact that it is intelligent, clear, and not beclouded is evidence of the emanation and revelation of the highest good. It is the original substance of the clear character which is called innate knowledge of the good. As the highest good emanates and reveals itself, we will consider right as right and wrong as wrong. Things of greater or less importance and situations of grave or light character will be responded to as they act upon us. In all our changes and movements, we will stick to no particular point, but possess in ourselves the Mean that is perfectly natural. This is the ultimate of the normal nature of man and the principle of things. There can be no consideration of adding to or subtracting from it. If there is any, it means selfish ideas and shallow cunning, and cannot be said to be the highest good. Naturally, how can anyone who does not watch over himself carefully when alone, and who has no refinement and singleness of mind, attain to such a state of perfection? Later generations fail to realize that the highest good is inherent in their own minds, but exercise their selfish ideas and cunning and grope for it outside their minds, believing that every event and every object has its own peculiar definite principle. For this reason the law of right and wrong is obscured; the mind becomes concerned with fragmentary and isolated details and broken pieces; the selfish desires of man become rampant and the Principle of Nature is at an end. And thus the learning of manifesting character and loving people is everywhere thrown into confusion. In the past there have, of course, been people who wanted to manifest their clear character. But simply because they did not know how to abide in the highest good, but instead

---

[19] The text of the *Great Learning*.   [20] *ibid*.
[21] *The Mean*, ch. 22.   [22] The text of the *Great Learning*.

drove their own minds toward something too lofty, they thereby lost them in illusions, emptiness, and quietness, having nothing to do with the work of the family, the state, and the world. Such are the followers of Buddhism and Taoism. There have, of course, been those who wanted to love their people. Yet simply because they did not know how to abide in the highest good, but instead sank their own minds in base and trifling things, they thereby lost them in scheming strategy and cunning techniques, having neither the sincerity of humanity nor that of commiseration. Such are the followers of the Five Despots[23] and the pursuers of success and profit. All of these defects are due to a failure to know how to abide in the highest good. Therefore abiding in the highest good is to manifesting character and loving people as the carpenter's square and compass are to the square and the circle, or rule and measure to length, or balances and scales to weight. If the square and the circle do not abide by the compass and the carpenter's square, their standard will be wrong; if length does not abide by the rule and measure, its adjustment will be lost; if weight does not abide by the balances, its exactness will be gone; and if manifesting clear character and loving people do not abide by the highest good, their foundation will disappear. Therefore, abiding in the highest good so as to love people and manifest the clear character is what is meant by the learning of the great man.

Question: "Only after knowing what to abide in can one be calm. Only after having been calm can one be tranquil. Only after having achieved tranquillity can one have peaceful repose. Only after having peaceful repose can one begin to deliberate. Only after deliberation can the end be attained."[24] How do you explain this?

Answer: People fail to realize that the highest good is in their minds and seek it outside. As they believe that everything or every event has its own definite principle, they search for the highest good in individual things. Consequently, the mind becomes fragmentary, isolated, broken into pieces; mixed and confused, it has no definite direction. Once it is realized that the highest good is in the mind and does not depend on any search outside, then the mind will have definite direction and there will be no danger of its becoming fragmentary, isolated, broken into pieces, mixed, or confused. When there is no such danger, the mind will not be erroneously perturbed but will be tranquil. Not being erroneously perturbed but being tranquil, it will be leisurely and at ease in its daily functioning and will attain peaceful repose. Being in peaceful repose, whenever a thought arises or an event acts upon it, the mind with its

[23] They were: Duke Huan of Ch'i (r. 685–643 B.C.), Duke Wen of Chin (r. 636–628 B.C.), Duke Mu of Ch'in (r. 659–619 B.C.), King Chuang of Ch'u (r. 613–589 B.C.), and Duke Hsiang of Sung (r. 650–635 B.C.). See *Mencius*, 6B:7.
[24] The text of the *Great Learning*.

innate knowledge will thoroughly sift and carefully examine whether or not the thought or event is in accord with the highest good, and thus the mind can deliberate. With deliberation, every decision will be excellent and every act will be proper, and in this way the highest good will be attained.

Question: "Things have their roots and their branches."[25] A former scholar [Chu Hsi] considered manifesting the clear character as the root (or fundamental) and renovating the people as the branch (or secondary), and that they are two things opposing each other as internal and external.[26] "Affairs have their beginnings and their ends."[27] The former scholar considered knowing what to abide in as the beginning and the attainment of the highest good as the end, both being one thing in harmonious continuity. According to you, "renovating the people" (*hsin-min*) should be read as "loving the people" (*ch'in-min*). If so, isn't the theory of root and branches in some respect incorrect?

Answer: The theory of beginnings and ends is in general right. Even if we read "renovating the people" as "loving the people" and say that manifesting the character is the root and loving the people is the branches, it is not incorrect. The main thing is that root and branches should not be distinguished as two different things. The trunk of the tree is called the root (or essential part), and the twigs are called the branches. It is precisely because the tree is one that its parts can be called roots and branches. If they are said to be two different things, then since they are two distinct objects, how can we speak of them as root and branches of the same thing? Since the idea of renovating the people is different from that of loving the people, obviously the task of manifesting the character and that of loving the people are two different things. If it is realized that manifesting the clear character is to love the people and loving the people is to manifest the clear character, how can they be split in two? What the former scholar said is due to his failure to realize that manifesting the character and loving the people are basically one thing. Instead, he believed them to be two different things and consequently, although he knew that root and branches should be one, yet he could not help splitting them in two.

Question: The passage from the phrase, "The ancients who wished to manifest their clear character throughout the world" to the clause, "first [order their state . . . regulate their families . . .] cultivate their personal lives,"[28] can be understood by your theory of manifesting the character and loving the people. May I ask what task, what procedure, and what effort are involved in the passage from "Those who wished to

[25] *ibid.*
[26] Chu Hsi, *Ta-hsüeh chang-chü.*
[27] The text of the *Great Learning.*
[28] *ibid.*

cultivate their personal lives would first rectify their minds . . . make their will sincere . . . extend their knowledge" to the clause, "the extension of knowledge consists in the investigation of things"?[29]

Answer: This passage fully explains the task of manifesting the character, loving the people, and abiding in the highest good. The person, the mind, the will, knowledge, and things constitute the order followed in the task. While each of them has its own place, they are really one thing. Investigating, extending, being sincere, rectifying, and cultivating are the task performed in the procedure. Although each has its own name, they are really one affair. What is it that is called the person? It is the physical functioning of the mind. What is it that is called the mind? It is the clear and intelligent master of the person. What is meant by cultivating the personal life? It means to do good and get rid of evil. Can the body by itself do good and get rid of evil? The clear and intelligent master must desire to do good and get rid of evil before the body that functions physically can do so. Therefore he who wishes to cultivate his personal life must first rectify his mind.

> *Comment*. The *Great Learning* clearly says that there is an order from "the investigation of things" to "bringing peace to the world," but Wang says they are but one affair. To the extent that he, like other Neo-Confucianists, depended on ancient Classics for authority and used ancient Confucian terminology, he was a conservative. But he used the *Great Learning* in his own way.

Now the original substance of the mind is man's nature. Human nature being universally good, the original substance of the mind is correct. How is it that any effort is required to rectify the mind? The reason is that, while the original substance of the mind is originally correct, incorrectness enters when one's thoughts and will are in operation. Therefore he who wishes to rectify his mind must rectify it in connection with the operation of his thoughts and will. If, whenever a good thought arises, he really loves it as he loves beautiful colors, and whenever an evil thought arises, he really hates it as he hates bad odors, then his will will always be sincere and his mind can be rectified.

However, what arises from the will may be good or evil, and unless there is a way to make clear the distinction between good and evil, there will be a confusion of truth and untruth. In that case, even if one wants to make his will sincere, he cannot do so. Therefore he who wishes to make his will sincere must extend his knowledge. By extension is meant to reach the limit. The word "extension" is the same as that used in the saying, "Mourning is to be carried to the utmost degree of grief."[30] In

---

[29] *ibid*. [30] *Analects*, 19:14.

the *Book of Changes* it is said: "Knowing the utmost, one should reach it."[31] "Knowing the utmost" means knowledge and "reaching it" means extension. The extension of knowledge is not what later scholars understand as enriching and widening knowledge.[32] It is simply extending one's innate knowledge of the good to the utmost. This innate knowledge of the good is what Mencius meant when he said, "The sense of right and wrong is common to all men."[33] The sense of right and wrong requires no deliberation to know, nor does it depend on learning to function.[34] This is why it is called innate knowledge. It is my nature endowed by Heaven, the original substance of my mind, naturally intelligent, shining, clear, and understanding.

Whenever a thought or a wish arises, my mind's faculty of innate knowledge itself is always conscious of it. Whether it is good or evil, my mind's innate knowing faculty itself also knows it. It has nothing to do with others. Therefore, although an inferior man may have done all manner of evil, when he sees a superior man he will surely try to disguise this fact, concealing what is evil and displaying what is good in himself.[35] This shows that innate knowledge of the good does not permit any self-deception. Now the only way to distinguish good and evil in order to make the will sincere is to extend to the utmost the knowledge of the innate faculty. Why is this? When [a good] thought or wish arises, the innate faculty of my mind already knows it to be good. Suppose I do not sincerely love it but instead turn away from it. I would then be regarding good as evil and obscuring my innate faculty which knows the good. When [an evil] thought or wish arises, the innate faculty of my mind already knows it to be evil. If I did not sincerely hate it but instead carried it out, I would be regarding evil as good and obscuring my innate faculty which knows evil. In such cases what is supposed to be knowledge is really ignorance. How then can the will be made sincere? If what the innate faculty knows to be good or evil is sincerely loved or hated, one's innate knowing faculty is not deceived and the will can be made sincere.

Now, when one sets out to extend his innate knowledge to the utmost, does this mean something illusory, hazy, in a vacuum, and unreal? No, it means something real. Therefore, the extension of knowledge must consist in the investigation of things. A thing is an event. For every emanation of the will there must be an event corresponding to it. The event to which the will is directed is a thing. To investigate is to rectify. It is to rectify that which is incorrect so it can return to its original cor-

[31] Commentary on hexagrams, no. 1, *ch'ien* (Heaven). Cf. Legge, trans., *Yi King*, p. 410.

[32] Chu Hsi, *Ta-hsüeh chang-chü*, commentary on the text.

[33] *Mencius*, 2A:6, 6A:6.   [34] Quoting *Mencius*, 7A:15.

[35] Paraphrasing the *Great Learning*, ch. 6.

rectness. To rectify that which is not correct is to get rid of evil, and to return to correctness is to do good. This is what is meant by investigation. The *Book of History* says, "He (Emperor Yao) investigated (*ko*) heaven above and earth below";[36] "[Emperor Shun] investigated (*ko*) in the temple of illustrious ancestors";[37] and "[The ruler] rectifies (*ko*) the evil of his heart."[38] The word "investigation" (*ko*) in the phrase "the investigation of things" combines the two meanings.

If one sincerely loves the good known by the innate faculty but does not in reality do the good as we come into contact with the thing to which the will is directed, it means that the thing has not been investigated and that the will to love the good is not yet sincere. If one sincerely hates the evil known by the innate faculty but does not in reality get rid of the evil as he comes into contact with the thing to which the will is directed, it means that the thing has not been investigated and that the will to hate evil is not sincere. If as we come into contact with the thing to which the will is directed, we really do the good and get rid of the evil to the utmost which is known by the innate faculty, then everything will be investigated and what is known by our innate faculty will not be deficient or obscured but will be extended to the utmost. Then the mind will be joyous in itself, happy and without regret, the functioning of the will will carry with it no self-deception, and sincerity may be said to have been attained. Therefore it is said, "When things are investigated, knowledge is extended; when knowledge is extended, the will becomes sincere; when the will is sincere, the mind is rectified; and when the mind is rectified, the personal life is cultivated."[39] While the order of the tasks involves a sequence of first and last, in substance they are one and cannot be so separated. At the same time, while the order and the tasks cannot be separated into first and last, their function must be so refined as not to be wanting in the slightest degree. This is why the doctrine of investigation, extension, being sincere, and rectification is a correct exposition of the true heritage of the Sage-Emperors Yao and Shun and why it coincides with Confucius' own ideas. (*Wang Wen-ch'eng Kung ch'üan-shu*, or Complete Works of Wang Yang-ming, SPTK, 26:1b-5a)

Comment. This is the most important of Wang's works, for it contains all of his fundamental doctrines—that the man of humanity forms one body with all things and extends his love to all, that the mind is principle, that the highest good is inherent in the mind, that to investigate things is to rectify the mind, and that the extension

[36] *History*, "Canon of Yao." Cf. Legge, trans., *Shoo King*, p. 15.
[37] *ibid.*, "Canon of Shun"; Legge, p. 41.
[38] *ibid.*, "The Charge to Ch'iung"; Legge, p. 585.
[39] *Great Learning*, the text.

of innate knowledge is the way to discover the highest good and to perfect the moral life. The theory of the unity of knowledge and action is not mentioned, but since he refuses to separate the internal and the external or substance and function, the theory is clearly implied. In fact, he explicitly says that manifesting the clear character, which may be equated with knowledge, and loving the people, which is action, are identical.

B. INSTRUCTIONS FOR PRACTICAL LIVING

3. I[40] said, "If the highest good is to be sought only in the mind, I am afraid not all principles of things in the world will be covered."

The Teacher said, "The mind *is* principle. Is there any affair in the world outside of the mind? Is there any principle outside of the mind?"

I said, "In filial piety in serving one's parents, in loyalty in serving one's ruler, in faithfulness in intercourse with friends, or in humanity in governing the people, there are many principles which I believe should not be left unexamined."

The Teacher said with a sigh, "This idea has been obscuring the understanding of people for a long time. Can they be awakened by one word? However, I shall comment along the line of your question. For instance, in the matter of serving one's parents, one cannot seek for the principle of filial piety in the parent. In serving one's ruler, one cannot seek for the principle of loyalty in the ruler. In the intercourse with friends and in governing the people, one cannot seek for the principles of faithfulness and humanity in friends and the people. They are all in the mind, that is all, for the mind and principle are identical. When the mind is free from the obscuration of selfish desires, it is the embodiment of the Principle of Nature, which requires not an iota added from the outside. When this mind, which has become completely identical with the Principle of Nature, is applied and arises to serve parents, there is filial piety; when it arises to serve the ruler, there is loyalty; when it rises to deal with friends or to govern the people, there are faithfulness and humanity. The main thing is for the mind to make an effort to get rid of selfish human desires and preserve the Principle of Nature."

I said, "Having heard what you said, sir, I begin to understand. However, the old theory still lingers in my mind, from which I cannot entirely get away. Take, for example, the matter of serving one's parents. The filial son is to care for their comfort both in winter and summer, and to inquire after their health every morning and evening.[41] These things in-

[40] Hsü Ai (1487-1518), Wang's favorite pupil, who recorded secs. 1-14 of the *Ch'uan-hsi lu*.

[41] Quoting the *Book of Rites*, "Summary of the Rules of Propriety." Cf. translation by Legge, *Li Ki*, ch. 1, p. 67.

volve many actual details. Should we not endeavor to investigate them?"

The Teacher said, "Why not endeavor to investigate them? The main thing is to have a basis. The main thing is to endeavor to investigate them by ridding the mind of selfish human desires and preserving the Principle of Nature. For instance, to investigate the provision of warmth for parents in the winter is none other than the extension of the filial piety of this mind to the utmost, for fear that a trifle of human selfish desires might creep in, and to investigate the provision of coolness for parents in the summer is none other than the extension of the filial piety of this mind to the utmost, for fear that a trifle of selfish human desires might creep in. It is merely to investigate this mind. If the mind is free from selfish human desires and has become completely identical with the Principle of Nature, and if it is the mind that is sincere in its filial piety to parents, then in the winter it will naturally think of the cold of parents and seek a way to provide warmth for them, and in the summer it will naturally think of the heat of parents and seek a way to provide coolness for them. These are all offshoots of the mind that is sincere in its filial piety. Nevertheless, there must first be such a mind before there can be these offshoots. Compared to the tree, the mind with sincere filial piety is the root, whereas the offshoots are the leaves and branches. There must first be roots before there can be leaves and branches. One does not seek to find leaves and branches and then cultivate the root. The *Book of Rites* says, 'A filial son who loves his parents deeply is sure to have a peaceful disposition. Having a peaceful disposition, he will surely have a happy expression. And having a happy expression, he will surely have a pleasant countenance.'[42] There must be deep love as the root and then the rest will naturally follow like this." (1:3a-4b)

5. I did not understand the Teacher's doctrine of the unity of knowledge and action and debated it back and forth with Huang Tsung-hsien[43] and Ku Wei-hsien[44] without coming to any conclusion. Therefore I took the matter to the Teacher. The Teacher said, "Give an example and let me see." I said, "For example, there are people who know that parents should be served with filial piety and elder brothers with respect but cannot put these things into practice. This shows that knowledge and action are clearly two different things."

[42] *ibid.*, "The Meaning of Sacrifices." Cf. Legge, ch. 21, pp. 215-216.
[43] The courtesy name of Huang Wan (1477-1551), Wang's pupil. His daughter was married to Wang Yang-ming's son.
[44] The courtesy name of Ku Ying-hsiang (1483-1565). He departed from the teaching of Wang Yang-ming in holding that knowledge and action were not identical.

The Teacher said, "The knowledge and action you refer to are already separated by selfish desires and are no longer knowledge and action in their original substance. There have never been people who know but do not act. Those who are supposed to know but do not act simply do not yet know. When sages and worthies taught people about knowledge and action, it was precisely because they wanted them to restore the original substance, and not simply to do this or that and be satisfied. Therefore the *Great Learning* points to true knowledge and action for people to see, saying, they are 'like loving beautiful colors and hating bad odors.'[45] Seeing beautiful colors appertains to knowledge, while loving beautiful colors appertains to action. However, as soon as one sees that beautiful color, he has already loved it. It is not that he sees it first and then makes up his mind to love it. Smelling a bad odor appertains to knowledge, while hating a bad odor appertains to action. However, as soon as one smells a bad odor, he has already hated it. It is not that he smells it first and then makes up his mind to hate it. A person with his nose stuffed up does not smell the bad odor even if he sees a malodorous object before him, and so he does not hate it. This amounts to not knowing bad odor. Suppose we say that so-and-so knows filial piety and so-and-so knows brotherly respect. They must have actually practiced filial piety and brotherly respect before they can be said to know them. It will not do to say that they know filial piety and brotherly respect simply because they show them in words. Or take one's knowledge of pain. Only after one has experienced pain can one know pain. The same is true of cold or hunger. How can knowledge and action be separated? This is the original substance of knowledge and action, which have not been separated by selfish desires. In teaching people, the Sage insisted that only this can be called knowledge. Otherwise, this is not yet knowledge. This is serious and practical business. What is the objective of desperately insisting on knowledge and action being two different things? And what is the objective of my insisting that they are one? What is the use of insisting on their being one or two unless one knows the basic purpose of the doctrine?"

I said, "In saying that knowledge and action are two different things, the ancients intended to have people distinguish and understand them, so that on the one hand they make an effort to know and, on the other, make an effort to act, and only then can the effort find any solution."

The teacher said, "This is to lose sight of the basic purpose of the ancients. I have said that knowledge is the direction for action and action the effort of knowledge, and that knowledge is the beginning of

[45] *Great Learning*, ch. 6.

action and action the completion of knowledge. If this is understood, then when only knowledge is mentioned, action is included, and when only action is mentioned, knowledge is included. The reason why the ancients talked about knowledge and action separately is that there are people in the world who are confused and act on impulse without any sense of deliberation or self-examination, and who thus behave only blindly and erroneously. Therefore it is necessary to talk about knowledge to them before their action becomes correct. There are also those who are intellectually vague and undisciplined and think in a vacuum. They are not willing at all to try to practice concretely. They only pursue shadows and echoes, as it were. It is therefore necessary to talk about action to them before their knowledge becomes true. The ancient teachers could not help talking this way in order to restore balance and avoid any defect. If we understand this motive, then a single word [either knowledge or action] will do.

"But people today distinguish between knowledge and action and pursue them separately, believing that one must know before he can act. They will discuss and learn the business of knowledge first, they say, and wait till they truly know before they put their knowledge into practice. Consequently, to the last day of life, they will never act and also will never know. This doctrine of knowledge first and action later is not a minor disease and it did not come about only yesterday. My present advocacy of the unity of knowledge and action is precisely the medicine for that disease. The doctrine is not my baseless imagination, for it is the original substance of knowledge and action that they are one. Now that we know this basic purpose, it will do no harm to talk about them separately, for they are only one. If the basic purpose is not understood, however, even if we say they are one, what is the use? It is just idle talk." (1:5b-8a)

> *Comment.* The relation between knowledge and action has been a perennial subject among Confucianists. Both Confucius[46] and the *Doctrine of the Mean*[47] insist that words and action should correspond. The whole doctrine of the rectification of names in ancient Chinese philosophy as well as the whole extensive discussion of the correspondence between names and actuality in ancient China[48] reinforced this tradition. In the entire Neo-Confucian movement, the equal emphasis on words and action was faithfully maintained.[49] The stress so far, however, had been on the correspondence and

[46] *Analects*, 5:9, 13:4, 14:4, 15:5, 18:8.
[47] *The Mean*, ch. 8.
[48] See above, ch. 2, comment on 13:3
[49] See above, ch. 34, secs. 20-24.

equal importance of knowledge and action but not their identity. Ch'eng I came nearest to it when he said that the extension of knowledge and actual demonstration should proceed simultaneously,[50] but he still thought of them as two. Wang's theory definitely struck a new note.

In spite of this identification, however, the Confucian tradition has always emphasized action. This tradition goes back to the *Book of History* where it is said that "it is not difficult to know but difficult to act."[51] Chu Hsi considered action more important than knowledge.[52] When Sun Yat-sen turned the ancient doctrine around and said that "it is difficult to know but easy to act,"[53] he was really upholding the ancient tradition of emphasizing action.

6. I said, "Yesterday when I heard your teaching about abiding in the highest good, I realized I had some grasp of this task. But I still feel that your teaching does not agree with Chu Hsi's doctrine of the investigation of things."

The Teacher said, "The investigation of things is the work of abiding in the highest good. Once we know what the highest good is, we know how to investigate things."

I said, "Yesterday when I examined Chu Hsi's doctrine of the investigation of things in the light of your teaching, I seemed to understand it in general. But I am still not clear in my mind, because Chu Hsi's doctrine, after all, has the support of what is called 'refinement and singleness of mind' in the *Book of History*, 'extensive study of literature and self-restraint by the rules of propriety' in the *Analects*, and 'exerting one's mind to the utmost and knowing one's nature' in the *Book of Mencius*."[54]

The Teacher said, "Tzu-hsia (507–420 B.C.) had strong faith in the Sage whereas Tseng Tzu (505–c.436 B.C.) turned to seek the highest good in himself.[55] It is good to have strong faith, of course, but it is not as real and concrete as seeking in oneself. Since you have not understood this idea, why should you cling to Chu Hsi's old tradition and not seek what is right? Even with Chu Hsi, while he respected and believed in Mas-

---

[50] *Ts'ui-yen* (Pure Words), 1:162b. in ECCS.
[51] *History*, "Charge to Yüeh," pt. 2. Cf. Legge, trans., *Shoo King*, p. 258.
[52] See above, ch. 34, sec. 20.
[53] *Sun Chung-shan ch'üan-chi* (Complete Works of Sun Yat-sen), 1928, vol. 2, p. 53ff.
[54] *History*, "Counsels of the Great Yü." Cf. Legge, *Shoo King*, p. 6; *Analects*, 6:25; *Mencius*, 7A:1; respectively.
[55] Quoting Chu Hsi, *Meng Tzu chi-chu* (Collected Commentaries on the *Book of Mencius*) ch. 3, comment on *Mencius*, 2A:2.

ter Ch'eng I, he would not carelessly follow him whenever he came to something he could not understand.[56] The teachings of refinement and singleness, extensive study and self-restraint, and exerting the mind to the utmost are basically harmonious with my doctrine. Only you have not thought about it.

"Chu Hsi's teaching on the investigation of things is not free from being forced, arbitrary, and far-fetched, and is not what the investigation of things originally meant. Refinement is the work of achieving singleness and extensive study the work of achieving restraint. Since you already understand the principle of the unity of knowledge and action, this can be explained in one word. As to exerting one's mind to the utmost, knowing one's nature, and knowing Heaven, these are the acts of those who are born with such knowledge and practice it naturally and easily. Preserving the mind, nourishing one's nature, and serving Heaven are the acts of those who learn them through study and practice them for their advantage. To maintain one's single-mindedness regardless of longevity or brevity of life, and to cultivate one's personal life while waiting for fate to take its own course, are the acts of those who learn through hard work and practice them with effort and difficulty.[57] But Chu Hsi wrongly interpreted the doctrine of the investigation of things. Because he reversed the above order, and thought that the higher attainments of exerting one's mind to the utmost and knowing one's nature are equivalent to the investigation of things and the extension of knowledge, he required the beginner to perform the acts of those who are born to know and who practice naturally and easily. How can that be done?"

I asked, "Why are exerting the mind to the utmost and knowing one's nature the acts of those who are born to know and who practice naturally and easily?"

The Teacher said, "Our nature is the substance of the mind and Heaven is the source of our nature. To exert one's mind to the utmost is the same as fully developing one's nature. Only those who are absolutely sincere can fully develop their nature and 'know the transforming and nourishing process of Heaven and Earth.'[58] Those who merely preserve their minds, on the other hand, have not yet exerted them to the utmost. Knowing Heaven is the same as knowing the affairs of a district or a county, which is what the titles prefect and magistrate mean. It is a matter within one's own function, and it means that one in his moral character has already become one with Heaven. Serving Heaven, on the other hand, is like the serving of the parents by the son and the serving

[56] See, for example, *Chu Tzu yü-lei* (Recorded Conversations of Chu Hsi), 1880 ed., 69:22a.

[57] Quoting alternately from *Mencius*, 7A:1 and *The Mean*, ch. 20.

[58] Quoting *The Mean*, ch. 22.

672

of the ruler by the minister. It must be done seriously and reverently to please them if it is to be perfect. Even then, one is still separated from Heaven. This is the difference between a sage [who exerts the mind to the utmost and knows Heaven] and the worthies [who preserve their minds and serve Heaven].

"As to allowing no double-mindedness regardless of longevity or brevity of life, it is to teach the student to do good with single-mindedness, and not to allow success or failure, longevity or brevity of life, to shake his determination to do good, but instead to cultivate his personal life and wait for fate to take its own course, realizing that success and failure, or longevity and brevity of life, are matters of fate and one need not unnecessarily allow them to disturb his mind. Although those who serve Heaven are separated from Heaven, they nevertheless already see Heaven right in front of them. Waiting for fate to take its own course, however, means that one has not yet seen Heaven but is still waiting for it, so to speak. It is the beginner's first step in making up his mind, involving a certain amount of effort and difficulty. But Chu Hsi reversed the order, so that the student has no place to start."

I said, "Yesterday when I heard your teaching, I vaguely realized that one's effort must follow this procedure. Now that I have heard what you said, I have no further doubt. Last night I came to the conclusion that the word 'thing' (*wu*) in the phrase 'the investigation of things' (*ko-wu*) has the same meaning as the word 'event' (*shih*), both referring to the mind."

The Teacher said, "Correct. The master of the body is the mind. What emanates from the mind is the will. The original substance of the will is knowledge, and wherever the will is directed is a thing. For example, when the will is directed toward serving one's parents, then serving one's parents is a 'thing.' When the will is directed toward serving one's ruler, then serving one's ruler is a 'thing.' When the will is directed toward being humane to all people and feeling love toward things, then being humane to all people and feeling love toward things are 'things,' and when the will is directed toward seeing, hearing, speaking, and acting, then each of these is a 'thing.' Therefore I say that there are neither principles nor things outside the mind. The teaching in the *Doctrine of the Mean* that 'without sincerity there would be nothing,'[59] and the effort to manifest one's clear character described in the *Great Learning* mean nothing more than the effort to make the will sincere. And the work of making the will sincere is none other than the investigation of things." (1:8a-10a)

7. The Teacher further said, "The word *ko* in *ko-wu* is the same as

---

[59] *The Mean*, ch. 25.

the *ko* in Mencius' saying that 'a great man rectified (*ko*) the ruler's mind.'[60] It means to eliminate what is incorrect in the mind so as to preserve the correctness of its original substance. Wherever the will is, the incorrectness must be eliminated so correctness may be preserved. In other words, in all places and at all times the Principle of Nature must be preserved. This is the investigation of principles to the utmost. The Principle of Nature is clear character, and to investigate the principle of things to the utmost is to manifest the clear character." (1:10a)

26. [The Teacher said,] "Knowledge is the beginning of action and action is the completion of knowledge. Learning to be a sage involves only one effort. Knowledge and action should not be separated." (1:22b)

32. [The Teacher said,] "The original mind is vacuous (devoid of selfish desires), intelligent, and not beclouded. All principles are contained therein and all events proceed from it.[61] There is no principle outside the mind; there is no event outside the mind." (1:24b)

33. Someone asked, "Master Hui-an (Chu Hsi) said that 'man's object of learning is simply mind and principles.'[62] What do you think of this saying?"

The Teacher said, "The mind is the nature of man and things, and nature is principle. I am afraid the use of the word 'and' makes inevitable the interpretation of mind and principle as two different things. It is up to the student to use his good judgment." (1:25a)

34. Someone said, "All people have this mind, and this mind is identical with principle. Why do some people do good and others do evil?"

The Teacher said, "The mind of the evil man has lost its original substance." (*ibid*)

---

[60] *Mencius*, 4A:20.

[61] The two sentences are paraphrases of Chu Hsi's *Ta-hsüeh chang-chü*, commentary on the text. According to Ōta Kinjō (1765-1825) (*Gimon roku*, or Records of Questioning, 1831 ed., p. 15a), the phrase "vacuous, intelligent, and not beclouded" comes from the *Ta-chih tu lu* (*Mahāprajñāpāramita śāstra*, Treatise on Great Wisdom) and was also used by Fa-tsang (643-712), but he gave no specific reference. It is probably derived from the common Buddhist phrase, "intelligent, knowing, and not beclouded," which was uttered by Zen Masters like Ch'eng-kuan (c. 760-838) (see *Ching-te ch'uan-teng lu*, or Records of the Transmission of the Lamp Compiled During the Cheng-te Period, 1004-1007, SPTK, 30:8a). The terms "intelligent and knowing" and "not beclouded" were also used by Tsung-mi (780-841) (in his *Ch'an-yüan chu-ch'üan chi tu-hsü* or General Preface to Collection of Source Material of the Zen School, TSD, 48:404-405). Chu Hsi considered the Buddhist concept too abstract and therefore added the second sentence. See *Chu Tzu yü-lei*, 1880 ed., 104:17a

[62] *Ta-hsüeh huo-wen* (Questions and Answers on the *Great Learning*), 1902 ed., 60a-b, in *Ssu-shu ta-ch'üan* (Great Collection of Commentaries on the Four Books). Hui-an was Chu Hsi's literary name.

53. T'ang Hsü[63] asked, "Does making up the mind mean retaining good thought at all times and wanting to do good and remove evil?"

The Teacher said, "When a good thought is retained, there is the Principle of Nature. The thought itself is goodness. Is there another goodness to be thought about? Since the thought is not evil, what evil is there to be removed? This thought is comparable to the root of a tree. To make up one's mind means always to build up this good thought, that is all. To be able to follow what one's heart desires without transgressing moral principles[64] merely means that one's mind has reached full maturity." (1:31b-32a)

78. I[65] asked, "The mind is the master of the body. Knowledge is the intelligence of the mind. The will is knowledge in operation. And a thing is that to which the will is directed. Is this correct?"

The Teacher said, "Generally correct." (1:39b-40a)

89. [The Teacher said,] "The various steps from the investigation of things and the extension of knowledge to bringing peace to the world[66] are nothing but manifesting the clear character. Even loving the people is also a matter of manifesting the clear character. The clear character is the character of the mind; it is humanity. The man of humanity regards Heaven and Earth and all things as one body.[67] If a single thing is deprived of its place, it means that my humanity is not yet demonstrated to the fullest extent." (1:41b)

93. I said, "Master Ch'eng Hao (Ch'eng Ming-tao, 1032-1085) said that 'the man of humanity regards Heaven, Earth, and all things as one body.' How is it that Mo Tzu's [fl. 479-438 B.C.] doctrine of universal love[68] is not considered one of humanity?"

The Teacher said, "It is very difficult to say. You gentlemen must find it out through personal realization. Humanity is the principle of unceasing production and reproduction. Although it is prevalent and extensive and there is no place where it does not exist, nevertheless there is an order in its operation and growth. That is why it is unceasing in production and reproduction. For example, at the winter solstice the first (active cosmic force) yang grows. There must be the growth of this first yang before all the six stages of yang (the six months between December and June) gradually grow. If there were not the first yang, could there

---

[63] Nothing is known of him.

[64] *Analects*, 2:4.

[65] Lu Ch'eng, Wang's pupil, whose courtesy name was Yüan-ching. He recorded secs. 15-94 of the *Ch'uan-hsi lu*.

[66] As taught in the *Great Learning*, the text.

[67] *I-shu*, 2A:2. See the following section.

[68] Mo Tzu was strongly attacked by Mencius because Mo Tzu did not acknowledge the special affection due a father. *Mencius*, 3B:9. For Mo Tzu's doctrine, see *Mo Tzu*, ch. 14-16, English translation by Mei, *Works of Motse*, p. 78ff.

be all the six? It is the same with the (passive cosmic force) yin. Because there is order, so there is a starting point. Because there is a starting point, so there is growth. And because there is growth, it is unceasing. Take a tree, for example. When in the beginning it puts forth a shoot, there is the starting point of the tree's spirit of life. After the root appears, the trunk grows. After the trunk grows, branches and leaves come, and then the process of unceasing production and reproduction has begun. If there is no sprout, how can there be the trunk, branches, or leaves? The tree can sprout because there is the root beneath. With the root the plant will grow. Without it, the plant will die, for without the root, how can it sprout?

"The love between father and son and between elder and younger brothers is the starting point of the human mind's spirit of life, just like the sprout of the tree. From here it is extended to humaneness to all people and love to all things. It is just like the growth of the trunk, branches, and leaves. Mo Tzu's universal love makes no distinction in human relations and regards one's own father, son, elder brother, or younger brother as being the same as a passer-by. That means that Mo Tzu's universal love has no starting point. It does not sprout. We therefore know that it has no root and that it is not a process of unceasing production and reproduction. How can it be called humanity? Filial piety and brotherly respect are the root of humanity.[69] This means that the principle of humanity grows from within." (1:42a-43a)

> *Comment.* The idea that humanity is life-giving is an important development in Neo-Confucianism. It was developed by Ch'eng Hao and his brother Ch'eng I.[70] Wang, however, made the idea clearer than ever.

94. I asked, "Yen-p'ing (Li T'ung, 1088-1163) said, 'Be in accord with principle and have no selfish mind.'[71] What is the difference between being in accord with principle and having no selfish mind?"

The Teacher said, "The mind is principle. To have no selfish mind is to be in accord with principle, and not to be in accord with principle is to have a selfish mind. I am afraid it is not good to speak of the mind and principle as separated."

I asked further, "The Buddhists are [internally] free from all kinds of selfishness of lust in the world and thus appear not to have a selfish mind.

[69] A saying in *Analects,* 1:2.

[70] See above, ch. 31, comment on sec. 11, and ch. 32, comment on 42. See also ch. 30, comment on sec. 1; ch. 31, comment on sec. 1; and ch. 34, comment on treatise 1.

[71] *Li Yen-p'ing chi* (Collected Works of Li T'ung), *Cheng-i-t'ang ch'üan-chu* (Complete Library of the Hall of Rectifying the Way) ed., 2:24a.

But externally they discard human relations and thus do not appear to be in accord with principle."

The Teacher said, "These are the same kind of things, all building up a mind of selfishness." (1:43a-b)

101. I[72] was pulling weeds out from among the flowers and thereupon said, "How difficult it is in the world to cultivate good and remove evil!"

The Teacher said, "Only because no effort is made to do so." A little later, he said, "Such a view of good and evil is motivated by personal interest and is therefore easily wrong." I did not understand. The Teacher said, "The spirit of life of Heaven and Earth is the same in flowers and weeds. Where have they the distinction of good and evil? When you want to enjoy flowers, you will consider flowers good and weeds evil. But when you want to use weeds, you will then consider them good. Such good and evil are all products of the mind's likes and dislikes. Therefore I know you are wrong."

I asked, "In that case, there is neither good nor evil, is that right?"

The Teacher said, "The state of having neither good nor evil is that of principle in tranquillity. Good and evil appear when the vital force is perturbed. If the vital force is not perturbed, there is neither good nor evil, and this is called the highest good."

I asked, "The Buddhists also deny the distinction between good and evil. Are they different from you?"

The Teacher said, "Being attached to the non-distinction of good and evil, the Buddhists neglect everything and therefore are incapable of governing the world. The sage, on the other hand, in his non-distinction of good and evil, merely makes no special effort whatsoever to like or dislike and is not perturbed in his vital force. As he pursues the kingly path and sees the perfect excellence,[73] he of course completely follows the Principle of Nature and it becomes possible for him to assist in and complete the universal process of production and reproduction and apply it for the benefit of the people."[74]

> *Comment.* Because Wang talked about the state of having neither good nor evil, he has been accused of being a Buddhist in Confucian garment. This passage makes the distinction between Confucianism and Buddhism quite clear. What is more important, Wang not only criticized the Buddhists for their escape from social responsibility, but also for their inability to be free from attach-

[72] Hsüeh K'an (d. 1545), Wang's pupil, who recorded secs. 95-129 of the *Ch'uan-hsi lu.*

[73] Quoting *History*, "Great Norm." Cf. Legge, *Shoo King*, p. 331.

[74] Quoting *Changes*, commentary on hexagram no. 11, *t'ai* (successful). Cf Legge, *Yi King*, p. 281.

677

ment. In other words, the Buddhists were incapable of handling the mind itself. Although he was not as hostile to Buddhism as many other Neo-Confucianists, he attacked the very foundation of Buddhism.[75]

"If weeds are not evil, they should not be removed."

"This, however, is the view of the Buddhists and Taoists. If they are harmful, what is the objection to your removing them?"

"What would be a case of making a special effort to like or to dislike."

"Not making special effort to like or to dislike does not mean not to like or dislike at all. A person behaving so would be devoid of consciousness. To say 'not to make a special effort' merely means that one's like and dislike completely follow the Principle of Nature and that one does not go on to attach to that situation a bit of selfish thought. This amounts to having neither likes nor dislikes."

"How can weeding be regarded as completely following the Principle of Nature without any attachment to selfish thought?"

"If weeds are harmful, according to principle they should be removed. Then remove them, that is all. If for a moment they are not removed, one should not be troubled by it. If one attaches to that situation a bit of selfish thought, it will be a burden on the substance of his mind, and his vital force will be much perturbed."

"In that case, good and evil are not present in things at all."

"They are only in your mind. Following the Principle of Nature is good, while perturbing the vital force is evil."

"After all, then, things are devoid of good and evil?"

"This is true of the mind. It is also true of things. Famous but mediocre scholars fail to realize this. They neglect the mind and chase after material things, and consequently get a wrong view of the way to investigate things. All day long they restlessly seek principle in external things. They only succeed in getting at it by incidental deeds of righteousness. All their lives they act in this way without understanding it and act habitually without examination."[76]

"How about loving beautiful color and hating bad odor?"

"This is all in accord with principle. We do so by the very nature of the Principle of Nature. From the beginning there is no selfish desire to make special effort to like or dislike."

"How can the love of beautiful color and the hatred of bad odor not be regarded as one's own will?"

"The will in this case is sincere, not selfish. A sincere will is in accord with the Principle of Nature. However, while it is in accord with the

[75] See comment on sec. 315.
[76] A quotation from *Mencius*, 7A:5.

678

Principle of Nature, at the same time it is not attached in the least to selfish thought. Therefore when one is affected to any extent by wrath or fondness, the mind will not be correct.[77] It must be broad and impartial. Only thus is it in its original substance. Knowing this, you know the state of equilibrium before feelings are aroused."

Meng Po-sheng[78] said, "You said that if weeds are harmful, according to principle they should be removed. Why should the desire to remove them be motivated by personal interest?"

"You must find this out yourself through personal realization. What is your state of mind when you want to remove the weeds? And what was the state of mind of Chou Mao-shu (Chou Tun-i, 1017-1073), when he would not cut down the grass outside his window?"[79] (1:47b-49b)

108. I asked, "A former scholar considered the mind in its tranquil state as substance and the mind in its active state as function.[80] What about it?"

The Teacher said, "The substance and function of the mind cannot be equated with its tranquil and active states. Tranquillity and activity are matters of time. When we speak of substance as substance, function is already involved in it, and when we speak of function as function, substance is already involved in it. This is what is called 'Substance and function coming from the same source.'[81] However, there is no harm in saying that the substance of the mind is revealed through its tranquillity and its function through its activity." (1:52a)

132. Your[82] letter says, "You teach us that knowledge and action should proceed simultaneously, that no distinction should be made as to which one should precede the other, and that this is the task of 'honoring the moral nature and following the path of study and inquiry' as taught in the *Doctrine of the Mean*,[83] in which the two nourish and develop each other and the internal and external, the fundamental and the secondary form one thread running through all. Nevertheless, in the performance of a task there must be a distinction between what is to be done first and what later. For example, one knows the food before he eats it, knows the soup before he drinks it, knows the clothes before he wears them, and knows the road before he travels on it. It is not true

[77] According to the *Great Learning*, ch. 7.
[78] Nothing is known of him except that his private name was Yüan.
[79] *I-shu*, 3:2a, in ECCS.
[80] Ch'eng I, *Wen-chi* (Collection of Literary Works), 5:12a, in ECCS. Wang Yang-ming said the same thing in *Wang Wen-ch'eng K'ung ch'üan-shu*, 5:62.
[81] Ch'eng I, preface to his *I chuan* (Commentary on the *Book of Changes*), in ECCS. See above, ch. 32, n.124.
[82] This refers to Ku Tung ch'iao (Ku Lin, 1476-1545), a high official and a renowned poet.
[83] Ch. 27.

679

that one performs an act without first of all knowing the thing to be acted on. The difference [between knowing first and acting later] is of course a matter of an instant. I do not mean to say that it is comparable to one's knowing today and then acting tomorrow."

Since you have said that the two nourish and develop each other, and the internal and the external, the fundamental and the secondary form one thread running through all, the idea that knowledge and action proceed simultaneously should no longer be doubted. You also say that in the performance of a task there must[84] be a distinction between what is to be done first and what later. Are you not self-contradictory? This is particularly clear and can easily be seen in your theories that one knows the food before he eats, but your understanding is obscured by recent opinions and you do not realize that it is obscured. A man must have the desire for food before he knows food. This desire to eat is the will; it is already the beginning of action. Whether the taste of the food is good or bad cannot be known until the food enters the mouth. Is there anyone who knows the taste to be good or bad before the food enters his mouth? A man must have the desire to travel before he knows the road. This desire to travel is the will; it is already the beginning of action. Whether the forks of the road are rough or smooth cannot be known until he himself has gone through them. Is there anyone who knows whether the forks of the road are rough or smooth before he has gone through them? The same can be said without a doubt about the theories that one knows the soup before he drinks it and that one knows the clothes before he wears them. The examples you have given are exactly those which show, as you say, that one first of all performs an act without knowing the thing to be acted on. You said also that the difference [between knowing first and acting later] is of course a matter of an instant and that you do not mean to say that it is clearly comparable to one's knowing today and then acting tomorrow. This shows that you have not examined the matter thoroughly. But even as you say, the fact that knowledge and action form a unity and proceed simultaneously is as a matter of course absolutely beyond any doubt. (2:3a-4b)

133. Your letter says, "[You say that] true knowledge is what constitutes action, and unless it is acted on it cannot be called knowledge. This idea is all right as an urgent doctrine for the student, meant to enable him to put his learning into actual practice. But if you really mean that knowledge and action are identical, I am afraid a student will only seek his original mind and consequently neglect the principles of things, and there will be points at which his mind will be closed to the outside world

---

[84] In the text there is the word *pu* (not) here. It is obviously a misprint and is therefore omitted from the translation.

and unable to penetrate it. Is this the established method of the Confucian school for the simultaneous advance of knowledge and action?"

Knowledge in its genuine and earnest aspect is action, and action in its intelligent and discriminating aspect is knowledge. At bottom the task of knowledge and action cannot be separated. Only because later scholars have broken their task into two sections and have lost sight of the original substance of knowledge and action have I advocated the idea of their unity and simultaneous advance. My idea that true knowledge is what constitutes action and that unless it is acted on it cannot be called knowledge can be seen in such ideas as those expressed in your letter that one knows the food before he eats it, and so forth. I have already stated this briefly. Although my idea arose as an urgent remedial measure, nevertheless the substance of knowledge and action is originally like this. It is not that I have promoted or suppressed either of them according to my own wishes, and purposely propounded such a doctrine carelessly to effect a temporary remedy. He who only seeks his original mind and consequently neglects the principles of things is one who has lost his original mind. For the principles of things are not external to the mind. If one seeks the principles of things outside the mind, there will not be any to be found. And if one neglects the principles of things and only seeks his mind, what sort of a thing would the mind be? The substance of the mind is nature, and nature is identical with principle. Consequently, as there is the mind of filial piety toward parents, there is the principle of filial piety. If there is no mind of filial piety, there will be no principle of filial piety. As there is the mind of loyalty toward the ruler, there is the principle of loyalty. If there is no mind of loyalty, there will be no principle of loyalty. Are principles external to the mind? Hui-an (Chu Hsi) said, "Man's object of learning is simply mind and principles. Although the mind is the master of the body . . . actually it controls all principles in the world. And although principles are distributed throughout the ten thousand things . . . actually they are not outside one's mind."[85] These are but the two aspects of concentration and diversification but [the way Chu Hsi put it] has inevitably opened the way to the defect among scholars of regarding the mind and principles as two separate things. This is the reason why later generations have the trouble of only seeking their original minds and consequently neglecting the principles of things. This is precisely because they do not realize that the mind is identical with principle. The idea that if one seeks the principles of things outside the mind there will be points at which the mind is closed to the outside world and cannot penetrate it is the same as Kao Tzu's (c.420–c.350 B.C.) doctrine that righteousness

---

[85] *Ta-hsüeh huo-wen,* 60a-b.

is external.[86] This is the reason why Mencius said that he did not know the nature of righteousness. The mind is one, that is all. In terms of total commiseration, it is called humanity. In terms of attainment of what is proper, it is called righteousness. And in terms of orderliness, it is called principle. If one should not seek humanity or righteousness outside the mind, should one make an exception and seek principles outside the mind? Knowledge and action have been separated because people seek principles outside the mind. The doctrine of unity of knowledge and action of the Confucian school means seeking principles in the mind. Why do you doubt it? (2:4b-6a)

135. Your letter says, "I have heard that you told students that following [Chu Hsi's] theory of the investigation of the principles of all things that we come into contact with[87] is to trifle with things and to lose one's purpose, and that you have also selected Chu Hsi's doctrines of rejecting the complex and preferring the simple,[88] cultivating the fundamental,[89] and so forth, to show students, labeling them as Chu Hsi's final conclusions arrived at late in life.[90] I am afraid this is also wrong."

What Chu Hsi meant by the investigation of things is "to investigate the principle in things to the utmost as we come in contact with them."[91] To investigate the principles in things to the utmost as we come in contact with them means to look in each individual thing for its so-called definite principles. This means to apply one's mind to each individual thing and look for the principle in it. This is to divide the mind and principle into two. To seek for the principle in each individual thing is like looking for the principle of filial piety in parents. If the principle of filial piety is to be sought in parents, then is it actually in my own mind or is it in the person of my parents? If it is actually in the person of my parents, is it true that as soon as the parents pass away the mind will lack the principle of filial piety? When I see a child fall into a well [and have a feeling of commiseration], there must be the principle of commiseration. Is this principle of commiseration actually in the person of the child or is it in the innate knowledge of my mind? Perhaps one cannot follow the child into the well to rescue it. Perhaps one can rescue it by seizing it with the hand. All this involves principle. Is it really in the person of the child or does it emanate from the innate knowledge of my mind? What is true here is true of all things and events. From this we know the mistake of dividing the mind and principle into two.

[86] See *Mencius*, 6A:4.
[87] *Chung-yung chang-chü* (Commentary on the *Doctrine of the Mean*), ch. 5.
[88] *Chu-tzu wen-chi* (Collection of Literary Works of Chu Hsi), CTTC, 35:26a.
[89] *ibid.*, 47:31a.
[90] *Wang Wen-ch'eng Kung ch'üan-shi.* 3:63a-80a.
[91] *Ta-hsüeh chang-chü*, ch. 5.

Such division is the doctrine of Kao Tzu who taught that righteousness is external to the mind, a fallacy which Mencius strongly attacked. You know the defects of devoting oneself to external things and neglecting the internal, and becoming broad but lacking essentials. Why are these defects? Is it not permissible to say that to investigate the principle of all things as we come into contact with them, as Chu Hsi has taught, is trifling with things and losing one's purpose in life? What I mean by the investigation of things and the extension of knowledge is to extend the innate knowledge of my mind to each and every thing. The innate knowledge of my mind is the same as the Principle of Nature. When the Principle of Nature in the innate knowledge of my mind is extended to all things, all things will attain their principle. To extend the innate knowledge of my mind is the matter of the extension of knowledge, and for all things to attain their principle is the matter of the investigation of things. In these the mind and principle are combined into one. As the mind and principle are combined into one, then all my humble opinions which I have just expressed and my theory that Chu Hsi arrived at his final conclusions late in life can be understood without discussion. (2:-8b-10a)

155. Your[92] letter says, "Innate knowledge is the original substance of the mind. It is what is called the goodness of human nature, the equilibrium before the feelings are aroused, the substance that is absolutely quiet and inactive, and the state of being broad and extremely impartial. When were ordinary people incapable of it and had to learn? Since equilibrium, absolute quiet, and impartiality are characteristics of the substance of the mind, then it must be innate knowledge. But as I examine the mind, I find that while knowledge is innate and good, it does not really have the characteristics of equilibrium, quiet, and impartiality. Can innate knowledge transcend substance and function?"

There is no human nature that is not good. Therefore there is no innate knowledge that is not good. Innate knowledge is the equilibrium before the feelings are aroused. It is the state of broadness and extreme impartiality. It is the original substance that is absolutely quiet and inactive. And it is possessed by all men. However, people cannot help being darkened and obscured by material desires. Hence they must study in order to get rid of the darkness and obscuration. But they cannot add or subtract even an iota from the original substance of innate knowledge. Innate knowledge is good. The reason why equilibrium, absolute quiet, broadness, and impartiality are not complete in it is that darkness and obscuration have not been entirely eliminated and its state of preservation is not yet complete. The substance and function [you refer to] are

---

[92] Referring to Lu Ch'eng. See n.65.

the substance and function of innate knowledge. How can it transcend them? (2:38a-39a)

228. I[93] asked, "Sir, you once said that good and evil are one thing.[94] But good and evil are opposed to each other like ice and burning coals. How can they be said to be only one?"

The Teacher said, "The highest good is the original substance of the mind. When one deviates a little from this original substance, there is evil. It is not that there is a good and there is also an evil to oppose it. Therefore good and evil are one thing."

Having heard our Teacher's explanation, I know that we can no longer doubt Master Ch'eng Hao's sayings, "Man's nature is of course good, but it cannot be said that evil is not our nature"[95] and "Good and evil in the world are both the Principle of Nature. What is called evil is not originally evil. It becomes evil only because of deviation from the Mean."[96] (3:12b-13a)

262. A friend who was engaging in sitting in meditation attained some insight. He ran to make an inquiry of the Teacher. The Teacher said, "Formerly, when I stayed in Ch'u-chou,[97] seeing that students were mostly occupied with intellectual explanations and debate on similarities and differences, which did them no good, I therefore taught them sitting in meditation. For a time they realized the situation a little bit (they saw the true Way) and achieved some immediate results. In time, however, they gradually developed the defect of fondness of tranquillity and disgust with activity and degenerated into lifelessness like dry wood. Others purposely advocated abstruse and subtle theories to startle people. For this reason I have recently expounded only the doctrine of the extension of innate knowledge. If one's innate knowledge is clear, it will be all right either to try to obtain truth through personal realization in a quiet place or to discover it through training and polishing in the actual affairs of life. The original substance of innate knowledge is neither tranquil nor active. Recognition of this fact is the basis of learning. From the time of Ch'u-chou until now, I have tested what I said several times. The point is that the phrase 'the extension of innate knowledge' is free from any defect. Only a physician who has broken his own arm can understand the causes of human disease."[98] (3:25a-b)

Comment. Under the influence of Zen Buddhism, most Neo-Confucianists taught sitting in meditation. Wang was no exception. In

[93] Huang I-fang, Wang's pupil, whose private name was Chih. He recorded secs. 222-236 and 317-343 of the *Ch'uan-hsi lu.* Otherwise nothing is known of him.
[94] *Ch'uan-hsi lu,* sec. 101.   [95] *I-shu,* 1:7b.
[96] *ibid.,* 2A:1b.
[97] In modern Anhui Province, near Nan-ch'ang.
[98] Quoting the *Tso chuan* (Tso's Commentary), Duke Ting, 13th years.

fact, in the first phase of his teaching, he emphasized it. However, it was soon replaced by an active approach, notably "polishing and training in actual affairs." This doctrine has exerted great influence on both China and Japan.

274. Chu Pen-ssu[99] asked, "Man has innate knowledge because he possesses pure intelligence. Have such things as plants and trees, tiles and stones innate knowledge also?

The Teacher said, "The innate knowledge of man is the same as that of plants and trees, tiles and stones. Without the innate knowledge inherent in man, there cannot be plants and trees, tiles and stones. This is not true of them only. Even Heaven and Earth cannot exist without the innate knowledge that is inherent in man. For at bottom Heaven, Earth, the myriad things, and man form one body. The point at which this unity manifests in its most refined and excellent form is the clear intelligence of the human mind. Wind, rain, dew, thunder, sun and moon, stars, animals and plants, mountains and rivers, earth and stones are essentially of one body with man. It is for this reason that such things as the grains and animals can nourish man and that such things as medicine and minerals can heal diseases. Since they share the same material force, they enter into one another." (3:29b-30a)

275. The Teacher was roaming in Nan-chen.[100] A friend pointed to flowering trees on a cliff and said, "[You say] there is nothing under heaven external to the mind.[101] These flowering trees on the high mountain blossom and drop their blossoms of themselves. What have they to do with my mind?"

The Teacher said, "Before you look at these flowers, they and your mind are in the state of silent vacancy. As you come to look at them, their colors at once show up clearly. From this you can know that these flowers are not external to your mind." (3:30a)

277. The Teacher said, "The eye has no substance of its own. Its substance consists of the colors of all things. The ear has no substance of its own. Its substance consists of the sounds of all things. The nose has no substance of its own. Its substance consists of the smells of all things. The mouth has no substance of its own. Its substance consists of the tastes of all things. The mind has no substance of its own. Its substance consists of the right or wrong of the influences and responses of Heaven, Earth, and all things." (3:31a)

308. I[102] asked, "In the discussion on the nature of man and things, the

---

[99] He was Chu Te-chih, Wang's pupil.

[100] The Hui-chi Mountain in present Chekiang.

[101] *Ch'uan-hsi lu*, sec. 6.

[102] Referring to Huang Mien-chih, who recorded secs. 248-316 of the *Ch'uan-hsi lu*.

ancients agreed in certain respects but differed in others. Which is the final and accepted conclusion?"

The Teacher said, "One's nature has no definite form. The discussion of nature also has no definite form. Some discussed it from the point of view of its original substance, some from the point of view of its emanation and functioning, some from the point of view of its source, and some from the point of view of the defects that may develop in the course of its operation. Collectively, they all talked about this one nature, but their depth of understanding it varied, that is all. If one held rigidly to one aspect as they did it would be a mistake. In its original substance, nature is in fact neither good nor evil. In its function it can indeed be made to be good or evil, and in its defects it is indeed definitely good or evil. It may be compared to the eyes. There are eyes when one is joyous and there are eyes when one is angry. When one looks straight ahead, the eyes see openly. When one looks stealthily, the eyes peep. Collectively speaking, they are all eyes. If one sees a person with angry eyes and forthwith declares that he has no joyous eyes, or if one sees a person with peeping eyes and forthwith declares that he has no openly seeing eyes, one is holding onto a fixed viewpoint and from this we know that one is making a mistake. When Mencius talked about nature, he discussed it directly from the point of view of its source and said only that generally speaking [nature is originally good]. Hsün Tzu's (fl. 298–238 B.C.) doctrine that nature is originally evil[103] was arrived at from the point of view of its defects and we should not say that he was entirely wrong, only that he did not understand the matter perfectly. As to ordinary people, they have lost the original substance of the mind." (3:42a-43a)

315. In the ninth month of the sixth year of Chia-ching (1527), our Teacher had been called from retirement and appointed to subdue once more the rebellion in Ssu-en and T'ien-chou[104] [when the earlier expedition under another official had failed]. As he was about to start, Ju-chung (Wang Chi)[105] and I (Ch'ien Te-hung) discussed learning. He repeated the words of the Teacher's instructions as follows:

In the original substance of the mind there is no distinction between good and evil.
When the will becomes active, however, such distinction exists.

[103] *Hsün Tzu*, ch. 17. See above, ch. 6. sec. 3. Hsün Tzu strongly criticized Mencius' doctrine of original goodness (*Mencius*, 2A:6).
[104] Both were counties in Kwangsi.
[105] Wang Chi (Wang Lung-hsi, 1498-1583), one of the two most prominent followers of Wang. He developed the intuitive tendency of Wang and had a large following.

The faculty of innate knowledge is to know good and evil.
The investigation of things is to do good and remove evil.

I[106] asked, "What do you think this means?"

Ju-chung said, "This is perhaps not the final conclusion. If we say that in the original substance of the mind there is no distinction between good and evil, then there must be no such distinction in the will, in knowledge, and in things. If we say that there is a distinction between good and evil in the will, then in the final analysis there must also be such a distinction in the substance of the mind."

I said, "The substance of the mind is the nature endowed in us by Heaven, and is originally neither good nor evil. But because we have a mind dominated by habits, we see in our thoughts a distinction between good and evil. The work of the investigation of things, the extension of knowledge, the sincerity of the will, the rectification of the mind, and the cultivation of the personal life is aimed precisely at recovering that original nature and substance. If there were no good or evil to start with, what would be the necessity of such effort?"

That evening we sat down beside the Teacher at the T'ien-ch'üan Bridge. Each stated his view and asked to be corrected. The Teacher said, "I am going to leave now. I wanted to have you come and talk this matter through. You two gentlemen complement each other very well, and should not hold on to one side. Here I deal with two types of people. The man of sharp intelligence apprehends straight from the source. The original substance of the human mind is in fact crystal-clear without any impediment and is the equilibrium before the feelings are aroused. The man of sharp intelligence has accomplished his task as soon as he has apprehended the original substance, penetrating the self, other people, and things internal and things external all at the same time. On the other hand, there are inevitably those whose minds are dominated by habits so that the original substance of the mind is obstructed. I therefore teach them definitely and sincerely to do good and remove evil in their will and thoughts. When they become expert at the task and the impurities of the mind are completely eliminated, the original substance of the mind will become wholly clear. Ju-Chung's view is the one I use in dealing with the man of sharp intelligence. Te-hung's view is for the second type. If you two gentlemen use your views interchangeably, you will be able to lead all people—of the highest, average, and lowest intelligence—to the truth. If each of you holds on to one side, right here you will err in handling properly the different type of

---

[106] Referring to Ch'ien Te-hung (Ch'ien Hsü-shan, 1496-1574). The other prominent follower of Wang's, he differed from Wang Chi radically and emphasized moral cultivation.

man and each in his own way will fail to understand fully the substance of the Way."

After a while he said again, "From now on whenever you discuss learning with friends be sure not to lose sight of my basic purpose.

In the original substance of the mind there is no distinction
of good and evil.
When the will becomes active, however, such distinction exists.
The faculty of innate knowledge is to know good and evil.
The investigation of things is to do good and to remove evil.

Just keep to these words of mine and instruct people according to their types, and there will not be any defect. This is indeed a task that penetrates both the higher and the lower levels. It is not easy to find people of sharp intelligence in the world. Even Yen Hui (Confucius' most virtuous pupil) and Ming-tao (Ch'eng Hao) dared not assume that they could fully realize the original substance of the mind as soon as they apprehended the task. How can we lightly expect this from people? People's minds are dominated by habits. If we do not teach them concretely and sincerely to devote themselves to the task of doing good and removing evil right in their innate knowledge rather than merely imagining an original substance in a vacuum, all that they do will not be genuine and they will do no more than cultivate a mind of vacuity and quietness [like that of the Buddhists and Taoists]. This defect is not a small matter and must be exposed as early as possible." On that day both Ju-chung and I attained some enlightenment. (3:45b-47b)

Comment. This conversation concerning the famous "doctrine in four axioms" raises a fundamental issue and led to a bitter controversy both inside and outside the Wang Yang-ming School. The issue is whether the mind in its original substance transcends good and evil, as the Buddhists would say, or is fundamentally good, as the Confucianists insist.

In his teachings Wang Chi interpreted the four axioms to mean the absence of distinction between good and evil and that sagehood comes through a direct intuition of reality in its totality. Ch'ien Te-hung, on the other hand, interpreted them to mean that the distinction exists and that sagehood comes only through moral efforts to do good and overcome evil. Actually Wang Yang-ming taught both, as the conversation clearly shows. It is only because they represented two sharply divergent tendencies within the Wang Yang-ming School, one emphasizing intuitive awakening and the other emphasizing moral endeavor, that they have given the doctrine a one-sided interpretation. Of the two, Ch'ien comes closer to the teacher, for the teacher definitely stated that the original nature of the mind is characterized by the highest good.[107] To him the mind is a unity and absolutely good and not divided between good and evil. Moral good and evil come in when our will becomes active, that is, when we begin to make a choice. Even accepting the one-sided views of the two pupils, there should have been no quarrel, for Ch'ien's understanding is on the moral plane whereas Wang's is on the religious plane, and the teacher's doctrine covers both.

For a hundred years outsiders, on the basis of Wang Chi's interpretation, attacked Wang Yang-ming's doctrine as a surrender to Buddhist indifference to good and evil. The attack kept the Confucian mind alert about the distinction between good and evil but only at the expense of a great injustice to Wang Yang-ming.

319. The Teacher said, "People merely say that in the investigation of things we must follow Chu Hsi, but when have they carried it out in practice? I have carried it out earnestly and definitely. In my earlier years[108] my friend Ch'ien[109] and I discussed the idea that to become a sage or a worthy one must investigate all things in the world. But how can a person have such tremendous energy? I therefore pointed to the bamboos in front of the pavilion and told him to investigate them and see. Day and night Mr. Ch'ien went ahead to try to investigate to the utmost the principles in the bamboos. He exhausted his mind and thoughts and on the third day he was tired out and took sick. At first I said that it was because his energy and strength were insufficient. Therefore I myself went to try to investigate to the utmost. From morning till night, I was unable to find the principles of the bamboos. On the seventh day I also became sick because I thought too hard. In consequence we sighed to each other and said that it was impossible to be a sage or a worthy, for we do not have the tremendous energy to investigate things as they have. After I had lived among the barbarians for [almost] three years,[110] I understood what all this meant and realized that there is really nothing in the things in the world to investigate, that the effort to investigate things is only to be carried out in and with reference to one's body and mind, and that if one firmly believes that everyone can become a sage, one will naturally be able to take up the task of investigating things. This idea, gentlemen, I must convey to you." (3:50b-51b)

[107] Ch'uan-hsi lu, sec. 318.
[108] According to the Nien-p'u (Chronological Biography), the following incident took place in 1492.
[109] This friend was not Ch'ien Te-hung, since he did not meet Wang until 1521.
[110] When he was banished to become an official in Kuei-chou between 1506 and 1508.

331. I said, "A former scholar said that the flying of the hawk, the leaping of fishes,[111] and the feeling that one must always be doing something[112] are all very lively and dynamic in the same way."[113]

The Teacher said, "Correct. The whole universe is very lively and dynamic because of the same principle. It is the unceasing universal operation of one's innate knowledge. To extend innate knowledge is the task of always doing something. Not only should this principle not be departed from, in reality it cannot be. The Way is everywhere, and so is our task." (3:56a)

337. I said, "The human mind and things form the same body.[114] In the case of one's body, blood and the vital force in fact circulate through it and therefore we can say they form the same body. In the case of men, their bodies are different and differ even more from those of animals and plants. How can they be said to form the same body?"

The Teacher said, "Just look at the matter from the point of view of the subtle incipient activating force of their mutual influence and response. Not only animals and plants, but heaven and earth also, form the same body with me. Spiritual beings also form the same body with me."

I asked the Teacher kindly to explain.

The Teacher said, "Among the things under heaven and on earth, which do you consider to be the mind of Heaven and Earth?"

"I have heard that 'Man is the mind of Heaven and Earth.' "[115]

"How does man become mind?"

"Clear intelligence and clear intelligence alone."

"We know, then, in all that fills heaven and earth there is but this clear intelligence. It is only because of their physical forms and bodies that men are separated. My clear intelligence is the master of heaven and earth and spiritual beings. If heaven is deprived of my clear intelligence, who is going to look into its height? If earth is deprived of my clear intelligence, who is going to look into its height? If earth is deprived of my clear intelligence, who is going to look into its depth? If spiritual beings are deprived of my clear intelligence, who is going to distinguish their good and evil fortune or the calamities and blessings that they will bring? Separated from my clear intelligence, there will be no heaven, earth, spiritual beings, or myriad things, and separated from these, there

---

[111] Quoting the *Book of Odes*, ode no. 239.

[112] Mencius' saying, in *Mencius*, 2A:2.

[113] Ch'eng Hao, *I-shu*, 3:1a.

[114] Undoubtedly a quotation of Wang's although it cannot be located. The idea is quite obvious in sec. 267.

[115] *Book of Rites*, "The Evolution of Rites." Cf. Legge, *Li Ki*, vol. 1, p. 382.

will not be my clear intelligence. Thus they are all permeated with one material force. How can they be separated?"

I asked further, "Heaven, earth, spiritual beings, and the myriad things have existed from great antiquity. Why should it be that if my clear intelligence is gone, they will all cease to exist?"

"Consider the dead man. His spirit has drifted away and dispersed. Where are his heaven and earth and myriad things?" (3:57a-58b)

36

THE MATERIALISM OF WANG FU-CHIH

IT HAS TAKEN two hundred years to appreciate the philosophical significance of Wang Fu-chih (Wang Ch'uan-shan, 1619-1692). Son of a scholar, he passed the civil service examination and obtained the first degree in 1642. By that time, the Manchus were already overrunning China. In 1648, as the Manchus oppressed his native province of Hunan, he raised a small army to fight them and to save the Ming dynasty (1368-1644). After his inevitable defeat, he retired at the age of thirty-three to the mountains near his home, and for forty years dedicated his life to writing, covering both ancient and modern periods, and Taoist and Buddhist as well as Confucian schools.[1] But he was practically forgotten until almost a century later, and his many works, of which seventy-seven have survived, were not published until the middle of the nineteenth century. Even then attention was attracted only to his bold political theory and unorthodox interpretation of history. It was not until our own time that his unique philosophy was appreciated. Because of his materialism, he has been praised in Communist China as one of the greatest philosophers in Chinese history.[2]

Aside from ideological considerations, his philosophy is significant in more senses than one. He was an independent thinker, attacking both the rationalistic Neo-Confucianism of Sung (960-1279) and the idealistic Neo-Confucianism of Ming and moving in a new direction. In so doing, he anticipated, though did not directly influence, Chinese thought in the following two centuries. One may even say that he inaugurated the modern era of Chinese philosophy.

Wang rejected the central thesis of both rationalistic and idealistic schools, namely, that principle (*li*) is a universal transcending and prior to material force (*ch'i*). Instead, he contended that principle is identical with the material force, not a finished product that can be grasped, but the order and arrangement of things. There are no such transcendental and abstract things as the Great Ultimate or the Principle of Nature (*T'ien-li*). They, along with the mind and the nature of things, are all within material force.

This philosophy is essentially similar to that of Chang Tsai (Chang Heng-ch'ü, 1020-1077), and Wang has been correctly described as Chang's successor. But he actually went beyond Chang. What he wanted

[1] For more information on his life, see Hummel, ed., *Eminent Chinese*, pp. 817-819.

[2] See below, ch. 44.

was not only materiality, but concreteness of materiality. To him, Chang's Great Vacuity is not an abstract entity but concrete. Because the Taoist idea of non-being was too abstract for him, he vigorously attacked it. Consequently, his most famous dictum is: "The world consists only of concrete things (ch'i)." This word ch'i is to be differentiated from the ch'i that means material force. The two words are represented by two different Chinese characters. Ch'i as material force means the general stuff of which things are made, but ch'i as concrete things means specific and tangible objects or systems. Literally implement, it means more than individual concrete objects but systems and institutions as well, so long as they are understood as being concrete.[3] A concrete thing is not just simple stuff; it possesses an order and exhibits definite principles inherent in it. Thus the Way or principle and ch'i are two aspects of an entity. As there is a concrete thing, there is always its principle in it, and there has never been a principle independent of a concrete thing.

Since he relegated principle to a secondary position, it is not surprising that he overthrew another major concept of Sung-Ming Neo-Confucianism, namely, the contrast between principle and human desires and the subordination of the latter. He refused to accept their opposition, although he conceded that desires should be correct. As to how the principle of correctness is to be obtained, he had to assume that concrete things have in them the tendency toward correctness.

In one respect he perpetuated the Sung-Ming Neo-Confucian tradition and pushed it further, notably the doctrine that things are daily renewed. Like Neo-Confucianists before him, he conceived of the universe as a process of continuous production and reproduction. In this process, the yin and yang elements (passive and active cosmic forces) of material force are in constant fusion and intermingling, so that both material force and principle are daily renewed.

Applied to government and history, this philosophy leads to some unorthodox and bold conclusions. Since principle is found only in concrete objects and systems, there is no Principle of Nature which Sung-Ming Neo-Confucianists employed as the model for history and society. Furthermore, since concrete things at present are different from those in the past, the past cannot be a pattern for today. This is the reason why he rejected feudalism. He also believed that the later the period, the more civilized society becomes. The ideas of progress and evolution are unmistakable. But he also felt that inasmuch as concrete things are never isolated but are always related and change from time to time, they

[3] For the translation of this ch'i as "concrete thing," see Appendix, comment on Ch'i.

follow certain principles in them. This being their tendency, it is wise for us to follow them. Here we have a conservative note in an essentially radical philosophy.

From the above, it is clear that while Wang clearly departed from Neo-Confucianism, he nevertheless continued its heritage to some extent. He is still close to Chu Hsi (1130-1200), though he is definitely opposed to Wang Yang-ming (Wang Shou-jen, 1472-1529). He was not the only one at his time, nor the first in Chinese history, to hold that principle is identical with material force. Liu Tsung-chou (1578-1645) had taught it[4] and Wang's contemporary, Huang Tsung-hsi (1610-1695) had said the same thing.[5] But none had built up a whole philosophical system on the basis of this concept. His revolt against principle in favor of concrete things and against the Principle of Nature in favor of human desires anticipated Yen Yüan (Yen Hsi-chai, 1635-1704) and Tai Chen (Tai Tung-yüan, 1723-1777). He also exerted considerable influence on T'an Ssu-t'ung (1865-1898).

Wang's ideas spread over many works. The following selections are from the *Ch'uan-shan i-shu* (Surviving Works of Wang Fu-chih).

1. THE WORLD OF CONCRETE THINGS

The world consists only of concrete things. The Way (*Tao*) is the Way of concrete things, but concrete things may not be called concrete things of the Way. People generally are capable of saying that without its Way there cannot be the concrete thing. However, if there is the concrete thing, there need be no worry about there not being its Way. A sage knows what a superior man does not know, but an ordinary man or woman can do what a sage cannot do. A person may be ignorant of the Way of a thing, and the concrete thing therefore cannot be completed. But not being completed does not mean that there is no concrete thing. Few people are capable of saying that without a concrete thing there cannot be its Way, but it is certainly true.

> *Comment.* Ch'eng Hao (Ch'eng Ming-tao, 1032-1085) also equated the Way with concrete things.[6] However, Ch'eng's emphasis is on the Way, while Wang's emphasis is on concrete things.

In the period of wilderness and chaos, there was no Way to bow and yield a throne. At the time of Yao and Shun,[7] there was no Way to pity the suffering people and punish the sinful rulers. During the Han (206 B.C.–A.D. 220) and T'ang (618-907) dynasties there were no Ways

---

[4] *Liu Tzu ch'üan-shu* (Complete Works of Master Liu), 11:3a.
[5] *Nan-lei wen-ting* (Literary Works of Huang Tsung-hsi), SPTK, 3:6b.
[6] See above, ch. 31, sec. 5.
[7] Legendary emperors (3rd millennium B.C.).

as we have today, and there will be many in future years which we do not have now. Before bows and arrows existed, there was no Way of archery. Before chariots and horses existed, there was no Way to drive them. Before sacrificing oxen and wine, presents of jade and silk, or bells, chimes, flutes, and strings existed, there were no Ways of ceremonies and music. Thus there is no Way of the father before there is a son, there is no Way of the elder brother before there is a younger brother, and there are many potential Ways which are not existent. Therefore without a concrete thing, there cannot be its Way. This is indeed a true statement. Only people have not understood it.

Sages of antiquity could manage concrete things but could not manage the Way. What is meant by the Way is the management of concrete things. When the Way is fulfilled, we call it virtue. When the concrete thing is completed, we call it operation. When concrete things function extensively, we call it transformation and penetration. When its effect becomes prominent, we call it achievement. . . .

By "what exists before physical form" [and is therefore without it][8] does not mean there is no physical form. There is already physical form. As there is physical form, there is that which exists before it. Even if we span past and present, go through all the myriad transformations, and investigate Heaven, Earth, man, and things to the utmost, we will not find any thing existing before physical form [and is without it]. Therefore it is said, "It is only the sage who can put his physical form into full use."[9] He puts into full use what is within a physical form, not what is above it. Quickness of apprehension and intelligence are matters of the ear and the eye, insight and wisdom those of the mind and thought, humanity that of men, righteousness that of events, equilibrium and harmony those of ceremonies and music, great impartiality and perfect correctness those of reward and punishment, advantage and utility those of water, fire, metal, and wood, welfare that of grains, fruits, silk, and hemp, and correct virtue that of the relationship between ruler and minister and between father and son. If one discarded these and sought for that which existed before concrete things, even if he spanned past and present, went through all the myriad transformations, and investigated Heaven, Earth, man, and things to the utmost, he would not be able to give it a name. How much less could he find its reality! Lao Tzu was blind to this and said that the Way existed in vacuity. But vacuity is the vacuity of concrete things. The Buddha was blind to this and said that the Way existed in silence. But silence is the silence of concrete things. One may keep on uttering such extravagant words to no end, but one can

<hr>

[8] *Changes*, "Appended Remarks," pt. 1, ch. 12. Cf. Legge, trans., *Yi King*, p. 377.

[9] *Mencius*, 7A:38.

never escape from concrete things. Thus if one plays up some name that is separated from concrete things as though he were a divine being, whom could he deceive? (*Chou-i wai-chuan*, or Outer Commentary on the *Book of Changes*, 5:25a-b, in *Ch'uan-shan i-shu*, 1933 ed.)

2. SUBSTANCE AND FUNCTION

All functions in the world are those of existing things. From their functions I know they possess substance. Why should we entertain any doubt? Function exists to become effect, and substance exists to become nature and feelings. Both substance and function exist, and each depends on the other to be concrete. Therefore all that fills the universe demonstrates the principle of mutual dependence. Therefore it is said, "Sincerity (realness) is the beginning and end of things. Without sincerity there will be nothing."[10]

What is the test for this? We believe in what exists but doubt what does not exist. I live from the time I was born to the time I die. As there were ancestors before, so there will be descendants later. From observing the transformations throughout heaven and earth, we see the productive process. Is any of these facts doubtful?. . . . Hold on to the concrete things and its Way will be preserved. Cast aside the concrete things and its Way will be destroyed. . . . Therefore those who are expert in speaking of the Way arrive at substance from function but those who are not expert in speaking of the Way erroneously set up substance and dismiss function in order to conform to it.

> *Comment.* That substance and function come from the same source is a persistent tradition in both Chinese Buddhism and Neo-Confucianism. Wang, however, obviously gives priority to function. Nowhere else in the history of Chinese philosophy is function stressed so strongly.

The state preceding man's birth when his nature is tranquil is beyond their knowledge. Sometimes when they happen to exercise their intelligence abnormally, they paint a picture out of the void, and perforce call it substance. Their intelligence gives them what they are looking for, surveys all things and gets an echo of them, and is therefore able to dismiss all functions completely. From this point on, they can indulge in their perverse doctrines. But how much better it is to seek in the realm where [the process of Change] is acted on and immediately penetrates all things,[11] daily observe its transformations and gradually dis-

---

[10] *The Mean*, ch. 25.

[11] The reference is to *Changes*, "Appended Remarks," pt. 1, ch. 10. Cf. Legge, trans., *Yi King*, p. 370.

cover their origin? Therefore if we get hold of descendants and ask for their ancestors, their genealogical lines will not be confused. But how can one correctly imagine the names of descendants when he passes by the ancestral temples and graves? (*ibid.*, 2:1a-1b)

3. BEING AND NON-BEING

Those who talk about non-being do so because they are roused by speakers of being and want to demolish it, and on the basis of what the speakers call being, they say that being does not exist. Is there really anything in the world that can be called non-being? To say that a tortoise has no hair is to talk about a dog [for example, which has hair] and not a tortoise. To say that a rabbit has no horn is to talk about a deer and not a rabbit. A speaker must have a basis before his theory can be established. Suppose a speaker wants to establish non-being in front of him as the basis. Even if he extensively searches for it throughout the universe and throughout history, there will be no end. (*Ssu-wen lu*, or Record of Thoughts and Questionings, "inner chapter," p. 7a, in *Ch'uan-shan i-shu*)

There will really be non-being only when there is nothing which can be described as non-being. Since non-being is so-called, it follows that it is merely a denial of being. Because the eye cannot see a thing or the ear cannot hear it, people hastily say that it does not exist. They are obscured because they follow their inferior faculties (eye and ear). Good and evil can be seen and heard but that which produces good and evil cannot be seen or heard. Therefore people hastily say that there is neither good nor evil. (*ibid.*, p. 9b)

Those who speak of non-self do so from the point of view of the self. If there were no self, who is going to deny the self? It is obvious that to speak of non-self is to utter extravagant and evasive words. (*ibid.*, p. 11a)

4. PRINCIPLE AND MATERIAL FORCE

Principle depends on material force. When material force is strong, principle prevails. When Heaven accumulates strong and powerful material force, there will be order, and transformations will be refined and daily renewed. This is why on the day of religious fasting an emperor presents an ox [to Heaven] so that the material force will fill the universe and sincerity will penetrate everything. All products in the world are results of refined and beautiful material force. Man takes the best of it to nourish his life, but it is all from Heaven. Material force naturally becomes strong. Sincerity naturally becomes solidified. And principle naturally becomes self-sufficient. If we investigate into the source of these phenomena, we shall find that it is the refined and beautiful transformation of Heaven and Earth. (*ibid.*, p. 12b)

At bottom principle is not a finished product that can be grasped. It is invisible. The details and order of material force is principle that is visible. Therefore the first time there is any principle is when it is seen in material force. After principles have thus been found, they of course appear to become tendencies. We see principle only in the necessary aspects of tendencies. (*Tu Ssu-shu ta-ch'üan shuo* or Discussions After Reading the *Great Collection of Commentaries on the Four Books*, 9:5a, in *Ch'uan-shan i-shu*)

Let us investigate principle as we come into contact with things but never set up principle to restrict things. What I dislike about the heterodoxical schools is not that they cannot do anything with principle, but that because they clearly have scarcely understood principle they set it up as a generalization for the whole world. . . . The heterodoxical schools say, "None of the myriad transformations can go beyond our basis." The basis is clearly what they have scarcely understood. But inasmuch as they say it is their basis, can it produce all the myriad transformations? If it cannot produce these transformations, then it is they who cannot go beyond their basis and not the myriad transformations. . . . They (natural phenomena) all follow principle to accomplish their work. It is permissible to say that their principle is identical with the order of their basis. But if they say that all that work is the construction and operation of their basis, who will believe them unless one is the most boastful talker in the world? (*Hsü Ch'un-ch'iu Tso-shih chuan po-i*, or Extensive Discussion to Supplement Tso's *Commentary on the Spring and Autumn Annals*, pt. 2, p. 4a, in *Ch'uan-shan i-shu*)

5. UNCEASING GROWTH AND MAN'S NATURE AND DESTINY

The fact that the things of the world, whether rivers or mountains, plants or animals, those with or without intelligence, and those yielding blossoms or bearing fruits, provide beneficial support for all things is the result of the natural influence of the moving power of material force. It fills the universe. And as it completely provides for the flourish and transformation of all things, it is all the more spatially unrestricted. As it is not spatially restricted, it operates in time and proceeds with time. From morning to evening, from spring to summer, and from the present tracing back to the past, there is no time at which it does not operate, and there is no time at which it does not produce. Consequently, as one sprout bursts forth it becomes a tree with a thousand big branches, and as one egg evolves, it progressively becomes a fish capable of swallowing a ship. . . . (*Chou-i nei chuan*, or Inner Commentary on the *Book of Changes*, 3:36a, in *Ch'uan-shan i-shu*)

> *Comment.* The power to change lies within material force itself. In the passage below, Wang seems to say that daily growth is due to the Mandate of Heaven. Actually, he is emphasizing that even the Mandate of Heaven grows every day.

By nature is meant the principle of growth. As one daily grows, one daily achieves completion. Thus by the Mandate of Heaven is not meant that Heaven gives the decree (*ming*, mandate) only at the moment of one's birth. . . . In the production of things by Heaven, the process of transformation never ceases. It is not that at the moment of birth there is no decree. How do we know that there is a decree? Without it, humanity, righteousness, propriety, and wisdom would be without any foundation. Similarly, when one grows from infancy to youth, from youth to maturity, and from maturity to old age, it is not that there are no [continual] decrees. How do we know that there are such decrees? For without further decrees, then as the years pass by, one's nature would be forgotten. A change in physical form is a change leading to excellence. A change through material force, however, is a change leading to growth. The evolution of the two material forces (yin and yang or passive and active cosmic forces) and the substance of the Five Agents (Water, Fire, Wood, Metal, and Earth) are first used to become an embryo and later for growth and support. In either case, there is no difference in the acquisition of the vital essence and the utilization of things, for they all come from the excellence of production by Heaven and Earth. The physical form gets its support every day, every day the material force enjoys its flourish, and principle attains completion every day. These things are received as one is born, but as one continues to live for a day, one keeps receiving them for a day. What one receives has a source. Is this not Heaven? Thus Heaven gives decrees to man every day and man receives decrees from Heaven every day. Therefore we say that by nature is meant the principle of growth. As one daily grows, one daily achieves completion. . . .

Since the mandate is never exhausted and is not constant, therefore nature repeatedly changes and is perpetually different. At the same time, as principle is fundamentally correct and is without any inherent defect, therefore it can return to its own principle without difficulty. What is not completed can be completed, and what has been completed can be changed. Does nature mean that once one has received a physical form, there cannot be any alteration? Therefore in nourishing his nature, the superior man acts naturally as if nothing happens, but that does not mean that he lets things take their own course. Instead, he acts so as to make the best choices and remain firm in holding to the Mean, and dares not go wild or make careless mistakes. (*Shang-shu yin-i*, or Elaboration on the Meanings of the *Book of History*, 3:6a-7b, in *Ch'uan-shan i-shu*)

6. THE PRINCIPLE OF NATURE AND HUMAN DESIRES

Although rules of propriety are purely detailed expressions of the Principle of Nature, they must be embodied in human desires to be seen. Principle is a latent principle for activities, but its function will become prominent if it varies and conforms to them. It is precisely for this reason that there can never be a Heaven distinct from man or a principle distinct from desires. It is only with the Buddhists that principle and desires can be separated. . . . Take fondness for wealth and for sex. Heaven, working unseen, has provided all creatures with it, and with it man puts the great virtue of Heaven and Earth into operation. They all regard wealth and sex as preserved resources. Therefore the *Book of Changes* says, "The great characteristic of Heaven and Earth is to produce. The most precious thing for the sage is [the highest] position. To keep his position depends on humanity. How to collect a large population depends on wealth."[12] Thus in sound, color, flavor, and fragrance we can broadly see the open desires of all creatures, and at the same time they also constitute the impartial principle for all of them. Let us be broad and greatly impartial, respond to things as they come, look at them, and listen to them, and follow this way in words and action without seeking anything outside. And let us be unlike Lao Tzu, who said that the five colors blind one's eyes and the five tones deafen one's ears,[13] or the Buddha, who despised them as dust and hated them as robbers. . . . If we do not understand the Principle of Nature from human desires that go with it, then although there may be a principle that can be a basis,[14] nevertheless, it will not have anything to do with the correct activities of our seeing, hearing, speech, and action. They thereupon cut off the universal operation of human life, and wipe it out completely. Aside from one meal a day, they would have nothing to do with material wealth and aside from one sleep under a tree, they would have nothing to do with sex. They exterminate the great character of Heaven and Earth and ruin the great treasure of the sage. They destroy institutions and eliminate culture. Their selfishness is ablaze while principles of humanity are destroyed. It is like the fire of thunder or a dragon. The more one tries to overcome

[12] *Changes*, "Appended Remarks," pt. 2, ch. 1. Cf. Legge, p. 381.
[13] *Lao Tzu*, ch. 12.
[14] Wang's own note: Like the Taoist emphasis on the supremely profound principle (*hsüan*) and the Buddhist seeing the Buddha-nature.

it, the more it goes on. Mencius continued the teaching of Confucius which is that wherever human desires are found, the Principle of Nature is found. (*Tu Ssu-shu ta-ch'üan shuo*, 8:10b-11a)

7. HISTORY AND GOVERNMENT

For the best way of government, there is nothing better than to examine the *Book of History* and modify it with the words of Confucius. But the central point is whether the ruler's heart is serious or dissolute. The danger lies in being too lax or too harsh. Those who are deficient are lazy, and those who are excessive are impatient. The great function of government is to make use of worthy men and promote education. In dealing with people, it should bestow humanity and love to the highest degree. Whether in the government of Yao and Shun, or in the Three Dynasties,[15] or from the Ch'in (221–206 B.C.) and Han down to the present, in no case can these principles not be extended and applied. Whether the administration or the selection of officials, the equalization of taxes and the conscription for service, the management of the army and weapons, the regulation of punishment, or the institution of law and ceremonies, they all depend on these principles to attain their appropriateness. As to setting up schemes or arranging for details, neither the *Book of History* nor Confucius said anything about them. Is it because they ignored substance and overlooked details? Probably because the ancient institutions were meant to govern the ancient world and cannot be generally followed today, the superior man does not base his activities on them, and because what is suitable today can govern the world of today but will not necessarily be suitable for the future, the superior man does not hand it down to posterity as a model. Therefore neither the *Book of History* nor Confucius talked about the regulations for the feudal system, the "well-field" system,[16] feudal lords' meetings and audience with the emperor, punitive expeditions, the establishment of offices, or the bestowing of emolument. How then dare anyone who is not equal in virtue to sage-emperors Shun and Yü[17] or Confucius determine the fundamental standards for ten thousand generations with what they have memorized and recited in books? There is a section entitled "The Tribute to Yü" in the "Book of Hsia" (of the *Book of History*) but the section is confined to Yü (founder of Hsia). Thus

[15] Hsia, 2183–1752 B.C., Shang, 1751–1112 B.C., and Chou, 1111–249 B.C.

[16] The system, most probably legendary, in which a piece of land was divided into nine squares, thus looking like the Chinese character for a well. Eight families would each cultivate a square for its own support and cultivate the central square jointly for the government.

[17] Founder of the Hsia dynasty, r. 2183–2175 B.C.?

the systems of the Hsia dynasty did not operate in the Shang or Chou. There is also a section entitled "Institutes of Chou" in the "Book of Chou," but this section is confined to the Chou dynasty. Thus the regulations of the Chou did not follow those of Shang or Hsia. . . . (*Tu T'ung-chien lun*, or Discussions After Reading the *Mirror of Universal History*, last chapter, p. 42-b, in *Ch'uan-shan i-shu*)

37

PRACTICAL CONFUCIANISM IN YEN YÜAN

IN REACTION to the speculative Neo-Confucianism of Sung (960-1279) and Ming (1368-1644) times and to some extent under the influence of Western knowledge introduced by Jesuits, Confucianists in the seventeenth century turned to practical learning and objective truth. Both Ku Yen-wu (1613-1682) and Yen Jo-ch'ü (1636-1704), the two leading Confucianists of the century, attacked Sung-Ming Neo-Confucianism and demanded practical and objective study. We have already seen Wang Fu-chih's (Wang Ch'uan-shan, 1619-1692) radical departure from earlier Neo-Confucianism. Yen Yüan (Yen Hsi-chai, 1635-1704)[1] went much further than all of them. In spite of the new spirit, the general tendency at the time was to compromise between the rationalistic Neo-Confucianism of Chu Hsi (1130-1200) and the idealistic Neo-Confucianism of Wang Yang-ming (Wang Shou-jen, 1472-1529). Yen, however, turned away from them completely and went directly back to Confucius and Mencius.

Yen Yüan considered the Neo-Confucian sitting in meditation and book learning as a waste of time and a sure cause for social degeneration. To him, principle (*li*), nature, destiny, and the sincerity of the will, and similar subjects close to the hearts of Sung-Ming Neo-Confucianists can be found only in practical arts like music, ceremony, agriculture, and military craft. He himself practiced medicine while he taught, and later he farmed with his students. He taught them mathematics, archery, weight-lifting, singing, dancing, and so forth. In his school, there were four halls for classics and history, literary matters, military craft, and practical arts. Like Wang Fu-chih, he believed that there is no principle apart from material force (*ch'i*). Opposed to Sung-Ming Neo-Confucianists, he insisted that physical nature is just as good as human nature itself. The investigation of things is to him not a study of principle, as in Chu Hsi, nor an examination of the mind, as in Wang Yang-ming, but learning from actual experience and solving practical problems. No one had so uncompromisingly opposed the several centuries of thought before him, and none had stressed practical experience so forcefully. Nevertheless, as in the case of Wang Fu-chih, he was not free from the

---

[1] Yen was a native of Chih-li. As a youth he studied fencing and later studied military craft. In his twenties he was first interested in the idealism of Wang Yang-ming but later shifted to the rationalism of Chu Hsi. He was a poor man. In 1696 he was invited to be the director of an academy. There he put his theory of practical learning into practice. For details of his life, see Hummel, ed., *Eminent Chinese*, pp. 912-915.

pattern of thought of his own day. He looked back to Confucius and Mencius. He advocated the return to the "well-field" system supposedly in practice in ancient times, in which land was equally divided into nine squares, thus resembling the Chinese character for a well, and in which eight families would cultivate a square each for its own support and jointly cultivate the central square for the government. What he called the practical affairs were the "six departments" dealing with water, fire, metal, wood, soil, and grains, the "six virtues" of wisdom, humanity, sageliness, righteousness, loyalty, and peace, the "six arts" of ceremonies, music, archery, carriage driving, writing, and mathematics, and the like taught in the ancient Classics. Tempered by this conservativism, his teachings, however dynamic, did not develop into a strong movement. He had few followers, although his pupil Li Kung (1659-1733), who reiterated his teachings, became as well known as he. But his school did not last, for all his targets of attack, like the doctrines of Chu Hsi, book learning, and literary composition, were still popular among Confucian scholars. And his attack on Chu Hsi was intolerable. Nevertheless his new ideas prepared for Tai Chen (Tai Tung-yüan, 1723-1777) and greatly strengthened the growing tendency toward practical learning.

Yen Yüan's philosophical ideas are quite naïve and superficial; he was really not much of a philosopher. The following selections are intended to bring out his most philosophical points.

1. IN DEFENSE OF PHYSICAL NATURE

Master Ch'eng [Hao (Ch'eng Ming-tao, 1032-1085)] said that in discussing human nature and material force, "It would be wrong to consider them as two."[2] But he also said, "Due to the material force with which men are endowed, some become good from childhood and others become evil."[3] Chu Hsi said, "As soon as there is the endowment by Heaven, there is the physical nature. They cannot be separated,"[4] but he also said, "Since there is this principle, why is there evil? What is called evil is due to material force."[5] It is regrettable that although they were highly intelligent, they were unwittingly influenced and confused by the Buddhist doctrine of the "Six Robbers" (the six senses, which avoid perception or give wrong perception), and said two different things in the same breath without realizing it. If we say that material force is evil, then principle is also evil, and if we say that principle is good, then material force is also good, for material force is that of principle and prin-

---

[2] *I-shu* (Surviving Works), 6:2a, in ECCS.
[3] *ibid.*, 1:7b.
[4] *Chu Tzu yü-lei* (Classified Conversations of Chu Hsi), 1880 ed., 4:9a.
[5] *ibid.*, 4:9b.

ciple is that of material force. How can we say that principle is purely and simply good whereas material force is inclined to be evil?

Take the eye, for example. Its socket, lid, and ball are its physical nature, whereas that which possesses vision and can perceive things is its nature. Shall we say that principle of vision sees only proper colors whereas the socket, lid, and ball see improper colors? I say that while this principle of vision is of course endowed by Heaven, the socket, lid, and ball are all endowed by Heaven. There is no need any more to distinguish which is the nature endowed by Heaven and which is physical nature. We should only say that Heaven endows man with the nature of his eyes. The fact that one can see through vision means that the nature of the eye is good. The act of seeing is due to the goodness of its feeling [which is the external expression of the nature]. Whether one sees distinctly or not and whether one sees far or not depends on the strength or weakness of its capacity. None of these can be spoken of as evil, for it is of course good to see distinctly and far, but to see near and indistinctly merely means that the goodness is not refined. How can we attribute any evil to them? It is only when vision is attracted and agitated by improper and evil colors which obstruct or becloud its clearness that there is evil vision, and only then can the term "evil" be applied. But is human nature to be blamed for the attraction and agitation? Or shall physical nature be blamed? If we blame physical nature, it surely means that the nature of the eye can be preserved only when the eye is eliminated. If this is not the Buddhist doctrine of "Six Robbers," what is it?. . .

> Comment. For several hundred years Neo-Confucianists had regarded physical nature as the source of evil. Yen threw this theory overboard. He still had to explain the origin of evil, of course, and he ascribed it to attraction and agitation from outside. These have to come through physical nature, and therefore it can be said that he is not entirely different from the Sung-Ming Neo-Confucianists. However, to them physical nature itself is the cause for evil. To Yen, on the other hand, it is only the means.

Originally Chu Hsi understood nature, but he was influenced by Buddhists and mixed up with the bad habits of people of the world. Had there been no doctrine of physical nature advocated by Ch'eng I (Ch'eng I-ch'uan, 1033-1107) and Chang Tsai (Chang Heng-ch'ü, 1020-1077),[6] we would surely distinguish man's nature, feeling, and capacity, on the one hand, and attraction, obscuration, and bad influence, on the other, and the fact that man's nature, feeling, and capacity are all good and that

6 See above, ch. 30, sec. 41.

evil originates later would be perfectly clear. But as these former scholars inaugurated this doctrine, they forthwith ascribed evil to physical nature and sought to transform it. Have they never thought that physical nature is a concentration of the two material forces (yin and yang or passive and active cosmic forces) and the Four Virtues (Origination, Flourish, Advantage, and Firmness)?[7] How can we say that it is evil? Evil is due to attraction, obscuration, and bad influence. . . .

> *Comment.* In saying that evil is due to bad influence and so forth, Yen is practically repeating Mencius. In fact, in his whole concept on human nature, he went directly back to Mencius. Later, Tai Chen did the same.

Scholars often compare human nature with water, material force with earth, and evil with turbidity.[8] They regard physical nature, which is the loftiest, as the most honorable and the most useful endowment given to man by Heaven and Earth, as if it were a burden to his human nature. They did not realize that if there were no physical nature, to what will principle be attached? Furthermore, if physical nature were discarded, then human nature would become an empty principle without any function in the world. . . .

Master Ch'eng Hao (using water as an analogy) said, "Although they differ in being clear or turbid, we cannot say that the turbid water ceases to be water."[9] Does this not mean that although good and evil are different, it is incorrect to regard evil not as nature? Is this not precisely to regard evil as the property of physical nature? Let me ask: Is turbidity the physical nature of water? I am afraid that clearness and calmness are the physical nature of water and that what is turbid is a mixture with earth which is originally absent from the nature of water, just as human nature is subject to attraction, obscuration, and bad influence. Turbidity may be of high or low degree, and may be of great or small quantity, just as attraction, obscuration, and bad influence may be heavy or light and deep or shallow. If it is said that turbidity is the physical nature of water, then it would mean that turbid water has physical nature but clear water is without it. How can that be?. . . .
(*Ts'un-hsing pien*, or Preservation of Human Nature, 1:1a-3b, in *Yen-Li ts'ung-shu* or Yen Yüan and Li Kung Collection, 1923 ed.)

[7] These are the characteristics of Change, the universal process of creation and existence. The Chinese term may be translated as "Four Powers," which would indicate that the four are dynamic in character, but "Four Virtues" retains the literal meaning of *te* and, furthermore, indicates that the four are good.

[8] For example, Cheng Hao. See above, ch. 31, sec. 7.

[9] *I-shu*, 1:7b.

2. THE IDENTITY OF PRINCIPLE AND MATERIAL FORCE

The nature of the ten thousand things is an endowment of principle, and their physical nature is a consolidation of material force. What is balanced is this principle and material force, what is unbalanced is also this principle and this material force, and what is mixed is none other than this principle and this material force. What is lofty and bright is this principle and this material force, and what is lowly and dark is also this principle and this material force. What is clear or sturdy is this principle and this material force, and what is turbid or slight is also this principle and this material force. The long and the short, the perfect and the imperfect, the penetrating and the obstructed, are none other than this principle and material force.

As to man, he is especially the purest of all things, one who "receives at birth the Mean of Heaven and Earth (balanced material force)."[10] The two material forces and the Four Virtues are man before his consolidation, and man is the two material forces and the Four Virtues after their consolidation. As the Four Virtues are preserved in man, they are humanity, righteousness, propriety, and wisdom. They are called the nature with reference to the internal existence of origination, flourish, advantage, and firmness. When externally manifested, they become commiseration, shame and dislike, deference and compliance, and the sense of right and wrong. These are called feelings with reference to the application of the Four Virtues to things. Capacity is that which manifests one's nature in feelings; it is the power of the Four Virtues. To say that feeling involves evil is to say that the Four Virtues before manifestation is not the same as the Four Virtues after manifestation. To say that capacity involves evil is to say that what is preserved is the Four Virtues but what can be aroused into action is not the Four Virtues. And to say that physical nature involves evil is to say that the principle of the Four Virtues may be called the Way of Heaven but the material force of the Four Virtues may not be so called. Alas! Is there in the world any material force without principle, or principle without material force? Are there principle and material force outside of yin and yang and the Four Virtues? (*ibid.*, 2:2b-3a)

3. LEARNING THROUGH EXPERIENCE

Knowledge has no substance of its own. Its substance consists of things. It is similar to the fact that the eye has no substance of its own;

[10] *I-shu*, 1:3a. Although it is not indicated whether this is an utterance by Ch'eng I or Ch'eng Hao, it is most likely by the latter. See above, ch. 31, sec. 4.

its substance consists of physical forms and colors. Therefore although the human eye has vision, if it does not see black or white, its vision cannot function. Although the human mind is intelligent, if it does not ponder over this or that, its intelligence will find no application. Those who talk about the extension of knowledge today mean no more than reading, discussion, questioning, thinking, and sifting, without realizing that the extension of one's knowledge does not lie in these at all. Take, for example, one who desires to understand the rules of propriety. Even if he reads a book on the rules of propriety hundreds of times, discusses and asks scores of times, thinks and sifts scores of times, he cannot be considered to know them at all. He simply has to kneel down, bow, and otherwise move, hold up the jade wine-cup with both hands, hold the present of silk, and go through all these himself before he knows what the rules of propriety really are. Those who know propriety in this way know them perfectly. Or take, for example, one who desires to know music. Even if he reads a music score hundreds of times, and discusses, asks, thinks, and sifts scores of times, he cannot know music at all. He simply has to strike and blow musical instruments, sing with his own voice, dance with his own body, and go through all these himself before he knows what music really is. Those who know music this way know it perfectly. This is what is meant by "When things are *ko* (investigated, reached, etc.), true knowledge is extended."[11]. . . . The word *ko* is the same as that in the expression, "*Ko* (submit and kill) fierce animals with one's own hands." (*Ssu-shu cheng-wu*, or Corrections of Wrong Interpretations of the Four Books, 1:2b, in *Yen-Li ts'ung-shu*)

> *Comment.* Several important points are indicated in these simple statements: Learning is an active pursuit through personal experience. The object of knowledge is not ideas but actual and concrete things, and knowledge and action form a unity. Without saying, he selected only those experiences that would support his case, but if his logic is defective, his outlook is extremely modern. As to his interpretation of *ko*, he comes close to Ssu-ma Kuang (1019-1086) and is diametrically opposed to Ch'eng I and Chu Hsi.[12]

[11] The text of the *Great Learning*.
[12] See above, ch. 32, comment on sec. 44.

38

TAI CHEN'S PHILOSOPHY OF PRINCIPLE
AS ORDER

IN EIGHTEENTH-CENTURY CHINA, the rationalistic Neo-Confucianism of Chu Hsi (1130-1200) was still influential, but the tide had turned against it. The movement, inaugurated by Ku Yen-wu (1613-1682) and Yen Jo-ch'ü (1636-1704), to search for objective truth and shun speculation had by this time become strong and extensive. Scholars refused to accept anything without evidence, and their sole interest was to get at the truth through concrete facts. Consequently, the movement has been called "Investigations Based on Evidence." Although their center of interest was still the Confucian Classics, they were deeply engaged in studying such concrete subjects as philology, history, astronomy, mathematics, geography, collation of texts, and the like. They revolted against the abstract learning of the Sung dynasty (960-1279) of which rationalistic Neo-Confucianism was the major product, and looked to the earliest studies of the Classics during the Han (206 B.C.–A.D. 220) for evidence. For this reason, the movement is also known as Han Learning. It is characterized philosophically by a revolt against Chu Hsi, and methodologically by objective, inductive, and critical methods. The towering figure in this whole movement was Tai Chen (Tai Tung-yüan, 1723-1777).

Actually Tai was better known as a Great Master of Investigations-Based-on-Evidence than as a philosopher. But his investigations and philosophy are really inseparable, for they reinforce each other. He was an expert in mathematics, astronomy, water-works, phonetics, collation of texts, and textual criticism, in which he employed critically the inductive and comparative methods. Unlike his contemporaries who pursued investigation-based-on-evidence for their own sake, he regarded them as primarily a means to reveal truth. At the same time, because of his method and concrete studies, he viewed truth as an order, a systematic arrangement of concrete, ordinary daily matters and human affairs. Obviously a thinker of this frame of mind would not entertain an abstract, transcendental concept of principle (*li*), which, he said, the Neo-Confucianists of Sung and Ming (1368-1644) looked upon "as if it were a thing." To him, principle was nothing but the order of things, and by things he understood "daily affairs such as drinking and eating."

The concept of principle as order goes back to Han times and so Tai was not original in this respect. But none had developed the idea as fully as he and none had pushed it more forcefully. With such a concept of principle as the premise, it follows that the way to investigate principle is not by intellectual speculation, as in the case of Chu Hsi, or by introspection of the mind, as in the case of Wang Yang-ming (Wang Shou-jen, 1472-1529), but by a critical, analytical, minutely detailed, and objective study of things.

His concept of principle led him also to oppose vigorously Sung-Ming Neo-Confucianists with regard to human feelings and desires, which he thought they had undermined. In his belief, principle can never prevail when feelings are not satisfied, for principle consists of "feelings that do not err." In point of fact, Sung-Ming Neo-Confucianists never condemned feelings and desires as such, only selfish and excessive ones, which are no different from those that err. It cannot be denied, however, that while Sung-Ming Neo-Confucianists contrast principle as good and desire as evil, Tai would not tolerate such an opposition. In this he drew support from Mencius' doctrine of the original goodness of human nature, and explains error in terms of selfishness. Since he maintained that principle is feelings that do not err, he had to postulate an unalterable, objective, and necessary principle as the standard. This is what he meant by "necessary" moral principles. He did not reject universal truth after all, except that he insisted that these are definite and inherent in concrete and ordinary things.

In another respect he perpetuated a major doctrine of Sung-Ming Neo-Confucianists but again interpreted it in terms of order. To him as to Sung-Ming Neo-Confucianists, the universe is an unceasing process of production and reproduction.[1] However, this process is not just a universal operation. In addition, it is a natural order, an order in which basic moral values can be seen.

Tai was perhaps the greatest thinker in the Ch'ing period (1644-1912). He was a poor man and never passed the higher civil service examinations.[2] He did not attack Chu Hsi until his late years. It was then that he wrote the *Meng Tzu tzu-i shu-cheng* (Commentary on the

[1] For this idea, see above, ch. 32, sec. 22, and ch. 34, sec. 84.
[2] He was a native of Anhui. The family being poor, he taught primary school in 1740-1742 in a place where his father was a cloth merchant. He continued studies and did tutoring and thus became acquainted with both established and potential scholars. His own scholarship was gradually making him famous. In 1762, he obtained the "recommended person" degree. But he failed in the metropolitan examinations several times. In 1773, he was appointed a compiler of the famous *Four Libraries* by imperial command. He failed once more in the metropolitan examination in 1775 but was bestowed the degree of "presented scholar" and made an academician in the Han-lin Academy, a position of high honor. He continued his compilation work until death. For more information on him, see Hummel, ed., *Eminent Chinese*, pp. 695-700.

Meanings of Terms in the *Book of Mencius*), from which the following selections are made. It is his most important work and one that contains his most philosophical ideas. But for a hundred years it did not exert any influence, partly because his doctrines are not really profound and partly because interest in philosophy during the whole Ch'ing dynasty was very slight. In the twentieth century, however, he has suddenly become popular, undoubtedly because his philosophy suits the temper of the age.

COMMENTARY ON THE MEANINGS
OF TERMS IN THE BOOK OF MENCIUS[3]

1. On Principle (Li)

Sec. 1. *Li* is a name given to the examination of the minutest details with which to make necessary distinctions. This is why it is called the principle of differentiation. In the case of the substance of things, we call it "fibre in muscle," "fibre in flesh," and "pattern and order" (*wen-li*).[4] When the distinctions obtain, there will be order without confusion. This is called order (*t'iao-li*). Mencius called Confucius a complete concert,[5] saying, "To begin the order (harmony of an orchestra) is the work of wisdom, and to terminate the order is the work of sageness."[6] Sageness and wisdom reached their height in Confucius merely in the sense that order was attained. The *Book of Changes* says, "With the attainment of ease and simplicity all principles in the world will obtain."[7] Ease and simplicity are mentioned here but not humanity (*jen*) and wisdom because the principle of *ch'ien* (Heaven) and *k'un* (Earth) are under discussion. The principle of *ch'ien* knows through the easy" means that it knows that humanity, love, justice, and altruism are the same. And "the principle of *k'un* accomplishes through the simple"[8] means that it accomplishes in such a simple way that nothing seems to happen. "He who attains to this ease will be easily understood. . . . He who is easily understood will have adherents. . . . He who has adherents can continue long. . . . To be able to continue long shows the virtue of the worthy."[9] One who answers to this description is a man of humanity. "He who attains to this simplicity will be easily followed. . . . He who is easily fol-

---

[3] This work consists of forty-three sections divided into three parts. Actually it is not a commentary on the *Book of Mencius*. Rather it is a discussion of philosophical concepts all of which are important in the *Book of Mencius*, which Tai quotes frequently. The edition used is that in Hu Shih's (1891-1962) *Tai Tung-yüan ti che-hsüeh* (Philosophy of Tai Chen), Shanghai, 1927.

[4] Tai's own note: Also called "pattern and grains" *wen-lü*, li and lü, being similar in pronunciation.

[5] *Mencius*, 5B:1. [6] *ibid.*

[7] "Appended Remarks," pt. 1, ch. 1. Cf. translation by Legge, *Yi King*, p. 349.
[8] *ibid.* [9] *ibid.*

lowed will achieve success. . . . He who achieves success can become great. . . . To be able to become great is the heritage of the worthy."[10] One who answers this description is a man of wisdom. When events and situations in the world are distinct in their order and clear in their details and one responds to them with both humanity and wisdom, can there even be the slightest error? The *Doctrine of the Mean* says, "Pattern, order, refinement, and penetration enable him (the perfect sage) to exercise discrimination."[11] The *Record of Music* says, "Music is [the sound of the human mind] penetrating the order (*li*) of human relations."[12] In his annotation Cheng K'ang-ch'eng (Cheng Hsüan, 127-200) said that "*li* means to differentiate." In the preface to his *Shuo-wen chieh-tzu* (Explanation of Words and Elucidation of Characters), Hsü Shu-chung (Hsü Shen, fl. A.D. 100) said, "[The inventor of the script] knew that [from the traces of birds and animals] patterns and order (*fen-li*) can be distinguished and differentiated." What the ancients understood as *li* was never anything like what is understood by latter-day scholars.

Sec. 2. *Question*: What did the ancients mean when they speak of the Principle of Nature (*T'ien-li*)?

Answer: Principle consists of feelings that do not err. Principle can never prevail when [correct] feelings are not satisfied. When one does something to others, one should examine oneself and think quietly to see whether he could accept if others did the same thing to him. When one gives some responsibility to others, one should examine himself and think quietly to see whether he could fulfill it if others give the same responsibility to him. When the measure of the self is applied to others, principle will become clear. The Principle of Nature (*T'ien-li*, Principle of Heaven) means natural discrimination.[13] With natural discrimination, one measures the feelings of others in terms of one's own, and there will be no injustice or imbalance. . . . When feelings are balanced and just, this means that like and dislike are in proper measure. It means accord with the Principle of Nature.[14] What the ancients understood as the

---

[10] *ibid.*

[11] Ch. 31.

[12] *Book of Rites*, "Record of Music." Cf. Legge, trans., *Li Ki*, vol. 2, p. 95.

[13] *Fen-li*, literally fibre in muscle, is extended to mean distinction and discrimination, especially between right and wrong.

[14] Tai's own note: In the *Chuang Tzu*, King Wen-hui's cook was cutting up a bullock. The cook himself said, "Following the natural fibres (*t'ien-li*), my chopper slips through the great cavities and slides through the great openings in accordance with the natural conditions. I did not attempt the central veins or their branches, or the connections between flesh and bone. How much less the great bones." *T'ien-li* is what he meant by cavities between the joints, and the chopper was not thick. To apply what is not thick to cavities is just like natural discrimination." (Prince Wen-hui was King Hui of Liang, r. 371-320 B.C. The story is found in *Chuang-Tzu*, ch. 3, NHCC, 2:2a. Cf. Giles, trans., *Chuang Tzu*, 1961 ed., p. 48).

Principle of Nature was never anything like what is understood by latter-day scholars.

> *Comment.* Tai's relentless attack on the doctrine of the Principle of Nature was partly motivated by the fact that the Yung-cheng emperor (r. 1723-1735) used it as justification for his oppressive measures.

Sec. 3. *Question*: If one measures the feelings of others by one's own without error, one will surely be in accord with principle in his deeds. What is the difference between feeling and principle?

Answer: Feelings are the same in oneself as in others. They become principle when they are neither excessive nor deficient. The *Book of Odes* says, "Heaven produces the teeming multitude. As there are things, there are their specific principles. When the people keep to their normal nature, they will love excellent virtue."[15] Confucius said, "The writer of this poem indeed knew the Way (Tao)."[16] Elaborating on the poem, Mencius said, "Therefore as there are things, there must be their specific principles, and since people keep to their normal nature, therefore they love excellent virtue."[17] Specific principle means to regard keeping to [normal nature] and holding on to it as the standard, principle means to be in accord with the distinction in each case, and excellent virtue means to demonstrate concretely in words and action. A thing is an affair or event. When we talk about an event, we do not go beyond daily affairs such as drinking and eating. To neglect these and talk about principle is not what the ancient sages and worthies meant by principle.

Sec. 10. *Question*: From the Sung dynasty on, those who talk about principle have maintained that what does not issue from principle issues from desire and what does not issue from desire issues from principle. They have therefore clearly drawn the line between principle and desire, and held that this is where the superior man and the inferior man are distinguished. Now, however, you hold that principle is feelings that do not err. This means that principle is contained in desires. Is it, then, wrong to have no desire?

Answer: Mencius said, "For nourishing the mind there is nothing better than to have few desires."[18] It is clear that men should not be without desires at all but should have only a few. There is no greater pain in man's life than being unable to preserve and fulfill one's own life. To desire to preserve and fulfill one's own life and also to preserve and fulfill the lives of others is humanity (*jen*). To desire to preserve and fulfill one's own life to the point of destroying the lives of others without

---

[15] Ode no. 260.
[17] *ibid.*
[16] Quoted in *Mencius*, 6A:6.
[18] *ibid.*, 7B:35.

any regard is inhumanity. . . . Therefore it is correct to say that what does not issue from correctness issues from perverseness and what does not issue from perverseness issues from correctness, but not correct to say that what does not issue from principle issues from desire and what does not issue from desire issues from principle. Desire is a fact, whereas *li* is its specific principle (its measure of right and wrong). . . . Whatever issues from desire is always concerned with life and its support. When desire is wrong, it is the result of selfishness and not of obscuration.[19] [The selfish person] thinks that he is in accord with principle but what he adheres to is erroneous. Consequently, he is obscured and unenlightened.

The greatest troubles of people in the world, whether past or present, are the two items of selfishness and obscuration. Selfishness is the product of error in desire, and obscuration is the product of error in knowledge. Desire is produced by blood and vital force (*ch'i*), while knowledge is produced by the mind. People blame desire because of selfishness, and blame blood and vital force because of desire. Likewise, they blame knowledge because of obscuration and blame the mind because of knowledge![20] This is why Lao Tzu said, "He (the sage) always causes his people to be without knowledge or desire."[21] [The Taoists] neglected their own bodies and honored the True Lord (Creator). Later the Buddhists held theories that seem different but are really the same. Neo-Confucianists of Sung times went in and out of Taoist and Buddhist schools[22] and therefore what they had to say is mixed with the words of Taoists and Buddhists. The *Book of Odes* says, "The people are secured.[23] They daily enjoy their drink and food."[24] And the *Book of Rites* says, "Man's greatest desires are for drink, food, and sexual pleasure."[25] In governing the world, the sage understands the feelings of the people, satisfies their desires, and the kingly way is thereby completed. . . .

> *Comment.* The theory that selfishness and obscuration are the causes of moral evil is reminiscent of Mencius.[26] But central to Tai's idea is also the Confucian doctrine of the Mean.

[19] Hu Shih's comment: "No one has expressed this idea before." *Tai Tung-yüan ti che-hsüeh*, Appendix, p. 54.

[20] The word "mind" is added, quite correctly, by Hu Shih. *ibid.*, p. 55.

[21] *Lao Tzu*, ch. 3.

[22] In a long note, Tai recounted how Ch'eng I (Ch'eng I-ch'uan, 1033-1107), Chang Tsai (Chang Heng-ch'ü, 1020-1077), and Chu Hsi studied Taoism and Buddhism.

[23] *Chih*, also interpreted as contended, simple, etc.

[24] Ode no. 166.

[25] "Evolution of Rites." Cf. Legge, *Li Ki*, vol. 1, p. 380.

[26] See *Mencius*, 6A:6-8.

Sec. 13. *Question*: From the Sung dynasty on, scholars have said that principle "is received from Heaven and completely embodied in the mind."[27] Since they considered it to have been received by all people, they have therefore ascribed the inequality of wisdom and stupidity to physical nature, and their doctrines of seriousness and dissoluteness, perverseness and correctness are all directed to give substance to their doctrine of [the contrast of] principle and desire. Lao Tzu's sayings, "Embracing the One"[28] and "Having no desire,"[29] and the Buddhist saying, "Be always alert"[30] refer to the [Taoist] True Lord and the Buddhist True Emptiness, respectively.[31] The Neo-Confucianists replaced them with the word "principle," and thought that was enough to be considered as the teachings of Confucius. Since they have regarded principle to have been received from Heaven, they therefore further invented the doctrine of principle and material force, and compare them to two things merged one with the other.[32] They described principle in a most elaborate manner, calling it "pure and vast."[33] They did no more than describe the principle of Heaven in terms of the Taoist True Lord and the Buddhist True Emptiness, and transfer the words of Lao Tzu, Chuang Tzu, and the Buddha to Confucius and Mencius in the Six Classics.[34] How can they be distinguished now so they absolutely cannot confuse or compound each other?

[27] This is Chu Hsi's utterance. See *Chu Tzu yü-lei* (Classified Conversations of Chu Hsi), 1880 ed., 98:9a.

[28] *Lao Tzu*, ch. 10.

[29] *ibid.*, ch. 57.

[30] A common Zen saying derived from a dictum by Zen Master Jui-yen (c.850-c.910). See *Wu-teng hui-yüan* (Five Lamps Combined), ch. 7, in *Zokuzōkyō* (Supplement to the Buddhist Canon), 1st collection, pt. 2, B, case, 11, p. 120b. The saying is quoted in *Ming-chiao Ch'an-shih yü-lu* (Recorded Sayings of Zen Master Ming-chiao, 980-1052), ch. 3, TSD, 47:690. This saying, however, is not found in the section on Jui-an in *Ching-te ch'uan-teng-lu* (Records of the Transmission of the Lamp Completed During the Ching-te Period, 1004-1007). See SPTK, 17:17b-18a.

[31] Here in an inserted note Tai cites *Chuang Tzu*, ch. 3, NHCC, 1:23a. Cf. Giles, *Chuang Tzu*, 1961 ed., p. 35, where "true Lord" is mentioned, and three Buddhist passages where "True Emptiness" is used, including one from Shen-hui's (670-762) treatise, *Hsien-tsung chi* (Elucidating the Doctrine) in *Ching-te ch'uan-teng lu*, SPTK, 30:7a. Cf. translation by Chan, in *Sources of Chinese Tradition*, ed. by de Bary, Chan, and Watson, p. 398.

[32] This refers to Chu Hsi's saying in *Chu Tzu ch'üan-shu* (Complete Works of Chu Hsi), 1713 ed., 49:5b. See above, ch. 34, sec. 110. According to the reference in the *Complete Works* this saying is from Chu Hsi's letter in reply to Liu Shu-wen in the *Chu Tzu wen-chi* (Collection of Literary Works by Chu Hsi), but there is no letter under such name.

[33] Chu Hsi's description. See *Chu Tzu yü-lei*, 1:3a.

[34] Originally these were: *Book of History, Odes, Changes, Rites, Spring and Autumn Annals*, and the *Book of Music*, which is now lost. Since the Sung dynasty, the *Chou-li* (Rites of Chou) has taken its place.

Answer: With respect to heaven, earth, men, things, events and activities, I have never heard of any of these to be without the principle which we can talk about [in contrast to True Emptiness, which is indescribable]. "As there are things, there are their specific principles."[35] This is what it means. The term "things" refers to concrete objects or concrete events, while the term "specific principles" refers to their unmixed purity and central correctness. Concrete objects and concrete events are what is natural. When they arrive at the state of what is necessary (according to moral laws) then heaven, earth, men, things, events, and activities will be in accord with principle. Heaven and earth are vast, men and things are numerous, and events and activities are complex and varied. But if they are in accord with principle, and are similar to something as straight as the plumb line, something level as the water-level, something round as the compass, and something square as the measuring square, then they will remain standard even if they are extended to the whole world and to ten thousand generations to come. The *Book of Changes* says, "He (the great man) may precede Heaven and Heaven will not act in opposition to him. He may follow Heaven but will act only as Heaven at the time would do. If even Heaven does not act in opposition, how much less will men! How much less will spiritual beings!"[36] The *Doctrine of the Mean* says, "It is tested by the experience of the Three Kings and found without error, applied before Heaven and Earth and found to be without contradiction in their operation, laid before spiritual beings without question or fear, and can wait a hundred generations for a sage without a doubt."[37] When men and things are like this, they will be in accord with principle and will be "what is common in our minds."[38] Mencius said, "The compass and the square are the ultimate standards of circles and squares. The sage is the ultimate standard of human relations."[39] When we talk about Heaven and Earth and, as a matter of refinement, we talk about their principle it is just as, in talking about the sage, we say that he can be our model. To exalt principle and say that Heaven and Earth, or yin and yang (passive and active cosmic forces) are not worthy of being its equal necessarily means that it is not the principle of Heaven and Earth or yin and yang. The principle of Heaven or Earth or yin and yang is similar to the sageness of the sage. Is it correct to exalt sageness and say that the sage is not worthy of being its equal? A sage is also a man. Be-

---

[35] Ode no. 260.

[36] Commentary on hexagram no. 1, *ch'ien* (Heaven). Cf. Legge, *Yi King*, p. 417.

[37] Ch. 29. The Three Kings were the founders of the Hsia (2183–1752 B.C.), Shang (1751–1112 B.C.) and Chou (1111–249 B.C.) dynasties.

[38] Mencius' saying, by which he meant moral principles. See *Mencius*, 6A:7.

[39] *ibid.*, 4A:2.

cause he completely fulfills the principle of man, all people praise him as sagely and wise. Completely fulfilling the principles of men does not mean anything other than completely fulfilling what is necessary (moral principles) in the daily activities in human relations. When we extend the principles to the ultimate point where they cannot be altered, we call them necessary. We are describing their ultimate character and not investigating their origin. Latter-day scholars have gone too far and have regarded opinions, words, ideas, and theories, which are merely describing the ultimate state, as a thing, and said that it attains its being by being merged with material force. Those who hear this theory keep hearing it habitually without examination, and none realizes that it is different from the teachings of Confucius and Mencius in the Six Classics. If we seek what is necessary and unalterable in heaven, earth, men, things, events, and activities, we shall find principle in them to be perfectly clear and evident. But if we exalt it and glorify it, not only calling it the principle of heaven, earth, men, things, events, and activities, but instead calling it omnipresent principle, regarding it as if it were a thing, the result will be that even until their hair turns white, students will be at a loss and will not be able to find this thing. It is not that the teachings of Confucius and Mencius in the Six Classics are hard to understand. It is rather that commentaries and annotations [of the Classics, such as those by Sung Neo-Confucianists] have followed one another, and people learned them from childhood without giving them any more thought.

> *Comment.* In Tai's theory, animals know what is natural but man knows what is necessary, that is, what is morally correct. It is the human mind alone that can direct the natural to the necessary. Since he considers blood, vital force, the mind, and intelligence[40] as components of human nature, it follows that blood and vital force lead man to error. Since these are physical nature, he virtually subscribes to the Neo-Confucian theory that physical nature is responsible for man's error, a theory he strongly criticized.

2. On Nature

Sec. 20. Nature means an allotment of yin and yang and the Five Agents (Water, Fire, Wood, Metal, Earth) which becomes blood, vital force, the mind, and intelligence, with which the ten thousand things are differentiated. All activities they engage in, all potentialities they possess, and all qualities they preserve from the time of their production are based on this fact. This is why the *Book of Changes* says, "That which

[40] See the next section.

realizes it is the individual nature."[41] It has been a long time since man and things were created through the transformation of material force and each flourishes within its own category, but the distinction of categories have been the same for a thousand ages. They simply follow the same old pattern. The transformation of material force is described in terms of yin and yang and the Five Agents. Their completion and transformation of things involves a great complexity and an infinite variation. Therefore in their changing configurations, not only are the ten thousand things different. Even within a category things are not the same. To receive an allotment of physical form and vital force from one's parents is the same as receiving an allotment from yin and yang and the Five Agents. The fact that men and things flourish according to their categories is natural in the process of the transformation of material force. The *Doctrine of the Mean* says, "What Heaven imparts (*ming*, orders) to man is called human nature."[42] Because life is limited by Heaven, we say "the Mandate of Heaven" (*T'ien-ming*, Heaven's order). The *Book of Rites of the Elder Tai* says, "What gets an allotment of the Way is called destiny (*ming*). What makes a thing assume one particular form is called nature."[43] To receive an allotment of the Way means to receive an allotment of yin, yang, and the Five Agents. Since assuming one particular form is spoken of as allotment, there is a limitation from the beginning, and things are unequal in their completeness or incompleteness, thickness or thinness, clearness or turbidity, darkness or brightness, each following its allotment and assuming one particular physical form, and each completing its nature. However, although the individual natures are different, they are generally differentiated by their categories. Therefore the *Analects* says, "By nature men are alike."[44] This is said from the point of view that men are alike. Mencius said, "All things of the same kind are similar to one another. Why should there be any doubt about men? The sage and I are the same in kind."[45] Since it says that things of the same kind are similar to one another, it is clear that things of different kinds are not similar. Therefore Mencius questioned Kao Tzu's (c.420–c.350 B.C.) theory that "what is inborn is called the nature,"[46] saying, "Then is the nature of a dog the same as the nature of an ox, and is the nature of an ox the same as the nature of a man?"[47] This was said to make clear that they cannot be confused or identified. The Way of Heaven is none other than yin and yang and the Five Agents. The natures of men and things are all allotments of the Way and each becomes different, that is all.

[41] "Appended Remarks," pt. 1, ch. 5. Cf. Legge, p. 356.
[42] Ch. 1.   [43] Sec. 80, SPTK, 13:3a.   [44] 17:2.
[45] *Mencius*, 6A:7.   [46] *ibid.*, 6A:3.   [47] *ibid.*

3. On Capacity

Sec. 29. Through capacity man and creatures assume physical form and solid substance in accordance with their nature, and their intelligence, and ability are thereby differentiated. This is what Mencius called "natural capacity endowed by Heaven."[48] Man and things are produced through the transformation of material force. Destiny is so called on the basis of their limitation of allotment. Man's nature is so called on the basis of the fact that the transformation of material force is the basic beginning of men and things. Capacity is so called on the basis of their physical substance. Because they each differ in their completed nature, therefore they each also differ in their capacity. Capacity is the manifestation of one's nature. Without capacity, how can one's nature be revealed?. . . Latter-day scholars ascribed evil to physical nature. What Mencius called nature and capacity both denote nothing but physical nature. Man's nature is endowment in its completeness and capacity is the physical substance in its completeness. There is no basis on which to describe endowment in its completeness. For example, the nature of a peach or an apricot is complete in the whiteness of their kernels. Their [potential] physical forms, colors, smells, and flavors are all contained therein, but they cannot be seen. But when the budding sprouts burst forth, the stems, branches, and leaves of the peach and apricot become different. From this to flowers and fruits, their physical forms, colors, smells, and flavors are all differentiated and distinguished. Although they are so because of their natures, they depend on the capacities of the plants to reveal them. As their natures are completed, there is this capacity. Separately, we speak of destiny, nature, and capacity, but totally speaking, it is called Heavenly endowed nature. . . .

4. On Humanity, Righteousness, Propriety, and Wisdom

Sec. 36. Humanity is the character of production and reproduction. "The people are secured. They daily enjoyed their drink and food."[49] All this is none other than how the way of man produces and reproduces. When one person fulfills his life and by extension helps all others to fulfill their lives, that is humanity. . . . If we trace the way of Nature from the way of man and trace the character of Nature from that of man, we shall know that the universal operation of the transformation of material force consists in unceasing production and reproduction. This is humanity. Because in the process of production and reproduction there is a natural order, and as we see in it a regular procedure, we can understand propriety. As we see that the order can never be confused, we

[48] *ibid.*, 6A:7.   [49] See n.24.

can understand righteousness. In Nature the virtue of humanity is the production and reproduction of the transformation of material force, and in man it is the mind to produce and reproduce. In Nature the virtue of wisdom is the order in which the transformation of material force operates, and in man it is the mind's realization that the order is without any confusion. Only because there is order that there are production and reproduction. Without it, the way of production and reproduction will cease. . . .

Comment. To regard humanity as production and reproduction is a Sung Neo-Confucian contribution.[50]

5. On the Variety of Circumstances

Sec. 41. Question: The Sung Neo-Confucianists knew also how to seek principle in things, but because they were attracted to Buddhism, they have applied what the Buddhists used to designate spiritual consciousness to designate principle. Therefore they look upon principle as if it were a thing. They not only talk about the principle of things, but also say that principle lies scattered through events and things. Since principle is that of things, it can be discovered only after things have been analyzed to the minutest detail. And since principle lies scattered through events and things, they therefore seek it through deep and quiet concentration of the mind. They said the substance [of principle] is one but [in function] it has ten thousand manifestations, and "Unroll it (extended) and it reaches in all directions. Roll it up (contracted) and it withdraws and lies hidden in minuteness."[51] Actually they got this idea by imitating the Buddhists, who say that "Universally manifested, it includes the whole Realm of Law. Collected and grasped, it is a single speck of dust."[52] Since they seek principle through a deep and quiet [concentration] of the mind, thinking they have understood that the substance of principle is one, they are quite confident that principle means having no desire. Even their partial opinions are regarded as issuing from principle but not from desire. Simply because they regard principle as if it were a thing, they could not help regarding it to be one principle. But since everything necessarily has its own principle, and principles change with things, therefore they also say, "The mind embodies all principles and responds to all things. The mind embodies principle and issues it forth."[53]

[50] See below, ch. 31, sec. 11 and ch. 32, sec. 42.

[51] Chu Hsi's introductory remark on *The Mean*. See above, ch. 5.

[52] I have not been able to trace the source of this quotation.

[53] Chu Hsi *Ta-hsüeh chang-chü* (Commentary on the *Great Learning*), commenting on the opening sentence of the text. Also in his *Meng tzu chi-chu* (Collected Commentaries on the *Book of Mencius*), ch. 13, commenting on *Mencius*, 7A:1. See above, ch. 35, n.61.

What could this be if it is not mere opinion? Furthermore, if all principles are contained in the mind, then when one event occurs, the mind issues one principle to respond to it. When another event occurs, it has to issue another principle to respond to it. And so on to hundreds and thousands and millions, there is no end. Since the mind contains all principles, they should be described in terms of number. There must be an explanation whether it is one or innumerable. Therefore they say, "Principle is one but its manifestations are many." The *Analects* twice mentions the one thread running through Confucius doctrines.[54] In his commentary on the chapter where Confucius told Tseng Tzu[55] about this, Chu Hsi said, "The mind of the Sage is one undifferentiated principle, but in its various responses and applications, it functions differently in each case. With respect to its functioning, Tseng Tzu had understood principle clearly as things occurred and had earnestly put it into practice, but he did not understand that its substance is one."[56] This interpretation must be wrong. Will you please tell us the original meanings of the two chapters?

Answer: By one thread running through the doctrines is not meant to run one certain thing through them. In understanding moral principle, efforts may differ in studying things on the lower level or in penetrating the higher level. In learning, people's objectives may differ in knowing the traces of moral principles or in discriminating the principles themselves. To say that there is a thread running through my doctrines means that the doctrines to be understood by penetrating the higher level are the same as those to be understood by studying the lower level. . . . Mencius said, "Study extensively and discuss thoroughly. This is in order to go back and discuss the most restrained."[57] By being restrained is meant the most correct. He further said, "Moral principles which, when held, are restrained, while their application is extensive, are good principles . . . The way the superior man holds these principles is to cultivate his personal life and peace will thereby prevail throughout the world."[58] To restrain means to cultivate one's person. When the Six Classics, the books of Confucius and Mencius, talk about restraining action, they aim at nothing more than the cultivation of one's personal life, and when they talk about restraining knowledge, they aim at nothing more than extending the intelligence of the mind to the utmost. They have never designated a One in a vacuum and tell people to understand and seek it. If one extends his intelligence to the

[54] *Analects*, 4:15, 15:3.

[55] Confucius' pupil, 505–c.436 B.C. The chapter referred to is *Analects*, 4:15.

[56] *Lun-yü chi-chu* (Collected Commentaries on the *Analects*), ch. 2, commenting on *Analects*, 4:15.

[57] *Mencius*, 4B:15. [58] *ibid.*, 7B:32.

utmost, he can naturally judge situations and does not make the slightest mistake. What is the need for understanding the One and seeking it?

> *Comment.* Sung-Ming Neo-Confucianists never looked upon principle as if it were a thing. They differentiated what exists before form [and is therefore with it] (*hsing-erh-shang*), such as principle, and what exists after physical form [and is therefore with it] (*hsing-erh-hsia*), such as a thing. Tai, however, would not accept this distinction. In this respect he resembles Wang Fu-chih (Wang Ch'uan-shan, 1619-1692) and Yen Yüan (Yen Hsi-chai, 1635-1704).

39

K'ANG YU-WEI'S PHILOSOPHY OF GREAT UNITY

LIKE MOST CONFUCIANISTS, K'ang Yu-wei (1858-1927)[1] attempted to put Confucian teachings into practice in government and society. But as no other Confucianist had ever done, he changed the traditional concepts of Confucius, of the Confucian Classics, and of certain fundamental Confucian doctrines for the sake of reform.

Several factors made this transformation unavoidable. In the last decades of the nineteenth century, the call for reform was getting louder and louder in China. The influence of Western science and Christianity was increasingly felt. Interest in Buddhism was being revived. The controversy between the Modern Script School of those who upheld the Classics written in ancient script, and the Modern Script School of those who accepted the Classics written in the script current during the second and first centuries B.C., which was modern at the time, arose once more. The Modern Script School was winning because instead of regarding Confucius as only a great teacher and the Classics as purely historical documents, it looked upon Confucius as an "uncrowned king" to reform the world and the Classics as containing "esoteric language and great principles" to support his reforms. K'ang promoted this current of thought

[1] K'ang was a native of the Nan-hai district of Kwangtung. Hence the honorary title "Master Nan-hai." At nineteen he became a pupil of Chu Tz'u-ch'i. In 1888 he addressed a memorial to the Kuang-hsü emperor (r. 1875-1908) for reform, but the memorial was prevented from reaching him. In 1891 he taught at Canton, with Liang Ch'i-ch'ao among his pupils. In 1895 he obtained the "presented scholar" degree in Peking and founded the Society for National Strength and New Learning there. When China was defeated by Japan in that year, he organized the graduates from eighteen provinces into a mass meeting to petition for rejection of the peace treaty with Japan but for reform instead. The petition never reached the emperor. Two years later he memorialized once more. The emperor now intended to start reform. In 1898, at the introduction of the imperial tutor, K'ang and the emperor met for two hours and decided on reform measures. Many edicts were rapidly issued ordering wholesale reform. But when Yüan Shih-k'ai (1858-1916), army commander guarding the capital, was asked to help the emperor and arrest a chief opponent, the Empress Dowager, he informed her instead. The reform movement collapsed.

K'ang fled to Hong Kong, and thence to Japan, the South Seas, America, and Europe, traveling for a period of sixteen years. While in Canada in 1899, he founded the Party to Preserve the Emperor who was then virtually under house arrest. With the establishment of the Republic in 1912, K'ang returned to China. In 1914 he advocated Confucianism as the state religion and in 1917 took part in the abortive attempt to restore the deposed Hsüan-t'ung emperor (r. 1909-1912) to the throne. He tried restoration and failed again in 1924. A radical reformer turned arch-reactionary, he died in disgrace, but because of his great scholarship and loyalty to Confucianism, he has been called Sage K'ang from his youth. For details of his life, see Lo, Jung-pang, ed., K'ang Yu-wei.

and eventually became the center of the school. In addition, the fire of the rationalistic Neo-Confucianism of Ch'eng I (Ch'eng I-ch'uan, 1033-1107) had burned out by this time. Scholars gradually turned to the idealistic Neo-Confucianism of Lu Hsiang-shan (Lu Chiu-yüan, 1139-1193) and Wang Yang-ming (Wang Shou-jen, 1492-1529), which is imbued with the spirit of purposeful action instead of Ch'eng-Chu's cold and abstract speculation. Not only was there this general trend toward Lu-Wang. He was also strongly influenced by his teacher, Chu Tz'u-ch'i (Chu Chiu-chiang, 1807-1881), a prominent scholar at the time, who was an enthusiastic follower of the Lu-Wang School. It was the combination of these factors that caused him to enunciate his extraordinary theories that Confucius was first and last a reformer, that history evolves through three stages toward utopia, or the Age of Great Unity, and that humanity (jen)[2] is ether and electricity.

K'ang presented Confucius as a reformer who purposely attributed institutional reforms to antiquity in order to have precedents, even to the extent of imagining great achievements of sage-emperors Yao and Shun[3] whose historicity is doubtful. This bold dismissal of the age-old Confucian idols virtually amounted to a revolution. Liang Ch'i-ch'ao (1873-1929), his outstanding disciple, was not exaggerating when he said that K'ang's three most important works were comparable to a cyclone, a mighty volcanic eruption, and a huge earthquake.[4] But it is interesting to note that K'ang the reformer had to look to the past for authority and that his authority, in turn, had to look to the past for authority also, even if he had to invent it.

Whatever conservatism he had, however, was more than offset by his novel concept of historical progress. The theory of three ages is not new. Tung Chung-shu (c.179–c.104 B.C.), for example,[5] great leader of the Modern Script School who had a tremendous influence on K'ang, had propounded it. But K'ang conceived of history not as a cycle, as Tung did, but as an evolution. The source of this idea is probably Western, but he insisted on tracing it to Confucius.

He set forth his theory of the Three Ages in his commentary on a passage in the Confucian Classic, the *Book of Rites*, in which Confucius is said to have taught that history progresses from the Age of Chaos to that of Small Peace and finally to that of Great Unity. K'ang advocated this doctrine not so much as an echo of the new idea of progress as to provide a philosophical foundation for his political reforms. In the 1880's, when he was still a young man, he plunged into reform move-

---

[2] For this translation, see Appendix, comment on *Jen*.
[3] Legendary rulers of 3rd millennium B.C.
[4] Liang Ch'i-ch'ao, *Intellectual Trends in the Ch'ing Period*, p. 94.
[5] See above, ch. 14, sec. E, 4.

ments. Together with other scholars, he repeatedly petitioned the emperor to reconstruct China. In 1898, he actually engineered the dramatic Hundred Days Reform. In this reform he was convinced that though China was not ready for the Age of Great Unity, she had to enter upon an Age of Small Peace. Edicts were issued in rapid order to reform the political, educational, economic, and military institutions, modeled after the West, only to be defeated by the conservative Empress Dowager and he had to flee for his life.

T'ang's ideas about the Age of Great Unity are so radical that the book in which he expresses them, the *Ta-t'ung shu* (Book of Great Unity) was kept unpublished until 1935, eight years after his death. There was already a hint of the idea in his commentary on the passage mentioned above. This commentary was written in 1884-1885. But the book, based on earlier drafts of the 1880's, was not finished until 1901-1902. Anyway, since he called for the total abolition of nations, families, classes, and all kinds of distinctions, his doctrine was too far ahead of his age to be accepted. Other philosophers had had utopias before. But different from them, K'ang drew inspiration from many sources—Confucian, Christian, and Buddhist—and spelled out in detail the organization and program of the ideal society, such as communal living, public nurseries for all children, and cremation and the use of ashes for fertilizer.

The philosophical bases for this utopia are two, namely, his theory of historical progress and his interpretation of the central Confucian ethical concept of humanity. He equates this with what Mencius called "The mind that cannot bear [to see the suffering of] others."[6] Humanity is also the power of attraction that unites all people as one. It is the force of origination permeating everywhere. It is ether and electricity. It is production and reproduction. It is universal love. In the traditional Confucian theory of love, one proceeds from affection for one's parents to being humane to all people, and finally to kindness to all creatures.[7] The Age of Great Unity is the logical culmination of this gradual extension. K'ang was certainly revolutionary in both vision and action, but in this as in other respects he remained within the main stream of Confucianism.

SELECTIONS

1. The Three Ages

In the progress of mankind there have always been definite stages. From the clan system come tribes, which in time become nations, and from nations the Great Unification comes into existence. From the indi-

[6] *Mencius*, 2A:6.   [7] See *ibid.*, 7A:45.

vidual man the rule of tribal chieftains gradually becomes established, and from the rule of tribal chieftains the correct relationship between ruler and minister is gradually defined. From autocracy gradually comes [monarchic] constitutionalism, and from constitutionalism gradually comes republicanism. From men living as individuals gradually comes the relationship between husband and wife, and from this the relationship between father and son is gradually fixed. From the relationship between father and son gradually comes the system in which blessings are also extended to all the rest of mankind. And from this system, that of Great Unity comes into being, whereby individuals again exist as individuals [in a harmonious world without the bonds of father and son, husband and wife, and so forth].

Thus in the progress from the Age of Disorder to the Age of Rising Peace, and from the Age of Rising Peace to the Age of Great Peace, their evolution is gradual and there are reasons for their continuation or modification. Examine this process in all countries and we shall find that the pattern is the same. By observing the infant one can foretell the future adult and further the future old man, and by observing the sprout one can foretell the future tree large enough to be enclosed with both arms and further the future tree high enough to reach the sky. Similarly, by observing what the Three Systems[8] of the Hsia (2193–1752 B.C.?), Shang (1751–1112 B.C.) and Chou (1111–249 B.C.) added to or subtracted from the previous period, one can infer the changes and modifications in a hundred generations to come.

When Confucius wrote the *Spring and Autumn Annals*, he extended it to embrace the Three Ages. During the Age of Disorder, he considered his own state (of Lu) as native and all other Chinese feudal states as foreign. In the Age of Rising Peace, he considered all Chinese feudal states as native and the outlying barbarian tribes as foreign. And in the Age of Great Peace, he considered all groups, far or near, big or small, as one. In doing this he was applying the principle of evolution.

Confucius was born in the Age of Disorder. Now that communications have extended throughout the great earth and important changes have taken place in Europe and America, the world has entered upon the Age of Rising Peace. Later, when all groups throughout the great earth, far and near, big and small, are like one, when nations will cease to exist, when racial distinctions are no longer made, and when customs are unified, all will be one and the Age of Great Peace will have come. Confucius knew all this in advance.

However, within each age there are Three Rotating Phases. In the Age of Disorder, there are the phases of Rising Peace and Great Peace,

[8] See above, ch. 14, n.41.

and in the Age of Great Peace are the phases of Rising Peace and Disorder. Thus there are barbarian red Indians in progressive America and primitive Miao, Yao, T'ung, and Li tribes in civilized China. Each age can further be divided into three ages. These three can further be extended (geometrically) into nine ages, then eighty-one, then thousands and tens of thousands, and then innumerable ages. After the arrival of the Age of Great Peace and Great Unity, there will still be much progress and many phases.

It will not end after only a hundred generations. (*Lun-yü chu*, or Commentary on the *Analects*, *Wan-mu ts'ao-t'ang ts'ung-shu* or Thatched Hall Surrounded by Ten Thousand Trees Series ed., 12:10b-11a)

> *Comment.* Coupled with the cycle theory, Confucianists have always looked upon history as a movement of ups and downs. In modifying his theory of the Three Ages with that of Three Rotating Phases, K'ang was in effect perpetuating this traditional outlook.

In his methods and institutions Confucius emphasized their adaptability to the times. If, in the age of primitivism and chaos, when the transforming influence of moral doctrines had not operated, one were to practice the institutions of Great Peace, it would surely result in great harm. But at the same time, if, in the Age of Rising Peace, one still clung to the institutions of the Age of Disorder, it would also result in great harm. At the present time of Rising Peace, for example, we should promote the principles of self-rule and independence and the systems of parliamentarianism and constitutionalism. If institutions are not reformed, great disorder will result. Confucius thought of these troubles and prevented them. He therefore inaugurated the doctrine of the Three Rotating Phases so that later generations may adapt and change in order to remove harm. This is Confucius' perfect humanity in establishing institutions. (*Chung-yung chu*, or Commentary on the *Doctrine of the Mean*, *Yen-K'ung ts'ung-shu* or Exposition of Confucianism Collection ed., p. 36b)

2. Confucius' Institutional Reforms

In high antiquity, people esteemed valor and competed in physical strength. Chaos was impending and misery prevalent. Heaven was sorry for them and decided to save them. It was not to save one generation alone but a hundred generations. Therefore Heaven produced the sagely king of spiritual intelligence. He did not become a ruler of men but a master of creation of institutions. The entire world followed him and all people, far or near, flocked to him. In the eight hundred years from the Warring States Period (403–222 B.C.) to Later Han (25-220), all scholars regarded Confucius as the king. . . . He had the actuality of people flocking to him. Therefore he had the actuality of a king. It is a matter of course that one who had the actuality of a king should have the name of a king. But the great Sage reluctantly followed the path of expediency. He humbly negated the reality of the rank and title of a king. He [promoted institutional reforms] by attributing them to ancient kings and the king of Lu,[9] and only assumed the role of a "king behind the scene" and an "uncrowned king." (*K'ung Tzu kai-chi k'ao* or An Investigation on Confucius' Institutional Reforms, *Wan-mu ts'ao-t'ang ts'ung-shu* ed., 8:1b-2a)

Founders of religions in all great lands have always reformed institutions and established systems. Even ancient Chinese philosophers did this. All Chinese moral institutions were founded by Confucius. His disciples received his instructions and transmitted his teachings, so that they spread over the whole empire and changed its traditional customs. Among the outstanding changes have been costumes, the three-year mourning (of one's parents' deaths), marriage ceremonies, the "well-field" land system,[10] the educational system, and the civil service examination system. (*ibid.*, 9:1a)

Confucius was the founder of a religion. He was a sagely king with spiritual intelligence. He was a counterpart of Heaven and Earth and nourished all things. All human beings, all events, and all moral principles are encompassed in his great Way. Thus he was the Great Perfection and Ultimate Sage the human race had never had. . . .

On what basis did he become founder of a religion and a sagely king with spiritual intelligence? *Answer*: On the Six Classics.[11] They are the works of Confucius. This was the unanimous opinion before the Han dynasty (206 B.C.–A.D. 220). Only when the student knows that the Six Classics are the works of Confucius does he understand why Confucius was a great sage, was the founder of a religion, encompassed ten thousand generations, and has been venerated as supreme. Only when a student knows that Confucius was founder of a religion and that the Six Classics are his works does he know Confucius' achievements in wiping out the Age of Disorder and bringing about the Age of Great Peace, and that everyone with blood and vital force is daily benefited by his great achievements and great virtue and should never forget it. (*ibid.*, 10:1a-b)

[9] Confucius' native state.

[10] For a description of this system, see above, ch. 3, no. 81. There is no evidence that the system was ever practiced, though many Confucianists and Neo-Confucianists insisted that it was the practice in high antiquity and urged its revival.

[11] Namely, the *Books of History, Odes, Changes, Rites, Music* (now lost) and the *Spring and Autumn Annals*. Since the Sung dynasty (960-1279) the *Book of Music* has been replaced by the *Chou-li* (Rites of Chou).

Comment. K'ang was the first to regard Confucius as the founder of a religion, and he vigorously advocated Confucianism as the state religion. Because of this he was branded in his late years as reactionary. He may also be so considered in his theory that Confucius wrote all the Six Classics. He was not so reactionary, however, when he devoted a whole book to show that all Classics in the ancient script were forgeries, for this theory uprooted the whole foundation of Ch'ing scholarship and forced scholars to reexamine the entire Confucian heritage in new lights.

All the Sage wanted was to benefit the world. Therefore "his words are not necessarily [literally] truthful. . . . He simply speaks what is right."[12] "Without evidence, they (ancient institutions) could not command credence, and not being credited, the people would not follow them."[13] Therefore he put all institutions into operation by citing the ancient kings of the Three Dynasties[14] as precedents and authority. If it is said that in his work a sage should not cite others as precedent and authority, then one would be equating Confucius, who possessed spiritual transforming power, with an obstinate inferior man. (*ibid.*, 11:1b)

3. The Mind That Cannot Bear to See the Suffering of Others

In consciousness and perception, forms and sounds of objects are transmitted to my eyes and ears. They rush against my soul. Chilly and cold, they attack the active aspects (yang, active cosmic force) of my existence. Dark and quiet, they enter my negative aspects (yin, passive cosmic force). They continue at moderate speed as if they could not stop. Of what are they the clue? Is it what Europeans call ether? Is it what the ancients called the "mind that cannot bear [to see the suffering of] others"? Do all people have this mind that cannot bear to see the suffering of others? Or do I alone have it? And why should I be deeply affected by this clue?

Thereupon Master K'ang says: Do I not have a body? If not, how do I have knowledge or affection? Since I have a body, can that which permeates my body as well as the material force (*ch'i*) of Heaven, the concrete stuff of Earth, and the breath of man be cut off or not? If it could be cut off, then one could draw a knife and cut water to pieces. If it cannot be cut off, then it is like material force filling space and being possessed by all things, like electricity operating through material force and penetrating everything, like water spreading all over the land and permeating everything, and like blood-vessels spreading through the

---

[12] *Mencius*, 4B:11.   [13] *The Mean*, ch. 29.   [14] Hsia, Shang, and Chou

body and penetrating every part of it. Cut the material force off the mountain and it will collapse. Cut the blood-vessels off the body and it will die. And cut the material force off the earth and it will disintegrate. Therefore if man cuts off the substance of love which is the mind that cannot bear to see the suffering of others, moral principles of mankind will be destroyed and terminated. If these are destroyed and terminated, civilization will stop and mankind will revert to barbarism. Furthermore, barbarism will stop and men will revert to their original animal nature.

Great is the material force of origination. It created Heaven and Earth. By Heaven is meant the spiritual substance of a thing (the universe), and by man is also meant the spiritual substance of a thing (the body). Although they differ in size, they are no different in partaking the great force of great origination, just as if both were scooping up small drops of water from the great sea. Confucius said, "Earth contains spiritual energy, which produces the wind and thunder. As a result of movements of wind and thunder, a countless variety of things in their changing configurations ensue, and the myriad things show the appearance of life."[15] Spirit is electricity with consciousness. The electric light can be transmitted everywhere, and spiritual energy can act on everything. It makes spiritual beings and gods spiritual. It produces Heaven and Earth. In its entirety it is origination; divided, it becomes man.[16] How subtle and how wonderful does spirit act on things! There is nothing without electricity, and there is nothing without spirit. Spirit is the power of consciousness, the consciousness of the soul, spiritual intelligence, clear intelligence, and clear character. These are different in name but the same in actuality. As there is consciousness, there is attraction. This is true of the lodestone. How much more is it with man! Not being able to bear to see the suffering of others is an instance of this power of attraction. Therefore both humanity and wisdom are stored in the mind, but wisdom comes first. Both humanity and wisdom are exercised (in action), but humanity is nobler. . . .

The love of those whose consciousness is small is also small, and the humanity of those whose consciousness is great is also great. (*Ta-t'ung shu* or Book of Great Unity, Peking, 1956, pp. 2-4)

4. The Age of Great Unity

Therefore all living creatures in the world only aim at seeking happiness and avoiding suffering. They follow no other course. There are

[15] *Book of Rites*, "Confucius at Home at Ease." Cf. Legge, trans., *Li Ki*, vol. 1. p. 282.

[16] The word *wei* here does not mean only but is interchangeable with *wei* (to become).

some who take a roundabout way, take an expedient way,[17] or zig-zag in their course, going through painful experiences without getting tired. They, too, only aim at seeking happiness. Although men differ in their nature, we can decidedly say that the way of mankind is never to seek suffering and avoid happiness. To establish institutions and inaugurate doctrines so as to enable men to have happiness but no suffering is the highest of goodness. To enable men to have much happiness and little suffering is good but not perfectly good. And to cause men to have much suffering and little happiness is no good. . . .

Having been born in an age of disorder, and seeing with my own eyes the path of suffering in the world, I wish to find a way to save it. I have thought deeply and believe the only way is to practice the way of Great Unity and Great Peace. Looking over all ways and means in the world, I believe that aside from the way of Great Unity there is no other method to save living men from their sufferings or to seek their great happiness. The way of Great Unity is perfect equality, perfect impartiality, perfect humanity, and good government in the highest degree. Although there are good ways, none can be superior.

The sufferings of mankind are so innumerable as to be unimaginable, changing from place to place and from time to time. They cannot be all listed, but let us roughly mention the major ones that are readily apparent:

(1) Seven sufferings from living: 1, rebirth, 2, premature death, 3, physical debilities, 4, being a barbarian, 5, living in frontier areas (on the fringe of civilization), 6, being a slave, and 7, being a woman.

(2) Eight sufferings from natural calamities: 1, famines resulting from floods or droughts, 2, plagues of locusts, 3, fire, 4, flood, 5, volcanic eruptions (including earthquakes and landslides), 6, collapse of buildings, 7, shipwrecks (including collisions of cars), and 8, epidemics.

(3) Five sufferings from conditions of life: 1, being a widow or widower, 2, being an orphan or childless, 3, being ill without medical care, 4, being poor, and 5, being humble in social station.

(4) Five sufferings from government: 1, punishment and imprisonment, 2, oppressive taxation, 3, military conscription, 4, the existence of the state, and 5, the existence of the family.

(5) Eight sufferings from human feelings: 1, stupidity, 2, hatred, 3, sexual love, 4, burden imposed by others, 5, toil, 6, desires, 7, oppression, and 8, class distinction.

(6) Five sufferings from being objects of honor and esteem: 1, a rich man, 2, a man of high station, 3, a man of longevity, 4, a king or emperor, and 5, a god, a sage, an immortal, or a Buddha. (*ibid.*, pp. 6-10)

---

[17] Literally, "borrow a way."

All these are sufferings of human life, not to mention the conditions of sufferings of the feathered, furred, or scaly animals. But if we broadly survey the miseries of life, we shall find that all sufferings originate from nine spheres of distinction. What are these nine? The first is the distinction between states [as a cause of suffering], because it divides the world into territories and tribes. The second is class distinction, because it divides people into the honored and the humble, the pure and the impure. The third is racial distinction, which divides people into yellows, whites, browns, and blacks. The fourth is the distinction between physical forms, because it makes the divisions between male and female. The fifth is the distinction between families, because it confines the various affections between father and son, husband and wife, and brothers to those personal relations. The sixth is the distinction between occupations, because it considers the products of farmers, artisans, and merchants as their own. The seventh is the sphere of chaos, because it has systems that are unfair, unreasonable, non-uniform, and unjust. The eighth is the distinction between species, because it divides them into human beings, birds, animals, insects, and fish. And the ninth is the sphere of suffering. Suffering gives rise to suffering, and so they pass on without end and in a way that is beyond imagination. . . .

> *Comment.* To consider life as suffering is Buddhistic and utterly un-Confucian, but the Buddhist outlook leads to compassion, and compassion is none other than the mind that cannot bear to see the suffering of others. K'ang was syncretic, but Confucianism remains in the center.

My way of saving people from these sufferings consists in abolishing these nine spheres of distinction. First, do away with the distinction between states in order to unify the whole world. Second, do away with class distinction so as to bring about equality of all people. Third, do away with racial distinction so there will be one universal race. Fourth, do away with the distinction between physical forms so as to guarantee the independence of both sexes. Fifth, do away with the distinction between families so men may become citizens of Heaven. Sixth, do away with the distinction between occupations so that all productions may belong to the public. Seventh, do away with the spheres of chaos so that universal peace may become the order of the day. Eighth, do away with the distinction between species so we may love all sentient beings. And ninth, do away with the sphere of suffering so happiness may reach its height. (*ibid.*, pp. 51-52)

In the world of Great Unity, the whole world becomes a great unity.

There is no division into national states and no difference between races. There will be no war. (*ibid.*, p. 255)

In the Age of Great Unity, the world government is daily engaged in mining, road building, reclamation of deserts, and navigation as the primary task. (*ibid.*, p. 264)

In the Age of Great Peace, all agriculture, industry, and commerce originate with the world government. There is no competition at all. (*ibid.*, p. 270)

In the Age of Great Peace, there are no emperors, kings, rulers, elders, official titles, or ranks. All people are equal, and do not consider position or rank as an honor either. Only wisdom and humanity are promoted and encouraged. Wisdom is to initiate things, accomplish undertakings, promote utility and benefits, and advance people, while humanity is to confer benefits extensively on all the people and bring salvation to them, to love people and to benefit things. There is no honor outside of wisdom and humanity. (*ibid.*, p. 275)

In the Age of Great Peace, since men's nature is already good and his ability and intelligence is superior, they only rejoice in matters of wisdom and humanity. New institutions appear every day. Public benefits increase every day. The humane mind gets stronger every day. And knowledge becomes clearer every day. People in the whole world together reach the realm of humanity, longevity, perfect happiness, and infinite goodness and wisdom. (*ibid.*, pp. 277-278)

In the Age of Great Unity, since there is no more state, there is therefore no severe military discipline. As there is no ruler, there is no rebellion or instigation of disturbance. As there are no husbands or wives, there is no quarrel over women, necessity to prevent adultery, suppression of sex desires, complaint, hatred, divorce, or the calamity of murder. As there are no blood relatives of clansmen, there is no reliance on others for support, [authoritarian] admonition to do good, or litigation over inheritance. As there are no ranks or positions, there is no such thing as relying on power or strength to oppress or rob others, or resorting to intrigue or flattery to get jobs. As there is no private property, there is no litigation over land, residence, or industrial or business property. As there is no burial [but cremation], there is no litigation over grave land. As there is no tax, customs, or conscription, there is no crime of cheating or desertion. And as there is neither title nor status, there is no insulting or oppression, or such things as offense or counterattack. (*ibid.*, p. 283)

In the Age of Great Peace, all people are equal. There are no servants or slaves, rulers or commanders, heads of religion or popes. (*ibid.*, p. 284)

In the Age of Great Unity, all people live in public dwellings. . . . There will be automatic boats and cars. . . . New inventions appear every day. . . . There will be no difference in dress between men and women. . . . There will be no disease. . . . People think of nothing because happiness will reach its limit. They only think of immortality on earth. (*ibid.*, pp. 294-300)

5. Humanity

The mind that cannot bear to see the suffering of others is humanity. It is electricity. It is ether. Everyone has it. This is why it is said that the nature of all men is originally good.[18] Since there is already this mind that cannot bear to see the suffering of others, when it is aroused and applied externally, it results in a government that cannot bear to see the people's suffering. If man were without this mind that cannot bear to see the suffering of others, then the sage ruler would be without this seed and that means that none of the benevolent governmental measures can be produced. Therefore we know that all benevolent governmental measures proceed from this mind that cannot bear to see the suffering of others. It is the seat of all transformations, the root of all things, the source of all things, the seed that will become the tree reaching up to the sky, the drop of water that will become the great sea. Man's feeling of love, human civilization, the progress of mankind, down to Great Peace and Great Unity all originate from it. . . .

The mind that cannot bear to see the suffering of others is a humane mind. The government that cannot bear to see the people's suffering is a humane government. Although they differ as inner and outer and as substance and function, their constituting the Way is the same. It is humanity, that is all. Humanity means "people living together."[19] Chuang Tzu said that in an empty valley "One is happy when he sees someone similar in appearance."[20] It is the natural feeling of men that when they see someone with a similar appearance, a similar form, or a similar voice, the feeling is inevitably aroused in their minds to love each other. . . . All people have the mind to love each other. All people work for each other. . . .

Confucius instituted the scheme of Three Ages. In the Age of Disorder, humanity cannot be extended far and therefore people are merely affectionate to their parents. In the Age of Rising Peace, humanity is extended to one's kind and therefore people are humane to all people. In the Age of Great Peace, all creatures form a unity and therefore

[18] This refers to *Mencius*, 2A:6, on which K'ang's present remarks are a commentary.

[19] This is the definition given by Cheng Hsüan (127-200) in his commentary on *The Mean*, ch. 20.

[20] *Chuang Tzu*, ch. 24, NHCC, 8:21b. Cf. Giles, trans., *Chuang Tzu*, 1961 ed., p. 233.

people feel love for all creatures as well.[21] There are distinction and gradation in humanity because there are stages in historical progress. . . . History goes through an evolution, and humanity has its path of development. As the path may be large or small, so humanity may be large or small. Before the time is ripe, it cannot be forced. (*Meng Tzu wei*, or Subtle Meanings of the *Book of Mencius, Wan-mu ts'ao-t'ang ts'ung-shu* ed., 1:2b-4b)

With respect to Heaven, humanity is the principle of production and reproduction, and with respect to man, it is the virtue of universal love. . . . Heaven is humane. It sustains and nourishes all things, transforming them, producing them, and further nourishing them and bringing them to completion. Man takes humanity from Heaven and thus becomes a man of humanity. . . .

The word *jen* consists of one part meaning man and another part meaning many. It means that the way of men is to live together. It connotes attraction. It is the power of love. It is really electrical energy. (*Chung-yung chu*, pp. 20b-21a)

> *Comment.* K'ang synthesized most Confucian concepts of humanity —humanity as the basic virtue, as "people living together," as universal love, and as "production and reproduction"[22]—and made it more emphatic by equating it with "the mind that cannot bear [to see the suffering of others]." He did more than just synthesizing, however. Under the influence of Western science, he identified *jen* with ether and electricity, thus for the first time in Chinese history extending *jen* to the realm of natural science. He added the new notes that *jen* is power of attraction and that it is based on the "feeling of the same kind," so that the gradual extension of love for one's parents to all men is not just a result of natural moral feelings as Mencius and Neo-Confucianists had thought, but also a result of the power of attraction.
>
> Fung Yu-lan thinks that K'ang's use of the concept of all-pervasive ether and electricity is no more than the Neo-Confucianist doctrine that all things form one body supplemented with theories of physics without his understanding them.[23] But he overlooked at least three new elements in the picture, namely, that forming one body is a process of some energy, that it is a result of mutual attraction, and that it is a natural phenomenon. The one drawback

[21] This refers to *Mencius*, 7A:45.

[22] For discussions on *jen*, see above, ch. 30, sec. 1; ch. 31, secs. 1 and 11; ch 32, sec. 42; ch. 34, treatise no. 1.

[23] Fung, *History of Chinese Philosophy*, vol. 2, p. 686.

in K'ang's treatment of *jen* is that he did not develop the Neo-Confucian idea of *jen* as the will to grow, although he has hinted at the idea of humanity as seeds.[24] If he had developed it, his theory would have been much more dynamic.

[24] See n.22 and also Chan, "K'ang Yu-wei and the Confucian Doctrine of Humanity (*Jen*)," in Lo, Jung-pang, ed., *K'ang Yu-wei*.

40

THE PHILOSOPHY OF HUMANITY (*JEN*)
IN T'AN SSU-T'UNG

T'AN SSU-T'UNG (1865-1898) is a replica of K'ang Yu-wei (1858-1927) on a small scale.[1] Like K'ang, he followed the idealistic Neo-Confucianism of Lu Hsiang-shan (Lu Chiu-yüan, 1139-1193) and Wang Yang-ming (Wang Shou-jen, 1472-1529), was a syncretist in lumping together Confucianism, Buddhism, Christianity, and Western science, was a reformer, and propounded a philosophy of universalism.

T'an's philosophy is presented and expounded in his *Jen-hsüeh* (Philosophy of Humanity). According to Liang Ch'i-ch'ao (1873-1929), it is an elaboration of K'ang's basic doctrine.[2] He never studied under K'ang and met him only during the Hundred Days Reform in 1898. When that movement collapsed, K'ang fled abroad but T'an became a martyr at the age of thirty-three. Two years before that, he had heard of K'ang's teachings through Liang and declared himself K'ang's pupil. Thus he was deeply influenced by K'ang, quickly became the elaborator and modifier of K'ang's basic philosophy of humanity, and wrote the *Jen-hsüen* in 1896-1897. There is no evidence that T'an had read K'ang's manuscript of the *Ta-t'ung shu* (Book of Great Unity), but it is difficult to imagine what else Liang could have told him.[3]

As an elaborator and modifier, T'an was neither thorough nor profound. His book is unsystematic and spotty and has been described as a confused dream. His ideas of humanity as universal love, as production and reproduction, as ether and electricity, and as power of attraction are no more than repetition of K'ang. However, he did refine them to some

[1] He was from Hunan. His courtesy name was Fu-sheng. After the Sino-Japanese war of 1895, he promoted new learning in Hunan. Attracted by the Society for National Strength and New Learning founded by K'ang Yu-wei in Peking, he went there to see him. K'ang had left for his native Kwangtung, but T'an met the secretary of the society, Liang Ch'i-ch'ao. In 1896 he was put on the waiting list to become a prefect, spending the year at Nanking where he studied Buddhism. In the next year he and Liang promoted modern education in Hunan. When the reform of 1898 was started by K'ang in Peking, they were called there to help. T'an was appointed one of four secretaries in the Grand Council to supervise the reforms. He was sent to persuade Yüan Shih-k'ai (1858-1916), commander of an army guarding the capital, to help the reformers and eliminate the opposition. Yüan promised him but betrayed the reformers. As a result T'an was arrested and executed. For greater details see Hummel, ed., *Eminent Chinese*, pp. 702-705.
[2] Liang Ch'i-ch'ao, *Yin-ping-shih wen-chi* (Collection of Literary Works of Yin-ping Study), 1st collection, 1936, 3:51a.
[3] On the question of K'ang's influence of T'an, see Chan, "K'ang Yu-wei and the Confucian Doctrine of Humanity (*Jen*)," in Lo, Jung-pang, ed., *K'ang Yu-wei*.

extent. For example, whereas K'ang brought in the idea of *jen* as penetration incidentally, T'an made it his basic concept, or "the first principle," as he put it. But the most important refinement is that while K'ang merely mentioned ether as *jen*, he attempted to formulate some sort of system and postulate *jen* in the sense of ether as the element of elements, as uncreated and indestructible, and as the source of all elements of existence and of all creatures. In doing so he was the first one to regard *jen* not only as a characteristic of reality but as reality itself. He is still the only one in Chinese history to have devoted a whole book to *jen*.

No other Chinese philosophical concept has gone through so many interesting phases of development as *jen*. Before Confucius' time, it was the specific virtue of benevolence. Confucius turned it into the universal virtue and basis of all goodness. In the Han times (206 B.C.–A.D. 220) it was interpreted as love, affection, and "people living together." In Han Yü (768-824), it became universal love. Neo-Confucianists of the Sung period (960-1279) understood it variously as impartiality, consciousness, unity with Heaven and Earth, the character of love and the principle of the mind, the character of production and reproduction, seeds that generate virtue, and so forth. And now K'ang describes it in terms of ether and electricity and T'an identifies it with the indestructible element of all elements of existence. In bringing the development to a higher stage, T'an has made a significant contribution.[4]

SELECTIONS

1. Ether and Humanity

Throughout the realms of elements of existence (dharmas),[5] empty space, and sentient beings, there is something supremely refined and subtle, which makes everything adhere, penetrates everything, and connects everything so that all is permeated by it. The eye cannot see its color, the ear cannot hear its sound, and the mouth and nose cannot perceive its flavor and fragrance. There is no name for it but we shall call it ether. As manifested in function, Confucius referred to it as humanity (*jen*), origination, and nature. Mo Tzu (fl. 479–438 B.C.) referred to it as universal love. The Buddha referred to it as ocean of ultimate nature (all-embracing reality) and compassion, Jesus referred to it as the soul and as loving others as oneself and regarding one's enemies as friends, and scientists refer to it as the power of love and power of attraction. They all refer to this thing. The realms of elements of existence, empty space, and sentient beings all issue from it.

[4] For comments on *jen*, see above, ch. 30, sec. 1; ch. 31, secs. 1 and 11; ch. 32, sec. 42; and ch. 34, sec. 1.
[5] For the translation of this term, see Appendix, comment on *Fa*.

There is nothing more intimate to man than his body. There are more than two hundred bones and in addition a great number of tendons, muscles, blood vessels, and internal organs. It is ether alone that produces them, makes them adhere, and causes them not to scatter apart. It is ether alone that causes men to go from individuals to the (five human relations) between husband and wife, father and son, elder and younger brothers, ruler and minister, and friends, and from individuals to families, states, and the world, and remain interrelated without scattering apart. It is ether alone that causes the earth . . . the moon . . . the planets . . . the infinite number of worlds . . . to attract each other and not to scatter apart. (*Jen-hsüeh*, or Philosophy of Humanity, in *T'an Liu-yang ch'üan-chi*, or Complete Works of T'an Ssu-t'ung, Shanghai, 1917, pt. 1, 3a-4a)

The most intelligent function of ether that can be shown by evidence is the brain in the case of man . . . and electricity in the case of empty space. Electricity is not confined to space, for there is nothing which it does not integrate and penetrate. The brain is one of the instances in which electricity assumes physical form and solid substance. Since the brain is electricity with physical form and solid substance, then electricity must be brain without physical form or solid substance. Since men know that it is the power of the brain that pervades throughout the five sense organs and the hundred bones and makes them one body, they should know that the power of electricity pervades throughout heaven, earth, the ten thousand things, the self and the other, and makes them one body. . . . Electricity is everywhere. It follows that the self is everywhere. Erroneously to make a distinction between the self and the other is to be without humanity. . . . Without humanity, the same body would be like different regions. . . . Therefore the distinction between humanity and inhumanity lies in whether there is penetration or obstruction. The basis of penetration or obstruction is simply humanity or inhumanity. Penetration is like electric lines reaching out in all directions, and there is nowhere which they do not reach. This means that different regions are like one body. . . . Unless I can penetrate heaven, earth, all things, myself and other selves as one body, I shall have no way to appreciate the knowledge of that which penetrates and I would regard it as strange. Actually, if there is penetration throughout the self, which knows all, there is nothing strange at all. The difference between having knowledge and having no knowledge depends on whether there is humanity or not. There is only humanity in the universe; there is no wisdom to speak of. (*ibid.*, 4a-6a)

Comment. Here T'an departs from K'ang. Instead of equally emphasizing humanity and wisdom, as K'ang did, T'an stresses humanity exclusively.

If humanity is violated, will ether become extinct? *Answer*: There is no extinction. Not only does ether not become extinct; humanity does not, of course. None can extinguish them and they cannot become extinct in any case. To violate it or to extinguish it means not to follow the order which it possesses. Who can arbitrarily make an existing thing nonexistent? By the same token, none can arbitrarily make a nonexistent thing existent. Since none can arbitrarily make a nonexistent thing existent, even a person as perfectly humane as Heaven cannot augment humanity by any degree. And since none can arbitrarily make an existent thing nonexistent, even a person as inhumane as beasts cannot diminish it by any degree. It cannot be augmented because there is no production, and it cannot be diminished because there is no extinction. Knowing that there is neither production nor extinction, we can then talk about human nature. . . . Nature is a function of ether. Since ether possesses the power to cause things to perfect each other and to love each other, therefore we say that human nature is good. (*ibid.*, 8a)

2. The Principle of Nature and Human Desires

Ordinary society and petty scholars regard the Principle of Nature (*T'ien-li*) as good and human desires as evil. They do not realize that without human desires there cannot be any Principle of Nature. I therefore feel sad that the world has erroneously made a distinction between them. The Principle of Nature is good, but human desires are also good. Wang Fu-chih (Wang Ch'uan-shan, 1619-1692) said that the Principle of Nature is within human desires and that without human desires the Principle of Nature cannot be revealed.[6] This agrees with the Buddhist doctrines that the Buddha and all sentient things are identical and that ignorance (*avidyā*) and Thusness (*Tathatā*, True Reality)[7] are the same.

Let us prove it. Function has been called evil, it is true. But a name is only a name and not an actuality. Function is also a name and not an actuality. How did names originate? When did function begin? Names are given by men and function is given its name by men. They are all products of men. "Function" is only one of many names. Why do we say this? Sexual intercourse is called lust. "Lust" is but a name. This name has been followed for long since the beginning of man, and has not been changed, and therefore people have customarily called lust evil. But suppose from the beginning of man there had been the custom of

6 See above, ch. 36, sec. 6.
7 For this concept, see above, ch. 24, n.19.

considering this lust as a great institution in imperial audiences and public banquets, practicing it in imperial temples, in cities, and in the midst of large crowds, like kneeling and bowing low in China and embracing and kissing in the West, and being followed as a tradition up to the present, who will know that it is evil? Somehow it was called evil and as a result people have considered it evil. (*ibid.*, 8b-9a)

> *Comment.* T'an was the first one to have launched such a frontal attack on Confucian moral dogmas. This is extraordinary, for he was essentially a Confucianist.

3. Neither Production nor Extinction

Is there any evidence that there is neither production nor extinction? *Answer*: You can see it everywhere. For example, take the principles of chemistry already referred to. Even if we study them to the utmost, they involve no more than analyzing a certain number of physical elements to divide and synthesizing to combine them. All we do is to make use of what elements there already and necessarily are and take into consideration their attraction or repulsion at the time, and adjust their proficiency or deficiency, and call the product this or that thing, that is all. How can we eliminate a physical element or create another one? (*ibid.*, 12b-13a)

4. Daily Renovation

What is seen by our eye or heard by our ear is not the real object itself. The eye has a lens. When the shape of the thing enters it, it makes an image. . . . By the time the image is made, the shape of the thing has long been gone. Furthermore, the image depends on the brain to be known. By that time the image itself has become a past image and the true image cannot be seen. . . .

When we view things in the opposite direction from those that are gone, we have what is called daily renovation. Confucius said, "The symbolism of the *ko* (change) hexagram means to cast away the old and the *ting* (caldron, symbolizing reform) hexagram means to take on the new."[8] He also said, "Its (the Way's) virtue is abundant because it renovates things every day."[9] Good reaches its limit when it is daily renewed, and evil also reaches its end when it does not daily renew. If heaven does not renew itself, how can it produce things? If the earth does not renew itself, how can it revolve? If the sun and moon do not renew themselves, how can they be bright? And if the four seasons do not renew themselves, how can there be the cold and warm seasons?. . .

---

[8] *Changes*, "Random Remarks on the Hexagrams." Cf. Legge, trans., *Yi King*, p. 443. *Ko* and *ting* are the 49th and 50th hexagrams in the *Book of Changes*.

[9] *ibid.*, "Appended Remarks," pt. 1, ch. 5. Cf. Legge, *ibid.*, p. 356.

If ether does not renew itself, all the elements of existence in the three realms (the threefold world of sensuous desire, of form, and of formless world of pure spirit, that is, our world) will become extinct. . . .

> *Comment.* The idea of daily renovation is a traditional one. In quoting Confucius about casting away the old, T'an is hinting at the idea of renovation not only as a new phase but as reform or even revolution, for that is what the caldron symbolizes. Unfortunately T'an did not develop this idea.

On what is daily renovation based? It is based on the activating power of ether. Have you not heard thunder? There is nothing in the vast and quiet empty space. Then suddenly cloud and rain meet, involving two charges of electricity. As there are two charges, there are the positive and the negative. As there are the positive and the negative, there are similarity and difference. Because of difference, there will be mutual attack, and because of similarity, there will be mutual attraction. Thus fleeting lightning and roaring thunder burst out. . . . Sweet rain follows and gentle wind moves back and forth. . . . As a result, all kinds of things flourish and thus grow and mature. Is this not because of the activity of ether which goes on indefinitely? This may be said to be the beginning of humanity. . . . Do those who govern the world well not follow this way? They advance and change, lead the people and work hard, create and promote things, raise what is neglected, and replace what is worn out. . . . (*ibid.*, 23a-b)

41

CHANG TUNG-SUN'S THEORY OF KNOWLEDGE

NOT SINCE the third century B.C. have there been "one hundred schools" of thought contending in China as in the twentieth century. The combination of Western thought and revolt against traditional heritage caused many intellectual currents to run in all directions. The introduction of modern Western philosophy began with Yen Fu's (1853-1921) translation of Huxley's *Evolution and Ethics* in 1898. His translation of works of Mill, Spencer, and Montesquieu soon followed. At the turn of the century, ideas of Schopenhauer, Kant, Nietzsche, Rousseau, Tolstoi, and Kropotkin were imported. After the intellectual renaissance of 1917, the movement advanced at rapid pace. In the following decade important works of Descartes, Spinoza, Hume, James, Bergson, Marx, and others became available in Chinese. Dewey, Russell, and Dreisch came to China to lecture, and special numbers of journals were devoted to Nietzsche and Bergson. Clubs and even schools were formed to promote a particular philosophy. Almost every trend of Western thought had its exponent. James, Bergson, Eucken, Whitehead, Hocking, Schiller, T. H. Green, Carnap, and C. I. Lewis had their own following. For a time it seemed Chinese thought was to be completely Westernized.

But that was not to be the case. Simultaneously with the propagation of Western thought, efforts were made to revive and reconstruct Chinese philosophy. We have already seen the attempt by T'an Ssu-t'ung (1865-1898). The great rebel Sun Yat-sen (1866-1925) himself incorporated part of Confucian ethics into his political ideology. In 1921, Liang Souming (1893-1962) championed Confucian moral values and aroused the Chinese to a degree seldom seen in the contemporary world. Both Ouyang Ching-wu (1871-1943) and Abbot T'ai-hsü (1889-1947) promoted the revival of the Buddhist Consciousness-Only philosophy for many years. While Liang created a strong current in reevaluating and revitalizing Confucianism, he did not develop a philosophy of his own. Neither Ou-yang nor T'ai-hsü added anything really new to Buddhist philosophy in spite of the latter's attempt to synthesize it with Western thought and modern science. The two outstanding philosophers who have achieved concrete success in reconstructing traditional philosophy and establishing a system of their own are Fung Yu-lan (1895—) and Hsiung Shih-li (1885-1968) who will be the subjects of the next two chapters. Significantly, they have derived their philosophies from the two

743

major Neo-Confucian tendencies, the rationalistic and the idealistic, respectively.

The number of scholars advocating Western philosophy has been far greater than those oriented toward Chinese thought, although they cannot match the latter group either in originality or in influence until Marxism overcame China. Pragmatism, introduced and advocated by Hu Shih (1891-1962), vitalism, materialism, and new realism were particularly strong. But these were but Western philosophy transplanted on Chinese soil without any fundamental change. Chin Yüeh-lin (1894 —), an expert in logical analysis and much influenced by T. H. Green, has developed his own system of logic and a metaphysics based on it. The one who has assimilated the most of Western thought, established the most comprehensive and well coordinated system, and has exerted the greatest influence among the Western oriented Chinese philosophers, however, is indisputably Chang Tung-sun (1886-1962).[1]

Chang is a self-educated man. From editor of newspapers and magazines, he rose to be a professor and dean of several universities. He has never been to the West but has translated Plato's *Dialogues* and Bergson's *Matter and Memory* and *Creative Evolution*, among others, into Chinese, and has read more of Western philosophy than perhaps any of his Chinese colleagues. He has written thirteen books, in which he has developed a system which may be called revised Kantianism, epistemological pluralism, or panstructuralism.

Chiefly formulated between 1929 and 1947, Chang's philosophy is derived from Kant but he rejects Kant's bifurcation of reality into the manifold and unity and the division of the nature of knowledge into the given and the innate. To him knowledge is a synthetic product of sense data, form, and methodological assumption. Perception, conception, mind, and consciousness are all syntheses or "constructs," and constructs are products of society and culture. He said that he has combined Western logic with modern psychology and sociology, but that his system is his own. He shows not only the influence of Kant and Hume, but also that of Dewey, Russell, and Lewis.

During World War II he shifted more and more from metaphysics to

[1] He was a native of Chekiang. Some say he was born in 1884. He did not study in Tokyo University as sometimes stated but did spend some time in Japan. After serving as an editor of various newspapers and magazines and as a university professor in Shanghai and Canton, he became a professor in Yenching University in Peking. Originally a leader of the Progressive Party, he later became a leader of the State Socialist Party and as such was opposed to both the Nationalist Party and the Communist Party. During World War II, he was imprisoned by the Japanese in Peking. After the war he left his party and joined the leftist Democratic League. In 1949 he became a member of the Central Committee of the People's Government in Peking. Soon afterward he retired. He died in 1962.

the sociology of knowledge and thus was drawn closer to Marxism. This is a far cry from his anti-Marxian stand in 1934 when he edited a symposium mostly critical of dialectical materialism. But his theory of concepts as products of culture made it easy, if not inevitable, for him to accept the Marxian philosophy.

The following selections are from his two most important philosophical works, the *Jen-shih lun* (Epistemology), Shanghai, 1934, and the *Chih-shih yü wen-hua* (Knowledge and Culture), Chungking and Shanghai, 1946.

SELECTIONS

In my theory, the knowing cannot be absorbed by the known, nor can the known be absorbed by the knowing. But my theory is different from epistemological dualism, for it only recognizes the opposition of subject and object, which seems to me to be too simple. Of course my theory is also a kind of epistemological criticism. . . . For example, critical realism is a tri-ism, for it holds that apart from mind or the knowing and matter or the known, there is also what is called "meaning as essence." The critical philosophy of Kant still resorts to bifurcation, although not obviously, for he separates sense data and form, except that the latter can advance progressively. My epistemological pluralism may be said to follow Kant's path generally. But there are important points of difference, and that is that I do not consider form as a subjective construction. Unlike Kant, I do not regard the external world as without order, or regard sense data as material for knowledge. I hold that sensation cannot give us orderly knowledge. Although I agree with Kant in this, I disagree with him in that I hold that order cannot be entirely the product of the synthesizing power of the mind. For this reason I hold that there is order in the external world and that there is also construction in the internal world. The construction in the internal world is further divided into two, namely, the a priori form of intuition and the a priori form of understanding. As to sensation, it is not really an existent. Therefore there are several aspects in my theory and I have therefore called it pluralism. (*Jen-shih lun*, pp. 45-46)

> *Comment.* Aside from these technical differences from Kant, Chang also thinks that Kant's theory of knowledge is within the limits of the Western type of knowledge and therefore has no universal validity. Since Chang's approach is fundamentally sociological, it is inevitable that he looks upon Kant's epistemology as having been conditioned by his time and culture.

As to the origin of knowledge, an epistemological pluralist thinks that it should not be generally discussed. Knowledge is a synthetic product of sense data, form, and assumption. There is no knowledge apart from sense data, form, or assumption. But as there are sense data, there must be an order behind them. . . . Therefore with respect to the nature of knowledge, we can hold the view that between two ends there is the middle section. At the one end is the knower, and at the other end the known. . . . At the end of the knower, there are external things which are absolutely unknowable but there is also an external world that is relatively knowable. At the end of the known there is the self which is absolutely unknowable but also an internal world which is relatively knowable. . . . Although epistemological pluralism adopts the theory of functionalism, nevertheless it does not hold that knowledge is produced only because of action. To regard knowledge as an instrument of action is an extreme of functionalism. Although knowledge cannot be separated from action or even restricted by it, nevertheless knowledge itself is not the product of action nor does it exist solely as an instrument of action. I hold that knowledge and action are intimately related but do not admit that action can absorb knowledge. . . .

In short, our universe has no substance of its own. It is only a construct. The process of construction is not entirely natural, and there must be the part of our knowing activity in it. For we cannot cast aside knowledge and see the true nature of this construct. Although in our knowledge this construct is not what it is originally, nevertheless it certainly does not deviate too much from its original nature. We can therefore say that the universe is a construct. (*ibid.*, pp. 123-133)

Scholars have generally divided knowledge into two general types. One is called direct acquaintance and the other indirect comprehension. . . . Of course we also accept this general distinction and use the common terms of sense perception and conception, but we prefer to regard one as perceptual knowledge and the other as interpretative knowledge. For example, when I see a lump of black stuff moving, accompanied by some rumbling noise, I immediately know that it is a train. For us adults this recognition is instantaneous. Surely we do not "see" it and at the same time do not "know" what it is. For the sake of analysis, however, we assign what appears as a dark lump that moves to "acquaintance" and the recognition that it is a train to "discrimination." Some hold that the former is the material for knowledge while the latter is the faculty of knowledge. Without material there is nothing for the faculty to work with and without the faculty material cannot function even if it was there. The former is sensation, whereas the latter is conception induced by sensation. Therefore this distinction between direct acquaintance and indirect discrimination is merely a kind of analysis. They are not two different independent parts. . . . Although (direct) acquaintance merely exists in (indirect)[2] discrimination, nevertheless there is no necessary relation between them. . . . There can be different understandings of the same perception. It seems that this point has been overlooked by the sensationistic empiricists. They think that all kinds of knowledge can be reverted back to direct acquaintance, thus wiping out all explanations and discriminations. In this way it is very difficult to explain why there is error. We must realize that there is error only because perception and thought do not agree. If our knowledge always depends on direct acquaintance and is in accord with its face value, then the question of error cannot be answered. It is because of this that new realism has been criticized. . . . In short, direct acquaintance and discrimination cannot be separated. There is no direct acquaintance which is not involved in discrimination, and there is no discrimination which does not involve direct acquaintance. . . .

In psychology, act and content are usually distinguished as two different aspects. . . . We must realize that act is involved in content and content is produced by act. The two cannot be separated, for they are but the two aspects of the same thing. . . . Modern science supports my view, namely, that content is produced by act. For this reason I feel that what Kant saw more than a hundred years ago is not inferior to what contemporary scholars see. The idea of threefold synthesis presented in his *Critique of Pure Reason* really cannot be shaken. Unfortunately he almost did not explain sensation at all. What I am doing is to amend his deficiency with the relatively reliable theories of modern psychology.

> *Comment.* One wonders if Chang's persistent refusal to accept any absolute bifurcation is not an influence of Chinese traditional thought, for the doctrines that "substance and function come from the same source"[3] and that knowledge and action form a unity have been major Chinese traditions. Chang is a profound student of both Neo-Confucianism and Buddhism.

On the basis of the ideas set forth above, we must first of all admit that "mind" or "consciousness" is merely an act of continuous and progressively advanced synthesis. Progress from psychological activities on the low level (such as sensing a shadow or form) to those on the high level (such as thought and judgment), form all but continuous stages in this synthesis. Synthesis can advance continuously to the degree of changing its nature. In other words, synthesis can advance from one

---

[2] These and the following parentheses are Chang's own.

[3] Ch'eng I (Ch'eng I-ch'uan, 1033-1107), preface to the *I chuan* (Commentary on the *Book of Changes*), in ECCS.

level to another and thus move up so that the content of each level becomes different. I call the result of this synthesis "the constructs." Even that which synthesizes is a product of synthesis.

We must realize that sensation is still only a synthesis, although it is on the lowest level, or a synthesis that tends to be biological. As to the ordinary person's idea that whiteness, hotness, or fragrance is a simple thing, that is wrong. Kant called this thoroughgoing synthesis a *Verbindung*, but I rather call it collectively "physical integration." Within it there are four levels, to each of which I have given a name. With respect to sensation I call it "fusion or sensory fusion." With respect to perception, I call it "configuration." With respect to conception, I call it "unification." And with respect to categories, I call it "regulation." (*Chih-shih yü wen-hua*, pp. 7-9)

Now we have to explain unification, or the nature of concepts. We must realize that sensation is necessarily related to perception and perception to conception. In their aspect of advancing upward, they are continuous. But in their special characteristics, perception involves meaning which sensation does not possess, and concepts can enter into another person's mind, which perception cannot do. . . .

According to Kant, no knowledge can be separated from concepts. This means that when we discriminate a thing or an event, we simply have to use concepts. Without concepts there will be no knowledge. What is called knowledge is simply the use of concepts we already have and concepts newly formed. Therefore it is quite natural that perception changes to concepts. But when we analyze them, we cannot help saying that conception is more advanced than perception, that is all. For a concept can detach itself from the immediate perception and goes from one's own mind into another person's mind.

Now our question is this: How is a concept produced? In other words, how is it formed? Of course concept is formed by "unification to become one. . . ." We learn in psychology that perception always leaves an image . . . . When the image becomes weaker and weaker, it naturally changes to be a sign. A sign means a vague and general outline. When the sign is transferred, it becomes a symbol. By transferring is meant that a sign for A becomes the sign for B. This is the mobility of signs. I believe that this is the origin of the concepts of things, because as soon as the sign appears, the concept is formed. What we ordinarily call a concept is really a sign. We talk about the origin of concepts purely from the point of view of psychological process. In reality a concept is the same as a sign, and a sign is the same as a concept. In short, a concept is not like what the new realists call the subsistent which subsists in things but exists in them as an independent entity. [On the contrary] a concept is formed when a concreta changes from a sign into a symbol and can be applied to another concreta so that it becomes an abstraction. . . .

The concreta from which the concept emerges is not limited to the object of perception. The most important concreta is the meaning of the perception, and relation is one of the meanings. All of these can be abstracted to be concepts. For example, when I see two things, I perceive that they coexist. This coexistence can become a concept. Or I perceive that A is larger than B. This comparative largeness can also become a concept. . . .

The reason why a concept can become a norm for other concepts is that when a concept arises, it immediately becomes a world or group of concepts, in which all concepts are related. In other words, in a group of concepts, the concept with the strongest normalizing power can cause other concepts to follow it and change their color (or become tainted by its color). Although this normalizing function only operates among the concepts themselves, it does definitely have a negative condition, and that is that the concept cannot conflict with perception or oppose it. If in perception there appears a phenomenon conflicting with it, the concept will immediately collapse. Then another concept must emerge to explain the phenomenon, so that the new phenomenon and other existing concepts will not conflict. This is why experimental knowledge can correct and revise concepts.

If it is necessary to give examples to show that concepts can be advanced to categories, we have some excellent ones. Take, for example, purpose. This concept arose from the fact that primitive people felt that they had the will to do something. Gradually this feeling is broadened until it is believed that all changes are due to a will. Take, for example, a man killed by lightning. Primitive people thought it was God's will that he died. The man's death is a fact. It remains the same but its interpretations are different. Explained in scientific terms, it is electric shock, and in terms of superstition, it is God's punishment. These two interpretations are completely compatible with the culture of their times. If in our day of scientific culture we still believe that it is God's punishment, we will be considered wrong. But in the whole of ancient culture, only the theory of God's punishment was compatible. Therefore it could not have been discovered by the people of the time that it was not the truth . . . . (*ibid.*, pp. 19-26)

Western religious concepts like God and Supreme Being and philosophical concepts like substance, ultimate stuff, the highest idea, oneness, and the absolute all serve to reflect society as a whole, so that when people believe in them they will feel more and more united with it and will be willing to sacrifice for it. For when society needs a centripetal force stronger than the centrifugal force, some theory or idea must arise to hold the people together so that they feel in their own minds that it is the truth and only then will they be willing to practice it and seek its realization. We must realize that any concept has a suggestive power. French scholars have called it the idea force. The term itself (that is, the concept) has a suggestive power to urge us to move toward a united society. On the other hand, philosophical concepts like freedom, personality, and dialectics all reflect social conflicts. When people believe in them, a psychology of conflict naturally arises in society. . . .

Since government is a "force," it is in itself a necessary evil. But the degree of its evil cannot be higher than the degree of goodness which society needs. Otherwise society will completely disintegrate. This is a natural check and balance. Therefore no matter in what evil society, when moralists promote social unity they always have an appeal to people, can exert their influence, and can prove their usefulness. What we have been talking about does not concern society as such but to show how social conditions are reflected in ideas so readers may realize that while ideas seem on the surface to be independent and represent laws of logic or the structure of the universe that we talk about, actually they are secretly controlled by social needs, that is all. . . . (*ibid.*, pp. 80-82)

42

THE NEW RATIONALISTIC CONFUCIANISM:
FUNG YU-LAN

THERE IS NO DOUBT that Fung Yu-lan (1895—) has been the most outstanding philosopher in China in the last thirty years.[1] He was already on the way to sure prominence when he published his two-volume *History of Chinese Philosophy*[2] in 1930, 1934. With the publication of his *Hsin li-hsüeh* (The New Rational Philosophy) in 1939, his position as the leading Chinese philosopher was firmly established. It is the most original Chinese philosophical work in this century. It has been the most discussed. Aside from Hsiung Shih-li's *Hsin wei-shih lun* (New Doctrine of Consciousness-Only) it is also the only work in twentieth-century China presenting a person's comprehensive philosophical system. Significantly, Fung's system is a reconstruction of rationalistic Neo-Confucianism while Hsiung's is a reconstruction of idealistic Neo-Confucianism.

The term *li-hsüeh*, literally "school of principle," is the usual name for the Neo-Confucianism of Sung (960-1279) and Ming (1368-1644) times. Fung explicitly said that his system is derived from, though does not follow, Neo-Confucianism.[3] It is based on four main metaphysical concepts, namely, principle (*li*), material force (*ch'i*), the substance of Tao, and the Great Whole.[4] Collectively, they are deduced from the statement that "Something exists." They are all formal concepts and logical implications, empty and without content.[5] Specifically, each of them is deduced from a proposition or a set of propositions developed chiefly in the rationalistic Neo-Confucianism of Ch'eng I (Ch'eng I-ch'uan, 1033-1107) and Chu Hsi (1130-1200) but also in Taoism.

The first concept, that of principle, is derived from the Ch'eng-Chu proposition that "As there are things, there must be their specific principles."[6] In order to be, a thing must follow the principle by which it is what it is.

---

[1] He is from Honan. After graduating from Peking University in 1919, he went to Columbia University and obtained a Ph.D. in 1923. Returning to China, he was a professor in various universities and from 1928 on was professor and dean of Tsing-hua University in Peking. In 1933, he lectured in England. During World War II, he was dean at the Southwest Associated University. He has been visiting professor at the University of Pennsylvania and University of Hawaii and has an LL.D. from Princeton. He is now professor at Peking University.

[2] See Bibliography.   [3] See also his *Spirit of Chinese Philosophy*, p. 204.

[4] *ibid.*, p. 205. For comments on the translation of the terms *li* and *ch'i* see Appendix.

[5] *ibid.*, p. 205; Fung, *Short History of Chinese Philosophy*, p. 335.

[6] *Hsin li-hsüeh*, p. 53; *Spirit of Chinese Philosophy*, p. 205.

Principle is self-existent, absolute, eternal, a universal as understood in Kung-sun Lung (b. 380 B.C.?)[7] and in Western philosophy. It is neither in nor above the world, for in itself it does not enter into any temporal or spatial relationship. A thing needs to follow principle but principle does not have to be actualized in a thing. It belongs to the realm of reality but not actuality.[8] Hence there are more principles than are actualized in the world. The sum total of principles is the Great Ultimate.[9]

The second concept, that of material force, is derived, as in the Ch'eng-Chu School, from the proposition that "If there is principle, there must be material force." This means that if a thing is to exist, there must be the material force by which it can exist.[10] This material, comparable to matter in Western philosophy, is the material force in Neo-Confucianism. Being the material of actualization, it has the characteristic of existence but itself does not exist either in principle or in the actual world. Like principle, it is only a formal logical concept.[11]

The third concept, that of the substance of Tao, is derived from the Neo-Confucian proposition of "The Ultimate of Non-being and also the Great Ultimate."[12] This means that the universe is a "universal operation" or a "great functioning" through the processes of "daily renewal"[13] and incessant change.[14]

The fourth concept is that of the Great Whole, Tao, or Heaven,[15] in which, according to Buddhism and Neo-Confucianism, one is all and all is one.[16] This is a formal concept, because it is merely the general name for all and not an assertion about the actual world.[17] It is the Absolute in Western philosophy, just as the concepts of principle, material force, and the substance of Tao may be compared to the concepts of being, non-being, and becoming, respectively.[18]

The Great Whole is the goal of life which is to be fulfilled through the investigation of things, the fulfillment of one's nature, and serving Heaven. When this is done, one will reach the highest sphere of life, that of "forming one body with all things," which is the sphere of "great *jen* (humanity)."

[7] *Hsin li-hsüeh*, p. 43.   [8] *ibid.*, pp. 10, 27-28.
[9] *ibid.*, pp. 38, 42, 47, 53-55, 61-62; *Spirit of Chinese Philosophy*, pp. 205-207.
[10] *Hsin li-hsüeh*, pp. 63-68.
[11] *Spirit of Chinese Philosophy*, pp. 207-209.
[12] Chou Tun-i (Chou Lien-hsi, 1017-1073), *T'ai-chi t'u-shuo* (An Explanation of the Diagram of the Great Ultimate). See above, ch. 28, sec. 1.
[13] A term originating from the *Great Learning*, ch. 2.
[14] *Hsin li-hsüeh*, pp. 97, 99, 100, 109-121; *Spirit of Chinese Philosophy*, pp. 209-211.
[15] *Hsin li-hsüeh*, pp. 36-38.   [16] *Spirit of Chinese Philosophy*, p. 211.
[17] *Hsin li-hsüeh*, p. 40; *Spirit of Chinese Philosophy*, p. 212.
[18] *ibid.*, p. 213.

Such is a bare outline of the *Hsin li-hsüeh*. Following it Fung wrote five books to complete his system in its various phases. The *Hsin shih-lun* (China's Road to Freedom, 1939) deals with social, political and cultural reconstruction and is an economic interpretation of Chinese civilization and history. The *Hsin shih-hsün* (A New Treatise on the Way of Life, 1940) presents his mainly Confucian but to some extent also Taoistic ethics. The *Hsin yüan-jen* (A New Treatise on the Nature of Man, 1943) offers a theory of four different spheres of living. The scheme involves an advance from the innocent sphere where one does not know what he is doing, to the utilitarian sphere where one lives primarily for self-benefit, to the moral sphere of serving society, and finally to the transcendental sphere when one becomes a "citizen of Heaven" and serves Heaven.[19] The *Hsin yüan-tao* (The Spirit of Chinese Philosophy, 1944) interprets the historical development of Chinese philosophy. In the *Hsin chih-yen* (A New Treatise on the Methodology of Metaphysics, 1946), Fung develops his own methodology. These works supplement but do not alter the fundamental position of his philosophy.

Fung frankly calls his own system a "new tradition," which to him not only represents a revival of Chinese philosophy but is also the symbol of a revival of the Chinese nation.[20] Thus his is not only a new system, but also one that continues and reconstructs the orthodox tradition from Confucius through the Sung Neo-Confucianists to himself. Quite aside from this confident sense of destiny, his system is new in the sense that he incorporates into the traditional rationalistic Neo-Confucianism the Western elements of realism and logic as well as the Taoist element of negativism and transcendentalism.[21]

Fung's greatest innovation is of course his conversion of Neo-Confucian ideas into logical concepts. In so doing he has transformed Neo-Confucianism fundamentally. Neo-Confucianism, which is essentially a philosophy of immanence, is now replaced by one of transcendence. In Neo-Confucianism, problems of the mind and the nature are basic, and metaphysical speculation about the universe is intended primarily to help understand them. Fung considers the mind and the nature to belong to the world of actuality, and does not seem to take them as seriously as logical concepts. In emphasizing universals, he found more of them in Chinese philosophy than there really are. To interpret Kung-sun Lung's *chih* (mark?) as a universal is no more than a conjecture. As to principle, if it only belongs to the realm of reality and does not imply actuality, is the actual world then an accident or even a mistake? How can reality be

---

[19] *Short History of Chinese Philosophy*, pp. 338-339.

[20] *Spirit of Chinese Philosophy*, ch. 10; *Short History of Chinese Philosophy*, p. 335.

[21] *Spirit of Chinese Philosophy*, pp. 203-204.

real without existence? How can principle be the moral nature of things and yet in our nature transcends the actual world? If principle is not immanent in things, it is difficult to conceive any direct relation between universal operation and principle. In rejecting the Neo-Confucian philosophy of immanence, he also undermines its practical and this-worldly character. This is in direct opposition to the persistent tendency of Chinese philosophy and raises the serious question whether Fung's claim of a new tradition is justified.

These questions call for answers. The more vital question, however, is whether Fung still holds this new rational philosophy. In 1950 he repudiated it, saying that it is but a twilight of old Chinese philosophy, just as Neo-Thomism is a twilight of Western philosophy. He regretted his neglect of the concrete and the particular, and compared Marxism-Leninism to modern medicine and traditional Chinese philosophy to medieval medicine.[22] Later in the year he specifically renounced the main thesis of his five books mentioned above. To him becoming a citizen of Heaven was no longer the highest sphere of living but escapism. As to the *Hsin li-shüeh* itself, he said that it over-stressed the universal and was too strongly influenced by Taoism and Buddhism, thus reflecting the crumbling feudal society.[23]

It is difficult to appraise utterances of this sort. Fung's attraction to Marxism is by no means an unlikely possibility. After all, as early as 1939, he wrote his *Hsin shih-lun* from the point of view of materialistic interpretation of history. Later he said that the Taoist idea of returning to the root or reversion and the whole concept of daily renewal are dialectic. In 1952, however, he maintained that the difference between the new philosophy and the old philosophy in China is that the former is close to the people. The old philosophy should be criticized, he added, but what is correct in it should be adopted.[24] In 1957, he argued that Confucius was not a materialist but an idealist who brought facts into harmony with abstract concepts, as when he said, "Let the ruler [fact] *be* a ruler [concept].[25] To defend both idealism and abstract concepts when these were under strong attack seems to indicate that much of traditional Chinese philosophy in general and his own philosophy in par-

[22] See his "I discovered Marxism-Leninism," *People's China*, 1, 1950, no. 6, p. 11.

[23] "*Hsin li-hsüeh ti tzu-wo chien-t'ao* (Self-appraisal about the *New Rational Philosophy*)," *Kuang-min jih-pao* (Bright Light Daily), Oct. 8, 1950; reprinted in *Hsin-hua yüeh-pao* (New China Monthly), 3, 1950, no. 1, pp. 193-197.

[24] "Philosophy in New China According to Fung Yu-lan," *East and West*, July. 1952, pp. 105-107. For a digest of the article, see *Far East Digest*, no. 66, 1952, pp. 12-13.

[25] Fung, "Problems in the Study of Confucius," *People's China*, 1957, no. 1, pp. 21-22, 27-31. The quotation is from *Analects*, 12:11.

ticular is still with him. More will be said about him in chapter forty-four. We are here concerned solely with his new rationalism for which the following selections have been made from his *Hsin li-hsüeh*, Changsha, 1939.

SELECTIONS

1. The World and Principle

What makes a thing square is the square. As explained before, the square can be real but not actual. If in fact there are no actual square things, the square is then not actual. But if in fact there are actual square things, they must have four corners. An actual square thing necessarily follows that which makes a square square; it cannot avoid this. From this we know that the square is real. Since the square is real but not actual, it belongs to the realm of pure reality. . . .

When we say "There is a square," we are making a formal affirmation about reality. The statement "There is a square" does not imply an actual square thing. Much less does it imply a particular actual square thing. Therefore the statement does not affirm anything about actuality, but merely makes a formal affirmation about reality. From the point of view of our acquisition of knowledge, we must in our experience see an actual square thing before we can say that there is a square. But since we have said that there is square, we see that even if in fact there is no actual square thing, we still can say there is a square. (pp. 27-28)

Chu Hsi regards principle as that by which actual things necessarily are what they are and the specific principle according to which they should be. Our idea of principle is the same. A square thing must follow the principle of the square before it can be square, and it must completely follow the principle of the square before it can be perfectly square. Whether a square thing is perfectly square depends on whether or not it follows the principle of the square completely. According to this reasoning, the principle of the square is the standard of all square things; it is the specific principle according to which they should be. The *Book of Odes* says, "Heaven produces the teeming multitude. As there are things, there are their specific principles."[26] This was often quoted by the Neo-Confucianists of the Sung period. Ch'eng I-ch'uan said, "As there are things, there must be their specific principles. One thing necessarily has one principle."[27] The principle of a class of things is the same as the specific principle of that class of things. We often say, "This square thing is more square or less square than the other square thing." In saying so we are following this standard. Without this standard

[26] Ode no. 260.
[27] *I-shu* (Surviving Works), 18:9a, in ECCS.

no criticism is possible. Those who do not accept the existence of principle have overlooked this point. (p. 53)

Sung Neo-Confucianists also have the theory that the "principle is one but its manifestations are many," which Chu Hsi also held. But when he talked about principle being one and its manifestations being many, the principle he talked about is already different from the principle when he discussed it [as such]. In commenting on the *Western Inscription* by Chang Heng-ch'ü (Chang Tsai, 1020-1077), Chu Hsi said, ". . . . There is nothing in the entire realm of creatures that does not regard Heaven as the father and Earth as the mother. This means that the principle is one. . . . Each regards his parents as his own parents and his son as his own son. This being the case, how can principle not be manifested as many?. . ."[28] The principle referred to here concerns the realm of that which exists after physical form and is with it (*hsing-erh-hsia*). It makes an affirmation about actuality. According to this theory, among individual, actual things there are certain internal relations. But this is a question about actuality. To say that there must be relations [among them] is to make an affirmation about actuality.

In our system we can still say that "the principle is one but its manifestations are many." But when we say so, the principle we are talking about is still the principle when we discuss it as such. Let us first take things in a certain class. The things in this class all follow one principle. However, although they all follow the same principle, they each have their own individuality. From the point of view of things of this class being related within the class, we can say that their principle is one but its manifestations are many. As we said before, the principle of a class implies the principle of a general class. From the point of view of specific classes within a general class, all specific classes belong to the general class but at the same time possess that which makes them specific classes. The relation among the specific classes within the general class can also be stated in terms that the principle is one but its manifestations are many. . . .

This is our theory that the principle is one but its manifestations are many. This theory is presented in its logical aspect. It only makes an affirmation about reality. It does not imply that there are internal relations among actual things, and therefore does not make any affirmation about actuality. (pp. 60-62)

Comment. The doctrine of principle being one and its manifestations being many is in Neo-Confucianism precisely taught to har-

[28] See above, ch. 30, sec. 1. See *Chang Tzu ch'üan-shu* (Complete Works of Master Chang), SPPY, 1:7a, Chu Hsi's comment following the *Western Inscription*.

monize the abstract universal and the concrete particular.[29] Instead, Fung applies the doctrine only to the realm of reality, thus leaving multiplicity in the realm of actuality still to be accounted for.

2. Principle and Material Force

There are two aspects in every actually existing thing, namely, its "what" and that on which it depends for its existence or to become actually what it is. For example, every round thing has two aspects. One is that "it is round." The other is that on which it depends for existence, that is, to become actually round. This "what" is the thing's essential element in the class to which it belongs and the thing's nature. The reason that it exists is the foundation of the thing's existence. Its "what" depends on the principle it follows. That on which it depends for existence is the material which actualizes the principle. . . .

Material is either relative or absolute. Relative material has the two aspects just described. Absolute material, on the other hand, has only one of these aspects, namely, that it can be material simple and pure. Take a building, for example. . . . Bricks and tiles are material for the building, but they are relative and not absolute material. Earth is material for bricks and tiles, but it is still relative and not absolute material, for it still possesses the two aspects described above. . . .

When the nature of the building is removed, it will cease to be a building but only bricks and tiles. When the nature of bricks and tiles is removed, they will cease to be bricks and tiles but only earth. The nature of earth can also be removed, *ad infinitum*. At the end there is the absolute material. This material is called matter in the philosophies of Plato and Aristotle. . . . Matter itself has no nature. Because it has no nature whatsoever, it is indescribable, inexplicable in speech, and unrealizable in thought. . . .

We call this material *ch'i* (material force). . . . In our system material force is entirely a logical concept. It is neither a principle nor an actual thing. An actual thing is that which is produced by what we call material force in accordance with principle. Those who hold the theory of principle and material force should talk about material force in this way. But in the history of Chinese philosophy, those who held the theory of principle and material force in the past never had such a clear view of material force. In Chang Tsai's philosophy, material force is entirely a scientific concept. If there is the material force which he talked about, it is a kind of an actual thing.[30] This point will be taken up in detail later. Even what Ch'eng I and Chu Hsi called material force does not seem to

[29] For this doctrine, see above, ch. 34, sec. 116.
[30] For Chang's doctrine of material force, see above, ch. 30, secs. 2-9, 16, 30, 36, 42, 43.

be a completely logical concept. For instance, they often described material force as clear or turbid.[31] The way we look at the matter, the material force that can be described as clear or turbid is no longer material force [as such] but material force in accordance with the principle of clearness or turbidity. When they talked about material force as clear or turbid, they did not make clear whether they were talking about material force itself or about material force achieving the principle of clearness or turbidity. (pp. 64-68)

> *Comment.* Only Buddhists characterize the absolute as indescribable or unthinkable. Fung definitely equates material force with the Taoist and Neo-Taoist "unnamable" or non-being.[32]

We shall first discuss [Chu Hsi's statement], "There has never been any material force without principle."[33] This can very easily be proved. When we said that [what Ch'eng I called][34] the material force of the true source has no nature whatsoever, we spoke entirely from the point of view of logic. From the point of view of fact, however, material force has at least the nature of existence. If not, it fundamentally does not exist. If material force does not exist, then there will not be any actual thing at all. If material force has the nature of existence, it means that it follows the principle of existence. Since it at least has to follow the principle of existence, therefore "There has never been any material force without principle."

(Chu Hsi also said), "There has never been any principle without material force."[35] This saying cannot be interpreted to mean that all principles are with material force, for if so, it would mean that all principles are actually exemplified and that there would be no principle which is only real but not actual. This statement merely says, "There must be some principles with material force," or "There has never been the time when all principles are without material force." This has been proved above, for at least the principle of existence is always followed by material force. (p. 75)

3. Tao, Substance and Function, and Universal Operation

What we call the material force of the true source is the Ultimate of Non-being, and the totality of all principles is the Great Ultimate. The process from the Ultimate of Non-being to the Great Ultimate is our world of actuality. We call this process "The Ultimate of Non-being and also the Great Ultimate." The Ultimate of Non-being, the Great Ultimate, and the Ultimate of Non-being-and-also-the-Great-Ultimate are,

---

[31] See above, ch. 32, sec. 63; ch. 34, secs. 57, 66, 69.
[32] *Spirit of Chinese Philosophy*, p. 209. [33] See above, ch. 34, sec. 100.
[34] See above, ch. 32, sec. 21. [35] See above, ch. 34, sec. 100.

in other words, the material force of the true source, the totality of principle, and the entire process from material force to principle, respectively. Collectively speaking, they are called Tao (the Way). . . .

Why have Tao in addition to the Great Whole or the universe? Our answer is that when we talk about the Great Whole or the universe, we speak from the aspect of tranquillity of all things, whereas when we talk about Tao, we speak from the aspect of activity of all things. . . .

The principle followed by "fact" (which includes all facts) is the Great Ultimate in its totality, and the material force depended on by "fact" is the Ultimate of Non-being in its totality. (Actually the Ultimate of Non-being has no totality to speak of. We merely say so.)[36] In the first chapter we said that according to the old theory (of Sung Neo-Confucianists), principle is substance while actual things that actualize principle are function. But according to the concept of "the Ultimate of Non-being and also the Great Ultimate," the Great Ultimate is substance and the "and also" is function. As all functions are included in this function, it is therefore (what Chu Hsi called) the total substance and great functioning. . . .[37]

All things (meaning both things and events) go through the four stages of formation, flourish, decline, and destruction. Old things go out of existence this way and new things come into existence this way. This successive coming-into-existence and going-out-of-existence is the universal operation of the great functioning. The universal operation of the great functioning is also called the process of creation and transformation. The formation and flourish of things are creation, while their decline and destruction are transformation. The creation and transformation of all things are collectively called the process of creation and transformation. At the same time each thing or event is a process of creation and transformation. Since all things are each a process of creation and transformation, they are collectively called ten thousand transformations (all things). The term "transformation" may also involve both meanings of creation and transformation. Therefore the process is also called great transformation. The universal operation of the great transformation is the same as the universal operation of the great functioning. Our actual world is a universal operation. (pp. 97-100)

The Lao Tzu and the "Appended Remarks" of the Book of Changes have a common idea, that is, that when things reach their limit, they return to their origin.[38] . . . . According to the law of circular movement described above, things in the universe come into existence and go out of

[36] Fung's own note.

[37] See above, ch. 4, Chu Hsi's commentary on sec. 5.

[38] Lao Tzu, chs. 16, 40, and 78; Changes, commentary on hexagram no. 11, t'ai (successfulness). See Legge, trans., Yi King, p. 81.

existence at all times. They are always in the process of change. This is the daily renewal of the substance of Tao.

The daily renewal of the substance of Tao can be seen from four points of view.... (1) We can, from the point of view of classes, see the production and extinction of their actual members. Looked at this way, the daily renewal of the substance of Tao is cyclical. (2) We can, from the point of view of principle, see whether its actual exemplification tends to be perfect or not. Looked at this way, the daily renewal of the substance of Tao is one of progress and retrogression. (3) We can, from the point of view of the universe, see the increase or decrease of classes which have members in the actual world. Looked at this way, the daily renewal of the substance of Tao is one of increase and decrease. (4) And we can, from the point of view of an individual entity, see the process of its movement from one class to another. Looked at this way, the daily renewal of the substance of Tao is one of transformation and penetration. (pp. 110-111)

4. Principle and the Nature

Principle is the moral nature of things. From one point of view, if the moral nature of things is perfectly good, then the physical nature of things is also good, for the physical nature of things is that by which things actually follow their principle. Their following may not be perfect, but since they are following the highest good, they should be good. They may be eighty percent good or seventy percent good or not very good, but we cannot say they are not good. . . .

If a thing can follow its principle perfectly, it can be said to have "investigated principle to the utmost." To get to the utmost of the principle which it follows means to develop its own nature fully. Therefore investigating principle to the utmost is the same as fully developing one's nature. According to the idea of destiny set forth in this chapter, investigating principle to the utmost and full development of one's nature are the same as getting to the point of fulfilling one's destiny.[39] I-ch'uan (Ch'eng I) said, "The investigation of principle to the utmost, the full development of one's nature, and the fulfillment of destiny are only one thing. As principle is investigated to the utmost, one's nature is fully developed, and as soon as one's nature is fully developed, destiny is fulfilled."[40] We also say the same. We further believe that this does not apply only to man but to things also. (pp. 134-136)

[39] These three points are derived from Changes, "Remarks on Certain Trigrams," ch. 1, and became common topics in Neo-Confucianism. Cf. Legge, Yi King, p. 422.

[40] See above, ch. 32, sec. 49.

5. Serving Heaven and Jen (Humanity)

From the point of view of Heaven (*T'ien*, Nature), every class of things has its own principle. Its principle is also its ultimate. With reference to the things in this class, their ultimate is the highest good, and their physical nature is that by which they actually follow principle. It is "what issues [from the Way]" and "is good."[41] From the point of view of Heaven, what things in a given class should do in the great process of "the Non-ultimate and also the Great Ultimate" is to follow their principle completely. To be able to do so is to develop their nature fully and to investigate their principle to the utmost. This point has been discussed in chapter four. There the investigation of things means the use of my knowing faculty to know the principle of things. Here the term has a different meaning; it means to direct my conduct to realize fully the principle I am following. To use my knowing faculty to know the principle of things enables me to transcend experience and be free from the restriction of experience. This is transcendence of and freedom from experience. To direct my conduct to realize fully the principle I am following enables me to transcend myself and be free from self-bondage. This is transcendence and freedom from the self.

From the point of view of Heaven, men are also a class, and what they should do in the process of "the Non-ultimate and also the Great Ultimate" is also to follow their principle completely. Shao K'ang-chieh (Shao Yung, 1011-1077) said, "The sage is the ultimate of man."[42] By the ultimate of man is meant the perfect man, one who can fully develop the nature of man and investigate the principle of man to the utmost.

Mencius said, "The sage is the ultimate standard of human relations."[43] Human relations means to carry on the social relations, and to carry out human relations means the social activities of men. We said in chapter four that man's nature is social and that his social life issues from his nature. Therefore the full development of our nature and our investigation of principle to the utmost must be carried out in society.

In social life man's most social conduct is moral conduct. We can approach moral conduct in two different ways, one from the point of view of society and the other from the point of view of Heaven. From the point of view of society, man's moral conduct consists in fulfilling one's social duty. From the point of view of Heaven, one's moral con-

---

[41] Quoting from *Changes*, "Appended Remarks," pt. 1, ch. 5. Cf. Legge, p. 356.
[42] *Huang-chi ching-shih shu* (Supreme Principles Governing the World), SPPY, 5:5b.
[43] *Mencius*, 4A:2.

duct consists in fulfilling his universal duty, that is, fulfilling the way of man. From this point of view, in doing something moral, one is serving Heaven. . . .

We said previously that viewing things from the point of view of Heaven gives us a sympathetic understanding of them. In the sphere where the self is transcended, sympathy toward things is also increasingly enlarged until the sphere of what Sung and Ming Neo-Confucianists called "forming one body with all things" is reached. They call this sphere that of *jen*.

The word *jen* has two meanings. One is moral, the *jen* (humanity) in the (Five Constant Virtues) of humanity, righteousness, propriety, wisdom, and faithfulness discussed in chapter five. The other meaning refers to the sphere we are discussing. Ch'eng Ming-tao (Ch'eng Hao, 1032-1085) said, "The man of *jen* forms one body with all things without any differentiation. Righteousness, propriety, wisdom, and faithfulness are all [expressions of] *jen*."[44] What he meant is this *jen*. In order to distinguish the two meanings, we shall call this *jen* "the great *jen*." (pp. 300-304)

> *Comment.* In spite of Fung's Taoistic tendencies, he remains a true Confucianist after all. His Tao is certainly more that of the Taoists than that of the Confucianists, and his highest sphere of serving Heaven is close to the Taoist identification with Tao. But Fung's serving Heaven is moral, and instead of rejecting knowledge as a way of reaching Tao, Fung, like all Neo-Confucianists, insists on the investigation of things.

[44] *I-shu*, 2A:3a.

43

THE NEW IDEALISTIC CONFUCIANISM:
HSIUNG SHIH-LI

JUST AS Fung Yu-lan has attempted to reconstruct rationalistic Neo-Confucianism, so Hsiung Shih-li (1883-1968) has tried to reconstruct idealistic Neo-Confucianism. He has written eight books on his philosophy.[1] The whole system is systematically presented in the *Hsin wei-shih lun* (New Doctrine of Consciousness-Only, 1944).[2]

According to its central thesis, reality is perpetual transformation, consisting of "closing" and "opening" which are a process of unceasing production and reproduction. The "original substance" is in perpetual transition at every instant, arising anew again and again, thus resulting in many manifestations. But reality and manifestation, or substance and function, are one. In its "closing" aspect, it is the tendency to integrate— the result of which may "temporarily" be called matter—while in its "opening" aspect it is the tendency to maintain its own nature and be its own master—the result of which may "temporarily" be called mind. This mind itself is one part of the "original mind," which in its various aspects is mind, will, and consciousness.

It can readily be seen that the ideas of closing and opening and production and reproduction come from the *Book of Changes*, which, Hsiung said, is the main source of his ideas. The analysis of the mind comes from the Buddhist school of Consciousness-Only, the idea of the unity of substance and function from Neo-Confucianism, and that of the primacy of the original mind from Wang Yang-ming (Wang Shou-jen, 1472-1529). Like all Neo-Confucianists, he characterizes the original mind as *jen* (humanity) and aims at Heaven (Nature) and man forming one body.

[1] He was a native of Hupei. He was at first interested in political revolution and science but later shifted to the study of Buddhism and Indian philosophy. As a young man he studied the *Ch'eng wei-shih lun* (Treatise on the Establishment of the Doctrine of Consciousness-Only) at the Institute of Buddhism at Nanking. But he soon became dissatisfied and turned to the *Book of Changes*. He became professor of philosophy at Peking University in 1925. He continued to write and died in Mainland China in 1968.

[2] This book is in three parts. The first deals with consciousness and transformation, the second with function, and the third with mind and matter. The first two parts were in classical Chinese and printed for private circulation in 1932. They were translated into colloquial Chinese and published in 1942. Later the third part was added and the whole book was published in Chungking in 1944 and again in Shanghai in 1947, both in one volume. In the same year, it was published in four volumes in Shanghai as part of the *Shih-li ts'ung-shu* (Hsiung Shih-li Collection), 1947.

Hsiung at first followed the Buddhist school of Consciousness-Only. Later he became dissatisfied, turned to Neo-Confucianism, criticized, synthesized, and transformed both, and borrowed elements from Western philosophy to constitute his "New Consciousness-Only Doctrine." As he has emphasized, the word "consciousness" here means not the mind or *ālaya* (storehouse) as in the Consciousness-Only School which evolves an apparent world but the original mind or the original substance of all existence, and the word "only" means "especially." He has subjected Buddhism to lengthy, careful, and profound criticism.[3] In fact, he is the first one in Chinese history to do so. Nevertheless, he has not been able to be free from one outstanding defect of Buddhism, and that is to consider the external world as "temporary" or *chia*. In Buddhism the word means tentative, transitory, or even false. Hsiung has not gone as far as the Consciousness-Only School which considers external objects to have only false existence. But since he considers concrete, physical things as a threat to the original nature of the mind, his tendency to subordinate the external world is clear. This weakens his theory of perpetual transformation, for unless concrete, physical things possess the true nature of original substance, transformation with and through them would be on a shaky foundation.

What Hsiung has benefited from Buddhism is not so much idealism as the concept of instantaneous transformation. He applies it to the doctrine of production and reproduction in the *Book of Changes* and reinforces it. The idea of dynamic change was already prominent in Neo-Confucianism, especially in Wang Yang-ming, but Hsiung provides it with a metaphysical basis. In this he was partly influenced by Western philosophy, notably that of Bergson. But he is more critical than appreciative of Western philosophy. Without knowledge of Western languages, he incorrectly asserts that there is in Western philosophy not enough emphasis on realization of truth through personal experience *(t'i-jen)*, too much pursuit after external things, and no understanding of the unity of substance and function.

In spite of these weaknesses, Hsiung has definitely made an advance in Neo-Confucianism, particularly in the identification of principle *(li)* and material force *(ch'i)*. The objection of Chu Hsi's (1130-1200) bifurcation of them and Wang Yang-ming's idea that material force is only an aspect of the mind is now overcome. It is true that he has not clarified the relationship between the mind and principle, but he has given idealistic Neo-Confucianism a more solid metaphysical basis and a more dynamic character.

Aside from Fung and Hsiung, there were others in the twentieth cen-

[3] For this see Chan, *Religious trends in Modern China*, pp. 126-135.

tury who have tried to reconstruct traditional philosophy, especially Ou-yang Ching-wu (1871-1943), Abbot T'ai-hsü (1889-1947), and Liang Sou-ming (1893—). Both Ou-yang and T'ai-hsü only revived the Consciousness-Only philosophy and added nothing new. Liang, in giving the Confucian concept of *jen* a new interpretation of dynamic intuition, exerted tremendous influence on the New Culture movement in the 1920's, but he did not evolve a philosophical system of his own. Hsiung has done this. Besides, he has influenced more young Chinese philosophers than any other contemporary Chinese philosopher. Most importantly, he has restated, as no other has done, his whole philosophy in a book since the Communist accession to power in 1949, and he has done so without employing Communist slogans or referring to Marx, Stalin, or Mao Tse-tung. Philosophically, this book, entitled *Yüan-ju* (An Inquiry on Confucianism, 1956)[4] has not altered the fundamental thesis of the *Hsin wei-shih lun*, but it indicates that Confucianism is very much alive in China. The following selections are made from these two books.

1. "CLOSING AND OPENING"

From one point of view transformation is closing and opening (*ho-p'i*).[5] The two terms in this expression merely indicate a difference in tendencies. Opening is merely a tendency and closing is also merely a tendency. We should not say that each has a substance of its own, nor should we say that closing comes first and then opening. In another respect, transformation means that as soon as there is coming-into-existence, there is going-out-of-existence. In other words, as soon as closing or opening takes place, it disappears, without preserving its former tendency in the slightest degree but at all times destroying the old and producing the new. If we want to understand the nature of transformation, we must carefully analyze and thoroughly understand these two aspects. Otherwise we shall never be able to appreciate transformation.

Let us now talk about closing and opening. What are they? As it has been said before, original substance becomes function when it reveals itself as many manifestations. Thus if we say that original substance is that which can transform, or call it perpetual transformation, we must realize that perpetual transformation is formless and is subtle in its movement. This movement is continuous without cease. This kind of unceasing movement is of course not a simple tendency. In each move-

---

[4] Published in two volumes in Shanghai. The first volume deals with "kingliness without" and the second volume with "sageliness within," the twofold ideal in Chinese, especially Confucian, philosophy.

[5] Referring to *Changes*, "Appended Remarks," pt. 1, ch. 11. Cf. Legge, trans., *Yi King*, p. 372.

ment there is always a sort of integration. Without it the movement would be aimless, drifting, and baseless. Therefore when the tendency to act begins, there is at the same time a sort of integration. This tendency to integrate is positive consolidation. Consequently, without anyone's intention, an infinite number of "physical becoming" come into being from which the physical universe is formed. The tendency from integration to physical becoming is called closing.

We must realize that original substance has neither physical form nor character, is not physically obstructed by anything, is absolute, whole, pure, strong, and vigorous. However, in the functioning of the original substance to become many manifestations, it is inevitable that there is what we called closing. This closing possesses a tendency to become physical forms and concrete stuff. In other words, through the process of closing individual concrete things obtain their physical form. As perpetual transformation manifests itself as a tendency to close, it almost has to be completely materialized as if it were not going to preserve its own nature. This may be said to be a reaction.

However, as the tendency to close arises, there is another tendency arising simultaneously. It rises with perpetual transformation as the basis. It is firm, self-sufficient, and would not change itself to a process of closing. That is to say, this tendency operates in the midst of closing but is its own master, thus showing its absolute firmness and causes the process of closing to follow its own operation. This tendency—strong, vigorous and not materialized—is called opening. . . .

> Comment. In the Buddhist school of Consciousness-Only, perpetual transformation is identified with consciousness (*ālaya*), whereas here it is identified with original substance. Also, in Consciousness-Only, the energy to transform comes from "seeds," which "perfume" or influence previous seeds to produce transformation, but Hsiung ascribes the cause of transformation to natural tendencies.[6]

The tendency to close is integrative and tends to form physical things. On the basis of what it is, we temporarily call closing "matter" or "the operation of matter." The tendency to open is strong and vigorous, operating in the midst of closing but makes it follow itself. On the basis of what it is, we temporarily call opening "mind," or "the operation of mind." (*Hsin wei-shih lun*, pp. 56-59)

2. THE UNITY OF PRINCIPLE AND MATERIAL FORCE

In my opinion the word *ch'i* (material force) means the tendency to produce and reproduce, or energy. It operates universally without com-

---

[6] For the Buddhist doctrines of *ālaya* and seeds, see above, ch. 23, sec. 3.

ing to a standstill. The character of activity falsely appears as if the material force is distributed. For this reason we call it material force. Please understand thoroughly what is called material force here is precisely what I have called function in this treatise. As to the myriad things or material force in physical forms, it is tentatively so called because it is the trace or manifestation of transformation. There is no material force in concrete, physical forms apart from the various tendencies.

The word *li* (principle) originally has the meaning of order or pattern. But we should not say, as Sung (960-1279) and Ming (1368-1644) Neo-Confucianists said, that it is order within material force. Many of them considered material force to be real being, and consequently considered principle to be merely order within material force. According to this, principle itself is an empty form and material force alone is real. This view was more prevalent among Ming Neo-Confucianists. Even within the [idealistic] Wang Yang-ming School scholars generally held this view. On the one hand, they talked about innate knowledge of the good and necessarily admitted that the mind is the master. On the other hand they said that material force is real being and principle is a form belonging to it. Their theory seems to be a dualism of mind and matter, which violates very much the fundamental teachings of Wang Yang-ming. Here I do not want to criticize them too much. I merely want to explain my idea of principle and material force. I believe they cannot be sharply divided into two pieces. The word "principle" is a general term for both substance and function, whereas the word "material force" refers only to function. When the meaning of the word *ch'i* was explained above, it was already made quite clear that material force is function.

Why is "principle" the general term for both substance and function? Because spoken from the point of view of substance, it is originally absolute quiet and without [distinguishing] character, but it manifests itself as the countless phenomena involved in closing and opening. It means that all principles are brilliantly present. Therefore this substance is also called principle.

Substance also means the source of all transformations, the foundation of all things, and the converging point of all principles. It should be called true principle or concrete principle. It can also be called ultimate principle. Spoken from the point of view of function, in the wonderful functioning of closing and opening, all characters and phenomena seem to be manifest. Here phenomena follow a certain order, easily pervasive without any obstruction. It is also called principle, for phenomena and principle are identical, that is, phenomena are principle. Principle in the first instance refers to substance. It is the one source, which actually involves all manifestations. Principle in the second instance derives its name from function. It is the many manifestations which returns to the one source. Although principle may be said to be two, essentially it is neither one nor two. As its meanings as substance and function differ, it is not one. But since it is at the same time substance and function, it is not two. (*ibid.*, pp. 157-158)

3. THE MIND AND HUMANITY (JEN)

The original mind is an absolute whole. But because of its manifestations it is differentiated and necessarily has many names. First of all, it is called the mind, which means master. It pervades the concrete substance of all things but is not matter itself. It consolidates to become the myriad things, but these are the means to manifest itself and not materialization in which it loses its own nature. Since it is not materialized, it always remains true to its nature. For this reason, it is called master with respect to things.

Secondly it is called the will. The will implies a definite direction. What is called the mind is the universal substance penetrating all things and not just the master of my own body. But my body is part of the myriad things, and the master pervading all things is the same master controlling my body. Things differ but their master is the same. Now, when I search for the master of my own body, I find that in a subtle way it always has a definite direction. Spoken this way, it is the will.

What is meant by a definite direction? It means that it always unfolds itself in accordance with its original nature of unceasing production and reproduction and refuses to be materialized. This definite direction means life, and unique and definite substance, on the basis of which the self is established. In spite of countless transformations, it always remains firm as one, for it is the master.

Thirdly, it is called consciousness. The mind and the will refer to substance, whereas consciousness refers to the function of substance. When the deep and quiet substance is acted on, immediately penetrates everything, and utilizes sense organs to understand sense objects, it is called sense consciousness. When its activity develops further and further and without depending on sense organs can initiate deliberation itself, it is called sense-center consciousness. (*ibid.*, pp. 282-283)

> *Comment.* Instead of dividing the mind into eight categories as the school of Consciousness-Only does, Hsiung divides it into three. The emphasis on the will comes from Wang Yang-ming who traced it back to the *Doctrine of the Mean.*

Humanity (*jen*) is the original mind. It is the original substance common to man, Heaven, Earth, and all things. . . . From Confucius and

Mencius to teachers of the Sung and Ming periods, all directly pointed to humanity which is the original mind. The substance of humanity is the source of all transformations and the foundation of all things. (*ibid.*, pp. 260-261)

4. THE UNITY OF SUBSTANCE AND FUNCTION

In Chinese studies when discussing substance and function in cosmology, it is considered that they are basically one and yet are different. Some do not understand this. I offer the analogy of water in the big ocean and the many waves so as to lead them to understand this principle. . . . Original substance has physical form but in its function it involves internally the two processes of strong movement and consolidation. Consolidation means concrete stuff, and strong movement means spirit. As the two processes revolve, there is unceasing universal operation. Therefore we say that the universal operation of the original substance is its great functioning. By functioning is meant putting substance into functioning, and by substance is meant the true character of function. Therefore substance and function are basically one. However, although they are one, yet in the final analysis they cannot but be different, for in universal operation there are physical forms which are fathomable, whereas the original substance of the universal operation has no physical form, is most hidden and subtle, and is difficult to know. (*Yüan-ju*, pt. 2, p. 32b)

> *Comment.* The analogy of the oceans and the many waves for the relationship between substance and function is a favorite Buddhist one. Chu Hsi preferred the use of the moon and its scattered light.[7]

Substance means the original substance of the universe. By function is meant the universal operation of the original substance, which is absolutely strong and unceasing, arising anew again and again, whose transformation results in many manifestations. This is called function. . . .

What is meant by arising anew again and again? The universal operation of the original substance is in perpetual transition at every instant. As soon as there is production, there is destruction, and as soon as there is destruction, there is production. There is not a single instant in which the operation comes to a standstill and produces something new without something destroyed. The *Book of Changes* says, "Change means production and reproduction."[8] We should ponder over the term "production and reproduction" carefully. In every passing instant there is a new production. This is why it is called production and reproduction.

[7] See above, ch. 34, sec. 116.
[8] "Appended Remarks," pt. 1, ch. 5. Cf. Legge, p. 356.

Since in every passing instant there is a new production, without saying, it is clear that in no instant does the operation come to a standstill. The universal operation of this great transformation never stops or is obstructed for a moment. This is why we say that it arises anew again and again; by that we mean that the operation does not stand still.

Someone may object and say, "According to you, sir, the universal operation of the original substance is in perpetual transition at every instant, arises anew again and again, without standing still for a moment. It would mean there is a sudden change at every instant, and transformation would seem to be baseless." I reply: Universal operation is not the operation which suddenly appears out of a vacuum but the universal operation of the original substance. This original substance is the true source of all transformations and changes. It embraces the entire universe and is infinite. The *Doctrine of the Mean* describes its wonderful functioning as "deep and unceasingly springing . . . coming forth at all times."[9] It is an excellent analogy. Precisely because the original substance is the true source, it is never exhausted. Therefore this great operation changes suddenly at every moment and is perpetually creating something new without being exhausted. Are you not mistaken in saying that it is baseless? We must realize that true source and universal operation cannot be divided into two sections. . . . The original substance and its wonderful operation can be compared only with water in the ocean and the many waves. They are basically one and yet are different. While different, they are really one. (*ibid.*, p. 48a-b)

The universe from the past to the present and from the present rushing into the infinite future is truly an undifferentiated great current, in perpetual transition at every instant, discarding the old and going toward the new, jumping [like fish] in a lively manner without cease, rich, and inexhaustible. We must realize that although this undifferentiated great current changes and is daily renewed, yet for every change there must be the cause for its occurrence. No matter how novel a development may be, it cannot occur without cause and suddenly evolve an extremely strange phenomenon. For example, the seed of a pea cannot produce hemp, for it is not the generating cause of hemp. Spirit and matter are the two aspects of the universal operation of original substance, which is *ch'ien* (Heaven), the Originator.[10] We should not regard spirit as part of matter. If we say that in the beginning of the universe there was only layers of physical obstruction and originally no manifestation of any spiritual phenomena and therefore conclude that spirit does not originally exist, then, if this theory is to be maintained, we must first of all affirm that

---

[9] *The Mean*, ch. 31.

[10] A reference to hexagram no. 1, *ch'ien* (Heaven) of the *Book of Changes*. See Legge, p. 213.

matter originally involves the character and nature of spirit. Otherwise there will be no cause from which organic matter and the function and manifestations of the mind can emerge. But I don't see how this theory can be maintained. We must also realize that matter is not fixed concrete stuff. As the *Book of Changes* has already said, as there is concrete stuff, there is function.[11] It further affirms spirit as brilliant, strongly active, moving forward, pure, and developing things. It is merged with matter as one but also controls and directs it. Is this theory erroneously formulated on the basis of fancy and imagination? (*ibid.*, 64b-65a)

Question: I have already learned the ultimate principle of the great *Book of Changes*, namely, substance is at the same time function and function is at the same time substance. But I still have some doubt. Are the ten thousand things in the universe the same as the great functioning or are they its products?

Answer: According to principle, the ten thousand things and the great functioning cannot be separated. Why is this the case? Because the ten thousand things are not separated from the universal operation of the great functioning and each independently possesses a concrete character of its own. From this we should say that the ten thousand things and the great functioning are basically one. Once this principle is ascertained, there should be no further doubt. If you say that the ten thousand things in the universe are produced by the great functioning, then I should ask you what you mean by the word "production." If it means the same as a mother producing a son, then it will be greatly mistaken. Fundamentally the word "production" means manifestation. According to this meaning, as the great functioning universally operates in a lively and dynamic manner, it manifests all kinds of traces and phenomena. These are called the ten thousand things. The ancients meant this when they said that the ten thousand things are traces of transformation. Spoken this way, the ten thousand things are traces and forms of the universal operation of great functioning. Put differently, the concrete self-nature of the ten thousand things consists in the great functioning which operates unceasingly and in a very lively and dynamic manner. Can they and the great functioning be said to be two?

Question: If the ten thousand things and the great functioning are one, then the ten thousand things will lose their own selves. Why is this the case? The reason is that if the ten thousand things are merely traces of transformations, how can they possess evidently independent selves? Lao Tzu sighed over [the fact that Heaven and Earth regard all things

---

[11] This refers to the general philosophy of the *Book of Changes* rather than to any particular saying in the book.

as] sacrificial straw dogs,[12] and Chuang Tzu theorized [that the Creator, after people die, turns them into] the liver of a rat or the arm of an insect.[13] They both wanted to merge all things with great transformation so they will lose their own selves.

Answer: How extremely deluded you are! In the universal operation of great functioning, there are forms clearly before us. Take, for example, lightning. With each flash some red light is manifested. The red lights are traces and forms. Do you think the lightning at this time is outside the red lights? Or take, for example, water in the ocean manifesting itself as lively and active waves. The many waves are also traces and forms. Do you think that the water is outside the waves? Or take, for example, a torrent bursting violently, with thousands and thousands of white drops lashing up and down. These white drops are also traces and forms. Do you think that they are outside the torrent? Please think it over. The ten thousand things manifest themselves and seem to be individual objects, but really their self-nature consists in the great functioning universally operating without cease. (*ibid.*, 72b-73a)

[12] *Lao Tzu*, ch. 5.
[13] *Chuang Tzu*, ch. 6, NHCC, 3:17a. Cf. Giles, trans., *Chuang Tzu*, 1961 ed., p. 79.

44

CHINESE PHILOSOPHY IN COMMUNIST CHINA

PHILOSOPHY in Communist China can be summed up in one word, "Maoism."

Mao Tse-tung (1893—) has not claimed to be a philosopher, and he has not been labeled as such. But his ideas have determined the directions in which philosophy has been developing in New China since its establishment in 1949. Of his many works, two are of extreme importance in this connection, namely, *On Practice* (1937) and *On New Democracy* (1940).[1] In the former, the nature of philosophy for New China is defined and in the latter the future of Chinese traditional philosophy is virtually decided.

The thesis of *On Practice*, which is the most philosophical of Mao's works, is simple and definite. In his own words:

"To discover truth through practice, and through practice to verify and develop truth. To start from perceptual knowledge and actively develop it into rational knowledge, and then, starting from rational knowledge, actively direct revolutionary practice so as to remold the subjective and the objective world. Practice, knowledge, more practice, more knowledge; the cyclical repetition of this pattern to infinity, and with each cycle, the elevation of the content of practice and knowledge to a higher level. Such is the whole of the dialectical materialist theory of knowledge, and such is the dialectical materialist theory of the unity of knowing and doing."[2]

The fact that Mao concluded his essay with the theory of the unity of knowledge and action is most interesting, for it is one of the most prominent theories in the history of Chinese philosophy.[3] However, the source of Mao's inspiration is Engels, Marx, Lenin, and Stalin and not the Confucianists. In his essay he repeatedly refers to Communist writings but not to Chinese culture. In his *On New Democracy*, however, he made his attitude toward Chinese culture abundantly clear:

"New-democratic culture is scientific . . . but it can never form a united front with any reactionary idealism. . . . A splendid ancient culture was created during the long period of China's feudal society. To clarify the process of development of this ancient culture, to throw away its feudal dross, and to absorb its democratic essence is a necessary con-

[1] These are included in his *Selected Works*, vol. 1, New York, International Publishing Co., 1954, pp. 282-297, and vol. 3, pp. 106-156, respectively.
[2] *ibid.*, vol. 1, p. 297.
[3] See above, ch. 32, comment on sec. 38.

dition for the development of our new national culture and for the increase of our national self-confidence; but we should never absorb anything and everything uncritically. We must separate all the rotten things of the ancient feudal ruling class from the fine ancient popular culture that is more or less democratic and revolutionary in character. As China's present new politics and new economy have developed out of her old politics and old economy, and China's new culture has also developed out of her old culture, we must respect our own history and should not cut ourselves adrift from it. However, this respect for history means only giving history a definite place among the sciences, respecting its dialectical development, but not eulogizing the ancient while disparaging the modern, or praising any noxious feudal element."[4]

From the foregoing, it is clear that philosophy in New China must be practical, scientific, democratic, and popular. There have been radical changes in New China on many fronts, but so far as philosophy is concerned, its direction has been definite and straight. At first philosophers confessed their mistakes. This was followed by their study of Marxism. Then they corrected their wrong views. Subsequently there were more attacks on revisionism and rightism. With the establishment of communes in 1958, both philosophy and philosophers have been put to work among the masses. Throughout all these various movements, the theme of philosophy has remained the same, namely, philosophy for practical use for the masses.

Since knowledge must come from practice, all abstract concepts, idealistic theories, and subjectivism of any kind are considered feudalistic and are to be totally rejected. Philosophy acquires its true meaning only in the discovery and solution of practical problems. Therefore the chief lesson of philosophy is the concrete development of society. Philosophy and production must be united, not only because philosophy can thus fulfill its function but also because objective analysis can best be carried out in production.

Furthermore, this practical application of philosophy must be done among and indeed through the masses, for philosophy must be popular as well as scientific. This is the logic behind sending philosophers to work in the communes. To be democratic, philosophers must work and study with the masses. In fact, the masses are their best teachers, for theirs is really the philosophy of the people. Therefore, just as thought and practice must be identical, so intellectuals and workers must be united.

In this situation, there can be no distinction between theory and practice. There are in Communist China courses and research on philosophy, departments of philosophy, philosophical journals, philosophical con-

[4] *ibid.*, vol. 3, pp. 154-155.

ferences, and many publications on philosophy. But these are regarded as only aids to the practical function of philosophy. The effort is not being devoted to the development of new theories of technical philosophy or the production of individual philosophical works but to the transformation of existing philosophy according to the Marxist pattern. It is significant that in a book which is virtually the official Communist history of Chinese philosophy in English, the section on contemporary philosophy, 1919 to 1959, is entirely devoted to the Communist political and social revolution with almost not a single word on technical philosophy.[5] We have noted that Hsiung Shih-li (1883-1968) published his *Yüan-ju* (An Inquiry on Confucianism) in 1956, a presentation of his Neo-Confucian philosophy without quoting any Communist writer or using any Communist terminology.[6] But Hsiung's is essentially a new statement of an old theme and he is entirely outside the main stream.

Like the distinction between theory and practice, that between the philosophical expert and the layman must also disappear, for philosophy is to be identified with the masses. To be sure, there are many teachers of philosophy and many writers on it. Among them Fung Yu-lan (1895 —) is still the most outstanding. Evidently he is not yet completely converted to Marxian philosophy, and therefore he has been the chief target of attack. The constant demand is that he must forsake the capitalist camp and serve the masses.

Under such circumstances what is the future of Chinese philosophy? In point of fact, research on Chinese philosophy is going on. Studies and commentaries on Chinese philosophical classics are being published. It can be said, however, that its fate is the same as that of philosophy in general, namely, that it must be reconstructed according to the Marxist pattern.

Nothing can show this tendency better than the conference on Chinese philosophy held on January 21–26, 1957 in which the nature of the history of Chinese philosophy and the question of the continuation of the Chinese philosophical heritage were vigorously debated on among more than one hundred participants. Materials presented at the conference have been published in a volume with subsequent statements. The following selections are made from this volume.

It may be said that since the conference took place shortly before the "Let one hundred schools contend" campaign in which relative freedom of thought was allowed, and since that campaign was short lived, the results of the conference may not be indicative of things to come. Fung Yu-lan, who upheld Chinese philosophy, was continuously criticized.

[5] Hou Wai-lu, *Short History of Chinese Philosophy*, pp. 108-169.
[6] See the preceding chapter.

More than a year later, he had to criticize himself as a member of the capitalistic class, an idealist, and one who used the metaphysical method.[7] Nevertheless, it is not Chinese philosophy as such that has been attacked. Rather, it is its idealism and abstract ideas. Fung's self-criticism serves to show that Marxian philosophy will dominate Communist China, but that Chinese philosophy will continue, although it will be reconstructed and directed to practical problems for the benefit of the masses. Confucius, Chu Hsi (1130-1200), Wang Yang-ming (1472-1529), and the rest may be branded as feudalists, but who can deny that they were primarily interested in the solution of practical problems for all?

SELECTIONS[8]

1. The Nature of the History of Chinese Philosophy

Fung Yu-lan:

There are many struggles in social and political thought, which are in reality struggles between materialism and idealism. For example, in the history of Chinese philosophy, the question whether human nature is good or evil has continuously aroused extensive controversy from the pre-Ch'in (221–206 B.C.) period to modern times. In the pre-Ch'in period, Mencius held that nature is good, believing that inborn nature is good because there is originally a moral principle endowed by "Heaven." This is of course the view of idealism. Hsün Tzu (fl. 298–238 B.C.), on the other hand, held that human nature is evil, believing "Heaven" to be merely "Nature" in which there is no moral principle and that man's moral qualities are acquired through education. Such an idea directly negating Mencius' idealism should be regarded as materialistic.

Later, the Neo-Confucianism of Sung (960-1279) and Ming (1368-1644) distinguished the Principle of Nature and human desire and emphasized that the former should control the latter. What was called the Principle of Nature is really feudalistic moral principles objectified and made absolute. Philosophers who opposed the Neo-Confucianism of Sung and Ming like Ch'en Liang (1143-1194), Wang Fu-chih (Wang Ch'uan-shan, 1619-1692) and Tai Chen (Tai Tung-yüan, 1723-1777), regarded the Principle of Nature as the correct development of human desires, denied that the Principle of Nature had any right to control human desires, and placed man's desires and feelings in the position of

---

[7] *Che-hsüeh yen-chiu* (Studies in Philosophy), 1958, no. 5, p. 42.

[8] These are made from the *Chung-kuo che-hsüeh shih wen-t'i t'ao-lun chuan-chi* (Proceedings of the Discussions on Problems Concerning the History of Chinese Philosophy), Peking 1957.

first importance. This is a direct negation of the idealism of Sung-Ming Neo-Confucianism. This type of thought should also be regarded as materialistic. . . .

In the past several years in our effort to settle the problem of the struggle between materialism and idealism in the history of Chinese philosophy, we have only emphasized their conflicts and have paid no attention to their mutual influence and mutual penetration. Of course this side of the story is a relative one, but to ignore it is an error of one-sidedness.

Let us take an example. In the beginning Sung-Ming Neo-Confucianism was fundamentally materialistic. In the philosophies of both Chou Tun-i (Chou Lien-hsi, 1017-1073) and Chang Tsai (Chang Heng-ch'ü, 1020-1077), material force was considered as primary. Later Ch'eng I (Ch'eng I-ch'uan, 1033-1107) and Chu Hsi (1130-1200) reverted to idealism. But Wang Fu-chih set aside the idealism of Ch'eng and Chu, directly continued the materialism of Chang Tsai, and thus established his great materialistic system of thought. This line of development is quite clear, and this is what we have said in instructing our students.

But this is only one side of the story. On the other side, while Wang continued Chang, he did not simply do so or revert to him without change. Similarly, while he set aside Ch'eng and Ch'u, he did not simply do so. What he did was to develop his own philosophy out of that of Ch'eng and Ch'u, then set them aside, and at the same time continued Chang Tsai. In the dialectical development of history and human knowledge, to go through something is not a simple matter. It involves absorbing its rational elements and throwing away its dregs. It involves an advance. . . .

In our recent work on the history of philosophy, we have generally employed the metaphysical and materialistic methods and have over-simplified and vulgarized the struggle between materialism and idealism in the history of philosophy, so that the history of philosophy, which is originally rich and active, has become poor and static. Actually the history of philosophy is what Lenin has described as a great development. . . . (pp. 14-23)

Chang Tai-nien:

What is the fundamental direction in the study of the history of Chinese philosophy since emancipation? Its essential expressions are three: First, the recognition that the problems of thinking and existence are basic in Chinese philosophy. Although the terminology employed in Chinese philosophy is different from that of the West, since these problems are also basic in Chinese philosophy [as in the West], the history of Chinese philosophy is also the history of the struggle between materialism and idealism [as in the West] and its area of struggle is also similar to that of the West. Second, the recognition that social consciousness is determined by social existence and that in philosophical studies the method of class analysis must be used. That is to recognize that the struggle between materialism and idealism is a reflection of class struggle. Third, learning from the enlightened experience of Russian philosophers and their method of studying the history of philosophy. . . . (p. 84)

2. The Chinese Philosophical Heritage

Fung Yu-lan:

To understand totally certain philosophical premises in the history of Chinese philosophy, we must pay attention to their two meanings, one abstract and the other concrete. In the past I have paid attention almost entirely to the abstract meaning of some of these premises. This, of course, is wrong. Only in the last several years have we paid attention to their concrete meaning. Without saying, it is correct to pay attention to their concrete meaning, but it would be wrong to pay attention to it alone. In trying to understand these premises in the history of philosophy we should of course place their concrete meaning in the position of first importance, for they have a direct relation to the concrete social conditions in which the authors of these premises lived. But their abstract meaning should also be taken into consideration. To neglect it would be to miss the total picture. . . .

Take for example Wang Yang-ming's doctrine of innate knowledge of the good (*liang-chih*). From the point of view of its concrete meaning, the content of what is called innate knowledge is the same as feudal morality and nothing new. The fact is that feudal morality at his time had become a dogma and not very effective. Wang therefore provided feudal morality with a new foundation. According to him, feudal morality was not imposed from the outside but something evolved from man's innate knowledge itself. . . .

Such a premise seems to advocate the emancipation of the individual, but the actual effect is that he is even more strongly bound by feudal morality. However, although this appraisal rests on a solid foundation, it concerns only one side of the matter, for aside from the concrete meaning of the premise, there is also its abstract meaning. . . . According to its abstract meaning, "Every one can become (sages) Yao and Shun,"[9]

[9] *Mencius*, 6B:2. Yao and Shun were legendary sage emperors of 3rd millennium B.C.

"People filling the street were all sages,"[10] and "All people are equal."[11] That is to say, in their original nature all men are equal. . . . From this point of view, the philosophy of the school of Lu Hsiang-shan (Lu Chiu-yüan, 1139-1193) and Wang should not be simply denied in its entirety. (pp. 273-277)

[*Later Fung added*:]

(1) What we have to continue is essentially the materialistic thought in the history of Chinese philosophy, the type of thought that is for the people, scientific, and progressive. I did not particularly mention this because I thought it was a matter of course. That shows that I believed in continuing anything abstract, regardless of whether it was idealistic or materialistic.

(2) According to my article, premises in the history of philosophy have both abstract and concrete meanings, as if they were arrayed in parallel before us, so that there seems to be a finished, concrete thing that we can take up and continue at any time without reconstructing it. . . .

(3) In my second statement I substituted general and special meanings for abstract and concrete meanings. My defect indicated above still remains.

What I said in my article is incomplete and my presentation of the problem is also incorrect. (p. 284)

Yang Cheng-tien:

There are three points in Mr. Fung's theory that are worth discussing:

(1) Philosophy as a form of social consciousness surely has its own special characteristics in the development of thought and the process of continuation, but it also has a universal principle which is unalterable, namely, that of partisanship. Instead of focusing his attention on the continuation of the materialistic tradition and proceeding from an analysis of the concrete substance of philosophical theories, Mr. Fung set aside the opposition and struggle of the two major camps in the history of philosophy and generally started with philosophical premises, reduced the problem of continuing the philosophical heritage to that of understanding the meanings of those premises. He thereby eliminated the historical content and class characteristics of philosophical thought and unconsciously separated the history of philosophy from Marxism in both objective and scope.

(2) Mr. Fung subjectively wishes to employ the Marxian method of thought to solve the problem of the continuation of philosophical herit-

---

[10] Wang Yang-ming, *Ch'uan-hsi lu* (Instructions for Practical Living), sec. 313.
[11] A common saying in Buddhism and Neo-Confucianism.

age, but the fact is that his method and Marxism have nothing in common. When dialectical materialism is used as a weapon in methodology, its principles and categories are intensely and organically united as one and will not allow any split or isolation. "Content and form" is merely one of the many categories in the system of dialectical materialism. "Abstractness and concreteness" is also merely one form of expression of the "generality and particularity" of things. To exaggerate abstractness and concreteness or form and content to the point of absolute contrasts, and to think that this method and these categories apply to all and embrace all, and even to use them as the only standard in determining the value of philosophical heritage, is unreasonable according to formal logic. . . .

(3) The process of historical development of Chinese philosophy itself shows that it is based on the principle of partisanship and the use [of the heritage] for reconstruction. In Chinese history the expression of the partisan spirit of philosophers has been extremely clear, although the expression was not necessarily completely conscious. For example, the *T'ai-hsüan ching* (Classic of the Supremely Profound Principle)[12] written by Yang Hsiung (53 B.C.–A.D. 18), a materialist of the Han dynasty (206 B.C.–A.D. 220) was slandered and rejected by Liu Hsin (c.46 B.C.–A.D. 23), an idealistic thinker who was a representative of the benefits of the ruling class. . . . But in his *Lun-heng* (Balanced Inquiries) Wang Ch'ung (27–100 A.D.?) praised him. . . . These historical facts and their direction of the continuation of thought show that there were already opposite camps and it was not a matter of accident. (pp. 325-327)

3. Guidance for Future Developments

Hsiao Sha-fu:

Classical writers on Marxism have shown us in detail the principles and methods for the study and continuation of philosophical heritage. Moreover, they have set examples by practicing those principles and methods themselves and have produced norms and standards for us. The profound studies and classical criticism of European philosophy by Marx, Engels, Lenin, and Stalin are forever models in our study. The philosophical writings of comrade Mao Tse-tung and his comrades-in-arms especially are most glorious examples showing us how to continue our philosophical heritage and to unify Marxian philosophy and the Chinese people's good traditions of thought. For example, to the problems of the relation between knowledge and conduct, the good or evil nature of man, of ethical ideals, of methods of cultivation and the like, about which inquiries and

[12] See above, ch. 15.

controversies have been carried on for a long time in the history of Chinese philosophy, they have given us the Marxian final conclusion and answer in such works as *On Practice*,[13] [Liu Shao-ch'i's] *On the Cultivation of Communist Party Members*,[14] and other writings. In his "On Contradictions"[15] Mao reconstructed and elaborated on the basis of the science of Marxian dialectics such dialectical ideas long discussed by [Chinese] philosophers throughout the ages as "When a thing reaches the limit in one direction, it will turn back to the other direction,"[16] "Opposition leads to mutual completion,"[17] and "If yin and yang do not exist, the one (the Great Ultimate) cannot be revealed. If the one cannot be revealed, then the function of the two forces will cease."[18] In this way he has enriched science of Marxian dialectics.

The direction given by the Party is the direction of our efforts and the compass for our work. (p. 436)

Ai Ssu-ch'i:

How do we understand the problem of philosophical heritage? I think we can use as reference Chairman Mao's viewpoint in his *On New Democracy* concerning the continuation of cultural heritage. He pointed out that the attitude of Marxists-Leninists toward the cultural heritage of the past is to select its quintessence and to throw away its dregs.[19] What is its quintessence? It is that part of the heritage that is democratic, scientific, and for the masses. What are the dregs? They are what is anti-democratic, anti-scientific, and anti-people or aristocratic. The culture we want to build up is that which is nationalistic, democratic, scientific, and for the masses. Therefore what we want to continue is that in the old culture which is democratic, scientific, and for the masses and we must throw away what is anti-democratic, anti-scientific, and anti-people. This should be the general attitude of Marxists-Leninists toward cultural heritage. This is a universal principle. In handling the history of Chinese philosophy we should also pay attention to this principle. . . . We must follow the principle enunciated by Chairman Mao. (p. 438)

[13] Mao Tse-tung, *Selected Works*, vol. 1, 1954, pp. 282-297.
[14] By Liu Shao-ch'i, written in 1949. English translation entitled *How to Be a Good Communist*, 2d ed., rev., 1952.
[15] Mao, *Selected Works*, vol. 2, 1954, pp. 11-53.
[16] Cf. *Ho-kuan Tzu*, sec. 5, the last sentence.
[17] cf. *Lao Tzu*, ch. 2.
[18] Chang Tsai, *Chang Tzu ch'üan-shu* (Complete Works of Master Chang), SPPY, 2:4b.
[19] *Selected Works*, vol. 3, p. 154.

ON TRANSLATING CERTAIN CHINESE
PHILOSOPHICAL TERMS

No TWO translators of Chinese terms will ever agree entirely on their translations. Since each Chinese character has several meanings, different emphases by different translators are inevitable. Some terms are so complicated in their meanings, like *yin* (dark, negative, passive, or female principle, force, or element) and its opposite, *yang*, that they have to be transliterated. Others call for interpretation rather than a literal translation. The title *Ta-hsüeh chang-chü*, for example, literally means punctuation and redivision of the *Great Learning*. But the work is actually a commentary containing some of Chu Hsi's (1130-1200) most important sayings. Therefore "Commentary" tells a better story than a literal rendering. Again, *i-shu* means a transmitted work. But transmission suggests a line of transmission which is totally absent from the term, which simply denotes a work which we still have today. Therefore it should be rendered as "surviving work" or "preserved work."

Some have to be translated variously. For example, *wen* means pattern, literature, signs, ornament, culture, and many more, and cannot be rendered in the same way. Likewise, *tzu-jan* means spontaneity, nature, to follow nature, etc. The word *ch'ü* generally means to take, but in Buddhism it means to cling to or to apprehend. *Shu* refers to number, truth, principle, the course of things, one's lot, repeatedly, etc. None of these can be rendered consistently. It is because Duyvendak failed to appreciate the correct idea of *shu* in the *Hsün Tzu* that he considered Hu Shih's translation of it as truth to be wrong.[1]

Without saying, in the choice of alternative renderings, one must choose the one intended by the writer or specific to the particular philosophical system. The title *Ts'ui-yen*, for example, can mean either "collected sayings" or "pure words." While the former is more general, it is clear from the preface of the book that the latter is intended. Again, *p'ing-teng* ordinarily means equality, but in Buddhism it expresses a much more refined idea, namely, sameness and absence of differentiation. *T'ung*, of course, is the word for penetration, but in Buddhism it has the special meaning of being free und unrestricted.

In a number of cases, the translation is difficult and controversial. While personal choice is in order, there should be adequate reasons behind it. The following sets forth the reasons for my own choice which I hope are sufficient:

[1] See above, ch. 6, n.31.

Chi, "subtle, incipient, activating force." Graham expresses the sense of the term most correctly in the phrases "inward spring of movement" and "incipient movement not yet visible outside."[2] Both Bodde's "motive force"[3] and Carsun Chang's "state of subtlety"[4] are correct but incomplete. See above, ch. 28, comment on sec. 2, ch. 3.

Ch'i, "concrete thing." This is a technical philosophical term that should not be understood in its popular meanings of an instrument, an implement, or a vessel, or be distorted to mean matter, substance, or material entity. Philosophically it means a concrete or definite object in contrast to Tao which has neither spatial restriction nor physical form. It also includes systems and institutions, or any thing or affair that has a concrete form.

Ch'i, "material force." Every student of Chinese thought knows that *ch'i* as opposed to *li* (principle) means both energy and matter, a distinction not made in Chinese philosophy. Both "matter" and "ether" are inadequate. Dubs' "matter-energy"[5] is essentially sound but awkward and lacks an adjective form. Unless one prefers transliteration, "material force" seems to be the best. In many cases, especially before the Neo-Confucian doctrine of *li* developed, *ch'i* denotes the psychophysiological power associated with blood and breath. As such it is translated as "vital force" or "vital power," and in the case of *hao-jen chih ch'i* as "strong, moving power." Such are the cases in *Mencius,* 2A:2.

Chin-ssu, "reflections on things at hand." The term *chin-ssu* refers to *Analects,* 19:6, in which Confucius said that what one thinks about should be matters near at hand, that is, matters of immediate application. *Chin* also refers to the self, as in *Analects,* 6:28, "To judge of others by what is near to ourselves." Bruce incorrectly translated it as "modern thought"[6] and he has been followed by others, such as Alfred Forke.[7] In a footnote Bruce cited for his support a saying by Chu Hsi to the effect that his *Chin-ssu lu* (Records of Reflections on Things at Hand) contains sayings of recent people and is therefore more to the point. This saying is quoted in the *Chu Tzu nien-p'u* (Chronological Biography of Chu Hsi) in the beginning of ch. 2, pt. 1. But in this saying Chu Hsi was not explaining the title of the *Chin-ssu lu* but was characterizing its contents. Evidently Bruce misunderstood the saying. The meaning of the title is quite clear from the comments of Lü Tsu-ch'ien (1137-1181),

[2] *Two Chinese Philosophers,* 1958, p. 35.

[3] In Fung, *History of Chinese Philosophy,* vol. 2, 1953, p. 450.

[4] *Neo-Confucian Thought,* 1957, p. 157.

[5] "Mencius and Sun-dz on Human Nature," PEW, 6 (1956), p. 219.

[6] *Chu Hsi and His Masters,* 1923, p. 74.

[7] *Neueren chinesischen Philosophie,* 1938, p. 170.

co-compiler with Chu Hsi, in the same paragraph of the *Nien-p'u*.[8]
Waley's "thinks for himself about what he has heard"[9] is entirely un-
justified. Likewise, Needham's "systematic thought"[10] is unsatisfactory.
Carsun Chang's "reflective thought"[11] and Vincent Yu-chung Shih's
"intimate thinking"[12] are interpretations. Legge's "reflecting with self-
application"[13] expresses well the meaning of self-application but not the
idea of nearness. I have struggled hard to choose from "thoughts for
immediate application," "reflections for immediate application," and
"reflections on things at hand," but finally settled on the latter because
it implies, at least, the idea of application also.

Ching, "seriousness." In ancient Confucianism the word *ching* is
often interchangeable with *kung* and means reverence but in Neo-Confucianism the two words are sharply different. As Ch'en Ch'un (1153-
1217) has pointed out, *kung* has to do with one's appearance and expression in respect for others while *ching* has to do with one's effort; the
former is external and the latter internal.[14] The main difference is that
reverence implies an object whereas *ching* is a state of mind. This seems
to be similar to the Buddhist calmness of mind and has probably led
Carsun Chang to translate it as "attentiveness" and "concentration,"[15] and
Graham to render it as "composure."[16] But the Neo-Confucianists emphasized making an effort in handling affairs, an effort not stressed by
the Zen Buddhists. As Ch'en Ch'un said, in ancient Classics the word
only denotes composure but the Neo-Confucianists stress making
effort in handling affairs. Chai Ch'u's "prudence" comes close to the
Neo-Confucian meaning[17] but Bruce's translation of "seriousness" is the
best.[18]

Chung-shu, "conscientiousness and altruism." This is open to many
possible translations but the central meaning must not be lost. As the
Confucian pupil Tseng Tzu said, it is the one thread of the Confucian

[8] See also discussion on the title by Olaf Graf, *Dschu Hsi Djin-sï Lu*, vol. 1,
1953, pp. 19-20.
[9] Waley, *Analects of Confucius*, 1938. 19:6.
[10] *History of Chinese Scientific Thought*, 1956, p. 459.
[11] *Neo-Confucian Thought*, p. 50.
[12] "The Mind and the Moral Order," MEB, 10, 1955, p. 352.
[13] Legge, *Confucian Analects*, 19:6.
[14] *Hsing-li tzu-i* (Meanings of Neo-Confucian Philosophical Terms), pt. 2,
sections on *ching* and *kung-ching*, and Liu Shih-p'ei (1884-1919), *Li-hsüeh tzu-i
t'ung-shih* (General Explanation of the Meanings of Neo-Confucian Terms), 1936,
p. 20a-b.
[15] *Neo-Confucian Thought*, pp. 197 and 222.
[16] *Two Chinese Philosophers*, p. 67.
[17] "Neo-Confucianism of the Sung-Ming Period." SR, 18 (1951), p. 389.
[18] *Philosophy of Human Nature by Chu Hsi*, 1922, p. 439ff.

doctrine.[19] In essence, *chung* means the full development of one's originally good mind and *shu* means the extension of that mind to others. In other words, it is the Confucian golden rule, or *jen* (humanity), with *chung* referring to the self and *shu* referring to others. Any translation must involve these two aspects.[20]

Fa. The word *fa* covers a wide range of meanings, such as law, punishment, custom, duty, discipline, method, technique, and model, and has to be translated variously. In the Legalist School, it involves the three concepts of law, statecraft, and power. In Buddhism, it means Buddhism itself, the Law preached by the Buddha, Reality, Truth. As a philosophical term, however, it is the Chinese rendering of *dharma*, which means "that which is held to." It connotes all things, with or without form, real or imaginary, the material or principle of an entity, something that holds onto its nature as a particular thing. In this connection it is a most difficult term to translate. The nearest English term to it is "element of existence," taking unreal dharmas as having a negative existence. It is best left untranslated except when it means the Law of the Buddha.[21]

Hsiang, "character." As a technical Buddhist term, *hsiang* (*lakshana* in Sanskrit) is related to *hsing* (*svabhāva*, nature) as characteristic is to nature or phenomenon to noumenon, although in some connections, such as *shih-hsiang* (true state), it means nature itself. Essentially the self-nature is *hsing* whereas what can be described is *hsiang*. Of course in ordinary usage it means a sign, feature, appearance, form, etc.

Hsing-erh-shang, "what exists before physical form [and is therefore without it]," *hsing-erh-hsia,* "what exists after physical form [and is therefore with it]." These phrases first appeared in the *Book of Changes,* "Appended Remarks," pt. 1, ch. 12.[22] K'ung Yung-ta (574-648) said in his commentary, "Physical form is established according to the Way. Therefore there is first the Way and then physical form and the Way exists before physical form. . . . Physical form is in objects, not in the Way. As there is physical form, there can be objects and functions." The relationship, then, is one of both sequence and attribute. Thus Legge's and Duyvendak's rendering of "antecedent" and "subsequent to the material form," Wilhelm's and Bodde's "what is above form" and "what is within form," Bruce's "the corporeal" and "the incorporeal," etc. are all correct only in one of these two aspects.[23] Boodberg is correct in

---

[19] *Analects,* 4:15. [20] See above, ch. 2, comment on 4:15.
[21] For the meaning of *fa-men,* see above, ch. 24, n.12.
[22] Cf. translation by Legge, *Yi King,* p. 377.
[23] See Bodde, "On Translating Chinese Philosophic Terms," FEQ, 14 (1955), 232-233. Also J. J. L. Duyvendak, trans., *Tao Te Ching, The Book of the Way and its Virtue,* 1954, p. 73.

believing that *erh* has the meaning of transition, but it is not a verb as he suggested, and *hsing-erh-shang* does not mean, as he thought, "what is shaped and transcends."[24] Rather it means "what is without shape and transcends." The meaning of sequence is important. Without it Chu Hsi's discussion of the terms cannot be understood.[25] In ordinary usage, however, *hsing-erh-shang* simply means before and *hsing-erh-hsia* simply means after. The *Daikanwa jiten* (Great Chinese-Japanese Dictionary) is correct in simply defining these phrases as "with form" and "without form."[26]

Hsing-ming, "actuality and name." The term is generally understood to mean the relation between name and actuality, which was a major topic of debate among ancient scholars. As Creel has pointed out, most translators have mistranslated *hsing* to mean punishment.[27] It is interchangeable with *HSING*, meaning form or body.[28] Creel maintains that *hsing-ming* means performance and title, especially in connection with the selection and appraisal of government officials, but he has not provided any etymological basis or any clear-cut collateral evidence to show that *hsing* means to perform. The most important passage bearing on the term *HSING-ming* is found in the *Yin Wen Tzu*, to which Creel has not referred. The book begins by saying, "The Great Way (Tao) has no *HSING* and what are called material objects have *ming*." Here *HSING* clearly means form and *ming* means name, and cannot be understood as performance and title. Creel also does not accept the traditional equation of *hsing-ming* or *HSING-ming* with *ming-shih* (name and actuality), but the *Yin Wen Tzu* definitely says that name is to examine form[29] also to examine *shih* (reality). Creel said that *HSING* (form or appearance) is opposed to *shih* (reality),[30] evidently forgetting that *HSING* also means body. He does not accept the interchange of *hsing* with *HSING* and thinks that scholars and copyists have simply confused them.[31] Where they are used interchangeably, as in the *Han Fei Tzu*, he arbitrarily chose the former to suit his thesis. In order to be consistent, he had to interpret *hsing* in the term *hsing-cheng* (government) in the *Mo Tzu* as a verb, to perform or to administer.[32] This would destroy the parallelism in such sentences as "the wealth of the country, the size of

[24] *Far Eastern Quarterly*, 13 (1954), p. 377.
[25] See above, ch. 34, sec. 101.
[26] *Daikanwa jiten*, vol. 9, p. 167.
[27] Creel, "The Meaning of Hsing-Ming," *Bernhard Karlgren Dedicata*, pp. 199-211.
[28] See, for example, *Han Fei Tzu*, chs. 5, 7, 8, SPTK, 1:8b, 2:5a, 6b, 7a.
[29] *Yin Wen Tzu*, SPTK, pp. 1b and 2b, respectively.
[30] *Bernhard Karlgren Dedicata*, p. 205.
[31] *ibid.*, p. 204.
[32] *ibid.*, p. 205.

the population, and the order of government,"[33] and make the phrase *wei* (act) *hsing-cheng* to mean to do the administering of government, a most extraordinary construction in Chinese for which there is no parallel. A title is of course one of many kinds of names, and performance (what one has actually done) is one form of actuality. But *hsing* is not a verb and the ancient interchange of *hsing* and *HSING* and the common equation of *hsing-ming* with *HSING-ming* are not mistakes, as Creel maintains. Chu Hsi condemned strategists, calculators, and *hsing-ming* alike because they used tricks and were opportunists. *Hsing-ming* does not seem to fit the description of rulers who demanded performance according to titles.[34] And Chu Hsi said they were based on Taoism rather than Legalism with which Creel has associated *hsing-ming*.[35] Chu Hsi was of course thinking of *Lao Tzu*, ch. 36, where it is said, "In order to grasp, it is first necessary to give," a technique used by strategists, calculators, and debaters alike and for which Confucianists have strongly condemned them as immoral.

Hsü, "vacuous." A Taoist term often used by Neo-Confucianists also. As a description of a state of mind, it means absolute peacefulness and purity of mind and freedom from worry and selfish desires and not to be disturbed by incoming impressions or to allow what is already in the mind to disturb what is coming into the mind. *Hsü-shih* means unreality and reality, but *hsü* also means profound and deep continuum in which there is no obstruction. It is not to be equated with the Buddhist term *k'ung* (empty). Although *k'ung* is not really nihilistic but means the absence of specific characters, *hsü* is a more positive concept. Even then, Neo-Confucianists used it sparingly.

Hsüan, "profound" or "mysterious." This word has as wide a range of meanings as any other Chinese word. It means dark, abstruse, deep, profound, secret, etc. In Taoist religion the aspect of mystery should be stressed, but in Taoist philosophy, the profound or metaphysical aspect is paramount. Thus *hsüan-hsüeh* should be "metaphysical school," while *hsüan-te* should be "profound and secret virtue." The word simply has to be understood in its context. *Hsüan-ming*, for example, is not just "profoundly dark," but means noumenon.

Jen, "humanity." *Jen* has been variously translated as benevolence, perfect virtue, goodness, human-heartedness, love, altruism, etc. None of these expresses all the meanings of the term. It means a particular virtue, benevolence, and also the general virtue, the basis of all goodness.

[33] *Mo Tzu*, ch. 8, SPTK, 2:1a.
[34] See above, ch. 34, sec. 135.
[35] *Bernhard Karlgren Dedicata*, p. 210.

In the *Book of Mencius* (6A:11), it is "man's mind." In Han times (206 B.C.–A.D. 220), Confucianists understood it to mean love or "men living together." To Han Yü (768-824) it was universal love. Neo-Confucianists interpreted it as impartiality, the character of production and reproduction, consciousness, seeds that generate, the will to grow, one who forms one body with Heaven and Earth, or "the character of love and the principle of mind." In modern times, it has even been equated with ether and electricity.[36] Etymologically, *jen* means man in society, as the Chinese character for *jen* consists of both the word for man and the word for two (signifying a group). In both the *Book of Mencius* (7B:16) and the *Doctrine of the Mean* (ch. 20) *jen* is equated with man. Waley's "Goodness,"[37] Hughes' "human-heartedness,"[38] Bodde's "love,"[39] and Dubs' "benevolent love,"[40] all fail to convey the etymological meaning, although they cover most of the other aspects. Furthermore, "love" is the correct translation for *ai,* and it would confuse *jen* and *ai* in Chu Hsi's dictum, "*jen* is the character of love,"[41] and Mencius' saying, "The man of *jen* loves others."[42] Boodberg's "humanity" and "co-humanity"[43] and Lin Yutang's "true manhood"[44] are good. My choice is "humanity," for it seems to express all meanings and also has an adjective form while "true manhood" does not. Of course it is absurd to say that humanity is ether or electricity, but these are used really as metaphors. "Humanity" takes care of all the Neo-Confucian interpretations, for humanity certainly possesses the characteristics of life-giving and the like, and it is man who forms one body with Heaven and Earth.[45]

Kuei-shen, "spiritual beings" and "positive spiritual force and negative spiritual force." Ch'en Ch'un said that *kuei-shen* should be discussed under four categories: that in the Confucian Classics, that in ancient religious sacrifices, that in latter-day religious sacrifices, and that referring to demons and gods.[46] By the Confucian Classics he meant the Classics as interpreted by the Neo-Confucianists, namely, *kuei-shen* as

[36] For comments on these interpretations, see above, ch. 30, sec. 1; ch. 31, secs. 1 and 11; ch. 32, sec. 42; ch. 34, treatise 1; ch. 40, Introduction.

[37] *Analects of Confucius,* p. 83.

[38] *Chinese Philosophy in Classical Times,* p. 13. Lucius Porter and Bodde also used this translation. See Fung, *History of Chinese Philosophy,* vol. 1, p. 69.

[39] "On Translating Chinese Philosophic Terms," FEQ, 14 (1955), 235-237.

[40] "The Development of Altruism in Confucianism," PEW, 1 (1951), 48-49.

[41] See above, ch. 34, treatise 1.

[42] *Mencius,* 4B:28.

[43] "The Semasiology of Some Primary Confucian Concepts," PEW, 2 (1953), 327-330; also book review in FEQ, 13 (1954), p. 334.

[44] *Wisdom of Confucius,* p. 184.

[45] For a succinct but excellent discussion on *jen* and Neo-Confucian interpretations, see Ch'en Ch'un, *Hsing-li tzu-i,* pt. 1, sections on *jen.*

[46] *op.cit.,* pt. 2, entry on *kuei-shen.*

positive and negative forces behind events. Thus expansion is *shen* while contraction is *kuei*. This naturalistic and philosophical meaning should always be kept entirely distinct from the other meaning in the first three categories, namely, *kuei-shen* as spiritual beings. In ancient times *shen* usually refers to heavenly beings while *kuei* refers to spirits of deceased human beings. In latter-day sacrifices, *kuei-shen* together refers to ancestors. In popular religion *shen* means gods (who are good) and demons (who are not always good). In Neo-Confucianism *kuei-shen* may refer to all these three categories but more often than not the term refers to the activity of the material force (*ch'i*). Chang Tsai's dictum, "The negative spirit (*kuei*) and positive spirit (*shen*) are the spontaneous activity of the two material forces (yin and yang),"[47] has become the generally accepted definition.

Li, "ceremony," etc. *Li* originally means a religious sacrifice but has come to mean ceremony, ritual, decorum, rules of propriety, good form, good custom, etc., and has even been equated with Natural Law.[48] Obviously the translation "rites" or "ceremony" is too narrow and misleading. I use "Book of Rites" for the *Li chi* simply because it is becoming common and because of want of a good translation. But the term *li* itself has to be rendered differently in different context. Boodberg is right in saying that "Form" understood as ritual form, social form, or good form serves best,[49] but in this case it is difficult to use a uniform translation.

Te, "virtue" or "character." *Te* ordinarily means moral character but in relation to Tao it means Tao particularized when inherent in a thing. The classical definition of it is to *te* (attain or be able to). Waley is correct in understanding it as a latent power, a virtue inherent in something and in rendering it as "power."[50] But "power" does not connote moral excellence which the word *te* involves. Both "virtue" and "character" seem to be better.

T'i-jen, "realization through personal experience." Literally "to recognize through one's own person," this basic Neo-Confucian term denotes a special method of knowledge, namely, to realize through sincere effort and personal experience in order to attain an intimate and genuine realization.

[47] See above, ch. 30, sec. 10.
[48] See Hu Shih, "The Natural Law in the Chinese Tradition," in *Natural Law Institute Proceedings,* 1953, 5:142-145. Hu is not inclined to accept the equation by Kenneth Scott Latourette and Joseph Needham, but he believes that *li* has time and again played the role of a higher law.
[49] "The Semasiology of Some Primary Confucian Concepts," PEW, 2 (1953), pp. 326-327.
[50] *The Way and Its Power,* 1934, p. 33.

T'i-yung, "substance and function." Variously rendered as "essence and application" or "operation." The term originated with Wang Pi (226-249) in his commentary on *Lao Tzu*, ch. 38.[51] There he equated *wu* (non-being) with *t'i*, thus providing the term with a metaphysical meaning. It became one of the most prominent terms in Buddhism and Neo-Confucianism and the metaphysical concept is a major one in those systems. In this connection the term is not to be understood in the sense of form or body as Boodberg has contended.[52]

Wu, "non-being." There is nothing wrong in rendering *wu* as a negative. However, in some cases it has to be interpreted. For example, *wu-hsin* is not just "no mind" but "no deliberate mind of one's own," and *wu-wei* is not simply "inaction" but "taking no unnatural action," or in Buddhist usage, "not produced from causes." Boodberg thinks *yu* and *wu* should not be rendered as "being" and "non-being," because they are essentially transitive verbs.[53] But in *Lao Tzu*, chs. 2, 40, etc., and in many places in the *Chuang Tzu*,[54] for example, they are not verbs and mean exactly "being" and "non-being."

[51] See above, ch. 19, sec. 3.
[52] *op.cit.*, pp. 335-336.
[53] Peter Boodberg, "Philosophical Notes on Chapter One of the *Lao Tzu*," *Harvard Journal of Asiatic Studies*, 20 (1957), pp. 598-618.
[54] For example, *Chuang Tzu*, chs. 2, 6 and 12, SPTK, 1:33b-34a, 3:15a; 5:9a. Cf. Giles, trans., *Chuang Tzu*, 1961 ed., pp. 41, 79, 122.

THIS BIBLIOGRAPHY is largely limited to the most essential titles. For a more extensive bibliography with specific page references on specific topics and with comments on works referred to, see Chan, *Outline and Annotated Bibliography*. For full titles and publication facts, see the alphabetical list at the end.

The best history of Chinese philosophy is Fung, *History*, 2 vols. Next come Fung, *Short History*, which is more technical, and Creel, *Chinese Thought*, which is more general, as are Day's *Philosophers of China* and Chai's *Story*. For short surveys, see Chan's "Chinese Philosophy," *Encyclopedia Britannica*, 1960, and "Story of Chinese Philosophy," in Moore, ed., *Philosophy East and West*, pp. 24-68. For the ancient period, add Hu, *Logical Method*, and Waley, *Three Ways of Thought*. Source materials are found in de Bary, Chan, and Watson, comp., *Chinese Tradition* (all periods); Hughes, *Classical Times* (ancient), and Lin Yutang, *Wisdom of China and India* (ancient).

CH. 1. THE GROWTH OF HUMANISM

The best accounts are found in Fung, *History*, vol. 1, pp. 7-42 and Hu, *Logical Methods*, pp. 1-9. Hughes, *Classical Times*, pp. xxiv-xxx gives some helpful additional information.

CH. 2. THE HUMANISM OF CONFUCIUS

Excellent studies are: Fung, *History*, vol. 1, pp. 43-75, *Short History*, pp. 38-48, *Spirit of Chinese Philosophy*, pp. 10-28, Hu, *Logical Methods*, pp. 22-27, Creel, *Chinese Thought*, pp. 25-45, Lin Yutang, *Wisdom of Confucius*, pp. 3-24, and Liu, *Confucian Philosophy*, pp. 13-25. For a general survey, see Chan, "Confucius," *Encyclopedia Britannica*, 1960. On Confucius' life, Lin, *Wisdom of Confucius*, pp. 53-100 contains a translation of the standard biography, and Creel, *Confucius*, pp. 75-141, offers some interesting theories, and Liu, *Confucius*, pp. 141-156, gives a general picture. For a discussion of Confucian humanism, see Chan, "Chinese Theory and Practice," in Moore, ed., *Philosophy and Culture*, pp. 80-95. For translations of the *Analects*, read Legge, *Confucian Analects*, in *Chinese Classics*, vol. 1, pp. 137-354, Waley, *Analects of Confucius*, and also selections by Lin Yutang, in *Wisdom of Confucius*, pp. 160-204.

CH. 3. IDEALISTIC CONFUCIANISM: MENCIUS

For general discussions, see Fung, *History*, vol. 1, pp. 106-131, *Short History*, pp. 68-79, Liu, *Confucian Philosophy*, pp. 59-89, Creel, *Chinese Thought*, pp. 68-93, and Waley, *Three Ways of Thought*, pp. 115-162. For a brief survey, see Chan, "Mencius," *Encyclopedia Britannica*, 1960. For translation, see Legge, *Works of Mencius*, Ware's *Sayings of Mencius* is a fairly free rendering.

CH. 4. MORAL AND SOCIAL PROGRAMS: THE *Great Learning*

The only instructive studies are Fung, *History*, vol. 1, pp. 361-369, and *Short History*, pp. 181-183. Good translations are Legge, "Great Learning," in *Chinese Classics*, vol. 1, pp. 355-381, and Lin Yutang, "The Great Learning," *Wisdom of Confucius*, pp. 135-152.

Ch. 5. Spiritual Dimensions: The *Doctrine of the Mean*

For helpful discussions, see Fung, *History*, vol. 1, pp. 369-377 and *Short History*, pp. 172-177. Legge's translation, "Doctrine of the Mean," in *Chinese Classics*, vol. 1, pp. 382-434, is sound and Ku Hung-ming's interpretative rendering in Lin Yutang, *Wisdom of Confucius*, pp. 100-134, is stimulating.

Ch. 6. Naturalistic Confucianism: Hsün Tzu

For profitable reading see Hu, *Logical Methods*, pp. 149-158, Fung, *History*, vol. 1, pp. 279-311, *Short History*, pp. 143-154, Liu, *Confucian Philosophy*, pp. 90-103, Dubs, *Hsüntze*, pp. xxv-xxxi, 48-56, and Creel, *Chinese Thought*, pp. 115-134. For translation, see Dubs, *Works of Hsüntze*. Compare his translation of ch. 22 on the rectification of names with those by Duyvendak, TP, 23, pp. 221-254 and by Mei, PEW, 1, pp. 51-66. For ch. 1, see Mei, "Hsün Tzu's Theory of Education," THJ, 2, pp. 361-377.

Ch. 7. The Natural Way of Lao Tzu

Good studies include Fung, *History*, vol. 1, pp. 170-191, *Short History*, pp. 93-103, Hu, *Logical Methods*, pp. 13-20, Chan, *The Way of Lao Tzu*, Introduction, Creel, *Chinese Thought*, pp. 94-114, T. C. Lin, "The Chinese Mind," JHI, 8, pp. 259-273, and C. Y. Ching, "Concept of Tao," RR, 17, pp. 126-130. For translations see Waley, *The Way and Its Power*, Chan, *op.cit.*, Lin Yutang, *The Wisdom of Laotse*, and Duyvendak, *Tao Te Ching*.

Ch. 8. The Mystical Way of Chuang Tzu

Fung, *History*, vol. 1, pp. 221-245, *Short History*, pp. 104-117, *Spirit of Chinese Philosophy*, pp. 65-80, Creel, *Chinese Thought*, pp. 94-114, and Waley, *Three Ways of Thought*, pp. 67-86, are all helpful. Herbert Giles' translation, *Chuang Tzu*, is complete but not good, while that of Fung, *Chuang Tzu*, is good but confined to chs. 1-7. Lin Yutang's version of chs. 1-6, 8-11, and 17 in *Wisdom of China and India* and of ch. 33 in *Wisdom of Laotse*, pp. 23-37, is excellent.

Ch. 9. Mo Tzu's Doctrines of Universal Love, Heaven, and Social Welfare

The best account is found in Hu, *Logical Methods*, pp. 63-82. Fung, *History*, vol. 1, pp. 76-105, *Short History*, pp. 49-59, *Spirit of Chinese Philosophy*, pp. 34-44, Creel, *Chinese Thought*, pp. 46-67, and Mei, *Motse*, pp. 183-195, are also authoritative. Mei's translation, *Works of Motse*, is good.

Ch. 10. Debates on Metaphysical Concepts: The Logicians

An original approach is found in Hu, *Logical Methods*, pp. 109-130. Fung offers a different approach in *History*, vol. 1, pp. 192-220, *Short History*, pp. 80-92, and *Spirit of Chinese Philosophy*, pp. 45-58. Mei, "Some Observations on the Problems of Knowledge," TJ, n.s. 1, no. 1, pp. 114-121, is suggestive, and Needham, *Scientific Thought*, pp. 189-197, dealing with science, is penetrating. Mei's translation, *Kung-sun Lung Tzu*, is the best.

CH. 11. THE YIN YANG SCHOOL

The best account is found in Fung, *Short History*, pp. 129-138. Also helpful is his *History*, vol. 1, pp. 159-169; vol. 2, pp. 7-16. For fundamental Yin Yang ideas of science, see Needham, *Scientific Thought*, pp. 232-278.

CH. 12. LEGALISM

For good discussions see Hu, *Logical Methods*, pp. 170-187, Fung, *History*, vol. 1, pp. 312-336, *Short History*, pp. 155-165, and Waley, *Three Ways of Thought*, pp. 199-247. Also consult Liang, *Chinese Political Thought*, pp. 113-138; John Wu, "Chinese Legal Philosophy," CC, 1, no. 4, pp. 7-48; and Chen En-cheng, "Han Fei's Principle of Government by Law," *ibid.*, pp. 91-103. For translations of Legalist works, see under "Han Fei Tzu" and "Shang Yang" in the alphabetical list below.

CH. 13. THE PHILOSOPHY OF CHANGE

Y. T. T'ang, "Wang Pi's New Interpretation of the *I-ching* and *Lun-yü*," HJAS, 10, pp. 124-161, is indispensable. An original treatment is Hu, *Logical Methods*, pp. 28-45, and so is Fung, *History*, vol. 1, pp. 379-395 (also *Short History*, pp. 138-142, and *Spirit of Chinese Philosophy*, pp. 81-103). On scientific thought, see Needham, *Scientific Thought*, pp. 304-340. A general and excellent survey is Hellmut Wilhelm, *Change*. The best translation is still Legge, *Yi King*. Richard Wilhelm's German version rendered into English, *I Ching*, is good but interpretative to some extent.

CH. 14. YIN YANG CONFUCIANISM: TUNG CHUNG-SHU

Fung, *History*, vol. 2, pp. 16-87, *Short History*, pp. 191-203, *Spirit of Chinese Philosophy*, pp. 117-125, and Liu, *Confucian Philosophy*, pp. 124-126, are all satisfactory. Yao, "Cosmological and Anthropological Philosophy," JNCBRAS, 73, pp. 40-68, is comprehensive and informative. Only a small amount of Tung's works has been translated, in *Lectures chinoises*, 1, pp. 1-17, de Bary, *Chinese Tradition*, pp. 178-183, and Hughes, *Classical Times*, pp. 293-308.

CH. 15. TAOISTIC CONFUCIANISM: YANG HSIUNG

The only reading really worth while on Yang Hsiung is Fung, *History*, vol. 2, pp. 136-150. There are a German translation of his *Fa-yen* (Model Sayings) by von Zach, "Fa-yen," in SB, 4, pp. 1-74, and a French version by Belpaire, *Yang-Hiong-tsé*.

CH. 16. THE NATURALISM OF WANG CH'UNG

Fairly good studies are found in Fung, *History*, vol. 2, pp. 150-167, Li, "Wang Ch'ung," THM, 5, pp. 162-184, 290-307, and Alfred Forke, in Wang Ch'ung, *Lun-Heng*, vol. 1, pp. 13-44. Needham, *Scientific Thought*, pp. 371-386, concerns science. Alfred Forke, "Wang-Chung and Plato on Death and Immortality," JNCBRAS, 31, pp. 40-60, is a critical study. Translation by Forke, *Lun-Heng*, is reliable.

Ch. 17. The Taoism of Huai-nan Tzu

See Fung, *History*, vol. 1, pp. 395-399, and *Spirit of Chinese Philosophy*, pp. 112-117. Morgan, *Tao, The Great Luminant*, is poor both in translation and in study.

Ch. 18. Negative Taoism in the *Lieh Tzu* and the Yang Chu Chapter

Fung, *History*, vol. 2, pp. 190-204 and *Short History*, pp. 232-235, are recommended. Needham, *Scientific Thought*, pp. 40-41, 53-54, is brief but significant. For translation, see Graham, *Book of Lieh Tzu*.

Ch. 19. Neo-Taoism

For Wang Pi, there are excellent studies: Y. T. T'ang, "Wang Pi's New Interpretations of the *I-ching* and *Lun-yü*," hjas, 10, pp. 124-161, Fung, *History*, vol. 2, pp. 168-189, and *Spirit of Chinese Philosophy*, pp. 135-138, 154, Kenneth Ch'en, "Neo-Taoism and the Prajña School," cc, 1, no. 2, pp. 38-41, and Wright, Review of Petro: *Wang Pi*, hjas, 10, pp. 75-88. For Kuo Hsiang, see Fung, *History*, vol. 2, pp. 205-236, *Short History*, pp. 220-230, *Spirit of Chinese Philosophy*, pp. 135-146, 154, and *Chuang Tzu*, comments on chs. 1 and 2, and pp. 145-157.

Ch. 20. The Seven Early Buddhist Schools

Fung, *History*, vol. 2, pp. 244-258, Liebenthal, *Book of Chao*, pp. 149-166, Kenneth Ch'en "Neo-Taoism and the Prajña School," cc, 1, no. 2, pp. 35-37, Zürcher, *Buddhist Conquest of China*, pp. 95-102, 116-137, 177-179, 184-204, Demiéville, "La pénétration du bouddhisme," chm, 1, pp. 25-27, 30-31, Link, "Problem of Buddho-Taoist Terminology," jaos, 77, pp. 1-14 (translation) are all top-notch works.

Ch. 21. Seng-chao's Doctrine of Reality

See Fung, *History*, vol. 2, pp. 258-270, *Short History*, pp. 246-248, *Spirit of Chinese Philosophy*, pp. 146-155, and Liebenthal, *Book of Chao*, pp. 46-66 (translation) and pp. 21-38 (study).

Ch. 22. The Philosophy of Emptiness: Chi-tsang of the Three-Treatise School

Basic references are: Fung, *History*, vol. 2, pp. 293-299, *Short History*, pp. 245-246, Takakusu, *Buddhist Philosophy*, pp. 96-107, and Chan, *Religious Trends*, pp. 102-103.

Ch. 23. Buddhist Idealism: Hsüan-tsang of the Consciousness-Only School

Fung, *History*, vol. 2, pp. 299-338, Takakusu, *Buddhist Philosophy*, pp. 80-95, Keith, *Buddhist Philosophy*, pp. 242-251, Thomas, *Buddhist Thought*, pp. 230-248, Chan, *Religious Trends*, pp. 105-135, are all important. Expert translation of Hsüan-tsang's work is La Vallée-Poussin's *Le siddhi de Hiuan-Tsang*, and those of Vasubandhu's works are Hamilton, *Treatise in Twenty Stanzas* and Lévi, *L'étude du système Vijñaptimātra*.

BIBLIOGRAPHY

CH. 24. THE T'IEN-T'AI PHILOSOPHY OF PERFECT HARMONY

Excellent accounts are given in Fung, *History*, vol. 2, pp. 360-386, Taka-kusu, *Buddhist Philosophy*, pp. 126-141, Chan, *Religious Trends*, pp. 95-105, and Petzold, *Tendai Teaching*, pp. 1-49. On the *Lotus Scripture*, see Chan, "The Lotus Sūtra," in de Bary, ed., *Approaches to the Oriental Classics*, pp. 153-165.

CH. 25. THE ONE-AND-ALL PHILOSOPHY: FA-TSANG OF THE HUA-YEN SCHOOL

For good discussions, see Fung, *History*, vol. 2, pp. 339-359, Takakusu, *Buddhist Philosophy*, pp. 29-56, 108-125, and Chan, *Religious Trends*, pp. 95-105.

CH. 26. THE ZEN (CH'AN) SCHOOL OF SUDDEN ENLIGHTENMENT

Much of the tremendous literature on Zen is inspirational rather than philosophical. Good systematic presentations are Fung, *History*, vol. 2, pp. 386-406, *Short History*, pp. 255-265, *Spirit of Chinese Philosophy*, pp. 156-174, Chen-chi Chang, *Practice of Zen*, *passim*, Takakusu, *Buddhist Philosophy*, pp. 153-165, and Chan, trans., *Platform Scripture*, Introduction. For historical and mystical approaches to Zen, see Hu, "Chan (Zen) Buddhism in China," PEW, 3, pp. 3-24, and Suzuki, "Zen: A Reply to Hu Shih," *ibid.*, pp. 25-46. A brief history of Zen is contained in Dumoulin, *Development of Chinese Zen*, pp. 3-44. Special topics are discussed in Suzuki's well-known series of *Essays in Zen Buddhism*. His *Studies in the Lankāvatāra* is an authoritative philosophical study. More general treatises on special subjects are his *Studies in Zen*, and *Zen Doctrine of No-Mind*, and also Chan's "Transformation of Buddhism in China," PEW, 7, pp. 107-116. For translations of Zen works, aside from Suzuki and Dumoulin mentioned above, see under *Lankāvatāra sūtra*, Hui-neng, Shen-hui, Hui-hai, Hsi-yün, and Chan. Also see Day, *Philosophers of China*, pp. 129-159.

CH. 27. THE REVIVAL OF CONFUCIANISM: HAN YÜ AND LI AO

Illuminating accounts are found in Fung, *History*, vol. 2, pp. 407-424, Carsun Chang, *Neo-Confucian Thought*, pp. 79-111, and Liu, *Confucian Philosophy*, pp. 138-143. Special problems are discussed in Chan, "Confucian Concept *Jen*," PEW, 4, pp. 303-304, de Bary, "Reappraisal of Neo-Confucianism," in Wright, *Studies in Chinese Thought*, pp. 83-88, and Rideout, "Context of the *Yüan Tao* and *Yüan Hsing*," BSOAS, 12, pp. 403-408.

CH. 28. THE NEO-CONFUCIAN METAPHYSICS AND ETHICS IN CHOU TUN-I

Systematic treatments have been given in Fung, *History*, vol. 2, pp. 434-451, *Short History*, pp. 269-272, Carsun Chang, *Neo-Confucian Thought*, pp. 137-158, Alfred Forke, *Neueren chinesischen Philosophie*, pp. 45-56, and Chow, *Philosophie morale*, pp. 80-140. For a French translation of the *T'ung-shu* (On Understanding the *Book of Changes*), see Chow, pp. 163-188, and for translations of selections, see Hsü, *Neo-Confucian Thought*, pp. i-vi, Graf, *Djin-sï lu*, vol. 2, *passim*, de Harlez, *L'école philosophique moderne*, pp. 25-32, and de Bary, *Chinese Tradition*, pp. 513-515.

CH. 29. THE NUMERICAL AND OBJECTIVE TENDENCIES IN SHAO YUNG

General surveys are: Fung, *History*, vol. 2, pp. 451-476, *Short History*, pp. 272-278, Carsun Chang, *Neo-Confucian Thought*, pp. 159-167, Liu, *Confucian Philosophy*, pp. 155-157, and Alfred Forke, *Neueren chinesischen Philosophie*, pp. 18-40. de Harlez, *L'école philosophique moderne*, pp. 82-110, and de Bary, *Chinese Tradition*, pp. 516-520, offer limited translations.

CH. 30. CHANG TSAI'S PHILOSOPHY OF MATERIAL FORCE

See Fung, *History*, vol. 2, pp. 477-498, *Short History*, pp. 278-280, *Spirit of Chinese Philosophy*, pp. 175-179, Carsun Chang, *Neo-Confucian Thought*, pp. 167-183, and Liu, *Confucian Philosophy*, pp. 157-159. C. I. T'ang, "Chang Tsai's Theory of Mind," PEW, 6, pp. 113-136, Chan, "The Concept of Man in Chinese Thought," in Radhakrishnan and Raju, ed., *Concept of Man*, pp. 177-182, and his "Neo-Confucian Solution of the Problem of Evil," BIHPAS, 28, pp. 780-783, are excellent discussions. Translations can be found in Eichhorn, "Die Westinschrift," AKM, 22, pp. 9-75, Hsü, *Neo-Confucian Thought*, pp. vi-xii, Graf, *Djin-sï lu*, vol. 2, *passim*, de Harlez, *L'école philosophique moderne*, pp. 36-76, and de Bary, *Chinese Tradition*, pp. 521-525.

CH. 31. THE IDEALISTIC TENDENCY IN CH'ENG HAO *and*
CH. 32. THE RATIONALISTIC TENDENCY IN CH'ENG I

Good studies are: Fung, *History*, vol. 2, pp. 498-532, *Short History*, pp. 281-293, *Spirit of Chinese Philosophy*, pp. 179-186, Graham, *Two Philosophers*, pp. 3-151, Carsun Chang, *Neo-Confucian Thought*, pp. 185-229, Liu, *Confucian Philosophy*, pp. 159-160, Chan, "Confucian Concept Jen," PEW, 4, pp. 311-314, and his "Neo-Confucian Solution of the Problem of Evil," BIHPAS, 28, pp. 784-791. Extensive translations are found in Ts'ai, *Philosophy of Ch'eng I*, and limited translation in Graf, *Djin-sï lu*, vol. 2, *passim*, and de Bary, *Chinese Tradition*, pp. 527-533, 559-564.

CH. 33. THE UNITY OF MIND AND PRINCIPLE IN LU HSIANG-SHAN

Fung, *History*, vol. 2, pp. 572-579, 585-592, Huang, *Lu Hsiang-shan*, pp. 30-97, Carsun Chang, *Neo-Confucian Thought*, pp. 146-151, 285-307, Creel, *Chinese Thought*, pp. 209-213, and Cady, *Lu Hsiang-shan*, pp. 348-415, are all excellent. There are extensive translations in Cady, pp. 95-115, 129-180, and brief selections in de Bary, *Chinese Tradition*, pp. 565-569.

CH. 34. THE GREAT SYNTHESIS IN CHU HSI

Valuable studies are Fung, *History*, vol. 2, pp. 533-571, *Short History*, pp. 294-306, *Spirit of Chinese Philosophy*, pp. 186-192, Carsun Chang, *Neo-Confucian Thought*, pp. 146-151, 243-283, 290-336, Liu, *Confucian Philosophy*, pp. 160-164, Creel, *Chinese Thought*, pp. 206-209, Bruce, *Chu Hsi*, pp. 99-314, Hsü, *Neo-Confucian Thought*, pp. 25-146, and Alfred Forke, *Neueren chinesischen Philosophie*, pp. 164-202. For superior discussions on special problems, see Needham, *Scientific Thought*, pp. 496-505, Bodde, "The Chinese View of Immortality," RR 6, pp. 369-383, Graf, *Djin-sï lu*, vol. 1, pp. 278-286, Chan, "Confucian Concept Jen," PEW, 4, pp. 307-314, his "Synthesis in Chinese Metaphysics," in Moore, *Essays*, pp. 163-177, and his "Neo-Confucianism and Chinese Scientific Thought," PEW, 6, pp. 301-310, Sargent, *Tchou Hi contre le Bouddhisme*, pp. 10-45, and his "Tchou Hi en matière de methodologie," JA, 243, pp. 213-228. For translations, see Bruce, *Philosophy of Human Nature*, Graf, vol. 2, Pang, *L'idée de Dieu*, pp. 73-119, Le Gall, *Tchou Hi*, pp. 81-123, de Harlez, *La Siao Hio*, Wieger, *Textes philosophiques*, pp. 187-254, Sargent, pp. 55-148, de Bary, *Chinese Tradition*, pp. 536-557.

CH. 35. DYNAMIC IDEALISM IN WANG YANG-MING

Enlightening discussions are given in Fung, *History*, vol. 2, pp. 596-620, *Short History*, pp. 308-318, Carsun Chang, "Wang Yang-ming's Philosophy," PEW, 5, pp. 3-18, and his *Wang Yang-ming*, pp. 13-73, Chan, *Instructions for Practical Living*, Introduction, his "How Buddhistic Is Wang Yang-ming," PEW, 11 (1962), 203-216, and his "Wang Yang-ming," *Encyclopedia Britannica*, 1960, Hsü, *Neo-Confucian Thought*, pp. 138-146, T. T. Wang, "La philosophie morale de Wang Yang-ming," pp. 38-119, Liu, *Confucian Philosophy*, pp. 167-173. Iki, "Wang Yang-ming's Doctrine of Innate Knowledge," PEW, 11, pp. 27-44, and Day, *Philosophers of China*, pp. 215-228. For translations, see Chan's rendering of Wang's works, which supplants Henke, *Philosophy of Wang Yang-ming*, and selections in de Bary, *Chinese Tradition*, pp. 571-581.

CH. 36. THE MATERIALISM OF WANG FU-CHIH

One can have a glimpse in Fung, *History*, vol. 2, pp. 641-643, 648-649. Lin Mousheng's *Men and Ideas*, pp. 200-214, deals with Wang's political thought. For translation, see de Bary, *Chinese Tradition*, pp. 597-606.

CH. 37. PRACTICAL CONFUCIANISM IN YEN YÜAN

Not much material. Fung, *History*, vol. 2, pp. 631-639, 644-648, and Creel, *Chinese Thought*, pp. 224-226 are satisfactory for a general survey.

CH. 38. TAI CHEN'S PHILOSOPHY OF PRINCIPLE AS ORDER

See Fung, *History*, vol. 2, pp. 651-672, and Creel, *Chinese Thought*, pp. 226-234 for good discussions. Summaries of Tai's philosophy are given in Chan's "The Story of Chinese Philosophy," in Moore, ed., *Philosophy East and West*, pp. 65-68, and his "Neo-Confucianism," in MacNair, ed., *China*, pp. 261-263. Hummel, *Eminent Chinese*, pp. 695-700 gives a general account of his life, works, and ideas.

CH. 39. K'ANG YU-WEI'S PHILOSOPHY OF GREAT UNITY

By far the best study is Hsiao, Kung-ch'üan's "K'ung Yu-wei and Confucianism," MS 18, 96-212. Fung, *History*, vol. 2, pp. 676-705 is good. Account of his life and translation of his *Ta T'ung-shu* (Book of Great Unity) is found in Thompson, *Ta T'ung-shu*. See also Lo, Jung-pang, ed., *K'ang Yu-wei* for good studies.

CH. 40. THE PHILOSOPHY OF HUMANITY (*Jen*) IN T'AN SSU-T'UNG

The best study is Fung, *History*, vol. 2, pp. 691-705. For comprehensive studies, see Oka, "The Philosophy of T'an Ssu-t'ung," POC, 9, pp. 1-47, and

Kiang Shao-yuen, "The Philosophy of Tang-Ssu-Tung," OP, 36, pp. 449-471. Talbott's "T'an Ssu-t'ung and the Ether," in Sakai, ed., *Studies on Asia*, 1960, pp. 20-34, dealing with science, is helpful. There is a general account in Hummel, *Eminent Chinese*, pp. 702-705.

CH. 41. CHANG TUNG-SUN'S THEORY OF KNOWLEDGE

Only one of Chang's works is available in English: "A Chinese Philosopher's Theory of Knowledge," *Etc.*, 9, pp. 203-226. There are short summaries of his thought in Chan, "Trends in Contemporary Philosophy," in MacNair, ed., *China*, pp. 319-320, and Brière, *Fifty Years of Chinese Philosophy*, pp. 66-72.

CH. 42. THE NEW RATIONALISTIC CONFUCIANISM: FUNG YU-LAN

For his own summary of his ideas, see his *Short History*, pp. 334-342. For a summary and discussion, see Chan, *Religious Trends*, pp. 43-53, and Day, *Philosophers of China*, pp. 330-346. Shorter summaries are found in Chan, "Philosophies of China," in Runes, ed., *Twentieth Century Philosophy*, pp. 562-567, or his "Trends in Contemporary Philosophy," in MacNair, ed., *China*, pp. 326-330, and Brière, *Fifty Years of Chinese Philosophy*, pp. 50-53. See also Sheehan, *A Summary of Fung Yu-lan's Hsin Yüan-jen*.

CH. 43. THE NEW IDEALISTIC CONFUCIANISM: HSIUNG SHIH-LI

Hsiung is virtually unknown in the West. For a summary of his philosophy and his criticism of Buddhism, see Chan, *Religious Trends*, pp. 32-43, 126-135. A very brief résumé is also found in Brière, *Fifty Years of Chinese Philosophy*, pp. 48-50, Day, *Philosophers of China*, pp. 327-330, and Chan, "Trends in Contemporary Philosophy," in MacNair, ed., *China*, p. 324.

CH. 44. CHINESE PHILOSOPHY IN COMMUNIST CHINA

There is a brief account in Brière, *Fifty Years of Chinese Philosophy*, pp. 75-85. Some reference, though little, is contained in T. K. David, *Philosophy in Contemporary China*, FECR, 23, pp. 35-37, and Willetts, "Philosophy in Changing China," *Humanist*, 71, no. 9, pp. 22-24. For Fung Yu-lan, see his "Philosophy in New China," EW, 1952, pp. 105-107; "I Discovered Marxism-Leninism," PC, 1950, no. 6, pp. 10-11, 21; and "Problems in the Study of Confucius," *ibid.*, 1957, no. 1, pp. 21-22, 27-31. Dai Shen-yu's comparative study in his *Mao Tse-tung and Confucianism*, is quite instructive.

The following list includes works in the European languages referred to in this work. For a longer list, see Chan, *Outline and Annotated Bibliography*.

Asanga, *Le somme du Grand Véhicule*, trans. into French by Étienne Lamotte, 2 vols., Louvain, Bureaux du Muséon, 1938-1939.

Aśvagosha, *Aśvaghosa's Discourse on the Awakening of Faith in the Mahāyāna*, trans. by Teitarō Suzuki. Chicago, Open Court, 1900.

Baynes, Cary F., trans. See *I ching*.

Belpaire, B., trans. See Yang Hsiung.

Blackney, R. B., trans. See Lao Tzu.

BIBLIOGRAPHY

Blofeld, John, trans. See Hsi-yün, Huang-po, and Hui-hai.

Bodde, Derk, "The Chinese View of Immortality: Its Expression by Chu Hsi and Its Relationship to Buddhist Thought," *Review of Religion*, 6 (1942), 369-383.

————, "On Translating Chinese Philosophical Terms," *Far Eastern Quarterly* 14 (1955), 235-237.

————, "A Perplexing Passage in the Confucian Analects," *Journal of the American Oriental Society*, 53 (1933), 347-351.

————, trans. See Fung Yu-lan.

Boodberg, Peter, "The Semasiology of Some Primary Confucian Concepts," *Philosophy East and West*, 2 (1953), 327-330.

Book of Changes. See *I ching*.

Book of History. See *Shu ching*.

Book of Mencius. See Mencius.

Book of Odes. See *Shih ching*.

Bruce, J. Percy, *Chu Hsi and His Masters*, London, Probsthain, 1923.

————, trans. See Chu Hsi.

————, "The Theistic Import of the Sung Philosophy," *Journal of the North China Branch of the Royal Asiatic Society*, 49 (1918), 111-127.

Cady, Lyman Van Law, "The Philosophy of Lu Hsiang-shan, A Neo-Confucian Monistic Idealist," typescript, 2 vols., New York, Union Theological Seminary, 1939.

Chai, Ch'u, "Neo-Confucianism of the Sung-Ming Periods," *Social Research*, 18 (1951), 370-392.

————, with Winberg Chai. *The Story of Chinese Philosophy*, paperback. New York: Washington Square Press, 1961.

Chan, Wing-tsit, Articles on *Ch'i, Jen, Li*, etc., in Dagobert D. Runes, ed., *The Dictionary of Philosophy*, New York, Philosophical Library, 1942, *passim*.

————, "The Chinese Concept of Man in Chinese Thought," in S. Radhakrishnan and P. T. Raju, ed., *The Concept of Man: A Study in Comparative Philosophy*, London, Allen and Unwin, 1960, pp. 158-205.

————, "Chinese Philosophy," *Encyclopedia Britannica*, 1960, vol. 5, pp. 581-584.

————, "Chinese Theory and Practice, with Special Reference to Humanism," in Moore, ed., *Philosophy and Culture*, pp. 80-95.

————, "Confucianism," *ibid.*, vol. 6, pp. 237-239.

————, "The Evolution of the Confucian Concept *Jen*," *Philosophy East and West*. 4 (1955), 295-319.

————, "How Buddhistic Is Wang Yang-ming?" *Philosophy East and West*, 12 (1962), pp. 203-216.

————, "The Lotus Sūtra," in Wm. Theodore de Bary, ed., *Approaches to the Oriental Classics*, New York, Columbia University Press, 1959, pp. 153-165.

————, "Mencius," *Encyclopedia Britannica*, 1960, vol. 15, pp. 239-240.

————, "The Neo-Confucian Solution of the Problem of Evil," *Studies Presented to Hu Shih on His Sixty-fifth Birthday, The Bulletin of the Institute of History and Philology, Academia Sinica*, 28 (1957), 773-791.

———, "Neo-Confucianism and Chinese Scientific Thought," *Philosophy East and West*, 6 (1957), 309-332.

———, *An Outline and an Annotated Bibliography of Chinese Philosophy*, New Haven, Far Eastern Publications, Yale University, 1961.

———, *Religious Trends in Modern China*, New York, Columbia University Press, 1953.

———, Review of A. C. Graham, *Two Chinese Philosophers: Ch'eng Yi-ch'uan and Ch'eng Ming-tao*, in *Journal of the American Oriental Society*, 79 (1959), 150-155.

———, "The Story of Chinese Philosophy," in Charles A. Moore, ed., *Philosophy—East and West*, pp. 24-68.

———, "Synthesis in Chinese Metaphysics," in Moore, ed., *Essays in East-West Philosophy*, pp. 163-177

———, "Transformation in Buddhism in China," *Philosophy East and West*, 7 (1957-1958), 107-116.

———, "Wang Yang-ming," *Encyclopedia Britannica*, 1960, vol. 23, pp. 320-321.

———, *The Way of Lao Tzu, a Translation and Study of the Tao-te ching*, paperback, New York, Bobbs-Merrill, 1963.

———, See also Wang Yang-ming, de Bary, Hui-neng, and Takakusu.

Chang, Carsun, *The Development of Neo-Confucian Thought*, New York, Bookman Associates, 1957.

———, *Wang Yang-ming, the Idealist Philosopher of the Sixteenth-Century China*, New York, St. John's University Press, 1962.

———, "Wang Yang-ming's Philosophy," *Philosophy East and West*, 5 (1955), 3-18; reprinted in *Asian Culture* (Spring 1959), 55-75.

Chang, Chen-chi, *The Practice of Zen*, New York, Harper, 1959.

Chang Chung-Yüan, "The Concept of Tao in Chinese Culture," *Review of Religion*, 17 (1953), 115-132.

Chang Tung-sun, "A Chinese Philosopher's Theory of Knowledge," *Etc.; A Review of General Semantics*, 9 (1952), 203-226; reprinted in S. I. Hayakawa, ed., *Our Language and Our World: Selections from Etc.: A Review of General Semantics*, New York, Harper, 1959, pp. 299-323.

Changes, The Book of. See *I ching*.

Chavannes, Édouard, trans. See Ssu-ma Ch'ien.

Chen En-cheng, "Han Fei's Principle of Government by Law," *Chinese Culture*, 1, no. 4 (1958), 91-103.

Ch'en, Kenneth, "Neo-Taoism and the Prajña School during the Wei and Chin Dynasties," *Chinese Culture*, 1, no. 2 (1957), 33-46.

Ch'en, L. T., trans. See Liang Ch'i-ch'ao.

Ch'eng I, "The Philosophy of Ch'eng I, A Selection of Texts from the *Complete Works*," Typescript, New York, Columbia University, 1950; Ann Arbor, University Microfilms, 1950.

Chou Tun-i, *Ein Beitrag zur Kenntnis der chinesischen Philosophie T'ung-Su des Ceu-tsi, mit Cu-hi's Kommentare*, trans. by Wilhelm Grube, 1890-1891, completed by Werner Eichhorn in *Asia Major*, 8 (1932), 23-104.

Chow Yih-ching, *La philosophie morale dans le Néo-Confucianisme (Tcheou Touen-Yi)*, Paris, Presses Universitaires de France, 1953.

Chu Hsi, *Djin-sï lu*, trans. into German by Olaf Graf, 3 vols., Tokyo, Sophia University Press, 1953.

————, *The Philosophy of Human Nature, by Chu Hsi*, trans. by J. Percy Bruce, London, Probsthain, 1922.

————, *La Siao Hio, ou morale de la jeunesse*, trans. into French by Ch. de Harlez (*Annales du Musée Guimet*, 15), Paris, Musée Guimet, 1889.

Chuang Tzu, *Chuang Tzu, A New Selected Translation with an Exposition of the Philosophy of Kuo Hsiang*, trans. by Yu-lan Fung, Shanghai, Commercial Press, 1933.

————, *Chuang Tzu, Mystic, Moralist, and Social Reformer*, trans. by Herbert A. Giles, reprinted, London, Allen and Unwin, 1961.

Ch'un-ch'iu, The Ch'un Ts'ew, with the Tso Chuen, trans. by James Legge, *The Chinese Classics*, vol. 5, London, Oxford University Press, 1895.

Chung-yung, "Central Harmony," trans. by Ku Hung Ming (originally published as *The Conduct of Life*, London, John Murray, 1906), in Lin Yutang, ed., *The Wisdom of Confucius*, pp. 104-134; also entitled "The Golden Mean of Tsesze," in Lin Yutang, ed., *The Wisdom of China and India*, pp. 845-864.

————, "The Doctrine of the Mean," trans. by James Legge, in his *The Chinese Classics*, vol. 1, Oxford, Clarendon Press, 1893, pp. 382-434; also in James Legge, trans., *The Four Books*.

————, "The Mean-in-Action," trans. by E. R. Hughes, in his *The Great Learning and the Mean-in-Action*, New York, Dutton, 1943, pp. 105-144.

Confucius, *The Analects of Confucius*, trans. by Arthur Waley, London, Allen and Unwin, 1938; paperback, Vintage.

————, *Confucian Analects*, trans. by James Legge, in his *The Chinese Classics*, vol. 1, Oxford, Clarendon Press, 1893, pp. 137-354; also in James Legge, trans., *The Four Books*.

————, *The Wisdom of Confucius*, ed. and trans. by Lin Yutang, New York, The Modern Library, 1938.

Conze, Edward, *Buddhist Wisdom Books*, London, Allen and Unwin, 1958.

Creel, H. G., *Chinese Thought: From Confucius to Mao Tse-tung*, Chicago, University of Chicago Press, 1953; paperback, New American.

————, "The Meaning of Hsing-Ming," *Studia Serica, Bernhard Karlgren Dedicata*, Copenhagen, International Booksellers, 1959, pp. 199-211.

Dai Shen-yu, "Mao Tse-tung and Confucianism," typescript, University of Pennsylvania, 1952; Ann Arbor, University Microfilms, 1953.

David, T. K., "Philosophy in Contemporary China," *Far Eastern Economic Review*, 23 (1957), 35-37.

Day, Clarence Burton, *The Philosophers of China, Classical and Contemporary*, New York, Philosophical Library, 1962; paperback, Citadel.

de Bary, Wm. Theodore, "A Reappraisal of Neo-Confucianism," in Arthur F. Wright, ed., *Studies in Chinese Thought*, pp. 81-111.

————, ed., *Approaches to the Oriental Classics*, New York, Columbia University Press, 1959.

————, Wing-tsit Chan, and Burton Watson, eds., *Sources of Chinese Tradition*, New York, Columbia University Press, 1960.

de Harlez, Ch., *L'École philosophique modern de la Chine ou système de la nature* (*Sing-Li*) (*Mémoires de L'Académie Royale des Sciences des Lettres et des Beaux-Arts de Belgique*, 49), 1890.

————, trans. See Chu Hsi.

Demiéville, P., "Enigmes taoïstes," in Kaizuka Shigeki, ed., *Silver Jubilee Volume of Zinbun-Kagaku-Kenkyusyo*, Kyoto, Kyoto University, 1954, pp. 54-60.

———, "La pénétration du bouddhisme dans la tradition philosophique chinoise," *Cahiers d'Histoire Mondiale*, 1 (1956), 19-38; an elaboration of the summary, "Résumé des cours et travaux de l'année scolaire 1946-47—langue et littérature chinoise," *Annuaire du Collège de France*, 47 (1947), 151-157.

———, "Le miroir spirituel," *Sinologica*, 1 (1948), 112-137.

Doctrine of the Mean. See *Chung-yung*.

Dubs, H. H., "The Archaic Royal Jou Religion," *T'oung Pao*, 46 (1959), 218-259.

———, "Comparison of Greek and Chinese Philosophy," *Chinese Social and Political Science Review*, 17 (1933), 307-327.

———, "The Date and Circumstances of the Philosopher Lao-dz," *Journal of the American Oriental Society*, 61 (1941), 215-221. Further discussions with Bodde, *ibid.*, 62 (1942), 8-13, 300-304; 64 (1944), 24-27.

———, "The Development of Altruism in Confucianism," in W. R. Inge *et al.*, eds., *Radhakrishnan, Comparative Studies in Philosophy*, London, Allen and Unwin, 1951, pp. 267-275; an expansion of "The Development of Altruism in Confucianism," in E. W. Beth, H. J. Pos, and J. H. A. Hollak, eds., *Proceedings of the Tenth International Congress of Philosophy*, Amsterdam, North-Holland Publishing Co., 1949, pp. 235-237; also in *Philosophy East and West*, 1 (1951), 48-55.

———, trans., See Hsün Tzu.

Dumoulin, Von Heinrich, *The Development of Chinese Zen after the Sixth Patriarch in the Light of Mumonkan*, trans. from the German by Ruth Fuller Sasaki, New York, The First Zen Institute of America, 1953.

Duyvendak, J. J. L., trans. See Hsün Tzu, Lao Tzu, and Shang Yang.

Eichhorn, Werner, "Die Westinschrift des Chang Tsai, ein Beitrag zur Geistesgeschichte der nördlichen Sung," *Abhandlungen für die Kunde des Morgenlandes*, 22 (1937), 1-85.

Erkes, E., "Ssu erh pu-wang," [on death], *Asia Major*, n.s. 3 (1952), 156-159; Note by H. H. Dubs, 159-161; Erkes' reply, 4 (1954), 149-150. All in English.

Filial Piety, Book of. See *Hsiao ching*.

Forke, Alfred, *Geschichte der neueren chinesischen Philosophie*, Hamburg, Friederichsen, de Gruyter and Co., 1938.

———, "Wang-Chung and Plato on Death and Immortality," *Journal of the North China Branch of the Royal Asiatic Society*, 31 (1896-1897), 40-60.

———, trans. See Mo Ti and Wang Ch'ung.

Fung Yu-lan, *A History of Chinese Philosophy*, trans. by Derk Bodde, 2 vols., Princeton, Princeton University Press, 1952-1953.

———, "I Discovered Marxism-Leninism," *People's China*, 1, no. 6 (1950), 10-11, 21.

———, "Philosophy in New China according to Fung Yu-lan," *East and West*, July, 1952, 105-107.

———, "Problems in the Study of Confucius," *People's China*, 1957, no. 1 (January), 21-22, 27-31.

————, *A Short History of Chinese Philosophy*, New York, Macmillan, 1948; paperback, Macmillan.

————, *The Spirit of Chinese Philosophy*, trans. by E. R. Hughes, London, Kegan Paul, 1947.

————, trans. See Chuang Tzu.

Gernet, Jacques, trans. See Shen-hui.

Giles, Herbert A., trans. See Chuang Tzu.

Graf, O., trans. See Chu Hsi.

Graham, A. C., *Two Chinese Philosophers; Ch'eng Ming-tao and Ch'eng Yi-ch'uan*, London, Lund Humphries, 1958.

————, trans. See Lieh Tzu.

Grube, Wilhelm, trans. See Chou Tun-i.

The Great Learning, "The Great Learning," trans. by E. R. Hughes in his *The Great Learning and The Mean-in-Action*, New York, Dutton, 1943, pp. 145-166.

————, "The Great Learning," trans. by James Legge, in his *The Chinese Classics*, vol. 1, pp. 355-381; also in James Legge, trans., *The Four Books*.

Hamilton, Clarence H., trans. See Vasubandhu.

Han Fei Tzu, *The Complete Works of Han Fei Tzu*, trans. by W. K. Liao, 2 vols., London, Probsthain, 1939 and 1960.

Henke, Frederick Goodrich, trans. See Wang Yang-ming.

History, Book of. See *Shu ching*.

Hou Wai-lu *et al.*, *A Short History of Chinese Philosophy*, Peking, Foreign Language Press, 1959.

Hsi-yün, *The Zen Teaching of Huang Po on the Transmission of Mind*, trans. by John Blofeld, London, Rider, 1958.

Hsiao ching, The Hsiao Ching, trans. by Mary Lelia Makra, New York, St. John's University Press, 1961.

————, "Hsiao King," trans. by James Legge, in *The Sacred Books of the East*, vol. 3, Oxford, Clarendon Press, 1879, 464-488.

Hsiao, Kung-ch'üan, "K'ang Yu-wei and Confucianism," *Monumenta Serica*, 18 (1959), 96-212.

Hsü, Immanuel C. Y., trans. See Liang Ch'i-ch'ao.

Hsü, P. C. *Ethical Realism in Neo-Confucian Thought*, Peiping, privately published, 1933.

Hsüan-tsang, trans., *Vijñaptimātratāsiddhi, le siddhi de Hiuan-Tsang*, 2 vols., trans. into French by Louis de La Vallée Poussin, Paris, Geuthner, 1928-1929.

Hsün Tzu, "Ein chinesischer Beamterspiegel aus dem 2 Jahrhundert v. Chr. *Hsün-tzi*, Abschnitt 13," trans. by H. Köster, *Oriens Extremus*, 3, no. 1 (1956), 18-27.

————, "Hsün-tzu on Terminology," trans. by Y. P. Mei, *Philosophy East and West*, 1, no. 2, (July, 1951), 51-66.

————, "Hsün-tzu on the Rectification of Names," trans. by J. J. L. Duyvendak, *T'oung Pao*, 23 (1924), 221-254.

————, *The Works of Hsüntze*, trans. by H. H. Dubs, London, Probsthain, 1928.

Hu Shih, "Ch'an (Zen) Buddhism in China: Its History and Method," *Philosophy East and West*, 3 (1953), 3-24.

———, *The Chinese Renaissance*, Chicago, University of Chicago Press, 1934.

———, "Chinese Thought," *Asia*, 42 (1942), 582-584.

·———, "Chinese Thought," in Harley Farnsworth MacNair, ed., *China*, Berkeley, University of California Press, 1946, pp. 221-230.

———, "A Criticism of Some Recent Methods Used in Dating Lao Tzu," *Harvard Journal of Asiatic Studies*, 2 (1937), 373-397.

———, *The Development of the Logical Method in Ancient China*, 3rd ed., Shanghai, The Oriental Book Co., 1928.

———, "The Natural Law in the Chinese Tradition," in Edward F. Barrett, ed., *Natural Law Institute Proceedings*, 5, Notre Dame, University of Notre Dame Press, 1953, pp. 119-153.

———, "Religion and Philosophy in Chinese History," in Sophia H. Ch'en Zen, ed., *Symposium on Chinese Culture*, Shanghai, China Institute of Pacific Relations, 1931, pp. 31-58.

Huai-nan Tzu, *Tao, The Great Luminant*, trans. by Evan Morgan, Shanghai, Kelly and Walsh, 1934.

Huang-po, *The Zen Teaching of Huang Po on the Transmission of Mind*, trans. by John Blofeld, London, Rider, 1958, paperback, Evergreen.

Huang, Siu-chi, *Lu Hsiang-shan, A Twelfth Century Chinese Idealist Philosopher*, New Haven, American Oriental Society, 1944.

Hughes, E. R. *Chinese Philosophy in Classical Times*, London, Dent, rev., 1954.

———, trans. See *Chung-yung*, Fung Yu-lan, and *Great Learning*.

Hui-hai, *The Path to Sudden Attainment,* trans. by John Blofeld, London, The Buddhist Society, 1948.

Hui-neng, "The Altar Sutra of the Sixth Patriarch," trans., by Lu K'uan-yu, in his *Ch'an and Zen Teaching*, Third Series, London, Ryder and Co., 1962, pp. 15-102.

———, "Das Sūtra des sechsten Patriarchen," trans. into German by Erwin Rousselle, *Sinica*, 5 (1930), 117-191; 6 (1931), 26-34; 11 (1936), 131-137, 202-210.

———, *The Platform Scripture, The Basic Classic of Zen Buddhism*, trans. by Wing-tsit Chan, New York, St. John's University Press, 1963.

———, *The Sūtra of Wei Lang*, trans. by Wong Mou-lam, London, Luzac, rev., 1953.

Hummel, Arthur W., ed., *Eminent Chinese of the Ch'ing Period*, Washington, D.C., Library of Congress, 1944.

I ching, The I Ching or Book of Changes, trans. by Cary F. Baynes from the German version of Richard Wilhelm, 2 vols., New York, Pantheon Books, 1950.

———, *The Yi King*, trans. by James Legge, *The Sacred Books of the East*, vol. 16, Oxford, Clarendon Press, 1882.

Iki, Hiroyuki, "Wang Yang-ming's Doctrine of Innate Knowledge of the Good," *Philosophy East and West*, 11 (1961), 27-77.

K'ang Yu-wei, *Ta T'ung Shu, The One-World Philosophy of K'ang Yu-wei*, trans. by Laurence G. Thompson, London, Allen and Unwin, 1958.

Kao Ming-k'ai, trans. See Tung Chung-shu.

Karlgren, B., trans. See *Shih ching*.

Keith, A. Berriedale, *Buddhist Philosophy in India and Ceylon*, Oxford, Clarendon Press, 1923.

Kern, H. trans. See *Lotus Scripture*.

Kiang Shao-yuen, "The Philosophy of Tang-Szu-Tung," *The Open Court*, 36 (1922), 449-471.

Köster, H., trans. See Hsün Tzu.

Ku Hung-ming, trans. See *Chung-yung*.

Kung-sun Lung. See Mei.

Kuo-yü, "Koue yü (Discours des Royaumes)," p. 1, *Journal Asiatique*, 9 (1893), 373-419, 3 (1894), 5-91; pt. 2, Louvain, 1895, pp. 1-268.

La Vallée Poussin, Louis, trans. See Hsüan-tsang.

Lamotte, Étienne, trans. See Asaṅga.

Laṅkāvatāra sūtra, trans. by Daisetz Teitarō Suzuki, London, Routledge, 1932.

Lao Tzu, *Tao Te Ching, The Book of the Way and Its Virtue*, trans. by J. J. L. Duyvendak, London, John Murray, 1954, paperback, Taplinger.

————, *Tao Teh Ching*, trans. by John C. H. Wu, New York, St. John's University Press, 1961.

————, *The Way and Its Power*, trans. by Arthur Waley, London, Allen and Unwin, 1935; paperback, Evergreen.

————, *The Way of Lao Tzu*. See Chan.

————, *The Way of Life; Lao Tzu*, trans. by R. B. Blakney, paperback, a Mentor Book, New York, The New American Library of World Literature, 1955.

————, *The Wisdom of Laotse*. See Lin Yutang.

Laufer, B., "Lun Yü IX, 1," *Journal of the American Oriental Society*, 54 (1934), p. 83.

Le Gall, Le P. Stanislas, *Tchou Hi, sa doctrine, son influence*, Shanghai, La Mission Catholique, 1923.

Lee, Shao Chang, *Popular Buddhism in China*, Shanghai, Commercial Press, 1939.

Legge, James, trans. See *Ch'un-ch'iu*, *Chung-yung*, Confucius, *Great Learning*, *Hsiao ching*, *Li chi*, Mencius, and *Shu ching*.

Leslie, D., "Contribution to a New Translation of the *Lun Heng*," *T'oung Pao* (1956), 100-149.

Lévi, Sylvain, trans. See Vasubandhu.

Li chi, The Li Ki, trans. by James Legge, *The Sacred Books of the East*, vols. 27 and 28, Oxford, Clarendon Press, 1885.

Li Shi-yi, "Wang Ch'ung," *T'ien Hsia Monthly*, 5 (1937), 162-184, 209-307.

Liang Ch'i-ch'ao, *History of Chinese Political Thought during the Early Tsin Period*, trans. by L. T. Ch'en, London, Kegan Paul, 1930.

————, *Intellectual Trends in the Ch'ing Period*, trans. by Immanuel C. Y. Hsü, Cambridge, Mass., Harvard University Press, 1959.

Liao, W. K., trans. See Han Fei Tzu.

Liebenthal, Walter, trans. See Seng-chao and T'ang Yung-t'ung.

Lieh Tzu, The Book of Lieh Tzu, trans. by A. C. Graham, London, John Murray, 1960.

Lin Mousheng, *Men and Ideas, An Informal History of Chinese Political Thought*, New York, John Day, 1942.

Lin Tung-chi, "The Taoist in Every Chinese," in *T'ien Hsia Monthly*, 11 (1940-1941), 211-225; reprinted as "The Chinese Mind: Its Taoist Substratum," *Journal of the History of Ideas*, 8 (1947), 259-273.

Lin Yutang, *The Wisdom of China and India*, New York, Random House, 1942.

————, *The Wisdom of Laotse*, New York, The Modern Library, 1948.

————, trans. See *Chung-yung* and Confucius.

Link, Arthur E., "Shyh Daw-an's Preface to Saṅgharakṣa's *Yogācārabhūmi-sūtra* and the Problem of Buddho-Taoist Terminology in Early Chinese Buddhism," *Journal of the American Oriental Society*, 77 (1957), 1-14.

Liu Shao-ch'i, *How to be a Good Communist*, 2d ed., rev., Peking, Foreign Language Press, 1952.

Liu, Wu-chi, *A Short History of Confucian Philosophy*, Baltimore, Penguin Books, 1955.

Lo, Jung-pang, ed., *K'ang Yu-wei, 1858-1927, A Symposium*, Seattle, University of Washington Press (in press).

Lotus Scripture, The Lotus of the Wonderful Law, or The Lotus Gospel, trans. by W. E. Soothill, Oxford, Clarendon Press, 1930.

————, *The Saddharmapuṇḍarīka or the Lotus of the True Law*, trans. by H. Kern, *The Sacred Books of the East*, vol. 21, London, Oxford University Press, 1884.

Lu K'uan-yu, trans. See Hui-neng.

Lü Pu-wei, *Frühling und Herbst des Lü Bu We*, trans. into German by Richard Wilhelm, Jena, Eugen Diederichs Verlag, 1928.

Makra, Mary Lelia, trans. See *Hsiao ching*.

Mao Tse-tung, *Selected Works*, 4 vols., New York, International Publishing Co., 1954.

Mean, The Doctrine of the. See *Chung-yung*.

Mei, Y. P., "Hsün Tzu's Theory of Education, with an English translation of the *Hsün Tzu*, Chapter I, An Exhortation to Learning," *Tsing Hua Journal of Chinese Studies*, n.s. 2, no. 2 (1961), 361-377.

————, "The Kung-sun Lung Tzu, with a Translation into English," *Harvard Journal of Asiatic Studies*, 16 (1953), 404-437.

————, *Motse, The Neglected Rival of Confucius*, London, Probsthain, 1934.

————, "Some Observations on the Problem of Knowledge among the Ancient Chinese Logicians," *Tsing Hua Journal of Chinese Studies*, n.s. 1, no. 1 (1956), 114-121.

————, trans. See Hsün Tzu and Mo Ti.

Mencius, *The Sayings of Mencius*, trans. by James Ware, paperback, New York, New American Library, 1960.

————, *The Works of Mencius*, trans. by James Legge, *The Chinese Classics*, vol. 2, Oxford, Clarendon Press, 1895 (previously published as *The Life and Works of Mencius*, London, Trübner, 1875).

Mo Ti, *The Ethical and Political Works of Motse*, trans. by Y. P. Mei, London, Probsthain, 1929.

————, *Me Ti des Sozialethikers und seiner Schüler philosophische Werke*, trans. into German by Alfred Forke, Berlin, Kommissionsverlag der Vereinigung Wissenschaftlicher Verlager, 1922.

Moore, Charles A., ed., *Essays in East-West Philosophy*, Honolulu, University of Hawaii Press, 1951.

————, *Philosophy and Culture—East and West*, Honolulu, University of Hawaii Press, 1962.

————, *Philosophy East and West*, Princeton, Princeton University Press, 1944.

Morgan, Evan, trans. See Huai-nan Tzu.

Nāgārjuna, *Die mittlere Lehre des Nāgārjuna nach des chinesischen version übertragen* (*Die Buddhistische philosophie in ihrer geschichtlichen entwieklung*, vol. 3), trans. into German by Max Welleser, Heidelberg, Winter, 1904.

Needham, Joseph, *Science and Civilisation in China, vol. 2: History of Scientific Thought*, Cambridge, Cambridge University Press, 1956.

Odes, Book of. See *Shih ching*.

Ogata, Sohaku, *Zen for the West*, London, Rider, 1959.

Oka, Takashi, "The Philosophy of T'an Ssu-t'ung," *Papers on China*, Harvard University Committee on Regional Studies, 9 (1955), 1-47.

Pang Ching-jen, *L'idée de Dieu chez Malebranche et l'idée de Li chez Tchou Hi*, Paris, Librairie Philosophique J. Vrin, 1942.

Petzold, Bruno, *The Chinese Tendai Teaching*, n.p., n.d.

Rideout, J. K., "The Context of the *Yüan Tao* and *Yüan Hsing*," *Bulletin of the School of Oriental and African Studies*, 12 (1947), 403-408.

Rites, Book of. See *Li chi*.

Rousselle, Erwin, trans. See Hui-neng.

Saddharmapuṇḍarika, see *Lotus Scripture*.

Sargent, Galen Eugène, "Les débats entre Meng-tseu et Siun-tseu sur la nature humaine," *Oriens Extremus*, 3 (1956), 1-17.

————, "Les débats personnels de Tchou Hi en matière de methodologie," *Journal Asiatique*, 243 (1955), 213-228.

————, *Tchou Hi contre le Bouddhisme*, Paris, Imprimerie Nationale, 1955.

Sasaki, Ruth Fuller, trans. See Dumoulin.

Seng-chao, *The Book of Chao*, trans. by Walter Liebenthal, Peiping, The Catholic University of Peking, 1948.

Shang Yang, *The Book of Lord Shang*, trans. by J. J. L. Duyvendak, London, Probsthain, 1928.

Sheehan, Joseph J., "A Summary of Fung Yu-lan's Hsin Yüan-jen," Typescript, Columbia University, 1950.

Shen-hui, "Entretiens du maître de Dhyāna Chen-houei du Ho-tsö," trans. by Jacques Gernet, *Publications de L'École Française d'Extrême-Orient*, 31 (1949), 1-126.

Shih ching, The Book of Odes, trans. by B. Karlgren, Stockholm, Museum of Far Eastern Antiquities, 1950.

————, *The Book of Songs*, trans. by Arthur Waley, Boston, Houghton, 1937; paperback, Evergreen.

Shih, Vincent Yu-chung, "The Mind and the Moral Order," *Mélanges chinois et bouddhiques*, 10 (1955), 347-364.

Shu ching, The Shoo King, trans. by James Legge, *The Chinese Classics*, vol. 3, Oxford, Clarendon Press, 1865.

Soothill, W. E., trans. See *Lotus Scripture*.

Spring and Autumn Annals. See *Ch'un-ch'iu*.

Ssu-ma Ch'ien, *Les mémoires historiques de Se-Ma Ts'ien*, 5 vols., trans. into French by Édouard Chavannes, Paris, E. Leroux, 1895-1905.

————, *Records of the Grand Historian*, trans. by Burton Watson, New York, Columbia University Press, 1961.

Stcherbastky, Th., *The Conception of the Buddhist Nirvāṇa*, Leningrad, Publishing Office of the Academy of Science of the U.S.S.R., 1927.

Suzuki, Daisetz, *Essays in Zen Buddhism*, First Series, London, Luzac, 1927; Second Series, 1933; Third Series, 1934.

————, *Studies in the Laṅkāvatāra Sūtra*, London, Routledge, 1930.

————, *Studies in Zen*, New York, Philosophical Library, 1955.

————, "Zen: A Reply to Hu Shin," *Philosophy East and West*, 3 (1953), 25-46.

————, *The Zen Doctrine of No-Mind*, London, Rider, 1949.

————, trans. See Aśvagosha and *Laṅkāvatāra sūtra*.

Ta-hsüeh. See *Great Learning*.

Takakusu, Junjirō, *The Essentials of Buddhist Philosophy*, ed. by Wing-tsit Chan and Charles A. Moore, Honolulu, University of Hawaii, 1947.

Talbott, Nathan, "T'an Ssu-t'ung and the Ether," in Robert K. Sakai, ed., *Studies on Asia, 1960*, Lincoln, Nebraska, University of Nebraska Press, 1960, pp. 20-34.

T'ang Chun-i, "Chang Tsai's Theory of Mind and Its Metaphysical Basis," *Philosophy East and West*, 6 (1956), 113-136.

T'ang Yung-t'ung, "On 'Ko-yi', the Earliest Method by Which Indian Buddhism and Chinese Thought were Synthesized," in W. R. Inge *et al.*, eds., *Radhakrishnan, Comparative Studies in Philosophy*, London, Allen and Unwin, 1951, pp. 276-286.

————, "Wang Pi's New Interpretation of the *I ching* and *Lun-yü*," trans. by Walter Liebenthal, *Harvard Journal of Asiatic Studies*, 10 (1947), 124-161.

Thomas, Edward J., *The History of Buddhist Thought*, London, Kegan Paul, 1933.

Thompson, Laurence G., trans. See K'ang Yu-wei.

Ts'ai Yung-ch'un, ed. and trans. See Ch'eng I.

Tso chuan. See *Ch'un-ch'iu*.

Tucci, Giuseppe, *Pre-Diṅnāga Buddhist Texts on Logic from Chinese Sources*, Beroda, Oriental Institute, 1929.

Tung Chung-shu, *Tch'ouen-ts'ieu fan-lu 44 et 74*, trans., Kao Ming-k'ai *et al.*, in *Lectures chinoises* (Paris, Université de Paris, Centre d'Études Sinologiques de Pékin), 1 (1945), 1-17.

Vasubandhu, *Trimśikā, Matériaux pour l'étude du système Vijñaptimātra*, trans. into French by Sylvain Lévi, Paris, Champion, 1932.

————, *Trimśikavijñapti des Vasubandhu mit bhāyśya des ācārye Sthiramati*, trans. into German by Hermann Jacob, Stuttgart, W. Kohlhammer, 1932.

————, *Vimsatikā, Wei Shih Er Shih Lun or the Treatise in Twenty Stanzas on Representation-Only*, trans. by Clarence H. Hamilton, New Haven, American Oriental Society, 1938.

von Zach, trans. See Yang Hsiung.

Waley, Arthur, *Three Ways of Thought in Ancient China*, London, Allen and Unwin, 1939; paperback, Anchor.

————, trans. See Confucius, Lao Tzu, and *Shih ching*.

BIBLIOGRAPHY

Wang Ch'ung, "Lun-Heng," trans. by Alfred Forke, *Mitteilungen des Seminars für Orientalische Sprachen*, 9 (1906), 181-399; 10 (1907), 1-173; 11 (1908), 1-188; 14 (1911), 1-536; also published in two volumes, entitled *Lun-Heng*, London, Luzac, 1907-1911.

Wang Tch'ang-tche, *La philosophie morale de Wang Yang-ming*, Shanghai, T'ou-Sè-Wè Press, 1936.

Wang Yang-ming, *Instructions for Practical Living, and Other Neo-Confucian Writings of Wang Yang-ming*, trans. by Wing-tsit Chan, New York, Columbia University Press, 1963.

———, *The Philosophy of Wang Yang-ming*, trans. by Frederick Goodrich Henke, Chicago, Open Court, 1916.

Ware, James, trans. See Mencius.

Welleser, Max, trans. See Nāgārjuna.

Werner, E. T. C., trans. See Wieger.

Wieger, Léon, *A History of the Religious Beliefs and Philosophical Opinions in China*, trans. by E. T. C. Werner, Hsien Hsien, Hsien Hsien Press, 1927.

Wilhelm, Hellmut, *Change, Eight Lectures on the I Ching*, trans. from the German by Cary F. Baynes, New York, Pantheon Books, 1960.

Wilhelm, Richard, trans. See *I ching* and Lü Pu-wei.

Willetts, William, "Philosophy in Changing China," *The Humanist*, 71, no. 9 (1956), 22-24.

Wong Mou-lam, trans. See Hui-neng.

Wright, Arthur, Review of A. A. Petrov's *Wang Pi (226-249): His Place in the History of Chinese Philosophy*, *Harvard Journal of Asiatic Studies*, 10 (1947), 75-88.

———, ed., *Studies in Chinese Thought*, Chicago, University of Chicago Press, 1953.

Wu, John C. H., "Chinese Legal Philosophy: A Brief Historical Survey," *Chinese Culture*, 1. no. 4 (1958), 7-48.

———, trans. See Lao Tzu.

Yang Hsiung, *Le catechisme philosophique de Yang-Hiong-tsé*, trans. into French by B. Belpaire, Brussels, Éditions de l'Occident, 1960.

———, "Yang Hsiung's *Fayen*: Wörter strenger Ermahnung," trans. into German by Erwin von Zach, *Sinologische Beiträge*, 4 (1939), 1-74.

Yao, Shan-yu, "The Cosmological and Anthropological Philosophy of Tung Chung-shu," *Journal of the North China Branch of the Royal Asiatic Society*, 73 (1948), 40-68.

Zen, Sophia H. Chen, ed., *Symposium on Chinese Culture*, Shanghai, China Institute of Pacific Relations, 1931.

Zücher, E., *The Buddhist Conquest of China*, Leiden, Brill, 1959.

A GLOSSARY OF CHINESE CHARACTERS

The names and titles of the same man are given in the same entry. Well-known place names and names of dynasties are omitted.

愛　　　*ai*: love;
衰　　　　　sorrow
文思奇　Ai Ssu-ch'i
安世高　An Shih-kao
詫　　　*ch'a*: to boast;
察　　　　　to examine
習楚　　*chai*
　　　　Chai Ch'u
辰禽　　Chan-ch'in
陳榮捷　Chan Wing-tsit
憚　　　Ch'an
禪源諸詮　*Ch'an-yüan chü-ch'üan*
集都序　　*chi tu-hsü*
張啟勘　Chang, Carsun
張湛　　Chang Chan
張澄基　Chang, Chen-chi
張鍾元　Chang Chung-yüan
張橫渠集　*Chang Heng-ch'ü chi*
張行成　Chang Hsing-ch'eng
張儀　　Chang I
章炳麟　Chang Ping-lin,
太炎　　　T'ai-yen
張伯行　Chang Po-hsing
張栻　　Chang Shih,
　南軒　　Nan-hsien,
敬夫欽夫　Ching-fu, Ch'ien-fu
張守節　Chang Shou-chieh
張岱年　Chang Tai-nien
張載　　Chang Tsai,
橫渠子厚　Heng-ch'ü, Tzu-hou
張東蓀　Chang Tung-sun
張子正蒙　*Chang Tzu Cheng-meng*
註　　　　*chu*
張子全書　*Chang Tzu ch'üan-shu*
常　　　*ch'ang*: always;

嘗　　　　　has been
長安　　Ch'ang-an
長沮　　Ch'ang-chü
長沙　　Ch'ang-sha
長梧子　Ch'ang-wu Tzu
昭　　　Chao
昭著　　*chao*: light;
　　　　　to attach
趙岐　　Chao Ch'i
著境　　*chao-ching*
趙景子　Chao Ching Tzu
肇論　　*Chao lun*
肇論註　*Chao lun chu*
肇論中夹　*Chao lun Chung-wu*
集解　　　*chi-chieh*
昭文　　Chao Wen
趙元任　Chao, Yuen Ren
韶州　　Ch'ao-chou
趙日明　*Ch'ao-jih-ming*
三昧經　　*san-mei ching*
者　　　*che*
哲學研究　*Che-hsüeh yen-chiu*
哲宗　　Che-tsung
真　　　*chen*
真覺　　Chen-chiao
真如　　*chen-ju*
真元　　*chen-yüan*
陳　　　Ch'en
陳杆　　Ch'en Chi
陳敬天　Ch'en Ch'i-t'ien
陳奇猷　Ch'en Ch'i-yu
陳建　　Ch'en Chien,
　清瀾　　Ch'ing-lan
陳景元　Ch'en Ching-yüan
陳淳北溪　Ch'en Ch'un, Pei-hsi

813

陳恩成 Ch'en En-cheng
陳傳良 Ch'en Fu-liang
陳相 Ch'en Hsiang
陳觀勝 Ch'en, Kenneth K. S.
陳立庭 Ch'en, L. T.
陳亮 Ch'en Liang
陳龍正 Ch'en Lung-cheng
陳陸州 Ch'en Mu-chou
陳摶 Ch'en Tuan
陳寅恪 Ch'en Yin-k'o
鄭 Cheng
正 cheng: ruler, cor-
徵 rect, rectifying,
standard;
政據 to collect, invite;
證玄 to control, leader,
鄭康成 government
正誼 cheng-chü
全書 Cheng Hsüan,
正觀論 K'ang-ch'eng
正理蒙 Cheng-i-t'ang
正蒙註 ch'üan-shu
正蒙會稿 Cheng-kuan lun
正蒙大義 cheng-li
蒙道歌 Cheng-meng
證成 Cheng-meng chu
程 Cheng-meng hui-kao
誠 Cheng-meng ta-i
成覯 fa-wei
程朱 Cheng-tao ko
成具 Ch'eng
尭明經 ch'eng: insect;
程顥明道 real, complete;
伯淳 sincerity
成玄英 Ch'eng Ch'ien
Ch'eng-Chu
Ch'eng-chü
kuang-ming ching
Ch'eng Hao, Ming-tao,
Po-ch'un
Ch'eng Hsüan-ying

程頤伊川 Ch'eng I, I-ch'uan,
正叔 Cheng-shu
程伊川 Ch'eng I-ch'uan
年譜 nien-p'u
澄觀 Ch'eng-kuan
程樹德 Ch'eng Shu-te
程子詳本 Ch'eng Tzu hsiang-pen
成唯識論 Ch'eng wei-shih lun
成唯識論 Ch'eng wei-shih lun
述記 shu-chi
冀 Chi: district;
季 king, family;
櫻 minister;
濟 river
箕 viscount
紀 chi: bond;
稽 commensurate;
incipient force,
幾 quantity;
機 moving power;
記 record;
制 system;
述 trace
擧壤歌 Chi-jang ko
季康子 Chi K'ang Tzu
郎色 chi-se
紀他藏 Chi T'o
吉 Chi-tsang
岐 Ch'i: mountain;
故 person;
淇 river
齊 state, district
詑器 ch'i: already;
齊 concrete thing;
equal;
material or
氣 vital force;
其 that;
起 to arise
七女經 Ch'i-nü ching

漆雕開 Ch'i Tiao-k'ai
齊物論釋 *Ch'i-wu lun shih*
器遠 Ch'i-yüan
假 *chia*
嘉靖 Chia-ching
賈誼 Chia I
家人 *chia-jen*
將聖 *chiang-sheng*
姜稟權 Chiang Shu-ch'üan
江永 Chiang Yung
較 *chiao*
焦竑 Chiao Hung
焦循 Chiao Hsün
校定古本 *Chiao-ting ku-pen*
　夫子 *Lao Tzu*
樂 Chieh
節 *chieh*: to fit;
　　to remove,
　　to understand
介然 *chieh-jan*
桀溺 Chieh-ni
解深密經 *Chieh shen-mi ching*
澗 *chien*: brook;
間 space
兼愛吾 *chien-ai*
肩吾 Chien-wu
錢 Ch'ien
乾 *ch'ien*
前漢書 *Ch'ien-Han shu*
錢穆 Ch'ien Mu
錢德洪 Ch'ien Te-hung,
　緒山升 Hsü-shan
錢子升 Ch'ien Tzu-sheng
止 *chih*: at ease;
直 classifier;
之 it;
指 mark;
質 secured;
　to abide, con-
　centrate, rest,
　stay, stop;
止直 uprightness

智顗 Chih-i
直隸 Chih-li
致良知 *chih liang-chih*
支愍度 Chih Min-tu
至命 *chih-ming*
知識與 *Chih-shih yü*
文化 *wen-hua*
支道林 Chih Tao-lin
志德 Chih-te
智儼 Chih-yen
知言 *Chih-yen*
晉 Chin
盡 *chin*: all;
近 near, alike
金剛經 *Chin-kang ching*
金獅子章 *Chin shih-tzu chang*
近思錄 *Chin-ssu lu*
近思錄 *Chin-ssu lu*
集註 *chi-chu*
金岳霖 Chin Yüeh-lin
秦 Ch'in
親 *ch'in*
親民 *ch'in-min*
景 Ching: duke;
荆 place
精 *ching*: essence,
　material force;
　reverence, seri-
　ousness;
敬 sphere
境
荆州 Ching-chou
景春 Ching Ch'un
經權 *ching-ch'üan*
經義叢鈔 *Ching-i ts'ung-ch'ao*
淨名 *Ching-ming*
經說 *Ching-shuo*
景德傳燈 *Ching-te ch'uan-teng*
　錄 *lu*
經典釋文 *Ching-tien shih-wen*
淨源 Ching-yüan
情 *ch'ing*
青寧 *ch'ing-ning*

815

ch'ing-shu
ch'ing-t'an
Ch'ing-t'ung shih-tai
Chiu-T'ang shu
chiu-yu
Ch'iu
Ch'iu K'ai-ming
Chou: duke, district; king
chou
Chou Hsien
Chou-i
Chou-i cheng-i
Chou-i chi-chieh
Chou-i chu
Chou-i lüeh-li
Chou-i nei-chuan
Chou-i wai-chuan
Chou Ju-teng
Chou-li
Chou Lien-hsi chi
Chou Ming-tso
Chou Tun-i, Lien-hsi, Mao-shu
Chou Tzu ch'üan-shu
Chow Yih-ching
Chu
chu
Chu Hsi, Yüan-hui, Hui-an
Chu Pen-ssu, Te-chih
Chu Pi
Chu Tao-ch'ien
chu-tsai
Chu Tzu i-shu
Chu-tzu k'ao-so
Chu Tzu nine-p'u
Chu-tzu p'ing-i
Chu Tzu ta-ch'üan
Chu Tzu wen-chi
Chu Tzu yü-lei

Chu Tzu-ch'i, Chiu-chiang
Ch'u
Ch'u-chou
Ch'u san-tsang chi-chi
Ch'u-tzu
chuan
Chuan-hsü
Ch'uan-hsi lu
Ch'uan-shan i-shu
Chuang
Chuang Tzu, Chou
Chuang Tzu chang-i
Chuang Tzu chi-chieh
Chuang Tzu chu
Chuang Tzu i
Chuang Tzu i-cheng
Chuang Tzu p'ing
Chuang Tzu pu-chu
Chuang Tzu shu
Chuang Tzu tsuan-chien
Ch'un-ch'iu fan-lu
Ch'un-ch'iu fan-lu chu
Ch'un-ch'iu fan-lu i-cheng
Ch'un-ch'iu Tso chuan cheng-i
Ch'un Ts'ew
Chung
chung: center, mean; conscientiousness
chung-hsin
Chung-hui
Chung-kuan lun shu
Chung-kuo che-hsüeh shih ta-kang
Chung-kuo che-hsüeh shih wen-t'i t'ao-lun chuan-chi

中國古代思想史的提要 *Chung-kuo chung-ku ssu-hsiang shih ti t'i-yao*

中國思想史 *Chung-kuo ssu-hsiang shih*

仲弓冉雍 Chung-kung, Jan Yung

中論 Chung lun

仲尼 Chung-ni

仲山甫 Chung Shan-fu

忠恕 *chung-shu*

中庸 *Chung-yung*

中庸章句 *Chung-yung chang-chü*

中庸正義 *Chung-yung cheng-i*

中庸註 *Chung-yung chu*

中庸或問 *Chung-yung huo-wen*

崇 Ch'ung

冲虛至德真經 *Ch'ung-hsü chih-te chen-ching*

據 *chü*

據梁 Chü-liang

鴻掇 *chü-t'o*

取去 *ch'ü*: to cling, take; to go

瞿鵲子 Ch'ü-chiao Tzu

渠孫皇 Ch'ü-sun-huang

屈萬里 Ch'ü Wan-li

曲園雜篡 *Ch'ü-yüan tsa-tsuan*

全祖望 Ch'üan Tsu-wang

均 Chün

君子 *chün-tzu*

戴震 Dai Shen-yu

大漢和典 Daikanwa jiten

辭錄

近思錄 *Djin-sï lu*

朱熹 Dschu Hsi

惡 e

耳 Erh

而 erh

二程全書 Erh-Ch'eng ch'üan-shu

二取 erh-ch'ü

二十二子 Erh-shih-erh tzu

二諦章 Erh-ti chang

法發 *fa*: dharma, model, standard; to issue, start

法家 Fa-chia

法相 *fa-hsiang*

法門 *fa-men*

法琛竺潛 Fa-shen, Chu Ch'ien

法藏 Fa-tsang

法遍 Fa-wen

法言 *Fa-yen*

范 Fan: lord

獎 state

獎遲須遲淹子 Fan Ch'ih, Hsü, Tzu-ch'ih

范仲宣子禹 Fan Chung-yen

范相 Fan Hsüan Tzu

范望 Fan Tsu-yü

范網經 Fan Wang

梵網經 *Fan-wang ching*

范曄 Fan Yeh

坊 *fang*

放光經 Fang-kuang ching

方內 *fang-nei*

方賓王 Fang Pin-wang

方生 *fang-sheng*

方外 *fang-wai*

廢 *fei*

非而謁搖有牛 *fei-erh-yeh, ying-yu-niu*

分理 *fen-li*

馮夷 Feng I

佛圖澄 Fo T'u-ch'eng

復 *fu*

復齊 Fu-chai

涪州 Fu-chou

伏羲伏戲 Fu-hsi

復性書 *Fu-hsing shu*

傅玄風 Fu Hsüan-feng

傅奕 Fu I

伏勝 Fu Sheng

傅斯年 Fu Ssu-nien

傅說 Fu Yüeh
福田直美 Fukuda, Naomi
馮友蘭 Fung Yu-lan
疑問錄 *Gimon roku*
漢 Han
罕 *han*
韓昌黎 Han Ch'ang-li
　全集 ch'üan-chi
韓非 Han Fei
韓非子 *Han Fei Tzu*
韓非子 *Han Fei Tzu*
　集解 chi-chieh
韓非子 *Han Fei Tzu*
　集釋 chi-shih
韓非子 *Han Fei Tzu*
　校釋 chiao-shih
韓康伯 Han K'ang-po
翰林 Han-lin
漢魏兩晉 *Han Wei Liang-Chin*
南北朝 *Nan-pei-ch'ao*
佛教史 *Fo-chiao shih*
漢魏叢書 *Han-Wei ts'ung-shu*
韓愈退之 Han Yü, T'ui-chih,
　文公 Wen Kung
郝懿行 Hao I-hsing
浩然之氣 *hao-jan chih-ch'i*
浩生不害 Hao-sheng Pu-hai
早川 Hayakawa
衡 Heng
玄奘 Hiuan-tsang
賀 Ho
鶡冠子 Ho-kuan Tzu
河南程氏 *Ho-nan Ch'eng-shih*
　遺書 *i-shu*
何平 *ho-p'i*
河上公 Ho-shang Kung
何叔京 Ho Shu-ching
荷澤 Ho-tsö
何晏 Ho Yen
後 *hou*
后稷 Hou-chi
后之邸 Hou-chih-ti

後漢書 *Hou-Han shu*
侯外廬 Hou Wai-lu
厚嚴經 *Hou-yen ching*
襲 Hsi
習 *hsi*: to follow;
息 to learn, practice;
羲 to stop;
　 what, how
稽康 Hsi K'ang
西銘 *Hsi-ming*
奚侗 Hsi T'ung
繫辭 *hsi-tz'u*
孫韋 Hsi-wei
惜陰軒 *Hsi-yin-hsien*
叢書 *ts'ung-shu*
　 Hsi-yün
布夏 Hsia Chi
夏侯玄 Hsia-hou Hsüan
夏禹 Hsia Yü
夏襄象相 Hsiang: duke;
　 Shun's brother
　 hsiang: character;
　 abstract meaning,
　 form, symbol, to
　 seem
象 Hsiang Hsiu
何秀山 *Hsiang-shan ch'üan-chi*
象孝經全集 *Hsiao ching, Shiao King*
孝己 Hsiao I
蕭公權 Hsiao, K'ung-ch'üan
蕭韋夫 Hsiao Sha-fu
謝良佐 Hsieh Hsi-shen
謝良蔡 Hsieh Liang-tso,
上 Shang-ts'ai
獻 Hsien
軒 *hsien*: elucidation;
鮮 fully;
仙 immortal;
咸 influence;
間 leisure
顯宗記 *Hsien-tsung chi*

革 心	Hsin	
心	hsin: mind;	
新	to renovate	
新知言	Hsin chih-yen	
心經	Hsin ching	
新州	Hsin-chou	
心法	hsin-fa	
新序	Hsin-hsü	
新華月報	Hsin-hua yüeh-pao	
新理學	Hsin li-hsüeh	
新理學的 自我檢討	Hsin li-hsüeh ti tzu-wo chien-t'ao	
新民	hsin-min	
新世訓	Hsin shih-hsün	
新事論	Hsin shih-lun	
新書	Hsin-shu	
新唐書	Hsin-T'ang shu	
新唯識論	Hsin wei-shih lun	
新原人	Hsin yüan-jen	
新原道	Hsin yüan-tao	
形	hsing: body, form, to contrast;	
性	nature;	
刑	punishment	
刑政	hsing-cheng	
形而下	hsing-erh-hsia	
形而上	hsing-erh-shang	
性理精義	Hsing-li ching-i	
性理學	Hsing-li hsüeh	
性理大全	Hsing-li ta-ch'üan	
性理字義	Hsing-li tzu-i	
形名	HSING-ming	
刑名	hsing-ming	
性命古訓	Hsing-ming ku-hsün	
性命古訓 辨證	Hsing-ming ku-hsün pien-cheng	
那昺壽	Hsing Ping	
邢	Hsing Shou	
修	hsiu	
熊十力	Hsiung Shih-li	
虛	hsii	

徐愛	Hsü Ai
胥敖	Hsü-ao
續近思錄	Hsü Chin-ssu lu
續春秋左 氏傳博議	Hsü Ch'un-ch'iu Tso-shih chuan po-i
徐中約	Hsü, Emmanuel C. Y.
許行	Hsü Hsing
徐幹	Hsü Kan
續高僧傳	Hsü kao-seng chuan
徐寶謙	Hsü, P. C.
徐辟	Hsü Pei
虛實	hsü-shih
許叔重慎	Hsü Shu-chung, Shen
虛堂語錄	Hsü-t'ang yü-lu
徐子融	Hsü Tzu-jung
許由	Hsü Yu
胥餘	Hsü Yü
宣	Hsüan
玄	hsüan
玄學	hsüan-hsüeh
玄冥	hsüan-ming
玄德	hsüan-te
玄奘	Hsüan-tsang
宣統	Hsüan-t'ung
玄同	hsüan-t'ung
薛	Hsüeh
學齋佔畢	Hsüeh-chai chan-pi
薛暄 敬軒	Hsüeh Hsüan, Ching-hsien
薛侃	Hsüeh K'an
學蔀通辨 循	Hsüeh-pu t'ung-pien
	hsün
荀子卿 況	Hsün Tzu, Ch'ing, K'uang
荀子集解	Hsün Tzu chi-chieh
荀子補註	Hsün Tzu pu-chu
荀子補釋	Hsün Tzu pu-shih
荀子詩説	Hsün Tzu shih-shuo
荀悦	Hsün Yüeh
胡	Hu
胡季随	Hu Chi-sui

嗶池	Hu-ch'ih
胡宏 五峯	Hu Hung, Wu-feng
胡廣	Hu Kuang
狐不偕	Hu Pu-chieh
胡適	Hu Shih
胡適論學 近著	*Hu Shih lun-hsüeh chin-chu*
胡瑗 安定	Hu Yüan, An-ting
華	Hua
華嚴	Hua-yen
華嚴經	*Hua-yen ching*
華嚴義海 百門	*Hua-yen i-hai po-men*
淮	Huai
淮南集證	*Huai-nan chi-cheng*
淮南鴻烈 集解	*Huai-nan hung-lieh chi-chieh*
淮南子	*Huai-nan Tzu*
淮南子註	*Huai-nan Tzu chu*
淮南王書	*Huai-nan Wang shu*
桓	Huan
懽	*huan*
桓魋	Huan T'ui
皇極經世 全書解	*Huang-chi ching-shih ch'üan-shu chieh*
皇極經世 觀物外篇 衍義	*Huang-chi ching-shih kuan-wu wai-p'ien yen-i*
皇極經世 釋義	*Huang-chi ching-shih shih-i*
皇極經世 書	*Huang-chi ching-shih shu*
皇極經世 書解	*Huang-chi ching-shih shu chieh*
皇清 經解	*Huang-Ch'ing ching-chieh*
皇甫謐	Huang Fu-mi
黃當	Huang Hsün
黃暉	Huang Hui
黃以方 直齋	Huang I-fang, Chih
黃榦 勉齋	Huang Kan, Mien-chai
皇侃	Huang K'an

黃軝	*huang-k'uang*
黃老	Huang-Lao
黃勉之	Huang Mien-chih
黃櫱	Huang-po
黃百家	Huang Po-chia
黃式三	Huang Shih-san
黃秀璣	Huang, Siu-chi
黃帝	Huang-ti
黃宗羲	Huang Tsung-hsi
黃宗賢 綰	Huang Tsung-hsien, Wan
黃粵洲	Huang Yüeh-chou
惠	Hui
惠	*hui*: kindness; understanding
慧海	Hui-hai
惠能	Hui-neng
惠施	Hui Shih
惠施公孫 龍	*Hui Shih Kung-sun Lung*
慧思	Hui-ssu
慧文	Hui-wen
慧遠	Hui-yüan
魂魄	*hun-p'o*
弘忍	Hung-jen
弘明集	*Hung-ming chi*
洪以	Hung, William
以	I: by; righteousness, moral principle, river; standard; then; to increase
義沂儀亦益	
一切之種智	*i-ch'ieh chung-chih*
夷	I Chih
易經	*I ching*
易傳	*I chuan*
伊川文集	*I-ch'uan wen-chi*
意而子	I-erh Tzu
義玄	I-hsüan
一貫	*i-kuan*

義理   *i-li*
伊洛淵源   *I-Lo yüan-yüan*
   錄   *lu*
頤輅   *i-lu*
遺書   *I-shu*
易牙   I Ya
伊尹   I Yin
猪城博之   Iki, Hiroyuki
染   *jan*
冉有求   Jan Yu, Ch'iu,
   冉子   Jan Tzu
任   *Jen*: ability;
仁   humanity;
人   person;
柾   to weaken
仁學   *Jen-hsüeh*
認識論   *Jen-shih lun*
壬子   *jen-tzu*
壬寅   *jen-yin*
仁の研究   *Jin no kenkyū*
若   *jo*
若教   Jo-ao
肇論研究   *Jōron kenkyū*
周   Jou
汝   Ju
如   *ju*: if, as;
入   to enter
入楞伽經   *Ju Leng-chia ching*
阮籍   Juan Chi
阮元   Juan Yüan
瑞巖   Jui-yen
榕村全書   *Jung-ts'un ch'üan-shu*
榕村全書   *Jung-ts'un ch'üan-shu*
   通書篇   *T'ung-shu p'ien*
貝塚茂樹   Kaizuka Shigeki
干   Kan
乾餘骨   *kan-yü-ku*
坎   *k'an*: pit, sinking;
看   to look
看敬   *k'an-ching*
堪杯   K'an-pi
康   K'ang
康有為   K'ang Yu-wei

高名凱   Kao Ming-k'ai
高僧傳   *Kao-seng chuan*
高蘇垣   Kao Su-yüan
告子   Kao Tzu
高誘   Kao Yu
華嚴   Kegon
艮   *ken*
江紹源   Kiang Shao-yuen
革   *ko*: change;
        to arrive, cor-
        rect, investigate
格   *格*
格心   *ko-hsin*
格義   *ko-i, ko-yi*
格物   *ko-wu*
克   *k'o*
公案   *koan*
古逸叢書   *Koitsu sōsho*
句踐   Kou-chien
國語   *Koue-Yü*
故   *ku*: fact, reason;
固   firm
辜鴻銘   Ku Hung-ming
瞽瞍   Ku-sou
顧東橋璘   Ku Tung-ch'iao, Lin
顧惟賢   Ku Wei-hsien,
   應祥   Ying-hsiang
顧炎武   Ku Yen-wu
卦辭   *kua-tz'u*
會稽   K'uai-chi
管   Kuan
觀   *kuan*
管仲   Kuan Chung
關內   Kuan-nei
管子   Kuan Tzu
觀物篇解   *Kuan-wu p'ien chieh*
觀音   Kuan-yin
光緒   Kuang-hsü
光明日報   *Kuang-ming jih-pao*
廣雅疏證   *Kuang-ya shu-cheng*
曠   K'uang: person;
臣   place
臣山   K'uang-shan
久保田量遠   Kubota Ryōon

公田	Kuda	國學基本	*Kuo-hsüeh chi-pen*
連太郎	Rentarō	叢書	*ts'ung-shu*
瞻兎	Kuei	國故論衡	*Kuo-ku lun-heng*
鬼	*kuei*: spirit;	郭沫若	Kuo Mo-jo
歸	to return	國語	*Kuo-yü*
竈山語錄	*Kuei-shan yü-lu*	萊	*lai*
鬼神	*kuei-shen*	老萊子	Lao Lai Tzu
睽	*k'uei*	老聃	Lao Tan
竅基	K'uei-chi	老子章句	*Lao Tzu chang-chü*
鯀	Kun	老子校詁	*Lao Tzu chiao-ku*
坤	*k'un*	老子註	*Lao Tzu chu*
崑崙	K'un-lun	老子翼	*Lao Tzu i*
躬	Kung	老子本義	*Lao Tzu pen-i*
恭	*kung*	老子道德	*Lao Tzu tao-te*
公案	*kung-an*	經註	*ching chu*
宮之奇	Kung Chih-ch'i	李紹昌	Lee, Shao Chang
公西華	Kung-hsi Hua,	麗	Li: king;
赤子華	Ch'ih, Tzu-hua	李	surname;
公明儀	Kung-ming I	黎	tribe
公孫丑	Kung-sun Ch'ou	里	*li*: distance;
公孫淢	Kung-sun Hsieh	驪	mixed;
公孫龍	Kung-sun Lung		separate, bright-
公孫龍子	*Kung-sun Lung Tzu*	離	ness;
公孫龍子	*Kung-sun Lung Tzu*		principle, pattern,
註	*chu*		order;
公孫尼子	Kung-sun Ni-tzu	理	propriety, rites
公孫段	Kung-sun Tuan	禮	
公孫鞅	Kung-sun Yang	李翱習之	Li Ao, Hsi-chih,
公孫衍	Kung-sun Yen	文公	Wen Kung
公都子	Kung-tu Tzu	麗姬	Li Chi
公羊	*Kung-yang*	禮記	*Li chi*
空	*k'ung*	禮記正義	*Li chi cheng-i*
孔安國	K'ung An-kuo	李之才	Li Chih-ts'ai
孔夫子丘	K'ung Fu-tzu, Ch'iu,	李耳	Li Erh
仲尼	Chung-ni	理學宗傳	*Li-hsüeh tsung-ch'uan*
孔子家語	*K'ung Tzu chia-yü*	理學字義	*Li-hsüeh tzu-i*
孔子改制	*K'ung Tzu kai-chi*	通釋	*t'ung-shih*
攷	*k'ao*	李頤	Li I
孔穎達	K'ung Ying-ta	禮記	*Li Ki*
過	Kuo: person;	李光地	Li Kuang-ti
虢	state	李軌	Li Kuei
郭象	Kuo Hsiang	李塨	Li Kung
		離婁	Li Lou

822

李伯敏 Li Po-mien
李思意 Li Shi-yi
李斯 Li Ssu
李田意 Li T'ien-yi
李侗延平集 Li T'ung, Yen-p'ing
李文公集 *Li Wen Kung chi*
李延平集 *Li Yen-p'ing chi*
梁 Liang
liang
梁敢超 Liang Ch'i-ch'ao
良止 Liang Chih
liang-chih
梁漱溟 Liang Sou-ming
廖文奎 Liao, W. K.
列子 Lieh Tzu
列子集解 *Lieh Tzu chi-chieh*
列子集釋 *Lieh Tzu chi-shih*
列子註 *Lieh Tzu chu*
臨濟 Lin-chi
臨濟慧照禪師語錄 *Lin-chi Hui-chao Ch'an-shih yü-lu*
林放 Lin Fang
林茂聖 Lin Mou-sheng
林擇之 Lin Tse-chih
林同濟 Lin Tung-chi
林語堂 Lin Yutang
靈 Ling
嶺南 Ling-nan
凌曙 Ling Shu
靈祐 Ling-yu
六 *liu*
劉安 Liu An
劉璣 Liu Chi
劉家立 Liu Chia-li
劉瑾 Liu Chin
柳下惠 Liu-hsia Hui
劉向 Liu Hsiang
劉歆 Liu Hsin
劉良 Liu Liang
劉盼遂 Liu P'an-sui
劉寶楠 Liu Pao-nan

劉少奇 Liu Shao-ch'i
劉師培 Liu Shih-p'ei
劉叔文 Liu Shu-wen
六祖壇經 *Liu-tsu t'an-ching*
劉宗周 Liu Tsung-chou
劉子政向 Liu Tzu-cheng, Hsiang
劉子全書 *Liu Tzu ch'üan-shu*
劉文典 Liu Wen-tien
柳無忌 Liu Wu-chi
羅香林 Lo Hsiang-lin
羅榮邦 Lo Jung-pang
羅根澤 Lo Ken-tse
洛陽 Lo-yang
魯 Lu
陸長庚 Lu Ch'ang-keng
陸澄元靜 Lu Ch'eng, Yüan-ching
陸賈 Lu Chia
陸象山九淵子靜 Lu Hsiang-shan, Chiu-yüan, Tzu-ching
魯可機 Lu K'o-chi
陸寬昱 Lu K'uan-yü
陸德明 Lu Te-ming
陸子美 Lu Tzu-mi
陸王 Lu-Wang
盧文弨 Lu Wen-ch'ao
論衡 *Lun-heng*
論衡集解 *Lun-heng chi-chieh*
論衡校釋 *Lun-heng chiao-shih*
論衡舉正 *Lun-heng chü-cheng*
論語 *Lun-yü*
論語正義 *Lun-yü cheng-i*
論語集解 *Lun-yü chi-chieh*
論語集註 *Lun-yü chi-chu*
論語集釋 *Lun-yü chi-shih*
論語解 *Lun-yü chieh*
論語註 *Lun-yü chu*
論語註疏 *Lun-yü chu-shu*
論語後案 *Lun-yü hou-an*
論語或問 *Lun-yü huo-wen*
論語義疏 *Lun-yü i-shu*

論語論仁論 *Lun-yü lun-jen lun*

論語筆解 *Lun-yü pi-chieh*

論語補疏 *Lun-yü pu-shu*

論語疏 *Lun-yü shu*

龍門 Lung-men

龍子 Lung Tzu

旅 Lü

呂柟 Lü Nan

呂不韋 Lü Pu-wei

呂氏春秋 *Lü-shih ch'un-ch'iu*

呂大臨與叔 Lü Ta-lin, Yü-shu

呂祖謙伯恭東萊 Lü Tsu-ch'ien, Po-kung, Tung-lai

馬叙倫 Ma Hsü-lun

馬融 Ma Jung

麻谷寶徹 Ma-ku, Pao-ch'e

毛嬙 Mao Ch'iang

毛詩正義 *Mao-shih cheng-i*

毛澤東 Mao Tse-tung

墨翟 Me Ti

梅賾 Mei Tse

梅貽寶 Mei, Y. P.

明治 Meiji

門 *men*

蒙 *meng*

孟季子 Meng Chi Tzu

孟諸 Meng-chu

孟仲子 Meng Chung Tzu

孟獻子 Meng Hsien

孟慈子 Meng I Tzu

孟賁 Meng Pen

孟伯生源 Meng Po-shang, Yüan

孟孫才 Meng-sun Ts'ai

孟子 Meng Tzu

孟子正義 *Meng Tzu cheng-i*

孟子集註 *Meng Tzu chi-chu*

孟子註 *Meng Tzu chu*

孟子註疏 *Meng Tzu chu-shu*

孟子反 Meng Tzu-fan

孟子字義疏證 *Meng Tzu tzu-i shu-cheng*

孟子微 *Meng Tzu wei*

孟武伯 Meng Wu-po

宓子賤 Mi Tzu-chien

苗 Miao

妙 *miao*

妙觀章 *Miao-kuan chang*

民 *min*

閔子騫 Min Tzu-ch'ien

冥 *ming*: dark;

命 fate, mandate, order;

暝 ignorance;

名 name;

明 understanding

名家 *Ming-chia*

明覺禪師語錄 *Ming-chiao Ch'an-shih yü-lu*

明儒學案 *Ming-ju hsüeh-an*

名辯 *ming-pien*

名僧傳抄 *Ming-seng chuan-ch'ao*

名實 *ming-shih*

明道全書 *Ming-tao ch'üan-shu*

明道文集 *Ming-tao wen-chi*

明瓚 Ming-tsan

莫 *mo*

摩訶衍論 *Mo-ho-yen lun*

墨子墨翟 Mo Tzu, Mo Ti

墨子註 *Mo Tzu chu*

墨子閒詁 *Mo Tzu chien-ku*

鏌鎁 *mo-yeh*

末有 *mo-yu*

畝 *mou*

牟宗三 Mou Tsung-san

穆 Mu

楊叔 Mu-shu

無門關 Mumonkan

中村元 Nakamura, Hajime

南鎮 Nan-chen

南海 Nan-hai

經墨真	*Nan-hua chen-ching*
副墨華	*Nan-hua fu-mo*
南郭子綦	Nan-kuo, Tzu-chi
南雷文定	*Nan-lei wen-ting*
南伯子葵	Nan-po Tzu-k'uei
南子	Nan-tzu
蜀缺	Nieh Chüeh
涅槃經	*Nieh-p'an ching*
年譜	*Nien-p'u*
甯	Ning
牛	Niu
女偶	Nü-yü
緒方宗博	Ogata, Sohaku
岡孝	Oka, Takashi
太田錦城	Ōta Kinjō
歐陽竟無仁	Ou-yang Ching-wu
龐景	Pang Ching-jen
暴	*pao*
寶徹	Pao-ch'e
包咸	Pao Hsien
北海	Pei-hai
本寂	Pen-chi
本體	*pen-t'i*
本無	*pen-wu*
彭祖	P'eng, P'eng-tsu
鵬	*p'eng*
畢戰	Pi Chan
比干	Pi-kan
祕思	Pi-ssu
碧巖集	*Pi-yen chi*
碧巖錄	*Pi-yen lu*
畢沅	Pi Yüan
表	*piao*
評合	*pien-ho*
豳	Pin
平	P'ing
平等	*p'ing-teng*
平原	P'ing-yüan
博	*po*: extensive;
薄	thin, to interfere
博愛	*po-ai*
伯成子高	Po-ch'eng Tzu-kao

伯夷	Po-i
百衲本	*Po-na-pen*
伯牛	Po-niu
伯有	Po-yu
魄	*p'o*
不	*pu*
不肖	*pu-hsiao*
卜梁倚	Pu-liang I
不說破	*pu-shuo-p'o*
樸	*p'u*
菩薩戒經	*P'u-sa chieh ching*
普曜經	*P'u-yao ching*
臨濟	Rinsai
坂井	Sakai
三正	*san-cheng*
三論	*San-lun*
三論玄義	*San-lun hsüan-i*
三論玄義誘蒙	*San-lun hsüan-i yu-meng*
三論	*sanron*
三統	*san-t'ung*
佐々木	Sasaki
色	*se*
司馬遷	Se-Ma Ts'ien
僧肇	Seng-chao
僧叡	Seng-jui
僧祐	Seng-yu
上	*shang*
尚書正義	*Shang-shu cheng-i*
尚書大傳	*Shang-shu ta-chuan*
尚書引義	*Shang-shu yin-i*
上帝	*Shang-ti*
上蔡語錄	*Shang-ts'ai yü-lu*
商鞅	Shang Yang
召	Shao
韶州	Shao-chou
紹熙	Shao-hsi
邵伯溫	Shao Po-wen
邵子全書	*Shao Tzu ch'üan-shu*
邵雍康節堯夫	Shao Yung, K'ang-chieh, Yao-fu
葉	She
詩經	*She King*

攝論 *She-lun*

攝大乘論 *She ta-ch'eng lun*

慎 *shen*: careful;
　　　expansion;
申　　　spirit

神氣 *shen-ch'i*

申鑒閣 *Shen-chien*

沈閣閣 Shen Hsien

神秀 Shen-hsiu

神會 Shen-hui

神會和尚遺集 *Shen-hui ho-shang i-chi*

神會語錄 *Shen-hui yü-lu*

沈桂 Shen Kuei

申不害 Shen Pu-hai

申生 Shen-sheng

慎到慎子 Shen Tao, Shen Tzu

神宗 Shen-tsung

申徒狄 Shen-t'u Ti

生 *sheng*

聖學宗傳 *Sheng-hsüeh tsung-ch'uan*

爽 Shih

始 *shih*: beginning;
事　　　fact;
適　　　near;
勢　　　power;
實　　　reality;
士　　　ruler;
恃　　　to depend;
識　　　to know

史記 *Shih chi*

史記正義 *Shih chi cheng-i*

史記索引 *Shih-chi so-yin*

詩經集註 *Shih ching chi-chu*

詩經釋義 *Shih ching shih-i*

螢 *shih-ho*

實相 *shih-hsiang*

施璜 Shih Huang

師曠 Shih-k'uang

十力叢書 *Shih-li ts'ung-shu*

什伯 *shih-po*

史綱祖 Shih Sheng-tsu

世碩 Shih Shih

世說新語 *Shih-shuo hsin-yü*

十地經 *Shih-ti ching*

家章 Shih-wei

尤友忠 Shih Yu-chung

支那儒道佛交涉史 *Shina judō-butsu kōshōshi*

支那儒道佛三教史論 *Shina judō-butsu sankyō shiron*

支那仁於ける佛教 *Shina ni okeru bukkyō*

ヤ儒教道教 *to jukyō dokyō*

書經 *Shoo King*

首陽 Shou-yang

恕 *shu*: altruism;
數　　　number, truth;
術　　　statecraft

叔齊 Shu-ch'i

書經 *Shu ching*

叔向 Shu-hsiang

叔孫武叔 Shu-sun Wu-shu

叔魚 Shu-yü

舜 Shun

順 *shun*

淳于髡 Shun-yü K'un

說文解字 *Shuo-wen chieh-tzu*

說無垢稱經 *Shuo Wu-kou-ch'eng ching*

說苑 *Shuo-yüan*

朱子學 *Shushigaku*

小學 *Siao Hio*

思 *ssu*: thought;
死　　　to die

思思 Ssu-en

死而不亡 *ssu erh pu-wang*

思想時代 *Ssu-hsiang yü shih-tai*

四庫全書珍本 *Ssu-k'u ch'üan-shu chen-pen*

司馬貞 Ssu-ma Chen

司馬遷 Ssu-ma Ch'ien

司馬光　Ssu-ma Kuang
司馬牛，向　Ssu-ma Niu, Hsiang
司馬溫公　Ssu-ma Wen Kung
文集　　　wen-chi
斯彌　　　ssu-mi
四部備要　Ssu-pu pei-yao
四部叢刊　Ssu-pu ts'ung-k'an
四書正誤　Ssu-shu cheng-wu
四書釋義　Ssu-shu shih-i
四書大全　Ssu-shu ta-ch'üan
駟帶　　　Ssu Tai
思問錄　　Ssu-wen lu
蘇季明　　Su Chi-ming
蘇軾，東坡　Su Shih, Tung-po
素問　　　Su-wen
蘇輿　　　Su Yü
巽　　　sun: bending;
　　　　　decreasing
孫奇逢　　Sun Ch'i-feng
孫中山　　Sun Chung-shan
全集　　　ch'üan-chi
孫星衍　　Sun Hsing-yen
孫詒讓　　Sun I-jang
孫人和　　Sun Jen-ho
孫奭　　　Sun Shih
孫逸仙，　Sun Yat-sen,
中山　　　Chung-shan
宋　　　　Sung
訟　　　sung
宋鈃　　　Sung Hsing
宋高僧傳　Sung kao-seng chuan
宋史　　　Sung shih
宋四子　　Sung ssu-tzu
抄釋　　　ch'ao-shih
宋元學案　Sung-Yüan hsüeh-an
鈴木大拙　Suzuki,
　　　　　Daisetz Teitarō
ta: great;
　　　　　to understand
大乘起信論　Ta-ch'eng ch'i-hsin
　　　　　lun

大乘止觀　Ta-ch'eng chih-kuan
法門　　　fa-men
大乘密藏　Ta-ch'eng mi-yen
經　　　　ching
大集經　　Ta-chi ching
大智度論　Ta chih-tu lun
大莊嚴　　Ta Chuang-yen
大小大　　ta-hsiao-ta
大學　　　Ta-hsüeh
大學章句　Ta-hsüeh chang-chü
大學或問　Ta-hsüeh huo-wen
大人先生　Ta-jen hsien-sheng
傳　　　　chuan
大垃　　　ta-pang
大通　　　ta-t'ung
大同書　　Ta-t'ung shu
大雅　　　Ta-ya
大愚　　　Ta-yü
大戴　　　Tai: surname;
代　　　　tribe
待　　　　tai
震東原　　Tai Chen, Tung-yüan
戴東原集　Tai Tung-yüan chi
戴東原的　Tai Tung-yüan ti
哲學　　　che-hsüeh
大正新脩　Taishō shinshū
大藏經　　daizōkyō
太　　　　T'ai: king;
泰　　　　mountain
泰　　　　t'ai
太極　　　t'ai-chi
太極圖說　T'ai-chi t'u shuo
太甲　　　T'ai-chia
太虛　　　T'ai-hsü
太虛　　　t'ai-hsü
太玄經　　T'ai-hsüan ching
太上感應　T'ai-shang kan-ying
篇　　　　p'ien
高楠　　　Takakusu,
順次郎　　Junjirō
聃　　　　Tan
曇濟　　　T'an-chi

827

譚劉陽 T'an Liu-yang
　全集同 　ch'üan-chi
譚嗣復 T'an Ssu-t'ung,
　　　生 　Fu-sheng
薰湯 tang
唐 T'ang: king;
唐荊川 　lord
　集 T'ang Ching-ch'uan
唐居毅 　chi
唐謫之 T'ang Chun-i
唐順代文化 T'ang Hsü
史 T'ang Shun-chih
湯同彤 T'ang-tai wen-hua
道 　shih
道安州 T'ang Yung-t'ung
道行經 Tao
道宣 Tao-an
道論 Tao-chou
道德經 Tao-hsing ching
道德經註 Tao-i
道藏 Tao lun
道統錄 Tao-te ching
陶 Tao-te ching chu
陶鴻慶 Tao-tsang
德 Tao-t'ung lu
得 T'ao
天台 T'ao Hung-ch'ing
藤帝 te: character, virtue;
底柱 　to attain, able
體 Tendai
體認物 T'eng
體用 ti
條理 Ti-chu
天 t'i
天機州 t'i-jen
田恒 t'i-wu
田 t'i-yung
t'iao-li
t'ien
t'ien-chi
T'ien-chou
T'ien Heng

天下 T'ien Hsia
天理 t'ien-li
天命 t'ien-ming
天台 T'ien-t'ai
天道 t'ien-tao
定 Ting
鼎 ting
多 to
帝鑑大定 Tokiwa Daijō
墩煌出士 Tonkō shutsudo
六祖壇經 　Rokuso dankyō
通報 T'oung Pao
雜 tsa
在 tsai
蔡 Ts'ai
才 ts'ai: ability;
材 　raw material
蔡李通 Ts'ai Chi-t'ung,
　元定 　Yüan-ting
蔡詠春 Ts'ai Yung-ch'un
臧文仲 Tsang Wen-chung
造物者 tsao-wu che
曹 Ts'ao
曹器之 Ts'ao Ch'i-chih
漕溪 Ts'ao-hsi
曹山本寂 Ts'ao-shan Pen-chi
禪師語錄 　Ch'an-shih yü-lu
曹拭遠 Ts'ao Shu-yüan
曹端月川 Ts'ao Tuan,
　　　 　Yüeh-ch'uan
則 tse
于思 Tse-sze
曾晳參 Tseng Hsi, Tien
曾子華 Tseng Tzu, Ts'an
清丘明 Tsing-hua
左 Tso Ch'iu-ming
左傳 Tso chuan, Tso Chuen
鄒 Tsou
鄒衍 Tsou Yen
粹言 Ts'ui-yen
塚本善隆 Tsukamoto Zenryū
存性篇 Ts'un-hsing p'ien

Tsung

Tsung-mi

Tu

Tu Kung-sun Lung Tzu

Tu-shu tsa-chih

Tu-shun

Tu Ssu-shu ta-ch'üan shuo

Tu T'ung-chien lun

tuan-chuan

tui

Tun-huang

Tung Chung-shu

Tung-kuo Tzu

Tung-lin

T'ung

t'ung: penetration; same; tree

t'ung-ch'u

t'ung-i-shih

T'ung Po-yü

T'ung-shu

tzu: honorific; to indulge; tree

Tzu-ch'an

Tzu-chang, Shih, Chuan-sun

Tzu Ch'in-chang

Tzu-erh

Tzu-hsia, Pu Sheng

tzu-jan

Tzu-kung, Tz'u, Tuan-mu Tzu

Tzu-lai

Tzu-li

Tzu-liang

Tzu-lu, Chih-lu, Chung Yu

Tzu-mo

Tzu Sang-hu

Tzu-ssu

 (Confucian)

 (In *Chuang Tzu*)

Tzu Ta-shu

Tzu-tu

Tzu-wen

Tzu-yu, Yu Yen

Tzu-yü

tz'u: affection; forthwith

Ui Hakuju

Wai-shu

Wan

Wan Chang

wan-k'ung

Wan-mu ts'ao-t'ang ts'ung-shu

Wan-yu wen-k'u

wang: kingly; to destroy; to forget

Wang An-shih

Wang Chi, Ju-chung, Lung-hsi

Wang Chih

Wang Ching-ch'u

Wang Ch'ung

Wang Fu-chih, Ch'uan-shan

Wang Hsien-ch'ien

Wang Hsien-shen

Wang I

Wang K'ai-yün

Wang Mang

Wang Mou-hung

Wang Nien-sun

Wang Pi

Wang Su

Wang-sun Chia

Wang Tch'ang-tche

Wang Wen-ch'eng Kung ch'üan-shu

王陽明
伯安 文成
　　新建

微衛

尚偽
咸惟
謂
韋昭
魏志
魏晉玄學
　論稿
雜摩詰
　所說經

唯識
未始
唯識二十
　論
唯識三十
　論
魏源
文

文問
文章
文集
文理
文縷
文子
文僵
文言
文我
黃茂林

武
吳惡

Wang Yang-ming,
　Po-an, Wen-ch'eng,
　Hsin-chien
Wei: feudal district;
　state
wei: act, activity,
　become;
　artifice, activity;
　powerful;
　to become;
　to say
Wei Chao
Wei chih
*Wei-Chin hsüan-hsüeh
　lun-kao*
*Wei-mo-chieh
　so-shuo ching*
wei-shih: Conscious-
　ness-Only;
　has not been
*Wei Shih Er Shih
　Lun*
*Wei-shih san-shih
　lun*
Wei Yüan
Wen
wen: culture, orna-
　ment, literature;
　to ask
wen-chang
Wen-chi
wen-li
wen-lü
Wen Tzu
Wen-yen
wen-yen
wo
Wong Mou-lam
Wu: king, emperor,
　empress;
　surname, state
wu: hate;

無
舞
吳澄
無極
無莊
無心
五行
吳經熊
務光
無名論
吳少大
五燈會元
武丁
吳斗南
王子近思
　錄證明
无妄
無為
雅
山崎闇齋
山口察常
陽
楊正典
楊朱昊
揚雄
陽虎
楊良我
楊龜山集
楊倞
楊聯陞
楊伯峻
揚時龜山
堯
猺
姚名達
姚鼐
姚善友
爻辭

耶
也

no, non-being;
　to dance
Wu Ch'eng
wu-chi
Wu-chuang
wu-hsin
wu-hsing
Wu, John C. H.
Wu Kuang
Wu-ming lun
Wu Pi-ta
Wu-teng hui-yüan
Wu-ting
Wu Tou-nan
*Wu-tzu chin-ssu
　lu fa-ming*
wu-wang
wu-wei
ya
Yamazaki Ansai
Yamaguchi Satsujō
yang
Yang Cheng-tien
Yang Chu
yang-hsi
Yang Hsiung
Yang Hu
Yang I-wo
Yang Kuei-shan chi
Yang Liang
Yang, Lien-sheng
Yang Po-chün
Yang Shih, Kuei-shan
Yao: emperor;
　tribe
Yao Ming-ta
Yao Nai
Yao, Shan-yu
yao-tz'u
yeh: final interrogative
　article;
　final positive article

Yeh Ts'ai
Yen
yen: salt;
    saying
Yen-ch'eng Tzu-yu
Yen-ching-shih chi
Yen Fu
Yen-K'ung ts'ung-shu
Yen-Li ts'ung-shu
Yen Shih-ku
Yen Yüan, Hsi-chai
Yen Yüan, Yen Tzu,
    Hui
Yenching
Yi King
Yin
yin
*Yin-ping-shih wen-
    chi*
Yin Po-ch'i
Yin Wen Tzu
Ying: capital;
    district;
    warden
Ying-lo ching
Yo-cheng
Yōmeigaku
Yu
yu
Yu Pen
Yu Tzu, Jo
yuishiki
yung: mean, ordinary,
    universal;
    use
Yung-chia
Yung-lo ta-tien
Yü: dynasty, state;
    king

yü: and, same, to
    give;
    happy;
    in, to;
    spatial continuum
Yü-ch'iang
yü-chou
Yü Fa-k'ai
yü-lu
Yü-lou tsa-tsuan
Yü-lung
Yü-p'ien
Yü Tao-sui
Yü-tou
Yü Yüeh
Yüan
yüan: first, origin,
    origination;
    source
Yüan Hsien
Yüan-hsing
Yüan-ju
Yüan-k'ang
Yüan-ku
Yüan Shih-k'ai
Yüan-tao
Yüeh: mountain;
    person;
    state
yüeh
Yüeh-chiao
Zen
Zen, Sophia H. Chen
*Zenshūshi ken-
    kyū*
Zinbun-Kagaku-
    Kenkyūsyo
*Zoku Yamazaki
    Ansai zenshū*
Zokuzōkyō

D

E

F

G

God, 637, 640; *see also* Lord on High
golden rule, 16-17, 27, 42, 100, 162,
see also p. 18
good and evil: Lao Tzu on, *see* p. 138;
Consciousness-Only School on, 384;
Chou Tun-i on, *see* p. 462; Ch'eng
Hao on, *see* p. 522; Ch'eng I on, *see*
p. 547; Chu Hsi on, 597-98, 600
Goose Lake Temple, 583
government: Confucius on, *see* p. 18;
Mencius on, *see* p. 51; in *Great Learning*, 86, 91-92; in the *Mean*, 104-7;
Hsün Tzu on, 130-34; Lao Tzu on,
see p. 138; Mo Tzu on, 229-31; Han
Fei on, 252-60; Chou Tun-i on, *see*
p. 462; Wang Fu-chih on, 693, 701-2;
K'ang Yu-wei on, 734
Graham, 461*n*, 785
Great Learning: discussed, 84-85; described, 85*n*; main ideas of, 85*ff*
  on cultivation of personal life, 86;
on extension of knowledge, 86; on
manifesting the clear character, 86, 87;
on highest good, 86, 88; on sincerity
of the will, 86, 89-90; on daily renewal, 87; on root and branches, 88;
on investigation of things, 89; on
watchful over oneself when alone,
89; on rectification of the mind, 90;
on regulating the family, 90; on order
of the state, 91-92; on internal and
external, 92; on bringing peace to the
world, 92-94; on humanity and righteousness, 93-94; on righteousness and
profit, 94
  compared with Mencius, 79; Chu
Hsi's arrangement of, 84; and Wang
Yang-ming, 84, 656; Chu Hsi's commentary on, 85-94; compared with the
Mean, 95-96; and Hsün Tzu, 96
"Great Norm," 8-11, 249, 548
Great Ultimate: in Neo-Confucianism,
14; in the *Changes*, 263, 271; in Chou
Tun-i, 472, 463-65; in Shao Yung,
see p. 484; in Ch'eng Hao, 535; in
Lu Hsiang-shan, 585; in Chu Hsi, *see*
p. 593; in Fung Yu-lan, 752, 758
"great unit," 233
Great Unity, Age of, 730-31
Great Whole, 752, 759
Greek philosophy, 143, 544, 611
Green, T. H., 743-44
growth, *see* production and reproduction

H

Han dynasty Confucianism, 22, 27, 122,
289, 316, 511, 709
Han Fei Tzu: and Hsün Tzu, 115, 254;
interpretation of Tao, 159, 260-61;
discussed, 251-52; criticism of Confucianism and Moism, 252-53; on
human nature, 253-54; on following
Nature, 254-55; on law and statecraft,
255-56; on names and actuality, 255-
57; on universal love, 257-58
Han Fei Tzu, 252-61, 787
Han Wen Kung, *see* Han Yü
Han Yü: discussed, 450-51; life of, 451*n*
  explanation of the *Analects*, 35, 38;
on nature and feelings, 451-54, 630;
on humanity, righteousness, Tao, and
virtue, 454-55; on rectification of the
mind and sincerity of the will, 455;
on universal love; 499; explanation
of *jen*, 789
  and ancient Classics, 450; and Li
Ao, 450; criticism of Hsün Tzu and
Yang Hsiung, 450; and Mencius, 450,
452; attack on Taoism, 453-56; attack on Buddhism, 453-56, 554; attack on Moism, 454-55; Ch'eng I's
criticism of, 559
hao-jen chi-ch'ih (strong moving
power), 784
Hao-sheng Pu-hai, 82
hardness and whiteness, 185, 240
hate, 25, 42, 93
Heaven (Lord), *see* p. 18 *and* Lord on
High
Heaven and hell, 362, 438
Heaven and man, *see* unity of Heaven
and man
Hegel, 183, 361
hexagram, explanation of, 721
Hīnayāna: criticized by the Three-
Treatise School, 365-66; and Consciousness-Only School, 384; in Shen-
hui, 441
history: Mencius on, 72; Yin Yang
School on, 245-47; Han Fei on, 257;
Tung Chung-shu on, 272, 287-88;
Wang Ch'ung on, 304; Kuo Hsiang
on, *see* p. 326; Shao Yung on, *see* p.
484; Wang Fu-chih on, 693, 701-2; as
cycles, 724, 727
History, Book of, 8-10, 17*n*, 81, 249,
701
ho-p'i (closing and opening), 765

Hsün Yüeh, 276, 296, 454
Hu An-kuo, 616*n*, 617*n*
Hu An-ting, *see* Hu Yüan
Hu Chi-sui, 616
Hu Hung, 467, 616*n*, 631
Hu Shih: on Mencius, 79; on Chuang
    Tzu, 204; on Logicians, 234; on
    Natural Law, 272, 519; on Huai-nan
    Tzu, 307; on Zen, 425, 430*n*; on
    scientific spirit, 611; and pragmatism,
    744; and Hsün Tzu, 783
Hu Wu-feng, *see* Hu Hung
Hu Yüan, 521
Hua-yen ching, 406
Hua-yen i-hai po-men, 408, 414-24
Hua-yen School: discussed, 406-8
    on universal causation, 407; on Ten
    Mysterious Gates, 407, 411-14; on
    Six Characters, 407, 413; on Three
    Natures, 409; on Five Doctrines, 410;
    on one and many, 411-13, 423; on
    principle and facts, 412-15, 420, 422,
    424; on substance and function, 414-
    15; on causation, 414-15, 420; on
    activity and tranquillity, 419; on mat-
    ter and Emptiness, 420
    and Consciousness-Only School,
    373, 406, 408-9; and T'ien-t'ai School,
    403, 406-7, 411; and Neo-Confucian-
    ism, 408; and Zen, 433
Huai-nan Tzu: and Wang Ch'ung, 305;
    discussed, 305; on Tao, 305-6; cosmol-
    ogy of, 305-8; macrocosm and micro-
    cosm in, 308
Huai-nan Tzu, 305-8
Huan T'ui, 32
Huang-chi ching-shih shu, 481, 483-94
Huang Chih, *see* Huang I-fang
Huang-fu mi, 4*n*
Huang Hsün, 615
Huang I-fang, 684*n*
Huang Kan, 461*n*
Huang K'an, 34
Huang-Lao, 314
Huang Mien-chai, *see* Huang Kan
Huang Mien-chih, 685*n*
Huang-po, 445-46, 448-49
Huang Po-chia, 461, 488
Huang Shih-nan, 35
Huang Tsung-hsi, 461*n*, 558, 562, 583,
    694
Huang Tsung-hsien, 668
Huang Wan, *see* Huang Tsung-hsien
Huang Yüeh-chou, 493
Hughes, 789
Hui, King, 60-61

Hui-neng, 426-27, 430-40
Hui Shih: and Chuang Tzu, 209; dis-
    cussed, 232-33; paradoxes of, 233-35;
    on similarities and differences, 233-35;
    on universal love, 234; on space and
    time, 234-35; on knowledge, 235; on
    names, 235
Hui-yüan, 363, 425
human heartedness (*jen*), *see* humanity
human relations, *see* p. 51 *and* Five Re-
    lations
humanism, 3-13, 14-18
humanity, 18, 51, 84, 115, 138, 212,
    285, 454, 462, 498, 522, 547, 593,
    603, 659, 719, 734, 738, 788
Hume, 382, 743-44
hun (soul), 12
Hung-jen, 425, 430, 432, 439
Hung, William, xvi
Huxley, 743

I

i (increase) hexagram, 477
I, Master, 60
I Chih, 70, 71
I chuan, 570-71
i-kan (one thread), *see* one thread
I-shu, 551, 600, 783
I-ya, 55
I-yin, 470
idealism, 370-95, 408, 737, 776-78
immortality, 11-13
immortals, 289-91, 564
immutability of things, 344-50
impartiality, 537, 552-53, 556, 635
inaction, *see* taking no action
Indian philosophy: significance of water
    in, 36; compared with Chuang Tzu,
    191; and Buddhism, 337, 343-44, 358,
    373; and meditation, 405, 425, 429
Indra's net, 412
infant, 144, 150, 154, 165, 602
inferior man, *see* superior man *and* p. 18
innate knowledge: Mencius on, *see* p.
    51; Shao Yung on, 509; Lu Hsiang-
    shan on, 575; Wang Yang-ming on,
    see p. 659.
"Inquiry on the *Great Learning*," 658-67
"Inquiry on Human Nature," 451-54
"Inquiry on the Way," 254-56
Instructions for Practical Living, xv
instruments (*ch'i*), *see* concrete things
internal and external: Mencius on, 52-
    53; in *Great Learning*, 92; in the
    Mean, 108; Chou Tun-i on, 461;
    Ch'eng Hao on, 521-22, 525-26, 531;

16, 318, 320-24; on destiny, 316; on
original substance, 316; on names and
form, 316, 322, 324-26; on having
no mind, 317; on one and many, 317;
on the sage, 317; on Tao, 317, 324;
on taking no action, 322; on substance
and function, 323; on numbers, 323

Han Fei's influence on, 261; Mo
Tzu's influence on, 315-16; Logician's
influence on, 316; the *Changes'* influence on, 316; and Buddhism, 336-37,
358, 415-16, 428, 433, 445

Neo-Thomism, 754

Nieh-p'an ching, 443

Nietzsche, 743

nihilism, 359, 396

Nine Categories, 9, 472

nine standards, 106

Nirgrantha, 378*n*

Nirvāṇa: in Three-Treatise School, 360;
entrance to, 348, 395, 404-5, 413; in
Consciousness-Only School, 380; discussed, 382, 418; in Zen, 427

Niu, 56

non-action, *see* taking no action

non-being: in Neo-Taoism, 315-16, 324;
Wang Ch'ung on, 320-24; Fung Yu-
lan on, 758; *see also* being and non-
being

non-ultimate, *see* Ultimate of Non-being

Northern and Southern Schools, 427-
28

numbers, 269, 323, *see also* p. 484

O

Ocean, analogy of, 769

Odes, Book of, 4*n*, 5-7, 17*n*

*On the Cultivation of Communist Party
Members*, 781

On New Democracy, 773-74, 781

On Practice, 773, 781

One, The: Lao Tzu on, *see* p. 138;
Chuang Tzu on, *see* Chuang Tzu;
Shao Yung on, 492-93

one and many: in Neo-Taoism, 317; in
Buddhism, 411-13, 423; in Neo-Confucianism, 460, 471, 571, 615, *see also*
p. 496; in Hsiung Shih-li, 756, 763,
765, 771; *see* one is all

one body, Heaven and man forming, *see*
unity of Heaven and man

one is all, all is one: in Neo-Taoism,
320; in Buddhism, 397, 403, 411-13;
see also one and many

one thread: Confucius on, *see* p. 18;
discussed, 27, 721; Lu Hsiang-shan
on, 574; Wang Yang-ming on, 679-80

One Vehicle, 410

origin: Tung Chung-shu on, 271-85;
Chou Tun-i on, 465-66; Ch'eng Hao
on, *see* p. 522; Ch'eng I on, 545, 560;
see also origination

original non-being, 336, 338-39, *see also*
being and non-being

original substance: in Neo-Taoism, 316;
in Buddhism, 357, 433; in Hsiung
Shih-li, 765-66, 769-70; *see also* Wang
Yang-ming

origination, 263; *see also* origin

Ōta Kinjō, 570*n*, 651*n*, 674*n*

Ou-yang Ching-yu, 374, 743, 765

P

Pao-ch'e, *see* Ma-ku

Paradise, 438, *see also* Heaven and hell

past and present, *see* history

P'eng, 31

P'eng-tsu, 186, 195, 313

permanence, *see* immutability of things

physical form: in the *Changes*, 267;
Shao Yung on, *see* p. 484; Ch'eng
Hao on, *see* pp. 522, 527, 537, 542;
Lu Hsiang-shan on, 577, 583, 587;
Chu Hsi on, 597, 634-36, 639;
Wang Fu-chih on, 695; discussed, 722

physical nature: Chang Tsai on, *see* p.
496; Chu Hsi on, *see* p. 593; Tai Chen
on, 715; Fung Yu-lan on, 760

Pi Chan, 68

Pi-kan, 54

Pin, 312

p'ing-teng (equality), 783

Plato, 49, 115, 640-41, 744, 757

Po-ch'eng Tzu-kao, 311

Po-ch'i, 498

Po-i, 593

Po-niu, 626

Po-yu, 12

p'o (soul), 12

portents, belief in, 292

pragmatism, 744

prajñā, 336, 344, 350, 428

pratyekabuddha, see Buddhas-for-themselves

principle: in the *Odes*, 5-6; in Neo-Con-
fucianism, 14; in the *Mean*, 97; in the
Changes, 269; Han Fei on, 260-61;
Wang Ch'ung on, 315-16, 318, 320-

U

Ultimate, Great, *see* Great Ultimate
Ultimate of Non-being, 154, 460, 463, 556, 577-78, 752, 758-9
unity of Heaven and man: in "Great Norm," 10; in Neo-Confucianism, 14; in Confucius, 40; in Han Confucianism, 292; Chang Tsai on, 516; Ch'eng Hao on, *see* p. 522; Lu Hsiang-shan on, *see* p. 574; Chu Hsi on, 595; Wang Yang-ming on, *see* p. 659; Fung Yu-lan on, 752, 762; Hsiung Shih-li on, 763
Universal Causation, 407-8
universal love: Mo Tzu on, 213-17; Logicians on, 233; Legalists on, 257-58; Han Yü on, 454-55; Chang Tsai on, 499; Ch'eng I on, 550, 559
universals, 751-52
utensils (*ch'i*), *see* concrete things
utilitarianism, 212, 226-31
utopia, K'ang Yu-wei's, 732-34

V

vacuity: in the *Analects*, 33; Lao Tzu on, 141-42, 147; Chu Hsi on, 142, 650; Taoist ideas of, 269, 344; Wang pi on, 322; Seng-chao on, 350; Yang Hsiung on, 291; Chang Tsai on, 501-4; Wang Fu-chih on, 693, 695
Vaiseshika, 378*n*
Variant School of Original Non-being, 337, 339; *see also* School of Original Non-being
Vasubandhu, 370, 372, 518
Vijñaptimātra, *see* Consciousness-Only School
Vijñatimātratātriṁsika, 370
Vimalakīrti, 446
Vimalakīrtinirdesa sūtra, see Scripture Spoken by Vimalakīrti
virtue: emphasis on, 6-8; Confucius' teaching of, *see* p. 18; Lao Tzu on, *see* p. 139; Han Yü on, 454-55
vitalism, 744
Void, Absolute, 357

W

Wai-shu, 518
Waley, 8, 785, 789, 790
Wang An-shih, 496, 518*n*
Wang Chi, 686-89
Wang Chih, 488
Wang Ching-ch'u, 444

Wang Ch'uan-shan, *see* Wang Fu-chih
Wang Ch'ung: discussed, 292-93; skepticism of, 292, 299-304, 309; naturalism in, 292-304; materialism of, 780
　explanation of the *Analects*, 29, 38; on human nature, 290, 293-96, 454; on material force, 290-99; on spontaneity, 296-99; on taking no action, 297-99; on death and spiritual beings, 299-302; on strange phenomena, 299-303; on accident and necessity, 302-3; on fate, 303-4; on equality of past and present, 304
Wang Fu-chih: life of, 692; discussed, 692-94
　on Principle of Nature, 692, 700-701, 776; on principle and material force, 692-95, 697-701; on daily renewal, 693, 698-99; on concrete things, 693-97; on substance and function, 696-97; on being and non-being, 697; on nature and destiny, 698-700; on history and government, 701-2; and Buddhism, 373
　reaction against Sung and Ming Neo-Confucianism, 692, 703; and Chu Hsi, 592; Chang Tsai, 504, 509, 692; and Ch'ing Confucianism, 694; compared with Tai Chen, 722; and T'an Ssu-t'ung, 740; and materialism, 777
Wang Ju-chung, *see* Wang Chi
Wang Lung-hsi, *see* Wang Chi
Wang Mang, 292
Wang Pi: discussed, 316-17
　on principle, 315-16, 318, 320-24; on the One, 318-19; explanation of hexagrams, 318-24; on yin yang, 319; on non-being, 320-24; on names and form, 322; on taking no action, 322; on numbers, 323; on substance and function, 323, 791; on one and many, 337; on original non-being, 339-40
　commentary on *Lao Tzu*, 156, 159, 321-24; commentary on the *Changes*, 320-21
Wang Po-an, *see* Wang Yang-ming
Wang Su, 4*n*, 19
Wang-sun Chia, 25
Wang Wen-ch'eng, *see* Wang Yang-ming
Wang Wen-ch'eng Kung ch'üan-shu, 659-66
Wang Yang-ming: discussed, 654-58;

Y

Z